Malaysia, Singapore & Brunei

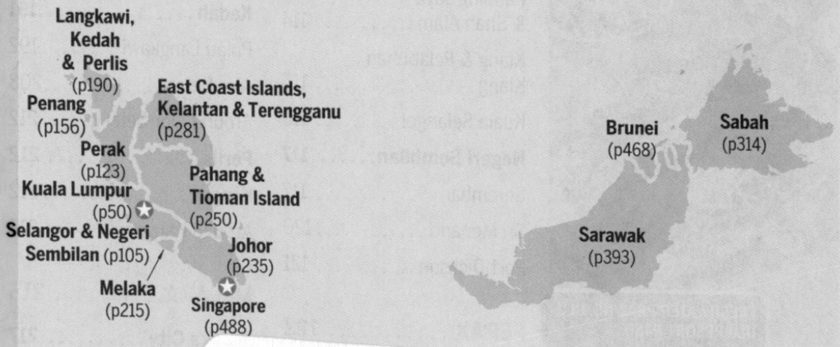

THIS EDITION WRITTEN AND RESEARCHED BY
Isabel Albiston, Brett Atkinson, Greg Benchwick,
Cristian Bonetto, Austin Bush, Anita Isalska, Robert Scott Kelly,
Simon Richmond, Richard Waters

PLAN YOUR TRIP

FRESHWATER PRAWNS, ULU ULU RESORT P486

PETRONAS TOWERS P57

ON THE ROAD

Contents

Contents

ON THE ROAD

ELENA ERMAKOVA /SHUTTERSTOCK ©

CHRISTOPHER CHAN/GETTY IMAGES ©

ORANGUTANS, SINGAPORE ZOO P509

Contents

BLUE MANSION, GEORGE TOWN P159

JAME'ASR HASSANIL BOLKIAH MOSQUE P473

UNDERSTAND

SURVIVAL GUIDE

SPECIAL FEATURES

Welcome to Malaysia, Singapore & Brunei

Entwined by shared history, Southeast Asia's terrific trio offer steamy jungles packed with wildlife, beautiful beaches, idyllic islands, culinary sensations and multi-ethnic culture.

Tropical Rainforests

For many people this region is defined by its equatorial rainforest. Significant chunks of primary jungle – among the most ancient ecosystems on earth – remain intact, protected by national parks and conservation projects. Seemingly impenetrable foliage and muddy, snaking rivers conjure up the 'heart of darkness' – but join a ranger-led nature walk, for example, and you'll be alerted to the mind-boggling biodiversity all around, from the pitcher plants, lianas and orchids of the humid lowlands, to the conifers and rhododendrons of high-altitude forests.

Sensational Wildlife

The icing on this verdant cake is the chance to encounter wildlife in its natural habitat. The most common sightings will be a host of insects or colourful birdlife, but you could get lucky and spot a foraging tapir, a silvered leaf monkey, or an orangutan swinging through the jungle canopy. The oceans are just as bountiful: snorkel or dive among shoals of tropical fish, paint-box tipped corals, turtles, sharks and dolphins. Even if you don't venture outside the urban centres, there's excellent opportunities for wildlife watching at the world-class Singapore Zoo or the KL Bird Park.

Urban Adventures

City lovers will be dazzled by Singapore, an urban showstopper that combines elegant colonial-era buildings with stunning contemporary architecture and attractions. Malaysia's capital, Kuala Lumpur (KL), is a place where Malay *kampung* (village) life stands cheek by jowl with the 21st-century glitz of the Petronas Towers, and shoppers shuttle from traditional wet markets to air-conditioned mega malls. Go off-radar in Brunei's surprisingly unostentatious capital Bandar Seri Begawan: its picturesque water village Kampong Ayer is the largest stilt settlement in the world.

Cultural Riches

Unesco World Heritage–listed Melaka and George Town (Penang) have uniquely distinctive architectural and cultural townscapes, developed over half a millennium of Southeast Asian cultural and trade exchange. Muslim Malays, religiously diverse Chinese, and Hindu and Muslim Indians muddle along with aboriginal groups (the Orang Asli) on Peninsular Malaysia and Borneo's indigenous people, scores of tribes known collectively as Dayaks. Each ethnic group has its own language and cultural practices which you can best appreciate through festivals and delicious cuisine.

Why I Love Malaysia, Singapore & Brunei

By Simon Richmond, Writer

For Southeast Asia in a microcosm you can't beat this trio of fascinating countries. From my first slurp of lip-smacking laksa noodles and taste of sizzling satay chicken at an outdoor food stall in Kuala Lumpur many years ago, to the continual thrill of watching the evolution of Singapore into an arts, architecture and culture heavyweight, the appeal of the region has been addictive. Whether exploring the heritage cityscape of George Town or riding longboats into the deepest recesses of Sarawak, it's all one huge adventure in the company of some of the region's friendliest people.

For more about our writers, see page 640

Above: Tea plantation, Cameron Highlands (p134)

Peninsular Malaysia & Singapore

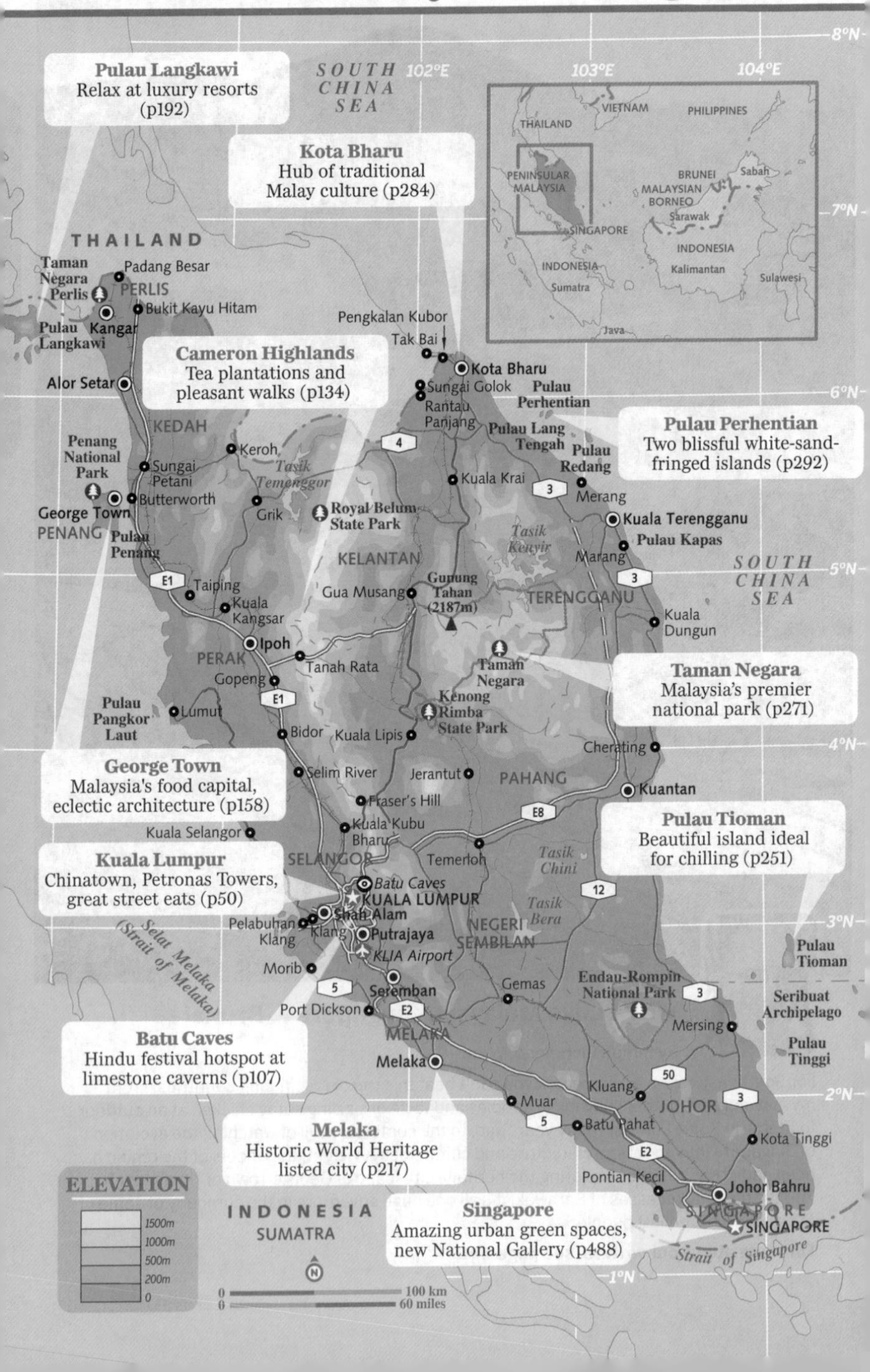

Malaysian Borneo & Brunei

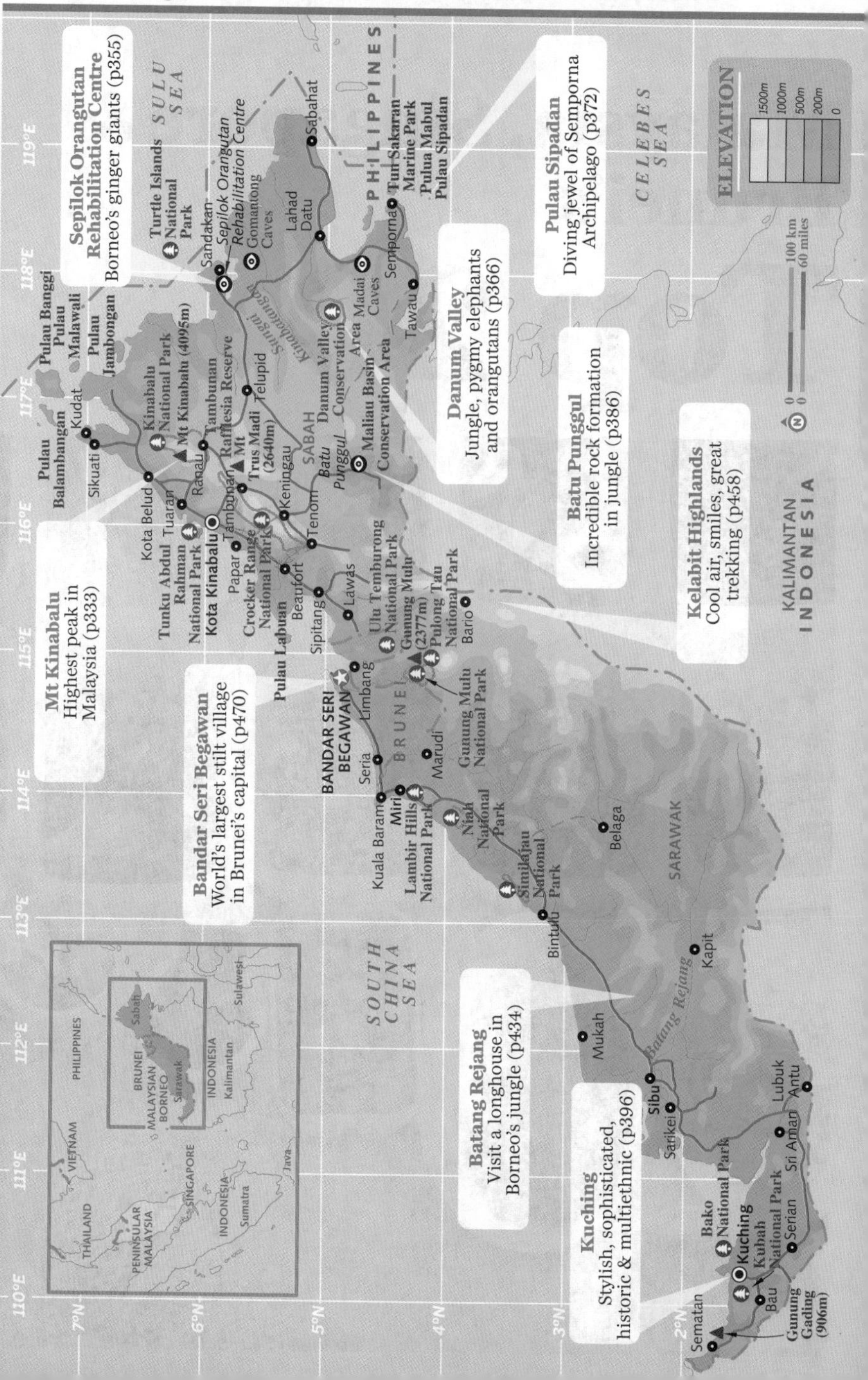

Malaysia, Singapore & Brunei's Top 20

1

Street Food

1 White tablecloth? Confounding cutlery? Snooty waiters? A roof? No thanks. In Malaysia, the best food is served in the humblest surroundings and involves the least amount of fuss. Countless vendors serve delicious dishes from mobile carts, stalls and shophouses, many still employing recipes and techniques handed down from previous generations. And in addition to informality, ubiquity and quality, you're also spoilt for choice – on a single street, such as Lorong Baru in George Town (p175), Penang, you're likely to encounter Malay, regional Chinese, South Indian and Western cuisines. Street food stall, Kota Kinabalu (p326)

Diving, Pulau Sipadan

2 Sometimes it seems as if the world's most colourful marine life considers the seawall of Sipadan (p372) to be prime real estate – from the commonplace to utterly alien fish, molluscs and reptiles, creatures seem to have swum through every slice of the colour wheel. They live here, play here, hunt here and eat here, and you, lucky diver, may dance an underwater ballet with them. For any diver, from the amateur to seasoned veterans, Sipadan is the ultimate underwater adventure.

LANO LAN/SHUTTERSTOCK ©

2

REINHARD DIRSCHERL/GETTY IMAGES ©

3

MATTHEW MICAH WRIGHT/GETTY IMAGES ©

4

PURIPAT LERTPUNYAROJ/GETTY IMAGES ©

George Town, Penang

3 Once abandoned by locals and dismissed by tourists, George Town (p158) has managed to cling to its relatively newfound reign as one of the region's hottest destinations. The 2008 Unesco World Heritage declaration sparked a frenzy of cultural preservation that continues to this day, and the city's charismatic shophouses have been turned into house museums, charming boutique hotels and chic cafes. And did we mention that George Town is also home to some of Malaysia's best food? George Town World Heritage Inc. Headquarters (p159)

Cameron Highlands

4 Misty mountains, Tudor-themed architecture, 4WDs, scones, strawberries and tea plantations all converge in this distinctly un-Southeast Asian destination. Activities such as self-guided hiking, nature tours and agricultural tourism make the Cameron Highlands (p134) one of Malaysia's more worthwhile and approachable active destinations. The area also represents a clever escape within a vacation, as the weather in the Cameron Highlands tends to stay mercifully cool year-round.

LAURIE NOBLE/GETTY IMAGES ©

R.M. NUNES/SHUTTERSTOCK ©

Snorkelling, Pulau Perhentian

5 Though eastern Peninsular Malaysia has several islands offering unparalleled underwater activities, amazing Pulau Perhentian (p292) wins flippers-down when it comes to attracting snorkellers. Perhaps it's the water itself: clear and ethereally blue, the seas surrounding Perhentian draw a huge variety of colourful marine life. Coral beds lie close to shore, and on most days you won't have to swim much further than the jetty at Long Beach before finding yourself inside a veritable rainbow cloud of fish of all shapes and sizes.

Mt Kinabalu

6 It is the abode of the spirits, the highest mountain in Malaysia, the dominant geographic feature of northern Borneo, the granite rock that has worn out countless challengers. Mt Kinabalu (p333) is all of this, and one of the most popular tourism attractions in Borneo. Don't worry though, you will still have moments of utter freedom, breathing in the only alpine air in Sabah and, if you're lucky, enjoying a horizon that stretches to the Philippines. Or it will be cloudy. Whatever: the climb is still exhilarating.

Kuching

7 Borneo's most sophisticated and stylish city (p396) brings together an atmospheric old town, aromatic waterfront, fine cuisine for all budgets, and chic nightspots that would be right at home in London. But the city's biggest draw is what's nearby: some of Sarawak's finest natural sites, easy to visit on day trips. You can spot semi-wild orangutans or search out a giant rafflesia flower in the morning, look for proboscis monkeys and wild crocs on a sundown cruise in the South China Sea, and then dine on superfresh seafood or crunchy midin fern tips. Jalan India (p397), Kuching

Chillin' on Pulau Tioman

8 What's your pleasure? Swimming off any of the dozens of serenely beautiful beaches that run north to south along Pulau Tioman's western shore? Challenging the serious surf that pounds the island's eastern beaches at Kampung Juara? If hiking is more your thing, Tioman's myriad trails will challenge your legs, lungs and internal compass. Care to chill out by a waterfall? Swing in a hammock all day with a good book? Or simply do nothing? All of these goals (and others) are infinitely obtainable on Pulau Tioman (p251). Welcome to paradise.

7

ANDREW WATSON/GETTY IMAGES ©

8

DIDIER MARTI/GETTY IMAGES ©

KJORGEN/GETTY IMAGES ©

MATT MUNRO/LONELY PLANET ©

KARL LEHMANN/GETTY IMAGES ©

Sepilok Orangutan Rehabilitation Centre

9 There is no primate quite like the orangutan. These great apes are a stirring combination: brawn and grace; raw power and gentle restraint; stupid amounts of cuteness and even more cuteness. And behind their sparkling eyes, deep reserves of what we can only call wisdom and, sometimes, sadness. All these complicated observations occur at once at the Sepilok Orangutan Rehabilitation Centre (p604), where visitors can see the ginger apes from an (admittedly often crowded) viewing platform, the highlight of many a Sabah trip.

Visiting Longhouses

10 Even though they include some modern amenities, there's no better way to get a sense of indigenous tribal culture than to visit a longhouse – or, better yet, stay overnight. Essentially a whole village under a single roof, these dwellings can be longer than two football pitches and contain dozens of family units, each of which opens onto a covered common verandah used for economic activities, socialising and celebrations. For longhouses least affected by modern life take a boat up the remote Batang Ai (p429). Longhouse in the Batang Ai region (p429)

Trekking, Kelabit Highlands

11 The air is clean and cool, the rice fields impossibly green, the local cuisine scrumptious and the trekking – from longhouse to longhouse – some of the best in Borneo. But the star attraction here is the people, justifiably famous for their ready smiles and easy way with visitors. Getting to Sarawak's remote northeastern corner (p458) is half the fun – you can either bust your butt on logging roads for 12 hours or take an exhilarating flight in a 19-seat Twin Otter turboprop.

12

JASON ISLEY - SCUBAZOO/GETTY IMAGES ©

13

GAVIN HELLIER/ROBERTHARDING/GETTY IMAGES ©

Batu Punggul

12 Not many travellers make it down here, deep in the Borneo interior, near the Maliau Basin Conservation Area (p382; pictured above). Their loss, because Batu Punggul (p386), an incredible rock formation that juts like a limestone knife into the air, and more importantly the primary jungle that surrounds it, is one of the most stunning sites on an island full of jaw-droppers. To get here you will travel via mud rivers, crossing under the canopies of ancient-growth trees. The reward: a sharp-tooth rock that presents a challenge to climbers, and deep travel Zen satisfaction for explorers.

Markets, Kota Bharu

13 A centre for Malaysian crafts, visitors to Kota Bharu (p284) can lose themselves shopping for traditional items such as batik, *kain songket* (handwoven fabric with gold threads), hand-crafted silverware, hand-carved puppets and locally made kites. Both the Central Market and the nearby Bazaar Buluh Kubuh are great places to buy spices, brassware and other local goods. For shoppers inclined to roam, the bikeable road from town to Pantai Cahaya Bulan (PCB) is dotted with factories and workshops dedicated to the creation of crafts of all sorts.

Taman Negara

14 To visit Taman Negara (p271) is to step back in time and experience the land as it was before civilisation came along and replaced primeval jungle with endless rubber trees and palm-oil plantations. Inside this shadowy, nigh-impenetrable jungle, ancient trees with gargantuan buttressed root systems dwarf luminescent fungi, orchids, and rare and beautiful flora. Making their home within are elephants, tigers and leopards, as well as smaller wonders such as flying squirrels, lizards, monkeys, deer, tapirs and serpents of all sorts.

Kampong Ayer

15 Borneo is modernising quickly, but even the most tech-savvy entrepreneur is only a generation removed from the *kampung ayer* (water village). Some grow up in these waterbound communities, and some still choose to live in them. That's the case in the water village (p470) that hugs Brunei's capital of Bandar Seri Begawan, the largest water village in the world. Some residents live humbly, while others park sports cars before catching a water taxi home, a fascinating juxtaposition of nostalgia and development all set on stilts.

CRAIG PERSHOUSE/GETTY IMAGES ©

16

YASMINE AWWAD/GETTY IMAGES ©

17

I'AM/GETTY IMAGES ©

18

PAUL KENNEDY/GETTY IMAGES ©

Melaka's Jonker Walk Night Market

16 The biggest party in Melaka is every Friday and Saturday night when Jln Hang Jebat hosts the massively popular Jonker Walk Night Market (p231). Start by the river across from the pink Stadthuys building that glows in the street lights and make your way through the crowds towards the karaoke stage at Jln Tokong Besi. Along the way you'll pass stalls selling everything from cheap underwear and trinkets to fresh sugarcane juice. Haggle, nibble and maybe stop by the Geographér Cafe (p230) for a cold beer and some people-watching.

Indulgence, Pulau Langkawi

17 Pulau Langkawi (p192) ain't called the Jewel of Kedah for nothin', and its white-sand beaches, isolated resorts, diving opportunities and pristine jungles live up to the metaphor. Cheap booze (Langkawi is duty-free) and a decent restaurant and bar scene provide just a hint of a party scene, while a glut of kid-friendly activities make it a great destination for families. And best of all, it's not just a holiday island – off-the-beaten-track–type exploration will reveal that Pulau Langkawi has managed to retain its endearing *kampung* (village) soul.

Festivals, Batu Caves

18 It's always a very busy and colourful scene at this sacred Hindu shrine, but if you can, time your visit for a holy day. The biggest event is Thaipusam (p108), when hundred of thousands of pilgrims converge on the giant limestone outcrop a few kilometres north of Kuala Lumpur. Guarding the 272 steps that lead up to the main Temple Cave is the 43m gilded statue of Lord Murugan, assisted by a platoon of lively macaques who show little fear in launching raids on tourists' belongings. *Vel kavadi* bearer

Singapore's Museums

19 Among the many things that Singapore does supremely well is its museums, galleries and heritage centres, which shine a light on the cultures and arts of its multi-ethnic population. Joining the outstanding National Museum of Singapore and Asian Civilisations Museum is the new National Gallery Singapore (p492; pictured below). The S$530 million gallery is housed in the historic City Hall and Old Supreme Court, which have been unified by a striking aluminium and glass canopy. Exhibitions draw from its 8000-plus collection of 19th-century and modern Southeast Asian art.

Kuala Lumpur's Chinatown

20 Plumes of smoke curl upwards from smouldering coils of incense, flower garlands hang like pearls from the necks of Hindu statues and the call to prayer punctuates the honk of traffic. The temples and mosques of the city's Hindus, Muslims and Buddhists are crammed shoulder to shoulder in this atmospheric neighbourhood (p51) along the Klang river that epitomises multicultural Malaysia. Don't miss eating at the daytime Madras Lane hawker stalls or savouring the bustle and fun of the night market along Jln Petaling.

Need to Know

For more information, see Survival Guide (p597)

Currency

Malaysian ringgit (RM), Singapore dollar (S$), Brunei dollar (B$)

Language

Bahasa Malaysia, English, Chinese dialects, Tamil

Visas

Generally not required for stays of between 60 days (Malaysia), 90 days (Singapore) and 30 to 90 days (Brunei).

Money

ATMs widely available. Credit cards accepted by most businesses.

Mobile Phones

Local SIM cards can be used in most phones. Other phones must be set to roaming.

Time

GMT/UTC plus eight hours

When to Go

High Season
(Dec–Feb)

- School holidays followed by Chinese New Year inflate prices and mean advance booking of transport and hotel rooms is important.
- It's monsoon season for the east coast of Peninsular Malaysia and western Sarawak.

Shoulder
(Jul–Nov)

- From July to August, vie with visitors escaping the heat of the Gulf States as the region enjoys what it calls Arab Season.
- It's monsoon season down the west coast of Peninsular Malaysia until September.

Low Season
(Mar–Jun)

- Avoid the worst of the rains and humidity.
- The chance to enjoy places without the crush of fellow tourists.

Useful Websites

Tourism Malaysia (www.tourismmalaysia.gov.my) Official national tourist information site.

Your Singapore (www.yoursingapore.com) Official tourism board site.

Brunei Tourism (www.bruneitourism.travel) Oodles of useful information.

Lonely Planet (www.lonelyplanet.com) Information, bookings, forums and more.

Important Numbers

Country code	Malaysia ☎60; Singapore ☎65; Brunei ☎673
International access code	Malaysia & Brunei ☎00; Singapore ☎001
Police	Malaysia & Singapore ☎999; Brunei ☎993
Ambulance & fire	Malaysia ☎994; Singapore ☎995; Brunei ☎991 (ambulance), ☎995 (fire)
Directory assistance	Malaysia ☎103; Singapore ☎100; Brunei ☎113

Exchange Rates

Australia	A$1	RM3.06
Brunei	B$1	RM2.95
Canada	C$1	RM3.30
Europe	€1	RM4.93
Japan	¥100	RM3.67
Singapore	S$1	RM2.95
UK	UK£1	RM6.71
US	US$1	RM4.40

For current exchange rates see www.xe.com

Daily Costs

Budget: Less than RM100

- Dorm bed: RM15–50/S$20–40/B$10–25
- Hawker centres and food-court meals: RM5–7/S$3–5/B$2–6
- Metro ticket: RM1–2.50/S$1.60–2.70

Midrange: RM100–400

- Double room at midrange hotel: RM100–400/S$100–250/B$70
- Two-course meal at midrange restaurant: RM40–60/S$50/B$10
- Cocktails at decent bar: RM30–40/S$20–30

Top End: More than RM400

- Luxury double room: RM450–1000/S$250–500/B$170
- Meal at top restaurant: RM200/S$250/B$20
- Three-day diving course: RM800–1000

Opening Hours

Banks 10am–3pm Monday to Friday, 9.30am–11.30am Saturday

Bars and clubs 5pm–5am

Cafes 8am–10pm

Restaurants noon–2.30pm and 6pm–10.30pm

Shops 9.30am–7pm, malls 10am–10pm

Arriving in Malaysia, Singapore & Brunei

Kuala Lumpur International Airport (p100) Trains (RM35) run every 15 minutes from 5am to 1am; 30 minutes to KL Sentral. Buses (RM10) leave every hour from 5am to 1am; one hour to KL Sentral. Taxis cost from RM75–100; one hour to KL.

Changi International Airport (p557) Frequent MRT train and public and shuttle buses to town from 5.30am to midnight, S$2.50–9. Taxis cost S$20–40, 50% more between midnight and 6am.

Brunei International Airport (p480) Buses (B$1) run frequently to Bandar Seri Begawan until 5.30pm. Taxis cost B$15. Both take around 15 minutes.

Getting Around

Bus There's hardly anywhere you can't get by bus on Peninsular Malaysia and Singapore, but they are more limited on Brunei.

Train and MRT Trains in Malaysia are slower than the bus and have a far less extensive network; still useful for access to a few remote locations. The MRT is the best way to get around Singapore.

Car Good idea to hire one to explore Malaysia and Brunei's hinterlands; avoid using in cities though.

Air Planes go to major cities, islands and more remote destinations.

For much more on **getting around**, see p606.

If You Like...

Amazing Architecture

Khoo Kongsi The most dazzling of George Town's collection of ornate clan houses. (p165)

Petronas Towers The steel-wrapped twin towers are the poster children of contemporary architecture in Malaysia. (p57)

Putrajaya A showcase for Malaysian urban planning and its vaulting architectural ambition. (p113)

Marina Bay Sands An astonishing feat of engineering that's a Singaporean show-stopper. (p530)

Baba House One of Singapore's best-preserved Peranakan heritage homes. (p499)

Stadthuys Melaka landmark that's believed to be the oldest Dutch building in Asia. (p217)

Istana Lama This beautiful black hardwood palace is perched on 99 pillars. (p120)

Temples & Mosques

Sri Veeramakaliamman Temple Dedicated to the goddess Kali, this visually stunning temple is in Singapore's Little India. (p501)

Thean Hou Temple Multilayered, highly decorated Chinese temple with splendid views of Kuala Lumpur. (p65)

Masjid Negara This modernist-style national mosque is where Malaysia's prime ministers are buried. (p62)

Masjid Ubudiah Gold-domed jewel of Kuala Kangsar designed by colonial-era architect AB Hubback. (p147)

Masjid Selat Melaka Best viewed early morning or at dusk, this Melaka mosque appears to float on water. (p224)

Kek Lok Si Temple Buddhist sanctuary watched over by a 36.5m bronze statue of the goddess of mercy. (p170)

Jame'Asr Hassanil Bolkiah Mosque Twenty-nine gold domes and an equally lavish interior at Brunei's biggest mosque. (p473)

Scenic Vistas

Boh Sungei Palas Tea Estate Enjoy your cuppa while gazing over a verdant patchwork of hills and tea plantations. (p139)

Southern Ridges Forest canopy, striking architecture and skyline views on this nature trail along Singapore's south coast. (p512)

Mt Kinabalu You can't beat the view from the top of Malaysia's tallest mountain when skies are clear. (p333)

Penang Hill Look clean across Penang and to the mainland from this cool retreat above George Town. (p166)

Menara Kuala Lumpur An open-air observation deck and revolving restaurant for 360-degree views of the city. (p51)

Panorama Langkawi Ride the cable car to the top of Gunung Machinchang for views across the island. (p193)

Legends, Traditions & Kitsch

Blue Mansion Refurbished George Town mansion that's a fascinating crash course in feng shui and local legend. (p159)

Endau-Rompin National Park While jungle trekking look out for the snaggle-toothed ghost – Malaysia's own yeti. (p447)

Melaka's trishaws Festooned with fairy lights and cartoon cut-outs, these are the glitziest things on three wheels. (p232)

Ancient megaliths These enigmatic rocks are scattered around Negeri Sembilan and Sarawak's Kelabit Highlands. (p120) (p459)

Gelanggang Seni Watch *silat* (a Malay martial art) and shadow-puppet shows at this Kota Bharu cultural centre. (p284)

Top: Gardens by the Bay (p489), Singapore
Bottom: Street art, George Town (p167), Penang

Haw Par Villa Garden of garish statues and dioramas recounting fantastical Chinese folk stories and fables. (p513)

Marvelous Museums

National Museum of Singapore Heritage architecture meets interactive ingenuity at this ode to Singaporean history, culture and food. (p492)

Asian Civilisations Museum An epic journey through the history, beliefs and creativity of the world's largest continent. (p493)

Islamic Arts Museum Marvel at how craftspeople and artists have been inspired by the Muslim faith to produce gorgeous objects. (p60)

Ethnology Museum Kuching storehouse spotlighting Borneo's incredibly rich indigenous cultures. (p397)

Baba & Nyonya Heritage Museum Lavish Peranakan mansion with lively guided tours shining a light on Melaka's past. (p221)

Sabah Museum Ideal introduction to Sabah's ethnicities and environments, with new signage and clear explanations. (p316)

Galleries & Street Art

George Town (p167), **KL** (p65) and **Chinatown, Kuala Terengganu** (p304) Canvases for young creatives.

Sekeping Tenggiri One of the best private collections of Malaysian contemporary art is in this KL guesthouse. (p75)

National Gallery Singapore Two historic buildings were connected and revamped for this major new art house. (p492)

Singapore Art Museum An excellent showcase of Asian contemporary art. (p493)

Gillman Barracks Former military camp transformed into a rambling outpost of galleries amid verdant grounds. (p513)

Melaka's art galleries Browse the small galleries scattered around the Unesco World Heritage district. (p223)

Hin Bus Depot Art Centre Hub for George Town's burgeoning art scene, its open-air areas plastered with street art. (p166)

Crafts & Shopping

Little Penang Street Market Popular open-air craft market held on the last Sunday of the month. (p180)

Orchard Road Megamalls, chic boutiques and retro gems fight for space on Singapore's legendary shopping strip. (p551)

Kuching's Main Bazaar Shop for handmade Dayak crafts, including textiles, baskets and masks. (p409)

National Textiles Museum Admire skilful weaving, embroidery, knitting and batik printing. (p57)

KL's Central Market Former 1930s wet market in an art deco building that's now a top shopping location. (p97)

Publika Innovative, artsy KL mall with several galleries and a monthly crafts market. (p99)

Gardens & Parks

Gardens by the Bay Singapore's new botanic gardens are a triumphant marriage of architecture and horticulture. (p489)

KL Forest Eco Park Traverse the new canopy walkway in this pocket of primary rainforest. (p51)

Perdana Botanical Garden Dating back to the 1880s, this serene park has sections devoted to orchids and hibiscus. (p62)

Art & Garden by Fuan Wong Weird and wonderful plants combine with contemporary art in this unique Penang garden. (p187)

Tropical Spice Garden Another Penang-based oasis, showcasing the region's rich crop of edible botanicals. (p185)

Taman Tasik Taiping Glide in a swan-shaped boat across this lush garden crafted from an old tin mine. (p149)

Island Escapes

Pulau Pangkor Laze on the beaches of this little-visited island on Malaysia's west coast. (p141)

Pulau Tioman Its steep green peaks are surrounded by turquoise, coral-rich waters. (p251)

Pulau Kapas Go beachcombing and snorkelling on this lovely east coast island. (p303)

Pulau Tinggi An extinct volcano that's part of the beautiful Seribuat Archipelago of 64 islands. (p446)

Tunku Abdul Rahman National Park Hop between the five islands that are easily accessible from Kota Kinabalu. (p330)

Semporna Archipelago A diver's delight and home to the floating communities of Sea Gypsies. (p372)

Incredible Caves

Ramayana Cave The most psychedelic and visually enjoyable cavern at the Batu Caves. (p107)

Ipoh's Temple Caves Remarkable Buddhist temple trio that can be easily seen on a half-day tour. (p129)

Stepping Stone Cave A narrow corridor through a limestone wall leads to a hidden grotto at this Kelantan cave. (p291)

Taman Negeri Perlis Park riddled with caves, rich in wildlife and home to Malaysia's only semideciduous forest. (p214)

Gunung Mulu National Park Explore caverns of mind-boggling proportions. (p453)

Niah National Park The caves here are a netherworld of stalactites and bats. (p442)

Gomantong Caves Cathedral-like chamber swarming with bats, cockroaches, scorpions and swiftlets. (p360)

Animal Encounters

Singapore Zoo (p509) and **Night Safari** (p510) Possibly the world's best zoo, with wildlife living in open-air enclosures.

KL Bird Park Fabulous aviary with some 200 species flying beneath an enormous canopy. (p60)

Cherating (p266), **Pulau Tioman** (p254) and **Perhentians** (p294) Do your bit to save the endangered turtles.

Kota Kinabalu Wetland Centre Mud lobsters, turtles, water monitors and a stunning variety of migratory birds. (p317)

Sepilok (p604), **Shangri La Rasa Ria Resort** (p344) and **Semenggoh Wildlife Centre** (p419) View cute ginger orangutans.

Month by Month

TOP EVENTS

Thaipusam, January or February

Chinese New Year, January or February

Hungry Ghost Festival, August

Chingay, February

George Town Festival, August

January

New Year is a busy travel period. It's monsoon season on Malaysia's east coast and Sarawak.

Thaipusam

Enormous crowds converge at the Batu Caves north of Kuala Lumpur (KL), Nattukotai Chettiar Temple in Penang and in Singapore for this dramatic Hindu festival involving body piercing. Falls between mid-January and mid-February. (p108)

February

Chinese New Year is a big deal throughout the region and a busy travel period. Book transport and hotels well ahead.

Chinese New Year

Dragon dances and pedestrian parades mark the start of the new year. Families hold open house. Celebrated on 28 January 2017, 16 February 2018 and 5 February 2019.

Chingay

Singapore's biggest street parade (www.chingay.org.sg), a flamboyant, multicultural event, falls on the 22nd day after Chinese New Year.

April

Petronas Malaysian Grand Prix

Formula 1's first big outing of the year in Southeast Asia is held at the Sepang International Circuit over three days, usually at the start of the month or end of March. Associated events and parties are held in KL.

May

Wesak (Vesak) Day

Buddha's birth, enlightenment and death are celebrated with processions in KL, Singapore and other major cities, plus various events including the release of caged birds to symbolise the setting free of captive souls. Celebrated on 10 May 2017 and 29 May 2018.

June

School holidays and one of the hottest months so get ready to sweat it out. Ramadan is also observed through most of this month in 2017 and 2018.

Gawai Dayak

Held on 1 and 2 June but beginning on the evening of 31 May, this Sarawak-wide Dayak festival celebrates the end of the rice-harvest season.

Dragon Boat Festival

Commemorates the Malay legend of the fishermen who paddled out to sea to prevent the drowning of a Chinese saint, beating drums to scare away any fish that might attack him. Celebrated from June to August, with boat races in Penang.

Hari Raya Aidilfitri

The end of Ramadan is followed by a month of breaking-the-fast parties, many public occasions where you can enjoy a free array of Malay culinary delicacies. The Malaysian prime minister opens his official home in Putrajaya to the public. (p584)

July

Busy travel month for Malaysian Borneo so book ahead for activities, tours and accommodation.

Rainforest World Music Festival

A three-day musical extravaganza (www.rainforestmusic-borneo.com) held in the Sarawak Cultural Village near Kuching in the 2nd week of July.

Singapore Food Festival

This month-long celebration of food includes events, cooking classes and food-themed tours.

Sultan of Brunei's Birthday

Colourful official ceremonies (www.royalbirthday.org.bn) are held on 15 July to mark the Sultan's birthday and include an elaborate military ceremony presided over by the supremo himself.

August

With a big influx of Arab and Europeans tourists to the region during this time, it pays to book ahead for specific accommodation.

George Town Festival

This outstanding arts, performance and culture festival (http://georgetown-festival.com) in Penang includes international artists, innovative street performances and also has a fringe component in Butterworth on the mainland.

Singapore National Day

Held on 9 August (though dress rehearsals on the two prior weekends are almost as popular), Singapore National Day (www.ndp.org.sg) includes military parades, fly-overs and fireworks.

Hungry Ghost Festival

Chinese communities perform operas, host open-air concerts and lay out food for their ancestors. Celebrated towards the end of the month and in early September.

Malaysia's National Day

Join the crowds at midnight on 31 August to celebrate the anniversary of Malaysia's independence in 1957. The 60th anniversary in 2017 will be a big one with parades and festivities the next morning across the country.

September

Haze from forest and field clearance fires in Indonesia create urban smog across the region.

Singtel Singapore Grand Prix

It's Singapore's turn to host the Formula 1 crowd with a night race (www.singaporegp.sg) on a scenic city-centre circuit. Book well in advance for hotel rooms with a view.

October

Start of the monsoon season on Malaysia's west coast, but it's not so heavy or constant to affect most travel plans.

Deepavali

Tiny oil lamps are lit outside Hindu homes to attract the auspicious gods Rama and Lakshmi. Indian businesses start the new financial year, with Little Indias across the region ablaze with lights.

December

A sense of festivity (and monsoon rains in Singapore and east coast Malaysia) permeates the air as the year winds down. Christmas is a big deal mainly in Singapore with impressive light displays on Orchard Rd.

Zoukout

Held on Siloso Beach, Sentosa, this annual outdoor dance party (www.zoukout.com) is one of the region's best such events with a 25,000-strong crowd bopping to international DJs.

Itineraries

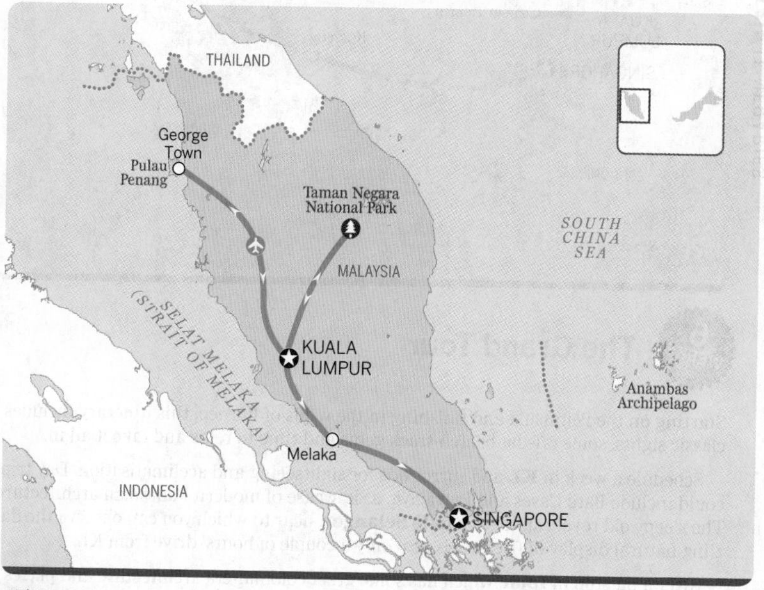

2 WEEKS Essential Malaysia & Singapore

This itinerary cherry-picks the best of the two countries with a focus on urban adventures but also with the chance to experience the region's amazing biodiversity.

Spend your first three days in Malaysia's capital **Kuala Lumpur (KL)**, where you can explore cultural diversity in Chinatown, marvel at the soaring steel-clad Petronas Towers and discover the treasures of the Islamic Arts Museum.

Next head inland to **Taman Negara National Park**. Even on a two-day visit to this magnificent national park you can clamber across the canopy walkway and do some short jungle hikes. Return to KL and hop on a flight to Penang where three days will give you a good taste of the Unesco World Heritage districts of **George Town** and other island highlights such as Kek Lok Si Temple.

Historic **Melaka**, another Unesco World Heritage Site, deserves a couple of nights but visit midweek to avoid the crowds. Then head across the causeway to **Singapore** where you can spend your final four days enjoying everything from maxing out your credit card at glitzy shopping malls and sampling delicious hawker food to visiting the eye-boggling space age architecture of Marina Bay and the excellent zoo and night safari.

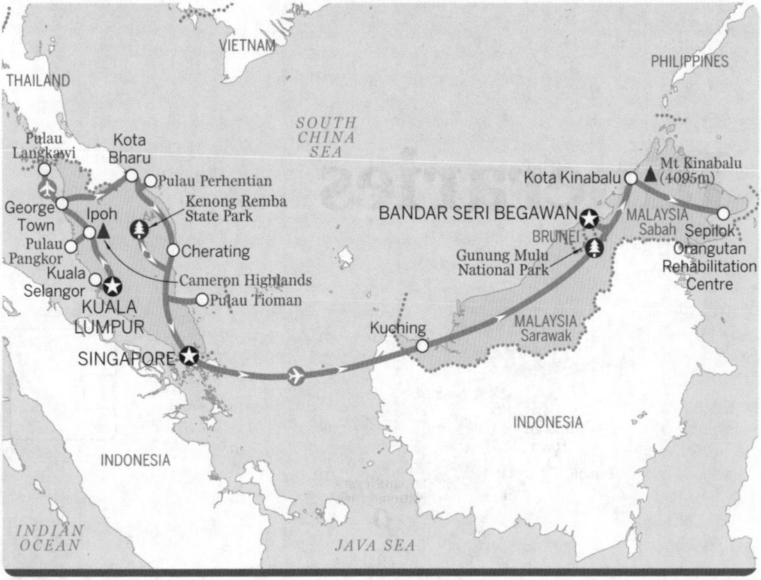

6 WEEKS

The Grand Tour

Starting on the Peninsula and finishing in the wilds of Borneo, this itinerary includes classic sights, some off-the-beaten-track gems and time to relax and take it all in.

Schedule a week in **KL** and surrounds for sightseeing and acclimatisation. Day trips could include Batu Caves and Putrajaya, a showcase of modern Malaysian architecture. The sleepy old royal capital of **Kuala Selangor**, near to which you can observe the dazzling natural display of fireflies, is also only a couple of hours' drive from KL.

After a pit stop in **Ipoh**, which has some great colonial-era architecture and places to eat, your second week is spent in the cooler climate of the **Cameron Highlands**, where you can take walks past verdant tea plantations. Return to the coast and hop across to **Pulau Pangkor**.

The urban delights of **George Town**, on Penang, are up next; the city's Unesco World Heritage district is packed with colourful, fascinating sights. This large island is also Malaysia's number-one food destination. A quick flight away are the resorts, gorgeous beaches and jungle hinterlands of **Pulau Langkawi**.

Into week four and it's time to cross the mountainous spine of the peninsula to **Kota Bharu**, a great place to encounter traditional Malay culture. Island- and beach-hop down the east coast, pausing at **Pulau Perhentian**, **Cherating** and **Pulau Tioman**. **Kenong Rimba State Park** offers jungle adventures without the crowds.

Singapore can easily swallow up a week of shopping, museum-viewing and world-class eating. From here you can fly to **Kuching** in Sarawak, a good base for a longhouse excursion or for arranging a trek in **Gunung Mulu National Park**. Rack up the visa stamps by taking the overland and river route from Sarawak to Sabah via Brunei, stopping in the capital **Bandar Seri Begawan**.

Having made it to Sabah's capital **Kota Kinabalu (KK)**, your final challenge, should you choose to accept it, is to climb **Mt Kinabalu**. Alternatively, it's difficult to resist the chance to eyeball close up the supercute ginger apes at **Sepilok Orangutan Rehabilitation Centre**.

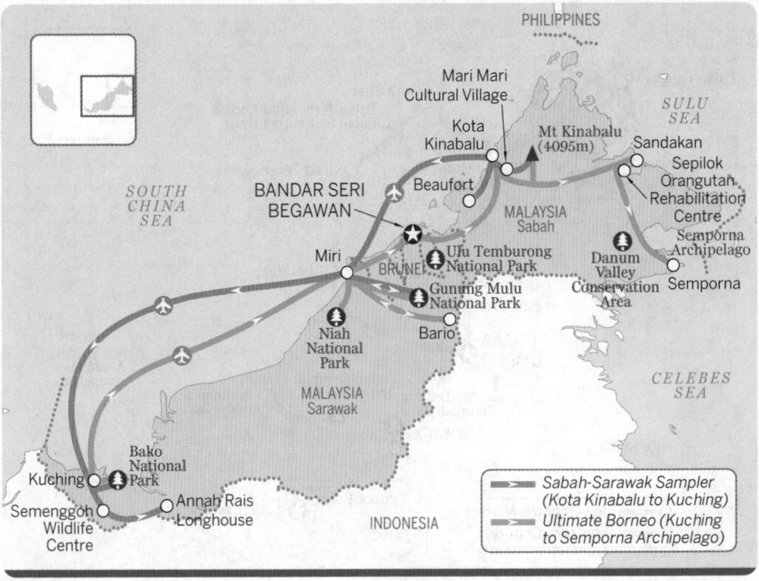

2 WEEKS Sabah–Sarawak Sampler

This abridged itinerary for the time-challenged offers a sample of the best of Malaysian Borneo, including top national parks, snaking rivers and time spent lounging on longhouse verandahs.

Start in **KK**, which encapsulates Southeast Asian city life on a manageable scale and where you'll be obliged to spend a day or two sorting permits to tackle Sabah's star attraction, **Mt Kinabalu**. Consider a day-trip cruise (including buffet dinner) down one of the tea-brown rivers in the **Beaufort Division**, or learn a little about the local culture at the **Mari Mari Cultural Village**.

Leapfrog by plane from KK to **Miri** and then on to **Gunung Mulu National Park**, home to the world's largest caves, and several challenging jungle treks, including the marathon Headhunters Trail. Pass through Miri once more for a flight down to **Kuching**. Sarawak's capital is a real charmer and will easily keep you occupied for several days. Break up your time in town with a visit to **Semenggoh Wildlife Centre**, **Bako National Park** and, if you have time, to a longhouse such as **Annah Rais Longhouse**.

4 WEEKS Ultimate Borneo

On this grand tour of Borneo tackle the island's top five treks and enjoy some world-class diving and snorkelling plus encounters with endangered wildlife.

From **Kuching** explore the local longhouses and **Bako National Park**. Fly to **Miri**, which is the base for trips to the impressive **Niah National Park**; **Gunung Mulu National Park** for more caves, the heart-pumping trek to the Pinnacles and along the Headhunters Trail; and **Bario**, in the vine-draped Kelabit Highlands.

Travel overland to **Bandar Seri Begawan**, Brunei's friendly capital. Also schedule in the sultanate's **Ulu Temburong National Park**, a pristine sliver of primary rainforest.

Chill out in **KK** before setting your sights on **Mt Kinabalu**. Catch some ape love in **Sepilok Orangutan Rehabilitation Centre**, followed by a layover in historic **Sandakan**. The mighty Sungai Kinabatangan offers wildlife enthusiasts plenty of photo fodder. If you've got the time trek through the **Danum Valley Conservation Area**. The magnificent dive sites of the **Semporna Archipelago** accessed from **Semporna** provide an ideal climax.

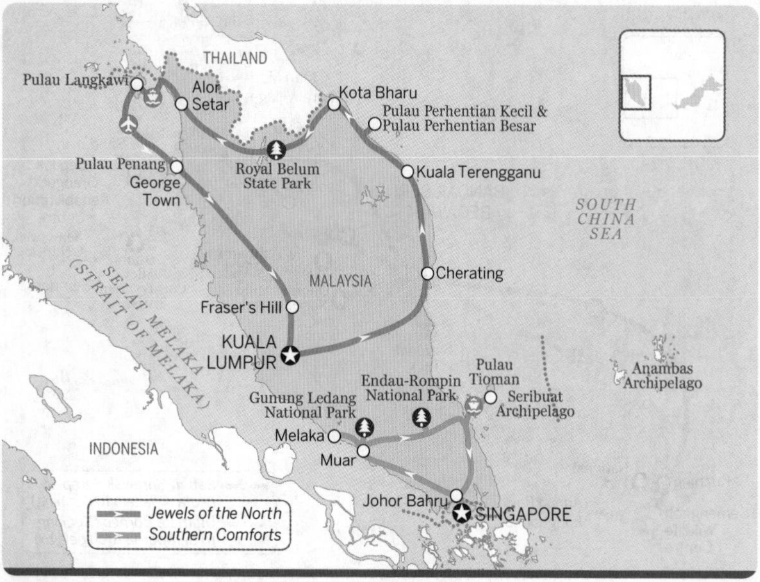

3 WEEKS Jewels of the North

Idyllic islands, Malay culture, rainforests and hill stations all feature on this tour around the north of Peninsula Malaysia.

Explore **KL** for a few days before heading to the east coast resort of **Cherating**. Move on to **Kuala Terengganu**, with its pretty Chinatown and the Kompleks Muzium Negeri Terengganu.

Next come the classic Perhentian islands, accessed from Kuala Besut. **Pulau Perhentian Besar** tends to be less crowded and just as gorgeous as its more popular twin, **Pulau Perhentian Kecil**. Back on the mainland, linger a day or two in **Kota Bharu**, for its museums, cultural events and night market, then head to the remote **Royal Belum State Park** in northern Perak.

Access more Malay culture in Kedah's capital **Alor Setar** before taking the ferry from Kuala Perlis to **Pulau Langkawi** for sunbathing, island-hopping and jungle exploration. Fly to **George Town**, the essential stop on Penang, then cool down in the hill station of **Fraser's Hill** (Bukit Fraser) before returning to KL.

3 WEEKS Southern Comforts

The southern end of Peninsular Malaysia is no slouch in offering up a diverse range of travel experiences, plus there's easy access to and from **Singapore**, the logical start and finish to this trip.

Leave yourself several days to soak up the island state's manifold attractions. If you're strapped for cash then **Johor Bahru**, just across the causeway, is a cheaper base. It's a decent hangout, not least for street food and duty-free booze.

The lethargic riverside town of **Muar** has a colonial-era district that's worth a look, and can be used as a base for assaults on Gunung Ledang, Johor's highest mountain, located within the **Gunung Ledang National Park**. Recover in Unesco World Heritage–listed **Melaka**, where you can spend several days enjoying the enduring Portuguese and Dutch influence.

Explore the last-remaining stands of lowland forest on the peninsula in **Endau-Rompin National Park**. Stunning **Pulau Tioman** is the epitome of an island paradise. Alternatively, indulge in some island-hopping and diving around the 64 gems of the **Seribuat Archipelago**.

Plan Your Trip

Outdoor Adventures

The region's national and state parks offer everything from easy-going nature trails to challenging hikes into the heart of virgin rainforests. There are also mountains to climb, caves to explore and tropical seas teeming with marine life to dive, as well as other aquatic-based activities such as surfing and white-water rafting.

Hiking

Fancy seeing what life might have been like 100 million years ago? Hiking into the deepest parts of the region's jungles will give you a clue as they were largely unaffected by the far-reaching climatic changes brought on elsewhere by the Ice Age. Significant chunks of these rainforests have been made into national parks, in which all commercial activities apart from tourism are banned.

The British established the region's first national park in Malaya in 1938. That was the basis for what is now Taman Negara (p271), the crowning glory of Malaysia's network of national parks, which crosses the borders of Terengganu, Kelantan and Pahang. In addition to this and the 27 other national and state parks across the country (23 of them located in Malaysian Borneo), there are various government-protected reserves and sanctuaries for forests, birds, mammals and marine life. Even in the heart of KL it's possible to stretch your legs in the KL Forest Eco Park (p51); alternatively, head a little north of the city to find a gorgeous network of forest trails and the tree-top canopy walkway at the Forestry Research Institute of Malaysia (p108).

Only 1 sq km of Brunei's 500-sq-km Ulu Temburong National Park (p486) is accessible to the public but what a treat it presents being one of the most pristine

Best Outdoors

Best Jungle Hikes

Taman Negara (p271), Maliau Basin (p382), Kelabit Highlands (p462), Endau-Rompin National Park (p247), Ulu Temburong National Park (p486)

Best Mountain Climbing

Mt Kinabalu (p335), Gunung Ledang (p242), Gunung Mulu (p452), Gunung Tahan (p273), Mt Trus Madi (p385)

Best Diving & Snorkelling

Semporna Archipelago (p372), Pulau Perhentian (p292), Pulau Redang (p301), Pulau Tioman (p251), Seribuat Archipelago (p245)

Best Caving

Gunung Mulu National Park (p453), Niah National Park (p442), Gomantong Caves (p360), Wind Cave Nature Reserve (p424)

slices of rainforest in the region. Even Singapore offers up trekking possibilities: the country's National Parks Board manages 10% of the island's total land area, which comprises over 300 parks and four nature reserves, including Bukit Timah Nature Reserve (p510).

When to Go

The region has wet months and less wet months. Global warming has also affected the monsoons so that year to year precipitation varies widely. In short, no matter where you go and when, you're likely to get wet – and if not from rain then certainly from sweating!

What is seasonal, however, is the number of other travellers you'll be competing with for experienced guides and lodgings. Northern hemisphere residents often come to the region during the summer holidays in their home countries, so if you plan to trek in July or August book a tour far in advance. Also watch out for regional travel high points such as Chinese New Year holidays and the so-called Golden Week of holidays that Japanese people usually take in late April or early May.

TOP WILDLIFE SPOTS

Taman Negara (p271) National Park Malaysia's oldest and most prestigious national park is home to everything from fireflies to elephants.

Royal Belum State Park (p154) Home to 10 varieties of hornbill and the majority of Malaysia's big mammals.

Sungai Kinabatangan (p360) Spot wild orangutans and pygmy elephants along the banks of Sabah's longest river.

Bako National Park (p413) The park's coves and trails are one of the best places to spot proboscis monkeys.

Singapore Zoo (p509) One of the world's best, along with the Night Safari and the newer River Safari experience.

Ulu Temburong National Park (p486) Breathtaking views from canopy walkway in Brunei's Temburong region.

Permits, Guides & Bookings

Many of the region's national parks and natural beauty spots charge a nominal entrance fee (around RM10). At a few, if you wish to trek or engage in other activities such as fishing or mountain climbing, then there may be additional permits to purchase and guides to hire. In particular, Mt Kinabalu (p333) has stringent visitor regulations, as does Gunung Mulu National Park (p452).

Accommodation is generally not a problem when visiting most national parks. Various types are available, from hostel to luxury resorts. Transport and accommodation operations are increasingly being handled by private tour companies, who require you to book in advance and pay a deposit.

Many national parks have well-marked day trails and can be walked unaccompanied. But for almost all overnights, only a fool would set out without a local guide. Remember, trail maps of any sort are completely unavailable and signage along remote trail networks is nonexistent. A good guide will be able to gauge your abilities and push you a little, rather than taking the easiest way as a matter of course. Try a shorter guided hike before setting off on an overnight adventure to get a sense of how you fare in tropical trekking conditions.

Especially in Sabah, Brunei and Sarawak, the national parks are very strict about allowing only licensed guides. We've heard stories of groups being turned back when they arrived with an uncertified leader. Before you fork over any cash, compare notes with other travellers and ask to see the guide's national-park certification.

Guides for day walks can sometimes be hired at national park HQ, but for overnights you'll need to contact either a freelance guide or a tour agency. Budget anything from RM50 to RM200 per day for a guide depending on the duration and difficulty of the trek you are planning.

Mountain & Rock Climbing

Towering above the forests of Borneo are some brilliant mountains. Even nonclimbers know about 4095m Mt Kinabalu, the

RESPONSIBLE HIKING

Jungle hiking can be one of the highlights of a trip to the region. However, to the uninitiated, it can be something of a shock – like marching all day in a sauna with a pile of bricks strapped to your back. To make the experience as painless as possible, it's necessary to make some preparations:

- On overnight trips, bring two sets of clothing, one for walking and one to wear at the end of the day (always keep your night kit separate and dry in a plastic bag). Within minutes of starting, your hiking kit will be drenched and will stay that way throughout your trip.
- If you'll be passing through dense vegetation, wear long trousers and a long-sleeved shirt. Otherwise, shorts and a T-shirt will suffice. Whatever you wear, make sure it's loose-fitting.
- Bring fast-drying synthetic clothes. Once cotton gets wet, it won't dry until you take it to the laundry back in town.
- It can be cool in the evening, so bring a fleece top to keep warm.
- Unless you like a lot of ankle support, consider hiking in running shoes with good traction. You could also go local and buy a pair of 'kampung Adidas' – a Malaysian jungle version of a hiking shoe, shaped like an Adidas soccer cleat but made out of rubber (like a souped-up Croc). They're cheap (under RM10 a pair) and popular with porters and guides.
- Buy a pair of light-coloured leech socks – they're not easy to come by in the region so buy them online before coming.
- Drink plenty of water. If you're going long distances, you'll have to bring either a water filter or a water-purification agent like iodine (most people opt for the latter to keep pack weight down).
- Get in shape long before coming to the region and start slowly, with day hikes before longer treks.
- Always go with a guide unless you're on a well-marked, commonly travelled trail.
- Wear loose underwear to help prevent chafing. Bring talcum powder to cope with the chafing caused by wet undergarments.
- If you wear glasses, treat them with an antifog solution (ask at the shop where you buy your glasses).
- Consider putting something waterproof over the back padding to keep the sweat out of your pack, or consider a waterproof stuff sack.
- Keep your camera in a waterproof container, with a pouch of silica gel or other desiccant.
- Pack sunscreen, insect repellent, a water bottle and a torch (preferably a head-lamp to keep your hands free).

The following points are also worth bearing in mind if you're planning a mountaineering or caving adventure:

- Hire a local guide – it's the best way to make sure you're in touch with local customs and concerns as you move through tribal lands.
- Follow the golden rule of rubbish: if you carried it in, carry it out. Never bury your rubbish – it may be out of sight, but it won't be out of reach of animals.
- Where there isn't a toilet, bury your waste in a small hole 15cm deep and at least 100m from any watercourse. Use toilet paper sparingly and cover everything with soil and a rock.
- Always stick to the marked trails, however indistinct they may be. Carving your own path through the jungle can disrupt local people, not to mention plants and wildlife.

ROBBIE SHONE/GETTY IMAGES ©

Caves in Gunung Mulu National Park (p452)

highest peak between the Himalayas and the island of New Guinea. This craggy monster simply begs to be climbed, and there is something magical about starting the ascent in humid tropical jungle and emerging into a bare, rocky alpine zone so cold that snow has been known to fall. But beyond the transition from hot to cold, it's the weird world of the summit plateau that makes Mt Kinabalu among the world's most interesting peaks. It's got a dash of Yosemite and a pinch of Torres del Paine, but at the end of the day, it's pure Borneo.

Sabah's second-highest peak, Mt Trus Madi (2642m), is a far more difficult peak to ascend than Mt Kinabalu – and a more difficult trip to arrange.

Gunung Mulu (2376m) isn't quite as high but it's almost as famous, thanks in part to being a Unesco World Heritage Site. If you're a real glutton for punishment, you'll probably find the five-day return trek to the summit of this peak to your liking. Those who make the journey experience a variety of pristine natural environments, starting with lowland dipterocarp forest and ending with rhododendron and montane forest.

Pulau Berhala in the Sandakan Archipelago is also a prime destination for rock climbers; Fieldskills Adventures (p321) arranges rock climbing tours here.

On the peninsula, Gunung Ledang (1276m) is a good introduction to tropical mountaineering. There are also several good climbs in Taman Negara, including Gunung Tahan (2187m), an expedition that can take between seven to nine days. At Juara on Pulau Tioman there's also a rock-climbing operation.

Costs

Guide fees could be anything between RM100 and RM200 per day. There will also be national park entry fees (RM1 to RM15) and climbing permits (RM106 in the case of Mt Kinabalu) to consider.

Pre-Trip Preparations

Climbing one of Malaysia's mountains is like a jungle trek except more – more physically exhausting, more psychologically challenging and especially more vertical. Be prepared for ascents that turn your legs to rubber and much colder weather.

As with longer treks, book well ahead. Many of the agencies that handle trekking also offer mountain ascents. Some of the more experienced guides in Sarawak's Kelabit Highlands can take you to two rarely climbed peaks: Batu Lawi and Gunung Murud.

Keen mountain climbers may want to search out a copy of *Mountains of Malaysia – A Practical Guide and Manual* (1988) by John Briggs. Online resources include Climb Malaysia (www.climb.my).

Caving

Slice one of Malaysia's limestone hills in half and chances are you'll find that inside it looks like Swiss cheese. Malaysians have been living, harvesting birds' nests, planning insurgencies and burying their dead in these *gua* (caves) for tens of thousands of years. These days, the country's subterranean spaces – including some of the largest caverns anywhere on earth – are quiet, except for the flow of underground streams, the drip of stalactites and the whoosh of the wings of swiftlets and bats.

Sarawak's Gunung Mulu National Park is a place of spelunking superlatives. It's got the world's second-largest cave passage (the Deer Cave, 2km in length and 174m in height), the world's largest cave chamber (the Sarawak Chamber, 700m long, 400m wide and 70m high) and Asia's longest cave (the Clearwater Cave, 107km in length). Several of the park's caves are – like their counterparts in Niah National Park – accessible to nonspelunkers: you can walk through them on well-maintained walkways.

Other caves open to the public include the Dark Cave at the Batu Caves; various caverns in and around Gunung Stong State Park; those in Taman Negara; and the Gomantong Caves in Sabah.

Pre-Trip Preparations

A pitch-black passageway deep in the bowels of the earth is not the ideal place to discover that you can't deal with narrow, confined spaces. Before heading underground, seriously consider your susceptibility to claustrophobia and fear of heights (some caves require scaling underground cliffs). If you have any concerns about a specific route, talk with your guide beforehand.

Be prepared to crawl through muck, including bat guano, and bring clothes you won't mind getting filthy (some guides and agencies supply these).

MALAYSIA'S TOP 10 NATIONAL & STATE PARKS

PARK	FEATURES	ACTIVITIES	BEST TIME TO VISIT
Bako	beaches, proboscis monkeys	coastline walks, trekking	May-Sep
Batang Ai	primary forest crawling with wild orangutans	trekking	year-round
Endau-Rompin	lowland forest, unique plants, waterfalls and rivers	trekking, wildlife spotting	Apr-Sep
Gunung Mulu	caves, the Pinnacles, Headhunters Trail	caving, trekking, mountain climbing	May-Sep
Kinabalu	Mt Kinabalu	mountain climbing	May-Sep
Niah	caves	caving, trekking	May-Sep
Penang	meromictic lake, monkeys	trekking	Apr-Jul
Perlis	Gua Wang Burma cave, stump-tailed macaques, Malaysia's only semi-deciduous forest	caving, trekking	Jun-Aug
Taman Negara	canopy walkway, hides, jungle trails, rivers	trekking, wildlife-spotting, river trips	Apr-Sep
Tun Sakaran	sand-fringed islands, technicolour reefs	snorkelling, diving	year-round

Aquatic Adventures

Diving & Snorkelling

Reasonable prices, an excellent variety of dive sites and easy access make Malaysia a great diving choice for both first-timers and old hands. Island-based boat dives are the most common, but a few areas, like Sabah's Pulau Sipadan, have some cracking sites right off the beach. You may also come across live-aboard boats to get you to more remote spots.

The standards of diving facilities in Malaysia are generally quite high and equipment rental is widely available. Most places offer the universally recognised Professional Association of Diving Instructors (PADI) certification.

When to Go

The northeast monsoon brings strong winds and rain to the east coast of Peninsular Malaysia from early November to late February, during which time most dive centres simply shut down. Visibility improves after the monsoon, peaking in August and September. On the west coast conditions are reversed and the best diving is from September to March. In Malaysian Borneo the monsoons are less pronounced and rain falls more evenly throughout the year, making diving a year-round activity.

Costs

Most dive centres charge around RM200 to RM300 for two dives, including equipment rental. A three-dive day trip at Sipadan costs between RM250 and RM500 (check whether park fees are included). PADI open-water courses range from RM800 to RM1200. Many resorts and dive operators also offer all-inclusive dive packages, which vary widely in price.

Pre- & Post-Trip

While it is possible simply to show up and dive at some of the larger dive centres like Pulau Tioman, it's a good idea to make arrangements in advance, if only to avoid waiting a day or two before starting. Diving at Sipadan is capped at 120 divers per day; book in advance.

Note that it is unsafe to dive directly after flying due to poorly pressurised cabins and dehydration. It's also a serious health risk to fly within 24 hours of your last dive.

Kayaking & White-Water Rafting

Malaysia's mountains plus rainforests equal fast-flowing rivers, which result in ideal opportunities for river-rafting and kayaking enthusiasts.

On the peninsula, Kuala Kubu Bharu has become the white-water hot spot, with rafting and kayaking organised along the Sungai Selangor; Pierose Swiftwater (p112) is a reputable company.

In Gopeng on Sungai Kampar, 20 minutes' drive north of Ipoh, rafting trips and other outdoor adventures are offered at **My Gopeng Resort** (☑016-549 3777, 05-242

RESPONSIBLE DIVING

Consider the following tips when diving or snorkelling, and help preserve the ecology and beauty of the reefs:

➡ Do not use anchors on the reef, and take care not to ground boats on coral.

➡ Avoid touching living marine organisms with your body, or dragging equipment across the reef.

➡ Be conscious of your fins. Clouds of sand or even the surge from heavy fin strokes can damage delicate organisms.

➡ Major damage can be done by divers descending too fast and colliding with the reef, so practice buoyancy control across your trip.

➡ Resist the temptation to collect (or buy) coral or shells from reefs of dive sites. Some sites are even protected from looting by law.

➡ Ensure that you take home all your rubbish and any litter you may find.

➡ Don't feed the fish; this can disturb their habits or be detrimental to their health.

3777; www.mygopengresort.com; per person RM150-288).

White-water rafting has become quite the craze in Sabah, with Kota Kinabalu-based operators taking travellers south of the city to the Beaufort Division for some Grade III to IIII rapids on the Sungai Padas (Padas River). Calmer water at Sungai Kiulu near Mt Kinabalu is a tamer option for beginners.

Kayaking is offered by **Kuching Kayak** (☎082-253005; www.kuchingkayak.com; 269 Jln Padungan) and Borneo Trek & Kayak Adventure (http://rainforestkayaking.com) in Kuching.

Boating

Yachting clubs offer chances for those interested in a sailing trip around the region or learning how to sail, including **Royal Langkawi Yacht Club** (☎04-966 4078; www.langkawiyachtclub.com), Kuah; **Royal Selangor Yacht Club** (☎03-3168 6964; www.rsyc.com.my), Pelabuhan Klang; and Avillion Admiral Cove (p121), Port Dickson.

Boating adventures can also be had on the region's lakes, rivers and mangrove-lined estuaries. Taking a sundown boat ride through the mangroves of Kuching Wetlands National Park to spot crocodiles and fireflies can be a magical experience. Firefly-spotting boat trips out of Kuala Selangor are also popular.

On larger rivers, transport is by 'flying coffin' – long, narrow passenger boats with about 70 seats, not including the people sitting on the roof. Thanks to their powerful engines, these craft can power upriver against very strong currents.

BIRDWATCHING

Malaysia's tropical jungles and islands are home to over 600 species of bird. The following are principal twitching destinations:

- ➡ Bako National Park (p413)
- ➡ Cape Rachado Forest Reserve (p121)
- ➡ Endau-Rompin National Park (p247)
- ➡ Fraser's Hill (p110)
- ➡ Gunung Mulu National Park (p453)
- ➡ Kenong Rimba State Park (p278)
- ➡ Lambir Hills National Park (p444)
- ➡ Mt Kinabalu (p338)
- ➡ Royal Belum State Park (p154)
- ➡ Taman Negara (p271)

Surfing

Malaysia is no Indonesia when it comes to surfing, but Cherating and Juara on Pulau Tioman in Malaysia receive a steady stream of surfers during the monsoon season when the swells are up. You can also rent paddleboards in Tioman and Cherating, kitesurfing gear in Cherating and take courses in all of those sports in both locations.

Although the blog hasn't been updated for a while, Surfing in Malaysia (http://surfingmalaysia.blogspot.com.au) has useful links to other sources of information for surfers.

Plan Your Trip

Eat Like a Local

Eating like a local in Malaysia, Singapore and Brunei is a snap. The food is absolutely delicious, hygiene standards are among the highest in Southeast Asia and most vendors speak English. And an almost perverse obsession with food among the locals means that visitors are often smothered in culinary companionship.

The Year in Food

As might be expected of a people consumed with food and its pleasures, Singaporeans, Malaysians and Bruneians mark every special occasion with celebratory edibles.

Chinese New Year (January/February)

In the weeks leading to Chinese New Year, every table is graced with *yue sang* (*yee sang* or *yu sheng;* 'fresh fish'), a mound of grated raw vegetables, pickles, pomelo pieces and crispy, fried-dough pieces topped with sliced raw fish.

Ramadan (June/August)

During Ramadan special food markets swing into action in the late afternoons, offering a wide variety of Malay treats.

Deepavali (October/November)

During the Indian Festival of Lights, make your way to a Little India, where you'll find special sweets such as *jalebi* (deep-fried fritters soaked in sugar syrup) and savoury snacks like *muruku* (crispy fried coils of curry-leaf-studded dough).

Food Experiences

Meals of a Lifetime

Teksen, George Town (p176) Shophouse-bound legend that does nearly faultless Chinese and Chinese/Malay fare.

Lim Ko Pi, Ipoh (p129) Both atmosphere and menu are equally nostalgic at this old-town restaurant in Ipoh; choose from well-executed *nasi lemak* (rice cooked in coconut milk served with sides), caramel-scented stewed pork and a smooth dessert custard.

Seng Huat Bak Kut Teh, Klang (p116) Slurp down a lightly flavored bowl of the famous and eponymous pork-rib soup in the town where it originated.

Night Market, Kota Bharu (p288) KB's evening food hub specialises in busy stalls selling spicy *ayam percik* (marinated chicken on bamboo skewers).

Alu-Alu Cafe, Kota Kinabalu (p325) The restaurant sources its delicious seafood from sustainable sources – no shark fin here.

Rebung, Kuala Lumpur (p90) The next best thing to Malay home cooking is the expansive buffet of Malay specialities at this rustically charming restaurant.

Dyak, Kuching (p407) Traditional Dayak home cooking and fresh jungle produce transformed into unusual dishes such as chicken with tapioca leaves, or pork intestines with pineapple.

Madame Bee's Kitchen, Kuala Terengganu (p308) In KT's compact Chinatown, laksa Terengganu (spicy noodle soup) is served in this heritage Peranakan shophouse.

Siti Fatimah, Langkawi (p206) One plate just isn't enough at this seemingly never-ending lunchtime banquet of *ikan bakar* (grilled fish), chicken and mutton curries, and exotic vegetable dishes.

Kocik Kitchen, Melaka (p228) Tamarind fish-head stew and coconut pineapple prawns top the menu at this authentic Peranakan place, tucked away in Melaka's Chinatown.

Restoran Ratha Raub, Raub (p279) Make a culinary pilgrimage to this provincial town to sample fish-head soup in a rustic country setting.

Ye Olde Smokehouse Fraser's Hill, Fraser's Hill (p111) English country-inn classics are served up in a charming colonial-era bungalow.

Luen Fong Restaurant, Tanjong Tualang (p133) Juicy freshwater prawns and expertly steamed fish make this restaurant a worthy detour on road trips through Perak's Kinta Valley.

Thiam Hock Restaurant, Bandar Seri Begawan (p479) A long-standing Chinese restaurant famous for its fish-head curry.

Ding Dong, Singapore (p536) Vibrant, zingy Southeast Asian retakes with terrific cocktails to boot.

Cheap Treats

Lg Baru (New Lane) Hawker Stalls, George Town (p177) Basically everything that's tasty and cheap about Penang all in one narrow lane.

Restaurant Lou Wong, Ipoh (p129) The signature dish of Ipoh, *ayam tauge* (juicy chicken served with a mountain of crisp bean sprouts), has been perfected at this local favourite.

Food Stalls, Jerantut (p271) Skip Jerantut's formal restaurants, heading instead to the food stalls on Jln Pasar Besar to sample excellent tom yum (hot and sour soup).

Reaz Corner, Johor Bahru (p239) Take a corner seat to watch the world go by in this little open-air curry house in the heart of town.

Asoka, Klang (p116) A favorite in Klang's Little India for the crispy *dosa* (paper-thin, rice-and-lentil crêpe) and a host of Indian sweets.

Kedai Kopi White House, Kota Bharu (p288) *Kaya* (coconut jam) toast served with runny eggs and iced coffee is a top breakfast at this sleepy historic cafe.

COOKING COURSES

A standard one-day course usually features a shopping trip to a local market to choose ingredients, followed by the preparation of curry pastes, soups, curries, salads and desserts.

- Nazlina's Spice Station, George Town (p166)
- Penang Homecooking School, George Town (p168)
- Nancy's Kitchen, Melaka (p224)
- Roselan's Malay Cookery Workshop, Kota Bharu (p285)
- Equator Adventure Tours, Kota Kinabalu (p321)
- LaZat Malaysian Home Cooking Class, KL (p67)
- Bumbu Cooking School, Kuching (p402)
- Food Playground, Singapore (p518)

Night Market, Kota Kinabalu (p326) A huge hawker centre where you can eat your way through the entirety of Malay gastronomy.

Imbi Market, KL (p76) Hands down the best local breakfast selection, which includes *popiah* (similar to a spring roll, but not fried), egg tarts and many types of noodles.

Akob Patin House, Kuantan (p264) This riverfront restaurant serves the local eponymous fish in a *tempoyak* (fermented durian sambal) sauce.

Kuah Night Market, Langkawi (p205) Graze your way from chicken satay stall to fruit seller to mee goreng stand at this roving night market held at a different location each day of the week.

Jonker 88, Melaka (p228) Dive into a vast dessert menu for variations on *cendol,* a shaved-ice dessert topped with pandan noodles, beans, coconut and more.

Summit Café, Miri (p449) Kelabit cuisine that comes fresh from the jungle; think wild boar and midin fern served with Bario's famous rice.

Haji Shariff's Cendol, Seremban (p119) Sample the namesake and classic Malay dessert or a unique take on *rojak* (a type of fruit salad).

Restaurant Bunga Suria, Tanah Rata (p140) Slather *idli* (savoury, soft, fermented-rice-and-lentil cakes) in coconut chutney or pop a button for big banana-leaf specials at this cheap Cameron Highlands canteen.

Tamu Selera, Bandar Seri Begawan (p477) An old-fashioned hawker centre in a shady park serving cheap but tasty *ikan bakar* (grilled fish) and *ayam penyet* ('smashed' fried chicken).

Chinatown Complex, Singapore (p535) Hawker classics, craft beers and a full-throttle Chinatown rush.

Dare to Try

Adventurous diners should seek out these specialties:

Bak kut teh Order this comforting stewed pork dish 'with everything' and be converted to porcine bits and bobs.

Kerabu beromak On Langkawi, coconut milk, chillies and lime juice dress this 'salad' of rubbery but appealingly briny sea-cucumber slices.

Perut ikan This Penang Nonya coconut-milk curry made with fish innards, pineapple and fresh herbs is spicy, sweet, sour and – yes – a little fishy.

Siat When stir-fried, plump sago grubs turn golden and crispy and boast a savoury fattiness recalling pork crackling.

Sup torpedo Malay bull's penis soup is – like many 'challenging foods' – said to enhance sexual drive.

Local Specialities

Malaysia, Brunei and Singapore have similar populations, share a tropical climate and were all at one time home to important trading ports along the spice route. As a result, their cuisines are characterised by comparable flavours and are built on a shared foundation of basic ingredients. Yet there are some regional differences.

DRINKING

Tipplers never fear: despite being a predominately Muslim zone, alcohol is generally available across the region. In Singapore and most of Malaysia, beer and spirits are easily available, if expensive. However, in Brunei, alcohol is banned, and is only found in hotel bars or if imported and declared.

Malaysia

Asam laksa Thick rice noodles in a tart, fish- and herb-packed broth; one of Penang's most famous dishes.

Ayam tauge Tender boiled chicken served with fat bean sprouts is a favourite in Ipoh.

Cendol Fine, short strings of green-bean flour dough in coconut milk sweetened with Melaka's famous palm sugar, and topped with shaved ice; the city's signature dessert.

Char kway teow Closely associated with Penang is this dish of silky rice noodles stir-fried with plump prawns, briny cockles, chewy Chinese sausage, crispy sprouts, egg and a hint of chilli.

Chicken rice balls Hokkien-style chicken and scented rice combined in the form of small globes; one of Melaka's most beloved dishes.

Curry debal A fiery curry with origins in Melaka's Kristang (Portuguese-Eurasian) community.

Hinava Raw fish marinated with lime juice and herbs; a dish associated with Sabah.

Maggi goreng Fried instant noodles; a late-night snack ubiquitous in KL.

Nasi kerabu Rice tinted light blue from a flower, tossed with herbs and seasonings, and served with various toppings; a dish beloved in Kelantan.

Sarawak laksa Thin rice noodles served in a curry broth topped with shrimp, chicken and a shredded omelette.

Tuak Rice wine brewed by Sarawak's indigenous inhabitants.

Brunei

Ambuyat Use a long bamboo fork to dip this sticky, stringy, sago-flour-derived 'porridge' into various dips.

Daging masak lada hitam A popular beef dish that combines elements of a stir-fry, curry and stew.

Udang sambal serai bersantan Prawns served in a rich coconut-milk-based curry.

Singapore

Chilli crab Eat the stir-fried crab with your fingers, then mop up the spicy, eggy chilli and tomato sauce with French bread or deep-fried *man tou* (Chinese-style buns).

Fish-head curry Allegedly invented by an Indian cook and relying on a cut of fish beloved by the

SZEFEI/SHUTTERSTOCK ©

INMAGINEASIA/GETTY IMAGES ©

Top: Maggi goreng
Right: Locals enjoying a meal

Chinese, this example of Singaporean fusion is much better than it sounds.

Kaya toast Grilled bread served with *kaya* (coconut jam), often accompanied by soft boiled eggs and strong coffee, is Singapore's emblematic breakfast.

Katong laksa Singapore's signature laksa has thick noodles cut into short segments (making chopsticks unnecessary), a rich coconut-milk-based broth and a unique garnish of fish cakes.

For more on the region's dishes, see p79.

How to Eat

What to Eat

Centuries of trade, colonisation and immigration have left their culinary mark on Malaysia, Singapore and Brunei in the form of cuisines so multifaceted it would take months of nonstop grazing to truly grasp their breadth. Nowhere else in Asia are the elements of three great culinary traditions – those of China, India and the Malay archipelago – so intertwined. The result is dishes both starkly monocultural (think Chinese wonton noodles and the south Indian rolled 'crêpes' called *dosa*) and confusingly – but delightfully – multicultural (such as curry *debal,* Melaka's Kristang (Portuguese-Eurasian) curry which marries European red wine vinegar, Indian black mustard seeds, Chinese soy sauce and Malay candlenuts).

DINING DOS & DON'TS

If eating with your hands, do:

➡ wash your hands first; in Malay restaurants use water from the 'teapot' on the table while holding your fingers over the tray.

➡ use only your right hand, and scoop food up with your fingers.

➡ serve yourself from the communal plate with utensils, never your fingers.

Don't:

➡ offer alcohol or pork to Muslims (and don't mention pork to Muslims).

➡ stick your chopsticks upright in a bowl of rice; it symbolises death to Chinese.

Rice The locals would be hard-pressed to choose between *nasi* (rice) and *mee* (noodles) – one or the other features in almost every meal. Rice is boiled in water or stock to make porridge (congee or *bubur*); fried with chillies and shallots for nasi goreng (fried rice); and packed into banana-leaf-lined bamboo tubes, cooked, then sliced and doused with coconut-and-vegetable gravy for the Malay dish *lontong*. Glutinous (sticky) rice – both white and black – is a common ingredient in local sweets. Rice flour, mixed with water and allowed to ferment, becomes the batter for Indian *idli* (steamed cakes) to be eaten with dhal (stewed lentils), and *apam* (crispy-chewy pancakes cooked in special concave pans). Rice-flour-based dough is transformed into sweet dumplings like *onde-onde* (coconut-flake-dusted, pandan-hued balls hiding a filling of semiliquid *gula* Melaka – palm sugar).

Noodles Many varieties of noodle are also made from rice flour, both the wide, flat *kway teow* and *mee hoon* (or *bee hoon;* rice vermicelli). *Chee cheong fun* (steamed rice-flour sheets) are sliced into strips and topped with sweet brown and red chilli sauces; stubby *loh see fun* (literally 'rat-tail noodles') are stewed in a claypot with dark soy sauce. Round yellow noodles form the basis of the Muslim Indian dish *mee mamak*. The Chinese favourite *won ton mee,* found anywhere in the region, comprises wheat-and-egg vermicelli, a clear meat broth and silky-skinned dumplings.

Curry The region's curries start with *rempah* – a pounded paste of chillies and aromatics like garlic, shallots, *serai* (lemongrass), *kunyit* (turmeric) and *lengkuas* (galangal). Dried spices – coriander seeds, fennel seeds, cumin, fenugreek – might also be included, especially if the dish is Indian-influenced.

Meat and fish A person's religion often dictates a dish's protein. *Babi* (pork) is *haram* (forbidden) to Muslims but is the king of meats for Chinese. *Ayam* (chicken) is tremendously popular in Malaysia and Singapore, but more of a special-occasion meat in Brunei (as is beef or buffalo). Tough local *daging* (beef) is best cooked long and slowly, for dishes like coconut-milk-based *rendang*. Chinese-style beef noodles feature tender chunks of beef and springy meatballs in a rich, mildly spiced broth lightened with pickled mustard. Indian Muslims do amazing things with mutton; it's worth searching out *sup kambing,* stewed mutton riblets (and other parts, if you wish) in a thick soup, flavoured with loads of aromatics and chillies that's eaten with sliced white bread. Lengthy coastlines

FRUIT FOR THOUGHT

Fruit such as *nenas* (pineapple), watermelon, papaya and green guava are available year-round. April and May are mango months, and come December to January and June to July, follow your nose to sample notoriously odoriferous love-it-or-hate-it durian. Should the king of fruits prove too repellent, other lesser-known tropical fruits you may come across at markets and street stalls include:

Buah nona The custard apple; a knobbly green skin conceals hard black seeds and sweet, gloopy flesh with a granular texture.

Buah salak Known as the snakeskin fruit because of its scaly skin; the exterior looks like a mutant strawberry and the soft flesh tastes like unripe bananas.

Cempedak The Malaysian breadfruit; a huge green fruit with skin like the Thing from the *Fantastic Four;* the seeds and flesh are often curried or fried.

Ciku The dull brown skin of the sapodilla hides supersweet flesh that tastes a bit like a date.

Duku Strip away the yellowish peel of this fruit (also known as *dokong* and *langsat*) to find segmented, perfumed pearlescent flesh with a lychee-like flavour.

Durian Due to its intense odour and weapon-like appearance, the durian is possibly Southeast Asia's most infamous fruit, the flesh of which can suggest everything from custard to onions.

Durian belanda Soursop has a fragrant but tart granular flesh and hard black seeds; it's only ripe when soft and goes off within days so eat it quickly.

Jambu merah Rose apple; elongated pink or red fruit with a smooth, shiny skin and pale, watery flesh. It's a good thirst quencher on a hot day.

Longan A tiny, hard ball like a mini lychee with sweet, perfumed flesh; peel it, eat the flesh and spit out the hard seeds.

Manggis A hard, purple shell conceals the mangosteen's delightfully fragrant white segments, some containing a tough seed that you can spit out.

Nangka Considered the world's largest fruit, jackfruit takes the form of a giant green pod with dozens of waxy yellow sections, the taste of which reminds us of Juicy Fruit chewing gum.

Limau bali Like a grapefruit on steroids, pomelo has a thick pithy green skin hiding sweet, tangy segments; cut into the skin, peel off the pith then break open the segments and munch on the flesh inside.

Rambutan People have different theories about what rambutans look like, not all repeatable in polite company; the hairy shell contains sweet, translucent flesh, which you scrape off the seed with your teeth.

Belimbing The yellow flesh of the starfruit is sweet and tangy and believed by many to lower blood pressure.

and abundant rivers and estuaries mean that seafood forms much of the diet for many of the region's residents.

Vegetables Vegetable lovers will have a field day. Every rice-based Malay meal includes *ulam*, a selection of fresh and blanched vegetables – wing beans, cucumbers, okra, eggplant and the fresh legume *petai* (or stink bean, so-named for its strong garlicky taste) – and fresh herbs to eat on their own or dip into sambal. Indians cook cauliflower and leafy vegetables like cabbage, spinach and roselle (sturdy leaves with an appealing sourness) with coconut milk and turmeric. Other greens – *daun ubi* (sweet potato leaves), *kangkong* (water spinach), Chinese broccoli and yellow-flowered mustard – are stir-fried with *sambal belacan* or garlic. Although vegetarians do indeed exist, it's probably worth mentioning that vegans will struggle in the region, as even vegetable dishes may include a bit of meat or fish sauce.

Sweets The locals are passionate about *kuih* (sweets); vendors of cakes and pastries lie in wait

FASTING & FEASTING

In general, there's no need to be deterred from visiting Malaysia during Ramadan, the Muslim holy month of sunrise-to-sunset fasting. Indian and Chinese eateries remain open during the day to cater to the country's sizeable non-Muslim population and, come late afternoon, Ramadan bazaars pop up all over the country. These prepared-food markets offer a rare chance to sample Malay specialities from all over the country, some of which are specific to the festive season or are rarely found outside private homes. One of the country's biggest Ramadan markets is held in KL's Malay enclave of Kampung Baru. Cruise the stalls and pick up provisions for an evening meal – but don't snack in public until the cry of the muezzin tells believers it's time to *buka puasa* (break the fast). The one exception is in Brunei, where during Ramadan, hotel room service is just about the only place that will serve food during the daytime.

on street corners, footpaths and in markets. Many *kuih* incorporate coconut, grated or in the form of milk, and palm sugar, often combining sweet and savoury flavours to fantastic effect.

When to Eat

To those of us used to 'three square meals', it might seem as if the locals are always eating. In fact, five or six meals or snacks is more the order of the day than strict adherence to the breakfast-lunch-dinner trilogy. Breakfast is often something that can be grabbed on the run: *nasi lemak* wrapped to go *(bungkus)* in a banana leaf or brown waxed paper, a quick bowl of noodles, toast and eggs, or griddled Indian bread.

Come late morning a snack might be in order, perhaps a *karipap* (deep-fried pastry filled with spiced meat or fish and potatoes). Lunch generally starts from 12.30pm, something to keep in mind if you plan to eat at a popular establishment.

The British left behind a strong attachment to afternoon tea, consumed here in the form of tea or coffee and a sweet or savoury snack like *tong sui* (sweet soups), various Indian fritters, battered and fried slices of cassava, sweet potato, banana and – of course – local-style *kuih*.

Where To Eat

Many locals would argue that the best (and best-value) food is found at hawker stalls, and who are we to argue? Most of these dishes can't be found in restaurants and when they are, they're rarely as tasty, so hawker-stall dining is a must if you really want to appreciate the region's cuisines in all their glory. To partake, simply head to a stand-alone streetside kitchen-on-wheels, a coffee shop or a food court; place your order with one or a number of different vendors; find a seat (shared tables are common); and pay for each dish as it's delivered. After you're seated you'll be approached by someone taking orders for drinks, which are also paid for separately. Hawker food in Malaysia and Brunei is perfectly safe to eat, but the squeamish may want to start slowly, in one of Singapore's sanitised hawker centres.

Kopitiam Generally refers to old-style, single-owner Chinese coffee shops. These simple, fan-cooled establishments serve noodle and rice dishes, strong coffee and other drinks, and all-day breakfast fare like soft-boiled eggs and toast to eat with *kaya*.

Restoran (restaurant) Eateries ranging from casual, decades-old Chinese establishments to upscale establishments boasting international fare, slick decor and a full bar. Between the two extremes lie Chinese seafood restaurants where the main course can be chosen live from a tank, as well as the numerous cafes found in Malaysia's many shopping malls.

Pasar (markets) Consider grazing at one or more *pasar*. Morning markets usually have Chinese-owned stalls selling coffee and Indian-operated *teh tarik* stalls offering freshly griddled roti. Triangular *bungkus* piled in the middle of tables contain *nasi lemak* served with *ikan bilis* (small, dried sardines or anchovies) peanuts and a curry dish; help yourself and pay for what you eat.

Pasar malam (night markets) Also good hunting grounds, where you'll find everything from laksa to fresh-fried sweet yeast doughnuts.

Regions at a Glance

Kuala Lumpur

Food
Shopping
Art Galleries

Fantastic Food
Allow your stomach to lead the way around Kuala Lumpur (KL). Tuck in with locals at the fantastic hawker stalls along Jln Alor, at Imbi Market or in Chinatown. Sample Indian food in Brickfields, Malay delights in Kampung Baru, and a brilliant array of international options in the Golden Triangle, KLCC and Bangsar.

Super Shopping
KL sports a multiplicity of malls, classic Southeast Asian fresh-produce day markets and several atmospheric night markets, the most famous of which is along Chinatown's Jln Petaling. The art deco Central Market is strong on arts and crafts.

Contemporary Art
Access Malaysia's vibrant contemporary art scene at the National Visual Art Gallery, the new ILHAM gallery or exhibitions at smaller commercial spaces such as Wei-Ling Gallery.

p50

Selangor & Negeri Sembilan

Wildlife
Food
Architecture

Wildlife Encounters
Encounter monkeys up close at FRIM and Batu Caves. Go bird-spotting at Fraser's Hill, Cape Rachado Forest Reserve near Port Dickson, and the coastal mangroves near Kuala Selangor.

Eating Adventures
Head to Klang's Little India for authentic tastes from the subcontinent and the flavourful pork soup *bak kut teh*. Seremban has taste sensations ranging from beef-ball noodles to *cendol*.

Architectural Wonders
Putrajaya is stacked with monumental contemporary architecture around an artificial lake. The Istana Lama is a beautiful black hardwood palace in Sri Menanti.

p105

Perak

Architecture
Food
Nature

Colonial-Era Architecture
Ipoh and the surrounding Kinta Valley are virtual time warps into colonial-era Malaysia. Taiping also has its share of visit-worthy historic buildings, while Kuala Kangsar sparkles with mosques and royal palaces.

Culinary Destination
Ipoh, Perak's largest city, is one of Malaysia's top culinary destinations, home to excellent regional Chinese food as well as some great Malay food and aritisan coffee shops.

Jungles & Mangroves
Perak is home to the deep jungles of Royal Belum State Park and the slightly muddier forests of Matang Mangrove Forest Reserve. Gopeng, outside of Ipoh, also has a burgeoning nature scene.

p123

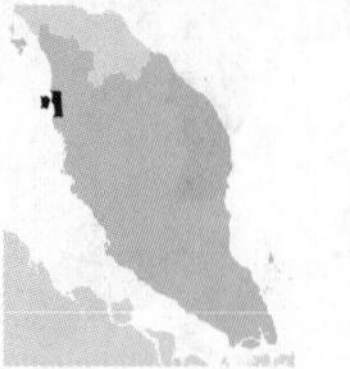

Penang

Architecture
Food
Museums

World Heritage

There's a good reason why George Town is a Unesco World Heritage Site: the city is home to countless protection-worthy antique shophouses, mansions, Chinese clan houses, markets and temples.

Food & Drink

George Town is the culinary capital of Malaysia and our favourite place to feed in Southeast Asia. Quality hawker centres, street vendors, and a contemporary eating and drinking scene.

Museums & Galleries

The streets of George Town are already something of an open-air museum, but the city's excellent museums and contemporary art galleries ensure you'll be both educated and entertained for days.

p156

Langkawi, Kedah & Perlis

Beaches
Nature
Eating

Splendid Beaches

Pulau Langkawi's beaches are world famous for a reason: the sand is white and fine, the water is clear, and there's been less development here than in other Southeast Asian destinations.

Mountainous Jungle

The ancient jungle on Pulau Langkawi isn't just a pretty backdrop; it can be explored from above, via the Panorama Langkawi cable car, or seen up close at one of the numerous waterfalls.

International Dining

Pulau Langkawi is home to an admirable spread of foreign restaurants, from Thai to Turkish. The island's duty-free status also means that the bar scene is less punishing to your wallet.

p190

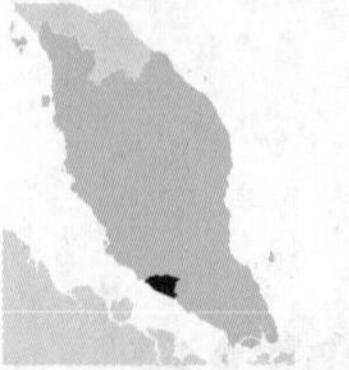

Melaka

Heritage
Food
Shopping

Walkable Heritage

Learn about the history, culture and architecture of Melaka at abundant museums. But better yet, experience it wandering past Chinese shophouses, Dutch colonial-era architecture, Chinese and Hindu temples, mosques and churches.

Sit-Down Meals

Take a dim sum breakfast, eat curry off a banana leaf for lunch and dine on Peranakan specialities for dinner. Melaka offers a great choice of international and regional cuisines.

Shopping Options

Shop Chinatown's trinkets and beaded Peranakan shoes, or go modern in massive air-con malls for electronics and name brands. Don't miss Jonker Walk Night Market.

p215

Johor

Nature
Diving
Nightlife

Malaysia's Wilds

Endau-Rompin National Park isn't nearly as well known as Taman Negara in Pahang, but that's what makes it so magical. Hike through dense rainforests and along clear rivers to several impressive waterfalls.

Off-Radar Islands

The Seribuat Archipelago is where all the in-the-know expats living in Singapore and southern Malaysia go. Here you'll find low-key beaches, spectacular diving and family-friendly lodgings.

Duty-Free Booze

The Zon is Johor Bahru's duty-free port, and several drinking holes and nightclubs clog the area. Hop from one to the next without spending all your ringgit.

p235

Pahang & Tioman Island

Beaches
Jungles
Food

Beach Life

Coastal Pahang offers the supremely chilled-out surf town of Cherating. Pulau Tioman has no less than eight great beach areas to choose from.

Jungle Adventures

The vast jungle preserve of Taman Negara offers plenty of hiking and wildlife-spotting opportunities. Pulau Tioman's trails will make you glad you packed hiking boots.

Culinary Travel

Kuantan is a food lover's city, from the cheap and delicious food stalls next to the bus station to the hard-to-find but oh-so-worth-it seafood paradise of Ana Ikan Bakar Petai restaurant. Culinary travellers will want to make a pilgrimage to taste Raub's famous fish-head curry.

p250

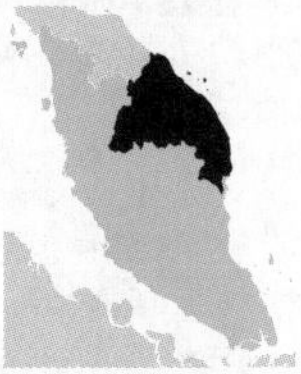

East Coast Islands, Kelantan & Terengganu

Islands
Jungles
Culture

Aquatic Adventures

Home to some of Southeast Asia's loveliest and most accessible islands, east coast Malaysia is a magnet for those looking to dive, snorkel and swim.

Off the Beaten Track

Travellers are few in Kelantan's wild interior. Make the pretty jungle town of Dabong your base for mountain treks, river tracing and caving, and visiting breathtaking waterfalls.

Cultural Insights

The geographical blending zone between Muslim Malaysia and Buddhist Thailand, Kelantan is amazingly rich in opportunities for cultural exploration. Further south, Terengganu offers visitors the chance to explore Malay culture.

p281

Sabah

Wildlife
Hiking & Trekking
Diving

Wildlife

Sabah is home to some of the world's rarest animal species such, as the iconic orangutan, while the surrounding seas are home to an abundance of colourful marine life.

Jungle Hiking

Sabah's mountainous hinterland is a hiker's delight, taking adventurers past raging rivers that flow out of and through some of the most primordial forests in the world.

Diving & Snorkelling

To say Sabah is known for its diving scene is like saying France is known for its cuisine. The diving in spots like Layang Layang and, of course, the famous Sipadan is – no hyperbole – some of the best in the world.

p314

Sarawak

Hiking & Trekking
Caves
Wildlife

Hiking

Hiking from Bario to Ba Kelalan or to the summit of Gunung Mulu will exhilarate experienced hikers, but even a relaxed stroll through one of the national parks around Kuching will envelope you in equatorial rainforest.

Cave Exploration

The Wind Cave, Fairy Cave and Niah National Park boast huge caverns with stalactites and bats, but for sheer size and spectacle you can't beat Gunung Mulu National Park, famed for the Deer Cave and the 700m-long Sarawak Chamber.

Jungle Wildlife

Wild proboscis monkeys munch leaves at Bako National Park, orangutans swing through Semenggoh Nature Reserve and estuarine crocodiles lurk in the muddy waters of Kuching Wetlands National Park.

p393

Brunei

Food
Architecture
Nature

Food Mad

Booze might be banned but there is no limit on gastronomic indulgence, a pleasure taken seriously in these parts. The sultanate is food mad and the opening of a restaurant is typically a major social event.

Grand Architecture

Between the Sultan's glittering palace, the opulent Empire Hotel, gaudy mosques and the largest water village in the world, this nation compensates for its small size with some huge construction projects.

Primary Jungle

The sultanate has done an admirable job of preserving its tracts of primary jungle. An excellent, tightly controlled national park gives green breathing space to Borneo's many beasties.

p468

Singapore

Food
Shopping
Museums

Ethnic Variations

Food in Singapore is both a passion and a unifier across ethnic divides, with Chinese, Indian, Indonesian and Peranakan specialities. Find legendary hawker centres and food courts, plus experimental, fine-dining hot spots.

Choice Shopping

All bases are covered, from lavish malls and in-the-know boutiques, to heirloom handicraft studios and galleries peddling contemporary local art.

History & Culture

World-class museums offer evocative insights into the region's history and culture. While giants like the National Museum of Singapore are a must, make time for lesser-known NUS Museums and the haunting Changi Museum & Chapel.

p488

On the Road

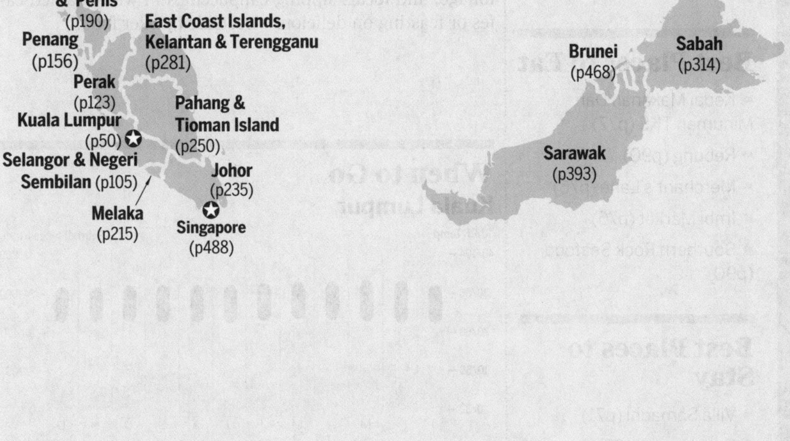

Langkawi, Kedah & Perlis (p190)
Penang (p156)
East Coast Islands, Kelantan & Terengganu (p281)
Perak (p123)
Kuala Lumpur (p50)
Pahang & Tioman Island (p250)
Selangor & Negeri Sembilan (p105)
Johor (p235)
Melaka (p215)
Singapore (p488)
Brunei (p468)
Sabah (p314)
Sarawak (p393)

Kuala Lumpur

☎ 03 / POP 1.63 MILLION / AREA 243 SQ KM

Includes ➡

Best Places to Eat

- ➡ Kedai Makanan Dan Minuman TKS (p77)
- ➡ Rebung (p90)
- ➡ Merchant's Lane (p76)
- ➡ Imbi Market (p76)
- ➡ Southern Rock Seafood (p90)

Best Places to Stay

- ➡ Villa Samadhi (p71)
- ➡ BackHome (p68)
- ➡ Aloft Kuala Lumpur Sentral (p75)
- ➡ Wolo Bukit Bintang (p70)
- ➡ E&O Residences Kuala Lumpur (p71)

Why Go?

Less than two centuries since tin miners hacked a base out of the jungle, Kuala Lumpur (KL) has evolved into an affluent 21st-century metropolis remarkable for its cultural diversity. Ethnic Malays, Chinese prospectors, Indian migrants and British colonials all helped shaped this city, and each group has left its indelible physical mark as well as a fascinating assortment of cultural traditions.

KL has few obvious sights; its quirky charm lies in historic temples and mosques rubbing shoulders with colonial architecture, mammoth shopping malls and soaring skyscrapers; traders' stalls piled high with pungent durians and counterfeit handbags; monorail cars zipping by lush jungle foliage; and locals sipping cappuccinos in wi-fi-enabled cafes or feasting on delicious streetside hawker food.

When to Go

Kuala Lumpur

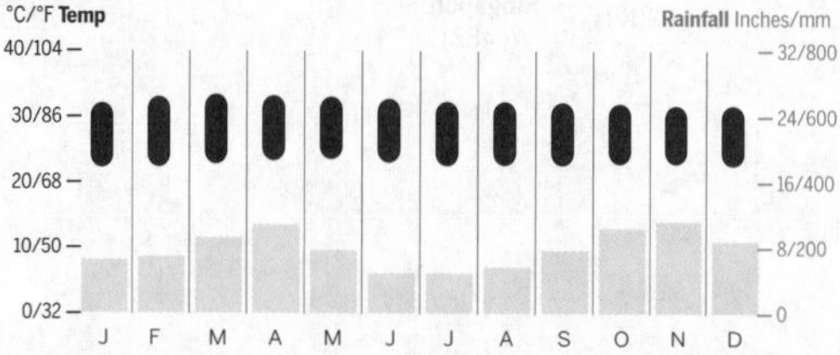

Jan & Feb Enjoy the Chinese New Year and the dramatic Hindu festival Thaipusam.

Mar & Apr Catch the first of the city's general sales and the Malaysian Grand Prix.

Aug & Sep Celebrate Independence and Malaysia Day then the arts festival DiverseCity.

History

In 1857, 87 Chinese prospectors in search of tin landed at the apex of the Klang and Gombak rivers and imaginatively named the place Kuala Lumpur, meaning 'muddy confluence'. Within a month, all but 17 of the prospectors had died of malaria and other tropical diseases, but the tin they discovered in Ampang attracted more miners and KL quickly became a brawling, noisy, violent boomtown.

As in other parts of the Malay peninsula, the local sultan appointed a proxy (known as Kapitan China) to bring the unruly Chinese fortune-seekers and their secret societies into line. The successful candidate Yap Ah Loy (Kapitan China from 1868 to 1885) took on the task with such ruthless relish that he's now credited as the founder of KL.

Yap had barely established control, however, when fighting broke out between local sultans for the throne of Perak. KL was swept up in the conflict and burnt to the ground in 1881. This allowed the British government representative Frank Swettenham to push through a radical new town plan that transferred the central government from Klang to KL. By 1886 a railway line linked KL to Klang; by 1887 several thousand brick buildings had been built; and in 1896 the city became the capital of the newly formed Federated Malay States.

After a brutal occupation by Japanese forces during WWII, the British temporarily returned, only to be ousted when Malaysia declared its independence here in 1957.

KL's darkest hour came on 13 May 1969, when race riots mainly between the Malays and Chinese communities claimed hundreds, perhaps thousands, of lives. A year later local government elections were suspended – ever since, KL's mayor has been appointed by the Federal Territories Minister. In 1974 the sultan of Selangor ceded the city's land to the state so it could officially become the Federal Territory of Kuala Lumpur.

Sights

KL's city centre is surprisingly compact – from Chinatown to Masjid India takes little more than 10 minutes on foot – and some sights are so close together that it's often quicker to walk than take public transport or grab a cab (which can easily become snarled in traffic and KL's tortuous one-way system).

Chinatown, Merdeka Square & Bukit Nanas

★Menara Kuala Lumpur TOWER
(KL Tower; Map p54; ☎03-2020 5444; www.menarakl.com.my; 2 Jln Punchak; observation deck adult/child RM52/31, open deck adults only RM105; ⌚observation deck 9am-10pm, last tickets 9.30pm; 🚝KL Tower) Although the Petronas Towers are taller, the 421m Menara KL, rising from the crest of Bukit Nanas, offers the best city views. Surrounded by a pocket of primary rainforest, this lofty spire is the world's fourth-highest telecommunications tower. The bulb at the top (its shape inspired by a Malaysian spinning toy) contains a revolving restaurant, an interior **observation deck** at 276m and, most thrilling of all, an **open deck** at 300m, access to which is weather dependent.

A free shuttle bus runs from the gate on Jln Punchak, or you can walk up through the KL Forest Eco Park and its new canopy walkway.

★KL Forest Eco Park NATURE RESERVE
(Taman Eko Rimba KL; Map p54; www.forestry.gov.my; ⌚7am-7pm; 🚝KL Tower) Don't miss traversing the lofty, newly constructed **canopy walkway** set in this thick lowland dipterocarp forest covering 9.37 hectares in the heart of the city. The oldest protected jungle in Malaysia (gazetted in 1906), the park is commonly known as Bukit Nanas (Pineapple Hill), and is also threaded through with short trails up from either Jln Ampang or Jln Raja Chulan. Pick up a basic map to the trails from the **Forest Information Centre** (Map p54; ☎03-2026 4741; www.forestry.gov.my; Jln Raja Chulan; ⌚9am-5pm; 🚝KL Tower) FREE.

Sri Mahamariamman Temple HINDU TEMPLE
(Map p54; 163 Jln Tun HS Lee; ⌚6am-8.30pm, till 9.30pm Fri; Ⓜ Pasar Seni) FREE This lively Hindu temple – the oldest in Malaysia and rumoured to be the richest – was founded in 1873. Mariamman is the South Indian mother goddess, also known as Parvati. Her shrine is at the back of the complex. On the left sits a shrine to the elephant-headed Ganesh, and on the right one to Lord Murugan. During the Thaipusam festival, Lord Murugan is transported to Batu Caves from the temple on a silver chariot.

Merdeka Square SQUARE
(Dataran Merdeka; Map p54; Ⓜ Masjid Jamek) The huge open square where Malaysian

Kuala Lumpur Highlights

1. Getting treetop views from the canopy walkway in **KL Forest Eco Park** (p51), followed by the thrill of being 300m high and outside on **Menara Kuala Lumpur** (p51).
2. Admiring the glittering exterior of the **Petronas Towers** (p57), then head up to the observation deck.
3. Day or night, Chinatown's **Petaling Street Market** (p97) is a dynamic place for eating, shopping and people watching.
4. Standing at KL's colonial heart on **Merdeka Square** (p51), surrounded by a handsome ensemble of heritage buildings.
5. Spotting all kinds of feathered beauties in **KL Bird Park** (p60), showpiece of the lush Tun Abdul Razak Heritage Park.
6. Admiring beautiful objects gathered from around the Islamic world in the **Islamic Arts Museum** (p60).
7. Diving into the streetside dining adventure of **Jln Alor** (p77).

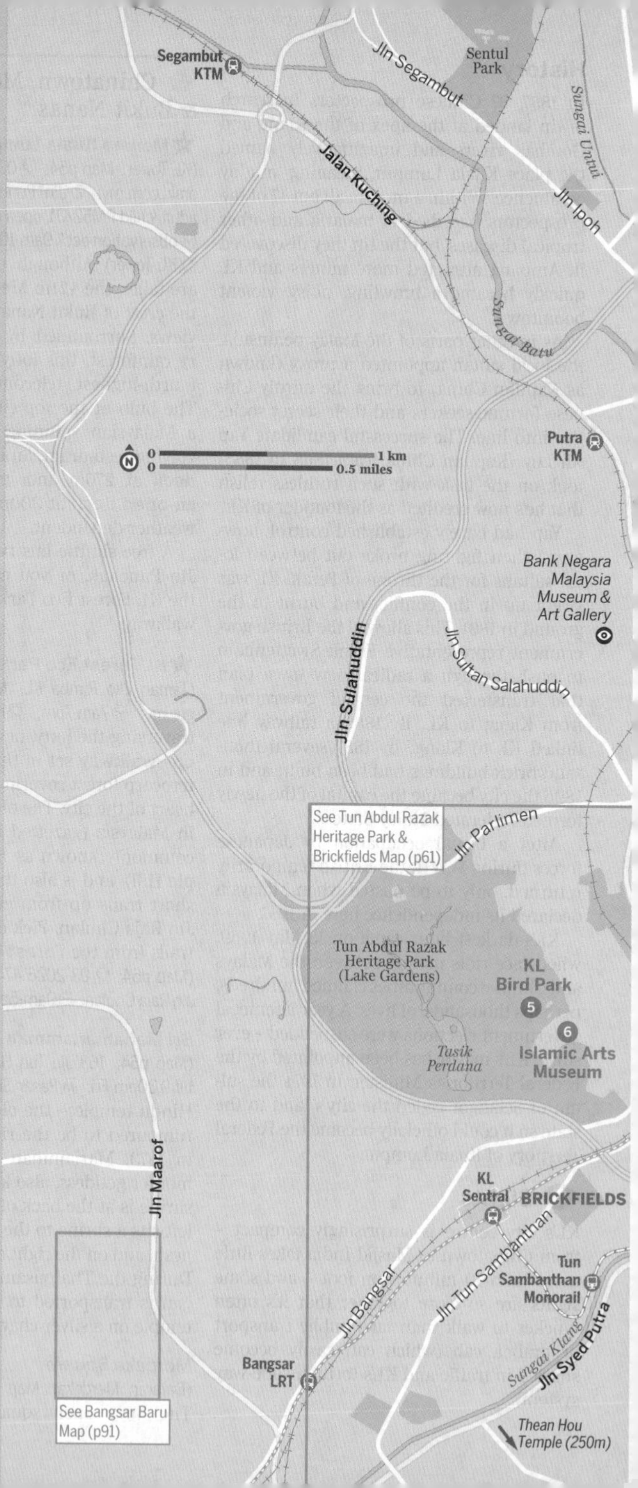

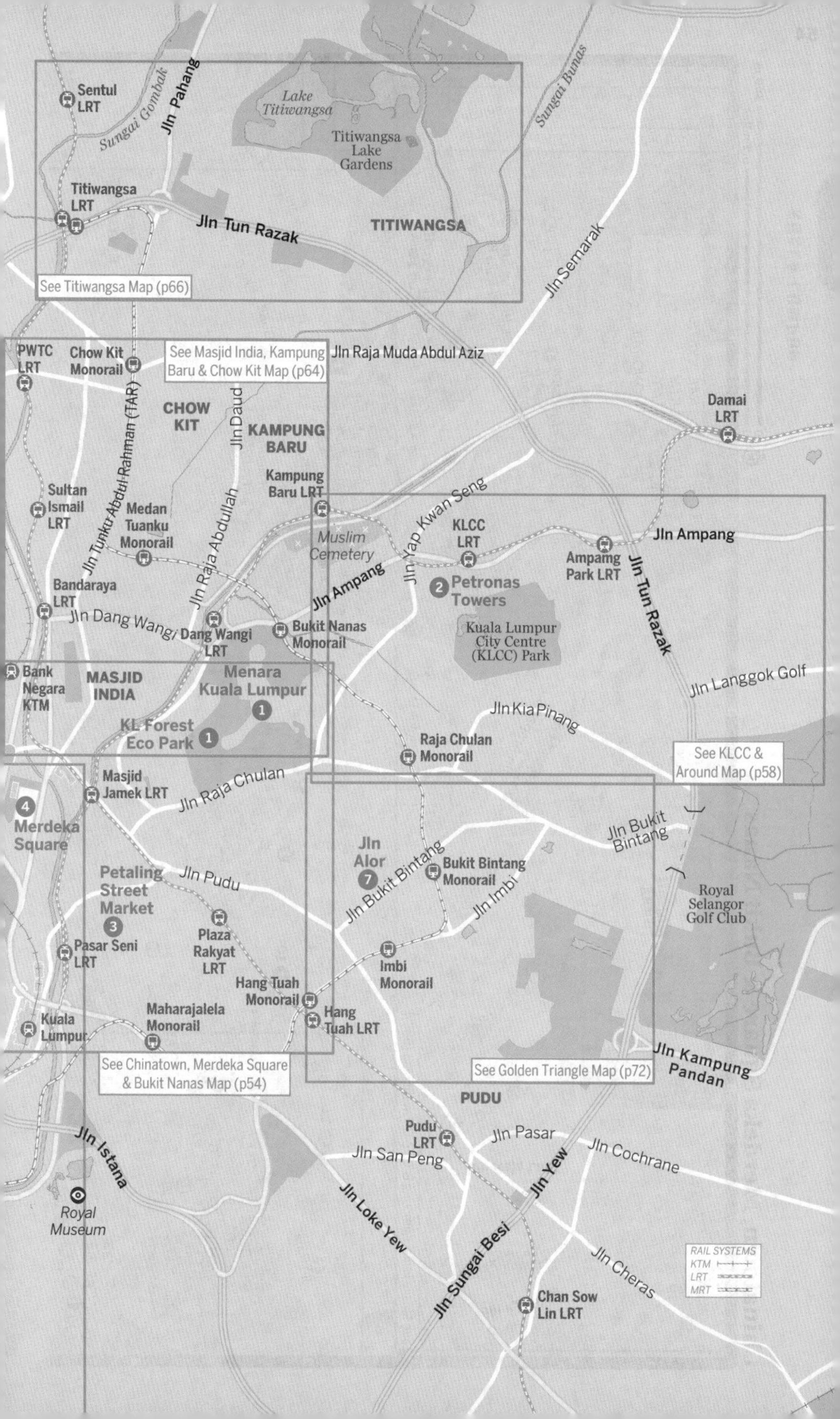

Sentul LRT
Sungai Gombak
Jln Pahang
Lake Titiwangsa
Titiwangsa Lake Gardens
Sungai Bunus
Titiwangsa LRT
Jln Tun Razak
TITIWANGSA
See Titiwangsa Map (p66)
Jln Semarak
PWTC LRT
Chow Kit Monorail
See Masjid India, Kampung Baru & Chow Kit Map (p64)
Jln Raja Muda Abdul Aziz
CHOW KIT
Jln Daud
KAMPUNG BARU
Jln Tunku Abdul Rahman (TAR)
Damai LRT
Sultan Ismail LRT
Medan Tuanku Monorail
Kampung Baru LRT
Jln Yap Kwan Seng
Muslim Cemetery
KLCC LRT
Jln Ampang
Ampang Park LRT
Jln Raja Abdullah
Jln Ampang
2 Petronas Towers
Jln Tun Razak
Bandaraya LRT
Jln Dang Wangi
Dang Wangi LRT
Bukit Nanas Monorail
Kuala Lumpur City Centre (KLCC) Park
Bank Negara KTM
MASJID INDIA
Menara Kuala Lumpur
1
Jln Langgok Golf
KL Forest Eco Park
1
Jln Kia Pinang
Raja Chulan Monorail
See KLCC & Around Map (p58)
Masjid Jamek LRT
Jln Raja Chulan
4 Merdeka Square
Jln Bukit Bintang
Jln Alor
7
Jln Bukit Bintang
Bukit Bintang Monorail
Petaling Street Market
3
Jln Pudu
Jln Imbi
Royal Selangor Golf Club
Plaza Rakyat LRT
Pasar Seni LRT
Imbi Monorail
Hang Tuah Monorail
Hang Tuah LRT
Maharajalela Monorail
Kuala Lumpur
See Chinatown, Merdeka Square & Bukit Nanas Map (p54)
See Golden Triangle Map (p72)
Jln Kampung Pandan
PUDU
Pudu LRT
Jln Pasar
Jln San Peng
Jln Cochrane
Jln Istana
Jln Yew
Jln Loke Yew
Royal Museum
Jln Sungai Besi
Jln Cheras
RAIL SYSTEMS
KTM
LRT
MRT
Chan Sow Lin LRT

Chinatown, Merdeka Square & Bukit Nanas

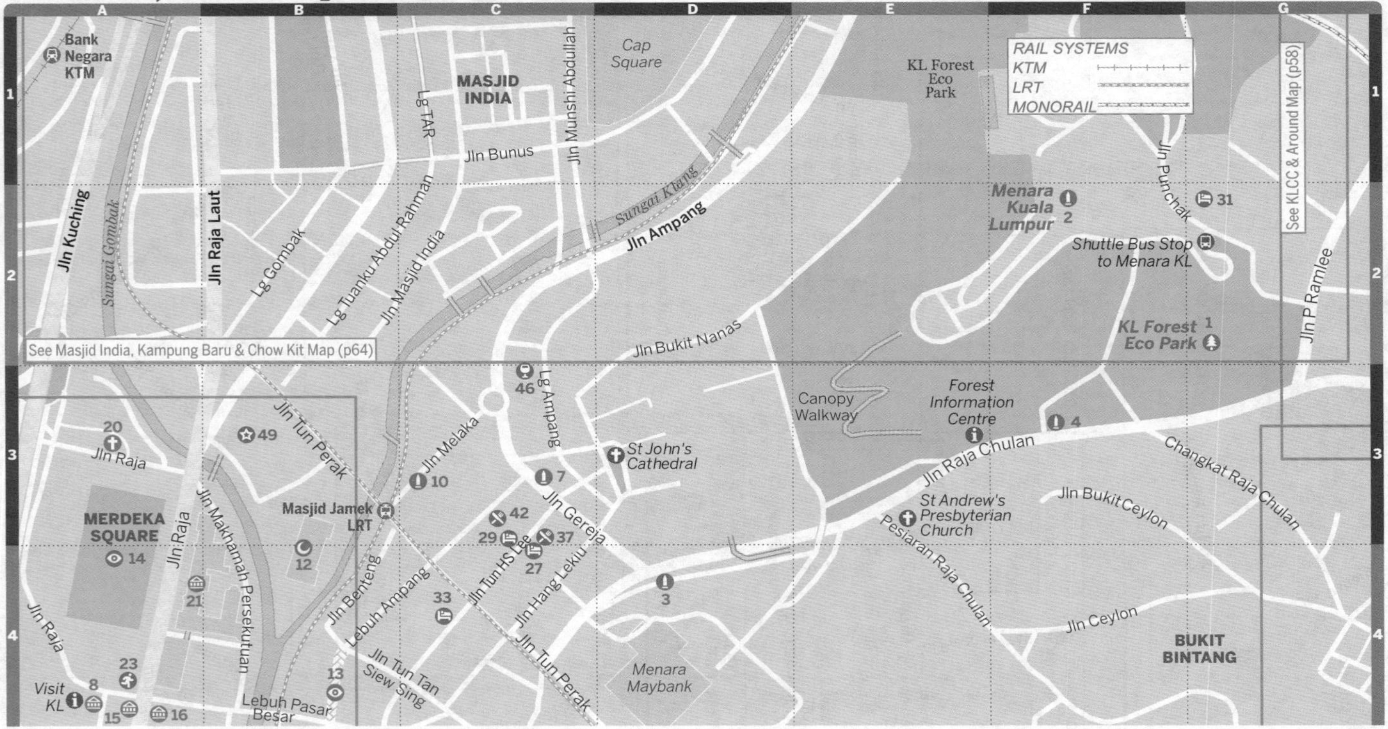

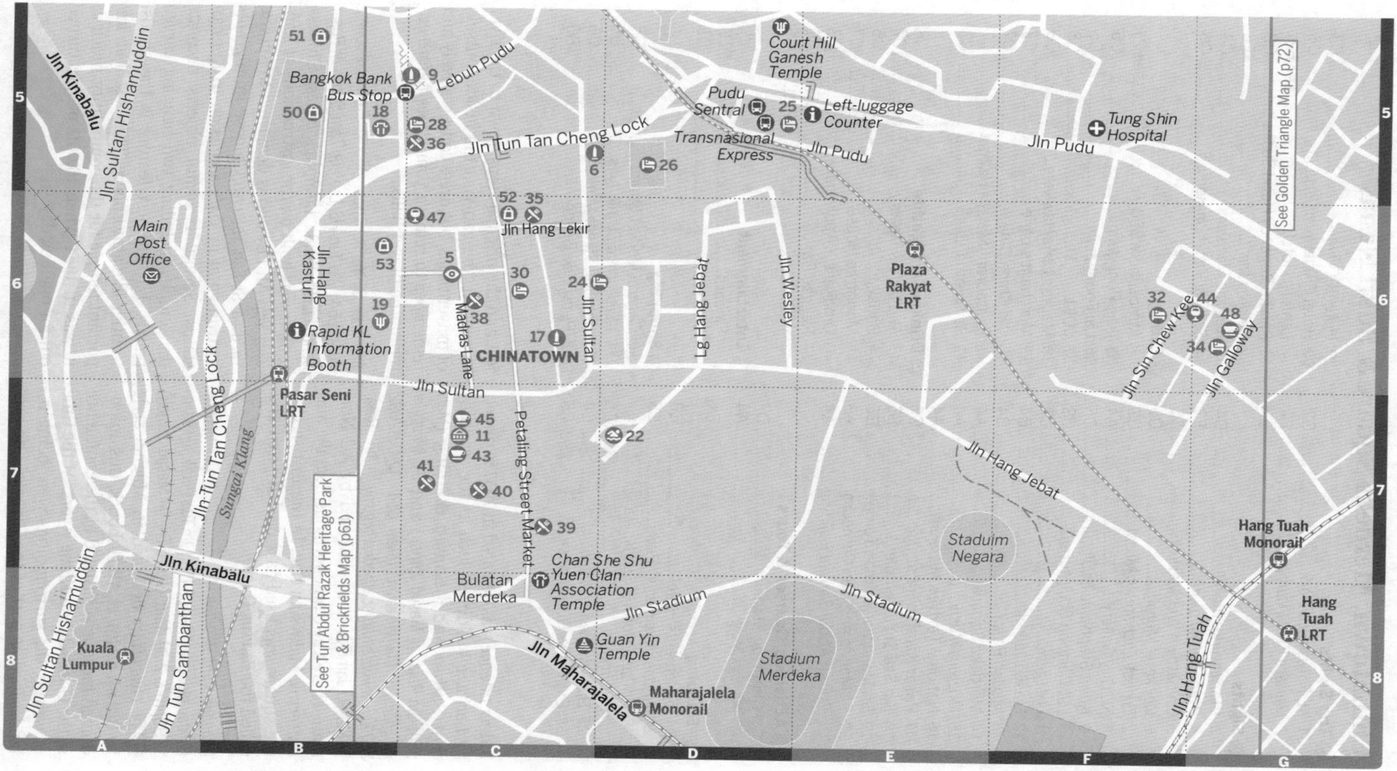
Jln Kinabalu
Jln Sultan Hishamuddin
51
Bangkok Bank Bus Stop
9
Lebuh Pudu
50
18
28
36
Jln Tun Tan Cheng Lock
6
26
Court Hill Ganesh Temple
Pudu Sentral
25
Left-luggage Counter
Transnasional Express
Jln Pudu
Tung Shin Hospital
See Golden Triangle Map (p72)
Main Post Office
47
52
35
Jln Hang Lekir
Jln Hang Kasturi
53
5
30
24
Lg Hang Jebat
Jln Wesley
Plaza Rakyat LRT
19
Rapid KL Information Booth
Madras Lane
38
17
CHINATOWN
Jln Sultan
Pasar Seni LRT
32
44
48
34
Jln Sin Chew Kee
Jln Galloway
Jln Tun Tan Cheng Lock
Sungai Klang
45
11
43
22
41
40
See Tun Abdul Razak Heritage Park & Brickfields Map (p61)
Petaling Street Market
39
Jln Hang Jebat
Stadium Negara
Hang Tuah Monorail
Jln Kinabalu
Bulatan Merdeka
Chan She Shu Yuen Clan Association Temple
Jln Stadium
Jln Stadium
Hang Tuah LRT
Jln Sultan Hishamuddin
Kuala Lumpur
Jln Tun Sambanthan
Guan Yin Temple
Jln Maharajalela
Maharajalela Monorail
Stadium Merdeka
Jln Hang Tuah
A
B
C
D
E
F
G
5
6
7
8

Chinatown, Merdeka Square & Bukit Nanas

independence was declared in 1957 is ringed by heritage buildings, such as the magnificent **Sultan Abdul Samad Building** (Map p54; Jln Raja; Ⓜ Masjid Jamek) and **St Mary's Anglican Cathedral** (Map p54; ☎ 03-2692 8672; www.stmaryscathedral.org.my; Jln Raja; Ⓜ Masjid Jamek), both designed by AC Norman. There's also an enormous flagpole and fluttering Malaysian flag. In the British era, the square was used as a cricket pitch and called the Padang (Field).

Masjid Jamek MOSQUE

(Friday Mosque; Map p54; off Jln Tun Perak; ⏰ 9am-12.30pm & 2.30-4pm, closed Fri; Ⓜ Masjid Jamek) FREE Gracefully designed in Mughal style by British architect AB Hubback, this onion-domed mosque is situated at the confluence of the Gombak and Klang rivers. At the time of writing the surroundings were being relandscaped as part of the River of Life project and the original steps down to the river reinstated. You can visit the inside, outside of prayer times, but dress conservatively and remember to remove your shoes before entering the prayer halls.

Sin Sze Si Ya Temple CHINESE TEMPLE

(Map p54; Jln Tun HS Lee; ⏰ 7am-5pm; Ⓜ Pasar Seni) FREE Kuala Lumpur's oldest Chinese temple was built on the instructions of Kapitan Yap Ah Loy and is dedicated to Sin Sze Ya and Si Sze Ya, two Chinese immigrants instrumental in Yap's ascension to Kapitan status. Several beautiful objects decorate the temple, including two hanging carved panels, but the best feature is the almost frontier-like atmosphere. This is still an important temple for the community, much as it was in 1864 when 10,000 people turned out for opening day.

National Textiles Museum MUSEUM

(Muzium Tekstil Negara; Map p54; ☎03-2694 3457; www.muziumtekstilnegara.gov.my; Jln Sultan Hishamuddin; ⏰9am-6pm; Ⓜ Masjid Jamek) FREE This excellent themed museum occupies an elegant Mughal-style building originally constructed for the railway works department. The lower floors cover the history of textiles, in particular Malaysian fabrics such as *songket* (silk or cotton with gold threading), and the traditional process and machinery used in manufacturing. Gorgeous examples of clothing and fabric abound. The upper floors cover Malaysian fabrics and design motifs in greater detail, as well as items for personal adornment such as jewellery and headgear.

KL City Gallery MUSEUM

(Map p54; ☎03-2691 1382; www.klcitygallery.com; 27 Jln Raja, Merdeka Sq; admission RM5; ⏰9am-6.30pm; Ⓜ Masjid Jamek) Pick up brochures and travel information at the information centre set in the former Government Printing Office (built 1898), before exploring the small exhibition on Kuala Lumpur's history. On the 2nd floor there's a large scale model of KL and you can watch a seven-minute film on the past, present and future of the city.

Muzium Musik MUSEUM

(Music Museum; Map p54; www.jmm.gov.my; Jln Raja, Merdeka Sq; ⏰9am-6pm; Ⓜ Masjid Jamek) FREE This new museum has one floor of exhibits on the history and variety of traditional music from the region. Among the things you'll learn from the displays is that Orang Asli believe music can ward off evil spirits. The building itself, one of the most striking around Merdeka Square, was formerly the Chartered Bank Building, built in 1891.

Lostgens' GALLERY

(Map p54; www.facebook.com/lostgens; 3rd fl, 8c Jln Panggung; ⏰1-7pm Tue-Sun; Ⓜ Pasar Seni) FREE A variety of solo and group artist exhibitions are held at this contemporary arts space, including intriguing installations and video work. Check its Facebook page for details of drawing courses and talks at the performance space Findars (p96), one floor above.

KLCC & Around

★ Petronas Towers TOWER

(Map p58; ☎03-2331 8080; www.petronastwintowers.com.my; Jln Ampang; adult/child RM84.80/31.80; ⏰9am-9pm Tue-Sun, closed 1-2.30pm Fri; 👪; Ⓜ KLCC) Resembling twin silver rockets plucked from an episode of *Flash Gordon*, the Petronas Towers are the perfect allegory for the meteoric rise of the city from tin-miners' hovel to 21st-century metropolis. Half of the 1440 tickets for 45-minute guided tours – which take in the Skybridge connection on the 41st floor and the observation deck on the 86th floor at 370m – are sold in

KUALA LUMPUR IN...

Two Days

Breakfast at **Imbi Market** then get your bearings of the city from atop **Menara Kuala Lumpur**, enjoying the view from the open-air deck if weather (and your head for heights) permits. Hike back down Bukit Nanas along the **canopy walkway**, keeping an eye peeled for monkeys.

Spend the afternoon exploring **Chinatown**, going souvenir shopping at the **Central Market** and admiring the heritage architecture around **Merdeka Square**. End the day at **Jalan Petaling** for food and the night market.

On day two, explore the Tun Abdul Razak Heritage Park, dropping by the **KL Bird Park** and the **Islamic Arts Museum** or **National Museum**. Hit the Kuala Lumpur City Centre (KLCC) at dusk to see the **Petronas Towers** beautifully illuminated. Browse the **Suria KLCC** mall, where there's plenty of places to eat, as there are at **Pavilion KL**. Trawl the night food stalls of **Jalan Alor**.

Three Days

There are great views of the city skyline from **Lake Titiwangsa**, where you can also visit the **National Visual Arts Gallery**. Amble through the Malay area of **Kampung Baru**, then take a taxi to the splendid **Thean Hou Temple**. Have dinner in **Bangsar**, then go see the musical show **Mud**, or check to see if there are concerts at the **Dewan Filharmonik Petronas** or **No Black Tie**.

KLCC & Around

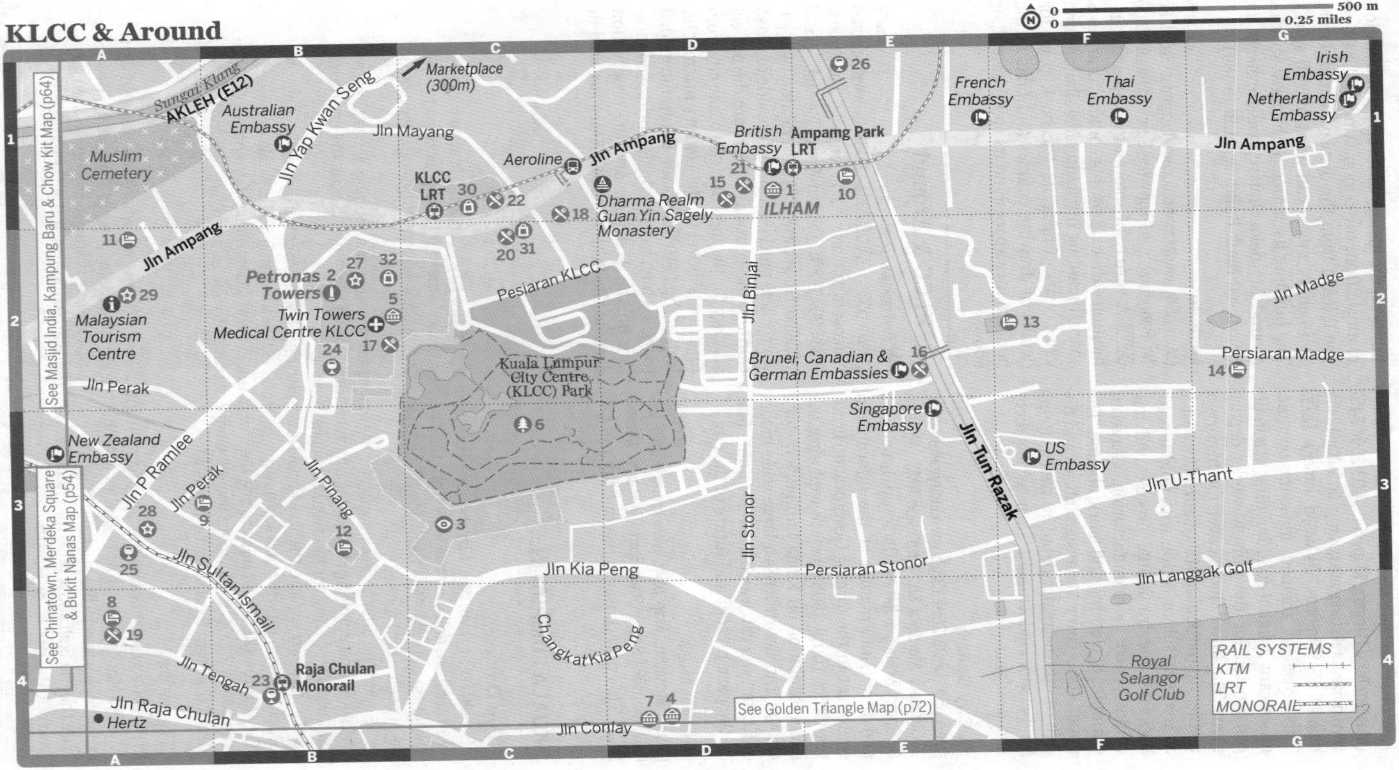
0 500 m
0 0.25 miles
Marketplace (300m)
Sungai Klang
AKLEH (E12)
Australian Embassy
Jln Yap Kwan Seng
Jln Mayang
Muslim Cemetery
Aeroline
Jln Ampang
KLCC LRT
30
22
18
Dharma Realm Guan Yin Sagely Monastery
British Embassy
Ampamg Park LRT
21
15
1
ILHAM
10
26
French Embassy
Thai Embassy
Irish Embassy
Netherlands Embassy
11
20
31
Pesiaran KLCC
Petronas Towers
2
27
32
5
29
Malaysian Tourism Centre
Twin Towers Medical Centre KLCC
17
24
Kuala Lumpur City Centre (KLCC) Park
6
Jln Binjai
13
Jln Madge
Persiaran Madge
14
16
Brunei, Canadian & German Embassies
Singapore Embassy
US Embassy
Jln Tun Razak
Jln U-Thant
Jln Perak
New Zealand Embassy
Jln P Ramlee
28
9
Jln Pinang
3
12
25
Jln Sultan Ismail
Jln Kia Peng
Jln Stonor
Persiaran Stonor
Jln Langgak Golf
8
19
Changkat Kia Peng
Jln Tengah
23
Raja Chulan Monorail
Jln Raja Chulan
Hertz
7
4
Jln Conlay
See Golden Triangle Map (p72)
Royal Selangor Golf Club
RAIL SYSTEMS
KTM
LRT
MONORAIL
See Masjid India, Kampung Baru & Chow Kit Map (p64)
See Chinatown, Merdeka Square & Bukit Nanas Map (p54)

KLCC & Around

Top Sights
1 ILHAM D1
2 Petronas Towers B2

Sights
3 Aquaria KLCC C3
4 Badan Warisan Malaysia D4
5 Galeri Petronas B2
6 KLCC Park C3
Petrosains .... (see 5)
7 Rumah Penghulu Abu Seman D4

Sleeping
8 E&O Residences Kuala Lumpur A4
9 Fraser Place Kuala Lumpur A3
10 G Tower Hotel E1
11 Hotel Maya A2
12 Impiana B3
13 MiCasa All Suite Hotel F2
14 Villa Samadhi G2

Eating
15 Acme Bar & Coffee D1
Cantaloupe .... (see 21)
Little Penang Kafé .... (see 32)
16 Living Food E2
17 Mama San B2
18 Nasi Kandar Pelita C1
Strato .... (see 21)
19 Sushi Hinata A4
20 Thai Syok C2
21 Troika Sky Dining D1
22 Wondermama C1

Drinking & Nightlife
Fuego .... (see 21)
23 Heli Lounge Bar B4
24 Marini's on 57 .... B2
25 Neo Tamarind A3
26 Tate E1

Entertainment
27 Dewan Filharmonik Petronas B2
28 KL Live A3
29 Saloma A2

Shopping
30 Avenue K C1
31 Prototype Gallery C2
32 Suria KLCC B2

advance online. Otherwise, turn up early to be sure of scoring a ticket to go up.

Even though completed back in 1998, the shimmering stainless-steel-clad towers, designed by Argentinian architect Cesar Pelli as the headquarters of the national oil and gas company Petronas, continue to epitomise contemporary KL. The 88-storey twin towers are the tallest pair in the world at nearly 452m and their floor plan is based on an eight-sided star that echoes arabesque patterns. Islamic influences are also evident in each tower's five tiers – representing the five pillars of Islam – and in the 63m masts that crown them, calling to mind the minarets of a mosque and the Star of Islam. They look particularly impressive when illuminated at night.

★ILHAM — GALLERY

(Map p58; www.ilhamgallery.com; 3rd & 5th fl, Ilham Tower, 8 Jln Binjai, 11am-7pm Tue-Sat, to 5pm Sun; Ⓜ Ampang Park) **FREE** KL's latest public art gallery provides an excellent reason to admire close up the slick 60-storey ILHAM Tower designed by Foster + Partners. With a mission to showcase modern and contemporary Malaysian art, ILHAM kicked off in style in August 2015 with a blockbuster show of works by Hoessein Enas (1924–1995). There's no permanent collection, with exhibitions changing every three to four months.

Talks, performances and classes are also planned. Outside the tower the giant copper-clad sculptures are the first permanent public work by Chinese artist Ai Weiwei to be installed in Southeast Asia.

KLCC Park — PARK

(Map p58; KLCC, Jln Ampang; ⏲7am-10pm; Ⓜ KLCC) The park is the best vantage point for eyeballing the Petronas Towers. In the early evening, it can seem like everyone in town has come down here to watch the glowing towers punching up into the night sky. Every night at 8pm, 9pm and 10pm the Lake Symphony fountains play in front of the Suria KLCC.

Aquaria KLCC — AQUARIUM

(Map p58; ☎03-2333 1888; www.aquariaklcc.com; Concourse, KL Convention Centre, Jln Pinang; adult/child RM53/42; ⏲10.30am-8pm, last admission 7pm; 👪; Ⓜ KLCC) The highlight of this impressive aquarium in the basement of the KL Convention Centre is its 90m underwater tunnel: view sand tiger sharks, giant gropers and more up close. Daily feeding sessions for a variety of fish and otters are complemented by ones for arapaimas, electric eels and sharks on Monday, Wednesday and Saturday (see website for schedule). Free dives (RM424), cage dives (RM211), and a Sleep With Sharks (RM211) program for kids aged six to 13 are also available.

Galeri Petronas GALLERY

(Map p58; ☎03-2051 7770; www.galeripetronas.com.my; 3rd fl, Suria KLCC, Jln Ampang; ⏲10am-8pm Tue-Sun; Ⓜ KLCC) FREE Swap consumerism for culture at this excellent art gallery showcasing contemporary photography and paintings. It's a bright, modern space with interesting, professionally curated shows that change every few months.

Petrosains MUSEUM

(Map p58; ☎03-2331 8181; www.petrosains.com.my; 4th fl, Suria KLCC, Jln Ampang; adult/13-17 year old/child RM26.50/21.20/15.90; ⏲9.30am-4pm Tue-Fri, to 5pm Sat & Sun; Ⓜ KLCC) Fill an educational few hours at this interactive science discovery centre with all sorts of buttons to press and levers to pull. Many of the activities and displays focus on the wonderful things that fuel has brought to Malaysia – no prizes for guessing who sponsors the museum. As a side note, 'sains' is not pronounced 'sayns' but 'science'.

Rumah Penghulu Abu Seman HISTORIC BUILDING

(Map p58; 2 Jln Stonor; suggested donation RM10; ⏲tours 11am & 3pm Mon-Sat; monorail Raja Chulan) This glorious wooden stilt house was built in stages between 1910 and the 1930s and later moved to the grounds of **Badan Warisan Malaysia** (Heritage of Malaysia Trust; Map p58; ☎03-2144 9273; www.badanwarisan.org.my; 2 Jln Stonor; ⏲10am-5.30pm Mon-Sat; monorail Raja Chulan) FREE. You can wander around outside tour times (and since it's built with ventilation in mind, you can easily look in). Check out the stunning hand-carved canoe under the house. The boat was used in religious ceremonies in Kelantan and has the head of a fantastic-looking bird carved into the prow.

Tun Abdul Razak Heritage Park & Brickfields

★Islamic Arts Museum MUSEUM

(Muzium Kesenian Islam Malaysia; Map p61; ☎03-2274 2020; www.iamm.org.my; Jln Lembah Perdana; adult/child RM14.85/7.40; ⏲10am-6pm; Kuala Lumpur) This outstanding museum is home to one of best collections of Islamic decorative arts in the world. Aside from the quality of the exhibits, which include fabulous textiles, carpets, jewellery and calligraphy-inscribed pottery, the building itself is a stunner, with beautifully decorated domes and glazed tilework. There's a good Middle Eastern restaurant and one of KL's best museum gift shops stocking beautiful products from around the Islamic world.

★KL Bird Park AVIARY

(Map p61; ☎03-2272 1010; www.klbirdpark.com; Jln Cenderawasih; adult/child RM50/41; ⏲9am-6pm; Kuala Lumpur) This fabulous 21-hectare aviary houses some 3000 birds comprising 200 species of (mostly) Asian bird. The park is divided into four sections: in the first two, birds fly freely beneath an enormous canopy. Section three features the native hornbills (so-called because of their

RIVER OF LIFE & HERITAGE WALKING ROUTES

It was the silt-laden Klang and Gombak rivers that gave Kuala Lumpur its name, which translates as 'muddy confluence'. That meeting of the two waterways, at the point graced by Masjid Jamek (p56), is now the central focus for the ambitious River of Life project. Budgeted at over US$1 billion, one of the aims is to make the currently badly polluted river water clean enough for leisure activities by 2020. The other is beautification of the central city riverbanks. The bridge carrying Lebuh Pasar Besar over the Klang river will be extended to turn it into a partly pedestrianised square, which along with riverside walkways will provide a place for events and to linger to admire the area's historic architecture.

The project also includes creating heritage walking routes through Chinatown, where **Medan Pasar** (Map p54; Ⓜ Masjid Jamek) has been pedestrianised. Along the routes, which were in the process of being signposted when we undertook research, look out for the red-painted metal **sculptures** (Map p54; www.kuenstephanie.com; Bangkok Bank Sq, Lebuh Pudu) based on artworks by Kuen Stephanie that depict scenes from Malaysian life in the style of paper cuttings. There are also life-sized **sculptures** (Map p54; Jln Melaka; Ⓜ Masjid Jamek) based on the cartoonist Lat's humourous characters on Jln Melaka beside Masjid Jamek LRT station.

Tun Abdul Razak Heritage Park & Brickfields

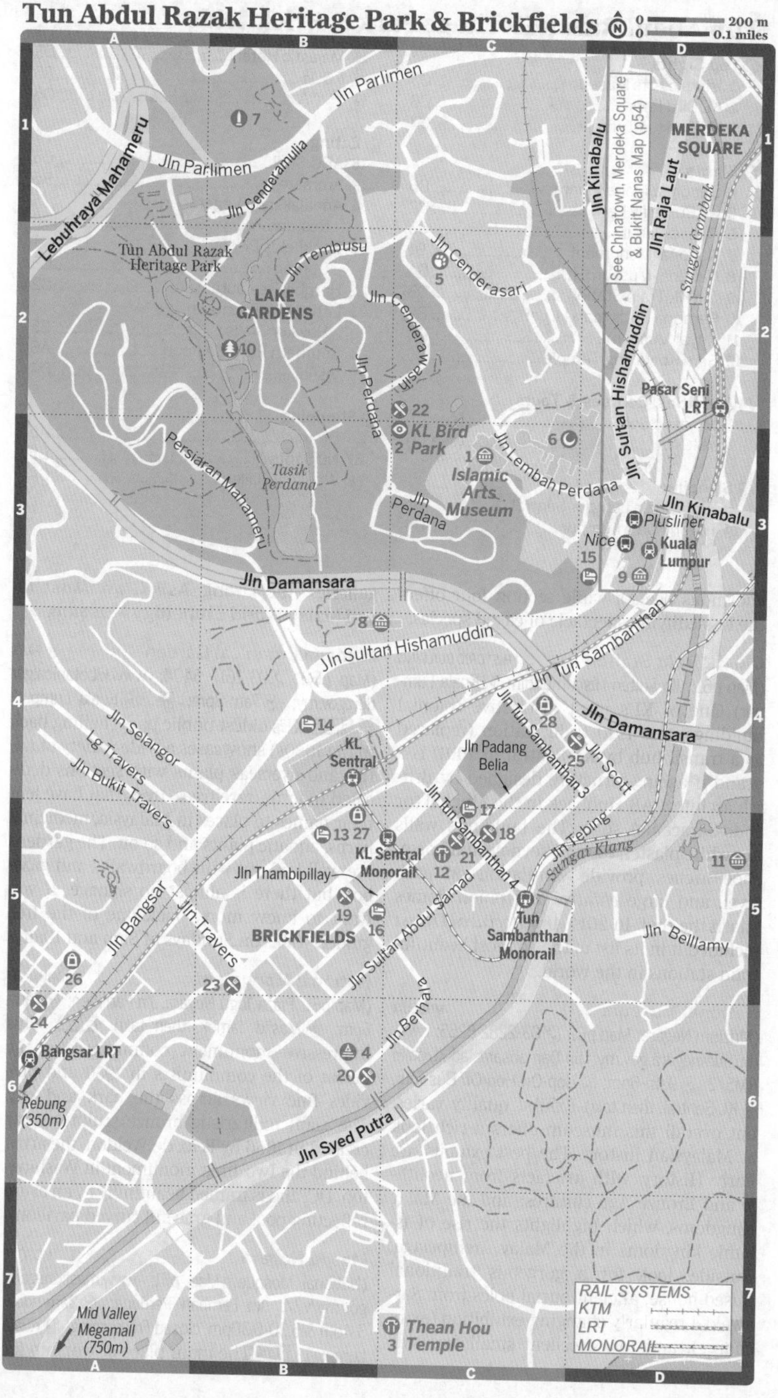

0 200 m
0 0.1 miles
A
B
C
D
1
2
3
4
5
6
7
Jln Parlimen
Lebuhraya Mahameru
Jln Cenderamulia
Tun Abdul Razak Heritage Park
LAKE GARDENS
Jln Tembusu
Jln Cenderasari
Jln Cenderawasih
Jln Perdana
Persiaran Mahameru
Tasik Perdana
KL Bird Park
Islamic Arts Museum
Jln Lembah Perdana
Jln Kinabalu
See Chinatown, Merdeka Square & Bukit Nanas Map (p54)
MERDEKA SQUARE
Jln Raja Laut
Sungai Gombak
Jln Sultan Hishamuddin
Pasar Seni LRT
Plusliner
Nice
Kuala Lumpur
Jln Damansara
Jln Tun Sambanthan
Jln Selangor
Lg Travers
Jln Bukit Travers
KL Sentral
Jln Padang Belia
Jln Tun Sambanthan 3
Jln Scott
Jln Tun Sambanthan 4
Jln Tebing
Sungai Klang
KL Sentral Monorail
Jln Thambipillay
Jln Sultan Abdul Samad
Tun Sambanthan Monorail
BRICKFIELDS
Jln Bangsar
Jln Travers
Jln Bellamy
Jln Berhala
Bangsar LRT
Rebung (350m)
Jln Syed Putra
Mid Valley Megamall (750m)
Thean Hou Temple
RAIL SYSTEMS
KTM
LRT
MONORAIL
1
2
3
4
5
6
7
8
9
10
11
12
13
14
15
16
17
18
19
20
21
22
23
24
25
26
27
28

Tun Abdul Razak Heritage Park & Brickfields

Top Sights
1 Islamic Arts Museum ... C3
2 KL Bird Park ... C3
3 Thean Hou Temple ... C7

Sights
4 Buddhist Maha Vihara ... B6
5 KL Butterfly Park ... C2
6 Masjid Negara ... C3
7 National Monument ... B1
8 National Museum ... B4
9 Old KL Train Station ... D3
10 Perdana Botanical Garden ... B2
11 Royal Museum ... D5
12 Sam Kow Tong Temple ... C5

Activities, Courses & Tours
Majestic Spa ... (see 15)
YMCA ... (see 17)

Sleeping
13 Aloft Kuala Lumpur Sentral ... B5
14 Hilton Kuala Lumpur ... B4
15 Majestic Hotel ... D3
16 PODs ... B5
17 YMCA ... C5

Eating
18 ABC Stall ... C5
19 Ammars ... B5
20 Annalakshmi Vegetarian Restaurant ... B6
21 Brickfields Pisang Goreng ... C5
22 Hornbill Restaurant ... C2
23 Little India Fountain Hawker Stalls ... B5
24 Southern Rock Seafood ... A6
25 Vishal ... D4

Shopping
26 DR.Inc ... A5
27 Nu Sentral ... B5
28 Wei-Ling Gallery ... C4

enormous beaks), while section four offers the less-edifying spectacle of caged species.

Old KL Train Station HISTORIC BUILDING
(Map p61; Jln Sultan Hishamuddin; Kuala Lumpur) One of KL's most distinctive colonial buildings, this 1910 train station (replaced as a transit hub by KL Sentral in 2001) is a grand if ageing structure designed by British architect AB Hubback in the Mughal (or Indo-Saracenic) style. The building's walls are white plaster, rows of keyhole and horseshoe arches provide ventilation on each level, and large *chhatri* and onion domes adorn the roof. In 2014 *Architectural Digest* included it in its list of the 26 most beautiful train stations in the world.

National Museum MUSEUM
(Muzium Negara; Map p61; 03-2282 6255; www.muziumnegara.gov.my; Jln Damansara; adult/child RM5/2; 9am-6pm; Hop-On-Hop-Off Bus Tour, KL Sentral, then taxi) Exhibit quality varies, but overall this museum offers a rich look at Malaysian history. The best exhibits are Early History, with artefacts from neolithic and Bronze Age cultures; and the Malay Kingdoms, which highlights the rise of Islamic kingdoms in the Malay Archipelago. Outside, look for a gorgeous traditional raised house; ancient burial poles from Sarawak; a regularly changing exhibition (extra charge); and two excellent small free side galleries, the **Orang Asli Craft Museum** and **Malay World Ethnology Museum**.

Perdana Botanical Garden PARK
(Map p61; 03-2617 6404; www.klbotanicalgarden.gov.my; 7am-8pm; ; Kuala Lumpur) FREE KL's oldest public park (hailing back to the 1880s) showcases a wide variety of native and overseas plants with sections dedicated to ferns, rare trees, trees that have lent their names to places in Malaysia, medicinal herbs, aquatic plants and so on. The gardens are well laid out with boardwalks and gazebos, but there is almost no signage. If you want to know more, book one of the free guided walks on Sundays at 8am and 10am.

National Monument MONUMENT
(Map p61; Plaza Tugu Negara, Jln Parlimen; 7am-6pm; Masjid Jamek, then taxi) FREE This impressive monument commemorates the defeat of the communists in 1950 and provides fine views across the park and city. The giant militaristic bronze sculpture was created in 1966 by Felix de Weldon, the artist behind the Iwo Jima monument in Washington, DC, and is framed beautifully by an azure reflecting pool and graceful curved pavilion.

Masjid Negara MOSQUE
(National Mosque; Map p61; www.masjidnegara.gov.my/v2/; Jln Lembah Perdana; 9am-noon, 3-4pm & 5.30-6.30pm, closed Fri morning; Kuala Lumpur) FREE The main place of worship for

KL's Malay Muslim population is this gigantic 1960s mosque, inspired by Mecca's Grand Mosque. Able to accommodate 15,000 worshippers, its umbrella-like blue-tile roof has 18 points symbolising the 13 states of Malaysia and the five pillars of Islam. Rising above the mosque, a 74m-high minaret issues the call to prayer, which can be heard across Chinatown. Non-Muslims are welcome to visit outside prayer times; robes are available for those who are not dressed appropriately.

KL Butterfly Park WILDLIFE RESERVE

(Taman Rama Rama; Map p61; ☎03-2693 4799; www.klbutterflypark.com; Jln Cenderasari; adult/child RM20/10; ⏰9am-6pm; Kuala Lumpur) Billed as the largest enclosed butterfly garden in the world, this is a great place to get up close with a hundred or so of the 1100-plus butterfly species found in Malaysia, including the enormous and well-named birdwings, the elegant swallowtails, and the colourful tigers and jezebels. There's also a bug gallery where you can shudder at the size of Malaysia's giant centipedes and spiders.

Sam Kow Tong Temple CHINESE TEMPLE

(Map p61; 16 Jln Thambapillai; ⏰7am-5pm; monorail KL Sentral) FREE Established in 1916 by the Heng Hua clan, the 'three teachings' temple has a beautiful Hokkien-style temple roof, with graceful curving ridgelines that taper at the ends like swallowtails. The colourful rooftop dragons, and other figures, are actually three-dimensional mosaics, another traditional decorative feature of southern Chinese temples (though these are new works). Inside look for photos of the original temple, a simple timber-frame structure with a thatched roof.

Buddhist Maha Vihara BUDDHIST TEMPLE

(Map p61; ☎03-2274 1141; www.buddhistmahavihara.com; 123 Jln Berhala, Brickfields; KL Sentral, monorail KL Sentral) Founded in 1894 by Sinhalese settlers, this is one of KL's major Theravada Buddhist temples. It's a particular hive of activity around Wesak Day, the Buddha's birthday, when a massive parade with multiple floats starts from here before winding round the city.

Masjid India, Kampung Baru & Chow Kit

Kampung Baru NEIGHBOURHOOD

The charm of this Malay area, gazetted by the British in the 1890s, lies in just wandering the streets, which you can also do with a guide on the city's free **Kampung Baru Walking Tour** (Map p64; ☎03-2698 0332; www.visitkl.gov.my/visitklv2; ⏰4.30-7pm Tue, Thu & Sun). Traditional Malay wooden houses stand amid leafy gardens and people go quietly about their daily lives as they have done for decades. Along the way enjoy tasty home-cooked Malay food at unpretentious roadside cafes and stalls.

Loke Mansion HISTORIC BUILDING

(Map p64; ☎03-2691 0803; 273a Jln Medan Tuanku; ⏰9am-5pm Mon-Fri; monorail Medan Tuanku) Rescued from the brink of dereliction by the law firm Cheang & Ariff, Loke Mansion was once the home of self-made tin tycoon Loke Yew. The Japanese high command also set up base here in 1942. After years of neglect, the mansion has been beautifully restored; access to the interior is by appointment only, but you're welcome anytime to pause in the driveway and admire the whitewashed exterior.

Bank Negara Malaysia Museum & Art Gallery MUSEUM

(☎03-9179 2784; www.museum.bnm.gov.my; Sasana Kijang, 2 Jln Dato Onn; ⏰10am-6pm; Bank Negara, then taxi) FREE This well-designed complex of small museums focuses on banking, finance and money, and is not dull in the least. Highlights include a collection of ancient coins and money (and a slick interactive screen to examine its history), a gallery of the bank's private art collection, a surreal 3m-long tunnel lined with RM1

GETTING TO THE TUN ABDUL RAZAK HERITAGE PARK

The Tun Abdul Razak Heritage Park, an area still best known by its colonial moniker of the Lake Gardens, can seem like an island of greenery cut off from the city by railway lines and highways. However, it is possible to walk here: take the pedestrian bridge across from the Central Market to Kompleks Dayabumi and then head south around the back of the post office to the underpass leading to the Masjid Negara. Another set of overhead pedestrian bridges lead into KL Station, from where you can also walk up to the gardens. Once in the park, you can use the hop-on, hop-off electric tram (adult/child RM2/1; 9am to 6pm) to get between the major attractions.

Masjid India, Kampung Baru & Chow Kit

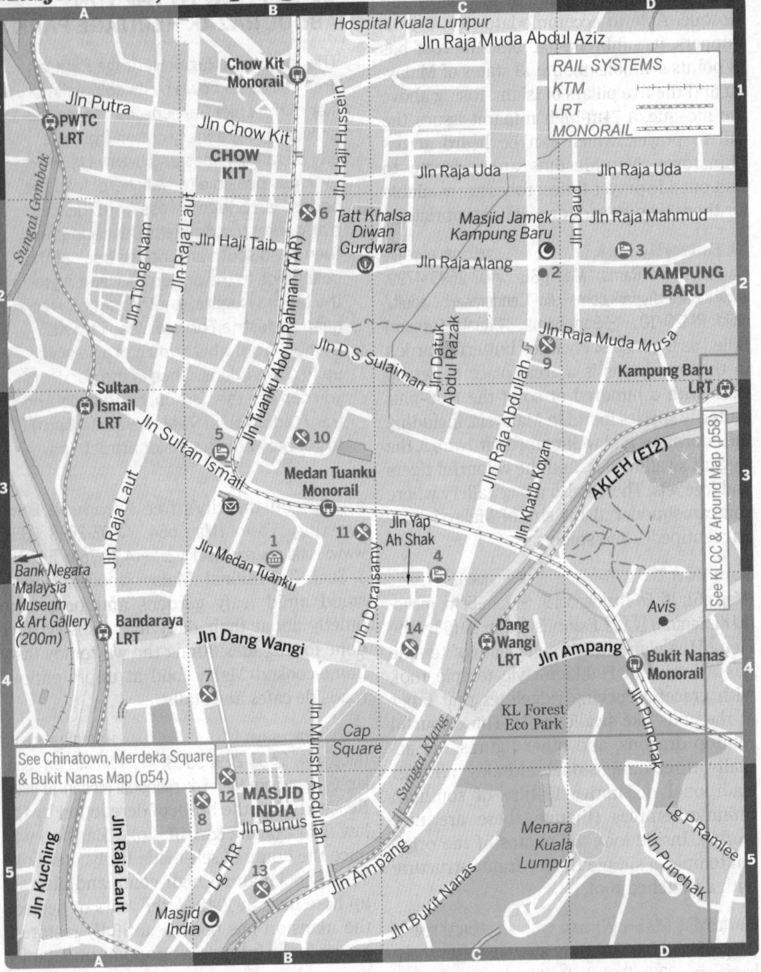

Masjid India, Kampung Baru & Chow Kit

Sights

1 Loke Mansion B3

Activities, Courses & Tours

2 Kampung Baru Walking Tour C2

Sleeping

3 Bagasta D2
4 The Reeds C3
5 Tune Hotel Downtown Kuala Lumpur B3

Eating

6 Bazaar Baru Chow Kit B2
7 Capital Café B4
8 Coliseum Cafe B5
9 Ikan Bakar Berempah C2
10 Kin Kin B3
11 Limapulo B3
12 Masjid India Pasar Malam B5
13 Saravana Bhavan B5
14 Yut Kee C4

Drinking & Nightlife

Butter & Beans .... (see 11)

KL'S NEW STREET ART

Following on from the successful street-art revolution in George Town, Penang, KL has seen a flurry of large-scale paintings on the sides of buildings, including one by Penang darling and Lithuanian artist **Ernest Zacharevic**. His giant mural of a **boy in a canoe** (Map p54; Wisma Allianz, 33 Jln Gereja; M Masjid Jamek) can be seen on the wall of Wisma Allianz, next to a car park on Jln Gereja.

The 2014 **#tanahairku** (my homeland) street-art project, sponsored by oil and gas conglomerate Petronas, saw six massive murals created around the city by 16 artists; you can still see ones on buildings along Jln Raja Chulan between Chinatown and Bukit Nanas, including a colourful one across a row of crumbling **shophouses** (Map p54; Jln Raja Chulan; KL Tower) at the foot of Bukit Nanas, and a massive wall **mural** (Map p54; Jln Raja Chulan; Muzium Telekom) of a boy in tiger hat.

Also in Chinatown, graphic artist turned street artist Kenji Chai painted a giant **cockerel** (Map p54; Jln Tun Tan Cheng Lock; M Plaza Rakyat) on the side of the Nando's building; and students from Kuala Lumpur Metropolitan College (KLMCU) have contributed a variety of fun murals along **Pasar Karat** (Map p54; alley btwn Jln Petaling & Jln Sultan; M Pasar Seni), where a flea market runs every day from 7am to 10am.

Also look out for the **#districtcreative #artforlife** (Map p72; Jln Imbi; monorail Imbi) explosion of colour overlooking a car park on Jln Imbi opposite the ParkRoyal Hotel and the ceiling murals in **Wisma Central** on Jln Ampang created by the folks behind Prototype Gallery (p98).

million (in the Children's Gallery), and a history of the little-known Islamic banking system (which must comply with sharia law, including prohibitions against usury).

Titiwangsa

★Titiwangsa Lake Gardens PARK

(Taman Tasik Titiwangsa; Map p66; Jln Tembeling; monorail Titiwangsa) For a postcard-perfect view of the city skyline, head to Lake Titiwangsa and the relaxing treed park that surrounds it. If you're feeling energetic, hire a row boat, go for a jog, play some tennis or explore the nearby neighbourhood of handsome bungalows. The park is a favourite spot for courting Malaysian couples. It's a 10-minute walk east of the monorail station.

National Visual Arts Gallery GALLERY

(Balai Seni Lukis Negara; Map p66; 03-4026 7000; www.artgallery.gov.my; 2 Jln Temerloh; 10am-6pm; monorail Titiwangsa) FREE Occupying a pyramid-shaped block, the NVAG showcases modern and contemporary Malaysian art. It's always worth turning up to see a variety of interesting temporary shows of local and regional artists, as well as pieces from the gallery's permanent collection of 4000 pieces, including paintings by Zulkifli Moh'd Dahalan, Wong Hoy Cheong, Ahmad Fuad Osman and the renowned batik artist Chuah Thean Teng. On the ground floor, the National Portrait Gallery also hosts regularly changing exhibitions.

Outside Central KL

★Thean Hou Temple CHINESE TEMPLE

(Map p61; 03-2274 7088; www.hainannet.com.my/en; off Jln Syed Putra; 8am-10pm; monorail Tun Sambanthan) Sitting atop leafy Robson Heights, this imposing multistorey Chinese temple, dedicated to Thean Hou, the heavenly queen, affords wonderful views over Kuala Lumpur. Opened in 1989 by the Selangor and Federal Territory Hainan Association, it serves as both a house of worship and a functional space for events such as weddings. In recent years it's also become a tourist attraction in its own right, especially during Chinese festival times and the birthdays of the various temple gods.

From the temple's upper decks you can get close-up views of the mosaic dragons and phoenixes adorning the eaves. To reach the temple, take either a taxi or the monorail to Tun Sambanthan station, cross Jln Syed Putra using the overpass and walk up the hill.

Royal Museum MUSEUM

(Muzium Diraja; Map p61; www.jmm.gov.my/en/muzium-diraja; Jln Istana; adult/child RM10/5; 9am-5pm;) With the opening in 2011 of the RM800-million Istana Negara, residence

Titiwangsa

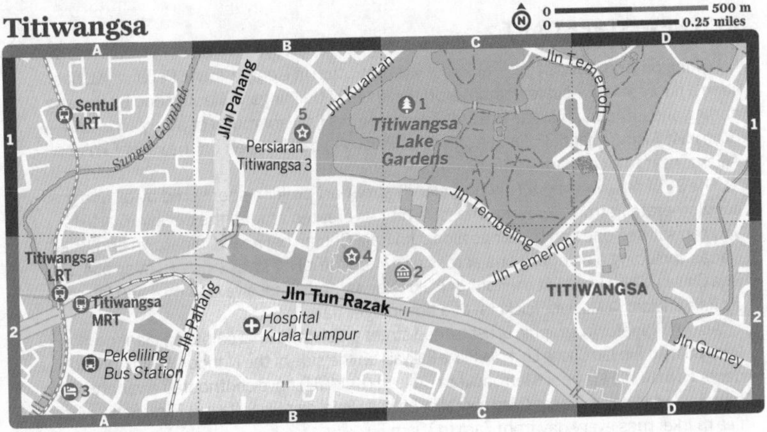

Titiwangsa

Top Sights

1 Titiwangsa Lake Gardens C1

Sights

2 National Visual Arts Gallery C2

Sleeping

3 Vistana A2

Eating

D'Istana Jalamas Café .... (see 4)

Entertainment

4 Istana Budaya B2
5 Sutra Dance Theatre B1

of Malaysia's head of state, in the north of the city, the former Royal Palace has become the Royal Museum. You can tour the first two floors of the mansion, originally built as a family home in 1928 by Chinese tin tycoon Chan Wing. The palace exterior, with its eclectic European style, looks much the same as it was in Chan Wing's day.

MAP ART GALLERY

(☎03-6207 9732; www.facebook.com/mapkl; Publika, 1 Jln Dutamas, Solaris Dutamas; ⏲10am-9pm; 🚗) The cultural anchor of the forward-thinking mall Publika, MAP hosts excellent art and photography exhibitions in its White Box space, while the Black Box space has everything from shows by Malaysian death-metal bands to major public events and product launches. Publika mall is located about 3km northwest of Tun Abdul Razak Heritage Park area.

Activities

Chin Woo Stadium SWIMMING

(Map p54; ☎03-2072 4602; www.chinwoo.org.my; Jln Hang Jebat; swimming adult/child RM5/2; ⏲2-8pm Mon-Fri, 9am-8pm Sat & Sun; Ⓜ Pasar Seni) This historic sports stadium sits atop a hill overlooking Chinatown. The highlight here is its 50m outdoor pool. Note that all swimsuits must be tight-fitting, ie no baggy shorts even with an inner mesh lining, and you need a cap as well. In the stadium itself various yoga classes are held every Monday at 7.30pm and there are badminton courts (racquets can be hired).

Spa Village SPA

(Map p72; ☎03-2782 9090; www.spavillageresort.org; Ritz Carlton, 168 Jln Imbi; treatments RM350-1000; ⏲10am-10pm; monorail AirAsia-Bukit Bintang) Indoor and outdoor beauty and massage treatments, a sensory room, and a second outdoor pool with waterfalls.

Asianel Reflexology Spa SPA

(Map p72; ☎03-2142 1397; www.asianel.com; Pamper fl, Starhill Gallery, 181 Jln Bukit Bintang; treatments from RM100; ⏲10am-9pm; monorail AirAsia-Bukit Bintang) Upmarket reflexology spa with a particular emphasis on foot treatments, though it also does complete body packages.

Kenko SPA

(Map p72; ☎03-2141 6651; www.kenko.com.sg; 5th fl, Pavilion KL, 169 Jln Bukit Bintang; treatments from RM39; ⏲10am-10pm; monorail AirAsia-Bukit Bintang) This popular branch of the Singapore-based reflexology and massage chain offers a variety of partial and full-body massage and acupressure therapies. There's also a popular and very hygienic fish spa should you wish skin to be nibbled off your tootsies.

Berjaya Times Square Theme Park AMUSEMENT PARK
(Map p72; ☎03-2117 3118; www.timessquarekl.com/themepark; Berjaya Times Sq, 1 Jln Imbi; adult/child RM51/41; ⏰noon-10pm Mon-Fri, 11am-10pm Sat & Sun; monorail Imbi) Despite the mall location, there's a full-sized looping coaster plus a good selection of thrill rides for teenagers and gentler rides for families. (Avoid the DNA Mixer unless you want to see your *nasi lemak* a second time.)

Courses

Check directly with each of the listings for prices and exact course times and details.

★LaZat Malaysian Home Cooking Class COOKING COURSE
(☎019-238 1198; www.malaysia-klcookingclass.com; Malay House at Penchala Hills, lot 3196, Jln Seri Penchala, Kampong Sg; ⏰10am-2pm Mon-Sat) A market tour is followed by a hands-on cooking course in a traditional Malay home in the leafy northwestern suburb of Penchala Hills.

Bayan Indah Culinary Retreat COOKING COURSE
(www.bayanindah.com) Learn to cook traditional Malaysian dishes at these hands-on classes run by friendly cookbook author Rohani Jelani in a beautiful countryside retreat where you can also stay the night. Each class ends with a sit-down meal of the dishes prepared that day.

Starhill Culinary Studio COOKING COURSE
(Map p72; ☎03-2782 3810; www.starhillculinarystudio.com; Starhill Gallery, Muse fl, 181 Jln Bukit Bintang; public classes Tue-Sun RM168-258; ⏰9am-6pm Tue-Sun; monorail AirAsia-Bukit Bintang) Sign up for a two- to three-hour class (focusing on a single dish usually) and you'll not only get top instruction in this gleaming, well-designed culinary-art studio, but you'll also be well fed. Classes vary daily and include Malay and Nonya (Peranakan) dishes, Japanese cuisine, and Asian and Western desserts. Private classes can also be arranged.

School of Hard Knocks COURSE
(☎03-4145 6122; http://visitorcentre.royalselangor.com/vc2; 4 Jln Usahawan 6, Setapak Jaya; 30-min classes RM63.60; ⏰9am-5pm; Ⓜ Wangsa Maju, then taxi) This famous pewter centre offers entertaining classes where you make your own pewter bowl; advance booking required.

YMCA LANGUAGE COURSE
(Map p61; ☎03-2274 1439; www.ymcakl.com; 95 Jln Padang Belia, Brickfields; monorail KL Sentral) Become a member, then you can join the Bahasa Malaysia classes as well as courses studying Thai, Mandarin, Cantonese and Japanese. You can also study martial arts and different types of dancing here.

Tours

Simply Enak FOOD TOUR
(☎017-287 8929; www.simplyenak.com; tours RM200-250) Daily tours to places such as Chow Kit, Petaling St and Kampung Baru to experience authentic Malaysian food with resident experts.

Food Tour Malaysia FOOD TOUR
(www.foodtourmalaysia.com; walking/driving tours RM110/160) Expert guides lead these walking tours around some of KL's best street-food and dining destinations. They also offer a full-day tour out to the foodie destination of Ipoh, plus food tours in Penang.

KL Hop-On Hop-Off BUS TOUR
(☎1800-885 546; www.myhoponhopoff.com; adult/child 24hr ticket RM45/24, 48hr ticket RM79/43; ⏰9am-8pm) This double-decker, wi-fi-enabled, air-con tourist bus makes a circuit of the main tourist sites half-hourly throughout the day. Stops include KLCC, Jalan Bukit Bintang, Menara KL, Chinatown, Merdeka Square and the attractions of Tun

FREE GUIDED WALKS

Visit KL (p100) offers two free guided walks, which are great for historical and local insight:

- Merdeka Square, 9am to 11.45am Monday, Wednesday and Saturday
- Kampung Baru, 4.30pm to 7pm Tuesday, Thursday and Sunday

Bookings can be made on ☎03-2698 0332 or via email at pelancongan@dblk.gov.my, ideally 24 hours in advance.

For self-guided walks, three signposted **heritage walking routes** that are part of the River of Life project are also being set up in the Chinatown and Bukit Nanas areas.

Abdul Razak Heritage Park. Tickets, which can be bought on the bus, last all day and you can get on and off as often as you like.

Festivals & Events

The capital puts on a show for Malaysia's major holidays and festivals, including Chinese New Year, Thaipusam, National Day and Deepavali.

Cooler Lumpur Festival ART
(www.coolerlumpur.com; Jun) Multidisciplinary arts festival with a different annual theme, usually held in June with events staged at Publika (p99).

DiverseCity CULTURAL
(http://diversecity.my; Sep) KL's international arts festival runs throughout September and offers a packed program from contemporary and traditional dance and music shows to literature readings, comedy and visual arts events.

KL International Jazz & Arts Festival JAZZ
(www.klinternationaljazz.com; Sep) A cracking line-up of artists perform at this festival held on the campus of the University of Malaya in September.

KL Tower BASE Jump ADVENTURE SPORTS
(www.kltowerjump.com; Sep-Oct) The only time you'll be able to see people legally flinging themselves off Menara KL is when the international BASE-jumping fraternity are in town in September/October.

Standard Chartered KL Marathon SPORTS
(www.kl-marathon.com; Oct) October sees over 17,500 runners take to the streets for this international marathon event.

Sleeping

KL is awash with accommodation, running the gamut from grubby fleapits with boxy, windowless rooms, appealing only for their rock-bottom rates, to expense-account pamper palaces.

Always ask about special deals as practically all midrange and top-end places offer promotions that can substantially slash rack rates; booking online will almost always bring the price down. The only time you should book ahead to be sure of accommodation is public holidays, when room discounts will not apply.

In KL budget ($) means places offering a dorm bed or a double room with attached bathroom for under RM100; midrange ($$) properties have double rooms with attached bathrooms for RM100 to RM400; top-end places ($$$) charge over RM400. At all budget places, prices will be net, but at many others, 10% service and 6% tax (expressed as ++) will be added to the bill.

Chinatown & Around

★**BackHome** HOSTEL $
(Map p54; 03-2022 0788; www.backhome.com.my; 30 Jln Tun HS Lee; dm/d/tr incl breakfast from RM53/134/192; M Masjid Jamek) This chic pit stop for flashpackers offers polished-concrete finishes, Zen simple decoration, fab rain showers and a blissful central courtyard sprouting spindly trees. It can be noisy on the street outside, but the hostel offers earplugs for light sleepers. Also check out its cool cafe, LOKL (p76).

Reggae Mansion HOSTEL $
(Map p54; 03-2072 6877; www.reggaehostelsmalaysia.com/mansion; 49-59 Jln Tun HS Lee; dm/d from RM50/150; M Masjid Jamek) Grooving to a beat that's superior to most backpacker places, including its own guesthouses in the heart of Chinatown, this is one cool operation. The decor is whitewashed faux colonial with contemporary touches including a flash cafe-bar, rooftop bar and mini cinema.

KUALA LUMPUR FOR CHILDREN

There are dozens of attractions around KL set up specifically to keep little ones entertained. A good starting point is the Tun Abdul Razak Heritage Park, particularly the KL Bird Park (p60) and the playground and boating pond in the Perdana Botanical Garden (p62). The waterfall splash pool in the KLCC Park (p59) is also great for waterbabies, as is the adjacent adventure playground and the Aquaria KLCC (p59).

Kids will also enjoy KL's malls. Berjaya Times Square has an indoor theme park (p67). There are more theme parks dotted around KL, including the wet and wild park at Sunway Lagoon (p114). For nature activities, head to the canopy walkways at KL Forest Eco Park (p51) and the Forestry Research Institute of Malaysia (p108).

Lantern Hotel HOTEL $
(Map p54; ☎03-2020 1648; www.lanternhotel.com; 38 Jln Petaling; r incl breakfast from RM98; ❄📶; Ⓜ Pasar Seni) You can't get more central to Chinatown than this slickly designed new hotel. The simple, whitewashed rooms with feature lime or tangerine walls all have their own bathrooms – the cheapest ones with no windows (but spared some of the noise from the market outside). A huge plus is the cool terrace with a bird's-eye view of Petaling Street Market.

Paloma Inn HOTEL $
(Map p54; ☎03-2110 6677; www.hotelpalomainn.com.my; 12-14 Jln Sin Chew Kee; dm/s/d incl breakfast from RM42/95/128; ❄@📶; monorail Hang Tuah) Set on a backstreet of painted prewar shophouses, Paloma is a great hang-out that's well run, quiet but also super central. VCR cafe (p92) is just around the corner for superb espresso, while the nightlife of Chankit Bukit Bintang is a 10-minute walk away. Rates are slightly higher Friday to Sunday.

Explorers Guesthouse HOSTEL $
(Map p54; ☎03-2022 2928; www.theexplorersguesthouse.com; 128-130 Jln Tun HS Lee; dm/d with shared bathroom incl breakfast from RM35/97.50; ❄@📶; Ⓜ Pasar Seni) One of Chinatown's more appealing hostels, the comfy, spacious lobby here leads on to clean, airy rooms, a roof terrace, colourfully painted walls and a few arty touches.

Hotel Chinatown (2) HOTEL $
(Map p54; ☎03-2072 9933; www.hotelchinatown2.com; 70-72 Jln Petaling; s/d from RM70/91; ❄@📶; Ⓜ Pasar Seni) If all you need is a cheap room to yourself, this place works. The cheapest rooms have no windows but are away from the noisy main street. The lobby offers a comfy lounge area, book exchange and piano.

Hotel 1000 Miles HOTEL $$
(Map p54; ☎03-2022 3333; 17 & 19 Jln Tun HS Lee; r incl breakfast from RM104; ❄@📶; Ⓜ Masjid Jamek) Channeling a vague 1960s feel (black-and-white photos of KL, a few modish pieces of midcentury modern furniture), this brightly painted newcomer has kerb appeal and friendly management. The rooms are all en suite and fine. At the time of writing they planned to add an elevator and a rooftop cafe.

5 Elements Hotel HOTEL $$
(Map p54; ☎03-2031 6888; www.the5elementshotel.com.my; lot 243, Jln Sultan; s/tw/d incl breakfast from RM150/180/190; ❄@📶; Ⓜ Pasar Seni) Offering a good range of rooms, some with views towards KL Tower, this hotel makes a credible stab at boutique stylings. We particularly liked the sensuous design motif snaking its way across the corridor and bedroom walls.

AnCasa Hotel & Spa Kuala Lumpur HOTEL $$
(Map p54; ☎03-2026 6060; www.ancasa-hotel.com; Jln Tun Tan Cheng Lock; d incl breakfast from RM258; ❄@; Ⓜ Plaza Rakyat) Promotional rates (including Friday to Sunday rates of RM160) make this one of Chinatown's best midrange options. The comfortable rooms are well equipped and there's an in-house Balinese-style spa. It also runs the functional business hotel **AnCasa Express @ Pudu** (Map p54; ☎03-2026 6060; www.ancasahotels.com; 4th fl, Pudu Sentral, Jln Pudu; r from RM90; ❄@📶; Ⓜ Plaza Rakyat) atop Pudu Sentral bus station.

Sarang Vacation Homes GUESTHOUSE $$
(Map p54; ☎012-210 0218; www.sarangvacationhomes.com; 6 Jln Galloway; s/d incl breakfast from RM130/150, minimum 2 night stay; ❄📶; monorail Hang Tuah) Michael and Christina run this appealing bed-and-breakfast operation. They have houses, apartments and rooms in five nearby locations and can accommodate single travellers (limited) and families alike. The furnishings are simple, the vibe is relaxed and welcoming and the location is excellent. It's a skip away from Jln Alor in a residential shophouse enclave.

Golden Triangle

Classic Inn HOSTEL $
(Map p72; ☎03-2148 8648; www.classicinn.com.my; 36 & 52 Lg 1/77a; dm/s/d incl breakfast from RM40/98/128; ❄@📶; monorail Imbi) Check-in is at the newer, more upmarket branch of Classic Inn at No 36 where there's spotless rooms all with private bathrooms and a pleasant veranda cafe. The original yellow-painted shophouse at No 52 continues to be a retro-charming choice with dorms and private rooms, a small grassy garden and welcoming staff.

Container Hotel DESIGN HOTEL $
(Map p72; ☎03-2116 4388; www.containerhotel.com; 1 Jln Delima; dm RM39, s with shared bathroom/d incl breakfast RM110/139; ❄📶; monorail AirAsia-Bukit Bintang) Stacked shipping containers turned into en suite rooms (sadly,

not too well maintained) are the basis of this inventive place. We preferred the singles in giant concrete cylinders. There's also a roof terrace and free bike rental. It's close by the excellent bakery cafe Levain and megaclub Zouk (p93).

Rainforest Bed & Breakfast GUESTHOUSE $

(Map p72; ☎03-2145 3525; www.rainforestbnbhotel.com; 27 Jln Mesui; dm/d/tw incl breakfast RM37/115/130; ❄@📶; monorail Raja Chulan) The lush foliage sprouting around and tumbling off the tiered balconies of this high-quality guesthouse is eye-catching and apt for its name. Inside, bright-red walls and timber-lined rooms (some without windows) are visually distinctive, along with the collection of Chinese pottery figurines. The location for nightlife, cafes and restaurants couldn't be better.

★ **Wolo Bukit Bintang** BOUTIQUE HOTEL $$

(Map p72; ☎03-2719 1333; www.thewolo.com; cnr Jln Bukit Bintang & Jln Sultan Ismail; r incl breakfast from RM270; ❄📶; monorail AirAsia-Bukit Bintang) Neon and mirror-clad elevators whisk you to dark corridors, the walls rippled with fabric, and on into rooms where the mattress sits on a blonde wood floor base, like a futon, and the shower and toilet are hidden behind faux padded leather doors. The vibe is rock-star glam and a change from the midrange norm.

At the time of research a new modern Asian restaurant was set to occupy the former penthouse suite, to be run by the folks behind Troika Sky Dining (p89).

The Mesui Hotel BOUTIQUE HOTEL $$

(Map p72; ☎03-2144 8188; www.themesuihotel.com; 9 Jln Mesui; r incl breakfast from RM277; ❄📶; monorail Raja Chulan) This low-scale gem is crafted from an old building that looks like it was made from a giant's set of building blocks. The Loft rooms allow you to peer out of the large signature circular windows onto the street. Other compact, functional rooms gain their light from the interior courtyard of which one wall is covered in lush greenery.

Anggun Boutique Hotel HOTEL $$

(Map p72; ☎03-2145 8003; www.anggunkl.com; 7-9 Tengkat Tong Shin; d incl breakfast from RM350; ❄📶; monorail Imbi) Two 1920s shophouses have been combined to create this antique-style, boutique property that oozes tropical charm with four-poster beds, dark-wood floors and local crafts. At the time of research a new ground-floor restaurant and bar was being planned with the rooftop becoming the spa. Avoid rooms facing the noisy street though – or bring earplugs.

The Yard Boutique Hotel HOTEL $$

(Map p72; ☎03-2141 1017; www.theyard.com.my; lot 623, 51d Tengkat Tong Shin; d from RM160; ❄@📶; monorail AirAsia-Bukit Bintang) This somewhat-hip oasis is steps away from both the eats of Jln Alor and the bars of Changkat Bukit Bintang. Contemporary-design rooms are comfortable and decent value for what they offer. Bring earplugs to block out the street noise.

YY38 Hotel HOTEL $$

(Map p72; ☎03-2148 8838; www.yy38hotel.com.my; 38 Tengkat Tong Shin; s/d/loft room from RM130/150/360; ❄📶; monorail AirAsia-Bukit Bintang) The bulk of the rooms here are fine but no-frills. However, the 7th floor offers 17 creatively designed duplexes, each sleeping three, with fun themes ranging from Marilyn Monroe to circus and tree house – a good one if you're travelling with kids.

Chaos Hotel HOTEL $$

(Map p72; ☎03-2148 6688; www.chaos-hotel.com; lot B1, Fahrenheit 88, 179 Jln Bukit Bintang; s/d from RM135/168; ❄📶; monorail AirAsia-Bukit Bintang) It might seem like tempting fate by calling your hotel Chaos, but this new place is actually well run with compact but smart, minimalist-styled rooms with concrete and exposed brick walls, wooden fixtures and snazzy graphic art.

Ceria Hotel HOTEL $$

(Map p72; ☎03-2143 1111; www.ceriahotel.com; 270 Jln Changkat Thambi Dollah; s/d RM98/138; ❄📶; monorail Imbi) An old shophouse has been cleverly converted into this 44-room hotel with exposed brick walls and some cool retro design features. Not all the rooms have windows but they're of a reasonable size with slightly better quality features than similar hotels at this price point. Plus there's a nice attached cafe for breakfast.

Sahabat Guest House GUESTHOUSE $$

(Map p72; ☎03-2142 0689; www.sahabatguesthouse.com; 39-41 Jln Sahabat; d incl breakfast from RM115; ❄@📶; monorail Raja Chulan) This blue-painted guesthouse is well run, offering 14 tidy bedrooms, with tiny en suite bathrooms and a feature wall plastered in vivid patterned wallpaper. There's a grassy front

SERVICED APARTMENTS

Some of the KL's best accommodation deals, particularly for longer stays, are offered by serviced apartments. Studios and suites tend to be far larger and better equipped than you'd get for a similar price at top-end hotels. There are quite a few of these complexes scattered across the city. For short stays breakfast is usually included. Our top picks:

Fraser Place Kuala Lumpur (Map p58; ☎03-2118 6288; http://kualalumpur.frasershospitality.com; lot 163, 10 Jln Perak; apt from RM370; ❄@🛜🏊; monorail Bukit Nanas) Good workspaces and walk-in closets feature in these colourfully designed apartments. The facilities, including an outdoor infinity pool, gym, sauna and games room, are top notch.

E&O Residences Kuala Lumpur (Map p58; ☎03-2023 2188; www.eoresidences.com; 1 Jln Tengah; 1-bed apt from RM461; ❄@🛜🏊; monorail Raja Chulan) Chances are once you spend a night in these elegantly designed apartments with their clean-line furnishings and striking contemporary art, you will not want to leave. There's a good gym and large outdoor pool in the landscaped courtyard garden. A buffet breakfast is served in the complex's Delicious Cafe.

MiCasa All Suite Hotel (Map p58; ☎03-2179 8000; www.micasahotel.com; 368b Jln Tun Razak; apt from RM420; ❄@🛜🏊; Ⓜ Ampang Park) A choice of one-, two- or three-bedroom suites – all reasonably priced, with wood floors and kitchens. Relax beside the large, palm-tree-fringed pool, or enjoy its small spa and the gourmet restaurant Cilantro.

Pacific Regency Hotel Suites (Map p54; ☎03-2332 7777; www.pacific-regency.com; Jln Punchak, Menara Panglobal; apt incl breakfast from RM465; ❄@🛜🏊; monorail Bukit Nanas) These upmarket self-catering studios and serviced apartments are good value compared with the rooms of a similar standard at KL's other five-star properties. Ask to see the newer rooms. Head up top to enjoy the rooftop pool and bar Luna.

Invito (Map p72; ☎03-2386 9288; www.invitohotelsuites.com.my; 1 Lg Ceylon; apt from RM550; ❄@🛜🏊; monorail Raja Chulan) A lively location and good facilities, including a decent-size pool, jacuzzi and gym, mark out this stylish hotel of self-catering studios and apartments. All units have balconies and the decor in purple and silver is reasonably classy.

garden in which to relax. Rates are slightly higher from Friday to Sunday.

KLCC & Around

Impiana HOTEL **$$**

(Map p58; ☎03-2141 1111; www.impiana.com; 13 Jln Pinang; d incl breakfast from RM350; ❄@🛜🏊; monorail Raja Chulan) This chic property offers spacious rooms with parquet floors and lots of seductive amenities including a spa and infinity pool. The newer and more pricey Club Tower rooms are the ones with views towards the KLCC.

★ Villa Samadhi HOTEL **$$$**

(Map p58; ☎03-2143 2300; www.villasamadhi.com.my; 8 Jln Madge; r from RM600; ❄@🛜🏊; Ⓜ Ampang Park) It's hard to believe you're in the heart of KL while staying at this gorgeous boutique property that epitomises Southeast Asian chic. The black polished concrete, bamboo and reclaimed-timber rooms with luxurious light fixtures, idyllic central pool, lush foliage, rooftop bar (serving complimentary cocktails) and intimate modern Malay restaurant Mandi Mandi combine to conjure an antidote to urban stress.

Hotel Maya HOTEL **$$$**

(Map p58; ☎03-2711 8866; www.hotelmaya.com.my; 138 Jln Ampang; r/ste incl breakfast from RM817/1160; ❄@🛜🏊; monorail Bukit Nanas) Still one of KL's most stylish hotels, even if there's wear and tear to some of its sleek timber-floored studios and suites. Rack rates include airport transfers, as well as a host of other goodies, while promotional rates – nearly half the official ones – include only breakfast and wi-fi. Its hydrotherapy pool is a plus.

G Tower Hotel HOTEL **$$$**

(Map p58; ☎03-2168 1919; www.gtowerhotel.com; 199 Jln Tun Razak; r from RM425; ❄@🛜🏊; Ⓜ Ampang Park) There's an exclusive atmosphere at

Golden Triangle

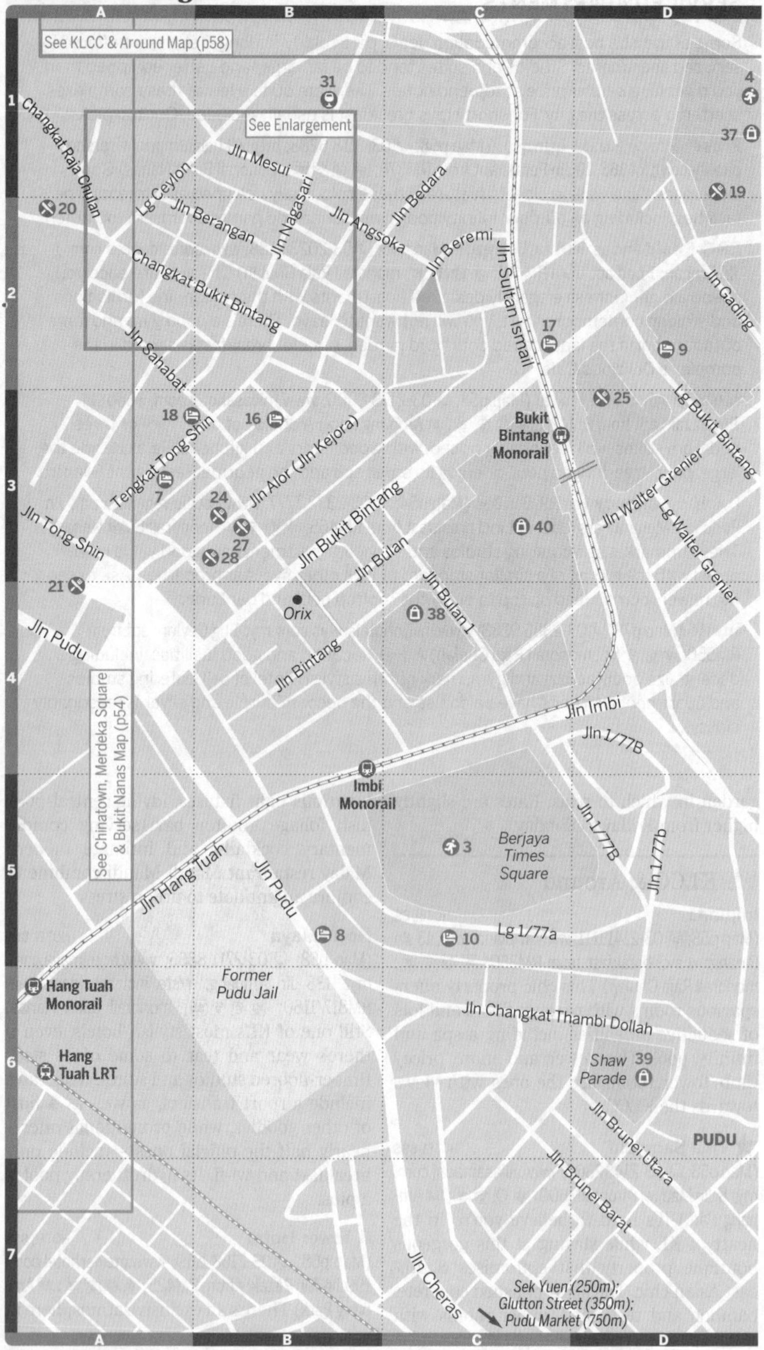

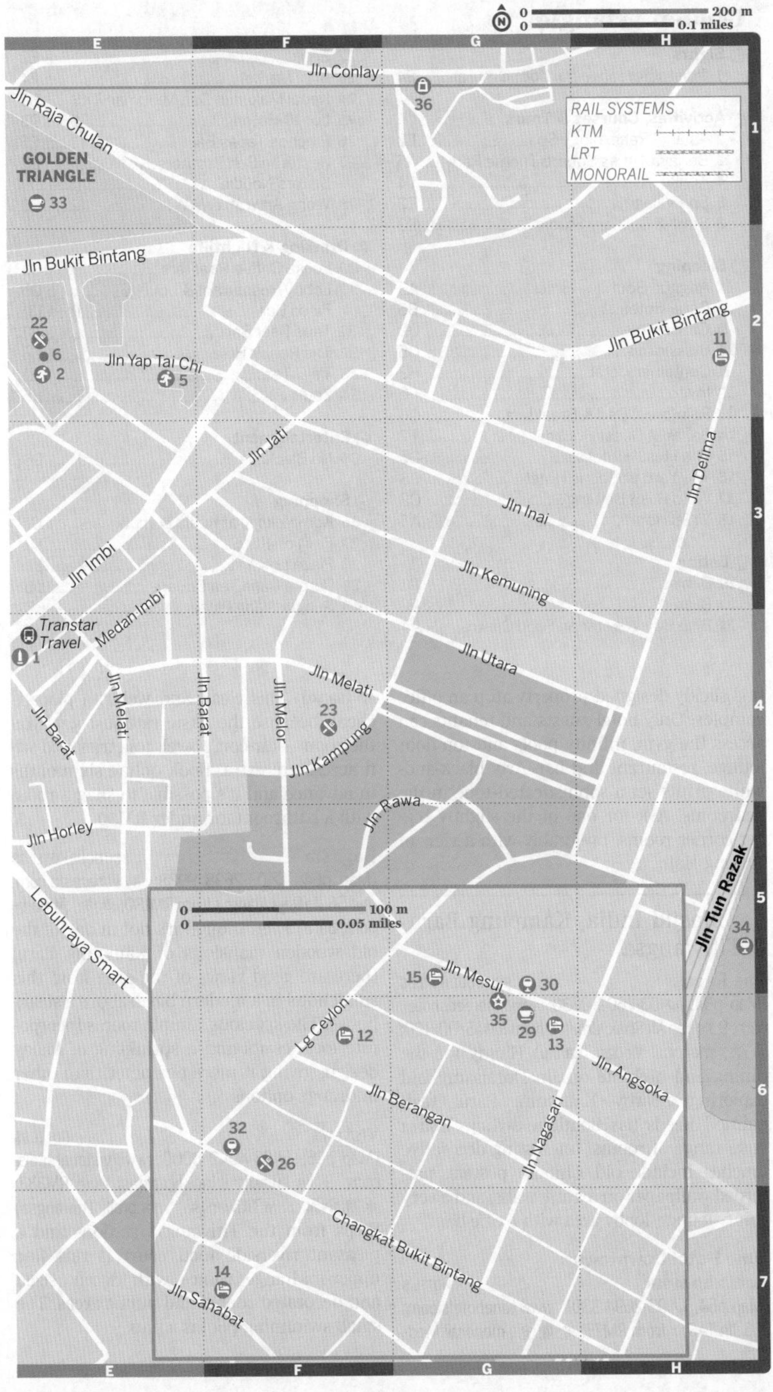

0 200 m
0 0.1 miles
E
F
G
H
1
2
3
4
5
6
7
RAIL SYSTEMS
KTM
LRT
MONORAIL
Jln Conlay
36
Jln Raja Chulan
GOLDEN TRIANGLE
33
Jln Bukit Bintang
22
6
2
Jln Yap Tai Chi
5
Jln Bukit Bintang
11
Jln Jati
Jln Delima
Jln Inai
Jln Imbi
Jln Kemuning
Medan Imbi
Transtar Travel
1
Jln Utara
Jln Melati
Jln Barat
Jln Melati
Jln Barat
Jln Melor
23
Jln Kampung
Jln Rawa
Jln Horley
Jln Tun Razak
Lebuhraya Smart
0 100 m
0 0.05 miles
34
15
Jln Mesui
30
35
29
13
Lg Ceylon
12
Jln Angsoka
Jln Berangan
Jln Nagasari
32
26
Changkat Bukit Bintang
14
Jln Sahabat

Golden Triangle

Sights
1 #districtcreative #artforlife mural E4

Activities, Courses & Tours
2 Asianel Reflexology Spa E2
3 Berjaya Times Square Theme Park C5
4 Kenko D1
5 Spa Village E2
6 Starhill Culinary Studio E2

Sleeping
7 Anggun Boutique Hotel A3
8 Ceria Hotel B5
9 Chaos Hotel D2
10 Classic Inn C5
11 Container Hotel H2
12 Invito F6
13 Rainforest Bed & Breakfast G6
14 Sahabat Guest House F7
15 The Mesui Hotel G5
16 The Yard Boutique Hotel B3
17 Wolo Bukit Bintang C2
18 YY38 Hotel A3

Eating
19 Ben's D1
20 Bijan A2
21 Blue Boy Vegetarian Food Centre A4
22 Enak E2
23 Imbi Market F4
24 Kedai Makanan Dan Minuman TKS B3
25 Lot 10 Hutong D3
26 Pinchos Tapas Bar F6
27 Restoran Beh Brothers B3
Sisters Noodle ....(see 27)
28 Wong Ah Wah (WAW) B3

Drinking & Nightlife
29 Feeka Coffee Roasters G6
30 Lobby Restaurant & Lounge G5
Pisco Bar ....(see 13)
31 Taps Beer Bar B1
32 The Rabbit Hole F6
33 TWG Tea E1
34 Zouk H5

Entertainment
35 No Black Tie G6

Shopping
36 Kompleks Kraf Kuala Lumpur G1
37 Pavilion KL D1
38 Plaza Low Yat C4
39 Purple Cane Tea Square D6
40 Sungei Wang Plaza C3

this slickly designed property atop an office complex. Only hotel guests and tenants can access the gym, infinity pools and top-floor lounge, restaurant and bar. Arty black-and-white prints set a sophisticated tone in the bedrooms. Ask for one of the slightly bigger corner rooms, preferably with a view of Tabung Haji.

Masjid India, Kampung Baru & Titiwangsa

The Reeds BOUTIQUE HOTEL **$**
(Map p64; ☎03-2602 0330; www.thereedshotel.com; 9 Jln Yap Ah Shak; dm/s/d from RM45/90/120; ❄ 📶; monorail Medan Tuanku) Handy for the dining and nightlife on Jln Doraisamy and exploring nearby Kampung Baru, teal-painted Reeds has boutique stylings and a wide range of rooms. Interesting decorative touches include old Chinese posters, patterned wallpaper on feature walls, and a very comfy lounge/lobby area with a cafe bar.

Tune Hotel Downtown Kuala Lumpur HOTEL **$**
(Map p64; ☎03-2694 3301; www.tunehotels.com; 316 Jln TAR; r from RM75; ❄ @ 📶; monorail Medan Tuanku) This clean and well-run place is cheap because the basic rate just gets you the room – air-con, towel, toiletries and wi-fi access are extra. Book online six months in advance and it's possible to snag a room with a bathroom for under RM50.

Bagasta BOUTIQUE HOTEL **$$**
(Map p64; ☎03-2698 9988; www.bagasta.com.my; 56 Jln Raja Alang; r from RM180; ❄ 📶; Ⓜ Kampong Baru) Even though it's not in one of the old wooden mansions of Kampung Baru, there are good views of the area from this small hotel in a modern block above a steakhouse. The spacious, simple rooms incorporate local crafts and a sprinkling of Malay design, giving it more character than other midrange options.

Vistana HOTEL **$$**
(Map p66; ☎03-4042 8000; www.vistanahotels.com; 9 Jln Lumut; r incl breakfast from RM333; ❄ @ 📶 🏊; Ⓜ Titiwangsa, monorail Titiwangsa) Steps from the Titiwangsa stations and a pleasant riverside food court is this fine upper-midrange choice with decent sized and decorated rooms and public areas. The small swimming pool is a plus.

🛏 Tun Abdul Razak Heritage Park, Brickfields & Bangsar Baru

PODs HOSTEL $

(Map p61; ☑ 03-2276 0858; www.podsbackpacker. com; 1-6, 30 Jln Thambipillay; dm/s/d with shared bathroom RM35/60/80; ❄ 🛜; ℝ KL Sentral, monorail KL Sentral) Broke? This basic backpackers offers free space on its couches in the common room on Tuesday. There's also the option of a six-hour stay for RM15. Note partitions between the rooms are flimsy and mattresses are on the floor. It has a pleasant cafe on the ground floor for breakfast.

★ Aloft Kuala Lumpur Sentral HOTEL $$

(Map p61; ☑ 03-2723 1188; www.starwoodhotels. com/alofthotels; 5 Jln Stesen Sentral; r from RM318; ❄ @ 🛜 🏊; ℝ KL Sentral, monorail KL Sentral) Designed for the Google generation of young creatives, Aloft is industrial chic meets plastic fantastic. Staff are superfriendly and you have to smile at the witty cartoon art in each of the spacious, well-designed rooms. Place a big tick against its infinity rooftop pool and bar with one of the best views in KL.

★ Sekeping Tenggiri GUESTHOUSE $$

(☑ 017-207 5977; www.sekeping.com; 48 Jln Tenggiri; r from RM330; ❄ 🛜 🏊; Ⓜ Bangsar) Providing access to architect Ng Seksan's superlative private collection of contemporary Malaysian art (displayed in the rooms of the adjoining house), this is a lovely place to stay. The rough luxe mix of concrete, wood and wire decor (with cleverly recycled materials making up lamp fixtures) is softened by abundant garden greenery and a cooling plunge pool.

YMCA HOTEL $$

(Map p61; ☑ 03-2274 1439; www.ymcakl.com; 95 Jln Padang Belia; d & tw RM116, tr with shared bathroom RM138; ❄ 🛜; ℝ KL Sentral, monorail KL Sentral) Handy for KL Sentral, the Y has spick-and-span rooms with TVs, telephones and proper wardrobes (not just hangers on a wall hook). There are laundry facilities, a shop and cafe, as well as tennis courts for hire if you become a member (RM85 per year), which will also give you 10% off the hotel rates.

Majestic Hotel HISTORIC HOTEL $$$

(Map p61; ☑ 03-2785 8000; www.majestickl.com; 5 Jln Sultan Hishamuddin; r incl breakfast from RM400; ❄ @ 🛜 🏊 🏊; ℝ Kuala Lumpur) Originally opened in 1932, and pre-WWII the KL equivalent of Raffles in Singapore, this long-shuttered hotel has been impeccably refurbished, although the bulk of the rooms are in the newly built Tower Wing. Lovely features include an orchid-filled conservatory, two swimming pools and a fine spa (treatments RM350–1000) with Charles Rennie Mackintosh–inspired decor. Its website provides the best booking deals.

Hilton Kuala Lumpur HOTEL $$$

(Map p61; ☑ 03-2264 2264; www.hilton.com; 3 Jln Stesen Sentral; d/ste from RM555/1856; ❄ @ 🛜 🏊; ℝ KL Sentral, monorail KL Sentral) Sharing a fabulous landscaped pool and spa with the Meridien next door, the Hilton offers beautiful contemporary design. Sliding doors open to join the bathroom to the bedroom, picture windows present soaring city views and rooms are decked out from floor to ceiling in eye-catching materials.

🍴 Eating

KL is a nonstop feast. You can dine in incredible elegance or mingle with locals at thousands of street stalls – it's all good and it's seldom heavy on the pocket. Often the best food is from the hawker stalls, cheap cafes (called *kopitiam*) and inexpensive restaurants *(restoran)*. Hygiene standards at hawker stalls are generally good and you should have little to fear from eating at them. However, if this is not your thing – or you just want air-con with your meal – there are plenty of good food courts in shopping malls.

🍴 Chinatown & Bukit Nanas

Madras Lane Hawkers HAWKER $

(Map p54; Madras Lane; noodles RM5-6; ⊙ 8am-4pm Tue-Sun; Ⓜ Pasar Seni) Enter beside the Guandi Temple to find this alley of hawker stalls. It's best visited for breakfast or lunch, with standout operators including the one offering 10 types of *yong tau fu* (vegetables stuffed with tofu and a fish and pork paste). The *bah kuh teh* (pork and medicinal herbs stew) and curry laksa stalls are also good.

Sangeetha INDIAN, VEGETARIAN $

(Map p54; ☑ 03-2032 3333; 65 Lebuh Ampang; meals RM10; ⊙ 8am-11pm; 🍴; Ⓜ Masjid Jamek) This well-run vegetarian restaurant serves lots of South Indian delights such as *idli* (savoury, soft, fermented-rice-and-lentil cakes) and *masala dosa* (rice-and-lentil crepes stuffed with spiced potatoes).

Lai Foong HAWKER $

(Map p54; Kedai Kopi Lai Foong, 138 Jln Tun Tan Cheng Lok; noodles RM8; 7am-3.30pm; M Plaza Rakyat) The stall that lends its name to this old-school hawker cafe has been dishing up beef ball noodles since 1956; on Mondays you can ask for its special 'steak and balls' soup made with beef penis and testicles.

Other stalls in the complex keep longer hours.

★**Merchant's Lane** FUSION $$

(Map p54; 03-2022 1736; Level 1, 150 Jln Petaling; mains RM20-30; 10.30am-6pm Thu & Sun-Tue, to 10pm Fri & Sat; ; monorail Maharajalela) Look for the narrow doorway at the end of the block for the stairs leading up to this high-ceilinged charmer of a cafe. The vibe is relaxed, the staff young, hip and friendly and the food a very tasty mash up of Eastern and Western dishes, such as Italian chow mein and its take on the Japanese savoury pancake *okonomiyaki*.

Old China Café MALAYSIAN $$

(Map p54; 03-2072 5915; www.oldchina.com.my; 11 Jln Balai Polis; mains RM11-21; 11am-11pm; M Pasar Seni) Housed in an old guild hall of a laundry association, this long-running restaurant continues to not only conjure retro charm but also serve good-value Peranakan food. Try the beef rendang, the succulent Nonya fried chicken, and tasty appetisers such as the top hats (a small pastry shaped like a hat and stuffed with veggies).

Ikan Panggang HAWKER $$

(Map p54; 019-315 9448; Jln Hang Lekir; mains RM15; 5-11pm Tue-Sun; M Pasar Seni) Tuck into spicy fish and seafood dishes and luscious chicken wings from this stall labelled only Ikan Panggang (which means grilled fish) outside Hong Leong Bank. Order ahead: it generally takes 20 minutes for your foil-wrapped pouch of seafood to cook, allowing time to explore the market.

LOKL INTERNATIONAL, MALAYSIAN $$

(Map p54; http://loklcoffee.com; 30 Jln Tun HS Lee; mains RM15-22; 8am-8pm Tue-Sun; ; M Masjid Jamek) From its clever name and slick design to its tasty twists on comfort foods, such as deep-fried Hainanese meatloaf sandwich and dessert toasties, LOKL ticks all the right boxes. This is also one of the few places in Chinatown to serve a Western breakfast (8am to 11am).

Restaurant Malaya Hainan MALAYSIAN $$

(Map p54; 019-329 7899; lot 16, section 24, Jln Panggong; mains RM12.50-17.50; 10am-10pm; M Pasar Seni) It's good to see this long-shuttered mock-Tudor-meets-the-tropics post office revamped as an appealing restaurant with a choice of breezy open-air and retro-themed indoor dining areas. Pick from a good range of colonial Hainanese and Nonya dishes such as roast chicken, sambal prawns and sweet sour fish.

Atmosphere 360 MALAYSIAN, INTERNATIONAL $$$

(Map p54; 03-2020 2020; www.atmosphere360.com.my; Menara Kuala Lumpur, 2 Jln Puncak; buffet lunch/afternoon tea/dinner RM92/60/208; 11.30am-3pm & 6.30-11pm; KL Tower) There are 360-degree views from this tower-top revolving restaurant. The lunch and dinner buffets offer ample choice of Malay dishes, though they can be hit-and-miss. Book ahead (you can do this online) for meals, especially sunset dining, but you can usually just drop in for High Tea. Note there's a smart-casual dress code.

Golden Triangle

★**Imbi Market** HAWKER $

(Pasar Baru Bukit Bintang; Map p72; Jln Kampung; dishes RM5-10; 6am-1pm Tue-Sun;) Breakfast is a cheerful affair in the courtyard of this walled traditional market. Time-tested stalls include Sisters Crispy Popiah for wraps; Teluk Intan Chee Cheung Fun for oyster-and-peanut congee and egg pudding and Ah Weng Koh Hainan Tea for coffee or tea.

The market is slated to move in 2017 as the area's developed into the Tun Razak Exchange financial district.

Lot 10 Hutong HAWKER $

(Map p72; Basement, lot 10, 50 Jln Sultan Ismail; dishes RM9-18; 10am-10pm; monorail AirAsia-

GOOD FOOD BLOGS

KLlites have strong opinions about their favourite places to eat – and they're very happy to share them online:

Fried Chillies (www.friedchillies.com) Spot-on reviews by some of the most enthusiastic foodies we've met, as well as video clips.

Eat Drink KL (http://eatdrinkkl.blogspot.co.uk) Hundreds of reviews for KL and Klang Valley, plus an app that gives you discounts at selected outlets.

DON'T MISS

JALAN ALOR

The restaurants and stalls lining Jln Alor haul in everyone, from sequined society babes to cash-strapped backpackers. From around 5pm till late every evening, the street transforms into a continuous open-air dining space with hundreds of plastic tables and chairs and rival caterers shouting out to passers-by to drum up business (avoid the pushiest ones!). Most places serve alcohol and you can sample pretty much every Malay Chinese dish imaginable, from grilled fish and satay to *kai-lan* (Chinese greens) in oyster sauce and fried noodles with frogs' legs. Thai food is also popular. Specific recommendations:

Wong Ah Wah (WAW; Map p72; 1-9 Jln Alor; small dishes RM10-15; ⏲5pm-4am; monorail AirAsia-Bukit Bintang) At the southern end of the street, and justly famous for its seriously addictive chicken wings, this is an ideal spot for a late-night snack with a bottle of beer. A wide variety of other dishes are also served here.

Restoran Beh Brothers (Map p72; 21a Jln Alor; dishes RM5-10; ⏲24hr; monorail AirAsia-Bukit Bintang) One of the few round-the-clock operations on this eats street. You can come here during the day for dim sum or drunken chicken *mee* (noodles) made with rice wine from the **Sisters Noodle** (Map p72; 21a Jln Alor; noodles RM6; ⏲7am-4pm; monorail AirAsia-Bukit Bintang) stall.

Kedai Makanan Dan Minuman TKS (Map p72; 32 Jln Alor; small mains RM15-35; ⏲5pm-4am; monorail AirAsia-Bukit Bintang) On KL's busiest food street is this nontouristy joint serving spicy Sichuan dishes. It's all good, from the chilli-oil fried fish to the gunpowder chicken buried in a pile of mouth-numbing fried chillies.

Bukit Bintang) Lot 10 Hutong was the first mall to encourage top hawkers to open branches in a basement food court. In its well-designed space it pulled in names such as Soong Kee, which has served beef noodles since 1945. Look also for Kong Tai's oyster omelets, Hon Kee's Cantonese porridge and Kim Lian Kee's Hokkien mee.

Blue Boy Vegetarian Food Centre — CHINESE $

(Map p72; ☎011-6695 0498; Jln Tong Shin; mains RM3-10; ⏲8am-6pm; 🌿; monorail Imbi) Run by Chung Ching Thye and his son for the last 40 years, this remarkable hawker-style cafe at the base of a backstreet apartment block serves vegetarian food. If you bypass a couple of stalls that use egg, it's also vegan. Try the *char kway teow* (noodles fried in chilli and black-bean sauce).

Pinchos Tapas Bar — TAPAS $$

(Map p72; ☎03-2145 8482; www.pinchos.com.my; 18 Changat Bukit Bintang; tapas RM14-30; ⏲food 5-11pm, bar to 3am, Tue-Sun; monorail Raja Chulan) This is the real deal for tapas, run by a Spaniard and packed with KL's approving Spanish-speaking community. A great place for a solo meal and drink or fun with a group when you can munch your way through the wide-ranging menu.

Ben's — INTERNATIONAL $$

(Map p72; ☎03-2141 5290; www.thebiggroup.co/bens; Level 6, Pavilion KL, 168 Jln Bukit Bintang; mains RM10-40; ⏲11am-10pm Sun-Thu, to midnight Fri & Sat; 📶; monorail AirAsia-Bukit Bintang) The flagship brand of the BIG group of dining outlets delivers on both style and substance. There's a tempting range of Eastern and Western comfort foods, appealing, trendy living-room design and nice touches such as a box of cards with recipes and talk topics on each table. Other branches are in Suria KLCC, Publika and Bangsar Shopping Centre.

★Bijan — MALAYSIAN $$$

(Map p72; ☎03-2031 3575; www.bijanrestaurant.com; 3 Jln Ceylon; mains RM30-90; ⏲4.30-11pm; monorail Raja Chulan) One of KL's best Malaysian restaurants, Bijan offers skilfully cooked traditional dishes in a sophisticated dining room that spills out into a tropical garden. Must-try dishes include *rendang daging* (dry beef curry with lemongrass), *masak lemak ikan* (Penang-style fish curry with turmeric) and *ikan panggang* (grilled skate with tamarind).

Enak — MALAYSIAN $$$

(Map p72; ☎03-2141 8973; www.enakkl.com; Feast fl, Starhill Gallery, 181 Jln Bukit Bintang; meals

WORTH A TRIP

PUDU DINING

Once a Chinese village on the edge of KL, Pudu is now firmly part of the city and is worth visiting not only for its lively fresh-produce market but also a wonderful alley of hawker stalls and one of the city's best Chinese restaurants.

Glutton Street (Pudu Wai Sek Kai; Jln Sayur; noodles RM5-10; 11am-midnight, most stalls open at 5pm; M Pudu) Off the tourist radar, but renowned locally, this hawker-stall alley near Pudu Market (p99) is best visited at night, although a few operations, such as the *hakka mee* stall, on the corner with Jln Pudu, are open through the day. Evening grazing could include addictive fried chicken and barbecued dried squid all, for bargain prices.

Sek Yuen (03-9222 0903; 315 Jln Pudu; mains RM20-40; noon-3pm & 6-10pm Tue-Sun; M Pudu) Occupying the same beautiful, time-worn, art-deco building for the past 60 years, Sek Yuen is a Pudu institution. Some of the aged chefs toiling in the wood-fired kitchen have served three generations the same old-school Cantonese dishes. The *kau yoke* (pork belly), village chicken and crispy-skin roast duck are all classics.

RM70-100; noon-midnight; monorail AirAsia-Bukit Bintang) Hidden at the back of Starhill's Feast floor, Enak is worth searching out for its finely presented Malay cuisine with a sophisticated twist.

KLCC & Around

Nasi Kandar Pelita MAMAK $
(Map p58; www.pelita.com.my; 149 Jln Ampang; dishes RM3-9; 24hr; M KLCC) There's round-the-clock eating at the Jln Ampang branch of this chain of excellent *mamak* (Muslim Indian-Malay) food courts. Among the scores of dishes available from the various stalls are magnificent *roti canai* (flat, flaky bread) and *hariyali tikka* (spiced chicken with mint, cooked in the tandoor).

Little Penang Kafé MALAYSIAN $
(Map p58; 03-2163 0215; Level 4, Suria KLCC, Jln Ampang; mains RM12-16; 11.30am-9.30pm; M KLCC) At peak meal times expect a long line outside this mall joint serving authentic food from Penang, including specialties such as curry *mee* (spicy soup noodles with prawns).

★ **Acme Bar & Coffee** INTERNATIONAL $$
(Map p58; 03-2162 2288; www.acmebarcoffee.com; unit G1 The Troika, 19 Persiaran KLCC; mains RM30-60; 11am-midnight Mon-Thu, to 1am Fri, 9.30am-1am Sat, to midnight Sun; M Ampang Park) Blink and you might be in a chic bistro in New York, Paris or Sydney. There are tasty nibbles such as root vegetable truffled fries and chilled sugar snap peas if you're not so hungry, and bigger dishes such as lamb shoulder marinated in *kicap* (a type of soy sauce) for larger appetites. It's a great choice for a lazy weekend brunch.

Thai Syok THAI $$
(Map p58; 03-2181 8314; basement, Wisma Central, Jln Ampang; mains RM12-26; 11.30am-9pm Mon-Sat; M KLCC) Fun street art is plastered across the walls of this basement venue beneath an old-school mall. Just as at Thai street stalls, you can squat on stools at low tables to enjoy traditional dishes such as pad Thai, pandan chicken, mango sticky rice and pineapple fried rice, served in a hollowed-out pineapple.

Mama San INDONESIAN $$
(Map p58; 019-787 5810; www.mamasankualalumpur.com; lot 46, ground fl, Suria KLCC, Jln Ampang; mains RM35-65; M KLCC) A KL offshoot of the original Bali Mama San, this stylish newcomer to the Suria KLCC's abundant range of eateries occupies a prime position overlooking the park's fountains. The menu is peppered with appealing Asian ingredients such as ginger flowers, lime leaves, tamarind and chilli. The dishes are a bit hit-and-miss, so choose carefully and don't over-order as portions are large.

★ **Sushi Hinata** JAPANESE $$$
(Map p58; 03-2022 1349; www.shin-hinata.com; St Mary Residence, 1 Jln Tengah; lunch/dinner set meals from RM77/154; noon-3pm & 6-11pm Mon-Sat; monorail Raja Chulan) It's quite acceptable to use your fingers to savour the sublime sushi, served at the counter one piece at a time, by expert Japanese chefs from Nagoya. There are also private booths for more intimate dinners. The *kaiseki*-style full course meals are edible works of art.

(Continued on page 89)

Regional Specialities

Malaysia, Singapore and Brunei collectively form a hungry traveller's dream destination – a multiethnic region boasting a wide-ranging cuisine shaped over centuries by the Muslim, European, Indonesian, Indian and Chinese traders, colonisers and labourers who have landed on its shores.

Above *Asam laksa* (a version of laksa that has a prawn paste and tamarind-flavoured gravy)

1

With the variety of ethnicities influencing local cuisine, you'll find yourself spoilt for choice come mealtime. Fancy breakfasting on Chinese dim sum? How about an Indian *dosa* (savoury pancake) for lunch, followed by a selection of rich Malaysian curries for dinner? It's all possible.

If the region has any single culinary constant at all, it's undoubtedly noodles. But even these differ from country to country, and coast to coast. *Asam laksa,* the Penang take on laksa, combines fantastically toothsome wide, flat rice noodles doused with a tart, fishy, herbal broth, while across the South China Sea in Sarawak, laksa is a breakfast food, and residents wake up to a spicy, coconut-rich curry soup packed with rice vermicelli, omelette strips, chicken and prawns. In Penang, Hokkien *mee* is a spicy noodle soup with bean sprouts, pork and prawns, but elsewhere in Malaysia it's a mound of thick stir-fried noodles with pork and cabbage in a dark soy sauce.

Rice also features prominently across the region. *Nasi lemak,* an unofficial 'national dish' of Malaysia, is rice steamed with coconut milk and cream, and topped with *ikan bilis* (small, dried sardines or anchovies), peanuts, sliced cucumber, sweet-hot sambal and half a hard-boiled egg (curry optional); banana leaf rice – rice served on a banana leaf 'plate' with a choice of curries – is daily Indian fare.

Penang is generally regarded as the region's gastronomic ground zero. KL residents have been known to make the four-hour drive to Penang for a single meal, and hungry Singaporeans pack

ANDREW TB TAN/GETTY IMAGES ©

BONCHAN/GETTY IMAGES ©

MIKHAELLA ISMAIL/GETTY IMAGES ©

1. Cooks preparing *asam laksa* **2.** *Ikan bilis* **3.** *Kuih*

out hotels on weekends. In addition to regional Chinese food, *mamak* (halal Indian) specialities, southern Indian treats and Malay dishes, the island is a hot spot for Peranakan or Nonya cooking, born of intermarriage between Chinese immigrants and local women. Culinary fusion is also a theme in Melaka, the former Portuguese outpost where you'll find Cristang (a blend of Portuguese and local cooking styles) dishes such as *debal*, a fiery Eurasian stew.

If it's all a bit too overwhelming, head to the peninsular east coast – the heartland of traditional Malay cooking. The states of Kelantan and Terengganu have been considerably isolated from the rest of the country, and have received few Chinese and Indian immigrants. Consequently, regional specialities have remained staunchly Malay. Graze the region long enough and you may develop a few cavities; local cooks excel at making all manner of *kuih* (Malay-style sweets) and even savoury dishes have a noticeably sweet edge.

If you're looking to diverge from the local cuisine altogether, then look no further than Singapore; the island nation's high-end dining scene is second to none in Southeast Asia. Whether you're hankering for handmade papardelle (pasta), steak frites, sparklingly fresh sashimi or a molecular gastronomic morsel quick-frozen in liquid nitrogen and bedecked with foam, you'll find it in one of Singapore's posh restaurants.

In this region, where the choices are endless, gastronomic malaise is unlikely to be a problem. That's a blessing, but also a curse of sorts – so many dishes, so little time.

SZEFEI/GETTY IMAGES ©

1. Hainanese chicken-rice **2.** *Sambal belacan* (shrimp-paste sauce)
3. Cooking *nasi kandar* **4.** *Hor fun*

2

KELVIN WONG/SHUTTERSTOCK ©

Penang

Penang is known for its Peranakan or Nonya cuisine, a fusion of Chinese and Malay (and sometimes also Thai) ingredients and cooking techniques. Examples include *kerabu beehoon,* rice vermicelli tossed with sambal and lime juice and garnished with fresh herbs, and *otak otak,* curried fish 'custard' steamed in a banana leaf.

It is also the home of *nasi kandar,* rice eaten with a variety of curries, a *mamak* speciality named after the *kandar* (shoulder pole) from which ambulant vendors once suspended their pots of rice and curry.

Penang's hawker food is a must. Wide, flat *kway teow* noodles are stir-fried with prawns, cockles, egg and bean sprouts for the hawker speciality *char kway teow.* Other don't-miss dishes include the laksa twins: *asam* (round rice noodles in a hot and sour fish gravy topped with slivered pineapple, cucumber, mint leaves and slightly astringent torch ginger flower) and *lemak* (with a coconut-milk-based broth).

4

Kedah, Perlis & Perak

Thai culinary influence extends to foods in Malaysia's west-coast states of Perlis and Kedah, where fish sauce is as common a seasoning as *belacan* (fermented prawn paste). Here, look for laksa *utara,* a lighter but still spicy and intensely fish-flavoured version of Penang's *asam laksa.*

Farther south is Ipoh, the mostly Chinese capital of Perak state and a town with a reputation for excellent eating. Pasta lovers rave over Ipoh's rice noodles, said to derive their exceptionally silky smoothness from the town's water. Judge for yourself with the local version of Hainanese chicken – served with a side of barely blanched bean sprouts and noodles instead of rice – and *hor fun,* rice-noodle soup with shredded chicken breast.

SZEFEI/GETTY IMAGES ©

1. *Nasi kerabu* 2. *Ayam percik* for sale at a Ramadan bazaar
3. *Mee rebus* 4. *Ikan patin* (silver catfish)

GRACETHANG/GETTY IMAGES ©

Melaka

Melaka's specialities include *ayam pong teh* (chicken cooked with soybean paste, dark soy sauce and sugar), *ikan cili garam* (fish curry), *satay celup* (skewered meat, seafood, and vegetables cooked at the table in a tub of peanut-based sauce) and Hainanese chicken served with rice moulded into balls.

Often overlooked here is Cristang cuisine, the edible result of intermarriage between Portuguese colonisers and locals that's an intriguing blend of Chinese/ Peranakan, Indian, Malay and, of course, European ingredients.

Johor & Pahang

Johor state boasts two tasty Malay noodle specialities: *mee bandung,* yellow noodles topped with a zippy, tomatoey shrimp gravy; and *mee rebus,* the same type of noodles doused with a sweet-savoury sauce thickened with sweet potatoes. The state also has its own variation on the laksa theme, consisting of spaghetti in a thin spicy fish gravy topped with chopped fresh herbs.

Pahang's rivers are known for *ikan patin,* known in English as silver catfish, a freshwater fish that's a local delicacy.

Kelantan & Terengganu

Kelantan state's capital, Kota Bharu, boasts Malaysia's most beautiful wet market, as well as plenty of places to try specialities like *ayam percik* (chilli paste-marinated chicken, grilled and doused with coconut sauce) and visually arresting *nasi kerabu* (rice tinted blue with natural colouring obtained from dried pea flowers).

In Terengganu state, a vendor dishing up mounds of red rice signals *nasi dagang.* The slightly nut-flavoured grain is cooked with coconut milk and eaten with fried chicken and sambal.

WWJE/GETTY IMAGES ©

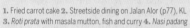

1. Fried carrot cake **2.** Streetside dining on Jalan Alor (p77), KL
3. *Roti prata* with masala mutton, fish and curry **4.** *Nasi padang*

LAURIE NOBLE/GETTY IMAGES ©

Kuala Lumpur, Selangor & Negeri Sembilan

Almost all of Malaysia's specialities can be found in KL, but two dishes in particular are more easily found here than elsewhere: *pan mee* (literally 'board noodles'), thick and chewy wheat noodles tossed with dark soy and garnished with chopped pork, *ikan bilis* and shredded cloud ear mushrooms; and *sang har mee* (fresh sea noodles), huge freshwater prawns in gravy flavoured with rice wine and prawn fat served over crispy noodles.

Farther south, in Negeri Sembilan state, descendants of Minangkabau, who immigrated from the Indonesian island of Sumatra hundreds of years ago, dish up a mean *nasi padang* – rice accompanied by a parade of fiery curries, *gulai* (fish and vegetables cooked in mild coconut milk gravy), soups and sambal.

Singapore

Singapore's culinary landscape is a near replica of Malaysia's, but in miniature. Still, Singaporeans do lay special claim to a few dishes, including crab stir-fried with black pepper, and fried carrot cake (squares of radish-flour cake stir-fried with bean sprouts, chilli sauce and salted radish). *Kari kepala ikan* (fish-head curry) was allegedly invented by a Singaporean-Indian cook playing to the Chinese love of fish cheeks. Hainanese chicken-rice, a plate of rice flavoured with garlic and broth, tender poached chicken, sliced cucumber and dipping sauces, assumes similarly iconic status here.

Singaporeans love their *roti prata* (the equivalent of Malaysia's *roti canai*) for breakfast, and have their own version of laksa – called Katong laksa for the neighbourhood that birthed it – noodles in a prawn and coconut-milk-based, highly spiced soup.

Seafood at the Filipino Barbecue Market (p325), Kota Kinabalu

Malaysian Borneo (Sarawak & Sabah)

Sarawak's highlanders specialise in dishes cooked in bamboo, like the chicken dish *ayam pansoh* (a special occasion dish of chicken wrapped in tapioca leaves and cooked with water inside a length of bamboo).

If you're in Kota Kinabalu, consider splurging on a meal of bounty from the South China Sea, chosen by your own self from a fish tank and cooked to order at one of the city's many seafood restaurants. Another seafood speciality worthy of mention is *hinava* (sometimes called *umai,* and also found in Sarawak), raw fish seasoned simply with lime juice, herbs and chillies.

Brunei

If Brunei had a national dish, it would be *ambuyat,* a glutinous mass made from the pith of the sago tree, ground to a powder and mixed with water. Served by twisting around chopsticks or long-twined forks, *ambuyat* is usually dipped into *cacah,* a *sambal belacan-* and tamarind-based sweet-and-tart sauce, and accompanied by boiled or smoked seafood and salads. *Ambuyat* itself doesn't have a taste – it's the sauce that gives it its zing. Shrimp-and-chilli mixes are the most popular, although you can technically dip the dish in anything you'd like.

If you are invited to a Bruneian home, you'll probably be served *buahulu* with your tea. This simple dessert is made from eggs, flour and sugar. *Kuripit sagu,* a biscuit-like version of *buahulu,* is jazzed up with mild coconut flavours.

(Continued from page 78)

Troika Sky Dining FRENCH, ITALIAN $$$
(Map p58; ☎03-2162 0886; www.troikaskydining.com; Level 23a, tower B, The Troika, Persiaran KLCC; Ⓜ Ampang Park) Sophisticated dining with outstanding views of KLCC's glittering high-rises are the highlights of the Troika complex of restaurants and bars. Try **Cantaloupe** (set lunch RM140, mains from RM75; ⏱noon-2pm Mon-Fri, 6.30-10.30pm daily) for modern French, and **Strato** (set lunch from RM50, pizzas RM30-50; ⏱noon-3pm & 6-11pm) for Italian that aims for homely authenticity (though we don't ever recall Mama making us Wagyu beef cheek and trotter ravioli).

Masjid India, Kampung Baru & Titiwangsa

★ **Yut Kee** CHINESE, INTERNATIONAL $
(Map p64; ☎03-2698 8108; 1 Jln Kamunting; meals RM6-15; ⏱8am-5pm Tue-Sun; monorailMedan Tuanku) A new location for this beloved *kopitiam* (in business since 1928) but still much of the same old furnishings and classic Hainanese and colonial-era food: try the chicken chop, *roti babi* (French toast stuffed with pork), toast with homemade *kaya* (coconut-cream jam) or Hokkien mee.

Kin Kin CHINESE $
(Map p64; 40 Jln Dewan Sultan Sulaiman; noodles RM7.50; ⏱7.30am-6.30pm; monorail Medan Tuanku) This bare-bones shop is famous throughout the city for its chilli *pan mee*. These 'dry' noodles, topped with a soft boiled egg, minced pork, *ikan bilis* (small, deep-fried anchovies), fried onion and a special spicy chilli sauce, are a taste sensation. If you don't eat pork, staff do a version topped with mushrooms.

Capital Café MALAYSIAN $
(Map p64; 213 Jln TAR; dishes RM4-6; ⏱10am-8pm Mon-Sat; Ⓜ Bandaraya) Since it opened in 1956, this truly Malaysian cafe has had Chinese, Malays and Indians all working together, cooking up excellent renditions of Malay classics such as mee goreng, *rojak* (salad doused in a peanut-sauce dressing) and satay (only available in the evenings).

Ikan Bakar Berempah HAWKER $
(Map p64; Jln Raja Muda Musa; meals RM5-10; ⏱7am-10pm; Ⓜ Kampung Baru) This excellent barbecued-fish stall sits within a hawker-stall market covered by a zinc roof and is one of the best places to eat in Kampung Baru. Pick your fish off the grill and add *kampung*-style side dishes to it off the long buffet.

D'Istana Jalamas Café MALAYSIAN $
(Map p66; Jln Tun Razak, Lake Titiwangsa; mains RM5-10; ⏱7am-8pm Mon-Fri; Ⓜ Titiwangsa, monorail Titiwangsa) A good eating option in the Titiwangsa area, this cafe at Istana Budaya (the national theatre) offers an appealing serve-yourself buffet of Malay and *mamak* favourites such as fish-head curry, as well as salads, snacks and fresh fruit. Try the local coffee: it's filtered here and not simply a powdered mix. Balcony seats are shaded by trees.

If there's a show at the theatre, the cafe is open on weekends.

Limapulo MALAYSIAN $$
(Map p64; ☎03-2698 3268; www.facebook.com/pages/Baba-Can-Cook/635621076504974; 50 Jln Doraisamy; mains RM17-45; monorail Medan Tuanku) Its tag line is 'baba can cook', the baba being genial Uncle John who is often to be found greeting guests at this atmospheric and justly popular restaurant. The Nonya-style cooking is very homely with dishes such as *ayam pongteh* (a chicken stew) and shrimp and petai beans cooked in sambal.

Coliseum Cafe INTERNATIONAL $$
(Map p64; ☎03-2692 6270; 100 Jln TAR; dishes RM13-49, weekday set lunches RM24-29; ⏱10am-10pm; Ⓜ Masjid Jamek) Little seems to have changed at Malaysia's longest-running Western restaurant (in business since 1921) since Somerset Maugham tucked into its famous sizzling steaks and Hainan Chicken Chops. Thoroughly retro, it's locally loved and the comfort food truly hits the spot. Even if you're not hungry, it's worth dropping by its attached bar, which is also a colonial time capsule.

Saravana Bhavan INDIAN $$
(Map p64; ☎03-2698 3293; www.saravanabhavan.com; Selangor Mansion, Jln Masjid India; meals RM10-20; ⏱8am-11pm; 🖉; Ⓜ Masjid Jamek) This global chain of restaurants offers some of the best-quality Indian food you'll find in KL. Their banana-leaf and mini-tiffin feasts are supremely tasty and you can also sample southern Indian classics such as *masala dosa*.

Tun Abdul Razak Heritage Park & Brickfields

Annalakshmi Vegetarian Restaurant INDIAN $
(Map p61; ☎03-2274 0799; www.facebook.com/AnnalakshmiVegetarianRestaurantKualaLumpur;

Temple of Fine Arts, 116 Jln Berhala; dinner mains RM10-15; 11.30am-3pm & 6.30-10pm Tue-Sun; ; KL Sentral, monorail KL Sentral) Inside the fancy main hall at the Temple of Fine Arts, this well-regarded vegetarian restaurant has set prices at night and a daily lunch buffet for RM16; or you can choose to eat at the humbler Annalakshmi Riverside next to the car park behind the main building, where it's 'eat as you wish, give as you feel'.

Vishal INDIAN $
(Map p61; 03-2274 1995; 22 Jln Scott; meals from RM5.80; 7.30am-10.45pm; ; monorail Tun Sambanthan) Sit at one of the tables and allow the army of servers to dollop out the great-tasting food on to a banana leaf for you. If you're hungry, supplement the standard meal with a good range of side dishes or a huge mound of chicken biryani. Good for tiffin snacks and a refreshing lassi too.

Hornbill Restaurant MALAYSIAN, INTERNATIONAL $$
(Map p61; 03-2693 8086; www.klbirdpark.com; KL Bird Park, 920 Jln Cenderawasih; mains RM13-27; 9am-8pm; ; Kuala Lumpur) Providing a ringside view of the feathered inhabitants of KL Bird Park, this rustic place offers good food without fleecing the tourists too much.

DON'T MISS

WEEKEND NIGHT MARKETS

Masjid India Pasar Malam (Night Market; Map p64; Lg Tuanku Abdul Rahman; street food RM5-10; 3pm-midnight Sat; Masjid Jamek) From around 3pm until late every Saturday, stalls pack out the length of Lg Tuanku Abdul Rahman, the alley between the Jln TAR and Masjid India. Amid the headscarf and T-shirt sellers are plenty of stalls serving excellent Malay, Indian and Chinese snacks and colourful soya- and fruit-based drinks.

Bangsar Sunday Market (Pasar Malam; Map p91; carpark east of Jln Telawi 2; hawker food RM4-6; 1-9pm Sun; Bangsar) This weekly market, though mostly for fresh produce, is also a fine hawker-food-grazing zone. Stalls sell satay, and a variety of noodles including *asam laksa* (laksa with a prawn paste and tamarind-flavoured gravy), *chee cheong fun* (rice noodles) and fried *kway teow*.

Go local with its *nasi lemak* (rice boiled in coconut milk, served with fried anchovies and peanuts) and fried noodles, or please the kids with fish and chips or the home-made chicken or beef burgers.

Bangsar Baru & Around

Chawan MALAYSIAN $
(Map p91; 03-2287 5507; http://site.chawan.com.my; 69g Jln Telawi 3; mains RM5-10; 8am-midnight; Bank Rakyat-Bangsar) A chic contemporary take on a *kopitiam* (coffee shop), offering megastrength coffees from all of the country's states to wash down dishes such as beef rendang and brown-paper-wrapped *nasi lemak*. There's also a branch in Publika (p99).

Bangsar Fish Head Corner HAWKER $
(Map p91; Lg Ara Kiri; mains RM3-20; 9am-6pm Mon-Sat; Bank Rakyat-Bangsar) If you don't fancy a fish head (various varieties of fish are available), you can still get the curry sauce poured over rice along with delicious fried chicken. There are other hawker stalls for different dishes on this strip.

Restaurant Mahbub INDIAN $
(Map p91; 03-2095 5382; www.restoranmahbub.com; 17 Lg Ara Kiri 1; mains RM7-15; 7am-2am; Bangsar) Tables spill out onto the street from this long-running operation famous for its luscious honey chicken biryani.

★ **Rebung** MALAYSIAN $$
(03-2283 2119; www.restoranrebungdatochefismail.com; 4-2 Lg Maarof; buffet lunch/high tea/dinner RM40/35/50; noon-10pm; ; Bangsar) The flamboyant celebrity chef Ismail runs the show at this excellent Malay restaurant, one of KL's best, respected for its authenticity and consistency. The buffet spread is splendid with all kinds of dishes that you'd typically only be served in a Malay home, several, such as *onde onde* (glutinous rice balls filled with jaggery), made freshly.

★ **Southern Rock Seafood** SEAFOOD $$
(Map p61; 03-2856 2016; www.southernrockseafood.com; 34 Jln Kemuja; mains RM35-52; ; Bangsar) The fishmonger to some of KL's top restaurants has opened its own operation and it's a corker. The fish and seafood – in particular a wide range of oysters – is top quality, simply prepared to allow the flavours to sing. The blue-and-white decor suggests nights spent on the sparkling Med rather than the muddy Sungai Klang.

★ Sri Nirwana Maju INDIAN $$

(Map p91; 03-2287 8445; 43 Jln Telawi 3; meals RM10-20; 10am-1.30pm; Bangsar) There are far flashier Indian restaurants in Bangsar, but who cares about the decor when you can tuck into food this good and cheap? Serves it all from roti for breakfast to banana-leaf curries throughout the day.

Wondermama MALAYSIAN $$

(Map p91; 03-2284 9821; http://wondermama.co; Bangsar Village I, 1 Jln Telawi 1; mains RM16-26; 9am-11pm Mon-Thu, to 11.30pm Fri & Sat, to 10.30pm Sun; Bangsar) Traditional meets contemporary at this family-friendly two-level restaurant serving Malaysian food with a modern twist. There's also a branch, **Wondermama X** (Map p58; http://wondermama.co; ground fl, Ave K, 156 Jln Ampang; mains RM16-26; 10am-10pm; KLCC), opposite the Petronas Towers.

Acme South AMERICAN $$

(Map p91; 03-2283 6288; www.acmesouth.com; lot 10, Bangsar Village I, Jln Telawi 1; mains RM19-59; 10am-midnight Mon-Fri, to 1am Sat & Sun; Bangsar) There's a Cajun flavour to the menu here, with recommended dishes including the tasty smoked chicken and Black Angus brisket as well as jambalaya, gumbo and chicken waffles. They also offer all-day breakfast – all served in a chilled space decorated with leafy plants.

Ashley's By Living Food INTERNATIONAL $$

(Map p91; 017-325 3663; www.ashleys.my; 11 Jln Telawi 3; mains RM25; 10.30am-11.30pm Mon-Fri, 8.30am-11.45pm Sat & Sun; Bangsar) Although not exclusively vegetarian, this arty, rustic place is where you can sample inventive and well-prepared veg-only dishes such as vegan laksa. They take care to use organic ingredients where possible and serve other rarities (for KL) such as gluten-free chocolate cake and 'raw food' cooked at under 40°C to preserve nutrients, texture and taste.

The same operators run **Living Food** (Map p58; www.livingfood.com.my; Menara Tan & Tan, Jln Tun Razak; mains RM20-30; 8am-5pm Mon-Fri, 9am-5pm Sun; Ampang Park) near the KLCC.

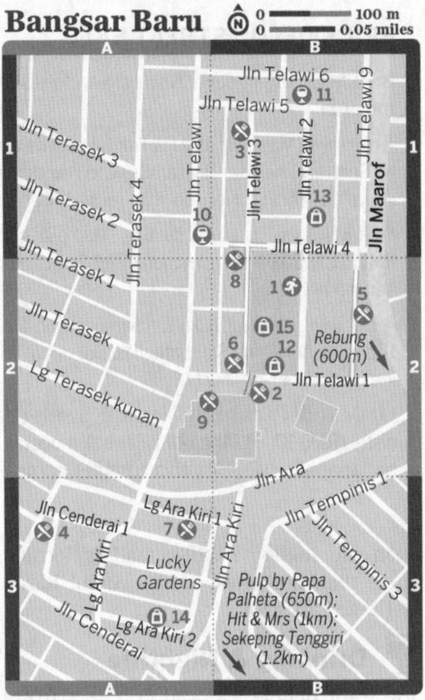

Bangsar Baru

Activities, Courses & Tours
1 Hammam Spa B2

Eating
2 Acme South B2
3 Ashley's By Living Food B1
4 Bangsar Fish Head Corner A3
5 Bangsar Sunday Market B2
6 Chawan B2
7 Restaurant Mahbub A3
8 Sri Nirwana Maju B2
9 Wondermama A2

Drinking & Nightlife
10 Bilique Bangsar A1
11 Ril's Bangsar B1

Shopping
12 Bangsar Village I & II B2
13 Never Follow Suit B1
14 Pucuk Rebung A3
15 Silverfish Books B2

Outside Central KL

The Bee INTERNATIONAL $$

(03-6201 8577; www.thebee.com.my; 36b, Level G2, Publika, 1 Jln Dutamas 1, Solaris Dutamas; mains RM15-20; 10am-midnight Mon-Thu, to 1.30am Fri, 9am-1am Sat, 9am-midnight Sun) Located in Publika mall, the Bee serves burgers and sandwiches that are the real deal, plus there are good salads, local gourmet ice creams and Two Man Tent coffee brewed just right. A stage is well used for various free events including live music, film screenings and

BRICKFIELDS STREET EATS

Brickfields offers several street vendors serving tasty snacks to sample as you explore the area:

Ammars (Map p61; Asia Parking, Jln Berhala; vadai RM1; ⌚7am-7pm; KL Sentral, monorail KL Sentral) The friendly family who run this stall fry up tasty Indian snacks, such as lentil *vadai* (fritters) flavoured with fennel seeds, in giant woks.

Brickfields Pisang Goreng (Map p61; cnr Jln Thambapillai & Jln Tun Sambanthan; fritters RM1.20; ⌚10am-6pm; monorail Tun Sambanthan) Tasty banana fritters and curry puffs are served here.

ABC Stall (Map p61; Jln Tun Sambanthan 4, outside 7-Eleven store; cendol RM1.90; ⌚10am-10pm; monorail Tun Sambathan) Cool down with fresh coconut water, *ais cendol* (shaved ice) and other desserts.

Little India Fountain Hawker Stalls (Map p61; Jln Tun Sambanthan & Lg Chan Ah Tong; dishes RM5-10; ⌚24hr; KL Sentral, monorail KL Sentral) For cheap eats like *roti canai* or banana-leaf meals, try this complex across from the gaudy central fountain.

open-mic nights. Publika mall is located about 3km northwest of Tun Abdul Razak Heritage Park area.

Drinking & Nightlife

You want bubble tea, iced *kopi-o*, a frosty beer or a flaming Lamborghini? KL's cafes, teahouses and bars can deliver it all.

Changkat Bukit Bintang in the Golden Triangle offers a nonstop party practically every night – though note that there have been reports of alcohol-fuelled violence here lately. For a more relaxed scene, hit up Bangsar Baru or see what's happening at The Row (www.therowkl.com), the revamped food and beverage strip along Jln Doraisamy.

Also under development at the time of research was TREC (http://trec.com.my), a major new complex of restaurants, cafes and bars on Jln Tun Razak, where you'll find the megaclub Zouk. For more on the clubbing scene read *Time Out* or *Juice*.

Chinatown & Around

★Aku Cafe & Gallery CAFE

(Map p54; ☎03-2857 6887; www.oldchina.com.my/aku.html; 1st fl, 8 Jln Panggong; ⌚11am-8pm Tue-Sun; Ⓜ Pasir Seni) This relaxed coffee haunt serves good hand-drip brews starting at RM10. There are also flavoured drinks such as mint and lemon iced coffee, cakes, and light *kopitiam*-style meals. Exhibitions change on a monthly basis and there are some nice local craft souvenirs for sale.

Reggae Bar BAR

(Map p54; www.facebook.com/reggaechinatown; 158 Jln Tun HS Lee; ⌚11.30am-3am; Ⓜ Pasar Seni) Travellers gather in droves at this pumping bar in the thick of Chinatown, which has outdoor seats if you'd like to catch the passing parade. There are beer promos, pool tables and pub grub served 'til late.

VCR CAFE

(Map p54; ☎03-2110 2330; www.vcr.my; 2 Jln Galloway; ⌚8.30am-10pm; ; monorail Hang Tuah) Set in an airy prewar shophouse, VCR serves first-rate coffee, excellent all-day breakfast and desserts. The crowd is young and diverse, but anyone will feel welcome here. Behind the shop, check out Jln Sin Chew Kee, a photogenic row of colourful shophouses.

Barlai COCKTAIL BAR

(Map p54; ☎03-2141 7850; http://thebiggroup.co/bignightout/barlai; 3 Jln Sin Chew Kee; ⌚4pm-midnight Tue-Thu, to 2am Fri, 9am-2am Sat & Sun; ; monorail Hang Tuah) On the ground floor of the ace rental apartment Sekeping Sin Chew Kee is this chilled bar that's a sophisticated place to sip a lemongrass G&T or a bacon bourbon Bloody Mary. There are cosy nooks inside and a leafy courtyard garden outside.

Golden Triangle

★Pisco Bar BAR

(Map p72; ☎03-2142 2900; www.piscobarkl.com; 29 Jln Mesui; ⌚5pm-late Tue-Sun; monorail Raja Chulan) Take your pisco sour in the cosy, exposed-brick interior or the plant-filled courtyard of this slick tapas joint. The chef is half Peruvian, so naturally the ceviche here is good. DJs regularly man the decks at the upstairs dance space on Friday and Saturday nights.

★Zouk CLUB

(Map p72; www.zoukclub.com.my; 436 Jln Tun Razak; admission from RM50; ⏲9pm-3am Tue-Sun; monorail Bukit Bintang, then taxi) If you're going to visit one club in KL, make it this one. Not only does Zouk's new location at the emerging TREC entertainment complex offer no fewer than around nine DJ spaces, bars and a cafe, if you bring your passport as a tourist you gain free entry to some of the enormous complex. Cover charges vary between venues.

Taps Beer Bar MICROBREWERY

(Map p72; www.tapsbeerbar.my; One Residency, 1 Jln Nagasari; ⏲5pm-1am Mon-Sat, noon-1am Sun; 📶; monorail Raja Chulan) Taps specialises in ale from around the world with some 80 different microbrews on rotation, 14 of them on tap. There's live music Thursday to Saturday at 9.30pm and an all-day happy hour on Sundays. Taps also serves pub grub (with a few Malaysian dishes) and a Sunday roast.

Feeka Coffee Roasters CAFE

(Map p72; www.facebook.com/feeka.coffeeroasters; 19 Jln Mesui; ⏲9am-10pm Mon-Thu, to 11pm Fri-Sun; 📶; monorail Raja Chulan) Set in a minimally remodelled shophouse on hip Jln Mesui, Feeka delivers both on its premium coffee (choose from microlot beans or espresso-based drinks) and its food (from omelettes and pulled-pork sandwiches to cakes). There's a lovely tree-shaded patio area and a gallery space upstairs, making this a place to linger.

The Rabbit Hole BAR

(Map p72; ☎010-899 3535; www.rabbithole.com.my; lot 14 & 16, Changkat Bukit Bintang; ⏲11am-2am Sun-Thu, to 3am Fri & Sat; monorail Raja Chulan) Not much evidence of Alice or a Wonderland here but it is one of the more convivial bars at the head of KL's rowdiest nightlife strip. There's plenty of seating and a variety of differently themed areas as well as a long bar and pool tables.

TWG Tea TEAHOUSE

(Map p72; www.twgtea.com; Level 2, Pavilion KL, 168 Jln Bukit Bintang; ⏲10am-10pm; monorail AirAsia-Bukit Bintang) Offering a mind-boggling range of over 450 teas and infusions, starting around RM21 a pot, this KL offshoot of the original Singaporean TWG is a luxurious and lovely place to refresh during your rounds of the mall. The teas are beautifully packaged for gifts too. Apart from afternoon tea (from RM30.50), it also serves breakfast (RM32) until noon.

KLCC & Around

★Heli Lounge Bar COCKTAIL BAR

(Map p58; ☎03-2110 5034; www.facebook.com/Heliloungebar; Level 34, Menara KH, Jln Sultan Ishmail; ⏲5pm-midnight Mon-Wed, to 3am Thu-Sat; 📶; monorail Raja Chulan) If the weather's behaving, this is easily the best place for sundowners in KL. Nothing besides your lychee martini and the cocktail waiter stands between you, the edge of the helipad and amazing 360-degree views. Steady your

SECRET BARS

The antidote to KL's many rooftop bars with expansive skyline views is its discrete crop of in-the-know watering holes serving premium libations and cocktails, speakeasy-style. Apart from the following, go online to discover the current whereabouts of 44 Bar (www.facebook.com/44Bar), a bar so secret it changes location every few months.

Omakase + Appreciate (Map p54; www.facebook.com/OmakaseAppreciate; basement, Bangunan Ming Annexe, 9 Jln Ampang; ⏲5pm-1am Tue-Fri, 9pm-1am Sat; 📶; Ⓜ Masjid Jamek) This cosy, retro cocktail bar is one of KL's top secret drinking spots. Sip sophisticated concoctions such as an Earl Grey Mar-tea-ni. Part of the fun is finding the entrance: look for the sign saying 'no admittance'.

Tate (Map p58; ☎03-2161 2368; http://thebiggroup.co/bignightout/tate; ground fl, Intermark, 182 Jln Tun Razak; ⏲5pm-2am Mon-Sat; 📶; Ⓜ Ampang Park) It's bordering on self-mockery to have a 'secret' speakeasy cocktail bar in a shopping mall, but once you get past that, Tate's sophisticated atmosphere, complete with cushy leather armchairs and a great cocktail menu, is perfect for a relaxing late-night drink.

hands as you have to buy your first drink at the somewhat-cheesy bar below and carry it up yourself. Weekends entry often requires your group to stump up for a bottle.

★Marini's on 57 BAR
(Map p58; ☎03-2386 6030; www.marinis57.com; Level 57, Menara 3, Petronas KLCC; ⏲5pm-1.30am Sun-Thu, to 3am Fri & Sat; Ⓜ KLCC) This is about as close as you can get to eyeballing the upper levels of the Petronas Towers from a bar. The stellar views are complemented by a sleek interior design and attentive service. When booking (advised) be aware that it's the lively bar not the laid-back whisky lounge that has the view of the towers. There's also a dress code.

★Fuego BAR
(Map p58; ☎03-2162 0886; www.troikaskydining.com; Level 23a, Tower B, The Troika, Persiaran KLCC; ⏲6.30pm-midnight; Ⓜ Ampang Park) Part of the Troika complex, Fuego shares the same sophisticated ambience and jaw-dropping views across the KLCC Park as the fine-dining restaurants. The bar specialises in innovative cocktails and tapas, while its sister venue, **Claret** (⏲4pm-1am) offers a curated wine list.

Neo Tamarind BAR
(Map p58; ☎03-2148 3700; www.tamarindrestaurants.com; 19 Jln Sultan Ismail; ⏲5pm-midnight; monorail Raja Chulan) Next to its sister operation, Burmese-Thai restaurant Tamarind Hill, this sophisticated restaurant-bar feels like a slice of Bali smuggled into the heart of KL. Sip cocktails by flickering lights and a waterfall running the length of the long bar. The Thai and Indochinese food is also lovely should you want to start with dinner.

Masjid India

Butter & Beans CAFE
(Map p64; ☎03-2060 2177; www.facebook.com/butterbeans.my; 42 Jln Doraisamy; ⏲9am-11pm; monorail Medan Tuanku) Jln Doraisamy's latest reinvention as The Row has thrown up a few cool cafes and restaurants to hang out in, including this one, handy for cold-brew coffee and other drinks. Next door is Slate, a space where events and music performances are held.

Bangsar Baru

Ril's Bangsar COCKTAIL BAR
(Map p91; ☎03-2201 3846; www.rils.com.my; 30 Jln Telawi 5; ⏲10am-2am; 📶; Ⓜ Bangsar) There's a premium-grade steak restaurant downstairs, but the main action is happening at the Prohibition-era-style cocktail bar upstairs, where the mixologists get creative and there's live music (jazz, blues, soul) on the weekends. Wednesdays there's selected free cocktails for women at their tiki-inspired night.

LGBT KL

KL has a small, but friendly LGBT scene that, with the exception of a few stalwarts, is fairly fluid. Check www.utopia-asia.com for the latest places to go.

Marketplace (☎03-2166 0750; http://mpkualalumpur.com/; 4a Lg Yap Kwan Seng; cover RM40; ⏲10pm-3am; Ⓜ KLCC) As Saturday night turns into Sunday morning at this restaurant, with a superb rooftop view of the Petronas Towers, KL's gay community dances and drinks like there's no tomorrow. Friday nights are also gay friendly.

Lobby Restaurant & Lounge (Map p72; ☎03-2141 3779; www.facebook.com/LobbyRestaurantLounge; One Residency 1, Jln Nagasari; monorail Raja Chulan) This otherwise-mediocre restaurant and bar comes into its own on Friday nights when a LGBT-friendly crowd descends to cheer on whoever is performing, be it the gloriously tacky and louche crew of the Funny Bone show or other drag divas. Entry is off Jln Mesui.

Bilique Bangsar (Map p91; www.facebook.com/biliquekl; 34a & 36a Jln Telawi; Ⓜ Bangsar) Every second Friday of the month, this Bangsar Baru venue hosts Rainbow Rojak (www.facebook.com/RainbowRojak), the most chilled LGBT-friendly party in town.

Moontree House (Map p54; www.moontree-house.blogspot.com; 1st fl, 6 Jln Panggong; ⏲10am-8pm Wed-Mon; 📶; Ⓜ Pasar Seni) Apart from being a quiet space for a well-prepared hand-drip or syphon coffee in an old Chinatown shophouse, Moontree also sells cute handicrafts and feminist literature and is probably the best central place to make enquiries about KL's discrete lesbian scene.

Hit & Mrs COCKTAIL BAR
(03-2282 3571; http://thebiggroup.co/bignightout/mrs; 15 Lg Kurau; 5pm-1am Tue-Sat; ; Bangsar) Above the Hit restaurant, on a quiet strip outside the main commercial area of Bangsar, you'll find the Mrs cocktail bar. It has cool but relaxed retro design with rattan chairs, and frosted glass and a very sophisticated list of cocktails and libations.

Pulp by Papa Palheta CAFE
(www.facebook.com/PULPbyPapaPalheta; 29-01 Jln Riong; 7.30am-10pm Tue-Fri, 9am-10pm Sat & Sun; ; Bangsar) Expect top-quality brews from this premium coffee roaster from Singapore. Their contemporary-style shed-like cafe is in the grounds of the media printers APW (www.apw.my/home), where exhibitions and various events are held. Apart from coffee, they also serve craft beer from Japan and tasty snacks such as truffle popcorn and croissant sandwiches.

☆ Entertainment

KL's entertainment options include a wide range of live music, theatre and dance. Mainstream movies are screened at the multiplexes in the malls. Tickets are around RM14. Cultural centres ocassionally screen art-house films.

★Dewan Filharmonik Petronas CONCERT VENUE
(Map p58; 03-2051 7007; http://mpo.com.my; Box Office, Tower 2, Petronas Towers, KLCC; box office 10am-6pm Mon-Sat; KLCC) Don't miss the chance to attend a show at this gorgeous concert hall at the base of the Petronas Towers. The polished Malaysian Philharmonic Orchestra plays here (usually Friday and Saturday evenings and Sunday matinees, but also other times), as do other local and international ensembles. There is a smart-casual dress code.

★Mud THEATRE
(Map p54; www.mudKL.com; Panggung Bandaraya, Jln Raja; tickets RM60; performances 3pm & 8.30pm; Masjid Jamek) A government-funded project, this lively musical show mixes a modern 1Malaysia theme with historical vignettes from KL's early days. The young, talented cast give it their all and there's some fun to be had with audience participation. It's staged in a beautiful historic theatre, the intimate auditorium based on the shape of a Malaysian kite.

★No Black Tie LIVE MUSIC
(Map p72; 03-2142 3737; www.noblacktie.com.my; 17 Jln Mesui; cover RM50; 5pm-1am Mon-Sun; monorail Raja Chulan) Blink and you'd miss this small live-music venue, bar and Japanese bistro, as it's hidden behind a grove of bamboo. NBT, as it's known to its faithful patrons, is owned by Malaysian concert pianist Evelyn Hii, who has a knack for finding the talented singer-songwriters, jazz bands and classical-music ensembles who play here from around 9.30pm.

Kuala Lumpur Performing Arts Centre PERFORMING ARTS
(KLPAC; 03-4047 9000; www.klpac.org; Jln Strachan, Sentul Park; Sentul) Part of the Sentul West regeneration project, this modernist performing-arts complex puts on a wide range of progressive theatrical events including dramas, musicals and dance. Also on offer are performing arts courses and free screenings of art-house movies (non-censored). Combine a show with a stroll in the peaceful leafy grounds and dinner. Sentul Park is 2.5km west of Titiwangsa Lake Gardens.

Istana Budaya PERFORMING ARTS
(National Theatre; Map p66; 03-4026 5555; www.istanabudaya.gov.my; Jln Tun Razak, Titiwangsa; tickets RM100-300; monorail Titiwangsa) Big-scale drama and dance shows are staged here, as well as music performances by the National Symphony Orchestra and National Choir. The building's soaring roof is based on a traditional Malay floral decoration of betel leaves, while the columned interior invokes a provincial colonialism. There's a dress code of no shorts, and no short-sleeved shirts.

KL Live LIVE MUSIC
(Map p58; 03-2162 2570; www.kl-live.com.my; 1st fl, Life Centre, 20 Jln Sultan Ismail; monorail Raja Chulan) A boon to KL's live-music scene, this spacious venue packs in rock and pop fans with an impressive line-up of overseas and local big-name artists and DJs.

Sutra Dance Theatre DANCE
(Map p66; 03-4021 1092; www.sutrafoundation.org.my; 12 Persiaran Titiwangsa 3, Titiwangsa; monorail Titiwangsa) The home of Malaysian dance legend Ramli Ibrahim has been turned into a showcase for Indian classical dance as well as a dance studio, painting and photography gallery and cultural centre near Lake Titiwangsa. See its website for upcoming events.

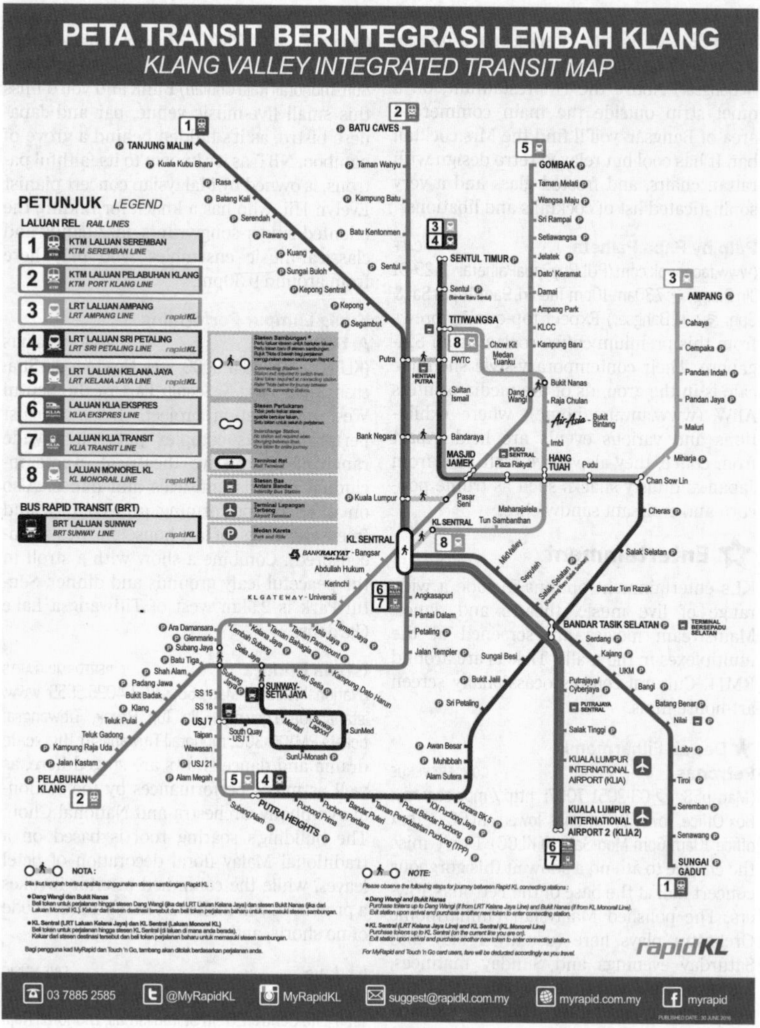

Saloma CABARET

(Map p58; ☎03-2161 0122; www.saloma.com.my; 139 Jln Ampang; show only RM60, buffet & show RM100; ⏰show 8.30-9.30pm; monorail Bukit Nanas) There's a chance for audience participation at this fun Malaysian dance and music show that can be combined with buffet dinner.

Findars LIVE MUSIC

(Map p54; www.facebook.com/FINDARS; 4th fl, 8c Jln Panggung; Ⓜ Pasar Seni) Check the Facebook page of this edgy, graphic arts space for details of gigs by local and visiting musicians and performance artists – they often happen on the weekends. The quirky street-art style cafe-bar is an installation in itself, complete with Darth Vader mask.

🛍 Shopping

Take your pick from street markets proffering fake-label goods to glitzy shopping malls (all open 10am to 10pm) packed with the real deal. Clothing, camera gear, computers and electronic goods are all competitively priced. You'll also find original handicrafts from all over the country, as well as interesting contemporary art. The shops in the

National Textiles Museum (p57) and Islamic Arts Museum (p60) are both packed with appealing items.

Chinatown

★ Peter Hoe Beyond ARTS, CRAFTS
(Map p54; ☎03-2026 9788; 2nd fl, Lee Rubber Bldg, 145 Jln Tun HS Lee; ⏰10am-7pm; Ⓜ Pasar Seni) On the 2nd floor of the historic Lee Rubber Building, Peter Hoe's charming emporium is a KL institution. Here you'll find all manner of original fabric products such as tablecloths, curtains and robes (many hand-printed in India directly for Peter Hoe), as well as woven baskets, hanging lanterns, embroidered cushions, silverware, candles, and knickknacks galore. There's also an excellent cafe.

Central Market Shops ARTS, CRAFTS
(Map p54; www.centralmarket.com.my; Jln Hang Kasturi; ⏰10am-10pm; Ⓜ Pasar Seni) This 1930s art deco building houses dozens of shops selling Malaysian arts and crafts, including batik clothing and hangings, *songket* (fine cloth woven with silver and gold thread), *wau bulan* (moon kites), baskets, Royal Selangor pewter, as well as vintage items from daily life. Don't miss the fascinating private Museum of Ethnic Arts in the Annexe where most items are for sale.

Museum of Ethnic Arts ANTIQUES
(Map p54; ☎03-2301 1468; 2nd fl, The Annexe, 10 Jln Hang Kasturi; ⏰11am-7pm; Ⓜ Pasar Seni) FREE Although billed as a museum, almost everything is for sale in this extraordinary private collection of tribal arts from Borneo. You'll also find Nonya ceramics, Tibetan thangka paintings, Chinese paintings and porcelain, embroidered wall hangings, hand-carved boxes and doors, and all manner of delights from Malaysia and the region. There's also a gallery of contemporary artworks.

Petaling Street Market MARKET
(Map p54; Jln Petaling; ⏰noon-11pm; Ⓜ Pasar Seni) Malaysia's relaxed attitude towards counterfeit goods is well illustrated at this heavily hyped night market bracketed by fake Chinese gateways. Traders start to fill Jln Petaling from midmorning until it is jam-packed with market stalls selling everything from fake Gucci handbags to bunches of lychees. Visit in the afternoon if you want to take pictures or see the market without the crowds.

Golden Triangle

★ Pavilion KL MALL
(Map p72; www.pavilion-kl.com; 168 Jln Bukit Bintang; ⏰10am-10pm; monorail AirAsia-Bukit Bintang) Pavilion sets the gold standard in KL's shopping scene. Amid the many familiar international brands, there are some good local options, including for fashion British India, offering well-made linen, silk and cotton clothing for men and women; and the more affordable Padini Concept Store. For a quick trip to Japan, head to the Tokyo Street of stalls on the 6th floor.

Kompleks Kraf Kuala Lumpur ARTS, CRAFTS
(Map p72; ☎03-2162 7533; www.kraftangan.gov.my/en/craft-complex-2; Jln Conlay; museum adult/child RM3/1; ⏰9am-8pm; monorail Raja Chulan, then taxi) A government enterprise, this huge complex mainly caters to coach tours, but it's worth a visit to browse the shops and stalls selling batik prints and fashion, wood carvings, pewter, basketware, glassware and ceramics. You can also watch artists and craftspeople at work in the surrounding Craft Village or take a look around the attached Muzeum Kraf.

Sungei Wang Plaza MALL
(Map p72; www.sungeiwang.com; Jln Sultan Ismail; ⏰10am-10pm; monorail AirAsia-Bukit Bintang) A little confusing to navigate but jam-packed with youth-oriented fashions and accessories, this is one of KL's more interesting malls with a focus of street fashion and bargains rather than glitzy international brands. Anchoring one corner is the Parkson Grand department store. There's also a post office, various fast-food outlets and a hawker centre on the 4th floor.

Purple Cane Tea Square TEA
(Map p72; ☎03-2145 1200; www.purplecane.my; 1st fl, Shaw Pde, Changkat Thambi Dollah; ⏰11am-9.30pm; monorail Imbi) All things to do with tea (especially the sale of good Pu-erh tea) are catered for at the main branch of this tea retailer. If you want to try tea-infused dishes, there is an attached restaurant. Purple Cane also sells recycled paper baskets and bags made by Salaam Wanita (www.ehomemakers.net), an organisation helping less fortunate women.

Plaza Low Yat ELECTRONICS

(Map p72; http://plazalowyat.com; 7 Jln Bintang, off Jln Bukit Bintang; ⏲10am-10pm; monorail Imbi) This is Malaysia's largest IT mall, with six floors of electronic goods and services. Head to the top-floor shops for repairs. There have been reports of credit-card details being recorded after transactions, so it's best to use cash here.

KLCC & Around

Suria KLCC MALL

(Map p58; ☎03-2382 2828; www.suriaklcc.com.my; KLCC, Jln Ampang; ⏲10am-10pm; Ⓜ KLCC) Even if shopping bores you to tears, you're sure to find something to interest you at this fine shopping complex at the foot of the Petronas Towers. It's mainly international brands but you'll also find some local retailers here too, including Royal Selangor for pewter, Vincci for shoes and accessories and Aseana for designer fashion.

My Batik Visitor Centre FASHION

(☎016-220 3190, 03-4251 5154; www.mybatik.org.my; 333 Persiaran Ritchie, off Jln Ritchie; ⏲8am-5pm; Ⓜ Ampang Park, then taxi) Founded by artist Emilia Tan and set in a pretty compound with frangipanni trees, My Batik sells colourful batik print fashions and offers demonstration sessions and DIY batik painting classes for adults and children (weekends are popular with families). The outdoor Green Tomato Cafe serves all-day Western breakfast. Call to arrange workshop bookings.

Prototype Gallery ARTS

(Map p58; www.facebook.com/prototypegallery; Level 2, Wisma Central, Jln Ampang; ⏲10am-6pm Tue & Thu-Sat; Ⓜ KLCC) Search out this small gallery of local arts products, ranging from 3D-printed items to prints and magazines, for the chance to also see the awesome murals freshly painted on the ceilings of this old-school mall. They also host the Junk-ED craft and flea market most weekends.

Avenue K MALL

(Map p58; www.avenuek.com.my; 156 Jln Ampang; ⏲10am-10pm; Ⓜ KLCC) Anchored by a huge branch of fast-fashion retailer H&M, Avenue K has undergone a serious revamp in recent years and is now packed with shops and appealing places to eat, as well entertainment such as a branch of the escape game Breakout and the interactive prehistoric exhibition Discoveria (discoveria.com.my).

Bangsar Baru & Brickfields

★**DR.Inc** HOMEWARES

(Map p61; ☎03-2283 4698; http://naladesigns.com; 8 Jln Kemuja; ⏲9am-7pm; 📶; Ⓜ Bangsar) Lisette Scheers is the creative force behind the Nala brand of homewares, stationary, accessories and other arty items. All her products embody a contemporary but distinctly local design aesthetic and are beautifully displayed at this Instagram dream of a concept shop and supercool cafe.

She also runs drawing and printing classes here; see the website for details.

★**Never Follow Suit** FASHION

(Map p91; ☎03-2284 7316; 28-2, Jln Telawi 2, Bangsar Baru; ⏲11am-9pm; Ⓜ Bangsar) You're guaranteed to find a unique piece at this extraordinary boutique hidden away on the 2nd floor. New and upcycled clothes and accessories are displayed like art works in a hipster, shabby-chic gallery.

★**Bangsar Village I & II** MALL

(Map p91; www.bangsarvillage.com; cnr Jln Telawi 1 & Jln Telawi 2, Bangsar Baru; ⏲10am-10pm; Ⓜ Bangsar) These twin malls are linked by a covered bridge and offer upmarket fashions, including local designers such as Richard Tsen at Dude & the Duchess, shoemaker Thomas Chan, and Desiree for women's clothing with a touch of Chinese styling. There's also a playcentre for kids, the excellent **Hammam Spa** (Map p91; ☎03-2282 2180; www.hammamspas.com; 3rd fl, Bangsar Village II, Jln Telawi 1; treatments from RM168; ⏲10am-10.30pm; Ⓜ Bangsar), and **Silverfish Books** (Map p91; ☎03-2284 4837; www.silverfishbooks.com; 2nd fl, Bangsar Village II, Jln Telawi 1, Bangsar Baru; ⏲10am-10pm; Ⓜ Bank Rakyat-Bangsar) stocking local titles and holding talks.

Wei-Ling Gallery ARTS

(Map p61; www.weiling-gallery.com; 8 Jln Scott, Brickfields; ⏲10am-6pm Mon-Fri, to 5pm Sat, by appointment only Sun; Ⓡ KL Sentral, monorail KL Sentral) The top two floors of this old shophouse have been imaginatively turned into a contemporary gallery to showcase local artists. Note the artwork covering the metal security gate in front of the shophouse next door.

Pucuk Rebung ARTS

(Map p91; ☎03-2094 9969; 18 Lg Ara Kiri 2, Lucky Gardens; ⏲10.30am-5pm Wed-Sun; Ⓜ Bangsar) Specialising in antiques and fine arts, this is

TRADITIONAL WET & DRY FOOD MARKETS

Western-style supermarkets are far more common in KL than the semioutdoor wet (produce) and dry food markets found across Asia. However, a few such traditional markets still exist and are worth searching out.

Pudu Market (Jln Pasar Baharu; 4am-2pm; Pudu) Arrive early to experience KL's largest wet market at its most frantic. Here you can get every imaginable type of fruit, vegetable, fish and meat – from the foot of a chicken slaughtered and butchered on the spot to a stingray fillet or a pig's penis.

Bazaar Baru Chow Kit (Chow Kit Market; Map p64; 469-473 Jln TAR; 8am-5pm; monorail Chow Kit) This daily, chaotic wet-and-sundry market serves the Chinese and Malay working class of Chow Kit. It's a warren of tight paths and hangers loaded with fruit, veggies, and all manner of cheap clothing and electronic items. You can also sample hawker and *kopitiam* food and drinks here in hole-in-the-wall outlets that haven't changed in decades.

Chinatown Wet Market (Map p54; off Jln Tun HS Lee; 7am-3pm; Pasir Seni) If you want your chicken freshly plucked, this is where to get it. The market is squished in darkened alleys between Jln Petaling and Jln Tun HS Lee and it's where locals shop for their groceries.

one of the best places in KL to find quality local crafts as well as pricier Malay ethnological items. It's worth dropping by for a browse and a chat with the affable owner, ex-banker Henry Bong.

Nu Sentral MALL
(Map p61; www.nusentral.com; 201 Jln Tun Sambanthan; 10am-10pm; KL Sentral, monorail KL Sentral) Providing the connection between the monorail and the main station at KL Sentral is this shiny, multilevel mall. Among many shops there's a branch of Parkson department store, MPH bookstore, a GSC multiplex and a food court, as well as the escape game complex Breakout (www.breakout.com.my).

Outside Central KL

★Publika MALL
(www.publika.com.my; 1 Jln Dutamas, Solaris Dutamas; 10am-9pm;) Art, shopping, dining and social life are all in harmony at KL's most innovative mall, 10 minutes' drive north of Bangsar. MAP (p66) acts as the cultural anchor with a wide variety of exhibitions, performances and talks. Free films are screened most Mondays in the central square and there's a good handicrafts market held on the last Sunday of the month.

Mid Valley Megamall MALL
(www.midvalley.com.my; Lingkaran Syed Putra; 10am-10pm; Mid Valley) Mega is the only way to describe this enormous mall, where you could easily lose yourself for days in the 300 stores, two department stores (Metrojaya and Jusco), an 18-screen cinema, a bowling alley, a huge food court and even a colourful Hindu temple. The KL Komuter Mid Valley station makes getting here a cinch.

Royal Selangor Visitor Centre ARTS, CRAFTS
(03-4145 6122; http://visitorcentre.royalselangor.com; 4 Jln Usahawan 6, Setapak Jaya; 9am-5pm; Wangsa Maju) Located 8km northeast of the city centre, the world's largest pewter manufacturer offers some very appealing souvenirs made from this malleable alloy of tin and copper. Also on sale are the company's silver pieces under the Comyns brand and its Selberam jewellery. Selangor's products are sold at its retail outlets in KL's malls including Suria KLCC and Pavilion KLCC.

Information

IMMIGRATION OFFICES

Immigration Office (03-6205 7400; 69 Jln Sri Hartamas 1, off Jln Duta; 7.30am-1.00pm & 2.00pm-5.30pm Mon-Fri;) Handles visa extensions; offices are opposite Publika mall.

INTERNET ACCESS

Internet cafes are rare these days, but if you're travelling with a wi-fi-enabled device, you can get online at hundreds of cafes, restaurants, bars and many hotels for free.

MEDIA

Juice (www.juiceonline.com) Free clubbing-oriented monthly magazine available in top-end hotels, restaurants and bars.

Time Out Kuala Lumpur (www.timeoutkl.com) What's on in KL.

Poskod Malaysia (http://poskod.my) Excellent online magazine about the city and Klang Valley area.

MEDICAL SERVICES

Pharmacies are all over town; the most common is Guardian, in most shopping malls.

Hospital Kuala Lumpur (Map p66; ☎03-2615 5555; www.hkl.gov.my; Jln Pahang; Ⓜ Titiwangsa, monorail Titiwangsa) City's main hospital, north of the centre.

Tung Shin Hospital (Map p54; ☎03-2037 2288; http://tungshin.com.my; 102 Jln Pudu; Ⓜ Plaza Rakyat) A general hospital with a Chinese traditional medicine clinic.

Twin Towers Medical Centre KLCC (Map p58; ☎03-2382 3500; http://ttmcklcc.com.my; Level 4, Suria KLCC, Jln Ampang; ⏲8.30am-6pm Mon-Sat; Ⓜ KLCC) Handily located in the mall attached to the Petronas Towers.

MONEY

You'll seldom be far from a bank/ATM. Moneychangers offer better rates than banks for changing cash and (at times) travellers cheques; they're usually open later hours and on weekends and are found in shopping malls.

POST

Main Post Office (Map p54; www.pos.com.my; Jln Raja Laut; ⏲6am-11.30pm; Ⓜ Pasar Seni) Across the river from the Central Market. Packaging is available for reasonable rates at the post-office store.

TOURIST INFORMATION

Visit KL (Map p54; ☎03-2698 0332; www.visitkl.gov.my; KL City Gallery, Merdeka Sq; ⏲9am-6.30pm; 📶; Ⓜ Masjid Jamek) Official city tourism office at the KL City Gallery (p57). In addition to tons of useful brochures and maps, it runs free walking tours of Merdeka Square and Kampung Baru.

Malaysian Tourism Centre (Map p58; ☎03-9235 4800; www.matic.gov.my/en; 109 Jln Ampang; ⏲8am-10pm; monorail Bukit Nanas) Information on KL and tourism across Malaysia. There's also a free traditional dance and music show staged at the theatre here (3pm to 3.45pm Monday to Saturday), plus a branch of the chocolate emporium Cocoa Boutique. The main office is housed in a handsome bungalow built in 1935 for rubber and tin tycoon Eu Tong Sen.

ℹ Getting There & Away

AIR

Kuala Lumpur International Airport (KLIA; ☎03-8777 7000; www.klia.com.my; Ⓡ KLIA) Kuala Lumpur's main airport has two terminals and is about 55km south of the city.

SkyPark Subang Terminal (Sultan Abdul Aziz Shah Airport; ☎03-7842 2773; www.subang-skypark.com; M17, Subang) Firefly, Berjaya Air and some Air Asia and Malindo Air flights go

INTERSTATE BUS FARES

DESTINATION	FARE	DURATION	STATION
Alor Setar	RM43	5hr	Pudu Sentral
Butterworth	RM35	4½hr	Pudu Sentral
Cameron Highlands	RM35	4hr	Pudu Sentral
Ipoh	RM28	2½hr	Pudu Sentral
Jerantut	RM18.40	3hr	Pekelining
Johor Bahru	RM34.30-40	4hr	Pudu Sentral, TBS
Kota Bharu	RM44	8hr	TBS
Kuala Terengganu	RM43	8hr	TBS
Kuantan	RM24.30	4hr	Pudu Sentral, Pekeliling
Lumut	RM27.70	4hr	Pudu Sentral
Melaka	RM10-12.50	2hr	Pudu Sentral, TBS
Mersing	RM30	5½hr	Pudu Sentral
Penang	RM30-40	5hr	Pudu Sentral
Seremban	RM6	1hr	TBS
Singapore	RM45-50	6hr	Pudu Sentral, TBS
Sungai Petani	RM40	5hr	Pudu Sentral
Taiping	RM35	3½hr	Pudu Sentral

from SkyPark Subang Terminal, around 23km west of the city centre.

BUS

KL has several bus stations, the main ones being Pudu Sentral, just east of Chinatown, and Terminal Bersepadu Selatan (TBS), 14.5km south of the city centre. Other long-distance bus services are operated by the following:

Aeroline (Map p58; ☎ 03-6258 8800; www.aeroline.com.my; Ⓜ KLCC) Daily services to Singapore (RM95, six daily), Penang (RM60, twice daily) and Johor Bahru (RM60, daily) leave from outside the Corus Hotel, Jln Ampang, just northeast of KLCC.

Nice (Map p61; ☎ 013-220 7867; www.nice-coaches.com.my; Ⓡ Kuala Lumpur) Services run from outside the old KL Train Station on Jln Sultan Hishamuddin to Singapore (from RM82, seven daily), Penang (from RM74, up to six daily) and Melaka (from RM33, three daily).

Transtar Travel (Map p72; ☎ 03-2141 1771; http://transtar.travel; monorail Imbi) Services to Singapore (from RM37, four daily) from 135 Jln Imbi, opposite Overseas Restaurant.

Pudu Sentral Bus Station

This crowded bus station remains the kind of place you want to get in and out of quickly. Close to the main entrance is an information counter. At the rear is a **left-luggage counter** (Map p54; per day per bag RM2-5; ⏲ 8am-11pm), as well as the tourist police.

Inside are dozens of bus company ticket windows. Staff will shout out destinations, but check to be sure the departure time suits you, as they sometimes try to sell tickets for buses that aren't leaving for many hours. Buses leave from numbered platforms in the basement.

On the main runs, services are so numerous that you can sometimes just turn up and get a seat on the next bus. However, tickets should preferably be booked at least the day before, and a few days before during peak holiday periods, especially to the Cameron Highlands and east-coast destinations which only have a few daily services.

Transnasional Express (Map p54; ☎ 1300-888 582; www.transnasional.com.my) is the largest operation here, with buses to most major destinations.

Terminal Bersepadu Selatan (TBS)

Connected to the Bandar Tasik Selatan rail hub, about 15 minutes south of KL Sentral, is the new **Terminal Bersepadu Selatan** (TBS; ☎ 03-9051 2000; www.tbsbts.com.my; Bandar Tasik Selatan; Ⓜ Bandar Tasik Seletan, Ⓡ Bandar Tasik Seletan), serving destinations south of KL (including Seremban, Melaka, Muar, Johor Bahru and Singapore) and the northeastern states of Kelantan and Terengganu.

> ### KLIA TRANSIT HOTELS
>
> If all you need to do is freshen up before or after your flight, KL has a couple of decent transit accommodation options.
>
> **Capsule by Container Hotel** (☎ 03-7610 2020; www.capsulecontainer.com; L1-2 & 3, Gateway, KLIA II; s for 3hr from RM50; ❄@📶; Ⓡ KLIA) Stacked transportation containers have been cleverly adapted into capsule-style rooms for short stays (from as little as three hours) in this contemporary-designed crash pad next to KLIA II.
>
> **Sama-Sama Express KLIA** (☎ 03-8787 3333; www.samasamaexpress.com; Mezzanine Level, Satellite A Bldg, KLIA I; d for 6/8hr RM382/435; ❄@; Ⓡ KLIA) Inside the terminal, all rooms here come with attached bathroom and TV. The company also runs a branch at KLIA II and a full-service top-end hotel just outside KLIA I.

Pasir Seni Station

From beside Pasar Seni LRT station in Chinatown, frequent buses head to destinations west of KL in the Klang Valley, including Shah Alam (RM3) and Petaling Jaya (RM3).

Pekeliling Bus Station

This bus station is next to Titiwangsa LRT and monorail stations, just off Jln Tun Razak. Buses leave here for Kuala Lipis (RM14.70, three hours, 11 daily) and Raub (RM9.20, two hours, 12 daily). Several companies, including **Plusliner** (Map p61; www.plusliner.com), run services to Kuantan (RM24.30, four hours, 12 daily); many go via Temerloh (RM12.40, two hours). Buses to Jerantut (RM18.40, three hours, nine daily) also go via Temerloh.

CAR

KL is the best place to hire a car for touring the peninsula. However, navigating the city's complex (and mostly one-way) traffic system is not for the timid.

Avis (Map p64; ☎ 03-2162 2144; www.avis.com.my; Rennaissance KL Hotel, 128 Jln Ampang; ⏲ 8am-6pm Mon-Fri, to 5pm Sat & Sun; monorail Bukit Nanas) There are also reservation counters at KLIA I & II.

Hertz (Map p58; ☎ 03-2026 2497; www5.hertz.com; Wisma MPL, Jln Raja Chulan; ⏲ 8am-

6.30pm Mon-Sat, to 1.30pm Sun; monorail Raja Chulan) Also has offices at KLIA I & II and at Skypark Subang Airport.

Orix (Map p72; ☎03-2142 3009; www.orix-auto.com.my; Ground fl, Federal Hotel, 35 Jln Bukit Bintang; monorail Imbi) Also has a rental counter at KLIA I.

TAXI

Long-distance taxis – often no faster than taking a bus – depart from upstairs at Pudu Sentral bus station. It you're not prepared to wait to get a full complement of four passengers, you will have to charter a whole taxi. Prices should include toll charges.

Fixed Fares For Whole Taxi

DESTINATION	FARE
Fraser's Hill (Bukit Fraser)	RM200
Cameron Highlands (Tanah Rata)	RM400
Genting Highlands	RM60
Ipoh	RM280
Johor Bahru	RM480
Lumut	RM400
Melaka	RM220
Penang	RM550

TRAIN

Kuala Lumpur is the hub of the **KTM** (Keretapi Tanah Melayu Berhad; ☎1300-885 862; www.ktmb.com.my; ⊙info office 9am-9pm, ticket office 6.30am-9.30pm) national railway system. All long-distance trains depart from KL Sentral; the information office in the main hall can advise on schedules and check seat availability.

There are daily departures for Butterworth, Johor Bahru and Thailand; fares are cheap, especially if you opt for a seat rather than a berth (for which there are extra charges), but journey times are slow. KTM Komuter trains also link KL with the Klang Valley, Ipoh and Seremban.

Getting Around

KL Sentral is the hub of a rail-based urban network consisting of the KTM Komuter, KLIA Ekspres, KLIA Transit, LRT and Monorail systems. Unfortunately the systems – all built separately – remain largely unintegrated. Different tickets generally apply for each service, and at stations where there's an interchange between the services, they're rarely conveniently connected. That said, you can happily get around much of central KL on a combination of rail and monorail services, thus avoiding the traffic jams that plague the inner-city roads. To coincide with the start of KL's new mass rapid transit system in 2017, it will be possible to use a single ticket to access all train services in the KL/Klang Valley area.

TO/FROM THE AIRPORTS

KLIA

The fastest way of reaching KL from KLIA I & II is on the **KLIA Ekspres** (www.kliaekspres.com; adult/child one way RM35/15), with departures every 15 minutes between 5am and 1am. From KL Sentral, you can continue to your destination by KMT Komuter, LRT, Monorail or taxi.

The **KL Transit train** (adult/child one way RM35/15) also connects KLIA with KL Sentral, but stops at three other stations en route (Salak Tinggi, Putrajaya and Cyberjaya, and Bandar Tasik Selatan).

If flying from KL on Malaysia Airlines, Cathay Pacific, Royal Brunei or Emirates, you can check your baggage in at KL Sentral before making your way to KLIA.

The **Airport Coach** (www.airportcoach.com.my; one way/return RM10/18) takes an hour to KL Sentral; for RM18, however, it will also take you to any central KL hotel from KLIA and pick-up for the return journey for RM25. The bus stand is clearly signposted inside the terminal. Other bus companies connecting KLIA to KL Sentral are **Skybus** (www.skybus.com.my; one way RM9.50) and **Aerobus** (www.aerobus.my; one way RM9).

TRAIN FARES FROM KUALA LUMPUR

DESTINATION	PREMIER	SUPERIOR	ECONOMY
Butterworth		RM34	
Gemas		RM20	
Ipoh		RM22	RM12
Johor Bahru	RM64	RM33	
Padang Besar		RM44	RM24
Taiping		RM28	RM18
Tampin	RM50	RM17	RM11

TRAVEL CARDS

There's a small discount on the cash price of fares if you use one of the following stored-value travel cards to pay for transport fares in the KL/Klang Valley area:

➡ MyRapid (www.myrapid.com.my) cards are valid on Rapid KL buses, the monorail and the Ampang and Kelana Jaya LRT lines. It costs RM20 (including RM5 in credit) and can be bought at monorail and LRT stations. Just tap at the ticket gates or when you get on the bus and the correct fare will be deducted. RapidKL also offers the Rapidpass Flexi Touch 'n Go, valid from one to 30 days (RM10 to RM150).

➡ Touch 'n Go (www.touchngo.com.my) cards can be used on all public transport, at highway toll booths across the country and at selected parking sites. The cards, which cost RM10 and can be reloaded with values from RM10 to RM200, can be purchased at My News outlets.

➡ KL TravelPass (www.kliaekspres.com/deals/kl-travelpass) cards are essentially a Touch 'n Go card which includes either a one-way/return trip on the KLIA Ekspres train plus RM10 of credit (RM50/RM85). They can be bought at both terminals of KLIA and KL Sentral.

Taxis from KLIA operate on a fixed-fare coupon system. Standard taxis cost RM75 (up to three people), premier taxis for four people RM103, and family-sized minivans seating up to eight RM200. The journey will take around one hour. Buy your taxi coupon before you exit the arrivals hall. Going to the airport by taxi, make sure that the agreed fare includes tolls; expect to pay at least RM65 from Chinatown or Jln Bukit Bintang.

SkyPark Subang Terminal

Taxis from the city centre to Subang will take between 30 minutes and one hour depending on traffic and cost RM40 to RM50.

Trans MVS Express (☎ 019-276 8315; http://klia2airporttransfer.com) runs buses on the hour from KL Sentral to Subang (RM10; one hour) between 9am and 9pm; and from Subang to KLIA I and II (RM10, one hour) roughly every two hours between 5am and 11pm.

BICYCLE

Rental bikes are also available at Titiwangsa Lake Gardens. Cycling Kuala Lumpur (http://cyclingkl.blogspot.co.uk) is a great resource with a map of bike routes and plenty of detail on how to stay safe on KL's roads.

KL By Cycle (Map p54; ☎ 03-2691 2382; www.myhoponhopoff.com; Dataran Merdeka Underground Mall, Merdeka Sq; per hour RM10, deposit RM100; ⏲ 9am-6pm; Ⓜ Masjid Jamek) rents basic bikes at the information desk in the underground mall across from the KL City Gallery. Rentals include a helmet.

BUS

Most buses are provided by either **Rapid KL** (☎ 03-7885 2585; www.rapidkl.com.my) or **Metrobus** (☎ 03-5635 3070). There's an **information booth** (Map p54; ⏲ 7am-9pm) near Pasir Seni station in Chinatown, where you can also board the free Go KL City Bus (www.gokl.com.my) services to the Golden Triangle and KLCC.

Rapid KL buses are the easiest to use as destinations are clearly displayed. They are divided into four classes. Bas Bandar (routes starting with B; RM2) services run around the city centre. Bas Utama (routes starting with U; RM3) buses run from the centre to the suburbs. Bas Tempatan (routes starting with T; RM1) buses run around the suburbs. Bas Ekspres (routes starting with E; RM3.80) are express buses to distant suburbs.

Local buses leave from half-a-dozen small bus stands around the city; useful stops in Chinatown include Jln Sultan Mohamed (by Pasar Seni), Bangkok Bank (on Lebuh Pudu) and Medan Pasar (on Lebuh Ampang).

KL MONORAIL

The air-conditioned **monorail** (www.myrapid.com.my; RM1.20-4.10; ⏲ 6am-midnight) zips from KL Sentral to Titiwangsa, linking up many of the city's sightseeing areas.

KTM KOMUTER TRAINS

KTM Komuter (www.ktmb.com.my; from RM1; ⏲ 6.45am-11.45pm) train services use KL Sentral as a hub. There are two lines: Tanjung Malim to Sungai Gadut, and Batu Caves to Pelabuhan Klang. Trains run every 15 to 20 minutes from approximately 6am to 11.45pm. Tickets start from RM1 for one stop.

LIGHT RAIL TRANSIT (LRT)

The **Light Rail Transit** (LRT; ☎ 03-7885 2585; www.myrapid.com.my; RM1.10; ⏲ every 6-10min, 6am-11.45pm, to 11.30pm Sun & holidays) system has three lines: Ampang/Sentul Timur, Sri Petaling/Sentul Timur and Kelana Jaya/Terminal Putra. The network is poorly integrated because the lines were constructed by different companies. As a result, to change from one line to another, you may also have to follow a series of walkways, stairs and elevators, or walk several blocks down the street.

KL'S NEW MRT

To give it its full title, the Klang Valley Mass Rapid Transit (KVMRT) project (www.mymrt.com.my) involves the construction of a rail-based public transport network which, together with the existing mass transit systems, aims to ease the road traffic congestion that plagues the Greater Kuala Lumpur/ Klang Valley region. Currently under construction is the new 51km Sungai Buloh–Kajang line; 9.5km of this link will run underground and drilling for the tunnels is causing disruption currently in parts of KL city centre. Phase one, from Sungai Buloh to Semantan, will be operational by the end of 2016. The remaining part of the line to Kajang will be finished in 2017.

You can buy tickets from the cashier or electronic ticket machines. Trains run every six to 10 minutes from 6am to 11.45pm. If you're going to be in KL for a while, consider getting one of the stored-value cards.

TAXI

➡ Air-conditioned taxis are plentiful and you can you usually flag one down easily during nonpeak, nonrainy hours.

➡ The red-and-white regular taxis *(teksi bajet)* charge RM3 for the first three minutes and 25 sen for each additional 36 seconds. From midnight to 6am there's a surcharge of 50% on the metered fare.

➡ Blue taxis are newer and more comfortable and start at RM6 for the first three minutes and RM1 for each additional 36 seconds. Night surcharges of 50% also apply.

➡ Some drivers have a limited geographical knowledge of the city and some also refuse to use the meter, even though this is a legal requirement. Taxi drivers lingering outside luxury hotels or tourist hot spots such as KL Bird Park are especially guilty of this behaviour.

➡ KL Sentral and some large malls such as Pavilion and Suria KLCC have a coupon system for taxis where you pay in advance at a slightly higher fee than the meter.

➡ Download the My Teksi booking app to your smartphone or tablet. My Teksi drivers have to use the meter and the service lets you know the approximate fare before you book.

➡ You can get right across the centre of town for RM10 on the meter even in moderate traffic.

Selangor & Negeri Sembilan

Includes ➡

Best for Architecture

- ➡ Putrajaya (p113)
- ➡ Sri Menanti (p120)
- ➡ Kampung Pantai & Terachi (p120)
- ➡ Seremban (p117)
- ➡ Rimbun Dahan (p109)

Best for Nature

- ➡ Chiling Waterfalls (p112)
- ➡ Cape Rachado Forest Reserve (p121)
- ➡ Forestry Research Institute of Malaysia (p108)
- ➡ Fraser's Hill (p110)
- ➡ Batu Caves (p107)

Why Go?

Venture beyond the urban sprawl of Kuala Lumpur (KL) and be rewarded with some of Malaysia's top attractions, from the holy Batu Caves to the lush Forestry Research Institute of Malaysia, both easy half-day trips from the capital. Rewarding stopovers include the lush Fraser's Hill (Bukit Fraser) and the old royal capital of Kuala Selangor, with its wildlife-watching and *kampung* (village) atmosphere.

South of KL, Malaysia's administrative capital of Putrajaya showcases its striking contemporary architecture and green urban planning. Further south, you can learn about Minangkabau culture and feast on local cuisine.

Consider hiring a car to explore beyond the big-hitters: cruise country lanes lined with stilt houses and ancient stone megaliths, explore colonial-era hill stations, and stop off to swim in waterfalls and dine at traditional roadside stalls.

When to Go

Kuala Selangor

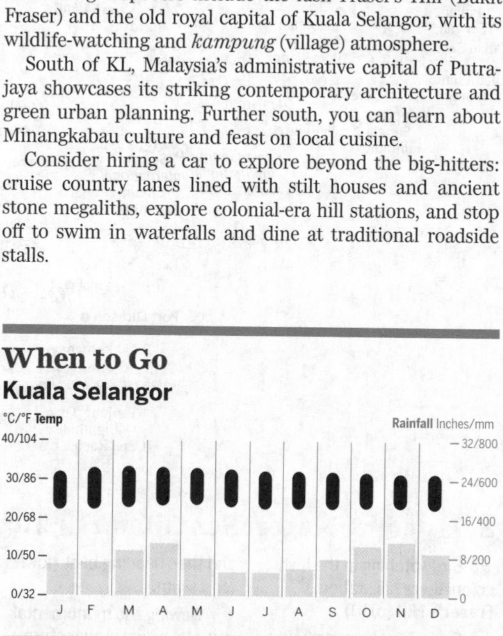

Jan & Feb During the festival of Thaipusam the Batu Caves are mobbed by pilgrims.

Mar & Apr Watch the raptors' annual northwards migration at the Cape Rachado Forest Reserve.

Jun Escape the lowland heat at Fraser Hill's International Bird Race.

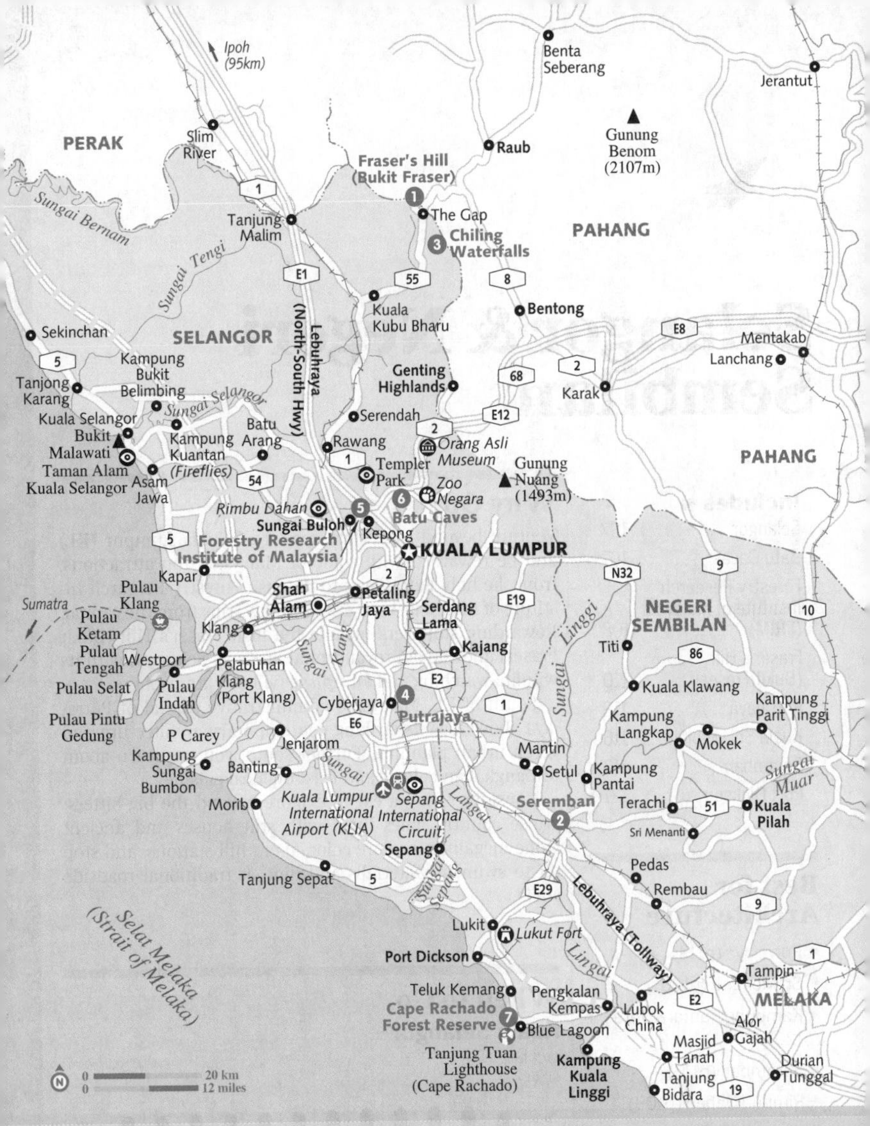

Selangor & Negeri Sembilan Highlights

1. Birdwatching in the lush colonial-era hill station of **Fraser's Hill** (p110).
2. Exploring Minangkabau villages, wood palaces and megaliths around **Seremban** (p117).
3. Hiking up to the 20m-high **Chiling Waterfalls** (p112) and then heading back down for a swim.
4. Viewing the monumental new Malaysian architecture of **Putrajaya** (p113) from a boat on its central lake.
5. Getting a treetop perspective on jungle life on the canopy walkway at the **Forestry Research Institute of Malaysia** (p108).
6. Exploring Hindu shrines and natural history at **Batu Caves** (p107).
7. Hiking through verdant jungle to the hidden beaches of **Cape Rachado Forest Reserve** (p121).

History

In the 15th century, all of what is now Selangor and Negeri Sembilan was controlled by Melaka. With the rising power of the Bugis (a seafaring group of warrior-like Malay settlers from Sulawesi) in Selangor, Minangkabau settlers from Sumatra felt increasingly insecure, so they turned to their former homeland for protection. Raja Melewar, a Minangkabau prince from Sumatra, was appointed the first *yang di-pertuan besar* (head of state) of Negeri Sembilan in 1773. Out of this initial union emerged a loose confederation of nine *luak* (fiefdoms). The royal capital of Negeri Sembilan was established at Sri Menanti.

After Melaka fell to the Portuguese in the early 16th century, control of Selangor was also hotly contested, partly because of its rich tin reserves. By the middle of the 18th century, the Buginese had established a sultanate, based at Kuala Selangor. A century later the success of the tin trade and the growing wealth of the Chinese communities in the fledgling city of Kuala Lumpur led to conflicts both among and between the Selangor chiefs and the miners. The outcome was a prolonged civil war, which slashed tin production and destroyed KL. In 1874, with the civil war over, the British took control. The sultan was forced to accede to the installation of a British Resident at Klang, and for the next 25 years the state prospered, largely on the back of another boom in tin prices.

Negeri Sembilan was also rich in tin, so for much of the 19th century it, too, suffered unrest and political instability motivated by greed. After Raja Melewar's death, the title of *yang di-pertuan besar* was taken by a succession of Sumatran chiefs, until a series of protracted tin-related wars from 1824 to 1832 led to the severance of political ties with Sumatra.

British Resident Frank Swettenham cajoled the sultans of Selangor, Negeri Sembilan, Perak and Pahang into an alliance that eventually became the Federated Malay States in 1896. The federation was centrally administered from a phoenix-like KL, which had become a well-ordered and prosperous city by the turn of the 20th century. In 1974 Selangor's sultan ceded KL as a federal territory, and Shah Alam took over the role of state capital. In the late 1990s the federal administrative capital of Putrajaya was also cleaved off from Selangor.

SELANGOR

Batu Caves

One of Malaysia's national treasures and holiest Hindu sites, this complex of giant limestone caves, just 13km north of KL, houses temples that have been drawing pilgrims for more than 120 years. The American naturalist William Hornaday is credited with discovering the caves in 1878, though they were known to Chinese settlers (who collected guano) and, of course, the local indigenous peoples.

Popular with monkeys as much as people, the caves are always a colourful (some might say joyfully tacky) and fascinating place to visit, and no more so than in late January or early February when hundreds of thousands of pilgrims converge during the three-day Thaipusam festival. Whenever you visit, plan enough time to tour the Dark Cave to learn about the area's natural history.

Note that each cave has a different admission price (the main Temple Cave is free) and opening hours vary.

Sights & Activities

Temple Cave CAVE, HINDU SHRINE

(8am-8.30pm; Batu Caves) FREE In 1890, K Thambusamy Pillai, founder of the Sri Mahamariamman Temple in KL, placed a statue of Lord Murugan inside the main Batu cavern, the so-called Temple Cave (actually two enormous caverns joined by a short flight of stairs). At the foot of 272 steps leading to the main dome-shaped cavern stands a 42.7m golden statue of Murugan. It was erected in 2006 and is said to be the largest in the world.

Inside the first cavern, at the top of the stairs, are the Murugan's six abodes carved into the walls. The second cavern holds the temple of Valli Devanai, Murugan's wife. Prayer times are held at 8.30am and 4pm.

Murugan, son of Shiva and Hindu god of war, is widely worshipped in Tamil, and Tamil diaspora, areas.

Ramayana Cave CAVE, HINDU SHRINE

(admission RM5; 8.30am-6pm; Batu Caves) Perhaps no cave at Batu is more spectacularly over-embellished and enjoyable to visit than the Ramayana Cave, which boasts gaudy dioramas of the Indian epic Ramayana. Near the entrance, look for the giant statue of Kumbhakarna, brother of Ravana and a deep sleeper (he once snoozed for six months). At the

DON'T MISS

THAIPUSAM AT BATU CAVES

Each year in late January or early February, hundreds of thousands of pilgrims converge at Batu Caves for the Hindu festival of Thaipusam. This is at once a moving, raucous and sublime display of devotion and community spirit. Lord Murugan's silver chariot takes pride of place as it makes its way from the Sri Mahamariamman Temple in KL's Chinatown. The slow procession begins around midnight and arrives some time in the early morning at the caves. Thousands of pilgrims follow the chariot, many in various states of trance.

As with Thaipusam festivals around the world, devotees of Murugan carry a *kavadi* (literally 'burden'). This burden, often a jug of milk, is an offering to Murugan for his blessings. Some pilgrims carry the jug on their head, and balance it with straps that are literally fastened to the skin on the chest and back with skewers. The most impressive acts of devotion involved carrying vel kavadi – massive metal cages, or altars, also fastened with skewers to the skin. The peacock feathers on these cages are symbols of Lord Murugan.

On arrival, pilgrims carry their *kavadi* up the 272 steps to the Temple Cave where their burden is relieved by Hindu priests. Those who have pierced their flesh will have the barbs removed and the wounds treated with ash and lemon.

Tens of thousands may be at the site at any one time. It's crowded but not intolerably so, and you can easily move through the masses for a picture of the procession.

It's good to arrive at the cave area before 8am (best is to follow the whole procession from Chinatown). If you wish to see the activities within the Temple Cave you should be there by 5am. Food and water are available outside the caves and at numerous stalls and shops (though bring your own if you are planning to be in the Temple Cave).

The exact date of Thaipusam is usually announced in the local papers, but you can also contact the Sri Mahamariamman Temple (p51).

top of the towering cave interior is a shrine to a naturally occurring linga. This phallic-like stalagmite is a symbol of Shiva.

Dark Cave TOUR

(☎012-371 5001; www.darkcavemalaysia.com; adult/child RM35/25; ⏰10am-5pm Tue-Fri, 10.30am-5.30pm Sat & Sun; 🚉Batu Caves) At step 204, on the way up to the Temple Cave, branch off to the Dark Cave to join a 45-minute guided tour along 800m of the 2km of surveyed passageways within the cave complex. The tour takes you through seven different chambers where you can witness dramatic limestone formations, including gorgeous flowstones, see pits used for guano extraction, and possibly spot two species of bat and hundreds of other life forms, including the rare trapdoor spider.

Tours run every 20 minutes and are organised by the Malaysian Nature Society. To get further into the cave on the three- to four-hour Adventure Tour you need a minimum of 10 people (RM80 per person); bookings must be made at least one week in advance.

Getting There & Away

KTM Komuter trains terminate at the Batu Caves station (RM2.60 from KL Sentral, 30 minutes, every 15 to 30 minutes).

A taxi from KL costs around RM20 to RM30.

Forestry Research Institute of Malaysia (FRIM)

Birdsong and wall-to-wall greenery replaces the drone of traffic and air-conditioning at the **Forestry Research Institute of Malaysia** (FRIM; ☎03-6279 7592; www.frim.gov.my; adult/child RM5.30/1.05, with DSLR camera extra RM5.30; ⏰8.30am-7.30pm; 🚉KTM Komuter to Kepong Sentral, then taxi). About 16km northwest of KL, and covering nearly 600 hectares, the institute was established in 1929 to research the sustainable management of rainforests. FRIM functions as a giant park, with quiet roads and well-established trails though the jungle landscape. There's also a wide variety of flora and native wildlife to discover, from leaf monkeys and colourful birds to indigenous fruit trees and rare, old dipterocarp.

Bring a picnic to enjoy in the park as the canteen has unreliable opening times.

Sights & Activities

Wooden Houses ARCHITECTURE

At the far end of the soccer field, look for a couple of handsome traditional raised houses built from hard cendol wood. Relocated from Melaka and Terengganu, the houses display regional variations such as in the use of roofing material (tile versus *atap*) and other features.

Canopy Walkway WALKING

(admission adult/child RM10.60/1.05; ⏲9.30am-1.30pm Tue-Thu, Sat & Sun) FRIM's highlight is this canopy walkway, hanging a vertigo-inducing 30m above the forest floor. The 200m walkway takes you right into the trees, offering views of the rainforest and, surprisingly, the towers of KL in the distance. The walkway is reached by a steep trail from **FRIM's One Stop Centre** (⏲8am-5pm Mon-Thu, 8am-12.15 & 2.45-5pm Fri, 9am-3pm Sat & Sun), on the right off the main road about a kilometre from the entrance gate.

As you head down from the walkway, the trail picks its way through the jungle to a shady picnic area where you can cool off in a series of shallow waterfalls. The return hike, incorporating the walkway, takes around two hours. Bring water with you.

The best time to walk the canopy is around 10am, which is after the morning rush and before the afternoon rains. Note that the canopy is closed during bad weather and during a three-week period every summer for maintenance.

Hiking & Biking

The quiet roads circling the park are pleasant for strolling though there are also clearly marked trails running through the forests. Basic bikes can be rented outside the park for RM5 to RM8 per day. Avoid renting within the park or you'll have to walk back to the gate at the end of the day when it's time to catch a taxi back to KL.

ℹ Getting There & Away

Take a KTM Komuter train to Kepong Sentral (RM2.50) and then a taxi (RM5); arrange for the taxi to pick you up again later.

Zoo Negara

Zoo Negara ZOO

(National Zoo; ☎03-4108 3422; www.zoonegaramalaysia.my; adult/child RM53/27, giant pandas RM85/43; ⏲9am-5pm) Laid out over 62 hectares around a central lake, Zoo Negara, 13km northeast of KL, is home to a wide variety of native wildlife, including tigers and animals from other parts of Asia and Africa. One of the most popular new exhibits is the giant pandas. Although some of the enclosures could definitely be bigger, this is one of Asia's better zoos.

It's possible to spend a day as a volunteer here; the website has details for arranging this.

Taxis charge around RM25 to RM35 from central KL or you can take Metrobus 16 from the Central Market.

Genting Highlands

☎03

Though referred to as a hill station, Genting is a modern and very heavily developed resort 2000m above sea level. About 50km north of KL, it's in stark contrast to the Old English style of other Malaysian upland resorts. There are no walks here, no quaint stone village, and in general little public space to stroll about and enjoy the mountain scenery. Genting's raison d'être is **Resort World Genting** (☎03-2718 1888; www.rwgenting.com), a glitzy casino billed as the only one in Malaysia.

Big changes are set for the end of 2016, though, when **20th Century Fox World** opens with a 10,000 seat stadium and a theme park based around movies such as *Ice Age*, *Life of Pi* and *A Night At the Museum*.

At the time of writing, you could get to Genting on a day package. This included a bus trip to the base of the hill where the 3.4km-long **Genting Skyway** (1-way RM6.30; ⏲7.30am-midnight) whisked you up in an 11-minute ride above the dense rainforest. There's no shortage of places to eat, including cheap fast-food outlets and noisy food courts, and if you want to stay overnight, the resort has a choice of six hotels (book online).

Expect Genting to look like a giant construction zone throughout 2016.

LOCAL KNOWLEDGE

RIMBUN DAHAN

Rimbun Dahan (http://rimbundahan.org) is a private property open to the public only a handful of times each year (check online for dates). The property boasts a 19th-century traditional Malay house and garden, and a gallery for traditional and contemporary art. Buildings are designed by Hijjas Kasturi, the architect of the striking Tabung Haji and Menara Maybank buildings in KL. It's about 20 minutes' drive west of Kepong and one hour from KL.

Getting There & Away

Assuming the new theme park continues with the current transport options, Genting Express Bus Services buses leave at 7.30am and then on the hour from 9am to 7pm from KL's Pudu Sentral bus station (adult/child RM11/9.90, 1½ hours). The same service is offered on the hour from 8am to 8pm from KL Sentral (RM10.70/9.60). The price includes the return trip on the Skyway cable car. At these locations you can also join the Go Genting Package Day Tour (RM70), which includes return transport from KL, the Skyway transfer and either a theme park pass or a combo meal.

A taxi from KL costs at least RM100.

Fraser's Hill (Bukit Fraser)

☎09

Of all Malaysia's hill stations, Fraser's Hill (Bukit Fraser), around 100km north of KL, retains the most colonial-era charm. Yet it attracts a fraction of the visitor numbers of a place like Cameron Highlands. Which is great news for you. Spread across seven densely forested hills of the Titiwangsa Range, this cool, quiet and relatively undeveloped station offers excellent hiking and birdwatching within a short stroll from the village centre. With some excellent old-world accommodation options, and surprisingly good food, Fraser's Hill is one of the best overnight retreats close to KL.

The station (at an altitude ranging from 1220m to 1524m) is named after Louis James Fraser, an adventurous Scotsman who migrated to Malaysia in the 1890s. Trying his luck in the country's booming tin-mining industry, Fraser set up a mule-train operation to transport the ore across the hills and ran gambling and opium dens. These had all vanished (along with Fraser himself) by 1917 when Bishop Ferguson-Davie of Singapore came looking for Fraser. Though he was unable to find the Scotsman, the bishop did recognise the area's potential as a hill station and wrote a report to the high commissioner on his return to Singapore. A couple of years later this 'little England' in the heart of the Malaysian jungle began to be developed.

Sights & Activities

Paddleboats can be hired (per 15 minutes RM8) to explore Allan's Waters, a former reservoir.

Fraser's Hill Golf Club GOLF

(☎09-362 2129; Jln Genting; green fees RM40, clubs RM40; ⏲8am-6.30pm) East of the village square is this picturesque nine-hole golf course, one of the oldest in the country. A 20% discount is often available for hotel guests in the area.

Paddock HORSE RIDING

(short ride adult/child RM5/4; ⏲9am-noon & 2-4.30pm Mon-Fri, to 7pm Sat & Sun) This small but charming paddock east of the golf course offers very short rides on gentle retired horses.

Birdwatching

The main attraction of Fraser's Hill is its abundant flora and fauna, particularly bird life – some 260 species have been spotted here, an astonishing 205 of which are endemic to Malaysia.

Bird Interpretation Centre MUSEUM

(⏲10am-5pm) FREE To get an overview of the birding scene, visit the Bird Interpretation Centre on the 2nd floor of the golf course clubhouse, across the village square.

Mr Durai BIRDWATCHING

(☎013-983 1633; durefh@hotmail.com; Shahzan Inn Fraser's Hill, Jln Lady Guillemard; per group half-/full day RM200/400) For one of Malaysia's top birding guides, contact the eagle-eyed Mr Durai at Shahzan Inn Fraser's Hill.

Hiking

A number of trails can be accessed from the main village area, or you can simply stroll alongside the main roads; traffic is light and Malaysian drivers tend to be very polite. Pick up a map with trail information from the front desk of Puncak Inn or snap a pic of the large map at the Bird Interpretation Centre. Most hikes, being former bridal paths, or survey trails, are pretty straightforward and clearly signposted so you won't get lost.

Jeriau Waterfall WATERFALL

About 4km northwest of the town centre, along Jln Air Terjun, is Jeriau Waterfall, where you can swim. It's a 20-minute climb up from the road to reach the falls.

Hemmant Trail HIKING

This relatively flat and wide path runs above the golf course for 1km. The trailhead is a few minutes' walk up from the village square.

Pine Tree Trail HIKING

The best-known trail in the Fraser's Hill area is the 5km Pine Tree Trail, which takes about

Fraser's Hill (Bukit Fraser)

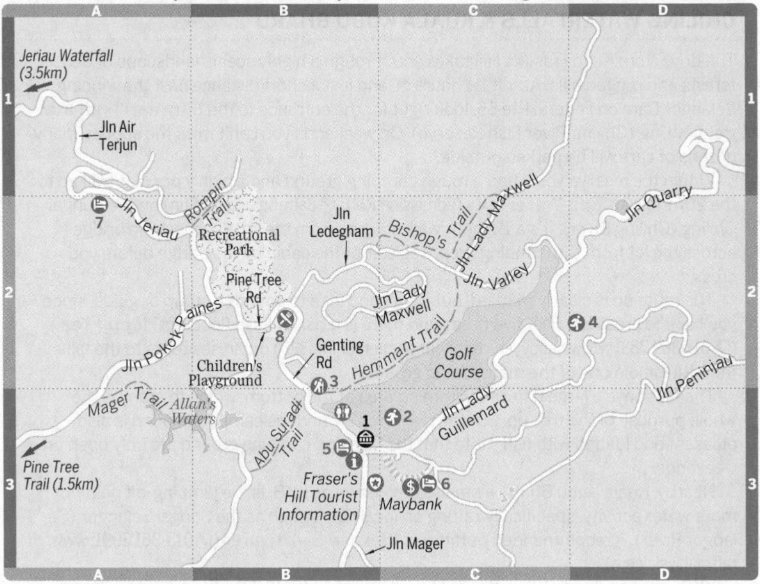

Fraser's Hill (Bukit Fraser)

eight to 10 hours return. You don't need a guide, but you must register at the police station in the village first. Note that it's a long walk to the trailhead if you don't have a vehicle.

Festivals & Events

International Bird Race FESTIVAL
In May or June Fraser's Hill hosts an International Bird Race in which teams of birdwatchers compete to observe and record the highest number of species in a set time period.

Sleeping

There's a good range of accommodation, from colonial-era bungalows to modern apartments; small discounts during the week are usual.

Check the website of Highland Resthouse Holdings Bungalows (www.hrhbungalows.com) for details about its range of rooms, chalets and bungalows, starting from RM220 for a room to between RM1400 and RM2000 for full bungalow hire.

★Ye Olde Smokehouse Fraser's Hill HOTEL $$
(☎09-362 2226; www.thesmokehouse.my; Jln Jeriau; d/ste incl breakfast from RM280/400; 📶) Exposed beams, log fires, four-poster beds and chintz – the Smokehouse goes for broke on its English-charm offensive. Even if you don't stay here, drop by for a pint at the bar, or a well-made pie or roast at lunch. Afternoon tea (RM18) is from 3pm to 6pm on the garden terrace overlooking a wooded valley.

WORTH A TRIP

CHILING WATERFALLS & KUALA KUBU BHARU

The drive from KL to Fraser's Hill takes you through a highly scenic landscape of dense forests and rugged hills. About 1½ hours in, and just a short distance past the winding Selangor Dam on Federal Rte 55, look right for the entrance to the **Santuari Ikan Sungai Chiling** (Chiling River Fish Reserve). On weekends you can't miss the spot as many dozens of cars will be parked outside.

Within the reserve you'll find a rough camping ground and a highly popular trail up to the 20m-tall **Chiling Waterfalls** (admission RM1; 8am-6pm Sat & Sun) on the Sungai Chiling (Chiling River). It's a 1½-hour walk starting from the small pedestrian bridge across the lot from the camping area. Register at the cabin by the bridge before you cross.

The route up is clearly marked, but it's a good idea to go with a group or guide, since you have to cross the river five times and there is a risk of flash flooding. **Happy Yen** (017-369 7831; www.happyyen.com; tour per person RM320) organises tours to the falls from KL, or join one of the many hiking groups.

The falls have a large natural swimming area at the bottom, which to many is the whole purpose of the trek up. But the river area around the camping ground is also pleasant and loaded with fish. Note that the falls and camping ground are only open on weekends.

Nearby, Kuala Kubu Bharu, a small town known as KKB, is the jumping-off point for more water activity, specifically rafting on local rivers such as the Sungai Selangor (Selangor River). A recommended outfitter is **Pierose Swiftwater** (013-361 3991; www.raftmalaysia.com).

KKB is connected to KL by the KTM Komuter train (RM8.70); you'll need to change at Rawang.

Puncak Inn HOTEL $$
(09-362 2007; puncakinn2@yahoo.com; Jln Genting; r incl breakfast RM100, cottages RM130-300;) This place offers the best-value rooms in Fraser's Hill and a handy central location. Apart from the hotel, they also offer studios, two- and three-bedroom apartments, and four cottages which can sleep between four and 15 people.

Puncak Inn has a pleasant patio restaurant overlooking the village square with a mix of Western and Malay dishes on offer.

Shahzan Inn Fraser's Hill HOTEL $$
(09-362 3300; shahzan7@yahoo.com; Jln Lady Guillemard; r from RM230;) Overlooking the golf course (where guests receive a 20% discount), this is the most contemporary accommodation at Fraser's Hill.

Eating & Drinking

As you come into Fraser's Hill you'll find a cloud of stores for self-catering supplies. There are also two hawker-stall complexes: one in the same complex as the Bird Interpretation Centre, next to the golf course, and the other a 10-minute walk up the hill from the village square.

All the hotels have restaurants; Ye Olde Smokehouse's (p111) the best of the bunch.

Hill View INTERNATIONAL, CHINESE $
(3 Food Garden, Pine Tree Rd; mains RM12-20; 10am-9pm) The family who have run this stall for a couple of generations serve up simple dishes. Find it in a hawker food court, a 10-minute walk uphill from the village square.

Scott's Pub & Restaurant BRITISH $$
(www.thesmokehouse.my; Jln Genting; mains RM18-25; 11am-10pm Thu-Tue) A slice of olde England is recreated at this pub (run by the same firm as the Ye Olde Smokehouse) where you can sink a pint and indulge in all-day breakfasts, stuffed chicken, steak or sandwiches.

Information

Fraser's Hill Tourist Information (09-517 1623; www.pkbf.gov.my; Puncak Inn, Jln Genting) Provides information, maps and brochures. Located in the Puncak Inn lobby.

Maybank (Shahzan Inn, Jln Lady Guillemard; 9.15am-4.30pm Mon-Thu, to 4pm Fri, ATM 6am-midnight) Accepts credit cards, exchanges foreign currency and travellers cheques, and has an ATM.

Getting There & Away

The route to Fraser's Hill is via Chiling Waterfalls and Kuala Kubu Bharu (KKB). You can take a KTM Komuter train to KKB and then a taxi (one way RM80). There are few taxis at KKB, however, so rather than showing up and hoping for the best have your hotel arrange one for you. From Kuala Lumpur a taxi will cost around RM200.

If driving yourself, note there's no petrol station in Fraser's Hill; the nearest ones are found at Raub and KKB.

Putrajaya

03 / POP 68,000

An eye-catching array of monumental architecture amid lush, manicured greenery is on display in Putrajaya, 25km south of KL and 20km north of KLIA. Covering 49.32 sq km of former rubber and palm-oil plantations, the Federal Government's administrative hub (almost exclusively Muslim in population) was but a twinkle in the eye of its principal visionary – former prime minister Dr Mahathir – as late as the early 1990s.

As a showcase of urban planning and vaulting architectural ambition, Putrajaya is impressive, but it's still a long way off its envisioned population of over 300,000 and a strange place to visit. Its heart is a 6-sq-km artificial lake fringed by landscaped parks and an eclectic mix of buildings and bridges, best viewed when illuminated at night.

Sights & Activities

Taman Wetland PARK

(03-8887 7773; park 9am-7pm, nature interpretation centre 9am-5pm Tue-Fri, 8.30am-5.30pm Sat & Sun, closed Fri 12.45-2.30pm) A short taxi ride from Dataran Putra (Putra Square) is this serene, contemplative space with peaceful nature trails, aquatic animals and water birds, fluttering butterflies and picnic tables overlooking the lake. Canoes, kayaks and bikes can be rented at the boathouse (from 9am to 7pm), which is about a kilometre from the Nature Interpretative Centre by road or walkway.

Taman Botani GARDENS

(03-8887 7770; Presint 1; 9am-1pm & 2-6pm Sat-Thu, 9am-noon & 3-6pm Fri) This 93-hectare site just north of town features attractive tropical gardens, a visitors centre, lakeside restaurant and a beautifully tiled **Moroccan Pavilion** (admission adult/child RM3/1). A tourist tram (RM4) trundles between the flower beds and trestles, and you can hire bicycles (RM4 per hour). You'll need to take a taxi to get here.

Cruise Tasik Putrajaya BOAT TOUR

(03-8888 5539; www.cruisetasikputrajaya.com; adult/child Perahu Dondang Sayang boat RM40/20, Belimbing cruise RM50/35; 10am-6.30pm Mon-Thu, to 9.30pm Fri-Sun) Located just beneath the Dataran Putra end of the Putra Bridge, this outfit offers two basic options for cruising Putrajaya Lake: the gondola-like Perahu Dondang Sayang boats, which depart any time for a 25-minute trip, and the 45-minute air-con cruise on the Belimbing boat, which leaves about every hour.

There are also shorter early bird air-conditioned cruises before 1pm (25 minutes in duration), and moonlight cruises at 8.30pm and 9.30pm on Saturday.

Putrajaya Sightseeing TOUR

(03-8890 4788; Putrajaya Sentral; adult/child RM20/10; 3pm Fri, 11am & 1pm Sat-Thu) Tours which stop at 12 sights in town. Tickets can be purchased on the spot (just after you exit the platform area) but call ahead to confirm departure times as they are changeable.

Architecture

Monumental buildings, sporting an array of designs, line the main boulevard of Persiaran Perdana, which runs from the circular Dataran Putra to the elevated spaceship-like **Putrajaya Convention Centre** (03-8887 6000; Presint 5), worth visiting for the views. In between, check out the Mughal-esque

SEPANG INTERNATIONAL CIRCUIT

The **Sepang Circuit** (03-8778 2222; www.sepangcircuit.com), 65km south of KL, is where Formula One holds the Malaysian Grand Prix every March or April. Tickets go for as little as RM80, though if you want to be in the main grandstand they start from RM340. During the three days of the grand prix, shuttle buses run from KLCC to the track.

Other car and motorcycle races are held here throughout the year – check the website for details. On weekdays call ahead to book a tour of the facilities including a run through the **auto museum** (www.jmm.gov.my/en/national-automobile-museum-sepang; museum free, circuit tour adult/child RM56/26.50; 9am-6pm Mon-Fri).

Istana Kehakiman (Palace of Justice; Persiaran Perdana); the striking modernist Islamic gateway (composed of a lattice of steel blades) fronting the **Kompleks Perdadanan Putrajaya** (Putrajaya Corporation Complex; Persiaran Perdana); and the **Tuanku Mizan Zainal Abidin Mosque** (Iron Mosque), which can be seen through the gateway across the **Kiblat Walk** skyway. During Ramadan the skywalk is the site of a large and colourful bazaar where you can sample speciality foods in a white tent city.

Framing Dataran Putra on two sides are **Perdana Putra**, housing the offices of the prime minister, and the handsome **Putra Mosque** (for non-Muslims 9am-12.30pm, 2-4pm & 5.30-6pm Sat-Thu, 3-4pm & 5.30-6pm Fri), which has space for 15,000 worshippers and an ornate pink-and-white-patterned dome, influenced by Safavid architecture from Iran. Appropriately dressed non-Muslim visitors are welcome outside prayer times.

There are nine bridges in Putrajaya, all in different styles. The longest, at 435m, is the **Putra Bridge**, which mimics the Khaju Bridge in Esfahan, Iran. Also worthy of a photo is the futuristic sail-like **Wawasan Bridge** connecting Presint 2 and 8.

The bridges and buildings look their best viewed from **Putrajaya Lake**.

Sleeping & Eating

Putrajaya Shangri-la HOTEL $$$
(03-8887 8888; www.shangri-la.com/kualalumpur/putrajayashangrila; Taman Putra Perdana, Presint 1; r from RM380;) This classy hotel has a great hillside view across to Putrajaya Lake. Good-value weekend packages are available, and there are frequent online promotions.

Pullman Putrajaya Lakeside RESORT $$$
(03-8890 0000; www.pullmanputrajaya.com; 2 Jln P5/5, Presint 5; r from RM350;) Close to the Convention Centre and beside Putrajaya Lake, this large resort complex incorporates traditional Malaysian architectural elements into its design. The rooms and resort facilities are good and include an alfresco seafood restaurant built over the lake.

Selera Putra FOOD COURT $
(meals RM10-15; 9am-9pm) Head to this food court beneath Dataran Putra and enjoy the lakeside view while enjoying a wide range of inexpensive Malaysian dishes.

Alamanda FOOD COURT $$
(www.alamanda.com.my; meals RM20; 10am-10pm) Putrajaya's swish shopping mall is home to several restaurants as well as an excellent food court where you can join the local bureaucrats for a meal. You'll need to take a taxi or your own wheels to get here.

Information

Tourist Information Booth (Dataran Putra; 8am-1pm & 2-5pm, closed 12.45-2.45pm Fri) A very helpful booth. Bicycles (RM6 per hour) can be rented here on weekends.

Getting There & Around

KLIA transit trains from KL Sentral (one way RM9.50, 20 minutes) and KLIA (one way RM6.20, 18 minutes) stop at Putrajaya Sentral.

Buses runs from the train station to close to Dataran Putra. A taxi is RM15; hiring one for an hour or two to tour the sights (the recommended option) is RM40/80.

Petaling Jaya & Shah Alam

03

Heading southwest of Kuala Lumpur along the Klang Hwy, the Kota Darul Ehsan ceremonial arch marks the transition between the city and Selangor. Just over the boundary, the suburb of Petaling Jaya blends into Shah Alam, the state capital. It can take hours to get to the sights as you need to pass through some of KL's worst traffic; make sure to factor this in when planning your visit.

Sights & Activities

Masjid Sultan Salahuddin Abdul Aziz Shah MOSQUE
(03-5159 9988; 9am-noon, 2-4pm & 5-6.30pm, closed 11.30am-3pm Fri) Known as the Blue Mosque, this is Southeast Asia's second-biggest mosque (it can hold up to 24,000 worshippers), and has the distinction of sporting the world's largest dome (for a religious building) and the tallest cluster of minarets, each over 140m.

Sunway Lagoon THEME PARK
(03-5639 0182; www.sunwaylagoon.com; 3 Jln PJS, 11/11 Bandar Sunway; adult/child RM150/120; 10am-6pm) Built on the site of a former tin mine and quarry, this multizone theme park has 80 attractions, including water slides, and the world's largest artificial surf beach.

WORTH A TRIP

ISLAND DAY TRIPS FROM KUALA LUMPUR

If you're looking for an off-the-beaten-track day trip from Kuala Lumpur, try Pulau Ketam, reached by ferry, or Pulau Carey, reached by road.

Pulau Ketam (Crab Island; www.pulauketam.com) This charming fishing village built on stilts sits over the mudflats. There's little to do here other than snap pictures and enjoy a Chinese seafood lunch at one of several restaurants, but most find this good enough.

Ferries depart from the ferry terminal across the street from Pelabuhan Klang Station, the end of the line for the KTM Komuter Train. Air-con ferries (adult/child return RM14/7, 30 minutes) depart roughly every hour starting from 7.45am for the ride through the mangroves. There are also open boats (RM10) that do the trip in 20 minutes. The last ferry back from Pulau Ketam is at 5.30pm (6pm on weekends).

Pulau Carey Though largely covered with palm-oil plantations, this island's Orang Asli village at Kampung Sungai Bumbon is worth a visit for the **Mah Meri Cultural Village** (http://mmcv.org.my; entry RM6; ⏲9am-6pm). If you don't have your own wheels, check out the tour packages available on the website (minimum two people) or hire a taxi to Pulau Carey from Klang (return with a couple of hours on the island RM120 to RM150).

The Mah Meri (also spelled Hma' Meri) are a subgroup of the Senoi people and live along the coast of Selangor. They are renowned for their masterful woodcarving, and comically expressive oversized masks. Drop by the village museum for excellent displays of their art with accompanying text explaining the local legends informing each piece (such as the story of a tiger trapped in a cage that inspired one of the people's most iconic wood sculptures).

You can order woodcarvings at the village centre, or pick up less expensive but still beautiful palm-leaf origami or woven baskets and mats made from pandanus leaves. You can also rent rickety bikes (RM15 per hour) to explore the rest of the island. Up the main road from the turn-off for Kampung Sungai Bumbon look for a sign for Kampung Sungai Rambai and turn left. At the sign for Balai Origami turn right for the **Pusat Origami** (Origami Centre), where you might be lucky to see displays of live origami making.

Klang & Pelabuhan Klang

☎03

About 30km west of KL lies Klang, Selangor's former royal capital. The town makes for a pleasant diversion, and if combined with a trip to nearby Pulao Carey and a sumptuous feast in the vibrant Little India, a good day out. Aficionados of mosque architecture should consider Klang a must-visit for the beautiful art deco Masjid Di Raja Sultan Suleiman.

Klang is easily accessed by the KTM Komuter train. Five stops further down the line trains terminate at Pelabuhan Klang. The main reason for coming here is to catch a ferry to either Sumatra or Pulau Ketam.

Sights

Klang is small enough to see on foot. Jln Tengku Kelana is the heart of Klang's colourful **Little India**. Especially frenetic around the Hindu festival of Deepavali, this Little India is always more vibrant and photogenic than the one in KL.

Galeri Diraja Sultan Abdul Aziz MUSEUM
(☎03-3373 6500; www.galeridiraja.com; Jln Stesen; ⏲10am-5pm Tue-Sun) FREE This grand whitewashed 1909 colonial-era building houses a mildly interesting royal gallery devoted to the history of the Selangor Sultanate (dating back to 1766). Inside there's a wide array of royal regalia, gifts and artefacts, including replicas of the crown jewels.

Heading straight out of the train station along Jln Stesyn you'll reach the museum on the left in about three blocks.

Istana Alam Shah PALACE
(Jln Istana) This was the Selangor sultan's palace before the capital was moved to Shah Alam. You can't enter but the pleasant park opposite offers a decent view.

Head out of the train along Jln Stesyn and continue walking as the road heads up the hill. The Istana Alam Shah is on the left across from a park.

Masjid Di Raja Sultan Suleiman MOSQUE
(Jln Kota Raja) This former state mosque, opened in 1934, is a striking blend of art

deco and Middle Eastern influences. Several sultans are buried here. Step inside to admire its stained-glass dome.

To get here head straight out from the train station along Jln Stesyn, and in a few blocks at the the four-way intersection, turn left. The mosque is a few more blocks up the road on the left.

Note that when we visited it was only possible enter the front gate of the compound but not the mosque itself, which was under repair.

Eating

Indian snack food is a highlight of Klang, but it's not the only thing on offer: the town's Chinese community is also famous for inventing *bak kut teh* (pork-rib soup with hints of garlic and Chinese five spice).

Seng Huat Bak Kut Teh MALAYSIAN, CHINESE $
(012-309 8303; 9 Jln Besar; mains RM11-20; 7.30am-noon & 5.30-8.30pm;) If you like your *bak kut teh* fragrant, but not overpowering, sample the pork stew at this eatery, two blocks to the right as you exit the train station (just beneath the Klang Bridge). Get here early as it tends to run out of meat towards the end of their opening sessions.

Asoka INDIAN $
(105 Jln Tengku Kelana; mains RM5-9; 8am-10pm) This parlour of Indian culinary goodness includes a great selection of sweets, juices and *dosai* (crispy pancakes) served with coconut chutney.

Sri Barathan Matha Vilas INDIAN, CHINESE $
(34-36 Jln Tengku Kelana; mains RM6-11; 6am-9pm) It's hard to resist a bowl of this restaurant's signature dish of spicy mee goreng (fried noodles). The chef prepares them in a giant wok beside the entrance.

Getting There & Around

KTM Komuter trains run from KL Sentral to Klang (RM5.40, one hour, every 20 to 30 minutes).

Klang's bus station is on the other side of the river from the sights. To get here from the train station head right and then cross the bridge. On the other side, the main bus station can be seen straight ahead. For buses to Kuala Selangor, turn left after crossing the bridge and wait under the overpass about a block past the 7-Eleven. Buses run every hour or so (RM6).

Taxis to Pulau Carey (RM120 to RM150 return) can be hired directly outside the train station.

Five stops down the KTM line from Klang is Pelabuhan Klang station (RM6.40), which is just a stone's throw from the ferry terminal to Pulau Ketam and also two locations in Sumatra, Indonesia: Tanjung Balai (one way RM155, four hours, one daily except Sunday) and Dumai (RM130, 3½ hours, Thursday and Saturday).

To check on ferry times call the **Pelabuhan Klang Ferry Terminal** (for Dumai 03-3167 7186, for Tanjung Balai 03-3165 2545).

Kuala Selangor

03

Off the beaten tourist track, Kuala Selangor has a friendly *kampung* (village) atmosphere and a few sights worth making the trek out here for, including a nature park in the mangroves, the remains of an old fort and a nightly light show of fireflies along the Sungai Selangor. If you have your own vehicle, the town makes for a relaxing retreat with plenty of pretty countryside to explore nearby.

The hilltop fort of this sleepy old royal capital was briefly conquered by the Dutch when they invaded Selangor in 1784; Sultan Ibrahim took it back a year later. The town later became embroiled in the Selangor Civil War (1867–73), which saw the fort partly destroyed. Its remains lie on Bukit Malawati, a green hill overlooking the town and sea.

Sights & Activities

Taman Alam Kuala Selangor Nature Park WILDLIFE RESERVE
(03-3289 2294; www.mns.org.my; Jln Klinik; adult/child RM4/1; 8am-6pm) On the estuary of Sungai Selangor, at the foot of Bukit Malawati, this 240-hectare park features three ecosystems to explore: secondary forest, an artificial lake and a mangrove forest with views out to sea. Cover them all on a 3km trail that includes a raised walkway above the mangroves and several raised lookouts. This is a wonderful place to spot a range of wildlife, including birds (September begins the migratory season), wild pigs, mudskippers and monkeys.

Bukit Malawati VIEWPOINT
It's a short walk through landscaped parklands to the top of Bukit Malawati, with views across the mangrove-dotted coastline. Once an administrative and military fort, all that remains today are sections of wall, cannons and a poisoned well used to torture traitors. At the summit is a picturesque British lighthouse (dating from 1910), and a podium for viewing the new moon. Further down the hill is the Royal Mausoleum, the

burial ground for the first three sultans of Selangor.

The road up Bukit Malawati starts basically from the edge of town. It does a clockwise loop of the hill; you can walk up and around in less than an hour.

Tame silvered leaf monkeys hang out here but resist feeding them.

Kampung Kuantan WILDLIFE WATCHING
(per boat RM53; ⌚7.45-10pm) The main place for viewing fireflies in the Kuala Selangor area is Kampung Kuantan, 9km east of town. Here Malay-style wooden boats (leaving on demand) take up to four people for a 45-minute river trip to the 'show trees' and their dazzling displays. Trips aren't recommended on full-moon or rainy nights as the fireflies are not at their luminous best. Bring insect repellent. It's easiest reached with your own vehicle.

Sleeping

Taman Alam Kuala Selangor Nature Park HUT $
(☎03-3289 2294; www.mns.org.my; Jln Klinik; hut RM30, wooden chalets RM60) Accommodation at the park entrance includes simple A-frame huts or two-bed (one single, one queen) wooden chalets with fan and attached bathroom. There's no food available for the individual traveller here, but the restaurants in town are only a few minutes' walk away.

De Palma Hotel Kuala Selangor HOTEL $$
(☎03-3289 7070; www.depalmahotel.com; Jln Tanjung Keramat; r incl breakfast from RM210; ❄@🛜🏊) Around 1.5km north of the entrance to Bukit Malawati (follow the signs) is this decent miniresort offering a range of accommodation in reasonably well-maintained wooden chalets. There are mountain bikes for guests and the resort can arrange an evening trip out to see the fireflies at Kampung Kuantan (RM90 for two people).

Eating

If seafood is what you're after, head to Pasir Penambang, a fishing village on the northern side of the river, where a number of chaotic seafood restaurants are clustered. If you don't have your own transport, ask your hotel to arrange a taxi (RM10 to RM15).

Auntie Kopitiam CHINESE, MALAYSIAN $
(No C3, Jln Sultan Ibrahim; meals RM5-12; ⌚6am-6pm) On the main road across from the entrance to Bukit Malawati, this old-style *kopitiam* (coffee shop; founded in 1935) serves Malaysian favourites such as *nasi lemak* (rice boiled in cocnut milk, served with *ikan bilis*, peanuts and a curry dish) and Hainanese chicken chop. Auntie's more modern sister establishment, Auntie Foo, just up the block, has wi-fi should you need it, plus the bus schedules to Klang and Kuala Lumpur.

Getting There & Away

In Klang catch bus 156 to Kuala Selangor (RM6, one hour, half-hourly). In KL catch bus 141 (RM7.40, two hours, half-hourly) at the Medan Pasar bus hub (just up from Central Market).

Once in Kuala Selangor, you'll need to take a short taxi ride to your destination. For this reason it might be better to either rent a taxi in KL for the day or half-day (it will be difficult to get a KL taxi to agree to take you one way to Kuala Selangor) or join a firefly tour from KL with a company like Viator (www.viator.com).

NEGERI SEMBILAN

Seremban

☎07 / POP 550,000

Like KL, Seremban's roots lay in the discovery of tin in the 19th century, which saw prospectors flock to the village originally known as Sungai Ujong. Today Negeri Sembilan's state capital, 64km southeast of KL, is a much more low-key place. While generally overlooked by international visitors, it's worth a stop if you're headed to the beachside resorts of Port Dickson. You could also use it as a base for exploring nearby villages, including Sri Menanti, Terachi and Kampung Pantai with their beautiful traditional wood houses.

Photographers will enjoy the town's eclectic architecture, which includes colonial-era lake gardens and whitewashed mansions, rows of shophouses as pretty as those in Melaka and some outstanding Minangkabau wood palaces. Seremban is home mostly to Chinese and Indian populations, evident in the tasty local specialities on offer here.

Sights

Muzium Negeri MUSEUM
(State Museum; Jln Sungai Ujong; ⌚10am-6pm Tue, Wed, Sat & Sun, 8.15am-1pm Thu, 10am-12.15pm & 2.45-6pm Fri) FREE This mildly diverting museum is worth a visit to learn a little about the megalith culture of Negeri Sembilan and

Seremban

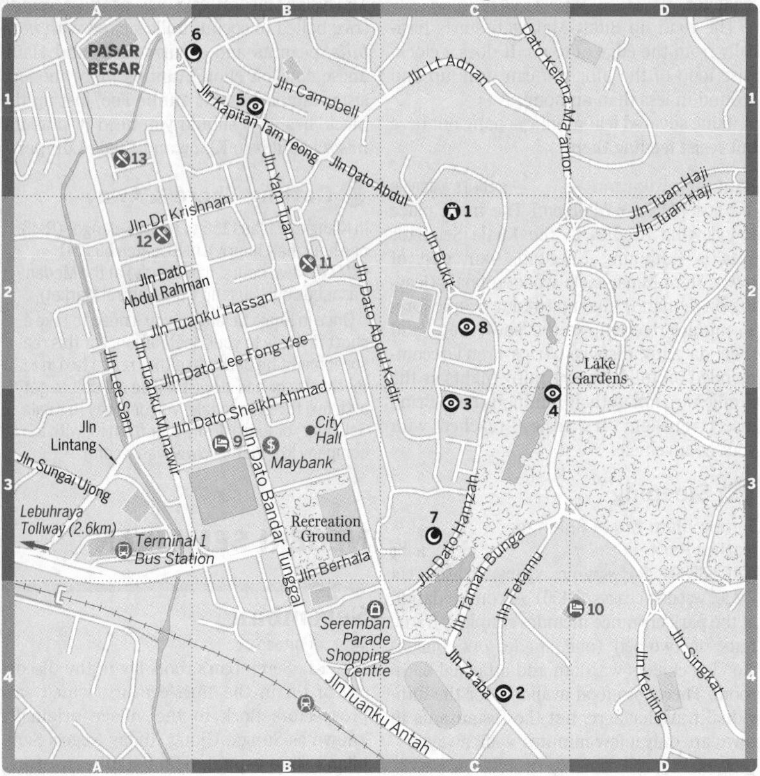

Seremban

Sights

1 Istana Besar C2
2 King George V School C4
3 Kompleks Kraf Negeri Sembilan C3
4 Lake Gardens C3
5 Liesheng Temple B1
6 Masjid Jamek B1
7 Masjid Negeri C3
8 State Library C2

Sleeping

9 Carlton Star Hotel B3
10 Royale Bintang Resort & Spa Seremban D4

Eating

11 Haji Shariff's Cendol B2
12 Kee Mei Siew Pao A2
13 Sin Yee Kee A1

to see the two gorgeous wood structures in the outside complex. The **Ampang Tinggi Palace** (1870) and the **Rumah Negeri Sembilan**, both transported and reconstructed here from elsewhere in the state, are superb examples of Minangkabau architecture and are sure to whet your appetite to see more around the state.

Both structures can be entered via short ladders, which you should do if only to understand the genius of traditional stilt housing with respect to ventilation. The Ampang Tinggi Palace also has beautifully carved foliage panels on the outer walls. At the far end of the Rumah Negeri Sembilan, which has the hallmark curved roof (like buffalo horns) of Minangkabau houses, check out the pretty etching of a traditional local mosque with a tiered pyramidal roof.

The park is 3km west of the city centre so if you don't have your own vehicle drop in on the way to Sri Menanti with your taxi.

Sleeping

Seremban lacks standout accommodation, so it's worth onsidering staying in KL and visiting for the day. Alternatively both Port Dickson and Melaka are only about an hour away by road.

Carlton Star Hotel HOTEL $
(07-762 5336; www.carltonstar.com; 47 Jln Dato Sheikh Ahmad; r from RM100;) Within walking distance of Terminal 1 bus station, this hotel has bland, ageing business-style rooms.

Royale Bintang Resort & Spa Seremban HOTEL $$
(07-766 6666; www.royalebintang-seremban.com; Jln Dato AS Dawood; r from RM300;) This four-star, resort-style business hotel has comfortable rooms, a good range of restaurants and amenities (including a swimming pool with water slides, fitness centre and a jogging track to the nearby lake gardens) and helpful staff.

Eating

★**Haji Shariff's Cendol** DESSERTS $
(44 Jln Yam Tuan; cendol/rojak from RM1.30/3.50; 11am-6.30pm Sat-Thu) Three generations of the Shariff family have been serving up refreshingly sweet bowls of *cendol* (a pandan-leaf-flavoured dessert served with shaved ice, red beans, jaggery syrup and coconut milk) to appreciative locals. Now installed in a distinctively green-painted 1919 shophouse, they also serve a local verison of *rojak* (a mixed vegetable dish with a thick shrimp-based sauce) with a spicy tomato rather than soy sauce.

★**Sin Yee Kee** CHINESE $
(Stall 742, upper fl, Pasar Besar Seremban, Jln Dato Bandar Tunggal; noodles RM6; 7.30am-3pm Fri-Wed) There's a good selection of hawker favourites dished up at the lively daytime food court above Seremban's main *pasar besar* (food market) at the edge of town in a warehouse-looking structure. This family-run beef-noodles stall has been going since the 1960s and is deservedly popular.

Kee Mei Siew Pao MALAYSIAN $
(cnr Jln Dr Krishnan & Jln Dato Bandar Tunggal; pork bun RM1.70; 8am-6pm, closed every 2nd & 4th Tue of month) This basic shop is a great place to pick up some of Seremban's famous *pao* (bun).

Getting There & Away

KTM Komuter trains (RM8.70, one hour 15 minutes, half-hourly) shuttle between KL Sentral and Seremban. There are also buses to/from KL and, surprisingly, most large centres in Malaysia

THE LAKE GARDENS & COLONIAL DISTRICT

Two thin lakes in the pleasantly wooded **Lake Gardens park** are the centrepiece of the old colonial-era district of Seremban. Popular with courting local couples, they make for a nice break as you walk a large loop from the train station. Start by heading east to **King George V School** (Jln Za'aba), the premier colonial-era academic institution for Seremban and still functioning as a local high school. Nearby is **Masjid Negeri** (Jln Dato Hamzah), the state mosque, with its nine external pillars representing the nine original fiefdoms of Seremban.

A short walk north is the now closed **Kompleks Kraf Negeri Sembilan** (cnr Jln Bukit & Jln Sehala) in a handsome 1912 mansion that was once home to British Resident Captain Murray. From the same era is the even grander neoclassical **State Library** (off Jln Dato Hamzah), once the offices of the colonial administration. It was built in 1912 and designed by AB Hubback, the architect responsible for many of KL's heritage buildings. While you can't enter, its position at the top of the hill at a junction of roads makes for a wonderful photo. Across the road is the **Istana Besar** (Jln Bukit; closed to the public), home of the Sultan of Negeri Sembilan.

If you continue east you'll soon reach the Chinese shophouse district. As is common in Malaysian towns, you'll find various houses of worship, including the Taoist **Liesheng Temple** (51 Jln Kapitam Tam Yeong; daylight hours). Just up the road in the arcade passageways look for a rare coloured advertisement of **Milk Maid Milk** condensed milk etched directly into the footpath. Further along check out **Masjid Jamek** (Jln Tun Dr Ismail), built in 1924 in the Melakan mosque style with a tiered pyramidal roof and a lighthouse-like minaret.

OFF THE BEATEN TRACK

MEGALITHS & MINANGKABAU

The countryside around Seremban is home to some of the most bucolic scenes in all of Malaysia. The hills are green and densely wooded, and rice fields spread across the valleys, but it's the villages that will steal your heart with their traditional wood houses, many in the charming Minangkabau style.

Hailing originally from western Sumatra, the Minangkabau people have lived in Peninsular Malaysia since at least the 15th century, settling primarily in the region now covered by Negeri Sembilan. Following Islam but also incorporating older animist beliefs and traditional customs (known as *adat*) into their daily lives, they have long since blended in with the Malay population. However, aspects of Minangkabau culture do remain. The most noticeable feature is the distinct traditional architecture of the region, such as homes with sweeping curved roofs and pointed gables that are supposed to resemble buffalo horns.

Good examples of this architectural style can been seen in Seremban's Muzium Negeri (p117), the old royal town of Sri Menanti, and especially in the dreamy villages of **Kampung Pantai** and **Terachi**. Kampung Pantai is just north of Seremban on Federal Rte 86, while Terachi is 27km east on Rte 51 at the turn-off to Sri Menanti. In addition to the highly photogenic houses of Terachi, don't miss the **ancient megaliths** which are indicated by the sign *Tapak Megalitik* just before the start of the village.

There are hundreds of megaliths scattered across Peninsular Malaysia, most concentrated in Melaka and Negeri Sembilan. Their origin and purpose remain obscure, as does their age, though they are often found in Muslim cemeteries (as in Terachi). The megaliths here could be a few hundred years old, from the time of the Minangkabau arrival, or they could be thousands of years old. Locals call them *Batu Hidup* (Living Stones), which may be a reference to the fact they seem to grow over the years, the result of land erosion around them. Surprisingly, megaliths aren't believed to be sacred.

If you have time, consider taking Rte 51 all the way to **Kuala Pilah**, a pretty town with rows of colourful Chinese shophouses and one of Malaysia's most interesting Chinese temples, the **Sansheng Gong** (Sansheng Temple; Jln Dato Undang Johol). The temple was the first in the country dedicated to Guan Gong, sometimes referred to as the god of war, and is adorned with painted mortar figures and wood sculpture. To the right as you enter the temple, look for a shrine featuring the two guards who escort the spirits of dead to the underworld. **Dua Di Ya Peh**, as they are known, are also worshipped as fortune gods in Malaysia, and you will see offerings of stout beer and cigarettes laid before them. Across the road from the temple is a *pailou* (archway) dedicated to Martin Lister, the first British Resident (1889–97) of Negeri Sembilan.

(even Singapore), though you are very unlikely to need to use them. Buses leave from the **Terminal 1 bus station** (Jln Sungai Ujong).

Long-distance taxis operate from outside both the train station and the bus station and have fixed prices to various destinations. A one-way fare to a beach resort at Port Dickson is RM60, while a round trip to Sri Menanti, including time in the village, costs RM100.

Sri Menanti

☎06

Tidy and placid Sri (or Seri) Menanti, 6km off Federal Rte 51 (the Seremban–Kuala Pilah road), is the old royal capital, first settled over 400 years ago by Minangkabau immigrants from Sumatra. Swathed in a silence only interrupted by birdsong, this sleepy, disengaged hamlet nestles in a highland valley surrounded by green jungle hills, fringed with simple dwellings and scampering chickens.

From Seremban a round-trip taxi with an hour in Sri Menanti costs RM100.

Sights

Istana Lama PALACE

(Old Palace; ⏲10am-6pm, closed Fri 12.30-2.45pm) FREE The magnificent Istana Lama, a black hardwood palace, was built at the beginning of the 20th century as a temporary replacement for an even older palace that was razed by British soldiers during the Bukit Putus War. Inside you can see the king and queen's bedchambers, the children's playroom, a large dining room and huge dining table, as well as kris weaponry and royal regalia.

Arranged over four floors, with long galleries, and a distinctive gabled tower in the centre, the palace was famously fashioned without the use of nails. It's elevated on 99 pillars, many of them carved with foliated designs, with each post said to represent one of the legendary 99 *luak* (clan) warriors of Negeri Sembilan. Climb to the top floor for views over the gardens.

In 2014 renovation work began on the palace to replace a number of ageing supports. Work is expected to last at least three years. Visitors can still tour the grounds and the outside of the palace.

Istana Besar PALACE

Just past Sri Menanti's own tiny Lake Gardens is Istana Besar, the impressive modern white palace of the Yamtuan Besar (the head of state) of Negeri Sembilan. It was originally built in the 1930s and is not open to the public.

Makam Di Raja CEMETERY

Towards the main road in the compound next to the mosque is the Makam Di Raja (Royal Cemetery), which has a distinctive Victorian/Moorish pavilion. The prominent grave of Tuanku Abdul Rahman, the first yang di-pertuan agong (king) of independent Malaysia, is immediately inside the gates.

Sleeping

Sri Menanti Resort HOTEL

(06-497 0049; r/chalets RM160/210) The Sri Menanti Resort, next to Istana Lama, has reasonably well-maintained rooms, including concrete chalets over an ornamental lake where you can go fishing. At the time of writing the resort did not have a restaurant open for individual guests but there were several small eateries down the road.

Port Dickson

06

The closest beach area to Kuala Lumpur, Port Dickson (PD) is popular with locals, Singaporeans and resident foreign expats. The coastline is lovely, and the area makes for a relaxing short break, or even day trip from the city, but it's difficult to get around here without your own vehicle.

Note that when people talk about Port Dickson they're usually referring to the coastline and not the actual Port Dickson, which is a small, uninteresting town slightly inland.

Sights & Activities

There's close to two dozen kilometers of coastline, much of it undeveloped, with several popular public beach areas outside the resorts. If you visit the latter be aware that local Malay rules of propriety prevail: don't dress skimpily, and if you're a couple, keep the PDA to a minimum.

Cape Rachado Forest Reserve NATURE RESERVE

(Tanjung Tuan Forest Reserve; admission RM1; 7am-8pm) The Port Dickson area's highlight is the 80-hectare Cape Rachado Forest Reserve. This jungle of towering lowland trees has secluded beaches that are ideal turtle laying grounds and is a stopover for over 300,000 migratory birds every year. A simple network of trails runs off the main path. Bring lots of water.

The reserve is 2km down a turn-off from the main road through PD. You can park at the Ilham Resort and then hike through the forest reserve for another kilometre to the **Tanjung Tuan lighthouse** (*rumah api*). The lighthouse, which was first built in 1528 by the Portuguese and is the oldest in Malaysia, isn't open to the public. You can, however, walk around to the front of it for great views and on a clear day see Sumatra, 38km away across Selat Melaka.

Avillion Admiral Cove BOATING

(03-2730 9988; www.avillionadmiralcove.com; Jln Pantai) This large resort and marina has various water-sport options for nonguests at the Eco-ride Centre to the right before the clubhouse. You can rent kayaks (per hour RM22) and banana boats (per person per hour RM27), take a boat cruise (per person RM180, 10.30am, 2pm and 5pm), or splash out on the sunset cruise and snorkelling package for RM425.

Sleeping

All the following rates reflect weekend prices. Rates are usually 15% lower on weekdays, and 10% higher on peak public holidays.

★ **Avillion Port Dickson** RESORT $$

(06-647 6688; www.avillionportdickson.com; Jln Pantai; r incl breakfast from RM385;)

DON'T MISS

MIGRATING RAPTORS

Around mid-February to mid-April, migrating raptors (birds of prey such as kestrels, falcons and eagles) make the crossing from Sumatra to the Asian continent via the Cape Rachado Forest Reserve (p121). Sightings are of course not guaranteed but you'll have the best luck seeing the birds from around the Tanjung Tuan lighthouse between 11am and 3pm, when the heat of the day creates thermals for the birds to soar on.

Some 25 species head north for the summer each year and, having used up most of their energy getting across the Straits of Melaka, are tired and fly so low that you can see them quite close up. The birds that arrive late in the afternoon or evening often rest and recuperate at the reserve for the night before heading off again on their long journeys. Without this precious forested rest area, naturalists say that many of the birds would die of exhaustion or starvation.

The **Raptor Watch Festival** (https://mnsraptorwatch.wordpress.com) is held during the height of the migratory period, usually during the first week of March. For more information and specific dates for the next festival go to the website, which is updated each year.

Beautifully designed and lushly planted with lily ponds, birds of paradise, bromeliads and palms, the accommodation highlight here is the over-the-water chalets that have big terraces you can swim from at high tide. Even the cheapest rooms here are classier than just about anywhere else, with hardwood floors, elegant wood furnishings, flagstone bathrooms and loads of natural light.

Several good restaurants, a huge pool with slides, a tennis court and a gym are also at hand.

Grand Beach Resort Port Dickson RESORT $$
(☎06-647 4090; www.grandbeachresortpd.com; Jln Pantai; r incl breakfast from RM320; ❄📶🏊) The name is a bit of an exaggeration, but this Minangkabau-style resort has sea-facing rooms, all with small balconies, and a particularly good stretch of beach all to itself. Admiralty Cove, with all its facilities and rental options, is just a a few minutes' walk away along the beach.

This place is popular with conference groups and so can feel rather busy at times. Note that during peak holidays the price of rooms nearly doubles.

PNB Ilham Resort RESORT $$
(☎06-662 6800; www.ilhamresort.com; Batu 10, Tanjung Biru; r incl breakfast from RM240; ❄📶🏊) Next to Cape Rachado Forest Reserve, Ilham is a massive resort on a calm bay with a quiet stretch of white-sand beach. English service is weak here compared with other resorts.

★**Thistle Port Dickson Resort** RESORT $$$
(☎06-648 2828; www.thistle.com/Malaysia; Jln Pantai; r incl breakfast from RM745; ❄@📶🏊) This exclusive resort set in 90 acres of landscaped grounds features a private 3km beach, golf course, magnificent pool, beautiful views, a fitness center and more.

✕ Eating

All resorts have restaurants (and some bars) on the premises, and most are open to nonguests.

If you have a vehicle you can also try the local food stalls which pop up at various places alongside the main road. Seafood is the speciality but you can also get Thai curries and Malay staples such as satay and fresh-fruit drinks.

Crow's Nest MALAYSIAN $$
(Avillion Port Dickson; mains RM35-55; ⏲7am-11pm; 📶) For excellent views of the coast, and good Malay food, try the airy restaurant at Avillion Port Dickson.

ℹ Getting There & Around

It's possible to use public transport to get to Port Dickson from KL. First take the KTM Komuter train to Seremban and then a taxi (RM60) from the Terminal 1 bus station to your destination. Taxi fares are fixed outside the bus station so you won't be overcharged.

There's little to no public transport around the beach areas, however. Get your resort to order you a taxi should you need one, and be prepared to wait an hour for it.

Perak

05 / POP 2,352,743 / AREA 21,035 SQ KM

Includes ➡

Best Places to Eat

- Restaurant Lou Wong (p129)
- Barracks Cafe (p141)
- Luen Fong Restaurant (p133)
- Lim Ko Pi (p129)
- Restoran Pasir Bogak (p146)

Best Places to Stay

- Sekeping Kong Heng (p127)
- Tiger Rock Resort (p145)
- Lakehouse (p139)
- Adeline's Villa (p134)
- Belum Eco Resort (p155)

Why Go?

Clifftop temples, dam-flooded wilderness, a mining town now famous for chicken with bean sprouts – Perak's highlights are as intriguing as they are varied, but somehow this rugged Malaysian region has never seized its share of the limelight.

Time spent unpeeling Perak's layers will reward you richly. Amble through Ipoh's old town for time-worn mansions, craft shops and excellent food. Beyond the city lie cave temples so precariously situated they'll make you sweat with awe and exertion. Cool off with rafting in Gopeng, tour Taiping's colonial architecture or head north to untouched Royal Belum State Park. The beaches on Pulau Pangkor don't rival Peninsular Malaysia's east coast, but the island has sun, sea and hornbill-spotting in abundance. Perak is also the best starting point to explore the Cameron Highlands (technically situated in Pahang state). Once beloved of colonial Brits seeking a breather, these breezy hill stations now lure travellers eager to escape the muggy lowlands – and sip tea straight from the source.

When to Go

Ipoh

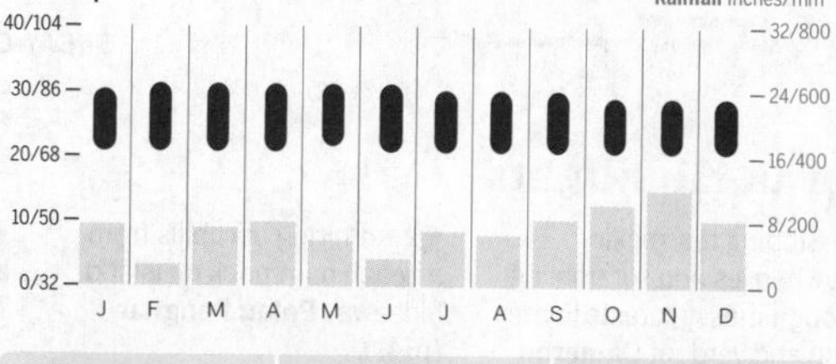

Dec–Feb Sizzle on Pangkor's beaches or cool down in Perak's high country.

Jun–Aug Seize binoculars for birdwatching in Belum or chill in the Cameron Highlands.

Sep–Nov During Perak's wetter months, skip to a city break in Ipoh or Taiping.

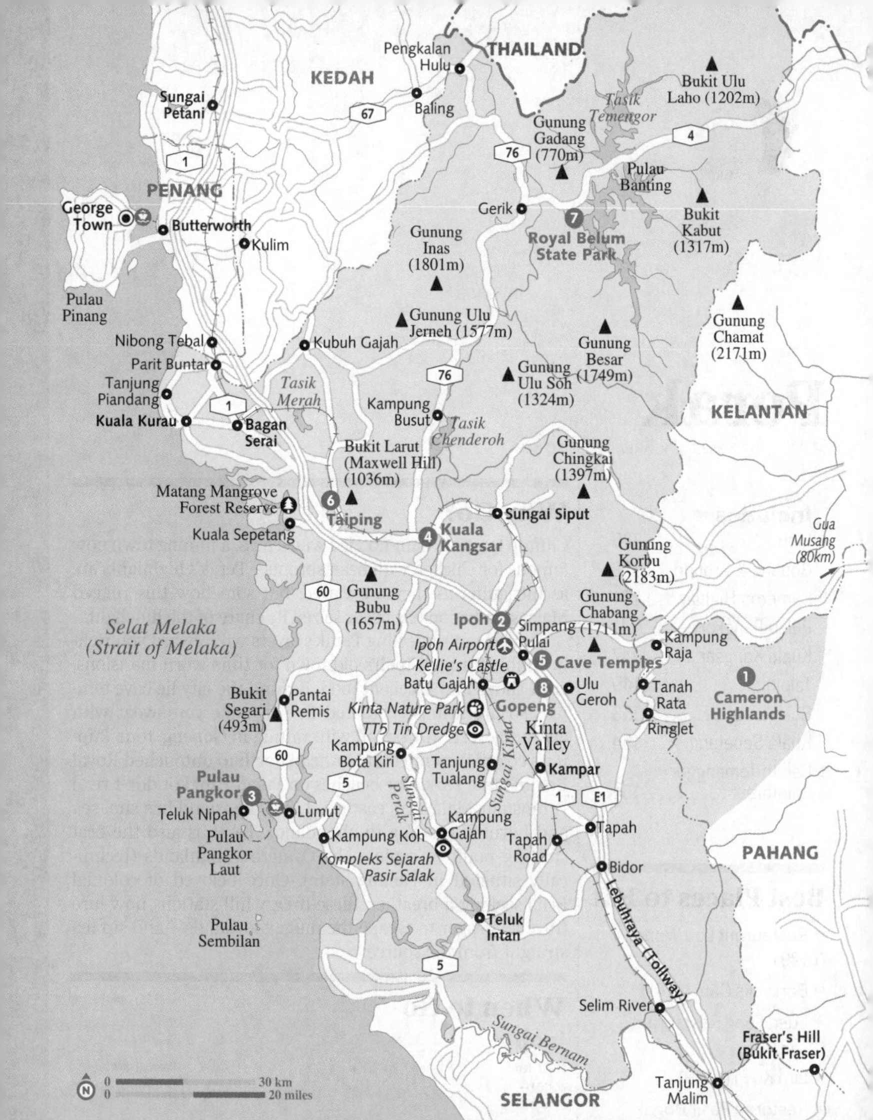

Perak Highlights

1. Sipping tea, picking strawberries and scrambling through mossy forests in the fresh and verdant **Cameron Highlands** (p134).
2. Gorging on food in revamped **Ipoh** (p131), from chicken and bean sprouts to excellent Indian cuisine.
3. Admiring hornbills from a beach hammock on island hideaway **Pulau Pangkor** (p141).
4. Being dazzled by the royal sights and rich architecture of **Kuala Kangsar** (p147).
5. Marvelling at the remarkable **cave temples** (p129) near Ipoh.
6. Perusing colonial buildings and luscious street food in **Taiping** (p149).
7. Muddying your hiking boots in the watery wonderland of **Royal Belum State Park** (p154).
8. Going rafting, caving and rambling around the wild terrain of **Gopeng** (p133).

History

Today's sultanate of Perak dates back to the early 16th century, when the eldest son of the last sultan of Melaka, Sultan Muzaffar Shah, began a new dynasty on the banks of Sungai Perak (Perak River). The state's rich tin deposits quickly made it a target of both covetous neighbours and foreign forces.

Dutch efforts in the 17th century to monopolise the tin trade were unsuccessful, but remains of their forts can still be seen on Pulau Pangkor (Pangkor Island) and at the mouth of Sungai Perak. In the 18th century, the Bugis from the south and the Siamese from the north made concerted attempts to dominate Perak, but British intervention in the 1820s trumped them both.

The British had remained reluctant to meddle in the peninsula's affairs, but growing investment in the Straits Settlements, along with the rich tin mines of Perak, encouraged their interest. The mines also attracted a great influx of Chinese immigrants, who soon formed rival clan groups allied with local Malay chiefs, all of whom battled to control the mines.

The Perak sultanate was in disarray, and fighting among successors to the throne gave the British their opportunity to step in, making the first real colonial incursion on the peninsula in 1874. The governor, Sir Andrew Clarke, convened a meeting at Pulau Pangkor at which Sultan Abdullah was installed on the throne instead of Sultan Ismail, the other major contender. The resultant Pangkor Treaty required the sultan to accept a British Resident, and be consulted on all issues other than those relating to religion or Malay custom. One year later, Sultan Abdullah was forced, under threat of deposition, to accept administration by British officials on his behalf.

Various Perak chiefs united against this state of affairs, and the Resident, James WW Birch, was assassinated at Pasir Salak in November 1875. Colonial troops were called in to fight the resulting brief Perak War. Sultan Abdullah was exiled and a new British-sanctioned sultan was installed. The next British Resident, Sir Hugh Low, had administrative experience in Borneo, was fluent in Malay and was a noted botanist – he even had a pitcher plant named after him *(Nepenthes Lowii)*. He assumed control of taxes from the tin mines and practised greater intervention in state affairs. In 1877 he introduced the first rubber trees to Malaysia, and experimented with planting tea and coffee as well. The sultans, meanwhile, maintained their status, but were increasingly effete figureheads, bought out with stipends.

The first railway in the state, from Taiping to Port Weld (now known as Kuala Sepetang), was built in 1885 to transport the wealth of tin; the result was rapid development in Taiping and Ipoh. In 1896, Perak, along with Selangor, Pahang and Negeri Sembilan, became part of the Federated Malay States. The system of British Residents (and later Advisers) persisted even after the Japanese invasion and WWII, ending only when Perak became part of the Federation of Malaya in 1948. Perak joined the new independent Malaysia in 1957.

IPOH

POP 710,000

Ipoh is undergoing a quiet renaissance. Until now, domestic tourists seldom lingered beyond a weekend sampling *ayam tauge* (chicken and bean sprouts) and Ipoh's famous white coffee. Backpackers considered this pleasant, midsized city an overnight stop between Kuala Lumpur and Penang. These days, renewed enthusiasm for Ipoh's heritage is seeing old shophouses restored, while new cafes and craft shops are springing up within historic buildings. Meanwhile, the ribbon is being cut on brand-new accommodation, from hostels to luxury hotels.

The key to enjoying Ipoh is tackling it by neighbourhood. Its pavements seem designed to shred sandals while its sights sprawl over a large area. Start with the old town's charismatic laneways and revived period buildings. Grab a trail map to seek out the best heritage structures and street art. South of here, Ipoh's Little India has glittering shops and some fine eateries.

East of the river in Ipoh's new town, a cluster of canteens serve up regional classics like *ayam tauge* and some of the creamiest bean-curd pudding around. Just north of this foodie hub are the city's more upmarket hotels alongside the shiny Parade shopping mall. As Ipoh's confidence grows, it's an exciting place for an urban interlude, not to mention a convenient gateway for travel to the Cameron Highlands or Pulau Pangkor.

Ipoh

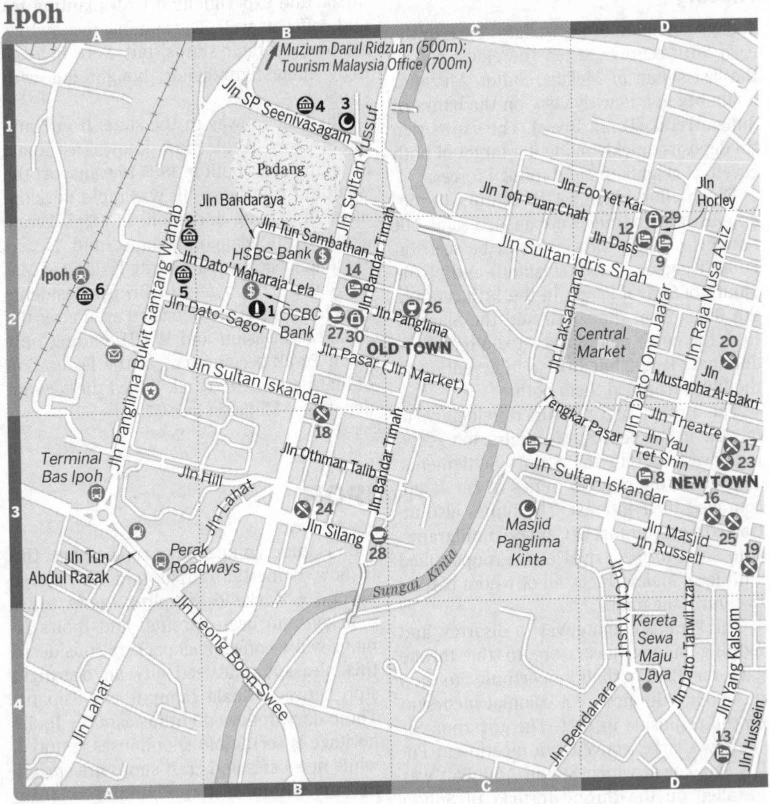

Sights

Most of Ipoh's grand colonial architecture is found in the old town, west of the Sungai Kinta.

Birch Memorial Clock Tower MONUMENT

(Jln Dato' Sagor) FREE The clock tower, with its 1.98m bell, was erected in 1909 in memory of James WW Birch, Perak's first British Resident. Birch was murdered in 1875 at Pasir Salak by local Malay chiefs. The friezes on the clock tower are meant to illustrate the growth of civilisation, featuring figures such as Moses, Buddha, Shakespeare and Charles Darwin. A figure representing Mohammed has since been erased.

The road on which this memorial stands has been renamed for one of Birch's killers. Today they are considered nationalists while Birch is remembered for his disregard of local custom.

Muzium Darul Ridzuan MUSEUM

(2020 Jln Panglima Bukit Gantang Wahab; 9.30am-5pm) FREE North of the *padang* (field), this museum is housed in a 1926 villa built for a wealthy Chinese tin miner. The museum features displays on the history of tin mining (downstairs) and forestry (upstairs) in Perak. Occasional temporary exhibitions are more interesting but most intriguing are the World War II–era bunkers behind the building. When we came by, the museum was undergoing renovation but was still accepting visitors.

Train Station HISTORIC BUILDING

(Jln Panglima Bukit Gantang Wahab) Dating from 1914 and known locally as the 'Taj Mahal', Ipoh's elegant domed train station is a blend of Moorish and Victorian architecture designed in the 'Raj' style.

Town Hall HISTORIC BUILDING

(Jln Panglima Bukit Gantang Wahab, Dewan Bandaran; 8am-5pm) Ipoh's gleaming white town hall

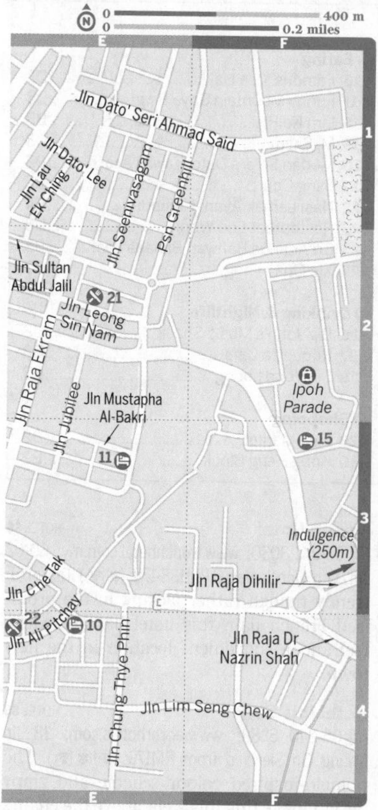

dates back to 1916 and is a popular spot for wedding photo shoots. Visitors are often allowed to wander inside; the upper floor has good views of the colonial train station.

Court House HISTORIC BUILDING
(Mahkanah Tinggi; Jln Panglima Bukit Gantang Wahab) Ipoh's courthouse was built in 1928 by AB Hubback, the same architect who designed Ipoh's train station and the town hall. Not open to the public.

Masjid India Muslim MOSQUE
(Jln SP Seenivasagam; ⏲8am-5pm) Built in the Mughal style in 1908 for the local Indian population. Only Muslims are allowed inside.

St Michael's Institution HISTORIC BUILDING
(Jln SP Seenivasagam) On the *padang's* northern flank is this neo-Gothic, three-storey colonial school with arched verandahs, founded by the Catholic La Salle brothers in 1912. Not open to the public.

Activities

A walking tour is the best way to cover all of the colonial-era architecture in Ipoh's old town. You can do a self-led tour, using the excellent *Ipoh Heritage Trail* maps 1 and 2, available at Ipoh's tourist information centre and on billboards around the Kong Heng Block (p130) area.

Regular guided heritage tours no longer run, but local guides **Mr Raja** (☎012-524 2357) and **Roselyn Lim** (☎012-500 9400) can lead walks for groups on request (from RM250).

Sleeping

The majority of lodgings are east of the Sungai Kinta, over in the new town.

Eloft HOSTEL $
(☎017-336 5592; 115 Jln Sultan Iskandar; dm incl breakfast RM30; ❄📶) Ipoh's friendliest backpacker accommodation opened its doors in July 2015. Partly run by volunteers, Eloft has one air-conditioned, 14-bed mixed dorm, a pleasant common area and a balcony overlooking busy Jln Sultan Iskandar. Bike rental is available (six/24 hours RM8/20). Ring the bell for access (the doorway is easy to miss).

Abby By The River HOSTEL $
(☎05-241 4500; www.abbyhotel.my; cnr Jln Laxamana & Jln Sultan Iskandar; dm/d/tr from RM35/100/125; P❄📶) Nestled right by Sultan Iskandar bridge, the Ipoh branch of this Perak chain is well positioned for exploration of the old or new towns. Choose from three-bed single-sex dorms, doubles or family rooms that sleep three. Rooms are comfy enough but the bland interior rather unfortunately evokes a hospital.

Hotel Robin HOTEL $
(☎05-242 1888; 100-110 Jln Mustapha Al-Bakri; r/ste from RM56/85; ❄📶) Zero charm, but rooms are clean and the owner speaks English.

★**Sekeping Kong Heng** BOUTIQUE HOTEL $$
(☎012-227 2745; www.sekeping.com/kongheng/home.html; 74 Jln Bandar Timah; r RM220-800; ❄📶🏊) Down an alleyway opposite Jln Panglima (Concubine Lane) lie rooms and apartments unlike anywhere else in Ipoh. Nostalgia resounds from every distressed wood panel and bare brick wall. The lovingly restored building is an architect's dream: high-ceilinged rooms overlooking laneways thick with creeping plants; apartments

Ipoh

Sights

1	Birch Memorial Clock Tower	B2
2	Court House	A2
3	Masjid India Muslim	B1
4	St Michael's Institution	B1
5	Town Hall	A2
6	Train Station	A2

Sleeping

7	Abby By The River	C3
8	Eloft	D3
9	French Hotel	D2
10	Hotel Ibis Styles	E4
11	Hotel Robin	E3
12	Pi Hotel	D2
13	Ritz Garden Hotel	D4
14	Sekeping Kong Heng	B2
15	WEIL Hotel	F3

Eating

16	Famous Mee Hakka	D3
17	Funny Mountain Soya Bean	D3
18	Lim Ko Pi	B3
19	M. Salim	D3
20	Medan Selera Dato' Tawhil Azar	D2
21	Ming Court	E2
22	Nasi Lemak Ayam Kampung	E4
23	Restaurant Lou Wong	D3
24	Sri Ananda Bahwan Banana Leaf	B3
25	Xin Quan Fang	D3

Drinking & Nightlife

26	Big John's Music Shack	C2
27	Roquette Cafe	B2
28	Sin Yoon Loong	B3

Shopping

29	Flea Market	D2
30	Kong Heng Block	B2

kitted out with hubcaps and other miscellany; a secret swimming pool; and zanily furnished common areas.

The menu of rooms spans a range of styles and rates. Be aware that some apartments are open air with mesh walls; not ideal for light sleepers. On our visit, the hotel was expanding with RM80 single rooms aimed at backpackers.

Pi Hotel HOTEL $$

(05-255 2922; http://hotelpi.com.my; Jln Veerasamy; d RM94-125; P) Rooms at this midrange place are comfortable and chic, and are decorated with black-and-white photographs, cushioned red headboards and inspirational catchphrases. Beaming staff help ensure an agreeable stay. The weekly flea market creates enjoyable chaos near the hotel each Sunday, so take advantage of the underground parking.

WEIL Hotel HOTEL $$

(05-208 2228; www.weilhotel.com; 292 Jln Sultan Idris Shah; d incl breakfast from RM290;) This brand-new upmarket hotel – 'WEIL' is the founder's name backwards – hadn't quite hit its stride on our visit. But staff are eager to please, dining spaces are achingly trendy and the breakfast buffet is lavish. Rooms feel more business than luxury, but beds are exceedingly comfortable and the bathrooms are rather chic. WEIL's location next to the Parade mall is superb for shoppers, though you might want a taxi to access the old town (around RM10).

French Hotel HOTEL $$

(05-241 3030; www.frenchhotel.com.my; 60-62 Jln Dato' Onn Jaafar; d RM138-178;) Tasteful, trendy though rather lacking in the promised French flair, this hotel has a modern feel and a convenient location in the new town.

Hotel Ibis Styles HOTEL $$

(05-240 6888; www.accorhotels.com; 18 Jln Chung On Siew; d from RM179; P) The pomelo-inspired colour scheme and zippy design make this Ibis a cut above the chain's usual offerings. Friendly staff and comfortable common areas make it a refreshing haven from the traffic-choked new town. Rooms are spotless and make excellent use of space.

Ritz Garden Hotel HOTEL $$

(05-242 7777; www.ritzgardenhotel.com; 86 Jln Yang Kalsom; d/tr/ste incl breakfast from RM145/200/260; @) Formerly fancy, now staunchly midrange, this hotel has seen better days and retains a stubbornly '80s feel. Rooms are functional and staff are friendly, though the quality of perks like wi-fi and pool leave a little to be desired.

Banjaran Hotsprings Retreat RESORT $$$

(05-210 7777; www.thebanjaran.com; 1 Persiaran Lagun Sunway 3; villas incl breakfast from RM1329; @) This is an exclusive spa resort at the base of limestone cliffs, 8km northeast of Ipoh. The 26 villas have features such as private pools and jacuzzi fed by the natural hot springs; spa activities include a thermal steam cave and an ice bath. Transport can be arranged by the resort.

Indulgence BOUTIQUE HOTEL $$$
(05-255 7051; www.indulgencerestaurant.com; 14 Jln Raja Dihilir; d/ste incl breakfast from RM340/540;) The seven rooms in this 1930s-era mansion span a variety of styles from Thai to rococo. If you can bear the somewhat-inconvenient location east of the city centre and a 10-minute walk from Parade shopping mall, these sumptuously decorated spaces offer a memorable stay.

Eating

★**Lim Ko Pi** CHINESE $
(05-253 2898; 10 Jln Sultan Iskandar; mains RM12; 8.30am-6pm) From its colourful tiles to the pretty inner courtyard, this relaxing cafe has a strong whiff of Ipoh's old glory days. Meals include generous portions of prawn fried rice, curry noodles and smoky-but-sweet stewed pork, best accompanied by a perfectly prepared white coffee. Service is wonderfully unrushed compared to many of Ipoh's eateries.

Lim Ko Pi is just as good as a dessert stop: choose between a mound of *cendol* (shaved-ice dessert with green noodles, syrups, fruit and coconut milk), peanut-strewn ice-cream sundaes, or (our favourite) wickedly fatty custard on a bed of caramel.

★**Restaurant Lou Wong** MALAYSIAN $
(05-254 4190; 49 Jln Yau Tet Shin; mains RM12; noon-10pm) This is the place to try Ipoh's esteemed signature dish, *tauge ayam* (chicken with bean sprouts). You'll have to fight for space on the plastic stools that spill out from Lou Wong onto the road, but it's worth it for a taste of smooth poached chicken served with generous mounds of rice and plump bean sprouts.

Sri Ananda Bahwan Banana Leaf INDIAN $
(05-253 9798; 7 Persiaran Bandar Timah; mains RM5; breakfast, lunch & dinner;) Some of Ipoh's best Indian food is cooked up in this simple cafeteria in Little India. Mop up chutney and dhal with a fluffy *dosa* (paper-thin rice-and-lentil crêpes) or order the generous banana-leaf special, with mountains of rice and spiced okra. Leave space to take away a box of the excellent *barfi*, fudge-like confectionery in flavours from cashew to chocolate.

IPOH'S CAVE TEMPLES

The rocky landscape in Ipoh's surrounds is a veritable honeycomb of caves, many of which have powerful spiritual associations. Several such clifftop meditation spots and stalactite-strewn temples grew into large complexes. While tricky to reach by public transport, these three temples make a convenient half-day trip by car or guided tour. Mr Raja (p127), a local guide, can take two or more travellers on a trip to all three cave temples for around RM350, including stops for breakfast and traditional white coffee.

Perak Tong (9.30am-4pm) Founded in 1926 by a Buddhist priest, this cave temple is Ipoh's most visited and offers spectacular views. Located 6km north of Ipoh, the temple extends into a warren-like complex of grottoes, with a gleaming 40ft seated Buddha the highlight. Bright murals of Buddhas and saints adorn the cave walls, some painted as recently as the 1990s. Outside, a steep walk up stairs and pathways accesses stunning views over Ipoh (arrive before 3.30pm for the climb).

From the local bus station, buses bound for Kuala Kangsar can stop at Perak Tong.

Gua Kok Look Tong (7am-5pm) Buddha statues glint out between shadowy stalactites in this serene temple away from the tourist trail. Three Sages dominate the central cavern, while towards the back a cheerful Chinese Buddha of Future Happiness sits in the company of three Bodhisattvas. Behind the cave is an ornamental garden with ponds and pagodas. The temple is a long walk from Sam Poh Tong; the easiest way to reach it is via by guided tour or taxi from Ipoh (around RM35 each way).

Sam Poh Tong (9am-3.30pm) First discovered by a monk in 1890, this cave 5km south of Ipoh now shelters Sam Poh Tong temple, which is still used today by nuns and monks pursuing solitary meditation. The temple contains a reclining Buddha flanked by smaller statues, but the main attraction is 'Turtle Pond', where locals release tortoises in the hope of balancing their karma. There's also a garden adorned with granite pillars and small bridges. The temple can be reached by Gopeng-bound buses from Ipoh's local bus station.

Funny Mountain Soya Bean CHINESE $
(49 Jln Theatre; mains RM1.20; from 10.30am;) Funny Mountain is immensely popular for two dishes: bean-curd pudding (*tau fu fah*) and soy-bean milk. The curd, served with a bit of syrup, is smooth and sweet, while the drink is rich and refreshing in original or grass-jelly flavours (RM2.50). Funny Mountain opens at 10.30am and shuts shop when the curd runs out; arrive early and prepare to queue.

M. Salim INDIAN $
(05-255 5786; cnr Jln Yang Kalsom & Jln Che Tak; mains RM7.50; 6.30am-9.30pm Sat-Thu, to 1pm & 2-9.30pm Fri) This busy, no-frills halal place offers great food. The occasionally brusque service is quickly forgotten over a forkful of biryani, fragrant with cloves, creamy korma chicken or its famous fish-head curry.

Medan Selera Dato' Tawhil Azar MALAYSIAN $
(Jln Raja Musa Aziz; mains RM2-8; dinner) Better known as Children's Playground, this hawker centre has mostly Malay stalls arranged around a small square filled with slides and swings.

Nasi Lemak Ayam Kampung MALAYSIAN $$
(43-45 Jln Ali Pitchay; mains RM5.50-30; 4.30pm-12.30am) This popular restaurant is the place to come for variations on *nasi lemak* (rice boiled in coconut milk, served with fried *ikan bilis* – dried sardines or anchovies – peanuts and a curry dish). Also gracing the extensive menu are battered octopus, tart and peppery eel soup, and mango sticky rice pudding with just the right balance of sweet and savoury.

HOW TO EAT AN IPOH ICE BALL

The fashion for nostalgia in Ipoh is producing vintage flourishes in everything from interior design to food. And one frosty snack, the ice ball (*ais kepal*), is making a comeback.

Part of the fun is seeing the making of this edible cannonball. It's pummeled roughly out of ice shavings, dowsed in syrups from lychee to *gula melaka* (cane sugar), then loosely wrapped in waxy brown paper. Turn the ice ball repeatedly as you suck out the syrup. Ice ball pros hold one sheet of paper in each hand (they tend to be served in two), flipping the rapidly melting ball between them. Wrap your sticky fingers around an ice ball at Bits & Bobs (RM3) at the Kong Heng Block in Ipoh's old town.

Drinking

Big John's Music Shack BAR
(05-241 1617; 24 Lg Panglima; 6pm midnight Fri, to 1am Sat) This loosely British-themed retro bar reverberates with live blues and rock music on Friday and Saturday nights. While away some time beneath the British Union flag with set menus (from RM12.95) and shooting the breeze over beers with gregarious owner John.

Roquette Cafe CAFE
(05-241 2616; 101 Jln Sultan Yussuf; coffee RM9; 10am-6pm;) At this enjoyably kitsch cafe, a soundtrack of pop and country music serves as the backdrop to Ipoh's most perfect flat white. Wooden floors, an old typewriter and a library packed with Chinese children's books give Roquette a distinctive charm, though most of the hip patrons will be engrossed in the free wi-fi. Coffees and cakes from macarons to pistachio gateau keep energy levels soaring.

Shopping

★**Kong Heng Block** CRAFTS
(75 Jln Panglima; 9am-10pm Wed-Mon) During the colonial era, these walls formed the city's large single shop block. Today a cluster of craft stalls has sprung up around this light-flooded atrium in Ipoh's old town. Colourful independent sellers here include Ipoh Craftnerds and Living Art, peddling everything from quirky jewellery and handmade postcards to antique suitcases and crockery. Don't miss pausing to slurp an ice ball at Bits & Bobs (RM3). Find them adjoining luxuriant chain cafe Plan B.

Flea Market MARKET
(Jln Horley; 6am-noon Sun) A busy flea market virtually engulfs the streets surrounding Pi Hotel every Sunday morning.

Information

Ipoh Hospital (05-208 5000; http://hrpb.moh.gov.my; Jln Hospital) Ipoh's main hospital is located about 1.5km northeast of the centre of town; a taxi here should cost about RM10.

Kinta Medical Centre (05-242 5333; www.kintamedicalcentre.com; 20a Jln Chung Thye Phin) This new town medical centre has a 24-hour emergency room.

IPOH'S BEST EATS

They say it's the water: Ipoh has a glowing reputation as a food city, and locals believe that deposits from the rich karst formations around town seep into the groundwater, giving the city's food a special quality. With this in mind, here are some of the city's best dishes and where to eat them:

Curry mee A combination of rice and wheat noodles in a spicy, rich and often-oily broth, served with chicken, pork and shrimp. Arguably the best place to eat it is is at **Xin Quan Fang** (174 Jln Sultan Iskandar Shah; mains from RM3.80; ⏲ breakfast & lunch), but be ready for a wait; the family here has been making the dish for decades, and didn't get their loyal following by rushing.

Ayam tauge Tender boiled chicken served with Ipoh's fat bean sprouts and rice (the latter cooked in chicken broth) or a bowl of rice noodles is probably the dish most closely associated with Ipoh. Restaurant Lou Wong (p129) serves the best in town, with several competing restaurants nearby also cooking tasty versions.

Kopi putih Known in English as Ipoh white coffee, this method of roasting beans with palm-oil margarine was allegedly invented at **Sin Yoon Loong** (15A Jln Bandar Timah; coffee drinks from RM1.40; ⏲ 7am-6pm Mon-Sat).

Hakka mee Flat wheat noodles topped with salty ground pork, and served with a side bowl of broth with fish and pork balls and tofu; best at **Famous Mee Hakka** (163 Jln Sultan Iskandar Shah; mains RM3; ⏲ 7am-noon).

Dim sum Ipoh's Chinese community is predominately of Cantonese origin, so it's not a surprise that dim sum is popular here. Although it's not as flashy as the other dim sum palaces nearby, locals eat at **Ming Court** (32-36 Jln Leong Sin Nam; dim sum RM3-5; ⏲ 6am-noon Wed-Mon).

Tourism Malaysia Perak (☎ 05-255 9962, 05-255 2772; www.tourism.gov.my; 12 Medan Istana 2 Bandar; ⏲ 8am-5pm Mon-Fri) Tourism Malaysia's Perak office is situated north of Ipoh's old town.

ℹ Getting There & Away

AIR

Ipoh's airport, Sultan Azlan Shah Airport (www.ipoh.airport-authority.com), is about 3km southeast of the city centre; a taxi here from central Ipoh costs RM20. At the time of writing there were three direct daily flights to Singapore (from RM209) with **Firefly** (☎ nationwide 03-7845 4543; www.fireflyz.com.my; Sultan Azlan Shah Airport), **Tiger Air** (☎ Singapore 0065 3157 6434; www.tigerair.com) or **Malindo Air** (☎ 03-7841 5388; www.malindoair.com) and one direct daily flight to Johor Bahru (from RM60).

BUS

For destinations in and around Perak, services run from Terminal Bas Ipoh (Medan Kidd) and Perak Roadways. For longer journeys and out-of-state travel, the correct station is Terminal Amanjaya.

Most travellers will arrive in Ipoh's long-distance bus station, **Terminal Amanjaya** (☎ 05-526 7818, 05-526 7718; www.peraktransit.com.my; Persiaran Meru Raya 5), approximately 8km north of Ipoh. Bus 116 (RM2) goes between Amanjaya and the more central Medan Kidd station, while taxis cost roughly RM20 to RM25. The following routes are among those leaving from Amanjaya.

DESTINATION	PRICE	DURATION	FREQUENCY
Cameron Highlands	RM18.50-20	2 hours	Frequent, 9.30am-5.30pm
Butterworth/George Town (Penang)	RM20	2 hours	Frequent, 8.30am-8.30pm
Kuala Lumpur (also KLIA/LCCT)	from RM20	2½-3 hours	Hourly, 4.30am-9.30pm
Alor Setar	RM29	4 hours	Frequent, 9am-4pm
Melaka	RM36-40	5 hours	Frequent, 9.30am-12.45am
Kota Bharu	RM40	6 hours	9.30am, 10am, 11.30am & 10pm
Hat Yai (Thailand)	RM55	6-7 hours	9.30am

Johor Bahru	RM60	7 hours	Frequent, 9am-11pm
Singapore	RM56-75	8 hours	Frequent, 8.30 10.30am & 8.30-11pm

Perak Roadways (☎ 05-254 4895; Jln Tun Abdul Razak), located near a Shell station southeast of Medan Kidd bus station, operates buses to Lumut and Gerik.

DESTINATION	PRICE	DURATION	FREQUENCY
Gerik (for Royal Belum State Park)	RM14.40-18	2½-3 hours	9am, 12.30pm, 3.30pm & 6.45pm
Lumut (for Pulau Pangkor)	RM8.50	2 hours	Eight daily (6.30am-7pm)

Nearby is the local station **Terminal Bas Ipoh** (Medan Kidd Bus Station; Jln Tun Abdul Razak, Medan Kidd), often referred to as Medan Kidd, off a roundabout south of the train station. Services around Perak leave from here.

DESTINATION	PRICE	DURATION	FREQUENCY
Gopeng	RM2.70	40 min	Every 15min, 6am-6.15pm
Kuala Kangsar	RM6.20	1½ hours	Every 15min, 5.30am-8.45pm
Taiping	RM10	1½ hours	Nine daily
Tanah Rata (for Cameron Highlands)	RM16.80	2½ hours	8am, 11am, 3pm & 6pm

TRAIN

Ipoh's train station is on the main Butterworth–Johor Bahru line which connects to Singapore via a shuttle train. Trains run to Kuala Lumpur (RM25-40, 2½-3½ hours, eight daily) and Butterworth (RM11-33, 2½-four hours, four daily). Some Butterworth-bound trains continue to Hat Yai in Thailand (RM46-90, eight hours, one daily). Check www.ktmb.com.my for the latest info on fares and schedules.

Getting Around

With hectic traffic and uneven pavements, Ipoh isn't the most pedestrian-friendly city around. Nonetheless its old and new towns are simple to explore on foot, and **taxis** (☎ 05-253 4188) can be used to zip between the two. For attractions out of town, you'll need public or hired transport.

For a car with driver, contact Mr Raja (p127), a local guide who charges around RM350 per day for destinations around Ipoh. Car hire is handled by **Kereta Sewa Maju Jaya** (☎ 05-255 5510, 019-556 2158, 012-520 3588; www.car-rentalipoh.com; Jln CM Yusuff; ⏲ 8am-8pm).

GOPENG & AROUND

When urban fatigue hits and your stomach won't stretch for another street-food binge, head for the hills in Gopeng. This former tin-mining outpost, 20km southeast of Ipoh, is a sleepy place but it borders a rippling region of caves, river rapids and jungle. Rafting, abseiling, hiking and other adrenalin-soaked escapades are all possible in these wilds.

Sights

Gua Tempurung CAVE

(☎ 05-318 8555; tours adult RM6-22, child RM2.50-11; ⏲ 9am-5pm Sat-Thu, 9am-12.30pm & 2.30-5pm Fri) The 'Coconut Cave', so-called for its dome-like interior, is located about 7km from Gopeng. Nearly 2km of grottoes snake beneath the hills. Within, you'll find plenty of huge stalactites and gnarled limestone pillars to fire your imagination. Visits are by guided tour; choose from the easy 40-minute Golden Flowstone walk or book ahead for 3½-hour trails where you can expect to get wet and muddy – not for the claustrophobic.

If you don't have your own transport, many resorts in Gopeng arrange tours. Last entry 4pm.

Gaharu Tea Valley FARM

(☎ 05-351 1999; www.gaharu.com.my; tours adult/child RM10/5; ⏲ 9am-6pm) This 300-acre *gaharu* (agarwood) plantation is a mini-Cameron Highlands right near Gopeng. It's touristy, with guides extolling the healing powers of *gaharu* and its role in Middle Eastern and Chinese cultures, plus contrived attractions like 'Lovers' Tree'. But with viewing platforms that overlook the plantations and a cafe serving snacks like tea eggs, it's a pleasant break from sweating it out in Gopeng's jungle.

Kinta Nature Park WILDLIFE RESERVE

FREE Bring your binoculars to spot stork-billed kingfishers, baya weavers, otters and butterfly lizards at this wildlife spot 6km south of Batu Gajah. Despite excellent bird-watching credentials, the park is yet to receive major tourist attention (or investment). Lookout points are underloved and there's

OFF THE BEATEN TRACK

KINTA VALLEY HERITAGE LOOP

Perak is thought to derive its name (Malay for 'silver') from shimmering tin ore, with much of the area surrounding Ipoh built on the tin trade. The Kinta Valley boom towns that sprang up during the 1870s may have lost their sheen (metallic and otherwise), but they form an interesting half-day excursion from Ipoh.

Leaving Ipoh, head south on Hwy 5, passing sparsely populated **Kampung Papan**. This small town has some attractive period houses, though most are depressingly dilapidated.

After about 20km you'll reach **Batu Gajah**, an important settlement since the early 19th century. The town's name, meaning 'stone elephant', comes from two pachyderm-shaped rocks submerged in the Kinta river. If arriving in the morning, make time for fresh roti and coffee at excellent **Restoran Ganapathi** (☎013-493 3006; 155 Jln Besar, Batu Gajah; mains RM2-6; ⏲6am-8pm).

Batu Gajah is rich in colonial buildings, including mansions, a splendid neoclassical **Court House** (1892), the custard-yellow **St Joseph's Church** (1882), the **Old Railway Station** and **Kinta Gaol**, built to hold more than 450 prisoners. Other photos ops include the modern gold-domed **mosque** and the well-kept **God's Little Acre Cemetery**. For an in-depth tour, consult the excellent *Batu Gajah Heritage Driving Trail* map, available in Ipoh tourism offices.

Leaving town, drive 9km south to the **TT5 Tin Dredge**. The now-defunct dredge dates back to 1938 and is one of the earliest of its type in Malaysia. This open-air museum was not accepting visitors when we came by, so check locally before you make a special trip.

Belly rumbling? Drive further south to the small town of **Tanjong Tualang**. **Luen Fong Restaurant** (☎05-360 9267; 19 Jln Pasar, Tanjong Tualang; mains RM20-48; ⏲noon-2pm & 5-8pm) serves impeccably steamed fish, freshwater prawns sizzled in garlic and ginger, and a host of other seafood treats (call ahead to avoid disappointment). Tanjong Tualang is 20km south of Batu Gajah or 12km south of the TT5 Tin Dredge.

Returning to Batu Gajah, head east along Hwy A8, where after about 7km you'll reach **Kellie's Castle** (adult/child RM5/3; ⏲9am-6pm). Also known as Kellie's Folly, this leftover of British eccentricity was commissioned by Scotland-born planter William Kellie Smith. Not only bricks, but artisans and labourers were sourced from India to build what would have been, if finished, one of the most magnificent residences in Malaysia. Smith died in 1926 and the house was abandoned; today, it's a well-tended tourist site.

About 500m from the castle is a **Hindu temple**, built for the artisans by Smith when a mysterious illness decimated the workforce. To show their gratitude to Smith, the workers placed a figure of him, dressed in a white suit and pith helmet, among the Hindu deities on the temple roof.

Continue east for about 7km until you reach Hwy 1. Either turn south to visit Gopeng – the town's historic centre is another remnant of the tin era – or turn north, where after 13km, you'll arrive back in Ipoh.

Public transport is infrequent so you'll need a car for a Kinta Valley circuit. Even better than a rental vehicle is hiring a driver; Mr Raja (p127) is a native of Batu Gajah, the capital of Kinta District, and can drive small groups to sights around the loop (from RM300).

no visitor or information centre. It is possible to visit independently by bike but we recommend using a guide with a 4WD in this overgrown and isolated spot; enquire at Gopeng hotels or try Ipoh-based Mr Raja (p127).

Heritage House MUSEUM
(Jln Pasar; admission by donation; ⏲9am-3pm Sat & Sun) A restored shophouse decorated with original furniture and explored via an informal tour. Located off Gopeng's monument roundabout.

Muzium Gopeng MUSEUM
(Jln Eu Kong; admission by donation; ⏲9am-5pm Fri-Tue) A somewhat-random collection of old-fashioned housewares and vintage furniture supplemented with displays on local history.

Activities

Resorts can arrange guided activities including rafting (half-day per person from RM150), wet abseiling (half-day per person

RM100), caving (half-day per person from RM40) and rafflesia-spotting (half-day per person from RM55), guided walks to the blooming site of this pungent, parasitic flower – though sightings aren't guaranteed. Rafting and some of the more advanced caving excursions are only for groups of eight or more; in general, prices are cheaper the larger your group is. If you're solo or in a small group, book a couple of weeks ahead as it is may be possible to join you to a larger group; the more flexible your dates, the better.

Sleeping & Eating

Four outdoorsy resorts are scattered about 6km south and east of Gopeng, all within walking distance to hiking, rafting and other activities. Rates include accommodation and meals, with the exception of Clearwater Sanctuary, a high-end resort west of Gopeng.

Nomad Adventure Earth Camp GUESTHOUSE $
(03-7958 5152; www.nomadadventure.com; Kampung Chulek; dm/tr/q incl meals RM50/210/280; P) Wilderness experts Nomad Adventure arranges high-adrenalin excursions for groups, including river rafting, waterfall abseiling, zip-lining and climbing. You have to book onto a half-day excursion to stay at its sustainably operated Earth Camp. There's a range of accommodation types, from 24-person dormitories constructed out of greenhouses to treehouses and simple three- and four-person bungalows.

Fans give relief from the heat and bathrooms are shared, except in the four-person Matahari Villas. Mosquito nets on request. Book accommodation and activities at least 24 hours in advance. It may be possible for solo and small-group travellers to join larger groups for excursions.

★ **Adeline's Villa** RESORT $$
(05-359 2833; www.adelinevilla.com; per person shared/tw bungalow incl meals RM220-273;) The most sophisticated accommodation in the area, this welcoming guesthouse takes the form of 10 rooms in cutesy wooden villas that can sleep up to nine people.

Gopeng Rainforest Resort RESORT $$
(012-516 8200; www.gopengrainforest.com; Kampung Geruntum; per person RM98-118) The location here is stunning, but accommodation is very basic – think mattresses in fan-cooled structures with shared bathrooms. The food and activities get good reports.

Clearwater Sanctuary RESORT $$$
(05-366 7433; www.cwsgolf.com.my; Batu Gajah; r RM250-475;) This vast, rural-feeling retreat calls itself a golf resort, but beyond the green there are tennis courts, a landscaped pool and a lake teeming with giant shrimp and catfish. Accommodation is comfortable and the wood-lined bungalows overlooking the lake are tranquil and pleasingly furnished. Staff can help arrange activities from archery to fishing.

Clearwater is located east of Batu Gajah, about 15km south of Ipoh; it's best to have your own car.

Getting There & Away

Gopeng's bus station is located about 300m east of Hwy 1. Frequent buses shuttle passengers the 15km between Gopeng and Ipoh from 6.30am to 10.30pm (RM3, 30 minutes). Sri Maju buses from Kuala Lumpur's Pudu Sentral towards Ipoh Amanjaya stop in Gopeng Town (RM19.30).

CAMERON HIGHLANDS

From your first lungful of fragrant highland air, sweat and stress evaporate. In Malaysia's largest hill-station area, the breeze is freshened by eucalyptus, fuzzy tea plantations roll into the distance, and strawberry farms snooze under huge awnings.

From north to south, the Cameron Highlands roughly encompass Tringkap, Brinchang, Tanah Rata, Ringlet and their surrounds. Though technically in the state of Pahang, they are accessed from Perak. Named after explorer Sir William Cameron, who mapped the area in 1885, the highlands were developed during the British colonial period. Gardens, bungalows and even a golf course sprang up during the 1930s, making the Cameron Highlands a refuge for heat-addled Brits to mop their brows.

Temperatures in these 1300m to 1829m heights rarely top 30°C. This fresh climate inspires convoys of visitors to pick strawberries and sip tea here each weekend. Tourism is big business, so expect quiet contemplation to be interrupted by the din of building sites, and hilltop views to be occasionally obscured by megaresorts.

But the highlands' combination of genteel tea culture, hiking trails and mild temperatures remains irresistible. With eco-conscious trekking, unexplored forests and some interesting temples, there is serenity to be found amid the touristic hubbub.

Cameron Highlands

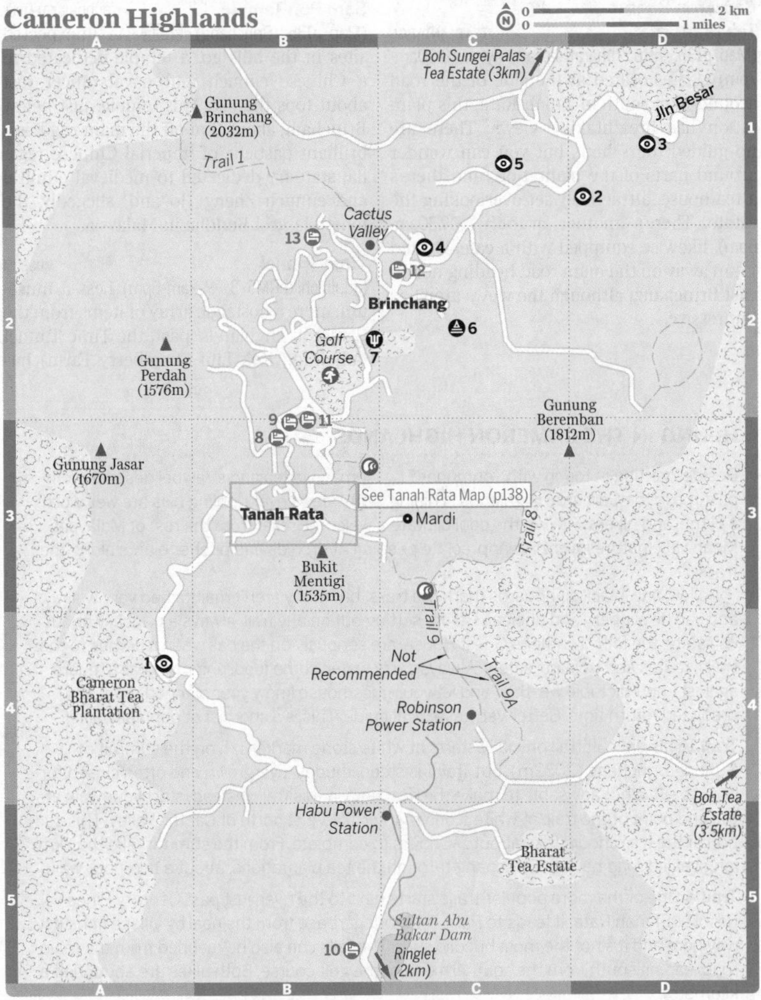

Cameron Highlands

Sights

1 Cameron Bharat Tea Plantation A4
2 Cameron Highlands Butterfly Farm D1
3 Ee Feng Gu Honey Bee Farm D1
4 Kok Lim Strawberry Farm C2
5 Raaju's Hill Strawberry Farm C1
6 Sam Poh Temple.................................... C2
7 Sri Tehndayuthapany Swamy B2

Sleeping

8 Bala's Holiday Chalet B3
9 Hotel De'La Ferns B3
10 Lakehouse B5
11 Smokehouse B3
12 Snooze C2
13 Strawberry Park Resort B2

Sights

Many attractions around the Cameron Highlands are glorified souvenir shops, peddling lavender or honey without much of a visitor experience. Tea plantations are as worthwhile for the views as the brews.

Cameron Bharat Tea Plantation TEA PLANTATION
(Map p135; http://bharattea.com.my; ⌚8.30am-7pm) FREE Located at the side of the road around 4km south of Tanah Rata, this plantation has breathtaking views. There are no guided tours here, but you can wander around parts of the plantation, and there's a tea house, attractively set overlooking the estate. There's another **branch** (⌚7.30am-6pm), likewise equipped with a cafe, located 12km away on the main road heading northeast Brinchang, although the views aren't as impressive.

Sam Poh Temple BUDDHIST TEMPLE
(Map p135; Brinchang) FREE As unexpected sites in the hills go, a temple dedicated to a Chinese eunuch and naval officer just about tops the list. This temple, just below Brinchang about 1km off the main road, is a brilliant pastiche of imperial Chinese regalia, statuary dedicated to medieval admiral and eunuch Zheng Ho and, allegedly, the fourth-largest Buddha in Malaysia.

Time Tunnel MUSEUM
(adult/child RM5/3; ⌚9am-6pm) Less a museum, more a nostalgic array of items from the Cameron Highlands' past, the Time Tunnel (adjoining Kok Lim Strawberry Farm) has

HIKING IN THE CAMERON HIGHLANDS

Besides getting in touch with your inner Englishman via tea and strawberries, the main pastime in the Cameron Highlands is hiking. Lofty views over rippling hills are well worth a climb, and hikers will find the cool climate a welcome relief from the rest of Malaysia. Meanwhile nature lovers will appreciate peeping at orchids and pitcher plants along the trails.

Yellow-and-black signboards mark the trails, but many aren't maintained very well and can be slippery and unclear. Before setting out on any trail, always ask locally about its safety; the folk at Father's Guest House, are seriously on the ball when it comes to the trails, routes and trekking safety. Always carry water, some food, and rain gear to guard against unpredictable weather, and let your guesthouse know your planned route and predicted return time. Better yet, get a local guide. This is a shortlist of popular walks:

Trail 1 This difficult trail officially starts at white stone marker 1/5 on the summit of Gunung Brinchang (2032m), but Trail 1 is steep, muddy, overgrown and often closed for repairs – it is not advisable to make the descent via this trail. Instead, start your walk at the end point of the trail, at white stone marker 1/48 just north of Cactus Valley. This section of the trail should take about 2½ hours to complete. From the summit take the 7km-long sealed road back to Brinchang through the tea plantations, about a two-hour walk.

Trail 4 One of the more popular trails starts next to the river, just past Century Pines Resort in Tanah Rata. It leads to Parit Falls, but garbage from the nearby village finds its way here and it's not the most bucolic spot. The falls can also be reached from the main road leading south from the southern end of the golf course. Both hikes are about half a kilometre.

Trail 8 This trail splits off Trail 9 just before Robinson Falls and is another steep three-hour approach to Gunung Beremban. Only experienced hikers should attempt this strenuous trail.

Mossy Forest If you're more partial to a stroll than a steep hike, an easy boardwalk wends through a short stretch of the Mossy Forest. Find the beginning at a pagoda 2km south of Gunung Brinchang's peak. At time of research the boardwalk was closed to tourists because of littering, but it was due to reopen after lying fallow for a few months. While it's off-limits, the best way to explore the area is by a guided hike via an operator like **Eco Cameron** (p137), which has exclusive access to a protected trail through part of the forest.

Warning: Trails 9 & 9A On our visit, hikers were being urged to avoid these trails because of a series of robberies and assaults targeting tourists. At the time of writing they were not considered safe and we strongly encourage you to avoid them. Always seek out local advice about the safety of a trail before you set out.

English-language displays on Malaysia's history amid rusty Horlicks signs, old barber's chairs and 1970s postcards of local towns.

Kok Lim Strawberry Farm FARM
(Map p135; Brinchang; ⊙9am-5pm) Just north of Brinchang, RM30 gets you the chance to be a labourer for a while and go home with half a kilo of hand-picked strawberries.

Ee Feng Gu Honey Bee Farm FARM
(Map p135; www.eefenggu.com; Brinchang; ⊙8am-7pm) FREE A working apiary about 3km northeast of Brinchang, with an indoor maze (adult/child RM3/2) for the kids and a royal selection of honey-themed gifts to take home.

Cameron Highlands Butterfly Farm FARM
(Map p135; http://cameronbutterflyfarm.com.my; Kea Farm; adult/child RM5/3; ⊙9am-6pm Mon-Fri, 8am-7pm Sat & Sun) This popular attraction is home to a fluttering collection of tropical butterflies, including the majestic Raja Brooke, and some rather depressed-looking reptiles.

Raaju's Hill Strawberry Farm FARM
(Map p135; ☎019-575 3867; Brinchang; ⊙8.30am-6.30pm) Locals whisper that Raaju has the sweetest strawberries in town. It's believed that the way the evening mist hits this valley-tucked berry farm is the reason its fruit tastes so good. If berry picking (RM30 for two people for half a kilo of strawberries) sounds like too much hard work, you're sure to find something – between tea and scone sets (RM16) and thick strawberry juice (RM6) – to tempt you in Raaju's cafe.

Sri Tehndayuthapany Swamy HINDU TEMPLE
(Map p135; Brinchang; ⊙6am-6pm) Located just south of Brinchang is this colourful Hindu place of worship. On our visit the temple's Tamil Nadu–style sculptures had enjoyed some recent renovation.

Tours

The distance between sights plus infrequent public transport makes guided tours popular in the Cameron Highlands. Most are half-day tours that focus on the tea plantation, strawberry picking and farm highlights of the area.

★ **Eco Cameron** TOUR
(Map p138; ☎05-491 5388; www.ecocameron.com; 72-A Psn Camellia 4, Tanah Rata; tours RM50-120; ⊙8am-9.30pm) This outfit specialises in nature tours of the Cameron Highlands: hiking, orchid walks, birdwatching and insect-spotting. Most enthralling are guided hikes through the Mossy Forest – Eco Cameron has exclusive access to a protected trail.

Jason Marcus Chin TOUR
(☎010-380 8558; jason.marcus.chin@gmail.com; half-/full-day tour from RM50/90) Exceptional nature guide Jason Marcus Chin leads guided hikes on request, sharing superlative knowledge of flora and fauna along the way.

CS Travel & Tours TOUR
(Map p138; ☎05-491 1200; www.cstravel.com.my; 47 Jln Besar, Tanah Rata; ⊙7.30am-7.30pm) This agency leads popular half-day 'countryside tours' of the Highlands, departing at 8.45am and 1.45pm (adult/child RM25/20). Longer tours, such as the full-day 'adventure tour' (adult/child RM80/70), take in Gunung Brinchang and an Orang Asli village.

Sleeping

Tanah Rata is the most popular place to stay in the Cameron Highlands, with its huge spread of hotels and proximity to endless restaurants and tour providers. Brinchang, 4km north, also has plenty of hotels, though most places are targeted at domestic tourists. Study a map before booking as many hotels, especially outside Tanah Rata, are only suited to travellers with a car.

The Highlands are at their busiest during the school holidays in April, August and December. During these times, book well in advance. Prices go up by around 25% at weekends and during holidays.

Air-con is not essential in the Cameron Highlands, and few hotels have it. Connectivity in the Cameron Highlands can be patchy so take wi-fi claims with a grain of salt.

★ **Father's Guest House** GUESTHOUSE $
(Map p138; ☎016-566 1111; www.fathersguesthouse.net; 4 Jln Mentigi, Tanah Rata; dm/d/tr/q from RM210/74/95/127; P@) Pleasant double rooms and clean 10-person dorms elicit sighs of relief from travellers checking in at Father's. Friendly staff ooze local knowledge, while hairdryers, good wi-fi, free tea and coffee, and a cafe are fine perks.

Snooze GUESTHOUSE $
(Map p135; ☎014-669 0108, 016-666 2102; chsnooze@gmail.com; 4 Jln Besar, Brinchang; d/tr/q from RM88/120/145;) The bright and cheery rooms at Snooze are excellent value. The cupcake wallpaper and buttercup

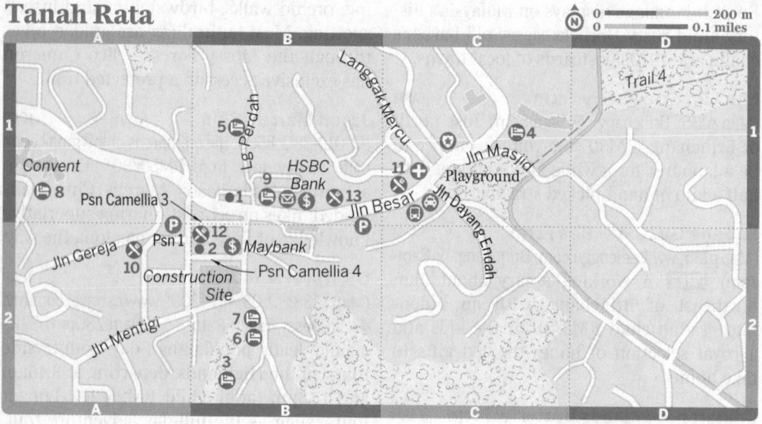

Tanah Rata

Activities, Courses & Tours
1 CS Travel & Tours B1
2 Eco Cameron B2

Sleeping
3 Arundina B2
4 Century Pines Resort C1
5 Daniel's Lodge B1
6 Eight Mentigi B2
7 Father's Guest House B2
8 Heritage Hotel A1
9 Planter's Hotel B1

Eating
10 Barracks Cafe A2
KouGen .... (see 9)
11 Lord's Cafe C1
May Flower .... (see 2)
12 Restaurant Bunga Suria B2
13 Restoran Sri Brinchang B1

bedsheets might be a little kitsch for some, but this clean guesthouse with friendly service is one of Brinchang's better places to stay. There are colourful sitting areas to chill or play, a fridge and laundry facilities, plus there are family rooms. Find more digs down the road at Snooze Too.

Eight Mentigi GUESTHOUSE $
(Map p138; ☎05-491 5988; www.eightmentigi.com; 8a Jln Mentigi, Tanah Rata; s/d/q from RM50/70/150; P @ wi-fi) The digs, from six-bed dorms to spacious family rooms, are simple. But your host Smith gives a welcoming ambience to this fuss-free hostel. The main drawback is the unsightly location, near a building site, though it's only a stone's throw from Tanah Rata's main drag. The better doubles cost around RM90.

Daniel's Lodge HOSTEL $
(Map p138; ☎05-491 5823; www.danielscameronhighlands.com; 9 Lg Perdah, Tanah Rata; dm RM15, r RM40-100, without bathroom RM20-60; @ wi-fi) The backpacker force remains strong at this long standing hostel, also known as Kang's. The accommodation won't win prizes for comfort, but despite the grungy feel it's a functional place with perks like wi-fi, a laundry service and a jungle-themed bar.

Bala's Holiday Chalet GUESTHOUSE $$
(Map p135; ☎05-491 1660; bala.reservations@gmail.com; r RM140-250, ste RM280-380; P @ wi-fi) This cluster of cottages oozes character from every ivy-strewn eave. Built as a 1930s boarding school, these mock-Tudor constructions feel a bit aged, with bathrooms rather prone to damp. Nonetheless, flowery gardens and wacky stone reliefs of Napoleon provide plenty of charm. Large split-level suites are suitable for families.

Bala's is up a steep road 1.5km north of Tanah Rata, so you need your own wheels to stay here.

Arundina GUESTHOUSE $$
(Map p138; ☎05-491 1129; www.arundina.com; 17 Jln Mentigi, Tanah Rata; d/tr incl breakfast from RM169/219; P wi-fi) This welcoming guesthouse on the outskirts of Tanah Rata has pleasant, high-ceilinged rooms, many of

which overlook a flower garden. The vibrant mauve colour scheme is a nod to *Arundina graminifolia*, the local bamboo orchid for which the guesthouse is named. Effervescent staff and communal balconies complete the guesthouse's cheery atmosphere. There's coffee and tea on tap.

Planter's Hotel HOTEL **$$**
(Map p138; ☎05-490 1001; www.plantershotel.com.my; 44a Jln Besar, Tanah Rata; d/tr/q RM125/185/225;) This is the place to stay if you don't need frills or atmosphere, and want to be in the middle of the action in Tanah Rata. Premier rooms are vast, while standard rooms don't have windows. Rates increase by about 20% from Friday to Sunday.

Heritage Hotel HOTEL **$$**
(Map p138; ☎05-491 3888; www.heritage.com.my; Jln Gereja, Tanah Rata; d/tr/ste from RM226/284/500;) This huge mock-Tudor hotel is a little faded in places but its rooms are ample. The most comfortable and modern are in the deluxe wing. The hotel's on-site amenities lift it above the competition: there's a kids' playroom, washing machines, pool tables, lounge areas with leather sofas, well-maintained gardens and an on-site bar, Vintage – ideal for the rainy days these highlands have in no short supply.

★ **Lakehouse** BOUTIQUE HOTEL **$$$**
(Map p135; ☎05-495 6152; www.lakehouse-cameron.com; incl breakfast r RM900, ste RM1050-1200; P) This hotel's English-country-manor vibe is the most authentic in the Cameron Highlands. Lakehouse has 19 sumptuous rooms with four-poster beds and wooden floors. This charming retreat, 2km north of Ringlet, is expensive but your wallet's whimpers of protest will be forgotten somewhere between cocktails by the lounge fireplace and dining at the classy British-themed restaurant (afternoon teas from RM24).

Wi-fi signal is downstairs at reception only.

Smokehouse BOUTIQUE HOTEL **$$$**
(Map p135; ☎05-491 1215; www.smokehousehotel.com; Ringlet; incl breakfast d RM440, ste RM520-870; P) This charismatic 1937 property looks as though it was lifted straight out of the English countryside with its exposed beams, four-poster beds and even a red phone box. Six of the rooms date to the 1930s, though the rest follow a similar style: expect heavy wooden furnishings and the occasional fireplace, plus modern comforts like mosquito screens.

There's also a fine restaurant serving cream teas and classic British fare, plus a range of vegetarian dishes. Smokehouse is

WORTH A TRIP

BREWS AND VIEWS AT BOH TEA ESTATE

Even if you're a dedicated coffee drinker, don't miss the breathtakingly beautiful **Boh Sungei Palas Tea Estate** (☎05-496 2096; www.boh.com.my; 9am-4.30pm Tue-Sun) FREE, set in an almost other-worldly green patchwork of hills and tea plants.

The narrow approach road leads past worker housing and a Hindu temple (tea pickers are predominantly Indian) to the modern visitor centre, where you can witness tea production first-hand, and a **cafe** (9am-4.30pm Tue-Sun) where you can sip a cuppa while gazing at the plantations below. Free 15-minute tours showing the tea-making process are conducted during opening hours. For true tea enthusiasts, we recommend the plantation's hour-long **Tea Appreciation Tours** (adult RM37.10; 9am & 11am Tue-Sun), which include a guided walk through tea plantations, a factory tour and tea sampling. Additional tours sometimes run at 1pm and 3pm; call ahead.

The estate is located in the hills north of Brinchang, off the road to Gunung Brinchang. Public buses running between Tanah Rata and Kampung Raja pass the turn-off to Gunung Brinchang. From there it's 4km along the winding road, after which it's another 15 minutes' walk downhill to the visitor centre.

Boh has another almost equally impressive **estate** (www.boh.com.my; 9am-4.30pm Tue-Sun) FREE southeast of Tanah Rata and 7km off the main road. There's a small cafe and tours are given every 15 minutes during opening hours. A taxi from Tanah Rata to either estate costs around RM40.

LOCAL KNOWLEDGE

PARTHIPAN RAMADASS: TEA EXPERT

We asked Parthipan Ramadass, tea expert and tour officer at Boh Sungei Palas Tea Estate (p139) about the art of preparing tea.

What's the sign of a good cup of tea? It all depends on your preferences. The aroma should not be too mild but it should not hit you too strongly either. No matter how strong the tea is, it should be orange in colour; if it's black, it is too strong or they've coloured it.

How do you prepare a perfect cup of tea? Always use loose tea, not teabags – the leaves are supposed to open. The measurement is a teaspoon – one for each person, and one for the pot. So if you are brewing for two people, three teaspoons. But for more than four people, add an extra teaspoon for the pot (seven teaspoons for five people). Preferably use a porcelain or clay pot. Glass and metal lose heat fast, they don't really give as good a brew.

What flavours can be added to tea? The only thing that makes sense in tea is milk, honey or lemon. A cup of tea should not have more than two teaspoons of milk in it. But do not follow the British way of making tea by adding milk first. It should be tea first, then milk, so the cup can absorb some heat.

located about 2km north of Tanah Rata on the road to Brinchang.

Strawberry Park Resort RESORT $$$
(Map p135; ☎05-491 1166; www.strawberryparkresorts.com; Brinchang; r RM600, ste RM800-2300; @ 🛜 🏊) If you're looking for a spot of pampering away from the town traffic, Strawberry Park retains a peaceful quality, despite being a favourite with big tour groups. Trim monochrome details give the well-kept villas a modern feel, while access to tennis courts, pool and spa allow plenty of opportunity for R&R. This resort is only viable if you have a car; it's 2km north from the main road along steep, winding roads.

Hotel De'La Ferns HOTEL $$$
(Map p135; ☎05-491 4888; www.hoteldelaferns.com.my; d/tr/q RM385/509/615, ste RM721-1908; P @ 🛜) A multistorey mock-Tudor behemoth it may be, but De'La Ferns is away from the town hubbub with special views and plenty of parking – bliss, in the increasingly built-up Cameron Highlands. Rooms are clean and well furnished and staff are superbly helpful. It's about 1.5km north of Tanah Rata, en route to Brinchang.

Century Pines Resort HOTEL $$$
(Map p138; ☎05-491 5115; www.centurypinesresort.com; 42 Jln Masjid; incl breakfast r RM320-450, ste RM450-900; P 🛜) Among so many vast Tudor-style mansions, this hotel complex at Tanah Rata's eastern edge stands out for its Malay feel, with elephant carvings, stained-glass mirrors and intricate rugs. Rooms don't quite live up to the splendour of the marbled reception, which positively groans with chandeliers, but they are well furnished and very comfortable.

Eating

Tanah Rata is home to the majority of the area's restaurants, with Chinese, Indian and Malay flavours jostling for attention alongside the colonial hangover of English breakfasts and scones. More upmarket fare can be found in hotel restaurants, though Tanah Rata's offerings have upped their game in recent years.

Restaurant Bunga Suria INDIAN $
(Map p138; 66a Persiaran Camellia 3, Tanah Rata; set meals RM6-10; ⏰7am-10pm; 🌱) The most crowd-pleasing (yet least manic) of Tanah Rata's Indian canteens has great-value banana-leaf meal specials and a good selection of curries. But where it really excels is at breakfast, when fresh *idli* (savoury, soft, fermented-rice-and-lentil cakes) pop out of the steamer, ready to surrender to a dunking in coconut chutney.

Restoran Sri Brinchang INDIAN $
(Map p138; 25 Jln Besar, Tanah Rata; mains RM4-20; ⏰7am-10pm; 🌱) This busy place heaps spiced aubergine, poppadoms and rice onto banana leaves for its filling lunches; it prides itself on spring chicken served straight from the tandoor.

Lord's Cafe CAFE $
(Map p138; Jln Besar, Tanah Rata; mains RM2.50-4.90; ⏰10am-9pm Wed-Fri & Mon, to 6pm Sat) Despite the neon threat from Tanah Rata's

controversial new Starbucks, Lord's Cafe, reassuringly decorated like your grandma's living room, lives on. Specialities include thick mango and banana lassis and apple pie, the standout star on a menu of cakes and ice-cream sundaes. Find the cafe by following the Christian signage to the floor above Marrybrown fast food.

★Barracks Cafe FUSION **$$**
(Map p138; ☎011-1464 8883; 1 Jln Gereja; mains RM15; ⊙10am-9pm Tue-Sun) This brand-new restaurant within a converted British military barracks suffers from an enjoyable identity crisis. Marble tables encircle a babbling fountain, and corrugated-iron walls are emblazoned with a mural of soldiers blasting butterflies from guns. Matching this eclectic decor are menu choices ranging from Indian masala lamb to burgers. The yoghurt smoothies and mason-jar mocktails (RM7.90) are exceptional.

KouGen JAPANESE, KOREAN **$$**
(Map p138; ☎012-377 0387; 35 Jln Besar, Tanah Rata; mains RM13-20; ⊙noon-9pm) A border-crossing selection of Japanese and Korean recipes are whipped up in the open kitchen of this friendly Tanah Rata eatery. Choose from sushi, *bibimbap* (a hot bowl of rice, egg, meat, veggies and more), fried rice in *kimchi* (fiery fermented cabbage) and a slurpable range of noodle dishes, topping them up with sides like *yakitori* (grilled chicken skewers) and freshly steamed soy beans.

May Flower CHINESE **$$**
(Map p138; ☎05-491 4793; 81a Psn Camellia 4, Tanah Rata; hotpot per person RM16, mains RM7-24; ⊙lunch & dinner; 📝) This place does a few versions of the hotpot (referred to as steamboat), so take your pick of seafood, meat and vegetarian options – ingredients are as varied as oyster, jellyfish and tofu – and set them simmering in the broth.

ℹ Information

The **post office** (Map p138), **hospital** (Map p138) and **police station** (Map p138) are all found on Jln Besar in Tanah Rata.

ℹ Getting There & Away

BUS

Tanah Rata's **bus station** (Map p138), known as Terminal Freesia, is located at the eastern end of Jln Besar. Daily bus and boat transfer packages also reach Taman Negara and the Perhentian Islands. Bus timetables are vulnerable to change but these services were operating on our visit.

DESTINATION	PRICE	DURATION	FREQUENCY
Brinchang	RM2	20 min	Every two hours, 6.30am-6.30pm
Ipoh	RM18	2 hours	8am & 2.30pm
Kuala Lumpur	RM35	4 hours	Six daily, 8.30am-5.30pm
Melaka	RM65	6 hours	9.30am
Penang	RM32	5 hours	8am & 2.30pm
Singapore	RM125-140	10 hours	10am

TAXI

Taxis (Map p138) wait at Terminal Freesia. During our visit, long-distance fares were set at RM160 to Ipoh, RM350 to KL and RM360 to Penang (Butterworth). A noticeboard lists standard fares for a number of destinations.

ℹ Getting Around

While we never recommend hitchhiking, some travellers do so to get between Tanah Rata, Brinchang and the tea plantations beyond.

BUS

Buses run between Tanah Rata and Brinchang between 6.30am and 6.30pm every two hours or so.

TAXI

Taxi services from Tanah Rata include Brinchang (RM8), Ringlet (RM25) and Boh (RM40); for prices on additional destinations, including hiking trailheads and tea estates, see the price list posted at the taxi stop at Terminal Freesia. For touring around, a taxi costs RM25 per hour.

PULAU PANGKOR

POP 25,000

From a swaying hammock on Coral Beach, it's hard to imagine Pulau Pangkor's turbulent past. But 'Beautiful Island' is a former pirate hideout and bit-player in the battle to control the Selat Melaka (Strait of Melaka). In the 17th century the Dutch built a fort here in their bid to monopolise the Perak tin trade, but they were driven out by a local ruler. In 1874 a contender for the Perak

Pulau Pangkor

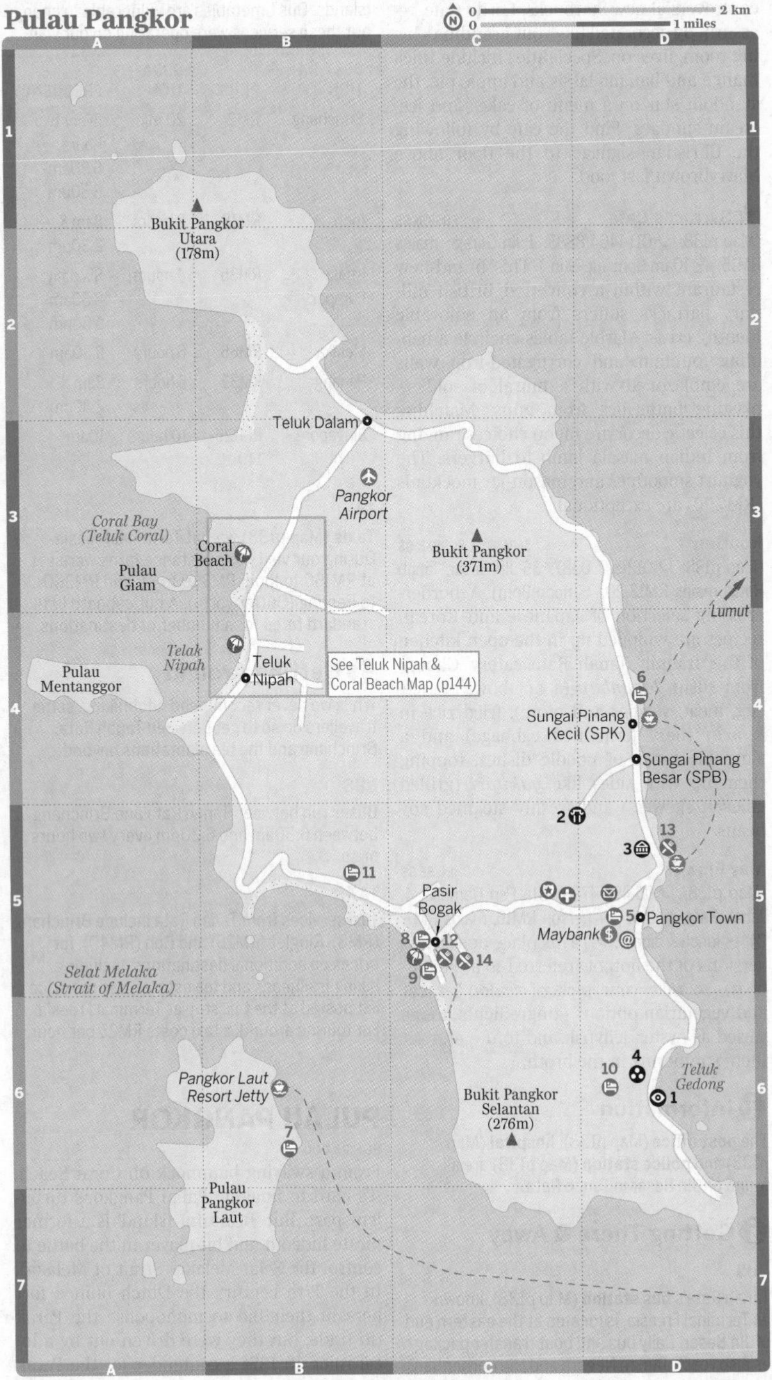

0
2 km
0
1 miles
A
B
C
D
1
2
3
4
5
6
7
Bukit Pangkor Utara (178m)
Teluk Dalam
Pangkor Airport
Bukit Pangkor (371m)
Coral Bay (Teluk Coral)
Coral Beach
Pulau Giam
Telak Nipah
Teluk Nipah
See Teluk Nipah & Coral Beach Map (p144)
Pulau Mentanggor
Lumut
Sungai Pinang Kecil (SPK)
Sungai Pinang Besar (SPB)
Pasir Bogak
Pangkor Town
Maybank
Selat Melaka (Strait of Melaka)
Pangkor Laut Resort Jetty
Pulau Pangkor Laut
Bukit Pangkor Selantan (276m)
Teluk Gedong
1
2
3
4
5
6
7
8
9
10
11
12
13
14

Pulau Pangkor

Sights
1 Batu Bersurat D6
2 Foo Ling Kong C5
3 Galeri Pangkor D5
4 Kota Belanda D6

Sleeping
5 BestStay Hotel D5
6 Pangkor Guesthouse SPK D4
7 Pangkor Laut Resort B6
8 Pangkor Sandy Beach Resort C5
9 Sea View Hotel C5
10 Tiger Rock Resort D6
11 Vikri Beach Resort B5

Eating
12 Guan Guan Seafood C5
13 Pangkor Kopitiam D5
14 Restoran Pasir Bogak C5

throne sought British backing and the Pangkor Treaty was signed, ushering in British Residents and the colonial period.

These days, the only ruckus is from chattering monkeys and hornbills. Wildlife is easy to spot around the island and a new eco-tourism mentoring program, kickstarted by NGO ECOMY (http://ecomy.org), seems sure to develop wildlife tourism here.

Pangkor's low-key villagey feel and beachside activities make it an agreeable place to escape. There's no shortage of Malaysian weekend warriors, though few foreign visitors wash ashore on Pangkor, probably because its beaches aren't among Malaysia's best.

To see a different side to Pangkor, stroll through villages like Sungai Pinang Kecil (SPK), with a pungent fish farm to its north, or colourful Teluk Gedong. That is, if you can bear to leave that beach hammock.

Sights

The island's east coast is its workaday side, home to **SPK** and **Sungai Pinang Besar** (SPB) – two fishing villages. The road that runs along the east coast turns west at Pangkor Town and runs directly across the island to **Pasir Bogak**, which has a good (though crowded) beach. From there the road runs north to the village of **Teluk Nipah**, another busy beach, and a good destination for water sports or snorkelling. Moving north, **Coral Beach** is the best (public) beach on Pangkor. The road then goes to the northern end of the island, past the airport.

Kota Belanda RUIN

(Map p142; 24hr) FREE At Teluk Gedong, 1.5km south of Pangkor Town, is the Dutch Fort, built in 1670 and sacked in 1690. The Dutch managed to rebuild the fort in 1743; only five years later they abandoned it for good after local warrior chiefs repeatedly attacked them. The old fort was totally swallowed by jungle until 1973, when it was reconstructed as far as the remaining bricks would allow.

Batu Bersurat HISTORIC SITE

(Map p142) FREE On the waterfront at Teluk Gedong is this mammoth stone carved with the symbol of the Dutch East India Company (Vereenigde Oost-Indische Compagnie; VOC) and other graffiti, including a faint depiction of a tiger stealing a child. Supposedly, the child of a local European dignitary disappeared while playing near the rock; the Dutch circulated the idea of a tiger abduction, although the kid was more likely nabbed by disenchanted locals.

Galeri Pangkor MUSEUM

(Map p142; 8am-5pm) FREE This single-hall gallery overlooking the jetty is a pleasant break from the sun. The gallery has a small collection of handicrafts and furnishings, including elaborately woven baskets and traditional music instruments, plus English explanations on island history.

Foo Ling Kong CHINESE TEMPLE

(Map p142; 7am-7pm) FREE With its brightly coloured bridges, cartoonish tiger statues and souvenir stands, this inland temple almost has the vibe of a theme park. Donations are encouraged; place them in the tin sentries at the entrance.

Lin Je Kong Temple TEMPLE

(Map p144; 24hr) FREE On the northern edge of Coral Beach, look out for this small, psychedelic temple, adorned with statues of giant mushrooms, a turtle, a mermaid and, of course, Donald Duck.

Activities

Snorkel gear, boats and jet skis can be hired at hotels or on the beach at Pasir Bogak and Teluk Nipah; a 15-minute **banana boat ride** costs RM15 to RM25, and a small boat to

Teluk Nipah & Coral Beach

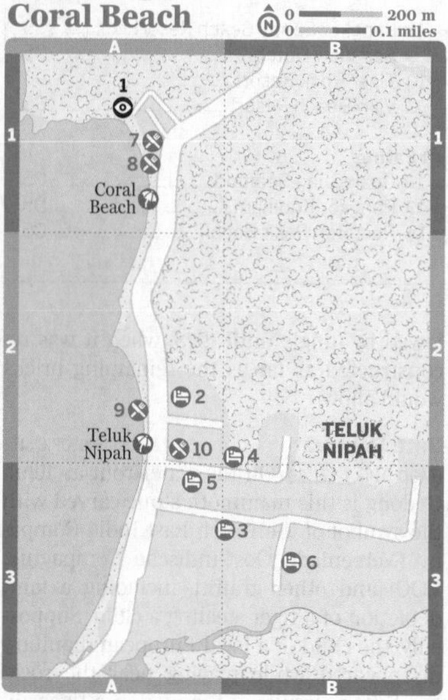

Teluk Nipah & Coral Beach

Sights

1 Lin Je Kong Temple A1

Sleeping

2 Anjungan A2
3 Budget Beach Resort B3
4 Nazri Nipah Camp B2
5 Pangkor Bayview A3
6 Seagull Beach Resort B3

Eating

7 Daddy's Café A1
8 Danny & Zharif Corner A1
9 Evening Seafood Stalls A2
10 Nasi Campur A2

take you **snorkelling** at small nearby islands costs around RM25 per person.

Sleeping

Teluk Nipah has the best beach and the biggest spread of accommodation choices on Pangkor. To the south, Pasir Bogak is home to several bigger midrange resorts. Lodgings in Pangkor Town and SPK offer a more local feel.

Rates at most places vary, often substantially, between peak (Friday and/or Saturday and Sunday, plus holidays) and off-peak periods; the following prices quoted are 'off-peak', available from Monday to Friday (or Sunday to Thursday) and in the low season. Finding a bed at any price during major holidays, such as Chinese New Year, can be near impossible without advance reservations.

Teluk Nipah

Nazri Nipah Camp GUESTHOUSE $
(Map p144; 017-604 4942; dm with fan/air-con RM25/30, r RM60-80;) Accommodation ranges from simple A-frames to bungalows with bathrooms at this reggae-themed backpacker favourite. Lodgings are basic, but Nazri Nipah is well loved for its relaxing ambience, helpful staff and secluded beer garden.

Budget Beach Resort HOTEL $
(Map p144; 05-685 3529; www.budgetbeachresort.com; d/tr/q RM80/100/120;) The somewhat self-deprecating name doesn't do justice to the simple but neat wood bungalows here, all equipped with air-con and TV. Friendly service and a pleasant outdoor area lift this choice above Pulau Pangkor's formulaic resorts.

Seagull Beach Resort GUESTHOUSE $
(Map p144; 05-685 2878; www.seagullbeachvillageresort.com; r from RM100;) Seagull's simple lodgings, tucked into the jungle away from Teluk Nipah's main road, are a decent no-frills choice. Monkeys prowl the free-standing huts and the helpful owners can organise activities. Family rooms are much more spacious than the bungalows that sleep three, so they're worth the extra RM10 per night.

Anjungan HOTEL $$
(Map p144; 05-685 1500; www.anjunganresortpangkor.com; d/tr/q from RM175/225/275;) The well-kept bungalows at Teluk Nipah's most stylish resort have simple tiled floors and nice trimmings like Dutch ceramic lamps and wicker chairs. The most stylish rooms encircle a pool shaped like a ship; there is also a kids' wading pool and family rooms. On the northern side of Teluk Nipah's main drag, Anjungan is quiet and family-friendly, with professional service.

Pangkor Bayview HOTEL $$
(Map p144; 05-685 3540; www.pangkorbayview.com; d/tr/q RM160/220/240;) The rooms won't win any beauty contests but this simple resort has a small pool and is a short walk from the beach.

Pasir Bogak

Vikri Beach Resort RESORT $$

(Map p142; ☎05-685 4258; www.vikribeach.com; d/tr/q RM90/150/180; ❄) Vikri has a dozen simple wooden and brick bungalows located in scrappy gardens across the road from the beach. It's a peaceful, homely environment, with a kitchen serving up home-cooked Indian food (with advance notice, and for hotel guests only). Ask staff about where best to spot wild boar, which venture near the resort each evening.

Pangkor Sandy Beach Resort RESORT $$

(Map p142; ☎05-685 3027; www.pangkorsandybeach.com; incl breakfast d/tr from RM210/265, bungalows RM315; ❄ 📶 🏊) A young resort in a 'hood filled with old-timers, Sandy Beach has rooms facing a small pool and three beachfront bungalows.

Sea View Hotel RESORT $$

(Map p142; ☎05-685 1605; www.seaviewpangkor.com; incl breakfast d/tr RM160/188, bungalows RM216-264; ❄ 📶 🏊) This beachfront resort has an old-school, seafront holiday vibe. There's an inviting pool, though the spartan brick bungalows have a somewhat institutional feel.

East Coast Villages

★ **Pangkor Guesthouse SPK** GUESTHOUSE $

(Map p142; ☎011-3551 4728; www.spkpangkorguesthouse.blogspot.com; Sungai Pinang Kecil; d/tr RM80/100; ❄ 📶) To steep yourself in local life, flee the beach resorts and bed down in barely touristed fishing village Sungai Pinang Kecil. Welcoming English-speaking host, Joyce Guok, is an ECOMY mentee and can advise on local places to eat and give tours around the village. As well as double and triple rooms, the guesthouse has family rooms that sleep five or six people (RM150 to RM180).

BestStay Hotel HOTEL $

(Map p142; ☎05-685 3111; www.beststay.com.my; Pangkor Town; d/tr RM130/180; ❄ 📶) Rooms in this budget hotel are plain but excellent value, with the bonus of quality wi-fi (a rarity on Pangkor). Hosts Simon and Rachel are helpful and kind, and the location is a fine choice for early or late ferry departures.

★ **Tiger Rock Resort** BOUTIQUE HOTEL $$$

(Map p142; ☎019-574 7183; www.tigerrock.info; Teluk Gedong; per person incl full board RM630-790; ❄ @ 📶 🏊) 🌿 This secluded retreat has eight ravishing rooms nestled into a jungle location. A library and terrace with bougainvillea-strewn views, exemplary service and 12.5-acre grounds strike a fine balance between eco and luxury. The hotel doesn't accept walk-ins, and reservations must be made at least seven days in advance.

The hotel was built in a sustainable low-impact way using all local materials and without the use of heavy machinery, and was designed to incorporate the landscape rather than bulldozing trees. The food served is strictly locally sourced. Tiger Rock is found in a somewhat-concealed location behind Kota Belanda at Teluk Gedong; get a taxi from the jetty when you arrive (RM15).

Pangkor Laut

Pangkor Laut Resort RESORT $$$

(Map p142; ☎05-699 1100; www.pangkorlautresort.com; r RM860-2310, ste RM2990-5500; ❄ @ 📶 🏊) The tiny, private island of Pangkor Laut, just opposite Pasir Bogak, is occupied by one of Malaysia's most exclusive tourist developments. This astonishingly luxurious resort is speckled with hillside, seafront and above-water villas stocked with king-sized beds, balconies and huge bathrooms.

Eating & Drinking

Teluk Nipah & Coral Beach

Evening Seafood Stalls MALAYSIAN $$

(Map p144; mains RM3-20; ⏰ dinner) Every night, the strip of road that backs Teluk Nipah plays host to several informal restaurants selling Malay-style dishes. Enjoy your pick of chilli crab, Thai steamed fish and sambal prawns, just some of the seafood dishes on offer. The best food is served from 5pm to 9.30pm, and pickings can be slim later into the evening.

Danny & Zharif Corner CAFE $

(Map p144; ☎017-561 5105; mains RM5; ⏰7.30am-7.30pm Sat-Thu) Seating at this friendly eatery spills right onto Coral Beach. Tuck into savoury pancakes stuffed with carrot and crab, or a small selection of rice and noodle dishes. Sweet-toothed travellers will prefer the dessert roti, drowned in honey or chocolate.

Nasi Campur MALAYSIAN $

(Map p144; mains RM2-6; ⏰ breakfast & lunch) Service can be gruff but this is a great-value stop for Western and Malay-style breakfasts, and cheap, filling lunches. Breakfasts start around 7am to 8am, and lunches from noon – arrive early for the best nosh.

Daddy's Café INTERNATIONAL $$
(Map p144; ☎013-208 0404; mains RM15-48; ⏰11am-11pm) If you're looking to sip a pineapple-topped beverage while gazing out at the sea, Daddy's is the ideal spot. This Coral Beach cafe serves a mix of local and international meals from meat-stuffed pitta to succulent satay chicken, with cocktails (RM21) to wash it all down. Meals are a little pricey for their size but the ambience and views compensate wonderfully.

Pasir Bogak

Restoran Pasir Bogak CHINESE $$
(Map p142; mains RM8-44; ⏰6-10pm) This is where locals go for a Chinese-style seafood splurge and a beer (we suspect they carry every local brand). The dry chilli chicken, served with a rich, spicy paste and curry leaves, is a Chinese-Indian-Malay fusion that works a treat. The steamed fish is expertly cooked but do your maths on the price-by-weight seafood menu, which can hit unsuspecting travellers in the wallet.

Guan Guan Seafood CHINESE, INTERNATIONAL $$
(Map p142; mains RM7-20; ⏰lunch & dinner) A simple Chinese-style seafood place doing solid versions of the usual beachy faves, as well as a few quasi-Western dishes.

Pangkor Town

There are a few busy Chinese *kedai kopi* (coffee shops) in Pangkor Town. Slightly north, the village of Sungai Pinang Besar is a great place for an old-school Chinese-style breakfast.

Pangkor Kopitiam MALAYSIAN $
(Map p142; mains RM4.50-18.90; ⏰8am-11pm; 📶) Meals at ferry terminals seldom inspire, but this jetty cafe whips up quality Thai and Malay rice dishes (RM4.50) and satisfying laksa (RM5). It's a well-air-conditioned spot with views of the boats crowding the shore, and there's wi-fi too.

Information

The island's **medical clinic** (Map p142; ☎05-685 4048) and **police station** (Map p142; ☎05-685 1222) are just west of Pangkor Town, on the road towards Pasir Bogak. There are a couple of banks and an internet cafe in Pangkor Town.

Getting There & Away

Lumut is the land gateway for Pulau Pangkor. The town is serviced by many buses, but if you get stuck, **Brezza Hotel** (☎05-683 3786; Lumut; d/tr RM88/130) is a convenient place to crash, a short walk west of the jetty.

BOAT

Boats leave from Lumut's jetty for Pulau Pangkor every 30 to 45 minutes between 7am and 8.30pm (round trip RM10). Many ferries from Lumut stop at SPK before reaching Pangkor Town, so don't hop off too soon. From Pangkor, boats run between 6.30am and 8.30pm. Tickets can be bought at either pier and outside of busy holidays, advance booking is not necessary.

Pangkor Laut Resort is served by its own ferry service from Lumut.

BUS

Lumut's scruffy bus station is a brief walk from the jetty to Pulau Pangkor and is well connected to points elsewhere in Malaysia and abroad.

DESTINATION	PRICE	DURATION	FREQUENCY
Butterworth	RM18	3½ hours	8 daily
Ipoh	RM8.50	2 hours	10 daily
Kota Bharu	RM44.40	8 hours	2 daily
Kuala Lumpur	RM37	4 hours	10 daily
Melaka	RM43.80	8 hours	4 daily
Singapore	RM67	8-9 hours	3 daily

Getting Around

There are no public buses available to tourists, so you will be obliged to use Pangkor's candy pink minibus taxis, which operate between 6.30am and 9pm. Set-fare services for up to four people from the jetty in Pangkor Town include Pasir Bogak (RM10) and Teluk Nipah (RM15), and RM20 for destinations in the north of the island. Travel between Teluk Nipah and Pasir Bogak will cost you RM10 to RM15.

The island is well suited to exploration by confident motorcyclists or bike riders. However, bendy roads and aggressive drivers mean it's not a good place for beginners. There are numerous places at Pangkor Town, Pasir Bogak and Teluk Nipah that rent motorcycles from around RM30 per day and bicycles for RM15. **Ah Toh Rental** (☎012-602 0409) loans cars for around RM80 per day.

KUALA KANGSAR

POP 39,300

This royal capital has been an epicentre for some of Malaysia's most defining moments. Kuala Kangsar (KK) was the first foothold of the British, who moved to control the peninsula by installing Residents at the royal courts here in the 1870s; birthplace of Malaysia's rubber industry; and site of the first Durbar, or conference of Malay sultans, in 1897.

While the growth of Ipoh and Taiping over the past century has left Kuala Kangsar lagging behind, this busy town still gleams with Perak's most ostentatious buildings. Colonial constructions are dotted around hectic central KK, while southeast of the town luxuriant royal palaces and a gold-topped mosque steal the spotlight. Sights may be few, but they are well maintained and the fusion architecture – melding Moorish, Renaissance and neoclassical styles – is worth a day trip from well-connected Ipoh or Taiping.

Sights

Kuala Kangar's top sights sprawl over an area southeast of the centre, best explored by car. If you arrive by public transport, consider asking a taxi driver to take you to the top trio – Istana Kenangan, Masjid Ubudiah and Sultan Azlan Shah Gallery – as a half-day excursion.

★Masjid Ubudiah MOSQUE
(Ubudiah Mosque; Jln Istana; admission by donation; 9am-noon, 3-4pm & 5.30-6pm) This grand gold-domed construction was commissioned by Perak's 28th sultan, Idris Shah, after his recovery from illness. Masjid Ubudiah – meaning the mosque of self-surrender to Allah – was masterminded by AB Hubback, the architect behind a number of Perak's colonial buildings. Marble imported from Italy adds bands of mauve to this bright white building. When works began in 1913, two fighting elephants damaged the marble, leading to a construction slowdown. The mosque was eventually completed in 1917.

The sultan didn't live to see Masjid Ubudiah finished. Almost a century later, in 2003, lavish restoration work was completed. Visitors are admitted, provided they are modestly dressed. Even if you don't step inside, it's well worth strolling through the grounds to admire the exterior.

RUBBERY FACTS

In the late 1870s, a number of rubber trees were planted by British Resident Sir Hugh Low in his gardens in Kuala Kangsar from seed stock allegedly smuggled out of Brazil or taken from London's Kew Gardens. However, it was not until the invention of the pneumatic tyre in 1888, and then the popularity of the motorcar at the start of the 20th century, that rubber suddenly came into demand and rubber plantations sprang up across the country. Almost all of the trees in the new plantations were descended from Low's original rubber trees or from the Singapore Botanic Gardens. You can still see one of those first trees in Kuala Kangsar's **District Office** (Jln Raja Chulan) compound.

Istana Kenangan MUSEUM
(Muzium Diraja Perak; Jln Istana; 9.30am-5pm Sat-Thu, 9.30am-12.15pm & 2.45-5pm Fri) FREE Also known as the Palace of Memories, Istana Kenangan is made entirely of wood and woven bamboo, without the use of a single nail. Built in 1926, it served as temporary royal quarters until the nearby Istana Iskandariah, the current residence of the sultan of Perak, was completed. It was also known as 'Palace of the Deceased' because of its use as a stopgap mausoleum for members of the royal family being prepared for burial.

On our visit it wasn't possible to visit the interior because of renovation work, but it was due to reopen with displays on state history and the Perak royal family.

★Sultan Azlan Shah Gallery MUSEUM
(Istana Kota; 05-777 5362; Jln Istana; adult/child RM4/2; 10am-5pm Sat-Thu, 10am-noon & 2.45-5pm Fri) This former royal palace, also known as Istana Kota and Istana Hulu, is a showy mash-up of Renaissance, neoclassical and Moorish styles. Completed in 1903, its marbled hallways now host exhibitions honouring the life of the 34th sultan of Perak, Sultan Azlan Shah: see his sunglasses, passport, shoes and a separate building harbouring Rolls Royces and other luxury vehicles.

Other royal family treasures include HRH's swords and *kris* (elaborate asymmetric daggers) and the fanciest baby cradle you've ever seen. State gifts are also

Kuala Kangsar

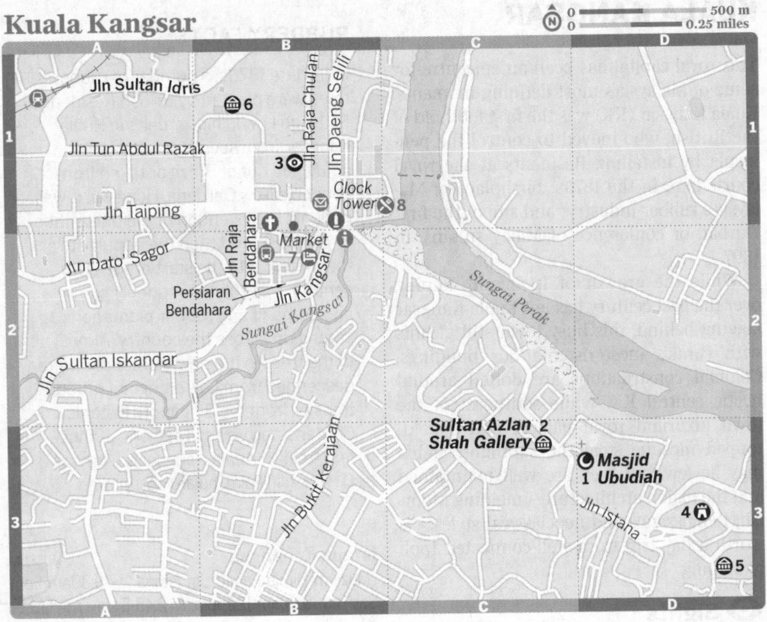

Kuala Kangsar

Top Sights

1 Masjid Ubudiah D3
2 Sultan Azlan Shah Gallery C3

Sights

3 District Office B1
4 Istana Iskandariah D3
5 Istana Kenangan D3
6 Malay College B1

Sleeping

7 Kangsar Hotel B2

Eating

8 Medan Cendol Dan Laksa C1

displayed, including a record-breaking 1.37m fungus. The royal reaction to this mighty mushroom is not described.

Istana Iskandariah PALACE

(Jln Istana) The official residence of the sultan of Perak is arguably the most attractive royal palace in Malaysia. Completed in 1933, this two-floor riverside palace is an intriguing mix of Arab and art-deco architectural styles; if you could combine the hotels in Miami's South Beach with a mosque, it might end up looking something like this. The palace is not open to the public but is worth cruising past.

Malay College HISTORIC BUILDING

(Jln Tun Abdul Razak) To the north of town lies the first Malay school to provide English education for the Malay elite destined for the civil service. Nicknamed 'the Eton of the East', it was established in 1905, and during the 1950s Anthony Burgess, who later authored *A Clockwork Orange*, wrote his first book while teaching here. Not open to the public.

Sleeping

Kuala Kangsar's sights are easily covered in a day, but if you do decide to linger, the hectic town centre has several budget hotels.

Kangsar Hotel HOTEL $

(☎05-776 7301; www.kangsar-hotel.com; 32 Jln Kangsar; d RM69-88, tr/q RM118/128; ❄️📶) This no-frills hotel offers simple but comfy rooms right in the centre of town. Room prices go up to RM79 to RM138 at weekends.

Eating

Medan Cendol Dan Laksa MALAYSIAN $

(cnr Jln Temenggong & Psn Sungai Perak; mains RM2-6; ⏰lunch) This cheerful open-air food hall is largely devoted to laksa dishes and *cendol*, a shaved-ice dessert lavished with coconut milk, pandan pasta, beans and palm-sugar syrup. There are also plenty of nasi goreng (fried rice) and noodle dishes on offer. Arrive early (from noon) for the freshest choice of food.

Information

There are banks with ATMs along Persiaran Bendahara and Jln Kangsar.

Tourist Information Centre (05-777 7717; Jln Kangsar; 8am-7pm Tue-Fri, to 2pm Sat) A privately run tourist office near the clock tower with helpful English-speaking staff.

Getting There & Away

The **bus station** (Jln Raja Bendahara) is located near the city centre. Timetables and prices are vulnerable to change.

DESTINATION	PRICE	DURATION	FREQUENCY
Taiping	RM4	1 hour	Frequent, 6am-7pm
Ipoh	RM6.20-15.50	2 hours	Nine daily, 7am-5pm
Butterworth	RM9.70	2 hours	11.15am & 4.15pm
Lumut (for Pulau Pangkor)	RM10.50	2 hours	11.30am, 5pm & 10pm
Kuala Lumpur (and KLIA)	RM22-25	3 hours	12 daily, 8.30am-11.45pm
Melaka	RM45	5 hours	11.45am
Kota Bharu	RM29.10	6 hours	10.15am & 10.45pm
Singapore	RM55	9 hours	9.30am

Kuala Kangsar's train station is located, less conveniently, to the northwest of town. There are three daily trains to Kuala Lumpur (RM26-44, 3½ to five hours) and four to Butterworth (RM17-23, 1½ to 2½ hours); check with www.ktmb.com.my for the latest info on fares and schedules.

TAIPING

POP 217,647

Locals laud Taiping ('city of peace') for trailblazing Malaysia's first museum, first railway and first newspapers in English, Malay and Tamil. But it's Taiping's 'rain city' title that has stuck. Verdant lake gardens and a refreshing hill station to its east, Bukit Larut, are both gifts of Taiping's weather, the wettest in Peninsular Malaysia. The city today seems ordinary, but a stroll exploring its well-preserved colonial buildings is rewarding, especially if you pause to nibble street food along the way. Foreign visitors are few, but Taiping's leisure-focused hotels and kid-friendly attractions have made it a favourite getaway for Malaysians with big families and even bigger umbrellas.

Sights & Activities

Taman Tasik Taiping GARDENS

(Lake Gardens; Jln Kamunting Lama) FREE Bob across Taiping's Lake Gardens in a swan-shaped boat (RM10 per person) or amble this beautiful 62-hectare site in between picnic stops. Built in 1880 on the site of an abandoned tin mine, the gardens owe their lush greenery to the fact that Taiping's annual rainfall is one of the highest in Peninsular Malaysia.

Muzium Perak MUSEUM

(05-807 2057; www.jmm.gov.my; Jln Taming Sari; adult/child RM5/2; 9am-6pm) Well-kept Muzium Perak harbours a moderately interesting series of collections about the region's wildlife, traditional crafts and multicultural customs. Model displays enliven rooms dedicated to Orang Asli traditions and Perak's rich fauna. Seemingly designed for one of Taiping's many rainy days, even the outdoor area, crammed with dugout canoes and the odd Rolls Royce, is sheltered. Displays have plenty of English-language explanation, though kids will head straight for the elephant skeleton.

Zoo Taiping & Night Safari ZOO

(05-808 6577; www.zootaiping.gov.my; Jln Taman Tasik; zoo adult/child RM16/8, night safari adult/child RM20/10; 8.30am-6pm daily, night safari 8-11pm Sun-Fri, 8pm-midnight Sat; P) As far as zoos go, this is a well-maintained space with notable native residents including elephants, tigers and Malayan sun bears. The night safari, billed as Malaysia's first, gets mixed reviews but offers a chance to see nocturnal animals beginning to stir. Zoo Taiping is located about 2km east of central Taiping; a taxi here will cost RM10.

All Saints' Church CHURCH

(Jln Taming Sari; 8am-noon Sun) This timbered church, dating back to 1886, is one of the oldest Anglican churches in Malaysia.

Taiping

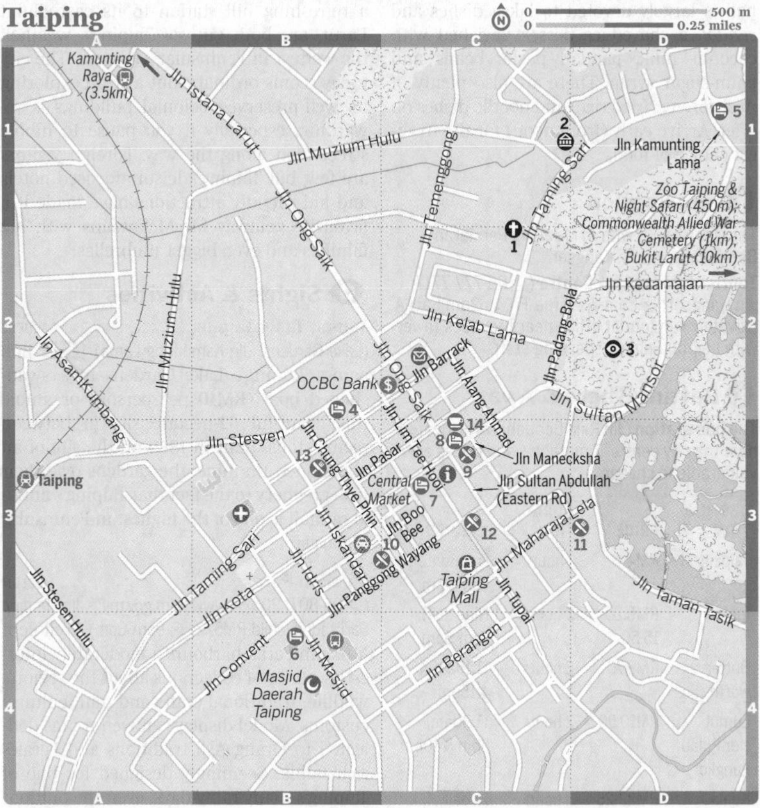

Taiping

Sights
1 All Saints' Church C2
2 Muzium Perak C1
3 Taman Tasik Taiping D2

Sleeping
4 Cherry Inn B2
5 Hotel Seri Malaysia D1
6 Legend Inn B4
7 Panorama Hotel C3
8 Sojourn Beds & Cafe C3

Eating
9 Kedai Kopi Prima C3
10 Larut Matang Food Court C3
11 Pusat Makanan Taman Tasik D3
12 Pusat Penjaja Taiping C3
13 Sri Annapoorana B3

Drinking & Nightlife
14 Espresso Yourself C3

The cemetery contains the graves of early colonial settlers, most of whom died of tropical diseases or failed to achieve the colonial pension needed to return home to Britain or Australia.

Commonwealth Allied War Cemetery CEMETERY
(Jln Bukit Larut; 24hr) This small cemetery has row upon row of headstones for the British, Australian and Indian troops killed during WWII. Arranged across two green spaces bisected by a main road, the cemetery is located about 2km east of central Taiping, along the way to Bukit Larut; a taxi here costs around RM10.

Burmese Pools RIVER
(Jln Bukit Larut) FREE This popular bathing spot is located about 3km east of central

Taiping, off the road that leads to Bukit Larut; a taxi here will cost RM10. Opening hours depend on the weather.

Sleeping

Sojourn Beds & Cafe HOSTEL $
(☎012-464 3443; www.sojournbc.com; 54 Jln Kota; dm RM35; wi-fi) Finally: a place for backpackers to rest, repose and socialise in central Taiping. Set in a 1930s shophouse, Sojourn's four-person dorms are a cut above standard creaky hostel bunks: each bed is part of a reinforced pod, allowing more privacy and less rocking from the top bunk. A balcony terrace and lounge area allow space to chat, locker access is included and there's wi-fi.

Cherry Inn HOTEL $
(☎05-805 2223; 17 Jln Stesyen; d/q from RM60/120; air-con, wi-fi) The exterior speaks of a comfy little inn, while the interior resembles a museum dedicated to Chinese kitsch. Once ushered inside by Cherry's affable owner, you'll find rooms that are large, clean and well-equipped. The cheaper rooms have shared bathrooms. A two-bedroom apartment is also available for RM250.

Sentosa Villa HOTEL $$
(☎05-805 1000; www.sentosa-villa.com; Jln 8, Taman Sentosa; r RM138-338, villa RM208-628; air-con, wi-fi) It's one of the most appealing places to stay in Taiping; the bad news is that you'll need private transport to get here. The attractive rooms are either in the main structure or in a handful of stand-alone and duplex wooden villas, all located at the foot of Bukit Larut. Woods, walking paths and running water lend the place a rural, natural feel.

Sentosa Villa is located about 3km east of the town centre, off the road that leads to Bukit Larut; follow the signs.

Panorama Hotel HOTEL $$
(☎05-808 4111; www.panoramataiping.com; 61-79 Jln Kota; r RM95.40-132.50, ste RM212; air-con, wi-fi) Its beige palette won't win points for style, but rooms at this midrange downtown hotel are huge and well maintained. Staff are helpful and the adjoining cafe has tasty eats and good service.

Legend Inn HOTEL $$
(☎05-806 0000; www.legendinn.com; 2 Jln Long Jafaar; r RM113.80-158.80, ste RM198.80-388.80; P air-con, wi-fi) Rooms are jazzily accessorised with gold throws and modern monochrome cushions, but this hotel isn't quite as clean and well furnished as we would like. Nonetheless, rooms are large, while the wi-fi and parking are adequate. Located across a busy road from the bus station, this modern hotel is handily located for both drivers and car-free travellers. Light sleepers should note the mosque across the road.

Hotel Seri Malaysia HOTEL $$
(☎05-806 9502; www.serimalaysia.com.my; 4 Jln Sultan Mansor; d/tr RM158/202; P air-con, wi-fi, pool) Rooms are a little mustier than the grand sculpted gardens suggest, but they are big, there's a pool, and wi-fi access is available at reception. Near the zoo and lake gardens, Seri is well located near family-friendly attractions but you'll need your own wheels to

STREET-FOOD CITY

Taiping is hot on the heels of foodie favourites Penang and Ipoh with its surprisingly rich street-food offerings.

Pusat Makanan Taman Tasik (Jln Maharaja Lela; mains from RM3; 24hr) This lakeside hawker court and coffee shop has a good selection of stalls serving dishes from *curry mee* (yellow noodles submerged in spicy broth) to *ikan bakar* (grilled fish).

Kedai Kopi Prima (cnr Jln Kota & Jln Manecksha; mains from RM5; 10am-midnight) This big, busy Chinese coffee shop spills out onto the street in the evenings, with several vendors selling a mix of Chinese and Malay dishes.

Pusat Penjaja Taiping (Jln Tupai; mains from RM3; 9am-11pm) Fish porridge, chicken chop and fruit-festooned ice-blended drinks are served up at this open-air food court.

Larut Matang Food Court (Jln Panggong Wayang; mains from RM3; 11am-7pm) Busiest and best at lunch, this gritty court is half Chinese and half Malay. Look out for local favourite Omar's Popiah stall, where you can chomp on large rolls of crisp veggies wrapped in a wheat pancake.

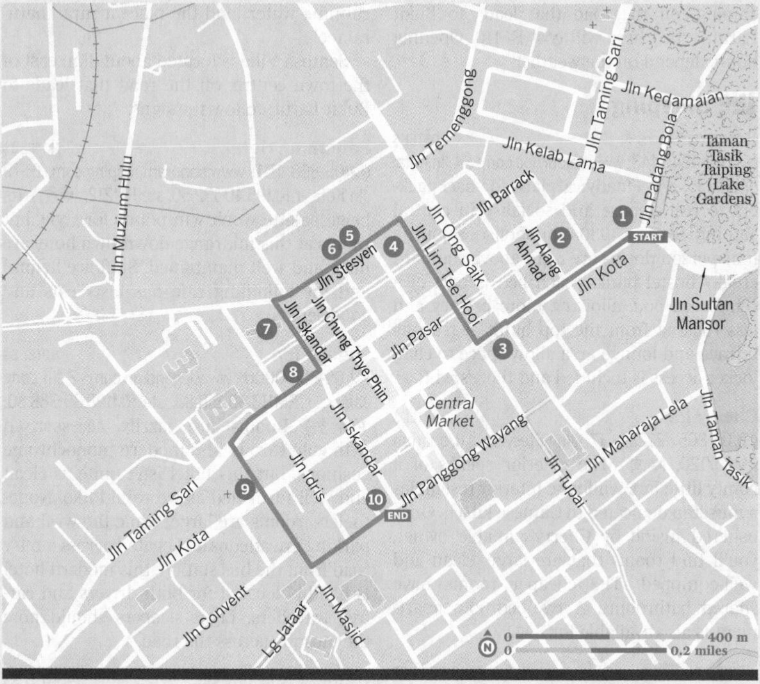

City Walk
Colonial Taiping

START PERPUSTAKAAN TAIPING
END HOTEL PEACE
LENGTH 2KM; ONE TO TWO HOURS

Taiping's former role as a prosperous and important colonial-era outpost is still palpable in the town's well-preserved architecture. This walking tour takes in Taiping's most notable colonial-era buildings, from religious monuments to state institutions.

Start at 1 **Perpustakaan Taiping** (1882), the red-roofed public library with imposing columns at its entrance. Nearby, the white neoclassical 2 **District Office** is on Jln Alang Ahmad. Continue south along Jln Kota until you reach 3 **Jam Besar Lama** (1890), the Old Clock Tower (undergoing restoration on our visit). It once functioned as Taiping's fire station and now houses a tourist information centre.

Turn right at Jln Lim Tee Hooi. Upon reaching Jln Stesyen, on your left is the 4 **Town Rest House** (1894), formerly the governor's residence (undergoing a lengthy restoration). Across Jln Stesyen is the colonial 5 **King Edward VII School** (1905), the classrooms of which were used as torture chambers by the Japanese during WWII. Taiping's original 6 **train station** is a few steps west; Taiping was the starting point for Malaysia's first railway line, now defunct. Opened in 1885, it ran 13.5km to Port Weld (Kuala Sepetang).

Walking further west on Jln Stesyen, you can see 7 **St George's School** (1915). Head south on Jln Iskandar, then turn right onto Jln Taming Sari; here you'll find Taiping's tiny 8 **Little India**. Follow the street west until Jln Masjid; opposite you'll see the 9 **Old Kota Mosque** (1897), the oldest in Taiping, mainly of note for its hexagonal design.

Moving south along Jln Masjid, turn left on Jln Panggong Wayang, where you'll see the 10 **Hotel Peace**; its Peranakan design features stained glass, stucco tiles and gold-painted lion heads roaring from stone columns. The scruffy hotel is better avoided, but the coffee shop downstairs is a good spot for *kway teow* (wide, flat noodles) and a soda.

stay here. Add an extra bed to a room for RM37.

Eating & Drinking

Sri Annapoorana INDIAN, NEPALESE $
(166 Jln Taming Sari; mains RM6; breakfast, lunch & dinner;) This shophouse restaurant offers a mix of southern Indian and Nepali dishes, including vegetarian banana-leaf specials (RM7) with hearty self-service choices from masala omelette to spinach and mutton curry.

Espresso Yourself COFFEE
(012-969 6765; 45 Jln Pasar; coffee RM5; 9am-9pm;) This friendly new place has schoolroom seating and quality Western-style coffees. The iced lattes, served quaintly in mason jars, are strong and smooth, putting most of Malaysia's watery blended coffees to shame. Wi-fi and air-con give you reason to linger, while the filled bagels (RM7.50) make a fine breakfast.

Information

There are several banks with ATMs along Jln Kota.
Tourist Information Centre (355 Jln Kota; 10am-5pm Mon-Sat, 2-6pm Sun) Located in the former clock tower, this office was closed for renovation when we stopped by. When open, it offers brochures and maps of the region.

Getting There & Away

Taiping's long-distance bus station, **Kamunting Raya** (Stesen Bas Ekspres Kamunting Raya; 05-891 5279; Taman Medan Kamunting), is 7km north of the town centre; hop on bus 8 (RM1.20, 6am to 8.30pm) to get to/from the local bus station, or take a taxi (RM10) to the town centre.

Prices and timetables are vulnerable to change but destinations include:

DESTINATION	PRICE	DURATION	FREQUENCY
Ipoh	RM8-13	1½ hours	Frequent, 6.30am-6pm
Butterworth	RM7	2 hours	Hourly, 6.30am-8pm
Kuala Lumpur	RM27-31	4 hours	13 daily
Kota Bharu	RM35	8 hours	10.10am
Singapore	RM101	9 hours	11am, 9pm, 10.30pm & 11pm

Local buses leave from the local bus station across the street from Masjid Daerah Taiping; taxis also depart from near the bus station. Destinations include Kuala Kangsar, with departures every half-hour from 6am to 8.30pm (RM3.90, one hour), and Lumut (for Pulau Pangkor), with one daily departure at 7am (RM10, three hours).

Taiping's train station is 1km west of the town centre, on the Kuala Lumpur–Butterworth line. There are three to four daily trains to Kuala Lumpur (RM28 to RM53, three to six hours) and three to Butterworth (RM15 to RM23, one to 1½ hours).

AROUND TAIPING

Bukit Larut

Northeast of Taiping and some 1036m above sea level is Bukit Larut (Maxwell Hill), the oldest hill station in Malaysia. This calming, fragrant place has none of the development of the Cameron Highlands, so its elegant bungalows and quiet lanes offer a more authentic glimpse of Perak's colonial past. Getting up to the hill station is half the fun, and once there, you've got excellent opportunities for walks and fine views over Taiping far below.

Sights & Activities

Most visitors go up and back by 4WD, but the hill is also a favourite with hikers. You need to be very fit to complete the walk, which spans more than 10km and can take as long as four hours. Plus you have to dodge 4WDs ferrying passengers up the steep and winding road.

On our visit, accommodation and other amenities at Bukit Larut were on pause following flood damage. Even so, the ride up the hill and strolls along the forest-fringed main road are good fun. We recommend hiring a guide if you want to tackle the additional 2km (30-minute) walk at the top of the hill, from which a rough, often-overgrown trail leads off the main road between the two transmission towers. The trail follows a practically abandoned path to Gunung Hijau (1448m). Due to thick vegetation, you can usually only follow the path for about 15 minutes, but even on this short walk there's a good chance of seeing monkeys and numerous birds.

Getting There & Away

Bukit Larut makes a pleasant half-day trip from Taiping. A taxi here from Taiping should cost RM10. Private cars are not allowed on the road up to Bukit Larut – it's only open to government Land Rovers, which run a regular service (round trip RM6) from the station at the foot of the hill. In theory, the Land Rovers operate roughly every hour on the hour from 8am to 3pm, but they usually only run when there are enough customers. The trip takes about 25 minutes.

Kuala Sepetang

Waterways fringed by mangrove trees snake out from the little town of Kuala Sepetang towards Penang. Mangrove forests, at the intersection of land and sea, support teeming ecosystems and are now understood to be crucial breakwaters, natural shields against tsunamis and flooding.

Matang Mangrove Forest Reserve near Kuala Sepetang is considered a shining example of environmental preservation. It is best known for fireflies, which sparkle like fairy lights each evening. The town itself – still shown on some maps under its old name of Port Weld – is unexciting, though it has a bank and a couple of restaurants.

Sights & Activities

Kuala Sepetang has a **charcoal factory** and a small **mosque**, but the main reason to venture this way is the forest reserve.

Matang Mangrove Forest Reserve NATURE RESERVE
(8am-5pm Mon-Fri) The entrance to the reserve is about 500m outside Kuala Sepetang. From here, a raised wooden walkway winds through a small section of the reserve. Smooth otters, leopard cats and macaques all inhabit this landscape, though you're unlikely to see much more than the odd bird and scampering lizard. If travelling here by bus from Taiping, ask the driver to let you off when you see the sign on your right reading 'Pejabat Hutan Kecil Paya Laut'.

If you wish to stay, there is very basic accommodation in the form of A-frame huts perched on stilts at the water's edge, which sleep between four and eight people. To pitch your own tent, enquire at the information centre as space is limited.

KS Eco Tours TOUR
(012-514 5023; www.kualasepetang.com) The company is passionate about preserving the delicate ecosystem and promotes low-impact exploration of the area. Packages include 30-minute boat rides around the old jetty and fishing villages (RM15 per person, minimum RM80), to firefly-watching half-day tours (RM350 for minimum 10 people).

Getting There & Away

Blue Omnibus 77 runs every 40 minutes from 6.05am to 7pm between Taiping's local bus station and Kuala Sepetang (30 minutes, RM2). Buses can drop you at the reserve on request.

Belum-Temenggor Rainforest

Perak's northernmost tip is home to Peninsular Malaysia's largest expanse of virgin jungle, the Belum-Temenggor Rainforest. Bordering Thailand to its north and the Malaysian state of Kelantan to the east, this area was partly inundated after Temenggor Dam was completed in 1972.

Within this green dream of wilderness is the 117.5-hectare Royal Belum State Park. The park is excellent for birdwatching, with all 10 species of hornbill cawing from its ancient trees. Tapirs, sun bears, tigers and panthers also make their home here. Spotting Belum's larger animals is a matter of luck, and odds are low unless you secure a guide for dawn or dusk. But even when the wildlife is shy, Belum's magic is revealed through the majesty of its forest, where tangled tree roots harbour orchids, and hand-sized katydids (crickets) zoom across the glades.

Sights

Royal Belum State Park PARK
(Belum-Temenggor Forest Reserve; www.royalbelum.my) This state park within Belum-Temenggor Rainforest was gazetted in 2007 to protect its rich menagerie of tigers, tapirs, panthers and the Sumatran rhino – though the latter is now feared extinct in Malaysia. A permit and guide are needed to explore; hotels can help with both. Book accommodation and excursions a fortnight in advance to allow time to secure the permit (you'll need to send a scan of your passport). If applying directly, contact **Perak State Park Corporation** (05-791 4543; 1st flr, Government Complex Building, Jalan Sultan Abd Aziz, Gerik).

LOCAL KNOWLEDGE

TIPS FOR GETTING THE BEST OF BELUM

Watery Royal Belum State Park requires guided tours by boat. Packages with accommodation, excursions and a park permit can be touristy, but offer good value. Common offerings include nature hikes and visits to the rafflesia site and Orang Asli village (only one village in the area receives visitors).

Some operators have meaningful links with Orang Asli villagers, but many travellers will be uncomfortable to witness the volume of tourists snapping cameras at locals. You may prefer to avoid these excursions. Rafflesia, heavy-weight parasitic blooms, are unpredictable so be wary of tours that guarantee sightings.

Locals say butterfly spotting is at its best in April, May, November and December. The best months to see hornbills are August and September, while migratory birds arrive in November and December. Otters and eagles can be seen year-round, along with an eye-popping variety of fungi, flowers and insect life.

Sleeping

Neither of the below are located in the state park, but each is well positioned for excursions in and around the protected area.

★Belum Eco Resort RESORT **$$**

(☎05-281 1288, 05-281 0834; www.belumecoresort.com.my; all-inclusive 3-day/2-night package per person RM590-650) This ecofriendly private island is well and truly off the grid. Accommodation at this isolated spot is very basic – choose from bungalows or bare rooms aboard a houseboat – but the atmosphere is friendly, communal meals are ample, and host Steve Khong is knowledgeable and helpful. The fee includes boat transport to and from the island, all meals, accommodation and excursions.

Bungalows are made of local and natural materials, electricity is switched off during daylight hours, and guided tours of the area emphasise minimal impact on the environment and strive to educate visitors about the local wildlife and ecosystem. Flinging open your bungalow door to see morning sunlight dappling Lake Temenggor is sure to linger in your memory; book ahead to ensure you get to enjoy it.

Belum Rainforest Resort RESORT **$$$**

(☎05-791 6800; www.belumresort.com; incl breakfast r RM700-900, ste RM1000-1100; P ❄ @ ☎ ≋) This resort's brick-and-bamboo aesthetic blends well with its location bordering the rainforest, and it has luxurious trappings and an atmospheric spa. Rooms are comfy but plain, so it's rather pricey for what you get – though we found substantial discounts by calling ahead. Visits to the protected area can be arranged here (short walk/full-day excursion RM90/370).

Getting There & Away

Driving offers the best flexibility when reaching Belum.

There are two ways by public transport: take a bus to Gerik (sometimes spelt Grik and pronounced 'Greek'), where taxis at the town's bus station will take you the remaining 40km to Jeti Pulau Banting for the boat to Belum Eco Resort (if you've prebooked) or other resorts (RM60).

Alternatively, from Butterworth, Ipoh, Kuala Kangsar or Taiping, board a Kota Bharu–bound bus and ask the driver to drop you off at Jeti Pulau Banting, or near Belum Rainforest Resort, located near Hwy 76. You'll be expected to pay the full fare to Kota Bharu.

Leaving Belum, buses from Kota Bharu are unpredictable, so you'll probably have to take a taxi to Gerik (RM60), and continue by bus from there. Departures from Gerik's bus station:

DESTINATION	PRICE	DURATION	FREQUENCY
Ipoh	RM13.10	3 hours	9am & 4pm
Kota Bharu	RM29.10	4 hours	11.45am
Kuala Lumpur	RM33.40	4-6 hours	10am, 5pm & 11.30pm

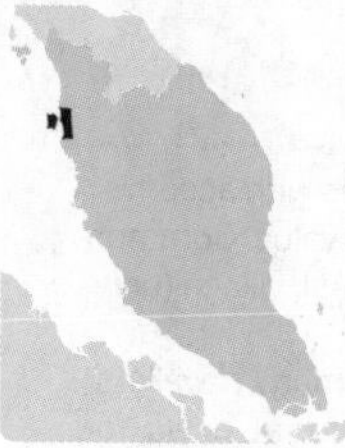

Penang

☎04 / POP 1.65 MILLION / AREA 293 SQ KM

Includes ➡

Best Places to Eat

- Teksen (p176)
- Lg Baru (New Lane) Hawker Stalls (p177)
- Pulau Tikus Hawker Stalls (p177)
- China House (p176)
- Hai Boey Seafood (p189)

Best Places to Stay

- Campbell House (p173)
- Museum Hotel (p174)
- 23 Love Lane (p173)
- Lone Pine Hotel (p185)
- Ren i Tang (p171)

Why Go?

Located at the intersection of Asia's great kingdoms and Europe's powerful colonial empires, the island of Penang has long served as the link between Asia's two halves and an important outlet to the markets of Europe and the Middle East.

This history has resulted in a culture that is one of Malaysia's most diverse, cosmopolitan and exciting. The culmination of this is undoubtedly George Town, Penang's main city, and an urban centre that delivers old-world Asia in spades; think trishaws pedalling past watermarked Chinese shophouses, blue joss smoke perfuming the air.

Yet it would be a shame to neglect Penang's abundant tropicalness, its palm-fringed beaches and fishing villages, its mountainous jungle and farms growing exotic produce such as nutmeg and durian.

If there's a more compact, convenient and exciting microcosm of the exotic East than Penang, we've yet to find it.

When to Go

George Town

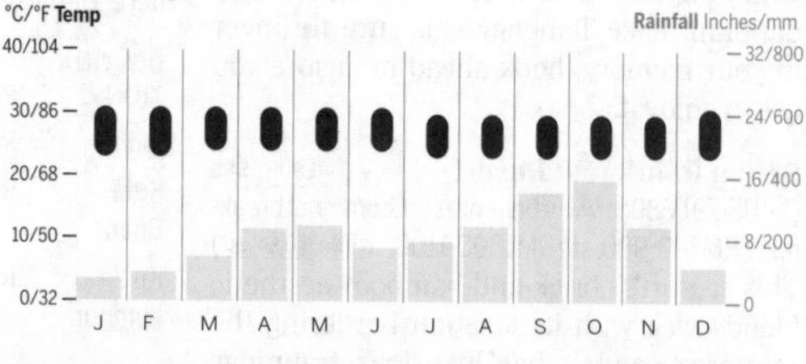

Jan–Feb Book accommodation in advance if visiting George Town during Chinese New Year.

Jun–Jul Penang's famous durian and other fruit are at their peak.

Nov–Dec Penang's 'winter' is the most comfortable time to visit the island.

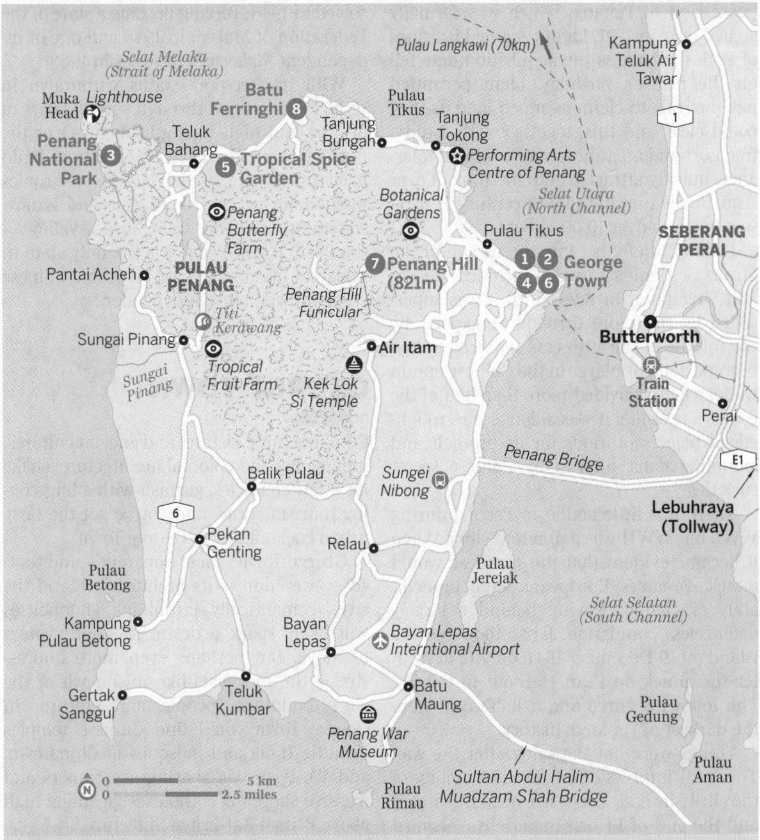

Penang Highlights

1. Gorging on George Town's seemingly never-ending spread of **hawker food** (p177).
2. Getting a virtual crash course in feng shui at **Blue Mansion** (p159).
3. Hiking through jungles to monkey-filled beaches at **Penang National Park** (p186).
4. Learning about the city's architectural heritage from street level via a **walking tour** (p164) of George Town.
5. Becoming familiar with the contents of your spice rack at the **Tropical Spice Garden** (p185).
6. Indulging in a stay at one of George Town's unique **heritage hotels** (p173).
7. Enjoying the cool breezes and fantastic views of the island from atop **Penang Hill** (p166).
8. Suntanning and cocktail drinking at a resort in **Batu Ferringhi** (p184).

History

Little is known of Penang's early history. Chinese seafarers were aware of the island, which they called Betelnut Island, as far back as the 15th century, but it appears to have been uninhabited. It wasn't until the early 1700s that colonists arrived from Sumatra and established settlements at Batu Uban and the area now covered by southern George Town. The island came under the control of the sultan of Kedah, but in 1771 the sultan signed the first agreement with the British East India Company, handing them trading rights in exchange for military assistance against Siam (present-day Thailand).

Fifteen years later, Captain Francis Light, on behalf of the East India Company, took possession of Penang, which was formally signed over in 1791. Light renamed it Prince of Wales Island, as the acquisition date fell on the prince's birthday. Light permitted new arrivals to claim as much land as they could clear and this, together with a duty-free port and an atmosphere of liberal tolerance, quickly attracted settlers from all over Asia. By the turn of the 18th century, Penang was home to over 10,000 people.

Penang briefly became the capital of the Straits Settlements (which included Melaka and Singapore) in 1826, until it was superseded by the more thriving Singapore. By the middle of the 19th century, Penang had become a major player in the Chinese opium trade, which provided more than half of the colony's revenue. It was a dangerous, rough-edged place, notorious for its brothels and gambling dens, all run by Chinese secret societies.

There was little action in Penang during WWI, but WWII was a different story. When it became evident that the Japanese would attack, Penang's Europeans were immediately evacuated, leaving behind a largely defenceless population. Japan took over the island on 19 December 1941, only 12 days after the attack on Pearl Harbour in the US. The following three and a half years were the darkest of Penang's history.

Things were not the same after the war. The local impression of the invincibility of the British had been irrevocably tainted and the end of British imperialism seemed imminent. The Straits Settlements were dissolved in 1946; Penang became a state of the Federation of Malaya in 1948 and one of independent Malaysia's 13 states in 1963.

With its free-port status withdrawn in 1969, Penang went through several years of decline and high unemployment. Over the next 20 years, the island was able to build itself up as one of the largest electronics manufacturing centres of Asia and is now sometimes dubbed the 'Silicon Valley of the East'. Today, Penang is the only state in Malaysia that has elected an ethnic Chinese chief minister since independence.

ISLAND OR STATE?

The strip of mainland coast known as Seberang Perai (or Province Wellesley) is the mainland portion of the state that many people don't even know is Penang. The state of Penang is divided both geographically and administratively into two sections: Pulau Pinang (Penang Island), a 293-sq-km island in the Strait of Melaka, and Seberang Perai, a narrow 760-sq-km strip on the peninsular mainland. George Town, on Penang Island, is the state capital, while Butterworth is the largest town in Seberang Perai. Confusingly, the city of George Town is often referred to as just 'Penang' or 'Pinang'.

GEORGE TOWN

POP 510,996

Combine three distinct and ancient cultures, indigenous and colonial architecture, shake for a few centuries, garnish with a burgeoning tourism scene, and you've got the tasty urban cocktail that is George Town.

George Town's most apparent – and touted – attraction is its architecture. And the city's romantically crumbling shophouses will likely spark a desire in some visitors to move. But perhaps even more impressive is the movie-set-like mishmash of the city's buildings, people and culture. In George Town you'll find Chinese temples in Little India and mosques in Chinatown, and Western-style soaring skyscrapers and massive shopping complexes gleaming high above British Raj–era architecture.

This eclectic jumble means that George Town is a city that rewards explorers. Dodge traffic while strolling past Chinese shophouses where people might be roasting coffee over a fire or sculpting giant incense for a ceremony. Get lost in the maze of chaotic streets and narrow lanes, past shrines decorated with strings of paper lanterns and fragrant shops selling Indian spices. Or you might be led to George Town's burgeoning art scene, its modern cafes or its fun bars.

Yet perhaps the greatest reward of all comes at the end of all this exploration: George Town is Malaysia's, if not Southeast Asia's, food capital. Home to five distinct cuisines, cheap and delicious open-air hawker centres, lauded seafood and legendary fruit, it's the kind of place that can boast both quality *and* quantity.

We'll drink to that.

UNESCO & GEORGE TOWN

In 2008, the historic centre of George Town was designated a Unesco World Heritage Site for having 'a unique architectural and cultural townscape without parallel anywhere in East and Southeast Asia'. A 'core' area comprising 1700 buildings and a 'buffer', which together span east from the waterfront to as far west as Jln Transfer and Jln Dr Lim Chwee Leong were drawn up, and the structures within these areas have been thoroughly catalogued and are protected by strict zoning laws.

Details about the Unesco designation can be seen at the **George Town World Heritage Inc. Headquarters** (www.gtwhi.com.my; 116-118 Lebuh Acheh; ⌚8am-1pm & 2-5pm Mon-Thu, 8am-12.15pm & 2.45-5pm Fri). *Value Your Built Heritage*, available here, is an informative and entertaining pocket guide to George Town's shophouse styles. Another excellent guide to the city's buildings is the 'George Town World Heritage Site Architectural Walkabout', available at the Penang Heritage Trust (p182).

The general consensus is that the Unesco listing has been a good thing for George Town, having helped the city safeguard its age-old feel while also reaping the benefits of a facelift. The designation seems to have sparked an interest in local culture among residents, and some claim that it has also had the effect of drawing younger locals back to the city, which suffered from a debilitating 'brain drain' during the 1980s and 1990s.

'In some ways, [the Unesco designation] has helped,' explains prominent heritage advocate and President of the Penang Heritage Trust, Khoo Salma. 'In some ways, [it] has hastened destruction. It has been a double-edged sword.'

The 2008 Unesco designation sparked a tourism boom that continues to this day. Old buildings, once abandoned, have been snatched up by developers hoping to cash in, and property values have skyrocketed. Today, there's rumours of shophouses selling for more than US$1M, and 'heritage' hotels and cutsey cafes can be found on just about every street in George Town.

'Investors expect quick returns,' explains Khoo Salma, 'and so heritage buildings are being converted into hotels and cafes. A few are well done but many involve hasty and illegal renovations which also undermine the tangible heritage.' According to Khoo Salma, the boom is beginning to have a negative impact on locals. 'Long-term tenants who can no longer afford the rent are moving out, some are actually being evicted for boutique hotels.'

'The challenge now is how to retain intangible cultural heritage,' explains Khoo Salma. 'It is urban residents who practise the traditions, festivals, etc. How [can we] preserve cultural heritage without residents?'

Sights

Inside the Unesco Protected Zone

★**Blue Mansion** HISTORIC BUILDING

(www.thebluemansion.com.my; 14 Lebuh Leith; adult/child RM16/8; ⌚tours 11am, 2pm & 3.30pm) The magnificent 38-room, 220-window 'Blue Mansion' was built in the 1880s and rescued from ruin in the 1990s. It blends Eastern and Western designs with louvred windows, art nouveau stained glass and beautiful floor tiles, and is a rare surviving example of the eclectic architectural style preferred by wealthy Straits Chinese. Its distinctive (and once-common in George Town) blue hue is the result of an indigo-based limewash.

Hour-long guided tours (included in the admission fee) provide a glimpse of the interior as well as an insight into traditional Chinese architecture.

The mansion was commissioned by Cheong Fatt Tze, a Hakka merchant-trader who left China as a penniless teenager and eventually established a vast financial empire throughout east Asia, earning himself the dual sobriquets 'Rockefeller of the East' and the 'Last Mandarin'.

★**Pinang Peranakan Mansion** MUSEUM

(www.pinangperanakanmansion.com.my; 29 Lebuh Gereja; adult/child RM21.20/10.60; ⌚9.30am-5.30pm) This ostentatious, mint green structure is among the most stunning restored residences in George Town. A self-guided tour reveals that every door, wall and

George Town

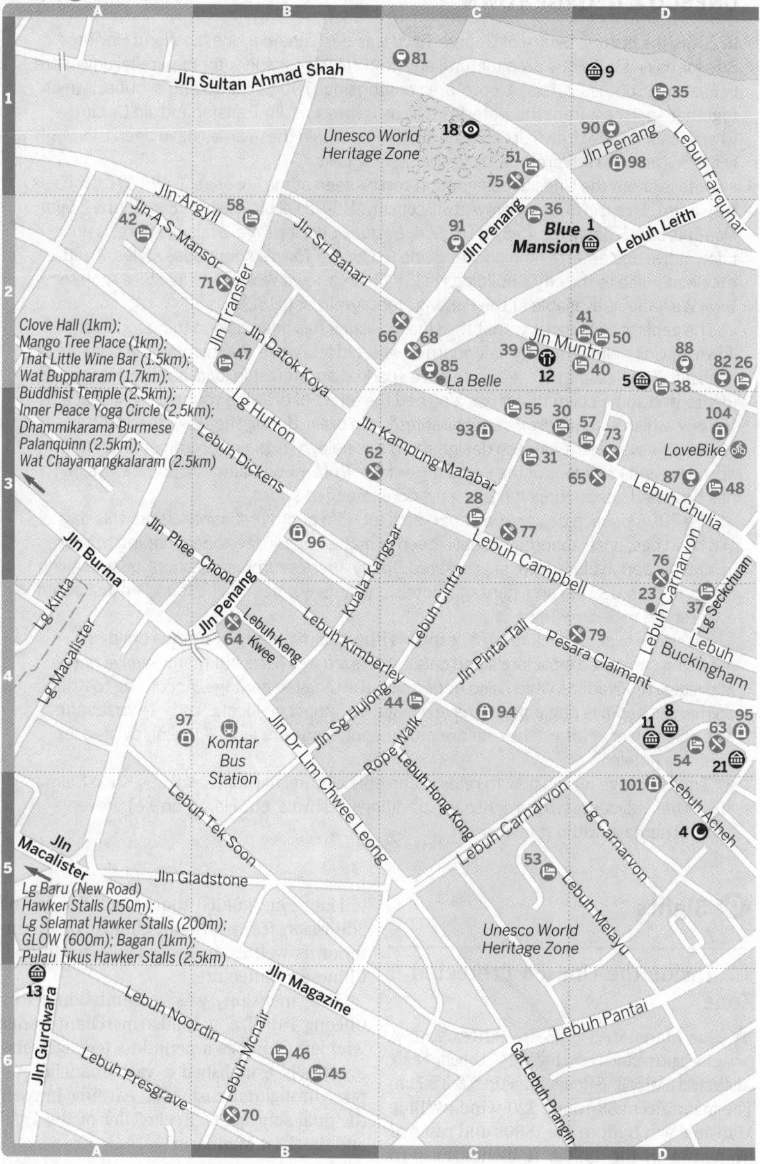

archway is carved and often painted in gold leaf; the grand rooms are furnished with majestic wood furniture with intricate mother-of-pearl inlay; there are displays of charming antiques; and bright-coloured paintings and fascinating black-and-white photos of the family in regal Chinese dress grace the walls.

The house belonged to Chung Keng Quee, a 19th-century merchant, secret-society leader and community pillar as well as being one of the wealthiest Baba-Nonyas of that era.

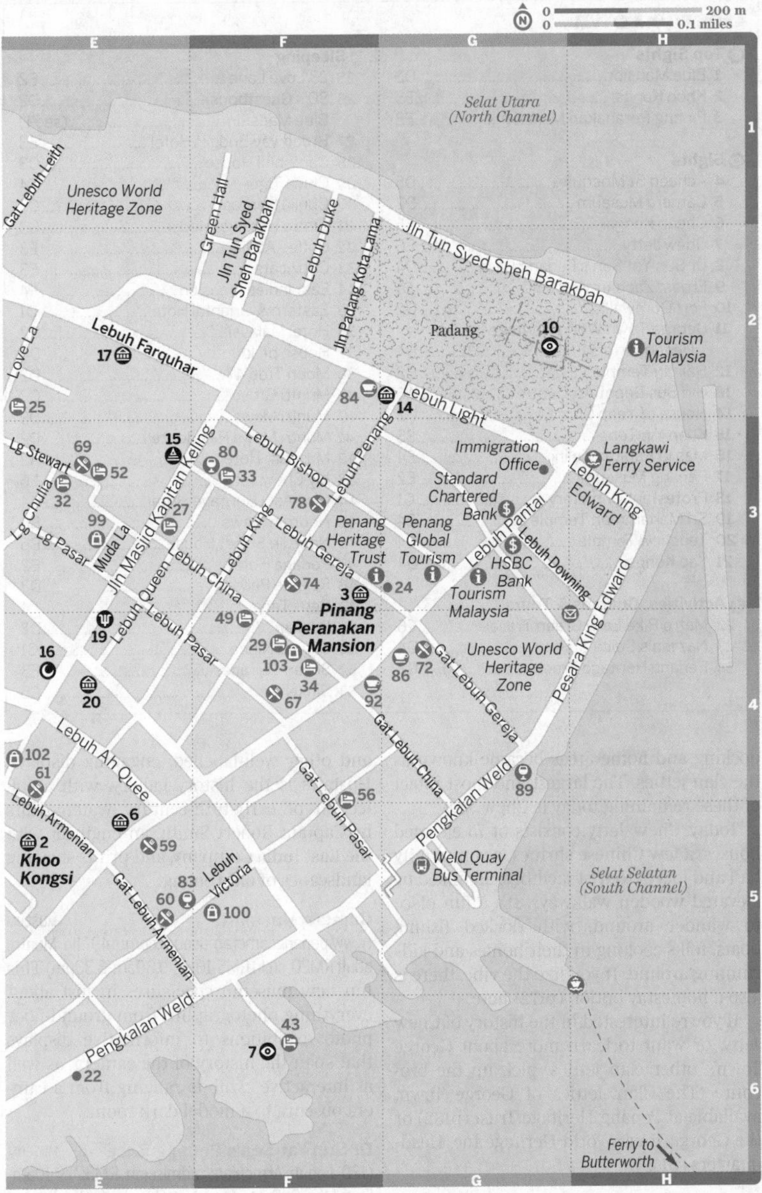

After visiting the house, be sure to also check out Chung Keng Kwi Temple, the adjacent ancestral hall.

Chew Jetty HISTORIC NEIGHBOURHOOD
(Pengkalan Weld) During the late 18th and early 19th centuries, George Town's Pengkalan Weld was the centre of one of the world's most thriving ports and provided plentiful work for the never-ending influx of immigrants. Soon a community of Chinese grew up around the quay, with floating and stilt houses built along rickety docks; these

George Town

Top Sights	
1 Blue Mansion	D2
2 Khoo Kongsi	E5
3 Pinang Peranakan Mansion	F3
Sights	
4 Acheen St Mosque	D5
5 Camera Museum	D2
6 Cheah Kongsi	E5
7 Chew Jetty	F6
8 Dr Sun Yat Sen's Penang Base	D4
9 Ernest Zacharevic x E&O	D1
10 Fort Cornwallis	G2
11 George Town World Heritage Inc. Headquarters	D4
12 Hainan Temple	C2
13 Hin Bus Depot Art Centre	A6
14 House of Yeap Chor Ee	G2
15 Kuan Yin Teng	E3
16 Masjid Kapitan Keling	E4
17 Penang Museum	E2
18 Protestant Cemetery	C1
19 Sri Mariamman Temple	E4
20 Teochew Temple	E4
21 Yap Kongsi	D4
Activities, Courses & Tours	
22 Metro Bike Easy Green Travel	E6
23 Nazlina's Spice Station	D4
24 Penang Heritage Trust	G3

Sleeping	
25 23 Love Lane	E2
26 80's Guesthouse	D2
Blue Mansion	(see 1)
27 Broadway Budget Hotel	E3
28 Campbell House	C3
29 China Tiger	F4
30 Chulia Heritage	C3
31 Cintra Heritage House	C3
32 Coffee Atelier	E3
33 Couzicats	F3
34 East Indies Mansion	F4
35 Eastern & Oriental Hotel	D1
36 Hotel Malaysia	C2
37 House of Journey	D4
38 Moon Tree 47	D2
39 Muntri Grove	C2
40 Muntri Mews	D2
41 Muntri Mews Residence	D2
42 Museum Hotel	A2
43 My Chew Jetty	F6
44 New Asia Heritage Hotel	C4
45 Noordin Mews	B6
46 Noordin Street House	B6
47 Penaga Hotel	B2
48 Reggae Penang	D3
49 Ren i Tang	F4
50 Ryokan	D2
51 Segara Ninda	C1
52 Seven Terraces	E3
53 Sinkeh	C5

docking and home areas became known as the clan jetties. The largest and most intact of these remaining today is Chew Jetty.

Today, Chew Jetty consists of 75 elevated houses, a few Chinese shrines, a community hall and lots of tourist facilities, all linked by elevated wooden walkways. It's a fun place to wander around, with docked fishing boats, folks cooking in their homes and kids running around. If you like the vibe, there is also a homestay option (p172) here.

If you're interested in the history of Chew Jetty, or want to learn more about George Town's other clan jetties, pick up the brochure 'The Clan Jetties of George Town', available at Penang Heritage Trust (p182) or the George Town World Heritage Inc. Headquarters (p159).

Penang Museum MUSEUM
(www.penangmuseum.gov.my; Lebuh Farquhar; admission RM1; 9am-5pm Sat-Thu) Penang's state-run museum includes exhibits on the history, customs and traditions of the island's various ethnic groups, with photos, videos, documents, costumes, furniture and other well-labelled, engaging displays. Upstairs is the history gallery, with a collection of early-19th-century watercolours by Captain Robert Smith, an engineer with the East India Company, and prints showing landscapes of old Penang.

Camera Museum MUSEUM
(www.penangcameramuseum.com; 49 Jln Muntri; adult RM20, child RM5-10; 9.30am-6.30pm) This fun new museum specialises in just about everything photographic, from ground-floor photo exhibitions to informative displays that span the history of the camera, as well as interactive exhibits ranging from a camera obscura to a model dark room.

Dr Sun Yat Sen's Penang Base MUSEUM
(120 Lebuh Armenian; admission RM5; 10am-5pm Mon-Sat) Dr Sun Yat Sen was the leader of the 1911 Chinese revolution, which established China as the first republic in Asia. He lived in George Town with his family for about six months in 1910; this house was the central meeting place for his political party. Today the structure is a museum documenting Dr Sun Yat Sen's time in Penang, and

54 Straits Collection D4
55 Time Capsule Hotel C3
56 Victoria Inn F4
57 Yeng Keng Hotel D3
58 Yes Hotel B2

Eating

59 BTB E5
China House .... (see 59)
60 Da Shu Xia Seafood House E5
61 Edelweiss E4
62 Hameediyah B3
63 Jawi House D4
64 Joo Hooi Cafe B4
65 Junk Cafe D3
66 Kafe Kheng Pin C2
67 Karai Kudi F4
68 Kashmir C2
69 Kebaya E3
70 Lebuh Presgrave Hawker Stalls B6
71 Nasi Padang Minang B2
72 Quay Café G4
73 Sky Cafe D3
74 Sri Ananda Bahwan F3
75 Sup Hameed C1
76 Teksen D3
77 Tho Yuen Restaurant C3
78 Veloo Villas F3
79 Yin's Sourdough Bakery D4

Drinking & Nightlife

80 Alabama Shake F3
81 Beach Blanket Babylon C1
82 Behind 50 Love Lane D2
83 Canteen E5
84 Constant Gardener F2
Farquhar's Bar .... (see 35)
85 Georgetown Wines C2
86 Jing-Si Books & Cafe G4
Kopi C .... (see 59)
87 Micke's Place D3
88 Mish Mash D2
89 QEII G4
90 Slippery Senoritas D1
91 Soho Free House C2
92 Ten Yee Tea Trading F4

Shopping

93 Ban Hin C3
94 Bee Chin Heong C4
95 China Joe's D4
96 Chowraster Bazaar B3
97 Komtar A4
98 Little Penang Street Market D1
99 Muda House E3
100 ottokedai F5
101 Rozanas Batik D5
102 Shop Howard E4
103 Tropical Spice Garden In Town F4
104 Unique Penang D3

even if you're not interested in history, is worth a visit simply for a peek inside a stunningly restored antique shophouse.

House of Yeap Chor Ee MUSEUM
(www.houseyce.com; 4 Lebuh Penang; adult/child RM13/free; 10am-6pm Mon-Fri) This museum, housed in an exquisitely restored three-storey shophouse mansion, is dedicated to a former resident, itinerant barber-turned-banker, Yeap Chor Ee. In addition to family photos and mementos, the museum has interesting exhibits on Chinese immigration to Penang.

Protestant Cemetery CEMETERY
(Jln Sultan Ahmad Shah; 24hr) FREE Under a canopy of magnolia trees you'll find the graves of Captain Francis Light and many others, including governors, merchants, sailors and Chinese Christians who fled the Boxer Rebellion in China (a movement opposing Western imperialism and evangelism), only to die of fever in Penang. Also here is the tomb of Thomas Leonowens, the young officer who married Anna – the schoolmistress to the King of Siam, made famous by *The King and I*.

For the stories behind the gravestones, consider picking up the informative brochure 'George Town's Northam Road Protestant Cemetery', available at the Penang Heritage Trust (p182) or the George Town World Heritage Inc. Headquarters (p159).

Ernest Zacharevic x E&O GALLERY
(www.facebook.com/ErnestZacharevicxEnO; ground fl, Eastern & Oriental Hotel, 10 Lebuh Farquar; 10am-5pm Wed-Mon) Like George Town's street art? Then buy a custom print to take home, or perhaps an original piece, from the gallery featuring the work of the man behind the murals, Ernest Zacharevic.

Acheen St Mosque MOSQUE
(Lebuh Acheh; 7am-7pm) FREE Built in 1808 by a wealthy Arab trader, the Acheen St Mosque was the focal point for the Malay and Arab traders in this quarter – the oldest Malay *kampung* (village) in George Town. It's unusual for its Egyptian-style minaret – most Malay mosques have Moorish minarets.

Hainan Temple CHINESE TEMPLE
(Jln Muntri; 9am-6pm) FREE Dedicated to Mar Chor Poh, the patron saint of seafarers,

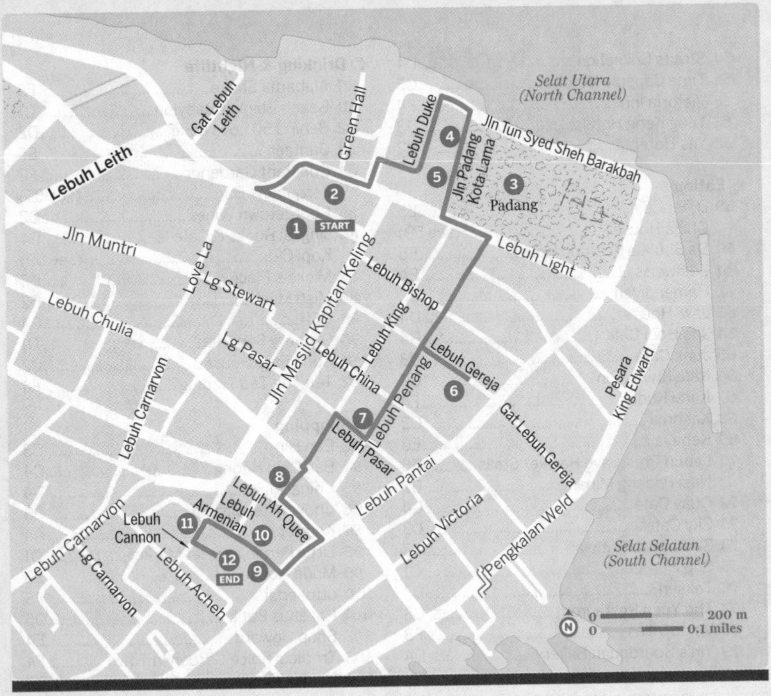

Town Walk
Five Cultures on Two Feet

START PENANG MUSEUM
END KHOO KONGSI
LENGTH 2.25KM; THREE TO FOUR HOURS

This walk will give you a glimpse of George Town's cultural mix: English, Indian, Malay, Baba-Nonya and Chinese.

Starting at **1 Penang Museum** (p162), head west and then north towards the waterfront, passing the **2 Supreme Court**. Note the statue of James Richardson Logan, advocate for nonwhites during the colonial era. Walk north along Lebuh Duke to the waterfront, then head south along Jln Padang Kota Lama past the vast **3 padang** (field) and grandiose architecture of the **4 City Hall** and **5 Town Hall**. Proceed east along Lebuh Light, then south on Lebuh Penang. A short detour east along Lebuh Gereja finds the impressive **6 Pinang Peranakan Mansion** (p159), the former digs of one of George Town's great Baba-Nonya merchant barons.

Returning to Lebuh Penang, head south into **7 Little India** and take a deep breath of all that spice; if it's around lunchtime, refuel with an authentic southern-Indian-style banana-leaf *thali* meal. At Lebuh Pasar, head west past shops selling milky South Asian sweets, then south at Lebuh King to the intersection of **8 Lebuh King and Lebuh Ah Quee**, a literal example of Penang's cultural crossroads. To your south is a Chinese assembly hall and rows of fading Chinese shopfronts; to your north is a small Indian mosque; and across the street is a large Malaysian restaurant.

Head east along Lebuh Ah Quee, then south along Jln Pantai; you're now at **9 Lebuh Armenian**. Among George Town's most gentrified streets today, it was formerly a centre for Chinese secret societies and was one of the main fighting stages of the 1867 riots. Stroll west along restored shophouses until you reach **10 Cheah Kongsi** (p165), home to the oldest Straits Chinese clan association in Penang.

Cross the street to the corner of Jln Masjid Kapitan Keling and the bright-green 1924 Hokkien clanhouse **11 Yap Kongsi** (p165). Head south on Lebuh Cannon and duck into the magnificently ornate **12 Khoo Kongsi** (p165), the most impressive *kongsi* in the city.

this temple was founded in 1870 but not completed until 1895. A thorough remodelling for its centenary in 1995 refreshed its distinctive swirling dragon pillars and brightened up the ornate carvings.

Fort Cornwallis HISTORIC SITE

(Lebuh Light; adult/child RM20/10; ⌚9am-7pm) It was here that Captain Light first set foot on the virtually uninhabited island of Penang in 1786 and established the free port where trade would, he hoped, be lured from Britain's Dutch rivals.

Between 1808 and 1810, convict labour replaced the then-wooden fort with stone; the unique star-profile shape of the walls allowed for overlapping fields of fire against enemies. Yet for all its size, the contemporary fort isn't particularly impressive; only the outer walls stand, enclosing a rather spare park within.

Light named the fort after Charles Cornwallis, perhaps best known for surrendering at the Battle of Yorktown to George Washington, effectively ending the American Revolution.

Sri Mariamman Temple HINDU TEMPLE

(Jln Masjid Kapitan Keling; ⌚7am-7pm) FREE Sri Mariamman was built in 1883 and is George Town's oldest Hindu house of worship. For local south Indians, the temple fulfils the purpose of a Chinese clanhouse; it's a reminder of the motherland and the community bonds

GEORGE TOWN'S CLANHOUSES

Between the mid-1800s and the mid-1900s, Penang welcomed a huge influx of Chinese immigrants, primarily from China's Fujian province. To help introduce uncles, aunties, cousins, 10th cousins, old neighbourhood buddies and so on to their new home, the Chinese formed clan associations and built clanhouses, known locally as *kongsi*, to create a sense of community, provide lodging and help find employment for newcomers. In addition to functioning as 'embassies' of sorts, clanhouses also served as a deeper social, even spiritual, link between an extended clan, its ancestors and its social obligations.

As time went on, many clan associations became extremely prosperous and their buildings became more ornate. Clans – called 'secret societies' by the British – began to compete with each other over the decadence and number of their temples. Due to this rivalry, today's Penang has one of the densest concentrations of clan architecture found outside China.

Khoo Kongsi (www.khookongsi.com.my; 18 Cannon Sq; adult/child RM10/1; ⌚9am-5pm) The Khoo are a successful clan, and their eponymous clanhouse is the most impressive one in George Town.

Guided tours begin at the stone carvings that dance across the entrance hall and pavilions, many of which symbolise or are meant to attract good luck and wealth. The interior is dominated by incredible murals depicting birthdays, weddings and, most impressively, the 36 celestial guardians. Gorgeous ceramic sculptures of immortals, carp, dragons, and carp becoming dragons dance across the roof ridges.

Yet, as impressive as all of this is, Khoo Kongsi was once even more ostentatious; the structure caught fire on the night it was completed in 1901, an event put down to divine jealousy. The present *kongsi* dates from 1906.

Cheah Kongsi (Lebuh Pantai; ⌚9am-5pm) Cheah Kongsi is home to the oldest Straits Chinese clan association in Penang. Besides serving as a temple and assembly hall, this building has also been the registered headquarters of several secret societies. Each society occupied a different portion of the temple, which became a focal point during the interclan riots that flared up in 1867. The fighting became so intense that a secret passage existed between here and Khoo Kongsi for a quick escape.

The Cheah Kongsi was being renovated when we were in town.

Teochew Temple (Han Jiang Ancestral Temple; Lebuh Chulia; ⌚9am-5pm) This 1870 clanhouse was renovated in 2005 by Chinese artisans and features informative displays on the immigration and culture of the eponymous Chinese group.

Yap Kongsi (71 Lebuh Armenian; ⌚9am-5pm) The main structure here, originally built in 1924 'Straits Eclectic' style and today painted a distinct shade of light green, is not always open to the public. Instead, stop in at the adjacent temple, Choo Chay Keong.

forged within the diaspora. It is a typically south Indian temple, dominated by the *gopuram* (entrance tower).

Penang's Thaipusam procession (p168) begins here, and in October a wooden chariot takes the temple's deity for a spin around the neighbourhood during Vijayadasami festivities.

The temple was being renovated when we were in town.

Masjid Kapitan Keling MOSQUE

(cnr Lebuh Buckingham & Jln Masjid Kapitan Keling; 7am-7pm) FREE Penang's first Indian Muslim settlers (East India Company troops) built Masjid Kapitan Keling in 1801. The mosque's domes are yellow, in a typically Indian-influenced Islamic style, and it has a single minaret. It looks sublime at sunset. Mosque officials can grant permission to enter.

Outside the Unesco Protected Zone

★Penang Hill HILL

(www.penanghill.gov.my; funicular adult/child RM30/15; 6.30am-11pm) The top of Penang Hill, 821m above George Town, provides a spectacular view over the island and across to the mainland.

The top is reached by a funicular, and on weekends and public holidays lines can be horrendously long, with waits of up to 30 minutes. From Weld Quay, Komtar or Lebuh Chulia, you can catch the frequent bus 204 (RM2.70) to Air Itam. A taxi here from the centre of George Town will set you back about RM25.

It's generally about 5°C cooler here than at sea level, providing a convenient retreat from the sticky heat below. There are some gardens, a food court, an exuberantly decorated Hindu temple and a mosque as well as David Brown's, a colonial-style British restaurant serving everything from beef Wellington to high tea. From the road that extends from the upper funicular station, you can walk the 5km to the Botanical Gardens in about 1½ hours.

Botanical Gardens GARDENS

(www.botanicalgardens.penang.gov.my; Waterfall Rd; 5am-8pm) FREE Once a granite quarry, Penang's Botanical Gardens were founded in 1884 by Charles Curtis, a tireless British plant lover who collected the original specimens and became the first curator. Today, the 30-hectare grounds include a fern rockery, an orchidarium and a lily pond. Or take the 1.5km Curtis Trail, which dips into the jungle.

The gardens are also known as the Waterfall Gardens after the stream that cascades through from Penang Hill, or the Monkey Gardens for the many long-tailed macaques that scamper around. Don't be tempted to feed them: monkeys do bite, and there's a RM500 fine if you're caught.

The Botanical Gardens are located about 8km northeast of George Town. To get there, take bus 10 (RM2.70) from Komtar or Weld Quay; a taxi will cost at least RM25.

Hin Bus Depot Art Centre GALLERY

(www.facebook.com/hinbusdepot; 31A Jln Gurdwara; noon-7pm) FREE This gracefully crumbling former bus terminal has become a centre for George Town's burgeoning art scene. The open-air areas are bedecked with street art, and the covered area spans exhibitions that change every couple months, and a cafe. Peruse the centre's Facebook page to see what's on when you're in town.

P Ramlee House MUSEUM

(4A Jln P Ramlee; 10am-5pm Tue-Thu, Sat & Sun, 10am-noon & 3-5pm Fri) FREE This museum compound is dedicated to Malaysia's biggest megastar, P Ramlee. Ramlee was particularly known for his singing; he also acted in and directed 66 films in his lifetime. Although visitors may not be familiar with his work, the grounds and displays are interesting, and there are a few kitschy souvenirs in the museum's gift shop.

P Ramlee House is about 5km west of George Town; a taxi here will cost RM15.

P Ramlee's music plays as a constant soundtrack throughout the compound, which consists of three zones: a performing arts centre, a small museum with artefacts and photos about P Ramlee's life, and Ramlee's birthplace, a humble, thoroughly restored *kampung* house built in 1926.

Courses

In addition to the following places, you can enrol in a cooking course at the Tropical Spice Garden (p185), a course in batik making at Rozanas Batik (p181) and pewter making at Royal Selangor (p181).

Nazlina's Spice Station COOKING COURSE

(012-453 8167; www.penang-cooking-class.com; 2 Lebuh Campbell; classes RM160; lessons 7.30am-12.30pm & 2.30-5.30pm) The bubbly and

DON'T MISS

GEORGE TOWN'S STREET ART

Forget shophouses and hawker stalls; the George Town of today is all about street art.

The trend goes back to 2010, when Penang's state government commissioned the studio Sculpture At Work (www.sculptureatwork.com) to do a series of cartoon steel art pieces across town. Affixed to George Town street walls, these 3D artworks detail local customs and heritage with humour, while also providing a quirky counterpoint to the natural urban beauty of the historic core.

Yet the real star of George Town's street-art scene is undoubtedly Lithuanian artist, Ernest Zacharevic (www.facebook.com/Ernestzachas). For the 2012 George Town Festival, Zacharevic was commissioned to do a series of public paintings in central George Town, some of which he chose to combine with objects such as bicycles, motorcycles and architectural features. The art has been a smash hit, with the piece on Lebuh Armenian having become a legitimate tourist destination, complete with long lines and souvenir stalls.

We spoke with Zacharevic in 2015; his comments have been edited for length and clarity.

What was the first piece of street art you did in George Town? It was a portrait of a local lady. It was my first or second day in Penang and I bumped into her while sketching on the street. We couldn't really communicate, but she had a very distinct look. I was inspired by that encounter and thought it would be nice to leave a painting. There was no plan, I just bought a bunch of crayons and did a sketch on a wall. It was gone a few days later.

Your paintings are a hit now, but how did people initially react to them? The initial reaction was surprise. There's not much of a street art scene in Malaysia, so people had a negative stigma about graffiti, and wondered what I was doing. I wasn't surprised that the paintings stood out, but I am surprised that they've lasted this long and have become so popular.

Do the scenes you paint come from your imagination or from photographs? A combination of both. I travel a lot and am always photographing situations and people I meet. Sometimes a painting is based on a specific photo, sometimes it's a combination of photos.

Your images are now found on shirts, notebooks and other souvenirs in George Town, ostensibly produced without your permission. How do you feel about this? I try to keep a distance and not interfere. I just want to carry on painting, I don't want to hire lawyers. I don't approve, but see it as free advertising, and it helps local businesses.

Now you have your own gallery (Ernest Zacharevic x E&O; p163), you're involved with a gallery in George Town (Hin Bus Depot Art Centre; p166), and you have your own studio. Are you moving away from street art? Working in the street is harder. It means working on your own, with more obstacles. But it's more challenging, more exciting. I'm always trying to channel people's interest and enthusiasm about public art, and encourage them to step away from souvenir shops.

Zacharevic's success has inspired similar works such as '101 Lost Kittens', a series of murals commissioned for the 2013 George Town Festival with the intent of bringing attention to the issue of stray animals, as well as many examples of privately-funded public art. It has also inspired more commercial knock-offs such as street-art-themed cafes and a '3D art' museum.

Marking George Town, a map showing the location of pieces by Ernest Zacharevic and the other the artists mentioned above, can be found at the office of Penang Global Tourism (p182).

enthusiastic Nazlina will teach you how to make those dishes you've fallen in love with while in Penang. A course begins with a visit to a morning market and a local breakfast, followed by instruction in three or four dishes. Afternoon lessons are vegan/vegetarian.

Penang Homecooking School COOKING COURSE
(www.penanghomecookingschool.com; classes RM270-320; ⏲Mon, Wed & Fri) Three times a week, Pearly and Chandra open their home to teach visitors how to make Indian, Nonya and street dishes. Courses are flexible in terms of scope and time (see the website), and the fee varies depending on how many dishes you want to make. A half-day course includes transportation and a visit to a market.

Inner Peace Yoga Circle YOGA
(☎016-411 0153; www.innerpeaceyogacircle.com; 293 Jln Burma; drop-in class RM20) Offers all types of yoga plus retreats and teacher-training programs. The class schedule is available on the website.

Tours

There's a huge variety of self-guided tours of George Town, from food walks to those focusing on traditional trades or architecture – pick up a pamphlet of the routes at the state tourist office or at the Penang Heritage Trust (p182). Likewise, the Penang Global Ethic Project (www.globalethicpenang.net) has put together a World Religion Walk that takes you past the iconography and houses of worship of Christians, Muslims, Hindus, Sikhs, Buddhists and Chinese traditional religion.

If walking isn't your thing, consider the **Hop-On Hop-Off** (www.myhoponhopoff.com/pg; adult/child per 24hr RM45/24, per 48hr RM79/43; ⏲9am-8pm) bus's city route, which winds its way around the perimeter of the Unesco protected zone. It's a good way to get a quick overview of the town, and you can get on and off at one of 17 stops.

George Town Heritage Walks WALKING TOUR
(☎016-440 6823; joannkhaw@gmail.com; tours from RM180) Discover George Town – and beyond – with Joann Khaw, a Penang native and heritage expert who also leads architecture and food tours of inland Penang, among others. Excursions require at least two people and advance notice.

Penang Heritage Trust WALKING TOUR
(PHT; ☎04-264 2631; www.pht.org.my; 26 Lebuh Gereja; tours RM200; ⏲9am-5pm Mon-Fri, to 1pm Sat) This conservation-minded entity leads well-regarded walking tours of George Town. There are four different walks, ranging from a religious-themed meander to an exploration of George Town's Little India, all led by experienced guides. Walks require at least two people, usually last around three hours, and need advance booking.

Metro Bike Easy Green Travel BICYCLE TOUR
(☎04-229 6434; www.metrobike.com.my; 8A Pengkalan Weld; tours from RM40) This outfit offers a variety of general and more specifically-themed bicycle (and trishaw) tours of George Town. Excursions depart from the company's bike-hire stall on Pengkalan Weld.

Food Tour Penang TOUR
(☎012-212 3473; www.foodtourpenang.com; tour per person RM160) Excellent brunch (9.30am–1.30pm) and dinner (5pm–9pm) tours take in around half a dozen George Town street-food markets and shophouse restaurants revered by locals. All food and drinks are included; come with an empty stomach.

EatingAsia Culinary Excursions WALKING TOUR
(www.eatingasiaculinaryexcursions.com; US$105) The folks behind the food blog EatingAsia offer private, three-hour food tours of George Town and beyond. The tour price drops to US$95 per person for groups of three or more.

Festivals & Events

A good resource for Penang festivals is the state's official tourism website, Visit Penang (www.visitpenang.gov.my). For smaller, more niche events, seek out the Penang Free Sheet, available online (www.facebook.com/TheFreeSheetPenang) or in the form of a newsletter at many guesthouses and cafes.

January–April

Thaipusam RELIGIOUS
(⏲Jan-Feb) This masochistic festival is celebrated as fervently as in Singapore and Kuala Lumpur (KL), but without quite the same crowds. The Sri Mariamman, Nattukotai Chettiar and Waterfall Hilltop temples are the main centres of activity.

Chinese New Year NEW YEAR
(⏲Feb) Celebrated with particular gusto in George Town. The Khoo Kongsi (p165) is done up for the event, and dance troupes and Chinese-opera groups perform all over the city.

Chap Goh Meh CULTURAL
(⏲Feb-Mar) The 15th day of the new year celebrations, during which local girls throw

DON'T MISS

TAKING IT TO THE STREETS

Perhaps taking cues from the city's street food scene, several culture-, art- and performance-related events have taken over George Town's streets in the last few years.

Occupy Beach Street (Legally) (www.facebook.com/occupybeachstreet; Lebuh Pantai; ⌚7am-1pm Sun) Every Sunday, a stretch of Lebuh Pantai (also known as Beach St) and linked side streets are closed to vehicular traffic and replaced by a carnival-like atmosphere of artists, performers and vendors.

Last Fri, Sat, Sun of the Month (www.facebook.com/LFSSPenang) As the name suggests, these are a series of activities and events that take place on the last weekend of each month, revolving around themes of heritage, entertainment, culture and nature. Previous events have included Chinese opera, live classical music, cemetery tours and guided walks of Penang's Botanical Gardens. Check the Facebook page to see what's on when you're in town.

Armenian Street's Got Talent (www.facebook.com/armeniansgt; Lebuh Armenian; ⌚5-10pm Sat) Every Saturday evening, Lebuh Armenian becomes an open-air, amateur Broadway hosting performances ranging from martial arts to drumming.

oranges into the sea. Traditionally the girls would chant 'throw a good orange, get a good husband' while local boys watched and later contacted their dream girl through matchmakers. The new year is also one of the only times to see Baba-Nonya performances of *dondang sayang* (spontaneous and traditional love ballads).

Penang World Music Festival MUSIC
(www.facebook.com/penangworldmusicfestival; ⌚Apr) Two-day festival featuring a line-up of international and local musicians.

May–August

Penang International Dragon Boat Festival CULTURAL
(www.facebook.com/penangdragonboat; ⌚May) A colourful and popular regatta on the Teluk Bahang Dam, featuring traditional dragon boats.

George Town Festival PERFORMING ARTS
(www.georgetownfestival.com; ⌚Aug) A month-long arts and performance festival celebrating the city's Unesco status.

Hungry Ghosts Festival (Phor Thor) CULTURAL
(⌚Aug-Sep) The gates of hell are said to be opened every year on the 15th day of the seventh month of the Chinese lunar calendar. To appease the hungry ghosts, Penangites set out food offerings and endeavour to entertain them with puppet shows and street-side Chinese-opera performances. This is a magical time to be in the city.

September–December

Lantern Festival CULTURAL
(⌚Sep) An islandwide festival celebrated by eating moon cakes, the Chinese sweets once used to carry secret messages for underground rebellions in ancient China.

Deepavali RELIGIOUS
(⌚Oct-Nov) The Hindu Festival of Lights is celebrated with music and dancing at venues in Little India.

Pesta Pulau Pinang CARNIVAL
(www.facebook.com/PestaPulauPinang; ⌚Nov-Dec) The annual Penang Island Festival features various cultural events, parades and a funfair in George Town.

Sleeping

The George Town of today has all the accommodation options you would expect of an established and growing tourism destination, from the grungiest hostels to the swankiest hotels and, in particular, some really charming boutiques.

The bulk of the city's budget hotels are located along Love Lane and Jln Muntri. If your budget is under RM100, that most likely means you'll be sleeping in a dorm bed, although a few places offer private rooms under the RM200 level. Moving up to midrange, dozens of George Town's shophouses have been converted into small 'heritage' hotels, although this moniker can mean just about anything nowadays. It's also worth noting that rooms in retrofitted shophouses

OFF THE BEATEN TRACK

BUDDHISM IN PENANG

While Malaysia is officially and predominantly Muslim, the Chinese population has remained mostly Buddhist. As one of Malaysia's most Chinese states, Penang has an uncommonly diverse and burgeoning Buddhist community that embraces not only traditional Chinese Buddhism but also the Thai and Burmese schools of Buddhist philosophy.

Kek Lok Si Temple (www.kekloksitemple.com; ⌚7am-9pm) The 'Temple of Supreme Bliss' is also the largest Buddhist temple in Malaysia and one of the most recognisable buildings in the country. Built by an immigrant Chinese Buddhist in 1890, Kek Lok Si is a cornerstone of the Malay-Chinese community, who provided the funding for its two-decade-long building (and ongoing additions).

The temple is in Air Itam, 8km from the centre of George Town. A taxi starts at about RM25, or you can hop on bus 204 (RM2.70).

To reach the entrance, walk through a maze of souvenir stalls, past a tightly packed turtle pond and murky fish ponds, until you reach **Ban Po Thar** (Ten Thousand Buddhas Pagoda; admission RM2), a seven-tier, 30m-high tower. The design is said to be Burmese at the top, Chinese at the bottom and Thai in between. A **cable car** (1-way/return RM3/6; ⌚8.30am-5.30pm) whisks you to the highest level, which is presided over by an awesome 36.5m-high bronze statue of Kuan Yin, goddess of mercy.

There are several other temples in this complex, as well as shops and a **vegetarian restaurant** (mains from RM5; ⌚10am-7pm Tue-Sun; ✎).

Wat Chayamangkalaram (Temple of the Reclining Buddha; Lg Burma; ⌚7am-6pm) The Temple of the Reclining Buddha is a typically Thai temple with it sharp-eaved roofs and ceiling accents. Inside it houses a 33m-long reclining Buddha draped in a gold-leafed saffron robe.

The temple is located about 2.5km northwest of central George Town; a taxi here will cost RM15.

Dhammikarama Burmese Buddhist Temple (Lg Burma; ⌚7am-6pm) A rare instance of a Burmese Buddhist temple outside Burma (now Myanmar). There's a series of panel paintings on the life of the Buddha lining the walkways, the characters dressed in typical Burmese costume, while inside typically round-eyed, serene-faced Burmese Buddha statues stare out at worshippers. This was Penang's first Buddhist temple, built in 1805; it has been significantly added to over the years.

The temple is located about 2.5km northwest of central George Town; a taxi here will cost RM15.

Wat Buppharam (8 Jln Perak; ⌚8am-6pm) This Thai temple is home to the 'Lifting Buddha', a renowned, 100-year-old, gold-leaf-encrusted Buddha statue about the size of a well-fed house cat.

As a seeker, kneel in front of the Buddha statue, pay respects to the figure with a clear mind and then ask, in your mind, the yes or no question you wish to have answered; ask also that you wish for the figure to become light for an affirmative answer. Try to lift the statue. To verify the answer, ask your question again, only this time ask that the statue become heavy. Lift again. When the statue is heavy it won't budge and when it's light it lifts off the platform like a butterfly.

To reach Wat Buppharam, heading northwest on Jln Burma, turn right on Jln Perak about 500m after Hotel 1926; the temple is about 150m down this road.

Kuan Yin Teng (Temple of the Goddess of Mercy; Jln Masjid Kapital Keling; ⌚24hr) This temple is dedicated to Kuan Yin – the goddess of mercy, good fortune, peace and fertility. Built in the early 19th century by the first Hokkien and Cantonese settlers in Penang, the temple isn't so impressive architecturally, but it's very central and popular with the Chinese community, and seems to be forever swathed in smoke from the outside furnaces where worshippers burn paper money, and from the incense sticks waved around inside.

often don't have en suite bathrooms. The top end is where George Town excels, with an impressive selection of unique and atmospheric small hotels.

In general, hotel prices increase on weekends and holidays. And despite all the accommodation options in George Town, just about everything fills up quickly, so be sure to book ahead – especially if a holiday, such as Chinese New Year, is approaching.

Inside the Unesco Protected Zone

Ryokan
HOSTEL $

(☑ 04-250 0287; www.myryokan.com; 62 Jln Muntri; incl breakfast dm RM34-50, r RM158; ❄ @ 🛜) This flashpacker hostel boasts a minimalist – if not particularly Japanese – feel. The dorms, which range from four to six beds (and two women-only rooms), are almost entirely white, and the communal 'Chillax', TV and reading rooms are similarly chic, and come equipped with iPads. Private rooms with en suite bathrooms have the same vibe yet, lacking windows and space, feel slightly overpriced.

80's Guesthouse
HOSTEL $

(☑ 04-263 8806; www.the80sguesthouse.com; 46 Love Lane; incl breakfast dm RM36-39, r with shared bathroom RM63-99; ❄ @ 🛜) The 1980s theme here rather confusingly includes film posters from the early 1950s, but that has no impact on the minimalist but comfortable dorms (which range from four to six beds) and rooms, all of which share central bathrooms.

Time Capsule Hotel
HOSTEL $

(☑ 04-263 0888; www.timecapsule.my; 418 Lebuh Chulia; dm incl breakfast RM55; ❄ @ 🛜) If you aspire to feel like a Japanese salaryman in the '80s – or just want to save some ringgit – consider a stay at this new and unique hostel. Upon checking in, you'll receive a bag of toiletries, slippers and, if needed, pyjamas, before being led to your bed: a futuristic pod equipped with TV, wi-fi, lights and a safe.

Broadway Budget Hotel
HOTEL $

(☑ 04-262 8550; www.broadwaybudgethotel.com; 35F Jln Masjid Kapitan Keling; r RM77-157; ❄ 🛜) If you're OK with sacrificing atmosphere for savings, consider the Broadway. Rooms are starkly bare and mostly small, but are clean and centrally located, and include en suite bathrooms.

House of Journey
HOSTEL $

(www.facebook.com/houseofjourney; 45 & 47 Lg Seckchuan; incl breakfast dm RM30-35, r RM100-120; ❄ 🛜) The dorms here are largely unremarkable, but the six private rooms, although cramped and not all boasting en suite bathrooms, represent a relative bargain.

Reggae Penang
HOSTEL $

(☑ 04-262 6772; www.reggaehostelsmalaysia.com; 57 Love Lane; dm incl breakfast RM30-40; ❄ @ 🛜) Perfect for the social traveller, this expansive heritage building holds several four- to 12-bed dorm rooms. Beds are double-decker pod style, and have individual lights, power point and free wi-fi. The lobby, outfitted with pool table and coffee shop, feels more like a bar than a hostel. There's another branch nearby on Lebuh Chulia.

Couzicats
HOSTEL $

(☑ 04-261 3296; 84 Lebuh Gereja; d/r RM25/65; ❄ 🛜 ≋) If the room names (Drunk, Absolute Vodka) aren't explicit enough, the owner's declaration that 'There's a party here every day' should give you a clear idea of the vibe of this self-professed 'party hostel'. As such, service standards may not be sky-high, but dorm beds and rooms are clean and relatively comfortable.

★ Ren i Tang
HOTEL $$

(☑ 04-250 8383; www.renitang.com; 82A Lebuh Penang; r incl breakfast RM218-455; ❄ 🛜) A lengthy and careful restoration has transformed this former Chinese-medicine wholesaler's into a warm, inviting small hotel. The rooms, which carry charming reminders of the building's former life, span several types, sizes and layouts; we particularly liked the corner Tub Room, equipped with a wooden soaking tub and fragrant bath salts.

Cintra Heritage House
HOTEL $$

(☑ 04-262 8232; www.cintrahouse.com; 1 Lebuh Cintra; incl breakfast r RM100-180, ste RM230; ❄ 🛜) Cool, spacious spacious rooms with en suite bathroom – under the RM200 barrier. Rooms aren't equipped with TV, but friendly staff and the attached cafe serve as ample distractions.

Sinkeh
HOTEL $$

(☑ 04-261 3966; www.sinkeh.com; 105 Lebuh Melayu; r incl breakfast RM198-280; ❄ 🛜) Yes, Sinkeh is located in an old shophouse, but unlike its counterparts, modern concrete, glass and steel set the tone. Despite this,

service is warm and the rooms are comfortable, if not particularly spacious.

Chulia Heritage BOUTIQUE HOTEL $$
(☎04-263 3380; www.chuliaheritagehotel.com; 380 Lebuh Chulia; r RM90-280; ❄📶) The White House would be a more apt name for this hotel. It's housed in an all-white former mansion, with smallish rooms also decked out in virginal white with, of course, white furnishings and amenities. It's all very pure and clean, if somewhat lacking in atmosphere (not to mention colour). The cheapest rooms lack windows and share bathrooms.

New Asia Heritage Hotel HOTEL $$
(☎04-262 6171; www.newasiahotel.net; 71 Lebuh Kimberley; r RM98-158, ste RM158; ❄📶) As we were told by the gruff-but-friendly manager here, 'The most important thing about this hotel is that everything is the same in every room'. And he's right; the 24 rooms in this plain but clean and comfortable midranger are similarly equipped with TV, air-con, and functional furniture, although some rooms are slightly larger and have vast balconies.

Moon Tree 47 HOTEL $$
(☎04-264 4021; moontree47@gmail.com; 47 Jln Muntri; r RM70-290; ❄📶) This rambling shophouse has a funky, retro vibe and friendly service, making it a fun choice for young couples or solo travellers. Yet it's worth mentioning that some might be put off by some of the hotel's rather rustic amenities and features. The three tight rooms in the main structure share a bathroom, while the remaining five rooms have more space and en suite bathrooms.

Victoria Inn HOTEL $$
(☎04-262 2278; www.victoriainn.com.my; 278 Lebuh Victoria; incl breakfast dm RM53, r RM121.90-159; ❄📶) There's just a hint of style here, from the faux wood floors, splashes of paint and arty Penang photos on the walls, but other than that it's really just a standard midranger with good beds, TV, air-con and attached bathrooms.

Hotel Malaysia HOTEL $$
(☎04-263 3311; www.hotelmalaysia.com.my; 7 Jln Penang; r incl breakfast RM140-190; ❄@📶) It's definitely not the sexiest hotel in town, but the spacious and recently-renovated rooms boasting crisp sheets, professional service and views to the Penang Bridge make this place a winner in the bland category, and a great deal for the price.

Yeng Keng Hotel HISTORIC HOTEL $$
(☎04-262 2177; www.yengkenghotel.com; 362 Lebuh Chulia; incl breakfast r RM286-423, ste RM423-495; ❄@📶🏊) The Yeng Keng is a revamp of a 150-year-old hotel. Its latest incarnation includes rather small rooms decked out in occasionally cheesy Chinese touches, but a convenient location and an inviting pool are incentives enough to overlook this.

Segara Ninda HOTEL $$
(☎04-262 8748; www.segaraninda.com; 20 Jln Penang; r RM100-180; ❄@📶) This elegant century-old villa was once the town residence of Ku Din Ku Meh, a wealthy timber merchant and colonial administrator. His home has been tastefully renovated, incorporating original features such as the carved wooden ventilation panels, staircase and tiled floors. By contrast, the 16 rooms are simply furnished, but the place boasts an inviting, home-like atmosphere.

My Chew Jetty HOMESTAY $$
(☎013-438 1217; www.mychewjetty.com; Chew Jetty; r incl breakfast RM148-168; ❄📶) For the epitome of a local experience, book one of the basic rooms in this pier-bound home at the edge of George Town's biggest clan jetty. You'll be crashing with a local family; bathrooms are shared and the noise from grandma's TV is included for free.

Penaga Hotel HISTORIC HOTEL $$$
(☎04-261 1891; www.hotelpenaga.com; cnr Lg Hutton & Jln Transfer; incl breakfast r RM370-501, ste RM549-954; ❄@📶🏊) This hotel takes up most of a city block, spanning three sections: a row of two-storey family-friendly minihomes, apartment-sized suites, and spacious rooms. All are decorated with a mix of original art, vintage-themed furnishings, and some charming touches such as cowhide rugs and midcentury furniture. The stack of amenities includes a pool, central gardens and a coffee shop.

Eastern & Oriental Hotel HOTEL $$$
(E&O; ☎04-222 2000; www.eohotels.com; 10 Lebuh Farquhar; ste incl breakfast RM960-3910; ❄@📶🏊) Dating back to 1885, the E&O is one of those rare hotels for which historic opulence has gracefully moved into the present day. We fancy the suites in the original Heritage Wing, which seamlessly blend modern comfort with colonial-era style using hardwood antiques and vintage-themed furnishings; those with a sea view are worth the extra outlay.

East Indies Mansion HOTEL $$$
(☎ 04-261 8025; www.eastindies.com.my; 25 Lebuh China; r incl breakfast RM285-650; ❄ 📶) This Chinese-style shophouse has been converted into a secluded-feeling small hotel. The seven rooms vary considerably, with some spanning two floors, but are united in a design theme that brings together retro touches and colourful, chunky furniture, not to mention the open-air courtyard and other inviting communal areas.

China Tiger APARTMENT $$$
(☎ 012-501 5360, 04-264 3580; www.chinatiger.info; 29 Lebuh China; r RM500; ❄ @ 📶) Fancy feeling at home even when you're away? Then consider a stay at one of China Tiger's two open-concept, self-catering, apartment-like rooms. They can accommodate up to five people, and include heaps of space, natural light and functional kitchenettes.

Muntri Mews HOTEL $$$
(☎ 04-263 5125; www.muntrimews.com; 77 Jln Muntri; r incl breakfast RM380; ❄ @ 📶) This building's original owners would no doubt be shocked to learn that their former stablehouse (mews) is today an attractive boutique hotel. The 13 rooms have a minimalist, studio-like vibe, with each boasting retro-themed furniture,

GEORGE TOWN'S BEST HERITAGE HOTELS

After decades of neglect, locals (and increasingly, outsiders) have come to realise the value of George Town's buildings, and have transformed many into some of the region's more unique accommodation.

Indeed, today's George Town is home to so many so-called 'heritage hotels' that the term is used to describe anything from a hostel to a featureless contemporary hotel. With this in mind, we list our favourite places that we feel embody the true meaning of 'heritage' by retaining the inherent old-world charm and atmosphere of the city's architecture.

Campbell House (☎ 04-261 8290; www.campbellhousepenang.com; 106 Lebuh Campbell; r incl breakfast RM350-460; ❄ @ 📶) This former hotel, dating back to 1903, is seeing a new life as a thoughtful, sumptuous boutique. The European owners have employed their extensive experience in the luxury world to include amenities such as fragrant, locally sourced toiletries, beautiful Peranakan tiles in the bathrooms, Nespresso machines and high-quality mattresses – this in addition to excellent service and overwhelmingly positive feedback from guests. Highly recommended.

23 Love Lane (☎ 04-262 1323; www.23lovelane.com; 23 Love Lane; r incl breakfast RM800-1200; ❄ @ 📶) The 12 rooms here, which are found both in the main structure (a former mansion) or the surrounding buildings (former kitchen and stables), tastefully combine antique furniture and fixtures with modern design touches and artsy accents. There's lots of open spaces and high ceilings to catch the breezes, inviting communal areas, a peaceful aura, and service that complements the casual, homely vibe.

Straits Collection (☎ 04-262 7299; www.straitscollection.com; 89-95 Lebuh Armenian; ste RM530-570; ❄ @ 📶) If, after having explored George Town, you have fantasies of living in a restored Chinese shophouse, then consider a stay here. Each residence is essentially a house (but with no cooking facilities), decorated with eye-catching art, regional antiques, bright-coloured cushions and rugs. Each is different but all have some sort of unforgettable detail such as light-well courtyards, wooden Japanese bathtubs or ancient sliding doors.

Blue Mansion (☎ 04-262 0006; www.thebluemansion.com.my; 14 Lebuh Leith; r incl breakfast RM800-1050; ❄ @ 📶 🏊) If you were impressed with the Blue Mansion (p159), you don't necessarily have to leave. This house museum is home to one of Penang's first boutique hotels, and after a recent renovation, holds its own among the city's best. Rooms are spacious and cool, and come outfitted with charming antique furniture. But best of all, you get the chance to eat, sleep and live in one of the city's most emblematic buildings.

Coffee Atelier (☎ 04-261 2261; www.coffeeatelier.com; 47-55 Lg Stewart; ste incl breakfast RM380-440; ❄ 📶) Unlike the rather slick heritage hotels you'll find elsewhere in town, the renovation of these two shophouses dating back to 1927 has left them feeling wonderfully rustic, and the peeling paint and quirky original furnishings provide heaps of character. Each house is divided into two units, with a second smaller bedroom on the first floor and huge courtyard-style bathrooms on the ground floor.

an attractive black-and-white tiled bathroom, and vast 'double queen' beds.

If full, consider the similar and associated rooms in **Muntri Grove** (☎04-261 5107; www.muntrigrove.com; 127 Jln Muntri; r incl breakfast RM400; ❄📶🏊), just up the road, or the spacious shophouse-bound rooms in **Muntri Mews Residence** (☎04-263 5125; www.muntrimewsresidence.com; 64 Jln Muntri; r incl breakfast RM550; ❄📶), across the street.

Seven Terraces HOTEL $$$
(☎04-264 2333; www.7terraces.com; Lg Stewart; ste incl breakfast RM550-2200; ❄@📶🏊) This hotel, crafted from a row of seven joined shophouses, has taken the crown as the most luxurious place to stay in central George Town. The 18 two-storey suites (including three even larger multiroom 'apartments') are vast and regal-feeling, and have been decorated with a mix of original antiques, reproductions and contemporary pieces, and surround a beautiful central courtyard.

Outside the Unesco Protected Zone

★**Museum Hotel** HOTEL $$
(☎04-226 6668; www.museumhotel.com.my; 72 Jln AS Mansor; r incl breakfast RM176-500; ❄@📶) Attractive, comfortable, boasting great service and representing good value, the Museum Hotel is a gem of a midranger. Located in a stately city block of restored shophouses, the 22 rooms here range from tight-but-comfy singles to larger rooms, all tastefully decorated with antique and vintage-themed design touches, and looked after by capable staff.

Noordin Street House HOTEL $$
(☎04-262 7173; www.noordinstreethouse.com; 71 Lebuh Noordin; r incl breakfast RM315-450; ❄@📶🏊) A charming, home-like boutique has been coaxed out of this rambling shophouse. Almost as noteworthy as the eight eclectic rooms are the inviting public spaces they share, which include a pool and restaurant.

GLOW HOTEL $$
(☎04-226 0084; www.glowbyzinc.com/penang; 101 Jln Macalister; r incl breakfast RM175-390; ❄@📶🏊) A chain with charm. And with lots of space. And a location near tonnes of street food. And it's great value. There's certainly a lot to like about this young-feeling hotel, located about 700m north of the intersection with Jln Penang.

Palanquinn BOUTIQUE HOTEL $$
(☎04-227 1088; www.palanquinn.com; 20 Lg Bangkok; r RM200-350; ❄@📶) Palanquinn comprises three houses dating back to 1927. We particularly liked the huge bathrooms – some with retractable roof – in most units. And you'd be hard-pressed to find a friendlier and more courteous host than Kelvyn.

Lg Bangkok is located just off Jln Burma, about 2.5km north of Jln Transfer, and a RM15 taxi ride from central George Town.

THE EASTERN & ORIENTAL HOTEL

Originally built in 1884, the stylish E&O (p172) was the archetypal 19th-century colonial grand hotel. It was established by two of the Armenian Sarkies brothers, Tigram and Martin, the most famous hoteliers in the East, who later founded the Raffles Hotel in Singapore.

In the 1920s, the Sarkies promoted the E&O as the 'Premier Hotel East of Suez'. High-ranking colonial officials and wealthy planters and merchants filed through its grand lobby, and the E&O was established as a centre for Penang's social elite. Rudyard Kipling, Noel Coward and Somerset Maugham were just some of the famous faces who passed through its doors.

The Sarkies almost closed the E&O when the rent was raised from £200 to £350 a month, but they kept it open largely at the insistence of Arshak Sarkies, the third brother (and a gambler by nature). Arshak's tastes were legendary – some observers said he ran the E&O not to make money, but to entertain. Shortly before his death, Arshak began lavish renovations to the hotel. This expense, coupled with loans to friends that were conveniently forgotten, finally bankrupted the family business in 1931.

In the 1990s, the E&O closed and fell into disrepair, but a huge renovation program came to its rescue. In 2001 it once again opened for business, as a luxury, all-suite grand hotel with elegant, spacious rooms decorated in the best of colonial style.

Yes Hotel HOTEL $$
(☎04-226 6501; yeshotelpenang@gmail.com; 60 Jln Transfer; r RM89-159; ❄📶) From the outside, the Yes is an unabashed architectural eyesore. But a peek inside reveals a midranger that delivers the goods – air-con, TV, en suite bathroom – in a new and tidy, if rather sterile-feeling, package.

Noordin Mews HOTEL $$
(☎04-263 7125; www.noordinmews.com; 77 Lebuh Noordin; incl breakfast r RM365, ste RM500-694; ❄@📶🏊) These two restored shophouses boast an attractive midcentury feel, down to the antique adverts and retro furniture. A pool and a secluded-feeling location away from the main tourist drag are additional draws.

Clove Hall HOTEL $$$
(☎04-229 0818; www.clovehall.com; 11 Jln Clove Hall; ste incl breakfast RM575-675; ❄📶🏊) An Edwardian Anglo-Malay mansion housing six luxury suites, Clove Hall is the place to go if you want to feel and be treated like a mogul of the early 1900s – hardly surprising giving that the structure was originally the Sarkies brothers' first Penang home.

Jln Clove Hall intersects with Jln Burma about 1km north of Jln Transfer; a RM15 taxi ride from central George Town.

Mango Tree Place HOTEL $$$
(☎04-246 2132; www.mangotreeplace.com.my; 29 Jln Phuah Hin Leong; r incl breakfast RM280-480; ❄@📶) Open spaces, primary colours, attractive furniture and natural light establish the vibe at these shophouses dating back to 1934. Ground-floor rooms have a garden terrace while the-upper floor rooms have two bedrooms.

Jln Phuah Hin Leong is located off Jln Burma, about 1km north of Jln Transfer; a long walk or a RM15 taxi ride from central George Town.

G Hotel HOTEL $$$
(☎04-238 0000; www.ghotel.com.my; 168 Persiaran Gurney; incl breakfast r RM763-923, ste RM1033-2383; ❄@📶🏊) The 303 rooms here are studies in minimalist, cubist cool. Collections of geometric form set off by swatches of blocky colour give the G a vibe that's as Manhattan as it is Malaysia. For something even hipper, consider the G's younger sibling, the adjacent G Kelawai.

The hotel is about 3.5km northwest of central George Town; a taxi here should cost around RM20.

Eating

We're just going to come out and say it: George Town is the best food city in Southeast Asia. It's easily the most diverse; in one block alone you can find Malay, regional Chinese, *mamak* (halal Indian/South Asian), regional Indian, Peranakan or Nonya (a blend of Chinese, Malay and sometimes Thai) and other unique blends of local and Chinese cuisines. Yet best of all, the quality's also there, and the locals are as crazy about the food as the visitors.

Another plus to George Town's food scene is its informality. As you'll see, eating in George Town doesn't necessary have to mean restaurants; the city is renowned for its hawker centres (p177), hubs of cheap, informal, delicious dining.

Inside the Unesco Protected Zone

Veloo Villas INDIAN $
(22 Lebuh Penang; mains from RM2, set meals RM5-9.50; ⌚7am-10pm; ✍) For one meal, set aside notions of service – and ambience – and instead focus on the vibrant, fun southern Indian cuisine. Come from approximately 11am to 4pm for hearty and diverse rice-based set meals, or outside of these hours for *dosa* (paper-thin rice-and-lentil crêpes) and other snacks.

Sup Hameed MALAYSIAN $
(48 Jln Penang; mains from RM3; ⌚24hr) On the surface, this is very much your typical *nasi kandar* (South Asian Muslim–influenced) shop found all over Malaysia, and we don't particularly recommend eating here during the day. But come night, Hameed sets out tables on the street and serves his incredibly rich and meaty soups (try *sup kambing* – goat soup), served with slices of white bread.

Sky Cafe CHINESE $
(Lebuh Chulia; mains RM1-6; ⌚11am-2pm) This gem sits in the middle of the greatest concentration of travellers in George Town, yet is somehow almost exclusively patronised (in enthusiastic numbers) by locals. Come on the early side of the three-hour open window for *char siew* (barbequed pork) and *siew yoke* (pork belly) that are considered among the best in town.

Hameediyah MALAYSIAN $
(164 Lebuh Campbell; mains RM5-35; ⌚10am-11pm Sat-Thu, 10am-12.30pm & 2-11pm Fri) Dating back to 1907 and allegedly the oldest *nasi*

kandar in Malaysia, Hameediyah looked it until a recent and much-needed facelift. In addition to rich curries served over rice, try the *murtabak*, a *roti prata* (flaky, flat bread) stuffed with minced mutton, chicken or vegetables, egg and spices.

Yin's Sourdough Bakery BAKERY **$**
(11 Pesara Claimant; mains RM4.50-25; 7am-6pm Mon-Fri, to 2pm Sat;) Tired of rice? Weary of noodles? Head here for some of the city's best bread, served in the form of creative sandwiches, pastries and breakfasts.

Tho Yuen Restaurant CHINESE **$**
(92 Lebuh Campbell; dim sum RM1-5; 6am-3pm Wed-Mon) Our favourite place for dim sum. It's packed with newspaper-reading loners and chattering groups of locals all morning long, but you can usually squeeze in somewhere. Servers speak minimal English but do their best to explain the contents of their carts.

Karai Kudi INDIAN **$**
(20 Lebuh Pasar; set meals RM8-18, mains RM3-24; 11am-11pm;) Come to this restaurant during lunchtime (11am to 4pm) for tasty, great-value, southern-Indian-style banana-leaf set meals, and breakfast or dinnertime for southern- and northern-Indian specialities.

Quay Café VEGETARIAN **$**
(2 Gat Lebuh Gereja; mains RM5-15; 11am-2.30pm Mon-Sat;) A modern-feeling cafeteria serving Asian-style meat-free dishes. Expect set meals, an emphasis on noodle dishes, and fresh juices and herbal teas.

Sri Ananda Bahwan INDIAN **$**
(55 Lebuh Penang; mains from RM3; 7am-10pm;) The local version of fast food – but much better – this place is busy and buzzy, and whips up everything from tandoori chicken to vegetarian Indian dishes.

★ **Teksen** CHINESE **$$**
(18 Lebuh Carnarvon; mains RM10-28; noon-3pm & 6-9pm Wed-Mon) There's a reason this place is always packed with happy locals: it's one of the tastiest, most consistent restaurants in town (and in a place like George Town that's saying a lot). You almost can't go wrong here, but don't miss the favourites – the 'double roasted pork with chilli padi' is obligatory and delicious – and be sure to ask about the daily specials.

Jawi House MALAYSIAN **$$**
(www.jawihouse.com; 85 Lebuh Armenian; mains RM16-27; 11am-10pm Wed-Mon;) This cosy, shophouse restaurant specialises in the type of unique Muslim dishes you'd be hard-pressed to find outside of a local home or celebration. We loved the fragrant, meaty 'Jawi briyani', but you may like the 'lemuni rice', which is seasoned with a type of flower.

Da Shu Xia Seafood House CHINESE **$$**
(Tree Shade Seafood Restaurant; cnr Gat Lebuh Armenian & Lebuh Victoria; mains RM10-50; 11am-3.30pm & 5-10pm Thu-Tue) In new digs that lack the shade of the eponymous tree, this open-air shack remains where locals go for cheap and tasty seafood. Pick your aquatic protein from the trays out front, and the staff will fry, steam, soup or grill it up for you.

Kashmir INDIAN **$$**
(105 Jln Penang; mains RM7.90-59.90; 11am-10pm;) A recent move has left this staple feeling more like a bar than a restaurant. But rest assured that this has had no impact on Kashmir's delicious tandoori. Attentive service, an assertive Indian soundtrack (with live music on Saturday and Sunday nights) and cocktails complete the package.

Junk Cafe AMERICAN **$$**
(401 Lebuh Chulia; mains RM19.50-22; noon-10pm Thu-Tue;) Some claim the burgers at this casual spot are the best in town. With a short drinks list and a fun, eclectic vibe, Junk also doubles as a bar.

Edelweiss SWISS **$$**
(38 Lebuh Armenian; mains RM18-39.50; noon-3pm & 6.30-10pm Tue-Fri, noon-10pm Sat, noon-7pm Sun;) Items like Currywurst and bratwurst may carry a German accent, but fondue and rösti (Swiss-style potato pancakes) solidify Edelweiss' Swiss-ness. The antique-filled dining room is a delight, and there's a selection of imported beers.

★ **China House** INTERNATIONAL **$$$**
(04-263 7299; www.chinahouse.com.my; 153 & 155 Lebuh Pantai; 9am-midnight) Where do we start? This complex of three cojoined shophouses features a dining outlet, a cafe/bakery, Kopi C (p180); and a bar, Canteen (p178), not to mention a shop and gallery.

BTB (mains RM44.52-76.32; 6.30-10.30pm;), the flagship dining venue, does a relatively short but exotic-sounding menu of Malaysian-, Middle Eastern- and Mediterranean-influenced dishes; think 'rack of lamb with cumin crust, smoked eggplant puree and eggplant gingerbud sambal'.

HAWKER-STALL HEAVEN

Not eating at a hawker stall in George Town is like missing the Louvre in Paris – you simply have to do it. There are tonnes of hawker centres in and around town, from shophouse-bound 'cafes' to open-air conglomerates of mobile stalls.

Keep in mind that hawker-stall vendors run flexible schedules, so don't be surprised if one isn't there during your visit. A good strategy is to avoid Mondays and Thursdays, when many vendors tend to stay at home.

Lg Baru (New Lane) Hawker Stalls (cnr Jln Macalister & Lg Baru; mains from RM3; ⏲dinner) Ask locals what their favourite hawker stalls are, and they'll always mention this night-time street extravaganza. Just about everything's available here, but we like the *char koay kak* stall, which in addition to spicy fried rice cakes with seafood, also does great *otak otak* (a steamed fish curry).

Lg Baru intersects with Jln Macalister about 250m northwest of the intersection with Jln Penang.

Pulau Tikus Hawker Stalls (cnr Solok Moulmein & Jln Burma; ⏲6am-2pm) Before yet another bland guesthouse breakfast gets you down, consider a visit to this busy morning market area. A cluster of cafes sell Hokkien *mee*, curry *mee*, *mie goreng* and other dishes that have earned die-hard fans.

The market is located across from Pulau Tikus's police station, about 2.5km north of Jln Penang; a taxi here will set you back about RM20.

Lebuh Presgrave Hawker Stalls (cnr Lebuh Presgrave & Lebuh Mcnair; ⏲4.30pm-midnight Fri-Wed) A famous Hokkien *mee* vendor draws most folks to this open-air hawker convocation, but there's lots to keep you around for a second course, from *lor bak* (deep-fried meats dipped in sauce) to a stall selling hard-to-find Peranakan/Nonya dishes.

Sea Pearl Lagoon Cafe (off Jln Tanjong Tokong; mains from RM8; ⏲5-10pm Thu-Tue) The unique location of this basic hawker centre – seemingly hidden in a Chinese temple complex looking out over the North Channel – and its excellent food make the Sea Pearl one of our favourite places to eat outside the city centre.

Sea Pearl Lagoon is located in Tanjong Toking, 7km northwest of George Town. A taxi here will set you back at least RM25.

Joo Hooi Cafe (cnr Jln Penang & Lebuh Keng Kwee; mains from RM3; ⏲11am-5pm) The hawker centre equivalent of one-stop shopping, this tiny shophouse has all of Penang's best dishes in one location: laksa, *rojak* (a 'salad' of crispy fruits and vegetables in a thick, slightly sweet dressing), *char kway teow* and the city's most famous vendor of *cendol* (a sweet snack of squiggly noodles in shaved ice with palm sugar and coconut milk).

Gurney Drive Hawker Stalls (Persiaran Gurney; mains from RM3; ⏲5pm-midnight) Penang's most famous food area sits amid modern high-rise buildings bordered by the sea. It's particularly known for its laksa stalls (try stall 11) and the delicious *rojak* at Ah Chye.

Persiaran Gurney is located about 3km west of George Town, near Gurney Plaza. A taxi here will set you back at least RM20.

Kafe Kheng Pin (80 Jln Penang; mains from RM4; ⏲7am-3pm Tue-Sun) The must-eats at this old-school-feeling hawker joint include a legendary *lor bak* and an exquisite Hainanese chicken rice (steamed chicken with broth and rice).

Lg Selamat Hawker Stalls (cnr Jl Macalister & Lg Selamat; ⏲noon-7pm Wed-Mon) The southern end of this eponymous strip is largely associated with Kafe Heng Huat, lauded for doing the city's best *char kway teow*, but adjacent stalls sell *lor bak*, *rojak*, *won ton mee* (wheat-and-egg-noodle soup) and other Chinese Penang staples.

Lg Selamat intersects with Jln Macalister about 500m northwest of the intersection with Jln Penang.

LOCAL KNOWLEDGE

BEE YINN LOW: FOOD WRITER

Bee is a native of Penang, a best-selling author, and the blogger behind popular cooking website Rasa Malaysia (www.rasamalaysia.com).

How is the food of Penang different than elsewhere in Malaysia? Penang is predominantly Chinese, so you will find myriad Chinese dishes. It's a Straits settlement, so one can find delicious Nonya (Peranakan) food, an extremely scrumptious and deeply flavourful cuisine that marries Chinese dishes with local herbs, spices, ingredients and produce. The surrounding sea in Penang also offers abundant fresh seafood such as shrimp, cockles and fish, which are widely used in local hawker fare.

What are a few dishes visitors to Penang should make a point of seeking out? *Char kway teow,* flat rice noodles fried with prawns, cockles, and Chinese sausage; Hokkien *mee,* a noodle dish with a rich, shrimp-based broth, and topped with shrimp, pork, and fried shallots; *asam laksa*, rice noodles in a spicy and sour fish broth, garnished with herbs and vegetables; and curry *mee*, noodles in spicy and aromatic curry broth with fried tofu puffs and cockles.

Which hawker centre should visitors not miss? In the evening, head to New Lane (also known as Lg Baru; p177) and try the street food sold by the hawkers in the area.

And what's a good all-around restaurant? I love Hai Boey Seafood (p189), a modest seafood restaurant by the beach at Teluk Kumbar. The food is good and you can't beat the views, especially during sunset.

Any particular fruit or produce visitors shouldn't miss? Penang offers some of the best durian in the region; it's absolutely creamy, rich and sweet.

Is there any sort of drink particularly associated with Penang? Nutmeg juice. You can get it at any coffeeshop.

Kebaya PERANAKAN $$$
(04-264 2333; www.seventerraces.com; Seven Terraces, Lg Stewart; set dinner RM120; 6-10pm Tue-Sun;) Kebaya sets the scene with a stately dining room decorated with a gorgeous collection of antiques, set to a soundtrack of live piano. The Peranakan-influenced cuisine – available only via a set dinner – is an appropriate visual counterpart, but flavour-wise, tends towards the timid end of the spectrum.

Outside the Unesco Protected Zone

Nasi Padang Minang INDONESIAN $
(92 Jln Transfer; mains from RM4; 11am-7pm) Serve-yourself, buffet-style restaurants generally opt for quantity over quality. But the Padang-style Indonesian curries, stir-fries, soups, salads and grilled dishes here are uniformly vibrant and delicious.

Nyonya Breeze Desire PERANAKAN $$
(1st fl, Straits Quay, Tanjung Tokong; mains RM9.90-44.90; 11am-10pm;) This long-standing go-to for Peranakan (or Nonya) cuisine has relocated to a rather charmless setting in a mall. But the food is better than ever, and ranges from several *kerabu* (salads) to staples such as *inche kabin* (deep-fried chicken).

Straits Quay is located about 7km northwest of George Town, in Tanjong Toking; a taxi here from central George Town will set you back about RM25.

Drinking & Nightlife

Between the largely hotel-based bars and some rather grungy pubs and clubs, Penang doesn't have much of a sophisticated bar scene. But it's growing, and there are a few fun places for a night out.

Bars are scattered throughout town, but the strip of road at the far northern end of Jln Penang is George Town's rather commercial-feeling entertainment strip. Another lively – if somewhat budget-oriented – nightlife area is the conglomeration of backpacker pubs near the intersection of Lebuh Chulia and Love Lane.

★Canteen BAR
(www.chinahouse.com.my; China House, 183B Lebuh Victoria; dishes RM10.60-61.48; 9am-11pm) This is about as close as George Town comes to a hipster bar – minus the pretension. Canteen

has an artsy/warehouse vibe, there's live music from 9.30pm, and there are great bar snacks. Canteen is also accessible via China House's entrance on Lebuh Pantai.

Mish Mash BAR
(www.mishmashpg.com; 24 Jln Muntri; ⌚2pm-midnight Tue-Sun) Mish Mash has brought some unique booze – not to mention some much needed panache – to George Town's drinking scene. Come for the city's most well-stocked bar, clever cocktails and some great nonalcoholic drinks (try the 'traditional ginger soda'), as well as a full tobacco counter. There's also food, although we hesitate to endorse Mish Mash as a dinner locale.

Alabama Shake BAR
(www.facebook.com/cjalabamashake; 92 Lebuh Gereja; ⌚4pm-late) Just your average American boozer – if your average American bar was located in Malaysia and was run by a gregarious Serbian and a local. Come to think of it, there's little ordinary about this bar, previously known as B@92, but it gets it right, from tasty American-themed cocktails to slow-cooked pulled-pork sandwiches.

Micke's Place BAR
(94 Love Lane; ⌚noon-late) This eclectic bar-restaurant is both the longest-standing and most fun of the area's backpacker bars. Pull up a grafittied chair, bump to the vintage soundtrack, suck on a shisha and make a new friend.

Behind 50 Love Lane BAR
(Lebuh Muntri; ⌚6pm-1am Wed-Mon) Pocket-sized, retro-themed bar-restaurant that draws a largely local following, despite being close to the backpacker strip. There's a classic rock soundtrack and a short menu of Western-style comfort dishes (RM14.90 to RM18.90).

Beach Blanket Babylon BAR
(32 Jln Sultan Ahmad Shah; ⌚noon-midnight) The open-air setting and relaxed vibe contrast with the rather grand building this bar is linked to. Pair your drink and alfresco views over the North Channel with tasty local dishes.

That Little Wine Bar WINE BAR
(www.thatlittlewinebar.com; 54 Jln Chow Thye; ⌚5pm-midnight Mon-Sat) A chic, cosy bar run by a German chef and his wife. Enjoy a selection of wine – glasses start at RM20 – and champagne cocktails, and consider accompanying your tipple with tapas (RM18 to RM58) or more substantial mains (RM28 to RM58).

Jln Chow Thye is located off Jln Burma, about 1.5km northwest of Jln Transfer. A taxi here will set you back about RM15.

Bagan Bar BAR
(Macalister Mansion, 228 Jln Macalister; ⌚5pm-1am) This sleek, dark, velvet-coated den is probably the most sophisticated bar in town – a fact seemingly verified by the rather strict dress code (no shorts, T-shirts or flip-flops). There's live music from 9pm.

Bagan is located about 1km north of the junction with Jln Penang.

Georgetown Wines BAR
(www.facebook.com/georgetownwines; 19 Lebuh Leith; ⌚5pm-midnight Tue-Sun) Wine bars are the flavour of the moment in George Town, and this one, cleverly built into a former stable, is among the more attractive. Take a walk through the cellar or order house wines by the glass; dinner is best left to another venue.

Gravity BAR
(Rooftop, G Hotel Kelawei, 2 Persiaran Maktab; ⌚6pm-1am) Yes, it's a hotel pool bar. But the breezy rooftop location and great views over the island make Gravity a legitimate drinks destination.

GEORGE TOWN STREET NAMES

Finding your way around George Town can be slightly complicated since many roads have both a Malay and an English name. While many street signs list both, it can still be confusing. We use primarily the Malay name. Here are the two names of some of the main roads:

Malay	English
Lebuh Gereja	Church St
Jln Masjid Kapitan Keling	Pitt St
Jln Tun Syed Sheh Barakbah	The Esplanade
Lebuh Pantai	Beach St
Lebuh Pasar	Market St

To make matters worse, Jln Penang may also be referred to as Jln Pinang or as Penang Rd – but there's also a Penang St, which may also be called Lebuh Pinang! Similarly, Chulia St is Lebuh Chulia but there's also a Lorong Chulia, and this confuses even the taxi drivers.

DON'T MISS

HIGH TEA

Penang's English, Chinese and Indian legacies have left an appreciation for tea that remains strong today. More recent immigrants to George Town have imported an enviable Western-style cafe culture (with good coffee to boot).

Suffolk House (www.suffolkhouse.com.my; 250 Jln Ayer Itam; high tea for 2 RM90; ⏲2.30-6pm) For the ultimate English tea experience, head to this 200-year-old Georgian-style mansion, where high tea, featuring scones and cucumber sandwiches, can be taken inside or in the garden.

Suffolk House is located about 6.5km west of George Town; a taxi here will cost around RM25.

David Brown's Tea Terrace (www.penanghillco.com.my; Penang Hill; afternoon tea RM24-70; ⏲9am-6pm) Located at the top of Penang Hill, this is probably the island's most atmospheric destination for colonial-style high tea (from 3pm to 6pm)

Ten Yee Tea Trading (33 Lebuh Pantai; ⏲9.30am-6.30pm Mon-Sat) Chinese teas are on sale here but the fun part is deciding which to buy. For RM20 you choose a tea (which you can share with up to five people), then Lim, the enthusiastic owner, shows you how to prepare it the proper way.

Jing-Si Books & Cafe (31 Lebuh Pantai; ⏲11am-7pm Mon-Sat, 8am-6pm Sun) An oasis of spiritual calm, this outlet for a Taiwanese Buddhist group's teachings is a wonderful place to revive in hushed surroundings over a pot of interesting tea or coffees – all of which go for RM5.

Kopi C (www.chinahouse.com.my; China House, 153 & 155 Lebuh Pantai; mains from RM10; ⏲9am-midnight) Located in the rambling China House complex, this cafe/bakery does good Western-style coffee and some of the best cakes and ice creams (don't miss the salted caramel) we've encountered in Southeast Asia.

Constant Gardener (www.constantgardener.coffee; 9 Lebuh Light; ⏲9am-6pm) A serious venue for serious coffee drinkers, this new place brews its lattes with coveted beans from Malaysia and beyond, and serves some pristine-looking pastries.

G Hotel Kelawai is about 3.5km northwest of central George Town; a taxi here should cost RM15.

Farquhar's Bar BAR
(Eastern & Oriental Hotel, 10 Lebuh Farquhar; ⏲11am-midnight) Colonial British-style bar inside the E&O Hotel, serving beer, traditional pub food and cocktails. There's live music Thursday to Saturday, and happy hour between 5pm and 8pm.

Soho Free House BAR
(50 Jln Penang; ⏲noon-midnight) This place starts rocking out early with cheesy '80s hits and a Chinese clientele noshing bangers and mash and swilling pints with a handful of expats.

QEII BAR, CLUB
(8 Pengkalan Weld; ⏲6pm-1am Mon & Tue, 1pm-2am Wed-Sat, 3pm-2am Sun) Located over water, open-air QEII boasts 360-degree views of the Strait of Melaka and a decent selection of booze and beers.

Slippery Senoritas CLUB
(2 Jln Penang) The longest-standing of the strip of pubs and clubs along upper Jln Penang. Come to this see-and-be-seen club for live music, lots of drinking and a Tom-Cruise-in-*Cocktail*-esque show put on by the bar staff.

Shopping

Little Penang Street Market MARKET
(www.littlepenang.com.my; ⏲10am-5pm last Sun of month) On the last Sunday of every month, the pedestrian section of upper Jln Penang hosts an open-air market, with wares including Malaysian arts and crafts (think dolls, batik, pottery, T-shirts and painted tiles), as well as items like bottled chutney.

Unique Penang HANDICRAFTS
(www.uniquepenang.com; 62 Love Lane; ⏲6pm-midnight Sun-Fri, 9pm-midnight Sat) This shophouse gallery features the work of the friendly young owners, Clovis and Joey, as well as the colourful paintings of the latter's young art students. As the couple point out,

paintings are notoriously hard to squeeze in a backpack, so nearly all of the gallery's art is available in postcard size.

ottokedai HANDICRAFTS
(174 Lebuh Victoria; ⏲10am-10pm) This tiny, charming shop has a carefully curated selection of local items, from edibles to literature.

Tropical Spice Garden In Town HANDICRAFTS
(Lebuh China; ⏲9am-5pm) Linked with Batu Ferringhi's Tropical Spice Garden (p185), this fragrant shop sells soaps, essential oils, dried spice and other spice-related goods.

Shop Howard HANDICRAFTS
(154 Jln Masjid Kapitan Keling; ⏲10am-6pm) Unique postcards, art, photos, handicrafts and books on local topics, all made by local artists.

Rozanas Batik HANDICRAFTS
(81B Lebuh Acheh; ⏲noon-6pm Mon-Sat) A shophouse workshop featuring the owner's beautiful handmade batik items. If you want to learn more about this craft, take a walk-in two-hour class in the adjacent studio (RM25 to RM100).

China Joe's HANDICRAFTS
(95 Lebuh Armenian; ⏲10am-7pm) Head here for fabrics – both new and antique – boxes, stationery, bags and other classy Asian bric-a-brac.

Muda House HANDICRAFTS
(8 Muda Lane; ⏲9am-6pm) If the owner's around, stop by to pick up some hand-painted Peranakan tiles (made in Vietnam) at this boutique in a restored shophouse. There's a few other interesting local-style knick-knacks available, and the profits go to help stray animals.

Straits Quay MALL
(www.straitsquay.com; Jln Seri Tanjung Pinang, Tanjung Tokong; ⏲10.30am-10pm) Penang's flashiest mall, built on reclaimed land just outside the city centre. If you're not into shopping, it's also home to the Performing Arts Centre of Penang (www.penangpac.org) and there are a couple decent restaurants and bars.

Straits Quay is located about 7km northwest of George Town. Buses 101 and 104 pass the mall (RM4), or a taxi here will cost about RM25.

Royal Selangor HANDICRAFTS
(www.visitorcentre.royalselangor.com; 3A-G-1, Straits Quay, Jln Seri Tanjung Pinang, Tanjung Tokong; 1-hour class RM63.60; ⏲10.30am-10pm) The top name in Malaysian pewter; this outlet stocks its current range, and holds pewter-making workshops (11am, 2.30pm and 4.30pm; RM63.60 for about one hour).

Straits Quay is located about 7km northwest of George Town. Buses 101 and 104 (RM4) will get you here, or a taxi will cost about RM20.

Ban Hin ANTIQUES
(Lebuh Chulia; ⏲9am-7pm) This old shophouse is literally stuffed full of old adverts, packages, tins, ceramics, toys and other quasi-antiques.

Chowraster Bazaar MARKET
(Jln Penang; ⏲8am-6pm) This sweaty old market hall is where to go for a frenetic, souk-like experience. It's full of food stalls and vendors selling headscarves, batik shirts, fabrics and *kebaya* (blouses worn over a sarong).

Bee Chin Heong ANTIQUES
(58 Lebuh Kimberley; ⏲10am-8.30pm) This interesting outlet sells a colourful, bewildering assortment of religious statues, furniture and temple supplies. If you're after a huge Chinese couch, a household shrine or have RM55,000 to spend on a 2m-tall carved-wood Buddha, this is the place to come. Even if you're not buying, it's still worth a look round.

Gurney Plaza MALL
(Persiaran Gurney; ⏲10am-10pm) In addition to more than 300 shops, Penang's biggest and boldest mall includes a cinema, mini theme park, fitness centre and a health spa.

Gurney Drive is located about 3km west of George Town; a taxi here costs about RM15.

Komtar MALL
(Jln Penang; ⏲10am-10pm) Penang's oldest mall is housed in a 64-storey landmark tower (at one time the tallest building in Malaysia). There are hundreds of shops in a place with the feel of an ageing bazaar. Komtar was being renovated when we were in town; future plans include a new rooftop dining complex.

ℹ Information

IMMIGRATION OFFICES

Immigration Office (☎04-250 3410; 29A Lebuh Pantai; ⏲7.30am-1pm & 2-5.30pm Mon-Thu, 7.30am-12.14pm & 2.45-5.30pm Fri)

GETTING TO & FROM BUTTERWORTH

Butterworth, the city on the mainland bit of Penang (known as Sebarang Perai), is home to Penang's main train station and is the departure point for ferries to Penang Island. Unless you're taking the train or your bus has pulled into Butterworth's busy bus station from elsewhere, you'll probably not need to spend any time here.

If you do find yourself in Butterworth, the cheapest way to get to George Town is via the **ferry** (per adult/car RM1.20/7.70; 5.30am-1am); the terminal is linked by walkway to Butterworth's bus and train stations. Ferries take passengers and cars every 10 minutes from 5.30am to 9.30pm, every 20 minutes until 11.15pm, and hourly after that until 1am. The journey takes 10 minutes and fares are charged only for the journey from Butterworth to Penang; returning to the mainland is free.

If you choose to take a taxi to/from Butterworth (approximately RM50), you'll cross the 13.5km Penang Bridge. There's a RM7 toll payable at the toll plaza on the mainland, but no charge to return. It's worth noting that 2014 saw the opening of a second span, the whopping 24km Sultan Abdul Halim Muadzam Shah Bridge, which connnects Batu Maung at the southeastern tip of the island to Batu Kawan on the mainland. There's a RM8.50 toll payable at the toll plaza on the mainland, but no charge to return.

INTERNET ACCESS

Internet cafes are a dying breed, and the only one we spotted was at La Belle (p183). Yet nearly all lodging options offer wi-fi and many also have a computer terminal for guest use. Wi-fi is also widely available at restaurants, cafes and in shopping malls.

MEDICAL SERVICES

Hospital Pulau Pinang (04-222 5333; http://hpp.moh.gov.my/v2/; Jln Hospital) The island's largest public hospital, with general health care and emergency services.

Loh Guan Lye Specialist Centre (04-238 8888; www.lohguanlye.com; 19 Jln Logan) For more specific health issues, head to this private hospital.

Penang Adventist Hospital (04-222 7200; www.pah.com.my; 465 Jln Burma) Not-for-profit hospital and health centre.

MONEY

Branches of major banks are on Lebuh Pantai and Lebuh Downing, near the main post office. Most have 24-hour ATMs. At the northwestern end of Lebuh Chulia there are a few money-changers open longer hours than banks and with more competitive rates.

POST

Post Office (Lebuh Downing; 8.30am-6pm Mon-Sat) The island's main post terminal.

TOURIST INFORMATION

Penang Global Tourism (04-264 3456; www.mypenang.gov.my; Whiteways Arcade, Lebuh Pantai; 9am-5pm Mon-Fri, to 3pm Sat, to 1pm Sun) This, the visitors centre of the state tourism agency, is the best all-around place to go for maps, brochures and local information.

Penang Heritage Trust (PHT; 04-264 2631; www.pht.org.my; Lebuh Gereja; 9am-5pm Mon-Fri, to 1pm Sat) Come to this tiny but excellent centre for information on the history and culture of Penang, conservation projects, self-guided walks, or to arrange one of the organisation's excellent guided tours.

Tourism Malaysia (04-262 0066; www.tourism.gov.my/en/my; 10 Jln Tun Syed Sheh Barakbah; 8am-1pm & 2-5pm Mon-Fri) The government tourist office provides general tourism information on the country as a whole; nearby, the agency's Penang branch (04-262 0202; 11 Lebuh Pantai; 8am-1pm & 2-5pm Mon-Fri) provides state-specific information.

Getting There & Away

AIR

Penang's **Bayan Lepas International Airport** (04-643 4411; www.penangairport.com) is 18km south of George Town. The airport is served by more than a dozen airlines with international destinations that include several cities in China, Indonesia and Thailand, as well as Hong Kong, Singapore and Taiwan, and numerous domestic destinations. The airport has the usual money-exchange and car-rental booths and a **Tourism Malaysia counter** (04-642 6981; Bayan Lepas International Airport; 7am-10pm) with a few basic brochures and maps.

BOAT

Several providers, including **Langkawi Ferry Service** (LFS; 04-264 2088; www.langkawi-ferry.com; PPC Bldg, Lebuh King Edward; 7am-5.30pm Mon-Sat, to 3pm Sun), have merged and operate a shared ferry service to

Langkawi (adult/child one way RM68.10/49.20, return RM136.20/98.40; 1¾ to 2½ hours). Boats leave at 8.15am, 8.30am and 2pm. Boats return from Langkawi at 10.30am, 2.30pm and 5.15pm. Book a few days in advance to ensure a seat.

BUS

All long-distance buses to George Town arrive at the Sungei Nibong Bus Station, just to the south of Penang Bridge, while buses bound for Butterworth arrive at the Butterworth Bus Station. A taxi from Sungei Nibong to George Town costs around RM25; a taxi from Butterworth can cost as much as RM50.

Buses to destinations in Malaysia can be boarded at Sungai Nibong and, more conveniently, at the **Komtar bus station** (www.rapidpg.com.my; Jln Penang); international destinations only at the latter. Note that transport to Thailand (except to Hat Yai) is via minivan. Transport can also be arranged to Ko Samui and Ko Phi Phi via a transfer in Surat Thani and Hat Yai respectively.

DESTINATION	PRICE	DURATION	FREQUENCY
Ipoh	RM25	2½ hours	5 departures 7am-7.30pm
Hat Yai (Thailand)	RM35	4 hours	4 departures 5am-4pm
Kuala Lumpur	RM38	5 hours	every 30min 7am-1am
Tanah Rata (for Cameron Highlands)	RM40	5 hours	8am & 2pm
Kota Bharu	RM45	7 hours	9am & 9pm
Melaka	RM50	7 hours	9am & 11.30pm
Kuala Terengganu	RM55	8 hours	8.20pm
Johor Bahru	RM60	9 hours	4 departures 8am-11pm
Singapore	RM60	10 hours	9pm
Bangkok (Thailand; transfer in Surat Thani)	RM130	20 hours	5am & 8.30pm

TRAIN

Penang's train station is next to the ferry terminal and bus and taxi station in Butterworth. There are four daily trains to Kuala Lumpur (six hours, RM19 to RM138) and two in the opposite direction to Hat Yai in Thailand (four hours, RM24 to RM156); check with www.ktmb.com.my for the latest info on fares and schedules.

Getting Around

TO/FROM THE AIRPORT

Penang's Bayan Lepas International Airport is 18km south of George Town. The fixed taxi fare to most places in central George Town is RM44.70; taxis take about 30 minutes to the centre of town. Bus 401 runs to and from the airport (RM4) every half-hour between 6am and 11pm daily, and stops at Komtar and Weld Quay, taking at least an hour.

BICYCLE

There are several places near the intersection of Gat Lebuh Armenian and Lebuh Victoria offering one-day hire of city bikes for around RM12. Alternatively, for something more specific, consider the more specialised bicycles at **LoveBike** (✆ 012-476 9918; 31 Love Lane; per 6hr RM10-25; ⏲9.30am-9.30pm).

BUS

Buses around Penang are run by the government-owned **Rapid Penang** (✆ 04-238 1313; www.rapidpg.com.my). Fares range from RM1.40 to RM4. Most routes originate at **Weld Quay Bus Terminal** (19-24 Pengkalan Weld) and most also stop at Komtar and along Jln Chulia.

DESTINATION	ROUTE NO	PICK-UP
Batu Ferringhi	101	Pengkalan Weld, Lebuh Chulia, Komtar
Bayan Lepas International Airport, Teluk Kumbar	401	Pengkalan Weld, Lebuh Chulia
Persiaran Gurney	103	Pengkalan Weld, Air Itam, Komtar
Penang Hill	204	Pengkalan Weld, Lebuh Chulia, Komtar
Sungei Nibong Bus Station	401	Pengkalan Weld, Lebuh Chulia, Komtar
Teluk Bahang	101, 102	Pengkalan Weld, Bayan Lepas International Airport

CAR

La Belle (✆ 04-262 7717; www.labelle.net.my; 440B Lebuh Chulia; per 24hr motorcycle RM30-70, car 24hr RM100-300; ⏲9am-1pm & 2-10pm) car hire operates out of George Town. There are also several companies based at Bayan Lepas International Airport, including:

Avis (☎04-643 9633; www.avis.com; ⌚7.30am-9.30pm)

Hertz (☎04-643 0208; www.hertz.com; ⌚7.30am-10pm Mon-Sat, 8am-4pm Sun)

Kasina (☎04-644 7893; www.kasina.com.my; ⌚7.30am-10pm Mon-Sat, 8.30am-5pm Sun)

New Bob Rent-A-Car (☎04-642 1111; www.bobcar.com.my; ⌚8am-10pm Mon-Fri, to 8pm Sat & Sun)

MOTORCYCLE

You can hire motorcycles from many places, including guesthouses and shops along Lebuh Chulia. Manual bikes start at about RM30 and automatic about RM40, for 24 hours.

TAXI

Penang's taxis all have meters, which nearly all drivers flatly refuse to use, so negotiate the fare before you set off. Typical fares to places just outside of the city centre start at around RM15. Taxis can be found on Jln Penang, near Cititel Hotel, at the Weld Quay Bus Terminal and near Komtar bus station.

TRISHAW

Bicycle rickshaws are a fun, if touristy, way to negotiate George Town's backstreets and cost around RM40 per hour – as with taxis, it's important to agree on the fare before departure. Drivers can be found waiting at the northern end of Jln Penang.

GREATER PENANG

Batu Ferringhi

For years, and no doubt aided by the tourism authorities, the lure of sun and sand at Batu Ferringhi was the main reason people came to Penang. In reality, the beach can't compare to Malaysia's best: the water isn't as clear as you might expect, swimming often means battling jellyfish, and the beach itself can be dirty, especially on weekends when hordes of day trippers visit. Still, it's the best easy-access beach stop on the island, and a pleasant break from the city.

Activities

There are plenty of **water sports** hire outfits along the beach; options include **wave runners** (RM70 for 15 minutes), **banana-boating** (RM25 per person) and **parasailing** (RM150 per ride) trips.

After which you might need a relaxing **massage**. All sorts of foot masseuses will offer you their services; expect to pay around RM40 for a 30-minute deep-tissue massage.

Festivals

Penang Island Jazz Festival MUSIC
(www.facebook.com/PenangIslandJazzFestival; ⌚Dec) Features local and international artists at changing venues in Batu Ferringhi.

Sleeping

Batu Ferringhi has lots of somewhat overpriced, chain-style resorts catering to families, and quite a few extremely overpriced, homestay-type budget places, but very little in between.

The vast majority of the area's accommodation and restaurants are located along Jln Batu Ferringhi, the town's main strip, which runs parallel to the beach. There's a cluster of midrange places near the petrol station intersection, and most of Batu Ferringhi's budget places are found behind the mosque, on the beach side of the main road.

Roomies HOSTEL $
(☎04-881 1344; www.roomiespenang.com; 4th fl, 76C-4 Jln Batu Ferringhi; incl breakfast dm RM35, r RM140-160; ❄📶) If you don't mind sleeping communally, Roomies is by far the most appealing budget option in Batu Ferringhi. The dorm spans 10 beds, is spacious, bright and clean, and Roomies also has two private rooms.

Roomies is located in the tall white structure opposite the Parkroyal, approximately in the centre of Batu Ferringhi.

Baba Guest House GUESTHOUSE $
(☎04-881 1686; babaguesthouse2000@yahoo.com; 52 Batu Ferringhi; r RM65-100; ❄📶) A ramshackle domestic compound belonging to a Chinese family. Rooms here are large and spotless – although bare. Half the rooms share bathrooms, while the dearer air-con rooms come with a fridge and shower.

Baba is located roughly in the centre of Batu Ferringhi, just behind the mosque.

Shalini's Guest House GUESTHOUSE $
(☎012-407 3822; www.shanilisguesthouse.blogspot.co; 56 Batu Ferringhi; r RM60-250; ❄📶) This old, two-storey house on the beach has a palpable homely atmosphere. Rooms are basic but neat and some have balconies, most with private bathrooms.

Baba is located roughly in the centre of Batu Ferringhi, just behind the mosque.

WORTH A TRIP

TROPICAL SPICE GARDEN

Between Teluk Bahang and Batu Ferringhi is the **Tropical Spice Garden** (☎04-881 1797; www.tropicalspicegarden.com; Jl Teluk Bahang; adult/child RM26/15, incl tour RM35/20; ⊙9am-6pm), an oasis of tropical, fragrant fecundity of more than 500 species of flora, with an emphasis on edible herbs and spices.

To get here by bus, take any Teluk Bahang-bound bus (RM4) and let the driver know that you want to get off here.

You can explore the grounds on your own, or join one of four daily guided tours at 9am, 11.30am, 1.30pm and 3.30pm.

The garden also offers **cooking courses** (adult/child RM233.20/116.60; ⊙lessons 9am-1pm Mon-Sat), there's a good shop, the restaurant is worth a visit, and just across from the gardens there's a beautiful roadside white-sand beach.

Tree Monkey (Tropical Spice Garden, Jln Teluk Bahang; mains RM16.80-48.89; ⊙9am-11pm) is alfresco dining at its best, surrounded by gorgeous gardens with a view of the sea. A Thai owner oversees a huge variety of tasty Thai dishes, including several 'tapas' sets (RM38 to RM168).

Tree Monkey is located at the Tropical Spice Garden; hop on bus 101 (RM1.40) or take a taxi from Batu Ferringhi (around RM10).

Roomies Suites HOTEL $$
(☎04-881 1378; www.roomiespenang.com; 4th fl, 1-9B Eden Parade, Lg Sungai Emas; r incl breakfast RM140-180; ❄📶) Maintaining the same standards as its sister property but emphasising private rooms, Roomies Suites is easily Batu Ferringhi's best midrange option. The 13 rooms here are stylish and spacious, and are looked after by a friendly host.

Roomies Suites is located on the 4th floor of the Eden Parade shopping complex, near Batu Ferringhi's petrol-station intersection.

EQ HOTEL $$
(☎04-885 1533; www.eqferringhi.com; 17 Lg Sungai Emas; r RM108-188; ❄📶) If you need a midrange hotel and are not fussed by zero character and not staying right on the beach, this is your place. Rooms are spacious and equipped with air-con, TV, large-feeling bathrooms with hot water – and a hat rack.

EQ is located behind the Eden Parade shopping complex, near the petrol-station intersection; there are a couple similar places nearby.

D'Feringghi HOTEL $$
(☎04-881 9000; www.dferingghihotel.com; 66 Jln Batu Ferringhi; r RM138-254; ❄📶) This hotel won't inspire any postcards home, but it's a contender within its price bracket. Rooms are clean and – for Batu Ferringhi, at least – inexpensive.

Located roughly opposite Tarbush restaurant, a brief walk to the beach.

★**Lone Pine Hotel** RESORT $$$
(☎04-886 8686; www.lonepinehotel.com; 97 Jln Batu Ferringhi; incl breakfast r RM480-800, ste RM900-2000; ❄@📶🏊) Dating back to the 1940s, the Lone Pine is one of Batu Ferringhi's oldest – and best – resorts. The 90 rooms are spacious and bright, and all have some kind of perk, such as personal plunge pools or private gardens. The grounds have a stately, national-park-like feel, with hammocks suspended between the pines (actually casuarina trees), and a huge 'spa salt' pool as a centrepiece.

Lone Pine is located roughly opposite Batu Ferringhi's petrol-station intersection

Rasa Sayang Resort RESORT $$$
(☎04-881 1966; www.shangri-la.com; Jln Batu Ferringhi; incl breakfast r RM835-1795, ste RM2425-8000; ❄@📶🏊) Penang's only five-star resort feels like something out of a South Sea dream. Rooms are large and decorated with fine hardwood furniture, and cloud-like white duvets float on the beds; all have balconies and many have sea views.

If approaching from George Town, the Raya Sayang is one of the first resorts you'll encounter in Batu Ferringhi.

Parkroyal RESORT $$$
(☎04-881 1133; www.parkroyalhotels.com; Jln Batu Ferringhi; incl breakfast r RM370-670, ste RM675-2400; ❄@📶🏊) The 1980s-era exterior here is a pretty good indicator of what's going on inside: 309 standard and comfortable, but nonflashy rooms. The grounds are more a

reason to stay, with two pools, lots of lawn to bask on and a great strip of beach out front.

Located roughly in the centre of Batu Ferringhi's strip, opposite the Holiday Inn.

Hard Rock Hotel RESORT $$$
(☎04-881 1711; www.penang.hardrockhotels.net; Jln Batu Ferringhi; incl breakfast r RM700-920, ste RM1000-3800;) If you can stomach the corny, hyper-corporate vibe (and the unrelenting gaze of Beatles memorabilia), this resort can be a fun place to stay. There's a particular emphasis on family friendliness, with child-friendly pools, kid-friendly suites and teen-themed play areas (complete with pool table and video games).

The Hard Rock is located just south of Batu Ferringhi's main strip.

Holiday Inn Resort RESORT $$$
(☎04-881 1601; www.holidayinnresorts.com/penang; 72 Jln Batu Ferringhi; r incl breakfast RM290-420;) A big, busy resort with accommodation blocks on either side of the main road. It's yet another place that's great for families, with expansive pools and themed 'kidsuites', which come with TV, video and Playstation. There are also tennis courts and a gym for the adults.

Located roughly in the centre of Batu Ferringhi's strip, next to the Parkroyal.

Eating & Drinking

You can get a beer at most nonhalal places, but outside of the hotels, toes-in-the-sand type beach bars are few – **Bora Bora** (Jln Batu Ferringhi; noon-1am Sun-Thu, to 3am Fri & Sat), located roughly in the centre of the strip, is the exception.

Long Beach MALAYSIAN $
(Jln Batu Ferringhi; mains from RM4; 6.30-11.30pm) This buzzy hawker centre has the usual selection of Chinese noodle dishes, Indian breads and meat curries, and Malaysian seafood dishes.

Long Beach is located approximately in the centre of Batu Ferringhi's main strip, not far from the petrol-station intersection.

Tarbush MIDDLE EASTERN $$
(www.tarbush.com.my; Jln Batu Ferringhi; mains RM25-60; 10am-1am;) Middle Eastern residents have brought their cuisine to Batu Ferringhi, and Lebanese restaurants line the town's main strip. The best of the lot is most likely this branch of a KL restaurant empire. We fancy the two meze platters, which bring together everything from hummus to *kibbeh* (lamb meatballs with bulgur).

Tarbush is located approximately in the middle of town.

Ferringhi Garden INTERNATIONAL $$
(Jln Batu Ferringhi; mains RM25-350; 5pm-midnight;) Everyone falls in love with the outdoor setting with its terracotta tiles and hardwoods surrounded by bamboo – not to mention the seafood-heavy menu. During the daytime hours, a linked cafe serves good breakfast and real coffee – a relative rarity in Batu Ferringhi.

Ferringhi Garden is located a block or so south of the Holiday Inn.

Getting There & Away

Bus 101 runs from Weld Quay and Komtar, in George Town, and takes around 30 minutes to reach Batu Ferringhi (RM4). A taxi to Batu Ferringhi from George Town will cost at least RM40.

Getting Around

Most of Batu Ferringhi is accessible on foot. If you want to go further afield, consider hiring a motorcycle at **Bike Discovery** (☎04-881 2820; 78 Jln Batu Ferringhi; per 24hr RM40-250), located at the southern end of town, opposite the mosque.

Teluk Bahang & Around

If Batu Ferringhi is Penang's version of Cancun or Bali, Teluk Bahang is the quiet (sometimes deathly so) beach a few kilometres past the party. Most come here for Penang National Park, although there are a few other attractions, and accommodation.

Sights

★**Penang National Park** NATIONAL PARK
(Taman Negara Pulau Pinang; ☎04-881 2016; 8am-5pm) FREE At just 23 sq km Penang National Park is the smallest in Malaysia; it's also one of the newest, having attained national-park status in 2003. A Penang highlight, it has some interesting and challenging trails through the jungle, as well as some of the island's finest and quietest beaches.

The park can be reached on Teluk Bahang-bound bus 101 (RM4) from George Town.

The park entrance is a short walk from Teluk Bahang's main bus stop. It's an easy 20-minute walk to the 250m-long canopy walkway, closed indefinitely for upgrading when we stopped by. From here, you have the choice of heading west to Muka Head or south to Pantai Kerachut.

The easiest walk is the 15-minute stroll west to **Teluk Tukun beach** where Sungai Tukun flows into the ocean. There are some little pools to swim in here. Following this trail along the coast about 10 minutes more brings you to the private University of Malaysia Marine Research Station, where there is a supply jetty, as well as **Tanjung Aling**, a nice beach to stop at for a rest. From here it's another 45 minutes or so down the beach to **Teluk Duyung**, also called Monkey Beach, after the numerous primates who scamper about here on the beach. It's another 30 minutes to **Muka Head**, the isolated rocky promontory at the extreme northwestern corner of the island, where on the peak of the head is an off-limits 1883 lighthouse and an Achenese-style graveyard. The views of the surrounding islands from up here are worth the sweaty uphill jaunt.

A longer and more difficult trail heads south from the suspension bridge towards **Pantai Kerachut**, a beautiful white-sand beach that is a popular spot for picnics and is a green turtle nesting ground. Count on about 1½ hours to walk to the beach on the clear and well-used trail. On your way is the unusual **meromictic lake**, a rare natural feature composed of two separate layers of unmixed fresh water on top and seawater below, supporting a unique mini-ecosystem. From Pantai Kerachut beach you can walk about 40 minutes onward to further-flung and isolated **Teluk Kampi**, which is the longest beach in the park; look for trenches along the coast that are remnants of the Japanese occupation in WWII.

Several operators near the park entrance can arrange boat pick-up at various locations; from Teluk Duyung (Monkey Beach) the cost is RM40, Pantai Kerachut RM80, and from Teluk Kampi RM90.

Art & Garden by Fuan Wong GARDENS, GALLERY
(adult/child RM30/15; ⏲9am-5.30pm Thu-Mon) Rising up a hillside on a part of the family's durian orchard is this amazing conceptual garden where Fuan Wong marries his superb collection of weird and wonderful plants with his glass sculptures and installations. Creative works by other artists are dotted throughout the garden, which also has a cafe, gift shop and breathtaking views of Penang Hill.

Tropical Fruit Farm FARM
(☎012-497 1931; www.tropicalfruitfarm.com.my; tour adult/child RM42.40/31.80; ⏲9am-5pm) About 8km south of Teluk Bahang is this 10-hectare hillside farm, which cultivates over 250 types of tropical and subtropical fruit trees, native and hybrid. Its one-hour **tours** include a fruit buffet and a glass of fresh juice.

The Tropical Fruit Farm can be reached on bus 501 from Teluk Bahang (RM2).

Escape AMUSEMENT PARK
(☎04-881 1106; www.escape.my; 282 Jln Teluk Bahang; adult/child RM60/50; ⏲9am-6pm Tue-Sun) Fun for all the family here, but be warned: adults report being more challenged than their kids by the adventurous games and attractions at this new eco-themed play park near the butterfly farm, some of which involve climbing and jumping.

Escape is located about 1km south of Teluk Bahang's roundabout, which can be reached via bus 101 (RM4).

Penang Butterfly Farm GARDENS
(www.butterfly-insect.com; 830 Jln Teluk Bahang; adult/child RM27/15; ⏲9am-5pm) Closed for renovations when we stopped by, this attraction is home to several thousand live butterflies representing over 150 species, as well as some fascinating beetles, lizards and spiders.

The Butterfly Farm is located about 1km south of Teluk Bahang's roundabout, and can be reached via bus 101 (RM4).

Sleeping & Eating

Several enterprising locals in Teluk Bahang take part in a homestay collective. Most are located on the side roads that link the sea and the road that leads to Penang National Park. Rooms run as little as RM18, and are generally basic, but clean, and there's the added bonus of cultural exposure.

The main shopping area along the road heading east to Batu Ferringhi has a few coffee shops where you'll find cheaper Chinese dishes and seafood, as well as a couple of *nasi kandar*–type places, such as **Restoran Khaleel** (Jln Teluk Bahang; mains from RM4; ⏲24hr), that sell *murtabak* and *dosa* (savoury Indian pancakes).

Hotel Sportfishing HOTEL $$
(☎04-885 2728; Jln Nelayan; r RM134-139; ❄📶) Probably Teluk Bahang's most comfortable

DON'T MISS

LAKSA BALIK PULAU

Locals have been known to cross the island for this town's signature dish: laksa Balik Pulau, a tasty rice-noodle concoction in a thick fish broth, with shredded lettuce, mint leaves, pineapple slivers, onions and fresh chillies. Get a bowl (coupled ideally with the local 'white' nutmeg juice) at the town's most famous vendor, **Nan Guang** (67 Jln Besar; mains from RM3; ⏲7.30am-5pm Wed-Sun), located just north of Balik Pulau's main roundabout.

place to stay, the two floors of plain-but-clean rooms are at the edge of the beach and look over the fishing pier.

Sea Princess Hotel HOTEL $$
(☎04-346 0981; 811A Jln Hassan Abas; r RM130-200; ❄📶) You can't miss this brightly coloured, three-storey block, located along Teluk Bahang's main drag. The 18 rooms are new, clean and spacious, if lacking character, and are overseen by an enthusiastic owner.

ℹ Getting There & Away

Bus 101 runs from George Town every half-hour all the way along the north coast of the island as far as the roundabout in Teluk Bahang (RM4). A taxi here from the centre of George Town will cost at least RM50.

Balik Pulau

Meaning 'on the other side of the island', Balik Pulau is Penang's main inland outpost. It's a busy but charming market town with a strip of antique shophouses surrounded by rice fields and durian, clove and nutmeg orchards.

Lack of accommodation in town means that Balik Pulau isn't exactly convenient for an overnight stay, but it functions as a good lunch stop if you're headed elsewhere on the island.

👁 Sights

My Balik Pulau, a brochure available for purchase in George Town at ottokedai (p181), and *Discover Balik Pulau*, a map available at the various tourism offices, are great guides to the area's smaller attractions, culture and history.

Holy Name of Jesus Catholic Church CHURCH
(Jln Bukit Penara; ⏲daylight hours) FREE Located just north of the centre of town, the current structure dates back to 1897. The floor tiles were designed by a French priest, the stained glass was imported from Belgium, the bell from France, and the church's twin spires stand impressively against the jungle behind.

🛏 Sleeping & Eating

There are a couple homestay options in Balik Pulau, but arranging accommodation is difficult if you don't speak Chinese. Yin, at Yin's Sourdough Bakery (p176) in George Town, may be able to help arrange a stay. Otherwise, the only accommodation in the area is Malihom, which is about 8km south of town.

Malihom RETREAT $$$
(☎04-261 0490; www.malihom.com; Kiri N/t 168 Bukit Penara Mukim 6; bungalows all-inclusive RM850-980; ❄@📶🏊) Accommodation here takes the form of nine 100-year-old rice barns, refurbished and united at the top of this 518m peak. But you won't want to stay inside; walk around the small complex to gawk at the 360-degree view over hills of jungle, the sea and several villages. Given its unique location, Malihom is isolated, and a stay is all-inclusive, including three meals.

The retreat is located off winding Rte 6 between Balik Pulau and Kampung Sungai Batu, at the top of a steep hill. You'll need to be shuttled up in the resort's 4WD.

ℹ Getting There & Away

You can reach Balik Pulau via bus 502 and 401E (tickets cost approximately RM4) from George Town and Bayan Lepas respectively, and bus 501 from Batu Feringghi (RM3.40).

Pulau Jerejak

Lying 1.5 nautical miles off Penang's southeast coast, thickly forested Pulau Jerejak has been home to a leper colony and a prison in its time. Displays on the island's former life can be seen at the George Town World Heritage Inc. Headquarters (p159).

Today the island is home to **Jerejak Resort & Spa** (☎04-658 7111; www.jerejakresort.com; r RM220-420; ❄@📶🏊), although guest feedback suggests that visiting the resort in the form of a **day-trip package** (adult/child

RM85/65), which allows access to the pool and other activities including archery and rock climbing, is probably a wiser approach than staying overnight.

The resort has its own jetty, with boats leaving roughly every two hours from 6.30am to 10.30pm (adult/child RM20/16). No buses run past the jetty; a taxi from George Town will cost around RM50.

Batu Maung

Batu Maung is Penang's deep-sea fishing port, and there are still some dilapidated, brightly painted boats along the coast. Yet encroaching development from the Bayan Lepas Industrial Zone and the completion of the second bridge to the mainland have erased any traces of the formerly biodiverse mangrove swamp that used to be found here.

The renovated seaside **Sam Poh Footprint Temple** (Jln Maung; daylight hours) FREE has a shrine dedicated to the legendary Admiral Zheng He, who was also known as Sam Poh. The temple sanctifies a huge 'footprint' on the rock that's reputed to belong to the famous Chinese navigator (local Hindus, on the other hand, believe the footprint to be that of Hanuman; Malays believe it was left by a giant).

Perched on top of the steep Bukit Batu Maung is the **Penang War Museum** (04-626 5142; www.facebook.com/PenangWarMuseum; Bukit Batu Maung; adult/child RM30/15; 9am-11pm). The former British fort, built in the 1930s, was used as a prison and torture camp by the Japanese during WWII. Today, the crumbling buildings have been restored as a memorial to those dark days. Barracks, ammunition stores, cookhouses, gun emplacements and other structures can be explored here, which also offers 'suspense and eerie' night visits and paintball (from RM75).

Also nearby is the **Penang Aquarium** (Pekan Batu Maung; adult/child RM5/2; 10am-5pm Thu-Tue), which houses 25 tanks filled with colourful fish.

Bus 307 leaves for Batu Maung every half-hour from Weld Quay and Komtar (RM4); a taxi here will cost about RM50.

Kampung Pulau Betong

This is a fishing village utterly off the beaten track with delightful *kampung* houses, flowers and colourful docked boats. At around 5.30pm the fishing boats come in and sell their fish at the little market near the dock. Bus 403 runs from Balik Pulau as far as the market (RM1.40) but if you walk another 1.5km you'll come to **Pantai Pasir Panjang**, an empty, pristine beach with white sand the texture of raw sugar – one of the prettier spots on the island for the few who make the effort to get here. The beach is backed by a National Service Training Centre for young graduates entering the army. Be vigilant if you go into the water – there's a heavy undertow.

Teluk Kumbar

Penangites come to Teluk Kumbar with one thing in mind: eating. While some housing estates have sprung up recently, the village is still calm and beautiful. Stop at one of the Malay food stalls for some *mee udang* (spicy noodles with prawns) or visit **Hai Boey Seafood** (013-488 1114; 29 MK9 Pasir Belanda; mains from RM10; 5.30-10.30pm), probably Penang's most famous destination for seafood; call ahead to reserve a table on weekends or holidays.

Buses 401 and 401E pass Teluk Kumbar (RM4); a taxi here will cost about RM60.

Langkawi, Kedah & Perlis

☎04 / POP 2.3 MILLION

Includes ➡

Best Places to Eat

- Muda Coffee Shop (p211)
- Siti Fatimah (p206)
- Nasi Lemak Ong (p211)
- Langkawi's Night Market (p205)

Best Places to Stay

- Bon Ton (p201)
- Temple Tree (p201)
- Ambong Ambong (p203)
- Tanjung Rhu Resort (p204)
- Datai Langkawi (p203)

Why Go?

The states of Kedah and Perlis represent a rural idyll that is central to the Malay identity. Limestone pillars thrust up through emerald paddy fields, which contribute to the harvest of over half of the country's domestic rice supply. Not that many foreigners see this. In fact, most travellers would draw a blank if you asked them about 'Kedah'. That's because almost everyone knows this state by its biggest island: Pulau Langkawi. And justifiably so. Langkawi's glorious clear waters and luxurious wide beaches warrant the attention they receive. Swathes of ancient rainforest reach right to the shore, while corners of the island mimic the green terrain of the mainland.

Perlis, Malaysia's smallest state, has an even lower profile. Like Kedah it borders Thailand, and most travellers simply rush through it on their way up there. Their loss; this friendly corner of the country is part of the Malay heartland, and well worth a look-in.

When to Go

Kuala Kedah

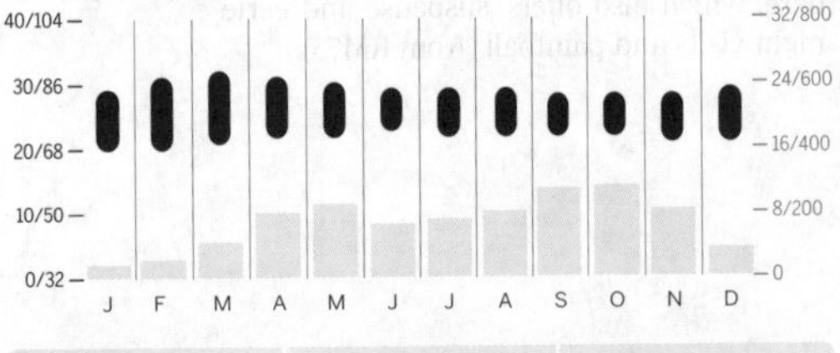

Feb & Mar Generally the region's driest months, although temperatures can be relatively high.

Apr–Oct The wettest time of year; the odd tropical storm is expected and tourist numbers are low.

Jul Typically Pulau Langkawi's coolest month.

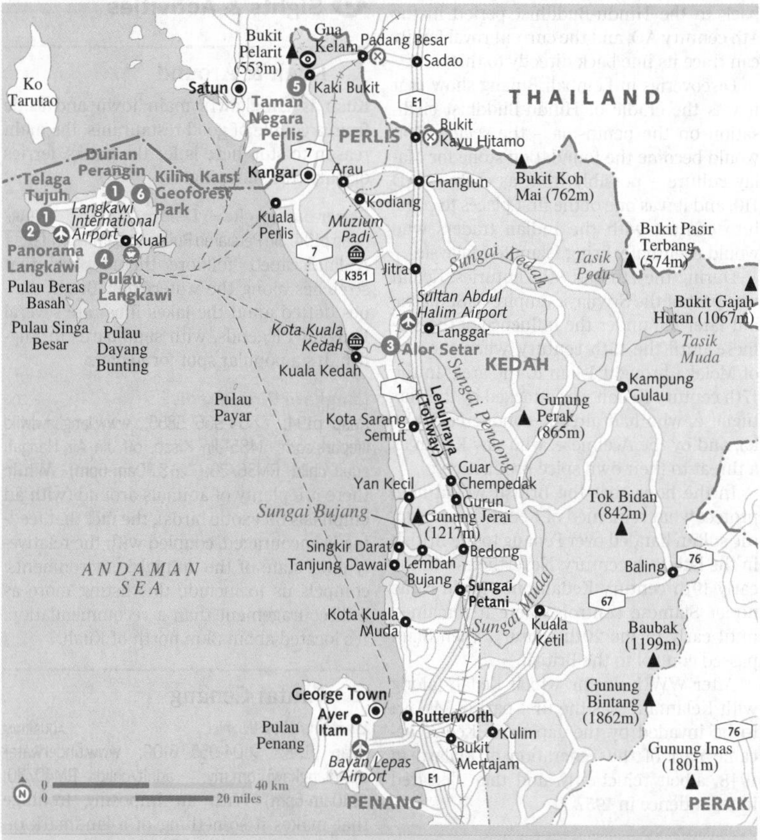

Langkawi, Kedah & Perlis Highlights

1. Cooling off in the freshwater pools at Langkawi's **Telaga Tujuh** (p195) or **Durian Perangin** (p196) waterfalls.
2. Riding the **Panorama Langkawi** (p193) cable car all 708m to the top of Gunung Machinchang to enjoy the spectacular views.
3. Revelling in the former glory days of royal Malaysia in **Alor Setar** (p208).
4. Relaxing on one of the stunning beaches of **Pulau Langkawi** (p192).
5. Exploring the limestone caves and remote border feel of **Taman Negeri Perlis** (p214).
6. Kayaking through the mangroves at **Kilim Karst Geoforest Park** (p195).

KEDAH

For travellers' purposes there are essentially two Kedahs: the tropical island of Pulau Langkawi and its surrounding islets, and the rural, little-visited mainland Kedah, known as Malaysia's 'rice bowl'.

Langkawi is the stuff of tourist brochures that don't skimp on descriptions such as 'sun-kissed' and 'paradise'. The good news is that the beaches generally live up to the hype, but it's also an island destination that continues to maintain its Malay roots. If, like most, you've only included Pulau Langkawi on your itinerary, you can rest assured that you'll still get the chance to experience both Kedahs.

History

Settlement in Kedah goes back to the Stone Age; some of the earliest excavated archaeological sites in the country are near Gunung Jerai. Recent finds in Lembah Bujang date back to the Hindu-Buddhist period in the 4th century AD, and the current royal family can trace its line back directly to this time.

Discoveries in Lembah Bujang show that it was the cradle of Hindu-Buddhist civilisation on the peninsula – the society that would become the foundation stone for Malay culture – possibly from as early as AD 110, and it was one of the first places to come into contact with the Indian traders who would eventually bring Islam to Malaysia.

During the 7th and 8th centuries, Kedah was part of the Srivijaya Empire of Sumatra, but later fell under the influence of the Siamese until the 15th century, when the rise of Melaka brought Islam to the area. In the 17th century Kedah was attacked by the Portuguese, who had already conquered Melaka, and by the Acehnese, who saw Kedah as a threat to their own spice production.

In the hope that the British would help protect what remained of Kedah from Siam, the sultan handed over Penang to the British in the late 18th century. Nevertheless, in the early 19th century Kedah once again came under Siamese control, where it remained until early in the 20th century when Siam passed control to the British.

After WWII, during which Kedah (along with Kelantan) was the first part of Malaya to be invaded by the Japanese, Kedah became part of the Federation of Malaya in 1948, albeit reluctantly, and then declared independence in 1957.

Pulau Langkawi

POP 94,777

Langkawi is synonymous with 'tropical paradise'. Since 2008 the archipelago's official title has been Langkawi Permata Kedah (Langkawi, the Jewel of Kedah), no doubt inspired by the island's clear waters, relatively pristine beaches and intact jungle. The district has been duty free since 1987 and pulling in tourists well before that. Yet, despite their immense drawing power, these 99 islands, dominated by 478.5-sq-km Pulau Langkawi, have not been overdeveloped beyond recognition. Get just a little way off the main beaches and this is idyllic rural Malaysia, with traditional *kampung* (villages) and a laid-back vibe. It's the kind of tropical island where there's no lack of spas, seafood restaurants and beach bars, but where the locals continue to go about their ways just as they have for generations.

Sights & Activities

Kuah & Around

Kuah is Langkawi's main town and aside from a couple of good restaurants, the main reason to stop here is for the banks, ferries or duty-free shopping.

Lagenda Langkawi Dalam Taman PARK
(Map p194; Jln Persiaran Putra; 9am-7pm) FREE A landscaped 'folklore theme park' that stretches along the waterfront. Bright statues dotted amid the lakes illustrate several Langkawi legends, with signboards in English. It's a popular spot for joggers.

Langkawi Bird Paradise ZOO
(Map p194; 04-966 5855; www.langkawiwildlifepark.com; 1485 Jln Kisap, off Jln Air Hangat; adult/child RM36/20; 8.30am-6pm) While there are plenty of animals around (with an emphasis on exotic birds), the fact that feeding is encouraged, coupled with the relatively poor state of the animals' environments, compels us to include this listing more as a discouragement than a recommendation. It's located about 3km north of Kuah.

Pantai Cenang

Underwater World AQUARIUM
(Map p198; 04-955 6100; www.underwaterworldlangkawi.com.my; adult/child RM40/30; 10am-6pm) With an imposing frontage that makes it something of a landmark on the main Cenang strip, this aquarium features 500 different species of marine and freshwater creatures as well as rockhopper penguins. Some exhibits (especially the rainforest walk) are well executed, while others seem small and in need of a clean.

Laman Padi MUSEUM
(Rice Garden; Map p198; 04-955 3225; lamanpadi@ladaeco.my; adult/child RM10/5, tour RM25/10; 9am-6.30pm) This somewhat-abandoned-feeling 'ecotourism' complex comprises rice paddies populated by water buffalo and ducks. Call in advance to arrange a tour to learn about, and even have a hand in, planting rice. There's also a basic museum dedicated to rice cultivation, a restaurant and **Nawa Sari Spa** (Map p198; 014-253 4489; Laman Padi; massage RM35-80; 11am-7pm), where you can contentedly watch rice paddies sway in the breeze while you're pummelled and oiled by Thai masseurs.

A CHEAT SHEET TO LANGKAWI'S BEACHES

Langkawi is big: almost 500 sq km. Kuah, in the southeast corner of the island, is the main town and the arrival point for ferries, but the beaches are elsewhere.

Pantai Cenang The busiest and most developed beach is the 2km-long strip of sand at Pantai Cenang. The beach is gorgeous: white sand, teal water and green palms. There are water sports on hand and the water is good for swimming, but beware of jellyfish (p201) and speeding jet skis ripping past.

There are some very fine top-end resorts at Cenang, as well as the bulk of Langkawi's budget and midrange accommodation. Come night-time, an odd mix of expats, domestic tourists, backpackers and package holidaymakers take to the main road to eat, drink, window-shop and generally make merry.

Pantai Tengah Head south and Langkawi gets a little more polished; as the road loops around a rocky headland, you're in upscale Pantai Tengah. It's a slightly smaller, narrower beach, with less noisy water-sports activity than on Pantai Cenang. There are a few big, all-inclusive resorts here, good restaurants and bars, and a few cheaper hotels too.

Pantai Kok (Map p194) On the western part of the island, 12km north of Pantai Cenang, Pantai Kok fronts a beautiful bay surrounded by limestone mountains and jungle. The beach here is popular with locals, who picnic under the trees. There are a handful of equidistantly located upscale resorts around here, many with their own small strips of beach.

Teluk Datai (Map p194) On the far northwestern corner of the island, the beaches at Teluk Datai are arguably some of the island's most beautiful and secluded, but are really only accessible if you're staying in one of the area's two luxury resorts.

Tanjung Rhu (Map p194) On the north coast, Tanjung Rhu is one of Langkawi's wider and better beaches, fronted by magnificent limestone stacks that bend the ocean into a pleasant bay. On clear days, the sunsets here give the word 'stunning' new meaning. The water is shallow, and at low tide you can walk across the sandbank to the neighbouring islands (except during the monsoon season). Accommodation is provided by two upscale resorts.

Pantai Tengah

The main strip along Pantai Tengah is home to many of the island's spas. Massages average about RM150 per hour, while facials and other treatments start at about RM60. Many also offer complimentary transfers; call for details.

Alun-Alun Spa SPA

(Map p198; ☎04-955 5570; www.alunalunspa.com; Jln Teluk Baru; ⏲11am-11pm) With three branches across the island, Alun-Alun is accessible and gets good reviews. The spa's blended aromatherapy oils are also available for purchase.

Ishan Spa SPA

(Map p198; ☎04-955 5585; www.ishanspa.com; Jln Teluk Baru; ⏲11am-8pm) Some pretty posh pampering is available here, with an emphasis on traditional Malaysian techniques – including an invigorating bamboo massage – and natural remedies, such as compresses made with herbs from the garden.

Sun Spa SPA

(Map p198; ☎04-955 9287; Jln Teluk Baru; ⏲1-10pm) An interesting repertoire of affordable packages is on offer here.

Pantai Kok & Around

Oriental Village AMUSEMENT PARK

(Map p194; ☎04-959 4959; www.orientalvillage.my; Burau Bay; ⏲most outlets 10am-7pm) There is a handful of fast-food restaurants and poor-quality souvenir shops at this Disneyland-like open-air mall, where the main attraction is the SkyCab cable cars at Panorama Langkawi.

Panorama Langkawi CABLE CAR

(Map p194; ☎04-959 4225; www.panoramalangkawi.com; Oriental Village, Burau Bay; SkyCab ticket adult/child RM35/25; ⏲9.30am-7pm) Panorama Langkawi encompasses a befuddling number of attractions with individual entrance prices (packages are available). But the star of the show, and one of the island's most worthwhile attractions, is the SkyCab

Pulau Langkawi

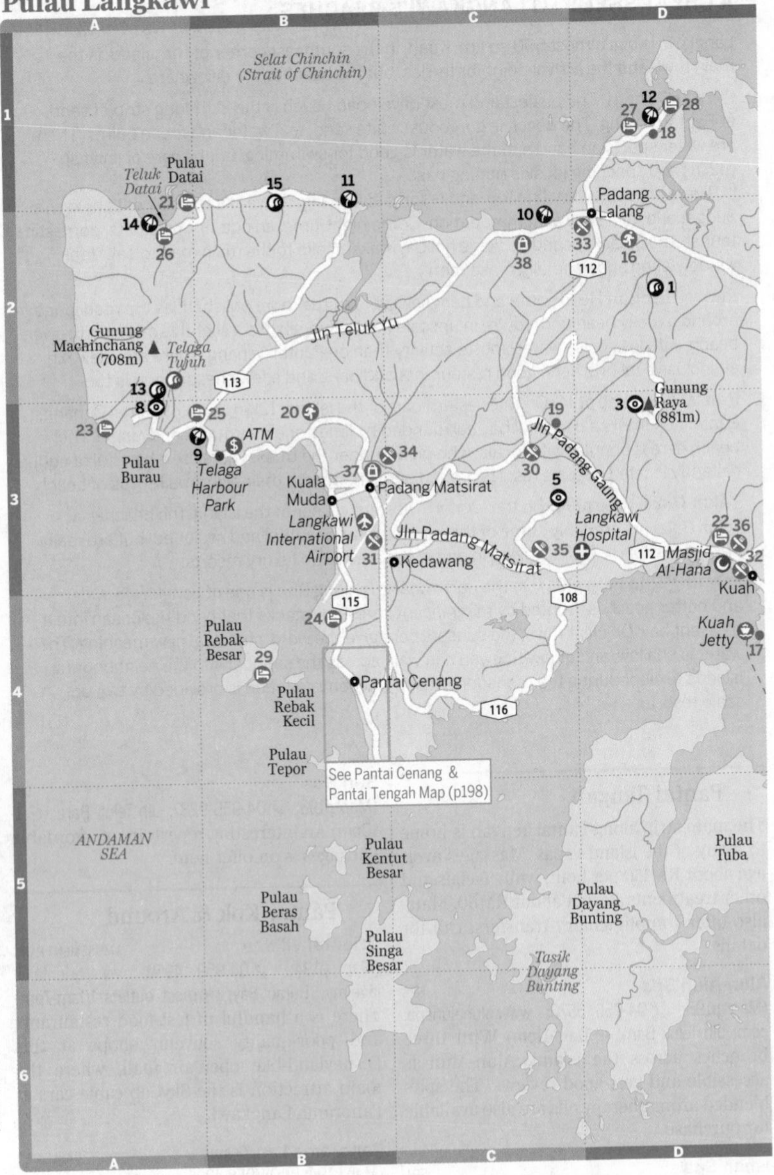

cable car that takes visitors on a vertiginous 20-minute trip to the top of the majestic Gunung Machinchang (708m). There are some incredible views along the way, and at the top, you can walk across the SkyBridge, a single-span suspension bridge located 100m above old-growth jungle canopy.

Other attractions here include an F1 simulator, 6D Cinemotion (a 3D movie simulator with splashes of water) and a 3D Art

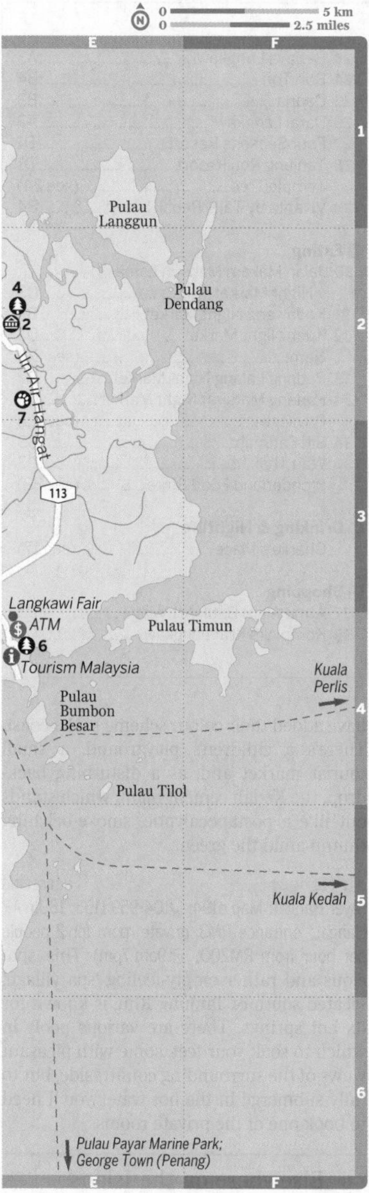

Museum where you can take selfies with murals of famous sights and artworks. Arrive early to avoid long queues at weekends and during school holidays. Once a month the SkyCab is closed for maintenance.

Telaga Tujuh WATERFALL

(Seven Wells; Map p194; Jln Telaga Tujuh) The series of freshwater rockpools at Telaga Tujuh, located at the top of a waterfall inland from Pantai Kok, makes a refreshing alternative to splashing about in the ocean. To get here follow the road from Pantai Kok past Oriental Village (SkyCab is well signposted) until it dead-ends at a car park. From here it's a steady 10-minute climb through the rainforest (stay to the right) to the wells at the top of the falls.

Connected by a thin trickle of refreshingly cool mountain water and surrounded by thick jungle that is home to a family of cheeky, and somewhat intimidating, monkeys (keep food out of sight), the pools also offer brilliant views of the island.

Teluk Datai & Around

Pantai Pasir Tengkorak BEACH

(Map p194; Jln Datai) This beautiful, secluded public beach, with its soft white sand, clear water, shady trees and jungle backdrop, is popular with locals on weekends; during the week it can be almost empty. The car park and entrance to the beach is on the 161 road, between Langkawi Crocodile Farm and Temurun waterfall. Note that the bathrooms here may or may not be open and there is nowhere to buy food or water.

There are several theories on the origins of the beach's name, meaning 'sandy skulls'. One eerie explanation relates to the legend of a nearby whirlpool which would swallow passing ships; the heads of the crew would later wash up on the shore.

Temurun Waterfall WATERFALL

(Map p194; Jln Datai) A brief walk from the main road up to Teluk Datai, the falls here – the island's tallest – are worth a look, though beware of food-stealing monkeys. The turn-off is on the left-hand side as you head east, 1km past Pantai Pasi Tengkorak.

Tanjung Rhu & Around

Kilim Karst Geoforest Park NATURE RESERVE

(Map p194; 1-4hr tour for a boat of up to 8 people per hour from RM150) The jetty near Tanjung Rhu is the main departure point for boat trips into the extensive mangrove forests with stunning limestone formations that edge much of the northeastern coast of Langkawi. Tours usually include a stop at Gua Kelawar (the bat cave, home to – you've guessed

Pulau Langkawi

Sights

1 Durian Perangin D2
2 Galeria Perdana E2
3 Gunung Raya D3
4 Kilim Karst Geoforest Park E2
5 Kota Mahsuri C3
6 Lagenda Langkawi Dalam Taman E4
7 Langkawi Bird Paradise E2
8 Oriental Village A3
Panorama Langkawi .... (see 8)
9 Pantai Kok B3
10 Pantai Pasir Hitam C2
11 Pantai Pasir Tengkorak B1
12 Tanjung Rhu D1
13 Telaga Tujuh A2
14 Teluk Datai A2
15 Temurun Waterfall B1

Activities, Courses & Tours

16 Air Hangat D2
17 Blue Water Star Sailing D4
East Marine .... (see 17)
18 JungleWalla D1
19 Langkawi Canopy Adventures C3
20 Rumah Holistic B3

Sleeping

21 Andaman Langkawi A1
22 Bayview Hotel D3
23 Berjaya Langkawi A3
24 Bon Ton B4
25 Danna B3
26 Datai Langkawi A2
27 Four Seasons Resort D1
28 Tanjung Rhu Resort D1
Temple Tree .... (see 24)
29 Vivanta by Taj – Rebak Island B4

Eating

30 Jalan Makam Mahsuri Lama Night Market C3
31 Kedawang Night Market B3
32 Kuah Night Market D3
Nam .... (see 24)
33 Padang Lalang Night Market D2
34 Padang Matsirat Night Market C3
Privilege .... (see 25)
35 Siti Fatimah C3
36 Wan Thai D3
Wonderland Food Store .... (see 32)

Drinking & Nightlife

Charlie's Place .... (see 17)

Shopping

37 Atma Alam Batik Art Vilage B3
38 Kompleks Kraf Langkawi C2

it – a colony of bats), lunch at a floating restaurant and eagle-watching.

Unfortunately, to attract eagles and please their camera-toting customers, many tour operators churn chicken fat or other foodstuff into the water behind the boats, disrupting the birds' natural feeding patterns and damaging the ecosystem. Dev's Adventure Tours (p200) is one outfit offering boat and kayaking trips that does not include eagle feeding.

Durian Perangin WATERFALL
(Map p194) The swimming pools here are a 10-minutes walk up paved steps through the forest, with pagoda-like shaded seating areas along the way. The water is always refreshingly cool, but the falls are best seen at the end of monsoon season, from late September and early October. The waterfalls are located 2km off the 112 road, just east of Air Hangat.

Pantai Pasir Hitam BEACH
(Map p194; Jln Teluk Yu) West of Tanjung Rhu is Langkawi's much touted but ultimately disappointing 'black-sand beach'. It isn't technically a black-sand beach, but mineral oxides have added their colour scheme to the coast. There's a children's playground, a small tourist market and, as a disturbing backdrop, the Kedah cement plant, which stands out like a postapocalyptic, smoke-belching thumb amid the green.

Air Hangat HOT SPRING
(Ayer Hangat; Map p194; ☎04-959 1195; 16 Jln Air Hangat; entrance RM3, private room for 2 people per hour from RM200; ⏰9am-7pm) This spacious and rather empty-feeling 'spa village', located south of Tanjung Rhu, is known for its hot springs. There are various pools in which to soak your feet, some with pleasant views of the surrounding countryside, but to fully submerge in the hot water you'll need to book one of the private rooms.

Elsewhere on the Island

Galeria Perdana MUSEUM
(Map p194; ☎04-959 1498; Jln Air Hangat; adult/child RM10/4; ⏰8.30am-5.30pm) Established by former prime minister Dr Mahathir Mohamad, who was born in Kedah and is credited with transforming the fortunes of Langkawi by granting it duty-free status,

this museum displays the sort of bizarre gifts that get passed between foreign nations and heads of state (Formula One race cars, Ming vases painted with Mahathir's face – that sort of thing). The vast collection is well displayed in this elegant gallery with magnificent, hand-painted ceilings. It's located 12km north of Kuah.

Gunung Raya MOUNTAIN

(Map p194) The tallest mountain on the island (881m) can be reached by a snaking, paved road through the jungle. It's a spectacular drive to the top with views across the island and over to Thailand from a lookout point and a small tea house (assuming there's no fog). In the evening there's a good chance of spotting the magnificent great hornbill near the road.

Kota Mahsuri SHRINE

(Mahsuri's Fort; Map p194; ☎04-955 6055; Kampung Mawat; adult/child RM15/5; ⌚8am-6pm) The story of Mahsuri, a Malay princess who was unjustly accused of adultery and put a curse on Langkawi in revenge, is commemorated at this historical complex that includes Mahsuri's shrine as well as a re-creation of a traditional house, a theatre, a 'diorama museum' and some simple food outlets. The site is west of Kuah, a few kilometres off the road to the airport.

As the legend goes, Mahsuri's punishment was to be executed by stabbing. With her dying breath she cursed Langkawi with seven generations of bad luck. This took place in around 1819. Not long after, the Siamese invaded the island, and some 160 years later, in 1987 (that's about seven generations), Langkawi took off as a tourism destination.

Rumah Holistic SPA

(Map p194; ☎019-339 1831; www.rumahholistic.com; massages from RM120; ⌚10am-6pm) This small retreat at the masseur's home, hidden in thick jungle, has just one treatment room for up to two people. While it is tricky to find (owner Eric will arrange to meet you and accompany you by car or send a local taxi driver to collect you), the rural, forest location is part of its charm. The approach here is holistic and full-day packages can include tai chi, yoga and meditation. Bookings must be made in advance.

Tours

Tours can be booked at any of the numerous travel agents at the jetty in Kuah and along Pantai Cenang, as well as at most hotels.

Cruises

There are several cruise operators in Langkawi, nearly all of which offer daily dinner, sunset and cocktail cruises.

LEGENDARY LANGKAWI

The name Langkawi combines the old Malay words *helang* (eagle) and *kawi* (reddish brown). Classical Malay literature claims the island as one of the resting places of Garuda, the mythological bird that became Vishnu's vehicle. The whole island is steeped in legends, and the favourite story is of Mahsuri, who was wrongly accused of infidelity by those jealous of her beauty. Before finally allowing herself to be executed, she put a curse on the island for seven generations. As proof of her innocence, white blood flowed from her veins, turning the sands of Langkawi's beaches white. Her tomb is known today as Kota Mahsuri.

A legacy of Mahsuri's curse is the 'field of burnt rice' at Padang Matsirat. There, villagers once burnt their rice fields rather than allow them to fall into the hands of the Siamese. It's said that to this day heavy rain sometimes brings traces of these grains to the surface.

Another legend concerns the naming of places around the island. Pulau Langkawi's two most powerful families became involved in a bitter argument over a marriage proposal. A fight broke out and all the kitchen utensils were used as missiles. The *kuah* (gravy) was spilt at Kuah and seeped into the ground at Kisap, which means 'to seep'. A pot landed at Belanga Perak (Broken Pot) and finally the saucepan of *air panas* (hot water) came to land where Air Hangat village is today. The fathers of these two families got their comeuppance for causing all this mayhem – they are now the island's two major mountain peaks. You can learn more at the intriguing Lagenda Langkawi Dalam Taman (p192) in Kuah.

Pantai Cenang & Pantai Tengah

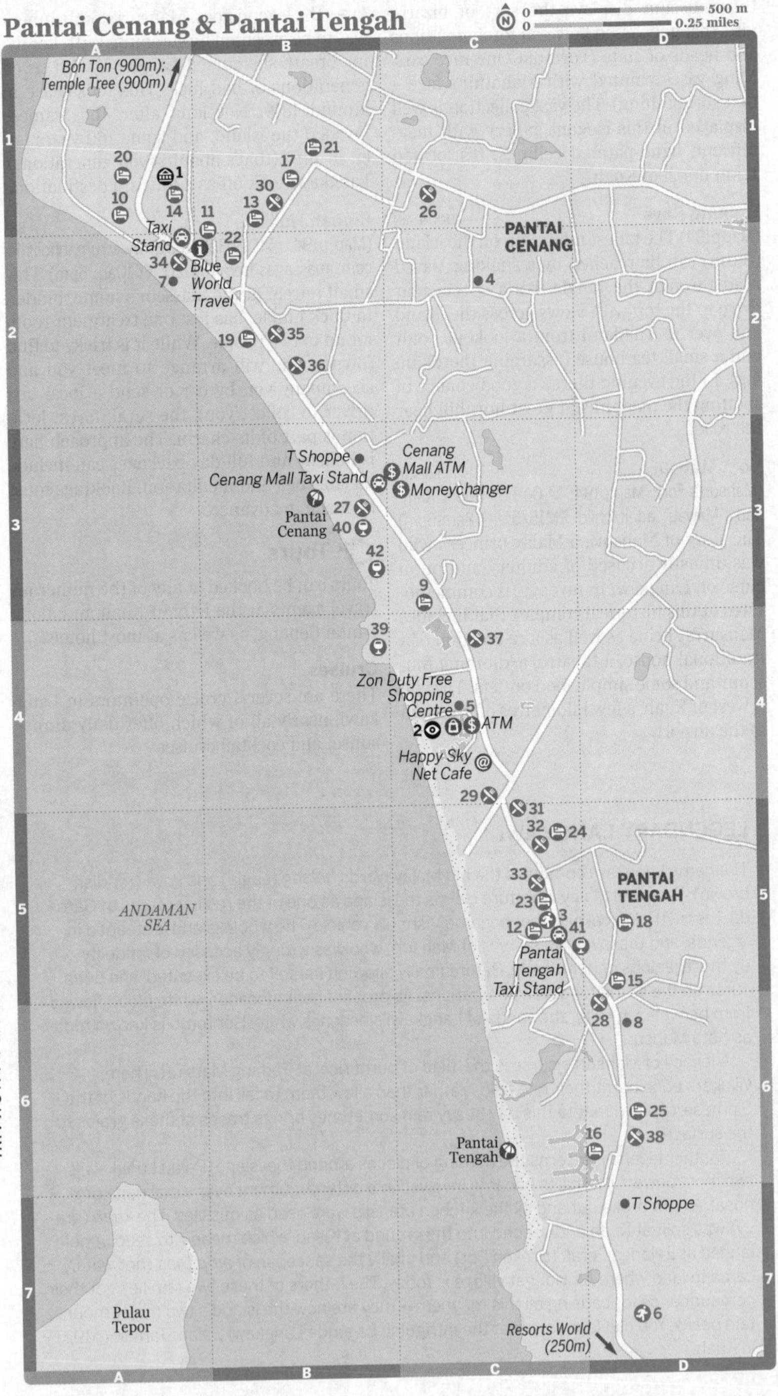

Pantai Cenang & Pantai Tengah

Blue Water Star Sailing CRUISE
(Map p194; ☎04-966 4868; www.bluewaterstarsailing.com; dinner cruise RM450) This outfit runs an infamously boozy dinner cruise every day from 3pm to 8pm. Boats depart from the yacht club in Kuah; transport here is not included.

Crystal Yacht Holidays CRUISE
(Map p198; ☎04-955 6545; www.crystalyacht.com; Pantai Cenang; dinner cruise RM280) Operates popular sunset dinner cruises. Boats depart from the pier at Resorts World, south of Pantai Tengah, and transport from most hotels is included.

Tropical Charters CRUISE
(Map p198; ☎012-588 3274; www.tropicalcharters.com.my; Pantai Tengah; cruises from RM260) Offers a variety of cruises. Boats depart from the pier near Resorts World, south of Pantai Tengah; transport from most hotels is included.

Diving & Snorkelling

Strung out like several green jewels in the teal sea are the four islands that make up **Pulau Payar Marine Park**, the focus of Langkawi's dive and snorkelling expeditions. Most trips come to 2km-long Pulau Payar, although you probably won't see the interior of the island – all the action centres on a diving platform and horseshoe-bend of coast. Enquire about the water conditions before you go, as it can get murky.

East Marine DIVING
(Map p194; ☎04-966 3966; www.eastmarine.com.my; Royal Langkawi Yacht Club, Jln Pantai Dato Syed Omar, Kuah; snorkelling/diving trips from RM300/320) Probably the most reputable diving outfit on the island. East Marine conducts full-day diving and snorkelling excursions to Pulau Payar Marine Park, as well as Professional Association of Diving Instructors (PADI) certification courses starting at RM1300.

Langkawi Coral SNORKELLING
(☎04-966 7318; www.langkawicoral.com; snorkelling/diving from RM300/320) Diving and snorkelling trips to Pulau Payar Marine Park include transfers from hotels to the departure point at Kuah pier, a buffet lunch and some time for sunbathing.

Island Hopping

The most popular day trip is the island-hopping tour, offered by most tour and diving companies and costing as little as RM30 per person. Tours usually take in **Dayang Bunting** (Lake of the Pregnant Maiden), located on the island of the same name. It's a freshwater lake surrounded by craggy limestone cliffs and dense jungle, and a good spot for swimming. Other destinations include the pristine beach at **Pulau Beras Basah**, sea stacks and sea caves and a stop for **eagle-watching**. As with the boat trips at Kilim Karst, many operators use food to attract the eagles, which disrupts their natural feeding patterns; the tours offered by JungleWalla (p200) do not include eagle feeding.

Nature & Adventure Tours

Dev's Adventure Tours ADVENTURE TOUR
(Map p198; ☎019-494 9193; www.langkawi-nature.com; Lot 1556, Tanjung Mali, Pantai Cenang; tour RM120-220) Cycling, birdwatching, mangrove excursions and jungle walks: this outfit offers a fat menu of options led by knowledgeable and enthusiastic guides. Book online or by phone. Transfers are provided from most hotels.

JungleWalla ADVENTURE TOUR
(Map p194; ☎019-590 2300; www.junglewalla.com; 1C, Lot 1392, Jln Tanjung Rhu; tours RM160-250) Since setting up this nature-tour company in 1994, Irshad Mobarak has become something of a celebrity naturalist in Malaysia. On offer are birdwatching excursions, jungle walks, and mangrove- and island-hopping trips, all with an emphasis on observing wildlife. Multiday itineraries are available on request.

Langkawi Canopy Adventures ADVENTURE TOUR
(Map p194; ☎012-466 8027; www.langkawi.travel; Lubuk Semilang; tour RM80-220) The highlight here is high-adrenalin 'air trekking' through the rainforest along a series of rope courses and zip lines. Excursions must be booked at least a day in advance and you'll need to arrange a taxi to take you to the site at Lubuk Semilang, in the middle of Langkawi.

Jet Skiing

Mega Water Sports WATER SPORTS
(Map p198; ☎012-200 2155; www.megawatersports.com; tour RM500-700) These guided jet-ski tours around the islands off the south coast of Langkawi get rave reviews. There are various difficulty ratings, from a family-friendly beginner level to one requiring wave-jumping experience. Tours start and end at the northern end of Pantai Cenang.

Festivals & Events

Langkawi International Maritime & Aerospace Exhibition AIR SHOW
(LIMA; www.lima.com.my) LIMA is considered one of the world's major air shows. Hotels fill up and prices soar during the biannual event held in March.

Sleeping

While there is plenty of decent accommodation on Langkawi, it isn't cheap. Luxury resorts here are some of the best around, but midrange places (and even some of the upscale ones) can feel lacklustre, and there are relatively few budget-oriented hostels and guesthouses.

During school holidays and the peak tourist season (approximately November to February), Pulau Langkawi can become crowded and advance bookings are generally necessary. At other times of the year supply far outstrips demand and prices are negotiable.

See our cheat sheet to the island's beaches (p193) to determine where to stay.

Kuah

Bayview Hotel HOTEL $$$
(Map p194; ☎04-966 1818; www.bayviewhotels.com; 1 Jln Pandak Mayah; r RM530-770, ste RM1200-1300, all incl breakfast;) This is your standard high-rise chain hotel. The rooms lack character but are spacious and functional, and there are great views from the higher floors and the outdoor pool area.

Pantai Cenang & Around

Sweet Inn HOTEL $
(Map p198; ☎04-955 8864; www.sweetinns.net; r RM80-100; P) One of the cleaner, brighter budget options in Pantai Cenang, with plain rooms that manage to keep cool in the heat. The wi-fi doesn't reach beyond reception and the place lacks a bit of atmosphere, but it does gain points for easy beach access.

Izz Room GUESTHOUSE $
(Map p198; ☎04-955 1397; www.izzroom.blogspot.com; r RM50-80;) Basic, sparsely furnished accommodation spread around a pleasant gravel courtyard with shady palm trees. The best rooms are in the brightly

coloured block opposite reception, while cheaper doubles have fans and shared bathrooms. Laundry service is available (RM4 per kilo).

Rainbow Lodge HOTEL $

(Map p198; ☎04-955 8103; www.rainbowlangkawi.com; dm RM22, r RM50-90; ❄@📶) Set a little way back from the beach, this friendly place has a sociable cafe area with views over neighbouring fields. Partitions and curtains give dorm beds some privacy. Popular with backpackers seeking a cheap place to rest between beers.

Cottage GUESTHOUSE $

(Map p198; ☎019-426 8818; www.thecottagelangkawi.blogspot.com; No 8, Kampung Haji Saad, Jln Pantai Cenang; dm RM25, r RM60-150; ❄📶) Turn down a narrow lane next to Laman Padi at the northern end of Pantai Cenang to reach this rustic guesthouse offering basic accommodation in a farmlike setting, complete with free-roaming chickens.

Gecko Guesthouse GUESTHOUSE $

(Map p198; ☎019 428 3801; rebeccafiott@hotmail.com; dm RM20, r RM45-75; ❄📶) Here you'll find a jungly collection of bungalows, chalets and rather dingy dorms, dreadlocked folk in the common area and very good chocolate milkshakes served at the bar.

Gemalai Village HOTEL $$

(Map p198; ☎04-955 3225; thegemalai@ladaeco.my; r incl breakfast RM350-430; P❄📶) A complex of six traditional *kampung* huts built on stilts over the paddy fields at Laman Padi. The authentically styled rooms are comfortable and well equipped, and the bathrooms are partially open air. An excellent Malay breakfast is served in your room.

Although the name Gemalai refers to the Bahasa Malaysia word for a gentle breeze that whispers across the paddy, light sleepers should beware that the huts' thin walls and close proximity to a road, as well as roosters and buffalo, might make their stay a little less than peaceful.

Malibest Resort HOTEL $$

(Map p198; ☎04-955 8222; www.malibestresort.com; r RM150-260; ❄📶) Malibest is a friendly place with rooms right on the busiest stretch of Pantai Cenang. These range from relatively modern brick bungalows to the undisputed king of the crop: 'treetop' chalets that sit atop tall wooden pylons (with steep steps up) and enjoy uninterrupted sea views.

> **JELLYFISH WARNING**
>
> Jellyfish can sometimes be present close to the shores of Langkawi. While stings can be painful, most are not dangerous. However, there have been infrequent reports of the presence of the potentially lethal box jellyfish. Some hotels display warning signs when jellyfish have been spotted; if in doubt ask around before entering the water. If you are stung, stay still and wash the affected area with seawater. Note that vinegar is no longer recommended for treating jellyfish stings, and putting alcohol or urine on the sting should also be avoided. If the sting is severe, or you have difficulty breathing, seek immediate medical assistance.

Cabin Resort HOTEL $$

(Map p198; ☎04-955 3189; www.thecabin.com.my; r RM160; ❄📶) With a vibe verging on caravan park, the Cabin features 10 cutesy bungalows a short walk from the beach. Rooms are pleasantly cosy (read: small) but, decked out with colourful furniture, have more character than most places in this price range.

Langkapuri Inn HOTEL $$

(Map p198; ☎04-955 1202; info@langkapuri-inn.com; r incl breakfast RM140-250; ❄📶) A pleasant clutch of connected chalets at the southern end of the beach. The pricier ones have sea views and a pinch of character; the cheapest are in need of a renovation and should be avoided.

★Bon Ton BOUTIQUE HOTEL $$$

(Map p194; ☎04-955 6787; www.bontonresort.com.my; villas incl breakfast RM750-1265; ❄📶🏊) Along with neighbouring Temple Tree, these two boutique hotels are our favourite places in Langkawi, if not in the region. Bon Ton takes the form of eight Malay stilt houses perched over a grassy, coconut-palm-studded plot of land, each one decked out with dark wood and positioned to catch the breeze. With its organic accents and traditional craftwork, it's somehow regal and rustic all at once.

★Temple Tree BOUTIQUE HOTEL $$$

(Map p194; ☎04-955 3937; www.templetree.com.my; r incl breakfast RM670-1515; ❄📶🏊) On the adjoining plot to Bon Ton, sister hotel Temple

LOCAL KNOWLEDGE

NARELLE MCMURTRIE: HOTELIER

Narelle has lived on Pulau Langkawi for 21 years and is the owner of Bon Ton (p201) and Temple Tree (p201).

How is Langkawi different from other beachy places in Southeast Asia? Development here is slow and the island is still very laid-back. People often return to Langkawi and by their second visit they feel at home. It's a real island with an easy-going lifestyle, and quite safe.

Your favourite beach? One of the deserted beaches on Dayan Bunting island: a beautiful little cove with clear water and a private beach.

A good place to eat? Lunchtime is the best time to eat local food – my favourite place is Siti Fatimah (p206). There can be up to 70 dishes on offer, buffet-style, for about RM10 with a drink. Nearly all the customers there are Malaysian.

A good bar? La Sal (p206) at Casa del Mar for an evening drink.

One must-do Langkawi activity? Rent a car and explore the island.

What's one way to gain an interesting peak into local life in Langkawi? If you happen to be here for Hari Raya at the end of the fasting month (Ramadan), you can sample amazing home cooking at the makeshift stalls that pop up all over the island from about 3pm.

Tree raises the stakes with a collection of antique structures relocated from various points in Malaysia. An imposing Chinese mansion, a wooden villa from Penang, colonial-style shophouses and other restored structures make up the stately, park-like compound.

Linking both locations is a common thread of class, style, thoughtful service and – take this as a warning if you don't care to share your villa with Felix – cats.

Casa del Mar BOUTIQUE HOTEL $$$
(Map p198; ☎04-955 2388; www.casadelmar-langkawi.com; r RM800-950, ste RM900-1770, all incl breakfast;) This is a sumptuous, vaguely Spanish-themed place on the quieter northern end of Pantai Cenang. Rooms are decked out with thoughtful design touches and techie amenities, as well as a small private garden or balcony. Various package deals are available. At peak times the 34 rooms can get booked up several months in advance.

Vivanta by Taj – Rebak Island RESORT $$$
(Map p194; ☎04-966 5566; www.vivantabytaj.com/rebak-island-langkawi; Rebak Besar; r RM440-900, ste RM740-1900, all incl breakfast;) Lying just off Pantai Cenang, the small island of Rebak Besar plays host to this exclusive resort, which offers spacious and elegant chalets in beautifully landscaped grounds. It has all the facilities you would expect, including gym, spa and restaurants. Access to and from the island is by speedboat and transfers from the airport are included.

The island is car free and has its own quiet stretch of beach, making it a good option for families with children.

Meritus Pelangi Beach Resort & Spa RESORT $$$
(Map p198; ☎04-952 8888; www.meritushotels.com; r/ste incl breakfast from RM810/1880;) An expansive, family-oriented resort with a full roster of facilities, kids' activities, restaurants and a seemingly never-ending swimming pool. A recent renovation has refreshed the traditional Malay-style rooms housed in wooden chalets with views of the gardens, pool or beach.

Pantai Tengah & Around

Zackry Guest House GUESTHOUSE $
(Map p198; zackryghouse@gmail.com; r RM60-110;) This ramshackle, family-run guesthouse has a homely, sociable atmosphere. Rooms are basic, yet clean and cosy, and the recently spruced-up communal areas include a small kitchen with a fridge but no cooking facilities. Note that there's a two-night minimum, no phone bookings, and only about half of the rooms have an attached bathroom.

★La Pari-Pari BOUTIQUE HOTEL $$
(Map p198; ☎04-955 3010; www.laparipari.com; r incl breakfast from RM330; P❄📶🏊) 🍃 Tucked away in a picturesque spot just off the main Pantai Tengah strip, La Pari-Pari has a laid-back vibe. The 12 immaculate rooms, with a slightly space-age feel and huge bathrooms, are housed in chic whitewashed chalets in attractive grounds, with day beds and a pond-side beach.

It's the type of place where guests exchange life stories over cocktails at the poolside bar and restaurant **fatCUPID** (Map p198; ☎04-955 3010; hello@fatcupid.com.my; 2273 Jln Teluk Baru; mains RM25-38; ⏲9am-10.30pm Tue-Sun).

Tropical Resort HOTEL $$
(Map p198; ☎04-955 4075; www.tropicalresortlangkawi.com; r incl breakfast RM200-250; ❄@📶🏊) Located by a quiet patch of beach, just a few minutes' walk down a sandy path to the seashore, is this string of spotless and well-run chalets. At night the soft lighting around the pool makes for a romantic setting.

Green Village HOTEL $$
(Map p198; ☎04-955 3117; www.greenvillagelangkawi.com; Jln Pantai Tengah; r incl breakfast RM140-220; ❄@📶🏊) Green Village takes the form of several linked, low-rise villas surrounding a pool and gardenlike grounds. Rooms are small, the decor is dated and some areas feel rather rundown, but bikes, treehouse and pool table make this a clever choice for a family on a budget.

★Ambong Ambong HOTEL $$$
(Map p198; ☎04-955 8428; www.ambong-ambong.com; studio/ste incl breakfast RM720/980; ❄📶🏊) This clutch of minimalist, contemporary structures perched on a jungly hillside form a pleasing contrast. Choose between one of six inviting studios, three large suites or one of the vast-feeling two-bedroom cottages; all are stylish and airy with balconies overlooking the rainforest and sea below. The steep access makes it unsuitable for people requiring wheelchair access and children under 12.

Frangipani RESORT $$$
(Map p198; ☎04-952 0000; www.frangipanilangkawi.com; r RM850-1200, ste 1500-1800, all incl breakfast; ❄@📶🏊) 🍃 Friendly service, genuine efforts towards ecological conservation and the location right on a quiet stretch of beach are the reasons to stay at this large resort, less so the slightly cramped rooms.

Villa Molek HOTEL $$$
(Map p198; ☎04-955 3605; www.villamolek.com; 2863 Jln Teluk Baru; ste incl breakfast from RM700; ❄📶🏊) Those looking for a quiet, home-like stay should head here. Accommodation takes the form of 12 classy, apartmentlike suites, each with living room and kitchenette. Rooms are slotted into a small, secluded garden across the road from the beach and, as children under 18 aren't welcome, draw a predominately mature clientele.

Holiday Villa RESORT $$$
(Map p198; ☎04-952 9999; www.holidayvillahotellangkawi.com; r RM540-590, ste RM1280-3630; ❄@📶🏊) A vast resort complex retaining a palpable '80s feel, not to mention tennis courts, gym, several restaurants and flash new infinity pool. Rooms are airy and brightly furnished, and look out over the lawns and the soft white-sand beach.

Pantai Kok & Around

Berjaya Langkawi RESORT $$$
(Map p194; ☎04-959 1888; www.berjayahotel.com; Karong Berkunci 200, Burau Bay; r RM750-860, ste 1190-1740, all incl breakfast; ❄@📶🏊) Located past the headland at the western end of Pantai Kok, the Berjaya has some 424 rooms spread over a vast area; guests are ferried between reception and their chalets in mini-buses. The waterfront suites are the most attractive, while others look out onto the lush rainforest. A stay includes a complimentary tour of the latter.

Danna HOTEL $$$
(Map p194; ☎04-959 3288; www.thedanna.com; Telega Harbour Park, Pantai Kok; r RM1200-2700, ste RM4500-5000, all incl breakfast; ❄@📶🏊) This imposing, sumptuous hotel embraces its colonial-era theme with details such as a billiard room, library and cigar room, tiffin lunches and speciality English afternoon teas. Rooms are huge and come decked out with attractive furniture and marble floors, and the hotel pool is the largest in Langkawi.

Teluk Datai

Datai Langkawi RESORT $$$
(Map p194; ☎04-950 0500; www.thedatai.com; Jln Teluk Datai; r RM1600-4500, ste RM3000-

15,000, all incl breakfast; P ❄ @ ≋ ≅) Tucked in a corner in the far northwest of the island surrounded by ancient rainforest, the Datai manages to feel both untamed and luxurious. Along with rooms and suites in the main hotel building, there are spacious and modern rainforest or seafront villas to choose from.

All have access to a small city's worth of amenities (spas, gyms, yoga – the works), not to mention one of the island's best beaches. A unique luxury experience.

Andaman Langkawi RESORT $$$
(Map p194; ☎04-959 1088; www.luxurycollection.com/andaman; Jln Teluk Datai; r RM800-1400, ste 1500-3000, all incl breakfast; P ❄ @ ≋ ≅) In a grand wooden Malay-style building seemingly dropped in the middle of the jungle is this luxurious retreat with the usual multi-star amenities and dining outlets, as well as its own stunning semiprivate beach. There are no villas or bungalows, but the rooms are large and inviting, many with great views.

Tanjung Rhu

★Tanjung Rhu Resort RESORT $$$
(Map p194; ☎04-959 1033; www.tanjungrhu.com.my; r RM1550-2800, ste RM3000-3500, all incl breakfast; P ❄ @ ≋ ≅) This beautifully situated resort has large and comfy rooms with balconies and great views of the limestone and green water at Tanjung Rhu. Service is a pleasant blend of competent and friendly, and two elegant 50m pools as well as a saltwater lagoon pool are added draws. With no water sports, the 2.5km private beach feels secluded and serene.

The only real downside is its distance from many of Langkawi's attractions, restaurants and nightlife; those seeking complete relaxation may view that as a plus.

Four Seasons Resort RESORT $$$
(Map p194; ☎04-950 8888; www.fourseasons.com/langkawi; r RM2900-3500, villa RM7000-25,000, all incl breakfast; P ❄ @ ≋ ≅) Sporting a youthful (at least for a Four Seasons resort) vibe and a Moroccan theme, this is among Langkawi's most unique and luxurious resorts. Amenities are everything you'd expect at this level and service is impeccable. Bathrooms-so-big-you'll-get-lost-in-them aside, we loved the manicured jungle setting and the semiprivate beach.

Eating

Around Kuah

Wan Thai THAI $$
(Map p194; ☎04-966 1214; 80 & 82 Persiaran Bunga Raya; mains RM12-55; ⏲11am-3.30pm & 6.30-10pm) A reminder that Langkawi is geographically closer to Thailand than the Malaysian mainland comes in the form of this buzzing restaurant serving excellent traditional Thai cuisine in a large dining room where the decorators didn't scrimp in their use of ornate polished wood. Popular dishes such as chicken cooked in pandan leaf sell out early. Booking is recommended.

Wonderland Food Store CHINESE $$
(Map p194; Lot 179-181, Pusat Perniagaan Kelana Mas, Kuah; mains from RM10; ⏲6-11pm Sat-Thu) Of the string of Chinese-style seafood restaurants just outside Kuah, Wonderland has been around longer than most and gets the best reviews. It's an informal, open-air place where the food is both cheap and tasty.

Pantai Cenang & Around

Padang Pasir INDIAN $
(Map p198; ☎04-966 6786; Jln Pantai Cenang; mains RM11-16; ⏲7am-1am) This well-positioned food stall with open-air seating on the main Cenang strip sells tempting chicken, lamb and naan bread fresh from the tandoor oven, as well as *nasi kandar* (rice with curry sauces) and rotis. It's open from 7am for breakfast to 1am at night, making it a good place to stop and refuel at any time of day.

Kasbah INTERNATIONAL $$
(Map p198; Pantai Cenang; mains RM7-23; ⏲9am-11pm) A relaxed, friendly cafe housed in a spacious, open-sided wooden structure constructed and furnished by the artistic owners using recycled materials. Reggae, hammocks, books and games attract a crowd of happy travellers, as does the menu of decent coffee, breakfasts, salads and sandwiches, and recommended daily Malaysian specials.

Brasserie MEDITERRANEAN $$
(Map p198; ☎04-955 1927; 27A Jln Pantai Cenang; mains RM24-118; ⏲noon-11pm Tue-Sun) A classy beachside restaurant and bar serving modern European food in a breezy, shaded outdoor dining area complete with ocean views and sand underfoot. There's a happy hour on cocktails from 4pm to 6pm.

DON'T MISS

LANGKAWI'S ROVING NIGHT MARKET

Local food can be tricky to find on Langkawi. Fortunately, for fans of Malay eats there's a rotating *pasar malam* (night market) held at various points across the island. It's a great chance to indulge in cheap, take-home meals and snacks, and is held from about 6pm to 10pm at the following locations:

Monday **Jalan Makam Mahsuri Lama** (Map p194), in the centre of the island, not far from the MARDI Agro Technology Park.

Tuesday **Kedawang** (Map p194), just east of the airport.

Wednesday & Saturday **Kuah** (Map p194), opposite the Masjid Al-Hana; this is the largest market.

Thursday **Bohor Tempoyak** (Map p198), at the northern end of Pantai Cenang.

Friday **Padang Lalang** (Map p194), at the roundabout near Pantai Pasir Hitam.

Sunday **Padang Matsirat** (Map p194), near the roundabout just north of the airport.

Red Tomato INTERNATIONAL **$$**
(Map p198; ☎04-955 4055; 5 Casa Fina Ave, Pantai Cenang; mains RM20-40; ⏲9.30am-10.30pm) Red Tomato is run by expats who crank out some of the best pizza on the island. It's also a popular breakfast spot; options include eggs cooked how you like them and served with homemade bread.

Nam INTERNATIONAL **$$$**
(Map p194; ☎04-955 6787; Bon Ton Resort, Jln Kuala Muda; mains RM30-94; ⏲11am-11pm; ✎) At Bon Ton resort (p201), Nam boasts a well-executed menu of fusion food, from chargrilled rack of lamb with roast pumpkin, mint salad, hummus and tomato jam, to a nine-dish sampler of Nonya cuisine. There are plenty of veggie options, and at night, amid Bon Ton's starry jungle grounds, the setting is superb. Reservations recommended during peak season (December and January).

Putumayo ASIAN **$$$**
(Map p198; ☎04-953 2233; Lot 1584, Pantai Cenang; mains RM10-100; ⏲1-11.30pm) Excellent service (the waiter folds your napkin on your lap) amid a beautiful open-air courtyard. The cuisine ranges from across Asia, looping from Malaysia through Thailand to China, with fresh fish and seafood (including prawns the size of your hand) priced by weight.

Orkid Ria CHINESE **$$$**
(Map p198; ☎04-955 4128; Lot 1225, Jln Pantai Cenang; mains from RM12; ⏲11.30am-3pm & 6-11pm) The place to go on Pantai Cenang for Chinese-style seafood. Fat shrimp, fish and crabs are plucked straight from tanks out front, but it doesn't come cheap.

Pantai Tengah & Around

Melayu MALAYSIAN **$**
(Map p198; ☎04-955 4075; Jln Teluk Baru; mains RM5-10; ⏲3-10.30pm) The comfortable dining room, pleasant outdoor seating area and efficient service here belie the reasonable prices. A good place to go for cheap, authentic Malaysian food in the evening, since most of the island's local restaurants are lunchtime buffets. Alcohol isn't served but you can bring your own for no charge.

Llawa MALAYSIAN **$$**
(Map p198; ☎04-955 3608; Lot 2863 Jln Teluk Baru; mains RM26-75; ⏲3-11pm Fri-Wed) First impressions of the 'dining lounge' at Llawa – low lighting, generously sized chairs with colourful cushions – are promising, and fortunately the ambience is matched by the flavoursome Malaysian food served here. We recommend the decadently rich beef rendang and the *udang percik* (grilled king prawns). The menu also features steaks and the like for the less adventurous.

Istanbul TURKISH **$$**
(Map p198; ☎04-955 2100; hungry_monkey@hotmail.com; Jln Pantai Tengah; mains RM22-60; ⏲6pm-midnight; 📶) Istanbul features a cosy dining room, friendly service and a menu that extends far beyond doner kebab. We loved the Adana lamb with eggplant dip that was filling and tasty, but if that doesn't sate your appetite try the 1m-long kebab served with rice, bread, a mixed meze plate, barbecue tomato and chilli (RM250).

Troppo Co INTERNATIONAL $$

(Map p198; ☎04-955 2602; Lot 1697 Kampung Tasek Anak, Jln Teluk Baru; sandwiches RM18-30; ⏲9am-5pm Wed-Mon; ✻📶) A cafe with tables outside, air-conditioned seating inside that serves real coffee and fruit smoothies, supplemented with a menu of hearty breakfast dishes and creative sandwiches on homemade bread.

La Chocolatine FRENCH $$

(Map p198; ☎04-955 8891; 3 Jln Teluk Baru; mains RM15-30; ⏲9am-9pm; ✻) Excellent French desserts – croissants, tarts and éclairs – as well as light salads, sandwiches and quiches. Did we mention coffees, teas and real hot chocolate? A sophisticated, air-conditioned snack stop.

Fat Mum CHINESE $$

(Map p198; ☎04-955 9882; Lot 62A Jln Teluk Baru; mains RM10-36; ⏲9am-10pm Wed-Mon) The eponymous proprietor here is a cheerful presence, serving up her brand of traditional Chinese home cooking, including homemade tofu and her speciality flaming noodles.

Unkaizan JAPANESE $$$

(Map p198; ☎04-955 4118; www.unkaizan.com; Jln Teluk Baru; mains RM30-100; ⏲6-11pm, closed 2nd Wed of each month) Lauded Japanese food, with seating in a cosy bungalow and on an open patio. The menu spans all that Japan is known for, but don't forget to ask for the specials board, which often includes dishes made with imported Japanese seafood. Reservations recommended.

Pantai Kok & Around

Privilege MALAYSIAN $$$

(Map p194; ☎04-956 1188; www.privilegerestaurant.com; B8, 1st fl, Perdana Quay; mains RM40-100; ⏲noon-11pm Mon-Sat) The intimate, jazzy dining room here has great views over Telaga Harbour. On the menu are international and modern Malaysian dishes and some excellent desserts including steamed *gula melaka* (sugar from the coconut tree) crème brûlée and homemade ice cream with exotic flavours like coconut and tamarind, pickled nutmeg and *gula melaka*.

Elsewhere on the Island

★ **Siti Fatimah** MALAYSIAN $

(Map p194; Jln Kampung Tok Senik, Kawasan Mata Air; mains from RM5; ⏲7am-4.30pm Thu-Tue) Possibly Langkawi's most famous destination for Malay food – and it lives up to the rep. Come midmorning, dozens of rich curries, grilled fish, dips, stir-fries and other Malay-style dishes are laid out in a self-service buffet. The flavours are strong and the prices low. It's located on Jln Kampung Tok Senik; most taxi drivers know the place.

Drinking & Nightlife

Langkawi's duty-free status makes it one of the cheapest places to buy booze in Malaysia, and alcohol at many restaurants and hotels is half the price as it is on the mainland. There are some decent beach-style bars along Pantai Cenang, including some informal candlelit and deckchair affairs that pop up on the sand as the sun goes down. Like the island itself, the bar scene here is pretty laid-back, and those looking to party hard may be disappointed.

Little Lylia's Chill Out Cafe BAR

(Map p198; Pantai Cenang; ⏲noon-1am) This long standing, chummy bar spills out onto Pantai Cenang until the late hours. The chairs and tables may be practically falling apart, but friendly service and a chilled-out vibe hold the place together.

Yellow Café BAR

(Map p198; Pantai Cenang; ⏲noon-1am Wed-Mon; 📶) A fun, breezy place with beanbags on the beach and a few imported beers. Come between 4pm and 6pm when beers are buy one get one free.

Cliff BAR

(Map p198; www.thecliff langkawi.com; Pantai Cenang; ⏲noon-11pm) Perched on the rocky outcrop that divides Pantai Cenang and Pantai Tengah, the Cliff is well located for a sunset cocktail. Expect a full bar, a good wine selection and an eclectic menu that spans from Europe to Malaysia (mains RM23 to RM72).

La Sal BAR

(Map p198; www.casadelmar-langkawi.com; Casa del Mar, Pantai Cenang) This open-air restaurant and cocktail bar has some creative drinks – who fancies a five-spiced poached apple and cinnamon mojito? Tom yum martini, anyone? Come evening, tables in the sand and torchlight make La Sal a sexy sunset drink destination.

Charlie's Place BAR

(Map p194; www.langkawiyachtclub.com; Jln Pantai Dato Syed Omar, Langkawi Yacht Club, Kuah;

9am-midnight) About 500m uphill from the jetty is this bar looking over the harbour. Yes, it's located at the Langkawi Yacht Club, but it's a friendly, unpretentious place that functions equally well as a restaurant (mains RM22 to RM60) or bar. It was being renovated at the time of research but should have reopened by the time you read this.

Sunba Retro Bar BAR
(Map p198; www.sungroup-langkawi.com; Jln Teluk Baru; 7pm-late) An in-house cover band, a DJ spinning tunes from the '60s, '70s and '80s, and a well-stocked bar fuel parties late into the night here.

Shopping

Duty-free shopping in Langkawi is a big draw for Malaysians, who flock here to stock up on cooking utensils, suitcases and chocolate. But unless you're planning to pick up a new set of saucepans or plates you are unlikely to be wildly excited by the duty-free shops; the greatest conglomeration of these is at Kuah jetty and at the southern end of Pantai Cenang, near Underwater World.

Atma Alam Batik Art Vilage HANDICRAFTS
(Map p194; 04-955 1227; www.atmaalam.com; Jln Padang Matsirat, near Petronas fuel station; 9am-6pm) A huge handicrafts complex with an emphasis on batik. Visitors can paint and take home their own swatch of batik for RM30. Atma Alam is located in Padang Matsirat, not far from the airport; most taxi drivers are familiar with it.

Kompleks Kraf Langkawi HANDICRAFTS
(Langkawi Craft Complex; Map p194; 04-959 1913; www.malaysiacraft.com.my; Jln Teluk Yu; 10am-6pm) An enormous handicrafts centre where you can watch demonstrations of traditional crafts and buy any traditional Malaysian product or craft you can imagine. There are also a couple of on-site exhibitions devoted to local legends and wedding ceremonies. The complex is located in the far north of the island, close to Pantai Pasir Hitam.

Information

INTERNET ACCESS

While most hotels and many restaurants offer wi-fi, the connection can be weak, especially in more jungly areas. Internet cafes are few and far between; one is **Happy Sky Net Cafe** (Map p198; Jln Pantai Cenang; per hour RM5; 9am-8pm).

MEDICAL SERVICES

Langkawi Hospital (Map p194; 04-966 3333; Jln Bukit Teguh) Located just west of Kuah, off the 112 road to the airport.

MONEY

The only banks are at **Kuah** (Map p194) and **Telaga Harbour Park** (Map p194), but there are ATMs at the airport, the jetty, at **Cenang Mall** (Map p198) and at **Underwater World** (Map p198). There are a couple of **money-changers** (Map p198) at Pantai Cenang.

TOURIST INFORMATION

Tourism Malaysia (Map p194; 04-966 7789; Jln Persiaran Putra, Kuah; 9am-5pm) With three offices in Langkawi – located opposite the ferry terminal entrance at Kuah jetty, on Jalan Persiaran Putra (next to the mosque) in Kuah Town, and in the airport arrivals hall (open until 10pm) – Tourism Malaysia offers comprehensive information on the whole island.

WEBSITES

A comprehensive source of island information is www.naturallylangkawi.my. Another source of island info is www.langkawi-info.com.

TRAVEL AGENCIES

There are travel agencies all along Pantai Cenang and at Kuah jetty that can organise the usual tours and tickets.

Blue World Travel (Map p198; 04-966 3637; www.theblueworldtravel.com.my; 3 Kedai Jln Pantai; 9am-11pm) This helpful travel company has stands on Pantai Cenang and at Kuah jetty.

Getting There & Away

AIR

Langkawi International Airport (Map p194; 04-955 1311; www.langkawiairport.com) is located in the west of the island near Padang Matsirat. It's well stocked with ATMs, currency-exchange booths, car-rental agencies, travel agencies, and a Tourism Malaysia office. A half-dozen airlines offer flights from Langkawi.

AirAsia (nationwide 600 85 8888; www.airasia.com) Daily flights to Kuala Lumpur, Penang and Singapore; four flights a week to Kuching.

Firefly (nationwide 03-7845 4543; www.firefly.com.my) Daily flights to Kuala Lumpur (Subang Airport) and Penang.

Malaysia Airlines (nationwide 1300-883 000; www.malaysiaairlines.com) Daily flights to Kuala Lumpur.

Malindo Air (nationwide 03-7841 5388; www.malindoair.com) Daily flights to Kuala Lumpur.

Silk Air (nationwide 03-2618 6333; www.silkair.com) Three flights a week to Singapore.

FERRY WARNING

During the wet season, from July to September, you may want to shelve any notions of taking the ferry to Langkawi, particularly from Penang. At this time of year the seas are typically very rough and the ferry ride can be a terrifying and quite literally vomit-inducing experience. Consider yourself warned.

Tigerair (☎Singapore office +65 3157 6434; www.tigerair.com) Three flights a week to Singapore.

BOAT

All passenger ferries operate from the busy terminal at Kuah jetty. Several ferry providers, including **Langkawi Ferry Service** (LFS; ☎04-966 9439; www.langkawi-ferry.com), have merged to operate a shared ferry service to the destinations below, with the exception of Ko Lipe, which is operated by Tropical Charters (p199).

DESTINATION	PRICE (ADULT/CHILD)	DURATION	FREQUENCY
Kuala Perlis	RM18/13	1¼ hours	Every 1½hr, 7.30am-7pm
Kuala Kedah	RM23/17	1¾ hours	Every 1½hr, 7.30am-7pm
Satun (Thailand)	RM30/23	1¼ hours	9am, 1pm & 5pm
Ko Lipe (Thailand)	RM118/100	1½ hours	9.30am & 2.30pm
George Town	RM60/45	2¾ hours	10.30am, 2.30pm & 5.15pm

Getting Around

TO/FROM THE AIRPORT/JETTY

Fixed taxi fares from the airport include Kuah jetty (RM30), Pantai Cenang or Pantai Kok (RM20), Tanjung Rhu (RM45) and Teluk Datai (RM70). The fare from Kuah jetty to Pantai Cenang is RM30. Buy a coupon at the desk before leaving the airport terminal and use it to pay the driver.

CAR

Cars can be rented cheaply and touts from the travel agencies at the Kuah jetty will assail you upon arrival. Rates start at around RM70 per day, but drop with bargaining.

T Shoppe (Map p198; ☎04-955 5552; Pantai Cenang) offers car and motorbike rentals as well as air tickets and the usual boat trips and snorkelling excursions. It also has branches in Pentai Tengah (Map p198) and Kuah.

MOTORCYCLE & BICYCLE

The easiest way to get around is to hire a motorbike for around RM35 per day. You can do a leisurely circuit of the island (70km) in a day. The roads are excellent, and outside Kuah it's very pleasant and easy riding. Motorbikes can be hired at stands all over the island. Many places also rent bikes for RM15 per day.

TAXI

As there is no public transport in Langkawi, taxis are the main way of getting around, but fares are relatively high so it can be worthwhile renting your own vehicle. There are taxi stands at the airport, Kuah jetty, **Pantai Cenang** (Map p198) and **Cenang Mall** (Map p198), and **Pantai Tengah** (Map p198), at Frangipani hotel. There are fixed rates for all destinations – displayed at the stand – and no taxi should use a meter. It's also possible to hire a taxi for four hours for RM120.

Alor Setar

POP 405,523

Most travellers use the capital of Kedah, also known as Alor Star, as a jumping-off point to Langkawi or southern Malaysia, but there's enough around to keep you exploring for a day. This is a very Malay city, culturally rooted in a conservative mindset that references a fairly strict interpretation of Islam and reverence for the local monarchy.

Sights

Mahathir's Birthplace MUSEUM
(Rumah Kelahiran Mahathir; ☎04-772 2319; 18 Lg Kilang Ais; ⏲10am-5pm Tue-Thu, Sat & Sun, 10am-noon & 3-5pm Fri) FREE Dr Mahathir Mohamad, Malaysia's fourth and longest-serving prime minister, was born the youngest of nine children in Alor Setar in 1925. Rumah Kelahiran Mahathir, his childhood home, is now preserved as a small but worthwhile museum, containing family effects, photos and the politician's old bicycle. Aside from providing an insight into Mahathir's early life, the museum is an interesting example of a traditional Malaysian house.

Menara Alor Setar TOWER
(Alor Setar Tower; ☎04-720 2234; www.menaraalorstar.com.my; Lebuhraya Darul Aman; adult/child RM15/8; ⏲9am-midnight) If the Petronas Towers in KL weren't enough for you, the second-tallest tower in the country is the Menara Alor Setar, which at 165.5m high

Alor Setar

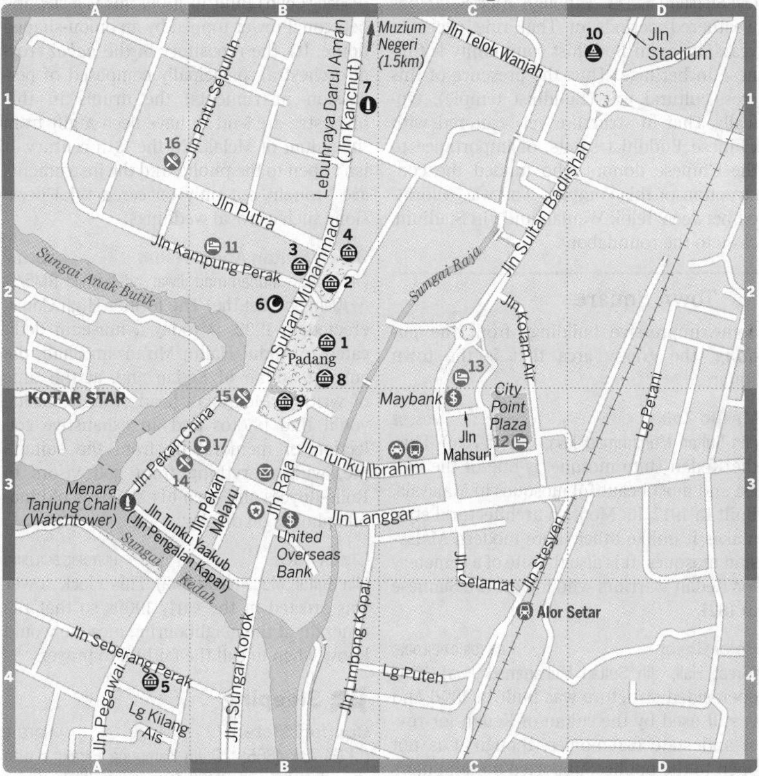

Alor Setar

Sights

1 Balai Besar B2
2 Balai Nobat B2
3 Clock Tower B2
4 Galeri Sultan Abdul Halim B2
5 Mahathir's Birthplace A4
6 Masjid Zahir B2
7 Menara Alor Setar B1
8 Muzium Diraja B2
9 State Art Gallery B3
10 Wat Nikrodharam D1

Sleeping

11 Comfort Motel B2
12 Holiday Villa C3
13 New Regent C2

Eating

14 Caffe Diem A3
15 Muda Coffee Shop B3
16 Nasi Lemak Ong A1

Drinking & Nightlife

17 Terrace Forty Eight B3

is by far the tallest structure in town. A glass-sided lift will take you to the observation deck for good views of Alor Setar and the surrounding countryside.

Muzium Negeri MUSEUM
(Kedah State Museum; ☎04-733 1162; Lebuhraya Darul Aman; ⏲9am-5pm Sat-Thu, 9am-12.30pm & 2.30-5pm Fri) **FREE** The State Museum is 2km north of the main square. The rather dry collection here includes early Chinese porcelain, background to the archaeological finds at Lembah Bujang, and dioramas of royal and rural life in Kedah. A taxi from the town centre costs RM10.

Wat Nikrodharam BUDDHIST TEMPLE

(Jln Stadium) FREE Although Alor Setar has weathered periods of Thai rule over the years, its main Buddhist community is Chinese in heritage. Thus the presence of this cross-cultural wat (Buddhist temple): typically Thai in structure yet scattered with Chinese Buddhist saints, of importance to the Chinese donors who funded the construction of this complex. The wat is located between Telok Wanjah and Jln Stadium, close to the roundabout.

Town Square

Some impressive buildings front the *padang*, the grassy area that is the town square.

Masjid Zahir MOSQUE

(Jln Sultan Muhammad Jiwa; 7am-7pm) This, the Kedah state mosque, is one of the oldest and most beautiful mosques in Malaysia. Built in 1912, its Moorish architectural style makes it unlike other more modern Malaysian mosques. It is also the site of a cemetery for Kedah warriors who fought the Siamese in 1821.

Balai Besar HISTORIC BUILDING

(Great Hall; Jln Sultan Muhammad Jiwa) This open-sided structure was built in 1896 and is still used by the sultan of Kedah for royal and state ceremonies, though it is not open to the public. Supported on tall pillars topped with Victorian iron lacework, the building also shows Thai influences in its decoration.

Muzium Diraja MUSEUM

(Royal Museum; Padang Court, Jln Raya; 9am-5pm Sat-Thu, 9am-12.30pm & 2.30-5pm Fri) FREE Now a museum, these connected structures with creaking wooden floorboards formerly served as the royal palace for the sultan and other members of the family from 1856. Among the royal paraphernalia on display is memorabilia from the historic joint wedding in 1904 of the five children (two princes and three princesses) of the 26th sultan of Kedah – the festivities lasted 90 days.

State Art Gallery ART GALLERY

(Jln Sultan Muhammad Jiwa; 9am-5pm Sat-Thu, 9am-12.30pm & 2.30-5pm Fri) FREE The elegant structure of this gallery, built in 1893 as a courthouse, is enough of a reason to visit, less so the rather uninspiring gallery of contemporary Malaysian art it holds.

Balai Nobat HISTORIC BUILDING

(Padang Court) Built in 1906, this is a striking octagonal tower topped by an onion-shaped dome. It's the repository of the *nobat* (royal orchestra), principally composed of percussion instruments; the drums in this orchestra are said to have been a gift from the sultan of Melaka in the 15th century. It isn't open to the public, and the instruments are brought out only on ceremonial occasions such as royal weddings.

Galeri Sultan Abdul Halim MUSEUM

(Jln Sultan Muhammad Jiwa; adult/child RM5/2; 10am-5pm Sat-Thu) The former High Court, erected in 1922, is today a museum dedicated to Abdul Halim Mu'adzam Shah, the current Sultan of Kedah and, at the time of writing, Malaysia's head of state. Inside you'll find photos and an exhaustive collection of memorabilia from the sultan's life, with everything from golf visors to Rolls-Royces and even his Majesty's old mobile phones on display.

Clock Tower HISTORIC BUILDING

(Jln Sultan Muhammad Jiwa) This clock tower was erected in the early 1900s so that the muezzin at the neighbouring mosque would know when to call the faithful to prayer.

Sleeping

Comfort Motel HOTEL $

(04-734 4866; 2C Jln Kampung Perak; r with shared bathroom RM28-40;) This is a good-value, Chinese-style budget hotel, located in a renovated wooden house across from a mosque. The rooms are tidy and come equipped with TV and air-con, but are otherwise bare and share bathrooms.

Holiday Villa HOTEL $$

(04-734 9999; www.holidayvilla.com.my; 162 Jln Tunku Ibrahim; r RM320, ste RM450-650, all incl breakfast;) This towering hotel adjoining the City Point Plaza shopping mall is easily the best place in town. It has spacious, tastefully furnished rooms with all the amenities, and a range of facilities, including gym, pool and spa. Online rates can be half those quoted here.

New Regent HOTEL $$

(04-731 5000; regentnew@gmail.com; 1536 Jln Sultan Badlishah; r RM165, ste RM270-320, all incl breakfast;) A recent makeover at this longstanding hotel has left the lobby area looking contemporary and jazzy. Though the rooms don't quite match up, they are clean and well equipped. Discounted promotional rates may be available.

Eating

★Muda Coffee Shop — CHINESE $

(Jln Pekan China; mains RM3-20; ⏲2.30-11pm) We should start by saying that this place is for adventurous eaters only: the staff don't speak much English, and the highlight is a dish of steamed fish head. But, oh, what a fish head. Accompanied with *lor mee* (noodles fried with dark soy sauce) and a beer, it was one of the tastiest meals we had in Malaysia. Located near the corner with Jln Sultan Muhammad Jiwa.

Nasi Lemak Ong — MALAYSIAN $

(☎012-498 3660; 24, ground fl, Jln Putra; mains RM5-12; ⏲10.30am-3.30pm Thu-Tue; ❄) This family-run *nasi lemak* (rice cooked in coconut milk and served with *ikan bilis*, peanuts and a curry dish) place, a popular lunch spot for office workers, is worth the queue. Once at the counter, select your rice and choice of accompaniments from the wide array of dishes laid out, including honey or spicy chicken, curry mutton and various fish options and vegetable dishes.

Caffe Diem — CAFE $$

(☎04-730 9328; 6 Jln Penjara Lama; mains RM14-16; ⏲noon-midnight; ❄📶) Alor Setar's answer to a hipster cafe is a quirky, friendly place serving coffee, sandwiches, pastas, salads and homemade cakes in a beautifully done-up old Chinese shophouse.

Drinking & Nightlife

Terrace Forty Eight — BAR

(48 Jln Penjara Lama, Pekan Cina; ⏲5pm-2am) An unexpectedly modern and rather flash bar with polished concrete walls, draught Guinness and other imported booze as well as a tapas menu (RM16 to RM48). The place to go to tap into Alor Setar's party scene.

Getting There & Away

AIR

Sultan Abdul Halim Airport is 11km north of town, just off the Lebuhraya. **AirAsia** (☎nationwide 600 85 8888; www.airasia.com), **Firefly** (☎nationwide 03-7845 4543; www.firefly.com.my) and **Malaysia Airlines** (☎nationwide 1300-883 000; www.malaysiaairlines.com) all offer daily flights to Kuala Lumpur (KLIA and Subang airports; from RM107, one hour).

> **GETTING TO THAILAND: BUKIT KAYU HITAM TO HAT YAI**
>
> **Getting to the border** The border at Bukit Kayu Hitam, 48km north of Alor Setar, is the main road crossing between Malaysia and Thailand, but as there are no taxis or local buses at this border, the only practical way to cross here is on a through bus from points elsewhere in Malaysia.
>
> **At the border** The Malaysian border post is open every day from 6am to midnight. All passengers must disembark to clear customs and immigration (both Thai and Malaysian) before reboarding.
>
> **Moving on** The lack of local transport means that you'll most likely pass this border on a bus already bound for Hat Yai.

BUS

The main bus terminal, **Shahab Perdana**, is 4km north of the town centre. A local bus links Shahab Perdana and Kuala Kedah (RM3, one hour, frequent departures from 7am to 10pm), passing through the city centre on the way. There is a **bus stop** (Jln Langgar) next to the taxi stand on Jln Tunku Ibrahim.

The bus to Shahab Perdana from the city centre costs RM1.30 and a taxi there costs RM10. Destinations include the following:

DESTINATION	PRICE	DURATION	FREQUENCY
Kangar	RM6.30	1 hour	Hourly, 6.45am-8.30pm
Kuala Kedah	RM3	1 hour	Hourly, 7am-10pm
Butterworth	RM10.80	1½ hours	Every 30min, 10am-8.45pm
Ipoh	RM29.40	4 hours	Frequent departures 9.30am-9pm
Kota Bharu	RM39.10	6 hours	10.15am & 10.15pm
Kuala Lumpur	RM43	7 hours	Every 30min, 9.30am-midnight
Melaka	RM56.70	8 hours	Frequent departures 9.30am-11.30pm
Singapore	RM80	12 hours	9pm, 9.45pm & 10pm

TRAIN

The **train station** (Jln Stesyen) is 850m south-east of the town centre. There is one daily north-bound train to Hat Yai (RM9 to RM48, 3½ hours, 7.56am) in Thailand and one to Bangkok (about RM110, 18½ hours, 2pm). There's one daily southbound train to Butterworth (RM8 to RM26, two hours, 11.09am) and one to Kuala Lumpur (9½ hours, RM39 to RM51, 7.55pm).

Getting Around

There's a **taxi stand** on Jln Tunku Ibrahim. A taxi to/from the airport costs RM30. The town centre is accessible on foot.

Around Alor Setar

Muzium Padi

Muzium Padi MUSEUM

(Paddy Museum; ☎04-735 1315; off Hwy K351; adult/child RM5/2; ⏲9am-5pm Sat-Thu, 9am-12.30pm & 2.30-5pm Fri) Muzium Padi is all about Kedah's main crop: rice. It's located 10km northwest of Alor Setar amid green rice paddies; a taxi costs RM25. The complex, which has a distinctly socialist, utopian feel, is supposed to emulate the gunny sacks used by rice farmers. And if you're *really* into rice, you'll love the exhaustive exhibits inside.

The main event is a top-floor, rotating observation deck that looks out onto a mural of the surrounding rice fields; the gimmick pays homage to Gunung Keriang, a nearby limestone hill that, according to local folklore, is also supposed to rotate.

Kuala Kedah

This busy fishing village, 11km from Alor Setar, is a departure point for boats to Langkawi (adult/child RM23/17). Ferries leave for the island approximately every hour from 7am to 7pm. A taxi to Kuala Kedah from Alor Setar costs RM20; hourly buses (one hour, RM3) also make the run between 7am and 10pm.

Kota Kuala Kedah FORT

(www.jmm.gov.my; Jln Marina Harbour; ⏲9am-7pm) FREE The fort, completed in 1780, is opposite Kuala Kedah town on the far bank of Sungai Kedah, a 10-minute taxi ride from the ferry terminal. The castle was once used as a base by the Portuguese in Melaka and was later a bastion of Malay independence against the Siamese until finally falling to the invaders in 1821. On the well-kept site there is also a museum providing background on the history of the fort and Kedah state.

Try to find Meriam Badak Berendam (the Wallowing Rhino), a cannon believed to be the abode of the fortress's guardian spirit.

PERLIS

Perlis is Malaysia's smallest state and doesn't tend to register on most travellers' radars except as a transit point to Thailand or Langkawi (via Kuala Perlis). Even Malays tend to regard it as essentially a rice-producing pocket along the Thai border. Though it isn't an area that's particularly heavy on sites of interest to tourists, it can be a kick just to hang out with the locals and improve your Bahasa Malaysia (because English definitely isn't widely spoken). Otherwise, small but beautiful Taman Negeri Perlis (p214) is worth exploring.

History

Perlis was originally part of Kedah, though it variously fell under Thai and Acehnese sovereignty. After the Siamese conquered Kedah in 1821, the sultan of Kedah made unsuccessful attempts to regain his territory until, in 1842, he agreed to Siamese terms. The sultan's position was restored, but Perlis became a separate principality with its own raja.

As with Kedah, power was transferred from the Thais to the British under the 1909 Anglo-Siamese Treaty, and a British Resident was installed at Arau. During the Japanese occupation in WWII, Perlis was 'returned' to Thailand, and then after the war it was again under British rule until it became part of the Malayan Union, and then the Federation of Malaya in 1957.

Kangar

POP 48,898

Kangar, 45km northwest of Alor Setar, is the state capital of Perlis and has a small-town vibe. Much like the state it's the capital of, there's not a whole lot to do here besides relax or chat, which are fine options for those awaiting an onward bus.

Sights

Muzium Kota Kayang MUSEUM

(☎04-977 0027; Al-Marhum Kayang; ⏲10am-5pm) FREE Around 7km southwest of Kangar, the small but impressive Muzium Kota Kayang houses displays on local history, including Neolithic tools, royal regalia and ceramics. There are some real treasures here, and facilities are surprisingly modern, with clear English descriptions. The museum is attractively located on a plot of land backed by limestone cliffs and shallow caves, as well as the modest mausoleums of two 16th-century sultans of Kedah. You'll need to catch a taxi from Kangar to get here (RM12).

Sleeping & Eating

There are many cheap restaurants and cafes dotted around the bus station.

Hotel Ban Cheong HOTEL $
(04-976 1184; 79 Jln Kangar; r RM40-65;) This long-standing Chinese hotel in the town centre has basic singles with fan and shared bathrooms and air-con doubles with private facilities. The rooms are in need of updating, not to mention a good dusting, but it's a reasonable budget option for an overnight stay.

Hotel Sri Garden HOTEL $$
(04-977 3188; www.hotelsrigarden.webs.com; 96 Persiaran Jubli Emas; r incl breakfast RM118-180;) Standard Malaysian midranger with clean and airy rooms.

Getting There & Away

BUS

The long-distance (express) bus station is on the southern edge of town on Jalan Bukit Lagi. Departures include the following:

DESTINATION	PRICE	DURATION	FREQUENCY
Alor Setar	RM6	1 hours	Every hour, 8am-7pm
Butterworth	RM15.10	3 hours	Every 30min, 7.30am-7.15pm
Ipoh	RM34.90-37.30	6 hours	9am, 2.30pm, 3.15pm, 8pm & 9.15pm
Kota Bharu	RM44-55	8 hours	8am, 8.15am, 8pm & 9pm
Kuala Lumpur	RM47.10-50	8 hours	Every 30min, 7.15am-11.30pm
Melaka	RM57.70-61	10 hours	8.15am, 9am, 9.30am, 3pm, 5pm, 8.30pm, 9.30pm & 10pm
Singapore	RM83	12 hours	7.30pm & 8.30pm

GETTING TO THAILAND: PADANG BESAR TO HAT YAI

Getting to the border There are four buses a day from Kangar to Padang Besar (RM4.20), stopping at an unmarked bus stop by a roundabout about 500m from the border.

At the border The Malaysian border post is open every day from 6am to 10pm. Few people walk the more than 2km of no-man's land between the Thai and Malaysian sides of the border. Motorcyclists shuttle pedestrian travellers back and forth for about RM2 each way. For train passangers, customs and immigration are dealt with at Padang Besar station.

Moving on Once in Thailand there are frequent buses to Hat Yai, 60km away. There are trains at 10.30am and 6.40pm connecting Padang Besar and Hat Yai (RM6 to RM13, 50 minutes).

Buses to Padang Besar (RM4.20, one hour) via Kaki Bukit leave from the local bus station beneath the shopping mall and bowling alley on Jln Tun Abdul Razak, at 8.45am, 11.45am, 2.45pm and 5.45pm. The bus waits 15 minutes before doing the return route from Padang Bedar to Kangar. There are also buses from Kangar local bus station to Alor Setar (RM6.30, about every two hours from 6.15am to 8pm) and there's a taxi rank here; drivers can take you to Padang Besar (RM36), Alor Setar (RM50) and Taman Negeri Perlis (RM50).

Kuala Perlis, about 10km southwest of Kangar, is a departure point for Pulau Langkawi. From Kangar, the pier can be reached by bus (RM3) or taxi (RM16), and ferries to Langkawi (adult/child RM17/13) leave approximately every hour from 7am to 7pm. From Kuala Perlis, there are buses to a number of destinations across Malaysia including Kuala Lumpur.

Around Kangar

Gua Kelam CAVE
(Cave of Darkness; Kaki Bukit; adult/child RM1/50 sen; 8am-5.30pm Sun-Fri, to 6pm Sat) Gua Kelam is a 370m-long cavern gouged out in the tin-mining days. Access is along a rickety gangway above a river that runs through the cave and emerges at a popular swimming spot in an attractive landscaped park, with a backdrop of craggy limestone hills. Gua Kelam is 1km from Kaki Bukit; the bus from Kangar to Padang Besar passes close to the entrance as it does a U-turn on the way back out of the one-street town.

Taman Negeri Perlis PARK
(Perlis State Park; ☎04-976 5966; Wang Kelian) The small state park in the northwest of Perlis runs for 36km along the Thai border. It comprises the Nakawan Range of limestone hills and the Mata Ayer and Wang Mu Forest Reserves, but the main draw for visitors is the vast system of **caves**. To visit them you must hire a guide (RM50), which can be arranged at the park visitor centre. There is no public transport to the park and a taxi from Kangar costs RM50.

This is a remote, wild-feeling place. A winding mountain road leads from Kaki Bukit to the tiny border village of Wang Kelian, 3km from the park visitor centre. There is very rustic, basic accommodation available, booked through the visitor centre, in the form of wooden chalets (RM50) and dorm beds (RM10); there is no restaurant but staff can prepare food.

The park is the country's only semi-deciduous forest and is rich in wildlife; this is the only habitat in Malaysia for the stump-tailed macaque. White-handed gibbons and a rich array of birds can also be found here. In the evening, as the sky glows orange with the setting sun, the forest's residents make their presence known with a crescendo of squawks and rustling leaves.

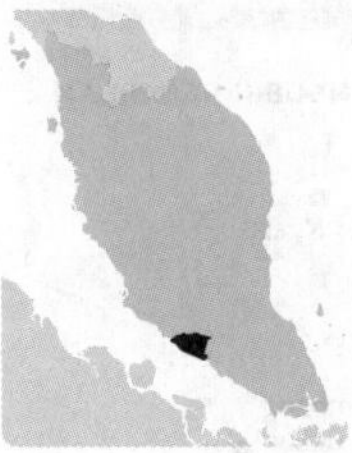

Melaka

☎06 / POP 860,000 / AREA 1652 SQ KM

Includes ➡

Best Places to Eat

➡ Nancy's Kitchen (p228)
➡ Pak Putra Restaurant (p228)
➡ Kocik Kitchen (p228)
➡ Selvam (p229)
➡ Le QUE (p228)

Best Places to Stay

➡ 45 Lekiu & The Stable (p226)
➡ Hotel Puri (p226)
➡ Majestic Malacca (p227)
➡ Apa Kaba Home & Stay (p227)
➡ Gingerflower (p226)

Why Go?

Centuries of vigorous conquests and maritime trade are now distant memories. But the last decade has seen Melaka capitalise on its swashbuckling history, asserting itself as one of Malaysia's most irresistible tourist draws.

Back when Kuala Lumpur was a muddy swamp and Penang was yet to become the 'Pearl of the Orient', Melaka was already one of Southeast Asia's greatest trading ports. Over time it lost favour to Singapore, but this slowdown in trade protected the ancient architecture of Melaka City, the state capital, from development. Much of it remains beautifully preserved to this day. When its historic centre was crowned a Unesco World Heritage Site in 2008, it kickstarted a decade of renewal. Modern Melaka swaggers once more, with visitors pouring in to experience the bustling weekend night market, heritage museums and famously glitzy trishaws. The rest of the state is a patchwork of forests, farmland and beaches, with a generous scattering of family-friendly attractions in smaller towns Alor Gajah and Ayer Keroh.

When to Go

Melaka

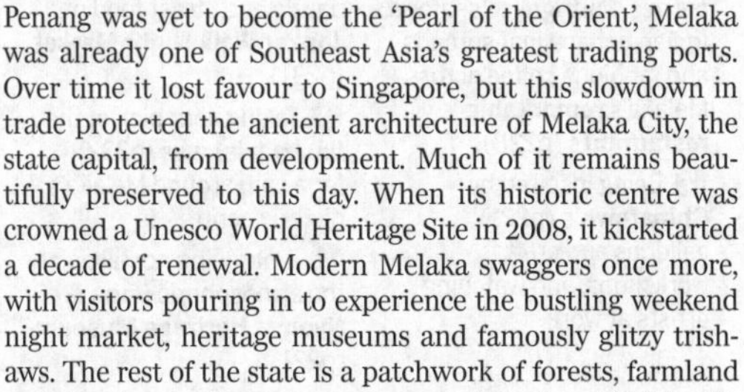

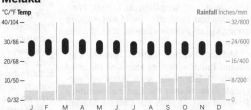

Jan & Feb Chinese New Year brings chaos and colour to the hot and dry months.

Apr–Jul Milder temperatures and festivals galore.

Nov & Dec Book ahead to see Christmas and Deepavali celebrations.

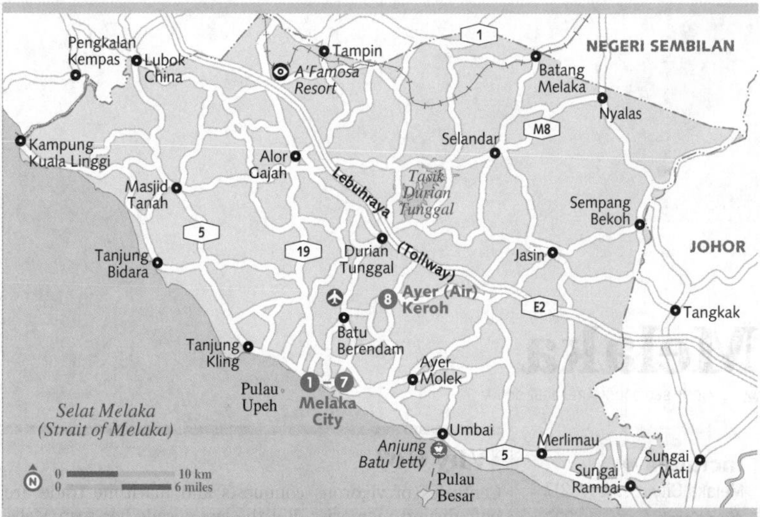

Melaka Highlights

1 Feasting on Peranakan curries, Portuguese seafood, Indian banana leaf spreads and fabulous coffee across Melaka's **remarkable restaurants** (p228).

2 Being inspired by **Chinatown's** (p221) galleries and craft workshops, and watching artists at work.

3 Experiencing the razzle-dazzle and street food of **Jonker Walk Night Market** (p231).

4 Taking your pick of the **flashy trishaws** (p232) for a spin around Melaka's historic centre.

5 Embracing nostalgia at the atmospheric **Baba & Nyonya Heritage Museum** (p221).

6 Delighting in vibrant colours and neck-craning temples on a stroll through **Kampung Chitty** (p223).

7 Watching the sun set over **Masjid Selat Melaka** (p224), the city's stately 'floating mosque'.

8 Ambling among traditional houses at open-air **Taman Mini Malaysia** (p233) in Ayer Keroh.

History

The modern city-state of Melaka bloomed from a simple 14th-century fishing village founded by Parameswara, a Hindu prince from Sumatra. According to legend, Parameswara was inspired to build Melaka after seeing a plucky mouse deer fending off a dog attack.

Melaka's location halfway between China and India, with easy access to the spice islands of Indonesia, soon attracted merchants from all over the East and became a favoured port. In 1405, the Chinese Muslim Admiral Cheng Ho arrived in Melaka bearing gifts from the Ming emperor and the promise of protection from Siamese enemies. Chinese settlers followed, who mixed with the local Malays to become known as the Baba and Nonya, Peranakans or Straits Chinese. By the time of Parameswara's death in 1414, Melaka was a powerful trading state. Its position was consolidated by the state's adoption of Islam in the mid-15th century.

In 1509, the Portuguese came seeking spice wealth and in 1511 Alfonso de Albuquerque forcibly took the city. Under the Portuguese, the fortress of A'Famosa was constructed. While Portuguese cannons could easily conquer Melaka, they could not force Muslim merchants from Arabia and India to continue trading there, and other ports in the area, such as Islamic Demak on Java, grew to overshadow Melaka.

Suffering attacks from neighbouring Johor and Negeri Sembilan, as well as from the Islamic power of Aceh in Sumatra, Melaka declined further. The city passed into Dutch hands after an eight-month siege in 1641 and the Dutch ruled Melaka for about 150 years. Melaka again became the centre for peninsular trade, but the Dutch directed more energy into their possessions in Indonesia.

When the French occupied Holland in 1795, the British (as allies of the Dutch) temporarily assumed administration of the Dutch colonies. In 1824, Melaka was permanently ceded to the British.

Melaka, together with Penang and Singapore, formed the Straits settlements, the three British territories that were the centres for later expansion into the peninsula. However, under British rule Melaka was eclipsed by other Straits settlements and then superseded by the rapidly growing commercial importance of Singapore. Apart from a brief upturn in the early 20th century when rubber was an important crop, Melaka returned again to being a quiet backwater, patiently awaiting its renaissance as a tourist drawcard.

MELAKA CITY

Melaka is the peacock of Malaysian cities. It's bright, loud, and almost preens with its wealth of homegrown galleries, crimson colonial buildings and showy trishaws.

The city's historic centre was awarded Unesco World Heritage status in 2008, and since then Melaka's tourism industry has developed at break-neck pace. Old shophouses and mansions have enjoyed makeovers as galleries and hotels, and Melaka's kaleidoscope of architectural styles – spanning Peranakan, Portuguese, Dutch and British elements – has been well preserved. Meanwhile restaurants have found a booming audience of weekend visitors, all eager to sample the varied cuisines that have spawned from Melaka's cultural mosaic of residents.

Inevitably, a strong whiff of commercialism has accompanied this success. A roaring trade in cheap trinkets and risqué T-shirts unfolds alongside artisan sellers and antiques shops. Meanwhile, big-name businesses skulk awkwardly next to faded shophouses. But Chinatown's charm still lingers, and is best represented by its resident artists, cooks and colourful trishaws.

The city today (as it has for centuries) exudes tolerance and welcomes cultural exchange. Locals are proud to nickname Chinatown street Jln Tokong Besi as 'Harmony Street', thanks to its mosque, Chinese temple and Hindu temple, all in close proximity.

It's easy to feel the town's old magic (and get a seat at popular restaurants) on quiet weekdays. Visiting at the weekend thrills and infuriates in equal measure: you'll experience the famed Jonker Walk Night Market, with music, shopping and street food galore, but you'll share the experience elbow-to-elbow with other travellers.

Sights

Historic Town Centre

Striking red buildings and a multitude of museums dominate Melaka's historic centre. Many of the museums are small, with a niche focus and an uninspiring diorama format. Start with more developed attractions like the Stadthuys and the Maritime Museum complex.

Stadthuys HISTORIC BUILDING

(☎06-282 6526; Dutch Sq; foreign/local visitor RM10/5; ⊙9am-5.30pm Sat-Thu, 9am-12.15pm & 2.45-5.30pm Fri) Melaka's most unmistakable landmark and favourite trishaw pick-up spot is the Stadthuys. This cerise town hall and governor's residence dates to 1650 and is believed to be the oldest Dutch building in the East. The building was erected after Melaka was captured by the Dutch in 1641, and is a reproduction of the former Stadhuis (town hall) of the Frisian town of Hoorn in the Netherlands. Today it's a museum complex, with the **History & Ethnography Museum** as the highlight. Admission covers all the museums. There is no fee for guided tours.

To gain a more in-depth acquaintance with Melaka past and present, you can also peruse the **Governor's House**, **Democratic Government Museum**, a **Literature Museum** focusing on Malaysian writers, **Cheng Ho Gallery** and the **Education Museum**.

Christ Church CHURCH

(☎06-284 8804; Jln Gereja; ⊙9am-5pm) FREE Built in 1753 from pink laterite bricks brought from Zeeland in Holland, this much-photographed church has Dutch and Armenian tombstones in the floor of its rather bare interior. The massive 15m-long ceiling beams overhead were each cut from a single tree.

Porta de Santiago RUIN

(A'Famosa; Jln Bandar Hilir; ⊙24hr) FREE A quick photo stop at Porta de Santiago is a must. Built by the Portuguese as a fortress

Melaka City

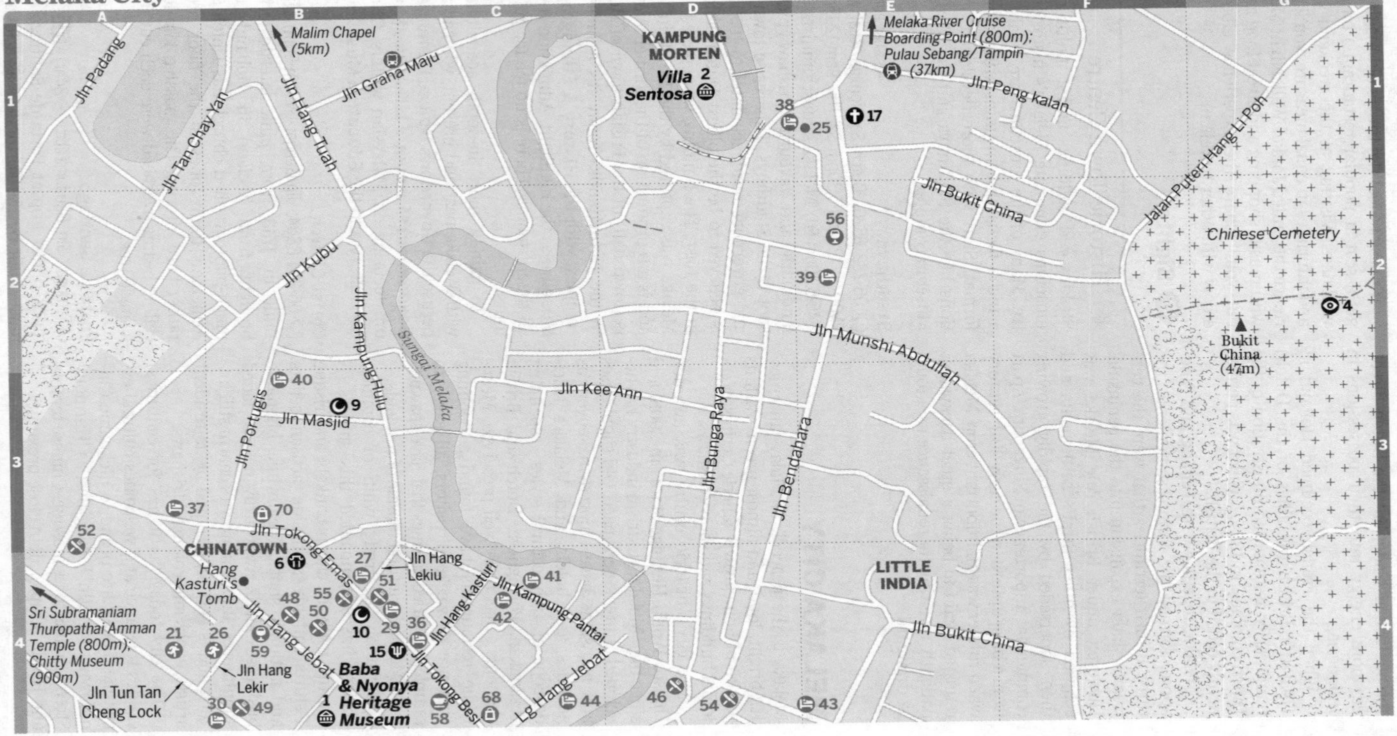
0 200 m
0 0.1 miles
N
A
B
C
D
E
F
G
1
2
3
4
Malim Chapel (5km)
Melaka River Cruise Boarding Point (800m); Pulau Sebang/Tampin (37km)
KAMPUNG MORTEN
Villa Sentosa
2
Jln Padang
Jln Tan Chay Yan
Jln Hang Tuah
Jln Graha Maju
Jln Peng kalan
Jalan Puteri Hang Li Poh
Jln Bukit China
Chinese Cemetery
Bukit China (47m)
4
17
38
25
56
39
Jln Kubu
Jln Kampung Hulu
Sungai Melaka
Jln Munshi Abdullah
Jln Kee Ann
Jln Bunga Raya
Jln Bendahara
40
9
Jln Masjid
Jln Portugis
37
70
52
Jln Tokong Emas
CHINATOWN
6
Hang Kasturi's Tomb
27
Jln Hang Lekiu
51
41
Jln Hang Kasturi
Jln Kampung Pantai
42
LITTLE INDIA
48
55
50
10
29
36
Sri Subramaniam Thuropathai Amman Temple (800m); Chitty Museum (900m)
21
26
59
Jln Hang Jebat
15
Jln Tokong Besi
Jln Hang Lekir
Jln Tun Tan Cheng Lock
30
49
1
Baba & Nyonya Heritage Museum
58
68
Lg Hang Jebat
44
46
54
43

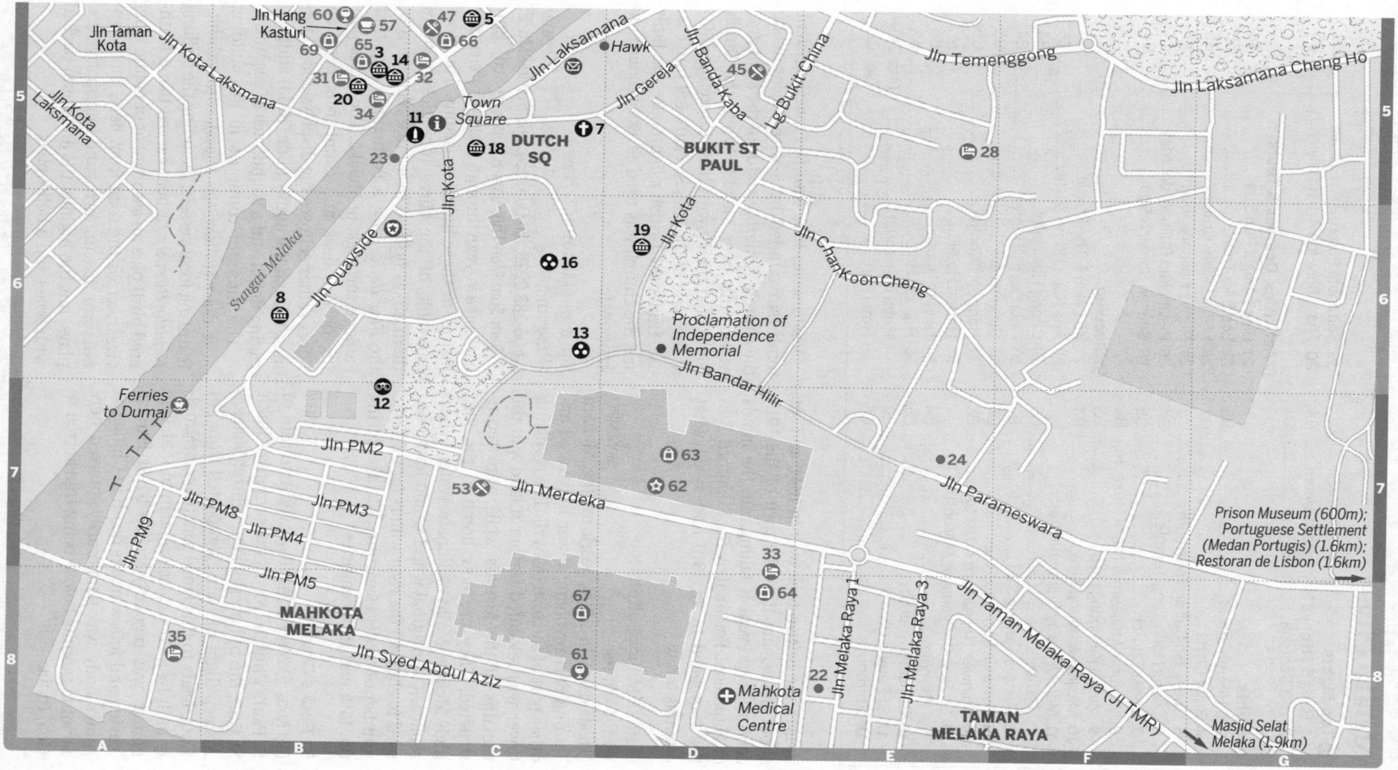
Jln Hang Kasturi
Jln Taman Kota
Jln Kota Laksmana
Jln Kota Laksmana
Jln Laksamana
Hawk
Jln Gereja
Jln Banda Kaba
Lg Bukit China
Jln Temenggong
Jln Laksamana Cheng Ho
Town Square
DUTCH SQ
BUKIT ST PAUL
Jln Kota
Jln Kota
Sungai Melaka
Jln Quayside
Jln Chan Koon Cheng
Proclamation of Independence Memorial
Jln Bandar Hilir
Ferries to Dumai
Jln PM2
Jln Merdeka
Jln PM8
Jln PM3
Jln PM9
Jln PM4
Jln PM5
MAHKOTA MELAKA
Jln Syed Abdul Aziz
Jln Parameswara
Prison Museum (600m); Portuguese Settlement (Medan Portugis) (1.6km); Restoran de Lisbon (1.6km)
Jln Melaka Raya 1
Jln Melaka Raya 3
Jln Taman Melaka Raya (Jl TMR)
Mahkota Medical Centre
TAMAN MELAKA RAYA
Masjid Selat Melaka (1.9km)
60
57
47
5
69
65
3
14
32
66
31
20
34
45
11
7
18
28
23
19
16
8
13
12
24
63
53
62
33
64
67
35
61
22
A
B
C
D
E
F
G
5
6
7
8

Melaka City

in 1511, the British took over in 1641, and set about destroying it at the turn of the 19th century to prevent it falling into the hands of Napoleon. Fortunately Sir Stamford Raffles happened by in 1810 and saved what remains today.

Melaka Malay Sultanate Water Wheel
MONUMENT

(Jln Merdeka) In 2006, work on the Menara Taming Sari revolving tower uncovered another part of the fortress wall. The revolving tower was relocated further inland and the remains of the fortress walls were reconstructed. They are now home to the 13m high Melaka Malay Sultanate Water Wheel replica. The original wheel would have been used to channel the river waters for the large number of traders swarming Melaka during the 15th and 16th centuries.

St Paul's Church
RUIN

(Jln Kota; 24hr) FREE The evocative ruin of St Paul's Church crowns the summit of Bukit St Paul, the hill overlooking central Melaka. A steep flight of stairs, signposted from Jln Kota, leads to this faded sanctuary, originally built by a Portuguese captain in 1521. The church was regularly visited by St Francis Xavier, and following his death in China the saint's body was temporarily interred here for nine months before being transferred to Goa, India.

Visitors can look into St Francis' ancient tomb (surrounded by a wire fence) inside the church. A marble statue of the saint gazes wistfully over Melaka. When the Dutch completed their own Christ Church in 1590 at the base of the hill, St Paul's fell into disuse. Under the British a lighthouse was built and the church was used as a storehouse for gunpowder.

Maritime Museum & Naval Museum
MUSEUM

(06-283 0926; Jln Quayside; adult/child RM6/2; 9am-5pm Mon-Thu, 9am-8.30pm Fri-Sun) Embark on a voyage through Melaka's maritime history at these linked museums. The most enjoyable of the three (one ticket covers them all) is housed in a huge recreation of the *Flor de la Mar,* a Portuguese ship that sank off the coast of Melaka. The fun of posing on the deck and clambering between floors rather eclipses the displays and dioramas, though the audio guide (RM3) adds engaging detail and a soundtrack of seagulls.

The museum continues in the building next door (follow the signs) with exhibits featuring local vessels, including the striking *Kepala Burung* (a boat carved like a feathered bird) plus an assortment of nautical devices. Across the road from here, the **Naval Museum** has uniforms and informative displays, but the highlight is an atrium packed with boats and a helicopter.

36 Jalan Jalan Guesthouse ... C4	**Drinking & Nightlife**
37 Jonker Boutique Hotel ... A3	56 Bulldog Cafe ... E2
38 Majestic Malacca ... D1	57 Calanthe Art Cafe ... B5
39 Ramada Plaza Melaka Hotel ... E2	58 Cheng Ho Tea House ... C4
40 Ringo's Foyer ... B3	59 Geographér Cafe ... B4
41 River One Residence ... C4	60 Me & Mrs Jones ... B5
42 Rooftop Guesthouse ... C4	61 Mixx ... C8
43 Sterling ... E4	Ola Lavanderia Café ... (see 58)
44 Tidur Tidur ... C4	
	Entertainment
Eating	62 Golden Screen Cinema Dataran Pahlawan ... D7
45 Capitol Satay ... D5	
46 Discovery Cafe ... D4	
47 Hoe Kee Chicken Rice Ball ... C5	**Shopping**
48 Jonker 88 ... B4	63 Dataran Pahlawan ... D7
49 Kocik Kitchen ... B4	64 Hatten Square ... D8
Le QUE ... (see 20)	Hueman Studio ... (see 55)
50 Limau-Limau Cafe ... B4	65 Joe's Design ... B5
51 Low Yong Mow ... B4	66 Jonker Walk Night Market ... C5
52 Poh Piah Lwee ... A3	67 Mahkota Parade Shopping Complex ... C8
53 Restoran Nyonya Suan ... C7	68 Orangutan House ... C4
54 Selvam ... D4	RazKashmir Crafts ... (see 29)
55 Shui Xian Vegetarian ... B4	69 Red Handicrafts ... B5
	70 Wah Aik Shoemaker ... B3

Menara Taming Sari VIEWPOINT
(☎06-288 1100; www.menaratamingsari.com; Jln Merdeka; adult/child RM20/10; ⏲10am-10pm) Melaka's revolving viewing deck looks worryingly like a theme park ride without the seat belts. Luckily, this is a leisurely thrill ride, and one with air-con. The UFO-shaped chamber atop this 80m-high tower slowly rotates as it ascends and descends, allowing panoramic views of Melaka. Binoculars are provided. Tickets are on sale in the adjacent building.

Sultanate Palace MUSEUM
(Jln Kota; adult/child RM2/1; ⏲9am-6pm Tue-Sun) This wooden replica of the palace of Sultan Mansur Shah, who ruled Melaka from 1456 to 1477, houses an open-air cultural museum. The fine recreations were crafted without the use of nails and closely follow descriptions of the original palace from *Sejarah Melayu* (*Malay Annals;* a chronicle of the establishment of the Malay sultanate and 600 years of Malay history).

Chinatown

Chinatown is the heart of Melaka and is by far the most interesting area to wander around. Stroll along **Jln Tun Tan Cheng Lock**, formerly called Heeren St, which was the preferred address for wealthy Peranakan (also known as Straits Chinese) traders who were most active during the short-lived rubber boom of the early 20th century. The centre street of Chinatown is **Jln Hang Jebat**, formerly known as Jonker St (or Junk St Melaka), that was once famed for its antique shops but is now more of a collection of clothing and crafts outlets and restaurants. On Friday, Saturday and Sunday nights, the street is transformed into the Jonker Walk Night Market (p231). Finally, the northern section of **Jln Tokong Besi** (also known as Harmony St) houses a mosque, Chinese temple and a handful of authentic Chinese shops.

★Baba & Nyonya Heritage Museum MUSEUM
(☎06-283 1273; http://babanyonyamuseum.com; 48-50 Jln Tun Tan Cheng Lock; adult/child RM16/11; ⏲10am-1pm & 2-5pm Wed-Mon) Touring this traditional Baba-Nonya (Peranakan) townhouse transports you to a time when women peered at guests through elaborate partitions, and every social situation had its specific location within the house. The captivating museum is arranged to look like a typical 19th-century Baba-Nonya residence. Tour guides enliven the setting with their arch sense of humour. Book ahead or arrive just before the strike of the hour. Last tour of the day is an hour before closing time.

8 Heeren Street HISTORIC BUILDING
(8 Jln Tun Tan Cheng Lock; ⏲11am-4pm Tue-Sat) FREE This 18th-century Dutch-period residential house was restored as a model conservation project. The project was partially chronicled in the beautifully designed coffee-table book *Voices from the Street,* which is for sale at the house, along with other titles. You can also pick up an *Endangered Trades: A Walking Tour of Malacca's Living Heritage* (RM5) booklet and map for an excellent self-guided tour of the city centre. Entry is free but donations are appreciated.

Cheng Hoon Teng Temple CHINESE TEMPLE
(Qing Yun Ting or Green Clouds Temple; 25 Jln Tokong Emas; ⏲7am-7pm) FREE Malaysia's oldest traditional Chinese temple, constructed in 1673, remains a central place of worship for the Buddhist community in Melaka. Notable for its carved woodwork, the temple is dedicated to Kuan Yin, the goddess of mercy.

Masjid Kampung Hulu MOSQUE
(cnr Jln Masjid & Jln Kampung Hulu) This is the oldest functioning mosque in Malaysia and was, surprisingly, commissioned by the Dutch in 1728. The mosque is made up of predominantly Javanese architecture with a multi-tiered roof in place of the standard dome; at the time of construction, domes and minarets had not yet come into fashion. It's not particulary well set up for visitors but this Chinatown icon is worth admiring from outside.

Masjid Kampung Kling MOSQUE
(Jln Hang Lekiu) FREE This Chinatown mosque dates to 1748. The 19th-century rebuild you see today mingles a number of styles. Its multi-tiered meru roof (a stacked form similar to that seen in Balinese Hindu architecture) owes its inspiration to Hindu temples, the Moorish watchtower minaret is typical of early mosques in Sumatra, while English and Dutch tiles bedeck its interior. Admission times to go inside vary; dress modestly and if you're female bring a scarf.

NO SMOKING

In 2011, Melaka's Chinatown and historic centre was declared a no-smoking zone. It's not heavily enforced but the air is noticeably more smoke-free than elsewhere in the city.

The proximity of Kampung Kling mosque to Cheng Hoon Teng temple and Hindu temple Sri Poyatha Moorthi has prompted locals to dub this area 'Harmony Street'.

Sri Poyatha Venayagar Moorthi Temple HINDU TEMPLE
(Jln Tokong Emas) FREE One of the first Hindu temples built in Malaysia, this temple was constructed in 1781 on the plot given by the religiously tolerant Dutch and dedicated to the Hindu deity Venayagar.

Cheng Ho Cultural Museum MUSEUM
(☎06-283 1135; www.chengho.org/museum; 51 Lg Hang Jebat; adult/child RM20/10; ⏲9am-6pm) The impressive exploits of Chinese Muslim seafarer Ming Admiral Cheng Ho (Zheng He) are celebrated by this museum's dioramas, maritime miscellany and an enormous giraffe, a model of the rather inconvenient animal gift brought overseas by the adventurer. Cheng Ho's tremendous voyages make for interesting reading, though the level of detail in this multi-floor museum wearies after a while. The museum is a good excuse to wander through a creaky old Chinese mansion, complete with swaying lanterns and mother-of-pearl embossed furnishings.

North of the City Centre

★Villa Sentosa HISTORIC BUILDING
(Peaceful Villa; ☎06-282 3988; Jln Kampung Morten; entry by donation; ⏲hours vary, usually 9am-1pm & 2pm-5pm) Malay village Kampung Morten is nestled right within central Melaka. The highlight of exploring the area, with its merry bridge and homes shaded by palm trees, is a visit to this living museum within a 1920s *kampung* (village) house. Visitors (or rather, guests) are welcomed by a member of the household who points out period objects including photographs, Ming dynasty ceramics and a century-old Quran. You're unlikely to leave without a photo-op on plush velvet furniture or a few strikes of the lucky gong.

Bukit China CEMETERY
(Jln Puteri Hang Li Poh) More than 12,500 graves, including about 20 Muslim tombs, cover the 25 grassy hectares of serene 'Chinese Hill'. Since the times of British rule, there have been several attempts to acquire Bukit China for road widening, land reclamation or development purposes. Fortunately, Cheng Hoon Teng Temple, with strong community support, has thwarted these attempts.

DON'T MISS

EXPLORING MELAKA'S GRASSROOTS GALLERIES

With its potent cocktail of cultures, Melaka inspires many an artist. Chinatown has an impressive concentration of independent galleries and craft workshops. Some are a delight for serious art collectors, with watercolours and sculptures to browse and buy. Others place their unique designs on handmade souvenirs and T-shirts (a little easier on the wallet). Take official opening hours with a grain of salt.

Tham Siew Inn Artist Gallery (www.thamsiewinn.com; 49 Jln Tun Tan Teng Lock; ⌚10am-6pm Thu-Tue) Vibrant watercolours of sunsets, street scenes and temples fill this art gallery arranged around an inner garden.

Shihwen Naphaporn Artist Studio (14 Jln Tun Tan Cheng Lock; ⌚10am-6pm Thu-Tue) Melaka-born Chiang Shihwen creates Cubo-futuristic works, while Naphaporn Phanwiset uses fish, fruit and the female form as her muse in marvellous neutral-toned pieces.

Red Handicrafts (Jln Hang Kasturi; ⌚11am-6pm Thu-Tue) Mr Ray Tan draws Japanese and Chinese-inspired designs that range from flowing organic patterns to quirky cartoons. Watch Mr Tan hand-print your favourite onto a 100% cotton T-shirt, or peruse his intricate paper-cutting art.

Hueman Studio (☎06-288 1795; 9 Jln Tokong Emas; ⌚10.30am-6pm) Woodblock prints, many with themes such astrology and calligraphy, take centre stage in this art studio-giftshop. Portable souvenirs include hand-painted rosewood jewellery (from RM16), buffalo horn pendants (RM35) and more.

In the middle of the 15th century, the sultan of Melaka imported the Ming emperor's daughter from China as his bride, in a move to seal relations between the two countries. She brought with her a vast retinue, including 500 handmaidens, to Bukit China and it has been a Chinese area ever since. Poh San Teng Temple sits at the base of the hill and was built in 1795. To the right of the temple is the King's Well, a 15th-century well built by Sultan Mansur Shah.

St Peter's Church CHURCH

(Jln Bendahara) FREE St Peter's Church is the oldest functioning Catholic church in Malaysia, built in 1710 by descendants of early Portuguese settlers.

Prison Museum MUSEUM

(☎06-281 3548; prmuzium@prison.gov.my; cnr Jln Parameswara & Jln Melati; adult/child RM6/3; ⌚9am-5pm Tue-Sun) This new, state-run museum fixes an unflinching gaze on Malaysian prisons, past and present. There is interesting detail on the 18th-century beginnings of the Malaysian prison system, how it was shaped under British rule, and famous jails like Pulau Jerjak, Malaysia's version of Alcatraz. Things get more disturbing with interactive displays on corporal punishment and the insides of lonely prison cells. Definitely not one for the kids.

The museum is isolated 2.5km east of Chinatown; a taxi should cost around RM10.

Kampung Chitty

As well as the Peranakan community, Melaka also has a small contingent of Chitty – Straits-born Indians, offspring of the Indian traders who intermarried with Malay women. Having arrived in the 1400s, the Chitties are regarded as older than the Chinese-Malay Peranakan community.

Their stomping ground, known as Kampung Chitty, lies west of Jln Gajah Berang, about 1km northwest of Chinatown; look for the archway with elephant sculptures opposite where Jln Gajah Berang meets Jln Kampong Empat. The best time to visit this delightfully colourful neighbourhood is in May, during the Mariamman Festival (Pesta Datuk Charchar).

Chitty Museum MUSEUM

(☎06-281 1289; Jln Gajah Berang; adult/child RM2/1; ⌚9am-1pm & 2-5pm Tue-Sun) The tiny Chitty Museum is a community effort with a collection of artefacts, including antique cendol makers and embroidered wedding garb. There's excellent English-language explanations about the Chitty language and rites of passage, plus news clippings about local efforts to preserve Chitty heritage.

WORTH A TRIP

MELAKA'S FLOATING MOSQUE

This gold-domed mosque gazes dreamily at the Strait of Melaka from its shoreside perch. Completed in 2006, the mosque's grand archways are panelled with intricate stained glass. When water levels are high, it appears to float. **Masjid Selat Melaka** (7am-7pm) is especially beautiful during morning or dusk light. Non-Muslim visitors are permitted provided they dress modestly and heed the 'no shoe' signs around different parts of this large complex. Women must bring a scarf or use a rental shawl to cover their head.

There are few attractions nearby and taxis don't always ply this part of town. If you don't have your own wheels, ask a taxi driver for a return trip (RM15 each way) plus waiting time.

Sri Subramaniam Thuropathai Amman Alayam TEMPLE
(Jln Gajah Berang, Kampung Chitty; 6.30am-9pm Mon-Fri, 7.30am-12pm Sat & Sun) FREE A huge *shikhara* (tower), as elaborate and pink as a tiered wedding cake, erupts from this temple. Few visitors come here, but if you shed your shoes, you can marvel at exterior statues of Surya with his chariot pulled by seven horses, plus a rainbow of enamelled decorations inside.

Little India

East of Chinatown on the opposite side of the river is Melaka's surprisingly plain Little India. While it's not nearly as charming as the historic centre or Chinatown, this busy area along Jln Bendahara and Jln Temenggong is a worthwhile place for soaking up some Indian influence and grabbing a banana-leaf meal.

Activities

Reflexology centres are plentiful in Chinatown. A half-hour foot massage costs from RM20 to RM25, but it's often worth paying a few extra ringgit for a good experience.

Biossentials Puri Spa SPA
(06-282 5588; www.hotelpuri.com/spa; Hotel Puri, 118 Jln Tun Tan Cheng Lock; on request) This spa in a sensual garden isn't a walk-in like Jonker St's casual reflexology outlets. The reward for booking ahead is the delicious menu of treatments, including steams, scrubs, facials and milk baths. Aromatherapy foot treatments (45 minutes) start at RM65, while body wraps and deep tissue massage cost around RM145 (one hour).

Season Sorvana Spa SPA
(06-286 8727; 5 Jln Hang Lekir; 11am-11pm) Handily situated just off Jonker St, this massage place offers good value to have your toes reset with a satisfying snap. A half-hour reflexology session costs RM23, while a full hour treating your shoulders and feet is RM48.

Courses

Nancy's Kitchen COOKING COURSE
(06-283 6099; 13 Jln KL 3/8, Taman Kota Laksamana; per person RM100) Nancy of this near-legendary Peranakan restaurant (p228) teaches cookery classes on request. Reserve well in advance.

Nonya Culinary Journey COOKING COURSE
(Hotel Equatorial 06-282 8333; Hotel Equatorial, Jln Parameswara; per person RM115) These two-hour cooking classes include a set lunch and a certificate of completion. You'll cook three Peranakan (Nonya) dishes, including specialities such as *ayam pong teh* (miso soy chicken) or *udang lemak nenas* (prawns with pineapple and spicy coconut), hands-on with the chef. Advanced booking required.

Peranakan Culinary Journey COOKING COURSE
(06-289 8000; www.majesticmalacca.com; Majestic Malacca Hotel, 188 Jln Bunga Raya; per person RM290) Learn about each ingredient and the history of each dish in a gorgeous kitchen with a master Peranakan chef at the Majestic Malacca Hotel. Book one week in advance.

Tours

Historic walking tours are offered through several hotels. The Majestic Malacca (p227) offers an especially good tour (RM150 for non-guests; book ahead) at 10am daily (except Wednesday).

Malacca Night Cycling BICYCLE TOUR
(016-668 8898; per person RM35) Pedalling through Melaka will test your trishaw-dodging skills, but evening is a pleasant time to tour the city. Tours leave by arrangement at 8.30pm and last 90 minutes (or longer, if you like). Call a day or two in advance to book.

Eco Bike Tour BICYCLE TOUR
(☎ 019-652 5029; www.melakaonbike.com; 117 Jln Tiang Dua; per person RM100) Explore the fascinating landscape around Melaka with Alias on his three-hour bike tour (minimum two people) through 20km of oil-palm and rubber-tree plantations and delightful *kampung* communities surrounding town. Flag your level of fitness when you book.

Melaka River Cruise BOAT TOUR
(www.melakarivercruise.com; adult/child RM15/7; ⏲9am-11.30pm) Frequent 40-minute river-boat trips (minimum eight people) along the Melaka River depart from two locations: the quay near the Maritime Museum and the 'Spice Garden' on the corner of Jln Tun Mutahir and Jln Tun Sri Lanang in the north of town. You won't learn a lot about the city but you will pass colourful shopfronts and get your bearings as you ply Melaka's waterways.

Festivals & Events

Melaka celebrates all the major Malaysian holidays, including Chinese New Year and Thaipusam. The tourist department creates new festivals all the time but few become annual events.

Easter RELIGIOUS
(⏲Mar/Apr) Good Friday and Easter Sunday processions are held outside at St Peter's Church.

Festa San Pedro RELIGIOUS
(⏲late Jun) Honouring this patron saint of the Portuguese fishing community, celebrations take place at St Peter's Church and normally include a float procession with cooking, fishing, handicrafts and a carnival atmosphere.

Festa San Juan RELIGIOUS
(⏲late Jun) This festival is celebrated by Melaka's Eurasian community by the lighting of candles in the Portuguese Settlement.

Dragon Boat Festival CULTURAL
(⏲Jun/Jul) This Chinese festival, marked by a dragon-boat race in the Strait of Melaka, commemorates the death by drowning of 3rd-century BC Chinese poet and statesman Qu Yuan.

Festa Santa Cruz RELIGIOUS
(⏲mid-Sep) This festival honours a miraculous cross with a candlelight procession of Melakan and Singaporean Catholics to Malim chapel, about 7km north of central Melaka.

Sleeping

With new places opening and established hotels rebranding or fading away, accommodation in Melaka is vulnerable to change, though the quality is the best it's been in years.

Chinatown

If you have the option of staying in Chinatown, do it. This is the vibrant historic centre of the city, although it can get both busy and noisy.

Ringo's Foyer GUESTHOUSE $
(☎ 06-281 6393, 016-668 8898; www.ringosfoyer.com; 46A Jln Portugis; dm/s/d/tr incl breakfast from RM15/18/30/60; ❄📶) This convivial hostel offers bike rental, laundry (RM8), guitars and the occasional rooftop barbecue: in short, this place has everything a weary backpacker could want. Slightly removed from central Chinatown's clamour, digs are as plain as the price suggests but they are clean and adorned with hilariously blunt etiquette signs. Rates for double rooms increase by RM5 at weekends.

Travellers will find a warm welcome and the hosts do a great job of keeping the atmosphere sociable. Ask about night cycle rides.

Chong Hoe Hotel HOTEL $
(☎ 06-282 6102; chonghoehotel@yahoo.com; 26 Jln Tokong Emas; s/d/q RM35/50/100; ❄📶) This plain guesthouse lacks charisma, but with private rooms in the heart of Chinatown, Chong Hoe is hard to beat on value and location. Air-con and wi-fi function well, though the lack of soundproofing in the rooms, and the call to prayer bellowing from nearby Masjid Kampung Kling, may interrupt light sleepers.

River One Residence GUESTHOUSE $
(☎ 06-281 0370; river1residence@gmail.com; 60 & 62 Jln Kampung Pantai; s/d RM60/88; ❄📶) Friendly service lifts this otherwise simple guesthouse above the competition. Rooms are plain, bathrooms are shared and it's not always the quietest place, but the upbeat vibe and riverside location make this excellent value. Shared kitchens are a nice perk.

Jalan Jalan Guesthouse GUESTHOUSE $
(☎ 06-283 3937; 8 Jln Tokong Emas; dm/s/d RM16/30/40; @📶) This agreeable hostel is

based within a restored old blacksmith's shop painted periwinkle blue. Fan-cooled rooms with one shared bathroom are spread around a tranquil inner garden-courtyard. As with some other older places, noise from your neighbours might keep you awake at night. Bike rental and laundry are available.

Tidur Tidur
GUESTHOUSE $

(☑ 014-928 3817; tidurtidurgh@yahoo.com; 92 Lg Hang Jebat; weekdays/weekends per person RM15/20; ☜) The name promises sweet dreams (*tidur* means 'sleep') but really you're here for the local feel and the hip riverside location of this simple guesthouse behind a T-shirt shop. The two- and four-bed dorm rooms aren't too airy but they are exceptional value.

Rooftop Guesthouse
HOSTEL $

(☑ 012-327 7746, 012-380 7211; rooftopguesthouse@yahoo.com; 39 Jln Kampung Pantai; dm/d/tr RM28/63/84; ✲) This hostel is simple but hits the spot with decent air-con, a choice of dorm-room and private accommodation, and a bird's-eye view from the roof terrace. Minimum two nights' stay.

★ Hotel Puri
HOTEL $$

(☑ 06-282 5588; www.hotelpuri.com; 118 Jln Tun Tan Cheng Lock; d/tr/q/ste incl breakfast from RM164/269/327/408; ✲☜) One of Chinatown's gems, Hotel Puri is an elegant creation in a superbly renovated Peranakan mansion dating to 1822. Its elaborate lobby, decked out with beautiful old cane and inlaid furniture, opens to a gorgeous courtyard garden where breakfast is served. Standard rooms have butter-yellow walls, crisp sheets, wi-fi and shuttered windows. There's also an on-site spa.

★ Gingerflower
BOUTIQUE HOTEL $$

(☑ 06-288 1331; www.gingerflowerboutiquehotel.com; 13 Jln Tun Tan Cheng Lock; d RM233-420; ✲☜) Rooms are small, but period fittings and immaculate housekeeping make this restored Peranakan town house an inspiring place to stay. It's a few paces from the Jonker St hubbub and well-placed for gallery and museum visits along Jln Tun Tan Cheng Lock.

Jonker Boutique Hotel
HOTEL $$

(☑ 06-282 5151; www.jonkerboutiquehotel.com; Jln Tokon; d/q incl breakfast from RM198/318; P✲☜) Perched where Jonker St meets Jln Tokong Emas, Jonker Boutique Hotel is located at ground zero for weekend night market mayhem. It's ideal if you want to step straight into a street food buffet, less enjoyable if you're a light sleeper. The cheaper rooms aren't too spacious but the accommodation is well-maintained and decorated in pleasing monochrome. Room rates go up by about 30% on weekends and holidays. There's wi-fi in the lobby.

Heeren House
GUESTHOUSE $$

(☑ 06-281 4241; www.heerenhouse.com; 1 Jln Tun Tan Cheng Lock; s/d/q incl breakfast from RM119/129/259; ✲☜) Lodging here positions you right in the heart of Chinatown, on the waterfront and within range of top local restaurants and sights. The traditional furnishings have a nostalgic air, while the family-run vibe and hearty breakfasts infuse this place with a homely feel. The six airy and clean rooms in this former warehouse largely overlook the river. Not all rooms pick up wi-fi signal from the lobby.

Courtyard@Heeren
BOUTIQUE HOTEL $$

(☑ 06-281 0088; www.courtyardatheeren.com; 91 Jln Tun Tan Cheng Lock; d RM200-250, ste RM300-800; ✲☜) Each room here is decorated with an individual touch, with light and bright decor paired with antique wood furniture. Some rooms have minimalist stained-glass details, modern takes on Chinese latticework or luxuriant drapes, but not all have windows. It's professionally run with great service.

Hangout@Jonker
HOTEL $$

(☑ 06-282 8318; www.hangouthotels.com; 19-21 Jln Hang Jebat; s/d/tr/q incl breakfast from RM90/140/180/200; ✲@☜) Halfway between a hostel and a budget hotel, Hangout@Jonker is surprisingly chic for its price. While its bare modern decor is at odds with the glitzy Peranakan mansions elsewhere in Chinatown, rooms are surgically clean and there's a roof terrace to ogle Melaka's skyline. Frills are few and far between; but with perks like wi-fi and laundry, you won't long for an in-room mini bar.

It's the second branch of a popular Singapore hostel. Prices go up 20% on weekends and holidays.

★ 45 Lekiu & The Stable
APARTMENT $$$

(☑ 012-623 4459; www.45lekiu.com; 45 Jln Hang Lekiu; weekdays/weekends RM1099/1299; ✲☜) These gorgeous restoration projects are in two different locations. 45 Lekiu is more upscale with four extremely comfortable storeys of big old beams and exposed original brick work, all within a clean, modern decor. **The Stable** is a smaller two-storey home with heritage-style doors, wooden floors, period tiles and timber beams. Both have cooking facilities. Highlights include a bougainvillea-filled courtyard with a dipping pool and an upper terrace overlooking the city.

Jalan Merdeka & Around

This area is in the heart of Melaka's mall shopping zone and is only a short walk to the historic centre and Chinatown.

Hatten Hotel HOTEL **$$**
(06-286 9696; www.hattenhotel.com; Hatten Square, Jln Merdeka; d weekday/weekend RM350/450; P ❄ wi-fi pool) A glossy marbled reception and lounges kitted out with velvet sofas set the tone for this marvellously well-equipped hotel perched over Hatten Square mall. Rooms are luxurious and many overlook the Strait of Malacca. The glamour continues with a rooftop infinity pool. Online offers can trim the room rates, sparing some of your budget for shopping in the surrounding malls.

Sterling HOTEL **$$**
(06-283 1188; www.thesterling.my; Jln Temenggong; d RM285-750; P ❄ wi-fi) You may need to shield your eyes against this blinding white behemoth of a hotel. Though billed as colonial-style, with rooms named after British icons like Churchill and Brighton beach, this brand-new hotel feels more business chic than awash in history. Despite the tenuous salutes to Britain, rooms are large, bathrooms positively gleam and there are great views from the rooftop restaurant.

Room rates vary according to how far ahead you book and how urgently you require an in-room spa bath.

Holiday Inn HOTEL **$$**
(06-285 9000; http://holidayinnmelaka.com; Jln Syed Abdul Aziz; r RM234-475; P ❄ @ wi-fi pool) Tourists rock up at the Holiday Inn for reliability and comfort. The generously sized rooms at this chain hotel don't disappoint (though they're thin on charm), while the staff are keen to assist; breakfast banquets are ample (RM22.50). An occasional courtesy shuttle bus putters the short journey from the hotel to Mahkota Parade and Dutch Sq.

Melaka's Holiday Inn is separated from the historic centre by a roaring main road that can be difficult to cross on foot.

Hotel Equatorial HOTEL **$$$**
(06-282 8333; http://melaka.equatorial.com; Jln Parameswara; d RM300-519, ste RM763-1653; P ❄ wi-fi pool) If you're looking to splurge, this lavish hotel is a quality choice. It has a refined air, elegantly decorated rooms, quality on-site restaurants and interconnected swimming pools for a dip with added va-va-voom. Good discounts online can slash room rates, so book ahead. Service is well mannered and the overall presentation is crisp.

Little India to Bukit China

This varied area allows a glimpse of Melaka's less touristed side without straying too far from the sights.

★ **Apa Kaba Home & Stay** GUESTHOUSE **$**
(012-798 1232, 06-283 8196; www.apa-kaba.com; 28 Kg Banda Kaba; d RM45-90, tr RM60-129; ❄ wi-fi) This tranquil homestay has rooms as low-key and relaxing as its *kampung* setting, despite being close to the roaring maelstrom of central Melaka. Rooms are simple (some have air-con) and there's a large garden to lounge in, complete with dangling mango trees and the occasional speeding chicken. The 1912 building is a mish-mash of Malay and Chinese styles.

The owners are long-term residents who treat guests like family. They are more than happy to impart the secrets of perfect chicken rice and where to find the best *cendol* (shaved-ice dessert with green noodles, syrups, fruit and coconut milk) in town.

Ramada Plaza Melaka Hotel HOTEL **$$**
(06-284 8888; www.ramadaplazamelaka.com; Jln Bendahara; d/ste incl breakfast from RM260/450; P ❄ @ wi-fi pool) This unexciting but competent chain hotel has spacious and well-furnished rooms with huge windows overlooking Melaka's skyline. There's a spa, squash courts and a choice of excellent restaurants within the complex. Parking costs RM5 per day.

★ **Majestic Malacca** HOTEL **$$$**
(06-289 8000; www.majesticmalacca.com; 188 Jln Bunga Raya; r RM550-2000; ❄ @ wi-fi pool) Claw-footed tubs and polished four-poster beds are just some of the trappings at this regal modern hotel. The bar, library and dining areas groan with nostalgia (think ornate Peranakan screens and gleaming teak furniture), while a small pool and richly endowed spa area add to the opulent feel.

Majestic Malacca is mere steps away from Kampung Morten, and a five-minute walk takes you to Little India. Book ahead and online for better bargains than the walk-up rate.

Eating

Peranakan cuisine is the most famous type of cooking here; it's also known as 'Nonya', an affectionate term for a Peranakan wife (often the family chef). There's also Portuguese Eurasian food, Indian, Chinese and more.

Chinatown

On Friday, Saturday and Sunday nights, Jln Hang Jebat turns into the not-to-be-missed Jonker Walk Night Market (p231).

★ Nancy's Kitchen PERANAKAN $

(06-283 6099; eat@nancyskit.com; 13 Jln KL 3/8, Taman Kota Laksamana; mains RM10; 11am-5pm Wed-Mon) The mouth-watering meals stirred up in this Peranakan (Nonya) restaurant are revered in Melaka, and Nancy's Kitchen lives up to the hype. Local diners crowd this small restaurant, especially at weekends, their bellies rumbling for a taste of signature dishes like candlenut chicken (succulent meat simmered in a nutty sauce, fragrant with lemongrass). The restaurant stays open until 9pm on public holidays.

If you want to take some Peranakan home-cooking flair away with you, call to arrange cooking courses (p224) with Nancy herself.

★ Pak Putra Restaurant PAKISTANI $

(012-601 5876; Jln Kota Laksmana 4; mains RM8-10; 6pm-1am, closed alternate Mondays;) Scarlet tikka chickens rotate hypnotically on skewers, luring locals and travellers to this excellent Pakistani restaurant. With aromatic vegetarian dishes, seafood and piquant curries, there's no shortage of choice (try the masala fish). The unchallenged highlights are oven-puffed naan bread and chicken fresh from the clay tandoor. Portions are generous and service is speedy.

Jonker 88 DESSERTS $

(88 Jln Hang Jebat; mains RM6; 11am-10pm Tue-Thu, to 11pm Fri & Sat, to 9pm Sun) Slurp-worthy laksa and decent Peranakan fare are served up at this efficient local canteen. But the highlight of this busy Jonker St eatery is its *cendol* menu. This frosty dessert, a mountain of shaved ice, coconut, pandan noodles, red beans and jaggery syrup, is as rainbow-coloured (and wacky) as it sounds. Jonker 88 has a fabulous selection of flavours and toppings, including sago pearl and durian (from RM5).

Low Yong Mow CHINESE $

(06-282 1235; Jln Tokong Emas; dim sum RM1-8; 5.30am-noon Wed-Mon) Famous across Melaka for its large and delectably well-stuffed *pao* (steamed pork buns), this place is Chinatown's biggest breakfast treat. With high ceilings, plenty of fans running and a view of Masjid Kampung Kling, the atmosphere oozes all the charms of Chinatown. It's usually packed with talkative, newspaper-reading locals by around 7am. Food offerings thin out by 11am, so arrive early.

Limau-Limau Cafe EUROPEAN $

(9 Jln Hang Lekiu; mains from RM7; 9am-5pm Thu-Tue;) Choose from healthy granolas and towering sandwiches, and wash it all down with tempting smoothies like dragon-fruit or papaya-banana blend (RM9 to RM13). The walls are crowded with artwork, giving this place a bright, inspiring feel.

Poh Piah Lwee PERANAKAN $

(14 Jln Kubu; mains from RM3; 9am-5pm) This lively hole in the wall has one specialist cook preparing delicious Hokkein-style *popiah* (lettuce, bean sprouts, egg and chilli paste in a soft sleeve), another making near-perfect *rojak* (fruit and vegetable salad in a shrimp paste, lime juice, sugar and peanut dressing), while the third whips up laksa.

★ Kocik Kitchen PERANAKAN $$

(016-929 6605; 100 Jln Tun Tan Cheng Lock; mains RM20-30; 11am-6.30pm Mon, Tue & Thu, 11am-5pm & 6-9pm Fri & Sat, 11am-7.30pm Sun) This unassuming little restaurant is hot on the heels of Melaka's other Peranakan (Nonya) specialists; try the creamy *lemak nenas* prawns, swimming in fragrant coconut milk with fresh chunks of pineapple.

Le QUE PERANAKAN, INTERNATIONAL $$

(012-601 5876; 21 Jln Tun Tan Cheng Lock; mains RM15-30; 1-11pm Mon-Thu, 2.30-11pm Fri, noon-11pm Sat & Sun) Rotating specials at this quirky halal place include Peranakan dishes like *asam pedas* (hot and sour stew with fish or chicken) alongside international classics like spaghetti carbonara and steak. Friendly staff blend a range of invigorating fruit and vegetable smoothies (RM9) plus

DON'T LEAVE MELAKA WITHOUT TRYING...

Chicken rice ball Steamed chicken and cannonballs of rice, often greased with stock or fat and served with a piquant dipping sauce.

Asam fish Freshwater fish dowsed in a mouth-burning stew of chilli and tamarind.

Laksa Melaka's version of this coconut milk and noodle soup, infused with a powerful lemongrass flavour.

Popiah Spring rolls without the crunch, stuffed with shredded veggies, prawns, garlic and more.

Satay celup Submerge your choice of tofu, fish and meat into a spicy bubbling soup.

Devil curry Scorching chicken curry that marries Portuguese and Malay flavours.

Cendol An addictive shaved-ice dessert with green tentacles (sorry, noodles) plus syrups, fruit and coconut milk.

Kuih Nonya Coconut milk and sticky rice sweets, too colourful to resist.

Pineapple tarts Buttery pastries with a chewy jam filling.

Malay thirst-quenchers like *teh tarik* (pulled tea).

Hoe Kee Chicken Rice Ball CHINESE $$
(4 Jln Hang Jebat; mains RM20; ⌚8.30am-3pm, closed last Wed of month) This is one of Melaka's top spots for juicy poached chicken served with wadded balls of rice, themselves sticky with chicken stock. A popular pilgrimage place for Hainanese chicken rice, don't expect a menu or deferential service. The queue allows plenty of time to decide if you're hungry enough for a quarter-chicken (RM14) or a whole one (RM40).

Jalan Merdeka & Around

Restaurants in the shopping mall district are mostly unexciting chains, but a lively food court serves Malay and Chinese fare just west of Mahkota Parade. East of the centre, the Medan Portugis (Portuguese settlement) has food stalls serving simple seafood dishes.

Restoran Nyonya Suan PERANAKAN $
(☎06-286 4252; 1336D Jln Merdeka; mains RM12; ⌚11am-2.30pm & 5-9.30pm) Fiery Peranakan specialties are served up at this large and pleasant restaurant, with *asam pedas* seafood (freshwater fish in a spicy tamarind sauce) and hot chicken rendang the standout dishes. Swaying lanterns and stained glass panelling give you something to admire while awaiting your towering *cendol*.

Restoran de Lisbon PORTUGUESE $$
(Medan Portugis; mains RM15-20; ⌚lunch & dinner, hours vary) The main reason to head to the Portuguese settlement is the food. On Friday and Saturday evenings, sample Malay-Portuguese dishes at Restoran de Lisbon's outdoor tables. Try the delicious local specialities: chilli crab (RM20) or Eurasian devil curry (RM10).

Little India to Bukit China

There's a string of local-style Chinese cafes around Jln Bunga Raya (ever-full of chattering locals) that serve chicken or duck rice as well as noodle and soup dishes at low prices.

★Selvam INDIAN $
(☎06-281 9223; 3 Jln Temenggong; mains RM6-9; ⌚7am-10pm; 🌿) This classic banana-leaf restaurant is excellent value, with efficient and amiable staff. Generous servings of aromatic chicken biryani are eclipsed by the vegetarian offerings, in particular the Friday afternoon veggie special.

Capitol Satay MALAYSIAN $
(☎06-283 5508; 41 Lg Bukit China; mains from RM8; ⌚5pm-midnight; 🌿) Famous for its *satay celup* (a Melaka adaptation of satay steamboat), this place is usually packed and is one of the cheapest outfits in town. Stainless-steel tables have bubbling vats of soup in the middle where you dunk skewers of okra stuffed with tofu, sausages, chicken, prawns and bok choy.

Shui Xian Vegetarian CHINESE $
(43 Jln Hang Lekiu ; mains RM5; ⌚7.30am-2.30pm Mon-Sat; 🌿) In a city where vegetable dishes so often arrive strewn with shrimp or

JONKER WALK NIGHT SIGHTS

Dr Ho Eng Hui (Jln Hang Jebat; 6.30-9pm Fri & Sat, hours vary), a kung fu master famed for piercing coconuts with a single gnarled finger, was once Jonker Walk Night Market's biggest draw. These days, Dr Ho's semi-retirement has spared many coconuts from a pummelling. Entertain yourself instead by walking north up Jonker Walk; a small Chinese temple (between Jln Hang Kasturi and Jln Hang Lekiu) often hosts traditional song and dance on weekend evenings. Shortly after the turn-off to Jln Hang Lekiu, join scores of visitors posing with the muscleman statue of Dr Gan Boon Leong, the founding father of Malaysian bodybuilding. Continue to Jonker Walk's northern end where the road meets Jln Tokong Besi. On market nights, karaoke enthusiasts take over the small stage.

pork, vegetarians can breathe a sigh of relief here. This no-frills canteen whips up meat-free versions of *nasi lemak*, laksa and even 'chicken' rice balls.

Drinking & Nightlife

Unlike much of Malaysia, there is no shortage of spots to cool down with a beer in Melaka. On Friday, Saturday and Sunday nights, Jonker Walk Night Market in Chinatown closes Jln Heng Lekir to traffic and the handful of bars along the lane become a mini street party with tables oozing beyond the sidewalks and live music.

Geographér Cafe BAR
(06-281 6813; www.geographer.com.my; 83 Jln Hang Jebat; 10am-1am Wed-Sun; wi-fi) Some come to socialise, others are drawn by the free wi-fi. Either way, a swinging soundtrack of Eurotrash, jazz and classic pop keeps the beers flowing at traveller magnet Geographér. This well-ventilated cafe-bar, strewn with greenery, feels like a haven despite bordering busy Jonker St. Monday nights have live jazz while Fridays and Saturdays bring a father-daughter vocal-keyboard duet (both 8.30pm).

Geographér also serves decent food, though it's pricey compared to other places on Jonker St (mains RM15); watch out for the chilli kick of the *kampung* fried rice.

Calanthe Art Cafe COFFEE
(13 States Coffee; 06-292 2960; 11 Jln Hang Kasturi; 10am-11pm; wi-fi) Full-bodied Johor or classic Perak white? Choose a Malaysian state's favourite coffee and this perky place, also known as '13 States', will have it blended with ice and jelly cubes for a refreshing caffeine kick. Breakfasts are served here too (10am to 11.45am).

Me & Mrs Jones PUB
(016-234 4292; 3 Jln Hang Kasturi; 7pm-12am Tue-Sun) This cosy pub is staunchly un-hip and all the more enjoyable for it. At weekends there is live blues and rock, often with retired co-owner Mr Tan leading a jam session. Relax into the atmosphere and grab a beer or juice (long menus are not the Jones' style).

Cheng Ho Tea House TEAHOUSE
(Jln Tokong Besi; 10am-5pm) In an exquisite setting that resembles a Chinese temple garden courtyard, relax over a pot of fine Chinese tea (from RM15) or nibble on a range of rice and noodle dishes (around RM12).

Ola Lavanderia Café CAFE
(012-612 6665; Jln Tokong Besi; 10am-6pm Mon-Sat; wi-fi) Backpacker salvation is here, in the form of the holy travel trinity: laundry, wi-fi and caffeine. This friendly Chinatown cafe does coffees (RM7.50) and croissants (RM5), and you can spin your laundry while you sip (RM4.80 per load, RM1 per item ironed).

Mixx CLUB
(2nd fl, Mahkota Arcade, Jln Syed Abdul Aziz; admission RM10; 10pm-late Tue-Sat) In a city where nightclubs are thin on the ground, Mixx dominates the scene with Paradox, a laser-lit warehouse-style venue where international DJs spin techno and electronica; and Arris, which has a garden area and live bands. It ain't KL, but this is definitely Melaka's best place to pound a dancefloor. Cover is charged on Friday and Saturday nights and includes one drink.

Bulldog Cafe BAR
(016-303 3970; 145 Jln Bendahara; 11.30am-2pm & 6-11pm Mon-Sat) Live music sets toes tapping in this monochrome-decorated cafe-bar every Friday and Saturday night from 9.30pm. A range of Peranakan, Chinese and Western dishes are on offer too.

Shopping

Chinatown's shopping spans antiques and cutting-edge art through to novelty flip-flops and keyrings. Best buys include Peranakan beaded shoes and clogs, Southeast Asian and Indian clothing, handmade tiles and stamps, woodblock-printed T-shirts and jewellery. Many shops double as art and craft studios, where you can glimpse a painter or silversmith busy at work. Where prices aren't marked, haggle firmly but always with a smile.

★ Jonker Walk Night Market MARKET
(Jln Hang Jebat; ⏲6-11pm Fri-Sun) Melaka's weekly shopping extravaganza keeps the shops along Jln Hang Jebat open late while trinket sellers, food hawkers and the occasional fortune teller close the street to traffic. It has become far more commercial, attracting scores of tourists, but it is an undeniably colourful way to spend an evening shopping and grazing.

★ RazKashmir Crafts ACCESSORIES
(www.razkashmir.com; 12 Jln Tokong Emas; ⏲10am-7pm) This little boutique is packed floor-to-ceiling with authentic Kashmiri crafts, jewellery and clothing. Peruse embroidered cotton tunics, enamelled teapots and attention-seizing labradorite pendants among the glittering shelves. The laidback owner is just as pleased to share cultural insights as he is to make a sale. Find it opposite Sri Poyatha temple.

★ Orangutan House CLOTHING
(☎06-282 6872; www.absolutearts.com/charlescham; 59 Lg Hang Jebat; ⏲10am-6pm Thu-Tue) Even on colourful Lg Hang Jebat, it's hard to miss the yellow-and-peach orangutan mural above artist Charles Cham's T-shirt store. Spirited designs range from Chinese astrology animals to uplifting slogans and 'play safe' banners above condoms.

Wah Aik Shoemaker SHOES
(56 Jln Tokong Emas) The Yeo brothers continue the tradition begun by their grandfather in the same little shoemaker's shop that has been in the family for generations. The beaded Peranakan shoes here are considered Melaka's finest and begin at a steep but merited RM300. The most unusual souvenirs are tiny bound-feet shoes (from RM95).

This minute footwear harks back to China's now-defunct tradition of foot binding, where women endured lifelong pain and deformity to attain the 'golden lotus' ideal of feet no longer than four inches.

Joe's Design JEWELLERY
(☎06-281 2960; 6 Jln Tun Tan Cheng Lock; ⏲10am-5pm Wed-Mon) Owl-shaped ornaments, iridescent floral necklaces and beautifully curled copper wire creations are some of the stock at this lovely craft jewellery shop.

Dataran Pahlawan MALL
(☎06-281 2898; www.dataranpahlawan.com; Jln Merdeka; ⏲10am-10pm) Melaka's largest mall, with a collection of upscale designer shops and restaurants in the western half and an odd, nearly underground-feeling craft-and-souvenir market in the eastern portion. Find the **Golden Screen Cinema** (☎06-281 0018; www.gsc.com.my; Dataran Pahlawan) on the fifth floor.

Mahkota Parade Shopping Complex MALL
(☎06-282 6151; www.mahkotaparade.com.my; Lot B02, Jln Merdeka; ⏲10am-10pm) For practical needs such as books, cameras, pharmacy goods or electronics, head to this shopping complex.

Hatten Square MALL
(Jln Merdeka) A fashion-heavy mall topped with the glamorous Hatten Hotel (p227).

Information

Most hotels and guesthouses have wi-fi and several cafes in Chinatown have a computer for clients and charge around RM3 per hour.

GETTING TO INDONESIA: MELAKA TO DUMAI

Getting to the border High-speed ferries make the trip from Melaka to Dumai in Sumatra daily at 10am (one way/return RM110/170, 1¾ hours; child tickets are half-price). The quay is walking distance or a short taxi ride from most hotels and guesthouses. Tickets are available at **Indomal Express** (☎06-281 6766, 019-665 7055) and other ticket offices near the wharf.

At the border Citizens of most countries can obtain a 30-day visa on arrival (US$35).

Moving on Dumai is on Sumatra's east coast and is a 10-hour bus ride from Bukittinggi.

There are plenty of ATMs at the shopping malls but fewer in Chinatown. Moneychangers can be found throughout Chinatown.

Mahkota Medical Centre (☎06-281 3333, emergency 06-285 2991; www.mahkotamedical.com; Jln Merdeka) A private hospital offering a full range of services including accident and emergency.

Post Office (Jln Laksamana; ⏲8.30am-5pm Mon-Sat) The post office is north of Dutch Sq.

State Tourism Office (☎06-281 4803; www.melaka.gov.my; Jln Kota; ⏲9am-2pm & 3-6pm) Tourism office diagonally across Dutch Sq from Christ Church.

Tourist Police (☎06-282 2222, 06-281 4803; Jln Kota; ⏲24hr) Melaka's tourist police office is available by phone around the clock.

Getting There & Away

Melaka is 144km from Kuala Lumpur, 220km from Johor Bahru and 94km from Port Dickson.

AIR

Melaka International Airport (☎06-317 5860; Lapangan Terbang Batu Berendam) is 12km north of Melaka. At the time of research, **Malindo Air** (☎03-7841 5388; www.malindoair.com) offered flights from Melaka to Penang (from RM99, daily) and Pekanbaru (Indonesia; from RM180, daily).

BUS

Melaka Sentral, the huge, modern long-distance bus station, is 5km north of the city. Luggage deposit at Melaka Sentral is RM2 per bag. There is also an ATM and restaurants.

A taxi into town should cost RM20 to RM25, or you can take bus 17 (RM1.40).

A medley of privately run bus companies make checking timetables a herculean feat; you can scout popular routes on www.expressbusmalaysia.com/coach-from-melaka. You can buy bus tickets in advance from downtown Melaka (not a bad idea on busy weekends or if you have a plane to catch) at **Discovery Cafe** (☎012-683 5606, 06-292 5606; www.discovery-malacca.com; 3 Jln Bunga Raya) – there's a small commission, dependent on the ticket fare.

DESTINATION	PRICE	DURATION	FREQUENCY
Cameron Highlands	RM37.50	5 hours	daily (9am)
Ipoh	RM35-41	5 hours	daily (9.30am)
Johor Bahru	RM20-24	3½ hours	10 daily
Kuala Lumpur	RM10-17	2 hours	every half hour
KLIA/LCCT airports	RM24-28	2 hours	hourly
Kota Bharu	RM51	10 hours	daily (8.30am)
Mersing	RM28	4½ hours	3 daily
Penang	RM45-50	7 hours	3 daily
Singapore	RM24-27	4½ hours	4 daily

CAR

Car-hire prices begin at around RM150 per day. If driving, Melaka's one-way traffic system requires patience. Try **Hawk** (☎06-283 7878; www.hawkrentacar.com.my; 52 Jln Cempaka 1; ⏲8am-5.30pm Mon-Fri, 8am-1pm Sat), north of town.

TAXI

At Melaka Sentral, follow signs to the taxi booking kiosk to ensure standard rates. Long distance fares at the time of writing were Johor Bahru (RM250), Mersing (RM300), KL (RM170) and KL airport (RM160).

TRAIN

The closest train station is inconveniently located for travellers to Melaka. Known as **Pulau Sebang/Tampin Station** (☎06-441 1034), the railway stop is 38km north of Melaka. Destinations from here include KL (RM17-29, two hours, three daily), Penang (Butterworth; RM42-85, seven hours, one daily), Johor Bahru (RM25-46, six hours, one daily) and Ipoh (RM17-42, five to six hours, three daily). Taxis from Melaka to Pulau Sebang/Tampin station cost around

PSYCHEDELIC TRISHAWS

First you hear a distant blare of horn-honking and hip-hop. Then suddenly, a convoy of three-wheeled vehicles is careening your way, in a blur of fairy lights and cartoon cut-outs. Melaka's trishaws are the glitziest you'll see anywhere in Malaysia, decorated with paraphernalia from papier mâché models of colonial buildings to Disney princesses and Christmas trees. Local opinion is divided over whether Melaka's blinged-up trishaws help preserve this historic mode of transport or hideously distort it. But it's hard to imagine a trip to Melaka without at least one ride. And it's impossible not to raise a smile when tourist groups hire them en masse, forming a carnivalesque, cycle-powered conga line.

RM60. Alternatively there's a half-hourly bus from Melaka Sentral (RM5, 1½ hours).

Getting Around

Melaka is small enough to walk around or, for the traffic-fearless, you can rent a bike for around RM3 per hour from guesthouses around Chinatown. A useful service is town bus 17, running every 15 minutes from Melaka Sentral to the centre of town, past the huge Mahkota Parade shopping complex, to Taman Melaka Raya and on to Medan Portugis. You can find local bus route information on www.panoramamelaka.com.my/routes.

Taking to Melaka's streets by trishaw is a must – by the hour they should cost RM40, or RM15 for any one-way trip within town, but you'll have to bargain.

Taxis should cost around RM15 for a trip anywhere around town.

AROUND MELAKA CITY

Ayer Keroh

About 13km northeast of Melaka, Ayer Keroh (also spelled Air Keroh) has a handful of kid-friendly attractions that are largely deserted on weekdays. Some feel a little contrived, but there's no denying this area is a fine family day-trip from Melaka City. Ayer Keroh can be reached on bus 19 from Melaka Sentral (RM2, 30 minutes), or a taxi will cost around RM45.

Sights

Taman Mini Malaysia & Mini ASEAN CULTURAL CENTRE

(☎06-234 9988; adult/child RM24/15; ⏰9am-6pm; P) This open-air museum exhibits traditional houses from all 13 Malaysian states, as well as neighbouring Southeast Asian countries. Visitors can tiptoe through a long-roofed fishing house from Perlis and peruse rice-pounding equipment from Langkawi at numerous recreations across the site. It's family-focussed and a little twee, but the houses are beautifully decorated with plenty of explanation about local traditions, foods and languages. Less interesting are the fairground attractions at the site.

Melaka Zoo ZOO

(www.melakazoo.com; adult/child RM24/18; ⏰9am-6pm daily, night zoo 8-11pm Fri & Sat; P) Malaysia's second-largest zoo is home to more than 200 species, from tigers and lions to less ferocious critters like capybaras, monkeys and mouse deer. The zoo takes pride in its conservation focus and most enclosures are large, though cages for some birds and smaller animals are still rather poky.

The night safari on Friday and Saturday evenings allows the chance to spot nocturnal animals at their most active, though visitors give mixed reviews about the wildlife-spotting and live shows at this event.

Hutan Rekreasi Air Keroh PARK

(Air Keroh Recreational Forest) FREE The Hutan Rekreasi Air Keroh is a good place for an easy ramble; this green space is part jungle, part landscaped park with paved trails.

Pulau Besar

This small island, 10km off the coast southeast of Melaka, was once a retreat for Muslim mystics. Pilgrims still arrive to seek out Pulau Besar's meditation caves and the graves of prominent Islamic teachers. If you're planning to hit the beach, we recommend modesty (slip a T-shirt over your bathing suit).

Plans to establish Malaysia's largest independent oil storage terminal here didn't materialise. Dreams of turning the island into a mega-resort and golf course also never hit their stride. So for tourism and industry, Pulau Besar is a placid spot. There are fine beaches, but amenities are few and some areas of the shore are scattered with as many cola bottles as coconut shells.

Sights

Turning left from Pulau Besar jetty, follow the shore to palm-shaded beaches. During peak season, a few street food stands serve Malay snacks and there's a small bazaar. Near here lie a few well-tended graves and shrines, including the **Tomb of Tok Janggut**, who spread a self-defence art on Pulau Besar.

Muzium Pulau Besar MUSEUM

(adult/child RM5/2; ⏰9am-5pm) This small museum illuminates the island's culture, history and spiritual significance, in particular its role as a rest point for sailors between China and Europe. Follow the paved road from the jetty uphill and to the left.

Getting There & Away

Exploring Pulau Besar is best done as a full or half-day excursion from Melaka City. Boats (return trip RM14, 20 minutes) depart from Anjung Batu jetty every two to three hours from 8am (last boat returns at 7pm, or 9pm on weekends). Inclement weather can disrupt schedules, so check ahead with Melaka's **tourism office** (p232).

For Anjung Batu, take bus 6 from Melaka Sentral towards Merlimau and ask to be let off at Anjung Batu jetty (RM2.50). The jetty is a 15-minute walk from the bus stop. Taxis from central Melaka to Anjung Batu should cost around RM40.

Alor Gajah

Just off the road to KL, 24km north of Melaka, is the countryside town of Alor Gajah. Though the town has some gaily painted shophouses and interesting mosques, in particular Masjid Al-Rasyidin Daerah, the main draw is nearby A'Famosa Resort with its huge water park.

Many Melaka–KL buses stop in Alor Gajah so it's possible to pause here between the two cities if you're willing to change buses. A taxi from Alor Gajah to A'Famosa should cost around RM22.

Activities

A'Famosa Resort WATER PARK
(06-552 0888; www.afamosa.com) The 520-hectare A'Famosa Resort is wildly popular with Malay and Singaporean tourists. While it's a little cheesy, you'd be hard pressed not to have fun at **Water World** (adult/child RM48/36; 11am-7pm Mon-Fri, 9am-7pm Sat & Sun), which has two seven-storey-high speed slides, a tube ride plus an artificially constructed beach with wave pool. There is also a **recreation area** with games and sports, including go-karts and archery, plus a good 27-hole **golf course** (weekday/weekend RM118/198). **Safari Wonderland** (9am-5pm) offers elephant rides and animal performances; activities which have been proven to be harmful for animals.

The resort is less than an hour's drive from Melaka and 90 minutes from Kuala Lumpur.

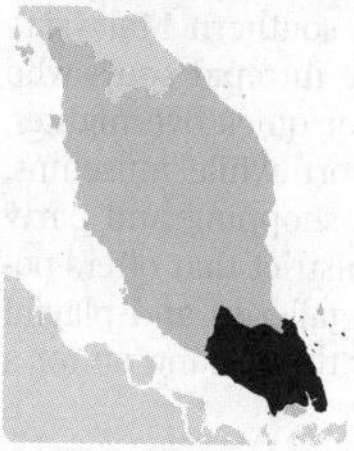

Johor

06, 07 / POP 3.3 MILLION / AREA 19,984 SQ KM

Includes ➡

Why Go?

Johor is Malaysia's most populous state and a growing economic power player. Most travel itineraries skip it, but those who stray into the southern gateway to Malaysia will be rewarded with the blissful solitude of its postcard-perfect islands and wild jungles, while getting access to a taste of authentic Malaysian culture and character not easily found in bigger tourist hot spots.

The top draw is without a doubt the ridiculously gorgeous white sand islands of the Seribuat Archipelago, where you'll find world-class diving, lost-beach trails and plenty of relaxation time with a fraction of Tioman's crowds. Inland, Endau-Rompin National Park offers the same rich flora, very elusive fauna (rhinos! elephants!) and swashbuckling action that visitors flock to experience at Taman Negara in Pahang, but can get here in a more pristine setting.

And then there's Johor Bahru, the working-class capital with a handful of worthwhile religious sites and museums that plays sister-city to neighbouring Singapore.

Best Outdoor Adventures

- Upeh Guling & Buaya Sangkut Falls (p248)
- Pulau Tinggi (p246)
- Takah Berangin & Takah Pandan Falls (p249)
- Pulau Sibu (p246)
- Gunung Ledang (p242)

Best Places to Stay

- Rimba Resort (p246)
- Thistle Johor Bahru (p239)
- Rawa Island Resort (p246)
- Mirage Island Resort (p245)
- Kampung Peta (p249)

When to Go

Johor Bahru

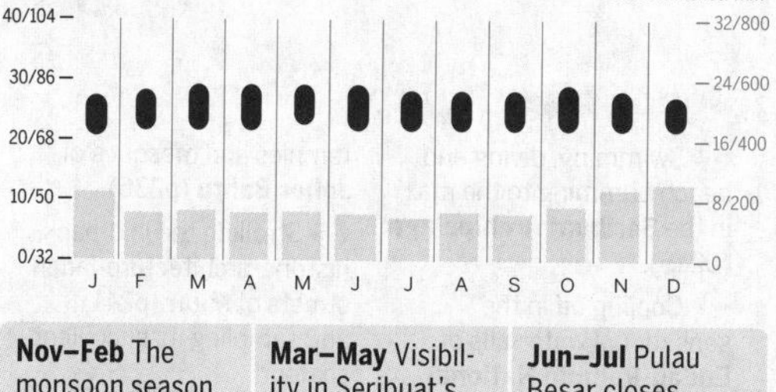

Nov–Feb The monsoon season brings bargain deals, rain and bugs. Surfers head to Rawa for rollers.

Mar–May Visibility in Seribuat's already translucent waters is at its best for diving and snorkelling.

Jun–Jul Pulau Besar closes for Expedition Robinson. Expect high temperatures everywhere.

Johor Bahru

07 / POP 1,371,000

After years of being criticised as a dirty, chaotic border town, Johor's capital city of Johor Bahru (JB for short) has been repaved and replanted and is well on the way to rebranding itself.

Most travellers skip southern Malaysia's largest city, but for the intrepid souls who stop for an afternoon or quick overnighter, there's a handful of worthwhile museums, temples and mosques, shopping and party zones, and a heritage district that offers poetic street scenes, hip galleries and playful cafes. If that ain't your thing, hang on for a

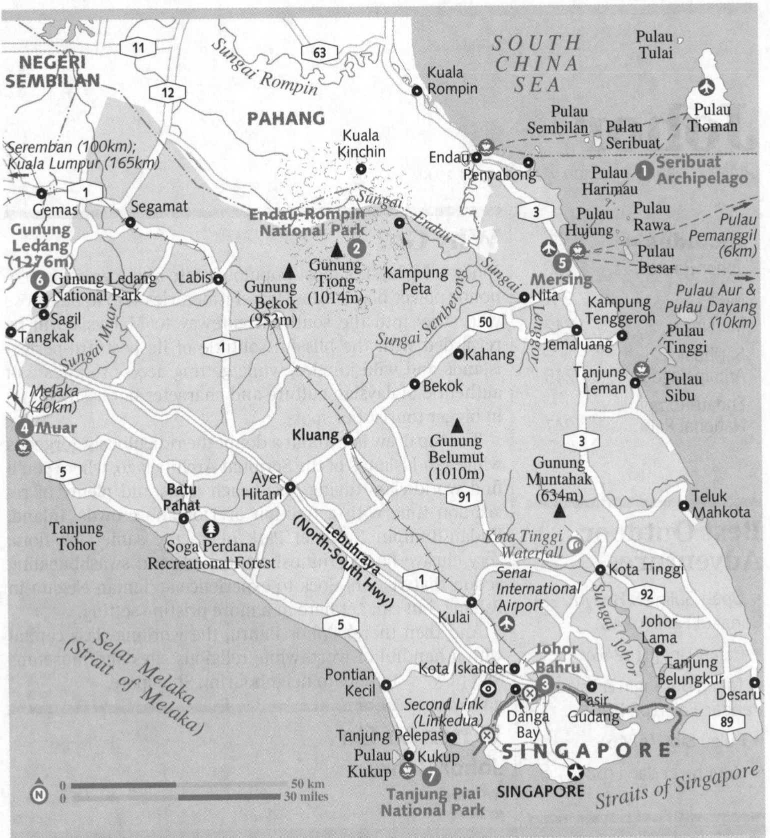

Johor Highlights

1 Swimming, diving and beach bumming to the max in the **Seribuat Archipelago** (p245).

2 Cooling off in the sensational waterfalls of **Endau-Rompin National Park** (p247) after hiking through dense jungle.

3 Discovering the colonial backstreets and ornate temples and mosques of **Johor Bahru** (p236).

4 Strolling the laid-back, historic-architecture-laden streets of **Muar** (p241) and sampling its succulent seafood.

5 Ambling the streets and riverwalk of **Mersing** (p242).

6 Sweating your way to the top of **Gunung Ledang** (p242), Johor's highest peak.

7 Taking the road less travelled to offbeat parks and preserves such as **Tanjung Piai National Park** (p244).

trip to Legoland, where 'everything is awesome'.

JB is conveniently connected to Singapore by the 1038m-long Causeway, and many people choose to work in Singapore and sleep in Johor Bahru.

As one of the five 'economic zones' of the Iskandar development project, which will radically change southern Malaysia over the next decade, JB is in for one hell of a makeover. The 720-hectare Danga Bay area, 5km from the Causeway, is poised to be a financial and commercial centre with lofty ambitions of emerging as something of a mini-Marina Bay. Work on the Iskandar development began in 2006 and is expected to be completed in 2025. For now Danga Bay is just a bleak sprawl of construction, but many remember Singapore looking a bit like that too in the not-so-distant past.

WORTH A TRIP

LEGOLAND!

Got kids? Opened in 2012, Southeast Asia's first **Legoland** (☎07-597 8888; www.legoland.com.my; Medini, Nusajaya; adult/child RM207/165; ⏲10am-6pm) offers more than 70 rides and attractions, plus a water park that can be visited separately or as part of a package. Nearly everything is hands-on, and it's not just about the bricks. Expect to crawl around, pull yourself up a tower with ropes, ride a dragon-coaster and shoot lasers at mummies. The centrepiece is Miniland, where you'll find regional landmarks including the Petronas Towers and Singapore's Merlion built in miniature out of Lego.

Sights

Sultan Abu Bakar Mosque MOSQUE
(Jln Gertak Merah) The stunning whitewashed walls and blue-tiled roof of this Victorian-inspired mosque speak of a mix of architectural influences. Built between 1892 and 1900, it is rightly hailed as one of the most magnificent mosques in the area. Non-Muslims are not permitted to enter the building.

Arulmigu Sri Raja Kalliamman HINDU TEMPLE
(Glass Temple; 22 Lorong 1; RM10; ⏲7am-noon, 6-10pm Mon-Fri, 7am-10pm Sat & Sun) FREE Step through the looking glass into this wonderland temple built from mirrors, glass and metal. Not a single inch of the vaulted roof or wall goes unadorned. The temple is dedicated to Kali, known as the goddess of time, change, power and destruction.

Heritage District ARCHITECTURE, AREA
Wandering around the heritage area between Jln Ibrahim and Jln Ungku Puan is a real highlight of Johor Bahru. Walk past old colourful shophouses filled with sari shops, barbers, Ayurvedic salons, gorgeous temples, a few modern-art galleries and old-style eateries.

Sri Raja Mariamman Devasthanam HINDU TEMPLE
(4 Jln Ungku Puan) FREE This beautiful Hindu temple, with ornate carvings and devotional artwork, and a tall, brightly painted *gopuram* (tower) entrance way, is the heart of JB's Hindu community. Photos are allowed, but be respectful of devotees.

Royal Abu Bakar Museum MUSEUM
(☎07-223 0555; Jln Ibrahim; adult/child RM21/9; ⏲9am-5pm Sat-Thu) The marvellous Istana Besar, once the Johor royal family's principal palace, was built in Victorian style by Anglophile sultan Abu Bakar in 1866. It was opened as a museum to the public in 1990 and displays the incredible wealth of the sultans. It's now the finest museum of its kind in Malaysia, and the 53-hectare palace grounds (free entry) are beautifully manicured.

At the time of research the museum was getting an extensive remodelling, with plans to reopen in 2016.

Bangunan Sultan Ibrahim ARCHITECTURE
(Bukit Timbalan, State Secretariat Bldg; ⏲Tue-Sat) Sitting magnificently atop Bukit Timbalan, the imposing Bangunan Sultan Ibrahim is a mighty melange of colonial pomp, Islamic motifs and indigenous design. Completed in 1942, the city landmark was employed as a fortress by the Japanese as they prepared to attack Singapore. Plans to convert it into a museum are in the works, though opening hours are still sporadic.

Chinese Heritage Museum MUSEUM
(42 Jln Ibrahim; RM5; ⏲8:30am-5pm Tue-Sun) Well-laid-out exhibits chronicling the history of Chinese immigrants in this part of the Malay peninsula are the highlight of this three-storey museum. Learn how the Cantonese brought their carpentry skills to this area, while the Hakkas traded in Chinese medicines and the Hainanese kick-started a

Johor Bahru

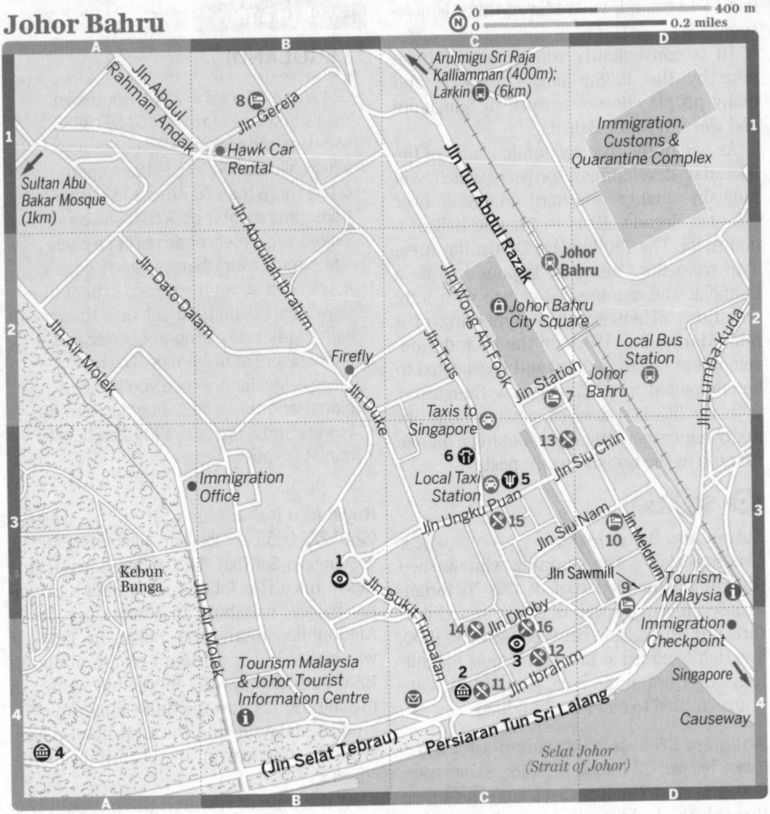

Johor Bahru

Sights

1 Bangunan Sultan Ibrahim B3
2 Chinese Heritage Museum C4
3 Heritage District C4
4 Royal Abu Bakar Museum A4
5 Sri Raja Mariamman Devasthanam C3
6 Tokong Cina C3

Sleeping

7 Citrus Hotel C2
8 Hilton Double Tree B1
9 J.A. Residence Hotel D3
10 Meldrum Hotel D3

Eating

11 Annalakshmi C4
12 Hiap Joo Bakery & Biscuit Factory C4
13 Medan Selera Meldrum Walk C3
14 Reaz Corner C4
15 Restoran Nilla C3
16 Roost Juice & Bar C4

trend in coffee shops, which lasts to this day. There's good English signage.

Tokong Cina CHINESE TEMPLE
(Johor Ancient Temple; Jln Trus) FREE This Chinese temple was established in 1870, primarily for the veneration of Yuan Tian Shang Di, the supreme lord of the dark heaven.

Sleeping

Meldrum Hotel HOTEL $$
(07-227 8988; www.meldrumhotel.com; 1 Jln Siu Nam; d RM131-189, q 225-260;) All options here are air-conditioned, clean, spacious and freshly painted, and the rooms have TVs, free drinking water and kettles. It's worth upgrading to a superior room with free wi-fi

and requesting a non-smoking room if you don't puff. Back rooms will save on street noise.

Thistle Johor Bahru HOTEL $$
(☎07-222 9234; www.thistle.com; Jln Sungai Chat; r from RM350; P❄@📶🏊) Overlooking the Straits of Johor, the Thistle is one of the poshest options this side of the Causeway. What puts it in a class above the rest are marble bathrooms, a lovely curving swimming pool and airy, light ambience.

The location, near Danga Bay, is a little out of the way, about 4km from the town centre, just off the main road, Jln Lingkaran Dalam.

Citrus Hotel HOTEL $$
(☎07-222 2888; www.citrushoteljb.com; 16 Jln Station; d RM159-189 incl breakfast; ❄📶) Rooms are small but clean with white walls and bright accents of green and orange – citrusy indeed. Breakfasts are tasty, staff are helpful and the location, just next to JB City Square, couldn't be better.

J.A. Residence Hotel HOTEL $$
(☎07-221 3000; www.ja-residencehotel.com; 18 Jln Wong Ah Fook; r/tr RM130/170, ste RM150-250; ❄@📶) Right in the heart of town, this is a comfortable and modern high-rise hotel offering good value for money, though the bathrooms and hallways are rather bleak and rundown. Its cream-coloured paint and polished wood interiors have some design flair and the staff are really friendly. Angle for a room on the upper floors for million-dollar views over the Causeway.

Hilton Double Tree BUSINESS HOTEL $$$
(☎07-268 6868; www.doubletree3.hilton.com; 12 Jln Ngee Heng; r from RM400; P❄@📶🏊) While it lacks the intimacy of the small boutiques in town, the Double Tree does deliver business-class comfort with well-tailored ample rooms, several restaurants and a 13th-floor pool and bar terrace that gives you a bird's-eye view of the city. Hit the internet for big savings. The lighting system in the rooms is confusing as hell.

Eating & Drinking

The streets sizzle with some of the country's best seafood (try the area around KSL City Mall), as well as local specialities including a curry-heavy version of laksa. Diners seeking European meals may want to hit up the restaurants in the Thistle or DoubleTree hotels.

Reaz Corner INDIAN $
(Jln Duke; RM8-12.50) You can't go wrong with the yellow rice topped with a spicy chicken curry at this clean, open-air curry joint. The ginger tea is a not-to-be-missed-nor-soon-forgotten accompaniment.

Annalakshmi INDIAN $
(☎07-227 7400; 39 Jln Ibraham; meals by donation; ⏰11am-3pm Mon-Sat; 🖉) An authentic vegetarian Indian restaurant run by volunteers of the Temple of Fine Arts, with the motto 'eat what you want and give as you feel'. Meals are a set and the ambience is classy.

Hiap Joo Bakery & Biscuit Factory BAKERY $
(13 Jln Tan Hiok Nee; buns from RM2.50; ⏰7am-5.30pm Tue-Sat) For over 80 years this little bakery has prepared delicious buns, cakes and biscuits in a charcoal oven just as the founder had done in his native Hainan, China.

Restoran Nilla INDIAN $
(Jln Ungku Puan, cnr Jln Trus; mains from RM2; ⏰7am-10pm; 🖉) An excellent South Indian eatery with some of the best chicken you've ever had. Ask for the 'vegetarian chicken' – it is, in fact, tofu but it's so good you'll hardly believe it.

Medan Selera Meldrum Walk HAWKER $
(Medan Selera Meldrum; meals from RM3; ⏰dinner) Every late afternoon, the little food stalls crammed along this alley (parallel to Jln Meldrum) start frying up everything from *ikan bakar* to the local curry laksa. Wash down your meal with fresh sugar-cane juice or a Chinese herbal jelly drink. Nothing here is excellent, but it's all good.

Roost Juice & Bar INTERNATIONAL $$
(Jln Dhoby; mains RM8-28, juice from RM7.90; ⏰noon-4pm Mon-Sat, 6pm-midnight daily) JB's most chillable spot uses recycled wood, bottles and more to create a cafe/bar that feels like someone's (very hip) living room.

DANGERS & ANNOYANCES

Although travelling in Johor Bahru is generally safe, visitors should be alert to motorcycle-riding bag-snatchers and, as in any city, avoid walking alone down dark alleyways. If you have any troubles call the **police hotline** (☎07-225 6699).

And the food is great too. Try the Hainanese noodles, fish 'n' chips, mutton ribs or Nyonya fish fillets, and finish it off with fresh juice or a cold beer.

Zon BAR, CLUB
(www.zon.com.my; Zon Ferry Terminal) Three words: duty-free booze. About 10 bars and clubs surround the courtyard of this happening spot.

Shopping

The mall is where it's at. Expect decent food courts, blaring air-con and plenty of visiting Singaporeans looking for deals. Top malls include **KSL City Mall** (www.kslcity.com.my; 33 Jln Seladang), **Johor Premium Outlets** (www.premiumoutlets.com.my; Indahpura, Kulaijaya; ⏲10am-10pm), **Tebrau City Shopping Centre** and **Plaza Pelangi** (Jln Tebrau).

Information

ATMs and banks are everywhere in the central areas. Moneychangers infest Jln Wong Ah Fook, and have competitive rates

Immigration Office (☎07-233 8400; www.imi.gov.my; Jln Setia Tropika, Kempas) For visa extensions.

KPJ Johor Specialist Hospital (☎emergency 07-220 7505, 07-227 3000; www.kpjjohor.com; 39-B Jln Abdul Samad) A squeaky clean, state-of-the-art, private hospital.

Tourism Malaysia & Johor Tourist Information Centre (☎07-223 4935; www.johortourism.com.my; 3rd fl, Jotic Bldg, 2 Jln Air Molek; ⏲9am-5pm Mon-Sat) One of two Tourism Malaysia offices in JB; the other is at the CIQ complex, right after you pass through immigration from Singapore.

Getting There & Away

AIR

JB is served by the **Senai International Airport** (☎07-599 4500; www.senaiairport.com), 32km northwest of JB. Prices are much lower to/from here than Singapore.

AirAsia (☎1300-889 933; www.airasia.com) Has low-cost flights to KL, Penang, Kuching, Kota Kinabalu, Sibu and Miri.

Firefly (☎03-7845 4543; www.firefly.com.my) Flies to Kuala Lumpur's Subang Airport and Kota Bahru. Tickets to KL start as low as RM79.

Malaysia Airlines (☎1300-883 000; www.malaysiaairlines.com; mezzanine fl, Persada Johor International Convention Center, Jln Abdullah Ibrahim) Flights to Kuching and Kuala

GETTING TO SINGAPORE FROM JOHOR BAHRU

At JB Sentral you can clear immigration and travel across the Causeway to Singapore.

At the border: All buses and taxis stop at Malaysian immigration. You'll need to disembark from your vehicle with your luggage (and ticket), clear immigration and reboard. Vehicles then stop at Singapore immigration; again, you'll clear immigration with your luggage, before getting back in your vehicle for the last leg to Queen St bus station. There are **tourism information offices** (CIQ Complex; ⏲9am-5pm Mon-Sat) and money exchanges at the border.

By bus: From central JB, board your bus after clearing Malaysian immigration just before the Causeway – you can buy your tickets on board. There are also frequent buses between JB's **Larkin bus terminal**, 5km north of the city, and Singapore's Queen St bus station. Causeway Link (www.causewaylink.com.my) is the most convenient service: from JB/Singapore RM3.40/S$3.30, 6.30am to midnight, every 10 minutes. Trans Star Cross Border Coaches (www.regentstar.travel/crossborder) run between the Larkin terminal in Johor Bahru and Singapore's Changi International Airport, embarking in the Terminal 2 coach area: from JB/Singapore RM10/S$9; every hour 5am to 11pm.

Registered taxis: These depart from the Plaza Seni Taxi Terminal in the centre of town, with taxis to Orchard Rd or Queen St terminal costing around RM60. Local city taxis cannot cross the Causeway.

By train: KTM Intercity trains (RM3) take you from JB Sentral to Woodlands in Singapore, leaving JB at 5:50am, 6:55am, 2:20pm and 9pm. You go through passport checks and switch to the Singapore metro system at Woodlands.

In Singapore: At Queen St there are buses, taxis and an MRT (light rail) system that can take you almost anywhere you need to go in the city.

GETTING TO INDONESIA: BATAM & BINTAN (RIAU ISLANDS)

Boats: There are several daily departures to Batam (one way RM69, 1½ hours) and Tanjung Pinangon Bintan (one way RM86, 2½ hours), part of Indonesia's Riau Islands. Ferries depart from the **Berjaya Ferry Terminal** (Zon Ferry; www.berjayawaterfront.com.my; 88 Jln Ibrahim Sultan), which is serviced by several buses from downtown Johor Bahru. **Tuah Ferry Services** (www.ferrytuah.comoj.com; Terminal Antarabangsa Kukup) depart from Kukup, southwest of JB, for Tanjung Balai on Karimun (three times daily, RM130) and for Sekupang, Batam (twice daily, RM165). Buses travel to Kukup from Johor Bahru (RM7, 1½ hours) and KL (RM26, 3½ hours). A taxi from Johor Bahru to Kukup is RM80.

At the border: You'll be charged a RM10 seaport tax and stamped out of Malaysia before you board the boat in JB; from Kukup the fee is RM25 per person.

From the Riau Islands there are ferry connections to Sumatra, Indonesia.

Lumpur with easy connections to a variety of destinations.

BUS

Larkin bus terminal (Jln Garuda) is about 5km north of town.

DESTINATION	PRICE	DURATION
Butterworth	RM62.60	9 hours
Melaka	RM21	2½ hours
Muar	RM17	2 hours
Kuala Lumpur	RM31	4 hours
Mersing	RM13	2 hours
Kuantan	RM20	5 hours
Kuala Terengganu	RM33	8 hours

TAXI

JB's main long-distance taxi station is at the Larkin bus station, 5km north of town, but there's a handier terminal on Jln Wong Ah Fook.

Some regular taxi destinations and approximate costs (share taxi with four passengers):

- KL (RM460)
- Kukup (RM80)
- Melaka (RM280)
- Mersing (RM160)
- Senai Airport (RM50).

TRAIN

Three daily express trains on **KTM Intercity** (☎300-885862; www.ktmintercity.com.my; JB Sentral) leave from the sparkling JB Sentral station in the CIQ complex, running to KL (6.30am, 2.56pm and 8.25pm). The line passes through Tampin (for Melaka), Seremban, KL Sentral, Tapah Rd (for Cameron Highlands), Ipoh, Taiping and Butterworth. The line splits at Gemas so you can board the 'jungle train' for Jerantut (for Taman Negara), Kuala Lipis and Kota Bharu (portions of this line were closed at research due to flooding).

Getting Around

TO/FROM SENAI INTERNATIONAL AIRPORT

Senai International Airport, 32km northwest of town, is linked to the city centre by regular shuttle buses (RM8, 45 minutes) that run from the bus station at Kotaraya 2 Terminal.

A taxi between the airport and JB is RM60, taking 30 to 45 minutes, depending on traffic.

BUS

Local buses operate from several stops around town, the most convenient being the stop in front of Public Bank on Jln Wong Ah Fook. From Larkin bus station, bus 39 goes into central JB (RM1.80).

CAR

Car hire in JB is considerably cheaper than in Singapore, but check that the hire firm allows cars to enter Singapore. Prices run about RM177 to RM233 per day, inclusive of insurance and tax. Many rental companies have cars for hire at Senai International Airport.

Hawk Car Rental (☎07-224 2854; www.hawkrentacar.com.my; Puteri Pacific Hotel)

TAXI

Taxis in JB have meters, and drivers are legally required to use them. Flagfall is RM3, with an average trip costing RM10. Taxis can be hired at around RM35 per hour for sightseeing.

Muar

☎06

A lethargic riverside town, languorously Malaysian in mood, Muar was historically an important commercial centre but today it's a very sleepy backwater. Most of the action is in the central Chinatown, which shows off cool historic architecture and a few temples. It makes for an off-the-beaten-path (though not very action-packed) stop between Melaka and Johor Bahru.

Sights

Colonial District AREA

The graceful colonial district by the river turns up several buildings of note. Walk around the area and look out for the customs house, the courthouse, the high school (built in 1914) and Masjid Jamek, a Victorian fantasy in much the same style as Johor Bahru's Sultan Abu Bakar Mosque.

Sleeping & Eating

Muar is known for its Nonya-style *otak-otak* (fish cakes) and satay breakfasts. You'll find hawker stalls on Jln Haji Abu just off Jln Ali.

Hotel Leewa HOTEL $

(06-952 1605; 44 Jln Ali & 75 Jln Arab; d without/with air-con & bathroom RM50/65; P) The owners love children, and the hotel attracts a lot of families. All rooms are simple, ageing and clean – though they can be a bit dank.

Hotel Classic BUSINESS HOTEL $$

(06-953 3888; 69 Jln Ali; r RM148-193, ste RM228-292; P) The ginormous rooms come with satellite TV and soft-like-Wonderbread mattresses. The difference between standard and deluxe is only room size.

Getting There & Away

Regular buses to JB (RM17, 2½ hours) and KL (RM18, 2½ hours) depart from the Muar long-distance bus station by the river. Buses to/from Melaka (RM6, one hour), and Gunung Ledang/Segamat (RM5, one hour) operate from the local bus station. The taxi station is just to the right of the bus station.

Mersing

07

This busy, compact fishing town has everything that travellers passing through on their way to the islands might need: cheap internet, OK sleeping options, grocery stores, cold beer and a pharmacy. The river is clogged with colourful fishing boats, and though most people only stay long enough to hop a ferry to Tioman, this is a relaxed village with a surprisingly lyrical air. Take an afternoon to revel in views of the hilltop mosque, hike out to the nearby green areas or just reconnect with mainland life.

Sights

Masjid Jamek Bandar Mersing MOSQUE

(Jln Masjid) Walk the 15 minutes to this hilltop mosque with stunning blue and white architecture, and take in views of the South China Sea, river and village. Night-time prayers are broadcast over a mega-super-charged hi-fi system.

Hock Soon Temple TAOIST TEMPLE

FREE This century-old Taoist temple is dedicated to Tua Pek Kong, the god of prosperity.

Sri Subramaniam Temple HINDU TEMPLE

FREE While you're waiting for your ferry, idle over to this ornate Hindu temple.

WORTH A TRIP

GUNUNG LEDANG NATIONAL PARK

According to legend, the highest mountain in Johor is the fabled home of Puteri Gunung Ledang, a mythical princess whose presence is said to still permeate the jungle slopes. Climbing Gunung Ledang (also called Mt Ophir; 1276m) is extremely popular with Malaysian and Singaporean groups but few foreigners visit the area. It's a very demanding – yet rewarding – two-day return trip from the National Park Office to the summit. While you are there, consider taking a side trip to the **Puteri Waterfalls**, which feature a cool bathing pool at the bottom.

There are several camp sites along the way up the mountain. Pre- and/or post-trek you can stay in one of the park's **accommodation options** (07-266 1301; www.johorparks.blogspot.com; Jln Muar; camp site RM10, dorm RM25, chalet from RM75), or at the more comfortable **Gunung Ledang Resort** (06-977 2888; www.ledang.com; Jln Segamat, sales office BT 28, Sagil, Tangkak; cabin RM50, standard/deluxe tw RM150/250;) a few kilometres down the road. Most camp sites and accommodation book out over the weekends – plan your trip on a weekday or reserve well in advance.

There's a park entrance fee of RM3 and an additional daily hiking fee of RM23. Mandatory guides cost RM140 per day. To get to the park take a bus or train to Segamat then hop on a local bus to Segil (RM5, 45 minutes), ask to get off at Gunung Ledang.

Mersing

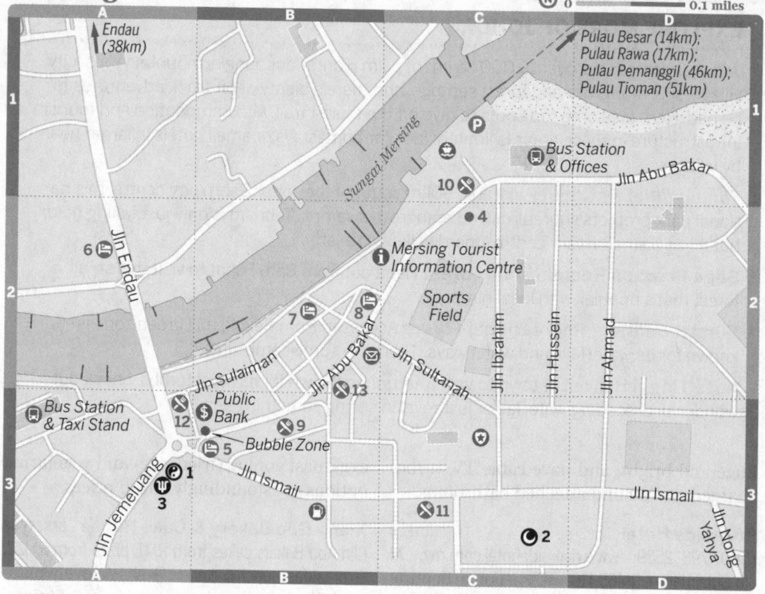

Tours

Several places around the port work as booking offices for islands in the Seribuat Archipelago and Tioman Island, and can arrange packages. There were no day tours to the Seribuat Archipelago when we passed through. Inquire near the ferry terminal.

Pure Value Travel Agency TOUR
(☎07-799 6811; www.purevalue.com.my; Jln Abu Bakar) This small operator by the ferry dock offers day trips to Endau-Rompin for RM200 per person (minimum four people). Overnight trips start at RM350 per person.

Sleeping

You may end up spending a night or two in Mersing waiting for ferries (due to weather or tides).

Avoid arriving during the Chinese New Year and other holiday periods, when midrange hotels can be booked solid.

Zeeadam Backpacker House HOSTEL $
(☎07-799 1280; ahmadzamani_77@yahoo.com; 10-1 Atas Jln Abu Bakar; dm RM20; @📶) The only true dorm-bed backpacker place in town, the Zeeadam has just two dorm rooms, sleeping six to eight people on ultra-firm beds. There's a little TV and a hangout chill area at this second-storey spot that is short on charms but long on value.

Mersing

Sights

1 Hock Soon Temple ...A3
2 Masjid Jamek Bandar Mersing...C3
3 Sri Subramaniam Temple ...A3

Activities, Courses & Tours

4 Pure Value Travel Agency...C2

Sleeping

5 Hotel Embassy ...B3
6 Hotel Timotel...A2
7 Riverside Hotel...B2
8 Zeeadam Backpacker House...B2

Eating

9 Loke Tien Yuen Restaurant ...B3
10 Port Café & Bistro...C1
11 Restoran Al-Arif ...C3
12 Seafood Stalls ...A3
13 Xiang Guo Bakery & Cake House ...B2

Hotel Embassy HOTEL $
(☎07-799 3545; 2 Jln Ismail; r RM55; ❄📶) This is a fabulous choice compared with the other cheapies in town, and is a great place to clean up and get back to reality after bumming it on island beaches. All rooms are

OFF THE BEATEN TRACK

EXPLORE MORE OF JOHOR

Johor encompasses over 19,000 sq km of palm plantations, jungle, mountain tops, city, village, sea, mangrove and forest settings, and there's plenty of off-track adventures to be had. Here are some top spots to dive off the tourist trail. Accommodation and tourist infrastructure in these areas is limited; look for homestays or small hotels in larger nearby villages.

Tanjung Piai National Park Just 90km south of the Johor Bahru city centre, this national park protects shorebirds and mangrove swamps. Tourism is only just taking hold, but it has a small visitor centre, boardwalks and a jetty.

Soga Perdana Recreational Forest Head out from Batu Pahat to visit this small forest that's popular with local birders.

Sungai Bantang Recreational Forest Accessed from Bekok, this green zone is known for its waterfalls and waterways. There are some camp sites.

Kota Tinggi Hop out of town to visit a *kampung* known for its royal tombs, check out a wonderful cascading waterfall or just revel in seeing something new.

huge and bright, and have cable TV, turbo-charged air-con and attached bathrooms.

Riverside Hotel HOTEL $
(07-798 2589; www.riversidehotel.com.my; 74 Jln Sulaiman; r RM65-110;) For a fleeting view of the river try this solid budget option that offers clean basic rooms and ever-so-slightly-awkward service. The rooms can be slightly musty, and river views cost double.

Hotel Timotel HOTEL $$
(07-799 5888; www.timotel.com.my; 839 Jln Endau; r RM165; @) Just across the bridge, this fading, business-style hotel is a step above, but shabby nevertheless. Doubles are clean, spacious and have satellite TV.

Eating

Seafood stalls open up nightly near the bus station along the river.

Loke Tien Yuen Restaurant CHINESE $
(55 Jln Abu Bakar; mains RM3.50-15; lunch & dinner;) Mersing's oldest Chinese restaurant is one of the friendliest and busiest places in town. You may have to wait for a marble table to enjoy the deliciously prepared prawn and pork dishes. The specialty, whole steamed fish that you'll see all the locals eating, isn't on the English menu so ask your server.

Restoran Al-Arif INDIAN $
(44 Jln Ismail; mains around RM6; breakfast, lunch & dinner;) Serving up *roti canai* (flaky, flat bread), *roti telur* (roti with an egg), nasi goreng (fried rice) and vegetarian options at astoundingly cheap prices.

Xiang Guo Bakery & Cake House BAKERY $$
(Jln Abu Bakar; cakes from RM1, pizza from RM22; breakfast, lunch & dinner;) A lovely place to chill out in the air-con with a meal (pizza, Malay-style noodles, rice dishes and more), a coffee and something sinful such as tiramisu or rich cheesecake.

Port Café & Bistro INTERNATIONAL $$
(Jln Abu Bakar; mains RM10-30; lunch & dinner;) A little open-air bar and eatery right at the jetty, with surprisingly good international grub such as pizza (from RM24) and grilled chicken salad with balsamic dressing (RM12).

Information

There are several banks with ATMs along Jln Ismail.

Mersing Tourist Information Centre (Jln Abu Bakar; 8am-5pm Mon-Sat) On the road to the pier. Stop in for helpful info, bus schedules and pamphlets.

Bubble Zone (Jln Abu Bakar; per load RM10;) Self-service.

Getting There & Away

Most buses as well as long-distance taxis depart from the bus station near the bridge on the river, although a few long-distance buses leave from bus company offices near the pier. Some buses will drop you off at the pier when you arrive in Mersing if you ask nicely. For buses to Cherating, travel first to Kuantan.

DESTINATION	PRICE	DURATION	FREQUENCY
Johor Bahru	RM13	2½ hours	2 per day
Kahang	RM7	1 hour	3 per day
Kuala Lumpur	RM40	5½ hours	5 per day
Kuala Terengganu	RM34	9 hours	2 per day
Kuantan	RM17	5 hours	2 per day
Melaka	RM25	4 hours	3 per day
Singapore	RM16	3 hours	2 per day

Taxi destinations and costs (per car):

- Johor Bahru (RM160)
- Kuantan (RM220)
- Pekan (RM150).

Local buses run to Endau (RM5, 45 minutes).

For boats to Sibu Island, take a taxi to Tanjung Leman (RM70).

Seribuat Archipelago

07

The Seribuat Archipelago, off the east coast of Johor, is a constellation of some of Malaysia's most beautiful islands. Of the cluster of 64 islands, most people only know of Pulau Tioman (p251), the largest, which is actually a part of Pahang. This leaves the rest of the archipelago as far less-visited dots of tranquillity.

Divers can expect to see excellent coral and an array of marine life, from butterfly fish and parrot fish to barracuda, giant clams and more. The waters around the archipelago are frequently whipped into foam during the monsoon (November to February), so ferry services can be patchy, especially during the high monsoon (November and December).

Pulau Besar

07

Easy to get to and perfect for a day or two of serious beach lounging, Pulau Besar's long white-sand beach is fronted by a veritable swimming pool when the sea is calm. If you tire of vegging out, explore the trails to hidden beaches and through plenty of jungle. Note that the coral isn't great and there is no dive operator, so you'll have to spend your water time frolicking in the sandy-bottomed turquoise seas or snorkelling along the scattered bits of reef.

You can visit Pulau Besar on a day trip by hopping on the resort's shuttle boats. At the time of research there were no public boats, although there have been some in the past – inquire at the Mersing jetty.

The island's resorts are situated along the beach on the west of the island. All have restaurants and provide transfers to/from Mersing for guests for around RM110 return.

Mirage Island Resort RESORT **$$**

(07-799 2334; www.mirageislandresort.com.my; r per person incl transfers & all meals RM385-600) Cheaper digs are in stylish A-frames while the more expensive options are in huge, louvred wood bungalows – all exude a tropical-colonial charm. The staff are young and fun, and there's a bar and pool table in the restaurant area.

Aseania Resort RESORT **$$**

(019-736 1277; www.pulaubesar.net; chalets incl breakfast from RM300;) Rooms are big, clean and have dark-wood interiors. The service is stellar and the jungle pool,

SURVIVING EXPEDITION ROBINSON

It will seem a little ironic while you're sipping your cocktail on a white-sand beach, but other visitors to your island paradise might have munched on bugs and scrounged for water. This is because the Seribuat Archipelago is the location of *Expedition Robinson*, the original Swedish reality TV show that inspired *Survivor*. The program first aired in 1997 and the sets now host several groups (for different versions of the show) from countries such as Belgium, the Netherlands, Denmark and South Africa.

Base camp is on Pulau Besar, while many of the rougher 'survivor' locations are on the smaller, more remote islands. The *Robinson* TV crew begins setting up around April and filming takes place around June and July. During these two months Pulau Besar's hotels are shut to the public but you can still make a day trip to the island by hitching a ride with one of the many crew boats going back and forth to the mainland. Enquire at the Pulau Besar hotel offices at the Mersing jetty.

surrounded by a stylish wood deck, is a shady alternative to the beach.

Pulau Sibu

07

Apart from Tioman Island, this cluster of several islands (**Pulau Sibu Besar**, **Pulau Sibu Kukus**, **Pulau Sibu Tengah**, **Pulau Tengah** and **Pulau Sibu Hujung**) is the most popular destination in the archipelago – particularly with expat families living in Singapore. The bulk of the accommodation is on Pulau Sibu Besar, a tiny island around 7km by 1km. Its main attractions are good diving and even better beaches.

Boats for Pulau Sibu do not depart from Mersing, but from the jetty at Tanjung Leman around 30km south of town. There are no public boats so you'll have to organise transport with your resort (included in package prices).

★Rimba Resort RESORT **$$**
(012-710 6855; www.resortmalaysia.com; Sibu Besar; bungalow per person from RM220) Welcome to a super-chilled-out beachy paradise, with comfy thatched huts all overlooking the island's best swimming and snorkelling beach. The spacious digs are quite stylish with canopy mosquito nets, cushion-clad lounging spaces and sunken semi-open-air bathrooms.

Guests from the other resorts are often lured here by the lovely white beach and loungable deck bar. There's a dive centre and massage hut, and the staff are delightful.

Sea Gypsy Village Resort RESORT **$$**
(07-222 8642; www.siburesort.com; Sibu Besar; A-frames RM180, bungalows RM220, family bungalow for 2 adults & 2 children RM700) This resort is one of the best, most affordable places to relax with kids in Malaysia. Special children's meals are served throughout the day; there's a fun kids' club, a mini-playground and even an ingenious worm composting system for ecological nappy disposal. The beach is better for playing in the waves than for swimming.

Huts are dark but beds are comfortable and most units have a terrace, bathroom and fan. A-frames close to the jungle are the cheapest options. There's also a dive centre and plenty of activities on offer.

Batu Batu RESORT **$$$**
(017-755 2813; www.batubatu.com.my; Pulau Tengah; d incl breakfast & transfers from RM780) This upscale ecoresort offers 22 private villas on a shimmering coral sand island. It also runs a turtle sanctuary and takes volunteers (who pay for lodging), rents all sorts of watercraft and has a PADI dive centre.

Sibu Island Resort RESORT **$$$**
(07-799 5555; www.sibuislandresort.com.my; Pulau Sibu Tengah; 2 people incl breakfast from RM520) On isolated Pulau Sibu Tengah, this relatively plush resort has all the mod cons and good snorkelling. There's a full spa, a dive centre, tennis courts and a ropes course for team-building corporate groups. The beaches are good but the restaurant and rooms are closed-in air-con-style and, thus, short on sea breezes. Expect karaoke on weekends.

WORTH A TRIP

PULAU TINGGI

About 10km northeast from Pulau Sibu Besar, jungle-clad Tinggi is an impressive sight when seen from a distance – it's an extinct volcano (*tinggi* means 'tall') with a 600m-high cone that creates a dreamy silhouette. Most resorts offer day trips around the island which include excellent snorkelling and a trek to a beautiful waterfall.

The island supports three village populations: Kampung Tanjung Balang, Kampung Pasir Panjang and Kampung Sebirah Besar. The main place to stay is the overpriced but beautifully located **Tad Marine Resort** (012-908 9929; www.tadmarineresort.com; incl meals per person from RM315), which caters mostly to Singaporean divers.

Pulau Rawa

07

Edged by a fine white-sand beach, and luring bands of sunseekers, surfers and snorkellers, the tiny island of Rawa pokes out of the sea 16km from Mersing. Its resorts arrange transport for guests.

Rawa's two resorts are right next to each other on one of the prettiest beaches in the Seribuat Archipelago, with sugary white sand leading to a bowl of perfect blue.

Rawa Island Resort RESORT **$$$**
(07-799 1204; www.rawaislandresort.com; full board per person RM550-675) The is-

land's main resort has basic, ageing accommodation scattered over the hillsides and on the beachfront. But you won't remain indoors. This is a lively, family-style heaven with paddle boats and a trampoline. There's a restaurant, dive centre and a wide range of facilities and activities.

Alang's Rawa Resort RESORT **$$$**
(☎016-729 7383; www.alangsrawa.com; two-nights per person incl meals & transfers from RM680) Cheerful white huts with sky-blue shutters line the best part of the beach: the destination for a perfect do-nothing escape. Service is non-existent – but in this setting, who cares? There are 14 rooms, including chalets and A-frames.

Pulau Aur, Pulau Dayang & Pulau Pemanggil

☎07

These three islands are so far from the mainland (four to six hours by boat) that you'll need to devote a few days here to make it worth the trip. In fact, you may not be able to get here at all outside of weekends and holidays, when the resorts run boats to pick up groups of Singaporean divers.

Eighty kilometres from the mainland, Pulau Aur has crystal-clear azure water, excellent coral and a few wrecks off its coast. **Diver's Lodge** (www.friendlywaters.com.sg; 3-day/2-night dive packages from S$365), bookable through Singaporean dive tour operators, is where most folks go, although there's not much of a beach.

About 300 beds are available on Pulau Dayang, across the channel from Pulau Aur, at the scenic beach at **Dayang Blues Resort** (☎in Singapore 65-6536 6532; www.dayangnow.com; from S$400) in Kampung Pasir Putih.

Forty-five kilometres east of Mersing, beautiful Pulau Pemanggil supports a sparse population. Needless to say, the water is beautiful. **Lanting Resort** (☎07-799 1939; www.lantingresort.com.my; 3-day/2-night package RM298) has a variety of bungalow, longhouse and suite accommodation, and offers lots of fishing adventures in a rustic, family-run setting.

Endau-Rompin National Park

The forest here dates back 260 million years – talk about the echo of the ancients. Endau-Rompin National Park is that pristine, waterfall-laden jungle teeming with animals that comes to mind when you hear the phrase 'deep Malaysian interior'. Straddling the Johor-Pahang border, the 870-sq-km park is the second-largest on the peninsula after the much more developed Taman Negara. In fact, there are few trails in Endau-Rompin so exploration is limited – unless you're gonna bust out some serious Bungalow Bill machete skills – but what you can see is spectacular.

The park's lowland forests are among the last in Peninsular Malaysia and have been identified as harbouring unique varieties of plant life including enormous umbrella palms, with their characteristic fan-shaped leaves, and *Livinstona endanensis,* a species of palm with serrated circular leaves.

The park is also Malaysia's last refuge of Sumatran rhinoceros and tigers, although these roam only within the park's remote areas. Herds of elephants are sometimes spotted near Kampung Peta around sunset. The park's birds include red jungle fowl, the black hornbill and the grey wagtail. Monkeys cackle in the trees.

The majority of travellers arrive on tours arranged by private operators but it's just as easy (and less expensive) to organise a trip through the park itself. A good first stop is the **Johor National Parks Corporation**

LOCAL KNOWLEDGE

SNAGGLE-TOOTHED GHOSTS

Johor's famed *hantu jarang gigi* (snaggle-toothed ghost) is a tall, hairy, camera-shy biped that's possibly stuck in the same evolutionary cul-de-sac as the Yeti or Sasquatch. The primate has been tracked unsuccessfully for decades, despite regular Orang Asli sightings of the 3m-tall brown-haired 'missing link' and discoveries of oversize footprints. A slew of sightings were reported in 2005 near a river in the jungle around Kota Tinggi, when an entire family of primates was reportedly glimpsed by labourers. This instigated a giant and unsuccessful hunt for the beasts in 2006 and since then there have been no reports.

So if you encounter a fugitive Yeti-like creature stumbling from the bushes, have your camera ready – and *no sudden movements*.

Endau-Rompin National Park

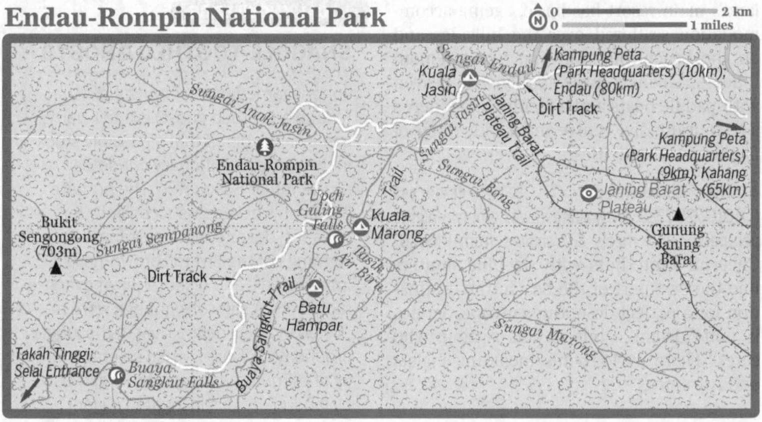

(johorparks.blogspot.com; Jln Sulaiman, Mersing; ⏲8am-1pm & 2-5pm Mon-Sat) office, who can help you get in touch with the appropriate park office.

There are two main entryways to the park, the principal one at Kampung Peta, accessed from Kahang, and a less-developed one at Selai, about a 40-minute drive from the town of Bekok. No trails link the the two areas so you have to choose to base yourself at one or the other. A third, lesser-used entry is in Pahang province 26km from Kuala Rompin and is not managed by the Johor Parks Corporation.

Guides

Officials of the Johor National Parks Corporation generally require that you hire a guide to explore the park. Guides can be hired for RM60 per day at the park headquarters at Kampung Peta, or at the Selai office, and are usually Orang Asli who come from the nearby villages and who have grown up in these jungles. A conservation fee (RM20) is also required.

Sights & Activities

Kampung Peta Entrance

The park office and lodging here is right next to a charming Orang Asli village whose residents often give demonstrations on local games (mostly puzzles – get ready to use your brain) and animal-trapping techniques. It's a lush setting a short walk from the river. To go on walks you'll need to first take a scenic boat trip about half an hour up river (RM140 for up to 10 people) – from here it's about a half-hour walk to **Kuala Jasin base camp**, from where all the trails lead. To organise lodging and activities from this entrance, call the **Endau-Rompin Peta Office** (☎07-888 2812; 11 Jln Bawall, Kahang).

Upeh Guling Falls HIKING

The main walk in the park follows the Sungai Jasin from Kuala Jasin base camp. On a one-day walk you'll go to these multi-tiered falls, an easy, mostly flat walk with a few river crossings through pristine jungle. There's a nice leech-free picnic spot on a rock facing the falls.

Batu Hampar HIKING

For a two-day trek you'll continue for a further 40 minutes to the flat rocks and camp site of Batu Hampar. It's about 4km of a challenging uphill slog over several ridges from Batu Hampar to the the top of the falls (a 40m drop) at Buaya Sangkut. Because the path is quite faint, only attempt this hike with a guide.

Tasik Air Biru SWIMMING

On the way back from one- or two-day treks, most people stop for a swim at this bright blue, clear and refreshing swimming hole a few minutes' walk from Kuala Jasin base camp.

Selai Entrance

Selai has far fewer facilities than Kampung Peta – notably, you have to bring your own food. Treks from **Lubuk Tapah base camp** in the west of the park follow the Sungai Selai to explore the many waterfalls along the river. To organise a trip from this entrance directly through the park, call the **Endau-Rompin Selai Office** (☎07-922 2875; 8 Jln Satrio 1, Bekok).

About a 1½-hour walk from base camp up a steep hill you'll reach the tall, single-drop **Takah Berangin Falls** where you can plop in for a dip and some body pummelling from the rapids. Thirty minutes on from here are the tall and slender **Takah Pandan Falls** where you can dive into a much calmer pool (around 2m deep).

From base camp at the parks office, trek about 1½ hours along a good trail to the roaring, low-slung **Takah Tinggi Falls.** Along the way you'll cross a few suspension bridges.

Sleeping & Eating

There are fan dorms and bungalows, in good condition, available in Kampung Peta (dorm bed RM25, bungalow RM80 to RM150) and simple A-frames at Kuala Jasin.

At Selai, simple chalet accommodation (from RM60) is available at Lubuk Tapah base camp.

You can camp at designated sites for RM5 per night per person.

Kampung Peta has a canteen where three good Malaysian-style meals per day (including a packed lunch if you're hiking) cost RM37. There's no canteen at Selai but there are simple cooking facilities.

Getting There & Away

Unless you have your own 4WD, getting to Endau-Rompin will require you to either book a tour in Mersing (try **Pure Value,** p243) or make arrangements independently through the park itself.

For Kampung Peta take a bus to Kahang and ask to be let off at the park office. Call the **Endau-Rompin Peta Office** (p248) in advance to charter one of the park's 4WDs with a driver (RM370) from here. It's a 56km ride through palm-oil plantations to Kampung Peta.

For Selai take a train to Kampung Bekok station. Call the **Endau-Rompin Selai Office** (p249) in advance to arrange a 4WD (RM120) pick up for the 45-minute drive over rough road to base camp.

Pahang & Tioman Island

☎09 / POP 1.45 MILLION / AREA 36,137 SQ KM

Includes ➡

Best Places to Eat

- ➡ Restoran Ratha Raub (p279)
- ➡ Ana Ikan Bakar Petai (p264)
- ➡ Duyong Restaurant (p268)
- ➡ ABCD Restaurant (p257)

Best Places to Stay

- ➡ Swiss Cottage Resort (p255)
- ➡ Rainbow Chalets (p257)
- ➡ Mutiara Taman Negara Resort (p275)
- ➡ Villa de Fedelia (p267)
- ➡ Coconut Grove (p258)

Why Go?

For many visitors, a journey to Peninsular Malaysia's largest state begins and ends on the enchanted isle of Pulau Tioman. Between its exhilarating diving, brilliant beaches, gnarly jungle treks and spirited villages, its tropical-island allure is impossible to resist.

Pahang's other big ticket – the primordial jungles of Taman Negara National Park – lies tucked up in the state's north. Its virgin tracts of rainforest, home to a howling, twittering, trumpeting (and occasionally roaring) rabble of elusive wildlife, offer a direct connection with nature as nature intended it: wild, unrelenting, raw.

Between these big acts, you'll find reggae beach parties at the surf-bum centre Cherating, royal splendour in Pekan, wild jungle nights outside Kuala Lipis and Tasik Chini, and plenty of culinary delights, colonial architecture and cultural insights.

When to Go

Endau

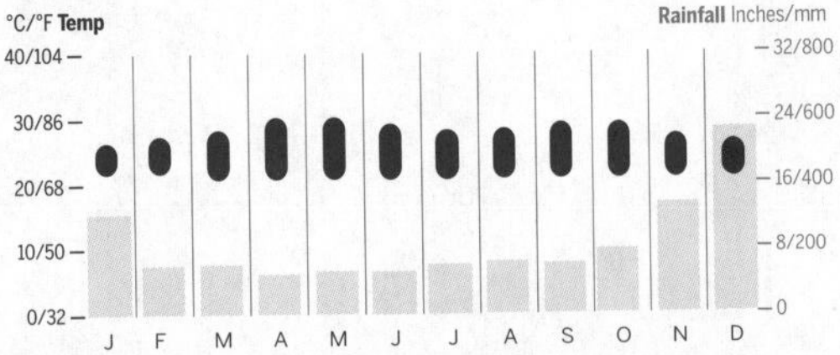

Jan–Apr The weather is at its warmest and driest. Crowds are at their peak.	**May–Dec** Prepare to sweat: the thermometer hovers between 21°C and 32°C, and humidity exceeds 82%.	**Nov–Feb** Monsoon season. Some places close, the surf is up in Cherating, and discounts abound.

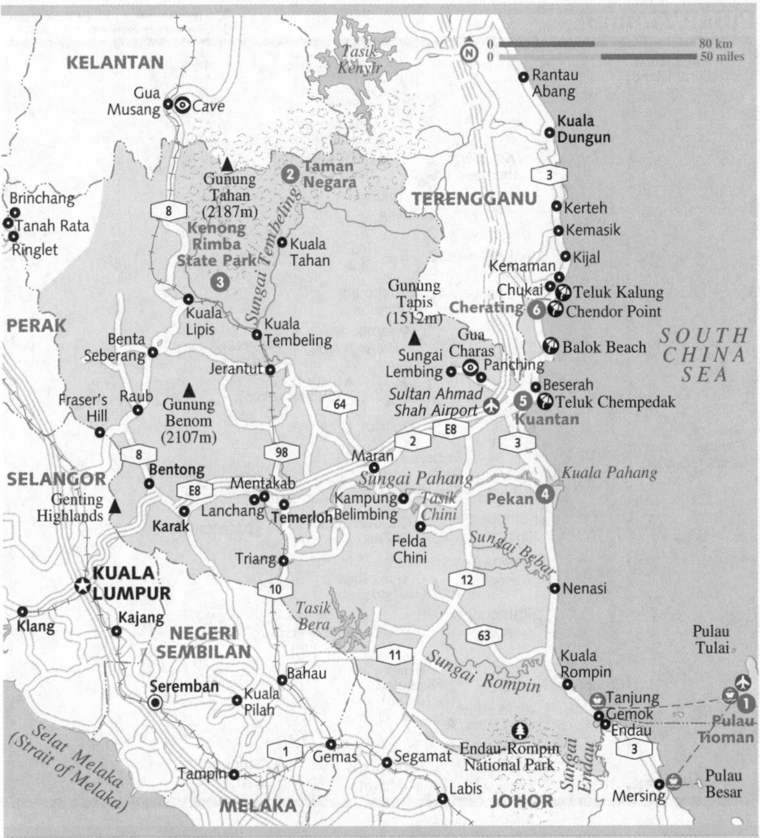

Pahang & Tioman Island Highlights

1. Village hopping, diving, snorkelling and jungle hiking on **Pulau Tioman** (p251).
2. Getting wet, muddy and covered in bug bites in deep, dark and undeniably adventurous **Taman Negara** (p277).
3. Leaving the tourist track for an expedition from Kuala Lipis to **Kenong Rimba State Park** (p278).
4. Being stared at by curious **Pekan** (p260) locals, who find visitors as interesting as we find their regal architecture and charming *kampung* houses.
5. Enjoying amazing food and day trips to nearby beaches and natural areas in **Kuantan** (p262).
6. Surfing, snorkelling and sand-floored beach-bar partying in footloose **Cherating** (p265).

PULAU TIOMAN

Sitting like an emerald dragon guarding the translucent waters of the South China Sea, Tioman Island offers every possible shade of paradise. There are cascading waterfalls, rigorous jungle hikes that take you past orange blossoms under an evergreen canopy, and a wide sampling of laid-back villages that present a tapestry of cultures and curiosities. And then there's the sea. That gorgeous sea of greens, blues and chartreuse swirls that beckons you to paddle, snorkel, dive and sail.

At 20km long and 11km wide, the island is so spacious that your ideal holiday spot is surely here somewhere. And despite its growing popularity, Tioman retains an unspoiled feel, with pristine wilderness and friendly, authentic village life.

Pulau Tioman

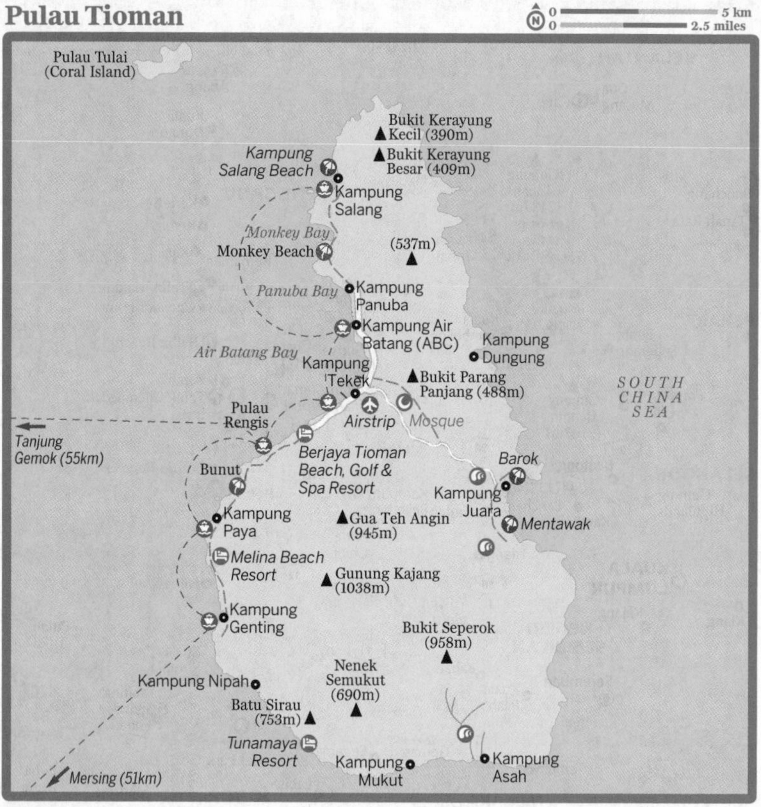

A short stretch of road runs along the western side of the island from the Berjaya Resort to the northern end of Tekek, where it is interrupted by steps before continuing as a path to the end of Air Batang (known as ABC). A winding road links Tekek with the dozy east-coast idyll of Juara. For walkers, there are jungle-road-trail combos that connect most of the west coast, from Salang to Genting.

Tekek is Tioman's largest village and its administrative centre. The airport is here, as is the island's only cash machine. Bear in mind that everything stocked in shops on Tioman is shipped from the mainland and tends to be expensive (except beer and tobacco), so stock up on essentials before you arrive.

Sights & Activities

Water Sports

The underwater world around the island offers some of the best (and most accessible) diving and snorkelling in Malaysia. It's also one of the few places in the country where you have a good chance of seeing pods of dolphins.

There is good snorkelling off the rocky points on the west coast of the island, particularly those just north of ABC, but the best snorkelling is around nearby Pulau Tulai, better known as Coral Island. Snorkelling equipment for hire is easy to find (masks and snorkels are typically RM15 per day) at many places on the island. Snorkelling trips with boat transfers cost RM40 to RM100.

There are plenty of excellent dive centres on Tioman, and Open Water Diver (OWD) certification courses are priced competitively. Expect to pay about RM1100 to RM1200 for a four-day Professional Association of Diving Instructors (PADI) OWD course and RM115 to R130 for fun dives. Discover dives (beginner dives that do not require precertification and include basic instruction), cost RM200 to RM250 for a half-day course.

Above water, you may wish to try your hand at **paddleboarding**. Swiss Cottage (p255) in Tekek rents boards for RM25 for two hours. A round-trip **Island Boat Tour** costs about RM150.

Marine Park Information Center MUSEUM
(Tekek; 8am-1pm & 2-5pm Mon-Fri, 8am-12.15pm & 2.45-5pm Sat;) FREE This centre has a few informative TV programs, a coral display and plenty of information on marine flora and fauna. It's a good stop for families and divers.

B&J DIVING
(09-419 1218; www.divetioman.com; ABC) This ABC shop is a PADI 5-Star Dive Centre with its own pool and a course director. It offers DSAT Tec and IANTD courses, nitrox blends and other high-end dive options, along with open-water courses (RM1100) and fun dives (RM110).

Tioman Dive Centre DIVING
(09-419 1228; www.tioman-dive-centre.com; Swiss Cottage Resort, Tekek) This place has a stellar reputation for its very responsible dive practices.

Ray's Dive Adventures DIVING
(019-330 8062; http://raysdive.com; ABC) Run by local couple Ray and Chloe, Ray's offers a four-day open-water PADI course for RM1200 and has various dive packages as well.

Hiking

Nautical pleasures aside, jungle-swathed Tioman offers plenty of excellent hikes to keep the intrepid landlubber exhausted and happy. You'll see more wildlife than in most of Malaysia's national parks, including black giant squirrels, long-tailed macaques, brush-tailed porcupines and – if you're out with a torch at dawn or dusk and incredibly lucky – the endangered, nocturnal binturong (bear cat).

While you can easily take on most hikes by yourself, guided jungle trips (arranged through your hotel) give you a curated look at the island's unique flora and fauna, and cost RM100 for a half-day. If you're setting out on foot, be wary of entering the jungle after around 4.30pm, as it's easy to get lost in the dark.

The 7km **Tekek to Juara Jungle Walk** offers an excellent feel for the richness of the spectacular interior, not to mention the added bonus of bringing the hiker to

CHOOSING A SLICE OF PARADISE

The hardest part of your Tioman adventure may well be deciding where to go. We've broken the major options down for you, counter-clockwise from north to south:

Salang The most backpacker-esque of Tioman's *kampung* (villages). Come to snorkel off nearby Coral Island, stay for the beach parties.

Air Batang (ABC) Slightly more upscale than Salang, ABC has a good choice of budget restaurants and accommodation. Though the beach isn't all that spectacular, the narrow trails that lead you through town give the feel of a paradise lost and found again.

Tekek Tioman's commercial hub is a good central location from which to explore the rest of the island, and the beach at the southern end of town is lovely.

Kampung Paya With two moderately priced resorts offering all-inclusive packages, Paya is popular with Singaporean students and the organised-tour set looking to snorkel off Paya beach.

Genting The beach is fairly built up, but is surrounded by a local village with an appealing *kampung* atmosphere. A good spot for meeting local fishing folk.

Nipah Beautiful, rugged and isolated, Nipah is an amazing choice for those wanting to bliss out on Tioman's serenest beach. The waters of Nipah are home to phosphorescent seaweed, and actually glow at night.

Mukut This traditional *kampung* may be one of the prettiest towns on the island, and the beach is lovely. If it's traditional Malaysian life you're after, Mukut is your spot.

Juara This east-coast village has the best surfing beach in Tioman and enough restaurants and accommodation to make it well worth the trip. The beachfront bungalows are out of this world.

beautiful Juara at hike's end. While the walk isn't too strenuous, parts of it are steep, and hiking in tropical heat can be taxing. Carry plenty of water; if you lose the trail, follow the power lines overhead. You'll find signs for the jungle walk about 1km north of the main jetty in Tekek. You can also walk along the recently paved road to Juara, a longer and somewhat less satisfying hike. A car back from Juara will cost around RM70 to RM90.

The 3.5km **ABC to Salang Trail**, which runs inland from the coast, is shorter but more difficult. The trail isn't well marked but it does lead to some excellent empty beaches. Climb up to Bamboo Hill Chalets at the northern end of ABC bay for a 10-minute hike over the next headland to Panuba Bay.

From there it's another 40 minutes through the rainforest to **Monkey Beach**. The trail continues from the far end of the beach across the next headland to the white-sand beach at Monkey Bay. From here, it's a long, steep climb over the headland to Salang.

An easier 30-minute hike heads south from **Tekek to Berjaya Tioman**, either by the road or by rock-hopping around the headland at low tide. From there you can walk through the golf course; just before the telecommunications tower there is a trail to the deserted beach of Bunut. From the end of the beach, the occasionally faint trail continues over the headland to Paya. The trail from Paya to Genting is easy to follow and there are houses along the way where you can ask directions.

If you head north from Tekek, you can walk all the way to Salang. Boat transport for the return journey can be arranged at most of the guesthouses in ABC or Salang if you don't feel like walking.

Another beautiful but harder-to-reach trek can be found on Tioman's southern tip, Mukut, accessible by boat from Genting. The **Asah Waterfall Trek** leads to a stunning waterfall with a beautifully polished swimming hole.

TRAIL SAFETY

Don't let Tioman's laid-back vibe fool you into forgetting you're in the jungle.

- Carry enough water – many a day tripper has learned too late the folly of heading out with insufficient fluids.
- Rethink your hiking plans if it's been raining – especially during monsoon season, when nearly every trail becomes unpleasantly muddy at best and impossible to follow at worst.
- Take a headlamp – if you think there's even the slightest chance you'll be out past sundown.
- Tell someone where you are going and when you expect to be back.
- Watch for snakes – don't freak out, but there are 25 snake species on Tioman, including the king cobra and reticulated python. Closed shoes are a wise choice.

Other Activities

Juara Turtle Project VOLUNTEERING

(☎09-419 3244; www.juaraturtleproject.com; Juara; tour RM10, volunteering with breakfast, lunch & dm, min 4 nights, RM120; ⏲10am-5pm) On the southern end of Juara, this voluntourism operation works to protect declining sea-turtle populations by collecting eggs and moving them to a hatchery, and patrolling the beaches for poachers and predators. Volunteers get basic dorm accommodation. They also work patrols and give information seminars. Daily activities including sea kayaking, treks and cooking classes are also offered.

Nonvolunteers can tour the facility, check in on the resident turtle, Joe, who is blind and unable to return to the wild, and learn more about the area's turtles, which nest here February to October, with public releases June through November.

Tioman Volcanic Rock Climbing ROCK CLIMBING

(☎012-956 1326; Juara) Offers climbing courses (RM1000), rappelling (RM80) and top-rope climbs (RM70 to RM120).

Sleeping & Eating

From Salang to Mukut, all towns and beaches with accommodation are serviced by regular ferries from Mersing. To get to Juara, take a ferry to Tekek, then taxi it over the hill.

Budget accommodation largely comprises small wooden 'chalets' (bungalows) and longhouse-style rooms, typically with a bathroom, fan and mosquito net. More expensive rooms have air-con and hot showers. Most operations have larger family rooms

TIOMAN'S TOP DIVE SITES

The leeward side of Tioman offers a remarkable variety of killer dive and snorkel sites, while the east coast's offerings are more limited. Most dives have a maximum depth of 30m.

Renggis Island Good for snorkelling and beginner dives, this spot just off the Berjaya Resort pier boasts blacktip reef sharks, turtles and lionfish.

Tiger and Labas Heading off Labas Island, advanced divers can spot reef fish, rays and schools of barracuda and jackfish at Tiger Reef.

Coral Island Head here for stunning soft coral, reef fish and an occasional pufferfish. This is a top half-day boat excursion for snorkellers.

WWII wreck sites Experienced divers won't want to miss two famous WWII-era wreck sites 45 nautical miles north of Tioman, HMS *Repulse* and HMS *Prince of Wales*. Both sites are astounding for their historical significance and wide array of marine life. They're challenging – best suited for those with more than a few dives under their belts – but you don't need certification aside from your open water.

for those with children, and many have restaurants.

Tekek

All accommodation options lie close to each other on the excellent southern beach.

Babura Seaview Resort BUNGALOW $
(☑ 017-715 4663; www.baburaseaviewresort.com; r with fan RM80, with air-con RM108-205; ❋ ☏) This family-run place on the end of the beach offers longhouse fan rooms and a selection of newer rooms and chalets with air-con and hot-water bathrooms. Alas, only a few rooms have beach views.

Cheers HOTEL $
(☑ 013-931 1425; s/d with shared bathroom RM50/60, r RM120-200; ☏) If you don't mind skipping the beach views, this is a solid Tekek budget option, with some of the cheapest rooms in this section of the island. The gardens are lovely, and you are a hop away from the water.

Coral Reef Holidays BUNGALOW $
(☑ 09-419 1868; dm RM25, d incl breakfast RM45, r RM130-160; ❋ ☏) Adik and Hasnizah's lovely beachfront longhouse has rooms facing the sea, all with individually crafted stonework, raised platform beds, air-con and colour TVs. The couple also offer air-con and fan dorms, and operate an excellent restaurant serving Western and local food.

★ **Swiss Cottage Resort** BOUTIQUE HOTEL $$
(☑ 09-419 1642; www.swiss-cottage-tioman.com; r with fan RM110-170, with air-con & breakfast RM145-215; ❋ ☏) This resort is clearly operated by creative folk. The rooms to nab are the sea-view chalets, which have breezy bamboo and wood interiors alongside colourfully painted walls and comfy deck furniture. Other options are nestled in a shady back garden, including the newly renovated beachside bungalow. There are just 15 rooms in all, giving it a boutique feel.

Tioman Cabana HOTEL $$
(☑ 013-717 6677; www.tiomancabana.com; r RM150-220; ☏) While it's a bit difficult to locate (right next to Coral Reef Holidays), this funked-out restaurant and beach bungalow has sharp ocean-front rooms with modern rugs and mozzie nets. The beautiful patios are literally steps from the lapping waves of the sea.

Delima MALAYSIAN $
(mains RM7-10) With two locations – one right by the Tekek pier and the other up the road by the Berjaya Resort, this friendly Malaysian joint offers up wholesome fare, big smiles and waterfront views.

Chinese Sarang Seafood CHINESE $$
(☑ 013-706 6484; mains RM20; ◷ lunch & dinner) This spot does a particularly tasty sizzling hotplate with bean curd and serves beer.

Air Batang (ABC)

ABC's beach is usually best at the southern and northern ends, although the sands are constantly shifting so this is changeable. Most of the beachfront is rocky with little sand.

TIOMAN'S RESORTS

Tioman resorts have exclusive beaches, pools, restaurants and private jetties. Your best bet for booking most resorts is going through travel aggregators (skip the all-inclusives if you have access to a nearby village). Note that many of these resorts offer amazing deals (up to 50% off listed price) during the monsoon season (November to February).

Melina Beach Resort (☎09-419 7080; www.melinabeachresort.com; Genting; chalets for 4-8 people incl breakfast RM200-495) Melina is located on a remote beach with photogenic boulders and white sand. Each sleeping option is unique, creatively designed from wood, thatch and Plexiglas to create a certain Crusoe chic – the most interesting is a tree house that hovers right over the beach.

Meals are served at the resort or you can walk for 20 minutes to Genting and try the restaurants there. The owners have set up a successful turtle hatchery, and plenty of activities are organised to keep folks entertained; there's also a beachside bar and BBQ. The relaxed atmosphere attracts lots of families.

Panuba Inn Resort (☎09-419 1424; ABC; r per person from RM355; ❄) Peaceful Panuba Inn, over the headland from ABC, has a pier and restaurant and 30 chalets built on a hill overlooking the bay. All rooms face the sea and range from simple fan affairs to chalets with hot shower, air-con and plenty of mod cons.

Berjaya Tioman Beach, Golf & Spa Resort (☎09-419 1000; www.berjayahotel.com/tioman; Berjaya; r from RM200; ❄@📶≋) Easily accessible from Tekek, Berjaya is the biggest resort on Tioman. For those seeking a resort experience on a budget, this is the best spot on the island. Accommodation ranges from chalets and suites to entire villas, not to mention standout attractions including tennis, a kids' playground and an arcade.

There are two swimming pools (one with great water slides), two restaurants and a beach bar. And – oh yes – there's 18-hole golf.

Tunamaya Resort (☎07-798 8108; www.tunamayaresort.com; Genting; r per person from RM388; ❄📶≋) Tunamaya is operated by the same folks who run the highly regarded Tuna Bay (p297) on Perhentian. The resort overlooks white-sand beaches and provides high-quality amenities including spas and a bar with beers from around the world.

Mokhtar's Place BUNGALOW $
(☎019-704 8299; www.mohktarplace.blogspot.com; s/d with fan RM50/60, q with air-con RM220; ❄📶) Great budget value, this cluster of 16 bungalows along the beach south of town features little patios and mozzie nets. If the wind's just right, you can catch a cooling ocean breeze at night.

Johan's Resort BUNGALOW $
(☎09-419 1359; dm/chalet/f RM20/40/100) A friendly, welcoming place offering tons of information. The two four-bed dorms up the hillside are decent value; the chalets are pretty much the same as other cheapies on the beach.

Sri Nelayan BUNGALOW $
(☎019-732 6373 r RM50; 📶) This family-run place north of the jetty has four clean, fan-cooled chalets facing a well-manicured lawn. The family also owns a small grocery store and arranges tours.

My Friend's Place BUNGALOW $
(☎09-419 1152; d/tr/q RM40/50/75; 📶) Just south of the jetty, this place is busy, social, clean and priced a whisker lower than the competition. All bungalows face a lovely garden.

Bamboo Hill Chalets BUNGALOW $$
(☎09-419 1339; www.bamboohillchalets.com; r RM90-140; @📶) These six well-kept chalets are in a stupendous location, perched on rocks on the northern end of the beach, surrounded by bougainvillea and humming cicadas alongside a waterfall and pool. It is almost always full, so call ahead.

B&J Dive Resort HOTEL $$
(☎09-419 1218; www.divetioman.com; d RM270-320, tr RM320-370; ❄@📶) This is easily the most high-class spot in ABC. All rooms have flat-screen TVs, air-con, safes, coffee makers and other touches that'll make you think you're back in a three-star hotel in KL. The lack of waterfront views is a bit of a downer.

Nazri's Place
GUESTHOUSE **$$**

(☑017-490 1384; www.nazrisplace.net; r incl breakfast RM120-200; ❄@🛜) At the far southern end of the beach, which has some of ABC's best sand, this place has clean rooms and a wide range of accommodation. The sea-view rooms are cheaper and more basic, while the upscale rooms have an almost business vibe, save for the pleasant patios that look onto a lush garden.

The restaurant is right on the water and serves an excellent seafood barbecue.

Nazri's II
BUNGALOW **$$**

(☑09-419 1375; d with fan/air-con RM80/140; ❄🛜) Similar to Nazri's Place, but on the north end of ABC and set in a particularly well-tended garden that spreads up the hillside.

Tioman House
HOTEL **$$**

(☑09-419 1021; tiomanhouse@yahoo.com; r RM50-150; ❄) At ABC's north end, this place offers rooms painted a happy yellow in classic modern hotel decor.

★ ABCD Restaurant
MALAYSIAN **$$**

(mains RM10-20; ☺breakfast, lunch & dinner) This restaurant is packed most nights with travellers who flock to enjoy ABCD's BBQ special (RM20), a tantalising array of freshly caught fish, prawn or squid. For less adventurous eaters, chicken will have to do. Beer is available.

Sunset Corner
INTERNATIONAL **$$**

(pizza from RM16; ☺2pm-late) The last spot before the stairs leading south, Sunset serves beer, booze, milkshakes and pizza. The wildly popular happy hour is from 5pm to 7pm.

🛏 Salang

Salang has more of a party vibe than elsewhere on the island. A very wide and inviting white-sand beach is just south of the jetty and is good for swimming. For many, Salang's star attractions are the monstrous monitor lizards that lurk in the inky river that runs through the village centre.

Ella's Place
BUNGALOW **$**

(☑09-419 5004; bungalows RM60-120; ❄) There's usually a loungeable patch of sand at this cute-as-a-button family-run place at the quiet northern end of the beach. There are 10 clean bungalows (some with air-con) and a small cafe.

Khalid's Place
BUNGALOW **$**

(☑09-419 5317; salangpusaka@yahoo.com; d bungalow with air-con RM80; ❄) South of the jetty, behind the Salang Complex and across a festering section of Sungai Salang. It has 47 cleanish bungalows set in a large grassy area, back from the beach; air-con chalets come with fridge and hot shower.

Salang Indah Resort
RESORT **$$**

(☑09-419 5015; www.pulautioman.com.my/SalangIndahResort.php; r with fan/air-con RM60/240, bungalow RM140-170; ❄@🛜) The expanse of bungalows seemingly sprawls forever at this resort complex. Most rooms aren't in tip-top condition, but if you look at several you'll probably find one to your liking. The most interesting are the Popeye-like chalets on stilts over the sea.

🛏 Juara

Juara is a world of its own. It's the sole place to stay on the east coast of the island and exists in a constant sleepy state of remote-hideaway bliss. There are two long stretches of wide white sandy beach, separated by a small hill and boulder outcrop. The northern half of the beach (called Barok) is where most accommodation is found, while the southern strip (known as Mentawak) is less travelled, and kicks up some of the country's best surfing waves between mid-October and February.

Turtles nest on both beaches and the area has been proclaimed a 'green zone' by the Sultan of Johor. This means it is protected from development, including the building of any big new resorts. All the places to stay in Juara overlook the magnificent beach; a few places hire out kayaks (RM15 per hour), surfboards (RM20 per hour), paddleboards (RM35 per hour) and fishing rods (RM15 per hour). To get here, take a taxi from Tekek (about RM70 one way).

★Rainbow Chalets
BUNGALOW **$**

(☑012-989 8572; rainbow.chalets@gmail.com; r with fan/air-con RM60/100; ❄🛜) Eight colourful bungalows – three air-con and five fancooled – await you. All come with wooden porches and are decorated with shells and coral. The beach and views onto the South China Sea are frickin' glorious.

Bushman
BUNGALOW **$**

(☑09-419 3109; matbushman@hotmail.com; r with fan/air-con RM60/100; ❄🛜) Nabbing one

LOCAL KNOWLEDGE

LEARN BATIK MAKING!

Genting is the home of renowned Malaysian batik artist Suhadi Mahadi, whose **Suzila Batik Arts & Crafts Centre** (☎013-751 4312; suzilabatik@gmail.com) is just south of the jetty. Suhadi teaches batik making using traditional materials. Tuition varies from RM25 to RM80; a simple batik might take an hour or two to make, while a more complex pattern might take the afternoon. Suhadi also sells ready-made batik (RM30 to RM1200).

of Bushman's five varnished wood bungalows, with their inviting wicker-furnished terraces, is like winning the Juara lottery – reserve in advance! The location is right up against the boulder outcrop and a small river that marks the end of the northern beach.

Bushman's little cafe serves breakfast, lunch and dinner, and is a wondrously languorous place to chill out.

Mezani's Place BUNGALOW $
(☎019-792 9640; r RM60; 📶) On the southern section of beach, these simple and old-but-clean bungalows have fans, mosquito nets and attached bathrooms.

★**Coconut Grove** BUNGALOW $$
(☎010-766 4089; www.1511asia.com; d/q incl breakfast RM298/500) On the far south side of town by the turtle sanctuary, these boutique beach bungalows have slow ceiling fans, thatched roofs and gorgeous balconies that look out to sea. Hardwood floors mix with South China Sea touches to create a classic mishmash of styles.

Beach Shack HOTEL $$
(Beach Hut; ☎012-696 1093; timstormsurf@yahoo.au; A-frame RM60, r with fan RM100-120, with air-con RM150; ❄📶) Grab an upstairs room at this two-storey spot with thatched roofs, and a few budget A-frames that just might catch an ocean breeze. Construction was still going when we passed through, and budgeteers can probably do better, but you won't find a friendlier spot.

Mutiara Resort BUNGALOW $$
(☎09-419 3161/76; http://juaramutiararesort.blogspot.co.uk; s/d/q chalets RM100/150/180; ❄) Just south of the jetty, this place has lots of options and high standards.

Santai Bistro MALAYSIAN $
(mains RM12-15; ⏲9am-11pm) This bar/restaurant right next to the jetty plays classic rock and serves delights such as sambal prawns, tom yum (hot and spicy Thai seafood soup) and mixed vegetable salads. The beers are cold and the views hypnotising.

Kampung Paya

The short, wide, white-sand beach is jam-packed with two resorts and a few restaurants and food shacks. The rocky seabed and shallow water make it a poor choice for swimming.

Paya Resort RESORT $$
(☎07-799 1432; www.payabeach.com; r RM169, bungalow RM229-449; ❄📶🏊) Spacious chalets are linked by wooden bridges over a lily pond. There are also tidy, air-con standard rooms in the lodge at a decent price, plus a restaurant, full spa, dive centre, lounge and a range of activities.

Sri Paya Tioman Chalet BUNGALOW $$
(www.tiomanchalet.com; r incl all meals & activities per person from RM280; ❄📶🏊) Opened in 2010, this place has beautiful air-con chalets, an on-site dive shop and a waterfront restaurant. Package deals include meals and organised snorkelling tours.

Genting

Genting caters mostly to the weekend crowds from Singapore and KL, but its surrounding local village gives it a touch of authenticity.

Sun Beach Resort RESORT $$
(☎07-799 4918; www.sunbeachresort.com.my; r incl breakfast & lunch per person RM295-545; ❄) Sun Beach has plenty of ocean-front chalets ranging from simple to deluxe (featuring minibars and TVs) and a great restaurant. It focuses on three- or four-day package tours.

Golden Dish Cafe CHINESE $
(dishes from RM6; ⏲10am-midnight; 🖉) 🌿 This might be the only place on Tioman serving its own home-grown organic vegetables. There are also plenty of authentic Chinese seafood specialities and healing herbal drinks and, if that isn't your thing, it serves beer for RM5.

Riverside Cafe MALAYSIAN $

(mains from RM3.50; breakfast, lunch & dinner) This very inexpensive place right next to the jetty serves burgers, omelettes and Malay and Thai specialities such as *kampung* noodles and tom yum.

Nipah

Blissful, isolated Nipah Beach is long and white with an unusual stripe of black sand running through it. A river mouth at the southern end creates a deep blue swimming hole that's bordered on one side by a large, flat knuckle of sand with a volleyball pitch. This is the place to come to hang in a hammock, snorkel, or hike in the jungle.

Both Nipah's hotels are open year round, and can arrange transfers from the ferry stop in Genting for RM30 each way.

Bersatu Nipah Chalets HOTEL $

(07-797 0091; bersatunipah_tioman@yahoo.com; r with fan/air-con RM60/90;) This clean beachfront longhouse has great service (from the amiable Jalil and Amy) and an excellent riverside restaurant with dishes such as freshly caught fish (priced by weight) and calamari fritters. Jalil also runs a free river cruise for guests.

Nipah Beach Tioman BUNGALOW $

(019-735 7853; bungalow from RM70) Young, friendly host Abbas runs these rustic bungalows on stilts by the water's edge. They sit so close to the beach that the sound of waves lapping at the stairs will soothe you to sleep.

Mukut

On the southern tip of Tioman, Mukut may be the loveliest – and perhaps loneliest – *kampung* on the island. The beach at this secluded spot is a tad less amazing than the one in Juara, but this is made up for by the prettiness of the town, with its traditional homes and flower-lined paths.

Mukut Coral Resort BUNGALOW $

(07-799 2535, 07-799 2612; r/chalet RM25/88;) Traditional village-style chalets (all with air-con and hot water, some with TV) are set in a marvellous location beside Mukut's jetty. There's a sea-view restaurant serving Chinese and Western food.

Mukut Harmony Resort BUNGALOW $

(07-799 2275; bungalow from RM50) A dozen fan-cooled bungalows on a strip of grass next to the jetty.

Drinking & Nightlife

A Peace Place BAR

(ABC) Opposite Ray's Dive Centre, this chilled roots place has great ocean views and occasional live music.

Hallo Cafe BAR

(ABC) In front of Nazri's II, this tiny beach bar offers a three-beers-for-RM12 happy hour from 5pm to 7pm.

Information

Tioman's sole cash machine is across from Tekek's airport and takes international cards. It's been known to run dry, so consider getting cash in Mersing. There's a moneychanger at the airport.

There's a small post office not far north of the Babura Seaview Resort in Tekek.

The island's sole clinic is **Poliklinik Komuniti Tekek** (09-419 1880).

Getting There & Away

AIR

Tekek has an airport but there were no commercial operations as of press time.

BOAT

Mersing in Johor is the main access port for Tioman. **Island Connection Tours** (07-799 2535; return RM70) has an office in Mersing; other operators sell tickets by the jetty for the same price. Boats run from early morning until late afternoon, stopping at Genting, Paya, Berjaya Tioman, Tekek, ABC and Salang, returning in the reverse order on the return trip. Decide where you want to get off and tell the ticket inspector. On weekends and holidays it's a good idea to buy your tickets in advance since the boats fill quickly (queue up or you may miss a spot).

Boat departures during the monsoon season (November to February) can be erratic, with sailings become more regular during the low monsoon months (January and February).

Ferries also depart for Tioman from the Tanjung Gemok ferry terminal (return RM70), 35km north of Mersing near Endau. This route is useful if coming from the north. Call ahead and make sure the ferries are running before you arrive.

Getting Around

Typical sea taxi fares from Tekek:

- ABC/Panuba (RM25)
- Genting (RM50)
- Nipah (RM120)
- Mukut (RM150)
- Paya Beach (RM35)
- Salang (RM35).

Some sea taxis have a two-person minimum. Most hotels can arrange boat charter. Expect to pay around RM600 for a full day on a boat, and expect waters to be far rougher on the Juara side of Tioman.

If you have the time, you can explore some of the island on foot. Bicycles can be hired at guesthouses on all the main beaches (per hour/day RM5/30), and mopeds (per hour/day RM15/40) are a good bet for trips to Juara.

Taxis from Tekek to Juara cost RM70 to RM90.

THE COAST

Endau

There's little of interest in Endau, but fast boats speed to Pulau Tioman from nearby **Tanjung Gemok**. If you get stuck here, you can spend the night at the **Hotel Seri Malaysia** (☎09-413 2723; smrom@serimalaysia.com.my; d incl breakfast RM150; ❄☒) in Tanjung Gemok, a few minutes' walk from Endau.

Pekan

The seat of the Pahang Sultanate, Pekan has a regal air and is uncommonly scenic with its wide clean streets, spacious *padang* (city square) and many grand buildings surrounded by expansive pristine lawns. There is also a collection of old Chinese shophouses along a shady river, excellent Malaysian street food, beautiful mosques and several examples of non-Islamic houses of worship.

Sights

Museum Sultan Abu Bakar MUSEUM
(Jln Sultan Ahmad; admission RM1; ⏲9.30am-5pm Tue-Thu, Sat & Sun, 9am-12.15pm & 2.45-5pm Fri) This museum is housed in a wonderful building constructed by the British in 1929. Exhibits are largely about the Pahang royal family, with other displays featuring weapons, pottery (including Chinese porcelain and Arab ceramics unearthed on Pulau Tioman) and exhibits on wildlife in Pahang.

TASIK CHINI

Beautiful Tasik Chini (Lake Chini) is a series of 12 lakes linked by vegetation-clogged channels. It's one of Pahang's natural flood-retention basins, and environmentalists see increasing threat to the area as a result of decades of uncontrolled mining and logging. But there is much to bring travellers to this magnificent and fragile landscape and, as elsewhere in Malaysia, many hope that ecotourism will motivate the government to protect it.

Tasik Chini's shores are inhabited by the Jakun people, an Orang Asli tribe of Melayu Asli origin, and the surrounding jungle hills are some of the least-visited trekking areas in the country, still hiding tigers and elephants amid glorious waterfalls and caves. Locals believe the lake is home to a serpent known as Naga Seri Gumum, sometimes translated as a 'Loch Ness monster'. The best time to visit the lakes is from June to September when the lotuses are in bloom.

Tasik Chini offers two excellent all-inclusive options for travellers. **Rajan Jones Guest House** (☎017-913 5089; r per person incl breakfast & dinner RM35) lies nestled in flower-filled Kampung Gumum and acts as base camp for the titular Rajan Jones' excellent jungle and lake adventures. Rajan speaks perfect English, is close with the Orang Asli, has been leading treks for over 20 years and can arrange a spectrum of activities from jungle trekking to night hikes (RM30 to RM100).

A less rustic option is the magnificently landscaped **Lake Chini Resort** (☎09-468 8088; tasikchiniresort@hotmail.com; dm incl breakfast RM25, r incl breakfast from RM150), which has beautiful rooms facing the lake, an on-site restaurant and even karaoke. The 10-bed dorms are neat and often filled with student groups. Staff at the resort can arrange all activities for you.

The easiest way to get to Tasik Chini is to arrange transport from either Lake Chini Resort or Rajan Jones. The more complicated way involves taking a bus to Kampung Chini from either Kuantan (RM7, 2 hours) or Pekan (RM6, 1½ hours) and then taking a private car the remaining 7.5km to Kampung Gunum for about RM20. You can take a taxi from either Pekan or Kuantan for around RM80.

Pekan

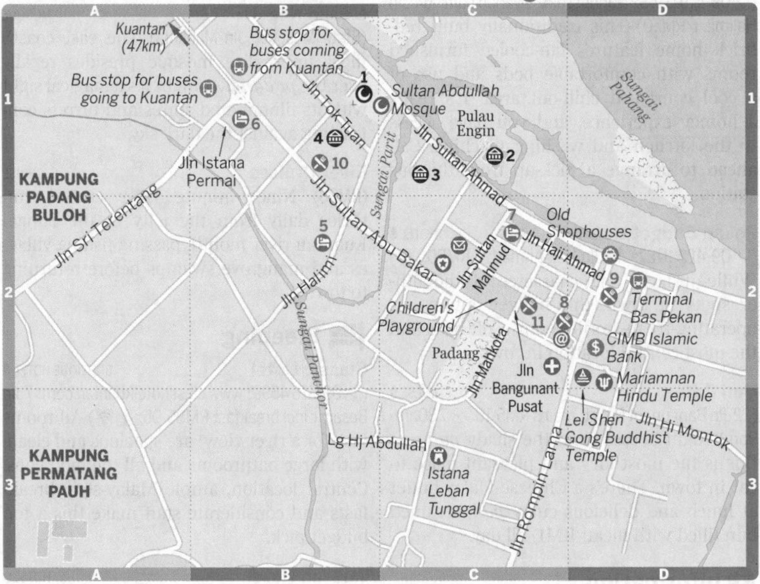

Galeri Pengangkutan Air MUSEUM
(admission RM1; 9.30am-5pm Tue-Thu, Sat & Sun, 9am-12.15pm & 2.45-5pm Fri) Displays traditional Malaysian watercraft. Look out for the fabulously carved craft with the head of a mythical beast.

Pekan Lama HISTORIC BUILDING
Behind the Sultan Abdullah Mosque stands this old tower fashioned from wood and stone.

Istana Abu Bakar PALACE
The grandiose sultan's palace is set on vast grounds of cow grass.

Abu Bakar Mosque MOSQUE
(Jln Sultan Ahmad) The active Abu Bakar Mosque is crowned with gold domes. Non-Muslims are not allowed to enter.

Istana Permai PALACE
The focus of Pekan's palm-lined royal quarter is the Regent of Pahang's palace.

Sleeping & Eating

A few restaurants, food stalls and fruit stalls can be found in the grid of streets between the Padang and Sungai Pahang and along the riverfront Jln Sultan Ahmad. Also, a handful of spicy Thai-style *ikan bakar* (grilled fish) and tom yum seafood restaurants open for dinner along Jln Sultan Abu Bakar.

Pekan

Sights

1	Abu Bakar Mosque	B1
2	Galeri Pengangkutan Air	C1
3	Museum Sultan Abu Bakar	C1
4	Pekan Lama	B1

Sleeping

5	Beach Shack Homestay	B2
6	Chief's Rest House	B1
7	Pekan Budget Hotel	C2

Eating

8	Food Stalls	C2
9	Fruit Stalls	D2
10	Restaurants	B1
11	Umi Café	C2

Chief's Rest House HISTORIC HOTEL $
(09-422 6941; Jln Istana Permai; d RM55-70;) This circa-1929 colonial wooden building exudes atmosphere and style, and is reason enough to stop in Pekan. All the rooms have wood floors, towering ceilings, TV and air-con. It's nearly 1km from the bus terminal, so let the driver know that you want to get off near the resthouse.

Beach Shack Homestay HOMESTAY $
(☑ 09-419 3148; izanhussain2@yahoo.com; 64 Jln Halimi; r RM50) This traditionally built redbrick home features fan-cooled furnished rooms with comfortable beds and use of a cool courtyard chill-out area. It's really a homey experience, and you have access to the kitchen and washing machine. Call ahead to arrange a pick-up from the bus station.

Pekan Budget Hotel HOTEL $
(☑ 09-422 3727; 40 Jln Haji Ahmad; r RM50; 🛜) While it lacks the character of the other spots in town, this budget option has operating-room-sterile rooms, soft beds and the most central location in town.

Umi Café CHINESE $
(22 Jln Bangunant Pusat; mains RM5-10; ⊙ 7.30am-9pm) Right across from the shady *padang*, this is the most airy and pleasant place to eat in town. There's a Chinese-Malay buffet at lunch and delicious curry *pao* (steamed bun filled with meat; RM1) all day.

ℹ Information

10 Net Cyber Café (Jln Sultan Abu Bakar; per hour RM3; ⊙ 10am-7pm) Internet access.
CIMB Islamic Bank (Jln Rompin Lama) has an ATM that accepts foreign cards.

ℹ Getting There & Away

Buses leave from **Terminal Bas Pekan** (Jln Engku Muda Mansor). **Utama Express** (☑ 09-422 8694) and **Cepat Express** (☑ 1300-88 842538) both have offices here. Regular local buses run to/from Kuantan (RM7, one hour), Kuala Rompin (RM7, two hours) and to Chini Village (RM6, 1½ hours). Long-distance buses run to Kuala Terengganu (RM24) and to KL (RM30).

The taxi station is at the bus station. A taxi to/from Kuantan costs RM50; to Tasik Chini it's RM60.

Kuantan

Most travellers only stop in busy Kuantan, Pahang's capital and Malaysia's second-biggest port, to break up long bus trips. We think this is a shame; while the city isn't geared towards tourism, it is definitely interesting enough to warrant a day or two's exploration, even just to make the most of the coast's best eating opportunities. The nearby beach of Teluk Chempedak gives you resort living without a backpacker in sight.

◉ Sights & Activities

Masjid Negeri MOSQUE
(State Mosque; Jln Mahkota) The east coast's most impressive mosque presides regally over the *padang*. At night it's a magical sight with its illuminated spires and turrets contrasting against the dark sky.

River Cruises CRUISE
(RM38) Ninety-minute river cruises run thrice daily from the jetty to the Sungai Kuantan river mouth, passing fishing villages and mangrove swamps before returning to town.

🛏 Sleeping

Classic Hotel BOUTIQUE HOTEL $
(☑ 09-516 4599; www.classhotelkuantan.com; 7 Jln Besar; r incl breakfast RM85-95; ❄🛜) All rooms (ask for a river view) are spacious and clean, with large bathrooms and all the mod cons. Central location, ample Malay-style breakfasts and considerate staff make this a top budget pick.

Tai Wah Hotel HOTEL $
(☑ 016-922 1377; 29 Jln Haji Abdul Aziz; s/d with fan RM48/60, with air-con RM60/68; ❄🛜) This Chinese-run hotel has spartan doubles, singles and triples with TVs – it's good value for the price, though rooms can be a bit cramped and smoky.

Hotel Kosma HOTEL $
(☑ 09-516 2214; 59 Jln Haji Abdul Aziz; s/d RM55/70; ❄@🛜) Among the better of the budget choices, the ageing Kosma lacks the boutique vibe of some of the newer mid-priced hotels but is centrally located.

★**Hotel Sentral Kuantan** BOUTIQUE HOTEL $$
(☑ 09-565 9999; www.hotelsentralkuantan.com.my; 45 Jln Besar; r RM128-168; ❄🛜) This new boutique hotel has a slick, ultra-modern lounge downstairs with turbo-charged air-con and plenty of bling-bling – and the chromed-out stylings continue over the six floors. The standard rooms are pretty small, but deluxe rooms feature floor-to-ceiling views of the riverway.

Mega View Hotel BUSINESS HOTEL $$
(☑ 09-517 1888; Lot 567, Jln Besar; d RM125-160, q RM180-255; ❄) This business hotel has professional service and designer studios with funky murals and padded bedheads (ask for a view...or go big with a megaview). Its 21st-century-take-on-art-deco feel puts it a step up from the crowd in the midrange category.

Kuantan

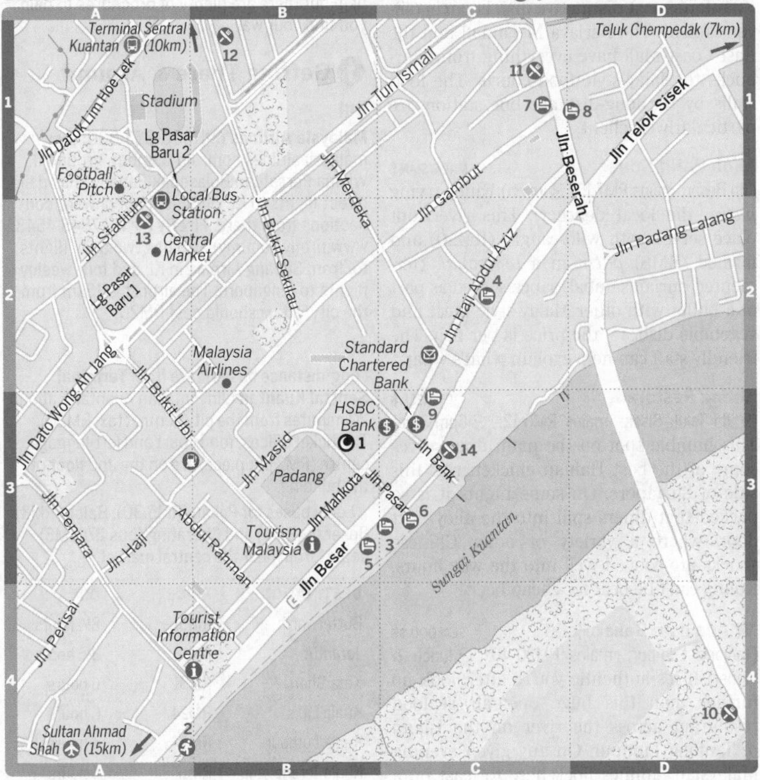

Kuantan

Sights

1 Masjid Negeri B3

Activities, Courses & Tours

2 River Cruises A4

Sleeping

3 Classic Hotel C3
4 Hotel Kosma C2
5 Hotel Sentral Kuantan B3
6 Mega View Hotel C3
7 MS Garden Hotel C1
8 Signature Hotel D1
9 Tai Wah Hotel C3

Eating

Akob Patin House .... (see 5)
10 Ana Ikan Bakar Petai D4
11 Berjaya Megamall C1
12 East Coast Mall B1
13 Food Stalls A2
14 Kohng Restoran C3

MS Garden Hotel HOTEL $$

(☎09-555 5899; www.msgarden.com.my; Lots 5 & 10, Lg Gambut, off Jln Beserah; r incl breakfast from RM292-304, ste RM410-430;) Like a 1980s business hotel without the neon and big hair, this sprawling spot has huge rooms that are just a bit too dark and stale for the price. The real reason to come is the garden pool, which is awesome!

Signature Hotel BOUTIQUE HOTEL $$

(☎09-513 2919; signaturehotel2012@gmail.com; 41 Jln Beserah; s RM88, d RM118-148;) With adorable lobby staff and cool modern lines, this is a solid entrant in the lower mid-range tier. The rooms can be pretty small, but feature boutique stylings and contemporary trimmings.

Eating & Drinking

Kuantan's most distinctive dish is *patin* (silver catfish). The Berjaya Megamall and the East Coast Mall have everything from Starbucks to Malay-style food courts. The food stalls by the long-distance bus station are particularly excellent.

Akob Patin House MALAYSIAN $
(Jln Besar; mains RM7-15; ⏲lunch) Fancy trying *patin,* the local delicacy? This riverfront place serves both wild-caught (RM20) and farmed (RM8) *patin* in a *tempoyak* (fermented durian sambal) sauce served as part of a buffet with other Malay-style meat and vegetable dishes – the price is per fish. The friendly staff can help explain what's what.

Kohng Restoran CHINESE $
(9 Jln Teluk Sisek; mains RM6-12; ⏲6pm-3am) This humble spot on the main drag serves some of the best Hainan chicken rice this side of Singapore. On some nights it is so packed that diners spill into the alley next door, where a variety of other Chinese snacks are cooked well into the wee hours. Kohng can't be beat for cheap beer.

★**Ana Ikan Bakar Petai** SEAFOOD $$
(Tanjong Lumpur; mains RM20-40; ⏲lunch & dinner) If it's authentic you're after, look no further than this huge open-air seafood restaurant across the river on the island of Tanjong Lumpur. On any given evening Malaysian families flock here to feast on a plethora of traditional Malay seafood dishes.

An extraordinary selection of freshly caught fish, crab and shrimp is priced by weight and cooked to your specifications in small kitchens along the side of the dining area, while a larger kitchen in the back prepares traditional Malaysian rice and noodle dishes. No beer is needed – an amazing assortment of fresh juices is available for whistle wetting.

Information

Lots of banks (many with 24-hour ATMs) are on or near the aptly named Jln Bank. You'll find wi-fi in most hotels. There are internet cafes at the Berjaya Megamall and East Coast Mall.

Post Office (Jln Haji Abdul Aziz)

Tourist Information Centre (☎09-516 1007; Jln Mahkota; ⏲8am-5pm Mon-Fri) Has particularly helpful staff and a range of useful leaflets.

Tourism Malaysia (☎09-517 7111; 601 Pejabat Nesi Pahang; ⏲8am-1pm & 2-5pm Mon-Thu, 8am-noon & 2.45-5pm Fri) Staff aren't much help but there are plenty of brochures to help you find your way.

Getting There & Around

AIR

Malaysia Airlines (☎1300-883 000; www.malaysiaairlines.com; Jln Gambut, ground fl, Wisma Persatuan Bolasepak Pahang) has daily direct flights to KL with plenty of onward connections from there. **Firefly** (☎03-7845 4543; www.firefly.com.my) also has two daily flights to/from Subang Airport in KL and four weekly flights to Singapore. The airport is 15km from the city; a taxi should cost RM20.

BUS

Long-distance buses leave from **Terminal Sentral Kuantan** (Jln Pintasan Kuantan), about 20 minutes from the city centre (taxi RM20). The ticket offices, food court and left-luggage centre (RM2 per piece) are on the 2nd floor of the building.

Local buses for Pekan (RM5.30), Balok (RM3), Beserah (RM3) and Cherating (bus 27; RM5) depart from near the central market.

DESTINATION	PRICE	DURATION
Butterworth	RM51	8½ hours
Jerantut	RM18	3½ hours
Kota Bharu	RM31	6 hours
Kuala Lipis	RM24	6 hours
Kuala Lumpur	RM24	4 hours
Kuala Terengganu	RM17	4 hours
Melaka	RM35	6 hours
Mersing	RM34	3 hours
Singapore	RM30	6 hours
Temerloh	RM12	2 hours

CAR

Hawk (☎09-538 5055; www.hawkrentacar.com.my; Sultan Ahmad Shah Airport, Kuantan)

TAXI

Ask your hotel to order a long-distance taxi or grab one from in front of the Terminal Sentral Kuantan. Approximate costs (per car):

- Cherating (RM50 to RM70)
- Jerantut (RM200)
- Johor Bahru (RM350)
- KL (RM280)
- Kuala Terengganu (RM200)
- Mersing (RM200)
- Pekan (RM60).

Prices may vary, and bargaining is possible.

OFF THE BEATEN TRACK

CAVE OF THE SLEEPING BUDDHA

Twenty-six kilometers north of Kuantan the limestone karst containing **Gua Charas** (Charas Caves/Charah Caves; admission RM1) towers above the surrounding palm plantations. The caves owe their fame to a Thai Buddhist monk who came to meditate here about 50 years ago. A steep climb up a stairway leads to the colossal **Sleeping Buddha Cave** (Wofo Dong), decorated with small altars to Kuanyin Puxian, other bodhisattvas and Buddhist idols. The main attraction is the Sleeping Buddha in the rear of the cavern.

A taxi from Kuantan to the caves costs RM40, or you can take the Sungai Lembing–bound bus 500 (RM3, one hour) from the local bus station in Kuantan and get off at the small village of **Panching** just past the sign reading 'Gua Charas 4km'. You can walk or get someone in Panching to give you a lift on a motorcycle for RM2.

Continue to **Sungai Lembing** to take in a small regional museum (RM2) that covers mining top to bottom, or head into the hills for a claustrophobic tour of neighbouring mines (RM15 to RM30).

Teluk Chempedak

Light waves crash on the shore of Teluk Chempedak and several walking tracks wind along the park jungle area at this strip of coast 6km east of Kuantan. From November to around February the beach break becomes surfable; surfboards are rented for RM50/100 per hour/day from the Gandom Club next door to the Hyatt Regency.

Sleeping

Pine Beach Hotel HOTEL $
(013-940 4458; s/d incl breakfast RM50/60;) About 200m from the beach just beyond McDonald's is this unremarkable but clean hotel. Its newish rooms all have aircon, TVs and hot-water showers. Groundfloor rooms are windowless.

Hyatt Regency Kuantan RESORT $$
(09-518 1234; www.kuantan.regency.hyatt.com; r from RM340;) A spacious, breezy and effortlessly luxurious place, with amenable staff, lovely views and a solid list of amenities (including two pools, two very good restaurants, three tennis courts, squash courts, a spa, a children's play area and a water-sports centre).

Rooms are sumptuous and a whole bevy of activities is on offer, including walks along the cliffs to Methodist Bay.

Getting There & Away

To get to Teluk Chempedak, take bus 200 from in front of Kuantan's Berjaya Megamall (RM2). A taxi between the two towns costs RM15.

Cherating

With a sweeping white beach bordered by coconut palms, and a small village of guesthouses and shops with more monkeys, monitor lizards and cats walking around than humans, Cherating is a popular spot for surfing and general beachfront slacking. It has plenty of beach bars and the best nightlife on Pahang's coast.

Sights & Activities

Batik making (canvas drawing with local dyes) is a Cherating speciality. **Limbong Art** (Main Rd) offers courses (from RM30) where you can make your own batik handkerchief or sarong.

Water Sports

Cherating's bay has a long sandy shelf, making this a peaceful spot for **swimming**. Watch out for jellyfish in June and July.

Some of Malaysia's best **surfing** waves kick up here during monsoon season, from late October to the end of March. In town, a point break rolls across the bay, with up to 2m waves and rides that last 400m. Rent a car to find more spots north of here.

Cherating beach isn't great for snorkelling but places all around town offer half-day **snorkelling tours** (RM60) to the aptly named Coral Island.

You can rent **kayaks** (sea or river, per hour RM15 to RM30) at Villa de Fedelia (p267) and Payung Guesthouse (p267) to cruise around on your own.

Kam's Surf Shack WATER SPORTS
(Cherating Beach; 8am-10pm) This surf shop rents every board imaginable, and doubles

Cherating

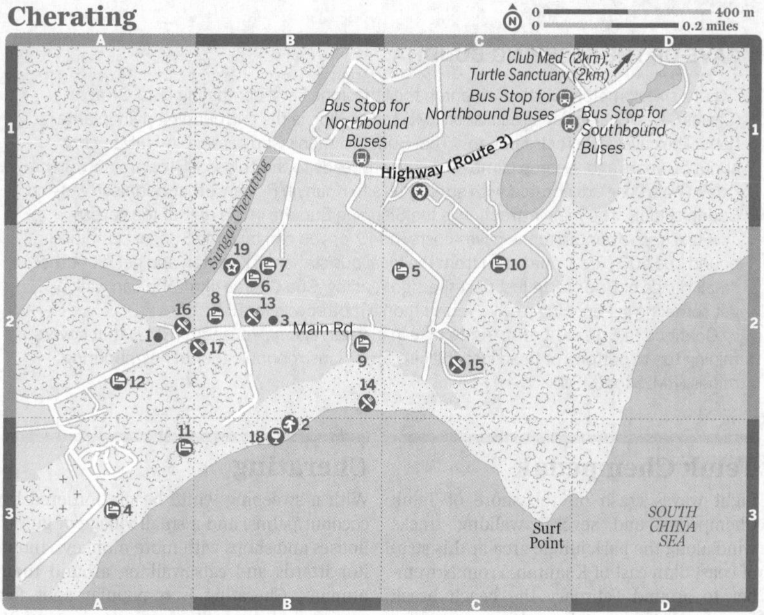

Cherating

Activities, Courses & Tours
- Cherating Point Surf School ... (see 6)
- 1 Hafiz's Cherating Activities ... A2
- 2 Kam's Surf Shack ... B3
- 3 Limbong Art ... B2

Sleeping
- 4 Cherating Bayview Resort ... A3
- 5 Lilo's Travelers Home ... C2
- 6 Matahari Holiday Huts ... B2
- 7 Maznah's Guest House ... B2
- 8 Payung Guesthouse ... B2
- 9 Ranting Beach Resort ... B2
- 10 Residence Inn ... C2
- 11 Tanjung Inn ... A3
- 12 Villa de Fedelia ... A2

Eating
- 13 Cherating Cottage Café ... B2
- 14 Don't Tell Mama ... B2
- 15 Duyong Restaurant ... C2
- 16 Matahari Restaurant ... A2
- 17 Nabill Café ... B2

Drinking & Nightlife
- 18 Cherating Beach Bar ... B3
- Eco Bar ... (see 14)

Entertainment
- 19 Little Bali ... B2

as a bar come sunset. Rent kitesurfing gear for RM100 (experienced riders only); lessons cost RM250. Windsurf rentals are RM60, while a class costs RM100; paddle-boards are RM50/80 for an hour/half-day. You can also rent a little sailboat (one hour/half-day RM100/460) or surfboards (RM40 to RM80).

Cherating Point Surf School SURFING
(www.cheratingpoint.com; Matahari Holiday Huts) Only open during monsoon season, this surf shack offers 1½-hour surf classes (RM110 to RM130), and rents boards (half-/full day RM40/70).

Wildlife Viewing

Several places around town run river mangrove tours, firefly tours, turtle-watching (April to September), nature walks and other activities.

Turtle Sanctuary ANIMAL SANCTUARY
(RM30; ⏲9am-5pm Tue-Sun) The turtle sanctuary next to Club Med has a few basins with

baby and rehabilitating green turtles, and can offer information about the laying and hatching periods.

Hafiz's Cherating Activities BOAT TOUR
(☎017-978 9256; www.cheratingbeachinfo.com.my; tours from RM30) Night-time firefly boat tours along the mangroves upriver are a Cherating activity *par excellence*. The best tours are led by Hafiz, a long-time firefly enthusiast and self-made expert at Cherating Activities. Tours leave around 7:30pm. Hafiz also offers river fishing (RM500) and deep-sea fishing (RM900).

Sleeping

Budget digs tend to fill up with surfers during the monsoon (November through January), and midrange places tend to fill up on the weekends year-round. Book in advance.

★**Villa de Fedelia** BUNGALOW $
(Tanjung Inn; ☎09-581 9081; www.tanjunginn.com; r with fan RM70, with air-con RM170-400; ❄@📶) This highly recommended place offers wooden bungalows with decks set around a stunning lilypad-bedazzled pond surrounded by tall grass and fruit trees. All the bungalows have hot showers, and there's an excellent lending library in the reception area. The family-friendly atmosphere and grounds are the real draw.

Payung Guesthouse BUNGALOW $
(☎09-581 9658; d/q RM60/120, d with air-con RM80; ❄📶) This friendly main-drag choice backs onto the river with a neat row of bungalows and well-manicured gardens. The bungalows all have mozzie nets, and this is an excellent spot to get information on local happenings.

Its owners are working on a jungle camp site nearby, and until it's completed you may be able to exchange a few hours' labour for free board.

Lilo's Travelers Home GUESTHOUSE $
(☎019-996 1723; r RM50) Located on a little dusty back road, this broad-smiling spot is just getting going. But you'll get superclean basic white rooms, a shared kitchen and cool central hang-out. Plans are in place to build a community garden.

Matahari Holiday Huts BUNGALOW $
(☎017-924 7465; d without/with bathroom RM30/50, q RM80, r/q with air-con RM80/150; ❄📶) Built on a large lot, this friendly spot has a shared kitchen, free coffee and an array of accommodation, running from budget shared-bathroom bungalows, to slightly more upmarket (but still budget) bungalows with private bathrooms and air-con.

Maznah's Guest House BUNGALOW $
(☎09-581 9307; s/d with shared bathroom RM30/35, r RM70, r with air-con RM120-150, all incl breakfast; ❄📶) Spirited kids happily chase chickens around the collection of sturdy wooden bungalows at this rather barren spot. The owners speak little English and a delicious *nasi lemak* (rice boiled in coconut milk, served with fried *ikan bilis*, peanuts and a curry dish) is served for breakfast. A clutch of new rooms sit over a rather stagnant pond.

Tanjung Inn BUNGALOW $$
(☎09-581 9081; www.tanjunginn.com; r RM200) Run by the folks at Villa de Fedelia (and sharing a lobby at least for now) these new chalets have doors that open right onto the beach, pitched ceilings and clean lines. They are still finishing the landscaping but we have big hopes for this new addition.

Ranting Beach Resort BUNGALOW $$
(☎09-581 9068; d with fan RM120, d with air-con RM160-250; ❄) The best bungalows are the wooden fan-cooled ones right on the busiest strip of the beach. More expensive chalets have air-con, and a four-room house that sleeps 10 can be rented for RM500.

Residence Inn HOTEL $$
(☎09-581 9333; ricresun@ric.my; r incl breakfast RM240-320; ❄📶🏊) Surrounding a pretty swimming pool, the rooms are a bit dated with button-down business-standard stylings. You do get flat-screen TV and air-con, but without beach access, you may shop elsewhere.

Cherating Bayview Resort BUNGALOW $$
(☎09-581 9248; http://cheratingbayviewresort.blogspot.com; r RM100-220; ❄📶🏊) The concrete rooms look onto the sea but do little to take advantage of their lovely location. There's no alcohol and no unmarried couples allowed.

Impiana RESORT $$
(☎09-581 9000; www.impianaresortcherating.com; 3km north of Cherating; r RM207-280, deluxe incl breakfast r RM365-385; P❄📶🏊) This Polynesian-inspired resort with its own secluded beach has a gorgeous lily pond in the

lobby that cascades to a circular pool. On-site there's a bar, expensive-but-recommended restaurant, kids club and fitness centre.

While the rooms could use a bit of updating, with their hardwood treatments and excellent beach views they are a solid offering for resort-goers who are OK being a little isolated from Cherating's bar and restaurant scene.

★Club Med RESORT $$$
(☎09-581 9133; www.clubmed.com.sg; all-incl package from RM550; P ❄ ≋ ≋) Crafted to look like a particularly beautiful Malaysian *kampung* with wooden buildings on stilts, this resort comes fully equipped with its own stretch of beach, immaculate sprawling lawns, international restaurants, nightclub, kids club, nearby turtle sanctuary and sports facilities. It's about 2km north of town.

Eating

Most of the town's guesthouses have on-site restaurants.

Cherating Cottage Café CAFE $
(mains RM5-9; ⊙breakfast, lunch & dinner; ≋) Almost always the first spot to open in the mornings (around 8am). The breakfasts are great.

Don't Tell Mama BURGERS $
(Cherating Beach; burger RM5-10; ⊙till late) Don't Tell Mama was relaunching when we passed through, relocating next to Eco Bar. It's bound to be a hit with a full menu and its legendary burgers still on offer. Ask to see the cool hydroponic garden set-up.

Nabill Café MALAYSIAN $
(mains RM6-9; ⊙dinner) Eat where the locals do and save a handful of ringgit. Choose your fresh seafood then watch it get grilled in a delicious spicy sambal.

Duyong Restaurant MALAYSIAN $$
(mains RM10-23; ⊙lunch & dinner; ≋) Raised on stilts at the western end of the beach, Duyong offers unbroken views around the bay. There's a large selection of seafood, steaks, poultry and vegetables, but it's the setting that is superlative. Try the tom yum (hot and spicy Thai seafood soup).

Matahari Restaurant MALAYSIAN $$
(mains RM10-20; ⊙breakfast, lunch & dinner) This seafood barbecue joint has cool wood tables and a peaced-out vibe.

Drinking & Entertainment

★Eco Bar BAR
(Rhana Pippin; Cherating Beach; ⊙noon-4am) Grab a low-slung table at this superfriendly beach bar and feel the sand between your toes as you check out the quirky local characters who spice up Cherating's nightlife scene.

The young owners built the bar themselves, using mainly repurposed materials – and they know how to throw a party.

Cherating Beach Bar BAR
(Cherating Beach; ⊙3pm-late) This beachfront option feels a little removed from the hippie earthbound energy of Cherating. But depending on where the town decides to party, it can get going after sunset, offering good cocktails and a fun crowd.

Little Bali LIVE MUSIC
(Sungai Cherating) Party late at night on the river with live music and plenty of camaraderie.

Information

There are no banks or ATMs in Cherating, so be sure to get plenty of cash in Kuantan or Pekan.

Getting There & Away

From Kuantan's local bus station catch a bus marked 'Kemaman' and ask to be dropped at Cherating Lama (look for a sign by the road that reads 'Pantai Cherating'). Buses leave every 30 minutes (RM5, one hour). When coming from the north, any bus heading for Kuantan will drop you on the main road. A taxi from Kuantan should cost about RM80.

From Kuala Lumpur, it's best to get a direct bus to Kemaman and ask to be dropped in Cherating Lama (Old Cherating).

From Cherating to Kuantan, wave down a Kuantan-bound bus from the bus stop on the highway (Rte 3).

For taxis from Cherating call the **Cherating Taxi Service** (☎09-581 9355). Expect to pay around RM55 for a taxi to Kuantan and RM280 for a trip to Taman Negara. Taxis to resorts outside town cost about RM30.

THE INTERIOR

Temerloh

An old town on the banks of the enormous Sungai Pahang, Temerloh has hints of colonial style and a colourful Sunday market.

As the main city of central Pahang, it serves as a transport hub. The bus station is in the centre of the shop-and-restaurant-filled new town (which is just a few minutes' walk from the old). The train station (currently not operating) is 12km away at Mentakab, a thriving satellite of Temerloh with a bustling nightly market.

Temerloh is a decent place to chill, especially if you're craving some modernity after a few days in the jungle. Budget lodgings are limited but there are a few midrange options.

Sleeping & Eating

Green Park Hotel HOTEL $
(09-296 3333; www.greenpark.com.my; Jln Terkukur, off Jln Merbah; r RM88-125;) This tall hotel towers over the town and offers clean, pretty rooms with hot showers and coffee- and tea-making facilities. The rooms are oh-so-sterile but have the occasional Polynesian print to spice things up.

Rumah Rehat Temerloh GUESTHOUSE $$
(09-296 3218; Jln Hamzah; r RM100-110;) In a quiet corner of town surrounded by green trees, this hotel is well worn but clean and friendly. Ten rooms are spread over two floors.

E Station Cafe JAPANESE $$
(Jln Pak Sako 1; RM6-21) Come on, admit it – after weeks of *mee sup* and laksa, you're craving something different. While this Japanese restaurant no longer offers sushi, you can still sample a variety of Japanese faves.

Getting There & Away

Terminal Bas Utama Temerloh (Jln Sudirman) is where you'll find buses to various spots on the peninsula.

DESTINATION	PRICE	DURATION
Jerantut	RM6.20	1½ hours
Kuala Lipis	RM17	3 hours
Kuala Lumpur (Pekeling)	RM11	3 hours
Kuantan	RM12	2 hours
Melaka	RM17	4 hours
Penang	RM55	6 hours

Taxis from the bus station. Approximate costs:

- Jerantut (RM60)
- Kuantan (RM160)
- KL (RM160)
- Mentakab (RM12)

Around Temerloh

Sights

Kuala Gandah Elephant Conservation Centre ANIMAL SANCTUARY
(09-279 0391; www.wildlife.gov.my/index.php/en; Kuala Gandah, Lanchang; entry by donation; 10am-3:15pm) This is the base for the Department of Wildlife and National Parks' Elephant Relocation Team, which helps capture rogue elephants from across Southeast Asia and relocate them to other suitable habitats throughout the peninsula, such as Taman Negara.

From 10:30am to noon observe elephants (behind an electric fence) on a small interpretive trail. Videos at 1pm and 1:30pm explain the plight of wild elephants (there are fewer than 1200 remaining in Peninsular Malaysia). The elephants get a bath at 2:15pm, and are introduced to the crowd from 2:45pm to 3:15pm. Most of the elephants at the centre are work elephants from Myanmar, India and Thailand. No rides are offered here.

A taxi ride from Temerloh costs RM120 round trip. You can make a full day of a trip here.

Sleeping & Eating

Buman Suri Biopurpose Resort HOMESTAY $
(013-377 3838; http://bumansuriresort.blogspot.com; d RM68) Family-run accommodation in a basic *kampung*-style house on the roadside.

Getting There & Away

The town of Lanchang is west of Mentakab and about 150km east of KL. Most people visit this area on tours (including a visit to Kuala Gandah Elephant Conservation Centre) from KL, Jerantut, Cherating and other tourist hubs on the peninsula. The most cost-efficient way to explore this area is to combine a visit with your return trip to KL from Taman Negara with Han Travel (www.taman-negara.com).

Jerantut

This small town is the gateway to Taman Negara, and most travellers do little more than spend a night before heading into the jungle (perhaps stocking up on booze at one of the Chinese-owned liquor stores on Jln Diwangsa before heading to dry Kuala Tahan). The town is pleasant enough to spend an afternoon in.

Jerantut

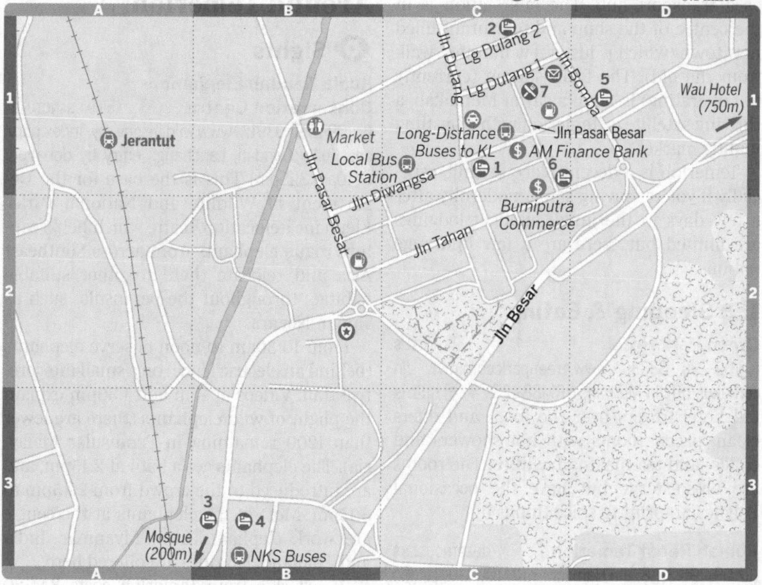

Jerantut

Sleeping

1 Greenleaf Guesthouse C1
2 Hotel Chet Fatt C1
3 Hotel Sri Emas B3
4 NKS Hostel B3
5 Sakura Castle Inn D1
6 Town Inn Hotel C1

Eating

7 Food Stalls C1
NKS Café .... (see 4)

Sleeping

Most places offer luggage storage, are open 24 hours and can arrange transport to Taman Negara. Hotels can get very busy around July and August.

Sakura Castle Inn HOTEL $
(09-266 5200; http://sakuracastleinn.blogspot.com; 51-52 Jln Bomba; r RM55-75;) This is the classiest place in town, and has clean, comfortable rooms all with TVs, hot water and air-con. The people who work here are as friendly and helpful as it gets.

Town Inn Hotel HOTEL $
(09-266 6811; www.towninn-hotel.com; Jln Tahan, Lot 3748; d/tr/q RM55/70/80;) The bright clean rooms (with flat-screen TVs) are a big step up from the backpacker-oriented places. Service is friendly.

Wau Hotel HOTEL $
(09-260 2255; www.wauhotels.com; K1 Pusat Perniagaan Sungai Jan; r incl breakfast RM78-90;) While these are the best rooms in town, the fact that they are a 15-minute walk (or RM6 taxi ride) from the centre makes them less appealing for travellers without their own wheels. The place is very new, with clean rooms, cheery halls decorated in yellow, peach and red, and deluxe rooms with flat screens.

Greenleaf Guesthouse HOTEL $
(09-267 2131; www.greenleaf-tamannegara.com; 3 Jln Diwangsa; dm/r RM10/30;) A quiet choice with simple, clean rooms and dorms, owned by a sweet woman and her family who also run a travel agency from here. The rooms are airy but the beds just might break your back.

Hotel Sri Emas HOTEL $
(09-266 4488; www.taman-negara-nks.com; 46 Jln Besar; dm RM8, r RM25-45, with shared bathroom RM15-35;) Very small fan doubles with shared hot-water bathrooms have saggy mattresses but are clean. Pricier private rooms are bigger and have attached

bathrooms and air-con. Across the street, the **NKS Hostel** (21-22 Jln Besar; d with/without shower incl breakfast RM50/35), serviced from the Sri Emas lobby, has dorm rooms. Luggage storage is offered.

Hotel Chet Fatt HOTEL $

(☎09-266 5805; 177 Jln Diwangsa; dm/d with shared bathroom RM10/40; @) If you arrive late at night you can stumble across the street from the bus station to this low-grade place with windowless rooms and springy beds.

Eating

On Jln Pasar Besar there are excellent food stalls specialising in tom yum, while cheap *kedai kopi* (coffee shops) serving Chinese food and Malay favourites are scattered around town.

NKS Café MALAYSIAN, INTERNATIONAL $

(NKS Hostel, 21-22 Jln Besar; mains RM10; ⏲7.30am-9pm, to 6pm low season) Serves mediocre Western breakfasts, Malay staples, *dou fu* (tofu) meals, sandwiches and beer. It's popular with backpackers, especially as it's the departure point for tours and buses.

Information

Several banks in town can change cash and travellers cheques (change money before heading into Taman Negara). The ATMs dry up sometimes so it's best to get money before reaching Jerantut.

AM Finance Bank (Jln Diwangsa; ⏲9.30am-4pm Mon-Fri, to noon Sat) Has an ATM that accepts most foreign cards, including Visa.

Bumiputra Commerce (Jln Tahan; ⏲9.30am-4pm Mon-Fri, to noon Sat) The ATM accepts MasterCard and Cirrus.

Police (☎09-266 2222; Jln Besar)

Getting There & Away

BUS

Long-distance buses leave from the ticket offices near the taxi stand. **Perwira Ekspres** (☎09-266 3919) and **SE Ekspres** (☎09-266 3188) both have offices here.

Local buses depart from the station not far away on the same street.

DESTINATION	PRICE	DURATION
Kuala Lipis	RM5	1½ hours
Kuala Lumpur (Pekeliling)	RM55	4 hours
Kuantan	RM18	4 hours
Temerloh	RM6.60	1½ hours

NKS Hostel (21-22 Jln Besar; ⏲7.30am-9pm, to 6pm low season) arranges minibuses and buses to a variety of destinations, including Tembeling jetty for boats to Taman Negara (RM15), KL (RM40), Kuala Besut (RM90) and the Cameron Highlands (RM80). Buses leave from the NKS Café. NKS can also help you to arrange a river trip to the national park from the jetty in Kuala Tembeling. If you want to skip the riverboat, take one of their minibuses directly from Kuala Tahan for Taman Negara (RM15, 8am and sometimes 1pm).

Public buses go to the jetty at Kuala Tembeling (RM2, 45 minutes) every hour from 7.45am to 5pm, although schedules are unreliable and don't necessarily coincide with boat departures.

TAXI

Taxi fares:

- Cherating (RM240)
- Kampung Kuala Tahan (RM65)
- KL (RM200)
- Kuala Lipis (RM65)
- Kuala Tembeling (RM20)
- Kuantan (RM180)
- Temerloh (RM50).

A surcharge of RM30 is enforced after 3pm.

TRAIN

Jerantut train station (☎09-266 2219) is on the Tumpat–Gemas railway line (also known as the jungle railway) – currently closed for repairs. All northbound trains go via Kuala Lipis and Gua Musang. If service resumes, trains should run daily to Singapore (2am, 12.30pm) via Johor Bahru. For KL Sentral, take the 12.30am express; there are four trains for Kuala Lipis.

For an up-to-date timetable and list of fares, consult KTM (www.ktmb.com.my).

Taman Negara

Taman Negara National Park blankets 4343 sq km (from Pahang to Kelantan and Terengganu) in shadowy, damp, impenetrable jungle. Inside this buzzing tangle, ancient trees with gargantuan buttressed root systems dwarf luminescent fungi, orchids, two-tone ferns and even the giant rafflesia (the world's largest flower).

Hidden within the flora are elephants, tigers, leopards and rhinos, as well as smaller wonders such as flying squirrels, but these animals stay far from the park's trails and sightings are extremely rare. Even if they do come close, you're not likely to see them through the dense thicket. What you might see are snakes (dog-toothed cat snakes,

Taman Negara

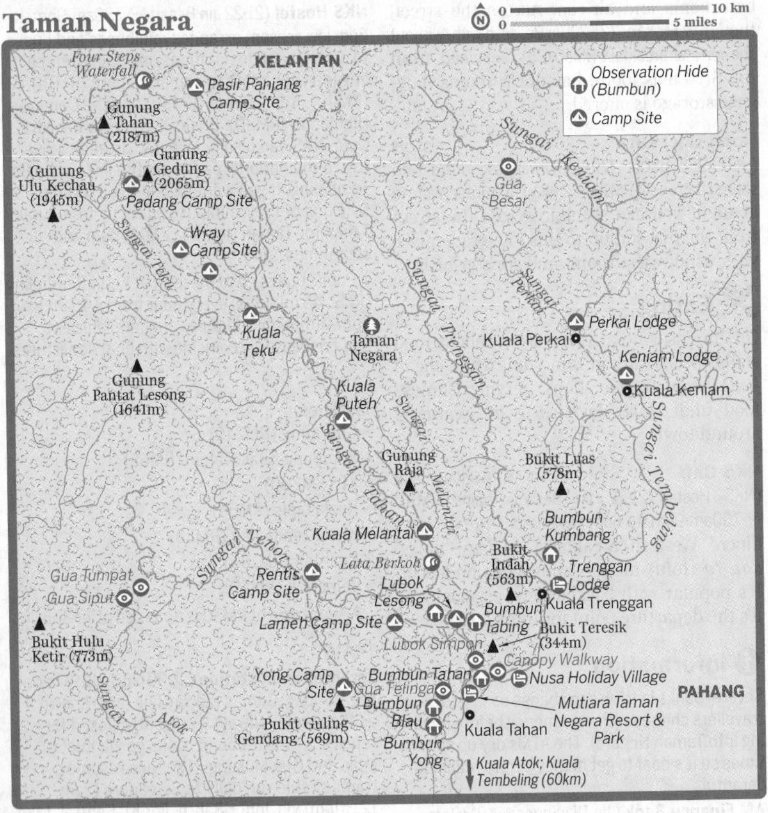

reticulated pythons, temple pit vipers and red-headed kraits), lizards, monkeys, small deer, loads of birds and perhaps tapir. Nearly everyone who visits Taman Negara gets an up-close-and-personal meeting with leeches and an impressive array of flying and crawling insects.

The more time you put into a visit to Taman Negara, the more you'll get out of it. Though they're feasible, fleeting visits only scratch the surface. Consider an overnight trek or at least a long boat trip up one of the park's rivers. Whether coming for an afternoon hike or a multiday trek, you'll need to buy a permit at the Tourist Information Counter (p276).

The park headquarters and the privately run Mutiara Taman Negara Resort (p275) are at Kuala Tahan at the edge of Taman Negara National Park; other accommodation and restaurants are across the Sungai Tembing at Kampung Kuala Tahan. River taxis buzz between the two sides of the river (RM1 each way) throughout the day.

Activities

There are a wide variety of trekking possibilities, from an hour's stroll with a romp on the canopy walk to nine arduous days up and down 2187m-high Gunung Tahan. You can shorten your hiking time in most cases by taking riverboat services or tours that include boat transport.

The trails around the park headquarters are convenient but heavily trafficked. Relatively few visitors venture far beyond the headquarters, and longer walks are much less trammelled.

Treks from Kuala Tahan

Easy-to-follow trails around park headquarters are signposted and marked with approximate walking times; enquire at the information office for details on other routes.

Canopy Walkway & Around HIKING
(adult/child RM5/3; ⏲10am-3.30pm Sat-Thu, 9am-noon Fri) This is easily the area's most popular hike. It begins east of park headquarters and leads along the Sungai Tembeling to the Canopy Walkway, 30 minutes away. The walkway is suspended between huge trees and the entire circuit takes around 40 minutes. Get here early for the best birding and wildlife watching.

From behind the Canopy Walkway a trail leads to Bukit Teresik (344m), from the top of which are fine views across the forest. The trail is steep and slippery in parts but is easily negotiated and takes about an hour up and back. You can descend back along this trail to the Mutiara Taman Negara Resort or, near the Canopy Walkway, take the branch trail that leads across to Lubok Simpon, a swimming area on Sungai Tahan. From here it is an easy stroll back to park headquarters. The entire loop can easily be done in three hours.

Past the Canopy Walkway, a branch of the main trail leads to Bukit Indah (563m), another steep but rewarding hill climb offering fine views across the forest and the rapids in Sungai Tembeling.

Kuala Trenggan HIKING
The well-marked main trail along the bank of Sungai Tembeling leads 9km to Kuala Trenggan, a popular trail for those heading to the Bumbun Kumbang hide. Allow five hours. From here, boats go back to Nusa Holiday Village (p275) and Kampung Kuala Tahan, or it's a further 2km walk to Bumbun Kumbang.

An alternative longer trail leads inland, back across Sungai Trenggan from Bumbun Kumbang to the camp site at Lubok Lesong on Sungai Tahan, then back to park headquarters (six hours). This trail is flat most of the way and crosses small streams. Check with park headquarters for river levels.

Lata Berkoh HIKING
North from park headquarters, this day hike leads to Gunung Tahan, but you can do an easy day walk to Lata Berkoh, the cascading rapids on Sungai Tahan. The trail passes the Lubok Simpon swimming hole and Bumbun Tabing, 1¼ hours from Kuala Tahan.

There is one river crossing before you reach the falls, which can be treacherous if the water is high. Do not attempt the river crossing in high water – you should hail one of the boat operators waiting on the opposite side to ferry you across.

Kuala Keniam HIKING
The trail from Kuala Trenggan to Kuala Keniam is a popular day hike. It's normally done by chartering a boat to Kuala Keniam and then walking back to Kuala Trenggan (six hours). The trail is quite taxing and hilly in parts, and passes a series of limestone caves.

This walk can be combined with one of the Kuala Tahan–Kuala Trenggan trails to form a two-day trip, staying overnight in the Trenggan Lodge or at Bumbun Kumbang. It is also possible to walk from Kuala Keniam to the lodge at Kuala Perkai, an easy two-hour walk.

Gunung Tahan HIKING
Really adventurous travellers climb Gunung Tahan (2187m), the highest peak in Peninsular Malaysia, 55km from park headquarters. It takes nine days at a steady pace, although it can be done in seven.

A guide is compulsory (RM700 for seven days plus RM75 for each day thereafter). There are no shelters along the way so you have to be fully equipped. Try to organise this trek in advance so you don't have to hang around park headquarters for a couple of days.

Rentis Tenor HIKING
From Kuala Tahan, this trek takes roughly three days, and takes you to remote corners of the park where you are more likely to see wildlife. Hiring a guide for this hike is highly recommended.

Day one: take the trail to Gua Telinga, and beyond, for about seven hours, to Yong camp site. Day two is a six-hour walk to the Rentis camp site. On day three cross Sungai Tahan (up to waist deep) to get back to Kuala Tahan: roughly a six-hour walk, or you can stop over at the Lameh camp site, about halfway.

Fishing

Anglers will find the park a real paradise. Fish found in the park's rivers include the superb fighting fish known in India as the *mahseer* and here as the *kelasa*.

Popular fishing rivers include Sungai Tahan, Sungai Keniam (north of Kuala Trenggan) and the remote Sungai Sepia. Simple fishing lodges are scattered through the park and can be booked at park headquarters. The best fishing months are February,

March, July and August. Fishing permits are RM10; rods can be hired across the river for between RM20 and RM30 per day. You can hire a three-day boat tour for up to three people with a guide for about RM1500.

River Bus & Boat Trips

The Mutiara Taman Negara Resort has daily boats that go upriver to Kuala Trenggan at 10am and 2.30pm. In the reverse direction, boats leave Kuala Trenggan at 11.15am and 3.15pm. These services are intended for guests only, but there are boat trips into the park from Mutiara Taman Negara dock that are open to the public.

DESTINATION	PRICE	TRIPS PER DAY	FIRST BOAT
Bunbun Yong	RM5	3	8.30am
Canopy Walkway	RM15	2	10.15am
Gua Telinga	RM15	4	8.30am
Kuala Tembeling	RM30	1	9am

Tours

There is a wide variety of thematic tours offered by nearly every hotel and a few independent operators in town. Some are doable on your own while others are more easily taken on with a guide and group.

Guides who are licensed by the Wildlife Department have completed coursework in forest flora, fauna and safety. Often the Kuala Tahan tour operators offer cheaper prices than those available at the Tourist Information Counter at park headquarters (whose guides are licensed), but talk with these guides first to find out what training they've had. Guides cost RM180 per day (one guide can lead up to 12 people), plus there is a RM100 fee for each night spent out on the trail.

Top tours include canopy and jungle treks that last a couple of hours (RM35 to RM50), night jungle trips with lots of insect viewing (RM25 to RM45), Lata Berkok hike (RM200), and motorboating through Class I rapids (RM40 to RM80).

Many travellers sign up for tours to an Orang Asli settlement (RM45 to RM80). Tribal elders give a general overview of life there and you'll learn how to use a long blowpipe and start a fire. While local guides insist that these tours provide essential income for the Orang Asli, most of your tour money will go to the tour company. A small handicraft purchase in the village will help spread the wealth.

Sleeping

Kampung Kuala Tahan, directly across the river from park headquarters and the Mutiara Resort, is where most of Taman Negara's lodging, restaurants and shops are found. There is a handful of secluded places just 10 minutes' walk south and north of Kampung Kuala Tahan that are worth checking out if you are looking for a little more tranquillity.

Kampung Kuala Tahan

Mahseer Chalet BUNGALOW $
(019-383 2633; mahseerchalet@gmail.com; dm with fan/air-con RM15/20, r RM70-100;) The best part of this clutch of jungle bungalows is its location just by the river. The rooms and bungalows have spankin' new sheets; the hostel rooms are hot and buggy (yes, the extra RM5 for air-con is well worth it). Cats patrol the grounds and there's a cool, friendly vibe.

Tembeling Riverview Lodge LODGE $
(09-266 6766; www.trvtamannegara.blogspot.com; dm/d/tr RM10/50/60) Straddling the thoroughfare footpath, this place has fan-cooled rooms with cold showers and mosquito netting and pleasant communal areas overlooking the river. Staff are friendly, and there's a lovely restaurant serving *roti john* (a Malaysian sandwich made with local bread, meat, cheese and vegetables; RM6).

Teresek View Motel MOTEL $
(09-266 9744; teresekviewmotel@gmail.com; r with fan/air-con RM70/90;) You can't miss this eyesore of a cement building in the 'centre' of Kuala Tahan. The rooms have leather headboards and playful cartoon-sheep sheets, and are spick and span with clean pink tiles throughout. Ask for one of the few rooms with a view; number 19 is our favourite.

Yellow Guesthouse GUESTHOUSE $
(017-946 3357; myusofth@gmail.com; d/tr/q RM80/100/120; @) Up and over the top of the hill (behind the school), this guesthouse consists of a single-storey house and a two-storey building that are cleaner and in better shape than most of the others. All

PAHANG & TIOMAN ISLAND TAMAN NEGARA

rooms have hot showers and private balconies. It's a very friendly spot.

Tahan Guesthouse GUESTHOUSE $
(017-970 2025; r RM50) Far enough from 'town' to feel away from it all but close enough to be convenient, this place has a great playful air with murals, colourful rooms and a big garden. The rooms can get a bit hot, but come with mozzie nets. Floors are covered with plastic sheets (bed-bug control or something else?).

Dakilih House HOTEL $
(010-919 3658; camping/d RM5/15, r RM50-80) Festive and colourful outside and in, this place sits on a hill overlooking the river a few minutes from the information centre. Cheaper rooms have shared bathrooms. There's a cute little restaurant that serves breakfast, lunch and BBQ from RM25 to RM40.

Aki Chalet BUNGALOW $
(dm/d/chalet RM13/60/90;) Nice-looking bungalows and decent dorm rooms surrounding a leafy garden. The staff don't speak any English.

Han Rainforest Resort HOTEL $$
(09-266 7244; www.tamannegara.com; 1km east of town; dm RM35, r incl breakfast RM320-350;) A little stream runs through this 'resort-like complex' just east of town. While the buildings do little to organically flow with nature, it does have some pretty sharp – though markedly bland – rooms and an expansive dining room. The dorms are cramped as hell but come with air-con.

★Mutiara Taman Negara Resort RESORT $$$
(in KL 03-2782 2222; www.mutiarahotels.com; camp site RM10, dm/chalet/ste/bungalow incl breakfast RM100/450/650/1500;) Conveniently located right at park headquarters, this eco-minded resort spreads over a large area of riverfront property. There are simple dorm rooms that sleep eight and come with air-con; little bungalow and 'chalet' cabins with dramatic lighting, rustic roofs and gorgeously modern showers; plus a fun grassy camping area with its own kitchen section.

The best part is you're in the park proper – with right-out-your-door access to afternoon hikes. That said, if you want to get across to town for dinner (the food here is great but very expensive), you'll need to shell out the RM1 fee for the crossing.

South of Kampung Kuala Tahan

Several peaceful places lie removed from the action just off the main Kampung Kuala Tahan–Jerantut road south of Kampung Kuala Tahan.

Park Lodge BUNGALOW $
(019-733 1661; bungalow RM60) The setting below a verdant hill 500m south of town is tranquil and idyllic. There are just eight fan-cooled back-to-basics bungalows, making this a welcome retreat.

TRV Motel & Lodge MOTEL $$
(127-984 7043; www.trvtamannegara.blogspot.com; d with air-con RM150, q with fan RM100;) TRV is operated by the same people who run the Tembeling Riverview Lodge, with more upscale lodgings than the Tembeling and a bit further out of town. Free shuttles in and out of town are available.

Holiday View Inn HOTEL $$
(012-952 9069; www.viewinn.com.my; 1km south of Kuala Tahan; r RM140;) This hillside offering has clean, high-ceilinged rooms with tile floors and plenty of air-con. You get nice views and are in a unique country setting, but there's no real common area and we wish the staff were just a bit less gruff.

North of Kampung Kuala Tahan

Mat Leon Village BUNGALOW $
(013-998 9517; dm with fan RM15, bungalow with fan RM60-80, bungalow with air-con & breakfast RM180;) This spot boasts a supreme forest location with river views, a good restaurant and free boat pick-up from the Kampung Kuala Tahan jetty (7am to 9:45am). To get here on foot go past Durian Chalet for around 350m to the sign at the edge of the forest; follow the forest path for 200m and you will see the bungalows on the far side of a small stream.

It has a barge on the river in Kuala Tahan that offers gear hire and information. Dorm rooms sleep four.

Nusa Holiday Village HOTEL $
(09-266 2369; www.tamannegara-nusaholiday.com.my; dm RM15, r with fan RM55-90, with air-con RM110;) About a 15-minute boat ride upriver from park headquarters, Nusa Holiday Village is more of a 'jungle camp' than anything. The isolation paired with the staff's

GEAR HIRE & LEECHES

Leeches are everywhere inside the park (but are rarely found in Kampung Kuala Tahan). Wearing boots with gaiters or long socks tucked over your trousers and doused in DEET will make hiking more pleasant.

You can hire camping, hiking and fishing gear at Mat Leon Village (p275). Approximate asking prices per day:

- sleeping bag RM10
- rucksack RM30
- tent RM25
- fishing rod RM30
- sleeping pad RM8
- stove RM8
- boots RM8.

general lack of English skills makes this a difficult place to stay unless you're on a packaged itinerary. The double cottages are the best value.

Kuala Perkai & Kuala Keniam

The Kuala Keniam Lodge (about an hour's boat ride upstream from Kuala Trenggan) and Kuala Perkai (a further two hours' walk past Kuala Keniam) are both officially closed and do not offer lodging; however, people still do camp there. If camping at either of these places, bring your own tent.

Eating

Floating barge restaurants line the rocky shore of Kampung Kuala Tahan, all selling the same ol' cheap, basic noodle and rice meals plus bland Western fare. All are open from morning until late, though most take rest breaks between 2pm and 4pm.

Family Restaurant MALAYSIAN $
(mains RM6-15) This floating restaurant serves a dish called *kerabu,* finely diced meat and vegetables with a light lemongrass sauce that's got way more local cred than the standard banana pancakes. It also serves banana pancakes.

Mama Chop MALAYSIAN $
(mains RM6-9; 🌿) Mama's serves Indian vegetarian meals at lunchtime and has very good clay-pot dishes for dinner. It's the most isolated of the river barges.

Wan's Floating Restaurant MALAYSIAN $
(mains RM7-10) Here you'll find some of the best *kway teow* (flat noodles) in town; a large bowl of *ayam kway teow* (noodles with chicken and gravy) will hit the spot.

Mutiara Restaurant INTERNATIONAL $$
(Mutiara Taman Negara Resort; RM20-40; ⌚ breakfast, lunch & dinner) Salads, sandwiches/burgers, pizza, local dishes and a small kiddies' menu. Breakfast is filling. This is bit more luxurious than the average, and is also the only place in the area where you can get a beer.

Information

MEDICAL SERVICES

For health care, the **Poliklinik Komuniti** (Community Clinic; ⌚ 24hr) is adjacent to Agoh Chalets in Kampung Kuala Tahan, opposite the school.

Dengue fever was on the rise in the deep jungle of Peninsular Malaysia when we last passed through. To avoid this and other mosquito-borne illnesses such as malaria, the best precaution is to avoid being bitten. Wear light long-sleeved clothes and cover up with DEET. Dengue-carrying mozzies generally bite between 6am and 9am and then again between 6pm and 9pm. Malaria meds are recommended by international travel clinics for the park.

POLICE

Police Station (☎ 09-266 6721) Three hundred metres up from the Teresek View Motel.

TOURIST INFORMATION

Information Centre (⌚ 9am-11pm) At the riverside end of the road in Kuala Tahan. It provides information on onward transport and tours, though it's run by private interests, so selling tours is more important than giving out information.

Tourist Information Counter (park entrance/camera/fishing/canopy/blinds RM1/5/10/5/5; ⌚ 8am-10pm Sun-Thu, 8am-noon & 3-10pm Fri) Register here before heading off into the park. The counter, located in the building 100m north of the Mutiara Taman Negara Resort's reception, also offers park information and guide services. A short video plays at 10am and 4pm, and there's a small aquarium on-site. Get here by crossing the river with a water taxi (RM1).

Getting There & Away

Most people reach Taman Negara by taking a bus from Jerantut to the jetty at Kuala Tembling, then a river boat to Kampung Kuala Tahan (the main entrance to the park). Many are now opting to head up to Taman Negara by minibus from

Jerantut and returning by boat. The bold of spirit can get here on foot.

BOAT

The 60km boat trip from Kuala Tembling (18km north of Jerantut) to Kuala Tahan is a beautiful journey – though recent floods did some major damage to riverfront trees. Still, it remains a highlight for many visitors. The boat ride is three hours to the park and two hours in the other direction.

Boats (one way RM35) depart daily at 9am and 2pm (9am and 2.30pm Friday). Extra boats are laid on during the busy season, and service can be irregular from November to February. Boats are run by NKS Hostel (p271) and a few other operators. On the return journey, regular boats leave Kuala Tahan at 9am and 2pm (2.30pm on Friday).

At the Kuala Tembeling Jetty you find tourist offices and a National Parks Information Office where you can purchase passes.

BUS

Minibus services go directly from several tourist destinations around Malaysia to Kampung Kuala Tahan. Han Travel (www.taman-negara.com), **NKS** (☎03-2072 0336; www.tamannegara.nks.com) and **Banana Travel & Tours** (☎04-261 2171; bananapenang.com; Information Centre, Kampung Kuala Tahan) run several useful private services, including daily buses to KL (RM35), a bus-boat combination (RM70) and minibuses to Penang (RM120), the Perhentian Islands (RM165 including boat) and the Cameron Highlands (RM95). These minibuses can also drop you en route anywhere in between.

WALKING

You can walk into or out of the park via Merapoh, at the Pahang–Kelantan border. The trail from Merapoh joins the Gunung Tahan trail, adding another two days to the Gunung Tahan trek. Guides are compulsory and can be hired in Merapoh to take you in. Popular and reputable travel guide Zeck, from Zeck's Traveller's Inn (p286) in Kota Bharu, can arrange a trip into the park from Kelantan that will definitely take you well off the beaten path.

Kuala Lipis

At the confluence of the Lipis and Jelai rivers, Kuala Lipis is a bustling little town with a charming colonial-era centre filled with Chinese shophouses. A large percentage of the population is Chinese or Indian, and their common language is English so it's easy to chat with the locals (who are also particularly friendly) and find your way around.

Lipis was a gold-mining centre long before the British arrived in 1887, but the town's heyday began in 1898 when it became the capital of Pahang. Grand colonial buildings date from this period, and trade increased when the railway came through in 1924. In 1957 the capital shifted to Kuantan and Kuala Lipis went into decline. The somewhat less charming 'New Town' is across the river from the old centre.

It's best known as a launching pad for visits to the nearby Kenong Rimba State Park, but Kuala Lipis also draws people for its lovely colonial-era architecture.

Sights

A very pleasant walk starts on the road behind the Lipis Centrepoint Complex. Follow the road up the hill where the sign says 'Driving Range Lipis'. You will soon pass the **Istana Hinggap** palace on your right; keep going uphill and the road forks. Take either branch and you will be led to a series of colonial-era houses, some in the process of being reclaimed by jungle.

A taxi around town for an hour to sightsee costs RM25.

District Offices HISTORIC BUILDING

Maroon and white and decorated with arches, the noble District Offices are located off Jln Lipis on a hill 1km south of the town centre.

The offices overlook the exclusive **Clifford School**, a grand public building that began life as the Anglo-Chinese School in 1913. During the occupation, the school served as the headquarters of the Kempetai (the Japanese secret police).

Pahang Club HISTORIC BUILDING

The road next to the Clifford School leads up a hill to the black-and-white wooden Pahang Club, off Jln Lipis, a stately and dignified bungalow with wide, open verandahs.

Night Market MARKET

If you're in town on Friday evening, be sure to visit the excellent night market in the parking lot next to the bus station. It extends until about noon the next day.

Activities

Kiara Holidays ADVENTURE TOUR

(☎016-446 6630; www.kiaraholidays.com; 4th fl, Centrepoint Hotel, Jln Pekeliling) Kiara plans tours all over the area, including whitewater rafting and canoe trips down the

Sungei Kesong (RM250 per person), treks into Kenong Rimba (RM225 per person) and a 4WD waterfall excursion (RM250).

Flora Shade Adventures ADVENTURE TOUR
(☎019-922 5361; cecawi@hotmail.com; Kompleks Alamanda) Try this nature guide for hikes into the nearby forests. Find it opposite the train station.

Hutan Lipur Terenggun Park HIKING
(⏰7am-6pm) For an afternoon romp, grab a taxi 7km out of town to the small 23-hectare Hutan Lipur Terenggun Park, which features a little lake and a few hiking tracks.

Empang Jaleh SWIMMING
Take a side trip to this lake and waterfall 14km west of Kuala Lipis. From here, you could also stage a climb of 2187m-high Gunung Tahan (p273).

Sleeping & Eating

There are busy and popular food stalls on either side of the northern end of the overhead walkway crossing Jln Pekeliling.

Appu's Guesthouse GUESTHOUSE $
(☎09-312 3142, 017-947 1520; jungleappu@hotmail.com; 63 Jln Besar, Hotel Lipis; r with shared bathroom RM20-40, q with shared bathroom RM60; ❄) Appu's is great for tourist info and guide services, and the rooms are some of the cheapest in town. They are doable, though some travelers have complained about the door locks.

Centrepoint Hotel & Apartments HOTEL $
(☎09-312 2688; www.centrepointhotel.com.my; Jln Pekeliling, Lipis Centrepoint; economy s/d RM48/50, deluxe d from RM108; ❄📶) You could film a horror movie in this rather bizarre high-rise complex. Economy rooms are slightly aged, while the deluxe options on the main floor are worth the upgrade.

Hotel London HOTEL $
(☎09-312 1618; 82 Jln Besar; r with fan/air-con RM25/40; ❄) This place is friendly enough. The rooms are cell-like but relatively clean, but the spongy, humid mattresses may be a challenge. Opposite the train station.

D'Valley Inn HOTEL $
(☎09-312 5868; www.dvalleyhotel.wix.com/valleyhotel; 44 Jln Bukit Bius; r RM56-68, ste RM98-128; ❄📶) D'Valley, located behind the high-rise Centrepoint, is pretty rough around the edges, though the terrace has worthwhile views. This hotel is giant and often vacant.

Residence Rest House HISTORIC HOTEL $
(☎09-312 2788; r RM60-150; ❄) This huge, homey colonial hilltop mansion once housed the British Resident. Rooms are massive, with floral wallpaper, big windows and garden grounds. The restaurant is only open for dinner and a taxi to town costs RM7.

Information

Hand-drawn maps of Kuala Lipis are available at Appu's Guesthouse. There are a few banks with ATMs on Jln Besar and the post office is east of the train station.

Watch out for fake police trying to extract bribes.

Getting There & Away

Buses run from the **bus station** (☎09-312 5055) in New Town to KL (RM13 to RM16, 4½ hours), Kuantan (RM28, 6 hours), Temerloh (RM16, 1 hour), Raub (RM6.50, 1½ hours) and Gua Musang (RM16, 1½ hours), from where you can catch onward buses to Kota Bharu.

Trains from Gemas to Tumpat have not been running since floods at the end of 2014 washed out bridges and destroyed infrastructure on much of the eastern line. Check locally for service; when it returns trains should run to Singapore, KL, Jerantut and Wakaf Baharu.

Taxis leave from the bus station. Approximate costs:

- Gua Musang (RM140)
- Jerantut (RM65)
- KL (RM180)
- Kuala Tahan (RM160)
- Kuantan (RM300)
- Temerloh (RM140).

Kenong Rimba State Park

A sprawling area of lowland forest rising to the limestone foothills bordering Taman Negara, this 120-sq-km forest park can be explored on three- or four-day jungle treks organised from Kuala Lipis. It's a much-less-visited alternative to Taman Negara. Sightings of big mammals are rare but expect to see monkeys, wild pigs, squirrels, civets and possibly nocturnal tapir; this is also a prime destination for birdwatching. The park is home to the Batek people, an Orang Asli tribe.

Visitors need to acquire a permit from the **Kuala Lipis District Forest Office** (☎09-312 1273). Park entry is RM50 per person. Guides are compulsory for entry to the park and can be arranged in Kuala Lipis. Appu of

Appu's Guesthouse in Kuala Lipis does tours for RM80 per person per day, plus RM150 (minimum three people) for the boat to and from Jeti Tanjung Kiara.

Tours include food and guide, but they are no-frills jungle experiences: you camp in the park, with all equipment and meals provided. Trips go when enough people are interested – and with the number of visitors to this area dropping extensively since the jungle train ended service, it's best to get a group together yourself.

You can also book similarly priced trips through Kiara Holidays (p277) in Kuala Lipis.

Access to Kenong Rimba is from Batu Sembilan, where you may be able to hire a boat (RM200) to Jeti Tanjung Kiara – though private ferry service is now very limited – taking you just across the river from Kampung Kuala Kenong.

ENVIRONMENTAL CONCERNS IN RAUB

Raub's Bukit Koman gold mine is a source of controversy, and multiple large-scale protests have been mounted by both Malaysian environmentalists and locals who claim to have been directly affected by cyanide used in a mining process called 'cyanide leach mining'. For the casual visitor, there should be no danger of cyanide poisoning from a short stay in Raub.

The negative impact of the area's other two major industries – palm oil and timber – are more noticeable. Trucks carrying timber roll through town with noisy regularity, and much of what was once jungle outside of Raub has been transformed into palm oil plantations.

Raub

Raub is Malay for 'scoop', which makes sense as this colonial town was built around a gold mine in the waning days of British Malaya. It's a pretty little town rarely visited by international tourists, boasting colonial-era charm and architecture along with one of our favourite restaurants in Pahang.

Sights & Activities

Like nearby Kuala Lipis, Raub also has both lovely colonial-era architecture and a more traditional *kampung* (village) on the outskirts. Raub is also a great base for exploring the nearby **Sungai Pasu Recreation Centre**, the **Jeram Besu Rapids**, **Fraser's Hill** and the **Bukit Telaga Waterfalls**. Expect to pay around RM150 for a taxi to nearby sites.

From town, hike (or taxi it) 4km north to the small **Raub Lake Garden** for an afternoon picnic. There are small **Hindu and Chinese temples** located just 1km west of the bus terminal on the road to Kuala Lipis.

Sleeping

Check around for homestays in the *kampung* on the outskirts.

Hotel Seri Raub HOTEL $
(09-355 0888; Jln Dato Abdullah; d/tr RM85/145;) Rooms are comfortable if a bit plain. They come with large flat screens and smiling English-speaking staff. Opposite the bus station.

Hotel Tai Tong HOTEL $
(09-356 1053; Jln Dato Abdullah; r with fan/air-con RM40/45;) Of a few budget places across from the bus station, this is one of the better ones (find it 100m south of the bus station). Rooms all have TV and hot shower, and the manager went to university in the US.

Rest House Raub HISTORIC HOTEL $$
(09-355 9668; Jln Dato Abdullah; d RM150-200, ste RM250 incl breakfast;) This historic guesthouse occupies the spacious grounds of a former colonial-era mansion. Ask for a room with a patio to watch over the town in the afternoon. The rooms and bathrooms are all very big and comfy, making this your top pick in town. It's 100m north of the bus station.

Eating

Sun Yen Cheong CAFE $
(Jln Tun Razak; snacks RM2-5; breakfast & lunch) This traditional Chinese-Malaysian coffee shop is bursting with customers every morning.

★ **Restoran Ratha Raub** INDIAN, MALAYSIAN $$
(Jln Tun Razak; mains RM20-40; lunch & dinner) Don't let the withered-looking fish head staring up from the buffet tray scare you – it's just for show. Though there are other dishes on the menu, what brings people from as

far away from KL is Ratha's kari kepala ikan Raub (Raub's famous fish-head curry).

All orders are prepared fresh and served in a metal tureen of fiery curry, green chilli, string beans, local eggplant and a special variant of light tofu that's been puffed with air – and, of course, the split head of a large red snapper out of which tender, bone-free cheek meat just spills. Ratha's also sells boxed 'curry in a hurry' home preparations.

Restoran Sentosa CHINESE **$$**
(Jln Padang; mains RM10-30; ⏲dinner) Sentosa specialises in whole fish prepared in Chinese fashion and served in a variety of ways – hot pot and grilled are quite popular. The building – a 100-year-old round pavilion with stained-glass windows and a lovely blue country facade 50m west of the bus station – is alone worth a visit. It charges by the pound, so meals can get pricey.

Information

Travel information is available from the friendly folks at Rest House Raub (p279).

There are several banks in town (some even sell gold), including an **HSBC** (Jln Tun Razak) with an ATM that accepts foreign cards.

Getting There & Away

Raub's bus station is on Jln Dato Abdullah. A number of companies, including **Transnasional** (☎09-355 1342) and **MARA** (☎09-355 1622), run several buses daily between Raub and KL's Pekeliling Station (RM9.20, four hours), Kuantan (RM21, four hours) and Bentong (RM4, 1 hour). A few buses also run to Kuala Lipis (RM6.25, 1 hour).

Taxi drivers tend to congregate at the bus station, offering rides to destinations all around Pahang.

East Coast Islands, Kelantan & Terengganu

☎ 09

Includes ➡

Best Places to Eat

- ➡ Kota Bharu Night Market (p288)
- ➡ Four Seasons (p288)
- ➡ World Cafe (p299)
- ➡ Madame Bee's Kitchen (p308)
- ➡ Restoran Golden Dragon (p308)

Best Places to Stay

- ➡ Pasir Belanda Homestay (p292)
- ➡ D'Lagoon Chalets (p299)
- ➡ Alunan Boutique Resort (p299)
- ➡ Terrapuri Heritage Village (p310)
- ➡ Kapas Turtle Valley (p303)

Why Go

Though Malaysia's east coast is beautiful, containing many lovely beaches and bucolic *kampung* (villages) well worth visiting, what brings folks back to the region time and again are the tantalisingly beautiful islands offshore. 'Paradise' barely does these gems justice, though that'll likely be the word that comes to mind when you first lay eyes on the white sands and swaying palms of the Perhentians or Pulau Kapas. Snorkellers and divers will find the coral and marine life beneath the azure waves among the planet's finest.

Cultural travellers, meanwhile, will find in cities like Kota Bharu and Kuala Terengganu a distinctively Malay vibe that's managed to remain fairly undiluted despite the nation's headlong rush to prosperity. And nature lovers will want to spend time exploring the vast and as yet largely untrammelled expanses of jungle that make up much of Kelantan's interior.

When to Go

Kuala Terrenganu

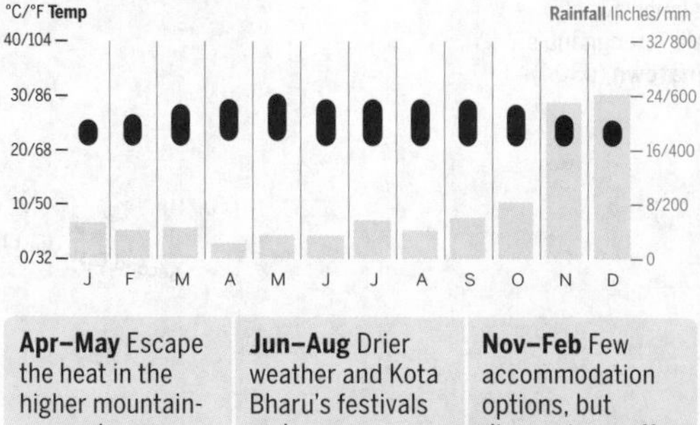

Apr–May Escape the heat in the higher mountainous regions.

Jun–Aug Drier weather and Kota Bharu's festivals make summer a great time to visit.

Nov–Feb Few accommodation options, but discounts on offer for those braving monsoonal rains.

East Coast Islands, Kelantan & Terengganu Highlights

1. Tempting your taste buds at the street stalls, markets and restaurants of **Kota Bharu** (p287)
2. Learning about Malay culture and history at the excellent museums in **Kota Bharu** (p284)
3. Checking out the Thai temples in the borderlands of **Tumpat** (p291)
4. Taking in sun, sand and sea on the diverse beaches of the **Perhentian Islands (Pulau Perhentian)** (p292)
5. Taking a night-time boat tour through the ghostly mangrove swamps and being surrounded by fireflies blinking in synchronisation at the **Penarik Firefly Sanctuary** (p310)
6. Snorkelling and beachcombing in the less visited tropical paradise of **Pulau Kapas** (p303)
7. Exploring the heritage alleys and laneways of Kuala Terengganu's **Chinatown** (p304)

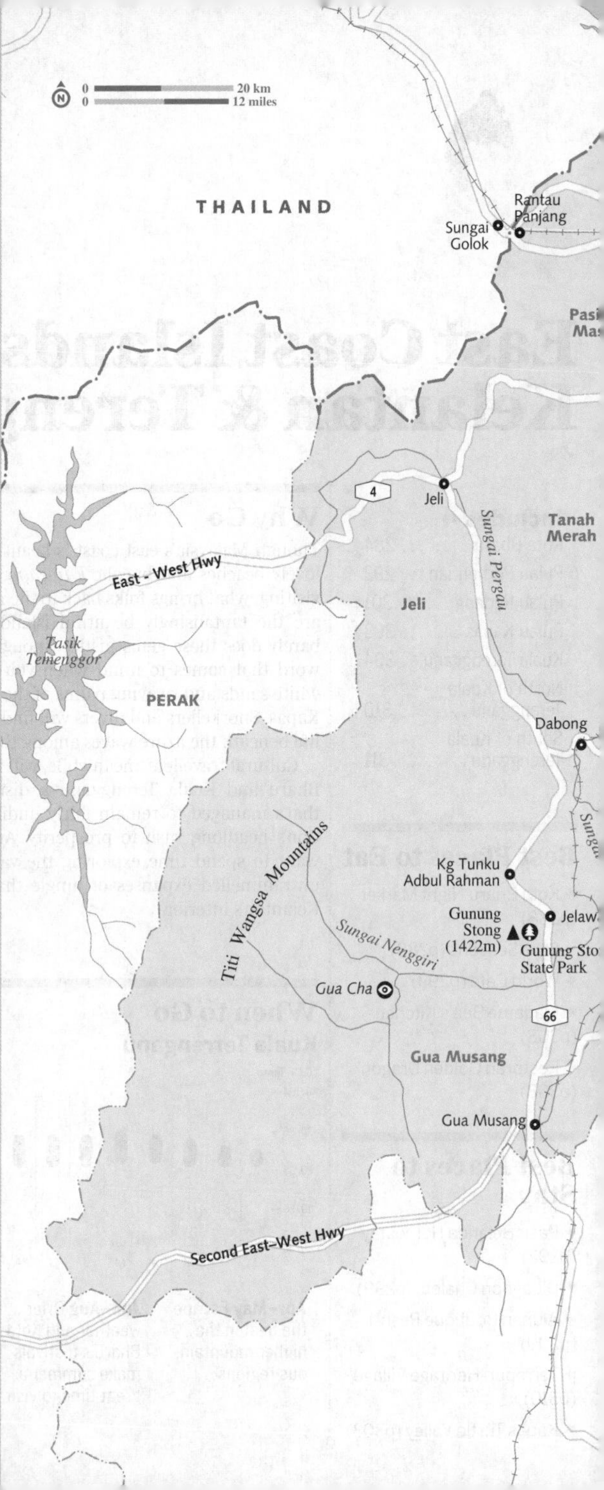

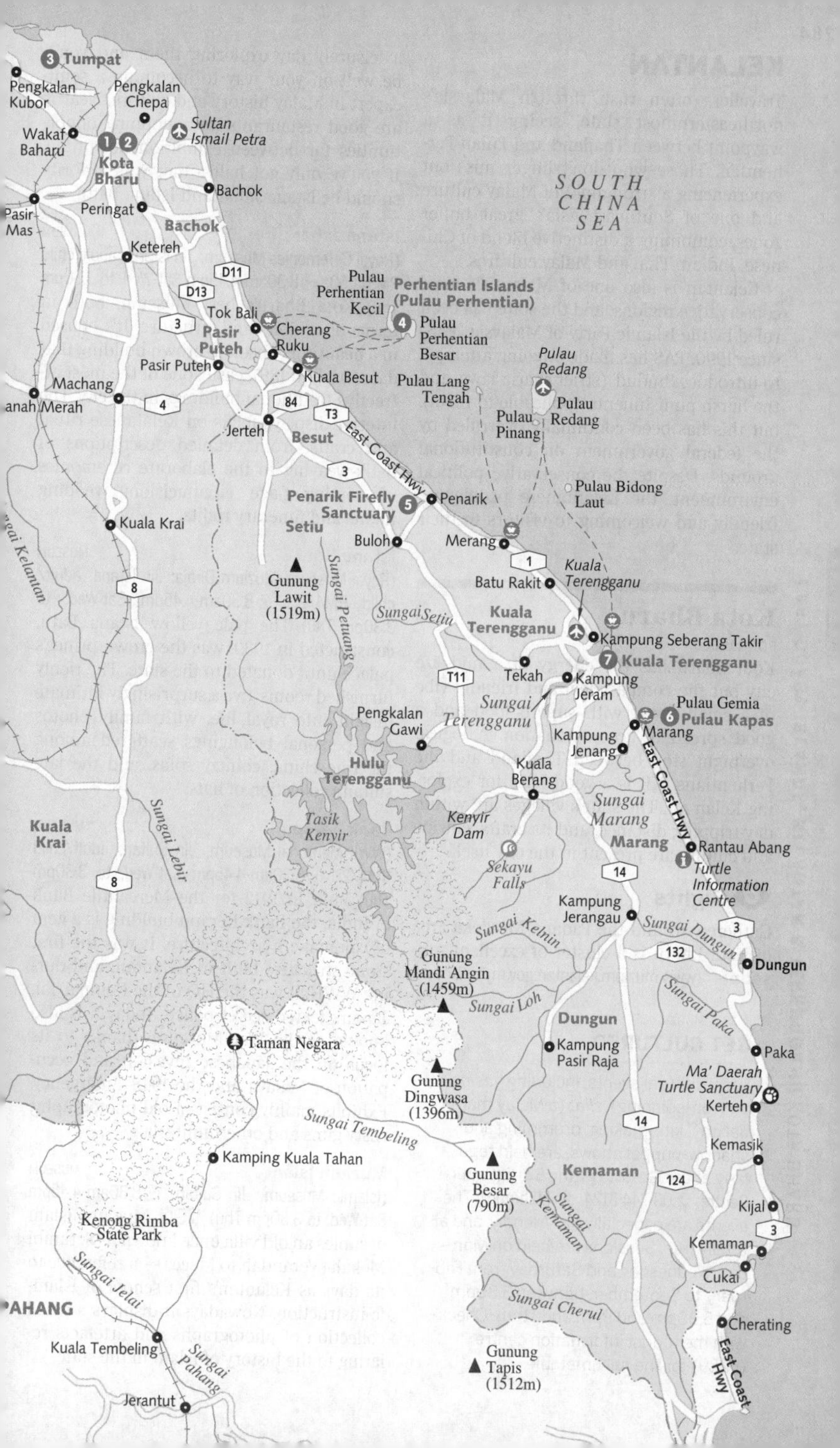

3 Tumpat
Pengkalan Kubor
Pengkalan Chepa
Sultan Ismail Petra
Wakaf Baharu
1 2
Kota Bharu
Bachok
Pasir Mas
Peringat
Bachok
Ketereh
D11
D13
3
Tok Bali
Pasir Puteh
Cherang Ruku
Pasir Puteh
Kuala Besut
Machang
4
Tanah Merah
84
T3
Jerteh
Besut
East Coast Hwy
3
SOUTH CHINA SEA
Pulau Perhentian Kecil
Perhentian Islands (Pulau Perhentian)
4 Pulau Perhentian Besar
Pulau Lang Tengah
Pulau Redang
Pulau Redang
Pulau Pinang
Pulau Bidong Laut
Penarik Firefly Sanctuary 5
Penarik
Setiu
Buloh
Merang
Kuala Krai
Sungai Kelantan
8
Gunung Lawit (1519m)
Sungai Petuang
Sungai Setiu
1
Batu Rakit
Kuala Terengganu
Kuala Terengganu
Kampung Seberang Takir
7 Kuala Terengganu
Tekah
T11
Kampung Jeram
Sungai Terengganu
Pengkalan Gawi
Pulau Gemia
6 Pulau Kapas
Marang
Kampung Jenang
East Coast Hwy
Hulu Terengganu
Kuala Berang
Tasik Kenyir
Kenyir Dam
Sungai Marang
Marang
Rantau Abang
Turtle Information Centre
Sekayu Falls
14
Kuala Krai
Sungai Lebir
8
Kampung Jerangau
Sungai Kelnin
Sungai Dungun
3
132
Dungun
Gunung Mandi Angin (1459m)
Sungai Loh
Sungai Paka
Dungun
Taman Negara
Kampung Pasir Raja
Paka
Gunung Dingwasa (1396m)
Ma' Daerah Turtle Sanctuary
Kerteh
Sungai Tembeling
14
Kemasik
Kamping Kuala Tahan
Gunung Besar (790m)
Kemaman
124
Sungai Kemaman
Kijal
3
Kenong Rimba State Park
Kemaman
Cukai
Sungai Jelai
PAHANG
Sungai Cherul
Cherating
Kuala Tembeling
Sungai Pahang
Gunung Tapis (1512m)
East Coast Hwy
Jerantut

KELANTAN

Travellers often rush through Malaysia's northeasternmost state, seeing it as a waypoint between Thailand and Pulau Perhentian. Those who don't linger miss out experiencing a stronghold of Malay culture and one of Southeast Asia's great buffer zones, combining a distinctive blend of Chinese, Indian, Thai and Malay cultures.

Kelantan is also one of Malaysia's most conservative regions, and the state has been ruled by the Islamic Party of Malaysia (PAS) since 1990. PAS has made ongoing attempts to introduce 'hudud' (strict sharia laws, and the harsh punishments applicable to them), but this has been continually overruled by the federal government on constitutional grounds. Despite the conservative political environment, the Kelantanese people are friendly and welcoming to visitors to their state.

Kota Bharu

POP 491,000

Kota Bharu has the energy of a mid-size city but the compact feel and friendly vibe of a small town, with superb food and a good spread of accommodation. A logical overnight stop between Thailand and the Perhentians, KB is a good base for exploring Kelantan. The state's villages are within day-tripping distance, and its crafts, cuisine and culture are present in the city itself.

Sights

Gathered around the Padang Merdeka area of Kota Bharu is a cluster of excellent **museums** (www.muzium.kelantan.gov.my). Spend a leisurely day exploring them and you'll be well on your way to becoming a semi-expert in Malay history and culture. Nearby are good restaurants and shopping opportunities for between exhibition downtime. If you've only got half a day, your priority should be Istana Jahar and Istana Batu.

GET CULTURED

Local cultural events, including *gasing uri* (top-spinning), *silat* (a Malay martial art), kite-making, drumming and shadow-puppet shows, are held regularly at the **Gelanggang Seni** (Cultural Centre; ☎03-744 3124; Jln Mahmud). The events are especially kid-friendly, and all totally free. Sessions are held on Monday, Wednesday and Saturday from February to September, between 3.30pm and 5.30pm and 9pm and 11pm. Check with the tourist information centre (p289) for the full timetable.

Istana Jahar MUSEUM

(Royal Ceremonies Museum; Jln Istana; adult/child RM3/1.50; ⏲8.30am-4.45pm Sat-Wed, to 3.30pm Thu) Kota Bharu's best museum, both in terms of exhibits and structure. It's housed in a beautiful chocolate-brown building that dates back to 1887, easily one of the most attractive traditional buildings in the city. The interior displays focus on Kelatanese ritual and crafts, from detailed descriptions of batik-weaving to the elaborate ceremonies of coming-of-age circumcision, wedding nights and funerary rights.

Istana Batu MUSEUM

(Royal Museum, Muzium Diraja; Jln Istana; adult/child RM4/2; ⏲8.30am-4.45pm Sat-Wed, to 3.30pm Thu) The pale yellow Istana Batu, constructed in 1939, was the crown prince's palace until donated to the state. The richly furnished rooms give a surprisingly intimate insight into royal life, with family photos and personal belongings scattered among the fine china, chintzy sofas, and the late sultan's collection of hats.

Bank Kerapu MUSEUM

(WWII Memorial Museum; Jln Sultan; adult/child RM4/2; ⏲8.30am-4.45pm Sat-Wed, to 3.30pm Thu) Built in 1912 for the Mercantile Bank of India, the Bank Kerapu building is a gem of colonial-era architecture. It was the first stone structure built in Kelantan, and during WWII, it was the HQ of the Kempai Tai, Japan's feared secret police. Today it is also known as the War Museum, thanks to its focus on the Japanese invasion and occupation of Malaya and the 1948 Emergency. Exhibits mainly consist of old photography, rusty guns and other militaria.

Muzium Islam MUSEUM

(Islamic Museum; Jln Sultan; ⏲8.30am-4.45pm Sat-Wed, to 3.30pm Thu) FREE Muzium Islam occupies an old villa once known as Serambi Mekah (Verandah to Mecca) – a reference to its days as Kelantan's first school of Islamic instruction. Nowadays it displays a small collection of photographs and artefacts relating to the history of Islam in the state.

Kota Bharu

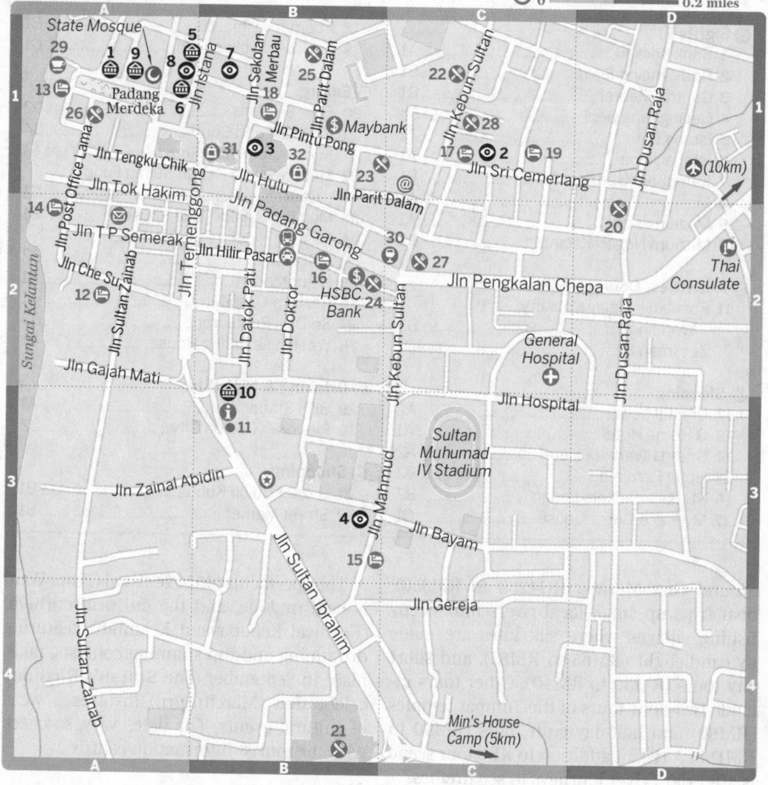

Kampung Kraftangan ARTS CENTRE
(Handicraft Village; Jln Hilir Kota; village admission free, museum adult/child RM2/1; ⏲ museum 8.30am-4.45pm Sat-Thu) This handicraft market, a touristy affair opposite Istana Batu, has a one-room museum with displays of woodcarving, batik-making and other crafts.

Muzium Negeri Kelanta MUSEUM
(State Museum; ☎ 09-748 2266; Jln Hospital; adult/child RM4/2; ⏲ 8.30am-4.45pm Sat-Wed, to 3.30pm Thu) This museum, next to the tourist information centre, is the official state museum. The exhibits on Kelantan's history and culture are interesting, but the accompanying signage is poor.

Courses

Some hostels can arrange cooking courses.

Zecsman Design BATIK PAINTING
(☎ 012-929 2822; www.facebook.com/zecsman; Jln Hilir Kota, Kampung Kraftangan; courses half-day RM50-70, full-day RM150; ⏲ 10am-5pm Sat-Thu) Buy ready-made batik or try your hand at batik painting at Zecsman Design's tutored four- to five-hour classes. Cost depends on the size and fabric used in your work.

Roselan's Malay Cookery Workshop COOKING COURSE
(☎ 012-909 6068; per person RM125, minimum group size of 2) The ever cheerful Roselan runs this popular Malay cookery workshop. Students are invited to a middle-class Malay home (Roselan's own or other locals'), and taught to cook typical Malay dishes. Contact Roselan by phone or ask for him at the tourist information centre. Call ahead for the address.

Tours

Most hostels and hotels can organise tours for their guests. Possible tours include two-day, three-night expeditions into the jungle

Kota Bharu

Sights

1 Bank Kerapu A1
2 Bird-Singing Field C1
3 Central Market B1
4 Gelanggang Seni B3
5 Istana Batu A1
6 Istana Jahar A1
7 Kampung Kraftangan B1
8 Museum Precinct A1
9 Muzium Islam A1
10 Muzium Negeri Kelanta B3

Activities, Courses & Tours

11 Roselan's Malay Cookery Workshop B3
Zecsman Design (see 7)

Sleeping

12 Crystal Lodge A2
13 G Home Hotel A1
14 Grand Riverview Hotel A2
15 Hotel Perdana B3
16 KB Backpackers Lodge B2
17 My Place Guest House C1
18 Room @ Zishi B1
19 Zeck's Traveller's Inn C1

Eating

20 Four Seasons D2
21 KB Mall Food Court B4
Kedai Kopi White House (see 6)
22 Medan Selera Kebun Sultan Food Court C1
23 Muhibah Aneka Cake House B1
24 Nasi Air Hideng Pok Sen Food Court B2
25 Night Market B1
26 Restoran Capital A1
27 Sri Devi Restaurant C2
28 West Lake Eating House C1

Drinking & Nightlife

29 Bike Station Cafe A1
30 Restoran Golden City C2

Shopping

31 Bazaar Buluh Kubu B1
32 Street Market B1

around Gua Musang (RM280 to RM350), boat trips up small local rivers into sleepy fishing villages where silk kites are made by candlelight (RM65 to RM85), and short city tours (RM30 to RM40). Other tours include two-hour tours of the Tumpat temples (RM80) and half-day craft tours (RM90 to RM115). A recent addition to KB's tour scene is after-dark river journeys to see fireflies.

Pawi at KB Backpackers Lodge, Zeck at Zeck's Traveller's Inn, and freelance tour guide **Roselan** (017-933 7242), who runs Roselan's Malay Cookery Workshop (p285), are all reputable and knowledgeable.

Festivals & Events

Kota Bharans love birdsong, to the point where they broadcast the chirping of birds in an abandoned building across loudspeakers set up through the city.

Each year around August the city holds a **bird-singing contest**, at Padang Perdana near the Sultan Muhumad IV Stadium, where Malay songbirds perform in ornate cages. Most Friday and Saturday mornings there's also a bird-singing contest at the **bird-singing field** (Jln Sri Cemerlang), where locals hang decorative bird cages up on long poles, then sit back and listen. Travellers are often invited to watch and even provide a bit of amateur judging.

The spectacular **kite festival** (Pesta Wau) is held in June, and the **cultural carnival** (Karnival Kebudayaan Kelantan), featuring drumming and top-spinning contests, takes place in September. The **Sultan's Birthday** celebration (March/April) involves a week of cultural events. The dates vary, so check with the tourist information centre.

Sleeping

There's plenty of cheap accommodation around town. Midrange and luxury options are aimed at business travellers.

Zeck's Traveller's Inn HOMESTAY $
(019-946 6655; zecktravelers@gmail.com; 7088-G Jln Sri Cemerlang; dm/s/d from RM12/15/25, r with air-con RM45-70;) Zeck and Miriam Zaki's home is located in a peaceful nook north of the city centre, with an attractive little garden to lounge about in and light meals and drinks always at hand. This family-owned place is a great way to get a feel for genuine Malaysian *kampung* (village) life in the heart of Kota Bharu.

The Zaki family are a mine of information and travel hook-ups, and will be glad to help you with your ongoing travel plans throughout Malaysia. Zeck also helps to arrange tours into Taman Negara through the park's far-less trammelled Kelantan entrance, and also to Gunung Stong State Park.

Room @ Zishi GUESTHOUSE $
(☎012-921 8103; theroom.zishi@hotmail.com; 67 Jln Pintu Pong; r/f from RM90/165; ❄📶) Stylish decor features at this well-run guesthouse located opposite Kota Bharu's central market. Rooms are furnished with an Asian Zen simplicity, and the shared downstairs area, complete with a full kitchen, has a cool relaxation space with lots of throw cushions and shag pile carpet. A key card system guarantees security. Note that cheaper rooms don't have windows.

KB Backpackers Lodge HOSTEL $
(☎019-944 5222, 09-748 8841; backpackerslodge2@yahoo.co.uk; 1872-D Jln Padang Garong; dm/r from RM15/35; ❄@) Owner Pawi is a wealth of information, dorms and rooms are simple but clean, there's a rooftop terrace, and local city tours can be arranged. Pawi is also a mad bicycling enthusiast and organises bike trips (on and off road) and rents out high-quality bicycles to guests. Make sure you've got the right place – a somewhat dingy hostel calling itself KB Backpackers Inn operates across the street.

My Place Guest House GUESTHOUSE $
(☎013-9011 463; myplacekb@yahoo.com; 4340-R2 Jln Kebun Sultan; s/d RM35/50; ❄📶) Just a short stroll from Chinatown, My Place Guest House is a welcoming and friendly spot. Retro posters including the Beatles and Che Guevara punctuate the eclectically furnished interior, and the rooms are simple but clean. Interesting shared spaces make it a good place to meet younger Malaysian travellers, and to get their local lowdown on where to travel to next.

G Home Hotel HOTEL $
(☎09-747 2219; www.ghomehotel.my; Pelangi Mall; s/d from RM60/100; ❄📶) Newly opened and featuring river views, G Home may well be KB's most colourful hotel. Rooms are decked out in a fetching shade of lime green, and bathrooms combine brown and white tiles. Some rooms are definitely compact, but the location is great with good restaurants nearby.

Grand Riverview Hotel HOTEL $$
(☎09-743 9988; www.grh.com.my; 9 Jln Post Office Lama; r/ste from RM270/1190; ❄@📶🏊) Perched on the river edge, this huge hotel offers high standards at reasonable prices; long-term 'promotions' will shave up to 50% off the published rates. Rooms at the back have some fine views across the water, and all have king-sized beds and big bathrooms with both showers and baths.

Min House Camp HOMESTAY $$
(☎013-922 5440; www.minkem.com; Lot 1287, Kg Pulau, Kubang Kerian; hut per person from RM20, apt RM110-180; ❄@📶) Around 6km from central Kota Bharu, Min House Camp combines a riverside location, complete with huge deck, and accommodation ranging from basic huts through to rooms and apartments perfect for groups and families. There's a strong emphasis on experiencing authentic Malay culture with opportunities for after-dark firefly cruises, handicraft workshops, and playing traditional games and sports.

Note that the property is popular with Malaysian school groups.

Crystal Lodge HOTEL $$
(☎09-747 0888; www.crystallodge.com.my; 124 Jln Che Su; s/d from RM100/150; ❄@📶) This clean and airy place is decent value, with comfortable rooms, free in-house movies and daily newspapers. There's an attractive rooftop restaurant with a great view over the river.

Hotel Perdana HOTEL $$
(☎09-7458 888; www.hotelperdanakotabharu.com; Jln Mahmud; d from RM300; ❄📶🏊) Reopened in 2014 after substantial renovations, the Moorish-accented Hotel Perdana is hands down the flashest accommodation in town. A glorious lobby with colourful examples of *wau bulan* (Malaysian kites) segues to spacious and stylish rooms. Additional services include a well-equipped gym, swimming pool, and five relaxing restaurants and cafes.

Eating & Drinking

Apart from KB's night market (p288), options for traditional Malay food are limited in the evening, and your best bet for dinner is to head to the Chinese restaurants and food courts along Jln Kebun Sultan.

Restoran Capital MALAYSIAN $
(Jln Post Office Lama; mains from RM5; ⊙7am-1pm) For our favourite breakfast, get here before 9am when the excellent *nasi kerabu* (blue rice with coconut, fish and spices) usually sells out. Nutty rice combines with a variety of subtle Kelantanese curries, and optional extras include eggs and crunchy crackers. It's also a top spot for an iced coffee or other snacks like *popiah* (fresh spring

QUICK EATS IN KOTA BHARU

One of the great things about KB is how well (and cheaply) you can eat without ever setting foot into a restaurant.

Night Market (Jln Parit Dalam; mains from RM4; ⊙5-9pm) The most popular spot for the best and cheapest Malay food in town is KB's night market, where stalls are set up in the evening. Specialties include *ayam percik* (marinated chicken on bamboo skewers) and *nasi kerabu*, squid-on-a-stick and *murtabak* (pan-fried flat bread filled with everything from minced meat to bananas). Say '*Suka pedas*' ('I like it hot') to eat as the locals do.

Nasi Air Hideng Pok Sen Food Court (Jln Padang Garong; mains from RM4; ⊙8am-5pm) The Nasi Air Hideng Pok Sen Food Court has several stalls serving Malay specialties and a self-serve buffet.

Medan Selera Kebun Sultan Food Court (Jln Kebun Sultan; mains from RM4; ⊙noon-11pm) The Medan Selera Kebun Sultan Food Court offers Chinese dishes like claypot chicken rice and *kway teow* (rice-flour noodles). They will also serve you an ice-cold beer, and are open late in a town that closes early.

KB Mall Food Court (Jln Hamzah; mains from RM4; ⊙noon-9pm) There's a food court serving international fast food (burgers, fried chicken) inside KB Mall. The mall is south of central KB, on the corner of Jln Hamzah and Jln Sultan Ibrahim.

rolls) from the other stallholders filling the heritage space.

Sri Devi Restaurant INDIAN $
(4213-F Jln Kebun Sultan; mains from RM5; ⊙7am-9pm ; 🅿) As popular with locals as it is with tourists, this is a great place for an authentic banana-leaf curry and a mango lassi. They also serve a great *ayam percik*, and terrific *roti canai* (flaky flat bread served with curry) in the morning and evening.

West Lake Eating House CHINESE $
(Jln Kebun Sultan; mains from RM5; ⊙10am-8pm; 🅿) Don't let the plain decor fool you. West Lake Eating House serves some of the tastiest Chinese fare in Eastern Malaysia. Esoteric dishes like stewed bean curd stuffed with fish cakes and lightly sautéed purple eggplant with garlic sauce share the steam table with more common (but no less delicious) dishes like braised pork ribs, roast duck and stir-fried vegetables.

Kedai Kopi White House CAFE $
(1329-L Jln Sultan Zainab; snacks from RM3; ⊙7am-3pm) For a classic local experience, pop into this old-school Chinese coffee shop for a tea or coffee while you're exploring Kota Bharu's museum precinct. The ambience is straight from decades past, and a lazy brunch of runny boiled eggs, crisp toast and homemade *kaya* (coconut jam) should definitely be considered. Don't forget a squirt of soy sauce.

Muhibah Aneka Cake House CAFE $
(Jln Pintu Pong; mains from RM5; ⊙8am-10pm) In addition to serving the best iced cappuccino in town (a good thing in a city where instant coffee is the rule), this lovely bakery also has great cakes, iced desserts and even doughnuts. Stop by for a green tea frappe and a chocolate and cashew doughnut for a mid-afternoon treat.

Four Seasons CHINESE $$
(www.fourseasonsrestaurant.com.my; 5670 Jln Sri Cemerlang; mains from RM15; ⊙noon-2.30pm & 6-10pm) The Four Seasons is packed nightly with locals enjoying seafood dishes like claypot prawn and dry cuttlefish with mango salad. The house speciality, deep fried soft-shell crab, should only set you back about RM40 for two people (it's priced by weight).

Restoran Golden City PUB
(Jln Padang Garong; ⊙4pm-midnight Sun-Fri; 📶) Your only options for a cold beer in KB are the restaurants and food centres in Chinatown, or this centrally located combination of pub and sports bar. The food's only average, but a cold pint of Tiger beer goes down very well during happy hour from 4pm to 9pm.

Bike Station Cafe CAFE
(Jln Sultan; ⊙2pm-midnight Thu-Tue) Look forward to elevated river views, a huge menu of hot and cold drinks, a tasty array of local

snacks (from RM3), and your best chance to meet some young English-speaking locals. Downstairs you can rent bikes to explore KB's riverfront esplanade (one/two hours RM20/25). The nearby area is often filled with local buskers on weekend afternoons from around 4pm.

Shopping

Kota Bharu is a centre for Malay crafts. Batik, *kain songket* (traditional handwoven fabric with gold threads), silverware, woodcarving and kite-making factories and shops are dotted around town.

One of the best places to see handicrafts is on the road north to Pantai Cahaya Bulan (PCB). There are a number of workshops stretched out along the road to the beach. Rent a bicycle from KB Backpackers Lodge (p287) or a scooter from Zeck's Traveller's Inn (p286) for the journey.

Central Market MARKET
(Pasar Besar Siti Khadijah; Jln Hulu; ⌚6am-6pm) One of the most colourful and active markets in Malaysia, KB's central market is at its busiest first thing in the morning, and has usually packed up by early afternoon. Downstairs is the produce section, while upstairs stalls selling spices, brassware, batik and other goods stay open longer. On the 1st floor, there's a tasty array of food stalls and it's a top spot for breakfast or lunch.

Bazaar Buluh Kubu HANDICRAFTS
(Jln Hulu; ⌚8am-6pm Sat-Thu) Near the central market, Bazaar Buluh Kubu is a good place to buy handicrafts such as batik, traditional Malay clothing and jewellery.

Street Market MARKET
(Jln Parit Dalam; ⌚6-10pm) A market selling fake designer clothes, imitation watches and bootleg DVDs takes over the street in the evenings.

Information

HSBC Bank (Jln Padang Garong; ⌚10am-3pm Sat-Wed, 9.30-11.30am Thu) Centrally located with ATM.

Maybank (Jln Pintu Pong; 10am-7pm Sat-Thu) Has an ATM.

Multimedia Internet (171 Jln Parit Dalam; per hr RM2.50) A short walk from the bus station.

Tourist Information Centre (☎09-748 5534; www.tic-kelantan.gov.my; Jln Sultan Ibrahim; ⌚8am-5pm Sun-Wed, to 3.30pm Thu, to 1.30pm Fri & Sat) Information on homestays, tours and transport.

Getting There & Away

AIR

Daily flights to major domestic destinations like Kuala Lumpur depart from Kota Bharu's Sultan Ismail Petra Airport. A number of airlines have offices inside the airport.

AirAsia (☎09-746 1671; www.airasia.com) To/from Kuala Lumpur, Kota Kinabalu, Johor Bahru and Kuching.

Firefly (☎03-7845 4543; www.fireflyz.com.my) To/from Kuala Lumpur, Penang and Johor Bahru.

Malindo Air (☎7841 5388; www.malindoair.com) To/from Kuala Lumpur, Melaka, Ipoh and Penang.

GETTING TO THAILAND: RANTAU PANJANG TO SUNGAI KOLOK

Getting to the Border

The Thailand border is at Rantau Panjang; bus 29 departs on the hour from Kota Bharu's central bus station (RM4, 1½ hours). Share taxis, also departing from the central bus station, cost around RM40 per car and take 45 minutes.

There's another border crossing at Pengkalan Kubor, on the coast, but transport links aren't as good and crossing here can be dodgy during periods of sectarian violence in southern Thailand. Enquire at the tourist information centre before using this crossing. During the day a large car ferry (RM1 for pedestrians) crosses the river to busy Tak Bai in Thailand. From Kota Bharu, take bus 27 or 43 (RM2.40) from the central bus station.

At the Border

From Rantau Panjang you can walk across the border to Sungai Kolok, where you can arrange ongoing transport to Bangkok. Trains to Bangkok depart at 11.30am and 2pm, buses at 8am, 11.30am and 3.30pm, and there are hourly minibuses from Sungai Kolok to Hat Yai.

Malaysia Airlines (☎09-771 4703; www.malaysiaairlines.com) To/from Kuala Lumpur.

BUS

Local buses and Transnasional express buses operate from the **central bus station** (☎09-747 5971, 09-747 4330; Jln Padang Garong). Other express and long-distance buses leave from **Lembah Sireh Bus Station** near the Kota Bharu Tesco; a taxi from this bus station to the centre of town is around RM15.

Most regional buses leave from the central bus station. Destinations include Wakaf Baharu (buses 19 and 27, RM1.60), Rantau Panjang (bus 29, RM5) and Tumpat (bus 19 and 43, RM3).

For the Perhentian Islands there are regular departures from 6am to 6.30pm to Kuala Besut (bus 639, RM6, around two hours).

Long-Distance Buses from Kota Bharu

DESTINATION	PRICE	DURATION
Alor Setar	RM43	7 hours
Butterworth	RM42	7 hours
Gua Musang	RM18	4 hours
Ipoh	RM40	6 hours
Kuala Lumpur	RM49	8 hours
Kuala Terengganu	RM19	3 hours
Kuantan	RM31	6 hours
Lumut	RM49	7 hours
Melaka	RM64	10 hours
Singapore	RM98	12 hours

CAR

Hire cars from **Hawk** (☎773 3824; www.hawkrentacar.com.my; Sultan Ismail Petra Airport) at the airport.

TAXI

The **taxi stand** is on the southern side of the central bus station. Avoid the unlicensed cab drivers who will pester you around town, and take an official taxi as these are cheaper and safer.

For early morning trains, arrange for the taxi to Wakaf Baharu the night before at your guesthouse. A taxi to Kuala Besut for boats to the Perhentian Islands is around RM45.

TRAIN

The nearest railway station is **Wakaf Baharu** (☎09-719 6986), around 10km west of Kota Bharu; it can be reached by local buses 19 or 17.

At the time of writing, trains to the south were suspended due to severe floods in December 2014. The service was scheduled to recommence in late 2016 and the following details reflect the timetable before the floods. Check with the **tourist information centre** (p289) in Kota Bharu or see the **Malaysian Railways** website, www.ktmb.com.my, for the latest.

A daily express train to KL (13 hours) leaves Wakaf Baharu at 6.45pm stopping at Kuala Lipis, Jerantut and Gemas. Two daily local trains stop at almost every station to Kuala Lipis (13 hours), and five local trains per day go as far as Gua Musang (five to six hours).

For details on the status of the Jungle Railway linking Kota Bharu to Dabong for the Gunung Stong State Park, contact local guide **Bukhari 'Bob' Mat** in Jelawang about alternative bus services.

ℹ Getting Around

Kota Bharu's Sultan Ismail Petra Airport is 9km outside the city centre. Bus No 9 (RM3, 20 minutes) leaves hourly from the main bus station. Taxis are around RM35.

Around Kota Bharu

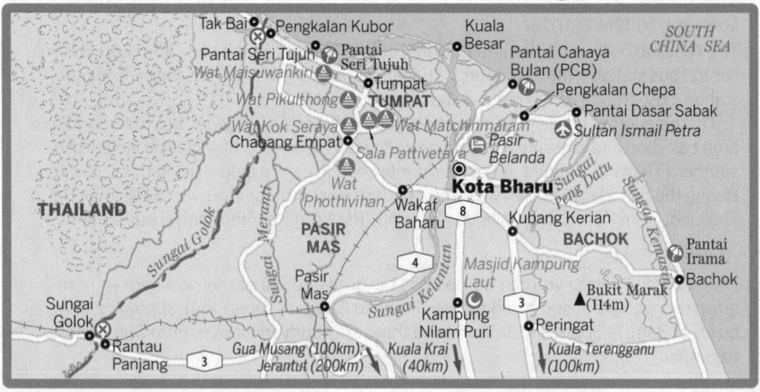

Trishaws can still be seen on the city streets, though they are not as common as they once were. Prices are negotiable but expect to pay around RM5 and upwards for a short journey of up to 1km.

Around Kota Bharu

Pantai Cahaya Bulan

Kota Bharu's main beach was once known as Pantai Cinta Berahi, or the Beach of Passionate Love. In keeping with Islamic sensibilities, it's now known as Pantai Cahaya Bulan (PCB), or Moonlight Beach, but most people call it PCB. Erosion over recent years has seen the installation of a concrete breakwater, but PCB's sandy sprawl is still worth considering for a seafood lunch and a day's escape from Kota Bharu's dusty streets.

The road leading to PCB is quite pretty, especially by bicycle, and there are batik shops and workshops along the way. To get here by public transport, take bus 10 (RM1.60) from behind Kampung Kraftangan in Kota Bharu. Buses also leave from the main bus station.

Tumpat's Temples

North of Kota Bharu, the Tumpat district is Malaysia's culturally diverse hinterland, neither wholly Malay nor Thai, with a dash of Chinese culture thrown in. Numerous

KELANTAN'S WILD INTERIOR

To really understand Kelantan, you need to penetrate its wild and woolly southern jungle interior, accessible via the so-called Jungle Railway ('so-called' since much of the once-verdant jungle has been hacked down to make way for palm-oil plantations). Some jungle does remain though, and peeks of peninsular Malaysia's mountainous backbone still evoke a feeling of tropical frontier adventure.

At the time of writing, the Jungle Railway linking Kota Bharu to Dabong had been suspended due to serious floods in December 2014; the service was scheduled to recommence by mid-2016. Alternative bus services via Kuala Krai or Jeli were running.

Lined with flowers, trees and a mixture of old- and new-style *kampung* (village) houses, the pretty jungle town of **Dabong** is an excellent exploration base. The town is about three hours by train from Tumpat and has restaurants, shops and guesthouses. The best place to stay is **Rose House** (☎019-9606 789; www.facebook.com/Rose.House.Dabong; Dabong; r RM60-100; ❄), a five-minute walk from the train station. Ask for Abang Din when you book.

The nearby village of **Jelawang** has the new **Jlawe Lodging House** (☎019-979 1099; bobtg6084@gmail.com; Jelawang; r RM35-80; ❄), around 10 minutes' walk from the entrance to Gunung Stong State Park.

There are several caves in the limestone outcrops a few kilometres southeast of Dabong; **Gua Ikan** (Fish Cave) is the most accessible, but the most impressive is **Stepping Stone Cave**, a narrow 30m corridor through a limestone wall that leads to a hidden grotto and on to **Kris Cave**. These latter two should not be attempted by those who experience claustrophobia.

About 15km from Dabong is **Gunung Stong State Park**. Named for the 1422m-high Gunung Stong mountain, the park offers amazing hiking, swimming and trekking. Next to the mountain, the park's star attractions are its waterfalls, located a 20-minute climb past the park's main resort. A further 45 minutes of climbing brings you to the top of the falls and a camp site, from which you can make longer excursions to the mountain's summit and the upper falls. Most tour companies divide the trek into three checkpoints. A combination of jungle mist and mountain fog can make for hazy conditions, but on good days you get the sense you're climbing over clouds humming with the calls of animals in the jungle below.

It is possible to explore the area via a tour organised in Kota Bharu, or just head down yourself and hire a taxi from Dabong train station. However, to get the most out of a visit, it's strongly recommended you contact the experienced and well-regarded **Bukhari 'Bob' Mat** (☎019-979 1099; www.kelantanature.blogspot.com) in Jelawang. With excellent English skills and boundless enthusiasm for the area, Bob leads caving, hiking and rafting tours, and has also launched river tubing on automotive tyre tubes. He is also the contact for Jlawe Lodging House and can provide the latest updates on the Jungle Railway.

DON'T MISS

PASIR BELANDA HOMESTAY

The **Pasir Belanda Homestay** (☎09-747 7046; www.kampungstay.com; Jln PCB, Pantai Cahaya Bulan; d RM175-210; ❄≋), around 4km from Kota Bharu, may well be one of Kelantan's nicest accommodation options. Three sizes of traditional Malay homes have been decked out with crisp bed linen and luxuries such as coffee makers. Explore a nearby beach, or just watch the stars from under your *kampung*–style awning. Cooking classes, batik and kite decoration workshops, and cycling and kayaking can also be arranged, and there's a spectacular swimming pool with river views.

To get here, take bus 10 (RM1.60) from behind Kampung Kraftangan in Kota Bharu. Buses also leave from the central bus station. A taxi costs around RM15. Pasir Belanda will arrange a pickup from Kota Bharu (RM15) or Sultan Ismail Petra Airport (RM30) with advance notice.

Buddhist temples are found all over the region, and **Wesak Day** (a celebration of Buddha's life, usually held in April or May) is a good time to visit. The area is serviced by some local buses. Alternatively, arrange a tour with Zeck's Travellers' Inn or KB Backpackers Lodge, or rent a scooter or car.

Supposedly one of the largest Buddhist temples in Southeast Asia, **Wat Phothivihan** boasts a 40m-long reclining Buddha statue, erected in 1973. There are some smaller shrines within the grounds, as well as a canteen and a rest house for use by sincere devotees, for a donation. Take bus 19 or 27 from Kota Bharu to Chabang Empat. Get off at the crossroads and turn left (southwest). Walk 3.5km along this road until you reach Kampung Jambu and the reclining Buddha (about one hour).

At Chabang Empat, if you turn to the right (north) at the light in front of the police station, you will come to **Wat Kok Seraya** after about 1km, which houses a modest standing female Buddha. While the temple's architecture is Thai, the female Buddha is more Chinese, which is probably attributable to most Buddhists here being of Chinese origin. Continuing north about 4km towards Tumpat is **Wat Pikulthong**, housing an impressive gold mosaic standing Buddha. You can get to both on bus 19; continue past Chabang Empat and ask the driver to let you off.

Around 4km north of Chabang Empat near the village of Kampung Bukit Tanah is **Wat Maisuwankiri**. A richly decorated dragon boat surrounded by murky water constitutes the 'floating temple', but of more interest is the preserved body of a former abbot on morbid public display. The bus from Kota Bharu's central bus station to Pengkalan Kubor (around 30 minutes) stops outside the temple.

Also worth a look is **Wat Matchinmaram** with its magnificent 50m-high seated Buddha (more Chinese than Thai, but also decorated with an Indian-origin dharma wheel), allegedly the largest of its type in Asia. Just across the road from here is **Sala Pattivetaya**, a Thai temple and village complex dotted with colourful statues. They are located about 2km south of Tumpat.

EAST COAST ISLANDS

Pulau Perhentian

The Perhentians boast waters simultaneously electric teal and crystal clear, jungles thick and fecund, and beaches with blindingly white sand. At night, beach bonfires and phosphorescence in the water illuminate the velvety black fabric of darkness, and myriad stars are mirrored above.

There are two main islands, Kecil ('Small'), popular with the younger backpacker crowd, and Besar ('Large'), with higher standards of accommodation and a more relaxed ambience. The quick hop between the two costs around RM20.

While you can usually find a beach party, the Perhentians are a long way from having a Thai-style party atmosphere. Alcohol is available at a few restaurants and bars.

Even paradise has its problems, though. The Perhentians are finding it increasingly difficult to deal with the by-product of increasing tourist traffic, and the sight (and smell) of burning piles of rubbish, especially plastic bottles, is unfortunately common. Fortunately, a passionate network of

Pulau Perhentian

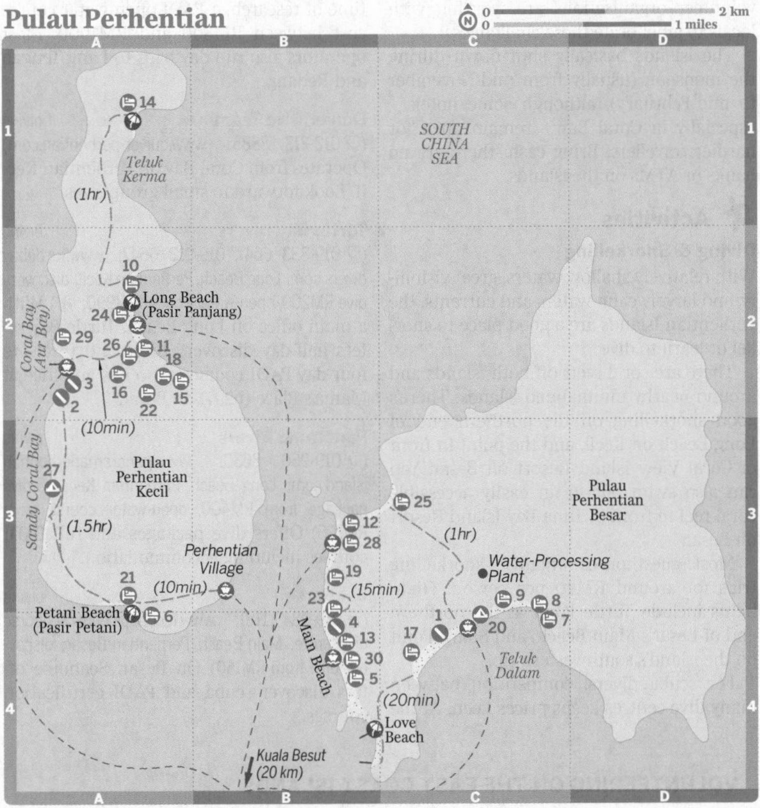

Pulau Perhentian

Activities, Courses & Tours

1 Alu Alu Divers C4
2 Angel Divers A2
Flora Bay Divers .... (see 17)
Leisure Divers .... (see 7)
Panorama Divers .... (see 24)
Pro Diver's World .... (see 12)
3 Quiver Dive Team A2
4 Seahorse B4
Turtle Bay Divers .... (see 19)
Turtle Bay Divers .... (see 14)

Sleeping

5 Abdul's Chalets B4
6 Alunan Boutique Resort A4
7 Arwana Perhentian Resort C4
Aur Bay Chalet .... (see 2)
8 Bayu Dive Lodge C3
9 B'First Chalet C3
10 BuBu Resort A2
11 BuBu Villa A2
12 Coral View Island Resort B3
13 D'Ayumni House B4
14 D'Lagoon Chalets A1
15 D'Rock Garden Resort A2
16 Ewan's Place A2
17 Flora Bay Resort C4
18 Lemon Grass A2
19 Mama's Place B3
20 Mandalica Beach Resort C4
21 Mari Mari Beach Bar & Resort A3
Maya Guest House .... (see 2)
22 Mohsin Chalet Bungalows A2
23 New Cocohut B3
24 Panorama Diver & Chalet A2
25 Perhentian Island Resort C3
26 Perhentian Tropicana Inn A2
27 RainForest Camping A3
28 Reef Chalets B3
Samudra Beach Chalet .... (see 8)
29 Shari-la Island Resort A2
30 Tuna Bay Island Resort B4

Eating

Santai .... (see 10)
World Cafe .... (see 11)

volunteer organisations are working with locals to ameliorate these challenges.

The islands basically shut down during the monsoon (usually from mid-November to mid-February), although some hotels – especially in Coral Bay – remain open for hardier travellers. Bring cash: there are no banks or ATMs on the islands.

Activities

Diving & Snorkelling

With relatively shallow waters, great visibility, and largely calm waters and currents, the Perhentian Islands are a good place to snorkel or learn to dive.

There are coral reefs off both islands and around nearby uninhabited islands. There's good snorkelling off the northern end of Long Beach on Kecil, and the point in front of Coral View Island Resort on Besar. You can also swim out to an easily accessible coral reef in front of Tuna Bay Island Resort on Besar.

Most guesthouses organise snorkelling trips for around RM40 per person. Highlights include Turtle Point at the northern end of Besar's Main Beach, and Shark Point on the island's southwestern tip.

For scuba divers, competition between many dive centres keeps prices keen. At the time of research, a PADI open-water course cost between RM800 and RM1000. Most operators also run day trips to Lang Tengah and Redang.

Quiver Dive Team DIVING
(012-213 8885; www.quiver-perhentian.com) Operates from Coral Bay on Perhentian Kecil. Look forward to small group sizes.

Turtle Bay Divers DIVING
(019-333 6647, 019-913 6647; www.turtlebaydivers.com; Long Beach, Perhentian Kecil; discovery dive RM200, open-water course RM990;) With a main office on Long Beach, Turtle Bay offers half-day discovery dives and three- to four-day PADI courses. Also has an office at Mama's Place (p297) on Besar.

Panorama Divers DIVING
(019-960 8630; www.panoramaperhentianisland.com; Long Beach, Perhentian Kecil; 5-dive package from RM400, open-water course from RM795) Offers dive packages and full PADI courses including accommodation.

Seahorse DIVING
(019-984 1181; www.facebook.com/Seahorsedivecentre; Main Beach, Perhentian Besar; discovery dive from RM150) On Besar, Seahorse offers discover scuba and PADI certification courses.

VOLUNTEERING ON THE EAST COAST ISLANDS

Keen to give back to the precious and varied marine life of Malaysia's East Coast islands? Consider signing up to one of the marine-focused volunteer projects on the Perhentians or Pulau Lang Tengah.

Blue Temple Conservation (www.bluetemple.co.uk; Perhentian Kecil; one/two weeks RM2500/4500) Combines diving and assisting with the sustainable management of the islands' marine resources. Volunteer activities include beach-cleaning and educating snorkelling groups about why hand-feeding fish is harmful to the marine ecosystem. Costs include all meals, transfers and accommodation in the funky village house at Blue Temple on Perhentian Kecil. Add RM400 for a PADI open-water course.

Perhentian Turtle Project (www.perhentianturtleproject.com; Perhentian Besar; one/two weeks RM1400/2300) The Perhentian Turtle Project is focused on supporting the islands' sea turtle population. Activities include daily snorkelling trips to identify and catalogue turtles, night beach patrols, and educating locals and visitors. See the website for how travellers can also play their part with underwater cameras and Instagram. Volunteer programs include meals and transfers, and accommodation is near Main Beach on Perhentian Besar.

Lang Tengah Turtle Watch (http://langtengahturtlewatch.org; Turtle Bay; per week US$240) Lang Tengah Turtle Watch works to safeguard the island's population of nesting turtles (mostly green). Volunteers assist with tasks such as beach patrols, egg collection and data maintenance, with the bonus of observing turtles come ashore to lay their eggs (April to October), and hatchlings emerge around 100 days later. Programs include basic accommodation and meals.

LOCAL KNOWLEDGE

LOCAL VOICE: BIRGIT WEBER

An instructor and assistant manager of the **Turtle Bay Divers**, Birgit Weber has been diving for over 25 years. Birgit chatted with us about different dive spots around the country.

What can I expect to see while diving around Perhentian? Everything from turtles to black-tipped reef sharks, many varieties of stingrays, and parrot fish – if it lives on the reef, you'll see it here.

What's the best spot for diving around the Perhentian Islands? Sugar Wreck is a huge shipwreck, and every year there seem to be more and more fish around it. It's only 18m deep, so any diver who's taken the open-water course can go down there. It's also only 20 minutes from Long Beach. The Pinnacle is also great. You can see a huge variety of marine life in one place.

What's the best spot in Malaysia for the advanced diver? Sipadan Island, off the coast of Sabah in Malaysian Borneo. It's an oceanic island as opposed to being on the continental shelf, so it drops down quite deep. You'll see dozens of turtles and sharks. The sheer number of marine animals you'll see is overwhelming. You need a permit to dive there, so book in advance.

How about for the beginner? Definitely Perhentian. The dive sites are shallow and generally have lighter currents. They're also nearby, meaning less time on the boat. One of them you can even swim to!

What's your take on Tioman diving? Tioman sites are a lot like those in Perhentian, but the dive sites are further from the shore, meaning more time in the boat. Plus, Tioman is closer to Singapore and KL, so the island tends to be more commercial and crowded. I prefer Perhentian myself.

Pro Diver's World DIVING
(☎09-691 1705; www.prodiversworld.com) Connected to Coral View Resort on Besar; offers accommodation and diving course specials in conjunction with the resort. Look forward to a special deal if it's your birthday.

Leisure Divers DIVING
(☎019-980 5977; www.divingperhentian.com.my; open-water course RM990) Offers underwater camera rental, dive packages and PADI certification courses. It's connected to Arwana Resort on Besar.

Angel Divers DIVING
(☎019-923 8840; www.facebook.com/angeldiversperhentian) Run from a red wooden hut at Coral Bay on Kecil.

Alu Alu Divers DIVING
(☎09-691 1650; www.alualudivers.com) Tuition is often from an experienced international crew. Located at Bayu Dive Lodge on Besar.

Flora Bay Divers DIVING
(☎09-691 1661; www.florabaydivers.com) At Teluk Dalam on Besar.

Hiking

There's plenty of hiking on both islands. On Kecil, the jungle track between Long Beach and Coral Bay is an easy 15-minute walk (around 1km) along a paved and signposted path through scrubby forest. A longer track (around 45 minutes, 2.5km) runs mostly along the shore between Coral Bay and Petani Beach. It's a lovely shaded walk with peeks of the ocean; keep an eye out for monitor lizards and local birdlife. An even longer and more rugged path (around one hour, 3km) goes between Long Beach and Teluk Kerma.

Besar has excellent hiking, including a long and hilly track (around one hour, 2.5km) cutting from north to south from close to Perhentian Island Resort to Teluk Dalam at Fauna Beach Chalet. The hike over the hill from Love Beach to Teluk Dalam (around 800m, 20 minutes) is also pretty steep and rugged, though somewhat shorter.

Some tracks can get washed out in heavy rains, so use common sense. Hot and humid is the norm, so bring plenty of water, and don't hike at night without a flashlight.

Sleeping & Eating

Besar

MAIN BEACH

Perhentian Besar's main beach stretches along the west coast of the island to the southern tip, interrupted by several rocky headlands – at low tide you can walk around them on the sand, otherwise you'll have to use a water taxi. A smaller beach taken up by Perhentian Island Resort is accessible via a footbridge on the northern end of the beach.

Reef Chalets BUNGALOW $$
(☎09-690 3669; www.facebook.com/The.Reef.Chalets; Main Beach; bungalow RM120-350; ❄📶) This family-owned resort offers 12 beautiful bungalows set along the beach, and surrounding a beautifully maintained jungle garden featuring trees filled with occasional lemurs, monkeys, birds and bats. The friendly owners rent out canoes and snorkelling equipment and can help you plan your stay. All bungalows have sea views; some are fan-cooled, while the more expensive ones have air-conditioning.

Coral View Island Resort RESORT $$
(☎09-697 4943; www.coralviewislandresort.com; Main Beach; r/ste from RM140/550; ❄📶) The ever-expanding Coral View has a great location at the northern end of Main Beach. Rooms range from simple fan-cooled, two-bed bungalows to rather smart air-conditioned beachfront suites. Coral View has good restaurants serving Asian and international dishes, shops, and a quiet beach at its northern edge.

FINDING THE RIGHT BEACH

With so many great options, your biggest dilemma on the Perhentians may well be choosing the right beach. Knowing the lay of the land will help you decide. A narrow strait separates Perhentian Besar from Perhentian Kecil, so hopping between the two is just a matter of flagging down a boat.

Main Beach (Besar)

A good selection of accommodation and a long stretch of white sand that's almost as lovely (and less prone to currents) as Long Beach on Kecil. There's no shortage of good spots to explore by walking either north or south. There's more of a family vibe happening on the big island than elsewhere.

Teluk Dalam (Besar)

The big island's 'southern bite,' this circular bay has white-sand beaches and excellent accommodation in all budget ranges. There are a few good restaurants, and good snorkelling spots on the bay's western edge.

Long Beach (Kecil)

Long Beach offers the best variety of budget accommodation and restaurants, from cookie-cutter BBQ beachfront joints to excellent cuisine at the World Cafe. It also has the prettiest beach and the most party-ish vibe. This brings crowds though, and Long Beach can sometimes feel overtouristed. This beautiful beach also has some serious rip currents, and in recent years there have been drownings.

Coral Bay (Kecil)

A good variety of accommodation in all budget ranges makes Coral Bay the spot for those wanting to stay within walking distance of Long Beach's party vibe without being in it. Coral Bay is more rocky than sandy. Note that a recent construction boom has diminished the quaintness of this once-quiet spot.

Teluk Kerma (Kecil)

Home to a single accommodation option, D'Lagoon Chalets (p299), this small bay has it going on when it comes to peace and quiet. There's great snorkelling, and a few equally isolated beaches within walking distance. But it's an hour's hike to your nearest neighbour (Long Beach), and if you stay out after dark your options for getting home will be limited and pricey (water taxis charge double after sundown).

New Cocohut BUNGALOW $$
(☎09-691 1811; www.perhentianislandcocohut.com; r RM 280-360; ❄📶) Cocohut has a good choice of rooms including pleasant beachside bungalows and a two-storey longhouse, which has some great views from the upstairs balcony. The cheapest rooms are in the rear and closest to the generator. Cocohut also manages another adjacent property called Cozy Chalet, which has loads of wooden accommodation cascading down a nearby hill. The attached restaurant at New Cocohut is popular.

Abdul's Chalets BUNGALOW $$
(☎019-912 7303; www.abdulchalet.com; r RM170-270; ❄📶) The once-humble Abdul's continues to upgrade to higher quality accommodation, and options range from garden view bungalows at the lower end of the price range to sea-view family rooms at the higher end. The dining area, where freshly caught fish and a variety of Malay and international dishes are served, is also pretty snazzy, and there's a handy minimart for snacks and drinks. The adjacent beach is safe and family-friendly.

Tuna Bay Island Resort RESORT $$
(☎09-690 2902; www.tunabay.com.my; Main Beach; d/tr/f from RM290/370/580; ❄@📶) This gathering of well-established bungalows perches on a lovely stretch of white sand, with others set in the pretty gardens or facing the jungle behind. Swim on a vibrant coral reef just offshore, or relax in the cocktail bar with a Long Island iced tea or cappuccino. For dinner, Tuna Bay serves multicourse BBQs featuring prawn, squid, barracuda, snapper and more.

D'Ayumni House BUNGALOW $$
(☎09-691 1680, 019-436 4463; http://d-ayumnihouse.blogspot.com; Main Beach; dm RM55, r RM140-180; ❄@📶) A pretty wooden house rises over a series of low-slung, chic teak bungalows. Popular with divers and those seeking a bit of a budget backpacker vibe on Besar. Owner Ms Lee is a fount of information, and can arrange ongoing travel all over Southeast Asia. She also has a little shop and cafe with a moonlight deck.

Mama's Place BUNGALOW $$
(☎013-984 0232, 019-985 3359; www.mamaschalet.com.my; Main Beach; bungalow RM80-170, f RM370; ❄📶) This sprawling property has 43 bungalows on the beach. All are comfortable and clean, and the more expensive ones have sea views and air-cons. Mama's also has an alcohol-free restaurant serving local dishes.

Perhentian Island Resort RESORT $$$
(☎691 1111; www.perhentianislandresort.net; Main Beach; r RM320-530; ❄📶🏊) Offering a bewildering variety of set three-day/two-night packages, this luxurious option overlooks perhaps the best beach on the islands – a beautiful half-moon bay with good coral around the points on either side. There's a huddle of comfortable bungalows and a first-class restaurant serving international and Malay dishes. Newly renovated garden bungalows are particularly comfortable.

TELUK DALAM

An easily missed track leads from behind the second jetty near Love Beach over the hill northeast to Teluk Dalam, a secluded bay with a shallow beach. It's easier to hire a boat than to walk.

Samudra Beach Chalet BUNGALOW $
(☎09-691 1677; www.samudrabeachchalet.com; Teluk Dalam; r RM60-160; ❄📶) Samudra has traditional Malaysian A-frame bungalows. They are slightly dark on the inside, and cheaper ones have fans. The air-conditioned family room with two double beds is a decent deal.

Mandalica Beach Resort CAMPGROUND $
(☎019-983 7690; Teluk Dalam; camping per person RM25, beach hut RM40) The lovely Halim family lives along sandy Teluk Dalam and offers covered camp sites and simple beach huts. Shared bathroom facilities are basic but clean. Pick ups from all over the Perhentians are available and fishing trips can be arranged; aquatic gear is also available for hire. There's a cafe serving juices, evening barbecues and amazing roti – Ida's banana chocolate roti is worth the walk across the island.

B'First Chalet BUNGALOW $
(☎013 9245946, 013 2955138; Teluk Dalam; r RM60-120; ❄) The Azman family runs this small resort and restaurant on the eastern edge of the beach. Fan-cooled bungalows are comfortable and have two beds; air-con bungalows have a double bed and a single. The popular restaurant serves Malaysian food and a seafood barbecue every night, and also has a cool little beachside bar with chilled beats, cocktails and cold beers.

Arwana Perhentian Resort RESORT **$$**
(☎09-778 0888; www.arwanaperhentian.com.my; Teluk Dalam; d RM160-370, f RM 270-340; ❄📶🏊) This huge resort occupies the eastern flank of Teluk Dalam, although it has no beach frontage itself. The cheaper 'standard' rooms are a bit pokey, but more expensive ones are decently furnished (some with balconies). Most comfortable are the recently refurbished standalone beachside bungalows. Facilities include a snooker room, karaoke booths and a dive centre.

Flora Bay Resort BUNGALOW **$$**
(☎09-691 1666; www.florabayresort.com; Teluk Dalam; r RM70-210; ❄@📶) The aptly named Flora Bay (flowers abound!) has a variety of options at the back of the beach, ranging from hill-view fan huts to 'deluxe' air-con beach bungalows. An extension of Flora Bay, with a smaller range of pretty much identical bungalows, is a little further along the beach. There's a decent, if overly large and impersonal, restaurant.

Bayu Dive Lodge BUNGALOW **$$**
(☎09-691 1650; www.bayudivelodge.com; Teluk Dalam; r RM95-290; ❄) A collection of smartly furnished, dark-brown bungalows are situated around a beautifully manicured central garden courtyard. All rooms are comfortable, with the more expensive ones having air-con and hot showers. Unfortunately the restaurant can sometimes be a letdown. The well-run Alu Alu Divers (p295) operates from here.

Pulau Perhentian Kecil

LONG BEACH

Panorama Diver & Chalet BUNGALOW **$**
(☎09-6911590; www.panoramaperhentianisland.com; Long Beach; r RM40-180; ❄@) A favourite with divers and snorkellers, this combination of accommodation, restaurant and dive shop (p294) is set back a short way from Long Beach. Rooms range from fan-cooled doubles to air-conditioned bungalows. The family room has two queen-sized beds, near-wraparound windows, and a balcony. What makes Panorama so special are the dive packages, with divers getting sweet deals (up to 40% off) on all rooms.

Panorama's restaurant is especially good, serving Asian and international cuisine, not to mention some of the best pizza in eastern Malaysia.

Lemon Grass BUNGALOW **$**
(☎019-981 8393; Long Beach; bungalow from RM50) At the southern tip of Long Beach, Lemon Grass has friendly management and 16 no-frills fan huts with shared bathrooms. There are great views from the verandah at reception and nice secluded spots to sit and gaze out to sea. All huts are the same price; try to get one with a sea view.

D'Rock Garden Resort BUNGALOW **$$**
(☎09-8922 2667, 013-928 9619; drockgarden@gmail.com; Long Beach; d RM130-300; ❄) Steep steps running up the southern end of Long Beach will get you to this vertiginous place on the rocks. Cheaper rooms are fan cooled, and only the deluxe ones have hot showers. The position of the huts (even the cheaper ones) overlooking the long sweep of Long Beach is fabulous.

D'Rock also has a little restaurant offering the usual cuisine and the same lovely view.

Mohsin Chalet Bungalows BUNGALOW **$$**
(☎012-932 1929; www.facebook.com/mohsinchalet; Long Beach; dm RM35, d RM140-170; ❄) Mohsin's bungalows are set on a steep hill on the southern end of the beach (to get here, take the path just behind the World Cafe and you'll arrive within a few minutes). The accommodation is fairly standard, but the ambience of the restaurant, the views, and the surreal friendliness of the staff – who'll greet you with a welcome drink in hand – make this place well worth spending a few days.

BuBu Villa VILLA **$$$**
(☎09-691 1333; www.buburesort.com; Long Beach; villa from RM820; ❄📶) These private villas are the most high-end option on the Perhentian Islands. The six air-conditioned units have private terraces, hot-water showers and huge, comfortable beds. Decor is chic and sophisticated, on-site spa and yoga services are available, and excellent food at the World Cafe is also right on hand. Room prices include breakfast for two and low-season discounts available.

BuBu Resort RESORT **$$$**
(☎03-2142 6688; www.buburesort.com; Long Beach; r from RM490; ❄📶) At the northern end of the bay, this top-end option offers 38 rooms in a modern, three-storey setting overlooking Long Beach itself and a gorgeous restaurant in *palapa* style (open-sided shelter, with a thatched roof made of dried palm leaves). All rooms face the beach

and offer similar mod cons, including air-con, hot showers and full wi-fi access.

Santai CAFE $$
(www.buburesort.com/santai-restaurant; BuBu Resort, Long Beach; mains RM30-60; ⏲noon-10.30pm) With a similar menu as the World Cafe, BuBu's Santai restaurant offers laid-back views that may see you staying for a second beer or cocktail before the dinner menu kicks off. Lighter dishes like burgers and wraps are complemented by more sophisticated Euro and Asian fare including rack of lamb or grilled prawns. There's also a popular nightly barbecue.

World Cafe CAFE $$
(www.buburesort.com/the-world-cafe; BuBu Villa, Long Beach; mains from RM30; ⏲7.30am-10.30pm; 📶) The best place to eat in the islands is this open-sided *palapa* restaurant where cool jazz bubbles away with sea breezes and beach views. Cocktails, fresh juices and smoothies, and a decent selection of beers are all on offer, and the menu features good pasta and salads. Our favourite is the smoked salmon sandwich combined with a chilled coconut juice.

There's also a popular 'catch of the day' barbecue each night.

PETANI BEACH

Mari Mari Beach Bar & Resort BUNGALOW $
(☎017-998 5462; Petani Beach; r RM50-150) Look no further if you're after a more remote Perhentians stay. Mari Mari is constructed solely of recycled and salvaged material, and there's a real Robinson Crusoe vibe to the simple beach huts with shared bathrooms and the more private treehouses with rustic ensuites. The attached beach bar and restaurant is also the real deal in laid-back island life.

Alunan Boutique Resort BOUTIQUE HOTEL $$$
(☎016-448 8297; www.alunanresort.com; Petani Beach; r/ste from RM500/950) Definitely raising the bar for Perhentian accommodation, Alunan's array of sleek designer pavilions cascade down a rocky, forested hillside to a compact cove. Translating to 'Waves' in Malay, the more remote southern coast location on Petani Beach is a quieter alternative to other parts of the islands, and stylish and spacious two-storey suites are complemented by the property's Bayu restaurant.

Note that water taxi fares will add up if you wish to head around to other beaches for alternative eating and drinking opportunities.

TELUK KERMA

D'Lagoon Chalets BUNGALOW $
(☎019-985 7089; www.dlagoon.my; Teluk Kerma; camp site RM15, dm RM25, r RM70-210) Teluk Kerma is a pretty, isolated bay with fine coral and a wonderfully tranquil location. Accommodation ranges from a longhouse with dorm beds to simple stilt bungalows and a honeymoon treehouse. Activities include snorkelling, shark- and turtle-watching trips, and jungle hikes to remote beaches. Management will also arrange local music at night on request.

There's an on-site restaurant serving decent international and Malay food for breakfast, lunch and dinner. Make sure you tell the boat captain to drop you here – otherwise it's an hour's hike from the Long Beach jetty.

CORAL BAY

A 15-minute walk west from the Long Beach jetty takes you to Coral Bay. A 20-minute walk south is Sandy Coral Bay.

RainForest Camping CAMPGROUND $
(www.facebook.com/rainforestcamping.perhentianisland.malaysia; Sandy Coral Bay; camping RM20) Simple tents equipped with compact bamboo decks sit in a sylvan rainforest glade. Shared toilets and bathrooms are rudimentary, but the real attractions here are the perfect arc of the private beach and the chilled vibe in the attached cafe. The semi-bright lights of Coral Bay are an easy 15-minute walk away north along the coast.

Ewan's Place HUT $
(☎014-817 8303; Coral Bay; d RM80) Cookie-cutter prefab huts on the path leading from Coral Bay to Long Beach. Rooms inside are clean and colourful, with comfortable double beds, mosquito netting and cold-water showers. The attached cafe serves the usual variety of Asian and international cuisine.

Perhentian Tropicana Inn BUNGALOW $
(☎09-6918 888; www.perhentiantropicana.com; Coral Bay; dm RM20, r RM250-500; ❄📶) Forty bungalows fill a hillside equidistant between Coral Bay and Long Beach. The cheaper rooms have double beds with mosquito netting and cold showers, and the more expensive but plain rooms feature air-conditioning. Dorms – dubbed Tivoli Backpackers – have eight beds, two bathrooms and screened-in windows for protection from bugs. Management also makes cash advances on Visa and Mastercard.

GATEWAY TO PARADISE: KUALA BESUT

Poor Kuala Besut! Though a lovely seaside town, most visitors only spend an hour or two here. Such is the fate of the transport gateway to one of Malaysia's best-known island paradises.

The restaurants and coffee shops are all located around the jetty (where you can rent snorkelling equipment for use on the islands). The town's few hotels are also scattered around the jetty. The best is **T'Lodge** (☎09-697 8777; Perkedaian MDB, Stesen Bas; r RM170), located near the bus station; it features large rooms with private bathrooms. On the road parallel to the beach, there's a helpful **Tourism Terengganu** (☎09-697 3166; www.tourism.terengganu.gov.my; Lot PT 85, Sebelah Syahbandar; ⌚8am-5pm Sun-Wed, to 3.30pm Thu, closed Fri) if you're planning on travelling further south. Hit them up for good maps and brochures for trip planning.

A taxi from Kota Bharu is around RM45. The bus from Kuala Terengganu is RM13, and a taxi around RM80. There are two daily buses from Kuala Lumpur (RM50, nine hours). Many travel agents run minibus services to Kuala Besut from tourist hotspots around Malaysia.

Aur Bay Chalet GUESTHOUSE $
(☎013-995 0817; Coral Bay; r RM50) Small but comfortable rooms with double beds, fans, cold showers and mosquito netting set in a longhouse structure just south of the Coral Bay jetty.

Maya Guest House GUESTHOUSE $
(☎019-970 4426; Coral Bay; r RM60-80) Twelve fan-cooled rooms just 100m back from Coral Bay. Leads ecofriendly snorkelling tours around the area and has an alcohol-free cafe.

Shari-la Island Resort RESORT $$
(☎09-691 1500; www.shari-la.com; r RM230-540; ❄@📶) Situated at Coral Bay's northern end, and sprawling into the jungle, this place offers a surprisingly posh package. A-frame bungalows are furnished with spacious wooden decks, and suites have satellite-equipped TVs and full bathrooms. Most bungalows are equipped with solar hot-water showers, and Shari-la has its own secluded beach. Also one of the few Coral Bay places with 24-hour electricity.

The on-site restaurant serving Malay, Thai and international dishes is also good.

ℹ Information

There's a RM5 conservation fee for everyone entering the marine park around the Perhentians. This is usually payable at a booth at the jetty in Kuala Besut.

EMERGENCY

The only medical facility on the islands is the very basic village clinic on Kecil. Dive operators and some of the bigger resorts can offer first aid if needed.

INTERNET ACCESS

Wi-fi is increasingly ubiquitous on Perhentian, at both accommodation and restaurants. A few spots on Long Beach and Coral Bay have expensive internet access for between RM20 to RM24 per hour.

If you're planning on using your own smartphone, Celcom has the best 3G broadband coverage in the islands.

MONEY

There are no banks or ATMs on the islands. If you run out of money, get a cash advance on your Visa or Mastercard at **Perhentian Tropicana Inn** (p299).

TELEPHONE

There are public telephones at all the main beaches. Mobile phone numbers for resorts may change from one season to the next, and some have no phone at all. **Tourism Terengganu** in Kuala Besut will have the latest contact details.

ℹ Getting There & Away

Speedboats run several times a day between Kuala Besut and the Perhentians (return trip adult/child RM70/35, 30 to 40 minutes) from 8.30am to 5.30pm. Tickets are sold by travel agents around Kuala Besut. The boats will drop you off at any of the beaches. Expect delays or cancellations if the weather is bad or if there aren't enough passengers.

In the other direction, speedboats depart from the islands daily at around 8am, noon and 4pm. Let your guesthouse owner know a day before you plan on leaving so they can arrange a pickup. If the water is rough or tides are low, you may be ferried from the beach on a small boat to your mainland-bound craft; you'll have to pay around RM5 for this.

Getting Around

While there are some trails around the islands, the easiest way to go from beach to beach or island to island is by boat. Accommodation owners can arrange a taxi boat. From island to island, the trip costs around RM20 per boat, and a jaunt from one beach to another on the same island usually costs about around RM15. Prices double at night.

Pulau Lang Tengah

Tiny, idyllic Lang Tengah lies roughly halfway between Pulau Redang and Pulau Perhentian, and with only three resorts to choose from, it's a much quieter, less-developed place than its better known neighbours. Diving and snorkelling trips are all on tap.

The island's three resorts are spaced out on the west coast, and offer a bewildering variety of package deals. **D'Coconut Lagoon** (☎03-4252 6686; www.dcoconutlagoon.com; r RM280-740; ❄📶🏊), the island's best accommodation, has two separate areas, separated by a forest track, and both with their own private beaches and swimming pools. Comfy rooms and bungalows have fridges, TVs and other mod cons. Our preferred area is the newer West Wing, especially the romantic cabanas – each with their own private garden – and the funky little beach bar. Note that the prices here are per night, but various package deals are also available. The other resorts on the island have a package-tour emphasis.

Nurul Boat Services (☎019-929 9587; www.boattoredang.com; Merang Jetty; per person RM80) has three daily boats departing Merang jetty for Lang Tengah at 8am, 10am and 3pm. Return boats leave Lang Tengah at 9am and noon, and there's also an 11am departure from Lang Tengah to Pulau Redang.

Pulau Redang

Redang's position within a marine park lends itself to excellent diving and snorkelling, and you can easily lose yourself to the golden sunlight, verdant jungle and lapping waves. Unfortunately, it can be difficult – and potentially more expensive – to visit independently, rather than as part of a package tour, which tend to be regimented affairs with arrival lectures and set times for meals, snorkelling and 'leisure'. It's popular with groups of young Malaysians and weekending Singaporeans.

Pulau Redang basically shuts down from the start of November and reopens at the start of March; the best time to visit is from mid-March to late September. There is a RM5 conservation fee for entering the marine reserve, usually payable as you catch the boat from Merang.

Sleeping & Eating

Accommodation on Pulau Redang needs to be arranged in advance. Tour companies sell packages for all the resorts, and several of the resorts have offices in Kuala Terengganu. Unless otherwise stated, all package prices given in this section are for three days and two nights and are per person, based on two sharing, and include boat transfer from Merang, all meals and two snorkelling trips.

Promotional packages are frequently offered; check hotel websites in advance. Off peak rates (usually for March and October) also attract significant discounts. Weekday (Sunday to Wednesday) rates are also cheaper than weekends (Thursday to Saturday).

Teluk Kalong

The more private beach of Teluk Kalong is to the southwest of Pasir Panjang.

Wisana Village BUNGALOW $$$
(☎012-629 7875; www.wisanaredang.com; Teluk Kalong Kecil; s/d full board per night from RM345/490; ❄📶) With a private beach location, Wisana Village is one of Redang's most alluring places to stay. Accommodation ranges from comfortable rooms to deluxe bungalows, all infused with an Asian design aesthetic. In contrast to other resorts, occupancy is limited to just 36 guests. Relaxation is maximised in the chic guest lounge and Wisana's cafe with views of nearby Pulau Kerengga.

Accommodation on a per-night basis is available.

Redang Kalong Resort RESORT $$$
(☎03-7960 7163; www.redangkalong.com; per person from RM430; ❄) This quiet place is set among the palm trees in a private bay where turtles often come to lay their eggs. Standard rooms have three double beds while sea-view rooms have two. Various diving and snorkelling packages can be booked online;

diving packages not including accommodation start at RM710 per person and include four dives.

⊨ Teluk Dalam

Teluk Dalam is in the north of the island, near a village with good local restaurants.

Taraas Beach & Spa Resort   RESORT **$$$**
(☑09-221 3997; www.thetaaras.com; per couple from RM2600; ✳@☱) One of Redang's most luxurious resorts, the Taraas offers sumptuous wooden bungalows in delightful, landscaped gardens and an excellent private beach. Personal pampering – spa and massage – are available. The two on-site restaurants, Asian All Day Dining and Beach Brasserie, serve meals all day, but only breakfast and dinner (plus boat transfers) are included in the package price.

⊨ Pasir Panjang

Most of the smaller resorts are built on a beautiful stretch of white-sand beach known as Pasir Panjang, on the east coast of the island.

Coral Redang Island Resort   RESORT **$$$**
(☑09-630 7110; www.coralredang.com.my; s/d per night RM380/450; ✳🛜☱) Towards the northern end of the beach, this recently renovated 31-room resort has a dive centre attached. A wide variety of snorkelling/diving packages starting at RM630/900 are on offer. Even if you're not staying here, it's worth considering the Matahari restaurant or a drink at the resort's Chicak Bar, both open to nonguests.

Redang Bay Resort   RESORT **$$$**
(☑09-620 3200; www.redangbay.com.my; dm/d per person from RM360/450; ✳🛜☱) At the southern end of the beach, this rather characterless resort has a mix of concrete block–style accommodation and bungalows. Rooms are neat and clean, if a little spartan. The karaoke lounge is open till all hours and there's a 'beach disco' on weekends, so don't come looking for a quiet island retreat.

Redang Holiday Beach Villa   BUNGALOW **$$$**
(☑09-624 5500; www.redangholiday.com; per person from RM400; ✳🛜) At the northern tip of the beach is this welcoming place, with a series of smart duplex bungalows climbing the rocks (bungalows S13 and S14 have the best outlooks). Larger bungalows sleep up to eight.

Redang Pelangi Resort   RESORT **$$$**
(☑09-624 2158; www.redangpelangi.com; per person from RM400; ✳🛜) This is a casual, resort-style affair that offers fairly simple two- and four-bed wooden bungalows. There's an on-site dive centre, a couple of shops, and a beachfront bar that usually has live music and decent happy hour prices most nights.

⊨ South of Pasir Panjang

The bay directly south of Pasir Panjang has an excellent white-sand beach.

Redang Reef Resort   RESORT **$$$**
(☑09-622 6181; www.redangreefresort.com.my; per person from RM430; ✳) This budget resort on the headland has a great location, though you'll get your feet wet going to and fro at high tide. The two-storey wooden bungalows are very basic but popular with student groups. The better bungalows on the rocks are more secluded and have fantastic bay views. It also has a tiny private beach and a dive centre.

Laguna Redang Island Resort   RESORT **$$$**
(☑09-630 7888; www.lagunaredang.com.my; per person RM630-1020; ✳🛜☱) Redang's biggest resort – a vast, 400-room complex – dominates this beach. It has luxurious sea-view suites with balconies, two restaurants, a dive centre and live music from Friday to Wednesday. Buildings are in traditional Malay style, but it definitely has a big-hotel vibe. From 5.30pm, a food court also operates. Check the website for good-value diving/snorkelling package deals.

Redang Beach Resort   RESORT **$$$**
(☑09-623 8188; www.redang.com.my; s/d per person RM690/450; ✳@) This place has an arrangement of modern double-storey bungalows and boasts a five-star PADI dive centre, a few shops and a regular beach disco, which makes it a bit intense for a quiet escape. The resort's two-night/three-day snorkelling /diving package includes all meals, boat transfer equipment and activities.

❶ Getting There & Away

Nearly all visitors to Redang come on packages which include boat transfer to the island. Independent travellers can hitch a ride on one of the resort boats (return RM110), but in the high season (April to September) room-only deals will be scarce.

Nurul Boat Services (☑019-929 9587; www. boattoredang.com; Merang Jetty) has speedboats departing from a newly expanded jetty along the river in Merang. Four daily boats depart from here for Redang (30 minutes, per person RM55) at 8am, 9.30am, 1pm and 3pm. Return boats leave Redang at 9am, 11am, 1pm and 4pm. There's also an 11am departure from Redang to Lang Tengah (per person RM80).

Slower ferries (around 1½ hours) also run from Shahbandar jetty in downtown Kuala Terengganu, but these are less frequent and generally must be arranged via your resort. It's also possible to visit Redang on a dive trip from Pulau Perhentian.

Pulau Kapas

More easily accessed than other East Coast islands – it's just 15 minutes by speedboat from the mainland – pretty Kapas is a worthy place to chill out for a few days. Try and visit during the week, as the island becomes overrun with day-trippers on holidays and long weekends. In the unlikely event that even Kapas seems too large, tiny Pulau Gemia (home to the Gem Island Resort & Spa) sits just off the north coast. All accommodation on Kapas is concentrated on three small beaches on the west coast, but you can walk or kayak to quieter beaches. During the east-coast monsoon season (November to March), the seas are too rough and the island largely shuts down.

Activities

Kapas is a snorkelling paradise, with the best coral to be found off the less accessible beaches on the northern end of the island and around tiny Pulau Gemia. The most impressive sites are best reached on a boat trip. North of Gemia, a sunken WWII Japanese landing craft, now carpeted in coral, is a popular dive site. Most resorts can arrange snorkeling and diving trips.

Aqua-Sport Divers DIVING
(☎019-983 5879; www.aquasportdiver.com.my; snorkelling RM35, one/two dives incl equipment RM110/180, open-water course RM1100) The only dive outfit on Kapas offers trips out to the Japanese wreck, snorkelling and a four-day PADI open-water course.

Sleeping & Eating

Though most come to Kapas on all-inclusive package tours, it's possible to rock up and find a place to stay during the week. The Jetty Cafe sells basic staples and serves meals.

Captain's Longhouse GUESTHOUSE $
(☎012-3770214; dm/r RM40/80) Formerly known as the Lighthouse, this superhip longhouse sits on the southernmost tip of the bay. Guests can enjoy art-covered walls, dorm beds bedecked in colourful batik blankets, and a sociable front porch with hammocks, chairs and even an out-of-tune piano. Surrounded by trees, it's pretty rustic but very comfortable.

Kapas Beach Chalet BUNGALOW $
(dm RM20, r RM50-80; 📶) The most laid-back spot on Kapas offers accommodation ranging from basic 'backpacker' rooms with outside (but private) toilets to comfortable A-frame huts. There's a great social vibe, courtesy of the hip shared spaces including 'The Big Chill,' a breezy beachfront pavilion equipped with hammocks and loads of cushions. Chilled beats bubble away, and most nights someone brings out a guitar. Walk-in guests only.

Ombak Kapas Resort BUNGALOW $
(☎017-985 9600, 019-951 4771; r RM80-130; ❄) Recently relaunched as the Ombak Kapas Resort, the former Mak Cik Gemul Resort has simple fan-cooled rooms and air-con bungalows, a handy store, and a decent restaurant with beachy views.

Pak Ya Seaview Resort BUNGALOW $
(☎019-960 3130; r RM90) Just north of the jetty, Pak Ya offers seven charming, fan-cooled A-frame bungalows with lovely sea-facing porches. Also rents kayaks and snorkelling gear, and has a little restaurant.

Kapas Turtle Valley RESORT $$
(☎013-354 3650; www.kapasturtlevalley.com; bungalow incl breakfast RM190, minimum 2 nights; ⏲open Mar–mid-Oct; 📶) In a rocky nook on the island's southern end, Kapas Turtle Valley is a hidden gem. Eight bungalows – all furnished with colourful local batik – sit above a white-sand beach perfect for swimming, lounging and snorkelling. There's an excellent on-site restaurant with a daily-changing menu, cold beer and good coffee. Dutch expat hosts Peter and Sylvia are very welcoming. Meals cost extra – expect to pay around RM30.

Qimi Private Bay BUNGALOW $$
(☎019-648 1714; www.facebook.com/QimiChalet; chalets RM250-350) In expansion mode since our last visit, Qimi now also offers more comfortable hillside bungalows with

excellent sea views and breezy outdoor bathrooms. There's also more rustic and cheaper bungalows that lack the hillside location, an exceptionally laid-back family-owned restaurant, and the opportunity to go snorkelling, kayaking and beachcombing on Qimi's sandy private cove.

Kapas Coral Beach BUNGALOW **$$**
(☎09-6181 976; r RM220-235; ❄) What this place lacks in character it makes up for in air-conditioning and hot showers. It's north of the jetty.

Gem Island Resort & Spa RESORT **$$$**
(☎09-688 2505; www.gemisland.com.my; Pulau Gemia; villa RM320-400, ste RM880 ; ❄) Perched on tiny Pulau Gemia, 800m north of Pulau Kapas, this resort offers airy wooden bungalows, a couple of small private beaches and a green turtle hatchery. Recently renovated rooms are particularly comfortable. The spa offers the usual pampering services, and all-inclusive package deals are available. The restaurant is pretty and the food gets good reviews.

ℹ Getting There & Away

Boats (return RM40) leave from Marang's main jetty whenever four or more people show up. You can usually count on morning departures at around 8am and 9am. The same boats will continue to Pulau Gemia if requested.

Onward transport leaving Marang can be difficult to secure, so if possible prebook a taxi to pick you up when you return to the mainland after visiting the island. Island accommodation or boat service companies can usually arrange this.

Both the following boat companies can also book accommodation on the island. See www.kapasisland.com for further information.

MGH Boat Service (☎09-6183 166, 016-922 5454; www.kapasisland.com) Offer a discount on boat costs for groups of six or more.

Suria Link Boat Service (☎019-983 9454, 09-618 3754; surialink@hotmail.com) Established operator at the Marang jetty.

COASTAL TERENGGANU

With so many amazing islands to chose from, Terengganu's coast is seen by many travellers as a mere pass-through to paradise. Travellers who take the time to explore between paradise-hops will find the region rich in culture, cuisine and scenery that is simply unavailable on the islands.

Kuala Terengganu

POP 396,433

A microcosm of Malaysia's economic explosion: fishing village strikes oil, modernity ensues. Kuala Terengganu is surprisingly attractive despite the number of newly built (with petro-wealth), sterile-looking skyscrapers. There's a boardwalk, a couple of decent beaches, a few old *kampung*-style houses hidden among the high rises, and one of eastern peninsular Malaysia's prettiest and most interesting Chinatowns. With seafood-heavy local cuisine and good transport links, KT is worth a day or two in between the islands and jungles.

Sights

★Chinatown NEIGHBOURHOOD
Centred on Jln Kampung Cina (also known as Jln Bandar), KT's picturesque and interesting Chinatown area features watermarked buildings and faded alleyways. Contemporary and quirky street art is slowly being added to the laneways of this compact neighbourhood, and other attractions include heritage buildings and temples. Pick up the Chinatown Heritage Trail brochure at the tourist information office.

Sleepy thoroughfares worth exploring are **Turtle Alley**, with mosaics telling the story of KT's now-endangered turtles, and **Pasar Payang** (Memory Lane), which commemorates local Chinese community leaders. Gentrification is slowly happening with cafes and gift shops opening up, but sleepy hardware shops and traditional Chinese medicinal herb shops still hold sway.

Ho Ann Kiong CHINESE TEMPLE
(Jln Kampung Cina; ⏰7.30am-7pm) FREE In Chinatown, this compact and colourful riot of red and gold architecture and decor dates back to 1796.

Teck Soon Heritage House HISTORIC BUILDING
(Jln Kampung Cina; ⏰10.30am-3pm Sat-Thu) FREE Painted a glorious trio of three shades of blue, this Chinatown house originally belonging to the Teck Soon trading company is now an interesting museum focusing on the history of Chinese Perakanan culture in Kuala Terengganu.

Perakanan Photo Gallery GALLERY
(Jln Kampung Cina; ⏰9am-5pm) FREE A compact Chinatown display of interesting B&W photos telling the story of KT's history.

Kuala Terengganu

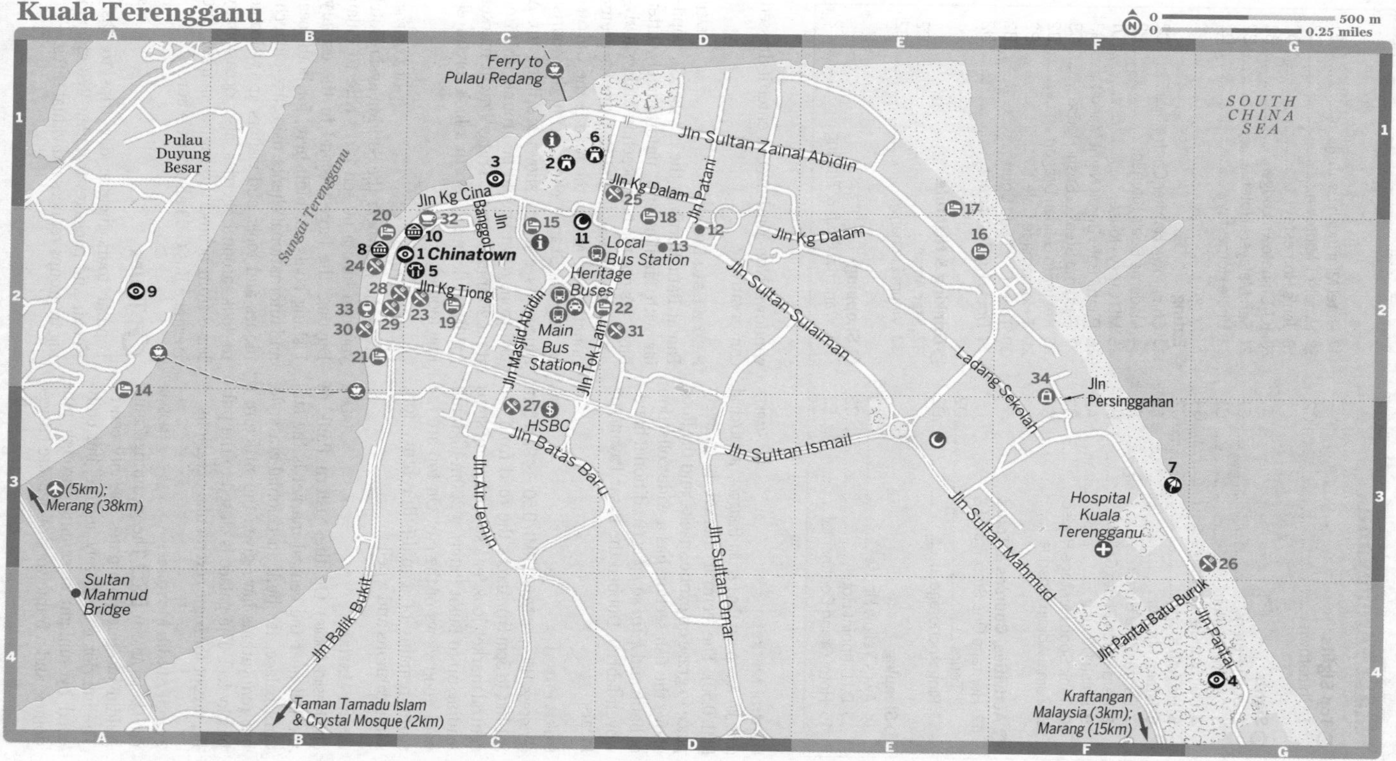

Kuala Terengganu

Central Market MARKET

(cnr Jln Kampung Cina & Jln Banggol; adult/child RM1/0.50) The central market is a lively place to graze on exotic snacks, and the floor above the fish section has a wide collection of batik and *kain songket* (traditional handwoven fabric). Dubbed the Pasar Payang by locals.

Bukit Puteri FORT

(Princess Hill; adult/child RM1/0.50; 9am-5pm Sat-Thu, to 3pm Fri) Across the road from the central market, look for a steep flight of steps leading up to Bukit Puteri, a 200m-high hill with good views of the city. On top are the scant remains of a mid-19th-century fort, some cannons and a bell.

Istana Maziah PALACE

(Jln Masjid Abidin) On the eastern flank of the hill near the central market is the sultan's palace. It's built in colonial-era style, but renovations have given the structure a blocky feel. The palace is closed to the public, except for some ceremonial occasions.

Zainal Abidin Mosque MOSQUE

(Jln Masjid Abidin) FREE The gleaming Zainal Abidin mosque dominates the city centre. The interior is relatively austere, but enlivened by sunlight streaming through nine domes, and a framework of delicate latticed windows. Non-Muslims can enter if dressed conservatively.

Pantai Batu Buruk BEACH

Pantai Batu Buruk is the city beach, popular with families and, unfortunately, litter bugs. It's not the best beach in Malaysia given the strong winds and rips, but it's pretty nonetheless. Across the road is the **Cultural Centre Stage**; check with the tourist office to see if any shows are lined up. A taxi from town should be around RM15 or it's a 20-minute walk. Friday's night market (p308) is definitely worth a look for travelling foodies.

Pulau Duyung HARBOUR, PORT

From the jetty near the Seri Malaysia Hotel you can take a 60-sen **ferry ride** to Pulau Duyung, the largest island in the estuary. Fishing boats are built here, for both local and international clients, using age-old techniques and tools, and visitors are welcome to look around. Ferries also occasionally leave from behind the central market, and Heritage Bus C-03 also travels here.

Tours

Popular tours include day trips to Tasik Kenyir and packages to Pulau Redang. Going in groups reduces individual rates.

Ping Anchorage TOUR
(☑09-626 2020; www.pinganchorage.com.my; 77A Jln Sultan Sulaiman) Organises numerous tours around Terengganu, including day trips to Tasik Kenyir and Sungai Terengganu. The latter takes in Pulau Duyung, the mangroves and stops at the tiny village of Kampung Jeram, with its exotic fruit trees and Chinese temple. Ping also manages Terrapuri Heritage Village (p310) in Penarik, and can arrange tours to the islands.

Heritage One Stop Travel & Tours TOUR
(☑09-631 6468; Jln Sultan Sulaiman, T009, Blok Teratai, Taman Sri Kolam; ☺9am-5pm) Offers tours to the islands, the jungles and around KT. Located on the ground floor of a housing complex on Jln Sultan Sulaiman.

🛏 Sleeping

Jen's Homestay APARTMENT $
(☑019-957 8368; www.jenhomestay.weebly.com; Jln Kampung Tiong, 8-12 Pangsapuri Kampung Tiong; s/d from RM60/80; ⊜❄🛜) Comprising two stylish bedrooms – choose between 'Paris' or 'Pisa' – and a shared lounge, the highlight of this rental apartment is the stunning view across the river and on to the ocean. The entire apartment can be rented, or just the bedroom. When we dropped by, the enterprising operators were looking to add additional accommodation one floor up.

Awi's Yellow House GUESTHOUSE $
(☑017-984 0337; r RM35, bungalow RM200) Awi's is (or sells itself as) what Terengganu once was: a wooden stilt house, the smell of fish paste, salt and chilli, no air-con and nights that stick to you like a wet kiss. Built over the Sungai Terengganu on Pulau Duyung, don't come here if you don't like roughing it a little, but do if you want a taste of *kampung* life. Rooms for two people are rustic, and there's a newer riverside bungalow for families and groups. From the ferry dock or Pulau Duyung bus stop, it's a short walk to Awi's; ask a local for directions.

KT Chinatown Lodge GUESTHOUSE $
(☑09-6221 938, 013-9316 194; lawlorenz@gmail.com; 113 Jln Kampung Cina; r RM90-110; ❄🛜) Right in the heart of Chinatown – and in proximity to nesting swiftlets – this two-storey guesthouse features simple but spotless rooms, and a friendly welcome from owner Lorenz. The cheapest rooms have no windows, but all include multichannel TV, private ensuites and air-con. Retro B&W

photos of Chinatown reinforce a heritage ambience.

Uncle Homestay GUESTHOUSE $
(☑016-953 7671; 77A Jln Tok Lam; r RM50; ❄🛜) Just around the corner from the bus station, location is everything at the welcoming Uncle Homestay. Rooms are prosaic (and can be windowless), but the shared bathrooms are clean and well kept. Brightly coloured floors and spacious, shared areas mean it's easily KT's best option for the really thrifty traveller.

DJ Citipoint Hotel BUSINESS HOTEL $
(☑09-630 9909; www.citipointhotel.com; 16 Pusat Niaga Paya Keladi, Jln Kampung Daik; r/ste from RM70/100; ❄🛜) Rooms are relatively compact and simple, but the team at reception is friendly and the location is just a short stroll to the attractions of Chinatown and the central market. OK for a night if you've just returned from an island visit on Kapas or Redang.

Hotel Mini Indah HOTEL $
(☑09-622 9053; 60 Jln Sultan Zainal Abidin; r from RM50; ❄🛜) The Mini Indah doesn't exactly drip with character, but it serves a very clean and functional purpose: getting you a pretty room within stumbling distance of the city beach.

Hotel YT Midtown HOTEL $$
(☑09-623 5288; ythotel@streamyx.my; 30 Jln Tok Lam; r RM115-145; ❄@🛜) The YT is a big, modern hotel in the centre of town with neat, good-value rooms that come with the regular mod cons such as TV, minifridge and kettle. On the higher view-friendly floors, the recently redecorated deluxe rooms are particularly comfortable. There's a decent cafe downstairs.

Seri Malaysia Hotel HOTEL $$
(☑09-623 6454; www.serimalaysia.com.my; 1640 Jln Balik Bukit; r RM190; ❄🛜) Part of a popular chain with branches all over Peninsular Malaysia, this reliable place offers the standard, comfortable, could-be-anywhere set-up. Rooms are a bit faded and dated, but the lobby and riverside terrace restaurant are lovely. Chinatown is just metres away.

Hotel Grand Continental HOTEL $$
(☑09-625 1888; www.grandcontinental-kt.com; Jln Sultan Zainal Abidin; d RM180-220, ste RM700-950; ❄🛜⛱) This reasonably swank high rise has comfortable rooms, some with excellent

beach views. There's a swimming pool on the 4th floor, a restaurant in the lobby, and location-wise, you're well placed near both KT town and the beach. A renovation is definitely overdue, but it's still worthwhile for a well-located overnight stay.

Eating & Drinking

Fish plays a big role in local cuisine, but the real local specialty is *kerepok* (a grey concoction of deep-fried fish paste and sago, usually moulded into sausages). Some restaurants in Chinatown serve local spins on Perakanan (Straits Chinese) cuisine including Terengganu laksa, a version of the Malay noodle classic.

Chinatown Hawker Centre HAWKER $
(off Jln Kampung Cina; ⏲7am-11pm) Chinatown's outdoor hawker centre is divided into Chinese and Malay sections, and sizzles with cooking and socialising at night. Turn left at the Ho Ann Kiang temple and follow your nose. There's often a small morning craft and produce market here too.

Town City Food Court HAWKER $
(Jln Kampung Cina; ⏲11am-9pm) Malay, Thai and Chinese hawker favourites and the best selection of cold beer in Kuala Terengganu.

T Homemade Cafe CHINESE, MALAY $
(Jln Kampung Cina; mains from RM5; ⏲10am-5pm) Right next to Chinatown's Dragon Arch, this place is a cooperative of a few food stalls. You can try Chinese and Malay dishes here, as well as clay pots and homemade juices. Take a seat under the faded Milo-branded bamboo shades and revive yourself before more Chinatown exploration.

MD Curry House MALAY, INDIAN $
(Jln Kampung Dalam; mains from RM5; ⏲11.30am-2.30pm & 5.30-9pm) Sometimes you just need a curry, and you need it served on a banana leaf by friendly locals. The MD has you covered in all regards.

Pantai Batu Buruk Night Market MARKET $
(mains from RM3; ⏲3-7pm) The aroma of charcoal grills wafts over Pantai Batu Buruk, the city beach, every Friday night.

★ **Madame Bee's Kitchen** CHINESE $$
(177 Jln Kampung Cina; mains RM12-20; ⏲9.30am-5pm Mon-Tue & Thu-Sun) In an interesting heritage-era space in the heart of Chinatown, Madame Bee turns excellent renditions of Perakanan dishes with local Terengganu influences. The award-winning chef's renowned dishes include Terengganu laksa (made with a richly flavoured fish broth) and *mee* Jawa (sweet and sour yellow noodles crammed with crunchy additions like *yao char kuai,* Chinese doughnuts, and peanuts).

Restoran Golden Dragon CHINESE $$
(198 Jln Kampung Cina; mains from RM12; ⏲11.30am-2.30pm & 5-11pm) The Golden Dragon seems constantly packed. There's ice-cold beer aplenty and one of the finest Chinese seafood menus in town. Anything steamed and off the fish list should serve you right. The sambal squid is particularly moreish. Friendly and prompt service – despite the restaurant's immense popularity – combine to make it one of KT's best.

Pertama Steak & Sushi House JAPANESE $$
(www.facebook.com/pertama808; 2A Jln Air Jernih; mains from RM12; ⏲noon-10pm) Excellent Japanese fare features at this friendly place just south of the town centre. Sashimi and sushi are both well prepared and super fresh, and robust bowls of rice and noodles are savoury antidotes to the often sweet local Malay food. Generous bento boxes offer a bit of everything, and salads, pasta and steak effortlessly quell any yearnings for international flavours.

Uncle Ng Restaurant CHINESE $$
(50E Jln Tok Lam; mains RM10-20; ⏲11.30am-2.30pm & 5.30-11.30pm) This family-owned restaurant turns out top Chinese eats just a short hop from the bus station. Try the butter-style mantis prawns with a cold beer or refreshing watermelon juice if you've just arrived in town.

Star Anise COFFEE, CAFE
(www.facebook.com/staranisekt; 82 Jln Kampung Cina; coffee & cake RM8-15; ⏲10am-midnight Mon-Thu & Sat, 3pm-midnight Fri;) KT's best coffee – including loads of variations on espresso and cappuccino – is the star at this chic and cosmopolitan cafe that's a real surprise in a largely conservative town. Secure a table in the front and admire gifts and local souvenirs including organic honey, or retire for conversation and blueberry cheesecake in the lounge out the back.

Vinum Exchange BAR
(www.facebook.com/thevinumXchange; 221 Jln Kampung Cina; ⏲11am-11pm) Equal parts cafe, bar and wine shop, Vinum Exchange is a

surprising addition to the gentrification slowly influencing Chinatown. With outdoor seating and a stylish interior, options include espresso, beers and ciders, and food ranges from bar snacks through to full meals. Wine is only available by the bottle, but there's an OK selection of smaller bottles perfect for sharing.

Shopping

Batik and *kain songket* are particularly good buys in Kuala Terengganu. Check out also the central market (p306) near the river.

Kraftangan Malaysia HANDICRAFTS
(09-622 6458; 9am-5pm Sun-Thu) About 4.5km south of town, this outlet sells high-quality *kain songket* costing as much as RM12,000 for 2.5 sq metres. There's also a tiny Songket Heritage Exhibition showing varying designs. Minibus 13 will take you here from the bus station.

Wanisma Craft & Trading HANDICRAFTS
(09-622 3311; Jln Persinggahan; 9.30am-6.30pm) Batik and local brassware can be purchased at this shop where you can also view artisans at work. Check with the tourist information office before heading there, as nearby real estate development may necessitate a change in location at some point.

Information

You'll find plenty of banks on Jln Sultan Ismail, most with 24-hour ATMs that accept international cards.

Hospital Kuala Terengganu (09-623 3333; Jln Sultan Mahmud) English-speaking and a good standard of care.

Tourist Information Office (09-622 1553; www.tourism.terengganu.gov.my; Jln Sultan Zainal Abidin; 9am-5pm Sat-Thu) Helpful staff and good brochures and maps.

Tourism Malaysia Office (09-630 9093; www.tourism.gov.my; Unit 11 Jln Kampung Daik; 9am-5pm Sat-Wed, 9am-3.30pm Thu) Good maps and English-language brochures.

Getting There & Away

AIR

A number of airlines have offices inside the Kuala Terengganu airport.

AirAsia (600 85 8888; www.airasia.com) To/from Kuala Lumpur.

Malaysia Airlines (09-662 6600; www.malaysiaairlines.com) To/from Kuala Lumpur.

Firefly (03-7845 4543; www.firefly.com.my) To/from Subang (Kuala Lumpur).

Malindo Air (03-7841 5388; www.malindoair.com) To/from Subang (Kuala Lumpur).

BUS

At the time of writing, the **bus station** on Jln Masjid Abidin was the terminus for both local buses and longer-distance express buses. There has been discussion of an express bus station near Shahbandar jetty also being used, so check your departure location when you book. Express bus companies at the station include **Transnasional** (090 581 582; www.transnasional.com.my), **MARA Liner** (1300 88 842538; www.maraliner.com.my), **Sani Express** (3341 1201; www.saniexpress.com.my) and **SP Bumi** (623 7789; www.spbumi.com.my).

Buses from Kuala Terengganu

DESTINATION	PRICE	DURATION
Dungun	RM10	2 hours
Johor Bahru	RM48	8 hours
Kota Bharu	RM17	3 hours
Kuala Besut (Perhentians)	RM13	2 hours
Kuala Lumpur	RM43	8 hours
Kuantan	RM20	6 hours
Melaka	RM48	8 hours
Merang (Redang)	RM5	1 hour
Penang	RM51	9 hours
Rantau Abang	RM7	1.5 hours
Singapore	RM74	11 hours

TAXI

Kuala Terengganu's **main taxi stand** is near the local bus station, but taxis can be found throughout the city. Destinations include Marang (RM30), Kota Bharu (RM110), Kuala Besut (RM80), Rantau Abang (RM60), Merang (RM50) and Tasik Kenyir (RM180).

Getting Around

Local buses leave from the **main bus station** (Jln Masjid Abidin) in the town centre.

Looking like heritage houses, KT's network of local **Heritage Buses** (per person RM1.50) runs across four separate lines. All four routes begin and end at Shahbandar jetty and also stop at the local bus station. Timings can be somewhat irregular, but these services are handy for getting to Pulau Duyung (number C-03), and the Muzium and Taman Tamadu Islam (number C-02).

Taxis around town cost a minimum of RM5. There are also a few bicycle rickshaws plying their trade through town. Prices are highly negotiable. A taxi to the airport, around 11km north of the city, costs around RM35.

Around Kuala Terengganu

Kuala Terengganu is the natural base for exploring Terengganu state. The museums are close to the city, and Sekayu Falls and Tasik Kenyir are to the southwest.

Sights

Kompleks Muzium Negeri Terengganu MUSEUM
(Terengganu State Museum; ☎09-622 1433; http://museum.terengganu.gov.my; adult/child RM15/10; ⏲9am-5pm Sat-Thu, 9am-noon & 3-6pm Fri) Comprised of interconnected buildings on 26 hectares of land, around 6km west of Kuala Terengganu, exhibits range from the historically interesting (a Jawi – traditional Malay text – inscription that essentially dates the arrival of Islam to the nation) to the mildly bizarre (a wildlife exhibit featuring somewhat threadbare taxidermy). The complex of traditional houses that fronts the grounds is worth the price of admission. English signage is sparse, however. To get here, catch Heritage Bus C-02 from the main bus station. A taxi will cost around RM10.

Masjid Tengku Tengah Zaharah MOSQUE
FREE The most famous religious structure in the state is the 'Floating Mosque,' located 4.5km southeast of Kuala Terengganu. It's not really floating, just set on a man-made island, but its white, traditional Moorish design is beautifully blinding in the strong daylight and warmly enchanting as the sun sets. Bus 13 from Kuala Terengganu's main bus station will drop you outside (RM1.50).

Taman Tamadu Islam AMUSEMENT PARK
(☎09-627 8888; www.tti.com.my; adult/child RM21/16; ⏲10am-7pm Mon-Thu, 9am-7pm Fri-Sun) Touted as the world's first 'Islamic civilisation park,' Taman Tamadu Islam, 2.5km west of Kuala Terengganu, is essentially a series of miniature models of famous Islamic landmarks from across the world, including Jerusalem's Dome of the Rock and Mecca's Masjid al-Haram. The highlight of the park is the **Crystal Mosque**. Widely considered among the world's most beautiful mosques, it features a particularly striking steel, glass and crystal exterior. Heritage Bus C-02 runs here, and a taxi will cost around RM15.

River cruises (adult/child RM21/16) spend around one hour exploring the nearby waterways, but regular departures can be dependent on the number of other visitors in the park.

North of Kuala Terengganu

North of Kuala Terengganu the main road (Route 3) leaves the coast and runs inland to Kota Bharu, 165km north, via Jerteh. The quiet coastal back road (Route 1) from Kuala Terengganu to Kuala Besut runs along a beautiful stretch of coast and is popular with cyclists.

Merang

Not to be confused with Marang (which it often is), the sleepy little fishing village of Merang is the gateway to the island of Redang. The beach is attractive if you have to spend some time waiting for ferry connections to Redang.

Kembara Resort (☎09-653 1770; http://kembararesort.tripod.com; dm RM15, r RM40-70; ❄@) is a cheap and friendly place whose plain but homely bungalows are popular with the student crowd. There are organised activities and a common kitchen. Follow the signs from the main road from the village.

Regular buses run from the main bus station in Kuala Terengganu to Merang (RM5). Taxis from Kuala Terengganu cost RM50 per car. Coming from the north is more difficult and it is easiest to go south as far as Kuala Terengganu and then backtrack. Otherwise, taxis from Kota Bharu cost around RM70.

Penarik

With its windswept beach and charmingly low-key population of farmers and fisher folk, the village of Penarik is as lovely a spot for a taste of coastal Malaysian culture as you could wish for. But for something truly magical, stick around until the sun goes down and charter a boat to take you down the Penarik river for a journey through the **Penarik Firefly Sanctuary**, where on certain nights (the darker the better) you'll be treated to a most unusual sight: thousands of fireflies blinking in near-perfect synchronisation. This synchronised flashing pattern is unique to the area, and entomologists suspect it is mating behaviour. The night-time boat trip through the ghostly and ethereal mangrove forest is unforgettable.

For somewhere to stay, the manicured grounds of **Terrapuri Heritage Village** (☎09-624 5020; www.terrapuri.com; house RM600-

LIVING HISTORY: BIDONG ISLAND

As the Vietnam War ended, millions of Vietnamese citizens decided to take to the high seas rather than face communist rule in newly reunified Vietnam. Dubbed 'boat people' by the international community – the first time this now-common and poignant phrase was coined – many of these refugees wound up in Malaysia. In 1978, Bidong, a tiny island off the coast of Terengganu, was designated a refugee camp. For the next two decades, Bidong served as a temporary home and transit point for tens of thousands of refugees, who endured unsanitary living conditions in shelters made from salvaged materials. At one point, the tiny island held 40,000 people, making it the most densely populated place on the planet. The camp was closed in 1990, and Bidong has since returned to a pristine state. Small groups occasionally visit Bidong for day trips (there is no accommodation on the island); divers in particular are drawn to the fantastic coral lanscapes surrounding Bidong.

Trips to Bidong can be arranged through Ping Anchorage (p307) in Kuala Terengganu.

RM1100, minimum 2 nights;) resemble a film set about the lives of sultans of yore. Meaning 'Land of Palaces', Terrapuri is equal parts conservation and restoration museum, and resort. The resort features 29 classically furnished antique houses painstakingly restored and is laid out to resemble a Terengganu palace c 1850 (though all are fully equipped with modern amenities).

The land on which Terrapuri sits is equally regal, flanked by the South China Sea (with stunning views of Pulau Perhentian, Lang Tengah and other islands) on one side, and the Setiu Wetland mangrove river on the other. By night, the flashing of fireflies is reflected in Terrapuri's long swimming pool, and during the summer months visitors may see green turtles laying their eggs on the sandy shore. Terrapuri offers delicious traditional meals and many activities.

A wide range of activities is offered at the Terrapuri Heritage Village resort, including excursions into local villages and and boat trips to the Firefly Sanctuary and outlying islands. Nonguests can book these same activities through Ping Anchorage (p307), who can also help arrange low-cost homestays with villagers in Penarik. From Kuala Terengganu, a Firefly Sanctuary tour with Ping costs RM130 per person (dependent on group size and minimum of two people) including dinner and transport.

Buses from Kuala Terengganu to Kuala Besut will let you off at the Penarik mosque in the village for RM6. From the other direction, buses from Kota Bharu to Kuala Terengganu are RM17. Taxis from either city are also available.

South of Kuala Terengganu

Marang

Marang is the jump-off point for ferries to Pulau Kapas. If you are in town on Sunday be sure to check out the excellent **market**, which starts at 3pm near the jetty. There are a few international restaurants and a couple of basic *kedai kopi* (coffee shops) in the town centre, and you can also find some **food stalls** (Jln Kampung Paya) near the jetties.

The most upscale spot in town to overnight is the bright, modern chain **Hotel Seri Malaysia** (09-618 2889; www.serimalaysia.com.my; 3964 Jln Kampung Paya; r RM190;) on the coast north of the centre. It offers rooms that any Western traveller in need of mod cons will be comfortable with.

It is sometimes possible to flag down through buses travelling to Kuala Terengganu (RM4) and Dungun/Rantau Abang (RM7/5), but often these services are express buses and will not always stop in Marang. The main bus stop is near the traffic roundabout on the main road (Route 3, the East Coast Highway), in front of the mosque.

If you're sure of the exact timing of your departure from Kapas, it's a good idea to prearrange a taxi to pick you up at the Marang jetty. Another option is to get your accommodation on the island to book one for you before you leave.

For travel further afield, such as to Kuala Lumpur or Cherating, the most straightforward option is to return to Kuala Terengganu, and catch an express bus from there.

SEKAYU FALLS

Located 56km southwest of Kuala Terengganu, Sekayu Falls are part of the Sekayu Recreational Forest, a large park popular with locals on Friday and public holidays. The falls extend down a mountainside; the main falls are a 15-minute walk from the entrance, but a further 20 minutes will bring you to the more attractive upper falls. There's also an orchard with a huge variety of seasonal tropical fruit.

The falls are best visited on a trip through Ping Anchorage (p307); it's possible to combine the falls with a visit to the Kenyir Dam. Costs are around RM140 to RM170 per person (dependent on group size and minimum of two people).

Kemasik

Kemasik's palm-fringed beach has some of the clearest water on the east coast. The nearest accommodation is at the gargantuan, five-star **Awana Kijal Golf, Beach & Spa Resort** (☎09-864 1188; www.awana.com.my; r/ste from RM195/440; ❄@🛜≋) on the beach around 1km south, towards Kijal, stacked with the usual golf courses, tennis courts, spa etc. Discounts are often available, especially if you book over the internet. Take a local bus running between Kemaman/Cukai and Dungun, or if you're driving, turn off Route 3 (East Coast Highway) at the 'Pantai Kemasik' sign.

Tasik Kenyir

The construction of the Kenyir Dam in 1985 flooded some 2600 sq km of jungle, creating Southeast Asia's largest man-made lake, with clumps of wild overgrowth gasping over the water's surface. Today Tasik Kenyir (Lake Kenyir) and its 340 islands constitute Terengganu's most popular inland tourism destination.

Unfortunately, a newly opened children's water park, and special islands dedicated to contrived displays of orchids and butterflies, have diminished the remote appeal of the area. Future planning also includes an island dedicated to duty-free shopping, and new resorts and carparks to cater to busloads of organised groups.

Factor in poor public transport links and the fact that some attractions are only available to groups, and the area is best visited by independent travellers on a tour from Kuala Terengganu. Another option is to stay at the relaxing Lake Kenyir Resort, and join in on activities with other guests.

Despite the area's increasing development, zipping about on the spectacular lake is still very enjoyable, but it's recommended independent travellers avoid weekends and public holidays when the serenity can often be ambushed.

Sights

Waterfalls and caves are high on the list of Kenyir's attractions. Among these, a journey up **Sungai Petuang**, at the extreme northern end of the lake, is a highlight of a Kenyir visit. When the water is high, it's possible to travel several kilometres upriver into beautiful virgin jungle.

Tours booked with Ping Anchorage in Kuala Terengganu incorporate a visit to the **Lasir waterfall**, including the opportunity to hike further into the jungle and enjoy a picnic lunch, and also visit the interesting **Herb Island**, where medicinal and therapeutic plants cover a compact islet. By arrangement, tours can also include **bird-watching**, and visiting the **Kenyir Elephant Village** where a spectacular elevated walkway allows excellent viewing of pachyderms that have been rescued and relocated from problem situations in the wild.

Fishing is also popular, and the lake is rich in species including *toman* (snakehead), *buang* (catfish), *kelah* (a type of carp), *kelisa* (green arowana) and *kalui* (giant gouramy). You will need a fishing permit (RM10) which can be arranged at Lake Kenyir Resort. Other attractions that can be visited with Lake Kenyir Resort include the **Kelah fish sanctuary**, and the **Bewah** and **Taat caves** near the lake's southern edge.

The lake's water level varies considerably, peaking at the end of the rainy season in March or April and gradually decreasing until the start of the next rainy season in November. When the water is high, the tops of submerged trees poke through the surface. When low the lake is a series of canals through partially denuded jungle hills. The high water is far more beautiful, so come in late spring or early summer.

Sleeping

Lake Kenyir Resort (☎09-666 8888; www.lakekenyir.com; chalet from RM500; ❄📶🏊) is the only option for independent travellers. This peaceful resort has spacious chalets with balconies overlooking the lake or the rainforest. The restaurant serves Malay and international dishes, and the swimming pool has a great view of the lake. The resort also has tennis courts, a gym and organised activities. A makeover of chalets was ongoing when we dropped by, so ask for a newly renovated one.

Other accommodation will only deal with groups of six or more people.

Information

There is a small **tourist information office** (☎09-626 7788; ⏲9am-5pm) near the jetty in Pengkalan Gawi, the lake's main access point. They can supply maps and brochures, but only book tours and activities for groups.

Getting There & Away

The main access point is the jetty at Pengkalan Gawi on the lake's northern shore. A taxi from Kuala Terengganu should cost around RM1280, but it can be expensive arranging boat transport once you reach the jetty at Pengkalan Gawi. Your best bet is to book an all inclusive package or day trip with **Ping Anchorage** (p307) in Kuala Terengganu (around RM220 to RM260 per person, dependent on group size and minimum of two people). Another option is to explore Kenyir's remote regions by houseboat, but you'll need around 10 people to make a trip economical; Ping Anchorage can also arrange this.

Sabah

POP 3.12 MILLION / AREA 76,115 SQ KM

Includes ➡

Best Places to Eat

- Kohinoor (p326)
- Sim Sim Seafood Restaurant (p353)
- Alu-Alu Cafe (p325)
- KK Night Market (p326)

Best Places to Stay

- Shangri-La's Tanjung Aru Resort & Spa (p324)
- Mañana (p345)
- Lupa Masa (p342)
- Tampat Do Aman (p347)
- Orou Sapulot (p386)

Why Go?

Pint-sized Sabah occupies a relatively small chunk of the world's third largest island, yet what a colourful punch it packs: the treasure of turquoise-fringed desert islands with coral reefs swarming with marine biodiversity; trekkers' paradise Mt Kinabalu reaching 4095m into the clouds; and jungles pulsing with a menagerie of bug-eyed tarsiers, gibbons, pythons, clouded leopards and huge crocs. Around 55% of Sabah is forest, and protected areas like the Maliau Basin and the Danum Valley Conservation Area are more accessible than ever.

Given its compact size, getting from one of Sabah's highlights to the next is eminently doable, plus as a former British colony, English is commonly spoken here, making it extremely traveller friendly. Whether it's pearl hunting in Kota Kinabalu, watching baby orangutans learning to climb at Sepilok, beach flopping on the northern Tip of Borneo, or diving or trekking, your time here will feel like five holidays condensed into one.

When to Go

Kota Kinabalu

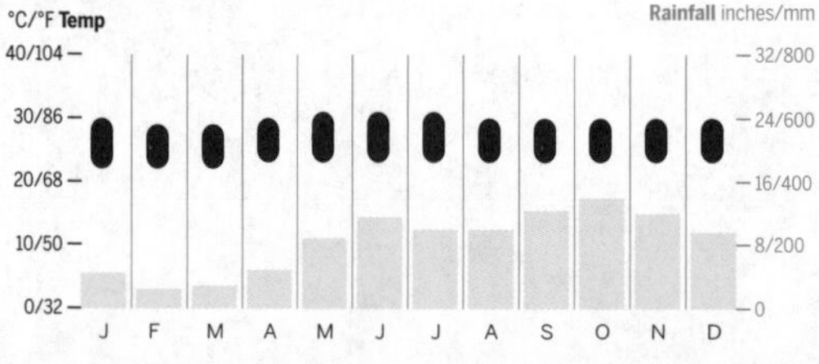

Jan–Apr A dry, pleasant time, exploding with celebrations for Chinese New Year.

Mar–Jul The water calms; this is the best time for diving.

Jun–Sep Hot and often (but definitely not always) rainy.

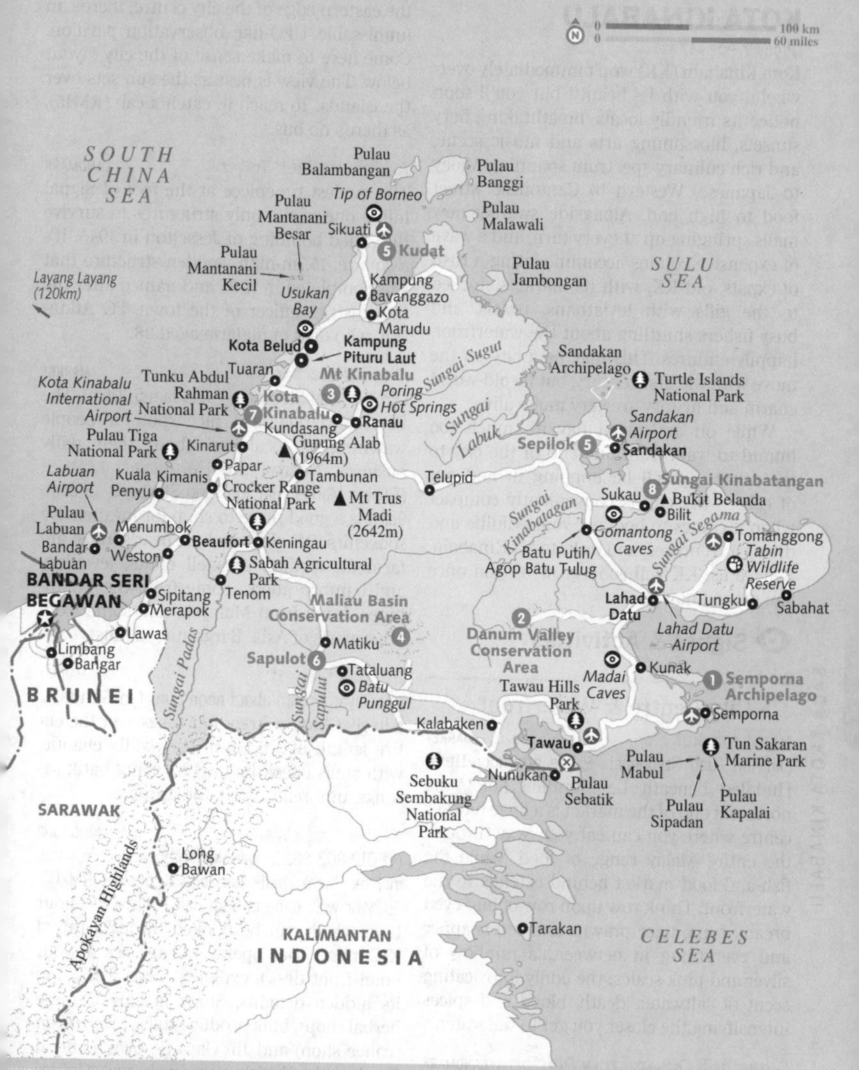

Sabah Highlights

1. Diving among wild sea turtles and sharks on the multicoloured reefs of the **Semporna Archipelago** (p372).
2. Exploring the misty wilderness of the **Danum Valley Conservation Area** (p366), between scoping for tarsiers, clouded leopards and orangutans.
3. Hoofing it over granite moonscapes for the ultimate Bornean sunrise atop **Mt Kinabalu** (p333).
4. Breathing in the air of an actual virgin rainforest in the **Maliau Basin Conservation Area** (p382).
5. Watching rescued orangutans and sun bears in **Sepilok** (p355).
6. Floating down a river through primary jungle to the Batu Punggul rock formation in **Sapulot** (p386).
7. Enjoying the thriving art scene of **Kota Kinabalu** (p316).
8. Facing off with very large crocs while cruising in a little tin boat down the **Sungai Kinabatangan** (p360).

KOTA KINABALU

☎088 / POP 457,325

Kota Kinabalu (KK) won't immediately overwhelm you with its beauty, but you'll soon notice its friendly locals, breathtaking fiery sunsets, blossoming arts and music scene, and rich culinary spectrum spanning Malay to Japanese, Western to Cantonese, street food to high end. Alongside swanky new malls springing up at every turn, and a wave of expensive condos accommodating a rush of expats, old KK, with its markets stocked to the gills with leviathans, pearls, and busy fishers shuttling about the waterfront, happily endures. This may be a city on the move with the 21st century, but its old-world charm and history are very much alive.

While on any given day it's much too humid to walk from one end of the city to the other – you'll be hopping in and out of cabs – the city is conveniently compact when it comes to booking your wildlife and diving adventures, and treks to Mt Kinabalu. Believe us, KK will soon grow on you once you get to know it.

Sights & Activities

City Centre & Waterfront

Night Market MARKET

(Jln Tun Fuad Stephens; late afternoon-11pm) Huddled beneath Le Méridien hotel, the northeast end of the market is a huge hawker centre where you can eat your way through the entire Malay range of food, while the fish-and-food market behind extends to the waterfront. Think row upon row of bug-eyed bream, tuna, tiger prawns and red snapper and everything in between...a rainbow of silver and pink scales; the oddly intoxicating scent of saltwater, death, blood and spices intensifying the closer you get to the water.

Signal Hill Observatory Platform LANDMARK

(Jln Bukit Bendera; 8am midnight) Up on Signal Hill, among the art deco mansions at the eastern edge of the city centre, there's an unmissable UFO-like observation pavilion. Come here to make sense of the city layout below. The view is best as the sun sets over the islands. To reach it, catch a cab (RM15), as there's no bus.

SUNDAY MARKET WARNING

During KK's big Sunday Market, animals lovers may prefer to avoid the market area where Jln Gaya intersects Beach St; overheating, thick-furred Persian kittens and gasping puppies in mesh cages are likely to distress.

Atkinson Clock Tower LANDMARK

The modest timepiece at the foot of Signal hill is one of the only structures to survive the Allied bombing of Jesselton in 1945. It's a square, 15.7m-high wooden structure that was completed in 1905 and named after the first district officer of the town, FG Atkinson, who died of malaria aged 28.

Central Market MARKET

(Jln Tun Fuad Stephens; 5.30am-5.30pm) The Central Market is a nice spot for people watching as locals go about their daily business. Nearby, the **Handicraft Market** (Filipino Market; Jln Tun Fuad Stephens; 8am-9pm) is a good place to shop for inexpensive souvenirs. Offerings include pearls (most are farmed), textiles, seashell crafts, jewellery and bamboo goods, some from the Philippines, some from Malaysia and some from other parts of Asia. Bargaining a must.

Sunday Market MARKET

(Jln Gaya; 6am-about noon Sun) On Sundays, a lively Chinese street fair takes over the entire length of Jln Gaya. It's vividly chaotic, with stalls cheek by jowl hawking batik sarongs, umbrellas, fruit and antiques.

KK Heritage Walk WALKING TOUR

(☎012-802 8823; www.kkheritagewalk.com; walk incl tea break, batik bandana & booklet RM200; 2½hr walk departs 9am daily) This 2½-hour tour, which can be booked through any of KK's many tour operators (just ask at your hotel front desk), explores colonial KK and its hidden delights. Stops include Chinese herbal shops, bulk produce stalls, a *kopitiam* (coffee shop) and Jln Gaya (known as Bond St when the British were in charge). Guides speak English, Chinese and Bahasa Malaysia.

There's also a quirky treasure hunt at the end leading tourists to the Jesselton Hotel.

Beyond the City Centre

Some of KK's best attractions are located beyond the city centre, and it's well worth putting in the effort to check them out.

Sabah Museum MUSEUM

(Kompleks Muzium Sabah; ☎088-253 199; www.museum.sabah.gov.my; Jln Muzium; admission

KK'S ART SCENE

KK is buzzing with festivals and gigs, you just need to keep an eye out for them. While the free and widely available monthly glossy magazine *Sabah* lists upcoming events, it's also worth checking out **SPArKS** (Society of Performing Arts Kota Kinabalu; www.sparks.org.my). SPArKS works with the US Embassy to bring world-famous acts over here to play gigs in intimate venues, as well as organising the hugely popular **Jazz Festival** in June or July (check out http://kkjazzfest.com), and the **KK Arts Festival**, which also runs through June and July.

Look out too for the new and quirky street market, **Tamutamu**, which is part arts and crafts, part eclectic gathering, with artists, musos and tarot readers. Happening on the third Sunday of every month from 10am to 5pm, it also features the work of the brilliant Cracko Art Gallery (p327). Enquire at Biru Biru restaurant (p324).

RM15; ⏲9am-5pm Sat-Thu; P) About 2km south of the city centre, this refurbished museum is the best place to go in KK for an introduction to Sabah's ethnicities and environments, with new signage and clear explanations. Expect tribal and historical artefacts, including ceramics and a centre-piece whale skeleton, and replica limestone cave. The **Heritage Village** has traditional tribal dwellings, including Kadazan bamboo houses and a Chinese farmhouse, all nicely set on a lily-pad lake.

The adjoining **Science & Education Centre** has an informative exhibition on the petroleum industry, from drilling to refining and processing. The **Sabah Art Gallery** features regular shows and exhibitions by local artists. Hold on to your ticket: it also includes entry to the Museum of Islamic Civilisation, and Agnes Keith House in Sandakan.

Mari Mari Cultural Village MUSEUM
(☎088-260 501; www.traversetours.com/sabah/marimari-cultural-village; Jln Kiansom; adult/child RM160/130; ⏲tours at 10am, 2pm & 6pm; P) With three-hour tours, Mari Mari showcases various traditional homes of Sabahan ethnic communities – the Bajau, Lundayeh, Murut, Rungus and Dusun – all of which are built by descendants of the tribes they represent. Along the way you'll get the chance to see blowpipe making, tattooing, fire-starting, and an insight into the mystical belief systems of each of these groups, as well as a notable culinary nibble from each tribe! It's touristy, sure, but good fun – especially for families.

A short dance recital is also included in the visit. The village is a 20- to 30-minute drive north of central KK. There is also a small waterfall – **Kiansom Waterfall** – about 400m beyond the cultural village, which is easily accessible by private transport or on foot. The area around the cascade lends itself well to swimming and it's a great place to cool off after a visit to Mari Mari.

Monsopiad Cultural Village MUSEUM
(☎088-774 337; www.monsopiad.com; Kg Kuai/Kandazon, Penampang; adult/child RM75/free; ⏲9am-5pm; P) Monsopiad is named after a legendary warrior and head-hunter. The highlight is the House of Skulls, which supposedly contains the ancient crania of Monsopiad's unfortunate enemies, as well as artefacts illustrating native rituals from the time when the *bobolian* (priest) was the most important figure in the community. The village is 16km from KK; to get here independently, take bus 13 from central KK to Donggongon (RM1.50), where you can catch a minivan to the cultural village (RM1). Taxis from KK cost RM40.

Kota Kinabalu Wetland Centre BIRD SANCTUARY
(☎088-246 955; www.sabahwetlands.org; Jln Bukit Bendera Upper, Likas District; admission RM15; ⏲8.30am-6pm Tue-Sun; P) Featuring 1.4km of wooden walkways passing through a 24-hectare mangrove swamp, expect to see scuttling fiddler and mangrove crabs, mud lobsters, mudskippers, skinks, turtles, water monitors and mangrove slugs (sadly, there are also plastic bottles.). For many, the big attraction is a stunning variety of migratory birds. To get here, take the bus towards Likas from the bus stations in front of City Hall or Wawasan Plaza in the city, to Likas Sq. A taxi from KK costs around RM15.

Museum of Islamic Civilisation MUSEUM
(☎088-538 234; admission RM15; ⏲9am-5pm Sat-Thu; P) This museum consists of six galleries devoted to Muslim culture and

Kota Kinabalu

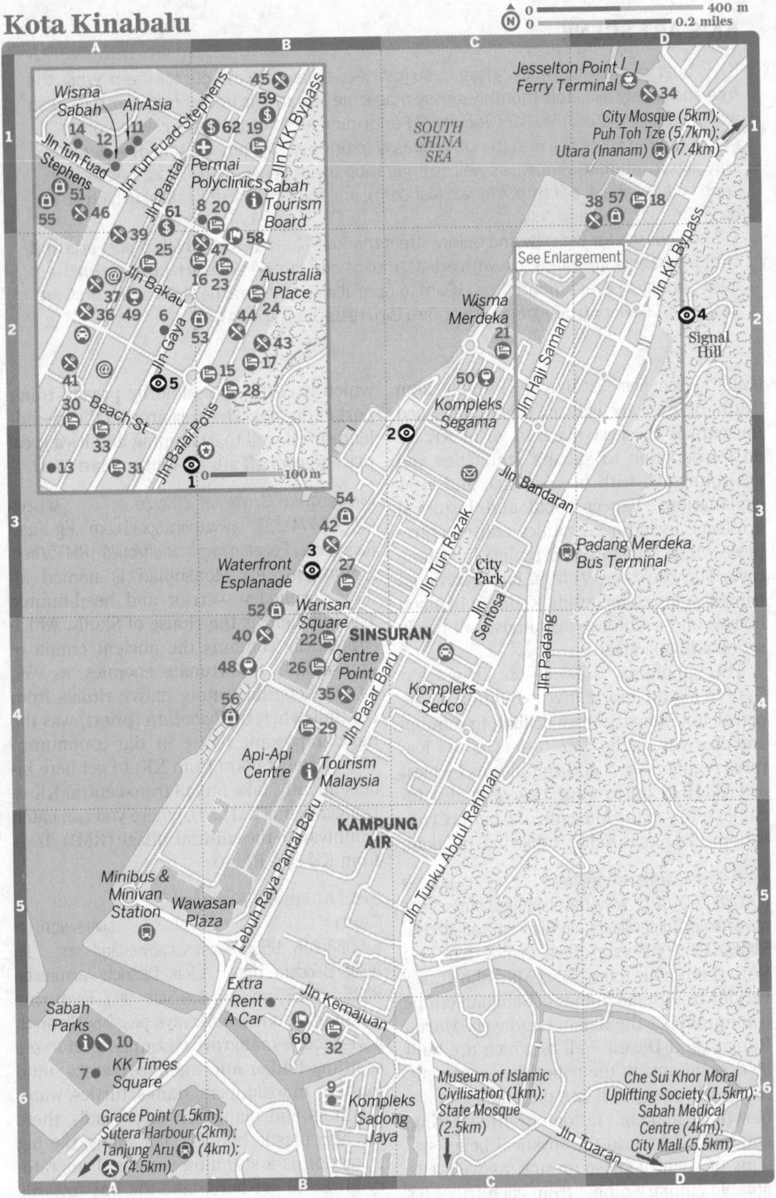

Malaysian history. The five domes represent the holy Five Pillars of Islam. It's in need of a facelift and an update, but can fill up an hour or two of a slow afternoon.

To get to the museum, 2km south of the city, catch a bus (RM1) along Jln Tunku Abdul Rahman and alight just before the mosque. It's a short but steep walk uphill to the museum. A taxi will cost around RM10 to RM15.

Bus 13 also goes right round past the Queen Elizabeth Hospital and stops near Jln Muzium (look for the Sacred Heart Church).

Kota Kinabalu

Sights
1 Atkinson Clock Tower A3
2 Central Market C3
3 Night Market B3
4 Signal Hill Observatory Platform D2
5 Sunday Market A2

Activities, Courses & Tours
6 Adventure Alternative Borneo A2
7 Borneo Adventure A6
8 Borneo Divers B1
9 Borneo Nature Tours B6
10 Downbelow Marine & Wildlife Adventures A6
11 GogoSabah A1
12 River Junkie A1
Riverbug/Traverse Tours .... (see 14)
Scuba Junkie .... (see 11)
13 Sticky Rice Travel A3
14 Sutera Harbour A1

Sleeping
15 Borneo Backpackers B2
16 Borneo Gaya Lodge B2
17 Bunibon B2
Celyn City Hotel .... (see 26)
18 Grandis Hotel D1
19 Hotel Eden 54 .... B1
20 Hotel Sixty3 .... B1
21 Hyatt Regency Kota Kinabalu C2
22 Imperial Boutec Hotel B4
23 Jesselton Hotel B2
24 Kinabalu Backpackers B2
25 Kinabalu Daya A2
26 Klagan Hotel B4
Le Hotel .... (see 26)
27 Le Méridien Kota Kinabalu B3
28 Lucy's Homestay B2
29 Pod's Backpackers B4
30 Rainforest Lodge A2
31 Seasons Street Lodge A3
32 Sky Hotel B6
33 Summer Lodge A3

Eating
7-Eleven .... (see 36)
34 Alu-Alu Cafe D1
Biru Biru .... (see 15)
35 Centre Point Food Court B4
36 Chili Vanilla A2
37 El Centro A2
38 Grazie D1
39 Kedai Kopi Fatt Kee A2
40 Kohinoor B4
41 Milimewa Superstore A2
Nagisa .... (see 21)
42 Night Market B3
43 October Cafe B2
44 Print Cafe B2
45 Tong Hing Supermarket B1
46 Wisma Merdeka Food Court A1
47 Ya Kee Bah Kut Teh B2

Drinking & Nightlife
48 Bed B4
49 Black World A2
El Centro .... (see 37)
Hunter's .... (see 25)
Shamrock .... (see 40)
Shenanigan's .... (see 40)
50 Upperstar C2

Entertainment
Suria Sabah .... (see 38)

Shopping
51 Borneo Shop A1
52 Borneo Trading Post B3
53 Cracko Art Gallery B2
54 Handicraft Market B3
55 Natural History Publications A1
56 Oceanus Waterfront Mall B4
57 Suria Sabah Shopping Mall D1

Information
Australian Consulate .... (see 20)
58 British Honorary Consul B2
59 HSBC B1
60 Indonesian Consulate B6
61 Maybank A1
62 Standard Chartered Bank B1

Puh Toh Tze Buddhist Temple BUDDHIST TEMPLE
(Mile/Batu 5.5, 20min north of KK; ⌚8am-5pm) FREE This impressive temple features a stone staircase-pavilion flanked by 10 Chinese deities leading up to a main temple complex dominated by Kwan Yin, Goddess of Mercy. A Chinese-style reclining Buddha rests inside. The temple is on a small hill west of the main highway junction north; you can get here by taking the Jln Tuaran bus or, more easily, by hiring a taxi; a round-trip shouldn't be more than RM36.

Che Sui Khor Moral Uplifting Society RELIGIOUS SITE
(Jln Tuaran) FREE About four minutes north-east of KK, this complex has an 11-storey pagoda that shimmers in orange and green. The Society espouses believing in the best Islam, Taoism, Buddhism and Christianity have to offer. Get here via the bus terminal at Wawasan Plaza going north on the Jln Tuaran route (RM3). To get home, just stand outside the temple on the main road and a minibus or regular bus will pick you up. A return taxi should cost around RM30.

City Mosque MOSQUE
(off Jln Tun Fuad Stephens) Built in classical style, this mosque is far more attractive than the State Mosque in both setting and design. Completed in 2000, it can hold up to 12,000 worshippers. It can be entered by non-Muslims outside regular prayer times, but there's not much worth seeing inside. It's about 5km north of the centre. To get here, take bus 5A from Wawasan Plaza going towards UMS (RM1.50). Ask the conductor to drop you off outside the City Mosque after the Tanjung Lipat roundabout.

Entry is free but robe hire will set you back a few ringgit.

State Mosque MOSQUE
(Jln Tunku Abdul Rahman) Sabah's State Mosque is a perfect example of contemporary Malay Muslim architecture: all modernist facade and geometric angles. The building is south of the city centre past the Kampung Air stilt village, not far from the Sabah Museum; you'll see the striped minaret and chevronned dome on your way to or from the airport. Non-Muslim visitors are allowed inside, but should dress appropriately.

Tanjung Aru BEACH
This pretty sweep of sand begins around the Shangri-La's Tanjung Aru Resort and stretches south to the airport. Tanjung Aru is a locals' beach, full of picnic spots and swoony-eyed couples. Food stalls are plentiful, most closing up come dark. We would advise against swimming here; the water may look pretty, and some locals may tell you it's fine, but others claim it's tainted by run-off from KK and nearby water villages.

Orchid De Villa FARM
(☎088-380 611; www.orchid-de-villa.com.my; Jln Kiansom; ⏲8am-5pm; P) If you're crazy about flora, head to this farm, located about 20km from central KK, along the road to Penampang. The farm specialises in rare Bornean orchids, hybrid orchids, cacti and herbal plants, and provides all of the five-star hotels in the region with flower arrangements. At the last count there were 300 different kinds of orchids.

Lok Kawi Wildlife Park ZOO
(☎088-765 710, 088-765 793; Jln Penampang; adult/child RM25/10; ⏲9.30am-5.30pm, last entry at 4.30pm; P) About an hour from KK (20km), a visit to this zoo offers a chance to see Sabah's creatures if you are unable to spot them in their natural environment. We warn you, however, that the tiger and sun bear enclosures are lamentably bare and small, and the orangutans are made to peel coconuts for tourists. Other animals include tarsiers, proboscis monkeys, pygmy elephants and rhinoceros hornbills, and there's a train which carts you around the park (RM2).

Bring plenty of water, hats and snacks (there's no shop in the park but there is a store outside), and order a cab from your hotel. It should cost around RM130 there and back, plus waiting time. The 20A minibus goes to Lok Kawi (RM2). Visitors with a private vehicle can access the park via the Papar–Penampang road or the Putatan–Papar road.

Tours

KK has a huge number of tour companies, enough to suit every taste and budget. Head to Wisma Sabah – this office building on Jln Haji Saman is full of agents and operators.

★ **Sticky Rice Travel** ADVENTURE TOUR
(☎088-251 654; www.stickyricetravel.com; 3rd fl, 58 Jln Pantai; ⏲9am-6pm) *National Geographic* prefers this outfit for a reason: they're organised, original in their choice of tours and have excellent knowledgeable guides. Responsible community-based tourism; expect adventure, culture and something very different. Sticky Rice will sit down with you and tailor your experience around your interests, fitness and budget; your trip may last four days or a few weeks.

★ **Adventure Alternative Borneo** ADVENTURE TOUR
(☎019-802 0549; www.aaborneo.com; 1st fl, 97 Jln Gaya; ⏲9am-6pm) Sustainable and ethical travel are key to this British-owned company, which works closely with Sabah Tourist Board, and run tours to Lupa Masa rainforest camp, close to Mt Kinabalu. If you're looking for remote natural immersion, they also operates trips to Sapulot.

★ **Borneo Divers** DIVING
(☎088-222 226; www.borneodivers.net; 9th fl, Menara Jubili, 53 Jln Gaya; ⏲9am-6pm) Top-notch dive outfit with a strong pedigree as the longest operator in Sabah, and excellent authoritative dive instructors who are especially good at teaching Professional Association of Diving Instructors (PADI) courses. Also based on Mabul island, it can take you diving all over Sabah. Good kit, great safety record, nice people.

★ Scuba Junkie DIVING
(☎088-255 816; www.scuba-junkie.com; Ground fl, lot G7, Wisma Sabah, Jln Haji Saman; ⊙9am-6pm) Also based on Mabul island, Scuba Junkie is the most ecologically progressive dive outfit, ploughing part of their profits into their turtle hatchery and turtle rehab centre, as well as employing a shark conservationist and an environmentalist. SJ tends to attract a younger, Western crowd. Great vibe, friendly instructors. Along with Borneo Divers, these are your go-to-guys on Mabul.

River Junkie RAFTING
(☎088-255 816 017-601 2145; www.river-junkie.com; Ground fl, lot G7, Wisma Sabah, Jln Haji Saman) Diving operator Scuba Junkie's affiliated river-rafting outfit, River Junkie, comes highly recommended by travellers. Day trips out of KK (costing from RM200 to RM400 per person with transfers) include leisurely boat tours and proboscis-monkey spotting through to more expensive white-water rafting expeditions and side trips to sites like the Mari Mari Cultural Village. Bookings normally require 24 hours' advance notice.

Equator Adventure Tours CULTURAL TOUR
(☎013-889 9535, 088-766 351; www.facebook.com/equator.tours; ⊙9am-6pm) Equator runs the Hajah Halimah Traditional cooking course (RM175), giving you the chance to get savvy with Malaysian cuisine in an authentic environment. You'll be picked up at 9am from your hotel and spirited to the wet market for ingredients, then learn how to make two memorable dishes. Runs until 12.30pm, transfers included.

GogoSabah TOUR
(☎012-838 5566; www.gogosabah.com; Lot G4, ground fl, Wisma Sabah, Jln Haji Saman; ⊙9am-6pm Mon-Sat) Gogo is useful for car and motorbike rentals and has a range of 150cc enduro bikes for tackling dirt roads (RM80 per day), as well as small cars (RM120 per day).

Bike Borneo BICYCLE TOUR
(☎088-484 734; www.bikeborneo.com; City Mall, Jln Lintas, Kota Kinabalu; 1-day tours from RM245; ⊙9am-6pm) Fieldskills Adventures, who operate Bike Borneo, run their mountain-biking activities largely out of Tuaran; packages include a one-day ride in the vicinity of town that crosses three swinging bridges, and a four-day cycling adventure across the foothills of Mt Kinabalu. Groups are small with a maximum of six persons. Bikes are well maintained, guides experienced. City Mall is about 6km east of central KK.

> **FIND YOUR WAY IN KK**
>
> Downtown KK is a dense grid of concrete buildings nestled between the waterfront and a range of low, forested hills to the east. It's compact, walkable (when not too humid) and easy to navigate – most of the restaurants, markets, accommodation, tourist offices and tour operators are located here. Transport terminals bookend the city on either side.

Riverbug/Traverse Tours ADVENTURE TOUR
(☎088-260 511, 088-260 501; www.riverbug.asia/sabah; Lot 227, 2nd fl, Wisma Sabah, Jln Tun Fuad Stephens; ⊙9am-6pm) An excellent and forward-thinking operator that makes admirable efforts to engage in sustainable travel practices. Runs a wide variety of tours across Sabah, including white-water rafting trips down the Sungai Padas from Beaufort.

The rafting day trip starts in KK at 5.20am, involves a three-hour train journey to Beaufort, then riding seven separate grade 3 & 4 rapids over 9km of the muddy-brown Padas river. Riverbug deliver you back to KK for 6pm, dog-tired but fully exhilarated!

Fieldskills Adventures ADVENTURE TOUR
(☎088-484 734; http://fieldskills.com.my; City Mall, Jln Lintas; ⊙9am-6pm) If you're into outdoor activities and adventure, get in touch with this outfit, which leads well-regarded cycling, rock climbing, trekking and diving trips across Sabah. City Mall is about 6km east of central KK.

Borneo Adventure ADVENTURE TOUR
(☎088-486 800; www.borneoadventure.com; block E-27-3A, Signature Office, KK Times Sq; ⊙9am-6pm) Award-winning Sarawak-based company with very professional staff, imaginative sightseeing and activity itineraries and a genuine interest in local people and the environment. Get in touch if you're heading to the Maliau Basin.

Borneo Authentic BOAT TOUR
(☎088-773 066; www.borneo-authentic.com; Lot 3, 1st fl, Putatan Point, Jln JKR) A friendly operation offering a variety of package tours including day-trip cruises on the Sungai Klias, as well as diving and cycling options. Located in Putatan, about 11km south of central KK.

Downbelow Marine & Wildlife Adventures DIVING
(☎012-866 1935; www.divedownbelow.com; Lot 67 & 68, 5th fl, KK Times Sq Block; ⏰9am-6pm) A well-respected dive outfit, with an office in KK and a PADI Centre on Pulau Gaya, that can arrange all kinds of travel packages across Borneo.

Borneo Eco Tours TOUR
(☎088-438 300; www.borneoecotours.com; Pusat Perindustrian Kolombong Jaya, Mile 5.5 Jln Kolombong; ⏰9am-6pm) Arranges tours throughout Malaysian Borneo to Danum Valley, Mt Kinabalu, the Crocker Range and Maliau Basin, as well as a new community-based program at Camp Lemaing (near Mt Kinabalu). Its office is about 6km northeast of the city centre.

Borneo Nature Tours NATURE TOUR
(☎088-267 637; www.borneonaturetours.com; Block D, lot 10, Kompleks Sadong Jaya, Ikan Juara 4; ⏰9am-6pm) Borneo Nature Tours runs Danum Valley's luxurious Borneo Rainforest Lodge, as well as operating tours to the Maliau Basin. Its office building is on the corner near a canal.

Sutera Harbour TREKKING
(Sutera Sanctuary Lodges; ☎088-308 914/5; www.suteraharbour.com; Ground fl, lot G15, Wisma Sabah, Jln Haji Saman; ⏰9am-6pm) Sutera runs a lot of the tourism activities in Sabah, and has a monopoly on accommodation in Mt Kinabalu National Park (p333). Make this your first stop in KK if you're planning to climb Kinabalu and didn't book your bed in advance.

Borneo Dream DIVING
(☎088-244 064; www.borneodream.com; F-G-1 Plaza Tanjung Aru, Jln Mat Salleh) Operating out of Kota Kinabalu and at the Gaya Island Resort (p332), on Pulau Gaya, this outfit has a good name and can take you diving on a try dive excursion or take you through your PADI paces to become an open-water diver. Near terminal 2 of the airport, southeast of town.

THE SABAH LOOP

A decent sealed road makes a frowning arc from KK to Tawau, passing Mt Kinabalu, Sepilok, Sandakan, Lahad Datu and Semporna (the gateway to Sipadan) along the way. So, getting from KK to Tawau via the northern half of the island, via a big frown, is simple. And now, thanks to the recent completion of the road between Sapulot and Tawau, the same can be said of the south side of the loop (going back to KK from Tawau). Sealed in 2015, it passes right by the formerly elusive Maliau Basin, dropping explorers right by the park entrance, and will save you bags of time.

Sleeping

Check out the Sabah Backpacker Operators Association (www.sabahbackpackers.com), which was set up in an effort to help shoestring travellers in the region. KK's midrange options proliferate less than the many high-end and backpacker choices, but there are deals to be found off-peak.

★Pod's Backpackers HOSTEL $
(☎088-287 113; admin-kk@podsbackpacker.com; 1st fl, Api-Api Centre, Jln Centre Point; dm/s/d RM35/60/80; ❄📶) Everyone's rightly talking about Pod's. This uber-friendly hostel is clean, helps you with forward travel and organising trips, and has six fresh avocado-green rooms with a zen-like simplicity (three doubles, three dorms), free wi-fi and free safety lockers. But most of all, we love the easy vibe they've created here; they want you to feel like you're at home.

★Borneo Backpackers HOSTEL $
(☎088-234 009; www.borneobackpackers.com; 24 Lg Dewan; dm/s/d incl breakfast from RM37/60/80; ❄📶) Turquoise and chic with Hoi An lanterns, choice art, wood floors and an excellent cafe down below firing up Asian fusion cuisine, this is one of KK's best backpacker haunts. Dorms and rooms are immaculate, with art-stencilled walls, a balcony and reading room to chill in, and constantly whirring fans. Better still, it's the HQ of Sticky Rice Travel (p320).

Borneo Gaya Lodge HOSTEL $
(☎088-242 477; www.borneogayalodge.com; 1st fl, 78 Jln Gaya; dm incl breakfast from RM25, d/q with bathroom RM85/119; ❄@📶) This friendly hostel pipes air-con through its entirety – phew! With a cosy communal lounge, the place is quiet and clean, while the friendly staff are happy to help you book tours and give you general advice.

Lucy's Homestay HOSTEL $
(Backpacker's Lodge; ☎088-261 495; http://borneohostel.wix.com/lucyshomestay; Lot 25, Lg Dewan, Australia Pl; dm/s/d incl breakfast RM28/58/68; 📶) Lucy's welcomes with brightly muralled walls, a book exchange (lots of travel tomes) and a plant-filled balcony

to flop on. There's a house-proud kitchen and basic wood floor, and fan-only rooms and dorms, all with shared bathroom. It's calm, quiet and without a hint of laddish noise. Check out the 100-year-old banyan tree towering above you out the back.

Seasons Street Lodge HOSTEL $
(☑088-253 867; seasonsstreet123@gmail.com; 123 Jln Gaya; dm/s/d/f incl breakfast RM40/50/75/130; 🅿@🛜) This popular new digs has a busy, happening vibe and thumping soundtrack in reception. There's a TV room, plenty of places to sit in the breezy lobby, fresh basic dorms and rooms with stencilled artwork, colourful walls, free lockers, and clean bathrooms.

Bunibon HOSTEL $
(☑088-210 801; www.bunibonlodge.com; Lot 21, Lg Dewan; dm RM30, r without/with bathroom 70/85; 🅿🛜) This friendly hostel has large double rooms, uncramped dorms, a great kitchen area and chilling/TV lounge with loads of DVDs. The staff can help you book trips around Sabah. While the decor is unimaginative, there is, however, air-con throughout.

Kinabalu Backpackers HOSTEL $
(☑088-253 385; www.kinabalubackpackers.com; Lot 4, Lg Dewan; dm/s/d from RM25/55/68; 🅿🛜) Despite lacking any vibe whatsoever, this bland hostel is clean, icy-cool and OK to kip for the night while trying to get in to a more atmospheric option. They can organise onward travel and tours.

Summer Lodge HOSTEL $
(☑088-244 499; www.summerlodge.com.my; Lot 120, Jln Gaya; dm/d RM35/65; 🅿🛜) Summer Lodge, compared to the new backpacker haunts, feels unloved and decrepit. That said, it's cheap, central and just above the booming Beach St bar complex.

★ Hotel Sixty3 HOTEL $$
(☑088-212 663; www.hotelsixty3.com; Jln Gaya 63; r/f from RM276/452; 🅿@🛜) This fabulous hotel has an international feel in its 100 rooms, with glossy floors, evocative black-and-white photos on the walls, dark-wood fittings, subtle down-lighting, olive colour schemes, flat screens and safety deposit boxes. Stylish.

Klagan Hotel HOTEL $$
(☑088-488 908; www.theklagan.com; Block D, Warisan Sq, Jln Tun Fuad Stephens; r/f RM313/470; 🅿🛜) Superfresh rooms with thick carpets, rain showers, tangerine-hued walls, large beds and attractive furniture. Rooms also boast comfy

work chair, desk, flat screen and downlighting. There's a nice cafe/bakery in the lobby, but the real ace card is the restaurant on the 11th floor with widescreen views of the sea and nearby islands. The buffet breakfast is superb; for nonresidents it costs RM30.

Hotel Eden 54 BOUTIQUE HOTEL $$
(☑088-266 054; www.eden54.com; 54 Jln Gaya; d/f RM139/239; 🅿🛜) In the shadow of Signal Hill, this dinky hotel boasts plenty of boutique flair, with stylish rooms decked in chocolate drapes, glass-topped desks, contemporary bedheads and burgundy or peacock-green walls. Eden is fragrant, like walking into a perfume factory, and there's a communal kitchen area behind the lounge. A fine choice for flashpackers, couples, even families. Avoid windowless rooms.

Jesselton Hotel HOTEL $$
(☑088-223 333; www.jesseltonhotel.com; 69 Jln Gaya; r RM215-239; 🅿🛜) The time-worn stucco facade may suggest faded grandeur, but within, all is sumptuous; think thick carpets, Rungus bed runners, marble-heavy bathrooms and sleek two-tone walls. The lobby is deliciously welcoming, the restaurant bright and airy. The oldest hotel in KK doesn't need to manufacture character – it fairly drips with it.

Sky Hotel HOTEL $$
(☑154-876 1941; www.skyhotelkk.com; Lg Kemajuan Karamunsing; r/f from RM208/418; 🅿⊖🅿@🛜🏊) In the business district close to the city centre, this skyscraping, modern hotel is great value if there's more than one of you. With cool, spacious suites enjoying modern fittings, amazing city views, self-catering facilities, flat screens, huge beds and, even better, a rooftop swimming pool and an excellent vegetarian breakfast buffet crammed with fresh fruits, yoghurt, cereal and eggs.

Le Hotel HOTEL $$
(☑088-319 696; www.lehotel.com.my; Block B, 3rd fl, Warisan Sq, Jln Tun Fuad Stephens; r RM120-158, f RM195; 🅿🛜) Up on the 3rd floor you'll find this colourful, pint-sized hotel with friendly staff. The rooms, while decidedly spacious for hobbits, are not so for anyone else. That said, they're nicely finished with upscale touches. Ask for one with a view of the water.

Kinabalu Daya HOTEL $$
(☑088-240 000; www.kkdayahotel.com; Lot 3-4, block 9, Jln Pantai; r/ste incl breakfast from RM146/320; 🅿🛜) While it won't win any design awards, this basic midtier hotel is solid,

with tastefully finished, comfy, clean rooms with fridges, flat screens, desks and contemporary bathrooms. Doubles are cramped.

Rainforest Lodge HOTEL $$
(088-258 228; www.rainforestlodgekk.com; Jln Pantai; dm/s/d/ste from RM40/115/135/165;) Located in the swinging centre of the 'Beach Street' complex, the Rainforest is all of a stairward stumble from some of KK's best nightlife. Rooms are refreshingly chic, a nice mix of modern and Sabah-tribal style, and many have cool balconies that look onto the Beach St parade below. Just be warned: it gets loud at night.

Imperial Boutec Hotel HOTEL $$
(088-525 969; 7th fl, Warisan Sq; r RM175-220;) This hotel has almost 100 rooms of varying sizes with laminate floors, flatscreens, contemporary fittings and modern bathrooms. Everywhere you look there's an overpowering theme of orange. Up on the 7th floor of Warisan Sq, it feels a little cut off and bland, but the rooms are nonetheless adequate.

Celyn City Hotel HOTEL $$
(088-448 787; www.celyns.com; Lot 21, Warisan Sq; r from RM150-180;) Located in a mall, this 72-room hotel has decent rooms with contemporary furniture, safety deposit box and flat-screen TVs. The walls and carpets feel fresh. Though perhaps lacking in overall character, the hotel has a handy, central location.

★ **Shangri-La's Tanjung Aru Resort & Spa** RESORT $$$
(STAR; 088-327 888; www.shangri-la.com/kotakinabalu/tanjungaruresort; Tanjung Aru; r from RM550;) Located in the Tanjung Aru area about 3km south of the city centre, this may be the finest hotel in Sabah; think beautifully stylish rooms with huge baths, comfy-as-cloud beds, sea-view balconies looking out over manicured, flower-filled gardens, spa treatments, a chic breakfast bar, plus lashings of water sports available. Pure, unblemished bliss; this is the place to relax.

★ **Grandis Hotel** HOTEL $$$
(088-522 888; www.hotelgrandis.com; Grandis Hotels & Resorts, Suria Sabah Shopping Mall 1, Jln Tun Fuad Stephens; r from RM368-498;) Attached to the Suriah Sabah Shopping mall, this four-star hotel is unfailingly clean and stylish. Standard rooms are huge, while family suites are large enough to tenpin bowl in. The last word in style, rooms have soaring views of the waterfront, baths, plush modern fittings, downlighting and flat-screen TVs. Another ace is the Sky Bar on the rooftop with unblemished views and a swimming pool.

Hyatt Regency Kota Kinabalu HOTEL $$$
(088-221 234; www.kinabalu.regency.hyatt.com; Jln Datuk Salleh Sulong; r from RM560;) Built in '67, from the outside the Hyatt looks decidedly dated; however inside it's a marble oasis of soaring ceilings, dark-wood chic and an inviting open-plan restaurant and lounge in the lobby. Lowlit rooms are huge, stylish affairs with all the mod cons: flat screen, rainshower, fine linen. Be sure to ask for discounts outside of peak season.

Le Méridien Kota Kinabalu HOTEL $$$
(088-322 222; www.lemeridienkotakinabalu.com; Jln Tun Fuad Stephens; r from RM450-500;) Five-star comfort with a freshly refurbished lobby contrasting sober dark woods with soothing lighting seguing blue to pink. Rooms are less inventive with international, somewhat anonymous decor, and minibar, flat screens and cable TV. That said, at the time of research rooms were due a date with the makeover wizard, so watch this space. Prices come down in low season.

Eating

KK is one of the few cities in Borneo with an eating scene diverse enough to refresh the noodle-jaded palate. Besides the ubiquitous Chinese *kedai kopi* (coffee shops) and Malay halal restaurants, you'll find plenty of interesting options around the city centre.

City Centre

★ **Print Cafe** CAFE $
(013-880 2486; 12 Lg Dewan; mains RM12; 8.30am-10.30pm) In the backpacker street of Lg Dewan, this brilliant cafe is a cool (in both senses of the word) place to catch your breath, read a book or play Jenga at one of its tables. Excellent coffee, papaya and orange shakes, a selection of cakes and waffles, pizza and lovely service. Keep an eye out for ingeniously foamed cappuccinos.

Biru Biru FUSION $
(24 Lg Dewan; mains RM9-13; 9am-late) Based at Borneo Backpackers, this blue joint is Asian fusion galore, with dishes like fish cooked in lime and ginger, huge tacos and an ever-evolving menu. Try the Lihing rice wine (aka rocket fuel). With its parasols and bikes on the wall, and lovely manager Jules, it's easy to fall in love with this place.

October Cafe CAFE $
(☎016-810 1274; Lg Dewan; bagels RM5; ⏰11am-10pm) Adding more appeal to backpacker street Lg Dewan, October is fresh with a wood-accented interior and upstairs balcony; great coffee, herbal teas, French toast, juices, cakes and bagels.

Ya Kee Bah Kut Teh CHINESE $
(☎088-221 192; 74 Jln Gaya; mains from RM8; ⏰4-11pm) Expect brisk service at this rammed plastic-chair joint spilling noisily onto the pavement in the centre of the old town. The buffet counter bubbles with noodles and glistens with sauce-laden pork. That's right, Cantonese-style pork, in herbal soup, fatty pork ribs…every which way you can. It's hot, crowded and delicious.

El Centro INTERNATIONAL $
(☎019-893 5499; www.elcentro.my; 32 Jln Haji Saman; mains RM15; ⏰11am-midnight Tue-Sun; 📶) Turquoise-and-orange-walled El Centro is superfriendly and cool, with a menu spanning Malysian and Mexican fare: tacos, pizza, chorizo wraps, chicken and beef burgers. They even do bangers and mash. Occasional live music.

Kedai Kopi Fatt Kee CHINESE $
(28 Jln Bakau; mains from RM8; ⏰noon-10pm Mon-Sat) The woks are always sizzlin' at this popular Cantonese joint next to Ang's Hotel. Look out for sweet-and-sour shrimp and oyster-sauce chicken wings.

Wisma Merdeka Food Court FOOD COURT $
(Wisma Merdeka, Jln Haji Saman; mains from RM5; ⏰9am-5pm) For cheap, excellent eats, head to the top floor of the Wisma Merdeka mall and get stuck into stalls serving mainly Asian street food; the Chinese dumpling stand is particularly delicious. In general this is a breakfast and lunch food court.

★Alu-Alu Cafe SEAFOOD $$
(Jessleton Point; mains from RM15-30; ⏰10.30am-2.30pm & 6.30-10pm; ❄) Drab on the outside, perhaps, but this restaurant wears its stripes in the tastiness of its food, and the fact it gets its seafood from sustainable sources – no shark-fin soup here. Alu-Alu

MAKAN: KK-STYLE

Kota Kinabalu's (KK's) melting pot of cultures has fostered a lively dining scene that differentiates itself from the rest of Malaysia. KK's four essential eats:

Sayur Manis Also known as 'Sabah veggie', this bright-green jungle fern can be found at any Chinese restaurant worth its salt. It's best served fried with garlic, or mixed with fermented shrimp paste. The *sayur manis* plant is a perennial and can grow about 3m high. It is harvested year-round, so it tends to be very fresh. Adventurous eaters might want to try other local produce like *tarap*, a fleshy fruit encased in a bristly skin, or *sukun*, a sweet-tasting tuber used to make fritters.

Filipino Barbecue Located at the north end of the KK Night Market (p326), the Filipino Barbecue Market is the best place in town for grilled seafood at unbeatable prices. Hunker down at one of the crowded tables and point to your prey. Once one of the waitstaff has sent your order off to the grill, they'll hand you a cup (for drinking), a basin (to wash your hands) and a small plate to prepare your dipping sauce (mix up the chilli sauce, soy sauce, salt and fresh lime for your own special concoction). No cutlery here! Just dig in with your bare hands and enjoy steaming piles of fresher-than-fresh seafood. Figure around RM15 for a gut-busting meal.

Hinava Perhaps the most popular indigenous appetiser, colourful *hinava* is raw fish pickled with fresh lime juice, *chilli padi*, sliced shallots and grated ginger. The melange of tangy tastes masks the fishy smell quite well. The best place to try *hinava* is Grace Point, a posh local food court near Tanjung Aru. You'll find it at the 'Local Counter' for around RM2 per plate (the portions are small – the perfect size for a little nibble).

Roti Canai The ubiquitous *roti canai*, a flaky flat bread fried on a skillet, is served from dawn till dusk at any Indian Muslim *kedai kopi* (coffee shop) around town. Although the dish may appear simple, there's actually a lot of skill that goes into preparing the perfect platter. The cook must carefully and continuously flip the dough (à la pizza chef) to create its signature flakiness. *Roti canai* is almost always served with sauce, usually dhal (lentil curry) or another curry made from either chicken or fish.

DON'T MISS

KK'S HAWKER CENTRES & FOOD COURTS

As in any Southeast Asian city, the best food in KK is the street food and hawker stalls. If you're worried about sanitation, you really shouldn't be, but assuage your fears by looking for popular stalls, especially those frequented by families.

Night Market (Jln Tun Fuad Stephens; satay RM1, fish/prawn per 100g from RM4/15; ⏲5-11pm) The night market is the best, cheapest and most interesting place in KK for barbecued squid, ray and a vast selection of delicious seafood cooked up right before your eyes.

Centre Point Basement Food Court (Basement, Centre Point Shopping Mall, Jln Raya Pantai Baru; mains from RM3; ⏲9am-9.30pm; 🖉) Your ringgit will go a long way at this popular and varied basement food court in the Centre Point mall. There are Malay, Chinese and Indian options, as well as drink and dessert specialists.

Grace Point (Jln Pantai Sembulan; mains RM2-8; ⏲11am-3pm) Take bus 15 out near Tanjung Aru for some local grub at this KK mainstay. The development is actually quite chic compared to the smoke-swathed food courts in the city centre – KKers joke that the public bathrooms here are Borneo's nicest (and it's true!). Go for the Sabahan food stall (located in the far right corner when facing the row of counters) and try *hinava* (raw fish pickled with fresh lime juice, *chilli padi*, sliced shallots and grated ginger).

excels in taking the Chinese seafood concept to new levels, with dishes such as lightly breaded fish chunks doused in a mouth-watering buttermilk sauce, or simmered amid diced chillies.

★Kohinoor INDIAN $$
(✆088-235 160; Lot 4, Waterfront Esplanade; mains RM17-30; ⏲11.30am-2.30pm & 5.30-11pm; ❄🖉) Come to this silk-festooned waterfront restaurant for northern Indian cuisine and classic dishes ranging from chicken tikka masala to prawn biryani and lamb rogan josh. The aromas from its tandoori oven are mouth watering, the naan bread pillowy-soft, and the service pure old-world charm. You'll be back more than once.

Grazie ITALIAN $$
(✆019-821 6936; 3-36, 3rd Fl, Suria Sabah Shopping Mall; mains from RM20; ⏲noon-10pm Mon-Sun; ❄) Delightful Italian cuisine in a stylish restaurant with exposed-brick walls and mozaic floors. Dishes span from ravioli with spinach to spaghetti bolognaise, seafood risotto, heavenly thin-crust pizza and melt-in-the-mouth panna cotta.

Chili Vanilla FUSION $$
(35 Jln Haji Saman; mains RM20-30; ⏲10am-10.30pm Mon-Sat, 5-10.30pm Sun; ❄📶) This cosy bijoux cafe is run by a Hungarian chef and is a real fave with travellers thanks to its central location. The menu makes an eclectic voyage through goulash, spicy duck tortillas, Moroccan lamb stew and gourmet burgers. Inside it's dinky, tasteful and peaceful.

Nagisa JAPANESE $$$
(✆088-221 234; Hyatt Regency, Jln Datuk Salleh Sulong; mains RM40-220; ⏲noon-10pm; ❄🖉) Superswanky Nagisa exudes class and executes Japanese cuisine with élan, with a wealth of sushi dishes from California *temaki* (crabstick, avocado and prawn roe) and *ebi tempura maki* (crispy prawn rolled with rice) to *agemeon* (deep-fried dishes) and noodles. Located in the Hyatt Regency.

Self-Catering

There is a variety of places to stock up on picnic items and hiking snacks, including the centrally located **Milimewa Superstore** (Jln Haji Saman; ⏲9.30am-9.30pm) and **Tong Hing Supermarket** (Jln Gaya); **7-Eleven** (Jln Haji Saman; ⏲24hr) is conveniently open throughout the evening.

Tanjung Aru

In the early evening, head to Tanjung Aru, at the south end of town near the airport, for sunset cocktails and light snacks along the ocean. The area has three beaches: First Beach offers up a few restaurants, Second Beach has steamy local stalls, and Third Beach is a great place to bring a picnic as there are no establishments along the sand. A taxi to Tanjung Aru costs RM20, or you can take bus 16, 16A or city bus 2 from Wawasan Plaza (RM2).

Drinking & Nightlife

Get ready for loads of karaoke bars and big, booming nightclubs, clustered around the

Waterfront Esplanade, KK Times Sq, where the newest hot spots are congregating, and Beach St, in the centre of town, a semipedestrian street cluttered with bars and eateries.

★El Centro BAR
(32 Jln Haji Saman; ⏲5pm-midnight, closed Mon) El Centro is understandably popular with local expats and travellers alike; it's friendly, the food is good and it makes for a nice spot to meet other travellers. With cool tunes, and a laid-back vibe, nonsmokey El Centro also hosts impromptu quiz nights, costume parties and live-music shows.

Bed CLUB
(☎088-251 901; Waterfront Esplanade; admission Fri & Sat incl drink RM20, beer from RM21; ⏲8pm-2am, to 3am Fri & Sat) KK's largest club thunders with pop, gyrating Filipino musicians, shrill teenagers and boasts guest DJs nightly. It's overcrowded and cheesy, but if you're looking for a party, this is it. Bands play from 9pm.

Shenanigan's BAR
(☎088-221 234; Hyatt Regency Hotel, Jln Datuk Salleh Sulong; ⏲5pm-1am Mon-Fri, to 2am Sat) Shani's, as it's affectionately known, enjoys a loyal crowd who are happy to pay the high prices. Below the Hyatt at street level, it has a beer garden and pool table, plus live bands from the Philippines. Head here for happy hour (daily 5pm to 9pm) to avoid being fleeced.

Shamrock BAR
(☎088-249 829; 6 Anjung Samudra, Waterfront Esplanade; ⏲noon-1am Sun-Thu, to 2am Fri & Sat) About as Irish as a Made-in-China leprechaun, this is, however, a good spot for a bit of rock music in its wood-panelled interior. Cool Guinness on tap, but best of all is the alfresco, sea-fronting terrace when the sunset douses the sky with bloody fire.

Hunter's BAR
(☎016-825 7085; Kinabalu Daya Hotel, Jln Pantai; ⏲11am-2am) A favourite for local guides and expats, Hunter's offers up karaoke, sport on the plasma TV and balmy outdoor seating in the heart of the city.

Upperstar BAR
(Jln Datuk Salleh Sulong; mains RM10-25; ⏲noon-11pm) Festooned with eclectica from Bruce Lee pics to musical instruments, Upperstar has a fine balcony that's a breezy place for a sundowner come evening, plus if you're feeling peckish, there's a Western-leaning menu featuring grilled meats and fish and chips.

Black World BAR, KARAOKE
(Jln Pantai; ⏲24hr) We know. This is the only spot that stays open past 2am in central KK. But here's what to expect: cheap beer served in iced buckets, ear-shredding karaoke and dance music, sleazy male clientele, ladies of negotiable affection and bathrooms from the deepest pits of hell.

☆ Entertainment

Suria Sabah CINEMA
(Suria Sabah Shopping Mall, Jln Haji Saman) The Suria Sabah mall houses a huge multiplex that shows all the Hollywood hits, usually in the original English with subtitles.

Shopping

KK is fast becoming a shopaholic's heaven, with leading brands in uber smart malls across the city. The latest is the Oceanus Waterfront Mall, chock-full of designer brands, and Western coffee and food outlets.

★Cracko Art Gallery ARTS
(www.facebook.com/crackoart; cnr Jln Bakau & Jln Gaya; ⏲noon-8pm) Made up of a group of brilliantly talented KK artists, high up on the 3rd floor (look for the Cracko sign outside on the street), you'll find a vivid working studio of abstract and figurative art, stunning jewellery, and sculpture from Manga-style figurines to mannequin-art. Affordable and original work, a visit here makes for a great hour.

In the same space, keep an eye out for Lost At Sea, a boutique tattoo parlour with amazing designs by Taco Joe and his ink men.

Oceanus Waterfront Mall SHOPPING CENTRE
(Jln Tun Fuad Stephens; ⏲10am-10pm; 📶👪) The city centre's newest mall, this gleaming palace of consumerism has all the top Western brands, from sunglasses shops to coffee-house chains, beauty products to fashion.

Natural History Publications BOOKS
(☎088-240 781; www.nhpborneo.com; 9th fl, Wisma Merdeka Mall, Jln Haji Saman; ⏲9am-8pm Mon-Sat) Easily the best resource in the country for pictorial and textual books on Sabah's culture, ethnicity, traditions, and wildlife and flora, at a fraction of the price you'll pay elsewhere.

Borneo Trading Post CRAFTS
(☎088-232 655; Lot 16, Waterfront Esplanade, Jln Tun Fuad Stephens) Upmarket tribal art and souvenirs.

Borneo Shop BOOKS
(☎088-241 050; Shop 26, ground fl, Wisma Merdeka Phase 2, Jln Haji Saman; ⌚10am-8pm Mon-Sun) Books, gifts, prints and postcards. There's a wealth of wildlife and flora books all focused on Borneo.

Information

Free maps of central KK and Sabah are available at almost every hostel or hotel.

EMERGENCY

Ambulance (☎088-218 166, 999)

Fire (☎994)

Police (☎088-253 555, 999; Jln Dewan, near Australia Pl)

INTERNET ACCESS

The majority of accommodation options have some form of wi-fi internet connection.

Borneo Net (Jln Haji Saman; per hour RM4; ⌚9am-midnight) Twenty terminals, fast connections and loud head-banger music wafting through the air.

Net Access (Lot 44, Jln Pantai; per hour RM5; ⌚9am-midnight) Plenty of connections and less noise than other net places in KK. LAN connections are available for using your own laptop.

IMMIGRATION OFFICES

Immigration office (☎088-488 700; Kompleks Persekutuan Pentadbiran Kerajaan, Jln UMS; ⌚7am-1pm & 2-5:30pm Mon-Fri) In an office complex near the Universiti Malaysia Sabah (UMS), 9km north of town. Open on weekends, but only for Malaysian passport processing.

MEDICAL SERVICES

Permai Polyclinics (☎088-232 100; www.permaipolyclinics.com; 4 Jln Pantai; consultation weekday RM60, Sat & Sun RM80; ⌚doctors on duty 8am-6pm, emergency 24hr) Excellent private outpatient clinic.

Sabah Medical Centre (☎088-211 333; www.sabahmedicalcentre.com; Lg Bersatu, off Jln Damai) Good private hospital care, located about 6km southeast of the city centre.

MONEY

Central KK is chock-a-block with 24-hour ATMs.

HSBC (☎088-212 622; 56 Jln Gaya; ⌚9am-4.30pm Mon-Thu, to 4pm Fri)

Standard Chartered Bank (☎088-298 111; 20 Jln Haji Saman; ⌚9.15am-3.45pm Mon-Fri)

POST

Main Post Office (Jln Tun Razak; ⌚8am-5pm Mon-Sat) Western Union cheques and money orders can be cashed here.

MAIN DESTINATIONS & FARES FROM KOTA KINABALU

The following bus and minivan transport information was provided to us by the Sabah Tourism Board and should be used as an estimate only: transport times can fluctuate due to weather, prices may change and the transport authority has been known to alter departure points.

DESTINATION	DURATION	PRICE	TERMINAL	FREQUENCY
Beaufort	2hr	RM15	Padang Merdeka	7am-5pm (frequent)
Keningau	2½hr	RM25	Padang Merdeka	7am-5pm (8 daily)
Kota Belud	1hr	RM10	Padang Merdeka	7am-5pm (frequent)
Kuala Penyu	2hr	RM20	Segama Bridge	8-11am (hourly)
Kudat	3hr	RM22	Padang Merdeka	7am-4pm (frequent)
Lahad Datu	8hr	RM55	Inanam	7am, 8.30am, 9am, 8pm
Lawas (Sarawak)	4hr	RM25	Padang Merdeka	8am
Mt Kinabalu National Park	2hr	RM15-20	Inanam & Padang Merdeka	7am-8pm (very frequent)
Ranau	2hr	RM20	Padang Merdeka	7am-5pm
Sandakan	6hr	RM45	Inanam	7am-2pm (frequent) & 8pm
Semporna	9hr	RM75	Inanam	7.30am, 8.30am, 2pm & 7.30pm
Tawau	9hr	RM80	Inanam	7.30am, 8am, 10am, 12.30pm, 4pm & 8pm
Tenom	3½hr	RM25	Padang Merdeka	8am, noon, 2pm & 4pm

DON'T MISS

RIDING THE BORNEO RAILS

Back in the late 19th century, colonials used to swan around the western Sabah coast on the **North Borneo Railway**, which eventually fell into disuse and disrepair. Recently, the old iron horse has been restored, with natural wood interiors and the original exterior colour scheme of green and cream, set off with the railway's old brass emblem of a crown surmounting a tiger holding a rail wheel.

While it's not an unmissable great train journey of the world, and yes it's a bit twee, it's still great family fun. The train leaves KK at 9.30am and arrives in Papar at 11.45am, taking in mountains and rice paddies, with stops for a look at a Chinese temple and the Papar wet market. On the trip back to KK (12.20pm to 1.40pm), a smashing colonially inspired tiffin lunch of cucumber sandwiches and satay is served.

The railway is operated by Sutera Harbour (p322); adult/child tickets cost RM318/159. The train leaves the station in Tanjung Aru twice a week, on Wednesday and Saturday. It's worth mentioning, however, that the old train occasionally runs out of steam (literally), forcing passengers to taxi back to KK from wherever the train retires. For more information or to book tickets, contact Sutera Harbour (www.suteraharbour.com/north-borneo-railway).

TOURIST INFORMATION

Sabah Parks (☎088-486 430, 088-523 500; www.sabahparks.org.my; 1st-5th fl, lot 45 & 46, block H, Signature Office KK Times Sq; ⊙8am-1pm & 2-4.30pm Mon-Thu, 8-11.30am & 2-4.30pm Fri, 8am-12.50pm Sat) Source of information on the state's parks.

Sabah Tourism Board (☎088-212 121; www.sabahtourism.com; 51 Jln Gaya; ⊙8am-5pm Mon-Fri, 9am-4pm Sat, Sun & holidays) Housed in the historic post-office building, KK's tourist office has plenty of brochures, maps and knowledgeable staff keen to help you with advice tailored around your needs – they won't just try and sell you a package tour! Their website, packed with helpful information from accommodation to sights, is equally worth a visit. Organised.

Tourism Malaysia (☎088-248 698; www.tourism.gov.my; Ground fl, Api-Api Centre, Jln Pasar Baru; ⊙8am-4.30pm Mon-Thu, 8am-noon & 1.30-4.30pm Fri) This office is of limited use for travellers, but does offer a few interesting brochures on sights in Peninsular Malaysia.

Getting There & Away

AIR

KK is well served by **Malaysia Airlines** (☎1300-883 000; www.malaysiaairlines.com) and **Air-Asia** (www.airasia.com; ground fl, Wisma Sabah, Jln Haji Saman; ⊙8.30am-5.30pm Mon-Fri, to 3pm Sat), which offer the following international flights to/from KK: Brunei, Shenzhen, Jakarta, Manila, Singapore and Taipei. Within Malaysia, flights go to/from Johor Bahru, Kuala Lumpur and Penang in Peninsular Malaysia, and Kuching, Labuan, Lawas, Miri, Kudat, Sandakan, Lahad Datu and Tawau in Borneo. **Jetstar** (www.jetstar.com) and **Tiger Airways** (www.tigerairways.com) both offer flights to Singapore.

BOAT

All passengers must pay an adult/child RM3.80/1.90 terminal fee for ferries departing from KK. Passenger boats connect KK to Pulau Labuan twice daily at 8am and 1.30pm (adult 1st/economy class RM41/36, child 1st/economy class RM28/23), with onward service to Brunei and to Tunku Abdul Rahman National Park. Ferries depart from Jesselton Point, located a little way north of the **Suria Sabah shopping mall** (Jln Haji Saman).

BUS & MINIVAN

Several different stations around KK serve a variety of out-of-town destinations. There is a bus to Brunei.

In general, land transport heading east departs from Inanam (Utara Terminal; 9km north of the city), while those heading north and south on the west coast leave from Padang Merdeka (Merdeka Field) Bus Station (also called Wawasan or 'old bus station'; at the south end of town). Local buses (RM1.80) from Wawasan can take tourists to Inanam if you don't want to splurge on the RM20 taxi. Have your hotel call ahead to the bus station to book your seat in advance. Same-day bookings are usually fine, although weekends are busier than weekdays. It's always good to ring ahead because sometimes transport will be halted due to flooding caused by heavy rains.

TAXI

Share taxis operate from the Padang Merdeka Bus Station. Several share taxis do a daily run between KK and Ranau, passing the entrance road to the Kinabalu National Park office. The fare to Ranau or Kinabalu National Park is RM30 or you can charter a taxi for RM120 per car (note that a normal city taxi will charge around RM250 for a charter).

Getting Around

TO/FROM THE AIRPORT

The international airport is in Tanjung Aru, 7km south of central KK and takes around 25 to 40 minutes to reach by taxi. Note that the two terminals of Kota Kinabalu International Airport (KKIA) are not connected, and at rush hour it can take a while to get from one to the other in the event you go to the wrong one. Most airlines operate out of Terminal 1, but an increasing number of carriers, including Air Asia, depart from Terminal 2.

Airport shuttle buses (adult/child RM5/3) leave Padang Merdeka station hourly between 7.30am and 8.15pm daily, arriving first at Terminal 2 then Terminal 1. Public transport runs from 6am to 7pm daily.

Taxis heading from terminals into town operate on a voucher system (RM30) sold at a taxi desk on the terminal's ground floor. Taxis heading to the airport should not charge over RM40, if you catch one in the city centre.

CAR

Major car-rental agencies have counters on the first floor at KKIA and branch offices elsewhere in town. Manual cars start at around RM120 to RM140 per day and most agencies can arrange chauffeured vehicles as well.

Borneo Express (☎016-886 0793, in Sandakan 016-886 0789; http://borneocar.com/; Lot 1-L01 C4, Kota Kinabalu Airport)

Extra Rent A Car (☎088-218 160, 088-251 529; www.e-erac-online.com; 2nd fl, Beverly Hotel, Jln Kemajuan)

Kinabalu Heritage Tours & Car Rental (☎088-318 311; www.travelborneotours.com; Block F, Tanjung Aru Plaza)

MINIVANS

Minivans operate from several stops, including Padang Merdeka Bus Station, Wawasan Plaza, and the car park outside Milimewa Superstore (near the intersection of Jln Haji Saman and Beach St). They circulate the town looking for passengers. Since most destinations in the city are within walking distance, it's unlikely that you'll need to catch a minivan, although they're handy for getting to the airport or to KK Times Square. Most destinations within the city cost RM4 to RM6.

TAXI

Expect to pay a minimum of RM15 for a ride in the city centre (even a short trip!). Taxis can be found throughout the city and at all bus stations and shopping centres. There's a stand by Milimewa Supermarket (near the intersection of Jln Haji Saman and Beach St) and another 200m southwest of City Park.

AROUND KOTA KINABALU

Tunku Abdul Rahman National Park

Whenever one enjoys a sunset off KK, the view tends to be improved by the five jungly humps of Manukan, Gaya, Sapi, Mamutik and Sulug islands. These swaths of sand, plus the reefs and cerulean waters in between them, make up **Tunku Abdul Rahman National Park** (adult/child RM10/6), covering a total area of just over 49 sq km (two-thirds of which is water). Only a short boat ride from KK, the islands are individually quite pretty, but in an effort to accommodate the ever-increasing tourist flow (especially large numbers of Chinese), barbecue stalls and restaurants now crowd the beaches. On weekends the islands can get *very* crowded, but on weekdays you can easily find some serenity. Accommodation tends to be expensive, but most travellers come here for day trips anyway, and there are camping options.

Diving in the park (especially around Gaya and Sapi) – with a dizzying 364 species of fish found here – may bring you into contact with blue-ringed octopus, black-tip reef shark and shape-shifting cuttlefish. And, if you're here between November to February, it's possible you might sight a whale shark. Borneo Dream (p322) and Downbelow (p322) both run PADI Open Water diving programs on Pulau Gaya.

Getting There & Away

Boats to the park leave from 8.30am to 4.15pm when full from KK's Jesselton Point Ferry Terminal (commonly known as 'The Jetty' by locals and taxi drivers); the last boats leave the islands for KK around 5pm. Service is every 30 minutes, but on slower days this can be every hour. Enquire at the counter for the next available boat, sign up for your chosen destination and take a seat until there are enough passengers to depart. Boats also run from Sutera Harbour – more convenient for those staying near Tanjung Aru (or for those wanting to reach Pulau Gaya).

Return fares to Mamutik, Manukan and Sapi hover around RM23. You can also buy two-/three-island passes for RM33/43.

The set fee for charter to one island is RM250, but this can be negotiated. Try to deal directly with a boat person if you do this – don't talk to the touts who prowl the area. And don't consider paying until you return to the dock.

A terminal fee of RM7.20 is added to all boat journeys, and a RM10 entrance fee to the marine park, paid when you purchase your ticket (if you are chartering a boat this should be included).

Pulau Manukan

Though this dugong-shaped island may not lay claim to as beautiful a beach as Sapi, beneath its waters you'll find far richer coral, and therefore more marine life, attracting snorkellers and divers. It is the second-largest island in the group, its 20 hectares largely covered in dense vegetation. There's a good beach with coral reefs off the southern and eastern shores, a walking trail around the perimeter and a network of nature trails; if you want to thoroughly explore all of the above it shouldn't take more than two hours, and you don't need to be particularly fit. There are little clouds of tropical fish swimming around. When you depart the boat, you'll likely be pointed towards a kiosk that hires equipment masks and snorkels (RM15), beach mats (RM5) and bodyboards (RM10).

Manukan Island Resort (☎017-833 5022; www.suterasanctuarylodges.com; r from RM800; ❄☸), managed by Sutera Sanctuary Lodges, has the only accommodation on the island. It comprises a restaurant, swimming pool and tennis courts, and 20 dark-wood villas, all overlooking the South China Sea and decked out in tasteful Bali-chic style.

Pulau Mamutik

Mamutik is the smallest island out here, a mere 300m end to end. A sandy 200m beach runs up and down the east coast, although beware of razor-sharp coral beneath the water that can cut your feet. Visibility can often be poor due to strong waves but on a still day the snorkeling is great. Better still, Pulau Mamutik picks up a small portion of the day-tripper footfall, so if you're here during the week, it will be mercifully quiet.

There's no resort here, but camping (RM40 per tent) is available – bring your own mozzie repellent. You'll also find a small store-restaurant-snorkel-rental place, barbecue stalls, resting pavilions, gift shop and public toilets. The last boat to Kota Kinabalu leaves at 5pm.

Pulau Sapi

The tiny sibling to Pulau Gaya, separated by a 200m channel, enjoys huge loads of day trippers to its lovely beach and can get a little overwhelmed on weekends. There are now lifeguards keeping vigil on the beach, and clearly defined areas for swimming. Disgorged from your ferry, expect to see busy clouds of fish swirling around the turquoise dock. There are multiple things to do, including bar flopping on the fine sand and hunting for monitor lizards (coralled behind a fenced area next to the main entrance; don't feed them).

Just back from the beach, you'll find **Borneo Sea Walking** (☎016-801 1161; www.borneoseawalking.com; Sapi dock; 30min sea-walk adult/child RM300/190; ⏲8.30am-3pm), giving nondivers the chance to go 5m deep among clownfish, breathing through a space-age helmet connected by a tube fed with air from

WATER MONITORING

If you look around the edge of the barbecue pits on Sapi, you may spot a fence cordoning off some of the jungle, and at said fence you'll usually find a hissing band of great, grey-green dragons: water monitor lizards, known locally as *biawak*. They're some of the largest reptiles in the world, with males averaging a length of 1.5m to 2m, sometimes growing as large as 3m, weighing anywhere from 19kg to 50kg. Within the lizard family they are only outstripped by Komodo dragons.

These mini-Godzillas are found all over Malaysia, but on Pulau Sapi they are the king of the jungle – and the waves. It's amazing watching these lumbering beasts take to the water, where they instantly transform into graceful sea monsters reminiscent of aquatic dinosaurs (which, indeed, are believed to be the ancestors of monitor lizards).

Warning: don't try and feed them or take a selfie next to one; their bite is poisonous (which can cause swelling and excessive bleeding) and their claws are very sharp.

the boat above. It's perfectly safe and kids love it. You'll also find **Seasport** (Sapi dock; fins, mask & snorkel per day RM15; ⊙8am-4pm) nearby, where you can hire snorkelling equipment. Snorkelling off the main beach is popular, though drifts of plastic in the water can make the experience less idyllic.

Finally, a zip line connects Pulau Sapi with Pulau Gaya. The **Coral Flyer** (☑011-2984 2023; www.coralflyer.com; Sapi Dock; adult/child RM64/30; ⊙10am-3.30pm) is 250m long, and gathers speeds up to 60km/h. Better still, there are two lines, so you can race a friend. Intrepid kids can go in tandem with a parent. The zip line starts in Gaya and ends in Sapi, so if on Sapi, catch the free transfer boat over the water.

Alternatively, you can explore the trails through Sapi's forest; it takes about 45 minutes to walk around the island. There are changing rooms, toilets, barbecue pits and a small snack kiosk, plus an outfitted campsite (RM40 per tent), but you'll need to bring most supplies from the mainland.

Pulau Gaya

With an area of about 15 sq km, Pulau Gaya is the Goliath of KK's offshore islands, rising to an elevation of 300m. It's also the closest to KK and covered in virtually undisturbed tropical forest. The bays on the east end are filled with bustling water villages, inhabited by Filipino immigrants (legal and otherwise) who live in cramped houses built on stilts in the shallow water, with mosques, schools and simple shops, also built on stilts. Residents of KK warn against exploring these water villages, saying that incidences of theft and other crimes have occurred. Recently, thanks to Sabah Police establishing an office here, crime has reduced considerably.

Three high-end resorts make up the accommodation options on Gaya.

🛏 Sleeping

Bunga Raya Island Resort   RESORT $$$
(☑088-380 390; http://bungarayaresort.com; villas from RM1200; ❀☎☲) Well-spaced villas boasting mod-cons such as satellite TVs, safe-deposit boxes, iPod docks and Bose sound systems, are spread around this tasty resort. The Plunge Pool has its own deep body of water that overlooks the beach, while the romantic Treehouse, reached by a private walkway, perches over a jacuzzi, lounge and its own natural jungle pool. Operated by the owners of Gayana Eco Resort.

Gaya Island Resort   RESORT $$$
(☑in KL 03-2783 1000; www.gayaislandresort.com; villas from RM800; ❀☎☲) Around 100-odd beautifully finished villas set in either lush jungle foliage, atmospheric mangrove, or looking out on the greens and blues of the nearby sea. This is a beautiful spot to fish, snorkel and dive, kayak, practise yoga, go on a sunset cruise or take a relaxing spa at the treatment centre. Or, alternatively, swim in its 40m-long pool.

Gayana Eco Resort   RESORT $$$
(☑088-380 390; www.gayana-eco-resort.com; villas from RM800; ❀☎☲) ∥ Fifty-two stunning villas stuffed with modern amenities and 'island-chic' touches make up posh Gayana. The Bakau (mangrove) Villa overlooks a series of tangled flooded forests, while the Palm Villa's deceptive simplicity masks steps that lead into the warm heart of Tunku Rahman's protected waters.

While here check out their inspiring on-site Marine Ecology Research Centre (MERC), which restores and rehabilitates different forms of marine wildlife; it has had great success in propagating giant clams. Also don't miss the excellent new Alu Alu Seafood restaurant, the sibling of the famous haunt in KK, with fish fresh from its organic farm.

Pulau Sulug

Shaped like a cartoon speech bubble, Sulug has an area of 8.1 hectares and is the least visited of the group, probably because it's the furthest away from KK. It only has one beach, on a spit of land extending from its eastern shore. Unfortunately, the snorkelling is pretty poor and rubbish often washes up on the beach and is not removed. If you want a quiet getaway, Sulug is a decent choice, but you'll have to charter a boat to get here as the normal ferries don't stop here. If you want a secluded beach and don't want to lay out for a charter (at least RM300), you'll do better by heading to Manukan and walking down the beach to escape the crowds.

NORTHWESTERN SABAH

The northern edge of Sabah manages to compact, into a relatively small space, much of the geographic and cultural minutiae that makes Borneo so special. The ocean? Lapping at miles of sandy beach, sky blue to stormy grey, and concealing superlative dive sites. The people? Kadazan-Dusun, Rungus, rice farmers, mountain hunters, ship builders and deep-sea fishers. And then, of course, 'the' mountain: Gunung Kinabalu, or Mt Kinabalu, the focal point of the island's altitude, trekkers, folklore and spiritual energy. For generations, the people of Sabah have been drawn to the mountain; don't be surprised when you fall under its spell too.

Mt Kinabalu & Kinabalu National Park

Gunung Kinabalu, as it is known in Malay, is more than the highest thing on the world's third-largest island. And it is more than scenery. Mt Kinabalu is ubiquitous in Sabah to the point of being inextricable. It graces the state's flag and is a constant presence at the edge of your eyes, catching the clouds and shading the valleys. It is only when you give the mountain your full attention that you realise how special this peak, the region's biggest tourist attraction, truly is.

The 4095m peak of Mt Kinabalu may not be a Himalayan sky-poker, but Malaysia's first Unesco World Heritage Site is by no means an easy jaunt. The main trail up is essentially a very long walk up a very steep hill, past alpine jungle and sunlit moonscapes, with a little scrabbling thrown in for good measure. If you don't feel up to reaching the mountain top, its base has some worthy attractions, including a large network of nature trails.

That said, the main detriment to climbing is not the physical challenge, but the cost. Things are expensive within Mt Kinabalu National Park. Bottled water costs four or five times what it goes for in KK, and Sutera Sanctuary Lodges has a monopoly on accommodation. You'll have to decide if you want to accept these fees, because they are basically the cost of climbing the mountain.

Amazingly, the mountain is still growing: researchers have found it increases in height by about 5mm a year. On a clear day you can see the Philippines from the summit; usually, though, the mountain is thoroughly wreathed in fog by midmorning.

History

Although it is commonly believed that local tribesmen climbed Kinabalu many years earlier, it was Sir Hugh Low, the British colonial secretary on Pulau Labuan, who recorded the first official ascent of Mt Kinabalu in 1851. Today Kinabalu's tallest peak is named after him, thus Borneo's highest point is ironically known as Low's Peak.

In those days the difficulty of climbing Mt Kinabalu lay not in the ascent, but in getting through the jungle to the mountain's base. Finding willing local porters was another tricky matter – the tribesmen who accompanied Low believed the spirits of the dead inhabited the mountain. Low was therefore obliged to protect the party by supplying a large basket of quartz crystals and teeth, as was the custom back then. During the subsequent years, the spirit-appeasement ceremonies became more and more elaborate, so that by the 1920s they had come to include loud prayers, gunshots, and the sacrifice of seven eggs and seven white chickens. You have to wonder at what point explorers started thinking the locals might be taking the mickey… These days, the elaborate chicken dances are no more, although climbing the mountain can still feel like a rite of passage.

On June 5 2015 an earthquake struck the mountain (p336), savagely taking the lives of 18 people.

Geology

Many visitors to Borneo assume Mt Kinabalu is a volcano, but the mountain is actually a huge granite dome that rose from the depths below some nine million years ago. In geological terms, Mt Kinabalu is still young. Little erosion has occurred on the exposed granite rock faces around the summit, though the effects of glaciers that used to cover much of the mountain can be detected by striations on the rock. There's no longer a snowline and the glaciers have disappeared, but at times ice forms in the rock pools near the summit.

Orientation & Information

Kinabalu National Park HQ is 88km by road northeast of KK and set in gardens with a magnificent view of the mountain. At 1588m the climate is refreshingly cool compared to the coast; the average temperatures are 20°C in the day and 13°C at night. The hike to the summit is difficult.

On the morning of your arrival, pay your park entry fee, present your lodging reservation slip to the Sutera Sanctuary Lodges office to receive your official room assignment, and check in with the Sabah Parks office to pay your registration and guide fees. Advance accommodation bookings are *essential* if you plan on climbing the mountain.

Mt Kinabalu Summit Trail

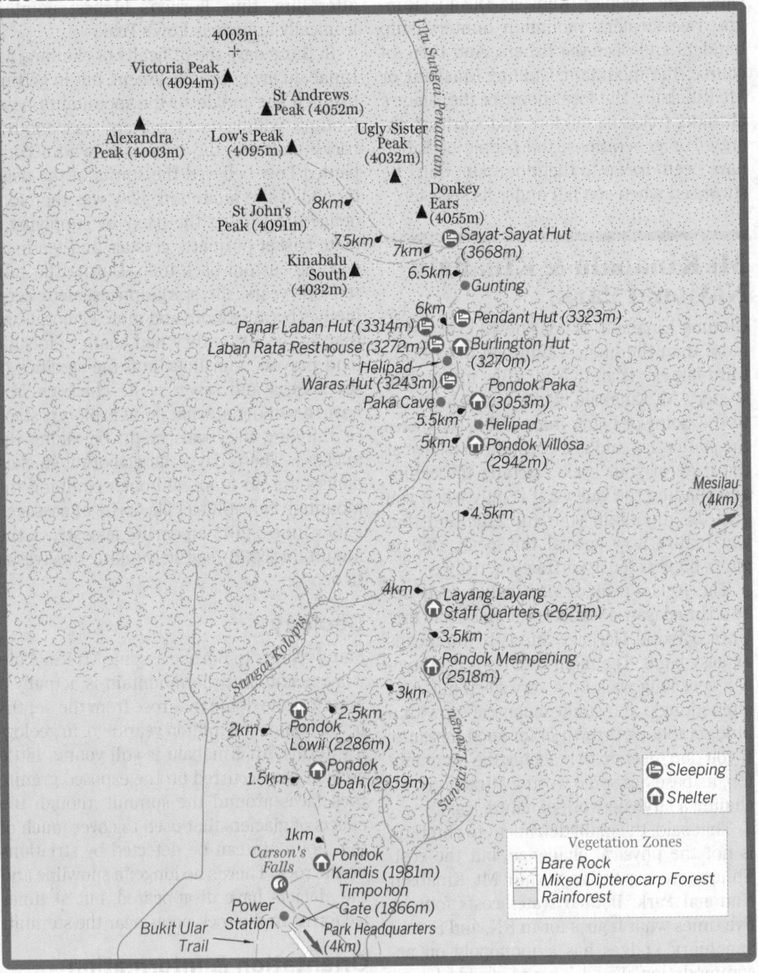

Permits, Fees & Guides

A park fee, climbing permit, insurance and a guide fee are *mandatory* if you intend to climb Mt Kinabalu. All permits and guides must be arranged at the **Sabah Parks office** (⏰7am-7pm), which is directly next door to the Sutera Sanctuary Lodges office, immediately on your right after you pass through the main gate of the park. Pay all fees at park HQ before you climb and don't ponder an 'unofficial' climb as permits (laminated cards worn on a string necklace) are scrupulously checked at two points you cannot avoid passing on the way up the mountain. Virtually every tour operator in KK can hook you up with a trip to the mountain; solo travellers are often charged around RM1400. It's possible, and a little cheaper, to do it on your own – but plan ahead. Packages are obviously easier.

All visitors entering the park are required to pay a park entrance fee: RM15 for adults and RM10 for children under 18 (Malaysians pay RM3 and RM1 respectively). A climbing permit costs RM106/RM42 for adults/children, while Malaysian nationals pay RM31.80/RM12.70. Climbing insurance costs a flat rate of RM7 per person. Guide fees for the summit trek cost RM203 for a group of one to five people. Climbers ascending Kinabalu along the Mesilau trail (when it reopens) will pay an extra RM18 (small group) or RM28 (large group) for their guide.

Your guide will be assigned to you on the morning you begin your hike. If you ask, the park staff will try to attach individual travellers to a group so that guide fees can be shared. Couples can expect to be given their own guide. Guides are mostly Kadazan from a village nearby and many of them have travelled to the summit several hundred times. Try to ask for a guide who speaks English – he or she (usually he) might point out a few interesting specimens of plant life. The path up the mountain is pretty straightforward, and the guides walk behind the slowest member of the group, so think of them as safety supervisors rather than trailblazers.

All this does not include at least RM669 for dorm-and-board or RM1349 for private room and board on the mountain at Laban Rata. With said lodging, plus buses or taxis to the park, you're looking at spending around RM900 for the common two-day, one-night trip to the mountain. It's no longer possible to do a one-day hike to the summit.

Optional extra fees include the shuttle bus (RM33, one way) or taxi (RM18, per person, group of four) from the park office to the Timpohon Gate, a climbing certificate (RM10) and a porter (RM80 per trip to the summit or RM65 to Laban Rata), who can be hired to carry a maximum load of 10kg.

If you need a helicopter lift off the mountain for emergency reasons, the going rate is RM6000.

Equipment & Clothing

No special equipment is required to successfully summit the mountain, however a headlamp is strongly advised for the predawn jaunt to the top – you'll need your hands free to climb the ropes on the summit massif. Expect freezing temperatures near the summit, not to mention strong winds and the occasional rainstorm. Don't forget a water bottle, which can be refilled at unfiltered (but potable) tanks en route. The average temperature range at Kinabalu Park is 15°C to 24°C. Along the Timpohon (the Summit trail), it's about 6°C to 14°C, and can sometimes drop to as low as 2°C.

The Climb to the Summit

This schedule assumes you're doing a two-day/one-night ascent of the mountain. You'll want to check in at park headquarters at around 9am – 8.45am at the latest for *via ferrata* (p337) participants – to pay your park fees, grab your guide and start the ascent (four to six hours) to Laban Rata (3272m), where you'll spend the night before finishing the climb. On the following day you'll start scrambling to the top at about 2.30am in order to reach the summit for a breathtaking sunrise over Borneo.

A climb up Kinabalu is only advised for those in adequate physical condition. The trek is tough, and *every step you take* will be uphill. You will negotiate several obstacles along the way, including slippery stones, blinding humidity, frigid winds and slow-paced trekkers. Mountain Torq (p337) compares the experience to squeezing five days of hiking into a 38-hour trek.

There are two trail options leading up the mountain – the Timpohon Trail and the Mesilau Trail. If this is your first time climbing Kinabalu, we advise taking the Timpohon Trail – it's shorter, easier (but by no means easy!), and more convenient from the park headquarters (an hour's walk or short park shuttle ride to the Timpohon Trail start. If

KINABALU PACKING LIST

- ☐ Headlamp (with spare batteries)
- ☐ Comfortable running or hiking shoes
- ☐ Whistle
- ☐ Energy food (Dextrasol tablets, sweets, chocolate, energy bars)
- ☐ Wool socks and athletic socks
- ☐ Hiking shorts or breathable pants
- ☐ Three T-shirts (one made of lightweight synthetic material)
- ☐ Fleece jacket
- ☐ Lightweight shell jacket, poncho or rain jacket
- ☐ Fleece or wool hat and fleece gloves
- ☐ Hand towel
- ☐ Water bottle
- ☐ Sunscreen and sunglasses
- ☐ Insect repellent
- ☐ Light, high-energy snacks
- ☐ Camera
- ☐ Money
- ☐ Earplugs for dorms

you are participating in Mountain Torq's *via ferrata,* you are required to take the Timpohon Trail in order to reach Laban Rata in time for your safety briefing at 4pm. The Mesilau Trail offers second-time climbers (or fit hikers) the opportunity to really enjoy some of the park's natural wonders. This 8km trail is less trodden so the chances of seeing unique flora and fauna are higher.

As you journey up to the summit, you'll happen upon signboards showing your progress – there's a marker every 500m. There are also *pondok* (rest shelters) at regular intervals, with basic toilets and tanks of unfiltered (but potable) drinking water. The walking times that follow are conservative estimates: don't be surprised if you move at a slightly speedier pace, and certainly don't be discouraged if you take longer – everyone's quest for the summit is different.

Timpohon Gate to Layang Layang

'Why am I sweating this much *already?*'

The trip to the summit officially starts at the Timpohon Gate (1866m) and from there it's an 8.72km march to the summit. There is a small bathroom outhouse located 700m before the Timpohon Gate, and there's a convenience shop at the gate itself for impulse snack and beverage purchases.

After a short, deceptive descent, the trail leads up steep stairs through the dense forest and continues winding up and up for the rest of the trip. There's a charming waterfall, **Carson's Falls**, beside the track shortly after the start, and the forest can be alive with birds and squirrels in the morning. Five *pondok* are spaced at intervals of 15 to 35 minutes between Timpohon Gate and Layang Layang and it's about three hours to the Layang Layang (2621m) rest stop. Near **Pondok Lowii** (2286m), the trail follows an open ridge giving great views over the valleys and up to the peaks.

Layang Layang to Pondok Paka

This part of the climb can be the most difficult for some – especially around the 4.5km marker. You've definitely made some headway but there's still a long trek to go – no light at the end of the jungly tunnel quite yet. It takes about 1¾ hours to reach Pondok Paka (3053m), the seventh shelter on the trail, 5.5km from the start.

Pondok Paka to Laban Rata

Also known as the 'can't I pay someone to finish this for me?' phase, this part of the climb is where beleaguered hikers get a second wind as the treeline ends and the summit starts to feel closer. At the end of this leg you'll reach Laban Rata (3272m), your 'home sweet home' on the mountain. Take a good look at the slender signpost announcing your arrival – it's the propeller of the helicopter once used to hoist the construction materials to build the elaborate rest station. This leg takes around 45 minutes.

Laban Rata to Sayat-Sayat Hut

It's 2am and your alarm just went off. Is this a dream? Nope. You're about to climb the

THE DAY THE MOUNTAIN SHOOK

On 5 June 2015 at 7.15am, an earthquake measuring 6.0 on the Richter scale struck Mt Kinabalu. It was until then a glorious morning, the sky a rich blue, the mountain teeming with trekkers. Massive landslides and huge rockfalls followed, even one of the famous 'Donkey's Ears' rock formations snapped off. The strongest to affect Malaysia since 1976, the quake lasted 30 seconds and tragically took the lives of 18 people, many of them students from Singapore. There were 137 people stranded on the mountain but later saved. That first evening alone three massive aftershocks were felt, and by 23 June, 90 had been felt as far away as Kota Kinabalu.

The 15-million-year-old mountain's name is derived from the Kadazan-Dusun tribe's phrase 'Aki Nabalu', meaning 'the resting place of the souls of the departed'. The Kadazan Dusun consider it a sacred temple and believe the earthquake was caused by 'Aki' (the mountain's protectors), who were enraged at the loutish behaviour of 10 Westerners (who allegedly stripped and urinated, insulted their guide, and two of their cohort even managed to have sex on their ascent of the mountain) on 30 May.

The trail from Timpohon to Laban Rata reopened to climbers in September 2015, with business as usual, and the trail from Laban Rata to the summit reopened on 1 December. At the time of research, the Mesilau Trail was closed until further notice. The number of climbers per day allowed on the mountain has also been reduced from 193 to 135.

VIA FERRATA

Mountain Torq (☎088-268126; www.mountaintorq.com; Low's Peak Circuit RM870, Walk the Torq RM650) has dramatically changed the Kinabalu climbing experience by creating an intricate system of rungs and rails crowning the mountain's summit. Known as *via ferrata* (literally 'iron road' in Italian), this alternative style of mountaineering has been a big hit in Europe for the last century and is just starting to take Asia by storm. In fact, Mountain Torq is Asia's first *via ferrata* system, and, according to the *Guinness Book of World Records*, it's the highest 'iron road' in the world.

After ascending Kinabalu in the traditional fashion, participants use the network of rungs, pallets and cables to return to the Laban Rata rest camp area along the mountain's dramatic granite walls. Mountain Torq's star attraction, the **Low's Peak Circuit** (minimum age 17), is a four- to five-hour scramble down metres upon metres of sheer rock face. This route starts at 3766m, passing a variety of obstacles before linking up to the Walk the Torq path for the last part of the journey. The route's threadlike tightrope walks and swinging planks will have you convinced that the course designers are sadistic, but that's what makes it such fun – testing your limits without putting your safety in jeopardy. Those who don't want to see their heart leaping out of their chest should try the **Walk the Torq** (minimum age 10) route. This two- to three-hour escapade is an exciting initiation into the world of *via ferrata*, offering dramatic mountain vistas with a few less knee-shaking moments. No matter which course you tackle, you'll undoubtedly think that the dramatic vertical drops are nothing short of exhilarating.

At the time of research a new *via ferrata* route was being established to replace Walk the Torq, due to the summit trail being rerouted after the earthquake. For more information, check out www.mountaintorq.com.

last part of the mountain in order to reach the summit before sunrise.

Most people set off at around 2.45am, and it's worth heading out at this time even if you're in great shape (don't forget your torch). The one-hour climb to Sayat-Sayat hut (3668m) involves a lot of hiker traffic and the crossing of the sheer Panar Laban rock face. There is little vegetation, except where overhangs provide some respite from the wind. It is one of the toughest parts of the climb, especially in the cold and dark of the predawn hours. Note that on some particularly steep sections, you have to haul yourself up specially strung ropes (gloves essential).

Sayat-Sayat Hut to Summit

After checking in at Sayat-Sayat, the crowd of hikers begins to thin as stronger walkers forge ahead and slower adventurers pause for sips from their water bottle. Despite the stunning surroundings, the last stretch of the summit ascent is, of course, the steepest and hardest part of the climb.

From just beyond Sayat-Sayat, the summit looks deceptively close and, though it's just over 1km, the last burst will take between one and three hours depending on your stamina. You might even see shattered climbers crawling on hands and knees as they reach out for the top of Borneo.

The Summit

This is it – the million-dollar moment. Don't forget the sunrise can be glimpsed from anywhere on the mountain. The summit warms up quickly as the sun starts its own ascent between 5.45am and 6.20am, and the weary suddenly smile; the climb up a distant memory, the trek down an afterthought.

Consider signing up with Mountain Torq to climb back to Laban Rata along the world's highest *via ferrata*.

The Journey Back to the Bottom

You'll probably leave the summit at around 7.30am and you should aim to leave Laban Rata no later than 12.30pm. The gruelling descent back down to Timpohon Gate from Laban Rata takes between three and four hours (if you're returning to the bottom along the Mesilau Trail it will take more time than descending to the Timpohon Gate). The weather can close in very quickly and the granite is slippery even when dry. During rainstorms the downward trek feels like walking through a river. Slower walkers often find that their legs hurt more the day after – quicker paces lighten the constant pounding as legs negotiate each descending step. If you participated in the *via ferrata* you will be absolutely knackered during your descent and will stumble into

FLORA & FAUNA OF MT KINABALU

Mt Kinabalu is a botanical paradise, designated a Centre of Plant Diversity as well as a Unesco-listed World Heritage Site. The wide range of habitats supports an even wider range of natural history, and over half the species growing above 900m are unique to the area.

Among the more spectacular flowers are orchids, rhododendrons and the *Insectivorous nepenthes* (pitcher plant). Around park HQ, there's dipterocarp forest (rainforest); creepers, ferns and orchids festoon the canopy, while fungi grow on the forest floor. Between 900m and 1800m, there are oaks, laurels and chestnuts, while higher up there's dense rhododendron forest. On the windswept slopes above Laban Rata vegetation is stunted, with *sayat-sayat* a common shrub. The mountain's uppermost slopes are bare of plant life.

Deer and monkeys are no longer common around park HQ, but you can see squirrels, including the handsome Prevost's squirrel and the mountain ground squirrel. Tree shrews can sometimes be seen raiding rubbish bins. Common birds are Bornean treepies, fantails, bulbuls, sunbirds and laughing thrushes, while birds seen only at higher altitudes are the Kinabalu friendly warbler, the mountain blackeye and the mountain blackbird. Other wildlife includes colourful butterflies and the huge green moon moth.

Timpohon Gate just before sunset (around 6pm to 6.30pm).

A 1st-class certificate can be purchased for RM10 by those who complete the climb; 2nd-class certificates are issued for making it to Laban Rata. These can be collected at the park office.

Walks Around the Base

It's well worth spending a day exploring the marked trails around park headquarters; if you have time, it may be better to do it before you climb the mountain, as chances are you won't really feel like it afterwards. There are various trails and lookouts.

The base trails interconnect with one another, so you can spend the day, or indeed days, walking at a leisurely pace through the beautiful forest. Some interesting plants, plenty of birds and, if you're lucky, the occasional mammal can be seen along the **Liwagu Trail** (6km), which follows the river of the same name. When it rains, watch out for slippery paths and legions of leeches.

At 11am each day a **guided walk** (per person RM5) starts from the Sabah Parks office and lasts for one to two hours. The knowledgeable guide points out flowers, plants, birds and insects along the way. If you set out from KK early enough, it's possible to arrive at the park in time for the guided walk.

Many of the plants found on the mountain are cultivated in the **Mountain Garden** (admission RM5; ⌚9am-1pm & 2.30-4pm) behind the visitors centre. Guided tours of the garden depart at 9am, noon and 3pm and cost RM5.

Sleeping

Laban Rata (On the Mountain)

Camping is not allowed on the mountain, and thus access to the summit is limited by access to the huts on the mountain at Laban Rata (3272m). This *must* be booked in advance, the earlier the better. In order to have any hope of clear weather when you reach the summit you must arrive around dawn, and the only way to do this is by spending a night at Laban Rata.

Sutera Sanctuary Lodges (☎088-287 887; http://suterasanctuarylodges.com.my; Lot G15, ground fl, Wisma Sabah; dm/tw incl 3 meals & bedding RM669/1349, nonheated dm incl 3 meals RM587) in Kota Kinabalu operates almost all of the accommodation here, but space is limited. Be mindful that travellers often report frustration with booking huts on the mountain – claiming the booking system is disorganised and inefficient, the huts are often full, or aren't full when they're told they are. Bookings can be made online (but only if you book at least two nights), in person or over the phone – our experience was that it was best to book at Sutera's offices in KK if you haven't done so in advance.

The most common sleeping option is the heated dormitory (bedding included) in the Laban Rata Resthouse, which sells for RM669 per person. If you need privacy, twin shares are available for RM1349. Three meals are included in the price. Nonheated facilities surrounding the Laban Rata

Kinabalu National Park Headquarters & Trails

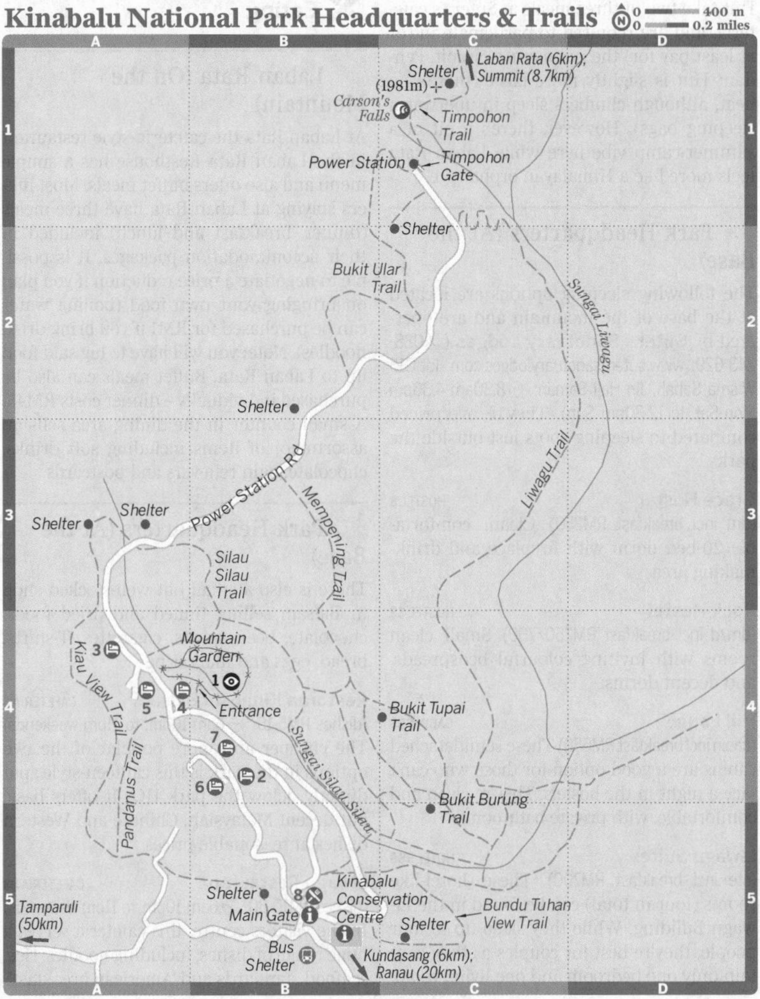

Kinabalu National Park Headquarters & Trails

Sights
1 Mountain Garden B4

Sleeping
2 Grace Hostel B4
3 Hill Lodge A4
4 Liwagu Suites A4
5 Nepenthes Villa A4
6 Peak Lodge B4
7 Rock Hostel B4

Eating
Liwagu Restaurant .... (see 4)
8 Restoran Kinabalu Balsam B5

building are also available for RM587 per person (meals included).

The other option at Laban Rata is to stay at Pendant Hut, which is owned and operated by **Mountain Torq** (☎088-268 126; www.mountaintorq.com; suite 1-3/4, Level 2 Menara MAA, 6 Lg Api Api 1, Kota Kinabalu; r incl via ferrata RM850-4000). All guests sleeping at Pendant

Hut take two of three meals at Sutera's cafeteria, and are required to participate in (or at least pay for) the *via ferrata* circuit. Pendant Hut is slightly more basic (there's no heat, although climbers sleep in uberwarm sleeping bags). However, there's a bit of a summer-camp vibe here while Laban Rata feels more like a Himalayan orphanage.

Park Headquarters (At the Base)

The following sleeping options are located at the base of the mountain and are operated by **Sutera Sanctuary Lodges** (☎088-243 629; www.suterasanctuarylodges.com; lot G15 Wisma Sabah, Jln Haji Saman; ⊙8.30am-4.30pm Mon-Sat, to 12.30pm Sun). They're overpriced compared to sleeping spots just outside the park.

Grace Hostel HOSTEL $
(dm incl breakfast RM250) Clean, comfortable 20-bed dorm with fireplace and drink-making area.

Rock Hostel HOSTEL $$
(dm/d incl breakfast RM250/700) Small clean rooms with inviting colourful bedspreads, and decent dorms.

Hill Lodge CABIN $$$
(cabin incl breakfast RM650) These semidetached cabins are a good option for those who can't face a night in the hostels. They're clean and comfortable, with private bathrooms.

Liwagu Suites HOTEL $$$
(ste incl breakfast RM700) These hotel-like rooms (four in total) can be found in the Liwagu Building. While they sleep up to four people, they're best for couples as they contain only one bedroom and one living room.

Nepenthes Villa HOTEL $$$
(lodge incl breakfast RM1100) These attached two-storey units fall somewhere between hotel rooms and private lodges. They have two bedrooms (one with a twin bed, one with a queen) and verandahs offering limited mountain views.

Peak Lodge UNIT $$$
(lodge incl breakfast RM980) These semidetached units have two bedrooms (one with a bunk bed and one with two twin beds), pleasant sitting rooms, fireplaces and nice views from their verandahs.

Eating

Laban Rata (On the Mountain)

At Laban Rata the cafeteria-style restaurant in the Laban Rata Resthouse has a simple menu and also offers buffet meals. Most hikers staying at Laban Rata have three meals (dinner, breakfast and lunch) included in their accommodation packages. It is possible to negotiate a price reduction if you plan on bringing your own food (boiling water can be purchased for RM1 if you bring dried noodles). Note: you will have to lug said food up to Laban Rata. Buffet meals can also be purchased individually – dinner costs RM45. A small counter in the dining area sells an assortment of items including soft drinks, chocolate, pain relievers and postcards.

Park Headquarters (At the Base)

There is also a small but well-stocked shop in Balsam selling tinned and dried foods, chocolate, beer, spirits, cigarettes, T-shirts, bread, eggs and margarine.

Restoran Kinabalu Balsam CAFETERIA $
(dishes RM5-15; ⊙6am-10pm, to 11pm weekends) The cheaper and more popular of the two options in the park is this canteen-style spot directly below the park HQ. It offers basic but decent Malaysian, Chinese and Western dishes at reasonable prices.

Liwagu Restaurant CAFETERIA $$
(dishes RM10-30; ⊙6am-10pm, to 11pm weekends) In the visitors centre, this cafeteria serves a huge range of dishes, including noodles, rice, seafood standards and 'American breakfast'.

Getting There & Away

It is highly advised that summit-seekers check in at the park headquarters by 9am, which means if you're coming from KK, you should plan to leave by 7am, or consider spending the night somewhere near the base of the mountain.

BUS

Express buses (RM30) leave KK from the Utara Terminal bus station every hour on the hour from 7am to 10am and at 12.30pm, 2pm and 3pm and leave at the same times in the reverse direction; alternatively take a Ranau-bound minivan (RM25) from central KK at Padang Merdeka bus terminal, asking the driver to drop you outside the gate at Kinabalu National Park. Minivans leave when full and run from early morning till around 2pm. We recommend leaving by 7am for the two-hour trip.

Express buses and minivans travelling between KK and Ranau (and Sandakan) pass the park turn-off, 100m uphill from the park entrance. You can go to Sandakan (RM40) if the bus has room.

JEEP

Share jeeps park just outside of the park gates and leave when full for KK (RM200) and Sandakan (RM500); each jeep can hold around five passengers, but they can be chartered by individuals.

TAXI

Share taxis leave KK from Inanam and Padang Merdeka Bus Stations (RM200).

Around Mt Kinabalu

Kinabalu National Park is home to Borneo's highest mountain and some of the island's best-preserved forest. Most travellers make a beeline for the mountain and the main park headquarters area, but there are some surrounding spots also worth exploring.

Sights & Activities

Kundasang War Memorial MEMORIAL
(Kota Kinabalu–Ranau Hwy; admission RM10; 8.30am-5pm) The junction for the Mesilau Nature Resort on the KK–Ranau Hwy is the site of the Kundasang War Memorial, which commemorates the Australian and British prisoners who died on the infamous Sandakan Death Marches (p352). While other memorials in Sabah often seem neglected and forgotten, the Kundasang gardens are remarkably touching. Four gardens, manicured in that bucolic yet tame fashion that is so very English, are separated by a series of marbled pavilions.

In the Anzac Garden you can see a full list of the deceased and at the back of the gardens is a stunning viewpoint of Mt Kinabalu.

The memorial is in Kundasang, 10km east of Kinabalu National Park headquarters. You'll know you're in Kundasang when you see the market stalls on either side of the road. Take the turn on the left for Mesilau Nature Resort. The memorial is on the right 150m after the turn-off. Look for the flags and the stone fort-like structure above the road.

Ranau Night Market MARKET
(central Ranau; Sat) Packed with aromas and produce from all over the region, this is where locals come to haggle and barter every Saturday evening; especially photogenic come dusk.

Sabah Tea Garden TEA PLANTATION
(088-440 882; www.facebook.com/sabahtea; KM17, Jln Ranau–Sandakan; admission free, guided tour RM12, with set lunch RM34, 2-day, 1-night package from RM190; 8am-4pm) A pretty tea plantation huddles in the mountains near Ranau. Contact the tea garden to arrange tours of both the plantation and surrounding rainforests and river valleys. Overnight packages are available in a cosy bungalow, a traditional longhouse or campsite. Also offers tours of the facilities coupled with a trip for a fish foot massage (RM110).

Mesilau Nature Resort TREKKING
(088-871 519; Kudasang, Ranau; adult/child RM15/10, guided nature walk RM10; 9am-4pm) Just 30 minutes' drive from Kinabalu Park, this peaceful resort, nestled amid lush jungle, sits at 6172m and is the highest point you can reach by car. The resort is terrific for walking trails, and is also an alternative starting point for ascending Mt Kinabalu, often favoured by trekkers as it's more challenging than the main route and much less crowded than park headquarters.

Tagal Sungai Moroli MASSAGE
(088-878 044; Kampung Luanti, Ranau; full body 'massage' RM25; 9am-5pm) After your epic Kinabalu climb, head to Tagal Sungai Moroli for a relaxing massage, courtesy of thousands of nibbling fish. The term 'tagal' means 'no fishing' in the local Kadazan-Dusun language, as the fish in the river (a species known locally as *ikan pelian*) are not to be captured – they are special massage fish.

The townsfolk claim that they've trained the little swimmers to gently nibble at weary feet (and more, if you're up for it). Kampung Luanti is half an hour's drive east of Ranau (24.5km).

Poring Hot Springs HOT SPRINGS
(Poring, Ranau; adult/child incl Kinabalu National Park RM15/10; entrance gate 7am-5pm, park until 8pm, Butterfly Garden & Canopy Walk closed Mon) One of the few positive contributions the Japanese made to Borneo during WWII, Poring Hot Springs has become a popular weekend retreat for locals. Located in a well-maintained forest park with nature paths that the elderly and children can enjoy, the springs steam with hot sulphurous

water channelled into pools and tubs, some of which feel a little rundown. Remember your towel and swimming trunks.

For our ringgit, the highlight of the place is actually way above the springs: a **Canopy Walkway** (admission RM15; ⏱9am-4pm) that consists of a series of walkways suspended from trees, up to 40m above the jungle floor, providing unique views of the surrounding forest. Get there early if you want to see birds or other wildlife. A **tropical garden** (⏱9am-4pm), **butterfly farm** (adult/child RM4/2; ⏱9am-4pm Tue-Sun) and **orchid garden** (adult/child RM10/5; ⏱9am-4pm) are also part of the Poring complex. Rafflesia sometimes bloom in the area; look out for signs in the visitors centre and along the road.

Part of Kinabalu National Park, the complex is 43km from park headquarters, east of Ranau.

Sleeping & Eating

It's worth spending a night around the base of Kinabalu before your ascent, and there are plenty of accommodation options suiting everyone's budget, which all come with attached restaurants.

The accommodation at Mesilau and Poring is run by Sutera Sanctuary Lodges with a notable exception. There are privately owned sleeping options looping around Kinabalu's base. Most of these are located along the road between the park headquarters and Kundasang (east of the park's entrance). Two homestays in Kundasang, **Walai Tokou** (☎019-860 2270, 088-888 166; koch_homestay@yahoo.com; Ranau; packages from RM240) and **Mesilou Atamis** (☎013-886 2474, 019-580 2474; www.facebook.com/Mesilou-Atamis-Homestay; 2-day/1-night package from RM350; P), are another option.

Mountain Guest House GUESTHOUSE $
(☎016-837 4040, 088-888632; KM53, Jln Tinompok, off Kinabalu Park, Ranau; dm/s/d/q incl breakfast from RM30/60/70/80) This friendly but clean guesthouse is endearingly ramshackle and sits (or hangs?) on different levels up the side of the mountain. About five minute's walk from the park entrance, houseproud basic rooms have a few sticks of furniture and spotless bathrooms. Breakfast included and vegetarian dinners (RM8) available. Run by lovely Anna.

★ **Lupa Masa** ECO-CAMP $$
(☎016-806 8194, 012-845 1987; http://lupamasa.com; Poring; per person incl meals tent/chalet RM90/250) This incredible eco-camp is surrounded by forest and has two gin-clear rivers to bathe in, with waterfalls and natural jacuzzis. Lupa Masa isn't for everyone though…no electricity or wi-fi, but bugs and leeches at no extra cost. Accommodation is on mattresses in tents on raised platforms, or the delightful new chalets with striking river views.

Seasonally it even has its own flowering rafflesias. Meals, mostly vegetarian, are included. The camp can also help with booking onward travel and offers mountain biking and day and overnight trips to the jungle, river tubing and hidden caves. Lupa Masa contribute generously to local communities. About a 45-minute walk/10-minute drive from Poring.

Wind Paradise YURT $$
(☎088-714 563, 012-820 3360; http://windparadise2011.blogspot.com/; Jln Mesilau, Cinta Mata, Kundasang; d/tr RM170/200, 4-person yurt RM300; P) With staggeringly pretty views of the valley and town of Kundasang far below, these Mongolian yurts, and rooms in a central lodge – both set in pleasant lawns – are delightful. There's self-catering and a great lounge, and barbecue facilities to lap up the mountain view. Yurts have comfy beds and make for a great sleep with natural ventilation.

D'Villa Rina Ria Lodge LODGE $$
(☎088-889 282, 011-601 6936; www.dvillalodge.com.my; KM53, Jln Tinompok, off Kinabalu Park, Ranau; dm/d/q RM30/120/220; @ 📶) Close to the Kinabalu National Park entrance, with 'traveller magnet' tattooed across its open restaurant and balconied rooms with jaw-dropping valley views. This is a great one-stop shop – literally – stock up on everything from batteries to chocolate, and socks to ponchos here. Rooms are basic with yellow walls, cosy quilts and piping-hot showers.

Poring Hot Springs Resort RESORT $$
(Poring Hot Springs, Ranau; ⏱dm/r US$35/42) At the base of Mt Kinabalu, this hotel boasts a range of accommodation from clean dorms to fine rooms with lacquered wood floors, separate living room, big beds, stylish bathroom, private balcony, and satellite TV. Close to the forest pools, and the rest of the park.

Mesilau Nature Resort RESORT $$
(☎088-871 519; Pekan Ranau, Ranau; 3-bed chalet RM1285) Sitting at over 6000m and nestled in thick lush jungle makes for an atmospheric

DON'T MISS

THE ORANGUTANS OF SHANGRI-LA

The **Sanctuary** at Shangri-La's Rasa Ria Resort (p344), located near Tuaran, is a makeshift wildlife reserve owned and managed by the resort. There are all kinds of daily activities, from birdwatching trips to night walks (there are civets and loris on the reserve) to viewing the Sanctuary's orangutans from a canopy walkway. The red apes here are just as cute as the ones at Sepilok (p355), and it's way less crowded as well. Plus, your money is still going towards a preservation organisation. There's different rates for all of the above activities depending on whether or not you're a guest at the hotel.

For more information, visit: www.shangri-la.com/kotakinabalu/rasariaresort/sports-recreation/nature/nature-reserve-activities or call ☎088-797 888.

The two-hour orangutan viewing occurs daily at 10am. Kids between 5 and 12 years can help out the rangers responsible for feeding the orangutans.

spot to stay. The lodging is in functional dorms and doubles, with attractive though basic rooms with desks and colourful quilts (which you'll be glad of – it gets chilly), plus three-bedroom chalets. There's also a pleasant restaurant terrace where buffet-style dinner and breakfast is served.

J Residence BUNGALOW **$$$**
(☎012-869 6969; www.jresidence.com; r/tr RM88/99, villa RM480) Just 300m from Mt Kinabalu Park's entrance, this tasteful accommodation clinging to the mountainside is redolent with the scent of surrounding pine trees, fresh and peaceful. There are eight rooms with wood floors, balcony and bathroom, plus tasteful linen and soaring views. Note the prices listed are weekday prices; add an additional 40% at the weekend.

Nikgold Garden BUNGALOW **$$$**
(☎088-888 112; www.facebook.com/NikgoldGarden; Jln Tinompok, off Kinabalu Park, Ranau; r/f RM98/400; P 📶) Set on the side of Mt Kinabalu opposite a vegetable farm, this new dark-wood building has a flavour of Swiss chalet to it. Its 10 sunrise-facing rooms are minimalist chic, while the chalets are huge affairs with two bedrooms, lounge, flat screen, DVD player, and balcony. It's on the road to Kundasang, five minutes' drive after the park entrance.

ℹ Getting There & Around

KK round-trip buses stop in front of park headquarters and in Ranau (RM15 to RM20, two hours) from 7am to 8pm. Minivans operate from a blue-roofed shelter in Ranau servicing the nearby attractions (park HQ, Poring etc) for RM5. The national park operates a van service between the headquarters and Poring for RM25 – it leaves the park HQ at noon.

Northwest Coast

The northwest coast of Sabah is criminally underexplored. The A1 runs north from KK to Kudat and the Tip of Borneo past wide headlands, rice paddies and hidden beaches. This is a good area for renting a car or motorbike – the roads are pretty level, and public transport links aren't reliable for getting off the main road.

Tuaran

Tuaran, 33km from KK, is a bustling little town with tree-lined boulevard-style streets and the distinctive nine-storey **Ling Sang Pagoda**, the approaches of which are dominated by vividly painted guardian deities. There's little point stopping in the town itself unless you happen to pass through on a market day (Tuaran is likely named for the Malay word *tawaran*, meaning 'sale', reflecting its history as a trading post), but the surrounding area conceals a few cool sights. You'll see signs for **Mengkabong Water Village**, a Bajau stilt village built over an estuary, but development and pollution has diminished this spot's charms.

Sights

Rumah Terbalik & the 3D Wonders Museum HOUSE
(The Upside Down House; ☎088-260 263; www.upsidedownhouse.com.my; Kg Telibong, Batu 21, Jln Telibong Tamparuli; Upside Down House adult/child RM19/5, 3D Wonders Museum RM35/15, Combo ticket RM48/19; 8am-10pm; P) Sabah has few 'quirky' sights... Enter 'Rumah Terbalik': the Upside Down House; a modern, tastefully decorated house, but...upside down! Even the furniture and the car parked in the

garage *sticks to the ceiling*. In the same compound is the equally odd 3D Wonders Museum, which allows you to poke your heads in aperture on painted scenes of turtles and swinging orangutans and join the fun.

Sleeping & Eating

Given the town's proximity to KK (with its many accommodation options), you probably won't need to stay in town. However, if for some reason you need a room, try **Orchid Hotel** (088-793 789, 012-820 8894; 4 Jln Teo Teck Ong; r from RM40-100;). It's somewhat overpriced but it'll do the trick for a night. Just a few doors away is **Tai Fatt** (Jln Teo Teck Ong; meals RM4; 7am-10pm), the best *kedai kopi* in Tuaran. It excels at *char mien/mee goreng*, the local, mouth-watering take on Chinese fried noodles, overflowing with vegetables, pork, oil, pork, egg, pork, wheat noodles and, yes, pork.

Shangri La Rasa Ria Resort RESORT **$$$**
(088-792888; www.shangri-la.com; Pantai Dalit; r incl breakfast from RM730;) Occupying a fine stretch of peach-hued dunes about 45 minutes north of KK's airport, this beautiful resort boasts its own 18-hole golf course, several fine restaurants, a lovely pool (plus a great kids pool with a twirly slide) and a relaxing spa. While the resort may be more comfy than heaven, its best feature is the small nature sanctuary (p343).

Getting There & Away

All buses north pass through Tuaran, and minivans shuttle regularly to and from KK (RM5 to RM10, 30 minutes). Minivans to Mengkabong are less frequent and cost RM2. Regular minivans go from Tuaran to Kota Belud (around RM15, 30 minutes).

Kota Belud

You could be forgiven for missing Kota Belud off your 'must see' list, but this bustling town makes for a useful stopover if you're en route to Mañana beach, Mantanani or Kudat. Other than the gold mosque on the hill, and the presence of cows blithely wandering the streets, the town's Sunday *tamu* (market) – a congested, colourful melee of vendors, hagglers and hawkers – is definitely worth your camera's time.

Once a year in October, Kota Belud hosts the famous **Tamu Besar** – the biggest *tamu* organised in Sabah. The highlight is a procession of fully caparisoned Bajau horsemen from the nearby villages, decked out, along with their steeds, in vivid, multicoloured satin 'armour' and embroidered barding.

Visitors looking for tribal handicrafts and traditional clothing may find a prize here, but it's cheaply made stuff for tourists. Ironically, the best way to experience this commercial event is to come not expecting to buy anything – soak up the convivial, occasionally manic atmosphere, enjoy a good meal at the lovely food stalls and just potter about like Grandma at a Sunday flea market.

Activities

Big Fin Divers DIVING
(014-679 3679; www.bigfindivers.com; Mañana Borneo Resort, Kota Belud; 2 dives RM250, PADI 4-day Open Water Course RM990) This new outfit offers PADI courses and diving on a near-

THE BEACH

Travellers are currently whispering about a beach of silky sand backdropped by thick jungle, fiery sunsets and turquoise green waters home to whale sharks and manta rays. Intrepid types regularly tramp across rising tides, through jellyfish, rocks and vines to reach it, knowing full well its only accommodation is booked up. OK, enough of the prelude, **Mañana Beach** is its name, and for once, here's a place that's all it's cracked up to be, and more.

Reached by boat from tiny **Pituru Laut village** (rather than walking through the jungle cliffs and rising tide!), the journey takes all of 10 minutes. However, on arrival you feel as if it's taken you back in time to a place of simplicity: kids playing happily on the sand, glassy waves and bobbing surfers, the sound of music piping from the nearby guesthouse, divers returning from the deep with smiles on their faces.

Currently there's only Mañana you can stay at; simple it may be but the easy vibe it's created combined with the nearby unchartered reef, surfable waves and paradisial setting, have got travellers saying things like: 'Thailand twenty years ago...', plus a few names from Hollywood thinking of buying plots of land here.

by reef within the 'coral triangle'; a reef so large it's not yet been charted. Mayne Point has huge granite boulders, while Ella's Garden is coral-rich and bursting with squid, cuttlefish, nurse and leopard sharks, stingrays, barracuda, and – if you're here around April till June – whale sharks.

Dive sites are close by, one of which is a downed WWII Japanese tanker, so you waste little time getting there, and on a clear day as you ascend from the depths you can clearly see Mt Kinabalu in the distance. Based at Mañana.

Sleeping & Eating

Most people visit Kota Belud as a day trip from KK, since you can make it there and back with plenty of time for the market. There are no great places to stay, nor is it much of a gastronome's delight, but tasty snacks can be picked up at the Sunday market.

TD Lodge HOTEL $

(013-880 3833; block D, lot D20-D24, Kompleks Alapbana; r RM82-92, f RM106) This Soviet-style flat-top building is fine for a night with its pleasant rooms with bright walls, TV, bathroom, laminate floors, coffee-making facilities, desk and fresh linen. Certainly the cleanest central option in town.

★**Mañana** GUESTHOUSE $$

(014-679 3679, 014-679 2679; www.mananaborneo.com; chalet/villa/family villa from RM120/180/350) Imagine a hidden beach and chilled vibe where young and old swap stories late into the night. Run by lovely Yan and Nani, Mañana's cabanas boast soulful views over an aquamarine bay. You can also learn yoga, paddle-board, surf, or dive with Big Fin Divers. The restaurant serves hot and cold food, and there's also a new bar. It's a special place.

Mañana feels as if it's on an island, given that you have to catch a boat from Kampung Pituru Laut to reach it. *Always* book ahead. It's possible to arrange a cab from KK with a trusted driver recommended by Mañana. If it is fully booked (which is highly likely), it's possible to rent a tent until a chalet becomes free.

Getting There & Away

Minivans and share taxis gather in front of Pasar Besar, the old market. Most of these serve the Kota Belud–KK route (RM10, two hours) or Kudat (RM20, two hours), departing from 7am to 5pm. To get to Kinabalu National Park, take any minibus going to KK and get off at Tamparuli, about halfway (RM10, 30 minutes). There are several minivans from Tamparuli to Ranau every day until about 2pm; all pass the park entrance (RM10, one hour). To go all the way to Ranau costs RM20 (the trip takes just over an hour).

Kudat

With its sunburnt stilted buildings, fishing boats out in the bay and slow tropical pace, there's a dreamy, end-of-the-world feeling in Kudat that will soon grow on you. Believe it or not, sleepy Kudat used to be an important trading post and capital of Borneo back in the late 19th century. You may notice some of the streets have Chinese names, harking back to the British adminstration's request to the Chinese to come and run their coconut plantations. Many of their descendants are still here today, along with a warm Bajau, Rungus and Filipino cast.

Kudat town's impressive **Chinese temple** FREE by the main square is worth a look, or you might visit **Tamu Kudat** (6am-2pm Tue & Wed) market with its tropical fruits, dried fish and edible seaweed. But it's the country that leads up to the Tip of Borneo that you really want to explore; think blood and vermilion sunsets, mile upon mile of powder-fine sand and cobalt blue water deserted but for the occasional fishing boat or local walking beneath her umbrella in the midday heat.

Swing by **New Way Car Rental & Souvenir Centre** (088-625 868; 40 Jln Lo Thien Chok) if you want to explore the area under your own steam. Staff can also book your accommodation on Pulau Banggi (p348).

Sleeping & Eating

Ria Hotel HOTEL $$

(088-622 794; http://riahotel.blogspot.com; 3 Jln Marudu; r RM135-146, f RM315;) Ria is central, has pleasant rooms with desk, comfy beds, fresh linen, TV and bathroom. The real boon though is the funky cafe downstairs which sells lovely pastries, sandwiches, cakes and decent coffee.

Kudat Golf Marina Resort HOTEL $$

(088-611 211; www.kudatgolfmarinaresort.com; off Jln Urus Setia; r RM166-186; P) Opposite a little marina, this faded dame has a huge banana-hued lobby complete with massage chairs and helpful staff, and large bedrooms with bathroom, decent fittings and TV. Breakfast is a buffet and egg station affair. Best of all is the huge alfresco swimming pool.

Getting There & Away

The bus station is in Kudat Plaza in the western part of town, very close to the Ria Hotel. Bus destinations include KK (RM25, three hours, twice daily), Kota Belud (RM15, 1½ hours, twice daily) and Sandakan (RM60, one daily). Minivans and jeeps also operate from here; a ride to KK in a full van will cost around RM50.

Around Kudat

The area around Kudat includes many hidden **coves**, **beaches** and **hill trails** that are almost all tucked away down hidden or unmarked roads. You'll want to get in touch with the folks at Tampat Do Aman or Tip of Borneo Resort to find the best spots. The Rungus **longhouses** (Bavanggazo Rungus Longhouses/Maranjak Longhouse; ☎088-612 846, 088-621 673; per person per night from RM70) of Kampung Bavanggazo, 44km south of Kudat, are highly touted by Sabah Tourism, but were in a bit of a neglected state when we visited them.

Tip of Borneo

Sabah's northernmost headland, at the end of a wide bay some 40km from Kudat, is known as Tanjung Simpang Mengayu, or the Tip of Borneo. Magellan reputedly landed here for 42 days during his famous 16th-century round-the-world voyage. Once a wild promontory, this windswept stretch where the cliffs meet the sea has been co-opted as a tourist attraction – there's a large, truncated globe monument dominating the viewpoint. A sign warns visitors not to climb down onto the rocks that form the mainland's actual tip due to lethal currents.

There's no public transport, so you'll need to negotiate a taxi from Kudat (around RM90, including waiting time upon arrival) or drive yourself. The area surounding the tip is also known as the Tip of Borneo, and it's here you'll find the best accommodation, diving and surfing. Of eight beaches, there are three of note: the northernmost Tip of Borneo Beach, otherwise known as Kosuhui Beach, where there are restaurants, dive shops and surfboards to hire; next up, the inaccessible private beach by dreamy Hibiscus Beach Resort; and finally, beautiful Bavang Jamal Beach, where you'll find a couple of excellent spots for refreshments.

Sights & Activities

Kudat Turtle Conservation Society WILDLIFE RESERVE

(☎013-839 7860; www.ktcs-borneo.org; Lupa Masa Bavang Jamal Homestay, Kampung Bavang Jamal; conservation fee RM15) Run by Roland, the Kudat Turtle Conservation Society is based at the Lupa Masa Bavang Jamal Homestay. An education centre has just been built here and it's possible to assist the society on night vigils of local beaches to protect the eggs of green and hawksbill turtles. Check the website for a list of long-term voluntary positions.

To get here from Kudat, call Driver Peter on ☎019-802 0084. It should cost around RM50.

Borneo Dive Centre WATER SPORTS

(☎016-830 0454; www.tipofborneoresort.com; Tip of Borneo Resort; fishing per boat RM400, snorkelling RM40, 2 dives RM300, surfboard hire RM80; ⊙9am-7pm) Based at the Tip of Borneo Resort, this funky-muralled dive hut is a tardis of surfboards, windsurfing and fishing equipment and diving paraphernalia. Also rents kayaks and bikes.

CATCHING THE MORNING TUBE

Surfing is beginning to take off on the west coast of Sabah, thanks to swells produced by the southwest and northeast monsoons – November to January being the best time to catch a glassy wave. The top spot is the northern Tip of Borneo, and its beautiful white-sand beaches and turquoise water are not the only pull; when the conditions are right, there's some very clean surf with glassy lefts and rights, perfect peels, and faces varying in size from 2ft to 9ft. Also there's no bad-tempered, overcrowded line-up; but for the odd local, the waves are yours and board hire is easy.

For surf lessons, get in touch with **Deep Borneo Adventures** (☎088-231 233; www.deepborneo.com; Lot 3.2, 2nd fl, Grace Sq, Lg Grace Square 1, Jln Pantai, Sembulan, Kota Kinabalu; private surf lessons RM180), which uses the smaller waves at Tanjung Aru or Kudat, depending on swells. Boards can be hired at Tip of Borneo Resort.

Sleeping

★ Lupa Masa Bavang Jamal Homestay HOMESTAY $
(019-802 0549; http://lupamasa.com; Kampung Bavang Jamal; r incl breakfast RM45; P) This stunning Rungus-inspired longhouse has ventilated sleeping areas, and simple private rooms within its high-beamed expanse – no mod cons, just mozzie net, mattress and shared bathroom. Nearby is La Playa Beachfront Bar on Bavang Jamal Beach. Kudat Turtle Conservation Society is based here. It's also possible to visit Banggi Island from here on an overnight snorkelling trip (RM280).

★ Tampat Do Aman HOMESTAY $$
(013-880 8395; http://tampatdoaman.com; r from RM43, chalet/family chalet RM160/220;) With its vernal maze of walkways, atmospheric Rungus longhouse rooms and powder-blue villas overlooking hibiscus-rich gardens, this is a fine place to stay. Owner Howard and his Rungus wife pour the profits into local initiatives like school building and nature conservation. There's an on-site museum, wildlife reserve, and the food is terrific. A new longhouse is currently being built. Recommended.

Take a hike, go snorkelling or hire a bike; Howard can hook you up with loads of activities.

Tip of Borneo Resort RESORT $$
(Tommy's Place; 088-493 468, 013-811 2315; http://tipofborneoresort.com/; r RM180-230, villa RM280;) With its welcoming cafe, dive and windsurf centre, as well as Tommy's wildlife conservation efforts, this is a cool place to stay. There's a new row of lovely mint-green triple rooms with balconies and bathroom, and the villas on the hill have widescreen views, huge beds, flat screen and cable. A new restaurant is in the making.

★ Hibiscus Beach Retreat BUNGALOW $$$
(019-895 0704; www.hibiscusbeachretreat.com; 2-person bungalow RM525-625) Perched on a hill overlooking a beautiful 1.5km swath of sand lapped by teal-green sea, this bijou one-bedroom cabana has a high thatch roof, fan-only rooms, self-catering facilities, sundeck and loungers, contemporary art and choice furniture. Order a fresh fruit breakfast, snorkel, then kick back and witness the purple and amber sunset. Exquisite!

Hibiscus Villa Borneo VILLA $$$
(019-895 0704; www.hibiscusvillaborneo.com; per night US$900-1100;) With its infinity pool, dark-wood floors, moody subdued lighting, and exquisitely chosen furniture, this fine 3-bedroomed villa is on a private beach and leaps straight from the pages of a glossy interiors magazine. There's daily maid service but otherwise you'll feel like you have died and gone to heaven. Perfect for families in search of privacy and escape.

Eating & Drinking

The Secret Place Cafe MALAYSIAN $
(Bavang Jamal Beach; mains RM9; 10am-9pm) This family-run joint on Bavang Jamal Beach is popular for its *nasi goreng* (fried rice), fresh fish, chicken wings and barbecued food. Whatever's been caught finds its way to the grill. There are hammocks to lounge on and drink up the sea view. You can even rent a tent (RM25). Look for the wood sign on the main road.

Tip Top Restaurant INTERNATIONAL $$
(013-880 8395; www.tampatdoaman.com/tiptop-menu; Kosuhui Beach; mains RM17; 8am-8pm) Just metres from the beach, here you can expect terrific food ranging from burgers to swordfish steak, curries, sweet-and-sour chicken, breakfasts, carrot cake and fresh juices. The restaurant has a shaded section and an outdoor decked area to chill. Run by the excellent Tampat Do Aman.

★ La Playa Beachfront Bar BAR
(southern end of Bavang Jamal Beach; mains RM10) Next to the Kudat Turtle Conservation Society, this lantern-lit open-decked bar is one of the most peaceful, best located watering-holes in Sabah. Tibetan prayer flags flutter as you recline on loungers, scatter cushions and hammocks, sipping fresh coconut juice and cocktails, gobbling pizza cooked in the wood-fired oven and gazing at the equatorial fiery sunset. Perfection.

On Saturday mornings, locals sell handmade beaded jewellery and fresh fruit here.

Offshore Islands

The real highlights of northwestern Sabah lie offshore. The first gem is Pulau Mantanani, which is actually two perfect tropical islands lying about 40km northwest of Kota Belud. The second is Layang Layang, a diving mecca about 300km northwest of KK, basically an airstrip built on a reef way out in the middle of the South China Sea. Famous for great visibility, seemingly endless wall dives and the occasional school of hammerheads, it's second only to Sipadan on Malaysia's list of top dive spots.

Pulau Mantanani

The 3km-long **Pulau Mantanani Besar** (Big Mantanani Island) and **Pulau Mantanani Kecil** (Little Mantanani Island) are two little flecks of land fringed by bleach-blond sand and ringed by a halo of colourful coral, about 25km off the coast of northwest Sabah (about 40km northwest of Kota Belud). Dugongs are spotted here from time to time, as is the rare Scops owl. The 1000-odd islanders are Bajau sea gypsies, who have been in the news recently because of their opposition to resorts buying up land for development and the imminent possibility they might be forcibly relocated by the government.

Overnight options include the excellent **Mari Mari Backpackers Lodge** (☎088-260 501; www.riverbug.asia; dm RM442, tw per person RM552), operated by Riverbug. Guests are placed in raised stilt chalets around a white-sand beach. There are also dorms with shared bathrooms. Diving and snorkelling activities feature high on the itinerary list, but this is also a lovely tropical escape if you just want to chill. It's possible to be picked up from KK and taken to Kota Belud from where you catch a speedboat (included) to the island for one night before being returned to Kota Belud for 6.30pm the next day. Rates start at RM442 for a dorm and RM552 per person for a twin room. Mari Mari also has its own dive centre offering PADI courses.

For more luxury, head to **Bembaran Dive Lodge** (☎088-728 702; www.bembarandivelodge.com; 2-day, 1-night package incl 3 dives RM575; ❋) with larger, more comfortable cabanas and a private beach and cafe. They too have a decent dive school and offer refresher courses, open-water courses and snorkelling.

Wi-fi is very iffy on the island and there are just a few shops, but this is a chance to cut free of the outside world for a few days. You can kayak and night-dive at night here, birdwatch or take a sunset cruise.

Pulau Banggi

If you want to fall off the map, head to Pulau Banggi, some 40km northeast of Kudat where the Sulu and South China Seas meet. The Banggi people, known locally for their unusual tribal tree houses, are Sabah's smallest indigenous group, and speak a unique non-Bornean dialect. The island is a postcard-esque slice of sand, tropical trees and clear water, and is actually the largest offshore island in all Malaysia.

Firmly in the 'Coral Triangle', one of the most biodiverse submarine habitats on earth, the diving here is superb, but be warned, due to its proximity to the Balabic Straight Corridor, the currents are a challenge and only experienced drift divers should dive here. You'll possibly see whale sharks, turtles, dolphins and a colourful mix of coral such as gorgonian fan, staghorn and bubble. Amidst this are batfish, clownfish, squid and moray eels. Keep an eye out too here for dugong, thanks to the presence of the island's mangrove and seagrass.

Accommodation is available at the modest **Bonggi Resort** (☎088-671 572, 019-587 8078; Waterfront, Karakit; r fan/air-con RM65/80, huts RM85; ❋), which can arrange boat trips and other activities. The small huts have kitchens and twin beds – make sure you request the charming tree-house hut. This place can get fully booked on weekends, so reserve in advance. Ask staff about the trails that lead into the small jungle interior of the island.

Kudat Express (☎088-328118; 1-way 1st class/economy RM18/15) runs a ferry between Kudat and the main settlement on Pulau Banggi. It departs the pier (near the Shell station) at 1pm daily. In the reverse direction, it leaves Pulau Banggi daily at around 7.15am.

Layang Layang

This turquoise-haloed coral atoll, some 300km northwest of KK, is actually artificial, constructed for the Malaysian Navy, and debated between scubaholics as one of the top 10 dive sites in the world. However, what lies beneath what is now an exclusive diving resort could only have been created by nature: think Technicolor reefs teeming with gorgonian fans, excellent visibility, and impossibly steep walls down to 2000km. Beyond the macro fish found in its 20m deep lagoon (seahorses, pipefish, cuttlefish and batfish) large pelagics to the outer walls include hammerhead, grey reef, leopard, thresher, silvertip and whale sharks; as well as orcas, dolphins, manta and devil rays.

Keep in mind that there is no decompression chamber at Layang Layang, so don't press your luck while underwater. The resort only provides air – no nitrox.

The island's location offers absolute isolation; luckily there is an airstrip with regular flights from Kota Kinabalu, which is the only mode of transport for guests visiting Layang Layang. Isolation doesn't come cheap, especially when mixed with high luxury.

Avillion Layang Layang Resort (☎in KL 03-2170 2185; www.avillionlayanglayang.com; 5-day, 4-night all-incl package, twin-share per person from US$985; ❄☒) is the only digs and it's all about scuba, with five daily meals scheduled around dives. The standard rooms are very comfortable, with air-con, TV, private verandahs and hot-water showers. The all-inclusive packages include accommodation, food, 12 boat dives and tank usage. Be warned, nondivers: besides a little snorkelling, there's nothing for you to do here but sunbathe.

The resort operates its own Antonov 26 aircraft, which flies every Tuesday, Thursday, Friday and Sunday between KK and Layang Layang. The flight over from KK in this barebones Russian prop plane is a big part of the adventure. The return flight costs US$408, which is not included in the accommodation-food-dive package.

EASTERN SABAH

Eastern Sabah takes nearly everything that is wonderful about the rest of Borneo and condenses it into a richly packed microcosm of the island consisting of equal parts adventure, wildlife, undersea exploration and flat-out fun. Let's tick off some of the natural wonders of this relatively tiny corner of the island: the great ginger men – ie the orangutans – of Sepilok; pot-bellied, flop-nosed proboscis monkeys in Labuk Bay; the looming vine tunnels and muddy crocodile highway of the Sungai Kinabatangan; pygmy elephants and treetop canopies that scratch the sky in the Danum Valley and Tabin; plunging sea walls rainbow-spattered with tropical marine life in the Semporna Archipelago; a forest as old as human civilisation in the Maliau Basin.

Did we just pique your travel appetite? Thanks to decent flight connections, travel up and down the eastern seaboard is a cinch, plus a newly sealed road between Tawau on the southeast coast and KK on the west, finally makes it possible to access the interior of the Maliau Basin without a headache.

Sandakan

☎089 / POP 392,288

Looking out across the teal-blue bay of Sandakan dotted with Chinese trawlers and distant isles, it's hard to believe its population was once composed of such an exotic cast of foreign interests: German traders, Dutch and Chinese planters, Arab and Indian traders, and pearl divers. Sadly it was razed to the ground during WWII by the British in an attempt to shake off the grip of the invading Japanese. After the war, a roaring timber trade blossomed here with wood from Borneo imported all over the world, so much so that for a time, there were more millionaires per head here than anywhere in the world. Today this little city is buzzing again with the success of the palm-oil industry, its drab, hastily erected postwar buildings enjoying a much needed 21st-century makeover – particularly the waterfront area and Four Points hotel.

Curiously, a completely new city centre is currently being built 2.5km west of the city, set to be completed within a few years.

As well as being a gateway to the Sungai Kinabatangan and Sepilok, Sabah's second city is dotted with religious relics, haunting cemeteries and stunning colonial mansions. You'll find loads of things to see here, most of them a short cab ride away.

Sights

Central Sandakan is light on 'must-see' attractions, although history buffs will appreciate the *Sandakan Heritage Trail* brochure available at the tourist office. The centre, where you'll find most hotels, banks and local transport, consists of a few blocks squashed between the waterfront and a steep escarpment from where you can look out over the bay, Teluk Sandakan.

We're glad to report that the Sandakan Crocodile Park is currently closed until it improves the conditions for its 3000 scaled and feathered occupants, following a plethora of complaints.

Chinese Cemetery CEMETERY

Sandakan's Chinese Cemetery is huge. As you wander further along the cemetery, you'll notice the graves become older and more decrepit – many have been claimed by the jungle. You will also see some charnel houses that accommodate the important members of Sandakan's major Chinese

Sandakan

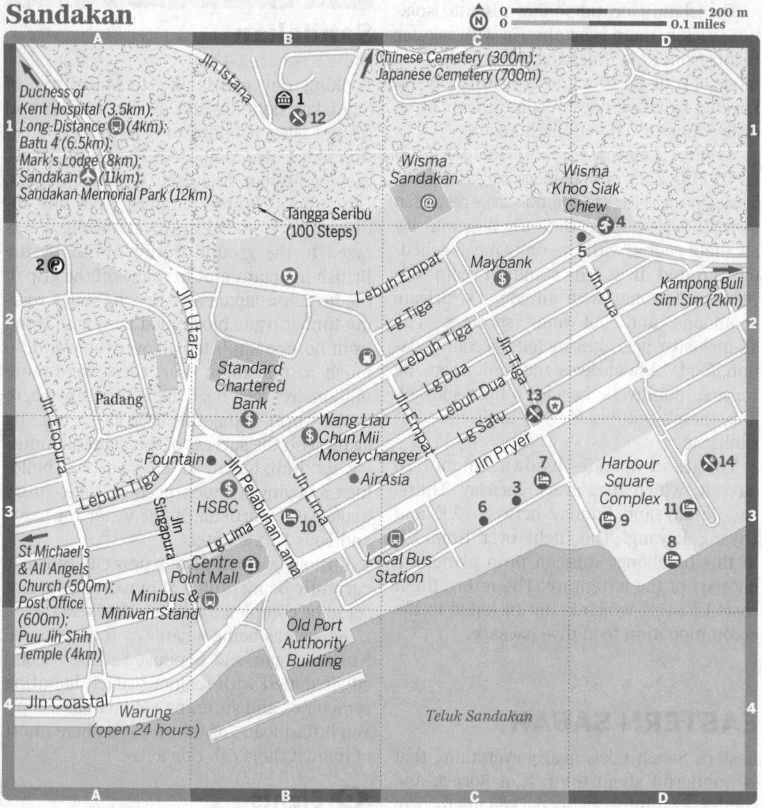

Sandakan

Sights

1 Agnes Keith House B1
2 Sam Sing Kung A2

Activities, Courses & Tours

3 Myne Travel C3
4 Ocean Quest D1
5 Sepilok Tropical Wildlife Adventure D2
6 SI Tours C3

Sleeping

7 Borneo Sandakan Backpackers C3
8 Four Points by Sheraton Sandakan D3
9 Ibis Styles Sandakan Waterfont D3
10 Nak Hotel B3
11 Sea View Sandakan D3

Eating

12 English Tea House & Restaurant B1
13 Habeeb Restaurant C2
14 Sandakan Central Market D3

Drinking & Nightlife

Balin Roof Garden .... (see 10)

clans. Across the road from the cemetery is a cremation ground for Hindus and Sikhs.

Japanese Cemetery CEMETERY

(Jln Istana) A poignant piece of Sandakan's ethnic puzzle, the cemetry was founded in the 1890s by Kinoshita Kuni, known as the successful madam-manager of Sandakan's lucrative 'Brothel 8'. Today's cemetery is small, but at one time there were hundreds of prostitutes buried here. A monument to the fallen Japanese soldiers of WWII was erected in the cemetery in 1989. To get here, climb the Tangga Seribu (100 Steps) to Jln

Residensi Dr and turn right, following signs to the cemetery.

Agnes Keith House MUSEUM

(☎089-221 140; www.museum.sabah.gov.my; Jln Istana; admission RM15; ⏰9am-5pm) This atmospheric two-storey wooden villa, and former British colonial quarters, is now renovated as a museum. Living in Sandakan in the 1930s, Amercian Agnes Keith wrote several books about her experiences here, including the famous *Land Below the Wind*. The villa documents Sandakan in all its colonial splendour.

To reach the museum, head up the Tangga Seribu to Jln Istana and turn left. Also on the grounds is the English Tea House & Restaurant (p353).

Sandakan Memorial Park HISTORIC SITE

(⏰9am-5pm) A beautiful forest orchard and series of gardens mark the unlikely site of a Japanese POW camp and starting point for the infamous WWII 'death marches' (p352) to Ranau. Of the 1800 Australian and 600 British troops imprisoned here, the only survivors by July 1945 were six Australian escapees. Rusting machines testify to the camp's forced-labour program, and a pavilion includes accounts from survivors and photographs from personnel, inmates and liberators. See www.sandakan-deathmarch.com for more details of the death-march route.

To reach the park, take any Batu 8 (or higher-numbered) bus from the local bus station on the waterfront in the city centre (RM1.50); get off at the 'Taman Rimba' signpost and walk down Jln Rimba. A taxi from downtown costs about RM30 one way.

Puu Jih Shih Temple CHINESE TEMPLE

(off Jln Leila) **FREE** Wrapped in the usual firework display of reds, golds and twining dragons, festooned with lanterns illuminating the grounds like a swarm of fireflies, this is one of the finest Chinese temples in Sabah. The temple is about 4km west of the centre. Take a bus to Tanah Merah and ask for directions. A taxi shouldn't cost more than RM10 one way, but don't be surprised if cabbies try to charge RM25 for a round trip plus waiting at the temple.

St Michael's & All Angels Church CHURCH

(off Jln Puncak; admission RM10) **FREE** As if airlifted from England's home counties, this pretty stone church sits like a relic of colonial times and monument to Christian worship, on a hillside high above Sandakan. Its construction reportedly involved prisoner labourers dragging huge stones across the Bornean jungle. The church avoided major damage during WWII. Notice its stunning stained-glass windows donated by Australians to commemorate the 60th anniversary of the end of this conflict.

Although the church is officially off Jln Puncak, many people call the street 'Church Rd'.

Sam Sing Kung TAOIST TEMPLE

(Jln Padang) **FREE** The Sam Sing Kung temple (also pronounced 'Sam Sing Gong') dates from 1887, making it the oldest building in Sandakan. The temple itself is a smallish, if attractive affair – a lovely example of a house of worship dedicated to the traditional Chinese Taoist pantheon.

Kampong Buli Sim Sim VILLAGE

This traditional stilt village, located about 3km east of the town centre, is the original settlement Sandakan grew from. You'll likely be grinned at as you wander around the wooden boards built over the water, as much an oddity to locals as their water village is to you, but please don't take pictures of people without asking permission. You can take a taxi here for no more than RM20.

☞ Tours

It is possible to visit many of the attractions around Sandakan independently, but if you want to stay at the river lodges on the Kinabatangan, you'll need to prebook accommodation. It's advisable to do so in Sandakan or in KK. Sandakan also has plenty of general tour operators offering packages to Sepilok and the Gomantong Caves. Hotels in Sandakan and Sepilok are all capable of booking tours as well, as are many of the tour companies listed in KK.

Sabah Holidays NATURE TOUR

(☎089-225 718; www.sabahholidays.com; Ground fl, Sandakan Airport; ⏰9am-6pm) Rents cars and minivans, and can arrange tours and accommodation in Kota Belud, the Danum Valley, Maliau Basin and Sepilok.

Sepilok Tropical Wildlife Adventure NATURE TOUR

(☎089-271 077; www.stwadventure.com; 13 Jln Tiga; ⏰9am-6pm) This midpriced tour specialist is connected to Sepilok Jungle Resort and Bilit Adventure Lodge on the Sungai Kinabatangan.

SI Tours NATURE TOUR
(☎089-213 502; www.sitoursborneo.com; lot 59, block HS-5, Sandakan Harbour Sq Phase 2; ⌚9am-6pm) This full-service agency operates Abai Jungle Lodge and Kinabatangan River Lodge and runs overnight turtle-spotting trips to the Sandakan Archipelago.

Myne Travel NATURE TOUR
(☎089-216 093; www.myne.com.my; 57 Harbour Sq; ⌚8am-5pm, closed Sun) Myne sells river trips on the Kinabatangan, and excursions to Turtle Island (RM880 including guide, boat, meals and one night's accommodation), as well as a 'fireflies and mangrove' local cruise in Tanjung Arung.

Sleeping

If you're only passing through Sandakan to see the orangutans, it's better to stay at Sepilok itself. Sandakan has a few upscale options; on the opposite end of the luxe spectrum, it also has some friendly hostels.

★Borneo Sandakan Backpackers HOSTEL $
(☎089-215 754; www.borneosandakan.com; 1st fl, 54 Harbour Sq; dm/s/d RM30/55/70;) These brilliant new digs are superclean with warm orange walls, a welcoming lobby, air-con in every room and – get this – flat screen and Xbox! Also, fresh sheets, safety lockers and a decent breakfast. There are six rooms and two well-sized dorms. There's a great vibe and helpful staff who are also qualified guides and run a number of tours.

Sea View Sandakan HOSTEL $
(☎089-221 221; 1st fl, lot 126, Jln Dua, Harbour Sq 14; dm RM25, d with fan & shared bathroom/d with bathroom & air-con RM66/84, breakfast incl;) You won't get any sea views and the rooms are a bit airless and need painting. That said, it's a nice vibe here, and the Lemongrass cafe on the 3rd floor has a cool mural and misted glass, and dishes up pumpkin curry.

★Four Points by Sheraton Sandakan HOTEL $$
(☎089-244 888; www.fourpointssandakan.com; Harbour Sq, Jln Pryer; r incl breakfast from RM240;) This new luxury option exudes international chic with a palatial lobby commanding great bay views, and even lovelier rooms with sleep-inducing ambient lighting, down pillows, uber-thick mattress, flat screen, desk and minibar. The Eatery Restaurant has arguably the best buffet breakfast in Sabah, while the Best Brew Bar serves great cocktails in sumptuous surroundings. Plus…a giant alfresco pool!

THE SANDAKAN DEATH MARCHES

Sandakan was the site of a Japanese prisoner-of-war camp during WWII, and in September 1944, 1800 Australian and 600 British troops were interned here. What is not widely known is that more Australians died here than during the building of the infamous Burma Railway.

Early in the war, food and conditions were bearable and the death rate stood at around three per month. However, as the Allies closed in, it became clear to the officers in command that they didn't have enough staff to guard against a rebellion in the camps. They decided to cut the prisoners' rations to weaken them, causing disease to spread and the death rate to rise.

It was also decided to move the prisoners inland – 250km through the jungle to Ranau, on a route originally cut by locals to hamper the Japanese invaders, passing mainly through uninhabited, inhospitable terrain. On 28 January 1945, 470 prisoners set off; 313 made it to Ranau. On the second march, 570 started from Sandakan; just 118 reached Ranau. The 537 prisoners on the third march were the last men in the camp.

Conditions on the marches were deplorable: most men had no boots, rations were less than minimal and many men fell by the wayside. The Japanese brutally disposed of any prisoners who couldn't walk. Once in Ranau, the surviving prisoners were put to work carrying 20kg sacks of rice over hilly country to Paginatan, 40km away. Disease, starvation and executions took a horrendous toll, and by the end of July 1945 there were no prisoners left in Ranau. The only survivors from the 2400 at Sandakan were six Australians who escaped, either from Ranau or during the marches.

As a final bitter irony, it emerged postwar that a rescue attempt had been planned for early 1945, but intelligence at the time had suggested there were no prisoners left at the camp.

Nak Hotel HOTEL $$
(☎089-272 988; www.nakhotel.com; Jln Pelabuhan Lama; s/d/f incl breakfast from RM88/138/218; ❄📶) We like Nak for its quirky lobby of ox-blood walls, Chinese lanterns, giant birdcages and oriental vases. Rooms are dinky but stylish; gunmetal-grey walls, retro elements and tasteful en suites. Best of all is the city's coolest cafe, the irresistible rooftop oasis Balin – a must even if you aren't staying here. Breakfast is pancakes and eggs. Look for the black Soviet facade.

Mark's Lodge HOTEL $$
(☎089-210 055; www.markslodge.com; Lot 1-7, block 36, Bandar Indah; r incl breakfast RM146-178; ❄📶) Peaceful and cool, just 8km from the centre, Mark's has some boutique elements and art-deco-style desks, as well as flat screens and a few movie channels, subtle lighting and sparkling bathrooms. The wood-panelled restaurant-bar is also inviting. It's a RM20 taxi ride into town.

Ibis Styles Sandakan Waterfont HOTEL $$
(☎089-240 888; www.ibisstyles.com; Harbour Sq; r RM158-173, f RM208; ❄📶) Contemporary, ice-cool and immaculate is a fair description of this popular French hotel chain's new acquisition on the waterfront. Tangerine-hued rooms are large and fresh with international-standard bathrooms, snow-white linen, flat screens and modern fittings. With widescreen views of the Sulu Sea and breakfast on the verandah, this place makes for a great stay.

Eating

For an authentic Malay meal, head to the waterfront Harbour Square Complex, where the restaurants surrounding it are cheap and flavourful. Most are standard Malay *kedai kopi*, with prices that rarely top RM6 per mains; all are open from roughly 9am to 9pm. **Habeeb Restaurant** (Jln Tiga; ⏲7am-3pm) is good for a cheap curry; it's actually part of a chain that serves good Indian Muslim food, so if you see other branches around town, consider them a solid bet.

Sandakan Central Market HAWKER $
(Jln Dua; mains RM1-8; ⏲7am-3pm) Despite being located in what looks like a multistorey car park, this is the best spot in town for cheap eats and food stalls. Upstairs you'll find strictly halal food stalls, with a mix of Chinese, Malay, Indonesian and Filipino stalls. Hours given for the food stalls are a bit flexible, but by 3pm most are empty.

Sim Sim Seafood Restaurant SEAFOOD $
(Sim Sim 8; dishes RM5; ⏲8am-2pm) Located in the heart of the stilt village of Kampong Buli Sim Sim, 3km east of the centre, this 'restaurant' is more of a dockside fishery, where the daily catch is unloaded and prepared for immediate consumption. Grab a red plastic seat and point to your prey! Ask a cab to drop you off at 'Sim Sim Bridge 8' (they'll very likely know where you're going).

English Tea House & Restaurant BRITISH $$
(☎089-222 544; www.englishteahouse.org; Jln Istana; mains RM15.50-55, cocktails RM16.80-20; ⏲10am-11pm) More English than a Graham Greene novel, this beautiful stucco-pillared villa, with its manicured croquet lawn, wood-blade fans and wicker chairs parked under a giant mango tree, is great for lunch. The menu spans fish 'n' chips to Oxford stew, enjoyed with a serene view of the bay below and a pot of tea.

Imagine staff dressed like Harrogate tea ladies and scones on triple-tiered cake trays. Sadly the dilatory service would induce paroxysms of purple rage in a Victorian gentleman, as the place is often saturated with overbearing package types and understaffed.

Drinking & Nightlife

Bandar Indah, commonly known as Mile 4 or Batu 4, is a buzzing grid of two-storey shophouses and the playground of choice for locals and expats alike, packed with restaurants, bars, karaoke lounges and nightclubs. It comes alive at night in a way that makes central Sandakan seem deader than the morgue in a ghost town. Bars generally close around 1am or 2am, music venues slightly later. A taxi to Bandar Indah should cost around RM20.

★**Balin Roof Garden** BAR
(Balin; ☎089-272 988; www.nakhotel.com; 18th fl, Nak Hotel, Jln Pelabuhan Lama; mains RM20, cocktails RM20-25; ⏲7.30am-1am, happy hour 2-8pm; 📶) A hidden treat at the top of the Nak Hotel, this stylish restaurant/bar has retro bubble lights, a '70s wicker swing-chair, and swallow-you-up couches. Eat inside or out; on the shaded verandah or up on the rooftop. Pizza, marinated New Zealand lamb, grass-fed burger and a wealth of juices and classy cocktails that any boutique 'mixologist' bar would be justifiably jealous of. Cool.

Information

INTERNET

Cyber Café (3rd fl, Wisma Sandakan, Lebuh Empat; per hour RM3; ⏲9am-9pm)

MEDICAL SERVICES

Duchess of Kent Hospital (☎089-248 600; http://hdok.moh.gov.my; Batu 2/Mile 2, Jln Utara; ⏲8am-10pm) Best private care in the area.

MONEY

Maybank (Lebuh Tiga) In addition to a full-service bank and ATM, a pavement currency-exchange window is open 9am to 5pm daily for changing cash and travellers cheques.

Wang Liau Chun Mii Moneychanger (23 Lebuh Tiga; ⏲8.30am-4.30pm) Cash only.

POST

Main Post Office (☎089-210 594; Jln Leila; ⏲8.30am-6pm Mon-Fri, to 12:30pm Sat)

Getting There & Away

AIR

Malaysia Airlines (www.malaysiaairlines.com)/**MASwings** (☎1300-883 000; www.maswings.com) has seven flights per day to/from KK and KL (RM248); two per day to/from Tawau (RM192) and two per week to Kudat (RM117). **AirAsia** (☎089-222 737; www.airasia.com; 1st & 2nd fl, Sandakan Airport) operates direct daily flights to/from KL and KK.

BUS

Buses and minibuses to KK, Lahad Datu, Semporna and Tawau leave from the long-distance bus station in a large car park at Batu 2.5, 4km north of town. Most express buses to KK (RM43, six hours) leave between 7am and 2pm, plus one evening departure around 8pm. All pass the turn-off to Kinabalu National Park headquarters.

Buses depart regularly for Lahad Datu (RM22, 2½ hours) and Tawau (RM43, 5½ hours) between 7am and 8am. There's also a bus to Semporna (RM40, 5½ hours) at 8am. If you miss it, head to Lahad Datu, then catch a frequent minivan to Semporna.

Minivans depart throughout the morning from Batu 2.5 for Ranau (RM30, four hours) and Lahad Datu (some of those continuing to Tawau). Minivans for Sukau (RM15) leave from a lot behind Centre Point Mall in town.

Getting Around

TO/FROM THE AIRPORT

The airport is 11km from the city centre. Batu 7 Airport bus (RM1.80) stops on the main road about 500m from the terminal. A coupon taxi to the town centre costs RM35; going the other way, around RM35.

BUS & MINIVAN

Buses run from 6am to 6pm on the main road to the north, Jln Utara, designated by how far from town they go, ie Batu 8. Fares range from RM2 to RM5.

Local minivans wait behind Centre Point Mall; fares cost from RM2. Use for the harbour area, about 7km west of town.

To reach the long-distance bus station, catch a local bus (RM1.50) from the stand at the waterfront; it takes about 20 minutes. The same bus leaves when full from the bus station for the city centre.

CAR

Borneo Express (☎016-886 0789; http://borneocar.com/; Lot GL 08 (A), ground fl, Terminal Building, Sandakan Airport), in KK, has an office at Sandakan airport, as does **Sandakan Car Rental** (☎019-823 7050, 016-815 0029; http://sandakancarrental.com; Bandar Maju Batu 1, Jln Utara).

TAXI

Short journeys around town should cost RM15; it's about RM20 to Bandar Indah and RM50

GETTING TO THE PHILIPPINES: SANDAKAN TO ZAMBOANGA

Getting to the border Standard Marine (☎089-216 996) links Sandakan with Zamboanga (economy/cabin RM280/320) on the Philippine island of Mindanao. Ferries depart Sandakan harbour at 10pm every Monday, arriving at 8pm the next day (22 hours). There are now no ferries to Jolo because of insurgency problems.

At the border Because of lawlessness, including kidnappings of foreign nationals, and Islamist insurgency, Western embassies warn against travel to or through Zamboanga, so check local conditions before you sail. Travellers we spoke to said you don't need an onward ticket to enter the Philippines; however, the Filipino government says otherwise, so it may be wise to have one.

Alternative route A ferry passenger service from Kudat to Palawan Island in the Philippines is expected to start operating by late 2016.

to Sepilok. A taxi from the long-distance bus station to town (or vice versa) will probably run RM20.

Sepilok

A visit to the world's most famous place to see orangutans in their natural habitat just became even more compelling thanks to the addition of an outdoor nursery for youngsters in the same complex, and the nearby, excellent Sun Bear Conservation Centre. On top of this, there's a stylish new restaurant and cafe that's recently opened.

What makes Sepilok work so well is its organisation, special-needs-friendly paths, and the fact that, with the exception of the nearby Labuk Bay Proboscis Monkey Sanctuary, it is all within walking distance. There are also some beautiful places to stay here in the clasp of the jungle.

Sights & Activities

Sepilok Orangutan Rehabilitation Centre ANIMAL SANCTUARY
(SORC; ☎089-531 189, emergency 089-531 180; sorc64@gmail.com; Jln Sepilok; adult/child RM30/15, camera fee RM10; ⏲ticket counter 9am-noon & 2-4pm Sat-Thu, 9-11am & 2-4pm Fri) Around 25km north of Sandakan, and covering some 40 sq km of the Kabili-Sepilok Forest Reserve, this inspiring world-famous centre welcomes orphaned and injured orangutans for rehabilitation before returning them to forest life. There are currently between 60 and 80 living here. The new showstopper is the recently opened **outdoor nursery,** just two minutes' walk from the feeding platforms, where abandoned toddlers are taught the building blocks they'll need to keep them alive back in the wild.

The youngsters you'll be charmed by are between six and nine years, and in the refrigerated cool of the nursery viewing area, you can sit and watch them focusing on their swinging skills; it's a laugh a minute as they tumble comically into one another and do their best to irritate the trainers by walking on the ground instead of climbing. Try and get here early in the morning before they're fed and become sleepy.

➡ Platform Feeding

Feedings at the platforms are at 10am and 3pm and last 30 to 50 minutes. Schedules are posted at the visitor reception centre. Tickets are valid for one day, although you can see two feedings in the same day. Watching the trees begin to shake, the cat's cradle of ropes vibrating, the first swatch of orange shifting through the branches, is a moment you'll never forget.

Also worth noting is that only around two to four of the population will feed at any one time. The larger males almost never congregate here. In order to get a good spot for your camera or kids, get here 20 minutes early. Finally, the morning feeding tends to be more tour-group heavy, so if you want a quieter experience, try the afternoon. It's

Sepilok

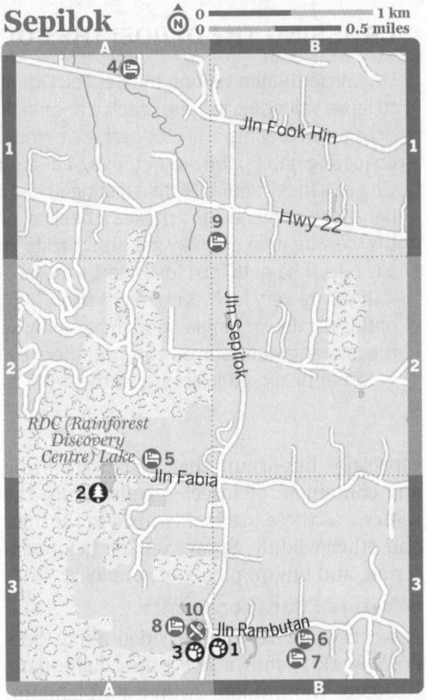

Sepilok

Sights
1 Borneo Sun Bear Conservation Centre ... B3
2 Rainforest Discovery Centre ... A3
3 Sepilok Orangutan Rehabilitation Centre ... A3

Sleeping
4 Paganakan Dii Tropical Retreat ... A1
5 Sepilok B&B ... A2
6 Sepilok Forest Edge Resort ... B3
7 Sepilok Jungle Resort ... B3
8 Sepilok Nature Resort ... A3
9 Uncle Tan Guesthouse ... B1

Eating
10 Lindung Gallery Cafe ... A3

CROSSING THE DIVIDE: THE COLLECTORS!

Be warned, when visiting the Sepilok Orangutan Rehabilitation Centre (SORC), it's better to leave valuables in your coach, car or locker (available on request) before entering the orangutan feeding area, for certain members of their population are renowned for their collecting habits; they're not fussy, Leica cameras and Ray Ban sunglasses will suffice. One ape in particular (with a distinguished black face) usually singles out a female member of the audience and makes a beeline, only to cross the divide between the arboreal to the viewing area. He may get attached to you, literally, and has been known to occasionally bite. If he gets too close, alert a member of staff.

If you're very lucky, you might spot C.I.D, a fully flanged large male and resident king of this particular jungle, though he's only seen once or twice a year. To learn more about these orangutans so you can spot them by name, check out the following link: www.orangutan-appeal.org.uk/about-us/meet-the-orangutans.

especially important that you don't bring any containers of insect repellent into the reserve, as these are highly toxic to the apes and other wildlife. Spray yourself before entering, and put on plenty of sunblock.

➡ **Nature Education Centre**

A worthwhile 20-minute video about Sepilok's work is shown five times daily (9am, 10.30am, 11am, noon, 2.10pm and 3.30pm) opposite reception in the auditorium here.

➡ **Walking Trails**

If you want to explore the sanctuary further, several walking trails lead into the forest; register at the visitor reception centre to use them. Trails range in length from 250m to 4km, and different paths are open at different times of year. Guided night walks can be arranged through the centre or at the various lodges. There's also a 10km trail through mangrove forest to Sepilok Bay; this is quite a rewarding walk, and if you're especially fit you may be able to complete it between feeding times. A permit from the **Forestry Department** (☎089-213 966, 089-660 811; Jln Leila) is required in advance for this route. The department can also arrange basic overnight accommodation at the bay (RM100) or a boat back to Sandakan. Some travel or tour agencies can assist with the permit and other arrangements.

Borneo Sun Bear Conservation Centre ANIMAL SANCTUARY
(BSBCC; ☎089-534 491; www.bsbcc.org.my; Jln Sepilok; adults/child under 12yrs RM30/free; ⏲9am-4pm) These rescued loveable pint-sized bears recently found a home here at Sepilok with the fantastic new Borneo Sun Bear Conservation Centre (BSBCC), which opened in 2014. The centre has full access for the disabled, and it's possible to see the bears from an elevated glassed viewing area as they climb up trees close by you. There are also telescopes set up for micro examination. There's also a gift shop that sells T-shirts, toys, and has an educational video-lounge.

So called because of the golden bracelet of fur around their necks, the bears' Rorschach-like pattern is never duplicated, varying as they do in colour from cream to orange. At a maximum of 150cm and 60kg in weight, they are are little larger than 'Paddington' and are the smallest of the world's bears. Sun bears are found throughout Southeast Asia in eastern India, southern China, Myanmar, Laos, Vietnam and Borneo, usually at an altitude of around 2700m. An average male sun bear needs at least 39 sq km of forest to find sufficient food. They're excellent climbers, equipped with long claws to scale high trees in search of beehives. As they rip a cavity in the trunk to get to their honey, they create a safe place for hornbills and other birds to nest at a later date. They also control the forest's destructive population of termites, as they are a critical part of the bears' diet.

Across Asia the sun bear is caught and slaughtered for meat and Chinese medicine. In countries like China and Vietnam, the poor beasts are strapped in tiny cages and hooked to IVs that pump bile from their gall bladders. Thankfully this does not happen in Sabah, although the bears are still under enormous threat from habitat loss. Animals donated to the centre are first checked for diseases they may have caught as humans' pets, before being transferred to the training pen. A new arrival will learn to climb, build nests and forage before its eventual release into the wild. Sadly while we were researching, a female was struck by lightning and fell from high in a tree and died on impact.

For RM100, it's possible to adopt a bear, and there are around 30 to choose from. If you wish to volunteer here as a keeper, it costs RM7060 for a month or RM4150 for two weeks, including accommodation and meals. Contact Mr Wong Siew Te, BSBCC's founder, for more info on ☎016-555 1256.

Rainforest Discovery Centre NATURE RESERVE
(RDC; ☎089-533 780; www.forest.sabah.gov.my/rdc; adult/child RM15/7; ⏱ticket counter 8am-5pm, park until 8pm) The RDC, about 1.5km from SORC, offers an engaging graduate-level education in tropical flora and fauna. Outside the exhibit hall filled with child-friendly displays, a botanical garden presents samples of tropical plants. There's a gentle 1km lakeside walking trail, and a series of eight canopy towers connected by walkways to give you a bird's-eye view of the tops of the trees; by far the most rewarding element of a trip here.

Paddle boats (RM5) are available to ride around the inviting lake near the centre's entrance. You can also book night walks, which afford the chance to spot nocturnal animals like tarsiers and wild cats.

It's best to get here either at 8am or 4pm, as wildlife tends to hibernate during the sweltering hours in the middle of the day. A proper visit along the trails and towers takes around 1½ hours. This is a good spot to while away time between feedings at the SORC.

Labuk Bay Proboscis Monkey Sanctuary ANIMAL SANCTUARY
(☎089-672 133; www.proboscis.cc; admission adult/child RM60/30, camera/video RM10/20; ⏱8am-6pm) A local palm-plantation owner has created a private proboscis monkey sanctuary, attracting the floppy-conked locals with sugar-free pancakes at 9.30am and 2.30pm feedings at Platform A, and 11.30am and 4.30pm at Platform B, a kilometre away. An estimated 300 wild monkeys live in the 6-sq-km reserve. The proboscis monkeys are enticed onto the main viewing platform so tourists can get better pictures, which may put you off if you're looking for a more ecologically minded experience. Also keep an eye out for the delicately featured silver leaf monkeys.

Proboscis monkeys *(Nasalis larvatus)* are found only on Borneo, although if you take a close look at them, you'd swear you've spotted one in the corner of a dodgy bar. Named for their long bulbous noses, proboscis monkeys are pot-bellied and red-faced, and males are constantly, unmistakably... aroused. With the arrival of Europeans, Malays nicknamed the proboscis *monyet belanda* (Dutch monkey).

Food and accommodation are provided at the Nipah Lodge, on the edge of the oil-palm plantations that surround the sanctuary; the lodge is quite comfortable, a collection of bungalows that are simply adorned, airy and inviting in a tropical-chic way. Guests can also venture out on mangrove

THE WILD MAN OF BORNEO & HOW TO HELP HIM

The term 'orangutan' literally means 'man of the wild', or 'jungle man' – a testament to the local reverence for these great ginger apes. Traditionally, orangutans were never hunted like other creatures in the rainforest; in fact, Borneo's indigenous people used to worship their skulls in the same fashion as they did the heads taken from enemy tribesmen. Orangutans are the only species of great ape found outside Africa. A mature male is an impressive creature with an arm span of 2.25m, and can weigh up to 144kg. Dominant males also have distinctive wide cheek pads to reinforce their alpha status. It was once said that an orangutan could swing from tree to tree from one side of Borneo to the other without touching the ground. Sadly this is no longer the case, and hunting and habitat destruction continue to take their toll; it's estimated 50,000 to 60,000 specimens exist in the wild.

If you'd like to get involved with the work of the Sepilok Orangutan Rehabilitation Centre, contact Sepilok Orangutan Appeal UK (www.orangutan-appeal.org.uk), a UK-based charity. The Appeal's orangutan adoption scheme is a particular hit with visitors: for UK£30 a year, you can sponsor a ginger bundle of fun and receive updates on its progress; see the Appeal's website for details. If you're really taken with the place, Sepilok has one of the most popular overseas volunteer programs in Malaysia. Apply through Travellers Worldwide (www.travellersworldwide.com); as of recently, the cost of an eight-week volunteer package, including accommodation, meals and a number of excursions, was UK£3345.

treks into the surrounding jungle, night treks with guides, and are often invited to give basic English lessons at a nearby village schoolhouse.

Independent travel here is difficult unless you have your own vehicle, as Teluk Labuk (Labuk Bay) sits 15km down a rough dirt track off the main highway. If you're staying here, Nipah Lodge will handle all transfers; otherwise your lodging in Sepilok will be able to arrange transport for around RM120. You can also look for minivans and taxis in the car park of SORC; travellers who want to go to Teluk Labuk should be able to negotiate shared taxis and vans to the proboscis feeding for around RM150 (round trip from Teluk Labuk back to your Sepilok lodging).

🛏 Sleeping & Eating

If you came to Sandakan for the orangutans of Sepilok, do yourself a favour and stay near the apes. The lodging here tends to have more character than Sandakan. Most accommodation options are scattered along Jln Sepilok, the 2.5km-long access road to the rehabilitation centre.

Sepilok B&B   HOSTEL $
(☑ 089-534 050, 019-833 0901; www.sepilokbedn breakfast.com.my; Jln Fabia; dm with fan/air-con RM35/45, d fan only RM68, d with air-con RM108-188) Located opposite the Rainforest Discovery Centre, this place has an authentic hostel vibe with a cosmo cast of backpackers. Dorms are spartan but clean. Rooms are nice with white walls, colourful curtains and fresh linen. Pitta Lodge has self-catering facilities for families and fan-only rooms. Camping here is better in March and April when there's less rain.

★**Paganakan Dii**
Tropical Retreat   BOUTIQUE HOTEL $$
(☑ 089-532 005; www.paganakandii.com; dm/s/d RM35/60/155, 2-/4-person bunaglow RM175/236; ❄🛜) Popular with families wanting a taste of nature, this place has hammocks at every turn, and brick-and-wood bungalows with balcony and nicely crafted furniture, wood floors and step-in showers. Make sure you ask for one with a view of the lake and mountains. There are also eight new box-standard rooms with shared bathroom. Transfers to Sepilok are included. Perfect.

Sepilok Nature Resort   RESORT $$
(☑ 089-674 999, 089-673 999; http://sepilok.com; r from RM265; ❄@) Beside an ornamental pond, this beautiful wood-accented hotel is a study in comfort: think mature rubber plants shading its two-tiered central lodge, carriage lamps casting their glow on its welcoming lounge. Chalets are roomy with sumptuous bathrooms, huge beds and private balconies. The Pan-Asian menu is superb with dinner on the candlelit terrace. Romantic.

Uncle Tan Guesthouse   GUESTHOUSE $$
(☑ 016-824 4749; www.uncletan.com; Jln Batu 14; dm RM51, d without/with bathroom RM106/116; ❄@🛜) The Uncle Tan empire is one of the oldest backpacker/adventure travel outfits in Sabah. Dorms are boxy, rooms have lino floors and bare walls, though both are clean. It's a summer camp vibe here, and the owners can hook you up with trips to places like the Sungai Kinabatangan (RM265).

Sepilok Forest Edge Resort   RESORT $$
(☑ 089-533 190, 013-869 5069; www.sepilokforest edgeresort.com; Jln Rambutan; dm/d RM48/100, chalets RM265; ❄🛜🏊) Set within manicured lawns, this stunning accommodation is

---

PROBOSCIS MONKEY: PROFILE OF A BIG NOSE

Proboscis monkeys are a curiosity, and not just because of those Cyrano de Bergerac hooters. Dominant males have a harem of wives while the other males form a lacklustre bachelor group trying to impress the ladies with their erections and gymnastic displays; often dejectedly resorting to one another as a source of pleasure. The more wobbly and huge the nose, the more attractive a male is to the comparatively smurf-nosed female. Sworn enemy of the aggressive domineering macaque monkey, the proboscis is also a favourite meal of crocodiles. Pursued by the former, they vault as far as they can across forest tributaries, land with an audible splash and swim like hell to the other side before they become lunch. Nature has kindly improved the probability factor of survival by endowing them with webbed fingers. Because of their diets, proboscis monkeys tend to have severe flatulence, another attractive element of this already most graceful of species. In the wild a group of these monkeys can number as many as 80 individuals.

choking on plants and flowers and has chalets fit for a colonial explorer, with polished-wood floors, choice art, and private balcony with wrought-iron chairs. There's also a dorm and double rooms located in a pretty longhouse, plus a relaxing tropical pool/jacuzzi. Around 15-minutes' walk from the Orangutan Rehabilitation Centre.

Sepilok Jungle Resort RESORT $$
(089-533 031; www.sepilokjungleresort.com; Jln Rambutan; dm RM37, r RM120-190;) Recently refurbished rooms with more colour on the walls and quilts than a bird of paradise. Rooms are tile-floored with desk, bathroom, TV and fan or air-con. There's a boardwalk over an ornamental pond and plenty of birdlife here. Pleasant staff.

Lindung Gallery Cafe INTERNATIONAL $$
(Jln Sepilok; mains RM16-24; 10am-10pm) Sitting on a hill close to the Borneo Sun Bear Conservation Centre, this new spaceship-shaped restaurant leaps from a design magazine, with its steel-raftered ceiling, buffed-cement floor, tin chairs and exposed brick interior. Thankfully the food easily lives up to the decor, with a menu featuring eggs Benedict, gourmet burgers, stone-baked pizza and fish 'n' chips, as well as cocktails and fresh juices.

Information

Sepilok is located at 'Batu 14', 14 miles (23km) from Sandakan. The street connecting the highway to the centre is lined with various accommodation options.

It's best to get money in Sandakan, but an ATM has been installed in a Petronas Station on the road between Sandakan and Sepilok. The next-closest ATM is in Sandakan Airport. Money can be changed at upmarket sleeping spots for a hefty change fee.

Getting There & Away

BUS

Bus 14 from Sandakan (RM3) departs hourly from the city centre. If coming from KK, board a Sandakan-bound bus and ask the driver to let you off at 'Batu 14'. You will pay the full fare, even though Sandakan is 23km away.

TAXI

If you are coming directly from Sandakan, a taxi should cost no more than RM45 (either from the airport or the city centre). If you want one to wait and return you to Sandakan, you're looking at RM100. Taxi 'pirates', as they're known, wait at Batu 14 to give tourists a ride into Sepilok. It's RM3 per person for a lift. Travellers spending the night can arrange a lift with their accommodation if they book ahead of time. Walking to the SORC is also an option – it's only 2.5km down the road.

VAN

You can usually organise a pick-up (in a shared minivan from the Kinabatangan operators) from Sepilok after the morning feeding if you are planning to head to Sungai Kinabatangan in the afternoon.

Sandakan Archipelago

While everyone knows about the Semporna Archipelago, it seems hardly anyone wants to visit the Sandakan Archipelago, off the coast of its namesake port. Don't they like fluffy specks of emerald sprouting like orchids out of the Sulu Sea, or tales of POW derring-do?

The archipelago is made up of a number of large islands like Libaran and Berhala, while islands Selingan, Bakungan Kecil and Gulisan comprise the national park. All three have turtle hatcheries, however the only one you can visit is Selingaan.

Recent reports of Turtle Island Park suggest that the former circus of gawping visitors watching a mother hawksbill or green turtle shuffling up the beach and laying her eggs, has become much more considerate of the reptiles' needs, with smaller numbers and stricter regulation on how close you get. For your part, please don't shine lights in the hatching mother's eyes in pursuit of a photo, nor allow any of your party to touch hatchlings – however cute they are – as they are released from their 50-day incubation. You may have to wait a while for the mothers to come, but come they will, often late in the night. Your ticket includes simple air-con accommodation on **Pulau Selingan**, boat transfer and meals. You leave Sandakan Jetty at 9.30am for Selingan (an hour away), and return the next morning.

To organise a trip here, book through **Ocean Quest** (089-212 711; cquest1996@gmail.com; Jln Buli Sim-Sim; boat transfer from Sandakan, accommodation & dinner on Selingaan Island RM800, camera fee RM10, entrance fee RM60), or SI Tours (p352), based in Sandakan.

Pulau Lankayan

Pulau Lankayan isn't just photogenic, it's screen-saver material. Water isn't supposed to get this clear, nor sand this squeaky

WORTH A TRIP

PULAU BERHALA

Part of the Sandakan Archipelago, Pulau Berhala is supremely serene, an exemplar of a rare genre: a lovely tropical island hardly touched by tourists. Sandstone cliffs rise above the Sulu Sea, hemming in quiet patches of dusty, sandy prettiness. The vibe is so sleepy it's narcoleptic, an atmosphere accentuated by a quiet water village inhabited by fishing families, loads of migrating birds (their presence is heaviest in October and November) and...well, OK. There's not a lot else, except some very big rocks.

But, oh, what rocks. Rock climbers grade the formations here F5a – F6b, which is jargon for a mix of slow sloping walls and vertical cliff faces. Fieldskills Adventures (p321) in Kota Kinabalu runs two-day/one-night rock-climbing trips out here for RM500 per person.

Berhala was a leper colony during the colonial period, and the Japanese used the island as a civilian internment centre and POW camp during WWII. American writer Agnes Newton Keith was kept here awhile, as was a group of Australian POWs who managed to escape the island by boat and sail to Tawi Tawi in the Philippines.

clean. A spattering of jungle, a few swaying palms...sigh. No wonder so many lovers come here for their honeymoons, which are often (but not necessarily) accompanied by dive expeditions at **Lankayan Island Resort** (☎088-238 113, 089-673 999; http://lankayan-island.com/; Batu 6; r diver/nondiver RM3350/RM2728), the one accommodation option on Lankayan. There are a few dozen cabins dotted along the sand where the jungle meets the sea, decked out in flowing light linens and deep tropical hardwood accents. Transfers from Sandakan are included in your accommodation.

Sungai Kinabatangan

The Kinabatangan River is Sabah's longest: 560km of chocolatey-brown water, coiling like the serpents that swim its length far into the Bornean interior. Riverine forest creeps alongside the water, swarming with wildlife that flee ever-encroaching palm-oil plantations. Lodges are tastefully scattered along the banks, while homestay programs pop up with the frequency of local monkeys.

Dozens of tin boats putter along the shores offering tourists the opportunity to have a close encounter with a wild friend. This is the only place in Sabah where you can find a concentration of 10 primates including: orangutan, Bornean gibbon, long-tailed and short-tailed macaque, three kinds of leaf monkey, western tarsier, slow loris and proboscis monkey. Add to this eight different kinds of hornbill, herds of pygmy elephants, crocs, wild boar and perhaps – if you're superlucky – a clouded leopard.

Sights

Gomantong Caves CAVE
(☎089-230 189; www.sabah.gov.my/jhl; Gomantong Hill, Lower Kinabatangan; adult/child RM30/15, camera/video RM30/50; ⏱8am-noon & 2-4.30pm, closing periods apply) Imagine a massive crack in a mountain, a cathedral-like inner chamber shot with splinters of sunlight and swarming with cockroaches and scorpions, and you have the Gomantong Caves. Yes, the smell is disgusting thanks to the ubiquity of bat shit, but these caves are magnificent. The forested area around the caves conceals plenty of wildlife – we spotted, and met many other travellers, who saw orangutans here. The most accessible cave is **Simud Hitam** (Black Cave). Rotate counterclockwise on the raised platform over a steaming soup of guano and roaches.

A 45-minute uphill trek beyond the park office leads to **Simud Putih** (White Cave), containing a great abundance of prized white swiftlets' nests. Both trails are steep and require some sweaty rock climbing.

The majority of visitors to Gomantong come as part of an add-on to their Kinabatangan tour package. It is possible to visit the caves under one's own steam though, usually by private vehicle. The turn-off is located along the road connecting Sukau to the main highway and is quite well signposted. Minivans plying the route between Sandakan and Sukau (RM20) can drop you off at the junction, but you'll have to walk the additional 5km to the park office.

Due to dwindling swiftlet bird populations, the caves are closed over certain periods, so check before planning your visit.

Bukit Belanda
HILL

Bukit Belanda – Dutch Hill – is a 420m hill located behind the village of Bilit. The land is owned by the citizens of Bilit, who, despite pressures from logging companies, have not opened the hill to the timber industry, preferring to maintain it as a haven for wildlife. Hike to the top early in the morning – before it gets hot – where you'll be rewarded by lovely views of Sungai Kinabatangan and, if you're lucky, glimpses of local wildlife.

There's no official infrastructure when it comes to visiting the hill; just ask someone in your lodge or Bilit itself to guide you to the beginning of the ascent path. So only attempt it if you're physically fit.

Batu Tulug
CAVES

(☎ 089-565 145; http://museum.sabah.gov.my; above Batu Putih village; adult/child RM5/3; ⏲ 9am-5pm, closed Fri) This hill is studded with caves housing the ancestors of local Chinese and Orang Sungai (People of the River). Because the Kinabatangan has a habit of frequently flooding, the final resting place of the dead has traditionally been located in cave complexes. Heavy wooden coffins are interred in the Batu Tulug caves with spears, knives, gongs, bells and Chinese curios, making the hill one of the most important archaeological sites in Sabah. An interpretive information centre is also located on-site.

Wooden staircases snake up the 40m hill. There are two main caves to explore, but if you climb the stairs to the top, you'll be rewarded with a nice view of the surrounding jungle and the Kinabatangan River.

The easiest way to get here is to include the caves in your package tour of the Kinabatangan. If you've got your own vehicle, look for signs indicating the turn-off to Batuh Putih or Muzium Batu Tulug on the Sandakan–Lahad Datu road. The village is south of Sukau Junction, about 1½ hours from Sandakan and 45 minutes from Lahad Datu. GPS coordinates are N 5024.935° E 117056.548°.

Kinabatangan the Orangutan Conservation Project (KOCP)
RESEARCH CENTRE

(☎ 088-413 293; www.hutan.org.my; Sukau) Inside Sukau village, this conservation camp, run in partnership with a French NGO, is dedicated to studying and protecting the orangutan. They also establish environmental-education programs, reforestation initiatives and an elephant-conservation project in the Sukau-Bilit area. It's not open to casual visitors, but staff may be willing to hire out guides for tracking wild orangutans. Ask for Dr Isabel.

Activities

Wildlife River Cruises

A wildlife cruise down the Kinabatangan is unforgettable. In the late afternoon and early morning, binocular-toting enthusiasts have a chance of spotting nest-building orangutans, nosy proboscis monkeys, basking monitor lizards and hyper long-tailed macaques. The reason so many animals are here though is depressing: the expansion of oil palm plantations has driven local wildlife to the riverbank. They simply have nowhere else to live. Add to this that the Green Belt rule, established to ensure a safe corridor of cover next to the river for animals to pass by new plantations, is being regularly broken by greedy farmers who want to maximise every centimetre of their land, and it's even more concerning.

THE BUSINESS OF BIRD NESTS

The Gomantong Caves are Sabah's most famous source of swiftlet nests, used for one of the most revered dishes of the traditional Chinese culinary oeuvre: the eponymous bird's-nest soup, made from dried swiftlet spit, which when added to the broth dissolves and becomes gelatinous.

There are two types of soupworthy bird nests: black and white. The white nests are more valuable and Gomantong has a lot of them. A kilogram of white swiftlet spit can bring in over US$4000, making nest-grabbing a popular profession, despite the perilous task of shimmying up bamboo poles.

In the last few years visiting has been restricted due to dwindling bird populations (cash-hungry locals were taking the nests before the newborn birds had enough time to mature). Today, the caves operate on a four-month cycle, with closings at the beginning of the term to discourage nest hunters. It's worth asking around before planning your visit – often the caves are empty or off limits to visitors. The four-month cycles are strictly enforced to encourage a more sustainable practice of harvesting.

Mammals can be seen all year, moving around in small groups. Colourful birds are a huge draw: all eight varieties of Borneo's hornbills, plus brightly coloured pittas, kingfishers and, if you're lucky, a Storm's stork or the bizarre Oriental darter all nest in the forests hugging the Kinabatangan. Avian wildlife is more numerous and varied during rainier months (usually October to late March), which coincides with northern-hemisphere migrations. Though friendly for birds, the rainy season isn't accommodating for humans. Flooding has been a problem of late and a couple of lodges will sometimes shut their doors when conditions are severe.

The success rate of animal-spotting largely depends on luck and the local knowledge of your guide. In the late afternoon you'll be looking for proboscis monkeys and crocs. River cruises by night are even more dramatic, the sky a silent theatre of electric-yellow lightning, or jeweller's cloth of glittering gems, as you sign a waiver of rights at your lodge (in the event you get eaten by a croc... just kidding!), then set out into the black mass of the Kinabatangan River. Your life and the success of the cruise is in the hands of your multitasking driver who scopes the trees with his torch whilst driving. You'll possibly see sleeping Stork kingfishers with their eyes open, pygmy elephants in the river, pythons coiled in trees, civet cats, egrets hanging like phantom pods from branches, buffy fish owls, flat-headed cats, and the red eyes of crocodiles emerging like periscopes as they slyly chart your progress.

River tours should always be included in lodge package rates. If you prefer to explore independently, contact local homestay programs, which will be able to hook you up with a boat operator. Or ask about renting a boat in Sukau – everyone in the village is connected to the tourism industry either directly or through family and friends, and someone will be able to find you a captain. Another option: just before the entrance to Sukau village is a yellow sign that says 'Di sini ada boat servis' (Boat service here); different river pilots hang out here throughout the day. Whatever way you choose to find a boat and a guide, expect to pay at least RM100 for a two-hour river cruise on a boat that can hold up to six people (ie you can split the cost with friends).

Hiking

Depending on the location of your lodge, some companies offer short hikes (one to three hours) through the jungle. Night hikes are some of the best fun to be had on the Kinabatangan – there's something magical about being plunged into the intense, cavernlike darkness of the jungle at night. Headlamps should be carried in your hand rather than on your head – wasps and bats tend to be attracted to light sources.

Sleeping & Eating

You'll need to book at the river lodges in advance. In Kinabatangan lingo, a 'three-day, two-night' stint usually involves the following: arrive in the afternoon on day one for a cruise at dusk, two boat rides (or a boat-hike combo) on day two, and an early morning departure on day three after breakfast and a sunrise cruise. When booking a trip, ask about pick-up and drop-off prices – this is usually extra.

Sukau

Tiny Sukau sits on the river across from massive stone cliffs seemingly lifted from a Chinese silk-scroll painting.

Sukau Greenview B&B B&B $

(089-565 266, 013-869 6922; www.sukaugreenview.net; dm/r RM45/60, 3-day, 2-night package incl breakfast & 3 x 2hr river trips per person RM499) Run by locals, this lime-green wooden affair had OK dorms and basic rooms. There's also a pleasant cafe looking out on the river. Greenview runs special elephant-sighting trips, and also crocodile trips in the early morning and at night (both priced at RM250).

★ **Sukau Rainforest Lodge** LODGE $$$

(088-438 300; www.sukau.com; 3-day, 2-night package RM1688;) One of *National Geographic's* 'Top 30 Lodges in the World', this is the most upscale digs on the river. Think beautifully appointed split-level rooms with wood and terrazzo floors, rain shower, lounge area and mozzie nets. There's a fine restaurant, an onsite naturalist who gives wildlife talks and night walks, plus a welcome plunge pool to cool off in. Romantic.

The Rainforest Lodge participates in tree-planting projects aimed at reviving degraded portions of riverine forest and is pioneering the use of quiet electric motors on its river cruises. Don't miss the 440m boardwalk in the back that winds through the canopy.

Kinabatangan Riverside Lodge LODGE $$$

(089-213 502; www.sitours.com; 2-day, 1-night packages incl visit to Sepilok's Sun Bear Conservation Centre & Orangutan Nursery from US$510; ❄📶) Come here to fall gently asleep in a series of luxury chalets, adrift in simple white sheets and polished wood floors, all connected by a series of shady raised walkways through the jungle. A looping nature trail is out the back and an adorable dining area abounds with stuffed monkeys, faux foliage and traditional instruments. It's managed by SI Tours, which charges in US$.

Bilit

Bilit is a friendly village with a number of homestays. River lodges are located on both the Bilit side of the Kinabatangan River and the opposite bank. There's a jetty from which boats depart to lodges on the other side of the river, and across the street is a small yard where you can park a car if you drove here; the family that owns the house charges RM20 a day for the privilege. A small banana orchard acts as a magnet for pygmy elephants.

★Myne Resort RESORT **$$**
(☎089-216 093; www.myne.com.my; longhouse/chalet RM250/280; ❄📶) Situated on the bend of the river, Myne has an open, breezy reception, games room and restaurant festooned with lifeguard rings, and is vaguely reminiscent of an old wooden ship. Chalets are beautiful with peach drapes, river-facing balcony, glossed wood floors, comfy beds, dresser, flat screen and cable TV. Night cruises cost RM75, transfers RM100.

Nature Lodge Kinabatangan LODGE **$$**
(☎088-230 534, 013-863 6263; www.naturelodgekinabatangan.com; 3-day, 2-night package dm/chalet RM402/583) Located close to Bilit, this backpacker jungle retreat has two sections: the Civet Wing with dorm-style huts, and the Agamid Wing with twin-bed chalets with high ceilings and wood floors. The activity schedule is fantastic: the three-day, two-night packages include four boat tours, one guided hike *and* all meals, which is as good value as you'll find in these parts.

Proboscis Lodge Bukit Melapi LODGE **$$**
(☎088-240 584; www.sdclodges.com; 2-day, 1-night package tw share per person RM350, river cruises RM95; ❄) Based on a promontory that saw a battle between local *Orang Sungai* (People of the River) and the Japanese in WWII, this lodge's fruit-luxuriant grounds are popular with sweet-toothed elephants. There's a games room and pleasant lounge here, while rooms are huge with river-facing balcony, cable TV, bathroom, desk and comfy beds. Watch out for the hornbills. Staff are superfriendly.

The two-day, one-night packages include three meals, one river cruise and a pick-up from the Lapit jetty.

Kinabatangan Jungle Camp LODGE **$$**
(☎013-540 5333, 019-843 5017, 089-533 190; www.kinabatanganjunglecamp.com; 2-day, 1-night package RM550) This earth-friendly retreat caters to birders and serious nature junkies; facilities are functional, with the focus on quality wildlife-spotting over soft, comfortable digs, with fan-only rather than air-con rooms. Packages include three meals, two boat rides, guiding and transfers. The owners also run the Labuk B&B in Sepilok, and four out of five travellers opt for a Kinabatangan–Sepilok combo tour.

Borneo Nature Lodge LODGE **$$$**
(☎088-230 534; www.naturelodgekinabatangan.com; Kampung Bilit, Kinabatangan District; 3-day, 2-night stay incl 3 boat rides RM1057) 🍃 Welcoming staff and deliciously cool, cosy rooms await in this fine eco-conscious lodge. The food is particularly tasty and there's an open lounge to read or watch DVDs (don't you dare!). The guides here are top-notch and know every centimetre of the river. Watch out for nosy macaques – keep your windows shut!

Last Frontier Resort RESORT **$$$**
(☎016-676 5922; www.thelastfrontierresort.com; 3-day, 2-night package RM600; ❄@📶) Maybe they should rename this place the Last Breath Resort after the torturously steep hill you have to ascend via an infinity of steps to reach the place. Only the fit should attempt it, however your reward is a serene view of the flood plains and a sense of absolute escape with boutique-style rooms with chocolate-brown walls, dark-wood beds and red linen. There's also the dinky Monkey Cup Cafe which serves pasta bolognese, chicken curry and pancakes.

The price includes two river cruises and one trek. The transfer here costs RM40 extra. You'll also be glad to hear there's a store room at the bottom of the 538 steps, to leave your heavy bag while you carry up the bare essentials.

Bilit Rainforest Lodge LODGE **$$$**
(☎088-448 409; http://bilitrainforestlodge.com; 2-day, 1-night package incl meals & 1 night river cruise RM420; ❄📶) Rainforest has 24 rooms

DON'T MISS

HOMESTAYS ON THE KINABATANGAN

Homestay programs are popping up with increasing frequency in Sukau, Bilit and other villages, giving tourists a chance to stay with local *Orang Sungai* and inject money almost directly into local economies. Please note the contacts we provide are for local homestay program coordinators who will place you with individual families.

The villagers of **Abai** love hosting guests and chatting with you – you can expect to be asked to participate in the local village volleyball matches! A homestay is best arranged through Adventure Alternative Borneo (p320) in Kota Kinabalu, which maintains direct contact with the villagers. It should cost RM870 for a two-night package that includes meals, guided village walk and jungle walk, one day and night river cruise, plus boat from Sandakan and room and meals.

In **Sukau**, **Bali Kito Homestay** (☎013-869 9026, 089-568 472; http://sukauhomestay.com; 3-day, 2-night package for 4 persons RM650, 1 night incl 2 meals RM50) can connect you with several different families and, for additional fees, hook you up with cultural programs, fishing trips, opportunities to work on traditional farms, treks, wildlife cruises and other fun. A special walk-in rate of RM30 is also available if you just rock up at the village (meals are RM10 each). A four-person three-day, two-night package that includes meals, four river cruises, transport to and from Sandakan and a visit to the Gomantong Caves costs RM650 per person, but different packages can be arranged for smaller groups.

Homestays in **Bilit** are on a rotation system of nine households so they all get a fair crack of the whip. The houses we visited were all fiercely houseproud with mattresses on clean floors (expect squat loos). You can just turn up here or look for the official 'Homestay Malaysia' sign. Alternatively, call **Mr Janggai** (☎013-891 2078; www.bilithomestay.wordpress.com; Bilit) the **Bilit Homestay Coordinator**. Three-day, two-night rates, which include river cruises and trekking, costs RM840 per person.

Near **Batu Puti** (the village adjacent to the Batu Tulug caves), **Miso Walai Homestay** (☎089-551070, 019-582 5214, 012-889 5379; www.mescot.org; r RM70) is one of the oldest, best-run community ecotourism initiatives in the area and works with the excellent KOPEL, a village co-operative managed and run by the local people themselves. We've had really glowing reports from travellers who have stayed and worked here on the volunteer program planting trees. You'll be encouraged to learn to cook, take part in village sports and farming as part of the experience. By dint of its location, this homestay also happens to be outside the tourist crush in Sukau and Bilit, so your chances of spotting wildlife are much better.

When staying in a homestay, it is important to act as a guest in someone's home. Privacy will be reduced, and you may be expected to help with chores, cooking, cleaning etc (this depends on the family you stay with). Men and women should dress modestly and couples will want to avoid overt displays of affection, which locals tend to frown on. English may not be widely spoken. The experience is a different one, one which many visitors absolutely love, but it's certainly not everyone's cup of tea. That said, we strongly encourage giving homestays a shot if you haven't done so before.

with stained-wood floors, balcony complete with hammock, armoire and bathroom. Comparatively bland compared with some of the competition, the service is warm, the grounds large. There's also a handsome central building with a nice bar come evening. An additional cruises cost RM120 per person.

Bilit Adventure Lodge LODGE $$$
(☎089-271 077; www.stwadventure.com; 2-day, 1-night package from RM665, with air-con RM740; ❄) Built 10 years ago, this cosy lodge has 16 air-con and eight fan rooms. It feels authentic with its river-bar cafe and bamboo-accented rooms with colourful quilts. The fan-only rooms are less impressive. Set in 10 acres of untamed wilderness, the lodge's lights are kept low at night to encourage the presence of visitors.

For RM30 you can take a cooking class with a local person.

Upriver

★**Tungog Rainforest Eco Camp** CABIN $
(☎089-551 070, 019-582 5214; www.mescot.org; per night incl 3 meals RM95, river cruises RM45)

This eco camp faces a pretty oxbow lake by the Kinabatangan River. Luxurious it isn't – expect wooden shelters with mattress, fragrant sheets and pillows, plus a mozzie net and shared bathrooms; however, the immersion in nature and chance to put something back by planting trees is magical. Given there are no other camps for kilometres, you have the wildlife to yourself.

On the road between Sandakan and Lahad Datu, ask the bus to drop you at the Kinabatangan bridge, from where you catch a boat to the camp. The office of KOPEL Ltd, which manages the camp, is located under the Kinabatangan River bridge. Book ahead.

Uncle Tan's Jungle Camp LODGE **$$**

(☎089-535 784, 016-824 4749; www.uncletan.com; 2-day, 1-night packages from RM350, 3-day, 2-night packages from RM450) Uncle Tan was one of the earliest environmentalists working along the Kinabatangan. His legacy lives on in his lodges. As the website clearly explains, it is *not* the Hilton. Expect very basic digs but bags of enthusiasm from the great staff, knowledgeable guides and a warm atmosphere. Due to its isolated location, animal sightings are high.

Abai Jungle Lodge LODGE **$$$**

(☎089-213 502, 013-883 5841; www.sitoursborneo.com; 2-day, 1-night packages incl visit to Sepilok's Sun Bear Conservation Centre & Orangutan Nursery from US$510) Managed by SI Tours (p352), ecofriendly Abai Jungle Lodge sits 37km upstream from Sukau as the river emerges from secondary forest. While it's basic, rooms are comfortable fan-only affairs, and the food is nothing to get excited about either, the wildife here is terrific, and reports of Abai's guides tend to be that they go all out to find what you're looking for.

Getting There & Away

Transfers are usually arranged with your lodging as part of your package, but you can save by arriving independently. Arrange transport from any of the drop-off points with your tour operator or with a local minivan. Don't get on Birantihanti buses – they stop any time someone wants to get on or off, which could quadruple travelling time.

BUS & MINIVAN

From KK, board a Tawau- or Lahad Datu–bound bus and ask the driver to let you off at 'Sukau Junction', also known as 'Meeting Point' – the turn-off road to reach Sukau. If you are on a Sandakan-bound bus, make sure your driver remembers to stop at the Tawau-Sandakan junction, it's called 'Batu 32' or 'Checkpoint' (sometimes it's known as Sandakan Mile 32).

From Sepilok or Sandakan, expect to pay around RM20 to reach 'Batu 32', and around RM35 if you're on a Sandakan–Tawau bus and want to alight at 'Meeting Point'.

Arrange in advance with your Sepilok accommodation to be picked up from these drop-off points. The alternative is vastly overcharging taxis.

A minivan ride to 'Meeting Point' from Lahad Datu costs RM25. When buying your bus tickets, remember to tell the vendor where you want to get off so you don't get overcharged.

CAR

If you are driving, note that the Shell petrol station on the highway at Sukau Junction (at the turn-off to Sukau) is the last place to fill up before arriving at the river. The road to Sukau is pretty smooth, but as you get closer to Bilit you'll start running into some dirt patches. It is possible to get to Bilit via 2WD – just drive carefully, especially if it's been raining.

Lahad Datu

POP 105,620

This little coastal town has a fish market, dry goods market, wilting sun-scorched buildings and very little else to keep you here. Travellers wishing to visit Tabin Wildlife Park and the Danum Valley – if they haven't already booked – arrive in town, head to the respective offices and stay a night before leaving for the jungle the next morning. If you *have* booked, you'll likely arrive on an early flight and be spirited away by your guide from either **Borneo Nature Tours** (☎089-880 207; www.borneonaturetours.com; Lot 20, block 3, Fajar Centre), which runs the Borneo Rainforest Lodge (BRL), or the **Danum Valley Field Centre** (☎089-881 092, 088-326 300; rmilzah@gmail.com; Block 3, Fajar Centre). Both of these outfits have offices next to each other in the upper part of town – known as Taman Fajar, or Fajar Centre.

There's a major difference between the two Danum Valley sleeping options, and that's price and luxury. The Borneo Rainforest Lodge is upscale and very comfortable, the Field Centre, rough, ready and very authentic. The Field Centre's office can be slow about responding to emails or phone calls asking for lodging. They offer ample rooms and dorm space these days for non scientific types, but it's always best to book ahead by a few days. For groups you may have to book much earlier. You can just show up in person, and politely request to speak with someone about sleeping arrangements.

At the airport terminal building you'll find the efficient and friendly booking office of Tabin Wildlife Holidays (p369), a secondary forest sanctuary on the other side of Lahad Datu.

Sleeping

Full Wah HOTEL $
(☎089-884 100; Jln Anggerik; s/d from RM45/65; ❄) If you're on a tight budget, Full Wah will do. Rooms are exceedingly mediocre, but clean and mould free.

★**Bike & Tours B&B** GUESTHOUSE $$
(☎017-864 2016, 017-293 6376; www.bikeandtours.com; Lot 62, Taman Hap Heng, Batu 1 1/4, Jln Segama; s/d with shared bathroom RM160/184 incl breakfast, d with bathroom RM230; ❄📶🏊) Winning applause for their cycling excursions in the area, and the quality of their digs, B&T is run by a friendly Swiss/Malay couple and their five rooms are cool affairs with laminate floors and fresh linen. There's a pool in the garden, great breakfast and a complimentary pick-up from the bus station/airport.

B&T are all about mindfulness in nature; taking your time on two wheels to get to know the locals and the environment around you. Recommended.

Bay Hotel HOTEL $$
(☎089-882 801; Block O, lot 1 & 2, 7b Jln Panji; s RM95, d RM105-118) Fresh rooms with flat screen, swish decor, bathroom and air-con – plus a pleasant cafe downstairs serving Western food – make this a nice addition to the currently limited sleeping options in town.

Hotel De Leon HOTEL $$
(☎089-881 222; www.hoteldeleon.com.my; Darvel Bay Commercial Centre; s/d from RM148/178; ❄📶) Lahud Datu's plushest option, seaward Leon is cool, with a chic baroque-accented lobby and restaurant, and fresh, air-conditioned rooms. Perfect for those needing a night of comfort after the bush. Free wi-fi is available in all the rooms.

Eating

It's worth stopping by one of the convenience stores in Fajar Centre on Lorong Fajar to stock up on a couple of snacks before your trip into the Danum Valley.

Kak Tini Restaurant MALAYSIAN $
(cnr Jln Bunga Raya & Jln Teratai; mains RM3.50; ⏲24hr) This 24-hour mint-green restaurant close to the bus station is popular for its buffet of fried chicken, soups, fresh fish and noodle dishes.

MultiBake BAKERY $
(Fajar Centre; cakes from RM1.80; ⏲8am-10pm; 📶) Malaysia's franchised patisserie is located in Fajar Centre (it has free wi-fi too).

Dovist CHINESE $
(mains from RM5; ⏲9am-10pm) Around the corner from the Danum booking offices; a respectable spot for a more substantial meal of Chinese-style seafood dishes.

Getting There & Away

AIR

MASwings (☎1800-883 000, outside Malaysia 03-7843 3000; www.maswings.com) currently operates five daily flights to Lahad Datu from KK. The airport is in the upper part of town near Fajar Centre. You must take the first flight of the day (departing KK at 7.25am) if you don't want a one-day layover in town before heading to the Danum Valley.

BUS

Express buses on the KK–Tawau route stop at the Shell station (Fajar Centre) behind the Danum Valley office in the upper part of town. Other buses and minivans leave from a vacant lot near Tabin Lodge in the lower part of town. There are frequent departures for Sandakan (RM25, 2½ hours), Sukau (RM25, two hours), Semporna (RM22 to RM25, two hours) and Tawau (RM20, 2½ hours). Charter vehicles and 4WDs wait in an adjacent lot; these guys are difficult to hire after sunset.

Danum Valley Conservation Area

Flowing like a series of dark, mossy ripples over 440 sq km of central Sabah, the Danum Valley Conservation Area is like something out a children's story book: the sheer spectrum of furry and scaled friends you find within its dipterocarp forest is mind-blowing: orangutans, tarsiers, sambar deer, bearded pigs, flying squirrels, king cobras, proboscis monkeys, red-leaf monkeys, gibbons and pygmy elephants (to name a few). The area is also known for its medium-sized cats, with the beautifully marked clouded leopard spotted on night drives, as well as the flat-headed cat, marbled cat, leopard cat and cartoon-like bay cat. This almost impenetrable arboreal fortress is watered by Sungai Segama and shaded by 70m-high old-growth canopy and 1093m-high Mt Danum. Recognised as one of the world's most complex ecosystems, and astonishingly, a new species of plant is found by scientists here every week. Your alarm clock is the melodic ray gun 'zap' of dawn gibbons and the chainsaw drone of cicadas, your bedtime cue the shrill of crickets and your aching calves (which will have done so much trekking, they'll be marching you to sleep).

This pristine rainforest is currently under the protection of **Yayasan Sabah** (Sabah Foundation; www.ysnet.org.my), a semigovernmental organisation tasked with both protecting and utilising the forest resources of Sabah. They say that at any given time, there are over a hundred scientists doing research in the Danum Valley. Accommodation has been expanded so more travellers can experience its rare delights with a capacity of up to 135 people. See the website of the South East Asia Rainforest Research (www.searrp.org) for more information on research occurring in the valley.

There are two lodging options in the Danum Valley: the Borneo Rainforest Lodge (p368) (BRL), and the Danum Valley Field Centre (p368). You absolutely must have accommodation arranged with one of them before you visit – no dropping in. Danum is a jungle, and while one person's night drive/day walk might yield multiple sightings, another's can be sparse; it really is the luck of the draw.

Sights & Activities

Both the Borneo Rainforest Lodge and the Danum Valley Field Centre offer a variety of jungle-related activities. Only the BRL has official nature guides, whereas the Field Centre offers park rangers. If you're booked with a tour company however, you will be attached to a trained English-speaking guide.

Watching the World Wake Up

Getting out of bed while it's still dark and your clock reads 5.30am is no fun; the jungle quiet as a cemetery, the air shivery cold. But driving through the forest to a vertiginously high wooden watchtower, climbing to its top and waiting for the sun to appear over the rim of the earth below make it all worthwhile. As the first cicadas wake, the melodic call of the gibbon reaching out of the mist-veiled jungle, you feel like a privileged voyeur witnessing a sacred, primal moment. Then slowly the fireworks begin as a sliver of sun appears over the distant forest ridge, the sky seguing through ruby to salmon, orange to vermilion. Priceless. Tip: it's cold, so bring a jumper!

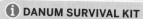

> **DANUM SURVIVAL KIT**
>
> We strongly recommend leech socks (especially if there's been rain), a stash of energy sweets, insect repellent, plasters for blisters, a strong torch and, if you're looking for that front-cover shot of a rhinoceros hornbill in flight, a powerful zoom lens. Sneakers are fine in dry weather; hiking boots, though heavier, provide better support in slippery conditions.

Trekking in the Valley

The main activities at the BRL and the Danum Valley Field Centre are walking on more than 50km of marked, meandering trails. Your average group is about six to eight persons and fitness will vary considerably; if you're in a troupe of superheroes and get left behind, don't be afraid to ask the guide to slow down. Depending on the zeal of your group, you might walk as much as 16km or more in one day over a series of short treks or one long and short one (excluding night walks); remember you're in the jungle and clambering over roots and fallen trees is hard work, so don't push yourself unnecessarily.

At the BRL, take advantage of the well-trained guides who can point out things you would have never seen on your own. The **Coffincliff Trail** is a good way to start your exploration and get your bearings. It climbs 3km to a cliff where the remains of some Kadazan-Dusun coffins can be seen (although the provenance of the coffins is unclear). After reaching a fairly eye-popping panoramic viewpoint 100m further up the way, you can either return the way you've come or detour around the back of the peak to descend via scenic **Fairy Falls** and **Serpent Falls**, a pair of 15m falls that are good for a quick dip.

The **Danum Trail**, **Elephant Trail** and **Segama Trails** all follow various sections of the Danum Valley and are mostly flat trails offering good chances for wildlife spotting. All can be done in an hour or two. The **Hornbill Trail** and **East Trail** have a few hills, but are still relatively easy, with similarly good chances for wildlife sightings. Finally, if you just need a quick breath of fresh air after a meal, the **Nature Trail** is a short plankwalk near the lodge that allows you to walk into the forest unmolested by leeches.

There are heaps of fantastic trails weaving around the Field Centre – you must bring a ranger along if you aren't a scientist (note that a guide is better than a ranger though, as rangers are not trained to work with tourists). About a two-hour hike away are the **Tembaling Falls**, a cool slice of tropical Edenic beauty. A more strenuous, four-hour trek gets you to the immensely rewarding **Sungai Purut** falls, a series of seven-tiered pools that are fed by waters that drop down 20m from the nearby mountains. The likelihood is you'll climb the 40m-high observation tower just behind the Field Centre at dawn, the mist like a veil over the canopy. The summit platform is reached via a rickety ladder with an ineffective cage around it. Hold on tight and don't look down; if you make it to the top, the view of the jungle is like a sea of green velvet, and is utterly stupendous.

At the Centre you'll also take **night walks**; these tend to be shorter, but give you the chance to see chameleons flopping on branches like drunken 'Rangos', bug-eyed tarsiers, various snakes and curious sambar deer.

Birdwatching

Birdwatchers from around the world come to see a whole variety of rainforest species including the great argus pheasant, crested fireback pheasant, blue-headed pitta, Bornean bristlehead and several species of hornbill, among many others. If you're serious about birding, it may be best to stay at the Borneo Rainforest Lodge. The canopy walkway here is ideal for birdwatching, and some of the guides are particularly knowledgeable about birds. The access road to BRL is also a good spot for birding, as is, frankly, your porch.

Canopy Walkway

As you'll probably know, most of the action in a tropical rainforest happens up in the forest canopy, which can be frustrating for earthbound humans. The BRL's 107m-long, 27m-high canopy walkway gives mere mortals a means of transcending the surly bonds of earth. The swinging bridges traverse a nice section of forest, with several fine *mengaris* and *majau* trees on either side. Birdwatchers often come here at dawn in hope of checking a few species off their master list. Even if you're not a keen birder, it's worth rolling out of bed early to see the sun come up over the forest from the canopy walkway – when there's a bit of mist around, the effect is quite magical. It's located on the access road, a 10-minute walk from the lodge. You need to be a guest at the BRL to access the walkway.

Night Drives

This is one of the surest ways to see some of the valley's 'night shift'. Expect to see one or two species of giant flying squirrels, sambar deer, civets, porcupines and possibly even leopard cats; lucky sightings could include elephants and slow loris.

Night drives leave the BRL and Field Centre most evenings; the best trips are the extended night drives, which depart at about 8.30pm and return at 1am or 2am. Things you'll be glad you brought: light waterproof jacket, binoculars and a powerful torch. It can be cold, too, so bring another layer.

Sleeping & Eating

Danum Valley Field Centre LODGE $$
(DVFC; ☎088-326 300, 088-881 688; rmilzah@gmail.com; resthouse r & board from RM180, camping RM30; ❄) An outpost for scientists and researchers, the field centre also welcomes wildlife enthusiasts. Accommodation is organised into four categories: hostel, resthouse, VIP and camping. We recommend the resthouse – with basic clean rooms, ceiling fans and twin beds – located by the canteen. Treks start from here, so if you're staying in the dorms you'll constantly be walking between the two.

Towels are provided for the cold-water showers. The simple hostel is about a seven-minute walk from the canteen, and the barracks-style rooms are separated by gender. If you want to camp, you can lay your sleeping kit (no tent needed) out on the walkways – bug spray recommended!

There are no professionally trained guides at the centre – only rangers who can show you the trails if you just turn up – but book with a tour company and they will provide you with one. We recommend Sticky Rice Travel (p320). Tourists take their meals in the cafeteria-style canteen (veggie friendly). Near the camp is a clear stretch of shallow river to cool off in.

Borneo Rainforest Lodge RESORT $$$
(BRL; ☎089-880 207, 088-267 637; www.borneonaturetours.com; d standard/deluxe 3-day & 2-night package per person RM3296/3190) Set beside the Danum River, Borneo Rainforest Lodge

is for Indiana Jones types with healthy wallets – adventure combined with luxury, if you will. If you can afford to splash out on one of their lovely 31 en suite chalets – the deluxe numbers have private balcony with hot tub overlooking the jungle – you won't be disappointed.

Crackling with classy atmosphere and having had a recent facelift, there are talks on wildlife and conservation, slide shows, and raised wooden walkways and a romantic outside terrace.

Getting There & Away

The Danum Valley is only accessible by authorised private vehicle. Borneo Rainforest Lodge guests depart from the lodge office in Lahad Datu at 9am, arriving by lunchtime. If you do not want to spend the night in Lahad Datu, take the 7.25am MASwings flight from KK.

Tourists staying at the Danum Valley Field Centre must board one of two jungle-bound vans that leave the booking office in Lahad Datu at 3.30pm on Mondays, Wednesdays and Fridays. Transport is around RM100 per person each way. Vans return to Lahad Datu from the Field Centre at 8.30am.

Tabin Wildlife Reserve

About an hour's drive from Lahad Datu, this 1205-sq-km reserve consists mainly of lowland dipterocarp forest with mangrove areas – most of it is technically secondary forest, but that doesn't seem to trouble the wildlife or visitors. The stars here are the elephants and primates: gibbons, red-leaf monkeys and macaques, plus a lot of orangutans. Rescued orangutans from Sepilok are actually released here, so you've got a pretty good chance of spotting some. Birdlife is particularly abundant with a staggering 260 species recorded here, including all eight of the hornbill family, from rhino through to helmeted.

Tabin has a number of mud volcanoes and salt licks where animals and birds gather for their precious minerals, and you can watch them, cameras poised, from viewing towers. Sadly you're unlikely to see the Sumatran rhino, which is now believed to be extinct in Borneo. The park is managed by **Tabin Wildlife Holidays** (088-267 266; www.tabinwildlife.com.my; Lahud Datu airport terminal; 2-day, 1-night package incl meals from RM1450), which runs the on-site Tabin Wildlife Resort, a pretty retreat with a clutch of upscale chalets. Fair warning: the chalets are attractive, but they're overpriced for what you get. Five trails snake out into the jungle from in front of the resort. Try the Elephant Trail (800m) if you're interested in seeing belching mud pits and improving your complexion by wiping it on your skin. The Gibbon Trail (2.8km) leads to the pretty Lipa Waterfall.

Tabin can be accessed with a rental vehicle (4WD is a must), but most people arrange transport with Tabin Wildlife, the office of which is now conveniently located at the airport terminal at Lahad Datu, which is around 2½ hours' drive from Tabin. There are several entrances to the reserve; the easiest one to navigate to is near the junction of Ladan Tungju and Ladang Premai.

Semporna

POP 62,640

You won't be using your camera's memory card up in the town of Semporna, which, but for its mosque, is not immediately captivating. There's a wet market and some pretty stilted water-hotels, but little reason to extend a stay beyond dumping your bags and going for a chat with one of the many dive companies – all conveniently located in the same street. They'll soon have you salivating over what lies waiting for you in the Semporna Archipelago, a short boat journey away. Many of these companies have a dive centre at the resorts on Mabul island. If you've booked your dive and stay from KK already, you'll be picked up from the airport by your respective tour company and spirited straight to Semporna's port to take you to your end destination, so no need to stay a night.

There are a couple of OK sleeping options, one or two restaurants worth a look, shops to stock up on supplies, and a few decent bars come happy hour, so it's not all bad if you do have to stay.

Sights & Activities

Scuba is the town's lifeline, and there's no shortage of places to sign up for it. Due to the high volume of interest, it is best to do your homework and book ahead – diving at Sipadan is limited to 120 persons per day. This means that if you're in a large group, it's impossible you'll be able to dive together at Sipadan the next day; however, if you're a couple or travelling solo, you're in with a better chance.

Semporna

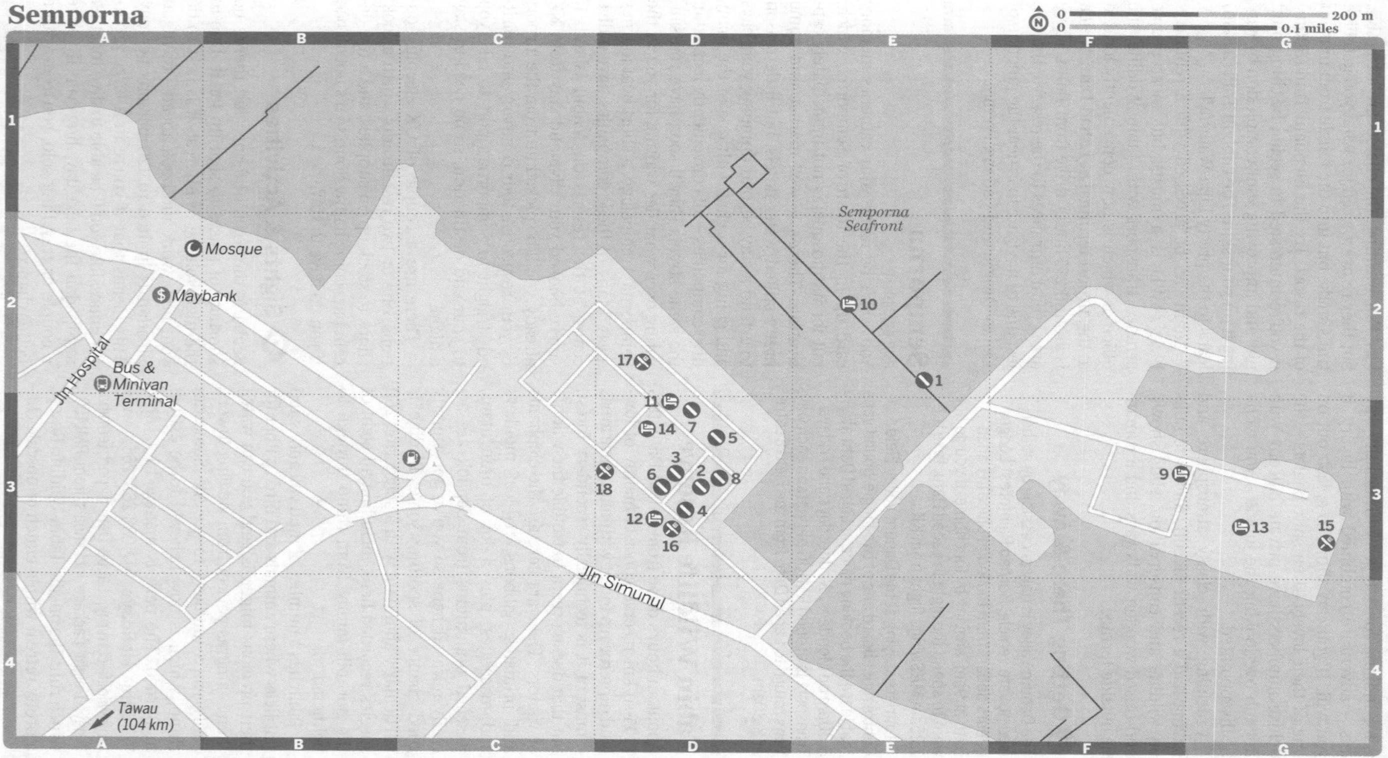
0 200 m
0 0.1 miles
A
B
C
D
E
F
G
1
2
3
4
Mosque
Maybank
Bus & Minivan Terminal
Jln Hospital
Jln Simunul
Semporna Seafront
Tawau (104 km)
1
2
3
4
5
6
7
8
9
10
11
12
13
14
15
16
17
18

Sleeping

★Scuba Junkie Dive Lodge HOSTEL $

(☎089-785 372; www.scuba-junkie.com/accommodations; Block B 36, 458 Semporna seafront; dm diver/nondiver RM25/50, r without bathroom diver/nondiver RM75/150, r with bathroom diver/nondiver RM95/190; ❄📶) Fresh yellow walls peppered with underwater shots of marine life, clean bathrooms and a variety of air-con rooms to choose from, make this a sure bet. Also it's directly opposite Scuba Junkie's office, and next to the Diver's Bar, a good spot for breakfast before you head of to the Semporna Archipelago.

Borneo Global Sipadan BackPackers HOSTEL $

(☎089-785 088; www.bgbsipadan.com; Jln Causeway; dm/tr/f incl breakfast RM27/99/130; ❄@📶) There are nine rooms comprising dorm, triples and family options with bathroom. The walls are fresh, the air is cool and there's a friendly lobby area to chill in. They also run three-day PADI Open Water courses for RM920. Run by energetic Max.

Sipadan Inn HOTEL $$

(☎089-781 766; www.sipadaninn-hotel.com; Block D, lot 19-24, Semporna seafront; d/f from RM110/170; ❄@📶) A slice of refrigerated comfort, the Inn has simple but tidy rooms with wood walls, fresh linen, bed runners, coffee-making facilities, spotless bathrooms and very friendly staff.

Holiday Dive Inn HOTEL $$

(☎089-919 128; www.holidaydiveinn.com; Lot A5-A7, Semporna seafront; r RM86-96, f RM168; ❄📶) This recent addition has spotless rooms with cheerful colours, fresh bathrooms, TVs and some rooms with balcony. Good value, it's affiliated with Sipadan Scuba nearby. There's also a nice sundowner roof lounge.

Seafest Hotel HOTEL $$

(☎089-782 333; www.seafesthotel.com; Jln Kastam; r/f RM135/250; ❄) Palatial in proportions, this white monolith at the far end of the 'Semporna seafront' neighbourhood is good value if there's two of you, with well-appointed rooms with desk, bathroom and an international feel. Plus there's a shop, adjacent fish restaurant by the water, and an outdoor pool. Atmosphere? We've been to more effervescent funerals.

Dragon Inn HOTEL $$

(Rumah Rehat Naga; ☎089-781 088; www.dragoninnfloating.com.my; 1 Jln Kastam, Semporna Ocean Tourism Centre; dm RM45, r incl breakfast from RM122, f RM170-190; ❄@📶) Arriving at Dragon Inn, built on stilts and connected by an infinity of a boardwalk over bottle-green water, the first thing you see is a taxidermied giant grouper outside its lobby. Rooms are simple but appealing with wood floors, TV and bathroom. There's also a peaceful shaded cafe to watch the harbour life buzzing by.

Semporna

Activities, Courses & Tours

1	Big John Scuba	E2
2	Billabong Scuba	D3
3	Blue Sea Divers	D3
4	Scuba Junkie	D3
5	Seahorse Sipadan	D3
6	Seaventures	D3
7	Sipadan Scuba	D3
8	Uncle Chang's	D3

Sleeping

9	Borneo Global Sipadan BackPackers	F3
10	Dragon Inn	E2
11	Holiday Dive Inn	D3
12	Scuba Junkie Dive Lodge	D3
13	Seafest Hotel	G3
14	Sipadan Inn	D3

Eating

15	Anjung Lepa	G3
16	Diver's Bar	D3
17	Fat Mother	D2
18	Mabul Steak House	D3

Eating

Various *kedai kopi* (coffee shops) line the 'Semporna seafront', while restaurants at the Seafest Hotel complex offer Chinese seafood. If you wanna go native, sample the *nasi lemak* or *korchung* (rice dumplings) – Semporna is well known for these two dishes.

★Fat Mother CHINESE $

(Semporna seafront; mains RM15; ⏲5-10pm) Mother's has terrific reviews for its warm service and wide-ranging seafood menu – your dinner will be glowering at you from the glass tanks. They'll even prepare your own fish if you've caught it. There's grouper and mango sauce, fish porridge, salted egg and squid, Malay curries and noodle dishes, plus free Chinese tea and melon dessert.

Anjung Lepa SEAFOOD $

(Jln Kastam; mains RM15; ⏲5-10pm) Parked beside the Seafest hotel, this is a lovely little spot to tuck into fresh fish and Malay dishes come early evening. Squid, prawns, crab... all the treasures of the deep.

Diver's Bar INTERNATIONAL $$

(Semporna seafront; mains RM18-32; ⌚7-9am & 1pm-midnight) Beside Scuba Junkie Dive Lodge and opposite the Scuba Junkie office, this terracotta-interiored, partially open-air joint is popular with divers and has a very underwhelming breakfast of fruit and cold eggs (RM10), but come lunch and dinner, it gets better with New Zealand beef and fries, Greek salad and various pasta dishes.

Mabul Steak House STEAK $$

(☎089-781 785; Semporna seafront; mains from RM15-20; ⌚noon-11pm) This breezy balcony with an easy vibe and phonebook-thick menu is heavy not just on steak but seafood, serving everything from grouper to parrot fish, mullet, lobster and squid, steak and lamb cutlets, as well as omelettes and glacial 'ice-blended juices'.

ℹ Information

If you're arriving in Semporna under your own steam, leave the bus and minivan drop-off area and head towards the mosque's minaret. This is the way to the waterfront. Follow the grid of concrete streets to the right until you reach 'Semporna seafront' – home to the diving outfitters, each stacked one next to the other in a competitive clump.

Decompression Chamber (☎089-783 100, 012-483 9572; www.navy.mil.my; Pangkalan TLDM, Semporna) There is a decompression chamber at the naval base 14km southwest of Semporna.

Maybank (☎089-784 852; Jln Jakarullah; ⌚9.15am-4.30pm) Expect small lines and the occasional beggar, especially in the evening.

ℹ Getting There & Away

AIR

Flights to Tawau from KK and KL land at Tawau Airport, roughly 28km from town. A private taxi from Tawau Airport to Semporna costs RM100, while Tawau–Semporna buses (RM20) will stop at the airport if you ask the driver nicely. Buses that do not stop at the airport will let you off at Mile 28, where you will have to walk a few (unshaded) kilometres to the terminal. Remember that flying less than 24 hours after diving can cause serious health issues, even death.

BUS

The 'terminal' hovers around the Milimewa supermarket not too far from the mosque's looming minaret. All buses run from early morning until 4pm (except Kota Kinabalu) and leave when full.

Kota Kinabalu (RM75, nine hours) leaves at around 7am or 7pm.

Lahad Datu (RM30, 2½ hours)

Sandakan (RM45 to RM40, 5½ hours)

Tawau (RM25, 1½ hours)

Semporna Archipelago

The stunning sapphires and emeralds of the Semporna Archipelago, home to copper-skinned Bajau sea gypsies in crayon-coloured boats and lush desert islands plucked from your deepest fantasies, are a sight for cynical souls. But no one comes this way for the islands, such as it were – rather, it is the ocean and everything beneath it, that appeals, because this is first and foremost a diving destination, consistently voted one of the best in the world.

Activities

In local speak Semporna means 'perfect', but there is only one island in the glittering Semporna Archipelago that takes this title. Miniature-sized Sipadan, moored 36km off the southeast coast, is perfection: turquoise water lapping sugar-fine sand, backdropped by a lush forest of palm trees and strangler fig trees. The island sits atop a pinnacle of rock and prompted world-famous diver Jacques Cousteau to describe it as 'An untouched piece of art'. With a virtual motorway of marine life passing on its way around you on any given day, locals include: parrotfish, batfish, octopuses and cuttlefish changing colour like underwater disco lights; reef sharks, lionfish and clownfish. Pelagic visitors include hammerhead and whale sharks and regular visits from majestic manta and eagle rays. And we haven't even gotten to the reef itself – think staghorn, black and sea-whip corals, barrel sponges and filigree coral fans all looking as if they've been dipped in funhouse paint.

Roughly a dozen delineated dive sites orbit the island, the most famous being **Barracuda Point**, where chevron and blacktail barracuda collide to form impenetrable walls of undulating fish. Reef sharks seem attracted to the strong current here and almost always swing by to say hello. **South Point** hosts the large pelagics like hammerhead and thresher sharks and manta, as well as bumphead parrotfish. Expect the current to be strong here too. The west side of the island features walls that tumble down to an impossibly deep 2000m – words can't do the sight of this justice. The walls are best appreciated from out in the blue on a clear afternoon.

Although Sipadan outshines the neighbouring sites, there are other reefs in the marine park that are well worth exploring. The macro-diving around **Mabul** (or 'Pulau Mabul') is world-famous, and on any given day you can expect to see blue-ringed octopuses, bobtail squid, boxer and orangutan crabs and cardinal fish. In fact, the term 'muck diving' was invented here. The submerged sites around **Kapalai**, **Mataking** and **Sibuan** are also of note.

It's unlikely you can rock up in Semporna and chance upon an operator willing to take you to Sipadan the following day, because you'll have to do an orientation dive on Mabul first. And if you're here in the peak months of July and August or the Christmas period and haven't booked in advance, you're likely to have a wait. Groups need to book many weeks in advance to get a shot at Sipadan.

The government issues 120 passes (RM40) to Sipadan each day (this number includes divers, snorkellers and day trippers). Bizarre rules and red tape, like having certain gender ratios, make the permit process even more frustrating. Each dive company is issued a predetermined number of passes per day depending on the size of its operation and the general demand for permits. Each operator has a unique way of 'awarding' tickets – some companies place their divers in a permit lottery, others promise a day at Sipadan after a day (or two) of diving at Mabul and Kapalai. No matter which operator you choose, you will be required to do a non-Sipadan intro dive unless you are a Divemaster who has logged a dive in the last six months. Permits to Sipadan are issued by day (and not by dive), so make sure you are getting at least three dives in your package.

A three-dive day trip costs between RM250 and RM500 (some operators include park fees, other do not – be sure to ask), and equipment rental (full gear) comes to about RM50 or RM60 per day. Cameras (around RM100 per day) and dive computers (around RM80 per day) are also available for rent at most dive centres. Top-end resorts on Mabul and Kapalai offer all-inclusive package holidays (plus a fee for equipment rental).

Although most of the diving in the area is 'fun diving', Open Water certifications are available, and advanced coursework is popular for those wanting to take things to the next level. Diving at Sipadan is geared towards divers with an Advanced Open Water certificate (currents and thermoclines can be strong), but Open Water divers should not have any problems (they just can't go as deep as advanced divers). A three-day Open Water course will set you back at least RM975. Advanced Open Water courses (two days) cost the same, and Divemaster certification costs around RM2800 and takes four weeks.

Several dive operators are based at their respective resorts, while others have shopfronts and offices in Semporna and/or KK. Please note we have listed the following dive operators alphabetically, not in order of preference.

Big John Scuba DIVING
(BJ Scuba; ☎089-785 399; www.bigjohnscuba.com; Jln Kastam; 3-dive day trip RM280, snorkelling day trip RM150-180) 'Big John' specialises in macro photography and muck diving. Has an office by the Dragon Inn (p371).

Billabong Scuba DIVING
(☎089-781 866; www.billabongscuba.com; Lot 28, block E, Semporna seafront) Accommodation can be arranged at a rickety 'homestay' on Mabul. And we mean rickety.

SNORKELLING IN SEMPORNA

Many nondivers wonder if they should visit Semporna. Of course you should! If you're travelling in a group or as a couple where some dive and some don't, the Semporna islands are a lot of fun; dive and snorkelling trips are timed so groups leave and come back at similar times, so you won't feel isolated from each other. If you're on your own and only want to snorkel, it's still great, but not as world class as the diving experience, and a bit pricey relative to the rest of Malaysia – snorkel trips cost around RM150, and you also have to factor in the relatively high cost of accommodation here and the price of getting out to the islands. Then again, you still have a good chance of seeing stingrays, sea turtles and all sorts of other macro-marine wildlife while in the midst of a tropical archipelago, so really, who's complaining?

DON'T MISS

REGATTA LEPA

The big annual festival of local Bajau sea gypsies is the Regatta Lepa, held in mid-April. Traditionally, the Bajau only set foot on mainland Borneo once a year; for the rest of the time they live on small islets or their boats. Today the Bajau go to Semporna and other towns more frequently for supplies, but the old cycle of annual return is still celebrated and marked by the regatta *lepa* (a traditional single mast sailing boat). For visitors, the highlight of the festival is the *lepa*-decorating contest held between Bajau families. Their already rainbow-coloured boats are further decked out in streamers, flags (known as *tapi*), bunting, ceremonial umbrellas (which symbolise protection from the omnipresent sun and rain that beats down on the ocean) and *sambulayang*, gorgeously decorated sails passed down within Bajau clans. Violin, cymbal and drum music, plus 'sea sports' competitions like duck catching and boat tug of war, punctuate the entire affair. The regatta occurs in mid-April; check www.sabahtourism.com/events/regatta-lepa-semporna-0 for details.

Blue Sea Divers DIVING
(☎089-781 322; www.blueseadivers-sabah.com; Semporna seafront) Budget day-trip operator in Semporna.

★Borneo Divers DIVING
(☎088-222 226; www.borneodivers.net; 9th fl, Menara Jubili, 53 Jln Gaya, Kota Kinabalu) The original and still one of the best dive outfits thanks to their high safety standards, quality equipment, excellent PADI teachers and divemasters. The office is located in Kota Kinabalu, plus a lovely resort on Mabul. Recommended.

★Scuba Junkie DIVING
(☎089-785 372; www.scuba-junkie.com; Lot 36, block B, Semporna seafront; 4 days & 3 nights on Mabul incl 3 dives per day at Kapilai, Mabul & 4 dives at Sipadan per person RM2385, snorkelling day trips incl lunch RM120; ⏱9am-6pm) The most proactive conservationists on Mabul, Scuba Junkie employ two full-time environmentalists and recycle much of their profits into their turtle hatchery and rehab centre and 'shark week' initiative. They're also a favourite with Westerners thanks to their excellent divemasters and comfortable, nonpackage type digs at Mabul Beach Resort (p376).

Scuba Jeff DIVING
(☎017-869 0218, 019-585 5125; www.scubajeffsipadan.com; Mabul Island) Jeff, a friendly local bloke, runs his adventures out of the local fishing village in Mabul. Accommodation is very basic.

Seahorse Sipadan DIVING
(☎089-782 289, 012-279 7657; www.seahorse-sipadanscuba.org; 1st fl, lot 1, Semporna seafront; 3-day, 2-night package incl 3 dives per day, accommodation, equipment & boat transfer RM690) Backpacker-oriented outfit with a new 1st-floor office on Semporna seafront, and accommodation on Mabul. Seahorse has been around for five years now.

Seaventures DIVING
(☎017-811 6023, 088-251 669; www.seaventuresdive.com; Lot 28, block E, Semporna seafront; 4-day, 3-night package incl 10 dives in total, with 3 dives on Sipadan, incl meals & transfers to island & airport RM2730) Based out of their funky blue/orange ocean platform close to Mabul island, this is a well-regarded outfit. Offices in Semporna and in KK's Wisma Sabah building.

Sipadan Scuba DIVING
(☎089-784 788, 089-781 788, 012-813 1688, 089-919 128; www.sipadanscuba.com; Lot 28, block E, Semporna seafront; 3-day & 2-night package incl dives, accommodation, transfer & equipment RM919) Twenty years' experience and an international staff make Sipadan Scuba a reliable, recommended choice. You can take your PADI Open Water course here for RM760.

Sipadan Water Village DIVING
(☎089-751 777, 089-950 023, 010-932 5783, 089-784 227; www.swvresort.com) A private operator based at the Mabul resort of the same name.

SMART DIVING
(☎088-486 389; www.sipadan-mabul.com.my) The dive centre operating at Sipadan-Mabul Resort and Mabul Water Bungalow; both are located on Mabul. Also has offices in KK.

Uncle Chang's DIVING
(Borneo Jungle River Island Tours; ☎089-781 002, 017-897 0002; www.ucsipadan.com; 36 Semporna seafront) Offers snorkelling day trips to Mataking (RM170), plus diving at Sipadan and digs at its basic lodge on Mabul.

Sleeping & Eating

From opulent bungalows to ragtag sea shanties, the marine park offers a wide variety of accommodation catering to all budgets, with most clustered on Mabul (Sipadan's closest neighbour), which is now threatening to become overcrowded. No one is allowed to stay on Sipadan. Note that prices rise in August and September. Nondivers are charged at different rates than divers.

At almost all of the places listed below, you're tied to a set schedule of three to five meals broken up by roughly three diving (or snorkelling) trips per day. Meals are included, drinks extra, although tea and coffee are often gratis. High-end resorts have their own bars and restaurants; you may be able to eat and drink there if you're staying in a budget spot and the person at the gate is in a good mood, but you'll pay for it. Remember there is still a 6pm curfew to be off the beach.

Divers and snorkellers can also opt to stay in the town of Semporna. That means slightly better bang for your buck, but no fiery equatorial sunsets. Perhaps more pertinently, it takes at least 30 minutes, and usually a bit longer, to get to dive sites from Semporna town.

Every one of the accommodation options listed below can arrange diving trips, including certification courses and trips to Sipadan.

Singamata

Not an island at all, but rather a floating village built onto a sandbar about 30 minutes from Semporna, **Singamata Reef Resort** (☎089-784 828; www.singamata.com; 3-day & 2-night incl diving & transfers RM1000-1200; ❄) is a pretty assemblage of stilt bungalows and decks with its own pool full of giant fish (which you can snorkel amid). If you feel like dipping into the water, you can literally just step out of your room (annoyingly, rubbish from Semporna sometimes still floats into the vicinity). Rooms are basic but pretty and breezy. You may feel isolated out here, but if you need an escape, this is a lovely option.

Mabul

Home to Bajau sea gypsies and a Malaysian village (where the budget accommodation is found), Mabul boasts a long sandy beach and is fairly crammed with resorts, a number of which are built out to sea on stilted water villages. With its excellent 'muck diving', fiery sunsets, desert island good looks and comfy resorts, the island makes for a nice play to chill, but really Mabul is your springboard for the neighbouring diving sites. For a little atmosphere, head to Scuba Junkie's bar at Mabul Beach Resort (p376).

It's worth having a walk around the island, passing a Bajau graveyard with its salt-worn wood-carved tombstones, and sidestepping giant monitor lizards. Behind the resorts are generators and barracks-style housing for resort staff. There are little shops in the villages that sell confectionery, crisps, cigarettes and other incidentals. Try to be sensitive if taking pictures of local people, we sensed that long zoom lenses and 'human zoo' behaviour from certain package-trip tourists was beginning to wear on the patience of islanders.

Sipadan Dive Centre (SDC) HOMESTAY $
(☎088-240 584, 012-821 8288; www.sdclodges.com; dm/r RM150/190, 3 dives RM280; ❄) Simple rainbow-coloured huts with attached bathroom, air-con, Caribbean-blue walls, fresh linen, wood floors, and a dive outfit – and less cramped quarters compared to other budget digs thanks to its spacious compound – make this a winner. Friendly management too; they cook up barbecue feasts by night.

Uncle Chang's GUESTHOUSE $
(☎089-781 002, 089-786 988, 017-895 002; www.ucsipadan.com; dm RM75, d with/without air-con & bathroom RM150/110; ❄) Shipwrecked amid the stilted weaveworld of the Malay village, if Chang's was an avuncular connection, he'd be a rough old seadog; think banana-yellow basic rattan-walled rooms in small chalets, a lively threadbare communal deck with occasional jam sessions and a happy, sociable vibe. There's also a well-known dive school here with seven daily dive permits to Sipadan.

Seahorse Sipadan Scuba Lodge GUESTHOUSE $
(☎Semporna 089-782 289; www.seahorse-sipadanscuba.com; dm/d from RM70/100) Seahorse has a few rooms showing their age with patchy lino floors, yellow walls and an open deck to catch the breeze. With nice little touches like conch shells on tables, there's also a dependable dive outfit here.

Scuba Jeff LODGE $
(☎017-869 0218, 019-585 5125; www.scubajeffsipadan.com; r with shared bathroom RM80; 📶) Crimson-walled Jeff is a fan-only, wood

affair with corridors darker than the Minotaur's labyrinth. There's a breezy open deck offering unblemished sea views, and budget dive centre. Basic accommodation with forgettable wooden box rooms – and don't think of getting steamy as there's a passion-killing gap at the top of the walls! – but indie travellers love this place.

Summer Friends Homestay HOMESTAY $

(☎013-557 1668; www.summerfriendshomestay.com; Malayan village; r RM50) This cheap as chips and not overly homely custard-yellow, wood affair is OK for a night if the island is full and you're waiting to get in elsewhere. There's a hammock out back, a shared bathroom and about as much atmosphere as the dark side of the moon. Fan only.

★ **Scuba Junkie Mabul Beach Resort** RESORT $$

(☎089-785 372; www.scuba-junkie.com; dm RM175, d with fan RM245-310, d with air-con RM320-380; ❄📶) Run by a lovely American couple, this place attracts a younger international crowd with a little cash to splash on semiluxe digs. Superfresh rooms come with porches and bathrooms, polished-wood floors and choice decor. Dorms are airy and of a good size, plus there's a welcoming central gazebo which houses the lively restaurant/bar. Prices include generous buffet meals.

There's also an exhibition of the many eco-marine causes Scuba Junkie is pioneering in the Semporna Archipelago. Divers (but not snorkellers) who book with Scuba Junkie get a 25% discount.

Billabong Scuba Backpackers GUESTHOUSE $$

(☎089-781 866; www.billabongscuba.com; Mabul; r with fan/air-con RM90/120, chalets with fan/air-con RM140-240, 3 dives at Sipadan RM700) Select from a choice of forgettable old rooms and dorm, faded chalets and brand new chalets

MEN IN BLACK: THE ONGOING SECURITY SITUATION

If staying in Mabul, you'll inevitably notice the presence of black-clad armed police patrolling the beach and the fact there's a 6pm curfew to be back in your resort. No doubt arriving at Sipadan after your first dive you'll also double-take at the dozen or so members of the Malaysian military stationed in a little hut with machine guns while you're diving. Try not to be alarmed, they're here for your safety and as a powerful deterrent. And so far it's working.

Here's a brief chronology of why their presence is so vital.

2000 The notorious Abu Sayyaf group abducted 21 people in Sipadan in April 2000.

2013 The Lahad Datu stand-off was a military conflict that arose after 235 Filipino armed militants arrived by boats in Lahad Datu claiming their objective was to assert the unresolved territorial claim of the Philippines over eastern Sabah.

2013 Two Taiwanese tourists were attacked in their room at the Sipadan Pom Pom Resort, off the coast of eastern Sabah; a male tourist was killed and his wife kidnapped.

2014 A Chinese tourist, and a Filipino hotel employee from Singamata Reef Resort, were taken in Semporna; a Malaysian fish breeder and his Filipino employee were seized by gunmen from their farm in Sabah.

2014 Armed men arrived by speedboat in Mabul with rocket launchers. In the ensuing crossfire with police, one officer was killed before the armed men, thought to be from Jolo island in the Phillipines, fled, taking another policeman hostage.

Esscom (Eastern Sabah Security Command; set up in 2013 and covering 1400km of the east coast of Sabah from Kudat to Tawau) claims there are 14 kidnap-for-ransom groups from southern Philippines, four of which have carried out kidnappings in Sabah's east coast.

So quite a litany of dramas. But is it now safe in the archipelago? Many international embassies recommend reconsidering your need to travel here, yet for the last year 120 divers per day have been enjoying one of the best dive sites in the world without incident. With the proactively beefed-up police numbers on the islands, the kidnappers are having to look elsewhere for their ransoms. Furthermore, a recent international assessment of the security situation in the Semporna Archipelago was judged to be positive. For now the curfew remains, but should you choose to come here you will be more than handsomely rewarded by its underwater treasures for any risks you may have taken.

with ox-blood-coloured walls and wood floors, which are built right out to sea (with great views). There's a communal decked area too. Billabong's diving outfit is only allocated seven diving permits per day for Sipadan, so try and book ahead.

★Borneo Divers Mabul Resort RESORT $$$ (☎088-222 226; www.borneodivers.net; 3-days, 2-nights incl transfer, food & dives per diver/nondiver RM1800/1400; ❄@📶) With flower-filled lawns, this charming accommodation has a pool, lovely chalets with wood floors and boutique accents, and a resident monitor lizard. The restaurant is terrific, the lounge open and comfy, their staff ever-friendly. Slow wi-fi is available in the dining room. Attracts a slightly older family-geared crowd.

Runs the archipleago's best dive centre; Borneo Divers introduced Cousteau to Sipadan back in '89.

Mabul Water Bungalow RESORT $$$ (☎088-486 389; www.mabulwaterbungalows.com; 3-day, 2-night dive package per diver/nondiver from RM3838/2339; ❄📶) Idyllically lapped by turquoise water, these Balinese-style stilted bungalows with their peaked roofs, fine interiors and palm-fronted porches are exquisite. When we say built out to sea we mean it – thoughtfully the hotel has a fleet of gleaming golf buggies to spirit your tired feet down the wooden walkway to your watery paradise. There's also a decent restaurant here.

Seaventures Dive Resort RESORT $$$ (☎088-261 669; www.seaventuresdive.com; 4-day, 3-night dive package per person twin share from RM2730; ❄) Moored beside nearby Mabul, this orange and polar-blue former oil rig accommodation platform, was made in Panama. The dive centre is terrific, as are the comfortable rooms and restaurant. Memorable digs and perfect for divers wanting to focus on their passion, eschewing noisy family joints. It sits on its own house reef, which is also ideal for beginners.

Sipadan-Mabul Resort RESORT $$$ (SMART; ☎088-486 389; www.sipadan-mabul.com.my; 7-day, 6-night dive package per diver/nondiver from RM4819/3643; ❄📶🏊) Winking with fairy lights and choking on palms, there's a welcoming restaurant here with belle epoque lights, glossed wood floors and a well-stocked shop. Bungalows are tastefully finished with art, private balcony and fresh linen. The stand-alone bungalows cost an extra RM112 per night, but are larger with fridge, private alfresco shower and settee.

Sipadan Water Village Resort RESORT $$$ (☎089-751 777; www.swvresort.com; 4-day, 3-night package diver/nondiver US$1215/835; ❄@) Set in a horseshoe design with a decent restaurant at the centre, these 42 stilted chalets perched on the turquoise water are connected by wooden walkways. Expect fresh, inviting rooms with bathroom and unblemished views of the Celebes Sea. Be prepared to be lulled to sleep by the lap of the waves.

Kapalai

Set on stilts on the shallow sandbanks of the Ligitan Reefs, this is one of the best macro dive sites in the world; on any given day you'll see blue-ringed octopuses, bobtail squid, cardinal fish and orangutan crabs. Although commonly referred to as an island, Kapalai is more like a large sandbar sitting slightly under the ocean surface. Upon it is based **Kapalai Resort** (☎088-316 011/3; http://sipadan-kapalai.com/; 4-day, 3-night package from RM2790; ❄@), a sumptuous water village with beautiful, upscale wood-accented rooms. Unlike busy Mabul, there's a sense of escape here with a long, thin powdery sandbar you can sunbathe on and snorkel from between dives.

Mataking

Mataking is also essentially a sandbar, two little patches of green bookending a dusty tadpole tail of white sand. **Mataking Island Resort** (☎089-786 045, 089-770 022; www.mataking.com; 2-day, 1-night package for divers/nondivers from RM1415/1235; ❄@) is the only accommodation here. This is an impeccably luxurious escape full of dark-wood chalets and gossamer sheets. This sandy escape has some beautiful diving – an artificial reef and sunken boats provide havens for plenty of sea life – and has a novel 'underwater post office' at a local shipwreck site. Mataking's eastern shore is a sloping reef and drops to 100m, making it great for sighting macro treasures as well as pelagics. Among the regular visitors large and small, expect to see trevally, eagle rays and barracuda, and pygmy seahorses and mandarin fish.

Pom Pom

About an hour from Semporna, and deep within the Tun Sakaran Marine Park, this pear-shaped idyll with its perfect azure water and white sand backed by pompom trees is a more attractive option than Mabul for those who want to dive *and* beach flop. With only two hotels on the island, it's far less crowded here; in fact, many come to get married and explore the underwater treasures as a secondary pursuit. That said, the diving is amazing.

There are two spots to stay: **Sipadan Pom Pom Island Resort** (089-781 918; www.pompomisland.com; 3-day, 2-night package RM1500-1800;) has a range of tasteful rooms, from garden chalets to dreamy stilted water cabanas, and resident turtles looking for a swimming date. There's also a solid dive school here. And just opened up is the splendid **Celebes Beach Resort** (089-782 828, 017-867 2232; www.celebescuba.com; 2-days, 1-night diver/nondiver RM730/610), with its deluxe seaview chalets exuding a zen minimalist decor. There's a great dive school here too offering PADI courses, and a fleet of three boats taking you to the best dive sites in the archipelago.

Roach Reefs

Roach Reefs Resort (089-779 332; www.roachreefsresort.com; 2-day, 1-night package for divers/nondivers per person US$185/148;) is built upon two sunken steel barges and an artificial reef at the edge of the Borneo shelf. Romantic water chalets with fresh, mint-white rooms with laquered wood floors, private bathroom and sea-view balconies are tempting, yes, but then there's the cosy bamboo bar, tasty Asian-fusion restaurant and excellent diving school. The waters are particularly fertile, with schools of bumphead parrotfish passing by at dawn and whale sharks visiting four months of the year. There's a cleaning station here too. Keep in mind boat transfers here come from Tawau, as opposed to Semporna.

Information

The Semporna Islands are loosely divided into two geographical sections: the northern islands (protected as Tun Sakaran Marine Park, gazetteered in 2004) and the southern islands. Both areas have desirable diving: Sipadan is located in the southern region, as is Mabul and Kapalai. Mataking and Sibuan belong to the northern area. If you are based in Semporna, you'll have a greater chance of diving both areas, although most people are happy to stick with Sipadan and its neighbours.

Consider stocking up on supplies (sunscreen, mozzie repellent etc) before making your way into the archipelago. Top-end resorts have small convenience stores with inflated prices. ATMs are nonexistent, but high-end resorts accept credit cards (Visa and MasterCard). Mabul has a small police station near the village mosque, as well as shack shops selling basic foodstuffs and a small pharmacy. Internet is of the wi-fi variety; most resorts now offer it, but service is spotty.

The closest decompression chamber (p372) is at the Semporna Naval Base.

Getting There & Around

With the exception of Roach Reefs, all transport to the marine park goes through Semporna. Your accommodation will arrange any transport needs from Semporna or Tawau airport (sometimes included, sometimes for an extra fee – ask!), which will most likely depart in the morning. That means if you arrive in Semporna in the afternoon, you will be required to spend the night in town.

Tawau

089 / POP 306,460

Sabah's third city, Tawau is not the most picturesque of places, despite its position beside the Celebes Sea and proximity to the Semporna Archipelago, but let's give it a break; poor Tawau has seen more conflict than a hard-bitten mercenary. Bombed by the British in 1944 to force out the invading Japanese army, today many of its hastily erected buildings don't merit much of a glance, but don't give up on it yet, for what the town lacks in photogenic charm, it more than makes up for with friendly locals and vibrant markets oozing pungent aromas and old-world atmosphere.

Tawau is Sabah's border crossing with Kalimantan and the only place where foreigners can get a visa to enter Indonesia.

Sights

Bukit Gemok Forest Reserve NATURE RESERVE
(adult/child RM5/1; 8am-5pm) About 10km from Tawau's centre, this reserve is great for a day visit, the jungle filled with chattering monkeys and popular with trekkers and tour groups. About an hour's hiking will bring you to the **Titian Selara canopy walkway**, which, at 231m long, offers terrific views of Tawau and the countryside. There are seven huts along the way for walkers to rest and relax. Be on the lookout for enormous flying seeds of the gourd *Alsomitra*

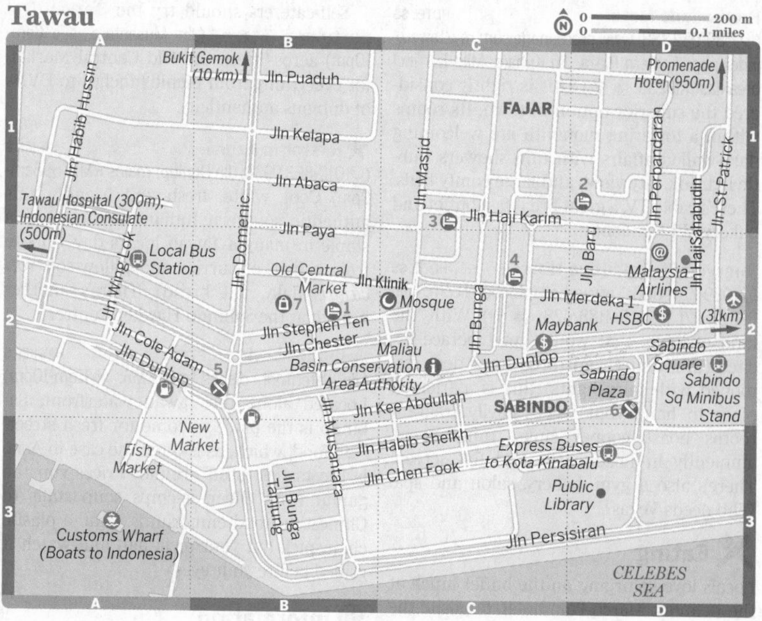

macrocarpa, gliding hundreds of metres through the forest.

A taxi to the park costs RM35; make sure your driver either sticks around to wait for you or is willing to come back and pick you up, as there's little public transport out this way.

Sleeping

Splurge for a midrange option in Tawau. Jalan Bunga and Jalan Haji Karim are packed with good-value accommodation. Budget accommodation tends to be pretty dire.

Tawau

Sleeping

1 Hotel Soon Yee B2
2 Kingston Executive Hotel D1
3 Monaco Hotel C1
4 Shervinton Executive Hotel C2

Eating

Restoran Azura .... (see 6)
5 Restoran Azura B2
6 Sabindo Hawker Centre D2

Shopping

7 Servay Department Store B2

Kingston Executive Hotel HOTEL $

(089-702 288; 4581-4590 Jln Haji Karim; d RM80;) Kingston's smoked-glass doors hide an arty lobby and gawping fish watching you check in. Rooms are clean with glass-topped desk, TV, coffee-making facilities and capacious bathroom. But can someone explain what those fake fireplace fixtures in the corridor are all about?

Monaco Hotel HOTEL $

(089-769 911/2/3; Jln Haji Karim; r from RM63;) With its crappy lobby, Monaco is not exactly evoking Camparis and film stars, but its en suite rooms are OKish wood-accented affairs with slightly thirsty walls but enough room for a barn dance. Expect a sofa, desk, TV and reading lamp. And plump for one away from the noisy road. The shuttle service to the airport costs RM40.

Hotel Soon Yee HOTEL $

(089-772 447; 1362 Jln Stephen Tan; r RM35-40;) On an atmospheric old street in the Central Market that's reminiscent of a Tintin cartoon, follow the steps up the bright turquoise stairway to the 1st floor and these distinctly budget but palatable rooms (air-con or fan) with colourful bedspreads and faintly Soviet bathrooms. The owner is a nice fella and the place is something of a magnet for indie travellers.

Promenade Hotel HOTEL $$
(☎089-982 888; www.promenade.com.my/tawau/index.php; Eastern Plaza, Jln Kuhara, Mile 1; r incl breakfast RM233; ❄📶) This is rightly considered the superior option in town. Its rooms within a towering monolith are welcoming dark-walled affairs with rain showers, subtle lighting, city views and large comfy beds. There's cable TV, a great breakfast buffet and bakery. Wi-fi in lobby.

Shervinton Executive Hotel HOTEL $$
(☎089-770 000; www.shervintonhotel.com; Jln Bunga; r/f from RM188/428; ❄📶) With the kind of lobby that would get Liberace excited (think kitsch mirrored front desk festooned with fairy lights) this is a friendly place to hang your wig. Heavily fragrant rooms boast copper sinks, rainshowers, ambiently lit headboards and flat screen. There's also a gym, bakery, salon and spa. Who needs Vegas?

Eating

Locals love splurging on the buffet lunch at the Belmont Marco Polo hotel, opposite the Old Central Market on Jln Klinik, which, for RM18 (RM33 on weekends), is a steal considering the variety of tasty bites. There are cheap Chinese *kedai kopi* along Jln Bunga; most open around 7am and close around 10pm.

Self-caterers should try the **Servay Department Store** (Jln Musantara; ⌚10am-10pm) across from the Old Central Market, for everything from picnic lunches to DVDs of dubious authenticity.

★ **Restoran Azura** INDIAN $
(☎012-863 9934; Jln Dunlop; mains RM7; ⌚8am-9pm) Cool, white, fresh and friendly, this authentic southern Indian restaurant is a staple in many a Tawau local's day. Choose from a host of curries and pillow-soft *roti canai* (flaky, flat bread). There's another branch at the Sabindo Hawker Centre.

Sabindo Hawker Centre HAWKER $
(Jln Waterfront; dishes from RM5; ⌚11am-10pm) Located along the Tawau waterfront, Sabindo is the place to come for fresh street-stall food, which, as is often the case in Asia, is the tastiest stuff around. Prices run the gamut from cheap-as-chips soup stalls to Chinese seafood emporiums. Grab a plastic chair, pick out your leviathan and watch it grilled before your eyes.

Information

BANKS

HSBC (Jln Perbandaran)
Maybank (☎089-762 333; Jln Dunlop)

TAWAU TREATS

Thanks to Tawau's proximity to Indonesia and large population of Indonesians, Filipinos, Bajau and Hakka Chinese, the town has developed some worthwhile culinary specialities. All of the following can be found in almost any of Tawau's *kedai kopi* and in the Sabindo Hawker Centre:

Mee jawa Javanese-style noodles, the Javanese take on Asia's ubiquitous noodle soup. This version comes with a yellowish broth swimming with bean sprouts, groundnuts, bean curd, fish balls, the occasional prawn and sometimes (interestingly) sweet potato, plus the usual garlic, shallots, chillies and shrimp paste.

Gado gado A deliciously simple Indonesian speciality: vegetable salad with prawn crackers and peanut sauce. The glory of *gado* is the variations of the standard recipe – every cook and hawker puts a different spin on it.

Nasi kuning Rice cooked with coconut milk and turmeric, hence the English translation of the name: 'yellow rice'. In Tawau, it is often wrapped and served in a banana leaf with deep-fried fish and eaten on special occasions.

Soto makassar Oh yes! *Soto* (also spelled *'coto'* and pronounced 'cho-to') *makassar* is buffalo/beef soup from southern Sulawesi, Indonesia. The dark broth is made incredibly rich by the addition of buffalo/cow blood, and enriched by a plethora of some 40 spices, plus beef heart, liver, tripe and brain. If you have a weak stomach, ignore those ingredients and trust us: this stuff is *delicious*, like liquid essence of beef spiced with all the wonderful herbs and spices of Southeast Asia.

GETTING TO INDONESIA: TAWAU TO TARAKAN

Getting to the border Tawau is the only crossing point with Kalimantan where foreigners can get a visa to enter Indonesia. The local **Indonesian consulate** (☎089-772 052, 089-752 969; Jln Sinn Onn, Wisma Fuji; ⏲8am-noon & 1pm or 2-4pm Mon-Fri, closed Indonesian and Malaysian public holidays) is known for being fast and efficient – many travellers are in and out in an hour. The consulate is in Wisma Fuji, on Jln Sinn Onn. Flag down a taxi (RM15) and ask the driver to drop you off in front of the consulate.

Visa applications are processed between 9.30am and 2pm Monday to Friday. You technically need to either provide proof of onward travel or a credit card, which consulate staff will make a copy of. A 60-day tourist visa will cost RM170 and require two passport photos. Bank on spending at least one night in town before shipping off to Indonesia, given the ferry departure schedule, and bring extra cash to the consulate, as there are no ATMs nearby.

Ferry companies Tawindo Express and Indomaya Express make the three- to four-hour trip to Tarakan (RM140; 11.30am Monday, Wednesday and Friday, 10.30am Tuesday, Thursday and Saturday) and the one-hour trip to Nunukan (RM65; 10am and 3pm daily except Sunday). We recommend showing up at least 60 minutes before departure to get a ticket; less than that is cutting it fine. A taxi ride to the ferry terminal costs RM10. MASWings flies from Tawau to Tarakan (RM135) five times per week.

At the border Blue minivans in Tarakan can get you around the city for Rp3000; expect to pay around Rp20,000 to get to the airport.

Moving On Ferry company Pelni (www.pelni.co.id) has boats to Balikpapan and the Sulawesi ports of Toli-Toli, Pare-Pare and Makassar.

INTERNET ACCESS

City Internet Zone (☎089-760 016; 37 Kompleks Fajar, Jln Perbandaran; per hour RM2-3; ⏲9am-midnight)

MEDICAL SERVICES

Tawau Hospital (☎089-773 533; Peti Surat 80; ⏲24hr)

TOURIST INFORMATION

Maliau Basin Conservation Area Authority (☎089-759 214; maliaubasin@gmail.com; 2nd fl, UMNO Bldg, Jln Dunlop) Can provide information on and help arrange visits to the Maliau Basin.

ℹ Getting There & Away

AIR

Malaysia Airlines (☎089-761 293; www.malaysiaairlines.com.my; Jln Haji Sahabudin; ⏲9am-6pm) and **AirAsia** (☎089-761 946; www.airasia.com; 1st fl, Tawau Airport Building, Jln Apas-Balung; ⏲9am-6pm) have daily direct flights to KK and KL. **MASwings** (☎1300-883 000; www.maswings.com.my) flies to Sandakan twice daily, the afternoon flight continuing to KK.

BUS

Kota Kinabalu Daily express buses for KK (RM60, nine hours) leave from behind the Sabindo area in a large dusty lot at 8am and 8pm (not in between).

Sandakan Departs hourly from Sabindo Sq (RM43, five hours, 7am to 2pm), one block on a diagonal from the KK terminus, behind the purple Yassin Curry House sign. That's also the spot for frequent minivans to Semporna (RM25, two hours) and Lahad Datu (RM20, three hours).

ℹ Getting Around

The airport is 28km from town along the main highway to Semporna and Sandakan. A shuttle bus (RM10) from the airport to the local bus station in Tawau's centre leaves six times daily. A taxi costs RM45.

Tawau Hills Park

Hemmed in by agriculture and human habitation, this small reserve has forested hills rising dramatically from the surrounding plain. The **park** (admission RM10) was gazetteered in 1979 to protect the water catchment for settlements in the area, but not before most of the accessible rainforest had been logged. Much of the remaining forest clings to steep-sided ridges that rise to 1310m Gunung Magdalena.

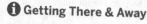

If getting into the Maliau Basin or Danum Valley feels like too much of an effort, consider Tawau Hills a user-friendly alternative. The forest here may not be as primevally awesome, but it's still impressively thick jungle, and the trails are quite easy on your feet. On a clear day the Tawau Hills Park's peaks make a fine sight.

The first trail leads along the Sungai Tawau (chattering with birds like a Disney movie when we attempted it) for 2.5km to **Bukit Gelas Falls**, which when not swarmed with school groups and tourists, is perfectly picturesque. Another track leads 3.2km to a group of 11 **hot springs** that are frankly as impressive as anything you'll see in Poring; locals believe the *ubat kulit* (skin medication) water has medicinal properties. If the above doesn't appeal, you can always take a quick 30-minute walk to **Bombalai Hill** (530m) to the south – the views from here are also quite rewarding. Another reason for coming here is to see the **world's tallest tropical tree** (88m). From the main entrance take the 900m trail. As well as macaques, red and white leaf monkeys, giant tree squirrels, civet cats and several kinds of hornbill you'll most likely come across leeches first. If it's been raining you absolutely must wear leech socks!

There's accommodation at **Tawau Hills Park** (Taman Bukit Tawau; ☎089-918 827, 089-768 719, 019-800 9607; camping/dm/chalet RM5/20/200). Rates are lower on weekdays. Both dorms and chalets are utilitarian, and there's not much reason to stay here unless you can't stomach a night somewhere else. If you want to camp, you'll need to bring all of your own equipment.

Tawau Hills is 28km northwest of Tawau. A taxi will cost around RM40.

Maliau Basin Conservation Area

This pocket of primeval wilderness tells the same untouched story it did millenniums ago. Hemmed in by mountains, separated by distance and altitude and expanse, the Maliau Basin Conservation Area (MBCA), known very appropriately as 'Sabah's Lost World', is something special. Beneath the canopy of its soaring dipterocarp trees, it's easy to imagine the emergent form of a brachiosaurus.

The basin, a 25km-wide bowl-shaped depression of rainforest, was unnoticed by the world until a pilot almost crashed into the walls that hem it off in 1947. Run by the Sabah Foundation, this is the single best place in Borneo to experience old-growth tropical rainforest. More than that, it is one of the world's great reserves of biodiversity, a dense knot of almost unbelievable genetic richness. A visit to the basin is always a poignant affair, as you'll share the road with a parade of logging trucks hauling trees out of the forest at an astonishing rate.

Unbelievably, there is no known record of human beings entering the basin until the early 1980s (although it is possible that indigenous peoples entered the basin before that time). It is only recently that the area has been opened up to a limited number of adventurous travellers.

Getting here became much more straightforward in 2014, with the sealing of the road that runs from KK to Tawau (five hours by car), passing by the entrance to the Maliau Basin. Within the reserve the roads are gradually improving, but a 4WD is still necessary.

Activities

Trekking

The trek through the Maliau Basin will likely be the most memorable hike of your Borneo experience. And possibly the hardest! The density of the old-growth forest is striking, and as it is more remote than the Danum Valley, the preserved wildlife is *even* better. Eighty species of mammal and counting have been recorded here, including the clouded leopard, Sumatran rhino, Malayan sun bear, pygmy elephant, Bornean gibbon, red- and grey-leaf monkeys and banteng. That said, you are in the jungle, and wildlife is not easy to spot. You may walk away without seeing anything (unlikely) but for some of Borneo's most ancient trees, which isn't so bad really, given the sheer outlandishness of the place.

Several treks are possible in the basin, ranging from short nature walks around **Agathis Camp** to the multiday slog to the rim of the basin via **Strike Ridge Camp**. The vast majority of visitors to the basin undertake a three-day, two-night loop through the southern section of the basin that we'll call the Maliau Loop. This brilliant route takes in wide swaths of diverse rainforest and four of the basin's waterfalls: **Takob Falls**, **Giluk Falls**, **Maliau Falls** and **Ginseng Falls**. Do not attempt the trek unless you are in excellent shape: adventure-tour operator Sticky Rice Travel (p320), one of a handful of companies operating here, insists that your travel insurance policy covers a helicopter evacuation.

Your tour operator will supply a forest ranger, guide and porters to carry your food.

INDEPENDENT EXPEDITIONS TO THE MALIAU BASIN

It's best to first contact the **Maliau Basin Conservation Area Authority** (☎089-759 214; maliaubasin@gmail.com; 2nd flr, UMNO Building, Jln Dunlop) in Tawau if you want to go there under your own steam. You may need to show up to the office in person, as this is not a tourism body accustomed to dealing with visitors.

To get into the park you need to pay an administration fee (RM50), a vehicle entry fee (RM5 per vehicle), a trekking fee (RM150) and, if you stay overnight, a conservation fee (RM50). If you plan to hike you *must* hire a guide, which costs RM150 per day. Breakfast, lunch and dinner can be taken in the guest camps for RM195. You can also arrange meals while trekking; this requires a porter (RM100, maximum 12kg per porter, additional weight, first 5kg RM40 per porter) and costs RM390 for breakfast/lunch/dinner. If you want to cook for yourself, bring your own supplies and rent their utensils for RM50 per day. Night safaris cost RM160, and night walks RM40 (lasting about an hour).

Ideally, if you're not buying the package tour, we advise prearranging your tour with the office in Tawau, now only 2½ hours away from the basin thanks to the new road.

You'll be in charge of your day pack, camera, leech socks, walking clothes and dry kit for the evening. You should also bring mozzie repellent, swimming outfit, powerful torch, sunscreen, poncho, sleeping sheet, a towel and energy sweets.

A **canopy walkway** stretches near the Basin study centre, and it is pretty astounding to walk its length amid rainforest canopy that has never felt a human cut.

Sleeping

Accommodation varies in standard from the upscale (VIP House/deluxe/standard RM1300/520/390) and regular resthouse rooms (from RM286 to RM325) to dorm beds (RM91) and camping in your own tent (RM39). To be honest, after a day on the trail fighting leeches, they'll all seem like paradise!

There are two ways to get here: with a trusted tour company or on your own. Among those who run treks here, we recommend Sticky Rice Travel (p320), Borneo Adventure (p321) and Borneo Nature Tours (p383), all of which offer four-day, three-night all-inclusive tours of the Maliau for around RM3700, or five-day, four-night options for RM4650 per person for two to three people (this can go as low as RM3696 per person for a group of 10 to 15).

Information

The Maliau Basin is located in the southern part of central Sabah, just north of the logging road that connects Tawau with Keningau. The basin is part of the Yayasan Sabah Forest Management Area, a vast swath of forest in southeastern Sabah under the management of Yayasan Sabah (www.ysnet.org.my), a semigovernmental body tasked with both developing and protecting the natural resources of Sabah.

The MBCA security gate is just off the Tawau–Keningau Rd. From the gate, it's a very rough 25km journey to the Maliau Basin Studies Centre, for researchers, and about 20km to Agathis Camp, the base camp for most visitors to the basin.

Getting There & Away

It's possible to drive yourself to the park, or take a public bus from Tawau or KK. Your tour company will handle all transport if you book through them. It will take around six hours to drive from KK, and 2½ hours from Tawau.

MINIBUS

Minibuses occasionally ply the route bringing loggers to their camps, but this isn't a regular service and cannot be relied upon.

VAN

If you've prearranged with the Maliau Basin Conservation Area Authority in Tawau, that office may get a minivan to take you to the park entrance for RM650. In the park, rangers can arrange vans to take you back to Tawau or Keningau (closer to KK) for a similar price.

SOUTHWESTERN SABAH

The Crocker Range is the backbone of southwestern Sabah, separating coastal lowlands from the wild tracts of jungle in the east. Honey-tinged beaches scallop the shores from KK down to the border, passing the turbid rivers of the Beaufort Division. Offshore you'll find Pulau Tiga, forever etched in the collective consciousness as the genesis site for the eponymous reality show *Survivor,* and Pulau Labuan, centre of the region's oil industry and the transfer point for ferries heading onto Sarawak and Brunei.

The Interior

Sabah's interior constitutes some of the wildest territory in the state, and the best place for accessing this largely unexplored hinterland is via the southwest part of the state.

The landscape is dominated by the Crocker Range, which rises near Tenom in the south and runs north to Mt Kinabalu. The range forms a formidable barrier to the interior of the state and dominates the eastern skyline from Kota Kinabalu down to Sipitang. Once across the Crocker Range, you descend into the green valley of the Sungai Pegalan that runs from Keningau in the south and to Ranau in the north. The heart of the Pegalan Valley is the small town of Tambunan, around which you'll find a few low-key attractions.

Crocker Range National Park

Much of the Crocker Range has been gazetteered as Crocker Range National Park. The main means of accessing this landscape by foot is via the **Salt Trail** (Salt Trails; ☎088-553 500; http://www.sabahparks.org.my/index.php/salt-trail-crp), a series of four treks that trace the path of traditional trade routes across the mountains. At their shortest the trails can be completed in half a day; the longest route, the **Inobong-Terian-Buayan-Kionop-Tikolod trail**, takes three days to finish (if you're fit!). At the time of writing the tourism infrastructure around the Salt Trails was quite minimal, making this an excellent adventure for DIY trekkers who want to get off Sabah's package tourism trail. You'll need to get in touch with Crocker Range National Park to organise guides.

Even if you're not trekking, the Crocker Range and Pegalan Valley make a nice jaunt into rural Sabah for those with rental vehicles. As you make your way over the range between KK and Tambunan, you'll be treated to brilliant views back to the South China Sea and onward to Mt Trus Madi.

Tambunan

Nestled among the green curves of the Crocker hills, Tambunan, a small agricultural service town about 81km from KK, is the first settlement you'll come to in the range. The region was the last stronghold of Mat Salleh, who became a folk hero for rebelling against the British in the late 19th century. Sadly Salleh later blew his reputation by negotiating a truce, which so outraged his own people that he was forced to flee to the Tambunan plain, where he was eventually killed.

Sights

Tambunan Rafflesia Reserve NATURE RESERVE
(☎088-898 500; admission RM5; ⏲8am-3pm) Near the top of the Crocker Range, next to the main highway 20km from Tambunan, is this park devoted to the world's largest flower. Rangers can guide you into the jungle reserve for the day for RM100. Keningau-bound buses will stop here if you ask the driver to let you off, but getting back to Tambunan will require hitching on the highway. A round-trip taxi from Tambunan costs RM120, which includes waiting time.

The rafflesia is a parasitic plant that grows hidden within the stems of jungle vines until it bursts into bloom, at which point it eerily resembles the monster plant from *Little Shop of Horrors*. It emits a stench of rotting flesh mimicking a newly dead animal, to attract carrion flies that help with pollination. The large bulbous flowers can be up to 1m in diameter. The 12 or so species of rafflesia here are found only in Borneo and Sumatra; several species are unique to Sabah, but as they only bloom for a few days, it's hard to predict when you'll be able to see one.

Sleeping

Tambunan Village Resort Centre RESORT **$$**
(TVRC; ☎087-774 076; http://tvrc.tripod.com; 24 Jln TVRC; r & chalets RM118-248; ❄) Also known as the Borneo Heritage Centre, this rural digs is 2km out of Tambunan, located by a pretty lake. There's boating, hiking, a nice cafe and a choice of basic rooms or self-catering family-size chalet rooms. Staff can help arrange trips up Mt Trus Madi.

If driving from KK, the centre's just south of the Shell station on the main road.

Getting There & Away

Regular minivans ply the roads between Tambunan and KK (RM10, 1½ hours), Ranau (RM15, two hours), Keningau (RM10, one hour) and Tenom (RM20, two hours). KK–Tenom express buses also pass through, though you may have to ask them to stop. The minivan shelter is in the middle of Tambunan town. Minivans to KK pass the entrance to the Rafflesia Reserve; you'll usually be charged for the whole trip to KK.

Mt Trus Madi

About 20km southeast of Tambunan town is the dramatic Mt Trus Madi, Sabah's second-highest peak, rising to 2642mm, and one of the best places in Malaysia to watch the sunrise. Ascents are possible, however, it's more challenging than Mt Kinabalu, and more difficult to arrange. Independent trekkers must be well equipped and bring their own provisions up the mountain. It is possible to go by 4WD (RM500) up to about 1500m, from where it is a five- to seven-hour climb to the top. The trail to the summit is about 4.9km but you'll have to climb three mountains to reach it!

There are two places to stay: **Mirad-Irad Riverside camp** (RM20) at base camp, and **SFD New Rest House** (RM100) halfway up the mountain. Before setting off, you are strongly advised to hire a guide (RM100) or at least get maps and assistance from **Forestry Department** (Jabatan Perhutanan; ☎089-660 811, 087-774 691) in Tambunan. Bring winter clothes, as it gets cold towards the peak, and be prepared for a long, muddy slog.

You can get here on your own, but it's far easier to organise with a tour company. **Tropical Mountain Holidays** (☎013-549 2730, 013-545 7643; www.tropicalmountainholidaysmalaysia.com), based in KK, specialises in Mt Trus Madi ascents. Their two-day, one-night climb up the mountain, which includes transfer from KK, runs US$380 per person, which is close to what you'll pay if you hire guides and your own vehicle to get out here.

Keningau

If you have a bent for the bucolic, you'll probably want to skip Keningau – this busy service town has a touch of urban sprawl about it, and most visitors only pass through to pick up transport, use an ATM or stock up on supplies. As far as attractions go, you might check out **Taipaek-gung**, a colourful Chinese temple in the middle of town, or the large **tamu** (market) held every Thursday.

For a sleepover, try **Hotel Juta** (☎087-337 888; www.sabah.com.my/juta; Lg Milimewa 2; standard/superior r RM175/275; ❄), which towers over the busy town centre. It's convenient to transport, banking and shopping needs, and rooms are nicely appointed in the Western business style. There is a restaurant on the premises. Shabbier options include the nearby **Crown Hotel** (☎087-338 555; Lg Milimewa; standard/superior d from RM40).

There are eight daily express buses to/from KK (RM15, two hours) and four to/from Tenom (RM10, one hour). These buses stop at the Bumiputra Express stop on the main road across from the Shell station. Minivans and share taxis operate from several places in town, including a stop just north of the express bus stop; they all leave when full. There are services to/from KK (RM50, two hours), Ranau (RM30, three hours) and Tenom (RM12, one hour).

Tenom

Tenom was closely involved in uprisings against the British in 1915, led by the famous Murut chief Ontoros Antanom, and there's a **memorial** to the tribe's fallen warriors off the main road. Most people pass through Tenom on their way to the nearby Sabah Agricultural Park.

If you somehow get stuck in town, spend the night at the **Orchid Hotel** (☎087-737 600; Jln Tun Mustapha; s/d RM40/80; ❄). Rooms are clean and well kept and good value for money. There are cheaper hotels in the vicinity, but they're all a bit musty.

Minivans operate from the *padang* (field) in front of the Hotel Sri Perdana. Destinations include Keningau (RM10, one hour) and KK (RM45, two to four hours depending on stops). There are also regular services to Tambunan (RM20, two hours). Taxis congregate at a rank on the west side of the *padang*.

Sabah Agricultural Park

Heaven on earth for horticulturalists, the vast **Sabah Agricultural Park** (Taman Pertanian Sabah; ☎087-737952; www.sabah.net.my/agripark; adult/child RM25/10; ⏲9am-4.30pm Tue-Sun), about 15km northeast of Tenom, is run by the Department of Agriculture and covers about 6 sq km. Originally set up as an orchid centre, the park has expanded to become a major research facility, tourist attraction and offbeat camp site (RM10), building up superb collections of rare plants such as hoyas, and developing new techniques for use in agriculture, agroforestry and domestic cultivation.

Flower gardens and nature paths abound and a minizoo lets you get up close and personal with some farm animals and deer. Exploring by bicycle would be a good idea, but the fleet of rental bikes here has just about rusted to the point of immobility; if they've been replaced by the time you arrive, rentals cost RM3. There is a free 'train' (it's actually more like a bus) that does a 1½-hour loop of the park, leaving from outside the reception hourly from 9.30am to 3.30pm. If you're truly taken with the park, there's a bare bones on-site hostel (dorm beds RM25), which is sometimes taken up by visiting school groups.

Take a minivan from Tenom heading to Lagud Seberang (RM5). Services run throughout the morning, but dry up in the late afternoon. Tell the driver you're going to Taman Pertanian. The park entrance is about 1km off the main road. A taxi from Tenom will cost around RM90.

Sapulot & Batu Punggul

Perhaps even more so than the Maliau Basin, this is as remote as it gets in Sabah. Not far from the Kalimantan border, Batu Punggul is a jungle-topped limestone outcrop riddled with caves, towering nearly 200m above Sungai Sapulot. This is deep in Murut country and the stone formation was one of several sites sacred to these people. Batu Punggul and the adjacent Batu Tinahas are traditionally believed to be longhouses that gradually transformed into stone. The view from the upper reaches of Batu Punggul may be the best in Sabah – in every direction is deep jungle, knifelike limestone outcrops and, if you are lucky, swinging orangutans. It can be difficult and expensive to get here, but this is a beautiful part of Sabah that few tourists visit, and it offers a chance to rub shoulders with the jungle Murut.

It is almost impossible to get out here on your own, as there is virtually no tourism infrastructure and English is almost nonexistent, but even the most independent traveller will likely enjoy booking through Orou Sapulot.

★ **Orou Sapulot** CULTURAL TOUR
(☎ 016-311 0056; www.orousapulot.com; 3-day/2-night per person for a group of 4 RM1122) The two- to three-night adventure encompasses **Romol Eco Village**, a longhouse homestay with the Murut; the **Pungiton Caves**, an extensive cavern system with underground rivers; an **eco-camp** by Pungiton located on the banks of a heavenly river; and finally, a sweat-inducing climb up Batu Punggul, followed by a rapid-shoot downriver all the way to the Kalimantan border.

Set up by Silas Gunting, a descendant of the local Murut, Orou is one of the most innovative eco-tourism projects in the state, and offers one of the most varied, best-value adventures in Sabah. By employing local Murut and encouraging their families to keep their lands for eco-tourism purposes rather than selling them to palm-oil and timber companies, Orou is providing a sustainable income for the communities of Sabah's interior.

The above prices are estimated rates that take in all/some of the activities mentioned above. To share costs, bigger groups are best but if you're a solo visitor, ask when booking if there are other groups to join. In KK, Adventure Alternative Borneo (p320) is Orou Sapulot's preferred booking agency.

Beaufort Division

This shield-shaped peninsula, popping out from Sabah's southwestern coast, is a marshy plain marked with curling rivers and fringed by golden dunes. Tourists with tight travel schedules should consider doing a wildlife river cruise at Klias (p388) or Garama (p388) if they don't have time to reach Sungai Kinabatangan. Yes, the Kinabatangan is better, but packs of proboscis monkeys can still be spotted here and it's only a day trip from KK. You can book trips to Beaufort, Weston and the Klias and Garama rivers in any KK travel agency.

Beaufort

Born as a timber town, Beaufort has reinvented itself with the proliferation of palm-oil plantations. A suitable pit stop for tourists travelling between Sabah and Sarawak, this sleepy township is the gateway to white-water rapids on the **Sungai Padas** and the monkey-filled Klias and Garama areas. The Sungai Padas divides Beaufort into two sections: the aptly named Old Town with its weathered structures, and New Town, a collection of modern shophouses on flood-phobic stilts. During WWII, Beaufort was the site of a major skirmish between the Japanese and Australians.

Sights & Activities

Memorial Stone MEMORIAL

(Jln Tugu) There's a small monument to Private Thomas Leslie Starcevich, an Australian WWII veteran. In 1945, Starcevich single-handedly overwhelmed a Japanese machine-gun position, for which he received the Victoria Cross, the British military's highest decoration. The stone is at the bottom of a small embankment and is marked by brown signs and an arch.

Rafting

White-water rafting enthusiasts can book a river trip with Riverbug (p321), the premier operator in the area. It also offers a combo paintball day!

Meanwhile, Scuba Junkie's affiliated river-rafting outfit, River Junkie (p321), also comes highly recommended by travellers. All trips include transfers by van, and normally require 24 hours' advance notice. Tourists who seek more serene waters can ride the rapids of Sungai Kiulu (bookable through the aforementioned operators), which is located near Mt Kinabalu and calm enough to be popular with families.

Sleeping & Eating

There's really no need to spend the night in Beaufort, but if you must, then try the **River Park Hotel** (☎087-223 333; Beaufort Jaya; r from RM130-160; P ❄). If you're stopping in town for a bite, make sure you try a pomelo (football-sized citrus fruit) and local *mee Beaufort* (Beaufort noodles) – both are locally famous.

Getting There & Away

BUS

Express buses operate from near the old train station at the south end of Jln Masjid (the ticket booth is opposite the station). There are departures at 9am, 1pm, 2.15pm and 5pm for KK (RM15, 1½ hours). There are departures at 9.10am, 10.30am, 1.45pm and 6.20pm for Sipitang (RM25, 1½ hours). The KK to Lawas express bus passes through Beaufort at around 3pm; the trip from Beaufort to Lawas costs RM30 and takes 1¾ hours.

MINIVAN

Minivans operate from a stop across from the mosque, at the north end of Jln Masjid. There are frequent departures for KK (RM20, two hours), and less-frequent departures for Sipitang (RM30, 1½ hours), Lawas (RM40, 1¾ hours) and Kuala Penyu (RM15, one hour, until around 2.30pm). To Menumbok (for Labuan) there are plenty of minivans until early afternoon (RM15, one hour).

TAXI

Taxis depart from the stand outside the old train station, at the south end of Jln Masjid. Charter rates include KK (RM120), Kuala Penyu (RM100), Sipitang (RM100), Menumbok (RM100) and Lawas (RM120).

Kuala Penyu

Tiny Kuala Penyu, at the northern tip of the peninsula, is the jumping-off point for Pulau Tiga, if you are not accessing 'Survivor Island' via the new boat service from KK. From Beaufort, minivans to Kuala Penyu (RM15) leave throughout the morning, but return services tail off very early in the afternoon, so you may have to negotiate a taxi or local lift back. A minivan to/from Menumbok costs RM90 per vehicle.

Tempurung

Set along the quiet coastal waters of the South China Sea, **Tempurung Seaside Lodge** (☎088-773 066; www.borneotempurung.com; 2-day, 1-night package per person from RM150, min 2 persons) is a good spot for hermits who seek a pinch of style. The main lodge was originally built as a holiday home, but friends convinced the owners that it would be a crime not to share the lovely property with the world. Rooms are scattered between several bungalows accented with patches of jungle thatch. The packages include fantastic meals. Nightly rates are also available.

Borneo Express (☎in KK 012-830 7722, in Limbang 085-211 384, in Miri 012-823 7722) runs buses from KK (departing from Wawasan) at 6.45am, 10am and 12.30pm daily. Ask the driver to let you off at the junction with the large Kuala Penyu sign. The bus will turn left (south) to head towards Menumbok; you want to go right (north) in the direction of Kuala Penyu. If you arranged accommodation in advance, the lodge van can pick you up here (it's too far to walk). Buses pass the junction at 9.30am and 3.30pm heading back to KK. If you're driving, take a right at the junction and keep an eye out for the turn-off on the left side of the road just before Kuala Penyu. We suggest calling the lodge for directions. A charter taxi from Beaufort will cost about RM55.

Klias

The tea-brown **Sungai Klias** looks somewhat similar to the mighty Kinabatangan, offering short-stay visitors a chance to spend an evening in the jungle cavorting with saucy primates. There are several companies offering two-hour river cruises. We recommend Borneo Authentic (p321), the first operator to set up shop in the region. Trips include a large buffet dinner and a short night walk to view the swarms of fireflies that light up the evening sky like Christmas lights. Cruises start at dusk (around 5pm), when the sweltering heat starts to burn off and animals emerge for some post-siesta prowling.

There is no accommodation in Klias, although Borneo Authentic can set you up with one of its comfy rooms at the Tempurung Seaside Lodge nearby. Tourists can make their own way to the row of private jetties 20km west of Beaufort; however, most trip-takers usually sign-up for a hassle-free day trip from KK (which ends up being cheaper since you're sharing transport).

Garama

Narrower than the river in Klias, the **Sungai Garama** is another popular spot for river-cruise day trips from KK. Chances of seeing fireflies are slim, but Garama is just as good as Klias (if not better) when it comes to primate life. Gangs of proboscis monkeys and long-tailed macaques scurry around the surrounding floodplain offering, eager tourists plenty of photo fodder.

Like Klias, the tours here start at around 5pm (with KK departures at 2pm), and after a couple of hours along the river, guests chat about the evening's sightings over a buffet dinner before returning to KK. There are several operators offering Garama river tours; we prefer **Only in Borneo** (☎088-260 506; www.oibtours.com; package tour RM190), an offshoot of Traverse Tours. It has a facility along the shores of Sungai Garama and offers an overnight option in prim dorms or double rooms.

It is technically possible to reach Garama with your own vehicle, but the network of unmarked roads can be tricky and frustrating. We recommend leaving early in the morning from KK if you want to get here on your own steam.

Weston

The little village of Weston – a couple of shacks clustered around a gold-domed mosque – is the jumping-off point for a gentle yet jungly patch of **wetlands** that is equal parts serene and overgrown. The area was bombed beyond recognition during WWII, but recent conservation efforts have welcomed groups of curious proboscis monkeys into the tidal marshlands, which are shaded by towering nipa palms and copses of spiderlike mangroves. As the tide rolls in and out, entire swaths of jungle are submerged and revealed. Monkeys, monitor lizards, otters and mud skippers flash through the aquatic undergrowth, and as the sun sets, clouds of flying foxes (ie *big* bats) flap in with the darkness.

Sights

Weston Wetland (☎088-485 103, 013-881 3233, 016-813 4300; www.westonwetlandpark.com) operates a variety of package tours including river-cruise day trips and sleepovers at its swampside longhouse (all-inclusive two-day, one-night package RM250). The dorm facilities are rustic at best, but the quality of the firefly show here is extremely high. Note that the folk at Weston Wetland insist you prebook before visiting.

While you're here, you can ask folk at the lodge to take you to **Che Hwa Schoolhouse**, the oldest wooden school building in Borneo and a fine example of antiquarian Chinese architecture.

Menumbok

The tiny hamlet of Menumbok is where you can catch car ferries to the Serasa Ferry Terminal in Muara, 25km northeast of Bandar Seri Begawan (Brunei), and to Pulau Labuan (adult/car RM30/80, departures every hour from 9.30am to 3.30pm).

On land, a charter taxi from Beaufort costs RM70, minivans from Kuala Penyu cost RM50 per vehicle. There is a direct bus service (RM15) connecting Menumbok to KK.

Pulau Tiga National Park

The name Pulau Tiga actually means 'three islands' – the scrubby islet is part of a small chain created during an eruption of mud volcanoes in the late 1890s. Over 100 years later, in 2001, the island had its 15 minutes of fame when it played host to the smash-hit reality TV series *Survivor,* so is commonly referred to now as as 'Survivor Island'. TV junkies still stop by for a look-see, although the 'Tribal Council' was destroyed in a storm and the debris was cleared after it turned into a home for venomous snakes. Whatever your viewing preferences, it's still a great place for relaxing on the beach, hiking in the forest and taking a cooling dip in burping mud pits at the centre of the island.

Sights & Activities

Pulau Kalampunian Damit is famous for the sea snakes (up to 150 per day) that come ashore to mate, hence the island's nickname, **Snake Island**. Enigmatically, the snakes are never seen on nearby Pulau Tiga. Pulau Tiga Resort runs boat trips to the island (RM50 per person), with a stop en route for snorkelling for RM30 extra. You can also dive off the island for RM100 per dive, or RM200 for a fun dive for those with no scuba experience.

Sleeping & Eating

Sabah Parks CAMPING $

(☎088-211 881; www.sabahparks.org.my; r from RM75) Sabah Parks runs basic lodging (ie block houses) on the island for less affluent survivalists. It's right next door to Pulau Tiga Resort, about 10m from where 'Tribal Council' was once held (sadly, tiki torches no longer line the way). Facilities are limited and there's no restaurant, though a cooking area is provided. Book through the KK Sabah Parks (p329) office.

Pulau Tiga Resort RESORT $$

(☎088-240 584; www.pulau-tiga.com; 2-day, 1-night package per person from Kuala Penyu RM305-360, from KK RM455-510; ❄) Built to house the production crew for the first series of *Survivor,* accommodation is available in dorm-style 'longhouse' rooms (three beds in each), while more luxurious private cabins have double beds and air-con. The beach-facing grounds offer amazing views of the sunset, while a map is available should you want to track down the beach where the Pagong Tribe lived (called Pagong-Pagong Beach).

Getting There & Away

From Kuala Penyu the boat ride (RM80 return ticket) takes about 20 minutes. Boats leave at 10am and 3pm. Most visitors to Pulau Tiga come as part of a package, in which case transport is included in the price. You can try showing up in Kuala Penyu and asking if you can board one of the day's boats out to the island (we don't recommend this option as priority is given to resort guests with bookings). For Sabah Parks' lodgings, try to hop a ride with the Pulau Tiga Resort boat – chartering your own craft costs RM600 at least.

Pulau Labuan

☎087 / POP 86,910

If you've ever wondered what a cross between a duty-free airport mall and a tropical island would look like, check out the federal district of Pulau Labuan. Some call this Sabah's Vegas, and in the sense that Labuan offers both duty-free sin and tacky family fun, we agree. By the way, everything here *is* duty free, because politically, Labuan is governed directly from KL. As such, a lot of the booze you consume and cigarettes you smoke in Sabah and Sarawak are illegally smuggled from Labuan. Thanks to financial deregulation, Labuan is now the home of some major offshore bank accounts, so you may also want to be on the lookout for men in sunglasses with big briefcases, although we suggest not taking pictures of them.

The sultan of Brunei ceded Labuan to the British in 1846 and it remained part of the empire for 115 years. The only interruption came during WWII, when the Japanese held the island for three years. Significantly, it was on Labuan that the Japanese forces in north Borneo surrendered at the end of the war, and the officers responsible for the death marches from Sandakan were tried here.

Bandar Labuan is the main town and the transit point for ferries linking Kota Kinabalu and Brunei.

Sights

Bandar Labuan

Labuan's main settlement is light on character but has a couple of passable attractions.

Labuan Museum MUSEUM

(☎087-414 135; 364 Jln Dewan; ⌚9am-5pm) FREE This museum on Jln Dewan takes a glossy, if slightly superficial, look at the island's history and culture, from colonial days, through WWII, to the establishment of

Bandar Labuan

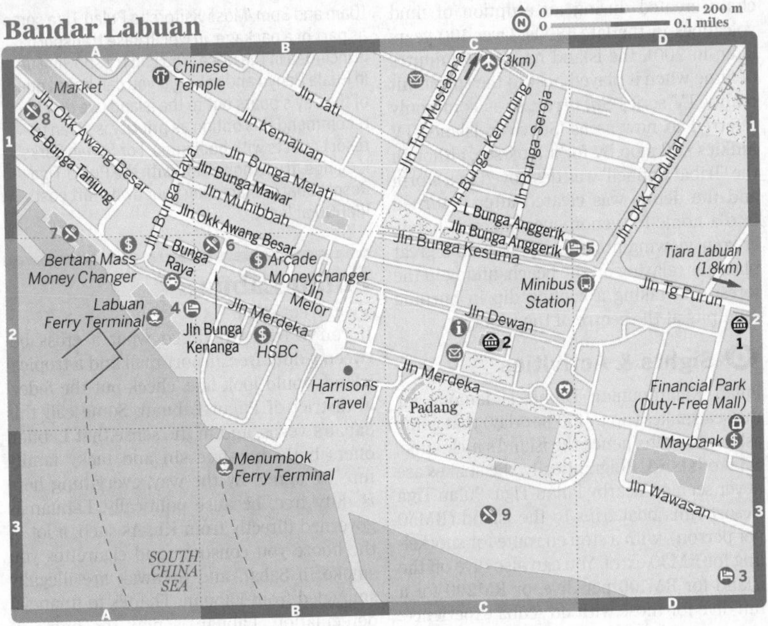

Bandar Labuan

Sights

1 Labuan Marine Museum D2
2 Labuan Museum C2

Activities, Courses & Tours

Borneo Star Dives ....(see 1)

Sleeping

3 Billion Waterfront Hotel D3
4 Grand Dorsett Labuan A2
5 Mariner Hotel.......................................D2

Eating

6 Choice Restaurant..................................B2
7 Port View Restaurant A1
8 Restoran Selera Farizah A1
9 The Chillout Cafe C3

Labuan as an independent federal territory. The most interesting displays are those on the different ethnic groups here, including a diorama of a traditional Chinese tea ceremony (the participants, however, look strangely Western).

Labuan Marine Museum MUSEUM
(☎087-425 927, 087-414 462; Jln Tanjung Purun; ⏰9am-6pm) **FREE** On the coast just east of the centre, the Labuan International Sea Sports Complex houses a decent little museum with a good shell collection and displays of local marine life. Head upstairs to find a 12.8m-long skeleton of an Indian fin whale. The real highlight, however, and a guaranteed hit with the kids, is the 'touch pool' opposite reception. This has to be the only shark-petting zoo we've ever seen (fret not: the sharks are less than a metre long).

Around Pulau Labuan

WWII Memorial (Labuan War Cemetery) CEMETERY
A dignified expanse of lawn with row upon row of headstones dedicated to the nearly 4000 Commonwealth servicemen, mostly Australian and British, who lost their lives in Borneo during WWII. The cemetery is near the golf course, about 2km east of town along Jln OKK Abdullah. A **Peace Park** on the west of the island at Layang Layangan commemorates the place of Japanese surrender and has a Japanese war memorial.

Labuan Bird Park WILDLIFE RESERVE
(☎087-463 544; adult/child/under 5yr RM3/1/free; ⏰10am-5pm, closed Fri) This pretty park offers refuge to a wide range of species in three geodesic domes, and a swath of rainforest – the birds look a little bored, but

healthy. The park is located at the north end of the island on Jln Tanjung Kubong.

Chimney LANDMARK
Believed to be part of an old coal-mining station, this is the only historical monument of its kind in Malaysia, and has good views along the coast. It's at the northeast tip of the island, best accessed by minibus or taxi.

Labuan Marine Park PARK
Pulau Kuraman, Pulau Rusukan Kecil and Pulau Rusukan Besar are uninhabited islands lying southwest of Labuan that are now protected by the federal government. The beaches are pristine, but dynamite fishing has destroyed much of the coral. You can hire boats from the jetty at the Labuan International Sea Sports Complex to explore the marine park. A day's charter costs around RM600 per group of six people.

If you want to dive here, enquire at Borneo Star Dives.

Sleeping

Labuan Homestay Programme HOMESTAY $
(☎013-854 0217, 016-824 6193, 087-422 622; 1/2 days incl full board RM70/150) This excellent service matches visitors with a friendly local in one of three villages around the island: Patau Patau 2, Kampong Sungai Labu and Kampong Bukit Kuda. If you want to be near Bandar Labuan, ask for accommodation at Patau Patau 2 – it's a charming stilt village out on the bay. If you want to enrol in the program, book at least a few days in advance.

★Tiara Labuan HOTEL $$
(☎087-414 300; www.tiaralabuan.com; Jln Tanjung Batu; r incl breakfast from RM250; ❄📶) Pulau Labuan's favourite hotel is a cut above the rest with its cobalt-blue outdoor pool nestled in manicured gardens at Tanjung Batu. There's an excellent Asian-fusion restaurant and open-range kitchen, plus large and very alluring wood-signatured rooms with bed runners, snow-white linen, spotless bathrooms and recessed lighting.

Billion Waterfront Hotel HOTEL $$
(☎087-418 111; leslbn@tm.net.my; 1 Jln Wawasan; r incl breakfast from RM350; ❄🏊) This large business hotel backs onto a lively port, has an open bar, and has large international-style rooms with comfy beds, reading lights, faux-wood floors and modern bathroom. Breakfast is a mix of Western and Malay.

Mariner Hotel HOTEL $$
(☎087-418 822; mhlabuan@streamyx.com; U0468 Jln Tanjung Purun; s/d RM120/140; ❄@📶) Mariner's rooms are spacious, with laminate floors, psychedelic art on the walls, fridges and clean bathrooms. Some rooms smelt a little smoky. Decent breakfast.

Grand Dorsett Labuan HOTEL $$$
(☎087-422 000; www.granddorsett.com/labuan; 462 Jln Merdeka; r from RM405; ❄@📶🏊) One of the most luxurious hotels in town, Dorset is palatial with a columned marble lobby, outdoor pool, pleasant carpeted rooms, fresh walls and bathroom, plus friendly staff. The breakfast buffet, which is packed with fresh fruit and pastry, is tip-top.

Eating

★The Chillout Cafe INTERNATIONAL $
(www.thechilloutco.com; unit 2-6, level 2, Labuan Times Sq; mains RM15; ⏲10am-10pm) Cosy, clean, cool and very inviting, the new little sister to its elder sibling on mainland Malaysia is perfect for reading a book while enjoying a cappuccino between tucking into its cakes, pasta dishes, sandwiches, nicely executed Western breakfasts and carefully concocted fruit juices.

Restoran Selera Farizah MALAYSIAN $
(Lg Bunga Tanjung; meals from RM3; ⏲8am-10pm) If you prefer a Muslim *kedai kopi* (coffee shop) you could try this place, which serves roti, curries and *nasi campur* (buffet of curried meats, fish and vegetables, served

DIVING

Labuan is famous for its **wreck diving**, with no fewer than four major shipwrecks off the coast (two from WWII and two from the 1980s). The only dive outfit operating here is **Borneo Star Dives** (☎087-429 278; stardivers2005@yahoo.com; Labuan International Sea Sports Complex, Jln Tanjung Purun; dive packages from RM438), which does island-hopping tours and can take you out to all four sites. Note that only the 'Cement Wreck' is suitable for novice divers; the 'Blue Water Wreck' (in our opinion, the most impressive of the bunch) requires advanced open-water certification, and the 'American' and 'Australian' wrecks are only recommended for those with a wreck diving course under their belt.

GETTING TO BRUNEI: BANDAR LABUAN TO BANDAR SERI BEGAWAN

Getting to the border Ferries depart Bandar Labuan for the Bruneian port of Muara (RM35, 1¼ hours) daily at 9am, 1.30pm, 3.30pm and 4pm.

At the border In Brunei, most visitors are granted a visa on arrival for free, although Australians must pay a fee.

Moving on You'll be dropped at Serasa Ferry Terminal; from here bus 37 or 39 can take you to central Bandar Seri Begawan for B$1 (one hour). A taxi should cost around B$30.

with rice), accompanied by pro wrestling videos.

Choice Restaurant INDIAN $
(☎087-418 086; 104 Jln OKK Awang Besar; dishes RM3-10; ⏲8am-10pm) Forget false modesty, the Choice simply proclaims 'We are the best', and this seems to be corroborated by the popularity of the authentic Indian meals with the authentic Indian residents who turn out for roti, fish-head curry and sambal.

Port View Restaurant SEAFOOD $$
(☎087-422 999; Jln Merdeka; dishes RM15-30; ⏲lunch & dinner) An outpost of the successful Chinese seafood franchise in KK, this waterfront restaurant has air-con indoor seating and outdoor seating that affords a nice view over Labuan's busy harbour, though service can be a little frosty.

Tiara Seafood Restaurant SEAFOOD $$
(seafoodrest@tiaralabuan.com; Tiara Labuan Hotel, Jln Tanjung Batu; mains RM20; ⏲10.30am-2.30pm & 6-10pm) Based at hulking Tiara Labuan Hotel, this glass-accented restaurant has great reports for its fresh seafood. Whether it's scallops, king prawns, salt-and-pepper squid and steamed lobster (frozen) with garlic, or their iced mango sago pudding, there's something for everyone's palate. Efficient service and oblique sea views.

ℹ Information

MONEY

Bertam Mass Money Changer (Jln Bunga Raya) Cash and travellers cheques. Near the ferry terminal.

HSBC (☎087-422 610; 189 Jln Merdeka)

TOURIST INFORMATION

Tourist Information Centre (☎087-423 445; www.labuantourism.com.my; cnr Jln Dewan & Jln Berjaya; ⏲8am-5pm Mon-Fri, 9am-3pm Sat) Tourism Malaysia office.

Harrisons Travel (☎087-408 096; www.harrisonstravel.com.my; 1 Jln Merdeka) Handy and reputable travel agency.

ℹ Getting There & Away

AIR

Malaysia Airlines (☎1300-883 000; www.malaysiaairlines.com.my) has flights to/from KK (45 minutes) and KL (2½ hours), which are usually booked full of oil prospectors. **AirAsia** (☎087-480 401; www.airasia.com) currently flies to KL only.

BOAT

Kota Kinabalu Passenger ferries (1st/economy class RM48/35, 3¼ hours) depart KK for Labuan from Monday to Saturday at 8am, and 1.30pm (3pm Sundays). In the opposite direction, they depart Labuan for KK from Monday to Saturday at 8am and 1pm, and 10.30am and 3pm on Sundays.

Sarawak There are daily speedboats to Limbang (two hours, RM31) and Lawas (2¼ hours, RM34) in Sarawak's Limbang Division.

ℹ Getting Around

MINIBUS

Labuan has a good minibus network based on a six-zone system. Minibuses leave regularly from the parking lot off Jln Tun Mustapha. Their numbers are clearly painted on the front, and fares range from 50 sen for a short trip to RM2.50 for a trip to the top of the island. Services are generally more frequent before sunset.

TAXI

Taxis are plentiful and there's a stand opposite the local ferry terminal. The base rate is RM15 for short journeys, with most destinations costing around RM20.

Sarawak

AREA 124,450 SQ KM

Includes ➡

Best Places to Eat

- Dyak (p407)
- Top Spot Food Court (p407)
- Summit Café (p449)
- Bla Bla Bla (p408)
- Choon Hui (p406)

Best Places to Stay

- Batik Boutique Hotel (p405)
- Dillenia Guesthouse (p448)
- Threehouse B&B (p404)
- Nanga Shanti (p418)

Why Go?

Sarawak makes access to Borneo's natural wonders and cultural riches a breeze. From Kuching, the island's most sophisticated and dynamic city, pristine rainforests – where you can spot orangutans, proboscis monkeys, crocodiles and the world's largest flower, the Rafflesia – can be visited on day trips, with plenty of time in the evening for a delicious meal and a drink by Kuching's waterfront. More adventurous travellers can take a 'flying coffin' riverboat up the 'Amazon of Borneo', the Batang Rejang, on their way east to hike from longhouse to longhouse in the cool environs of the Kelabit Highlands, or to the spectacular bat caves and extraordinary rock formations of Gunung Mulu National Park. Everywhere you go, you'll encounter the warmth, unforced friendliness and sense of humour that make the people of Malaysia's most culturally diverse state such delightful hosts.

When to Go

Kuching

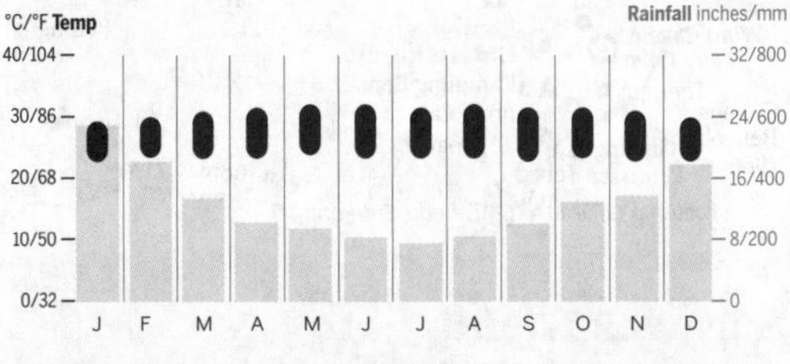

Jul Local bands and international artists jam at Kuching's Rainforest World Music Festival.

Jul–Sep It's tourist high season, so book flights and treks early.

Nov–Jan Rough seas can make coastal boat travel difficult or impossible.

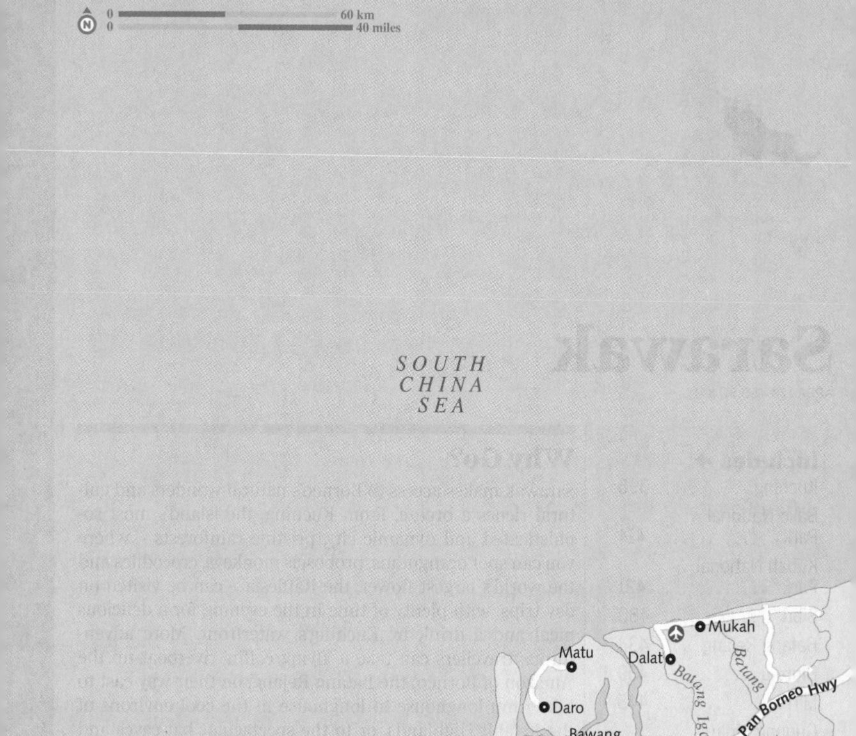

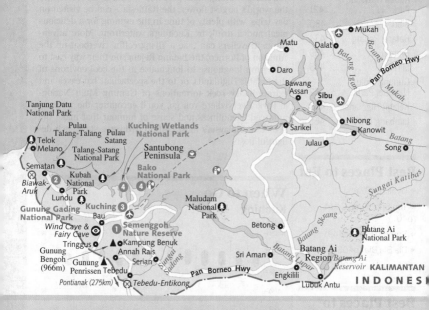

Sarawak Highlights

1. Watching semi-wild orangutans swing through the canopy at **Semenggoh Nature Reserve** (p419).
2. Seeing the elusive Rafflesia, the world's largest flower, at **Gunung Gading National Park** (p426).
3. Strolling the Waterfront Promenade in **Kuching** (p396).
4. Spotting endangered proboscis monkeys in **Bako National Park** (p413) or **Kuching Wetlands National Park** (p419).
5. Watching the jungle glide by as you make your way into

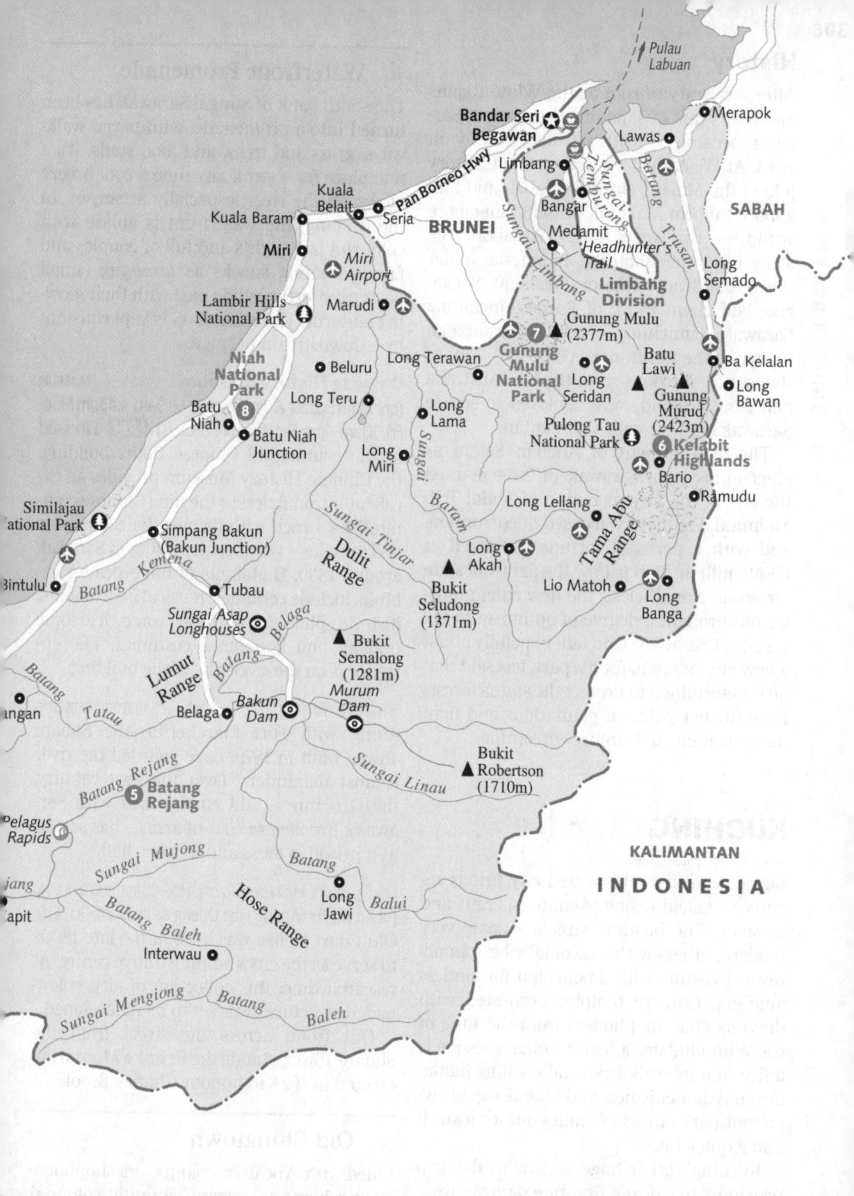

the very heart of Borneo along the **Batang Rejang** (p434), the 'Amazon of Borneo'.

6 Experiencing longhouse life and Kelabit hospitality in the **Kelabit Highlands** (p458).

7 Ascending to the summit of Gunung Mulu, the highest peak in **Gunung Mulu National Park** (p452), Borneo's best nature park, or going spelunking in its caves.

8 Entering a netherworld of stalactites and bats in the caves of **Niah National Park** (p442).

History

After a century of rule by the White Rajahs and four years of Japanese occupation, Sarawak became a British Crown colony in 1946. At Westminster's urging, the territory joined the Malay Peninsula, Sabah and Singapore to form Malaysia in 1963 (Singapore withdrew two years later). At about the same time, neighbouring Indonesia, under the leftist leadership of President Soekarno, laid claim to all of Borneo, including Sarawak, launching a military campaign known as the Konfrontasi (1962–66). Tens of thousands of troops from the UK, Australia and New Zealand were deployed to secure Sarawak's border with Kalimantan.

The appointment of Adenan Satem as chief minister of Sarawak in 2014 marked the end of the 13-year tenure of Abdul Taib Mahmud. Frequently accused of corruption, and with a personal fortune estimated at US$15 billion, Taib is now the Sarawak state governor. Nonetheless, the new chief minister has brought a degree of optimism to the people of Sarawak, who talk hopefully about a new era. Adenan, for his part, has said that he is determined to protect the state's forests from further palm-oil plantations and fight illegal logging and timber corruption.

KUCHING

082 / POP 600,000

Borneo's most sophisticated city brings together a kaleidoscope of cultures, crafts and cuisines. The bustling streets – some very modern, others with a colonial vibe – amply reward visitors with a penchant for aimless ambling. Chinese temples decorated with dragons abut shophouses from the time of the White Rajahs, a South Indian mosque is a five-minute walk from stalls selling half-a-dozen Asian cuisines, and a landscaped riverfront park attracts families out for a stroll and a quick bite.

Kuching's other huge asset is its day-trip proximity to a dozen first-rate nature sites.

Sights

The main attraction here is the city itself. Leave plenty of time to wander aimlessly and soak up the relaxed vibe and charming cityscapes of areas such as Jln Carpenter (Old Chinatown), Jln India, Jln Padungan (New Chinatown) and the Waterfront Promenade.

Waterfront Promenade

The south bank of Sungai Sarawak has been turned into a promenade, with paved walkways, grass and trees, and food stalls. It's a fine place for a stroll any time a cool breeze blows off the river, especially at sunset. In the evening, the waterfront is ablaze with colourful fairy lights and full of couples and families eating snacks as *tambang* (small passenger ferries) glide past with their glowing lanterns. The water level is kept constant by a downstream barrage.

Chinese History Museum MUSEUM
(cnr Main Bazaar & Jln Wayang; 9am-4.45pm Mon-Fri, 10am-4pm Sat, Sun & holidays) FREE Housed in the century-old Chinese Court building, the Chinese History Museum provides an excellent introduction to the nine Chinese communities – each with its own dialect, cuisine and temples – who began settling in Sarawak around 1830. Highlights of the evocative exhibits include ceramics, musical instruments, historic photographs and some fearsome dragon- and lion-dance costumes. The entrance is on the river side of the building.

Square Tower HISTORIC BUILDING
Along with Fort Margherita, the Square Tower, built in 1879, once guarded the river against marauders. Over the past century, the structure – still emblazoned with Sarawak's Brooke-era coat-of-arms – has served as a prison, a mess and a dance hall.

Old Court House Complex HISTORIC BUILDING
(btwn Jln Tun Abang Haji Openg & Jln Barrack) The Old Court House was built in the late 1800s to serve as the city's administrative centre. At research time, this collection of airy, colonnaded structures was set to be redeveloped.

Out front, across the street from the Square Tower, stands the **Brooke Memorial**, erected in 1924 to honour Charles Brooke.

Old Chinatown

Lined with evocative, colonial-era shophouses and home to several vibrantly coloured Chinese temples, Jln Carpenter is the heart of Kuching's Old Chinatown

Hong San Si Temple CHINESE TEMPLE
(Say Ong Kong; cnr Jln Wayang & Jln Carpenter; 6am-6pm) FREE Thought to date back to around 1840, this fine Hokkien Chinese temple with intricate rooftop dragons was fully restored in 2004. The new stone carvings,

done by stonemasons brought in from mainland China, are superb.

There is a big celebration here in April, when a long procession of floats, lion and dragon dancers and others wind their way through town following the altar of Kong Teck Choon Ong, the temple's diety.

Hin Ho Bio CHINESE TEMPLE
(36 Jln Carpenter; 6am-5pm) FREE It's easy to miss this temple, tucked away on the roof of the Kuching Hainan Association. Go up the staircase to the top floor and you come to a vivid little Chinese shrine, Hin Ho Bio (Temple of the Queen of Heaven), with rooftop views of Jln Carpenter.

Hiang Thian Siang Temple CHINESE TEMPLE
(Sang Ti Miao Temple; btwn 12 & 14 Jln Carpenter) FREE This temple, rebuilt shortly after the fire of 1884, serves the Teochew congregation as a shrine to Shang Di (the Emperor of Heaven). On the 15th day of the **Hungry Ghosts Festival** (mid-August or early September) a ceremony is held here in which offerings of food, prayer, incense and paper money are made to appease the spirits, blessed by a priest and then burned in a dramatic bonfire.

Sarawak Textile Museum MUSEUM
(Muzium Tekstil Sarawak; Jln Tun Abang Haji Openg; 9am-4.45pm Mon-Fri, 10am-4pm Sat, Sun & holidays) FREE Housed in a 'colonial Baroque'-style building constructed in 1909, this museum displays some superb examples of traditional Sarawakian textiles, including Malay *songket* (gold brocade cloth), as well as the hats, mats, belts, basketwork, beadwork, silverwork, barkwork, bangles and ceremonial headdresses created by the Iban, Bidayuh and Penan and other Dayak groups. Dioramas recreate the sartorial exuberance of Orang Ulu, Malay, Chinese and Indian weddings. Explanatory panels shed light on materials and techniques.

Jalan India Area

Once Kuching's main shopping area for imported textiles, brassware and household goods, pedestrianised Jln India – essentially the western continuation of Jln Carpenter – remains an exuberant commercial thoroughfare. The shops along the eastern section are mostly Chinese-owned; those to the west are run by Indian Muslims with roots in Tamil Nadu. It's *the* place to come in Kuching for cheap textiles.

Indian Mosque MOSQUE
(Indian Mosque Lane; 6am-8.30pm except during prayers) FREE Turn off Jln India (between Nos 37 and 39A) or waterfront Jln Gambier (between Nos 24 and 25A – shops selling spices with a heady aroma) onto tiny **Indian Mosque Lane** (Lg Sempit) and you enter another world. About halfway up, entirely surrounded by houses and shops, stands Kuching's oldest mosque, a modest structure built of *belian* (ironwood) in 1863 by Muslim traders from Tamil Nadu.

Notable for its simplicity, it is an island of peace and cooling shade in the middle of Kuching's commercial hullabaloo. There is usually someone sitting outside the mosque keeping an eye on things. If you would like to go inside, ask permission and he will probably offer to show you around. Women will be given a long cloak and headscarf to wear.

South of Padang Merdeka

The museums in the area just south of Padang Merdeka (Independence Square) contain a first-rate collection of cultural artefacts that no one interested in Borneo's peoples and habitats should miss. At research time, construction was underway on a new five-storey museum, located on the western side of Jln Tun Abang Haji Openg, due to be completed in 2020. The new modern building will bring the archaeology, ethnology, zoology and history collections under one roof, with state-of-the art interactive displays.

★ **Ethnology Museum** MUSEUM
(www.museum.sarawak.gov.my; Jln Tun Abang Haji Openg; 9am-4.45pm Mon-Fri, 10am-4pm Sat, Sun & holidays) FREE At the top of the hill, on the eastern side of Jln Tun Abang Haji Openg, the Ethnology Museum (the Old Building) – guarded by two colonial cannons – spotlights Borneo's incredibly rich indigenous cultures. Upstairs the superb exhibits include a full-sized Iban longhouse, masks and spears; downstairs is an old-fashioned natural-history museum.

At research time, there were plans to renovate the more than 100-year-old building, starting early 2016. During the renovations sections of the museum may be closed.

The museum was established in 1891 by Charles Brooke as a place to exhibit indigenous handicrafts and wildlife specimens, many of them collected by the naturalist Russell Wallace in the 1850s. The rajah's

Kuching

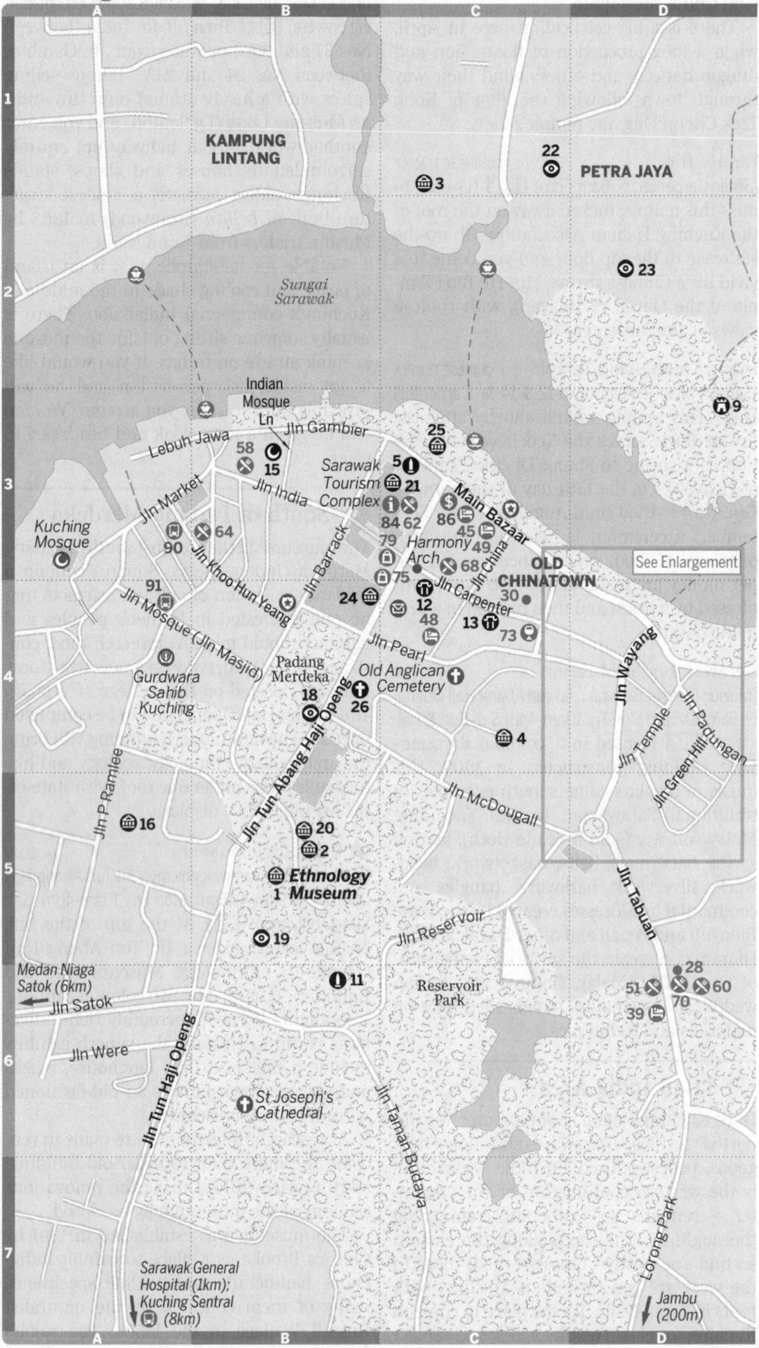

A
B
C
D
1
2
3
4
5
6
7
KAMPUNG LINTANG
PETRA JAYA
22
23
3
9
Sungai Sarawak
Indian Mosque Ln
Lebuh Jawa
Jln Gambier
58
15
25
5
Sarawak Tourism Complex
21
Main Bazaar
Jln India
Jln Market
Kuching Mosque
64
90
84
62
86
45
79
49
Harmony Arch
68
75
Jln China
OLD CHINATOWN
See Enlargement
Jln Barrack
Jln Khoo Hun Yeang
91
24
12
Jln Carpenter
30
48
13
73
Jln Mosque (Jln Masjid)
Jln Pearl
Jln Wayang
Padang Merdeka
Old Anglican Cemetery
Gurdwara Sahib Kuching
18
26
Jln Temple
Jln Padungan
Jln Green Hill
4
Jln Tun Abang Haji Openg
Jln P Ramlee
Jln McDougall
16
20
2
Ethnology Museum
1
Jln Tabuan
Jln Reservoir
19
11
Reservoir Park
28
51
70
60
39
Medan Niaga Satok (6km)
Jln Satok
Jln Were
Jln Tun Haji Openg
St Joseph's Cathedral
Jln Taman Budaya
Lorong Park
Sarawak General Hospital (1km); Kuching Sentral (8km)
Jambu (200m)

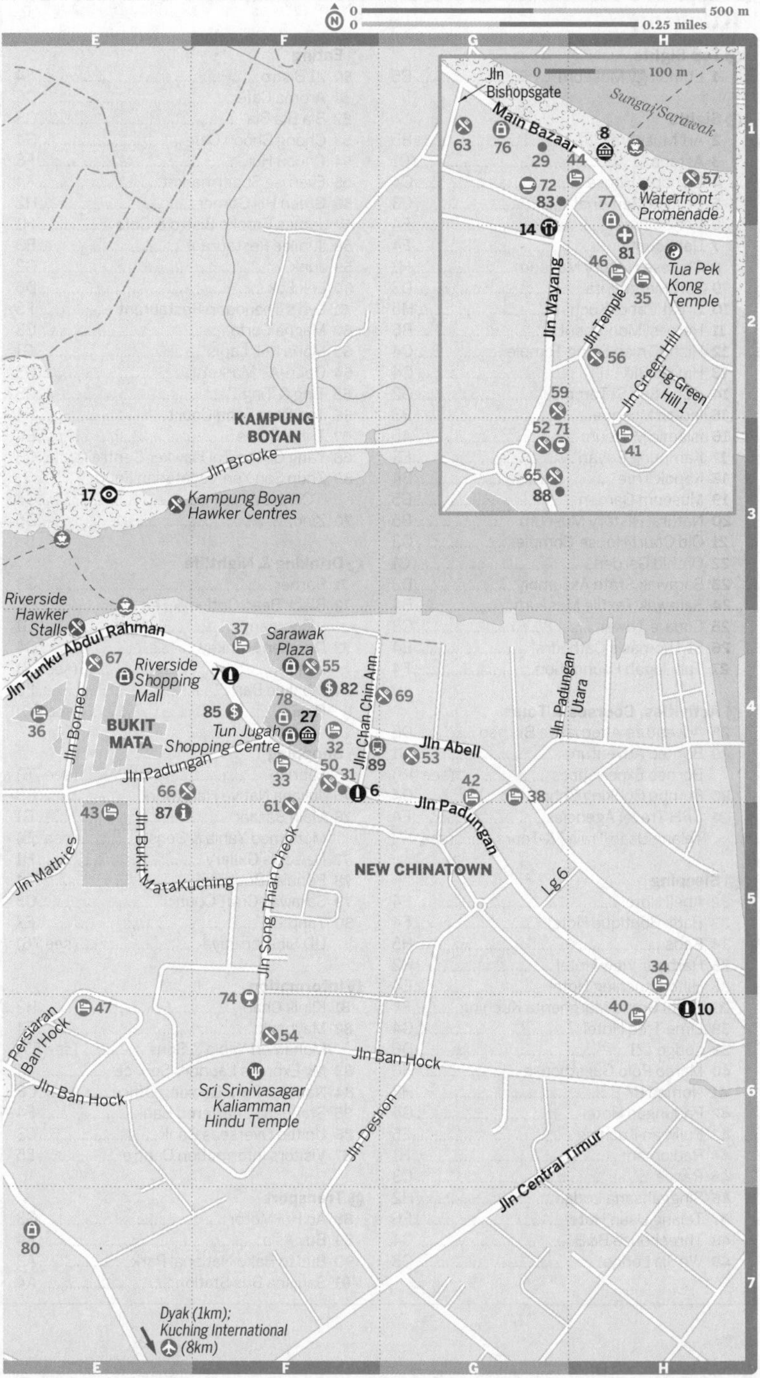

0
500 m
0
0.25 miles
Jln Bishopsgate
Main Bazaar
Sungai Sarawak
100 m
Waterfront Promenade
Jln Wayang
Jln Temple
Tua Pek Kong Temple
Jln Green Hill
Lg Green Hill 1
KAMPUNG BOYAN
Jln Brooke
Kampung Boyan Hawker Centres
Riverside Hawker Stalls
Jln Tunku Abdul Rahman
Sarawak Plaza
Riverside Shopping Mall
Tun Jugah Shopping Centre
BUKIT MATA
Jln Borneo
Jln Padungan
Jln Chan Chin Ann
Jln Abell
Jln Padungan Utara
Jln Song Thian Cheok
Jln Mathies
Jln Bukit MataKuching
NEW CHINATOWN
Lg 6
Persiaran Ban Hock
Jln Ban Hock
Sri Srinivasagar Kaliamman Hindu Temple
Jln Deshon
Jln Central Timur
Dyak (1km); Kuching International (8km)

Kuching

Top Sights
1 Ethnology Museum ... B5

Sights
2 Art Museum ... B5
3 Astana ... C1
4 Bishop's House ... C4
5 Brooke Memorial ... C3
6 Cat Column ... F4
7 Cat Fountain ... F4
8 Chinese History Museum ... H1
9 Fort Margherita ... D3
10 Great Cat of Kuching ... H6
11 Heroes' Monument ... B6
12 Hiang Thian Siang Temple ... C4
13 Hin Ho Bio ... C4
14 Hong San Si Temple ... G2
15 Indian Mosque ... B3
16 Islamic Museum ... A5
17 Kampung Boyan ... E3
18 Kapok Tree ... B4
19 Museum Garden ... B5
20 Natural History Museum ... B5
21 Old Court House Complex ... C3
22 Orchid Garden ... C1
23 Sarawak State Assembly ... D2
24 Sarawak Textile Museum ... B4
25 Square Tower ... C3
26 St Thomas's Cathedral ... B4
27 Tun Jugah Foundation ... F4

Activities, Courses & Tours
28 Adventure Alternative Borneo ... D6
29 Borneo Adventure ... G1
Borneo Experiences ... (see 46)
30 Bumbu Cooking School ... C4
31 CPH Travel Agencies ... F4
Telang Usan Travel & Tours ... (see 47)

Sleeping
32 Abell Hotel ... F4
33 Batik Boutique Hotel ... F4
34 Beds ... H5
35 Harbour View Hotel ... H2
36 Hilton Kuching Hotel ... E4
37 Hotel Grand Margherita Kuching ... F4
38 Lime Tree Hotel ... G4
39 Lodge 121 ... D6
40 Marco Polo Guesthouse ... H6
41 Nomad B&B ... H3
42 Padungan Hotel ... G4
43 Pullman Kuching ... E5
44 Radioman ... H1
45 Ranee ... C3
46 Singgahsana Lodge ... H2
47 Telang Usan Hotel ... E6
48 Threehouse B&B ... C4
49 Wo Jia Lodge ... C3

Eating
50 21 Bistro ... F4
51 Aroma Café ... D6
52 Bla Bla Bla ... G3
53 Chong Choon Cafe ... G4
54 Choon Hui ... F6
55 Everrise Supermarket ... F4
56 Green Hill Corner ... H2
57 James Brooke Bistro & Cafe ... H1
58 Jubilee Restaurant ... B3
59 Junk ... G2
60 Lok Lok ... D6
61 Lyn's Thandoori Restaurant ... F5
62 Magna Carta ... C3
63 Maria Kek Lapis ... G1
64 Open-Air Market ... B3
65 Ting & Ting ... G3
66 Top Spot Food Court ... E4
67 Tribal Stove ... E4
68 Yang Choon Tai Hawker Centre ... C3
69 Zhun San Yen Vegetarian Food Centre ... G4
70 Zinc ... D6

Drinking & Nightlife
71 Barber ... G3
72 Black Bean Coffee & Tea Company ... G1
73 Drunken Monkey ... C4
Lamin ... (see 47)
74 Monkee Bar ... F6
Ruai ... (see 60)

Shopping
Fabriko ... (see 76)
75 Juliana Native Handwork ... C3
76 Main Bazaar ... G1
Mohamed Yahia & Sons ... (see 55)
77 Nelson's Gallery ... H1
78 Popular Book Co ... F4
79 Sarawak Craft Council ... C3
80 Tanoti ... E7
UD Siburan Jaya ... (see 76)

Information
81 Klinik Chan ... H2
82 Maybank ... F4
Mohamed Yahia & Sons ... (see 55)
83 My Express Laundry Service ... G1
84 National Park Booking Office ... C3
85 Standard Chartered Bank ... F4
86 United Overseas Bank ... C3
87 Visitors Information Centre ... E5

Transport
88 An Hui Motor ... G3
89 Bus Asia ... F4
90 Bus to Bako National Park ... A3
91 Saujana Bus Station ... A4

French aide designed the building, modelling it on Normandy town hall.

The upstairs gallery is decorated with Kayan and Kenyah murals painted by local artists, forming the backdrop to exhibits that include basketry, musical instruments and a Bidayuh door charm for keeping evil spirits at bay, as well as information on native customs such as tattooing and the infamous *palang* penis piercing.

Downstairs in the natural-history gallery the highlight – remembered with horror by generations of Kuching children – is a hairball taken from the stomach of a man-eating crocodile, accompanied by the following explanation: 'human dental plate found attached to the hairball'. And if this isn't enough to put you off taking a dip in a muddy estuary, the 'watch found inside stomach' (the croc's stomach, of course) surely will – unless you'd like your smartphone to feature in some future exhibit.

Museum Garden GARDENS
(Jln Tun Abang Haji Openg; 9am-4.45pm Mon-Fri, 10am-4pm Sat, Sun & holidays) The landscaped Museum Garden stretches south from the hill, leading past flowers and fountains to a white-and-gold column called the **Heroes' Monument**, which commemorates those who died defending Sarawak.

Art Museum MUSEUM
(www.museum.sarawak.gov.my; Jln Tun Abang Haji Openg; 9am-4.45pm Mon-Fri, 10am-4pm Sat, Sun & holidays) FREE This museum features sculpture and paintings using traditional indigenous techniques as well as pieces inspired by Borneo's flora, fauna and landscapes. At research time the museum was closed for renovations but it will reopen with additional exhibits (previously contained in the now permanently closed Dewan Tun Abdul Razak gallery) on Sarawak's fascinating history, from the Brunei sultanate through to the Brooke era, prehistoric archaeology including important finds from the Niah Caves, and Chinese ceramics.

Natural History Museum MUSEUM
(www.museum.sarawak.gov.my; Jln Tun Abang Haji Openg) FREE This building, built in 1908 and adorned with a Wallace butterfly in reference to the naturalist it is named after, is currently being used to store zoological and archaeological specimens (including finds excavated in Niah) and as offices. It is not open to the general public, but researchers and students can apply for access to the collections.

Islamic Museum MUSEUM
(Jln P Ramlee; 9am-4.45pm Mon-Fri, 10am-4pm Sat, Sun & holidays) FREE This museum offers a pretty good introduction to Malay-Muslim culture and its long ties with the Muslim heartland far to the west. Displays range from Bornean-Malay architecture, musical instruments and wood carvings to Arabic calligraphy and astrolabes of the sort that helped Arab mariners travel this far east.

New Chinatown

Built starting in the 1920s, initially with money from the rubber boom, Kuching's liveliest commercial thoroughfare stretches 1.5km along Jln Padungan from Jln Tunku Abdul Rahman to the Great Cat of Kuching. It's lined with Chinese-owned businesses and noodle shops and a growing number of cafes, bars and restaurants. Covered arcades make it a fine place for a rainy-day stroll.

Tun Jugah Foundation MUSEUM
(082-239672; www.tunjugahfoundation.org.my; 4th fl, Tun Jugah Tower, 18 Jln Tunku Abdul Rahman; 9am-noon & 1-4.30pm Mon-Fri) FREE The textile gallery and museum of this charitable foundation, which aims to promote and preserve Iban culture, has excellent exhibits on Iban *ikat* and *sungkit* weaving, as well as beadwork. Iban women come here to make traditional textiles using handlooms.

North Bank of the River

To get to Sungai Sarawak's northern bank, take a *tambang* (river ferry; 50 sen) from one of the docks along the Waterfront Promenade.

Kampung Boyan AREA
This sedate, old-time Malay *kampung* (village), filled with joyously colourful houses and a profusion of flowering plants, is a world away from the glitz and bustle of downtown Kuching, to which it's connected by boat. The waterfront area has two roofed hawker centres as well as other Malay-style eateries.

Fort Margherita FORT
(Kampung Boyan; 9am-4.30pm) Built by Charles Brooke in 1879 and named after his wife, Ranee Margaret, this hilltop fortress long protected Kuching against surprise attack by pirates. It did so exclusively as a remarkably successful deterrent: troops stationed here never fired a shot in anger.

To get there from Kampung Boyan, follow the signs up the hill for 500m.

Inspired by an English Renaissance castle, whitewashed Fort Margherita manages to feel both medieval-European and tropical. At research time there were plans to add new exhibits on the Brookes to the almost empty fort.

Astana HISTORIC BUILDING

(Jln Taman Budaya; closed to public) Built by Charles Brooke in 1869, the Astana (a local word meaning 'palace') – conveniently labelled in giant white letters – and its manicured gardens still serve as the home of the governor of Sarawak. The best views are actually from the south (city centre) bank of the river, so it's not really worth taking a *tambang* across.

Sarawak State Assembly NOTABLE BUILDING

(Dewan Undangan Negeri, north bank of Sungai Sarawak, Petra Jaya) Inaugurated in 2009, the iconic home of Sarawak's State Assembly is an imposing structure whose soaring golden roof is said to resemble either a *payung* (umbrella) or a *terendak* (Melanau sunhat). The best views of the building (not open to the public) are from Jln Bishopsgate and the Waterfront Promenade.

Elsewhere in Kuching

St Thomas's Cathedral CHURCH

(www.stthomascathedralkuching.org; Jln Tun Abang Haji Openg; 8.30am-6pm Mon-Sat, to 7pm Sun) FREE Facing **Padang Merdeka** (Independence Sq), with its huge and ancient **kapok tree**, Kuching's Anglican cathedral (1954) has a mid-20th-century look and, inside, a bright red barrel-vaulted ceiling. Enter from Jln McDougall, named after Kuching's first Anglican bishop, who arrived here in 1848.

At the top of the hill, on the other side of the Parish Centre stands the **Bishop's House**. Kuching's oldest building, it was constructed – in 1849 with admirable solidness – by a German shipwright.

Kuching North City Hall NOTABLE BUILDING

(DBKU; Jln Semariang, Bukit Siol) Situated 8km north of the city centre is the hilltop Kuching North City Hall (known by its Malay abbreviation, DBKU), a landmark prestige project – some say it looks like a UFO – inaugurated in 1993. As well as being a local council building, the Cat Museum is on the ground floor.

To get here, take bus K15 from the Saujana bus station (p413). If you're going to the Santubong Peninsula by car, you can stop here on the way.

Orchid Garden GARDENS

(Jln Astana Lot; 9.30am-6pm Tue-Sun) FREE Sarawak's state flower, the Normah orchid, is just one of the 82 species growing in these peaceful gardens and greenhouse nursery. Other Borneo orchids to look out for are lady's slippers, identifiable by their distinct, insect-trapping pouches.

The easiest way to get here from the city centre is to take a *tambang* across the river to Pengakalan Sapi on the north bank (next to the Sarawak State Assembly building) and walk up the hill.

Medan Niaga Satok MARKET

(Satok Weekend Market; Jln Matang Jaya; 5.30am-7.30pm) Kuching's biggest and liveliest market has now moved to its spacious new digs 9km west of the city centre. It's open every day, but the main event is the larger weekend market, which begins around midday on Saturday, when rural folk, some from area longhouses, arrive with their fruits, vegetables, fish and spices. To get here, take the K7 bus.

The air is heady with the aromas of fresh coriander, ginger, herbs and jungle ferns, which are displayed among piles of bananas, mangoes, custard apples and obscure jungle fruits. If you smell something overpoweringly sickly sweet and pungent, chances are it's a durian. Vendors are friendly and many are happy to tell you about their wares, which are often divided into quantities worth RM1 or RM2.

Activities

Bumbu Cooking School COOKING COURSE

(019-879 1050; http://bumbucookingclass.weebly.com; 57 Jln Carpenter; per person RM150; 9am-1pm & 2.30-7pm) Raised in a Bidayuh village, Joseph teaches the secrets of cooking with fresh, organic ingredients from the rainforest. At the market you'll learn how to spot top-quality jungle ferns; back in the kitchen you'll prepare this crunchy delicacy, along with a main dish and a dessert that's served in a *pandan*-leaf basket you weave yourself. Maximum 10 participants.

The small shop that serves as the entrance to the cooking school is like a mini-museum full of pieces Joseph has collected: blow pipes, rattan baskets (one designed to be used as a baby carrier), a rice mill, and ceremonial blankets and masks from Iban and Orang Ulu longhouses.

KUCHING KITTIES

It's just a coincidence that in Bahasa Malaysia, Kuching means 'cat' (spelled '*kucing*'), but the city has milked the homonym for all it's worth, branding Sarawak's capital the 'Cat City' and erecting a number of marvellously kitschy cat statues to beautify the urban landscape.

Cat Fountain (Jln Tunku Abdul Rahman) An ensemble of polychrome cats who pose and preen amid the passing cars.

Cat Column (cnr Jln Padungan & Jln Chan Chin Ann) On the roundabout, the Cat Column features four cats around the bottom and four Rafflesia flowers near the top – the latter are just below the cat-adorned shield of the South Kuching municipality.

Great Cat of Kuching (Jln Padungan) A 2.5m-high white pussycat with blue eyes and wire whiskers is perched at the eastern end of Jln Padungan on a traffic island just outside the Chinese ceremonial gate.

Cat Museum (www.dbku.sarawak.gov.my; Jln Semariang, Bukit Siol; camera/video RM4/5; ⌚9am-5pm) This homage to the city's name, located 8km north of the centre, features hundreds of entertaining, surprising and bizarre *kucing* figurines – some the size of a cow, others tiny – alongside detailed presentations on 'Cats in Malay Society' and 'Cats in Chinese Art'. By the time you reach the exhibits on 'Cats in Stamps' and 'Cats in Film' (in which Bond villain Blofeld's mog features), you may feel it's all getting a little silly. To get here, take bus K15.

Hash House Harriers RUNNING
(☎Robin Kho 012-887 1420; www.kuchingcityhash.com) Kuching's various Hash House Harriers chapters hold about half-a-dozen one- to two-hour runs, over meadow and dale (and through thick jungle), each week.

Tours

Borneo Adventure TOUR
(☎082-245 175; www.borneoadventure.com; 55 Main Bazaar) Award-winning company that sets the standard for high-end Borneo tours and is the leader in cooperative projects benefitting Sarawak's indigenous peoples. Known for its excellent guides.

Adventure Alternative Borneo ADVENTURE TOUR
(☎082-248000, 019-892 9627; www.aaborneo.com; Lot 37, Jln Tabuan) Offers ethical and sustainable trips that combine 'culture, nature and adventure'. Can help you design and coordinate an itinerary for independent travel to remote areas, including the Penan villages of the Upper Baram.

Borneo Experiences TOUR
(☎082-429239; www.borneoexperiences.com; ground fl, No 1 Jln Temple; ⌚10am-7pm Mon-Sat, may also open Sun) Singgahsana Lodge's (p404) travel agency. Destinations include a remote Bidayuh 'village in the clouds' and an Iban longhouse in the Batang Ai area (two nights RM1370). Also offers cycling tours. Gets excellent reviews.

Borneo à la Carte TOUR
(☎082-236857; www.borneoalacarte.com) A Kuching-based agency offering innovative, tailor-made trips, mainly for a French-speaking clientele, to indigenous communities other agencies don't cover. Amélie, the owner, is known for having very reasonable prices and sharing receipts equitably with local communities.

One Wayang Tours BICYCLE TOUR
(☎082-238801; www.paradesaborneo.com; 1 Leboh Wayang) Specialises in bike tours, offering city tours (RM108) and off-road mountain biking (RM188).

Rainforest Kayaking TOUR
(Borneo Trek & Kayak Adventure; ☎082-240571, 013-804 8338; www.rainforestkayaking.com) Specialises in river trips, which can be combined with a trip to Semenggoh Nature Reserve.

Telang Usan Travel & Tours TOUR
(☎082-236945; www.telangusan.com; Telang Usan Hotel, Persiaran Ban Hock) A well-regarded, veteran agency based in the Telang Usan Hotel.

Festivals & Events

Chinese New Year NEW YEAR
(⌚late Jan or early Feb) The main festivities are along Jln Padungan.

Rainforest World Music Festival MUSIC
(www.rwmf.net; 1-/3-day pass adult RM340/130, child RM160/60; ⌚Jul or Aug) This three-day gathering, one of the world's great music festivals, is held in the Sarawak Cultural Village. International artists, who usually perform a type of music that is traditional in their country, hold informal workshops in the longhouses in the afternoon, while the main performances are held on the main stage at night. Accommodation gets booked out well in advance.

Kuching Food Fair FOOD
(Kuching City South Council, Jln Padungan; ⌚5-11pm for 1 month Jul-Aug) A huge food extravaganza with hundreds of stalls selling a whole range of meals and snacks – from Mongolian barbecues to Vietnamese spring rolls and deep-fried ice cream. Held in the park in front of the Kuching City South Council (the blue, teepee-shaped building just east of Jln Padungan, on the other side of the roundabout).

Mooncake Festival FAIR
(⌚Sep or early Oct) Musical performances and food stalls selling Chinese food, drink and, of course, mooncakes take over Jln Carpenter.

Sleeping

Kuching's accommodation options range from international-standard suites with high-rise views to windowless, musty cells deep inside converted Chinese shophouses. Many of the guesthouses – a great place to meet other travellers – are on or near Jln Carpenter (Old Chinatown), while the top-end spots are clustered a bit to the east in Kuching's high-rise district, on or near Jln Tunku Abdul Rahman. Cheap Chinese hotels can be found on or just off Jln Padungan and on the *lorong* (alleys) coming off L-shaped Jln Green Hill.

The majority of guesthouse rooms under RM50 have shared bathrooms; prices almost always include a very simple breakfast of the toast-and-jam variety. Rates at some guesthouses rise in July or from June to September.

★**Threehouse B&B** GUESTHOUSE $
(☎082-423499; www.threehousebnb.com; 51 Jln China; incl breakfast dm RM20, d without bathroom RM60-65; 📶) A spotless, family-friendly guesthouse in a great Old Chinatown location that is warm and welcoming – everything a guesthouse should be. All nine rooms are spaced over three, creaky wooden floors and share a bright-red colour scheme. Amenities include a common room with TV, DVDs and books, a laundry service and a kitchen.

★**Singgahsana Lodge** GUESTHOUSE $
(☎082-429277; www.singgahsana.com; 1 Jln Temple; dm/d incl breakfast RM31/RM112–132; ❄@📶) Setting the Kuching standard for backpacker digs, this hugely popular guesthouse, decked out with stylish Sarawakian crafts, has an unbeatable location, a great chill-out lobby and a sociable rooftop bar. Dorms have 10 beds and lockers.

Radioman HOSTEL $
(☎082 248816; 1 Jln Wayang; incl breakfast dm RM25, d without bathroom RM70; ❄📶) This centrally located, self-styled 'heritage hostel' occupies a century-old shophouse that was once used for radio repairs. The building still has the original ceilings, floors and fiendishly steep stairs, and it has been thoughtfully designed with nice touches like records on the walls, jungly plants and a courtyard garden.

When the new owners took over, they made use of all the radio equipment that was left behind to decorate the place – look out for lampshades made from pliers and large speakers that have been transformed into tables.

Marco Polo Guesthouse GUESTHOUSE $
(☎082-246679, Samuel Tan 019-888 8505; www.marcopolo.net.tf; 1st fl, 236 Jln Padungan; incl breakfast dm RM27, d without bathrooms RM56-60; ❄📶) A well-run, comfortable place with a breezy verandah and cosy indoor living room. The breakfast of fresh fruit, banana fritters and muffins is a popular bonus. Only some rooms have windows. Owner Sam is happy to give travel advice and sometimes brings guests to the market. Situated about 15 minutes' walk from the waterfront.

Nomad B&B GUESTHOUSE $
(☎082-237831, 016 856 3855; www.borneobnb.com; 1st fl, 3 Jln Green Hill ; incl breakfast dm RM20, with fan & without bathroom s/d RM50/60, d with air-con RM70-75; ❄@📶) There's a buzzing backpacker vibe at this relaxed, Iban-run place – guests often hang out in the lounge area with the friendly management. Breakfast times are flexible to suit late risers and there is a kitchen that guests can use. Of the 17 rooms, 10 have windows (the others make do with exhaust fans). Dorm rooms have eight beds.

Lodge 121 GUESTHOUSE $
(☎082-428121; www.lodge121.com; Lot 121, 1st fl, Jln Tabuan; dm/s/d/tr without bathroom, incl breakfast RM30/59/79/99; ❄📶) Polished concrete abounds in this former commercial space that has been transformed into a sleek, low-key guesthouse. The carpeted, 10-bed dorm room, with mattresses on the floor, is in the attic. All rooms share bathrooms that are on the small side.

Beds GUESTHOUSE $
(☎082-424229; www.bedsguesthouse.com; 229 Jln Padungan; dm RM20, s/d without bathroom RM40/55; ❄@📶) This guesthouse has attracted a loyal following thanks to comfy couches in the lobby, a kitchen you can cook in and 12 spotless rooms, nine with windows. Dorm rooms have six metal bunks of generous proportions. Located in New Chinatown, about 15 minutes' walk from the Main Bazaar.

Wo Jia Lodge GUESTHOUSE $
(☎082-251776; www.wojialodge.com; 17 Main Bazaar; incl breakfast dm/s/d/tr with air-con RM20/47/59/110, s/d with fan RM40/50; ❄@📶) A friendly, central spot to lay your head. The 18 neat rooms (five with windows, the rest with exhaust fans to the hallway) contain beds and nothing else. There is a small kitchen that guests may use. The dorm rooms, downstairs in the basement, are musty and dank, and best avoided.

Housed in an old Chinese shophouse – the lobby still has the original hardwood floors.

★ **Batik Boutique Hotel** BOUTIQUE HOTEL $$
(☎082-422845; www.batikboutiquehotel.com; 38 Jln Padungan; d incl breakfast RM280; ❄📶) A superb location, classy design and superfriendly staff make this a top midrange choice. The swirling batik design used on the hotel's facade is continued in the lobby and the 15 spacious rooms, each with a distinct colour theme. Some rooms have balconies overlooking the courtyard.

Lime Tree Hotel HOTEL $$
(☎082-414600; www.limetreehotel.com.my; Lot 317, Jln Abell; d incl breakfast RM170-250; ❄@📶) Dashes of lime green – a pillow, a bar of soap, a staff member's tie, the lobby's Cafe Sublime – accent every room of this well-run semi-boutique hotel. The 55 rooms are sleek and minimalist and offer good value; promotional room rates are lower than those quoted here. The rooftop bar has river views and happy hour prices from 5pm to 8pm.

Hotel Grand Margherita Kuching HOTEL $$
(☎082-423111; www.grandmargherita.com; Jln Tunku Abdul Rahman; d incl breakfast RM275; ❄@📶🏊) On a fine piece of riverfront real estate, this place will spoil you with a bright, modern lobby, 288 very comfortable rooms and amenities such as a fitness centre, a river-view swimming pool and a spa.

Padungan Hotel HOTEL $$
(☎082-257766; www.padunganhotel.com; 115 Jln Padungan; d RM100–115) A comfortable, modern hotel housed in a successfully redesigned commercial building (painted an unmissable orange) that offers good-value rooms in a convenient location.

Telang Usan Hotel HOTEL $$
(☎082-415588; www.telangusan.com; Persiaran Ban Hock; d incl breakfast RM130-150) A famously welcoming hotel with gleaming tile hallways and an old-school feel. The rooms are a little old fashioned with aging furniture, but the common areas are decorated with bright Kenyah and Kayan motifs.

The Lamin (p409) is the hotel's longhouse-style bar.

Harbour View Hotel HOTEL $$
(☎082-274666, 082-274600; www.harbourview.com.my; Jln Temple; s/d/f RM130/155/200; ❄@📶) If it's modern comforts you're after, this 243-room tower, is one of Kuching's best bargains, offering first-class facilities for reasonable prices. Breakfast is RM20 per person. Try to get a room with a river view.

Pullman Kuching HOTEL $$
(☎082-222888; www.pullmankuching.com; 1A Jln Mathies, Bukit Mata; d RM318-360; ❄@📶🏊) The 23-storey-tall Pullman stands on a hill, towering over its neighbours. The vast white lobby is so grandiose in its proportions that the rooms – in subdued tones of aquamarine, brown, white and green – feel small in comparison. The focus is on business travellers. Promotional rates available at less busy times.

Abell Hotel HOTEL $$
(☎082-239449; www.abellhotel.com; 22 Jln Tunku Abdul Rahman/Jln Abell; s RM145, d RM205–295; ❄@📶) This nonsmoking hotel offers 80 rooms that are stylish but not luxurious; the cheaper ones look out on an airwell. The name – like that of the street outside – is pronounced like the word 'able'.

★ **Ranee** BOUTIQUE HOTEL $$$
(☎082-258833; www.theranee.com; 6 & 7 Main Bazaar; d incl breakfast RM300-585; ❄📶) This

riverfront property, housed in an old shophouse that was completely rebuilt after a fire, has an urban-resort feel. All 24 rooms are different with plenty of design touches (the odd striped wall or globe-like lamp), high ceilings, hardwood floors and huge bathrooms with sleek, indirect lighting.

Hilton Kuching Hotel HOTEL $$$
(☎082-233888; www.hilton.com; cnr Jln Tunku Abdul Rahman & Jln Borneo; d RM405-485, ste RM755-790;) The Hilton has spacious, international-standard rooms in shades of cream, beige and maroon and all the amenities you would expect from this class of hotel. Most rooms have good views of the city; the best look out onto the river and rooftops of Old China Town. Rates vary and may be lower than those quoted here.

Eating

Kuching is the best place in Malaysian Borneo to work your way through the entire range of Sarawak-style cooking. At hawker centres, you can pick and choose from a variety of Chinese and Malay stalls, each specialising in a particular culinary tradition or dish, while Jln Padungan is home to some of the city's best noodle houses. The question of where to find the city's best laksa is a sensitive subject and one sure to spark a heated debate among Kuchingites. The only way to get a definitive answer is to try them all yourself.

★Choon Hui MALAYSIAN $
(34 Jln Ban Hock; laksa RM5-7; 7-11am Tue-Sun) This old-school *kopitiam* (coffee shop) gets our vote for the most delicious laksa in town, and we're not alone – the place can get crowded, especially at weekends. There is also a stall here selling excellent *popia,* a kind of spring roll made with peanuts, radish and carrot (RM3).

Open-Air Market HAWKER $
(Tower Market; Jln Khoo Hun Yeang; mains RM3-6.50; most stalls 6am-4pm, Chinese seafood 3pm-4am) Cheap, tasty dishes to look for include laksa, Chinese-style *mee sapi* (beef noodle soup), red *kolo mee* (noodles with pork and a sweet barbecue sauce), tomato *kueh tiaw* (a fried rice-noodle dish) and shaved ice desserts (ask for 'ABC' at stall 17). The Chinese seafood stalls that open in the afternoon are on the side facing the river.

From early mornings until mid-afternoon there is also a stall selling fish head and duck porridge, if that's your thing.

The market (which isn't strictly speaking open-air) has two sections, separated by a road, on the site of a former fire station; the yellow tower was once used as a fire lookout.

Yang Choon Tai Hawker Centre CHINESE $
(23 Jln Carpenter; mains RM3.50-8; 4am-midnight) Six food stalls, run by members of the Teochew Chinese community, serve up an eclectic assortment of native bites, including rice porridge with pork (3am to 9am), *kolo mee* (flash-boiled egg noodles; available from 6am to 2pm), super fish soup (3pm to 10pm) and – the most popular stall – pork satay (from 2pm).

Aroma Café DAYAK $
(☎082-417163; Jln Tabuan; mains RM10-16, buffet per plate RM5-6; 7am-10.30pm Mon-Sat, buffet 10am-2pm) A great place to try local indigenous specialities such as *ayam pansuh* (chicken cooked in bamboo; RM10), fried tapioca leaves (RM6) and *umai* (a Sarawakian version of sushi; RM10). The lunchtime buffet is good value.

Zhun San Yen Vegetarian Food Centre VEGETARIAN $
(Lot 165, Jln Chan Chin Ann; mains RM4.30-5.50; 8am-4.30pm Mon-Fri, 9am-4pm Sat;) A meat-free buffet lunch of Chinese-style curries, priced by weight, is served from 11am to 2pm (RM1.90 per 100g). When the buffet is over, you can order from a menu of dishes such as ginger 'chicken' (made with a soy-based meat substitute).

Lok Lok MALAYSIAN $
(7D Jln Ban Hock; mains RM5; 6pm-3am) This hugely popular nocturnal eatery specialises in *lok lok,* skewers (eg of fish, prawn, cuttlefish or bean curd; RM1.50 to RM2 each) that are either boiled or deep fried and eaten with sweet, sweet-and-sour, *belacan* (shrimp-paste sauce) or satay sauce. Also serves *rojak* (mixed vegetable dish with a thick shrimp-based sauce) and traditional mains such as curry chicken. Ideal for a late meal.

Chong Choon Cafe HAWKER $
(Lot 121, Section 3, Jln Abell; mains RM5-6; 7-11am, closed Tue) You'd never guess it from the picnic tables cooled by a fleet of overhead helicopter fans, but this unassuming, tile-floored cafe serves some of Kuching's best Sarawak laksa.

Jubilee Restaurant INDIAN $
(49 Jln India; mains RM5-11; 6.30am-5.30pm) A fixture in the heart of Kuching's Indian

Muslim district since 1974. Halal specialities include *nasi biryani* (rice with chicken, beef or lamb; RM9 to RM11) and *roti canai* (flatbread with egg and/or cheese; RM1 to RM2.50). The cook hails from Madras.

Green Hill Corner MALAYSIAN $
(cnr Jln Temple & Jln Green Hill; meals RM3-6; ⏲7am-10.30pm Mon-Sat, 7am-noon Sun) Look behind the green, Milo-sponsored awnings for the half-a-dozen stalls that crank out porridge, laksa, chicken rice and noodle dishes. Popular with locals.

★**Dyak** DAYAK $$
(☎082-234068; Jln Mendu & Jln Simpang Tiga; mains RM25-35; ⏲noon-11pm, last order 8.30pm; ✎) This elegant restaurant is the first to treat Dayak home cooking as true cuisine. The chef, classically trained in a Western style, uses traditional recipes, many of them Iban (a few are Kelabit, Kayan or Bidayuh), and fresh, organic jungle produce to create mouth-watering dishes unlike anything you've ever tasted. Situated 2km southeast of Old Chinatown.

The dining room is packed with unusual indigenous artefacts and the menu urges diners to have a walk around to view them. Vegetarian dishes, made without lard, are available upon request; staff are happy to explain the origin of each dish. A meal at the Dyak (the restaurant uses the colonial-era spelling of the word) is not to be missed.

★**Top Spot Food Court** SEAFOOD $$
(Jln Padungan; fish per kg RM30-70, vegetable dishes RM8-12; ⏲noon-11pm) A perennial favourite among local foodies, this neon-lit courtyard and its half-a-dozen humming seafooderies sits, rather improbably, on the roof of a concrete parking garage – look for the giant backlit lobster sign. Grilled white pomfret is a particular delicacy. Ling Loong Seafood and the Bukit Mata Seafood Centre are especially good.

★**Tribal Stove** DAYAK $$
(☎082-234873; 10 Jln Borneo; mains RM15-20; ⏲11.30am-10.30pm Mon-Sat; 📶✎) This laid-back restaurant serving delicious Kelabit food has somehow managed to capture something of the atmosphere of Bario, the Highland 'capital', and transport it to downtown Kuching. Specialities include *labo senutuq* (shredded beef cooked with wild ginger and dried chilli), *ab'eng* (shredded river fish) and pineapple curry. Popular dishes sometimes sell out by early evening. Food is prepared without MSG.

Junk ITALIAN $$
(☎082-259450; 80 Jln Wayang; mains RM28-68; ⏲6-10.45pm, bar to 2am, closed Tue; 📶) Filled to the brim with antiques, this complex of dining rooms (three) and bars (two) – housed in three 1920s shophouses – is a fashionable spot to see and be seen. Luckily, it's not a case of style over substance: the food here is very good. Pasta and other mains cost RM32 to RM68, pizzas are RM28 to RM48. Portions are generous.

21 Bistro FUSION $$
(64 Jln Padungan; mains RM10-48; ⏲4pm-2am or later Mon-Sat, food to 11pm) This self-consciously classy restaurant-cum-bar serves decent Western, Asian and fusion dishes such as pasta, grilled meats and fish (snapper is a speciality). Even the performance of the live band fails to inject much joy into the uptight crowd.

James Brooke Bistro & Cafe WESTERN $$
(☎082-412120; Waterfront Promenade opposite Jln Temple; mains RM10-39; ⏲10.30am-10.30pm,

KEK LAPIS – COLOURFUL LAYER CAKES

The people of Kuching – from all communities – love to add a dash of colour to festivities, so it comes as no surprise to see stalls selling *kek lapis* (striped layer cakes) sprouting up around town (especially along Main Bazaar and the Waterfront Promenade) during festivals, including Hari Raya.

Kek lapis is made with wheat flour, egg, prodigious quantities of either butter or margarine, and flavourings such as melon, blueberry or – a local favourite – *pandan* leaves. Since *kek lapis* are prepared one layer at a time and each layer – there can be 30 or more – takes five or six minutes to bake, a single cake can take up to five hours from start to finish.

Over 40 flavours of *kek lapis* are available year-round – to satisfy demand from Peninsular Malaysians – at **Maria Kek Lapis** (☎012-886 3337; 4 Jln Bishopgate; with butter RM15, with margarine RM20; ⏲8am-5pm). Free tastes are on offer. Cakes stay fresh for one or two weeks at room temperature and up to a month in the fridge.

LAKSA LUCK

Borneo's luckiest visitors start the day with a breakfast of Sarawak laksa, a tangy noodle soup made with coconut milk, lemongrass, sour tamarind and fiery *sambal belacan* (shrimp-paste sauce), with fresh calamansi lime juice squeezed on top. Unbelievably *lazat* ('delicious' in Bahasa Malaysia).

for drinks only to midnight) Gets consistently good reviews both for the cuisine and the lovely river views. Local dishes such as Sarawak laksa (RM12) and its own invention, uniquely flavoursome wild Borneo laksa (RM12), are quite reasonably priced. The beef stroganoff (RM25) has a following.

Jambu MEDITERRANEAN **$$**
(☎ 082-235292; www.jamburestaurant.com; 32 Jln Crookshank; mains RM28-55; ⏰ 5.30-10.30pm Tue-Thu & Sun, to 11.30pm Fri & Sat) Once the venue for elegant colonial parties (check out the photos on the way to the bar), this 1920s mansion, with teak floors and soaring ceilings, serves Mediterranean food and tapas. The terrace – with coloured lanterns and a pool table – is a romantic setting. The bar stays open until the last customer leaves. Situated 1.5km south of the centre.

Magna Carta ITALIAN **$$**
(Courthouse, Jln Tun Abang Haji Openg; mains RM10-28; ⏰ 10.30am-11pm Tue-Sun) For great Brooke-era atmosphere, you can choose between the breezy verandah with garden views, and the interior, whose decor is a mash-up of medieval England and 19th-century Straits Chinese. Good options include pasta, pizza with exquisitely thin crust (RM18), homemade bread and freshly squeezed orange juice.

Lyn's Thandoori Restaurant INDIAN **$$**
(☎ 019-889 7471; Lot 267, Jln Song Thian Cheok; mains RM16-34; ⏰ 10am-10pm Mon-Sat, 6-10pm Sun; 📶 ✍) This North Indian place, a Kuching fixture since 1994, sports a huge menu featuring tandoori chicken (of course) as well as delicious mutton, fish and veggie options (almost 50 of them, including 22 types of paneer cheese), all made with top-quality ingredients.

★ Bla Bla Bla FUSION **$$$**
(☎ 082-233944; 27 Jln Tabuan; mains RM22-90; ⏰ 6-11.30pm, closed Tue) Innovative and stylish, Bla Bla Bla serves excellent Chinese-inspired fusion dishes that – like the decor, the koi ponds and the Balinese Buddha – range from traditional to far-out. Specialities include *midin* (jungle fern) salad, mango duck (delicious), ostrich and deer, and pandan chicken. The generous portions are designed to be shared.

Zinc MEDITERRANEAN **$$$**
(☎ 082-243304; 38 Jln Tabuan; mains RM50-140; ⏰ 6-10.45pm) Well-to-do Kuchingites celebrated the recent opening of Zinc and its selection of European foods: Spanish Iberico ham, French cheeses and high-end wines that aren't available anywhere else in Borneo. Naturally, the finest imported ingredients don't come cheap, but you don't come to Zinc unless you're prepared to splurge. Often has live music; on Thursdays there's a jazz band.

Self-Catering

Ting & Ting SUPERMARKET **$**
(30A Jln Tabuan; ⏰ 9am-9pm, closed Sun & holidays) A good selection of wine, snack food, chocolate, toiletries and nappies.

Everrise Supermarket SUPERMARKET **$**
(Jln Tunku Abdul Rahman; ⏰ 9.30am-9.30pm) On the lower floor of the Sarawak Plaza shopping mall.

🍷 Drinking & Nightlife

Bars can be found along Jln Carpenter and Jln Tabuan.

Ruai BAR
(7F Jln Ban Hock; ⏰ 6pm-2.30am) This Iban-owned bar has a laid-back, welcoming spirit all its own. Decorated with old photos and Orang Ulu art (and, inexplicably, several Mexican sombreros), it serves as an urban *ruai* (the covered verandah of an Iban longhouse) for aficionados of caving, hiking and running. Has a good selection of *tuak* (local rice wine). Starts to pick up after about 9pm.

Barber BAR
(☎ 016-658 1052; Jln Wayang; ⏰ 5-11pm, to 1.30am Fri & Sat, closed Tue) The designers of this successfully repurposed barber's salon made use of the original tiled floor, mirrors and even old hairdryers to create a suitably hip hangout for Kuching's in-crowd. Serves a menu of burgers and American-diner-style food (mains RM16 to RM24) and a good selection of desserts (RM16). Beers are three for RM45 on Sunday, Monday and Wednesday.

Monkee Bar BAR

(www.monkeebars.com; Jln Song Thian Cheok; beer RM6.50-12, spirit & mixer RM13; ⏲ 3pm-2am) At Monkee Bar, 50% of profits go to the Orangutan Project, a wildlife conservation NGO that works at Matang Wildlife Centre (p422). If the idea of 'drinking for conservation' doesn't entice you, the prices might: Monkee Bar has some of the cheapest drinks in town. It's a smokey joint with a young local crowd interspersed with volunteers enjoying downtime from cage-cleaning.

Drunken Monkey BAR

(☎082-242048; 68 Jln Carpenter; ⏲ 2pm-2am) Despite its youthful name, this bar attracts a mature crowd of locals and tourists. The drinks list includes draught Guinness (RM19 per pint), a range of imported wines and a whole page of whiskys. There's a choice of outdoor seating in a fan-cooled alleyway or air-conditioned indoor tables. Happy hour prices, available until 8pm, offer meagre discounts.

Black Bean Coffee & Tea Company CAFE

(Jln Carpenter; drinks RM3-4.80; ⏲ 9am-6pm Mon-Sat; wi-fi) The aroma of freshly ground coffee assaults the senses at this tiny shop, believed by many to purvey Kuching's finest brews. Specialities, roasted daily, include Arabica, Liberica and Robusta coffees grown in Java, Sumatra and, of course, Sarawak. Also serves oolong and green teas from Taiwan. Has just three tables. Decaf not available.

Lamin BAR

(Persiaran Ban Hock; ⏲ 2-10pm Mon-Thu, noon-11pm Fri & Sat) This rustic, longhouse-style bar also serves a delicious range of homemade alcohol ice creams, including *tuak* and raisin, red wine and mango and Guinness stout (RM13).

Shopping

If it's traditional Borneo arts and crafts you're after, then you've come to the right place – Kuching is the best shopping spot on the island for collectors and cultural enthusiasts. Don't expect many bargains, but don't be afraid to negotiate either – there's plenty to choose from, and the quality varies as much as the price. Dubiously 'aged' items are common, so be sure to spend some time browsing to familiarise yourself with prices and range.

Most of Kuching's shops are closed on Sunday.

Juliana Native Handwork HANDICRAFTS

(☎082-230144; ground fl, Sarawak Textile Museum, Jln Tun Abang Haji Openg; ⏲ 9am-4.30pm) As well as her own Bidayuh beadwork pieces – most of which have been displayed in an exhibition in Singapore – Juliana sells quality rattan mats made by Penan artists (RM490) and *pua kumba* Iban woven cloths. The intricate, 50cm-long beaded table runners she sells (RM680) take her three months to complete.

Main Bazaar HANDICRAFTS

(Main Bazaar; ⏲ some shops closed Sun) The row of old shophouses facing the Waterfront Promenade is chock-full of handicrafts shops, some outfitted like art galleries, others with more of a 'garage sale' appeal, and yet others (especially along the Main Bazaar's western section) stocking little more than kitschy-cute cat souvenirs.

Handmade items worth seeing (if not purchasing) – many from the highlands of Kalimantan – include hand-woven textiles and baskets, masks, drums, brass gongs, statues (up to 2m high), beaded headdresses, swords, spears, painted shields and cannons from Brunei. At many places, staff enjoy explaining the origin and use of each item.

UD Siburan Jaya FOOD

(66 Main Bazaar; ⏲ 8.30am-9pm Mon-Sat, 9.30am-5pm Sun) Has an excellent selection of Sarawakian specialities such as pepper (black and white), laksa paste, sambal, Bario rice and even *tuak* (rice wine).

Fabriko CLOTHING

(56 Main Bazaar; ⏲ 9am-5pm Mon-Sat) This fine little boutique has a well-chosen selection of made-in-Sarawak fabrics and clothing in both traditional and modern Orang Ulu-inspired designs, including silk sarongs and men's batik shirts.

Nelson's Gallery ART

(54 Main Bazaar; ⏲ 9am-5pm) Upstairs, artist Narong Daun patiently creates vibrant jungle-themed batik paintings on silk.

Sarawak Craft Council HANDICRAFTS

(sarawakhandicraft.com.my; Old Courthouse, Jln Tun Abang Haji Openg; ⏲ 8.30am-4.30pm Mon-Fri) Run by a non-profit government agency, this shop has a pretty good selection of Malay, Bidayuh, Iban and Orang Ulu handicrafts – check out the cowboy hats made entirely of bark and the conical *terendak* (Melanau hats).

Tanoti HANDICRAFTS

(☎082-239277; www.tanoticrafts.com; Tanoti House, 56 Jln Tabuan; ⏲ 8am-5.30pm, closed public holidays) The group of women at Tanoti are the only people to practise a distinct Sarawakian form of songket weaving, a way of creating embroidered fabrics. Visitors are welcome to visit the workshop and see the weaving, but call first to arrange. There are a small number of pieces for sale in the gallery shop.

The women work to commission, weaving pieces such as *sampin* (a traditional male sarong) and decorative pieces – each one costs about RM10,000 to RM15,000.

Popular Book Co BOOKS
(Level 3, Tun Jugah Shopping Centre, 18 Jln Tunku Abdul Rahman; ⌚10am-9.30pm) A capacious, modern bookshop with a big selection of English titles, including works by local authors and travel guides.

Mohamed Yahia & Sons BOOKS
(☎082-416928; basement, Sarawak Plaza, Jln Tunku Abdul Rahman; ⌚10am-9pm) Specialises in English-language books on Borneo, including the four-volume *Encyclopaedia of Iban Studies*. Also carries Sarawak maps and travel guides.

ℹ Information

Kuching has Indonesian and Bruneian consulates and honorary consuls representing Australia and the UK.

DANGERS & ANNOYANCES

There are occasional incidents of bag snatching by motorbike-mounted thieves. Exercise reasonable caution when walking along deserted stretches of road (eg Jln Reservoir and Jln Tabuan), especially after dark.

In August and September Kuching and the surrounding areas suffer from periods of poor air quality, known as 'the haze'. What looks like a dense fog is actually smoke particles from forest fires, primarily in Indonesia. These are officially attributed to the traditional farming technique of slash and burn but are suspected by some to be caused by the clearing of forests for palm-oil plantations.

In 2015, the air-pollution index in Kuching reached levels deemed 'unhealthy'. Such levels can pose a risk to asthma sufferers, and provoke minor symptoms (stinging eyes, sore throat) in others.

Aside from health concerns, when the haze is bad it affects visibility in such a way as to make sight-seeing and national-park visits feel frustrating, even pointless; attractions do, however, stay open as normal. The haze usually clears after a few days, depending on weather conditions.

EMERGENCY

Police, Ambulance & Fire (☎999)

LAUNDRY

Most hotels have pricey laundry services with per-piece rates, but some guesthouses let you do your washing for just RM5 to RM10 per load, including drying.

My Express Laundry Service (Jln Wayang; 10kg cold/warm/hot RM5/6/7, dryer per 25min RM5; ⌚24hr) A convenient, self-service laundry.

MEDICAL SERVICES

Kuching has some first-rate but affordable medical facilities, so it's no surprise that 'medical tourism', especially from Indonesia, is on the rise. For minor ailments, guesthouses and hotels can refer you to a general practitioner, who may be willing to make a house call.

Klinik Chan (☎082-240307; 98 Main Bazaar; ⌚8am-noon & 2-5pm Mon-Fri, 9am-noon Sat, Sun & holidays) Conveniently central. A consultation for a minor ailment costs from RM35.

Normah Medical Specialist Centre (☎082-440055, emergency 082-311999; www.normah.com.my; 937 Jln Tun Abdul Rahman, Petra Jaya; ⌚emergency 24hr, clinics 8.30am-4.30pm Mon-Fri, to 1pm Sat) Widely considered to be Kuching's best private hospital. Has a 24-hour ambulance. Situated north of the river, about 6km by road from the centre. Served by the bus 1 from Saujana Bus Station (p413), departures on the hour from 7am to 5pm.

Sarawak General Hospital (Hospital Umum Sarawak; ☎082-276666; http://hus.moh.gov.my/v3; Jln Hospital; ⌚24hr) Kuching's large public hospital has modern facilities and remarkably reasonable rates but is often overcrowded. Situated about 2km south of the centre along Jln Tun Abang Haji Openg. To get there, take bus K6, K8 or K18.

Timberland Medical Centre (☎082-234466, emergency 082-234991; www.timberlandmedical.com; Jln Rock, Mile 2½; ⌚emergency 24hr) A private hospital with highly qualified staff. Has a 24-hour ambulance. Situated 5km south of the centre along Jln Tun Abang Haji Openg and then Jln Rock.

MONEY

The majority of Kuching's banks and ATMs are on Jln Tunku Abdul Rahman. If you need to change cash or traveller's cheques, moneychangers are a better bet than banks, which often aren't keen on handling cash or US$100 bills.

Maybank (Jln Tunku Abdul Rahman; ⌚9.15am-4.30pm Mon-Thu, to 4pm Fri) Has an ATM. Situated on the corner near KFC.

Mohamed Yahia & Sons (basement, Sarawak Plaza, Jln Tunku Abdul Rahman; ⌚10am-9pm) No commission, good rates and accepts over 30 currencies (including US$100 bills), as well as traveller's cheques in US dollars, euros,

Australian dollars and pounds sterling. Situated inside the bookshop.

Standard Chartered Bank (Jln Padungan; ⌚9.15am-3.45pm Mon-Fri) Has a 24-hour ATM.

United Overseas Bank (2 Main Bazaar; ⌚9.30am-4.30pm Mon-Fri) Has a 24-hour ATM around the corner on Jln Tun Abang Haji Obeng.

POLICE

Central Police Station (Balai Polis Sentral; ☎082-244444; 2 Jln Khoo Hun Yeang; ⌚24hr) In a blue-and-white building constructed in 1931.

Tourist Police (☎082-250522; Waterfront Promenade; ⌚8am-midnight) Most of the officers speak English. The pavilion is across the street from 96 Main Bazaar.

POST

Main Post Office (Jln Tun Abang Haji Openg; ⌚8am-4.30pm Mon-Fri, 8am-noon Sat) An impressive colonnaded structure built in 1931.

TOURIST INFORMATION

National Park Booking Office (☎082-248088; www.sarawakforestry.com; Jln Tun Abang Haji Openg, Sarawak Tourism Complex; ⌚8am-5pm Mon-Fri, closed public holidays) Sells brochures on each of Sarawak's national parks and can supply the latest newsflash on Rafflesia sightings. Telephone enquiries are not only welcomed but patiently answered. Bookings for accommodation at Bako, Gunung Gading and Kubah National Parks and the Matang Wildlife Centre can be made in person, by phone or via http://ebooking.com.my.

Visa Department (Bahagian Visa; ☎082-245661; www.imi.gov.my; 2nd fl, Bangunan Sultan Iskandar, Kompleks Pejabat Persekutuan, cnr Jln Tun Razak & Jln Simpang Tiga; ⌚8am-5pm Mon-Thu, 8-11.45am & 2.15-5pm Fri) Situated in a 17-storey federal office building about 3km south of the centre (along Jln Tabuan). Served by City Public Link buses K8 or K11, which run every half-hour or so. A taxi from the centre costs RM15.

Visitors Information Centre (☎082-410942, 082-410944; www.sarawaktourism.com; UTC Sarawak, Jln Padungan; ⌚8am-5pm Mon-Fri, closed public holidays) Usually located in the atmospheric old courthouse complex, at research time the Visitors Information Centre was about to move to a temporary new home in the UTC building on Jln Padungan while the Old Court House buildings were redeveloped.

The office has helpful and well-informed staff, lots of brochures and oodles of practical information (eg bus schedules).

Getting There & Away

As more and more Sarawakians have acquired their own wheels, public bus networks – especially short-haul routes in the Kuching area – have withered. For complicated political reasons, some services have been 'replaced' by unregulated and chaotic minibuses, which have irregular times, lack fixed stops and are basically useless for tourists.

The only way to get to many nature sites in Western Sarawak is to hire a taxi or join a tour. The exceptions are Bako National Park, Semenggoh Nature Reserve, Kubah National Park, Matang Wildlife Centre and, somewhat less conveniently, the Wind Cave and the Fairy Cave.

AIR

Kuching International Airport (www.kuchingairportonline.com), 11km south of the city centre, has direct air links with Singapore, Johor Bahru (the Malaysian city across the causeway from Singapore), Kuala Lumpur (KL), Penang, Kota Kinabalu (KK), Bandar Seri Begawan (BSB) and Pontianak.

MASwings, a subsidiary of Malaysia Airlines, is Malaysian Borneo's very own domestic airline. Flights link its hubs in Miri and Kuching with 14 destinations around Sarawak, including the lowland cities of Sibu, Bintulu, Limbang and Lawas and the upland destinations of Gunung Mulu National Park, Bario and Ba Kelalan.

The airport has three departure halls: 'Domestic Departures' for flights within Sarawak; 'Domestic Departures (Outside Sarawak)' for travel to other parts of Malaysia; and 'International Departures'.

Inside the terminal, there's a **Tourist Information Centre** (arrival level; ⌚8am-5pm Mon-Fri) next to the luggage carousels and customs.

GETTING TO INDONESIA: KUCHING TO PONTIANAK

Getting to the border A number of bus companies ply the route between Kuching Sentral bus terminal (and other cities along the Sarawak coast) and the West Kalimantan city of Pontianak (economy RM60, 1st class RM80, seven/10 hours via the new/old road), passing through the Tebedu-Entikong crossing 80km south of Kuching.

At the border Travellers from 64 countries can get a one-month Indonesian visa on arrival at the road crossing between Tededu (Malaysia) and Entikong (Indonesia), the only official land border between Sarawak and Kalimantan.

Moving on Pontianak is linked to other parts of Indonesia and to Singapore by airlines such as Batavia Air (www.batavia-air.com).

Foreign currency can be exchanged at the **CIMB Bank counter** (arrival level; ⌚7.30am-7.30pm), but rates are poor. Among the ATMs is one in front of McDonald's. For ticketing issues, drop by the **Malaysian Airlines & MASwings office** (departure level; ⌚5am-8pm).

BOAT

Ekspress Bahagia (☎016-889 3013, 016-800 5891, in Kuching 082-412 246, in Sibu 084-319228) runs a daily express ferry from Kuching's Express Wharf, 6km east of the centre, to Sibu. Departures are at 8.30am from Kuching and at 11.30am from Sibu (RM45, five hours). It's a good idea to book a day ahead. A taxi from town to the wharf costs RM35.

BUS

Every half-hour or so from about 6am to 6.30pm, various buses run by City Public Link (eg K9) and STC (eg 3A, 4B, 6 and 2) link central Kuching's Saujana Bus Station (p413) with the Regional Express Bus Terminal. Saujana's ticket windows can point you to the next departure. A taxi from the centre costs RM28 to RM30.

Kuching Sentral

This massive **bus terminal-slash-shopping mall** (cnr Jln Penrissen & Jln Airport) handles most of Kuching's medium-haul routes and all of its long-haul ones. Situated about 10km south of the centre, it's also known as Six-and-a-Half-Mile Bus Station. Amenities include electronic departure boards and cafes offering wi-fi. Book your ticket at a company counter, then pay at counter 2 or 3 (marked 'Cashier/Boarding Pass'). Before boarding, show your tickets to the staff at the check-in desk.

To Central Sarawak

From 6.30am to 10.30pm, a dozen different companies send buses at least hourly along Sarawak's northern coast to Miri (RM80, 14½ hours), with stops at Sibu (RM50, 7½ hours), Bintulu (RM70, 11½ hours), Batu Niah Junction (jumping-off point for Niah National Park) and Lambir Hills National Park. Bus Asia, for instance, has nine departures a day, the first at 7.30am, the last at 10pm; unlike its competitors, the company has a **city centre office** (☎082-411111; cnr Jln Abell & Jln Chan Chin Ann; ⌚6am-10pm) and, from Monday to Saturday, runs shuttle buses out to Kuching Sentral. Luxurious 'VIP buses', eg those run by **Asia Star** (☎082-456999), have just three seats across (28 in total), and some come with on-board toilets, and yet cost a mere RM10 to RM20 more than regular coaches. To get to Brunei, Limbang or Sabah, you have to change buses in Miri.

To Western Sarawak

Buses run to the Semenggoh Wildlife Centre, Bako National Park, Kubah National Park and the Matang Wildlife Sanctuary, all of which stop in town at or near Saujana Bus Station, and to Lundu (including the Wind Cave and Fairy Cave), whose buses use Kuching Sentral.

TAXI

For some destinations, the only transport option – other than taking a tour – is chartering a taxi through your hotel or guesthouse or via a company such as **Kuching City Radio Taxi** (p413). Hiring a red-and-yellow cab for an eight-hour day should cost about RM300 to RM350, with the price depending in part on distance; unofficial taxis may charge less. If you'd like your driver to wait at your destination and then take you back to town, count on paying about RM20 per hour of wait time.

Sample one-way taxi fares from Kuching (prices are 50% higher at night):

DESTINATION	PRICE
Annah Rais Longhouse	from RM90
Bako Bazaar (Bako National Park)	RM55
Express Wharf (ferry to Sibu)	RM35
Fairy Cave	RM70-80 (incl Wind Cave and 3hr wait RM150-200)
Kubah National Park	RM60
Matang Wildlife Centre	RM60
Santubong Peninsula Resorts	RM60
Sarawak Cultural Village	RM60
Semenggoh Nature Reserve	RM60-70 (round-trip incl 1hr wait RM120)
Wind Cave	RM40

ℹ Getting Around

Almost all of Kuching's attractions are within easy walking distance of each other, so taxis or buses are only really needed to reach the airport, Kuching Sentral (the long-haul bus terminal), the Express Wharf for the ferry to Sibu and the Cat Museum.

TO/FROM THE AIRPORT

The price of a red-and-yellow taxi into Kuching is fixed at RM30, including luggage; a larger *teksi eksekutiv* (executive taxi), painted blue, costs RM35. Coupons are sold inside the terminal next to the car-rental counters.

BOAT

Bow-steered wooden boats known as *tambang*, powered by an outboard motor, shuttle passengers back and forth across Sungai Sarawak, linking jetties along the Waterfront Promenade with destinations such as Kampung Boyan (for Fort Margherita) and the Astana. The fare for Sarawak's cheapest cruise is 50 sen (more from 10pm to 6am); pay as you disembark. If a *tambang* isn't tied up when you arrive at a dock, just wait and one will usually materialise fairly soon.

BUS

Saujana Bus Station (Jln Masjid & Jln P Ramlee) handles local and short-haul routes. Situated in the city centre on the dead-end street that links Jln Market with the Kuching Mosque. Three companies use the Saujana Bus Station:

City Public Link (☎082-239178) Has a proper ticket counter with posted schedules. Line numbers start with K. Urban services run from 6.30am or 7am to about 5.30pm. Buses K3 and K10 go to Kuching Sentral (the long-distance bus station) several times an hour.

Sarawak Transport Company (STC; ☎082-233579) The ticket window is in an old shipping container. Buses 2 and 3A go to Kuching Sentral about three times an hour. Bus 2 to Kuching's Sarawak General Hospital and Bau is run in conjunction with **Bau Transport Company**.

BICYCLE

On Jln Carpenter, basic bicycle shops can be found at Nos 83, 88 and 96. **Borneo Experiences** (p403) can rent out bicycles for RM50 per day.

CAR

Not many tourists rent cars in Sarawak. The reasons: road signage is not great; even the best road maps are a useless 1:900,000 scale; and picking up a vehicle in one city and dropping it off in another incurs hefty fees. That said, having your own car can be unbelievably convenient.

Before driving off, make sure the car you've been assigned is in good shape mechanically and has all the requisite safety equipment (eg seatbelts); some companies rent out vehicles that have seen better days.

Half-a-dozen car-rental agencies have desks in the arrivals hall of Kuching airport.

Ami Car Rental (☎082-427221, 082-579679; www.amicarrental.com)

Golden System (☎016-888 3359; www.gocar.com.my) We've received good reports on this outfit.

Hertz (☎082-450740; www.hertz.com) Backed by an international reputation.

Hornbill Tours & Car Rental (☎082-457948; hornbill.car.rental@gmail.com; counter 4, Kuching Airport arrivals hall) Rates start at RM80 per day.

MOTORCYCLE

Renting a motorcycle can be a great way to visit Kuching-area sights – provided you know how to ride, your rain gear is up to scratch and you manage to find your way despite the poor signage.

An Hui Motor (☎016-886 3328, 082-240508; 29 Jln Tabuan; ⏲8am-6pm Mon-Sat, 8am-10.30am Sun) A motorcycle repair shop that charges RM40 per day for a Vespa-like Suzuki RG (110cc) or RGV (120cc) and RM40 for a 125cc scooter (including helmet), plus a deposit of RM100. Insurance covers the bike but not the driver and may be valid only within an 80km radius of Kuching, so check before you head to Sematan, Lundu or Annah Rais.

TAXI

Kuching now has two kinds of taxis: the traditional red-and-yellow kind; and the larger, more comfortable – and pricier – executive taxis (*teksi eksekutiv*), which are painted blue.

Taxis can be hailed on the street, found at taxi ranks (of which the city centre has quite a few, eg at larger hotels) or ordered by phone 24 hours a day from the following:

ABC Radio Call Service (☎016-861 1611, 082-611611)

Kuching City Radio Taxi (☎082-348898, 082-480000)

T&T Radio Call Taxi (☎082-343343, 016-888 2255)

All Kuching taxis – except those on the flat-fare run to/from the airport (RM30) – are required to use meters; overcharging is not common, so taking a taxi is rarely an unpleasant experience. Flagfall is RM10; after the first 3km (or, in traffic, nine minutes of stop-and-go) the price is RM1.20 per km or for each three minutes. There's a RM2 charge to summon a cab by phone. Fares go up by 50% from midnight to 6am.

One-way taxi fares from central Kuching:

- Cat Museum (North Kuching): RM30
- Indonesian consulate: RM25 to RM30
- Kuching Sentral (long-distance bus terminal): RM30
- Visa Department: RM15

WESTERN SARAWAK

Western Sarawak offers a dazzling array of natural sights and indigenous cultures including a number of accessible longhouses, sandy beaches, rainforests and a chance to see their inhabitants – including proboscis monkeys and orangutans – up close.

Bako National Park

Occupying a jagged peninsula jutting into the South China Sea, Sarawak's oldest **national park** (☎Bako terminal 082-370434;

Around Kuching

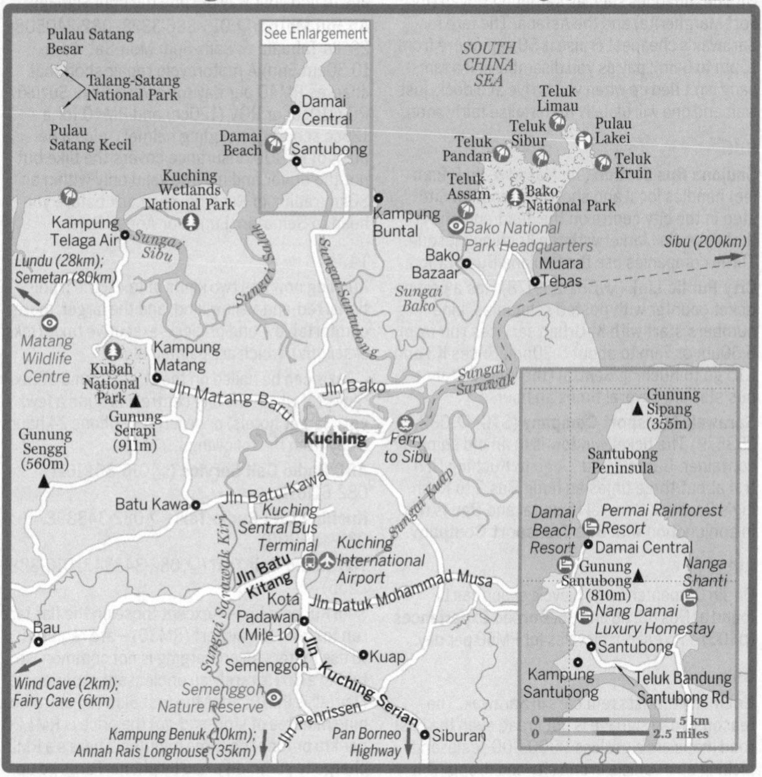

www.sarawakforestry.com; RM20; ⌚park office 8am-5pm) is just 37km northeast of downtown Kuching but feels like worlds away. It's one of the best places in Sarawak to see rainforest animals in their native habitats.

The coast of the 27-sq-km peninsula consists of lovely pocket beaches tucked into secret bays interspersed with wind-sculpted cliffs, forested bluffs and stretches of brilliant mangrove swamp. The interior of the park is home to streams, waterfalls and a range of distinct ecosystems, including classic lowland rainforest (mixed dipterocarp forest) and *kerangas* (heath forest). Hiking trails cross the sandstone plateau that forms the peninsula's backbone and connect with some of the main beaches, all of which can be reached by boat from park HQ.

Bako is notable for its incredible biodiversity, which includes almost every vegetation type in Borneo and encompasses everything from terrestrial orchids and pitcher plants to long-tailed macaques and bearded pigs. The stars of the show are the proboscis monkeys – this is one of the best places in Borneo to observe these endemics up close.

Bako is an easy day trip from Kuching, but it would be a shame to rush it – we recommend staying a night or two to really enjoy the wild beauty of the place. Getting to Bako by public transport is easy.

Sights & Activities

Interpretation Centre MUSEUM
(Bako National Park HQ; ⌚7.30am-5pm) Offers an old-fashioned introduction to the park's seven distinct ecosystems and an exposé of the co-dependent relationship between nepenthes (pitcher plants) and ants.

Wildlife Watching

Scientists estimate that Bako is home to 37 species of mammal, including silver-leaf monkeys, palm squirrels and nocturnal creatures such as the mouse deer, civet and colugo (flying lemur); 24 reptile species, among them the common water monitor, which can reach a length of over 1m; and about 190 kinds of bird, some of them migratory.

Jungle creatures are easiest to spot shortly after sunrise and right before sunset, so for the best wildlife-watching you'll have to stay over. Surprisingly, the area around park HQ is a particularly good place to see animals, including reddish-brown proboscis monkeys, whose pot-bellied stomachs are filled with bacteria that help them derive nutrients from almost-indigestible vegetation. You often hear them as they crash through the branches long before seeing a flash of fur – or a male's pendulous nose flopping as he munches on tender young leaves.

Proboscis monkeys, who show little fear of, or interest in, humans, can often be found on branches above the park's visitors cabins, around the mangrove boardwalk between the jetty and park HQ, in the trees along the Teluk Assam beach near park HQ, along the Teluk Paku Trail, where they forage in the trees lining the cliff, and along the Teluk Delima Trail.

The muddy floors of mangrove forests are home to an assortment of peculiar creatures, including hermit crabs, fiddler crabs and mudskippers (fish that spend much of their time skipping around atop the tidal mud under mangrove trees).

The Bornean bearded pigs, striking-looking creatures that hang around near the cafeteria and cabins with their piglets, are easy to spot.

Jungle Walks

Bako's 17 trails are suitable for all levels of fitness and motivation, with routes ranging from short strolls to strenuous all-day treks to the far end of the peninsula. It's easy to find your way around because trails are colour-coded and clearly marked with stripes of paint. Plan your route before starting out and aim to be back at park HQ before dark (by 6pm at the latest). It's possible to hire a boat to one of the far beaches and then hike back, or to hike to one of the beaches and arrange for a boat to meet you there.

Park staff are happy to help you plan your visit, provide updates on trail conditions and tides, help with boat hire and supply you with a B&W map that has details on each of the park's hiking options. A billboard near the Education Centre lists conservative time estimates for each trail. Even if you know your route, let staff know where you'll be going and make a note in the Guest Movement Register Book; sign back in when you return.

Take adequate water, a sun hat and sunscreen, as the *kerangas* (distinctive vegetation zone of Borneo) has precious little shade for long stretches. Sun-sensitive folks might consider lightweight long-sleeved shirts and trousers. Insect repellent is also a good idea.

Lintang Trail HIKING

If you have only one day in Bako, try to get an early start and take the Lintang Trail (5.8km, 3½ to four hours round-trip). It traverses a range of vegetation and climbs the sandstone escarpment up to the *kerangas*, where you'll find some grand views and many pitcher plants (especially along the trail's northeastern segment).

Teluk Pandan Kecil Trail HIKING

One of the most popular trails is the 2.6km path to **Teluk Pandan Kecil**, a gorgeous sandy beach surrounded by spectacular sandstone formations. The trail climbs

CHEEKY MACAQUES

That sign at Bako National Park's campground – 'Naughty monkeys around – watch out!' – is not a joke. The long-tailed macaques that hang about the park HQ are great to watch, but they are mischievous and cunning. Thanks to tourists who insist on offering them food (please don't!), they can become aggressive if they suspect you to be carrying anything edible, making running leaps at anything they think they can carry off. Keep the doors and windows of your room closed, zip your bags and do not leave valuables, food or drink – or anything in a plastic bag (known by macaques as the preferred human repositories for edibles) – unattended, especially on the beaches or on the cabin verandahs.

It's wise to leave the monkeys in peace – the males can be aggressive, and once you've seen a macaque tear open a drink can with his teeth you'll be happy that you didn't mess with them. Rangers advise against looking macaques in the eye (they'll think you're about to attack) or screaming (if they knows you're scared, they'll be more aggressive). Monkeys are not a problem after dark.

through the forest before emerging onto an open plateau covered in scrub. Pitcher plants can be seen on the trail down to the beach. On the way to Teluk Pandan Kecil, it's possible to do a 30-minute detour to a viewpoint overlooking **Teluk Pandan Besar**, an attractive stretch of sand accessible only by boat.

Around the point (to the northwest) of Teluk Pandan Kecil is the famous Bako Sea Stack, an islet that looks like a cobra rearing its head. To get close enough for a photo, though, you'll have to hire a boat (from HQ, RM35 one way or RM70 return for a boat for of up to five people).

Teluk Tajor Trail HIKING

A 3.5km trail leads across scrub, past Tajor waterfall (where you can have a dip) and on to Tajor beach, where it is possible to camp.

Boat Trips BOAT TOUR

(per boat for up to 5 people 1-way/return to Teluk Paku RM18/36, to Teluk Pandan Kecil RM35/70, to Teluk Tajor RM105/210) Catching a boat ride to or from one of the park's beaches is a good way to avoid retracing your steps on a hike. Arrangements can be made at the **Koperasi Warisan Pelancongan Bako Berhad** (Bako boat transfers; ☎011-2513 2711, 011-2509 5070; ⏰7.30am-4pm) counter at park HQ, although boatmen sometimes pass by the more popular beaches looking for tired hikers who might be tempted by a lift back.

Going out on the water is also the best way to view the unique sandstone sea stacks off Bako's coast, and the only way to get close enough to photograph them. Look out for sea snakes, sometimes visible in the water.

Night Walk WILDLIFE WATCHING

(per person RM10; ⏰8pm) The best way to see creatures that are out and about at night – we're talking spiders, fireflies, cicadas, frogs, anemones, owls and the like – is to take a night walk led by a park ranger trained in spotting creatures that city slickers would walk right by. These 1½- to two-hour night walks are not to be missed. Bring a torch.

Swimming

At Bako, it used to be popular to combine rainforest tramping, which quickly gets hot and sweaty, with a refreshing dip in the South China Sea. However, since a large saltwater crocodile was recently spotted on the sand, park staff no longer recommend it. Entering the water is not completely banned, but comes with an 'at your own risk' caveat. Staff recommend that you stay in shallow waters. Forget about taking a dip anywhere near the rivers, which are prime crocodile territory. To keep away the sandflies on the beach, use mozzie repellent.

Teluk Assam Beach BEACH

Some people risk entering the water at the beach near park HQ, but the water can be muddy. In the distance (to the west) you can see the wild east coast of the Santubong Peninsula.

Tours

Park HQ does not have enough permanent staff to accompany individual visitors, so if you'd like to hike with a **licensed guide** (☎Sabariman 019-469 2570; riman1978@gmail.com; Bako Bazaar; per group per hour/day RM35/120), enquire at the boat terminal at Bako Bazaar. The park is very strict about allowing only certified guides (unlicensed guides and the groups they're with are forced to leave).

Sleeping

Bako's accommodation is certainly not luxurious, but although basic its well-run and adequately equipped. There is a RM10 key deposit. Unlocked storage is available at park reception free of charge.

In-park accommodation often fills up, especially from May to September, so if you'd like to stay over book ahead. Some travel agencies reserve blocks of rooms that they release a week ahead if their packages remain unsold, and individual travellers also sometimes cancel, so week-before and last-minute vacancies are common.

Forest Lodge Type 5 CABIN $

(☎park booking office in Kuching 082-248088; ebooking.com.my; r RM100; ❄) 'Type 5' accommodation is in either two-room wooden lodges (three single beds in each) or a newer, concrete terraced block (four single beds in each). All rooms have attached bathrooms and air-con.

Forest Hostel HOSTEL $

(☎park booking office in Kuching 082-248088; ebooking.com.my; dm RM15, q RM40) Built of wood, the old hostel buildings are scuffed and dented but perfectly serviceable. Rooms have four single-storey beds lined up in a row, fridges and wall-mounted fans. Bring your own towel.

Forest Lodge Type 6 CABIN $

(☎park booking office in Kuching 082-248088; ebooking.com.my; d RM50, 2-room cabin RM75)

Each rustic, two-bed room has a wood-plank floor, a private bathroom, a fridge and a fan.

Camping CAMPGROUND $

(per person RM5) To avoid falling prey to raiding monkeys, tents can be set up at park HQ's fenced-in camping zone only after 6pm and must be taken down again early in the morning. You can also pitch your tent at Tajor, 3.5km from park HQ.

Eating

Cooking is not allowed in park accommodation. The nearest food shop is in Bako Bazaar.

Kerangas Café CAFETERIA $

(Canteen; meals RM8–10; ⏲7.30am-10.30pm) The cafeteria, designed to be macaque-proof, serves a varied and tasty selection of fried rice, chicken, fish, cakes, fresh fruit and packaged snacks. Buffet meals are available from 11.30am to 2pm and 6.30pm to 8pm.

Getting There & Away

Getting to the park by public transport is a cinch. First take one of the hourly buses from Kuching to Bako Bazaar, then hop on a motorboat to Teluk Assam jetty, about 400m along a wooden boardwalk from park HQ.

Kuching travel agencies charge about RM300 per person for a tour, including the boat ride.

BOAT

Boat transfers to Bako park HQ from Bako Terminal (at Bako Bazaar) are managed by Koperasi Warisan Pelancongan Bako Berhad, who have a counter at the terminal and at park HQ. The 20-minute journey from the terminal at Bako Bazaar to the park costs RM20 per person. From May to September, transfers are usually every hour from 8am to 4pm (ask at the counter for the day's schedule). The last boat back from Bako is at 4pm.

When the tide is low, boats may not be able to approach the jetty at Teluk Assam, so you may have to wade ashore. Boatmen may insist on an early afternoon return time to beat a late afternoon low tide – but bold outboard jockeys have been known to make the trip back to Bako Bazaar even at the lowest of tides.

From late November to February or March, the sea is often rough and scheduled boat trips may be less frequent.

BUS

Bus 1 (RM3.50) leaves from 6 Jln Khoo Hun Yeang in Kuching, across the street from the food stalls of the Open-Air Market. Departures from Kuching are every hour on the hour from 7am to 5pm, and from Bako Bazaar every hour on the half-hour from 6.30am to (usually) 5.30pm. If you miss the last bus, ask around the village for a minibus or private car (RM55) to Kuching.

In Kuching, bus 1 also picks up passengers at stops along the waterfront, on the river side of the street; motion to the driver to stop. These stops include bus shelters on Jln Gambier across the street from the Brooke Memorial; across the street from 15 Main Bazaar, next to the Chinese Museum; on Jln Tunku Abdul Rahman next to the 7-Eleven in the Riverside Suites; and on Jln Abell in front of Alliance Bank, a block northwest of the Lime Tree Hotel.

TAXI

A cab from Kuching to Bako Bazaar (45 minutes) costs RM55.

Santubong Peninsula

Like Bako National Park 8km to the east, the Santubong Peninsula (also known as Damai) is a 10km-long finger of land jutting out into the South China Sea. With some decent sandy strips, Santubong is the best place in Sarawak for a lazy, pampered beach holiday. The forested interior of the peninsula was declared a national park in 2007.

Sights & Activities

Sarawak Cultural Village MUSEUM

(SCV; ☎082-846411; www.scv.com.my; Damai Central; adult/child RM90/30; ⏲9am-4.45pm) This living museum is centred on seven traditional dwellings: three longhouses, a Penan hut, a Malay townhouse and a Chinese farmhouse. It may sound contrived but the SCV is held in high esteem by locals for its role in keeping their cultures and traditions alive.

Twice a day (at 11.30am and 4pm) a cultural show presents traditional music and dance. The lively Melanau entry involves whirling women and clacking bamboo poles, while the Orang Ulu dance includes balloons and a blowpipe hunter.

The dwellings are (supposed to be) staffed by members of the ethnic group they represent. Signage, however, is poor, so if you don't ask questions of the 'locals' – who demonstrate crafts – the subtle differences in architecture, cuisine, dress and music between the various groups may not be apparent. At the Penan hut you can try a blowpipe, while the Malay house offers top spinning.

It may be possible to book workshops in handicrafts (eg bead-making), music and dance – contact the SCV in advance. If you're planning to get married, you can choose to tie the knot here with a colourful Iban, Bidayuh, Orang Ulu or Malay ceremony.

Hotels and tour agencies in Kuching offer packages (per person RM 220), but it's easy enough to get out here by shuttle bus. The SCV is located at Damai junction.

Permai Rainforest Resort BEACH
(☎082-846490; www.permairainforest.com; Damai Beach; adult/child RM5/3; ⏲7am-7pm) The day rate at this bungalow complex is a real bargain. In addition to a safe, fine-sand beach with changing facilities, a variety of leisure and adventure activities are on offer, including a high-ropes course (per person RM60), a perfectly vertical climbing wall (RM48), sea kayaking (RM80 for three hours) and a bird-watching tower (RM45).

Damai Central Beach BEACH
A free beach with places to eat, situated across the parking lot from the Sarawak Cultural Village. Amenities include showers and lockers.

Jungle Walks HIKING
Several trails lead into the jungle interior of the peninsula. One, a challenging route with red trail markings, ascends towering **Gunung Santubong** (810m); the last bit is pretty steep, with steps and rope ladders, so it takes about three hours up and two hours down. The trail can be picked up at Bukit Puteri on the road to Damai Central.

Another trail, an easy-to-moderate circular walk (3km, two hours) with blue markings, passes by a pretty waterfall.

Tours

Coastal areas west and east of the Santubong Peninsula are home to a wide variety of wildlife. Oft-spotted species include endangered Irrawaddy dolphins, dragonflies, proboscis monkeys, estuarine crocodiles and all manner of birds.

Resorts on the peninsula, and guesthouses and tour agencies in Kuching, can make arrangements.

Sleeping

BB Bunkers HOSTEL $
(☎082-846835; www.bbbunkers.com; Damai Central; dm RM53; ❄📶) Situated a few metres from Damai Central Beach, this sleek hostel has the peninsula's only dorm beds. The industrial, hangar-like space is subdivided by curtains, creating cosy spaces for one to three beds, either twins or queens. Secure storage is available.

Nanga Shanti HOMESTAY $$
(☎011-2517 7108; www.nangashanti.weebly.com; Santubong Peninsula; d/tent incl breakfast RM120/170; ⏲Apr-Sep) 🍃 This unique beachside dwelling, located on the wild and undeveloped east side of Santubong Peninsula, is reachable only by boat (RM40 return) or a two-hour hike. Accommodation is in a four-room wooden longhouse or luxury tents. Solar panels provide 24-hour electricity and water comes (filtered) from a mountain stream. Operates as a homestay from April to September.

A 30-minute boat ride from Kampung Buntal, Nanga Shanti feels truly remote. It's run by a French couple who built it themselves using recycled materials where possible; the time and care put into the construction is evident in the details of the design, such as the dining room's *atap* roof and glass bottles used in some of the walls. Activities include walking or kayaking to a nearby beach. Lunch and dinner cost RM10 to RM45. There is a minimum stay of two nights.

Village House GUESTHOUSE $$
(☎016-860 9389, 082-846166; www.villagehouse.com.my; Lot 634, off Jalan Pantai Puteri, Kampung Santubong; incl breakfast dm/d RM102/278-552; ❄🏊) Tucked away in the quiet Malay village of Santubong, this place has an air of serenity and relaxation. Rooms with belian wood floors and four-poster beds are arranged around a gorgeous pool with frangipani trees at either end. A well-stocked bar and menu of local dishes (mains RM14 to RM60) means there is really no reason to leave.

Nanga Damai Luxury Homestay HOMESTAY $$
(☎019-887 1017; www.nangadamai.com; Jln Sultan Tengah, Kampung Santubong; d incl breakfast RM120-170; ❄@🏊) A beautiful garden with glimpses of jungle wildlife, friendly family dogs, hospitable owners, an 8m kidney-shaped pool and bright, comfortable rooms (six in total) make it easy to meet the two-night minimum stay. A delicious breakfast on the breezy verandah is included. Not suitable for children under 14. The Kuching-Santubong shuttles pass by here.

Permai Rainforest Resort BUNGALOW $$
(☎082-846490, 082-846487; www.permairainforest.com; Damai Beach; incl breakfast 6-bed cabin

with fan/air-con RM320/340, treehouse RM310, camping per person not incl breakfast RM15 ; @ 📶) This lushly forested bungalow complex, on a beach-adjacent hillside, hosts macaques and silver-leaf monkeys in addition to paying guests. Accommodation ranges from rustic, simply furnished cabins to air-con wooden bungalows towering 6m off the ground. Offers plenty of outdoor activities. Prices drop from Sunday to Thursday.

Damai Beach Resort RESORT $$$
(☎082-846999; www.damaibeachresort.com; Teluk Bandung, Kampung Santubong; incl breakfast d from RM487, ste from RM1044; ❄@📶🏊) This 252-room beach resort has enough activities and amenities to make you feel like you're on a cruise ship (in a good way), including boat excursions, sea kayaking and even an 18-hole **golf course** (www.damaigolf.com) designed by Arnold Palmer. Although in some areas the hotel sometimes falls short of four-star expectations, it's a reasonable option for families looking for a convenient beach location and a decent pool.

Eating

Food Court HAWKER $
(Damai Central; mains RM5-8; ⏲8am-10pm) A convenient food court with 10 stalls selling noodles, fried rice and cold drinks, as well as an excellent *roti canai* stall (RM2.50 to RM4).

Lim Hock Ann Seafood SEAFOOD $$
(Kampung Buntal; mains RM8-20, fish per kg RM46-74; ⏲11am-2pm & 5-10pm, closed Mon lunch) A sprawling, open-air shed on stilts with a wide-plank floor and a tin roof, this classic Chinese-style seafood restaurant is in Kampung Buntal, a fishing village 11km southeast of Damai Central (on the east coast of the base of the peninsula). The fresh, locally landed fish is superb.

Getting There & Away

MINIBUS

Kuching is linked to the Santubong Peninsula (45 minutes) by the slow K15 bus from Saujana Bus Station and minibuses operated by Damai Shuttle.

Damai Shuttle (☎082-846999; 1-way adult/child RM12/6) Has departures from Kuching's Grand Margherita Hotel to Damai Beach and Sarawak Cultural Village six times a day between 9am and 6.15pm. The last run back to Kuching leaves the Sarawak Cultural Village at 5.15pm.

TAXI

A cab from Kuching to Damai Central costs RM60 (about RM70 from the airport).

Kuching Wetlands National Park

The only way to see the majestic mangroves of 66-sq-km Kuching Wetlands National Park is – as you would expect – by boat. Situated about 15km northwest of Kuching (as the crow flies), the park doesn't have an office, just low-lying islands and saline waterways lined with salt-resistant trees that provide food and shelter to proboscis monkeys, silver-leaf monkeys and fireflies (above the water line); estuarine crocodiles and amphibious fish called mudskippers (at the water line); and countless varieties of fish and prawns (below the water line). Nearby open water is one of the finest places in Sarawak to spot snub-nosed Irrawaddy dolphins.

The morning (about 9am) is the best time to see the dolphins, while late-afternoon cruises are optimal for sighting a flash of reddish-brown fur as proboscis monkeys leap from tree to tree in search of the tenderest, tastiest young leaves. Sunset on the water is magical – and unbelievably romantic, especially if your guide points out an *api-api* tree (a 'firefly tree', surrounded by swirling green points of light). After dark, by holding a torch up at eye level, you can often spot the reflections of animalian eyes, including – if you're lucky – a crocodile.

Tours

CPH Travel Agencies BOAT TOUR
(☎in Kuching 082-243708; www.cphtravel.com.my; 70 Jln Padungan ; ⏲office 8.30am-5pm Mon-Fri, 8.30am-noon Sat) Offers a mangrove and Irrawaddy dolphin-sighting cruise (RM140 per person) at 8.30am and a wildlife cruise (RM165) at 4.30pm. Packages include transfers from and to your hotel. Boats usually set sail from the Sarawak Boat Club.

Semenggoh Nature Reserve

One of the best places in the world to see semi-wild orangutans in their natural rainforest habitat, swinging from trees and scurrying up vines, the **Semenggoh Wildlife Centre** (☎082-618325; www.sarawakforestry.com; Jln Puncak Borneo; adult RM10; ⏲8-11am &

2-4pm, feeding 9am & 3pm) can be visited on a half-day trip from Kuching or combined with a visit to Annah Rais Longhouse or Kampung Benuk.

Situated within the 6.8-sq-km Semenggoh Nature Reserve, the centre is home to 25 orangutans: 11 of whom were rescued from captivity or orphaned and their 14 Semenggoh-born offspring, some mere babes-in-arms who spend their days hanging onto their mother's shaggy chests. Four of the tree-dwelling creatures are completely wild (that is, they find all their own food), but the rest often swing by (literally) park HQ to dine on bananas, coconuts, eggs and – though they don't know it – medications. There's no guarantee that any orangutans, the world's largest tree-dwelling animal, will show up, but even when there are plenty of fruits in the forest the chances are excellent.

Hour-long feedings, in the rainforest a few hundred metres from park HQ, run from 9am to 10am and from 3pm to 4pm. When the feeding session looks like it's over, rangers sometimes try to shoo away visitors (especially groups, whose guides are in any case eager to get back to Kuching), but orangutans often turn up at park HQ, so don't rush off straightaway if everything seems quiet.

For safety reasons, visitors are asked to stay at least 5m from the orangutans – the animals can be unpredictable – and are advised to keep a tight grip on their backpacks, water bottles and cameras because orangutans have been known to snatch things in search of something yummy. To avoid annoying – or even angering – the orangutans, do not point at them anything that looks like a gun (such as a walking stick or camera tripod); do not scream or make sudden moves; and, when you take pictures, do not use a flash.

Rangers keep an eye out and radio back with news of the approach of Semenggoh's dominant male orangutan Ritchie, who is easily recognised by his cheek flanges. If he decides to stop by, his food must be ready for him when he arrives to avoid provoking his wrath.

Semenggoh Nature Reserve has two trails that pass through primary rainforest: the **Masing Trail** (Main Trail; red trail markings; 30 minutes), which links the HQ with the highway; and the **Brooke's Pool Trail** (yellow and red trail markings), a 2km loop from HQ, but they are not normally open to the public so as to limit the orangutans' contact with humans.

Getting There & Away

Two bus companies provide reliable public transport from Kuching's Saujana Bus Station to the park gate, which is 1.3km down the hill from park HQ (RM3, 45 minutes):

City Public Link (p413) Bus K6 (RM3) departs from Kuching at 7.15am, 10.15am and 1pm, and from Semenggoh at 8.45pm, 11.15am, 2.15pm and 4.15pm.

Sarawak Transport Company (p413) Bus 6 (RM3) has Kuching departures at 6.45am and 12.15pm; buses back to Kuching pass by Semenggoh at 10am and 3.45pm.

A taxi from Kuching costs RM60 to RM70 one-way or RM120 return, including one hour of wait time.

Tours are organised by Kuching guesthouses and tour agencies.

Kampung Benuk

This quiet, flowery **Bidayuh village** (adult RM6), where the loudest sound is often the crowing of a cock, attracted lots of tourists back when the road ended here. These days, it gets relatively few visitors, despite being a pleasant place to spend a few hours.

The traditional, 32-door **longhouse** (Lg 5), with bouncy bamboo common areas, is still home to a few families, though most of the villagers now live in attractive modern houses. In the **barok** (ritual hall), you can see about a dozen head-hunted skulls, bone-white but tinged with green, hanging from the rafters.

Sleeping

Kurakura Homestay HOMESTAY $$
(☎012-892 0051; www.kurakura.asia; Kampung Semadang; per person incl meals for 2 nights RM275; ❄) Run by Norwegian-born Lars and his Bidayuh wife Liza, this super-friendly, sustainable jungle homestay occupies a wooden house built on land that once belonged to Liza's grandfather. Meals are prepared using homegrown vegetables, fruits and herbs, and possible activities include hiking and kayaking. Situated about 30 minutes by boat from Kampung Semadang. Rates include transport to and from Kuching.

Kampung Annah Rais

Although this Bidayuh longhouse village has been on the tourist circuit for decades, it's still a good place to get a sense of what a longhouse is and what longhouse life is like.

The 500 residents of **Annah Rais** (adult/student RM8/4) are as keen as the rest of us to enjoy the comforts of modern life – they do love their mobile phones and 3G internet access – but they've made a conscious decision to preserve their traditional architecture and the social interaction it engenders. They've also decided that welcoming modern tourists is a good way to earn a living without moving to the city, something most young people end up doing.

Sights

Longhouse Veranda HOUSE
(Annah Rais longhouse) Once you've paid your entrance fee you're free to explore Annah Rais' three longhouses (Kupo Saba, Kupo Terekan and, across the river, Kupo Sijo).

The most important feature of a Bidayuh longhouse is the *awah*, a long, covered common verandah with a springy bamboo floor that's used for socialising and celebrations. Along one side, a long row of doors leads to each family's private *bilik* (apartment). Parallel to the *awah* is the *tanju*, an open-air verandah.

Headhouse HOUSE
(Annah Rais longhouse) Whereas the Iban traditionally hung head-hunted heads outside each family's *bilik*, the Bidayuh grouped theirs together in the community's *panggah* or *baruk* (communal meeting hall). The heads are no longer believed to protect the village – these days the people of Annah Rais are almost all Anglican (the Bidayuh of Kalimantan are mainly Catholic) – but about a dozen smoke-blackened human skulls still have pride of place in the headhouse, suspended over an 18th-century Dutch cannon.

Sleeping

Annah Rais is a peaceful, verdant spot to relax. Half-a-dozen families run homestays with shared bathrooms, either in one of the three longhouses or in an adjacent detached house. Standard rates, agreed upon by the community, are RM200 per person for accommodation and delicious Bidayuh board. It is also possible to arrange a package including activities such as hiking, rafting, fishing, (mock) blowgun hunting, soaking in a natural hot spring and a dance performance.

Akam Ganja HOMESTAY $$
(☎010-984 3821; winniejagig@gmail.com; per person incl meals RM200) Akam, a retired forestry official, and his wife Winnie, an English teacher, run a welcoming homestay at their comfortable detached house on the riverbank.

Getting There & Away

Annah Rais is about 40km south of Kuching. A taxi from Kuching costs RM90 one-way.

A variety of Kuching guesthouses and tour agencies offer four-hour tours to Annah Rais (per person from RM100).

Kubah National Park

Mixed dipterocarp forest, among the lushest and most threatened habitats in Borneo, is front and centre at this 22-sq-km **national park** (☎082-845033; www.sarawakforestry.com; admission incl Matang Wildlife Centre RM20; ⏲8am-5pm), which more than lives up to its clunky motto, 'the home of palms and frogs'. Scientists have found here an amazing 98 species of palm, out of 213 species known to live in Sarawak; and they have identified 61 species of frog and toad out of Borneo's more than 190 species. In 2012 researchers identified what they believe to be a new species of frog, adding it to a list that includes the aptly named (but oddly shaped) horned frog and a flying frog that can glide from tree to tree thanks to the webbing between its toes. The forest is also home to a wide variety of orchids.

Kubah's trails offer a good degree of shade, making the park ideal for the sun-averse. And when you're hot and sweaty from walking you can cool off under a crystal-clear waterfall.

Sights & Activities

Rainforest Trails HIKING
When you pay your entry fee, you'll receive a hand-coloured schematic map of the park's five interconnected trails. They're well-marked, so a guide isn't necessary. The park has about half-a-dozen rain shelters – keep an eye out for them so you'll know where to run in case of a downpour.

The **Selang Trail** (40 minutes to 60 minutes; trail-marked in yellow), linking the **Main Trail** (trail-marked in white) with the **Rayu Trail** passes by the **Selang Viewpoint**. Offshore you can see the turtle sanctuary of Pulau Satang.

The concrete-paved **Summit Road** (closed to non-official traffic), also known as the Gunung Serapi Summit Trail, runs along the park's southeastern edge from park HQ right up to the top of Kubah's highest peak, **Gunung Serapi** (911m), which holds aloft a

TV and telecom tower; on foot, it's 3½ hours up and a bit less coming down. As you ascend, notice that the mix of trees and plants (including pitcher plants and ferns) changes with the elevation. The summit is often shrouded in mist but near the top there's a viewing platform. When it's clear, there are stupendous views all the way from Tanjung Datu National Park on the Indonesian border (to the northwest) to Gunung Santubong and Kuching (to the east).

The **Waterfall Trail** (3km or 1½ hours from HQ one-way; trail-marked from the Summit Road in blue) passes by wild durian trees and belian trees, otherwise known as ironwood. This incredibly durable – and valuable, and thus endangered – tropical hardwood was traditionally used in longhouse construction. As you would expect, this trail ends at a waterfall and a natural swimming pool. Some visitors combine the Selang Trail and the Waterfall Trail to create a circuit that takes four to six hours.

The **Rayu Trail** (3.8km or 3½ hours) leads to Matang Wildlife Centre. Walked in the direction of Kubah to Matang the trail is mainly downhill.

Frog Pond WILDLIFE RESERVE

Situated 300m above sea level and about a half-hour's walk from park HQ, this artificial pool provides a breeding ground for numerous frog species. The delicate amphibians are especially active at night, more so when it's raining hard (during the day most prefer to hide in a hole in a tree), though their remarkable chorus begins about an hour before nightfall.

A track recorded at Kubah entitled 'Dusk at the Frog Pond' was recently voted the winner in a competition to find the most beautiful sound in the world.

Palm Garden GARDENS

In this labelled garden, near park HQ on the Main Trail, you'll find examples of the 98 species of palm growing in the park.

Sleeping

Kubah is a lovely spot to kick back and relax. While there's usually space, even on weekends, it's always a good idea to book ahead. The accommodation is often full on public and school holidays.

Forest Hostel HOSTEL $

(☎082-248088; ebooking.com.my; dm RM15) A comfortable, homely hostel with three small rooms containing four beds. Fan cooled.

Forest Lodge Type 5 CABIN $

(☎082-248088; ebooking.com.my; 10-bed cabin RM150) These attractive cabins have a living room with couch, chairs and a dining table, and three bedrooms with a total of 10 beds. Fan-cooled.

Forest Lodge Type 4 CABIN $$

(☎082-248088; ebooking.com.my; 6-bed cabin RM225; ❄) Two-storey, all-wood cabins that come with a balcony, a sitting room, a two-bed room and a four-bed room.

Eating

All accommodation options come with fully equipped kitchens, including a fridge, toaster and hob, but there is nowhere to buy food, so bring all you need.

Getting There & Away

Kubah National Park is 25km northwest of Kuching. A taxi from Kuching costs RM60.

From Kuching's Saujana Bus Station, bus K21 to the Politeknik stops on the main road 400m from park HQ, next to the Kubah Family Park (RM3.50, one hour). Departures from Kuching are at 8am, 11am, 2pm and 5pm, and from the main road (opposite the turn-off for Kubah), at 6.30am, 9.30am, 12.30pm and 3.30pm (be there at 3pm, the bus sometimes leaves early).

Matang Wildlife Centre

Situated at the western edge of Kubah National Park, the **Matang Wildlife Centre** (☎082-374869; www.sarawakforestry.com; admission incl Kubah National Park RM20; ⌚8am-5pm, animal encloure trail 8.30am-3.30pm) has had remarkable success rehabilitating rainforest animals rescued from captivity, especially orangutans. The highly professional staff do their best to provide their abused charges with natural living conditions on a limited budget, but there's no denying that the centre looks like a low-budget zoo plopped down in the jungle. Because of the centre's unique role, it's home to endangered animals that you're unlikely to see anywhere else in Sarawak.

Sights & Activities

Interpretation Centre MUSEUM

(⌚8am-1pm & 2-5pm Mon-Thu, Fri 8-11.30am & 2-5pm) FREE A good introduction to the wildlife centre and its residents. Most of the display panels provide information on orangutan rehabilitation. Inside the HQ building.

MATANG'S RESCUED ANIMALS

Some of the creatures at the Matang Wildlife Centre were orphaned, some were confiscated and others were surrendered by the public. Unless they're needed as evidence in court, all are released as soon as possible. During a quarantine period staff study the animals' behaviour and assess their suitability for release. Some – especially those that have been kept as pets – lack the necessary skills to survive in the wild. Releasing them would be a death sentence, since they would most likely starve, and having lost their fear of humans, they're liable to wander into a village and get into trouble.

Among the most celebrated residents of Matang is **Aman**, one of the largest male orangutans in the world. Known for his absolutely massive cheek pads, he hit the headlines in 2007 when he became the first of his species to undergo phacoemulsification (cataract surgery). The procedure ended 10 years of blindness, though it did nothing to restore his tongue, removed after he chomped into an electric cable, or his index finger, bitten off by a rival dominant male.

The orangutans that are deemed eligible for rehabilitation (that is, who don't display abnormal behaviours) are taken into the forest by their keepers and trained to forage for foods, build nests and improve their climbing technique. Sometimes they are joined by semi-wild orangutans, some of the 11 former residents at the centre now live nearby in the forest, and come over to join in the nest-building sessions.

Matang is home to three bearcats (binturongs), two of them females, that are too old to be released. This extraordinary tree-dwelling carnivore can tuck away a fertilised egg for months and perhaps years, delaying pregnancy until sufficient fruit is available (the trick is called embryonic diapause).

Other animals that live here include 10 of the happiest captive sun bears in the world. In horrific condition when brought here, they are undergoing a rehabilitation program that's the first of its kind anywhere. The whoops of three gibbons can be heard from the carpark.

Many of the centre's caged animals are fed from 9am to 10am. Orangutan life-skills training sessions are usually from 8am to 11am and 2pm to 4pm.

Trails HIKING

(animal enclosure trail 8.30am-3.30pm) The **Animal Enclosure Trail** takes visitors through the jungle past animals' cages. If they've got time, rangers are happy to guide visitors around. Pitcher plants can be seen on the 15-minute **Special Trail** loop.

The **Rayu Trail**, a 3.8km (three hour) uphill hike to Kubah National Park (p421), is now open. The starting point is near the park accommodation.

Volunteering VOLUNTEERING

(Leo Biddle 013-845 6531; projectorangutan.com; 2 weeks incl food & lodging US$2000) For details on volunteering – nothing glamorous: we're talking hard physical labour – contact Orangutan Project. In keeping with best practice, volunteers have zero direct contact with orangutans because proximity to people (except a handful of trained staff) will set back their rehabilitation by habituating them to humans. Placements are two or four weeks.

Sleeping & Eating

Matang's accommodation options are basic and rustic. Although there is usually no shortage of space, it's best to book in advance so that staff are expecting you and can make sure the room is ready. There is nowhere to buy food in the park, so bring your own. Cooking is forbidden inside the park accommodation, but an electric kettle is available on request and there are barbeque pits outside (but no utensils).

Forest Hostel HOSTEL $

(Kuching booking office 082-248088, Matang Wildlife Centre 082-374869; ebooking.com.my; dm/r RM15/40) The longhouse-style Forest Hostel is fan-cooled and has an attached bathroom. Rooms sleep four in either bunk beds or double beds.

Forest Hut CAMPGROUND

(Kuching Booking Office 082-248088, Matang Wildlife Centre 082-374869; ebooking.com.my; per person RM10) Open-air rain shelters in the jungle. There is no need to bring a tent, just bedding and a mosquito net.

Type 5 Forest Lodge CABIN $$
(☎Kuching booking office 082-242088, Matang Wildlife Centre 082-374869; ebooking.com.my; r/cabin RM100/150; ❄) There are two of these cabins, each with room for eight people (two double beds in each room), attached bathrooms and air-con.

ℹ Getting There & Away

Matang is about 33km northwest of Kuching. By the new road, it's 8km from Kubah National Park HQ.

A taxi from Kuching costs RM60 one-way.

Bau & Around

About 26km southwest of Kuching, the one-time gold-mining town of Bau is a good access point to two interesting cave systems and some Bidayuh villages.

ℹ Getting There & Away

Bau is 43km southwest of Kuching. The town is linked to Kuching's Saujana Bus Station (RM5, 1½ hours) by bus 2 (every 20 minutes from 6.20am to 6pm).

A taxi from Kuching costs around RM70.

Wind Cave Nature Reserve

Situated 5km southwest of Bau, the **Wind Cave** (Gua Angin; ☎082-765472; adult/child RM5/2; ⏲8.30am-4.30pm) is essentially a network of underground streams. Unlit boardwalks in the form of a figure eight run through the caves, allowing you to wander along the three main passages (total length: 560m) with chittering bats (both fruit- and insect-eating) swooping overhead. In January and February the cave may close if the water level is too high.

Near HQ, 300m from the cave entrance, you can cool off with a refreshing swim in the waters of Sungai Sarawak Kanan.

Flashlights/torches are available for rent (RM3) – if you get a feeble one, ask to exchange it. No food is sold at the reserve itself, though there is a drinks stand.

SEEING MOUNTAINS FROM THE INSIDE

Many of Sarawak's limestone hills are as filled with holes as a Swiss cheese. Boardwalks let you stroll around inside the Wind Cave, the Fairy Cave and the caverns of Niah National Park and Gunung Mulu National Park, but to get off the beaten track you need an experienced guide – someone just like UK-born James, who runs **Kuching Caving** (☎012-886 2347; www.kuchingcaving.com; per person from RM320). He knows more than almost anyone about the 467 cave entrances that have been found within two hours of Kuching, the longest of which is 11km. For an all-day caving trip, prices start at RM320 per person (minimum four people).

ℹ Getting There & Away

To get from Bau to the Wind Cave turn-off (a 1km walk from the cave), take BTC bus 3A. Departures are at 9am, 11am and 3pm.

A taxi from Kuching costs RM70 one-way, or RM150 to RM200 return including the Fairy Cave and three hours of wait time.

A tour from Kuching to both caves costs about RM150 per person.

Fairy Cave

About 9km southwest of Bau, the **Fairy Cave** (Gua Pari Pari; adult/child RM5/2; ⏲8.30am-4pm) – almost the size of a football pitch and as high as it is wide – is an extraordinary chamber whose entrance is 30m above the ground in the side of a cliff; access is by staircase. Outside, trees grow out of the sheer rock face at impossible angles. Inside, fanciful rock formations, covered with moss, give the cavern an otherworldly aspect, as do the thickets of ferns straining to suck in every photon they can.

Cliff faces near the Fairy Cave, many rated 6a to 7a according to the UK technical grading system, are popular with members of Kuching's **rock climbing** community. The sheer white cliff 300m back along the access road from the cave has three easy routes and about 15 wall routes with bolts. Nearest the cave is the Tiger Wall; nearby routes include the Orchid Wall and the Batman Wall. For information on guided rock climbing, contact **Outdoor Treks** (☎012-888 6460; www.bikcloud.com; full-day guided climb per person for groups of 1/2/4 RM300/220/180).

ℹ Getting There & Away

To get from Bau to the Fairy Cave turn-off (a 1.5km or 30-minute walk from the cave), take BTC bus 3, which departs at 8.40am, 10.30am, 11.40am and 3pm.

From Kuching, a taxi to the Fairy Cave costs RM70 to RM80 one-way, or RM150 to RM200 return including the Wind Cave and three hours of wait time. A tour from Kuching to both caves costs about RM150 per person.

Serikin

Serikin Weekend Market MARKET

(Pasar Serikin; Kampung Serikin; ⏲6am–4pm Sat, 6am–3pm Sun) Vendors from Kalimantan cross the mountains on motorbikes to sell fruit, electronics, handicrafts, rattan furniture and clothes at this sprawling weekend market, which occupies most of the otherwise quiet little border town of Serikin. The lack of a border or customs post here means that there is a free flow of cheap Indonesian produce; Kuchingites often make the drive down in search of a bargain. Serikin is 20km southeast of Bau; a taxi from Kuching is around RM80.

Gunung Bengoh

Inland from Bau, most of the population is Bidayuh. Unlike their distant relations on the eastern side of the Bengoh (Bungo) Range – that is, in the area around Padawan and Annah Rais – the Bau Bidayuh have never lived in longhouses. The area's Bidayuh speak a number of distinct dialects.

Tour agencies in Kuching can arrange treks into the valleys around **Gunung Bengoh** (966m) – including the fabled **Hidden Valley** (aka Lost World) – either from the Bau side or the Padawan side. Kuching's Borneo Experiences (p403), for instance, runs treks to the remote and very traditional Bidayuh longhouse community of **Semban**, where a few old ladies still sport brass ankle bracelets. A three-day, two-night trip, including transport, food and a guide, costs RM780 per person.

Lundu

The pleasant town of Lundu, an overgrown fishing village about 55km west of Kuching, is the gateway to Gunung Gading National Park.

The road north out of town leads not only to Gunung Gading National Park, but also to two beaches that are popular with Kuchingites on weekends and holidays. Romantic, coconut-palm-fringed **Pantai Pandan**, 11km north of Lundu, is one of Sarawak's nicest beaches (despite the sandflies), with a gentle gradient that's perfect for kids. A few beachfront huts sell eats and drinks. Camping is possible. **Pantai Siar**, 8km north of Lundu, is home to several small resorts that appeal mainly to the domestic market.

Sleeping

Lundu Gading Hotel HOTEL $

(☎082-735199; 174 Lundu Bazaar; d RM60; ❄) It may not be the most stylish hotel in Sarawak but Lundu's only hostelry – whose 10 rooms sport blue-tile floors and big windows – provides more than adequate lodgings. Situated diagonally across the street from the RHB Bank.

Pandan Beach Campground CAMPGROUND $

(☎082-735043, 013-820 5888; Pantai Pandan; per tent RM20, cabin fan RM60, air-con RM150) This simple campsite, located next to a beautiful sandy cove, has showers, toilets, and gas cylinders and barbecue areas for cooking. The cabin accommodation is shabby and overpriced.

There is not much food available in the tiny village – just a **food court** (waffles RM2.90; ⏲8am-7pm Mon-Fri, 10am-7pm Sat & Sun) selling instant noodles, packaged snacks and waffles – so bring your own.

★ **Retreat** RESORT $$

(☎082-453027; www.sbeu.org.my; Pantai Siar; cabin incl breakfast Sun-Fri from RM158, Sat from RM248; ❄📶🏊) Owned by the Sarawak Bank Employees Union, this is the ideal place to mix chilling on the beach with workers' solidarity. The grassy, family-friendly campus has 38 comfortable rooms, including 21 cabins, and gets enthusiastic reviews from travellers. Day use of the pool costs RM15 for adults and RM5 for children; the beach itself is free. Situated 8km from Lundu.

Eating

Pusat Penjaja Gading Lundu HAWKER $

(Lundu Hawker Centre; Jln Stunggang Malayu Baru; mains RM4-6; ⏲7am-5pm) Above the fruit and vegetable market is a hawker centre with 26 Chinese and Malay food stalls. The Malay buffet at stalls four and five includes delicious fresh crab as well as other local seafood.

Happy Seafood Centre SEAFOOD $$

(☎014-691 8577; Jln Blacksmith; mains RM5-15; ⏲7.30am-9pm Tue-Sun) Lundu's location on the edge of Sungai Stamin and just a few kilometres from the ocean makes for delicious fresh fish from both the river and sea. This informal eatery is a great place to sample it, as well as local jungle vegetables like *midin* (fern). Also serves chicken and pork. Located opposite the bus station.

Getting There & Away

Sarawak Transport Company (p413) runs Bus EP 7, which links Kuching Sentral long-haul bus station with Lundu (RM12, 1½ hours); departures from Kuching are at 7.30am, 10am, 1.30pm and 4pm. Buses from Lundu leave at 7.30am, 10.30am, 1.30pm and 4.30pm

At the Lundu bus station, it's possible to hire a private car to take you to Gunung Gading National Park (RM5 per person) or Sematan.

Gunung Gading National Park

The best place in Sarawak to see the world's largest flower, the renowned Rafflesia, **Gunung Gading National Park** (082-735144; www.sarawakforestry.com; adult RM20; 8am-5pm) makes a fine day trip from Kuching. Its old-growth rainforest covers the slopes of four mountains *(gunung)* – Gading, Lundu, Perigi and Sebuloh – traversed by well-marked **walking trails** that are great for day hikes. The park is an excellent spot to experience the incredible biodiversity of lowland mixed dipterocarp forest, so named because it is dominated by a family of trees, the Dipterocarpaceae, whose members are particularly valuable for timber and thus especially vulnerable to clear-cutting.

The star attraction at 41-sq-km Gunung Gading is the *Rafflesia tuan-mudae*, a species that's endemic to Sarawak. Up to 75cm in diameter, they flower pretty much year-round but unpredictably, so to see one you'll need some luck. To find out if a Rafflesia is in bloom – something that happens here only about 25 times a year – and how long it will stay that way (never more than five days), contact the park or call the National Park Booking Office (p411) in Kuching.

Sights & Activities

A variety of well-marked, often steep trails lead through the lush jungle. Park signs give one-way hike times. Except when instructed otherwise by a ranger, keep to the trails to avoid crushing Rafflesia buds underfoot.

Don't count on seeing many animals, as most species found here are nocturnal and wisely prefer the park's upper reaches, safely away from nearby villages.

Since these hikes must be done in one day (camping is permitted only at park HQ), you might want to arrive the day before to facilitate an early morning start. Sign in at park HQ before setting off.

Interpretation Centre MUSEUM
(Gunung Gading National Park HQ; 8am-5pm) FREE The well-presented displays provide detailed information on the Rafflesia, a parasitic plant with buds the size of cabbages and flowers with diameters measuring up to 75cm. The centre also highlights the dangers posed to this critically endangered species, and conservation efforts aimed at protecting it.

Rafflesia Loop Trail WALKING
(per hr for group of up to 10 RM30) This 620m-long plank walk, which begins 50m down the slope from park HQ, goes through a stretch of forest that Rafflesias find especially convivial. If the flower happens to be close to the trail, it is possible to go alone, but since most of the blooms are off the path, finding them requires a ranger or guide.

When the flowers are out, the local freelance (licensed) guide who usually takes groups is likely to already be at the park; if not, the office can give her a call.

Circular Route HIKING
For views of the South China Sea, you can follow a circuit that incorporates the **Viewpoint Trail** (follow the red-and-yellow stripes painted on trees), the **Lintang Trail** (red stripes) and the **Reservoir Trail** (a cement stairway).

Gunung Gading HIKING
Hiking up Gunung Gading (906m) takes seven to eight hours return, but don't expect panoramic views on the way up – the trail is thickly forested, so you'll see mainly the bottom of the rainforest canopy. Only once you reach the summit, where the British army cleared the jungle to make a camp during the Konfrontasi, are you rewarded with views.

At **Batu Berkubu** (10 to 12 hours return; trail marked in red and blue), you can see a communist hideout from the same period.

Waterfalls SWIMMING
Three lovely cascades are easily accessible along the **Main Trail** (marked in red and white). You can take a dip at **Waterfall 1**, **Waterfall 7** (1.5km from park HQ) and the **swimming hole**, fed by a crystal-clear mountain stream, at the beginning of the Rafflesia Loop Trail.

Sleeping & Eating

The busiest times are weekends, school holidays and when a Rafflesia is blooming, but even at quieter times park staff prefer advance bookings.

There is no food available at the park, so bring your own. Another dining option is driving or strolling about 2.5km to Lundu.

Hostel HOSTEL $
(☎Kuching booking office 082-248088, park HQ 082-735144; ebooking.com.my; Gunung Gading National Park HQ; dm/r without bathroom RM15/40) The hostel has four fan rooms, each with four beds (bunks). There is a kitchen with cooking utensils and a barbecue pit for cooking.

Camping CAMPGROUND $
(☎Kuching booking office 082-248088, park HQ 082-735144; www.sarawakforestry.com; Gunung Gading National Park HQ; per person RM5) The campground has a toilet and shower block and barbecue pits.

Forest Lodges CABIN $$
(☎Kuching booking office 082-248088, park HQ 082-735144; ebooking.com.my; Gunung Gading National Park HQ; per r/cabin RM100/150; ❄) Each three-bedroom cabin has one master bedroom with air-con and a double bed, while the other two rooms make do with single beds and a fan. There is a kitchen with cooking utensils and a dining area.

Getting There & Away

Gunung Gading National Park is 85km northwest of Kuching. Four public buses a day link Kuching Sentral long-distance bus station with Lundu, but from there you'll either have to walk north 2.5km to the park, or hire an unofficial taxi (about RM5 per person).

A tour from Kuching costs about RM350 per person including lunch (minimum two people). Groups could consider hiring a taxi for RM250 to RM300 including waiting time.

Sematan

The quiet fishing town of Sematan is Sarawak's westernmost town and the hometown of Sarawak's chief minister Adenan Satem. Most travellers who pass through are on their way to Tanjung Datu National Park, accessible by boat. The nearby Indonesian border – yes, those forested mountains are in Kalimantan – can be crossed at Biawak.

Sights & Activities

A grassy north-south **promenade** lines the waterfront, where a concrete **pier** affords wonderful views of the mouth of the river, its sand banks and the very blue, very clear South China Sea. The deserted beaches of **Teluk Pugu**, a narrow spit of land across the mouth of the Sematan River from Sematan's jetty, can be reached by boat (RM30 return).

At the northern end of the row of stores facing the waterfront, check out the shop called Teck Hunt (the furthest west of the waterfront stores), which hasn't changed in over a century. Built of *belian*, it still has wooden shutters instead of windows.

The sands of shallow **Pantai Sematan**, clean and lined with coconut palms, stretch along the coast northwest of town. It is home to several resorts that fill up with Kuchingites on the weekends.

Sleeping

Sematan Hotel HOTEL $
(☎011-2025 1078; 162 Sematan Bazaar; d RM50; ❄) The four basic rooms have tile floors and rudimentary furnishings. Bathrooms are attached but lack hot water. Situated 150m inland from the waterfront.

Eating

Sam Chai Seafood SEAFOOD $
(☎013-803 4892; Sematan waterfront; mains RM3-6 ; ⏰7am-7pm) A simple seafront *kopitam* serving delicious seafood *mee* (noodles) with fresh prawns (RM6).

Getting There & Away

Sematan is 107km northwest of Kuching, 25km northwest of Lundu and 30km (by sea) from Tanjung Datu National Park.

Buses link Kuching Sentral long-distance bus station with Lundu, and depart Lundu for Sematan (RM4) at 9.30am, 11.30am, 3pm and 5.30pm.

An unofficial taxi from Lundu bus station costs about RM30 one way.

Tanjung Datu National Park

Occupying a remote, rugged peninsula at Sarawak's far northwestern tip, this 14-sq-km **national park** (☎satellite phone for emergencies only 87077673978; www.sarawakforestry.com; adult RM20) features endangered mixed dipterocarp rainforest, jungle trails that hear few footfalls, clear seas, unspoilt coral reefs and near-pristine white-sand beaches on which endangered turtles – the green turtle and olive ridley turtle – occasionally lay their eggs. Few visitors make the effort and brave the expense to travel out here, but those who do often come away absolutely enchanted.

Activities

Park Trails WALKING

The park has four trails, including the **Teluk Melano Trail** from the Malay fishing village of Teluk Melano (a demanding 3.7km), linked to Sematan by boat; and the **Belian Trail** (2km), which goes to the summit of 542m-high **Gunung Melano** (2km, one hour) and affords breathtaking views of the coastlines of Indonesia and Malaysia.

To spot nocturnal animals, you can take a **night walk** on your own or with a ranger.

Snorkelling SNORKELLING

Snorkelling (but not scuba diving) is allowed in certain areas; details are available at park HQ. Bring your own equipment. Please don't touch the easily damaged coral, but bring water shoes just in case (the coral can be sharp).

Sleeping & Eating

For details of homestays in Teluk Melano, a steep, 3½-hour walk from park HQ, contact the National Park Booking Office (p411) in Kuching or ask around at the Sematan jetty.

There is no food at the park, so buy all you need in Sematan before getting the boat. Cooking equipment can be rented for RM11 a day; cooking gas costs RM6.

Guest Rooms CABIN $

(☎ Kuching booking office 082-248088; d without bathroom RM42) These four basic rooms, each with two single beds, share bathrooms and a kitchen.

Shelters HUT $

(☎ Kuching booking office 082-248088; per person RM5) These open-sided huts are as basic as they come, but the location – almost on the beach, looking out at the sea – makes a night here pretty special. The park can provide bedding and mosquito nets (RM16).

Getting There & Away

The only way to get to Tanjung Datu National Park or the nearby village of Teluk Melano, both about 30km northwest of Sematan, is by boat (one to 1½ hours). Weather and waves permitting, locals often (but not necessarily every day) pile into a motorboat and head from Teluk Melano to Sematan early in the morning, returning in the early afternoon (around 2pm or 3pm). If you join them, expect to pay RM30 to RM40 per person one way. Sea conditions are generally good from February or March to October. From October to February, rough seas make Tanjung Datu more or less inaccessible.

Walking from Sematan to Teluk Melano – the only other way to get there – takes a full day.

To hire a motorboat for up to seven people ask at Sematan jetty or contact **Mr Minhat** (☎ 013-567 9593) for trips to the park or Teluk Melano (RM450 to RM500 one way).

Talang-Satang National Park

Sarawak's first **marine park** (www.sarawakforestry.com), established in 1999 to protect four species of endangered turtles, consists of the coastline and waters around four islands: the two **Pulau Satang**, known as *besar* (big) and *kecil* (small), which are 16km west of the Santubong Peninsula; and, 45km to the northwest, the two **Pulau Talang-Talang**, also *besar* and *kecil*, situated 8km due north of Pantai Sematan.

Once every four or five years, female turtles (primarily green turtles but occasionally also hawksbill turtles, olive ridley turtles, and leatherback turtles) swim vast distances – sometimes thousands of kilometres – to lay their eggs on the exact same beach where they themselves hatched. Of every 20 turtles that come ashore in Sarawak to lay eggs, 19 do so on a beach in 19.4-sq-km Talang-Satang National Park. But of the 10,000 eggs a female turtle may lay over the course of her life, which can last 100 years, only one in a thousand is likely to survive into adulthood. To increase these odds, park staff patrol the beaches every night during the egg-laying season (mainly June and July, with fewer in August and a handful in April, May and September) and either transfer the eggs to guarded hatcheries or post guards to watch over them in situ.

Snorkelling and diving are permitted but only within certain designated areas, and divers must be accompanied by an approved guide.

Pulau Satang

While the national park's conservation area is managed by Sarawak Forestry, the islands themselves are the property of a family from Telaga Air – their 999-year lease, granted by the last White Rajah, Charles Vyner Brooke, expires in the year 2945. About 100 cousins now share ownership, but day-to-day management has devolved to Abol Hassan Johari, a retired accountant who lives in Telaga Air and is much more interested in conservation and research than in tourists. His family retains customary rights to the turtles' eggs, but these are 'sold' to the state government and the money donated to an orphanage.

The larger of the two islands, 1-sq-km **Pulau Satang Besar**, 14km northwest of Telaga Air, is the only island that is partially open to visitors. Groups are allowed to land but swimming is forbidden within the core protected zone (anywhere within a 2km radius of the islands' highest point).

The island has a fine beach and simple dorm accommodation with generator-powered electricity. Overnight visitors can sometimes watch fragile eggs being moved from the beach to a hatchery and, possibly, witness baby turtles being released into the wild. **CPH Travel** (☎in Kuching 082-243708; www.cphtravel.com.my; Damai Puri Resort & Spa) offers day trips (RM255) and overnight stays (RM695) on the island.

Pulau Talang-Talang

The two Pulau Talang-Talang, accessible from Sematan, are not open to the general public; visitors are only allowed within 2.8km of Pulau Talang Besar, Pulau Talang Kecil, Pulau Satang Kecil or the Ara-Banun Wildlife Sanctuary by special arrangement with Sarawak Forestry. Such permission is normally only granted to bona fide researchers, students, conservation organisations, and people participating in the **Sea Turtle Volunteer Programme** (4 days & 3 nights from RM2624; ⏲Jun-Sep).

With this programme, paying volunteers can stay on Pulau Talang-Talang Besar and help the staff of the Turtle Conservation Station patrol beaches, transfer eggs to the hatchery and even release hatchlings. For details, contact the National Park Booking Office (p411) in Kuching; booking is through Kuching-based tour agents such as Borneo Adventure (p403).

Getting There & Away

The easiest way to visit Pulau Satang is to book a tour with a Kuching-based agency. Day-trip charters cost RM400 per person and can be arranged through Kuching agencies. Boats usually set out from the coastal villages of Telaga Air, 10km northeast (as the crow flies) from Kubah National Park.

Batang Ai Region

Ask anyone in Kuching where to find old-time **longhouses** – that is, those least impacted by modern life – and the answer is almost always the same: Batang Ai, many of whose settlements can only be reached by boat.

As well as longhouses, Batang Ai is the best place in Sarawak to have a chance of seeing truly wild **orangutans**, or at least their nests. Sightings are not guaranteed, of course, but are not rare either; recent travellers report seeing a group of six of the ginger apes near their camp.

This remote region, about 250km (4½ hours by road) southeast of Kuching, is not really visitable without a guide, but if you're genuinely interested in encountering Iban culture, the money and effort to get out here will be richly rewarded. Trips to the Batang Ai region can be booked in Kuching, either through a tour operator (the four-day, three-night Borneo Adventure, p403, Menyang Tais longhouse to Nanga Sumpa trek, costing RM1590, gets rave reviews) or with a freelance guide.

Sights

Batang Ai National Park NATIONAL PARK

(☎National Park Booking Office in Kuching 082-248088; www.sarawakforestry.com; RM20) Batang Ai National Park's dipterocarp rainforests have the highest density of wild orangutans in central Borneo and are also home to gibbons, langurs and hornbills. Managed with the help of an Iban community cooperative, the park has various forest trails (ranging from an easy 1.8km walk to a strenuous 8.2km hike), but you must go with a guide. The only way to reach the park is by boat from Batang Ai jetty (two hours); there is no food or accommodation available.

The 240-sq-km park is part of a vast contiguous area of protected rainforest that includes the Batang Ai Reservoir (24 sq km) and Sarawak's Lanjak Entimau Wildlife Sanctuary (1688 sq km) as well as protected areas across the border in Kalimantan.

Getting There & Away

A daily shuttle bus goes at 8am from the Hilton Hotel in Kuching to Batang Ai jetty (RM145, four hours). Since nearly all of the longhouses and accommodation are only accessible by boat you will need to arrange to be met at the jetty.

A taxi from Kuching to Batang Ai costs RM400.

CENTRAL SARAWAK

Stretching from Sibu, on the lower Batang Rejang, upriver to Kapit and Belaga and northeastward along the coast to Bintulu and Miri, Sarawak's midsection offers some great river journeys, fine national parks and modern urban conveniences.

Sibu

☎084 / POP 255,000

Gateway to the Batang Rejang, Sibu has grown rich from trade with Sarawak's interior since the time of James Brooke. These days, although the 'swan city' does not rival Kuching in terms of charm, it's not a bad place to spend a day or two before or after a boat trip to the wild interior.

Situated 60km upriver from the open sea, Sibu is Sarawak's most Chinese city. Two-thirds of locals trace their roots to China, and many of them are descendents of migrants who came from Foochow (Fujian or Fuzhou) province in the early years of the 20th century. The city was twice destroyed by fire, in 1889 and 1928. Much of Sibu's modern-day wealth can be traced to the timber trade, which began in the early 1930s.

Sights

Strolling around the city centre is a good way to get a feel for Sibu's fast-beating commercial pulse. Drop by the tourist office for a brochure covering the **Sibu Heritage Trail**.

Features of architectural interest include the old **shophouses** along Jln Tukang Besi near the Visitor Information Centre and the old **Rex Cinema** (Jln Ramin), where art deco meets shophouse functionality.

Tua Pek Kong Temple TAOIST TEMPLE
(Jln Temple; ⌚6.30am-8pm) FREE A modest wooden structure existed on the site of this colourful riverfront Taoist temple as far back as 1871; it was rebuilt in 1897 but badly damaged by Allied bombs in 1942.

For panoramic views over the town and the muddy Batang Rejang, climb the seven-storey **Kuan Yin Pagoda**, built in 1987; the best time is sunset, when a swirl of swiftlets buzzes around the tower at eye level. Ask for the key at the ground-floor desk.

Anchored outside the temple and visible from the pagoda are 'floating supermarkets', boats used to transport supplies to upriver longhouses.

> **SWANS**
>
> No visitor to Kuching could miss the city's feline theme, but the state capital is not the only Sarawakian city with a mascot. Miri has adopted the seahorse, while Sibu's mascot is the swan, an 'ancient Chinese symbol of good fortune and health, an auspicious omen for a community living in harmony, peace and goodwill'. Keep an eye out for statues as you wander around town.

Sibu Heritage Centre MUSEUM
(Jln Central; ⌚9am-5pm, closed Mon & public holidays) FREE Housed in a gorgeously airy municipal complex built in 1960, this excellent museum explores the captivating history of Sarawak and Sibu. Panels, rich in evocative photographs, take a look at the various Chinese dialect groups and other ethnic groups, Sarawak's communist insurgency (1965–90), Sibu's Christian (including Methodist) traditions, and even local opposition to Sarawak's incorporation into Malaysia in 1963.

Don't miss the photo of a 1940s street dentist – it's painful just to look at.

Rejang Esplanade PARK
(Jln Maju) One of Sibu's 22 community parks – most donated by Chinese clan associations – this pleasant strip of riverfront grass affords views of the wide, muddy river and its motley procession of fishing boats, tugs, timber-laden barges and 'flying coffin' express boats.

Lau King Howe Memorial Museum MUSEUM
(Jln Pulau; ⌚9am-5pm Tue-Sun) One glance at this rather bizarre medical museum's exhibits and you'll be glad saving your life never required the application of early-20th-century drills, saws and stainless-steel clamps – or the use of a ferocious gadget called a 'urological retractor'. Another highlight: an exhibit on the evolution of local nurses' uniforms, which some visitors may find kinky.

Bawang Assan Longhouse Village VILLAGE
An Iban village one hour downstream from Sibu (by road the trip takes just 40 minutes), Bawang Assan has nine 'hybrid' longhouses (longhouses that combine traditional and 21st-century elements). To stay here without

Sibu

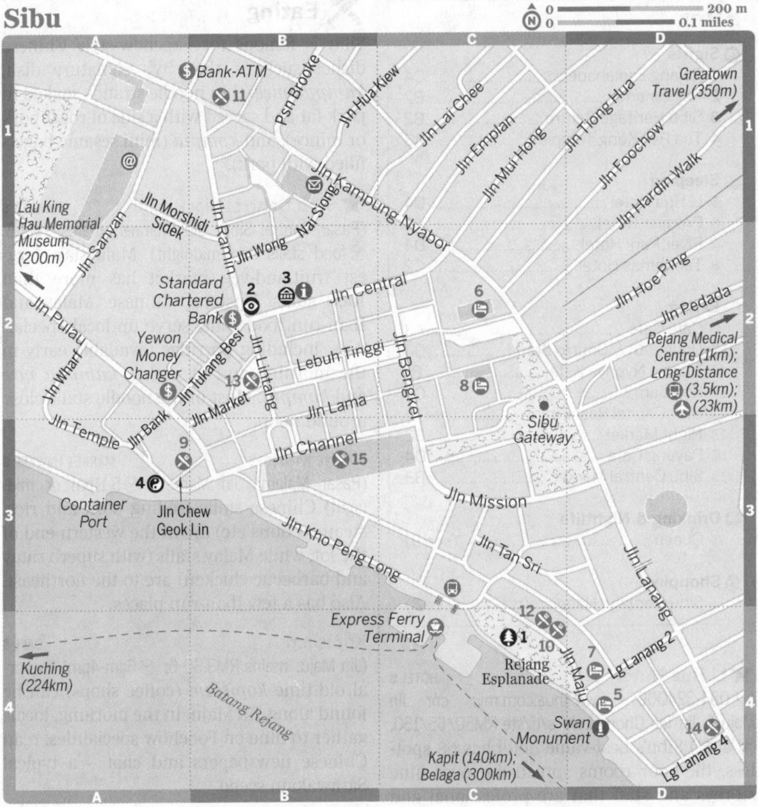

going through a Sibu-based tour company, contact the **Bawang Assan Homestay Programme** (☎014-582 8105; www.ibanlonghousestay.blogspot.com; per person incl 3 meals RM110); ask for Marcathy Gindau.

Tours

Greatown Travel TOUR
(☎084-211243, 084-219243; www.greatown.com; No 6, 1st fl, Lg Chew Siik Hiong 1A) A well-regarded tour company offering longhouse visits to Bawang Assan and around Sarikei, as well as trips to the 'Melanau heartland' around Mukah. Staff are happy to create an itinerary based on your interests and budget. The office is about 1km northeast of the centre along Jln Pedada.

Great Holiday Travel TOUR
(☎084-348196, 012-890 8035; www.ghtborneo.com; No 23, 1st fl, Pusat Pedada, Jln Pedada; ⏰8am-5pm Mon-Fri, 8am-1pm Sat) Based out near the long-distance bus station, this outfit can organise half-day walking tours of Sibu, visits to Bawang Assan Longhouse (half-day tour RM120, overnight stay RM290) and two-day trips up to the Kapit area, usually with an overnight stay at Rumah Jandok. Reasonably priced.

Festivals

Borneo Cultural Festival PERFORMING ARTS
(⏰Jul) A week-long festival of food, music and dance representing Central Sarawak's Chinese, Iban, Bidayuh, Orang Ulu and Malay-Melanau cultures and traditions.

Sleeping

Sibu has dozens of hotels, so there is no shortage of beds. Some of the ultra-budget places (those charging less than RM35 a room) are of a very low standard and double as brothels.

Sibu

Sights

1 Rejang Esplanade C4
2 Rex Cinema B2
3 Sibu Heritage Centre B2
4 Tua Pek Kong Temple A3

Sleeping

5 Li Hua Hotel D4
6 Premier Hotel C2
7 River Park Hotel D4
8 Tanahmas Hotel C2

Eating

9 Café Café A3
10 Doughnut & Churro Stand C4
11 Islamic Nyonya Kafé B1
12 Kopitiam C4
New Capital Restaurant .... (see 6)
13 Night Market B2
14 Payung Café D4
15 Sibu Central Market B3

Drinking & Nightlife

Queen .... (see 9)

Shopping

Sibu Heritage Handicrafts .... (see 3)

★Li Hua Hotel HOTEL $
(☎084-324000; www.lihua.com.my; cnr Jln Maju & Jln Teo Chong Loh; s/d/ste RM50/65/150;) Sibu's best-value hotel has 68 spotless, tile-floor rooms spread out over nine storeys and staff that are professional and friendly. It's especially convenient if you're arriving or leaving by boat. Light sleepers should avoid the rooms above the karaoke bars on Jln Teo Chong Loh that blare out music late into the night.

River Park Hotel HOTEL $
(fax 084-316688; 51-53 Jln Maju; d RM55-75;) A well-run, 30-room hotel in a convenient riverside location. The cheapest rooms don't have windows.

Premier Hotel HOTEL $$
(☎084-323222; www.premierh.com.my; Jln Kampung Nyabor; s/d incl breakfast from RM209/242;) This popular, midrange hotel offers 189 nice, spacious rooms in an excellent downtown location.

Tanahmas Hotel HOTEL $$
(☎084-333188; www.tanahmas.com.my; off Jln Kampung Nyabor; d from RM200;) As comfortable as it is central with rooms that are large and bright. Amenities include a small fitness centre and an open-air pool.

Eating

Sibu is famous for Foochow-style Chinese dishes such as the city's signature dish, *kampua mee* (thin noodle strands soaked in pork fat and served with a side of roast pork or mince), and *kompia* (mini sesame bagels filled with pork).

★Sibu Central Market HAWKER $
(Pasar Sentral Sibu; Jln Channel; mains RM3-5; food stalls 3am-midnight) Malaysia's largest fruit-and-veg market has more than 1000 stalls. Upstairs, Chinese, Malay and Iban-run food stalls serve up local specialities, including porridge (available early in the morning and at night), *kampua mee* and *kompia*. Most of the noodle stalls close around noon.

Night Market MARKET, HAWKER $
(Pasar Malam; Jln Market; 5-11pm or midnight) Chinese stalls (selling pork and rice, steamed buns etc) are at the western end of the lot, while Malay stalls (with superb satay and barbecue chicken) are to the northeast. Also has a few Iban-run places.

Kopitiam CAFE $
(Jln Maju; mains RM3.30-6; 6am-4pm) Several old-time *kopitiam* (coffee shops) can be found along Jln Maju. In the morning, locals gather to dine on Foochow specialities, read Chinese newspapers and chat – a typical Sarawakian scene.

Doughnut & Churro Stand HAWKER $
(27 Jln Maju; doughnuts 40 sen, churros RM1; 6am-7pm) A street stall selling freshly made douhgnuts and churros – perfect to bring on an upriver boat trip.

★Payung Café MALAYSIAN $$
(☎016-890 6061; 20F Jln Lanang; mains RM8-19; 11am-3pm & 6-11pm Mon-Sun) An exquisitely decorated cafe where diners feast on healthy local food (no re-used oil, deep frying or MSG) such as spicy *otak-otak* barbecued fish (RM13), deliciously fresh herb salad (RM8) and generous servings of the volcano-like Mulu icecream.

The walls of the semi-open air, garden-like dining room are adorned with intricate murals painted by the artistic owners, and the place is lit up with coloured lights and paper parasols (*payung* means umbrella in Bahasa Malaysia). The only thing we *didn't* love about this place was the Celine Dion soundtrack.

Café Café FUSION $$
(☎084-328101; 8 Jln Chew Geok Lin; mains RM18-44, set lunch RM12.90-19.90; ⏰noon-4pm & 6-11pm Tue-Sun) Café Café serves decent fusion fare, including Nonya-style chicken, daily specials and inventive desserts such as salted-caramel-apple-crisp cheesecake and Reese's-peanut-butter-chocolate cheesecake (RM10.90). With decor that mixes Balinese, Chinese and Western elements, this is a sophisticated urban dining spot.

Islamic Nyonya Kafé PERANAKAN $$
(141 Jln Kampung Nyabor; mains RM10-30; ⏰8am-11pm Tue-Sun, 4-11pm Sun; 📶✍) The highlight of the overwhelmingly extensive menu here are the deliciously spicy Nonya dishes, including *kari ayam* (chicken curry) and *kari kambing* (mutton curry).

New Capital Restaurant CHINESE $$
(☎084-326066; 46 Jln Kampung Nyabor; mains RM10-40; ⏰11am-2pm & 5-9pm) A classy, old-school Chinese restaurant. Foochow specialities include sea-cucumber soup (RM10) and white pomfret (RM70 to RM80 for a portion to share).

Drinking & Nightlife

Queen BAR
(12 Jln Chew Geok Lin; beer from RM10, cocktails RM22-38; ⏰6pm-12.30am Tue-Sun) Decked out like a Victorian sitting room, this dimly lit bar features plush couches and overstuffed wing chairs in black and burgundy velvet. Happy hour prices until 10pm. Sadly, the live music sessions have now been replaced by a karaoke machine.

Shopping

Sibu Heritage Handicrafts HANDICRAFTS
(☎084-333353; ground fl, Sibu Heritage Centre, Jln Central; ⏰8am-6pm) This great little store is so packed full of Kayan and Iban beads, Penan rattan baskets and Melinau and Kayan handicrafts that it is difficult to move around. Hidden behind the vintage photographs of Queen Elizabeth and her family in the shop window is a chaotic treasure trove. The more time you spend here the more you're likely to unearth.

Information

Terazone IT Centre (Level 4, Wisma Sanyan, 1 Jln Sanyan; per hr RM3; ⏰10am-9.45pm) Internet access.

Main Post Office (☎084-337700; Jln Kampung Nyabor; ⏰8am-4.30pm Mon-Fri, to 12.30pm Sat) Sibu's main post office.

Rejang Medical Centre (☎084-323333; www.rejang.com.my; 29 Jln Pedada; ⏰emergency 24hr) Has 24-hour emergency services, including an ambulance. Situated about 4km north-east of the city centre.

Sibu General Hospital (☎084-343333; hsibu.moh.gov.my; Jln Ulu Oya, Km 5½) Situated 8km east of the centre, towards the airport.

Visitors Information Centre (☎084-340980; www.sarawaktourism.com; Sublot 3a & 3b, Sibu Heritage Centre, Jln Central; ⏰8am-5pm Mon-Fri, closed public holidays) Well worth a stop. Has friendly and informative staff (ask for Jessie), plenty of maps, bus and ferry schedules, and brochures on travel around Sarawak.

Yewon Money Changer (8 Jln Tukang Besi; ⏰9.30am-5pm Mon-Sat, 2-4pm Sun) Changes cash. Look for the gold-on-red sign.

Getting There & Away

AIR

MASwings (☎084-307888, ext 2; www.maswings.com.my; Sibu Airport, Jln Durin; ⏰6am-8.30pm) Flights to Bintulu (twice daily), Kuching (five daily), Miri (four daily) and Kota Kinabalu (twice daily).

Malaysia Airlines (☎084-307799; www.malaysiaairlines.com; Sibu airport, Jln Durin) Two flights a day to Kuala Lumpur.

AirAsia (☎084-307808; www.airasia.com) Flies to Kuching and Kuala Lumpur.

BOAT

All boats leave from the **Express Ferry Terminal** (Terminal Penumpang Sibu; Jln Kho Peng Long; 📶). Make sure you're on board 15 minutes before departure time – boats have been known to depart early.

To Kapit & Belaga

'Flying coffin' express boats head up the Batang Rejang to Kapit (RM25 to RM35, 140km, three hours) hourly from 5.45am to 2.30pm. The 10.45am boat has an upper deck with non-air-con, semi-open seating. Water levels at the Pelagus Rapids permitting, one boat a day, departing at 5.45am, goes all the way to Belaga, 155km upriver from Kapit (RM55, 11 hours).

To Kuching

Unless you fly, the quickest way to get from Sibu to Kuching is by boat. **Ekspress Bahagia** (☎016-800 5891, in Kuching 082-429242, in Sibu 084-319228; ⏰from Sibu 11.30am, from Kuching 8.30am) runs a daily express ferry to/from Kuching's Express Wharf (RM55, five hours), which passes through an Amazonian dystopia of abandoned sawmills and rust-bucket tramp steamers. It's a good idea to book a day ahead.

BUS

Sibu's **long-distance bus station** (Jln Pahlawan) is about 3.5km northeast of the centre along Jln Pedada. A variety of companies send buses to Kuching (RM50 to RM60, seven to eight hours, regular departures between 7am and 4am), Miri (RM50, 6½ hours, roughly hourly from 6am to 3.30am) and Bintulu (RM30, 3¼ hours, roughly hourly from 6am to 3.30am).

Getting Around

TO/FROM THE AIRPORT

Sibu airport is 23km east of the centre; a taxi costs RM35.

From the local bus station, the Panduan Hemat bus to Sibu Jaya passes by the airport junction (RM3, every hour or two from 6am to 6pm), which is five minutes on foot from the terminal.

BUS

To get from the **local bus station**, in front of the Express Ferry Terminal, to the long-distance bus station, take Lanang Bus 21 (RM2, 15 minutes, once or twice an hour 6.30am to 5.15pm).

TAXI

Taxis (☎ 084-313658, 084-315440, 084-320773) can be ordered 24 hours a day. Taking a taxi from the city centre to the long-distance bus station costs RM15.

Batang Rejang

A trip up the tan, churning waters of 640km-long Batang Rejang (Rejang River) – the 'Amazon of Borneo' – is one of Southeast Asia's great river journeys. Express ferries barrel through the currents, eddies and whirlpools, the pilots expertly dodging angular black boulders half-hidden in the roiling waters. Though the area is no longer the jungle-lined wilderness it was in the days before Malaysian independence, it retains a frontier, *ulu-ulu* (upriver, back-of-beyond) vibe, especially in towns and longhouses accessible only by boat.

To get a sense of the extent of logging and palm-oil monoculture, check out Google Earth.

RIDING THE RAPIDS

When the water level in the Batang Rejang is too low for boats to make the trip upriver from Kapit, Belaga-based **Daniel Levoh** (p438) can arrange to collect you in his own small boat at **Punan Bah** longhouse – about halfway between Kapit and Belaga and the last stop before the **Pelagus Rapids**, which larger boats are unable to pass. He can take you to see the longhouse before continuing upriver to Belaga, with lunch on the way (RM500 for up to four people). The trip can also be done in reverse, from Belaga to Kapit.

Getting Around

For the time being, pretty much the only transport arteries into and around the Batang Rejang region are rivers. At research time, a new road from Kapit to Kanowit (already connected to Sarawak's highway network) was nearing completion and a rough logging road already connects Bintulu with Belaga. It seems that easy land access will soon change this part of Borneo.

Boats can navigate the perilous Pelagus Rapids, between Kapit and Belaga, only when the water level is high enough – these days, determined mainly by how much water is released from the Bakun Dam.

Express river boats – nicknamed 'flying coffins' because of their shape, not their safety record – run by half-a-dozen companies head up the broad, muddy Batang Rejang from Sibu with goods and luggage strapped precariously to their roofs. If you opt to ride up top for the view (not that we recommend it...), hang on tight! The passenger cabins tend to be air-conditioned to near-arctic frigidity.

From Sibu, boats to Kapit (140km, 2½ to three hours) leave every hour from 5.45am to 2.30pm; from Kapit, boats heading down to Sibu depart between 6.40am and 3.15pm. Boarding often involves clambering over boats and inching your way along a narrow, rail-less exterior gangway.

If the water level at the Pelagus Rapids (32km upriver from Kapit) is high enough, one 77-seat **express boat** (☎ 013-806 1333) a day goes all the way to Belaga, 155km upriver from Kapit, stopping at various longhouses along the way. Heading upriver, departures are at 5.45am from Sibu (RM85, 11 hours) and 9.30am from Kapit (RM55, 4½ hours). Coming downriver, the boat leaves Belaga at about 7.30am. When the river is too low, the only way to get to Belaga is overland via Bintulu.

Kapit

POP 14,000

The main upriver settlement on the Batang Rejang, Kapit is a bustling trading and transport centre dating back to the days of the White Rajahs. A number of nearby longhouses can be visited by road or river, but

Kapit

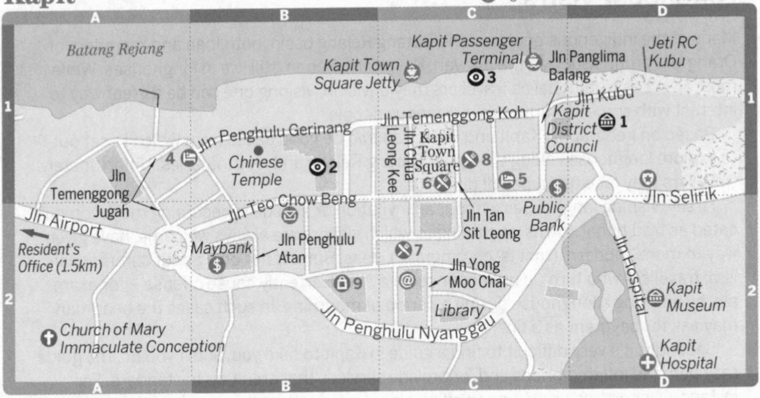

Kapit

Sights

1	Fort Sylvia	D1
2	Pasar Teresang	B1
3	Waterfront	C1

Sleeping

4	Hiap Chiong Hotel	A1
5	New Rejang Inn	C1

Eating

6	Famous Bakery	C1
	Gelanggang Kenyalang	(see 9)
7	Night Market	C2
8	Soon Kit Café	C1

Shopping

9	Sula Perengka Kapit	B2

the pickings are thin when it comes to finding a good local guide.

Fans of Redmond O'Hanlon's *Into the Heart of Borneo* may remember Kapit as the starting point of the author's adventures.

Sights

Fort Sylvia MUSEUM

(Jln Kubu; 10am-noon & 2-5pm, closed Mon & public holidays) Built by Charles Brooke in 1880 to take control of the Upper Rejang, this wooden fort – built of *belian* – was renamed in 1925 to honour Ranee Sylvia, Brooke's wife.

The exhibits inside offer a pretty good introduction to the traditional lifestyles of the indigenous groups of the Batang Rejang and include evocative colonial-era photographs. Also on show is the peace jar presented during the historical 1924 peacemaking ceremony between previously warring Iban, Kayan and Kenyah groups.

The museum also devotes space to the story of Domingo 'Mingo' de Rozario, the son of James Brooke's Portuguese Melakan butler and a man described by a contemporary as having 'a burly figure, dark kindly face, utter disregard for personal danger' and the tendency to 'look on life as a huge joke'. Rozario was sent to Kapit and charged with bringing it under the Rajah's control. He became an authority on Upper Rejang enthnography, describing life in the region in a series of colourful letters and reports.

Waterfront PORT

Kapit's waterfront is lined with ferries, barges, longboats and floating docks, all swarming with people. Porters carry impossibly heavy or unwieldy loads – we've seen 15 egg crates stacked in a swaying pile – up the steep steps from the wharfs.

Pasar Teresang MARKET

(5.30am-6pm) Some of the goods unloaded at the waterfront end up in this colourful covered market. It's a chatty, noisy hive of grass-roots commerce, with a galaxy of unfamiliar edibles that grow in the jungle, as well as handicrafts. Orang Ulu people sell fried treats and steamed buns.

Tours

Longhouse Tours

Longhouses, many of them quite modern and some accessible by road (river travel is both slower and pricier than going by minibus), can be found along the Batang

LONGHOUSE VISITS

Many of the indigenous people of the Batang Rejang basin, both Iban and members of Orang Ulu groups such as the Kenyah, Kayan and Punan, still live in longhouses. While most aren't as traditional as travellers may envision, visiting one can be a great way to interact with some of Sarawak's indigenous people.

Based on geography, Kapit and Belaga *should* be good bases from which to set out to explore longhouses along the upper Batang Rejang and its tributaries. Unfortunately, travellers may face two types of difficulties.

Firstly, visiting longhouses without an invitation or a guide is becoming more complicated as traditional norms, according to which visitors are always welcome, have given way to more 'modern' (that is, commercial) ideas. But it is not only about commercialism; travellers who turn up unannounced may inadvertently cause offense – for example, by entering a longhouse during a period of mourning. In such cases the headman may ask for payment as a fine.

Secondly, it's very difficult to find a guide in Kapit to take you, and if you do, the guide may demand inflated prices and/or provide services that aren't up to standard. For instance, visitors may be dropped off at a longhouse with nothing to do and no way to communicate with the residents until they're picked up the next day.

If you are flexible and have some time to spend in the area, you may well be lucky enough to be invited by locals to their longhouse. Otherwise, the best option is to make arrangements through one of the tour agencies based in Sibu (p431).

Baleh, which joins the Batang Rejang 9km upstream from Kapit, and the Sungai Sut, a tributary of the Batang Baleh. Longhouses along these rivers tend to be more traditional than their counterparts along the mainline Batang Rejang.

The problem is finding a good guide. Due to the lack of licensed guides in Kapit, and because many of Sarawak's unlicensed guides are competent and knowledgeable, we advise that you talk to other travellers and local hotel owners about which operators are recommended or best avoided. The safest bet is to arrange a tour with an established Sibu-based operator (p431).

Visiting Longhouses on Your Own

A few communities around Kapit are accustomed to independent travellers, charging between RM10 and RM40 for a day visit or RM50 to RM100 per person if you stay overnight, including meals. The headman may also expect a tip, and if you plan to stay overnight, you should also bring a gift. Remember that there may not be much to do at a longhouse, especially if there aren't any English speakers around.

Longhouses you may consider visiting:

Rumah Bundong One of the area's few remaining traditional Iban longhouses. Situated on Sungai Kapit a 45-minute (10km) drive from Kapit.

Rumah Jandok A traditional longhouse on Sungai Yong with quite a few English speakers, situated down the Batang Rejang from Kapit. The longhouse is one hour by road from Kapit and charges RM40 for a visit, plus RM10 for the headman and RM15 for taking photos of the skulls.

To arrange land transport, ask the car and van drivers outside Pasar Teresang (on Jln Teo Chow Beng). Alternatively, you could try joining the locals in the service-taxi minivans that hang out around Kapit Town Sq (at the corner of Jln Teo Chow Beng and Jln Chua Leong Kee) and at Pasar Teresang (on Jln Teo Chow Beng).

To get to longhouses accessible only by river, head to **Jeti RC Kubu** (Jln Kubu), the jetty facing Fort Sylvia, and negotiate for a longboat. These can be expensive – imagine how much fuel the outboard slurps as the boat powers its way upstream.

Festivals & Events

Baleh-Kapit Raft Safari WATER SPORTS

A challenging, two-day race recreating the experience of Iban and Orang Ulu people rafting downstream to bring their jungle produce to Kapit. Often held in April. For details, check with the **Resident's Office** (084-796230; www.kapitro.sarawak.gov.my; 9th fl, Kompleks Kerajaan Negeri Bahagian Kapit, Jln Bleteh; 8am-1pm & 2-5pm Mon-Thu, 8-11.45am & 2.15-5pm Fri) in Kapit or Sibu's Visitors Information Centre (p433).

Sleeping

New Rejang Inn HOTEL $
(084-796600, 084-796700; 104 Jln Teo Chow Beng; d RM78;) A welcoming and well-run hotel whose 15 spotless, good-sized rooms come with comfortable mattresses, hot water, TV, phone and mini-fridge. The best-value accommodation in town.

Hiap Chiong Hotel HOTEL $
(084-796314; 33 Jln Temenggong Jugah; d RM50;) The 15 rooms have outdated furniture but are clean and have tiny flat-screen TVs.

Eating & Drinking

Soon Kit Café CHINESE $
(13 Jln Tan Sit Liong; mains RM5-6; 5am-6pm) An old-time *kopitiam* (coffee shop) with laksa (RM5) in the morning and excellent chicken rice (RM5.50).

Gelanggang Kenyalang HAWKER $
(off Jln Penghulu Nyanggau; mains from RM3.50; 6am-5pm) An indoor food court with Malay and Chinese stalls. A good place for breakfast laksa or *roti canai*.

Night Market MARKET $
(Taman Selera Empurau; mains RM2.50-5; 5-11pm or midnight) Delicious satay and barbecue chicken are the highlight of this night market, which has tables to eat at. Situated a block up the slope from Kapit Town Sq.

Famous Bakery BAKERY $
(22 Jln Teo Chow Beng; pastries RM1-3.50; 5.30am-6pm) Freshly baked Chinese and Western-style pastries, cakes, mini-pizzas and other easy-to-pack day-trip picnic fare.

Shopping

Sula Perengka Kapit HANDICRAFTS
(off Jln Penghulu Nyanggau; 8am-4pm Mon-Sat, 8am-noon Sun) A tiny, Iban-owned handicrafts place (Shop 21) upstairs at the Gelanggang Kenyalang food court.

Information

Kapit Hospital (084-796333; Jln Hospital; 24hr) Has three ambulances and half-a-dozen doctors.

King Cyber Sky (Jln Penghulu Gerinang, 1st fl, above Public Cafe; per hr RM3; 10am-11pm)

Getting There & Away

BOAT

Express boats to Sibu (RM25 to RM35, 2½ to three hours, once or twice an hour) depart between 6.40am and 3.15pm from the **Kapit Passenger Terminal** (Jln Panglima Balang;), which has a nice verandah cafe with breezy river views.

Water levels permitting (for details, call **Daniel Levoh,** p438, in Belaga), an express boat heads upriver to Belaga (RM55, 4½ hours) from the **Kapit Town Square jetty** (Kapit Town Sq), two blocks downriver from the Kapit Passenger Terminal, once a day at about 9.30am. Be on board by 9.15am.

One express boat a day heads up the Batang Baleh, going as far as the Iban longhouse of Rumah Penghulu Jampi. It departs from Kapit at about 10am and from Rumah Penghulu Jampi at 12.30pm.

VAN

A small road network around Kapit, unconnected to the outside world, links the town to a number of longhouses. Vans that ply these byways congregate at Kapit Town Sq.

UPPER REJANG TRAVEL PERMITS

Theoretically, a free, two-week permit is required for all travel in the following places:

- Along the Batang Rejang to points upriver from the Pelagus Rapids (32km upstream from Kapit).
- Up the Batang Baleh, which flows into the Batang Rejang 9km upriver from Kapit.

In fact, we've never heard of anyone having their permit checked, and the whole arrangement seems to be a bureaucratic holdover from the time when the government sought to limit foreign activists' access to Orang Ulu communities threatened by logging or the controversial Bakun Dam. Permits are not required, even in theory, if you travel to Belaga overland from Bintulu.

Permits (unneccesary as they are) are issued in Kapit at the Resident's Office, in a nine-storey building 2km west of the centre. To get there, take a van (RM2) from the southeast corner of Pasar Teresang. To get back to town, ask the lobby guards for help catching a ride (offer to pay the driver).

Belaga

POP 2500

By the time you pull into Belaga after the long cruise up the Batang Rejang, you may feel like you've arrived in the very heart of Borneo – in reality, you're only about 100km (as the crow flies) from the coast. There's not much to do here except soak up the frontier vibe, but nearby rivers are home to quite a few Orang Ulu (primarily Kayan and Kenyah) longhouses.

Sights

To get a feel for the pace of local life, wander among the two-storey shophouses of the compact, mostly Chinese **town centre**, or stroll through the manicured **park** – complete with basketball and tennis courts – between Main Bazaar and the river. Along the riverfront, a wooden bridge leads downstream to **Kampung Melayu Belaga**, Belaga's Malay quarter, whose wooden homes are built on stilts. The town's 24-hour electricity is provided by generator – Belaga is not yet connected to the Bakun Dam grid.

Activities

The main reason travellers visit Belaga is to venture up a jungle stream in search of hidden longhouses and secret waterfalls. Possible destinations include the following:

Dong Daah A Kayan longhouse 10 minutes upriver by boat from Belaga.

Lirong Amo A Kayan longhouse half-an-hour's walk from Belaga.

Long Liten A huge, old Kejaman longhouse a ways upriver.

Long Segaham A Kejaman longhouse situated some way upriver.

Sekapan Panjang A traditional, all-wood Sekapan longhouse half-an-hour downstream by boat from Belaga.

Sihan A Penan settlement a two-hour walk from the other bank of the Batang Rejang.

Before you can share shots of *tuak* with the longhouse headman, however, you need to find a guide. A good package should include a boat ride, jungle trekking, a waterfall swim, a night walk and activities such as cooking and fruit harvesting.

Daniel Levoh GUIDE
(086-461198, 013-848 6351; daniellevoh@hotmail.com; Jln Teh Ah Kiong) A Kayan former school headmaster, Daniel is friendly and knowledgeable. Possible excursions include walking to Sihan, a Penan settlement across the river, and stopping at a waterfall (this can be done unguided at a cost of RM20 for the boat and a gift for the longhouse; Daniel will call ahead). Can also arrange private transport around Belaga and Bintulu.

Hamdani TOUR
(019-886 5770) Former guide Hamdini may be able to help arrange longhouse visits.

Events

Belaga Rainforest Challenge SPORTS
(Jul or Aug of even-numbered yrs) This five-day event combines a 17km jungle run with boat races and traditional music and dance performances.

Sleeping

Belaga's accommodation is of the cheap and shabby variety.

Daniel Levoh's Guesthouse GUESTHOUSE $
(013-848 6351, 086-461198; daniellevoh@hotmail.com; Jln Teh Ah Kiong; dm RM20, d without bathroom RM40;) The four simple rooms are on the 2nd floor, opening off a large open verandah decorated with a traditional Kayan mural. Owner Daniel Levoh is happy to share stories of longhouse life. Situated two blocks behind Main Bazaar.

Belaga B&B HOTEL $
(013-842 9760; freeland205@gmail.com; Main Bazaar; with fan dm/d RM25/15, with air-con d RM35;) Has seven basic rooms, some with air-con, and shared bathroom facilities. Don't let the name fool you: breakfast isn't included. Owned by Hasbee, a former longhouse guide who now runs the eponymous cafe downstairs. He is happy to help arrange longhouse visits.

Eating

There are a few simple cafes serving Chinese and Malay dishes along Main Bazaar.

Night Market HAWKER $
(block behind Main Bazaar; mains RM4.50-12; 3.30-10pm) An outdoor food court with six stalls selling Kayan, Kenyah and Malay food. Look for Robina's stall selling delicious ginger chicken (RM6).

Crystal Cafe MALAYSIAN $
(Jln Temenggong Matu; mains RM3.50-8; 7am-7pm) Owned by an Iban-Kenyah family,

Crystal Cafe is a good bet for a simple meal of mee goreng (RM3.50), laksa Sarawak (RM4.30), *nasi lemak ayam* (chicken with rice boiled in coconut milk; RM5.50) or *nasi ayam penyet* (smashed fried chicken with rice and sambal; RM8).

Information

The town's only ATM is often out of order; bring plenty of cash. The medical clinic has one doctor. Several places to stay have wi-fi.

Getting There & Away

When the express boat is running, it's possible to visit Belaga without backtracking, cruising the Batang Rejang in one direction and taking the logging road to/from Bintulu in the other.

BOAT

If the water levels at the Pelagus Rapids (32km upriver from Kapit) are high enough, you can take an express boat to Kapit (RM55, 4½ hours) departing at about 7.30am. To find out if the boat is running, call tour guide Daniel Levoh. When the river is too low, the only way to get out of Belaga is by 4WD to Bintulu.

LAND

A bone-jarring (and, in the rain, fiendishly slippery) logging road connects Belaga with Bintulu (160km). Part of the way the route follows the 125km-long paved road to the Bakun Dam.

4WD Toyota Land Cruisers link Belaga with Bintulu (RM50 to RM60 per person, RM400 for the whole vehicle, four hours) on most days, with departures from Belaga at about 7.30am and from Bintulu in the early afternoon (between noon and 2pm). In Belaga, vehicles to Bintulu congregate in front of Belaga B&B at about 7am. To arrange a vehicle from Bintulu, call Daniel Levoh.

If you're coming from Miri or Batu Niah Junction or heading up that way (ie northeast), you can arrange to be picked up or dropped off at Simpang Bakun (Bakun Junction), which is on the inland (old) highway 53km northeast of Bintulu and 159km southwest of Miri.

Upriver from Belaga

About 40km upstream from Belaga, the Batang Rejang divides into several rivers, including the mighty Batang Balui, which wends and winds almost all the way up to the Kalimantan border. Just below this junction, the controversial **Bakun Dam** generates electricity and provides locals with a place to catch fish, which they come down to the dam to sell on Wednesday and Saturday mornings. Belaga-based guides can arrange visits to area longhouses. The 15 longhouses in Sungai Asap are new – built to rehouse the communities displaced by flooding due to the dam – but traditional in style.

The dam is 40km (two hours) by road from Belaga.

Bintulu

086 / POP 190,000

Fifty years ago Bintulu was a small fishing village with a population of 5000; now, thanks to its offshore natural gas fields, it is a booming industrial town and Sarawak's most important centre for the production of LNG (liquefied natural gas) and fertiliser.

Most travellers who stop in Bintulu, roughly midway between Sibu and Miri (about 200km from each), plan to visit to Similajau National Park or travel overland to or from Belaga.

Sights

Tua Pek Kong CHINESE TEMPLE

(Main Bazaar; 7am-6pm) FREE This classic Chinese temple adds vibrant colours to the rather drab city centre. The serenity is somewhat marred by the sound of cock-a-doodle-doos drifting over from the paved area around back, where young fighting cocks are kept tethered to avoid strife.

Festivals

Borneo International Kite Festival SPORTS

(www.borneokite.com; Sep) An annual event, usually held over four or five days in September, that brings the world's top kite fliers to Bintulu to compete in the Borneo Sports Kite Championship. Also on the programme are kite-flying demonstrations and workshops.

Sleeping

There are quite a few hotels, some on the dodgy side, on and near Jln Keppel, its southern continuation, Jln Abang Galau, and parallel Jln Masjid.

Kintown Inn HOTEL $

(086-333666; 93 Jln Keppel; s/d RM80/86.25;) The carpeted rooms, though small and rather musty, are a reasonable option for those on a budget who aren't put off by a bit of peeling paint.

Riverfront Inn HOTEL $$

(086-333111; riverfrontinn@hotmail.com; 256 Taman Sri Dagang; s/d from RM81/104;) A long-standing favourite with business and

Bintulu

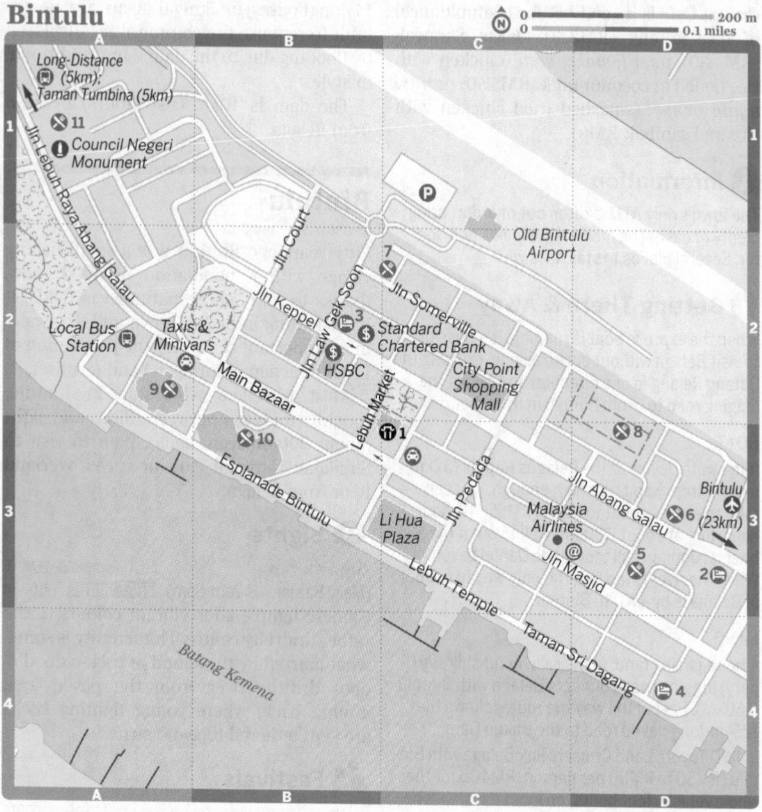

Bintulu

Sights

1 Tua Pek Kong C3

Sleeping

2 Kemena Plaza Hotel D3
3 Kintown Inn B2
4 Riverfront Inn D4

Eating

5 Ban Kee Café D3
6 Chef D3
7 Famous Mama C2
8 Night Market D3
9 Pasar Tamu A2
10 Pasar Utama B3
11 Popular Corner Food Centre A1

leisure visitors alike, the Riverfront is low-key but has a touch of class. Try to get a deluxe room (RM120) overlooking the river – the view is pure Borneo.

Kemena Plaza Hotel HOTEL $$
(086-335111; www.kemenahotelgroup.com; 116 Jln Abang Galau; d/ste incl breakfast RM170/290;) Recent renovations have refreshed the hotel's 162 rooms, which are spacious with wooden floors, neutral colours and small bathrooms; rooms on the upper floors overlook the river. The highlight here is a rooftop swimming pool and sun terrace, with spectacular views of the town and river and the ocean beyond them.

Eating & Drinking

Famous Mama MAMAK, HALAL $
(10 Jln Somerville; mains RM5-10;) Famous Mama does Mamak (halal Indian-Malay) cuisine and is a popular place for quick, cheap *nasi kandar* (rice served with side dishes of different curries) and *roti canai*.

Popular Corner Food Centre HAWKER $
(50 BDA Shahida Commercial Centre, Jln Abang Galau; mains RM7-12; 6am-5pm) If you've ever

wanted to try fresh frog porridge (RM12), this is the place to come. Less adventurous diners can chose from one of eight stalls selling dim sum and fresh seafood.

Night Market MALAYSIAN $
(Pasar Malam; off Jln Abang Galau; mains RM2-5; ⏲4-10pm) A good place to pick up snacks, fresh fruit and Malay favourites such as satay and *nasi lemak*.

Pasar Utama HAWKER $
(New Market; Main Bazaar; mains RM3-5; ⏲7am-4pm) Malay and Chinese food stalls fill the upper floor of this blue-coloured fruit and vegetable market. The cone-shaped roofs of Pasar Utama and the next door **Pasar Tamu** (Bintulu Market, Main Bazaar; ⏲7am-6pm) wet market represent *terendak*, the traditional headwear of the Melanau tribe.

Chef BAKERY $
(☎086-312964; 97 Jln Abang Galau; cakes from RM1; ⏲8.30am-9pm) Makes Chinese-inflected baked goods, including sweet and savoury bread rolls, sandwiches, pastries and surprisingly tasty Belgian chocolate cake. Ideal fare for a picnic lunch.

Ban Kee Café SEAFOOD $$
(off Jln Abang Galau; mains RM6-15; ⏲6.30am-11pm) An atmospheric Chinese seafood specialist with seating in a semi-covered outdoor courtyard, selling fresh fish and seafood (per kilogram RM40 to RM80) and breakfast noodles and laksa.

ℹ Information

Fi Wee Internet Centre (1st fl, 133 Jln Masjid; per hr RM2; ⏲9am-1am) Popular with gamers.

ℹ Getting There & Away

To arrange transport by 4WD Toyota Land Cruiser from Bintulu to Belaga (per person RM50, four hours) on some pretty rough logging roads, call Daniel Levoh (p438). Departures are generally in the early afternoon (between noon and 2pm).

AIR

AirAsia (www.airasia.com) and **Malaysia Airlines** (☎086-331349; www.malaysiaairlines.com) have direct flights to Kuching and Kuala Lumpur. **MASwings** (☎086-331349; www.maswings.com.my; Bintulu airport; ⏲7am-7pm) flies to Kota Kinabalu, Miri, Sibu and Kuching.

BUS

The long-distance bus station is at Medan Jaya, 5km northeast of the centre (aka Bintulu Town); a taxi costs RM20. About a dozen companies have buses approximately hourly to the following destinations:

- Kuching (RM70, 11 hours) via Sibu (RM25, four hours), from 6am to midnight.
- Miri (RM25, four hours) via Niah Junction (RM15, 2¾ hours), from 6am to 9.30pm.

ℹ Getting Around

There is no public transport to/from the airport, which is 23km from the centre by road. A taxi costs RM35.

Similajau National Park

An easy 30km northeast of Bintulu, **Similajau National Park** (☎Miri office 085-434184, Park office 086-489003; www.sarawakforestry.com; Kuala Likau; adult/child RM20/7; ⏲park office 8am-1pm & 2-5pm Sat-Thu, 8-11.45am & 2.15-5pm Fri) is a fine little coastal park with golden-sand beaches, good walking trails and simple accommodation. Occupying a narrow, 30km strip along the South China Sea, its 90 sq km encompasses littoral habitats such as mangroves, *kerangas* (heath forest) and mixed dipterocarp forest (classic lowland tropical rainforest). Four species of dolphin, including Irrawaddy dolphins, can sometimes be spotted out at sea, and green turtles occasionally trundle ashore to lay their eggs along Turtle Beach II and Golden Beach. The park is also home to gibbons, long-tailed macaques, mouse deer, barking deer and wild boars.

Bintuluans flock to Similajau (especially the beaches) on weekends and public holidays, but the park is gloriously deserted on weekdays.

Sights & Activities

Similajau Beach BEACH
(Similajau National Park) The casuarina-lined beach at Similajau park HQ, strewn with driftwood but clean, is a great place to chill

ℹ BEWARE CROCODILES!

Similajau's waterways are prime crocodile habitat, so do not swim or wade in the rivers or near rivermouths and be careful when walking near riverbanks, especially early or late in the day.

Swimming is forbidden at the two Turtle Beaches and at Golden Beach because of dangerous undertows.

out. It's also a popular spot for taking a dip – if the thought of estuarine crocodiles (those are the big ones) and jellyfish don't deter you, that is. If you do enter the water, make sure you are far away from the rivermouth.

Hiking Trails HIKING

(☎086-489003; Similajau National Park) Similajau's beautiful forest trails are easy to follow and clearly marked, so a guide isn't necessary, though it's possible to hire one (call in advance) for RM30 per hour (RM40 per hour for a **night walk**). Before setting off remember to sign in at park HQ and pick up the simple but useful trail map. Bring plenty of drinking water.

The gently undulating **Main Trail** (Coastal Trail) parallels the coast, starting at the suspension bridge that crosses Sungai Likau and ending at **Golden Beach** (10km, four hours one-way). The trail passes by rocky headlands, small bays and **Turtle Beach I** (6.5km, 2½ hours) and **Turtle Beach II** (7km, three hours). For a view back along the coast towards Bintulu and its natural-gas installations, head to the **View Point** (1.3km from HQ, 40 minutes).

Branching off to the right after crossing the suspension bridge, a 1.7km **Circular Trail** passes through brilliant estuarine mangroves and mixed dipterocarp forest.

Boat Trips BOAT TOUR

(☎086-489003, 019-861 0998; www.sarawakforestry.com; Similajau National Park; boat for up to 5 people to Turtle Beach 1-way/return RM195/245, to Golden Beach 1-way/return RM235/300; ⏲office 8am-5pm) To avoid retracing your steps on a hike, one option is to arrange a ride in the park boat to one of the beaches and walk back. The boat, with space for five passengers, can be hired for one-way or return trips. Sea conditions are often rough later in the day, so it's best to head out before 8am.

Options include a return trip to the rocky island of **Batu Mandi** (RM160), or making a 30-minute stop at the island before continuing on to **Golden Beach** to hike back from there (RM445). It is also possible to arrange a **night river cruise** (RM160) to see the crocs (reserve during office hours).

Sleeping

Similajau's rustic overnight options, just 100m from the beach, sometimes fill up on weekends.

Cabins CABIN $

(☎086-489003, 019-861 0998; www.sarawakforestry.com; Similajau National Park; r RM100, 2-room unit RM150; ❄) Each of the six simple but comfortable cabins has two rooms: one air-conditioned bedroom and a fan-cooled living room, each with a double and single bed (each unit sleeps six).

Hostel HOSTEL $

(☎086-489003, 019-861 0998; www.sarawakforestry.com; Similajau National Park; dm RM15) Each room has four beds (bunks in the case of Hostel 3) and a wall fan. Hostels 1 and 2 have attached bathrooms.

Campground CAMPGROUND $

(☎086-489003, 019-861 0998; www.sarawakforestry.com; Similajau National Park; per person RM5) Camping is only permitted next to park HQ. Showers are provided.

Rest House CABIN $$

(☎086-489003, 019-861 0998; www.sarawakforestry.com; Similajau National Park; 2-room unit RM300; ❄) The park's most luxurious accommodation is a self-contained, air-conditioned 'VIP' cabin with its own living room and verandah.

Eating

Cooking is not allowed in the park cabins or hostel, but there are designated sites for barbecuing.

Cafeteria CAFETERIA $

(mains RM5-13; ⏲7.30am-8.30pm; ☑) Serves simple rice and noodle dishes and can prepare packed lunches.

Getting There & Away

The HQ of Similajau National Park is about 30km northeast of Bintulu, 9km off the coastal road to Miri.

Count on paying RM55 one way to hire a taxi from Bintulu (there is no public bus).

To get back to Bintulu, you can pre-arrange a pick-up time or ask HQ staff to help you call for a taxi.

Niah National Park

The vast limestone caverns of 31-sq-km **Niah National Park** (☎085-737450, 085-737454; www.sarawakforestry.com; admission RM20; ⏲park office 8am-5pm) are among Borneo's most famous and impressive natural attractions. At the heart of the park is the Great Cave, one of the largest caverns in the world.

Niah's caves have provided groundbreaking insights into human life on Borneo way back when the island was still connected to mainland Southeast Asia. In 1958 archaeologists led by Tom Harrisson discovered the 40,000-year-old skull of an anatomically modern human, the oldest remains of a *Homo sapiens* discovered anywhere in Southeast Asia.

Rock paintings and several small canoe-like coffins ('death ships') indicate that the site was used as a burial ground much more recently. Some of the artefacts found at Niah are kept in Kuching; others (a handful) are in the park's own museum.

Niah's caves accommodate a staggering number of bats and are an important nesting site for swiftlets, some of whose species supply the vital ingredient for bird's-nest soup. Traditionally, the Penan are custodians and collectors of the nests, while the Iban have the rights to the caves' other commodity, bat and bird guano, which is highly valued as fertiliser (no prizes for guessing who got first pick). During the harvesting season (August to March), nest collectors can be seen on towering bamboo structures wedged against the cave roof.

Despite the historical significance of the sight, Niah has not been overly done-up for tourists. It's possible to visit the caves without a guide and during the week you may have the place to yourself. Travellers who have been (or are going) to Gunung Mulu National Park may feel caved-out at the thought of Niah, but for anyone with even a passing interest in human prehistory it is not to be missed.

Sights & Activities

Niah Archaeology Museum MUSEUM

(motor launch per person RM1, 5.30-7.30pm RM1.50; 9am-4.45pm Tue-Fri, 10am-4pm Sat & Sun) Across the river from park HQ, this museum has informative displays on Niah's geology, ecology and prehistoric archaeology, including an original burial canoe that's at least 1200 years old, a reproduction of the Painted Cave, a case featuring swiftlets' nests, and a replica of the 40,000-year-old 'Deep Skull'.

To get to the museum, cross Sungai Niah by motor launch. Torches – essential if you want to go any distance into the caves – can be rented at the museum (RM5).

Great Cave CAVE

A raised boardwalk leads 3.1km (3½ to four hours return) through swampy, old-growth rainforest to the mouth of the Great Cave, a vast cavern approximately 2km long, up to 250m across and up to 60m high. Inside, the trail splits to go around a massive central pillar, but both branches finish at the same point, so it's impossible to get lost if you stick to the boardwalk. The stairs and handrails are usually covered with guano, and can be slippery.

The rock formations are spectacular and ominous by turns, and you may find yourself thinking of Jules Verne's *Journey to the Centre of the Earth*. When the sun hits certain overhead vents, the cave is penetrated by dramatic rays of otherworldly light. When you're halfway through the dark passage known as Gan Kira (Moon Cave), try turning off your torch to enjoy the experience of pure, soupy blackness.

Painted Cave CAVE

After passing through Gan Kira, you emerge into the forest and another section of boardwalk before arriving at the Painted Cave, famed for its ancient drawings, in red hematite, depicting jungle animals, human figures and the souls of the dead being taken to the afterlife by boat. It can be tricky to make out the red hematite figures, as many have faded to little more than indistinct scrawls along a narrow 30m-strip at the back of the cave.

To return, retrace your steps, taking the stairs up to your left to close the loop in the Great Cave.

Bukit Kasut WALKING

This 45-minute trail, part of it a boardwalk through freshwater swamp forest, leads up to the summit of **Bukit Kasut** (205m). In the wet season, it can get muddy and treacherously slippery.

Sleeping & Eating

Bookings for park-run accommodation can be made at park HQ (in person or by phone) or through one of the **National Park Booking Offices** (in Kuching 082-248088, in Miri 085-434184). Lodges and rooms often fill up on Chinese, Malay and public holidays. Cooking is prohibited in park accommodation, but you can, boil water to make instant noodles, except at the hostel.

Batu Niah town, 4km from park HQ (3km if you walk), has a couple of basic hotels.

NIAH'S BATS & SWIFTLETS

The chorus of high-pitched sqwaking you'll hear as you enter the Great Cave is not the sound of bats but of Niah's resident swiftlets; further in, you'll detect the squeaking of bats. At one time, some 470,000 bats and four million swiftlets called Niah home. Current numers are not known, but the walls of the caves are no longer thick with bats and there are fewer bird's nests to harvest.

Several species of swiftlet nest on the cave walls. The most common by far is the glossy swiftlet, whose nest is made of vegetation and is therefore of no use in making soup. For obvious reasons, the species whose nests are edible (those that are made of salivary excretions that are considered by many to be a great delicacy) are far less abundant and can only be seen in the remotest corners of the cavern. Several types of bat also roost in the cave, but not in dense colonies, as at Gunung Mulu National Park.

The best time to see the cave's winged wildlife is at dusk (5.30pm to 6.45pm) during the 'changeover', when the swiftlets stream back to their nests and the bats come swirling out for the night's feeding. If you decide to stick around, let staff at the park HQ's Registration Counter know and make sure you either get back to the boat by 7.30pm or coordinate a later pick-up time with the boatman.

Hostel HOSTEL $
(Niah National Park HQ; r RM40, towel rental RM6) Each basic hostel room has space for up to four people.

Rumah Patrick Libau Homestay HOMESTAY $
(☎Asan 014-596 2757; Niah National Park; per person incl meals RM70; wi-fi) The traditional, 100-door Iban longhouse Rumah Patrick Libau, which is home to about 400 people, operates an informal homestay program. Accommodation is basic but the longhouse has wi-fi and 24-hour electricity. To get here, take the signposted turn off the main trail that leads to the caves. Villagers often sit at the junction selling cold drinks and souvenirs.

Campground CAMPGROUND $
(Niah National Park HQ; per person RM5) Camping is permitted near park HQ.

Forest Lodges CABIN $$
(Niah National Park HQ; with fan q RM100, with air-con d/q RM250/150) The park has six rustic, two-room cabins with attached bathrooms; each room can sleep up to four people. Two additional, more expensive air-con units each have two rooms with twin beds.

Getting There & Away

Niah National Park is about 115km southwest of Miri and 122km northeast of Bintulu and can be visited as a day trip from either city.

Park HQ is 15km north of Batu Niah Junction, a major transport hub on the inland (old) Miri–Bintulu highway. This makes getting to the park by public transport a tad tricky.

All long-haul buses linking Miri's Pujut Bus Terminal with Bintulu, Sibu and Kuching stop at Batu Niah Junction, but the only way to get from the junction to the park is to hire an unofficial taxi. The price should be RM30 (RM40 for a group of four), but you'll have to nose around the junction to find one. A good place to check: the bench in front of Shen Yang Trading, at the corner of Ngu's Garden Food Court. National park staff (or, after hours, park security personnel) can help arrange a car back to the junction.

From Batu Niah Junction, buses head to Miri (RM12, 1¾ hours) from about 8am to 1am and to Bintulu (RM16, two hours) from about 8am to 10.30pm. Other well-served destinations include Sibu (RM40, five to six hours) and Kuching (RM80, 12 hours). Kiosks representing various companies can be found at both ends of the building directly across the highway from Batu Niah Food Court Centre.

From Miri, a taxi to Niah costs RM150 one way or RM240 return, including waiting time.

It is also worth considering hiring a car or motorbike for the day. See p452 for Miri car and motorcycle hire companies.

Lambir Hills National Park

The 69-sq-km **Lambir Hills National Park** (☎085-471609; www.sarawakforestry.com; Jln Miri-Bintulu; RM20; ⏲8am-5pm, last entry 4pm) shelters dozens of jungle waterfalls, plenty of cool pools where you can take a dip, and a bunch of great walking trails through mixed dipterocarp and *kerangas* forests. A perennial favourite among locals and an important centre of scientific research, Lambir

Hills makes a great day or overnight trip out of the city.

The park encompasses a range of low sandstone hills with an extraordinary variety of plants and animals – perhaps even, as noted in Sarawak Forestry's publications, 'the greatest level of plant biodiversity on the planet'. Studies of a 52-hectare research plot (closed to visitors) have found an amazing 1200 tree species. Fauna include clouded leopards, barking deer, pangolins, tarsiers, five varieties of civet, 10 bat species and 50 other kinds of mammals, though you are unlikely to see many of them around park HQ. Lambir Hills is also home to an unbelievable 237 species of bird, among them eight kinds of hornbill, and 24 species of frog – and more are being found all the time.

Activities

Lambir Hills' interconnected, colour-coded trails branch off four primary routes and lead to 14 destinations – rangers, based in the HQ building, can supply you with a map and are happy to make suggestions. Make sure you get back to park HQ before 5pm – unless you're heading out for a **night walk**, that is, in which case you need to coordinate with park staff. Hiring a guide (optional) costs RM30 per hour for up to five people.

From HQ, the **Main Trail** follows a small river, Sungai Liam, past two attractive waterfalls to the 25m-high **Latak Waterfall** (1km, 15 minutes to 20 minutes one-way), which has a picnic area, changing rooms and a refreshing, sandy pool suitable for **swimming**. It can get pretty crowded on weekends and holidays.

You're likely to enjoy more natural tranquility along the path to **Tengkorong Waterfall**, a somewhat strenuous 6km walk (one way) from park HQ.

There are wonderful views from the top of **Bukit Pantu**, a 3.6km (one way) walk from HQ that is a good option for those on a day trip.

Another more challenging trail, steep in places, goes to the summit of **Bukit Lambir** (465m; 7km one way from HQ), which also affords fine views. Keep an eye out for changes in the vegetation, including wild orchids, as the elevation rises.

Sleeping & Eating

Camping CAMPING $

(☎085-471609; Jln Miri-Bintulu; per person RM5) Camping is permitted near the park HQ.

Cabins CABIN $

(☎085-471609; Jln Miri-Bintulu; 1-/2-bed r with fan RM50/75, with air-con RM100/150) The park's accommodation is in reasonably comfortable, two-room cabins; the old ones are wooden, the four new ones are made of concrete. Fan rooms have two beds, while air-con rooms have three. Individual dorm beds are not available. Cabins are sometimes booked out at weekends and during school holidays.

If you get in before 2pm (check-in time), bags can be left at the camp office.

Canteen CAFETERIA $

(Jln Miri-Bintulu; mains RM4-6; 8am-5pm or later) The park's canteen serves simple rice and noodle dishes. If you are staying in the park and would like to eat an evening meal at the canteen, inform staff in advance. May close early.

Getting There & Away

Park HQ is 32km south of Miri on the inland (old) highway to Bintulu. All the buses that link Miri's Pujut Bus Terminal with Bintulu, Sibu and Kuching pass by here (RM10 from Miri) – just ask the driver to stop. There is a bus stand on the main road by the turn-off for the park, from where you can flag down a bus to Miri for the return journey.

A taxi from Miri costs RM40 one way (RM80 to 120 return, including two hours of wait time).

Miri

☎085 / POP 300,500

Miri, Sarawak's second city, is a thriving oil town that is busy and modern. There's plenty of money sloshing around, so the eating is good, the broad avenues are brightly lit, there's plenty to do when it's raining and the city's friendly guesthouses are a great place to meet other travellers. The population is about 40% Dayak (mainly Iban), 30% Chinese and 18% Malay.

Miri serves as a major transport hub, so if you're travelling to/from Brunei, Sabah, the Kelabit Highlands or the national parks of Gunung Mulu, Niah or Lambir Hills, chances are you'll pass this way.

Sights

Miri is not big on historical sites – it was pretty much destroyed during WWII – but it's not an unattractive city. A walk around the centre is a good way to get a feel for the local vibe. Streets worth a wander include (from north to south) Jln North Yu Seng, Jln South Yu Seng, Jln Maju and Jln High Street.

Miri

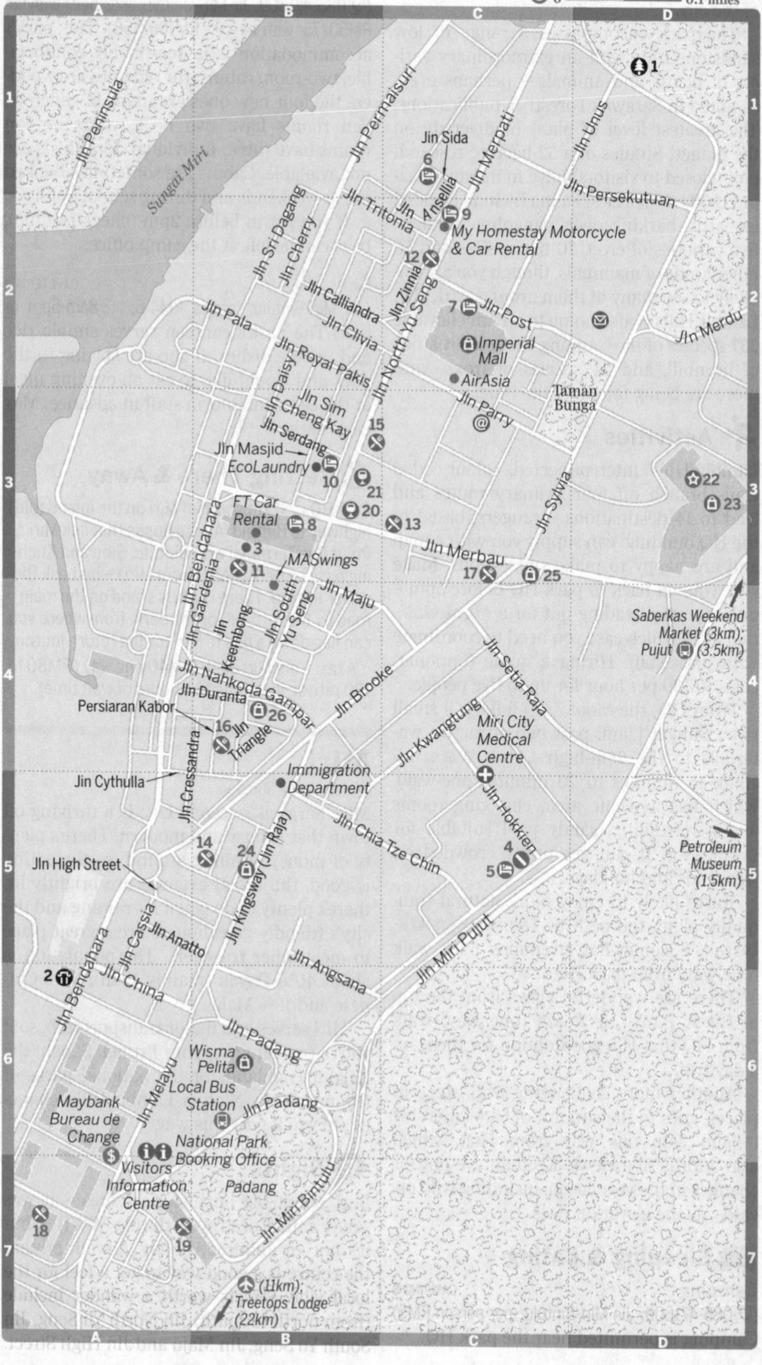

0 200 m
0 0.1 miles
A
B
C
D
1
2
3
4
5
6
7
Jln Peninsula
Sungai Miri
Jln Permaisuri
Jln Sida
Jln Merpati
Jln Unus
6
Jln Ansellia
9
Jln Tritonia
My Homestay Motorcycle & Car Rental
Jln Persekutuan
1
Jln Sri Dagang
Jln Cherry
12
Jln Zinnia
Jln North Yu Seng
Jln Calliandra
7
Jln Post
Jln Pala
Jln Clivia
Imperial Mall
Jln Merdu
Jln Royal Pakis
AirAsia
Taman Bunga
Jln Daisy
Jln Sim Cheng Kay
Jln Parry
Jln Serdang
15
Jln Masjid
EcoLaundry
10
21
Jln Sylvia
22
23
FT Car Rental
8
20
13
3
Jln Bendahara
Jln Merbau
17
25
11
MASwings
Jln Gardenia
Jln Keembong
Jln South Yu Seng
Jln Maju
Saberkas Weekend Market (3km); Pujut (3.5km)
Jln Nahkoda Gampar
Jln Brooke
Jln Setia Raja
Jln Duranta
26
Persiaran Kabor
16
Jln Triangle
Jln Kwangtung
Miri City Medical Centre
Jln Cythulla
Jln Cressandra
Immigration Department
Jln Hokkien
Jln Raja
Jln Chia Tze Chin
14
24
4
5
Jln High Street
Jln Kingsway
Petroleum Museum (1.5km)
Jln Cassia
Jln Anatto
Jln Miri Pujut
2
Jln Bendahara
Jln China
Jln Angsana
Jln Padang
Wisma Pelita
Jln Melayu
Local Bus Station
Jln Padang
Maybank Bureau de Change
National Park Booking Office
Visitors Information Centre
Padang
Jln Miri Bintulu
18
19
(11km); Treetops Lodge (22km)

Miri

Miri City Fan PARK

(Jln Kipas; 24hr) An attractive, open, landscaped park with Chinese- and Malay-style gardens and ponds that is a popular spot for walking and jogging. The complex also comprises a library, an indoor stadium and an Olympic-sized public swimming pool (RM1).

Petroleum Museum MUSEUM

(Bukit Tenaga; 9am-4.45pm Tue-Fri, 10am-4pm Sat & Sun) FREE The Petroleum Museum sits atop **Canada Hill**, a low ridge 2km southeast of the town centre that was the site of Malaysia's first oil well, the **Grand Old Lady**, drilled in 1910. Appropriately, the old derrick stands right outside the museum whose interactive exhibits, some designed for kids, are a good, pro-Big Oil introduction to the hugely lucrative industry that has so enriched Miri (and Malaysia's federal government).

The hill itself is a popular exercise spot, and it's worth coming here at sunset for the views across town to the South China Sea.

Saberkas Weekend Market MARKET

(Jln Miri Pujut ; 4-11pm Thu-Sat, 8am-noon Sun) One of the most colourful and friendly markets in Sarawak. Vendors are more than happy to answer questions about their produce, which includes tropical fruits and vegetables, BBQ chicken, satay and handicrafts. Situated about 3km northeast of the centre outside the Saberkas Commercial Centre. A taxi here costs RM15 (there is no bus).

San Ching Tian Temple TAOIST TEMPLE

(Jln Krokop 9; 8am-6pm) FREE This, one of the largest Taoist temples in Southeast Asia, was built in 2000. Set in a peaceful courtyard with soothing wind chimes, the temple's design features intricate dragon reliefs brought from China and majestic figures of the Three Pure Ones. Situated in the suburban neighbourhood of Krokop, 3km northeast of Miri town centre. A taxi here costs RM18.

Tua Pek Kong Temple CHINESE TEMPLE

(Jln Bendahara; 8am-6pm) FREE Miri's oldest Chinese temple – it was founded in 1913 – is a good spot to watch the river traffic float by. During the week-long celebration of Chinese New Year, virtually the whole of this area, including Jln China, is taken over by a lively street fair with plenty of red lanterns and gold foil.

Activities

Although the waters off Miri are better known for drilling than diving, the area – much of it part of the Miri-Sibuti Coral Reef Marine Park – has some excellent 7m- to 30m-deep scuba sites, including old oil platforms teeming with fish and assorted trawler and freighter wrecks. Water visibility is at its best from March to September.

The corals here are in good condition and the water unpolluted, despite the proximity of heavy industry. When visibility is good you might see giant cuttlefish, whale sharks and sting rays.

Coco Dive DIVING

(☎085-417053; www.cocodive.com.my; Lot 2117 Block 9, Jln Miri Pujut; 2 dives RM320, 3 dives RM370) A well-regarded dive company with a fat programme of dive packages and PADI-certification courses. Gets rave reviews for its friendly, professional staff and solid equipment.

Tours

Planet Borneo Tours TOUR

(☎085-414300, 085-415582; www.planetborneotours.com; Lot 273, 1st fl Brighton Centre, Jln Temenggong Datuk Oyong Lawai) Established tour operator with a head office in Miri offering a range of tours and activities in northeastern Sarawak and beyond. Longer itineraries include trekking in the highlands from Ba Kelalan to Bario via Gunung Murud (from RM2567) and a visit to a remote Kenyah longhouse in the upper Baram (four days, RM5880).

Borneo Tropical Adventure TREKKING

(☎085-419337; www.borneotropicaladventures.com; Lot 906, Shop 12, ground fl, Soon Hup Tower, Jln Merbau; ⏰9am-6pm) Veteran Miri-based company offering packages including the Headhunters Trail from Gunung Mulu National Park (five days, from RM1750) as well as longhouse visits and multiday Borneo-wide tours.

Borneo Trekkers TREKKING

(☎012-872 9159; www.borneotrekkers.blogspot.com) Guide Willie Kajan specialises in treks to Mulu along the Headhunters' Trail with the possibility of beginning or ending with a night at a longhouse in Limbang. Can also arrange treks in the Kelabit Highlands.

Festivals

Borneo Jazz MUSIC

(www.jazzborneo.com; Parkcity Everly Hotel, Jln Temenggong Datuk Oyong Lawai; 1-day pass adult/child RM70/30, 2-day pass adult/child RM130/50; ⏰2nd weekend in May) An outdoor jazz festival held over two nights featuring an eclectic ensemble of international talent. Prices quoted here are for door sales; there are hefty discounts for tickets bought online in advance.

Sleeping

Miri has some of Sarawak's best backpackers guesthouses, but if you're on a tight budget, choose your bed carefully – at the cheapie dives catering to oil-rig roustabouts (on and east of Jln South Yu Seng), many of the dreary rooms are windowless and musty, and Miri's brothel business booms at some of the shadier bottom-end digs.

★ **Dillenia Guesthouse** GUESTHOUSE $

(☎085-434204; www.sites.google.com/site/dilleniaguesthouse; 1st fl, 846 Jln Sida; dm/s/d/f incl breakfast, without bathroom RM30/50/80/110; ❄@📶) This super-welcoming hostel, with 11 rooms and lots of nice little touches like plants in the bathroom, lives up to its motto, 'a home away from home'. Incredibly helpful Mrs Lee, whose beautiful embroidered quilts adorn the walls, is an artesian well of travel information and tips – and even sells leech socks (RM20).

Coco House GUESTHOUSE $

(☎085-417051; www.cocodive.com.my; Lot 2117, Block 9, Jln Miri Pujut; incl breakfast dm/s/d RM35/55/80; ❄@📶) Coco House has bright, modern dorms with pod-like bunks and private rooms that are small but functional with splashes of colour. The spotless bathrooms have rainwater shower heads and there is a comfy common area with books, boardgames, DVDs and a microwave for heating food. There is talk of putting a barbecue on the roof terrace.

My Homestay GUESTHOUSE $

(☎085-429091; staymyhomestay.blogspot.com; Lot 1091, Jln Merpati; incl breakfast dm RM35, d RM55-120; ❄@📶) A friendly place in a good location with a spacious balcony overlooking the bustling street below. Most rooms, though clean and colourful, are windowless and a little stuffy. Prices are higher at weekends.

Next Room Guesthouse GUESTHOUSE $

(☎085-411422, 085-322090; 1st & 2nd fl, Lot 637, Jln North Yu Seng; incl breakfast dm RM28, d without bathroom RM55-85, d with bathroom RM85-95; ❄@📶) In the heart of Miri's dining and drinking district, this cosy establishment offers 13 rooms, a small kitchen, a DVD lounge and a great rooftop sundeck. Dorm rooms are pretty packed, with eight or 12 beds. Light sleepers be warned: the nightclub across the street pumps out music until 2am.

TreeTops Lodge LODGE $$

(☎019-865 6240; www.treetops-borneo.com; Lot 210, Kampung Siwa Jaya; d with air-con RM129-159, with fan & without bathroom RM99; ❄📶🏊) This mellow lodge surrounded by tropical fruit trees, run by Mike (a retired British pilot) and his Sarawakian wife Esther, has eight rooms – four of them in a basic wooden longhouse – set in a lovely, calming garden. Located in a small village 15km southwest of Miri along the coastal road to Bintulu; a taxi from Miri costs RM60.

There isn't much to do here besides take a walk to the nearby beach (2km away) or relax; nearby sights are difficult to reach without your own transport, but the lodge has cars available for hire (RM100 per day). A light lunch (RM12) and simple dinner (RM24) are served in a rustic wooden shelter overlooking the gardens. Bring insect repellent.

Imperial Hotel HOTEL $$
(☎085-431133; www.imperialhotel.com.my; Jln Post; incl breakfast d RM260-560, ste RM680-4000;) The city centre's poshest hotel boasts 23 floors, 266 rooms, business and fitness centres, a sauna and a swimming pool.

Mega Hotel HOTEL $$
(☎085-432432; www.megahotel.com.my; Lot 907, Jln Merbau; d RM330-380, ste RM700-4700; @) Don't judge a hotel by its tacky lobby – the 239 rooms here, spread over 16 storeys, are comfortable and spacious, if a bit old-fashioned. Amenities include a fitness centre (7th floor) and a 30m pool with sea views and a jacuzzi (4th floor). Promotional rates offer hefty discounts on prices quoted here.

Eating

★ **Summit Café** DAYAK $
(☎019-885 3920; Lot 1245, Centre Point Commercial Centre, Jln Melayu; meals RM8-15; 7am-4pm Mon-Sat;) If you've never tried Kelabit cuisine, this place will open up whole new worlds for your tastebuds. Queue up and choose from the colourful array of 'jungle food' laid out at the counter, including *dure* (fried jungle leaf), minced tapioca leaves, and *labo senutuk* (wild boar). The best selection is available before 11.30am – once the food runs out it closes.

Owner and chef Sally Bungan Bat uses only Bario salt and homegrown highland rice.

Khan's Islamic Restaurant INDIAN $
(☎012-878 9640; 229 Jln Maju; mains RM6-12; 6.30am-9pm;) This simple canteen is one of Miri's best North Indian eateries, serving up mouth-watering tandoori chicken (RM12), naan bread and mango lassi (RM4) as well as a variety of curries and vegetarian dishes.

Madli's Restaurant MALAYSIAN $
(☎085-426615; www.madli.net; Lot 1088, ground fl, Block 9, Jln Merpati; mains RM6-18.50; 8am-midnight Sun-Thu, 8am-1am Fri & Sat;) A long-running family business that started off as a satay stall in the 1970s; the first of three restaurants was opened in Miri in 1995. As well as lip-smackingly good chicken and lamb satay (RM1 per stick), the menu includes Malaysian dishes like *nasi lemak* and *kampung* (village) fried rice. Serves *roti canai* and Western breakfasts until noon.

Muara Restoran INDONESIAN $
(☎016-882 7370; Jln North Yu Seng; mains RM5-15; 11am-4am) Expat Indonesian oil workers in bright-yellow overalls flock to this tin-roofed shed for *lalapan* (tofu, tempeh, meat, spinach-like greens, raw cucumber and rice, eaten with spicy *sambal belacan*). Good for a late-night meal.

Miri Central Market HAWKER $
(Pasar Pusat Miri; Jln Brooke; mains RM2-6; 24hr, most stalls 4am-noon) Of the Chinese food purveyors selling *kari ayam* (chicken curry), porridge and the usual rice and noodle dishes, stall 6 (open 3.30am to 10am) is particularly popular. Stall 20 serves up vegetarian fare.

Persiaran Kabor CHINESE $
(Persiaran Kabor btwn Jln Duranta & Jln Cythulla; mains RM3-4.50; 6am-6pm) Come midmorning this atmospheric, covered courtyard, known locally as Old Folks' Street, is full of men of a certain vintage who congregate here to drink coffee, read the paper and play chess (the Chinese Chess Association is located in one of the shop lots). The surrounding coffee shops sell the usual rice and noodle dishes.

Tamu Muhibbah MARKET $
(Jln Padang; 2am-6pm or 7pm) Fruit and veggies, some straight from the jungle, are sold at stalls owned by Chinese, Malay, Iban and Orang Ulu people.

Rainforest Cafe CHINESE $$
(☎085-426967; 49 Jln Brooke; mains RM10-30; 10.30am-2pm & 5-11pm) Often packed with families tucking into a banquet of shared dishes, this breezy, open-air eatery specialises in Chinese-style dishes such as 'braised rainforest bean curd', 'crispy roasted chicken' and 'pork leg Philippine style'.

Meng Chai Seafood SEAFOOD $$
(☎085-413648; 11A Jln Merbau; meals from RM25; ⏲4pm-midnight) Discerning locals crowd this first-rate eatery, housed in two and unassuming adjacent buildings. There is no menu here – make your selection from the fishy candidates lined up on ice, decide how you would like it cooked and order any accompaniments such as rice or *midin* (fern). Seawater tanks hold live clams and prawns. Servings of fish are priced by weight.

Drinking

Ming Cafe BAR
(☎085-422797; www.mingcafe.com.my; cnr Jln North Yu Seng & Jln Merbau; ⏲10am-2am) This ever-busy corner bar stocks 16 imported bottled beers and has six on tap, including Guinness. The hefty menu also lists Australian and New Zealand wines and has a cocktail list covering several pages. Fresh juices and shakes cost RM5 to RM12. Also serves food ranging from Chinese, Malay and Indian to pizzas and burgers (RM5 to RM30).

Attracts a mixed crowd of local and expat drinkers and diners.

Soho Bar & Bistro BAR
(☎016-414 8883; Jln North Yu Seng; ⏲4pm-2am, happy hr 4-9pm) A vast, sportsbar-style place with outdoor seating at wooden tables and big screens showing football. Happy-hour offers include Tiger or Heineken beer towers (RM99 for one, RM180 for two). Also serves meals and bar snacks such as chicken wings, nachos and the house speciality 'Soho shrimp cocktail' served in a martini glass.

Shopping

Miri Handicraft Centre HANDICRAFTS
(cnr Jln Brooke & Jln Merbau; ⏲9am-6pm) Thirteen stalls, rented from the city, sell colourful bags, baskets, sarongs, textiles etc made by Iban, Kelabit, Kenyah, Kayan, Lun Bawang, Chinese and Malay artisans. Stall No 7 has some fine Kelabit beadwork from Bario. Some stalls are closed on Sundays.

Popular Book Store BOOKS
(2nd fl, Bintang Plaza, Jln Miri Pujut; ⏲10am-10pm) A mega-bookshop with a large selection of English books, and Lonely Planet titles in English and Chinese.

Bintang Plaza MALL
(Jln Miri Pujut; ⏲10am-10pm) A modern, multistorey, air-con mall with shops specialising in computers and cameras on the 3rd floor. Rainy-day entertainment comes in the form of **Megalanes East Bowling Alley** (3rd fl, Bintang Plaza; per game RM5.90-7.90, shoes RM3; ⏲9am-11.45pm) and a **cinema** (gsc.com.my; 4th fl, Bintang Plaza; adult RM7.50-11.50, children RM6.50).

Sin Liang Supermarket FOOD & DRINK
(Jln Duranta; ⏲8.30am-9pm) Well stocked with snacks, toiletries and Aussie wines. A good place to pick up supplies for a trek in Mulu or the Kelabit Highlands.

Miri Central Superstore SHOES
(998 Jln Raja; ⏲8am-6pm) Sells rubber 'kampung shoes' (RM7.50), which are perfect for jungle hikes.

Information

For some great tips and an outline of local history, see Miri's unofficial website, www.miriresort city.com.

ATMs can be found at the airport and all over the city centre.

It's a good idea to stock up on first-aid supplies before heading inland to Gunung Mulu National Park or the Kelabit Highlands.

INTERNET ACCESS

Sky Garden Cyber Cafe (☎085-418331; 1285 1st fl, 14B Jln Parry; per hr RM3; ⏲9.30am-noon Sun-Thu, 9am-2am Fri & Sat) Plenty of computers, coffee and snacks.

LAUNDRY

EcoLaundry (☎085-414266; 638 Jln North Yu Seng; per kg RM6; ⏲7am-6pm Mon-Sat, to 5pm Sun) Free pick up and delivery within the town centre.

MEDICAL SERVICES

Colombia Asia Hospital (☎085-437755; www.columbiaasia.com; Lot 1035-1039 Jln Bulan Sabit; ⏲24hr) A 35-bed private hospital with a 24-hour accident and emergency ward and a 24-hour ambulance. Situated 4km northeast of the city centre.

Miri City Medical Centre (☎085-426622; 916-920 Jln Hokkien; ⏲emergency 24hr) Has an ambulance service, a 24-hour accident and emergency department and various private clinics. Located in the city centre.

POST

Main Post Office (☎085-433423; Jln Post; ⏲8am-4.30pm Mon-Fri, to 12.30pm Sat)

TOURIST INFORMATION

National Park Booking Office (☎085-434184; www.sarawakforestry.com; 452 Jln Melayu; ⏲8am-5pm Mon-Fri) Inside the Visitors Information Centre. Has details on

Sarawak's national parks and can book beds and rooms at Niah, Lambir Hills and Similajau (but not Gunung Mulu).

Visitors Information Centre (☎085-434181; www.sarawaktourism.com; 452 Jln Melayu; ⏲8am-5pm Mon-Fri, 9am-3pm Sat, Sun & public holidays) The helpful staff can provide city maps, information on accommodation and a list of licensed guides. Situated in a little park.

VISAS

Immigration Department (Jabatan Imigresen; ☎085-442112; www.imi.gov.my; 2nd fl, Yulan Plaza, cnr Jln Kingsway & Jln Brooke; ⏲7.30am-5.30pm Mon-Thu, 8am-12.15pm & 2.45-5.30pm Fri) For visa extensions.

Getting There & Away

Miri is 212km northeast of Bintulu and 36km southwest of the Brunei border.

AIR

Miri's **airport** (www.miriairport.com; Jln Airport) is 10km south of the town centre.

There is a separate check-in area for MASwings 'Rural Air Service' which includes flights to Bario. If you are flying on a Twin Otter plane you'll be asked weigh to yourself on giant scales while holding your carry-on.

AirAsia (☎600 85 8888; www.airasia.com; Lot 946, Jln Parry; ⏲8.30am-5.30pm Mon-Fri, to 1pm Sat) Flights to Kuching, Kuala Lumpur, Singapore, Kota Kinabalu, Penang and Johor Bahru.

Malaysia Airlines (☎085-414155; www.malaysiaairlines.com; Lot No 10635 Airport Commercial Centre, Jln Airport) Daily flights to Kuala Lumpur. Office at airport.

MASwings (☎085-423500; www.maswings.com.my; ground fl, airport terminal; ⏲6am-9pm) The Malaysia Airlines subsidiary MASwings has flights within Sarawak to Mulu (for Gunung Mulu National Park), Kuching, Bintulu, Sibu, Lawas, Marudi and Limbang, and to Kota Kinabalu in Sabah. It also serves Sarawak's remote, rural communities of Bario, Ba Kelalan, Long Akah, Long Banga, Long Lellang, Mukah and Long Seridan.

BUS & VAN

Long-distance buses use the Pujut Bus Terminal, about 4km northeast of the centre.

About once an hour, buses head to Kuching (RM60 to RM90, 12 to 14 hours, departures from 7.15am to 8.30pm) via the inland (old) Miri–Bintulu highway, with stops at Lambir Hills National Park, Batu Niah Junction (access point for Niah National Park; RM10 to RM12, 1½ hours), Bintulu (RM20 to RM27, 3½ hours) and Sibu (RM40 to RM50, seven to eight hours). This route is highly competitive, so it pays to shop around. Taking a spacious 'VIP bus', with just three seats across, is like flying 1st class. Companies include **Bintang Jaya** (☎Kuching 082-531133, Miri 085-432178; www.bintangjayaexpress.com) and **Miri Transport Company** (MTC; ☎in Kuching 082-531161, in Miri 085-434161; www.mtcmiri.com).

Bintang Jaya also has services northeast to Limbang (RM45, four hours), Lawas (RM75, six hours) and Kota Kinabalu (KK; RM90, 10 hours). Buses leave Miri at 8.30am; departures from KK are at 7.30am. Borneo Express serves the same destinations at 7.45am; departures from KK are also at 7.45am. With both these companies, getting off in Brunei is not allowed.

Getting Around

TO/FROM THE AIRPORT

A taxi from the airport to the city centre (15 minutes, in traffic 25 minutes) costs RM25; a *kupon teksi* (taxi coupon) can be purchased at the taxi

GETTING TO BRUNEI: MIRI TO BANDAR SERI BEGAWAN

Getting to the border The only company that's allowed to take passengers from Miri's Pujut Bus Terminal to destinations inside Brunei is **PHLS Express** (☎in Brunei +673 277 1668, in Miri 085-438301), which sends buses to BSB (RM50) via Kuala Belait (RM38) and Seria (RM38) at 8.15am and 3.45pm. Tickets are sold at the Bintang Jaya counter. Another option for travel between BSB and Miri is a private transfer (which may be shared with other travellers) run by father-and-son team Mr Fu and Ah Pau (RM70 per person, three hours) Call Mr Fu on ☎013-833 2231.

At the border Border formalities are usually quick, and for most nationalities Bruneian visas are free, but the process can slow down buses. If you're eventually headed overland to Sabah, make sure you have enough pages in your passport for 10 new chops (stamps).

Moving on Brunei's Serasa Ferry Terminal, 20km northeast of BSB, is linked by ferry with Pulau Labuan, from where boats go to Kota Kinabalu in Sabah. Several buses a day go from BSB to Sarawak's Limbang Division and destinations in Sabah.

desk just outside the baggage-claim area (next to the car-rental desks). If you're heading from town to the airport, the fare is RM22. There is no public transport from the airport.

BUS

Local bus transport in Miri is handled by three companies: Miri City Bus, Miri Transport Company (MTC) and Miri Belait Transport. The **local bus station** (Jln Padang), next to the Visitors Information Centre, has schedules posted. Fares start at RM1; most lines run from 7am to about 6pm.

Buses 20 and 33A link the local bus station with Pujut Bus Terminal (RM1.60 to RM2.60, hourly until 6.30pm).

CAR

Most of Miri's guesthouses are happy to organise private transport to area destinations such as Lambir Hills National Park (RM85 return) and Niah National Park (RM240 return).

FT Car Rental (☎085-438415; www.ftcarrental.com; 3rd fl, Soon Hup Tower, Jln Maju) Also has a counter at Miri airport.

Golden System Car Rental (☎085-613359, 012-874 1200; www.gocar.com.my; counter 3, ground fl, Miri airport) Prices start at RM100 per day or RM500 per week.

Hertz (☎085-614740; www.hertz.com; arrivals hall, Miri airport; ⏰8am-5pm Mon-Sat) Has a range of vehicles available for hire.

Kong Teck Car Rental (☎085-617767; www.kongteck.com.my; arrivals concourse, Miri airport) Prices start at RM120 per day or RM600 per week.

My Homestay Motorcycle & Car Rental (☎085-429091; staymyhomestay@gmail.com; Jln Merpati) Offers car and motorcycle rentals.

TAXI

Taxi ranks are sprinkled around the city centre. A short cab ride around downtown is RM12, while a ride from the centre to the Pujut Bus Terminal costs RM20. Taxis run by the **Miri Taxi Association** (☎085-432277; ⏰24hr) can be summoned by phone 24 hours a day.

NORTHEASTERN SARAWAK

Gunung Mulu National Park

Also known as the **Gunung Mulu World Heritage Area** (☎085-792300; www.mulupark.com; 5-day pass adult/child RM30/10; ⏰HQ office 8am-5pm), this park is one of the most majestic and thrilling nature destinations anywhere in Southeast Asia. No surprise, then, that Unesco declared it a World Heritage Site in 2005.

Few national parks anywhere in the world pack so many natural marvels into such a small area. Home to caves of mind-boggling proportions, otherworldly geological phenomena such as the Pinnacles, and brilliant old-growth tropical rainforest (the park has 17 different vegetation zones), this is truly one of the world's wonders.

Among the remarkable features in this 529-sq-km park are its two highest peaks, Gunung Mulu (2376m) and Gunung Api (1710m). In between are rugged karst mountains, deep gorges with crystal-clear rivers, and a unique mosaic of habitats supporting fascinating and incredibly diverse wildlife. Mulu's most famous hiking attractions are the **Pinnacles**, a forest of razor-sharp limestone spires, and the so-called **Headhunters' Trail**, which follows an old tribal war path down to Limbang.

Some cave tours (especially the more difficult ones) and treks (especially the longer ones) may be booked out well in advance.

Sights & Activities

When you register, park staff will give you a placemat-sized schematic map of the park on which you can plan out your daily activities. HQ staff are generally very helpful in planning itineraries and are happy to accommodate special needs and interests like family-friendly activities.

The park's excellent website and the brochures available at park HQ have details of the full range of tours and activities available.

Mulu Discovery Centre MUSEUM
(Gunung Mulu National Park HQ; ⏰8am-6pm) FREE Offers a fine introduction to the park as a 'biodiversity hotspot' and to its extraordinary geology. Situated in the HQ building, between the park office and Café Mulu.

Activities Without Guides

Visitors are not allowed to go inside any of the caves without a qualified guide, but you can take a number of **jungle walks** unaccompanied so long as you inform the park office (or, when it's closed, someone across the path in the park security building). The trails are well marked and interconnected, so by using the park's map it's easy to join them up to create your own route.

GUIDES, RESERVATIONS & FEES

For almost all of the caves, walks and treks in **Gunung Mulu National Park** (Gunung Mulu World Heritage Area; ☎ 085-792300; www.mulupark.com; for five calendar days RM30), visitors must be accompanied by a guide licensed by Sarawak Forestry, generally supplied either by the park or by an adventure-tour agency (such as those based in Kuching, Miri or Limbang). Tours and activities booked directly through the park are cheaper and are often booked up well in advance; agencies charge considerably more but also supply extras, such as meals, and can often offer more flexibility when it comes to advance booking.

If you've got your heart set on **adventure caving**, or on trekking to the **Pinnacles** or up to the summit of **Gunung Mulu**, advance reservations – by phone or email (enquiries@mulupark.com) – are a must. They're doubly important if you're coming in July, August or September, when some routes are booked out several months ahead, and are essential if your travel dates are not flexible. If this is your situation, don't buy your air tickets until your trek or caving dates are confirmed.

That's not to say a last-minute trip to Mulu is impossible. The park may be able to reassign guides to accommodate you, so it's worth getting in touch. And if you are able to spend a week or so hanging out at the park (this usually means staying in a basic guesthouse outside the park's boundaries as in-park accommodation is in very short supply), trekking and caving slots do sometimes open up.

The park's own trekking and caving guides are well trained and speak good English, but there are only about 15 of them. Some travellers hire a freelance guide unattached to a tour agency, usually from a nearby village. Despite being licensed by Sarawak Forestry (they wouldn't be allowed to operate in the park if they weren't), such guides' nature knowledge and English skills vary widely, from excellent to barely sufficient. In addition, they may lack safety training and equipment (such as two-way radios, which the park supplies to all of its own guides) and, perhaps most importantly, are unlikely to have proper insurance, a factor that could be crucial if a helicopter evacuation is necessary.

A caving group must consist of at least four participants (including the guide) so that if someone is injured, one person can stay with them and the other two can head out of the cave together to seek help.

Park prices for caving and treks are on a straight per-person basis (minimum three people).

Paku Valley Loop WALKING

An 8km loop through the forest that passes alongside the Melinau River to the **Paku Waterfall** (3km) where it's possible to swim. The walk takes five to six hours at an easy-going pace.

Botanical Heritage Trail WALKING

This easy 1.5km boardwalk loop has accessible information panels on many of the fascinating plants it passes as it winds through the forest.

Tree Top Tower BIRDWATCHING

FREE Basically a 30m-high bird hide. The best time to spot our feathered friends is early in the morning (5am to 9am) or in the late afternoon and early evening (4pm to 8pm). Reserve a time slot and pick up the key (deposit RM50) at park HQ or, after 4.30pm, from Park Security (across the boardwalk from the park office). Situated about 500m from park HQ.

Guided Forest Walks

Garden of Eden Valley Walk WALKING

(per person RM140; ⏲ 9.30am-5pm) This memorable day hike takes you through the 2km-long **deer cave** to a seemingly enchanted, enclosed valley. There is a certain amount of walking on bat guano, scrambling over slippery rocks and wading through streams (rubber shoes are best; sandals are not suitable), but emerging into lush green forest surrounded by limestone is a fine reward.

A jungle trail leads up to a **waterfall** and **rock pools** perfect for swimming. Since the only way into – and out of – the garden of Eden is through the deer cave, you need to retrace your step back through the cave to the bat observatory where the walk ends in time to watch the bat exodus at dusk.

The price includes a packed lunch and afternoon tea.

Night Walk WALKING
(per person RM 20; ⏲7pm or 7.30pm, cancelled if raining) This 1½- to two-hour walk wends its way through alluvial forest. Creatures you're likely to see – after the guide points them out – include tree frogs just 1cm long, enormous spiders, vine snakes that are a dead ringer for a vine, and stick insects (phasmids), extraordinary creatures up to 30cm long that look like they've been assembled from pencils and toothpicks.

If you put your torch (bring one!) up to eye level and shine it into the foliage, the eyes of spiders and other creatures will reflect brightly back. Don't wear insect repellent or you risk repelling some of the insects you're trying to see. Mosquitoes are not a problem.

If you order dinner at the Wild Mulu Café before heading out, you can pick it up when you return (make sure you're back before 9.30pm). Eateries outside the park stay open later.

You can take the night walk trail on your own, without a guide after 8pm – make sure you inform either the park office or, when it's closed, someone in the park security pavilion. Between 5pm and 8pm, you can design your own night walk by taking trails the guided group isn't using.

Mulu Canopy Skywalk WALKING
(per person RM42.40; ⏲7am, 8.30am, 10am, 10.30am, 1pm & 2pm) Mulu's 480m-long skywalk, unforgettably anchored to a series of huge trees, has excellent signage and is one of the best in Southeast Asia. Often gets booked out early – for a specific time slot, reserve as soon as you've got your flight.

Climbing up into the rainforest canopy is the only way to see what a tropical rainforest is all about because most of the flora and fauna do their thing high up in the trees, not down on the ground, where less than 2% of the forest's total sunlight is available. Your guide can help point out the nuances of the surrounding forest, including traditional medicine plants that are still gathered and used in the nearby Penan settlement.

Show Caves

Mulu's 'show caves' (the park's name for caves that can be visited without specialised training or equipment) are its most popular attraction and for good reason: they are, quite simply, awesome.

Deer Cave & Lang Cave CAVE
(per person RM30; ⏲2pm & 2.30pm) A 3km walk through the rainforest takes you to these adjacent caverns. The Deer Cave – over 2km in length and 174m high – is the world's largest cave passage open to the public, while the Lang Cave – more understated in its proportions – contains interesting stalactites and stalagmites. Be sure to stay on for the 'bat exodus' at dusk.

The Deer Cave is home to two million to three million bats belonging to 12 species (more than in any other single cave in the world), who cling to the roof in a seething black mass as they gear up for their evening prowl. Every day between 4pm and 6pm (unless it's raining), millions of bats exit the cave in spiralling, twirling clouds that look a bit like swarms of cartoon bees. It's an awe-inspiring sight when viewed from the park's **bat observatory**, a kind of amphitheatre outside the cave. The bats' corkscrew trajectory is designed to foil the dinner plans of bat hawks perched on the surrounding cliffs.

We're not sure who did the calculations or how, but it's said that the Deer Cave's bats devour 30 tonnes of mosquitoes every night. If it's raining, the bats usually stay home because echolocation (the way they find prey) is not very good at homing in on flying insects amid an onslaught of raindrops.

Count on getting back to park HQ at around 7pm; bring a torch for the walk back.

Wind Cave & Clearwater Cave CAVE
(per person incl boat ride RM65; ⏲8.45am & 9.15am) Zipping along a jungle river in a longboat on your way to the caves is not a bad way to start the day. The Wind Cave, named for the cool breezes blowing through it, has several chambers, including the cathedral-like King's Chamber, filled with dreamlike forests of stalagmites and columns. There is a sweaty 200-step climb up to Clearwater Cave and the subterranean river there. The cave itself is vast: more than 200km of passages have been surveyed so far.

After visiting the caves, you can take a dip in the refreshingly cool waters of a sandy swimming spot.

Tours also include a stop at the riverside village of **Batu Bungan**, a Penan settlement set up by the government as part of a campaign to discourage their nomadic lifestyle. Locals sell trinkets and handicrafts.

The Wind Cave and Clearwater Cave tour takes about four hours, leaving time for another cave visit in the afternoon.

Langang Cave CAVE

(per person incl boat RM65; ⏲2pm) Langang Cave can be visited on the park's Fast Lane tour, which passes extraordinary stalactites and stalagmites. Keep an eye out for blue Racer Snakes, and 'moonmilk', a fibrous mineral formation – known to scientists as Lublinite – created when bacteria break down calcite, the main component of limestone. Don't touch it – it's very fragile.

Getting to the cave requires a 20-minute boat ride followed by a 1km walk to the cave entrance. The whole tour lasts three hours.

Adventure Caves

Cave routes that require special equipment and a degree of caving (spelunking) experience are known here as 'adventure caves'. Rosters for the seven half- or full-day options fill up early, so reserve well ahead. Groups are limited to eight participants. Heavy rains can cause caves to flood.

Caving routes are graded beginner, intermediate and advanced; guides determine each visitor's suitability based on their previous caving experience. If you have no background in spelunking, you will be required to do an intermediate route before moving on to an advanced one. Minimum ages are 12 for intermediate and 16 for advanced. Fees include a helmet and a headlamp; bring closed shoes, a first-aid kit and clothes you won't mind getting dirty.

Keep in mind that adventure caving is not for everyone, and halfway into a cave passage is not the best time to discover that you suffer from claustrophobia, fear the dark or simply don't like slithering in the mud with all sorts of unknown creepy crawlies.

Sarawak Chamber CAVING

(per person RM280; ⏲6.30am) This advanced level circuit is very demanding – getting to the entrance of the Good Luck cave involves a three-hour hike and it's an 800m wade through a river channel from there to the chamber. Moving around inside the cave requires some use of fixed ropes. There and back, the whole route takes 10 to 15 hours.

Measuring an incredible 700m long, 400m wide and 70m high, this chamber – discovered in 1981 – has been called the world's largest enclosed space. Don't count on seeing much, though – ordinary lights are no match for the ocean of black emptiness.

Clearwater Connection CAVING

(per person RM200) This 4.8km, four- to eight-hour advanced caving circuit starts at Wind Cave and heads into the wilds of the vast Clearwater Cave system. There's a good bit of scrambling and the route includes a 1.5km river section.

Racer Cave CAVING

(per person RM160) An intermediate caving session with some rope-assisted sections that require a bit of upper-body strength and a fair bit of climbing. It is named after the non-dangerous cave racer snake, which dines mainly on bats. Takes two to four hours.

Trekking & Climbing

Mulu offers some of the best and most accessible **jungle trekking** in Borneo. The forest here is in excellent condition and there are routes for every level of fitness and skill.

Expect rain, leeches, slippery and treacherous conditions, and a very hot workout – carry lots of water. Guides are required for overnights. Book well ahead.

Bring a first-aid kit and a torch.

Pinnacles TREKKING

(per person RM400; ⏲Tue-Thu & Fri-Sun) The Pinnacles are an incredible formation of 45m-high stone spires protruding from the forested flanks of Gunung Api. Getting there involves a boat ride and, in between two overnights at Camp 5 (p457), an unrelentingly steep 2.4km ascent. Coming down is just as taxing, so by the time you stagger back to camp, the cool, clear river may look pretty enticing.

Bring shoes that will give you traction on sharp and slippery rocks, and bedding (many people find that a sleeping bag liner or sarong is sufficient). If you book the tour through the park, you will also need to bring enough food for six meals; it is worth buying supplies in Miri, as the park shop sells only a limited selection of instant noodles and cans. You can buy a packed lunch from the park cafe for the first day, and it may be possible to buy fried rice from staff at Camp 5 (RM10), but don't count on it.

On the way to Camp 5 on day one you can stop off at Wind Cave and Clearwater Cave for a fee of RM30 (if you don't want to see the caves and you are in a group with others who do, you will need to wait for them). From the boat drop-off point it's an 8km hike to Camp 5 along an easy trail (though be prepared for leeches).

Since both nights are spent at Camp 5 you only need to carry a day pack on the Pinnacles climb on day two, but to be sure to bring plenty of water – at least two litres – in two separate containers (one bottle will be left half way up to pick up on the way down), as well as snacks and oral rehydration salts. If it's raining heavily, the guide may deem it necessary to cancel the climb, in which case you will be refunded RM80.

Right from the get-go the trail up to the Pinnacles is steep and rocky. There is plenty of clambering on all fours involved and the rocks are sharp. The final 400m section involves some serious climbing and use of ladders – most of them little more than spaced out metal brackets drilled into the rock, requiring a steady nerve and good balance to avoid falling onto the spikes below. The Pinnacles themselves are only visible from the very top. Factoring in the humidity, the climb is certainly an intense experience, but most people find it rewarding. What's more the trail passes through some gorgeous jungle and there are beautiful views of the valley below – if you dare look up from the track to admire it.

It is possible to continue along the Headhunters' Trail on day three, instead of returning to HQ.

Gunung Mulu Summit TREKKING

(per person RM500, minimum 3 people) The climb to the summit of Gunung Mulu (2376m) – described by one satisfied ascendee as 'gruelling' and, near the top, 'treacherous' – is a classic Borneo adventure. If you're very fit and looking for a challenge, this 24km, three-day, four-night trek may be for you. The climb must be booked at least one month in advance.

Bring proper hiking shoes, a sleeping bag (Camp 4 can get quite chilly, often dropping below 15°C), a sleeping pad (unless you don't mind sleeping on wooden boards), rain gear and enough food for four days. The camps along the way have very basic cooking equipment, including a gas stove. Bring water-purification tablets if you're wary of drinking the rainwater collected at shelters en route.

Near the summit you may spend much of your time inside clouds; a fleece jacket is the best way to ward off the damp and cold. Recent trekkers report having been visited by rats at Camp 3 and by squirrels who were 'keen on noodles' at Camp 4. The steep trail – which is slippery when wet – passes through limestone and sandstone forest. Fauna you might see on the way include gibbons, wild boar and even (possibly) sun bears.

Reaching the summit involves leaving Camp 4 at 3am to arrive at the top in time to see the spectacular sunrise.

Headhunters' Trail TREKKING

The physically undemanding Headhunters' Trail continues on from Camp 5 for 11km in the direction of Limbang and is an overland alternative to flying in or out of Mulu. The park does not offer guided trips along this trail, but several private tour operators do, and it is also (theoretically) possible to do it without a guide.

This backdoor route from Mulu to Limbang takes two days and one night and can be done in either direction, although most people start at the park. After climbing the Pinnacles (p455), it is possible to walk the Headhunters' Trail (unguided) on day three instead of returning back to Park HQ.

From Camp 5, the Headhunters' Trail continues through the forest to Kuala Terikan, from where you'll need to take a boat to Medamit, linked by road with Limbang. If you plan to do this trip without a guide, you must arrange road and river transport ahead of time – Borneo Touch Ecotour (p466) can organise a boat and van in either direction for about RM500. If you are starting in Limbang, remember to contact the park to reserve sleeping space at Camp 5.

The route is named after the Kayan war parties that used to make their way up the Sungai Melinau from the Baram area to the Melinau Gorge, then dragged their canoes overland to the Sungai Terikan to raid the peoples of the Limbang region. New roads mean that the trail is no longer much used, making it more likely to spot wildlife along the way.

Sleeping

Accommodation options range from five-star luxury to extremely basic. Camping is no longer permitted at park HQ, but you can pitch a tent at some of the guesthouses just outside the park (across the bridge from HQ). If you find accommodation within the park is fully booked, don't panic. There is always a bed of some kind available at one of the informal homestays just outside the park gates.

Inside the National Park

Park HQ, a lovely spot set amid semi-wild jungle, has 24-hour electricity and tap water that's safe to drink. All private rooms have attached bathroom. At research time, 12 new longhouse-style rooms were being constructed, which should go some way towards allieviating the accommodation shortage.

Rooms can be cancelled up to 48 hours ahead without penalty, which is why space sometimes opens up late in the game; phone for last-minute availability.

Hostel HOSTEL $

(dm incl breakfast RM52) All 20 beds are in a clean, spacious dormitory-style room with ceiling fans.

Garden Bungalows BUNGALOW $$

(s/d/tr incl breakfast RM253/294/341; ❄) These eight spacious units, the park's most luxurious accommodation, are light and modern and have their own private verandahs.

Cabins CABIN $$

(q incl breakfast RM387 ; ❄) Each of the two cabins has two rooms with four single beds and a huge living room. The minimum number of people per cabin is four (RM387) and the maximum is eight (RM648), with prices for five, six and seven people falling in between.

Longhouse Rooms GUESTHOUSE $$

(s/d/tr/q incl breakfast RM209/247/277/313; ❄) There are eight of these, four rooms – which are now starting to look a little dingy – in each of two wooden buildings. Rooms in Longhouse 1 have a double bed and two singles; in Longhouse 2 there are four single beds per room.

Camp 5 HUT $$

(per person incl boat ride RM190) A basic wooden 'forest hostel' or large hut divided into four dorms with sleeping platforms and mats, a kitchen (with gas for cooking and boiled water for drinking) and bathrooms with showers. Space is limited to 50 people; reservations are made at the park office. Most people find it's warm enough here without a sleeping bag (a sarong will do).

If you are doing the Pinnacles or Headhunters' Trail you will spend a night at Camp 5, whether you book through the park or a tour operator.

Outside the National Park

Several budget places, unaffiliated with the park, are located just across the bridge from park HQ, along the banks of the Melinau River. Reservations are not necessary, so if you don't mind very basic digs, you can fly up without worrying about room availability.

Mulu River Lodge HOSTEL $

(Edward Nyipa Homestay; ☎012-852 7471; dm/d/q incl breakfast RM35/70/140) Has 30 beds, most in a giant, non-bunk dorm room equipped with clean showers and toilets at one end. Electricity flows from 5pm to 11.30pm. One of the few guesthouses outside the park, if not the only one, with a proper septic system. Located a five-minute walk from park HQ, just across the bridge from the entrance.

D'Cave Homestay HOMESTAY $

(☎Dina 012-872 9752; beckhamjunior40@yahoo.com; incl breakfast dm RM30, d with/without bathroom RM120/RM80) A friendly, rather ramshackle place with mismatched patterned lino, beds crammed into small rooms and basic, outdoor bathrooms. Owner Dina cooks buffet-style lunches (RM15) and dinners (RM18), has tea and coffee, and has boiled water for water-bottle refills. Situated between the airport and the turning for the park – about a 10-minute walk from each.

Mulu Backpackers GUESTHOUSE $

(☎Helen 012-871 2947, Peter 013-846 7250; mulubackpackers@gmail.com; dm incl breakfast RM35) Mulu Backpackers, situated just past the airport, occupies a picturesque spot by the river but is a 15-minute walk from the park. There is a pleasant sheltered outdoor dining area with views of the water and electricity from 6pm to 6am. The 17 beds here are arranged in a large, barn-like space with some randomly positioned partition walls.

AA Homestay HOMESTAY $

(☎Albert 017-858 5241, Irene 017-805 3270; marygracealbert@gmail.com; d RM60) The four rooms here, housed in a wooden outbuilding near the family house, have attached bathrooms and mosquito screens. There is electricity from 6pm to about 10.30pm (later on request). Situated about 200m from the park entrance.

Mulu Marriott Resort & Spa RESORT $$$

(☎085-792388; www.marriott.com; d/ste incl breakfast from RM640/850; ❄📶🏊) Situated

3km from park HQ, this 101-room, largely wooden complex has been fully refurbished in a way that is both stylish and sympathetic to its jungle surroundings. Rooms come with all the amenities you would expect from a five-star resort and have balconies overlooking the forest or river.

The Balinese-style swimming pool is a real draw here after a sweaty day of caving and hiking. The resort also has its own jetty for river trips that bypass park HQ and go straight to the caves (booked through the hotel for much more than the park tours). A not wholly reliable wi-fi connection is available in the bar area only.

Eating

A handful of tiny shops sell a very limited selection of food items, such as instant noodles. Most food is flown in, which partly explains why prices are significantly higher than on the coast (RM6 for a large bottle of water).

Cooking is not allowed at any park accommodation except Camps 1, 3, 4 and 5.

Café Mulu INTERNATIONAL **$$**
(mains RM12.50-16; ⏲7.30am-8.30pm) This decent cafe serves excellent breakfasts and a varied menu with a few Western items, Indian curries and local dishes including Mulu laksa and *umai* (Sarawak sushi). A beer costs RM12. Staff are happy to prepare packed lunches.

Good Luck Cave'fe Mulu MALAYSIAN **$**
(mains RM8-10; ⏲11.30am-3pm & 5pm-midnight, kitchen closes at 9.15pm) The Good Luck Cave'fe Mulu (geddit?) is located right outside the park gates and stays open later than the park cafe, making it a good dinner option if you come back late from a night walk. Serves the usual noodle and fried-rice dishes. A beer costs RM8.

Information

For sums over RM100, the park accepts Visa and MasterCard. Staff can also do cash withdrawals of RM100 to RM300 (one transaction per day) for a 2% fee, but the machine is temperamental, so try to bring enough cash to cover your expenses (there is no ATM in Mulu).

The shop and cafe area at park HQ has an excruciatingly slow and unreliable wi-fi connection (RM5 per day).

The clinic in the nearby village of Batu Bungan is now staffed by a doctor and has a dispensary.

Getting There & Away

Unless you hike in via the Headhunters' Trail, the only way to get to Mulu is by MASwings plane.

AIR

MASwings (☎085-206900; www.maswings.com.my; ground fl, Mulu airport; ⏲8.30am-5pm) MASwings flies 68-seat ATR 72-500 turboprops to Miri (daily at 10.10am and 2.35pm), Kuching (Monday, Wednesday, Thursday and Saturday at 1.15pm; Tuesday, Friday and Sunday at 3.20pm) and Kota Kinabalu (Monday, Wednesday, Thursday and Saturday at 2.35pm via Miri; Tuesday and Friday at 11.25am; Sunday at 1pm).

Getting Around

Park HQ is a walkable 1.5km from the airport. Vans run by **Melinau Transportation** (☎012-852 6065, 012-871 1372) and other companies meet incoming flights at the airport; transport to park HQ and the adjacent guesthouses costs RM5 per person.

It's possible to hire local longboats for excursions to destinations such as the government-built Penan longhouse village of Long Iman (RM75 per person return, minimum three people), 40 minutes away by river.

Kelabit Highlands

Nestled in Sarawak's northeastern corner, the upland rainforests of the Kelabit (keh-*lah*-bit) Highlands are sandwiched between Gunung Mulu National Park and the Indonesian state of East Kalimantan, and home to the Kelabits, an Orang Ulu group who number only about 6500.

The main activity here, other than enjoying the clean, cool air, is hiking from longhouse to longhouse on mountain trails. Unfortunately, logging roads – ostensibly for 'selective' logging – are encroaching and some of the Highlands' primary forests have already succumbed to the chainsaw.

Bario

POP 1100

The 'capital' of the Highlands, Bario consists of about a dozen 'villages' – each with its own church – spread over a beautiful valley, much of it given over to growing the renowned local rice. Some of the appeal lies in the mountain climate (the valley is 1500m above sea level) and splendid isolation (the only access is by air and torturous 4WD track), but above all it's the unforced hospitality of the Kelabit people that will quickly

DON'T MISS

BARIO'S MYSTERIOUS MEGALITHS

Hidden deep in the jungle around Bario are scores of mysterious megaliths. The Cultured Rainforest Project (www.culturedrainforest.com), led by anthropologist Monica Janowski, involved a recent study of these sites as part of an investigation into how the people of the area interact with the rainforest.

The Kelabits believe in marking the landscape in order to establish rights over it, and these sites are viewed as spiritually significant. The markers include *perupan* (large mounds made from thousands of stones from the river bed), believed to have been built by rich men and women without heirs to bury their possessions and avoid fights breaking out over inheritance.

Pa' Umor Megaliths From Bario it's a 1½-hour walk to Pa' Umor, and another 15 minutes to Arur Bilit Farm, home to **Batu Narit**, an impressive stone carving featuring a human in a spread-eagled position among its designs.

Take the log bridge across the small river to reach **Batu Ipak**. According to legend, this stone formation was created when an angry warrior named Upai Semering pulled out his *parang* (machete) and took a wrathful swing at the rock, cutting it in two.

This circuit should take four or five hours – maybe a tad longer if your guide is a good storyteller.

Pa' Lungan Megaliths The trail from Bario to Pa' Lungan is walkable without a guide. About halfway along you'll see **Batu Arit**, a large stone featuring bird carvings and humanoid figures with heart-shaped faces.

At Pa' Lungan is **Batu Ritung**, a 2m stone table (probably a burial site, although no one is sure). Also near Pa' Lungan is **Perupun**, a huge pile of stones of a type assembled to bury the valuables of the dead who had no descendants to receive their belongings.

If you've got a bit more time, you could consider basing yourself for a day or two in Pa' Lungan, believed by many to produce the very best Bario rice.

win you over. A huge number of travellers find themselves extending their stays in Bario by days, weeks or even years. Do yourself a favour and get stuck here for a while.

Before the Konfrontasi, Bario consisted of only one small longhouse, but in 1963 residents of longhouses near the frontier fled raids by Indonesian troops and settled here for safety.

Except for a few places powered by a small hydroelectric dam and by photovoltaic cells (a large solar farm is planned), Bario has electricity – provided by private generators – only in the evening. It's hard to imagine life in hyper-social Bario without the mobile phone, a technology unknown in these parts until 2009.

Sights & Activities

The area around Bario offers plenty of opportunities for jungle exploration even if you're not a hardcore hiker. The nearby forests are a great place to spot pitcher plants, butterflies and even hornbills – and are an excellent venue for tiger leeches to spot you. Most guesthouses are happy to pack picnic lunches.

Bario Asal Longhouse HOUSE

(admission RM5) This all-wood, 22-door longhouse has the traditional Kelabit layout. On the *dapur* (enclosed front verandah) each family has a hearth, while on the other side of the family units is the *tawa'*, a wide back verandah – essentially an enclosed hall over 100m long – used for weddings, funerals and celebrations and decorated with historic family photos.

A few of the older residents still have earlobes that hang down almost to their shoulders, created by a lifetime of wearing heavy brass earrings. If you'd like a picture, it's good form to chat with them a bit (they may offer you something to drink) and only then to ask if they'd be willing to be photographed. Afterwards you might want to leave a small tip.

Bario Asal has 24-hour electricity (evenings only during dry spells) thanks to a micro-hydro project salvaged from a larger government-funded project that functioned for just 45 minutes after it was switched on in 1999 (it had been designed to operate on a much larger river).

Tom Harrisson Monument MEMORIAL

Shaped like a *sapé* (a traditional stringed instrument), this stainless-steel monument commemorates the March 1945 parachute drop into Bario by British and Australian troops under the command of Major Tom Harrisson. Their goal – achieved with great success – was to enlist the help of locals to fight the Japanese. The statue is across the first bridge heading west from the airport.

After the war, Harrisson stayed on in Borneo and was curator of the Sarawak Museum from 1947 to 1966. During this time, he and his wife Barbara began excavating the Niah caves, leading to the discovery of a 40,000-year-old human skull. For the life story of this colourful and controversial character, see *The Most Offending Soul Alive,* a biography by Judith M Heimann.

Junglebluesdream Art Gallery ART GALLERY

(www.junglebluesdream.weebly.com; Ulung Palang Longhouse; 9am-6pm) Many of artist Stephen Baya's paintings have traditional Kelabit motifs. In April 2013 his colourful illustrations of the Kelabit legend of Tuked Rini were featured at the Museum of Archaeology and Anthropology in Cambridge, England.

Kayaking KAYAKING

(for text messages 019-807 1640; roachas@hotmail.com; per kayak RM60, guide & transport RM200) A typical day trip involves a morning paddle upriver in inflatable kayaks, a barbecue lunch on a sandy river beach and an easy return trip downstream in the afternoon. Transport to the start point close to Pa Umur village is included. Also possible to arrange overnight camping trips in hammocks or tents. Advanced booking preferred.

Prayer Mountain HIKING

From the Bario Asal Longhouse, it's a steep, slippery ascent (two hours) up to the summit of Prayer Mountain, which has a cross that was erected in 1973, thickets of pitcher plants and amazing views of the Bario Valley and of the mixed Penan and Kelabit hamlet of Arur Dalan, with its three defunct wind turbines. Two-thirds of the way up is an extremely rustic church.

Festivals & Events

Bario Food Festival FOOD

(Pesta Nukenen Bario; www.facebook.com/pages/bariofoodfestival; Jul or Aug) Visitors flock to Bario for this three-day culinary festival celebrating traditional Kelabit food cultivation and cooking techniques. Delicacies on offer include plump wiggling grubs known as *kelatang,* river snails *(akep),* wild spinach, asparagus and ginger, and plenty of Bario pineapples.

Sleeping

Bario's various component villages are home to a whopping 19 guesthouses where you can meet English-speaking locals and dine on delicious Kelabit cuisine (accommodation prices almost always include board). Some of the most relaxing establishments are a bit out of town (up to 5km). Air-con is not necessary up in Bario, but hot water – alas, not yet an option – will some day be a nice treat. Almost all rooms have shared bathroom facilities. If you're on a very tight budget, enquire about renting a bed without board.

There is no need to book ahead – available rooms outstrip the space available on flights, and guesthouse owners meet incoming flights at the airport.

BARIO

Libal Paradise GUESTHOUSE $

(019-807 1640; d RM60) Surrounded by a verdant fruit and vegetable garden where you can pick your own pineapples, this sustainably run farm offers accommodation in two neat wooden cabins, each occupying their own idyllic spot in the greenery. Run by Rose and her Canadian husband Stu. From the airport terminal, walk eastward along the road that parallels the runway. Meals cost RM45 per day.

BARIO SALT

Along with pineapples and rice, another of Bario's celebrated local ingredients is salt, produced at the **main tudtu** under an hour's walk from Pa' Umor. Mineral-rich saline water is put in giant vats over a roaring fire until all that's left is high-iodine salt that goes perfectly with local specialities such as deer and wild boar. This traditional production technique is beginning to die out, but in Bario you can still purchase salt made the old way – look for a sausage-shaped 20cm-long leaf (RM17 to RM20).

Junglebluesdream GUESTHOUSE $
(☎019-884 9892; www.junglebluesdream.weebly.com; Ulung Palang Longhouse, Bario; per person incl meals RM90) Owned by artist and one-time guide Stephen Baya, a Bario native, and his friendly Danish wife Tine, this super-welcoming lodge (and art gallery) has four mural-decorated rooms, good-quality beds and quilts, a library of books on local culture and wildlife and fantastic Kelabit food. Guests can consult Stephen's extraordinary hand-drawn town and trekking maps.

Nancy & Harriss GUESTHOUSE $
(Hill View Lodge; ☎019-858 5850; nancyharriss@yahoo.com; per person incl meals RM70) This rambling place has seven guest rooms, a lovely verandah, a library-equipped lounge and endearingly tacky floor coverings. Situated 250m along a dirt track south of the main road. Prices include airport transfer.

Bario Asal Longhouse HOMESTAY $
(☎Julian 011-2508 1114; visitbario@gmail.com; per person incl meals RM80; Wi-Fi) There are various homestays in this traditional longhouse, including a six-room guesthouse at Sinah Rang Lemulun. Staying at Bario Asal – which is home to 22 families – is a great way to experience longhouse living. Transport from the airport costs RM30.

De Plateau Lodge HOMESTAY $$
(☎019-855 9458; deplateau@gmail.com; per person incl meals RM100) Situated about 2km east of the centre (bear left at the fork), this two-storey wooden cabin has eight rooms (including six triples) and a homey living room. It is owned by Douglas, a former guide whose son is a big fan of Liverpool FC. Price includes airport pickup.

Ngimat Ayu's House GUESTHOUSE $$
(☎013-840 6187; engimat_scott@yahoo.com; per person incl meals RM100) This spacious, two-storey family home has five comfortable rooms and paddy-field views. Situated on a slope 200m east of the yellow public library. Rates include transport from and to the airport.

Labang Longhouse Guesthouse GUESTHOUSE $$
(☎019-815 5453; lucysrb@yahoo.com; per person incl meals RM110) This 15-room, longhouse-style guesthouse, with valley views and a breezy verandah, is full of evocative photographs, each one with a story behind it that owner David will happily share. Prices include airport transport.

> **RICE & PINEAPPLES**
>
> Bario is famous throughout Malaysia for two things: Bario rice, whose grains are smaller and more aromatic than lowland varieties; and sweeter-than-sweet pineapples (RM2.50 in Bario), which are free of the pucker-inducing acidity of their coastal cousins. Outside the Kelabit Highlands, 1kg of Bario rice can cost RM18, and Bario pineapples are usually unavailable at any price.

PA' LUNGAN

Batu Ritung Lodge GUESTHOUSE $
(☎019-805 2119; baturitunglodge.blogspot.my; Pa' Lungan; per person incl meals RM90) Saupang and Nabu are welcoming hosts at their two-storey wooden lodge built on stilts over a pond, with gorgeous views of the mountains and paddy fields beyond. Plenty of space for larger groups. Meals are cooked using fresh jungle produce.

Mado Homestay HOMESTAY $
(☎019-854 9700; per person incl meals RM70) This family home is a peaceful spot to relax after a hike. After dinner, host Mado – a guide – likes to sit at the kitchen fire and tell stories of tourists who got lost in the jungle, a warning to anyone thinking of trekking alone.

Eating

Most guesthouses offer full board – almost always tasty local cuisine – but Bario also has several modest eateries. Pasar Bario, the town's yellow-painted commercial centre, is home to two or three **basic cafes** (mains RM6; 7am to about 10pm, closed Sunday morning) selling mainly generic fried noodle and rice dishes, though Kelabit food can sometimes be special-ordered.

Drinking

Finding a beer in Bario can be a bit of a challenge. This is a very evangelical town – you're as likely to hear Christian country music as the sound of the *sapé* (traditional stringed instrument) – so most establishments do not serve alcohol, and some of those that do keep it hidden.

Y2K BAR
(8am-1am) Local men quaff beer (RM4 to RM6) and play pool. Has karaoke in the evening.

Keludai BAR
(mains RM4; noon-1am) An all-wood saloon with beer (RM4), instant noodles, satellite TV and a pool table.

Shopping

Sinah Rang Lemulun HANDICRAFTS
(Bario Asal Longhouse; daily) Sinah sells lovely Kelabit beadwork, all locally made in the longhouse *dapur* (communal verandah). This is a good place to pick up a *kabo'* (RM50 to RM100, depending on the quality of the beads), a beadwork pendant shaped like a little beer barrel that's worn around the neck by Kelabit men.

Y2K FOOD, DRINK
(8am-1am) An old-fashioned, Old West-style general store that sells everything from SIM cards to something called Zam-Zam Hair Oil.

Information

INTERNET ACCESS

Bario Telecentre (www.unimas.my/ebario; Gatuman Bario; per hr RM4 ; 9.30-11.30am & 2-4pm, closed Sat afternoon & Sun) Solar-powered internet access.

MEDICAL SERIVES

Klinik Kesihatan Bario (085-786404, out of hrs emergencies 013-837 1996; Airport Rd intersection; 8am-1pm & 2-5pm Mon-Thu, 8-11.45am & 2.15-5pm Fri, emergency 24hr) Bario's innovative, ecologically sustainable rural health clinic, powered by solar energy, has one doctor, two paramedics, a dispensary (small pharmacy) and a helicopter on standby.

MONEY

At research time there were still no banks, ATMs or credit-card facilities anywhere in the Kelabit Highlands (although there was talk of installing an ATM in Bario), so bring plenty of small-denomination banknotes for accommodation, food and guides, plus some extra in case you get stranded. Commerce is limited to a few basic shops, some of them in Pasar Bario, the yellow commercial centre.

TELEPHONE

The best Malaysian mobile phone company to have up here is Celcom (Maxis works at the airport and in parts of Bario; Digi is useless). The airport has free wi-fi.

USEFUL WEBSITES

The Bario Experience (www.barioexperience.com) Kept up-to-date with the latest info on Bario.

Getting There & Around

AIR

Bario airport (Joanna 013-835 9009;) is linked with Miri twice a day by Twin Otters operated by MASwings (www.maswings.com.my). Weather, especially high winds, sometimes causes delays and cancellations. For flight updates, or if you're having a problem making a flight out of Bario, just ring the friendly staff at the airport.

Twin Otters have strict weight limits, so much so that checked baggage is limited to 10kg, hand luggage to 5kg and passengers themselves are weighed on a giant scale along with their hand-luggage when they check in.

The airport is about a 30-minute walk south of the shophouses, but you're bound to be offered a lift on arrival. As you'll notice, the people of Bario treat the air link to Miri almost like their own private airline and love dropping by the wi-fi-equipped airport terminal to meet flights, hang out with arriving or departing friends, and check emails.

CAR

The overland trip between Bario and Miri, possible only by 4WD (per person RM150), takes 12 hours at the very least and sometimes a lot more, the determining factors being the weather and the condition of the rough logging roads and their old wooden bridges. When things get ugly, vehicles travel in convoys so that when one gets stuck the others can push or winch it out.

In Bario, 4WD vehicles can be hired for RM250 or RM300 a day including a driver and petrol; guesthouses can make arrangements.

BICYCLE

Bike Rental (015-905 671, 013-514 0399; b333solutions_adventures@yahoo.com; per day from RM30) Mountain bikes for hire along with free maps showing suggested cycling routes.

Trekking in the Kelabit Highlands

The temperate highlands up along Sarawak's far eastern border with Indonesia offer some of the best jungle trekking in Borneo, taking in farming villages, rugged peaks and supremely remote Kenyah, Penan and Kelabit settlements. Most trails traverse a variety of primary and secondary forest, as well as an increasing number of logged areas. Treks from Bario range from easy overnight excursions to nearby longhouses to one-week slogs over the border into the wilds of Kalimantan.

While the Highlands are certainly cooler than Borneo's coastal regions, it's still hard work trekking up here and you should be in fairly good shape to consider a multiday trek. Be prepared to encounter leeches – many trails are literally crawling with them. Bring extra mobile-phone and camera batteries as charging may not be possible.

With so many trails in the area, there is ample scope for custom routes and creative planning beyond the most well-known routes.

BARIO TO BA KELALAN

The three- to four-day trek from Bario to Ba Kelalan covers a variety of terrain including paddy fields and primary rainforest – some of it on the Indonesian side of the frontier – and gives a good overview of the Kelabit Highlands.

The first day is an easy walk from Bario to **Pa' Lungan**. If you find a guide to take you from Pa' Lungan, it is possible to do this first day alone. The path follows an open trail for an hour and then continues through the jungle along what used to be the only route between the two villages. With the new logging road connecting Bario with Pa' Lungan, the jungle trail is less used and not as clear as it once was, but armed with directions it's straightforward enough.

From here there are two possible routes to Ba Kelalan. The first involves a night at a jungle shelter at **Long Rebpun** – your guide will find edible jungle mushrooms and ferns to cook for dinner – and on to Ba Kelalan (via Kalimantan) the following day. The alternative route is via the jungle shelter at **Long Pa Diit** and the Kalimantan village

HIRING A GUIDE: THE PRACTICALITIES

With very few exceptions, the only way to explore the Kelabit Highlands is to hire a local guide. Fortunately, this could hardly be easier. Any of the guesthouses in Bario can organise a wide variety of short walks and longer treks led by guides they know and rely on. Some of the best guides for longer treks live in Pa' Lungan, an easy walk from Bario. If you link up with other travellers in Bario or Miri, the cost of a guide can be shared.

Although there's a growing shortage of guides, in general it's no problem to just turn up in Bario and make arrangements after you arrive, especially if you don't mind hanging out for a day or two in Bario. If you're in a hurry, though, or your trip coincides with the prime tourism months of July and August, consider making arrangements with your guesthouse in advance by email or phone.

The going rate for guides is RM120 per day for either a Bario-based day trip or a longer trek. Some itineraries involve either river trips (highly recommended if the water is high enough) or travel by 4WD – naturally, these significantly increase the cost. The going rate for a porter is RM100 a day.

If you are connecting the dots between rural longhouses, expect to pay RM70 to RM80 for a night's sleep plus three meals (you can opt out of lunch and save RM10 or RM15). Gifts are not obligatory, but the people who live in remote longhouses are appreciative if, after you drink tea or coffee with them, you offer RM10 to cover the costs.

If your route requires that you camp in the forest, expect to pay approximately RM120 per night; in addition, you may be asked to supply food, which is provided for both you and your guide when you stay in a longhouse. Equipment for jungle camping (eg a sleeping bag, hammock, mozzie net and bed roll) cannot be purchased in Bario, so it's a good idea to bring your own, though Bario Asal Longhouse may be able to rent it out.

If you're trekking in one direction only (eg Bario to Ba Kelalan), you will need to hire a porter and continue paying the guide and porter's fee while they return home through the jungle (in this scenario, it would take them two days to trek from Ba Kelalan back to Bario). This is so that the guide does not have to spend a night alone in the forest.

Detailed topographical maps of Sarawak exist, but it's nearly impossible to get hold of them. According to one conspiratorial explanation, the government's calculation is that activists will find it harder to fight for native land rights if they lack proper maps.

of **Tanjung Karya** (where it is possible to spend the night at a homestay).

To avoid doubling back, you can trek from Bario to Ba Kelalan and then fly or take a 4WD down to the coast. Remember, though, that you'll have to pay the guide for the two days it will take him to walk back to Bario. It is possible to do the trek in either direction, but finding a guide is much easier in Bario or Pa' Lungan than Ba Kelalan.

BATU LAWI

If you were sitting on the left side of the plane from Miri to Bario, you probably caught a glimpse of the two massive limestone spires known as Batu Lawi, the taller of which soars to 2040m. During WWII they were used as a landmark for parachute drops.

While an ascent of the higher of the two rock formations, known as the 'male peak', is only for expert technical rock climbers, ascending the lower 'female peak' – described by one veteran trekker as 'awe-inspiring' – is possible for fit trekkers without special skills. It's a tough, four- or five-day return trip from Bario. Be prepared to spend the second day passing through areas that have been impacted by logging. Only a handful of guides are experienced enough to tackle Batu Lawi.

GUNUNG MURUD

Sarawak's highest mountain (2423m), part of 598-sq-km **Pulong Tau National Park**, is just begging to be climbed, but very few travellers make the effort to put the trip together. Since 1985, evangelical Christians in the area have made annual pilgrimages up the mountain for prayer meetings.

Gunung Murud is linked by trails with both Ba Kelalan and Bario. From Bario, the more common starting point, a typical return trip takes six or seven days. You can also walk from Bario via Gunung Murud to Ba Kelalan (five days one way), but as you approach Ba Kelalan you'll have to walk along a depressing logging road.

A rough logging road links the base of Gunung Murud with the lowland town of Lawas (five to eight hours by 4WD).

This is an adventure for the fittest of the fit: Planet Borneo Tours (p448) offers a seven-day trek from Ba Kelalan to Bario via Gunung Murud (from RM2567 per person).

CROSSING INTO INDONESIA

Thanks to an agreement between the Indonesian and Malaysian foreign ministries it is possible for Highland residents and tourists to cross from Ba Kelalan into Kalimantan on a trek to Bario (or vice versa), but you must bring your passport (it won't be stamped) and explain your plans. The immigration checkpoint outside Ba Kelalan is not an official border crossing and doesn't issue visas on arrival. If you want to continue your journey into Indonesia, you'll need to get a visa in advance.

Malaysian ringgits are very popular in this remote part of Kalimantan, but US dollars are not.

Ba Kelalan

Known for its rice, organic vegetables and apples, the Lun Bawang town of Ba Kelalan is a popular destination for treks from Bario.

The village is built on a hillside in an attractive valley; when the paddy fields are flooded, the effect of the mirror-like surface reflecting the surrounding mountains is spectacular. This is a deeply religious community; at the head of the large grassy playing field that acts as the town square sits the Borneo Evangelical Mission church, with Sunday services that last most of the day. The church seems incongruously large for such a small town, but at times it is filled to bursting with worshippers who come to Ba Kelalan to climb nearby **Gunung Murud** (2423m), known to some as prayer mountain.

Ba Kelalan is also one of the best places in Sarawak for birdwatching. Twitchers come here to spot ruddy cuckoo doves, oriental bay owls and broadbills, among others.

Sleeping & Eating

Apple Lodge GUESTHOUSE $
(085-435736, 013-286 5656; d RM60-120;)
A long-established guesthouse that was looking a little shabby when we visited, but is nonetheless a welcoming and comfortable place to stay. The owner, Tagal Paran, a former evangelical pastor who is now in his 80s, was the person first responsible for planting apples in Ba Kelalan and establishing the town's annual apple festival.

The walls of the lodge are papered with newspaper articles chronicling the festival's past successes, though sadly it has not been held for several years.

TREKKING WITH THE PENAN

The Penan, an indigenous group that was nomadic – surviving almost exclusively on hunting and gathering – until quite recently, has fared less well than other groups in modern Malaysia. Since independence, the Sarawak state government has often sold off rainforest lands to logging companies and evicted the Penan and other indigenous groups with minimal or no compensation. The **Penan Peace Park** is an unofficial, community-run nature reserve encompassing 18 villages in the remote Upper Baram area with the objective of establishing Penan land rights.

Community-based and sustainably managed, **Borneo Penan Adventure** (www.borneopenanadventure.org) is a pioneering, non-profit tourism initiative that offers intrepid trekkers a rare chance to visit the remote Penan villages of Long Kerong, Long Spigen and Long Sait in the Upper Baram, Penan Peace Park area. The villages are accessible by foot, river or 4WD from the Highland airports of **Long Lellang**, **Long Banga** and **Long Akah** (flights are from Miri with **MASwings**; p606). Itineraries are flexible (the minimum is three nights) and priced accordingly; typical expenses include a guide (RM100 per day), a porter (RM75 per day), boat hire (RM100 to RM250 one-way), hammock hire for jungle camping (RM25 per day) or a homestay (RM65 per person).

Recently returned travellers recommend doing a boat trip and bringing extra food (such as energy bars). There is a community fee of RM50 per person.

Juliasang Homestay HOMESTAY $
(www.homestayborneo.com; incl meals per person RM70) A large family house in the village's grassy main square opposite the church. Electricity from 6pm to 11pm only.

Ponook Santai Café MALAYSIAN $
(mains RM4.50-7; ⌚7pm-midnight) Opposite the airport (on the other side of the runway from the terminal building), this relaxed cafe's speciality is chicken rice. One of the main draws here seems to be the large flat-screen TV, which during our visit was showing Discovery Channel documentaries at full volume.

Getting There & Away

The only way to get from Ba Kelalan to Bario is on foot. A rough, 125km logging road links Ba Kelalan with Lawas (per person RM70 to RM80 by 4WD, seven hours, daily).

It's possible to get from Ba Kelalan to Long Bawan in Kalimantan by motorbike.

MASwings (www.maswings.com.my) flies Twin Otters from Ba Kelalan to Lawas and Miri three times a week.

Limbang Division

Shaped like a crab claw, the Limbang Division slices Brunei in two. Tourism is underdeveloped in these parts, but Bruneians love popping across the border to find shopping bargains, including cheap beer smuggled in from duty-free Pulau Labuan.

The area, snatched from the sultan of Brunei by Charles Brooke in 1890, is still claimed by Brunei.

Limbang

The bustling river port of Limbang (pronounced *lim*-bahng) is something of a backwater, but you may find yourself here before or after taking the Headhunters' Trail to or from Gunung Mulu National Park.

Sights

Limbang's old town stretches inland from riverfront Jln Wong Tsap En (formerly Main Bazaar) and southward along the riverbank.

Limbang Regional Museum MUSEUM
(www.museum.sarawak.gov.my; Jln Kubu; ⌚9am-4.30pm Tue-Fri, 10am-4.30pm Sat & Sun) This small museum features well-presented exhibits on Limbang Division's archaeology, culture and crafts, including Chinese ceramic jars that were a symbol of status and wealth for Orang Ulu communities. It is housed in a Charles Brooke–era fort originally built in 1897 and rebuilt (after a fire) in 1991. Located on the riverbank, about 1km south of the centre.

Limbang Raid Memorial MEMORIAL
(Jln Wong Tsap En) Commemorates four members of the Sarawak Constabulary and five members of the UK's 42 Commando Royal Marines killed during the Limbang Raid of 12 December 1962, which retook the town

from rebels of the pro-Indonesian North Kalimantan National Army. The memorial is 400m south of the centre, on the riverfront across the street from the police station.

Tours

Possible activities around Limbang include canoeing in the Limpaki Wetlands, where proboscis monkeys can sometimes be seen, and a self-spa at the Maritam Mud Spring, 39km outside town.

Borneo Touch Ecotour TREKKING
(013-844 3861; www.walk2mulu.com; 1st fl, 2061 Rickett Commercial Bldg) Run by the dynamic Mr Lim, this local company offers highly recommended treks along the Headhunters' Trail (p456) to or from Gunung Mulu National Park (for three days and two nights, including the Pinnacles: RM1150 per person for a group of two, RM900 per person for a group of three, RM780 per person for a group of four).

Can provide basic lodgings in Limbang (RM30 per person) and arrange for luggage to be sent by air cargo (RM70) so that you don't need to carry it on the trek. Advanced booking recommended.

A half-day trip to the Limpaki Wetlands including transport and two hours' canoeing costs RM60 per person.

Chua Eng Hin HIKING
(019-814 5355; chaulimbang@gmail.com) A well-known local personality with a passion for Limbang District's largely unknown charms. Specialises in climbing tours, but is happy to give advice on other local sights and activities, such as kayaking in the Limpaki Wetlands.

Sleeping

Metro Hotel HOTEL $
(085-211133; Lot 781-782, Jln Bangkita; s/d RM50/60;) Old-school, slightly shabby hotel offering reasonable budget accommodation. Centrally located.

Purnama Hotel HOTEL $$
(085-216700; www.purnamalimbang.com; Jln Buangsiol; s/d incl breakfast RM115/125-175;) Ensconced in Limbang's tallest building (12 storeys), this uninspiring hotel – ornamented with rainbow-hued balconies – has 218 spacious but aesthetically challenged rooms that come with big views and small bathrooms.

Eating

Diyana Cafe INDONESIAN $
(019-486 3342; Jln Wong Tsap Eng; mains RM5-15; 6am-11.30pm Mon-Sun) A buzzing little place with pavement tables and views of the river. Serves up tasty Indonesian fare including *nasi lalapan* (rice, vegetables and tofu served with a spicy sambal sauce).

Chinese Night Market HAWKER $
(Jln Bangkita; mains RM2.50-7; 2-10pm) Ten stalls selling quick, flavoursome bites such as *kolo mee* (RM5) and *wonton mee* (RM5) and fresh juices (RM4) in an attractive covered strip next to the town's football pitch.

Bangunan Tamu Limbang HAWKER $
(Jln Wong Tsap En; mains RM3.50-6; 6.30am-5.30pm) Houses Limbang's wet market, with an upstairs hawker centre where you can try the town's speciality, Limbang *rojak*, a mixed vegetable dish with a thick shrimp-based sauce.

Pusat Penjaja Medan Bangkita MARKET $
(Jln Bangkita; 6am-5pm) Bisaya, Lun Bawang and Iban stallholders sell jungle edibles, sausage-shaped Ba Kelalan salt and a dozen kinds of upland rice. The larger weekly *tamu* (market) takes place all day Thursday and until noon on Friday.

Pasar Malam MARKET $
(Night Market; Jln Wong Tsap En; mains RM3.50-7; 6-11pm) Come evening time the riverfront hawker centre is a good spot for a cheap, tasty meal of the usual Malay fare such as chicken satay, fried rice or noodles.

Information

Limbang has several international ATMs.

Sun City Cybercafe (Jln Bangkita, 1st fl; per hr RM2.50; 8.30am-midnight) A haven for gamers. On the corner of Jln Bangkita and Jln Tarap.

Getting There & Around

AIR

Limbang's small airport is 7km south of the centre. A taxi into town costs RM20. As there are too few taxis to meet flights, your driver may take other passangers in the same car (but still charge you the full rate).

MASwings (085-211086; www.maswings.com.my; Limbang Airport, Jln Rangau; 6.30am-5.50pm) Three flights a day to Miri.

BOAT

Express ferries from Limbang's immigration hall to Pulau Labuan (RM30, two hours, 8am daily) are run by **Royal Limbang** (☎013-882 3736). Tickets are sold at the jetty. Departures from Pulau Labuan are at 1.30pm. Bookings can be made by SMS/text message.

BUS

Borneo Express sends a bus to Miri's Pujut Bus Terminal (RM40, four hours) every day at 2.30pm. Tickets are sold at **Hock Chuong Hin Cafe** (Jln Bangkita). **Bintang Jaya** (☎016-859 4532) also sends daily buses to Miri (RM40) at 1.45pm, and to Lawas (RM30) and KK (RM50) at 12.30pm. You can buy tickets for Bintang Jaya at the coffee shop two doors up from Hock Chuong Hin Cafe.

A spot in a seven-seater unlicensed van to Miri costs RM50, departing from the tiny old bus station at the eastern end of Jln Wayang, two blocks inland from the river.

The only company that can drop you off inside Brunei is **Jesselton Express** (PHLS; ☎in Brunei +673-719-3835, +673-717-7755, +673-718-3838, in KK 016-836 0009, in Limbang 016-855 0222, 085-212990), which has daily buses to Bandar Seri Begawan (RM20) at 2.30pm; and to Bangar, Lawas (RM30, two hours) and KK (RM50) at 9.30am. Tickets are sold at **Wan Wan Cafe & Restaurant** (Jln Bangkita). Heading to Limbang, a bus departs from BSB every day at 8am.

TAXI & MINIBUS

Minibuses and red-and-yellow taxis hang out at the **Stesen Teksi** (☎085-213781; Jln Wong Tsap En; ⌚5am-6pm or later), on the waterfront. If you're heading towards BSB, one-way travel to the Kuala Lurah crossing costs RM60. From there public buses run to BSB until 5.30pm. If you're coming from BSB, taxis wait on the Malaysian side of the Kuala Lurah crossing.

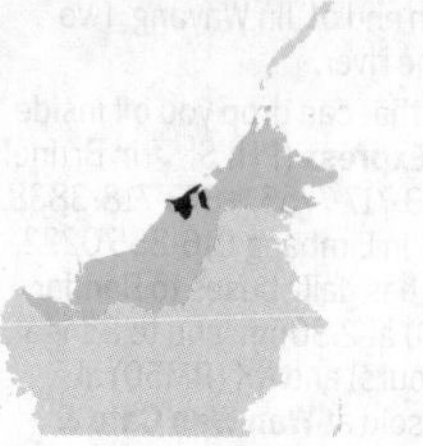

Brunei

POP 420,000 / AREA 5765 SQ KM

Includes ➡

Best Places to Eat

- ➡ Tamu Selera (p477)
- ➡ Pondok Sari Wangi (p478)
- ➡ Thiam Hock Restaurant (p479)

Best Places to Stay

- ➡ Ulu Ulu Resort (p486)
- ➡ Brunei Hotel (p476)
- ➡ Sumbiling Eco Village (p485)

Why Go?

Look beneath the surface of this well-ordered and tightly regulated sultanate and you'll see the underlying warmth of Brunei's people and the wildness of its natural environment.

This quiet *darussalam* (Arabic for 'abode of peace') has the largest oilfields in Southeast Asia, and thanks to the money they've generated, Brunei hasn't turned its rainforests into oil palm plantations. Old-growth greenery abounds, especially in verdant Ulu Temburong National Park.

The citizens of the capital, Bandar Seri Begawan (BSB), are mad for food and shopping (booze is banned). Here magnificent mosques contrast with the charmingly haphazard water village, while the nearby mangrove forest is home to proboscis monkeys and crocs.

This tranquil (sometimes somnolent) nation is the realisation of a particular vision: a strict, socially controlled religious state where happiness is found in pious worship and mass consumption. Visit and judge the results for yourself.

When to Go

Bandar Seri Begawan

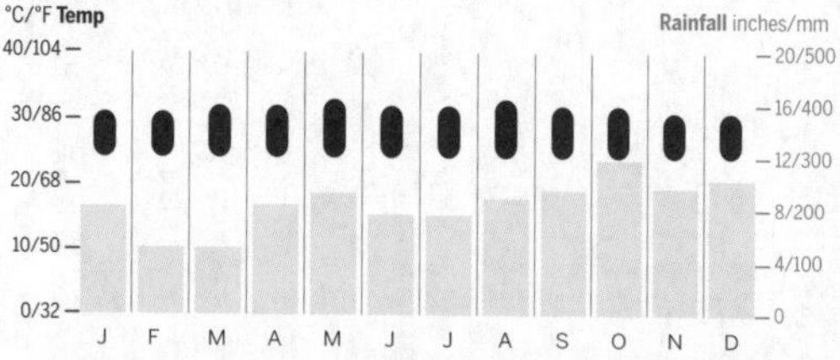

Oct–Dec The rainiest, if coolest, months of the year

Jan–May February and March are the driest months. National Day is celebrated on 23 February.

Jun–Aug It's *hot*. The sultan's birthday (15 July) is marked with festivities around the country.

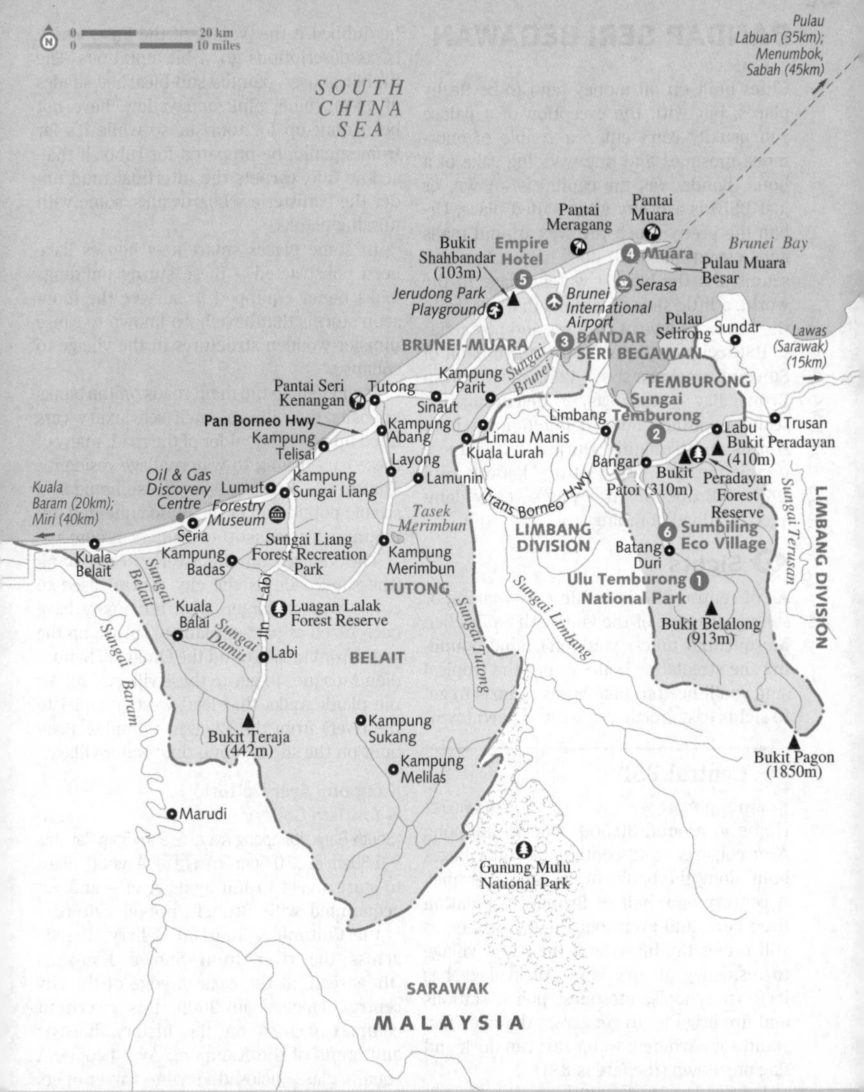

Brunei Highlights

1. Climbing high into the rainforest canopy and swimming in a cool jungle river at **Ulu Temburong National Park** (p486).
2. Tearing along mangrove-lined waterways on a **speedboat** (p484) from BSB to Bangar.
3. Taking a water taxi to the water village of **Kampong Ayer** (p470) and gorging on the culinary delights of **BSB** (p477).
4. Exploring the reefs and wrecks of Brunei's unspoilt **dive sites** (p474).
5. Enjoying the extravagance of the **Empire Hotel & Country Club** (p477) and cooling off in the pool.
6. Relaxing amid rural greenery at **Sumbiling Eco Village** (p485) in Temburong District.

BANDAR SERI BEGAWAN

POP 241,000

Cities built on oil money tend to be flashy places, but with the exception of a palace you usually can't enter, a couple of enormous mosques and one wedding cake of a hotel, Bandar (as the capital is known, or just BSB) is a pretty understated place. Urban life pretty much revolves around malls and restaurants. BSB does have a few museums and the biggest water village in the world, a little slice of vintage that speaks to the Bruneian love of cosiness and nostalgia.

BSB's city centre is on the north bank of Sungai Brunei at a spot – 12km upriver from Brunei Bay – that's easy to defend against seaborne attack and sheltered from both storms and tsunamis. During the Japanese occupation, the city centre – known until 1970 as Brunei Town – was severely damaged by Allied bombing.

Sights

All of central BSB is within easy walking or sailing distance of the Omar Ali Saifuddien Mosque, but unless you don't mind pounding the streets for hours under the tropical sun, you'll need to take buses or taxis to get to sights east, north and west of downtown.

Central BSB

Kampong Ayer WATER VILLAGE

Home to around 30,000 people, Kampong Ayer consists of 42 contiguous stilt villages built along the banks of the Sungai Brunei. A century ago, half of Brunei's population lived here, and even today many Bruneians still prefer the lifestyle of the water village to residency on dry land. The village has its own schools, mosques, police stations and fire brigade. To get across the river, just stand somewhere a water taxi can dock and flag one down (the fare is B$1).

Founded at least 1000 years ago, the village is considered the largest stilt settlement in the world. When Venetian scholar Antonio Pigafetta visited Kampong Ayer in 1521, he dubbed it the 'Venice of the East', which is, as descriptions go, a bit ambitious. The timber houses, painted sun-bleached shades of green, blue, pink and yellow, have not been done-up for tourists, so while it's far from squalid, be prepared for rubbish that, at low tide, carpets the intertidal mud under the banisterless boardwalks, some with missing planks.

In some places smart new houses have been constructed – these sturdy buildings looks better equipped to survive the monsoon storms that have been known to cause flimsier wooden structures in the village to collapse.

If you look to the main roads on the banks opposite the village, you'll see luxury cars lined up on the shoulder of the road; many of these cars belong to water-village residents. That said, Kampong Ayer is also home to a sizable population of the undocumented immigrants who constitute Brunei's underclass.

The villages on the river's **north bank** (the same side as the city centre) used to cover a much larger area, but many have been razed as part of plans to spruce up the waterfront area around the Omar Ali Saifuddien Mosque. To get to these villages, follow the plank walks that lead west (parallel to the river) from the Yayasan Complex, itself built on the site of a one-time water village.

> **FRIDAY OPENING HOURS**
>
> On Fridays all businesses and offices – including restaurants, cafes, museums, shops and even parks – are closed by law between noon and 2pm for Friday prayers.

Kampong Ayer Cultural & Tourism Gallery GALLERY

(South Bank, Kampong Ayer; 9am-5pm Sat-Thu, 9-11.30am & 2.30-5pm Fri) FREE A good place to start a visit to Kampong Ayer – and get acquainted with Brunei's pre-oil culture – is the Cultural & Tourism Gallery, directly across the river from Sungai Kianggeh (the stream at the eastern edge of the city centre). Opened in 2009, this riverfront complex focuses on the history, lifestyle and crafts of the Kampong Ayer people. A square, glass-enclosed **viewing tower** offers panoramic views of the scene below.

Omar Ali Saifuddien Mosque MOSQUE

(Jln Stoney; interior 8.30am-noon, 1.30-3pm & 4.30-5.30pm Sat-Wed, closed Thu & Fri, exterior compound 8am-8.30pm daily except prayer times) FREE Completed in 1958, Masjid Omar Ali Saifuddien – named after the 28th Sultan of Brunei (the late father of the current sultan) – is surrounded by an artificial lagoon that serves as a reflecting pool. This being Brunei, the interior is pretty lavish. The floor and walls are made from the finest Italian marble, the chandeliers were crafted in England and the luxurious carpets were flown in from Saudi Arabia. A 3.5-million-piece glass mosaic overlaying real gold leaf covers the main dome.

The mosque's 52m minaret makes it the tallest building in central BSB, and woe betide anyone who tries to outdo it – apparently the nearby Islamic Bank of Brunei building originally exceeded this height and so had the top storey removed by order of the sultan. The ceremonial stone boat sitting in the lagoon is a replica of a 16th-century *mahligai* (royal barge) where Koran-reading competitions were once held.

Come evening, the mosque is basically the happening centre of city life in Bandar; folks come for prayer, then leave to eat or shop, which is sort of Brunei in a nutshell.

Royal Regalia Museum MUSEUM

(Jln Sultan; 9am-5pm Sun-Thu, 9-11.30am & 2.30-5pm Fri, 9.45am-5pm Sat, last entry 4.30pm) FREE When called upon to present a gift to the sultan of Brunei, you must inevitably confront the question: what do you give a man who has everything? At this entertaining museum you'll see how heads of state have solved this conundrum (hint: you'll never go wrong with gold and jewels). Family photos and explanatory texts offer a good overview of the life of the sultan, who is himself depicted in myriad forms (including a hologram) in a series of portraits.

Also on display are the chariot used during the sultan's 1992 silver jubilee procession (the chariot is accompanied by an army of traditionally dressed headless mannequins representing those present on the day) and a second chariot used for the 1968 coronation.

East of Central BSB

Brunei Museum MUSEUM

(Jln Kota Batu; 9am-5pm Sat-Thu, 9-11.30am & 2.30-5pm Fri, last entry 30min before closing; P; 39) FREE Brunei's national museum, with its Islamic-art gallery, has exhibits depicting Brunei's role in Southeast Asian history from the arrival of the Spanish and Portuguese in the 1500s, and a natural-history gallery. It's a decent place to blow an hour of your time. It is 4.5km east of central BSB along the coastal road, at Kota Batu. At research time the museum was closed for ongoing renovations.

The oldest pieces here are ceramics from Iran and Central Asia and blown glass from Egypt and the Levant dating from the 9th and 10th centuries, as well as manuscripts of the Koran, tiny Korans the size of a matchbox and gold jewellery. Don't miss the collection of Brunei's famous ceremonial cannons, known as *bedil*, some with barrels shaped like dragon heads. It was not oil but these bronze-cast weapons that were once the source of the sultanate's wealth and power.

RAMADAN RULES

Brunei is an extremely religious, majority-Muslim country that takes Ramadan seriously. Under new laws introduced in 2014 as part of the first phase of the introduction of sharia law, during daylight hours for the month of Ramadan all eating, drinking and smoking in public is illegal. During the day, cafes and restaurants are open for takeaway only (bring food and drinks back to your hotel to consume).

If you're visiting during the holiest month of the Islamic year, it's a good idea to dress conservatively: men and women should cover their shoulders and wear clothes reaching below the knees. Museums close early (at 3pm Saturday to Thursday and noon on Friday) and other businesses may also operate for shorter hours. Mosques are closed to non-Muslim visitors for the whole month.

Brunei Darussalam Maritime Museum MUSEUM

(Muzium Maritim; Simpang 482, Jln Kota Batu; 9.30am-4.30pm Sat-Thu, 9am-noon Fri; P; 39) FREE A gleaming building, ship-like in both style and proportion, houses this interesting museum opened in 2015 at Kota Batu, 4.5km east of the city centre (take the 39 bus). On display are some of the more than 13,000 artefacts excavated from a shipwreck discovered by divers in 1997. The ship is believed to have set sail from China sometime in the late 15th or early 16th centuries before being struck by stormy weather as it approached Brunei.

Items exhibited in the well-presented shipwreck gallery include ceramics and glassware from China, Vietnam and Thailand, which would have been brought to Brunei to exchange for local products including spices, rattan, sago and camphor.

Bandar Seri Begawan

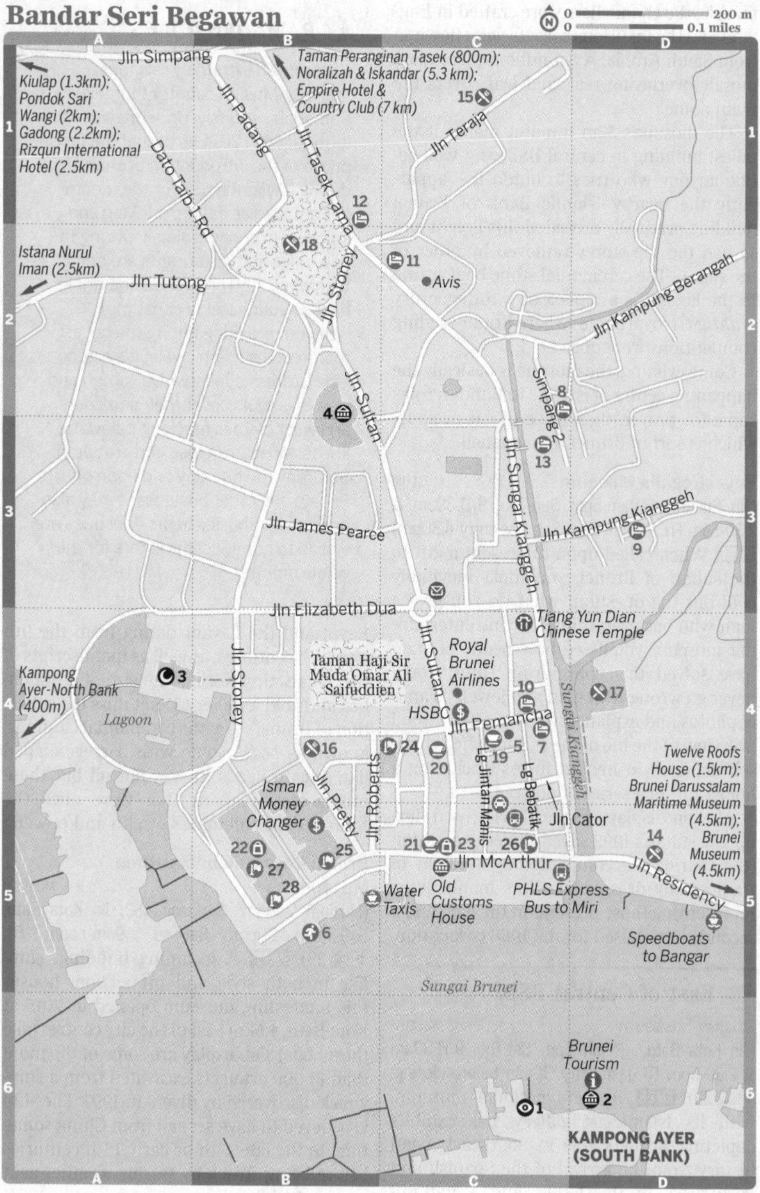

Malay Technology Museum MUSEUM

(Muzium Teknologi Melayu; Jln Kota Batu; ⌚9am-5pm Sun-Thu, 9-11.30am & 2.30-5pm Fri, 9.45am-5pm Sat, last entry 30min before closing) FREE Contrary to its misleading name, this museum focuses not on modern technology but on the traditional lifestyles and practices of Brunei's ethnic groups. The somewhat outdated displays on life in a Malay water village (stilt architecture, boat making, fishing techniques, handicrafts) and a Murut (Lun Bawang) longhouse have a certain charm

Bandar Seri Begawan

to them. The 39 bus passes along Jln Kota Batu, from where the museum is a five-minute walk down the hill.

Twelve Roofs House MUSEUM
(Bubungan Dua Belas; ☎224 4545; Jln Residency; ⏲9am-4.30pm Mon-Thu, 2.30-4.30pm Fri, Sat 9am-11.30am) FREE The one-time residence of Britain's colonial-era high commissioners, said to be the sultanate's oldest extant building, is now a museum dedicated to the longstanding 'special relationship' between Brunei and the UK. The evocative photos include views of Brunei as it looked a century ago. It's situated 1.5km southeast of the city centre, on a hilltop overlooking the river. When we stopped by in mid-2015 the museum was closed for ongoing extensive structural work (the building had been on the point of collapse).

North & West of Central BSB

Jame'Asr Hassanil Bolkiah Mosque MOSQUE
(Sultan Hassanal Bolkiah Hwy, Kampung Kiarong; ⏲8am-noon, 2-3pm & 5-6pm Mon-Wed & Sat, 10.45am-noon, 2-3pm & 5-6pm Sun, closed Thu & Fri; P) FREE Built in 1992 to celebrate the 25th year of the current sultan's reign, Brunei's largest mosque and its four terrazzo-tiled minarets dominate their surroundings. It's impossible to miss as you head towards Gadong, about 3km from the city centre. The number 1 bus goes here.

It's certainly an impressive building; because the sultan is his dynasty's 29th ruler, the complex is adorned with 29 golden domes. At night the mosque is lit up like a gold flame.

The mosque's interior more than matches its lavish exterior. The sheer volume of it is remarkable, not to mention the myriad woven rugs scattered across the men's prayer hall.

Look out for the sultan's own personal escalator at his private entrance to the mosque.

Istana Nurul Iman PALACE
(Jln Tutong) Istana Nurul Iman (Palace of the Light of Faith), the official residence of the sultan, is one of the largest habitations of any sort in the world – more than four times the size of the Palace of Versailles.

The palace is open to the public during the three-day Hari Raya Aidil Fitri festivities (p474) at the end of Ramadan. The best way to check it out on the other 362 days of the year is to take a water-taxi cruise.

Designed by Filipino architect Leandro Locsin, the palace mixes elements of Malay (the vaulted roofs) and Islamic (the arches and domes) design with the sweep and oversized grandeur of a 200,000-sq-m airport terminal. Nonetheless, it's relatively attractive from a distance or when illuminated in the evening. It is located 3km southwest of the town centre.

Taman Peranginan Tasek PARK
(Tasek Recreational Park; Jln Tasek Lama; ⏲6am-6pm Sun-Thu, 6-11am & 2-6pm Fri; Ⓟ) If you need a reminder that just beyond BSB's air-conditioned malls lies the Bornean jungle, this city park, with its background chorus of buzzing, chirping and rustling rainforest sounds, should do it. Well-marked paths lead to waterfalls, picnic areas and a hill-top *menara* (tower) offering views of the city and encroaching greenery. There are rougher jungle trails for longer walks (wear proper shoes). The park is 2km north of the city centre.

Muara

Peranginan Pantai Muara BEACH
(Muara Beach Recreational Park; Jln Pantai Muara; ⏲6am-6pm; Ⓟ) Muara Beach Recreational Park is a popular weekend retreat. It's pretty, but like many beaches in Borneo, it's littered with driftwood and other flotsam that comes in with the tide. Quiet during the week, it has picnic tables and a children's playground. A plaque commemorates the nearby Australian amphibious landings of 10 June 1945.

The beach lies just past Muara town, 27km from central BSB. Take bus 38 to Jln Pelempong, from where it is a 500m walk.

Activities

Diving

Though it's still relatively new, Brunei's burgeoning dive scene has the advantage of having some decent dive operators without the downside of crowds.

There are several interesting wrecks – some dating back to WWII – as well as plenty of undamaged reef here, including patches that are largely unexplored. On most of the shipwrecks and all the coral dive sites there is colourful hard and soft coral, such as large gorgonian fans and wide table corals. Marine life you are likely to see includes cuttlefish, octopus, morays, porcupine fish, giant puffers and sometimes a sea snake or two.

The best time to dive is between March and October; from May to mid-July the conditions are often ideal.

Poni Divers DIVING
(☎223 3655; www.ponidivers.com; Seri Qlap Mall, Unit L3/12, Kiulap; 2 fun dives B$150; ⏲9am-5pm) Brunei's largest dive centre offers a full range of PADI certification courses, recreational dives and various water sports including water skiing and banana boating. Operates from Serasa beach, with a booking office in BSB. Also puts together dive packages including airport transfers and accommodation at the dive centre's homestay.

A typical itinerary for fun dives includes three dives a day (B$180 including lunch) combining shallower reef dives with deeper

INSIDE THE SULTAN'S PALACE

If shaking hands with royalty is your thing, and you happen to be in Brunei for the Hari Raya Aidil Fitri festivities at the end of Ramadan, be sure to call in on the sultan at **Istana Nurul Iman** (p473), his 1788-room primary residence. In keeping with the local tradition of hosting an open house, during which guests are welcomed into the home and plied with a buffet of curries, dried fruit and cake, for three days the sultan receives members of the public at his palace in morning and afternoon sessions. There is no need for an invitation; simply turn up and join the queue (arriving early means a shorter wait). Bruneians will be dressed in their best clothes, some in outfits made especially for the occasion using brightly patterned materials, so wear something modest and reasonably smart.

After piling your plate high with a selection of curries and making multiple trips to the cake table at the free banquet, there is an hour or so of waiting involved. From here on, men and women are segregated. Seats are provided and Hari Raya pop songs played on a loop to keep the crowds entertained. You'll pass through a magnificent banquet hall before being ushered through to shake hands with the sultan (if you are a man) or the queen (if you are a woman), who receive guests in separate rooms. Each visitor is also given a gift.

If your moment with the sultan or queen feels all too fleeting, bear in mind that they will greet some 40,000 people a day during the festivities.

WORTH A TRIP

JERUDONG: PRINCE JEFRI'S PLAYGROUND

For much of the 1990s the sultan's younger brother and Brunei's then Finance Minister, Prince Jefri, was renowned for his extravagance in both his personal and public spending; the legacy of the latter lives on in the neighbourhood of Jerudong, an area so enveloped with Las Vegas–style bling that there is even a roundabout adorned with a giant replica diamond ring.

Amid the rows of mansions lie the **Jerudong Park Polo club** (the sultan himself is a keen polo player) and **Jerudong Park Medical Centre** (p480).

Back in the golden days, a concert hall hosted free shows by the likes of Whitney Houston and Michael Jackson, the latter to celebrate the sultan's 50th birthday in 1996. But in 1997 the party came to a halt when Prince Jefri (dubbed the Playboy Prince) was accused by the Brunei government of embezzling billions of dollars of state funds. After a long dispute involving a series of court cases, Prince Jefri now seems to have been welcomed back into the fold.

Nowhere sums up the legacy of Prince Jefri more than **Jerudong Park Playground** (www.jerudongpark.com.bn; Jerudong; adult/child B$20/10; ⏲4-11pm Wed, 3-11.30pm Fri, 10.30am - 11.30pm Sat & Sun, closed Mon, Tue & Thu; 👪), which reopened in 2014 with brand new rides for children after languishing for years in a poorly maintained state. It's a great place to bring kids, but despite the recent facelift the park continues to feel underused and rather empty. In its 1990s heyday, this B$1 billion attraction was the pride of Brunei, and the only major modern amusement park in Southeast Asia. Bruneians who were teenagers then have fond memories of the rides – all of them free – which included a giant roller coaster. Although the new attractions may be no match for the golden days, the place still evokes a feeling of nostalgia.

The **Empire Hotel & Country Club** (p477), commissioned by Prince Jefri at a cost of US$1.1 billion, is worth a visit if only to gawp at the cavernous, glass atrium and US$500,000 lamp made of gold and Baccarat crystal in the lobby. For B$25 you can use the sea-front swimming pool complex, and the hotel also has eight restaurants including the well-regarded **Pantai** (☎241 8888; Beachfront, level 1; buffet adult/child B$48/24; ⏲6.30-10pm Fri-Wed). The resort even has its own three-screen **cinema** (☎261 0001; www.timescineplex.com; adult B$4-8, child B$3-8; ⏲11am-2am).

Jerudong, which lies 20km northwest of BSB, is difficult to explore without private transport, although the 57 bus from the city centre will take you as far as the Empire Hotel.

wreck dives in locations chosen depending on water conditions and diving experience. PADI Open Water courses cost B$570; discounts are offered if booking more than one course.

Oceanic Quest Company DIVING
(☎277 1190; www.oceanicquest.com; No 6, Simpang 46, Jln Perusahaan, Kampong Serasa) Well-regarded company offering PADI certification courses (B$500) and dives to nearby reefs and wrecks (from B$40 per dive). Oceanic can also arrange airport transfers (B$60 return). Accommodation is available at the dive centre guesthouse in Muara (B$60 per person per night including meals).

Cruises

Water-Taxi Cruise BOATING
(1hr B$30-40) The best way to see BSB's water villages and the sultan's fabled palace, Istana Nurul Iman (p473), is from a water taxi, which can be chartered along the waterfront for about B$30 to B$40 (a bit of negotiating will occur, but at least you know the locals can't claim the petrol is expensive). Finding a boat won't be a problem, as the boatmen will have spotted you before you spot them.

After you admire the palace's backyard, your boatman can take you further upriver into the mangrove to see proboscis monkeys. Head out in the late afternoon if you can; the monkeys are easiest to spot around sunset.

Tours

A number of local agencies offer tours of BSB and trips to nature sites around the sultanate, including Ulu Temburong National Park (p486) and the mangroves of Pulau Selirong (p484), 45 minutes by boat from the city.

Some also offer night safaris where you can spot proboscis monkeys, crocs and fireflies.

★Borneo Guide TOUR
(☎718 7138, 242 6923; www.borneoguide.com; Unit 204, Kiaw Lian Building, Jln Pemancha; ⊙9am-5pm Mon-Thu, 9am-noon & 2-5pm Fri, 9am-1pm Sat & Sun) Excellent service, good prices and a variety of packages around Brunei and Borneo available. A day trip to Ulu Temburong National Park costs B$135 per person from BSB. Also offers overnight trips to Temburong with accommodation at Sumbiling Eco Village (p485; two days and one night from B$185) just outside the park. The office serves as a useful tourism information centre.

Sunshine Borneo Tours TOUR
(☎244 6812; www.bruneiborneo.com; No. 2 Simpang 146, Jln Kiarong; ⊙8am–5pm Mon-Thu & Sat, 8am–noon & 2–5pm Fri) Offers a range of tour packages in Brunei and Borneo, including birdwatching, river cruises, water-village tours and city night tours. Trips to Ulu Temburong National Park start at B$163 for a day trip and from B$330 for two days and one night with accommodation at the Ulu Ulu resort (p486). The office is 3km west of the city centre.

Intrepid Tours TOUR
(☎222 1685, 222 1686; www.bruneibay.net/intrepidtours; Unit G4, ground fl, Bangunan Sungai Akar Central) Offers a range of day tours and multiday packages, including trips to Ulu Temburong National Park (day trips B$100 to B$200 per person) and dawn tours of Pulau Selirong (B$67 to B$110 per person for a four-hour tour); the latter involves zipping across Brunei Bay as the sun rises and guided wildlife-spotting from a boardwalk.

Freme Travel Services TOUR
(☎223 4277; www.freme.com; 4th fl, office 403B, Wisma Jaya, Jln Pemancha) A bit corporate, but has plenty of options, as befits one of Brunei's largest travel agencies. Also has its own lodge close to Ulu Temburong National Park.

Sleeping

Budget options are thin on the ground. Upscale places often offer discounts online.

Youth Hostel HOSTEL $
(Pusat Belia; ☎222 2900, 887 3066; Jln Sungai Kianggeh; dm B$10; ❄📶🏊) Popular with backpackers, despite the fact that couples can't stay together. The five male and four female sex-segregated dorm rooms with functional furnishings and passable bathrooms are situated at the southern end of the Youth Centre complex, behind the cylindrical staircase. Reception is supposed to be open 7.30am to 4.30pm Monday to Thursday and Saturday, but staffing can be intermittent.

If the office is locked, hang around and someone should (eventually) find you. The hostel may fill up with government guests or school groups, so call ahead to check availability. The adjacent swimming pool costs B$1.

KH Soon Resthouse GUESTHOUSE $
(☎222 2052; http://khsoon-resthouse.tripod.com; 2nd fl, 140 Jln Pemancha; dm B$25, s/d B$40/50, without bathroom B$35/40; ❄) This basic guesthouse, in a converted commercial space with red cement floors, offers budget rates, huge but spartan rooms, and a central location. The reception level rooms that share bathrooms (squat toilets only) are probably a better bet than the ones upstairs, which have private facilities positioned awkwardly behind lower than ceiling-height partitions and dodgy looking electrical wires.

★Brunei Hotel HOTEL $$
(☎224 4828; www.thebruneihotel.com; 95 Jln Pemancha; r/ste incl breakfast B$140-175/240-320; ❄@📶) A chic, dare we say hip, hotel with clean lines, monochromatic colour schemes, geometric patterns and a general up-to-date style that is pretty unexpected in the sultanate. There's a decent breakfast buffet thrown into the deal served in the downstairs Choices Cafe.

★Capital Residence Suites HOTEL $$
(☎222 0067; www.capitalresidencesuites.com; Simpang 2, Kampong Berangan; d/ste incl breakfast B$80/180-280; ❄📶) This good value, rather blandly decorated hotel is lifted by friendly, helpful staff and a free shuttle service from 9am to 9pm, which transports guests all around BSB city and to the beaches and attractions beyond. The spacious suites are like small apartments with sofas, a kitchen and washing machine. Standard rooms, though comfortably furnished, are a little cramped.

Terrace Hotel HOTEL $$
(☎224 3555, 224 3554; www.terracebrunei.com; Jln Tasek Lama; d incl breakfast B$85-100; ❄📶🏊) A classic tourist-class hotel whose 84 rooms are a little dowdy (think 1980s) but clean, and come with marble bathrooms. It also has a great little swimming pool. In a good

LOCAL KNOWLEDGE

AMBUYAT – GUMMY, GLUEY & GLUTINOUS

Remember that kid in kindergarten who used to eat craft glue? Well, *ambuyat*, Brunei's unofficial national dish, comes pretty darn close. It's a gelatinous porridge-like goo made from the ground pith of the sago tree, which is ground to a powder and mixed with water, and eaten with a variety of flavourful sauces.

To eat *ambuyat*, you'll be given a special pair of chopsticks called *chandas* that's attached at the top (don't snap them in two!) to make it easier to twirl up the tenacious mucous. Once you've scooped up a bite-sized quantity, dunk it into the sauce. After your *ambuyat* is sufficiently drenched, place the glob of dripping, quivering, translucent mucilage in your mouth and swallow – don't chew, just let it glide down your throat.

location just 800m north of the waterfront, near the Tamu Selera hawker centre.

Jubilee Hotel HOTEL $$
(☎222 8070; www.jubileehotelbrunei.com; Jln Kampung Kianggeh; d/ste incl breakfast from B$95/120; ❄📶) The Jubilee's rooms aren't flash – they may remind you of your old aunt's seldom-used guest bedroom – but are liveable and clean. 'Superior' rooms come with kitchenettes. Prices include transfers to and from the airport, a short city overview tour and one further return trip within the city.

Empire Hotel & Country Club RESORT $$$
(☎241 8888; www.theempirehotel.com; Lebuhraya Muara-Tutong, Jerudong; d B$400-600, ste B$1000-16600, villas B$2200-3500; ❄@📶🏊; 🚌57) Pharaonic in its proportions and opulence, this 522-room extravaganza was commissioned by Prince Jefri as lodging for guests of the royal family and quickly transformed into an upscale resort (p475). Even the cheapest rooms have remote-control everything, hand-woven carpets, gold-plated power points and enormous bathrooms with marble floors. Online discounts offer substantial savings on the quoted rates.

Radisson Hotel HOTEL $$$
(☎224 4272; www.radisson.com/brunei; Jln Tasek Lama; d/ste B$170/350; ❄@📶🏊) This Radisson chain hotel, on the edge of the town centre, flies the flag for international standards. The sparkling lobby exudes comfort and wealth, as do the business-class rooms. Amenities include a pool, a fitness centre, a spa and two restaurants. Free shuttle service to Gadong and downtown three times daily.

Rizqun International Hotel HOTEL $$$
(☎242 3000; www.rizquninternational.com; Abdul Razak Complex; d incl breakfast from B$320; ❄📶🏊) The Rizqun is more sophisticated than you'd expect for something attached to a Gadong shopping mall and has all the usual business-class amenities on hand including a gym and a decent outdoor pool. The opulent lobby is pure Brunei (think marble, wood and stained glass) and the 7th-floor lounge has great views of the Jame'Asr Hassanal Bolkiah Mosque.

Eating

In the city centre, restaurants can be found along the waterfront and on Jln Sultan (south of Jln Pemancha). The big shopping malls, including those out in Gadong, have food courts. Just find a spot that looks busy and chow down.

★Tamu Selera HAWKER $
(cnr Jln Tasek Lama & Jln Stoney; mains B$2-6; ⏲5pm-midnight) At this old-fashioned hawker centre, set in a shady park, diners eat excellent, cheap Malaysian and Indonesian dishes under colourful tarps and ceiling fans. Options include satay, fried chicken, seafood, rice and noodle dishes, and iced drinks. Situated 1km north of the waterfront.

Pasar Malam Gadong MARKET $
(Gadong Night Market; Jln Pasar Gadong; ⏲4-10pm; 🚌1) Thanks to its authentic local snacks and dishes, this is Brunei's most popular night market. Unfortunately, it's geared to car-driving locals who take the food away, so there are almost no places to sit. It's 3km northwest of the city centre, served by bus, but after about 7pm the only way back to town is by taxi (B$15 until 10pm, then B$20).

Noralizah & Iskandar INDIAN $
(☎867 5781; 15 ground fl, Kompleks Awang Hj Ibrahim, Jln Berakas; mains B$3-7; ⏲7am-8pm; 🖉) It's all about the roti flatbreads at this busy spot, from flaky roti to deliciously oily paratha, stuffed with ground lamb and onions in a *murtabak*, or bananas and a dusting of sugar

LOCAL KNOWLEDGE

THANIS LIM: FOOD WRITER

Bruneian food writer and chef Thanis Lim lives in BSB and writes about the Brunei food scene for www.thanislim.com.

Describe the local attitude to food In Brunei our social life revolves around food and eating out. A typical night out here is to get together with friends for food or coffee at a restaurant or cafe, or go to a night market. Tamu Selera (p477) is one of my favourites. Go at about 7pm and order *ayam penyet* (Indonesian fried chicken with sambal).

What local foods should visitors try? *Ambuyat*, a kind of starchy, glutinous paste made from sago starch and hot water that is dipped into spicy sauces to give it flavour. *Ambuyat* became popular during the Japanese occupation in the 1940s when there wasn't enough rice to go around. The best place to try it is at Aminah Arif. The *ambuyat* set there comes with other typical local dishes like *belutak*, a sausage made with beef offal and local spices.

And drinks? *Teh tarik* – tea and condensed milk poured into the cup from a height. There used to be speakeasy-type places serving alcohol in Brunei, but they have closed now. Just across the Kuala Lurah border crossing, in Malaysia, there is a food court selling chicken wings and cheap beers that is popular with non-Muslims from Brunei. It's a 30-minute drive from BSB. Make sure you cross back into Brunei before the border closes at 10pm.

Any other tips? Bruneians are very friendly and love receiving visitors, so try to get in touch with locals via social media. Your new friends will probably be happy to show you around.

for a breakfast treat. Dip that deliciousness in one of several bowls of warming curry. The restaurant is located near the airport.

Gerai Makan Jalan Residency HAWKER $
(Jalan Residency Food Stalls; Jln Residency; mains B$2-5; 4pm-midnight) Along the riverbank facing Kampung Ayer, this grouping of food stalls features satay (B$1 for four chicken or three lamb skewers), various kinds of mee goreng and nasi goreng, and soups such as *soto* (noodle soup). Opening hours depend on the whim of the stall holder.

Tamu Kianggeh HAWKER $
(Kianggeh market; Jln Sungai Kianggeh; mains from B$1; 5am-5pm) The food stalls here serve Brunei's cheapest meals, including *nasi katok* (plain rice, a piece of fried or curried chicken and sambal; B$1) and *nasi lemak* (rice cooked in coconut milk and served with chicken, egg and cucumber slices; also B$1). The market feels endearingly chaotic and messy, something of a rarity in the sultanate.

★Pondok Sari Wangi INDONESIAN $$
(244 5403; Block A, No 12-13, Abdul Razak Complex, Jln Gadong; mains B$5-18; 10am-10pm;) Located in Gadong, Pondok Sari Wangi is a beloved Bandar institution. The extensive menu includes lots of gloriously rich, decadent, colourful grub like marinated 'smashed chicken', a fried fish with fiery sambal, sweet sauteed local greens and vegetables, mouth-watering satay with a heavily textured peanut sauce and the signature beef ribs, braised to something like perfection.

Seri Damai Restaurant PAKISTANI $$
(222 5397; ground fl, 144A Jln Pemancha; mains B$6-18; 9am-10pm;) This friendly, family-run Pakistani restaurant with an all-out green colour scheme (think wedding-style chair covers and plenty of satin) serves up some of the best biryanis, curries, naan breads and lassis in town. There is a good variety of vegetarian as well as meat and seafood dishes available. At B$6 the set menus are good value.

Lim Ah Siaw CHINESE $$
(222 3963; Jln Teraja; mains B$8-10; 6:30am-10pm) Though it's only a 10-minute walk from the main road, the jungly setting of the Lim Ah Siaw pork market and restaurant give it an underground feel. And while it might be located away from casual passersby – it must be the least Halal restaurant in Bru-

nei. Crispy braised pork knuckle, pork belly, pork dumplings; this place is Babe's hell.

Popular dishes include *kolo mee* (noodles cooked with pork lard) with pork ribs (B$8 to B$10).

Aminah Arif BRUNEIAN $$

(☎223 6198; Unit 2-3, Block B, Rahman Bldg, Simpang 88, Kiulap; mains B$4-28; ⏲7am-10pm; ❄✍) Aminah Arif is synonymous with *ambuyat* (thick, starchy porridge), Brunei's signature dish. If you're up for a generous serving of wiggly white goo, this is a good spot to do so (B$22 for a set meal for two people). Meals can be washed down with iced *kasturi ping* (calamansi lime juice; B$1.50).There are five branches of Aminah Arif in town; this one – located in Kiulap about 3km northwest of the waterfront – is the most central.

Kimchi KOREAN $$

(☎222 2233; Unit 19, Block B, Regent Sq, Kiulap; mains B$4.95-30; ⏲11am-10.30pm Sat-Thu, 2-10.30pm Sun; ❄) Korean restaurants are pretty ubiquitous in BSB, and Kimchi, in Regent Sq west of the centre, is the best in town. The titular *kimchi* (fermented cabbage) is delightfully smelly and spicy, rice cakes are drowned in a hot, rich sauce and the chicken wings...well, when are chicken wings a bad idea? The *bulgogi* (grilled marinated beef) is a lovely indulgence.

Thiam Hock Restaurant CHINESE $$$

(☎244 1679; 5 Yong Siong Hai Bldg, Gadong; mains from B$10-30; ⏲8.30am-10pm; ❄) This long-standing Chinese restaurant is famous for its curry fish head (some diners may find the blown-up photo of one such head looking back at them from the menu, mouth open and teeth bared, a little off-putting). Less challenging dishes here include delicious butter prawns. Thiam Hock is by the river on the block behind the Mall in Gadong.

Drinking

A double espresso is the most potent drink you're likely to find in Brunei, as the sale and public consumption of alcohol is banned. Locals are fond of the soft drink *air batu campur* (ice mix), usually called ABC, which brings together ice, little green noodles, grass jelly, sago pearls and red beans.

De Royalle Café CAFE

(38 Jln Sultan; ⏲24hr; 📶) With a living-room-style indoor area (complete with leopard-print armchairs) and outdoor pavement tables, this always-open establishment has a supply of perusable English-language newspapers and serves up an international menu (mains B$5.90 to B$15.90) and, of course, freshly brewed coffee. A fine place for a relaxed rendezvous with friends.

Another CAFE

(☎222 3012; G8 ground fl Wisma Jaya, Jln Pemancha; ⏲7.30am-6.30pm Mon-Sat; 📶) Corrugated metal walls, polished concrete floors and a wooden counter lend an industrial feel to this small, urban cafe. Coffee lovers (even the fussy ones) should be more than satisfied by the standard of flat whites served here, and there is a tempting selection of pastries, cakes (chocolate brownies and Dutch apple pie) and sandwiches (B$5 to B$7.50).

Piccolo Café CAFE

(☎224 1558; Lot 11, Jln McArthur; sandwiches RM3.50-6.90; ⏲7.30am-11pm Mon-Wed, 7.30am-1am Thu-Sat, 9.30am-11pm Sun; 📶) This cafe serves up lavender lattes (an original, if not completely delicious, drink) as well as more conventional coffees, teas and smoothies and a range of sandwiches, wraps and desserts, including an extremely tasty sea-salt chocolate tart (B$4.80).

☆ Entertainment

Locals often head to Gadong for a night out, which in Brunei usually amounts to dinner and perhaps a movie (which are censored so that even the kissing scenes are cut). Based on the enthusiasm locals have for Gadong, you might conclude that the area is a seething nightlife zone or at least a fine collection of smart restaurants. Unfortunately, it's neither – just some air-con shopping malls and commercial streets.

Shopping

Shopping is Brunei's national sport. Locals trail through the shopping malls scouting out the best deals while bemoaning the fact that their micro-nation doesn't have as much variety as Singapore.

Arts & Handicrafts Training Centre CRAFTS

(☎224 0676; Jln Residency; ⏲8am-5pm Sat-Thu, 8-11.30am & 2-5pm Fri) Sells silverwork, carved wood items, ornamental brass cannons (from B$500) and ceremonial swords (about B$500), made by the centre's students and graduates, for more than you'd pay in Sarawak or Kalimantan. Not bad for window-shopping, though. Check out the *jong sarat* (hand-woven cloth made from gold and silver threads). The centre is on the river 600m east of Sungai Kianggeh.

The Mall SHOPPING CENTRE
(Gadong; ⌚10am-10pm) Sure, this much-touted mall is sleek (the ceiling mural of Royal Brunei planes is an interesting touch), but as air-con malls go it's nothing remarkable: a collection of uninspiring outlets, a useful supermarket, a food court and an eight-screen **cineplex** (☎242 2455; www.themallcineplex.com; 3rd fl, adult B$4-10, child B$3-6; ⌚11am-midnight), the most popular cinema in Brunei!

Paul & Elizabeth Book Services BOOKS
(1st fl, 62 Jln McArthur; ⌚8.30am-8.30pm) Stocks a few books on Brunei, a street map of the entire sultanate and a small range of English-language paperbacks. There's also an internet cafe.

Hua Ho Department Store DEPARTMENT STORE
(Yayasan Complex, Jln McArthur; ⌚10am-10pm) A four-floor department store with a decent supermarket on the basement level.

Information

EMERGENCY

Ambulance (☎991)
Fire Brigade (☎995)
Police (☎993)

INTERNET ACCESS

Paul & Elizabeth Cyber Cafe (1st fl, 62 Jln McArthur; per hr B$1.80; ⌚8.30am-8.30pm) Old-style cybercafe with decent connections but a bad soundtrack.

> **GETTING TO SABAH: BANDAR SERI BEGAWAN TO KOTA KINABALU**
>
> **Getting to the border** At 8am daily a **Jesselton Express** (☎016-830 0722, 0060 88 751722; www.sipitangexpress.com.my) bus to runs KK (B$45, eight to nine hours) via Limbang, Bangar, Lawas and various towns in Sabah.
>
> **At the border** Make sure you have your passport ready if you're travelling overland to Sabah, because you'll be stopping at a whopping eight checkpoints. As long as your ID is in order you'll be fine; the trip is tedious rather than dodgy.
>
> **Moving on** Long-distance buses head to KK and drop you off close to the main stretches of hotels and restaurants.

MEDIA

Borneo Insider's Guide (www.borneoinsidersguide.com) Keep an eye out for the free, glossy magazine published four times a year.

MEDICAL SERVICES

Jerudong Park Medical Centre (☎261 1433; www.jpmc.com.bn; Tutong-Muara Hwy; ⌚24hr) Private medical facility with high standards of care. Located about 27km northwest of BSB centre.

RIPAS Hospital (☎224 2424; www.moh.gov.bn; Jln Putera Al-Muhtadee Billah; ⌚24hr) Brunei's main hospital, with fully equipped, modern facilities. Situated about 2km west of the centre (across the Edinburgh Bridge).

MONEY

Banks and international ATMs are sprinkled around the city centre, especially along Jln McArthur and Jln Sultan. The airport has ATMs.

HSBC (cnr Jln Sultan & Jln Pemancha; ⌚8.45am-4pm Mon-Fri, to 11.30am Sat) Has a 24-hour ATM. You must have an HSBC account to change travellers cheques.

Isman Money Changer (Shop G14, ground fl, Block B, Yayasan Complex, Jln Pretty; ⌚10am-8pm) Changes cash. Just off the central atrium.

POST

Main Post Office (cnr Jln Sultan & Jln Elizabeth Dua; ⌚8am-4.30pm Mon-Thu & Sat, 8-11am & 2-4pm Fri) The Stamp Gallery displays some historic first-day covers and blow-ups of colonial-era stamps.

TOURIST INFORMATION

Brunei Tourism (☎220 0874; www.bruneitourism.travel; Kampong Ayer Cultural & Tourism Gallery; ⌚9am-12.15pm & 1.30-4.30pm Mon-Thu & Sat, 9-11.30am & 2-4.30pm Fri) Free maps, brochures and information about Brunei. The website has oodles of useful information.

Getting There & Away

AIR

Brunei International Airport (☎233 1747; www.civil-aviation.gov.bn) Recent renovations, including new arrival and departure halls, have greatly improved the sultanate's small international airport. The arrival hall has an ATM and a tourist information desk (ground fl, arrival hall, Brunei International Airport; ⌚9am-5pm).

Air Asia (www.airasia.com) Two flights a day to Kuala Lumpur.

Cebu Pacific (www.cebupacificair.com) Flights from BSB to Manila on Monday, Wednesday, Friday, Saturday and Sunday.

Royal Brunei Airlines (☎222 5931; www.flyroyalbrunei.com; RBA Plaza, Jln Sultan; ⌚8am-4pm Mon-Thu & Sat, 8am-noon &

GETTING TO SABAH: BANDAR SERI BEGAWAN TO BANDAR LABUAN

Getting to the border Travelling by sea to Sabah is the easiest option, avoiding the hassles and delays of land borders – traffic at the Kuala Lurah crossing has been known to cause lengthy delays. **PKL Jaya Sendirian** (☎277 1771; www.pkljaya.com; 1st fl, Unit 7, Block A, Muara Centre, Jln Muara) runs daily car ferries from Serasa Ferry Terminal in Muara, about 25km northeast of BSB, to the Malaysian federal territory of Pulau Labuan (1½ hours), leaving Muara at 9am (adult/child/car B$17/10/58) and makes the return journey from Labuan at 4pm (adult/child/car RM38/18/120). Arrive at least an hour before sailing. To get to the ferry terminal by public transport, take the 38 bus to Muara town. From there, it's a short trip on the 33 bus (allow at least an hour for the journey).

At the border Most travellers to Malaysia are granted a 30- or 60-day visa on arrival.

Moving on From Bandar Labuan, twice daily ferries go to Kota Kinabalu (three hours).

2-4pm Fri) Direct flights from BSB to destinations including Bangkok, Kota Kinabalu, Kuala Lumpur, Melbourne and Singapore.

Singapore Airlines (www.singaporeair.com) Five flights a week from BSB to Singapore

TEMBURONG DISTRICT

Although a state-of-the-art bridge is being built that will link Muara and Temburong, for the time being the fastest way to get to Bangar is by speedboat (B$7, 45 minutes, at least hourly from 6am to at least 4.30pm – later on Sundays). The **dock** (Jln Residency) is about 200m east of Sungai Kianggeh.

BUS & VAN

BSB's carbon-monoxide-choked **bus terminal** (Jln Cator) is on the ground floor of a multistorey parking complex two blocks north of the waterfront. It is used by domestic lines, including those to Muara, and Kuala Lurah, but not to Sabah or Sarawak. Schematic signs next to each numbered berth show the route of each line.

There is no longer a public bus service to Tutong, Kuala Belait and Seria. The **PHLS express bus to Miri** stopping in Tutong (B$5), Seria (B$6) and Kuala Belait ($6) leaves BSB waterfront (near Sungai Kianggeh) at 7am and 1pm.

ℹ Getting Around

TO/FROM THE AIRPORT

The airport, about 8km north of central BSB, is linked to the city centre, including the bus terminal on Jln Cator, by buses 23, 36 and 38 until about 5.30pm. A cab to/from the airport costs B$25; pay at the taxi counter. Some hotels offer airport pick-up.

BUS

Brunei's limited public bus system, run by a variety of companies, is erratic and rather chaotic, at least to the uninitiated, so getting around by public transport takes effort. Buses (B$1) operate daily from 6.30am to about 6pm; after that, your options are taking a cab or hoofing it. If you're heading out of town and will need to catch a bus back, ask the driver if and when he's coming back and what time the last bus back is.

Finding stops can be a challenge – some are marked by black-and-white-striped uprights or a shelter, others by a yellow triangle painted on the pavement, and yet others by no discernible symbol. Fortunately, numbers are prominently displayed on each 20- or 40-passenger bus.

The bus station lacks an information office or a ticket counter, and while the schematic wall map may make sense to BSB natives, it's hard to decipher for the uninitiated. It may be best to ask about transport options at your hotel before heading to the bus station.

CAR

Brunei has Southeast Asia's cheapest petrol – gasoline is just B$0.53 a litre and diesel goes for only B$0.31. (Since a bottle of water costs B$1, petrol is cheaper than water.) If you're driving a car (eg a rental) with Malaysian plates and are not a Brunei resident, you'll be taken to a special pump to pay more (this is to prevent smuggling).

Hiring a car is a good way to explore Brunei's hinterland. Prices start at about B$85 a day. Surcharges may apply if the car is taken into Sarawak. Most agencies will bring the car to your hotel and pick it up when you've finished, and drivers can also be arranged, though this could add B$100 to the daily cost. The main roads are in good condition, but some back roads require a 4WD.

Avis (☎222 7100; www.avis.com; Raddison Hotel, Jln Tasek Lama 2203; ⏰8am-noon & 1.30-5pm Mon-Thu, 8am-noon & 2-5pm Fri, 8am-noon & 1.30-4pm Sat, 9am-noon & 1.30-3pm Sun) Also has an office at the airport (☎233 3298; airport; ⏰8.30am-5.30pm).

Hertz (☎airport 872 6000; www.hertz.com; airport arrival hall; ⏰8am-5pm) The international car-rental company has a counter at Brunei airport.

GETTING TO SARAWAK: BANDAR SERI BEGAWAN TO MIRI

Getting to the border Twice a day **PHLS Express** (☎277 1668) links BSB with Miri (B$20 from BSB, RM50 from Miri, 3½ hours). Departures from BSB's waterfront are at 7am and 1pm and from Miri's Pujut Bus Terminal at 8.15am and 3.45pm. Tickets are sold on board. Another option for travel between BSB and Miri is a private transfer (which may be shared with other travellers) run by father-and-son team Mr Fu and Ah Pau (B$25 or RM70 per person, three hours). Call Mr Fu on ☎013-833 2231 (Malaysian mobile) or ☎878 2521 (Brunei mobile). Departures from BSB are usually at 1pm or 2pm; departures from Miri are generally at 9am or 10am but may be earlier.

At the border Most travellers to Malaysia are granted a 30- or 60-day visa on arrival.

Moving on The bus will leave you at Miri's Pujut Bus Terminal, a 4km taxi ride from the city centre.

TAXI

Taxis are a convenient way of exploring BSB – if you can find one, that is. There is no centralised taxi dispatcher, and it's difficult or impossible to flag down a cab on the street. Hotels can provide drivers' cell-phone numbers. Most taxis have yellow tops; a few serving the airport are all white.

BSB's only proper **taxi rank** (Jln Cator) is two blocks north of the waterfront at the bus terminal on Jln Cator.

Some taxis use meters, although many drivers will just try to negotiate a fare with you. Fares go up by 50% after 10pm; the charge for an hour of wait time is B$30 to B$35. Sample day-time taxi fares from the city centre include the Brunei Museum (B$25), Gadong (B$15), the airport (B$25), the Serasa Ferry Terminal in Muara (B$40), the Empire Hotel & Country Club (B$35) and the Jerudong Park Playground (B$35). Fares increase after 10pm.

WATER TAXI

If your destination is near the river, water taxis – the same little motorboats that ferry people to and from Kampung Ayer – are a good way of getting there. You can hail a water taxi anywhere on the waterfront a boat can dock, as well as along Venice-esque Sungai Kianggeh. Crossing straight across the river is supposed to cost B$1 per person; diagonal crossings cost more.

TUTONG & BELAIT DISTRICTS

Most travellers merely pass through the districts of Tutong and Belait, west of BSB, en route to Miri in Sarawak, but there are a few worthwhile attractions here. Buses link Kuala Belait, Seria and Tutong with BSB, but if you want to really see the sights, the best way is to take a tour or rent a car.

Tutong

POP 20,000

About halfway between Seria and BSB lies Tutong, the main town in central Brunei. The town itself is neat and unremarkable, but the area is famous in Brunei for two things: pitcher plants and sand. Locals cook a variety of dishes in the insect-catching sacs of the area's six species of pitcher plants, while some of the sand near Tutong is so white that Bruneians take pictures with it, pretending it's snow (have your fun any way you can, Brunei). You can see *pasir putih* (white sand) in patches along the side of the Pan Borneo Hwy.

Sights

Pantai Seri Kenangan BEACH

(Pantai Tutong; Jln Kuala Tutong) Set on a spit of land, with the South China Sea on one side and Sungai Tutong on the other, the casuarina-lined beach is arguably the best in Brunei. Sandflies can be a problem here; if you plan to stay for sunset, be sure to bring repellent. The beach is 2km west of Tutong town, on Jln Kuala Tutong.

Getting There & Away

The PHLS express buses that link BSB with Seria, Kuala Belait and Miri stop here. Departures west to Seria, Kuala Belait and Miri are at 8am and 2pm and east to BSB at 10.45am and 6.15pm (arrive 15 minutes early as times are approximate and the bus doesn't wait).

Jalan Labi

A few kilometres after you enter Belait district (coming from Tutong and BSB), a road branches inland (south) to Labi and beyond, taking you through some prime forest areas. Now fully paved, the road leads to a number of Iban longhouses, which in these parts come complete with mod cons and parking lots.

Sights

Forestry Museum MUSEUM
(Simpang 50, Jln Labi; 8am-12.15pm & 1.30-4.30pm, closed Fri & Sun) FREE The Forestry Museum is located down the Simpang 50 turn-off (on the right as you head towards Labi). It's a small, simple place with seriously thorough information for visitors about the local forest. Exhibits detail the history of logging and conservation in the area with labelled examples of more than 50 types of wood found here, along with taxidermic examples of the resident wildlife – sadly, it's the closest you're likely to come to seeing a clouded leopard in Borneo.

Luagan Lalak Recreation Park PARK
(Jln Labi) If you're craving peace and serenity this is the place to find it: wooden walkways extend across alluvial freshwater swamp with tufts of greenery dotted like islands in mirror-like water. It's a beautiful spot for picnicking, birdwatching or meditating.

Following Jln Labi down from the main highway, the park is 20km before Labi (look for the sign marking this distance). There is no public transport here.

Labi Longhouses HOUSE
Labi is a small Iban settlement about 40km south of the coastal road with four longhouses: Rampayoh, Mendaram Besar, Mendaram Kecil and finally, at the end of the track, Teraja.

If you go without a guide, how much of the longhouse you are able to see will depend on whether there's an English speaker there to show you around. If so, the cost of such a tour might be B$2 per person. Mendaram Besar also has an informal **homestay programme** (Hensona 323 3019; Jln Labi; per person incl food B$55).

These longhouses are a mix of the modern and the traditional: you will see women weaving baskets, though nowadays they may be plastic rather than rattan, and the longhouses have 24-hour electricity. Outside, among the fruit trees and clucking chickens, there is a rustic shelter for a row of gleaming cars.

Seria

POP 34,000

Spread out along the coast between Tutong and Kuala Belait, low-density Seria is home to many of Brunei Shell's major onshore installations.

Sights

Oil & Gas Discovery Centre MUSEUM
(337 7200; www.ogdcbrunei.com; off Jln Tengah; adult/teenager/child B$5/2/1; 8.30am-5pm Mon-Thu & Sat, 9.30am-6pm Sun) Puts an 'edutainment' spin on the oil industry. Likely to appeal to young science buffs and Shell employees. About 700m northwest of Seria town centre.

Billionth Barrel Monument MONUMENT
Commemorates (you guessed it) the billionth barrel of crude oil produced at the Seria field, a landmark reached in 1991. Out to sea, oil rigs producing the sultanate's second billion dot the horizon. Situated on the beach directly in front of Seria town.

Sleeping

Roomz Hotel HOTEL $$$
(322 3223; www.roomz.com.bn; s/d incl breakfast B$150/160;) This sophisticated new hotel has slickly decorated rooms with wooden floors, balconies and sea views. The place is easy to find: it's the tallest building in town, situated one block north of the bus station.

Getting There & Away

Frequent purple minibuses go southwest to Kuala Belait (B$1). The PHLS express goes to Miri (B$15) via Kuala Belait at 9am and 2pm, and to BSB (B$6) via Tutong at 9.45am and 5.15pm (arrive 15 minutes early as times are approximate and the bus doesn't wait).

Kuala Belait

POP 35,500

Almost on the Sarawak frontier, coastal Kuala Belait is a modern, sprawling company town – that company being Brunei Shell – of one-storey suburban villas interspersed with grasshopper-like pump jacks, also known as nodding donkeys. Although there's a reasonable beach, most travellers just hustle through on their way to or from Miri.

Look out for the majestic **teapot roundabout** to the east of town, surely one of the region's finest. The four districts of Brunei are represented by four teacups.

Sleeping & Eating

In the town centre, restaurants can be found along Jln McKerron and, two short blocks east, on parallel Jln Pretty, KB's main commercial avenue.

Hotel Sentosa HOTEL $$
(☎333 1345; www.bruneisentosahotel.com; 92-93 Jln McKerron; d B$108; ❄@📶) Clean, well-run accommodation right in the centre of town. Situated one block south of the bus station.

Information

HSBC Bank (cnr Jln McKerron & Jln Dato Shahbandar) Has an international ATM. Situated diagonally opposite the bus station.

Getting There & Away

Frequent purple minibuses go to Seria (B$1). The PHLS express goes to Miri (B$15) via Kuala Belait at 9.30am and 2.30pm, and to BSB (B$6) via Tutong at 9.15am and 4.45pm (arrive 15 minutes early as times are approximate and the bus doesn't wait).

TEMBURONG DISTRICT

This odd little exclave (part of a country physically separated from the rest of the nation; feel free to take that to the next pub quiz night) is barely larger than Penang, but happens to contain one of the best preserved tracts of primary rainforest in all of Borneo. The main draw is the brilliant Ulu Temburong National Park, accessible only by longboat.

For now, at least, the journey from BSB to Bangar, the district capital, is an exhilarating speedboat ride: you roar down Sungai Brunei, slap through the nipah-lined waterways and then tilt and weave through mangroves into the mouth of Sungai Temburong. At research time, work had already begun on a 30km bridge, which will link the districts of Brunei-Muara and Temburong. Due to be completed in 2018, the bridge will no doubt put an end to the speedboat service.

How the Temburong bridge will effect this wild, remote area is hard to say. Look at Google Earth and the outline of Temburong District is easy to spot: at the Brunei frontier, Malaysia's logging roads – irregular gashes of eroded earth – and trashed hillsides give way to a smooth carpet of trackless, uninhabited virgin rainforest. Not long ago, almost all of Borneo looked like this.

Pulau Selirong

Pulau Selirong Recreational Park MANGROVE FOREST
At the northern tip of Temburong District lies this 25-sq-km mangrove-forested island reachable only by boat (45 minutes from BSB). Intrepid Tours (p476) runs half-day guided trips for around B$80 to B$100 per person depending on group size. Two kilometres of elevated walkways lead through the mangroves, the untamed habitat of proboscis monkeys and flying lemurs – if you're lucky you might spot one gliding down from the trees. Pulau Selirong is also known as Mosquito Island; bring repellent.

At certain times the tide levels are such that it is not possible to travel by boat to the island. Check with tour operators for current water levels.

Bangar & Around

Little Bangar, perched on the banks of Sungai Temburong, is the gateway to, and administrative centre of, Temburong District. It can be visited as a day trip from BSB if you catch an early speedboat, but you'll get more out of the town's easygoing pace if you stay over and explore the area, which has some fine rainforest.

Sights

Bukit Patoi Recreational Park PARK
(Taman Rekreasi Bukit Patoi) Within the protected **Peradayan Forest Reserve**, it is possible to do a 2km (one way) hike to the top of **Bukit Patoi** (310m). The well-marked trail, through pristine jungle, begins at the picnic tables and toilet block at the park entrance, about 15km southeast of Bangar (towards Lawas). To get here from Bangar ask around at the jetty for an unofficial taxi (about B$30 return). Bring plenty of water.

Once you reach the peak, enjoy the views then turn around and come back down; in theory it is possible to continue on to Bukit Peradayan (410m), but the path is poorly maintained.

If you want to explore the Bruneian rainforest without the logistics and expense of a trip further upriver, Peradayan Forest Reserve makes a good alternative that can easily be done as a day-trip from BSB.

Sleeping

Lukat Intan Guesthouse GUESTHOUSE $
(☎864 3766, 522 1078; Bangar; d incl breakfast B$50; P ❄) Run by a friendly couple, Lukat offers spic-and-span rooms and personable service. They're happy to give free rides to Bangar jetty. Call for directions.

Rumah Persinggahan Kerajaan Daerah Temburong GUESTHOUSE $
(☎522 1239; Jln Batang Duri, Bangar; s/d/tr/q B$25/30/40/50, 4-person chalets B$80; ❄ 📶) Set around a grassy, L-shaped courtyard, this government-run guesthouse has friendly, helpful staff and six spacious but slightly fraying rooms with rather more bathtub rust and somewhat cooler hot water than many would deem ideal. Situated about 200m west of the town centre, across the highway from the mosque.

Youth Hostel HOSTEL $
(Pusat Belia; ☎522 1694; Jln Bangar Puni-Ujong, Bangar; dm B$10; ⏲office staffed 7.30am-4.30pm, closed Fri & Sat; ❄) This basic hostel is in a bright-orange building across the road and about 100m downhill from the Bangar ferry terminal. The sex-segregated dorms, each with six beds (bunks), are clean and have air-con. The office is upstairs.

Eating

The fruit and vegetable market, behind the row of shops west of Bangar ferry terminal, has an upstairs **food court** (1st fl, Kompleks Utami Bumiputera; mains B$1-3; ⏲6am or 7am-8pm, closed noon-2pm Fri).

A handful of restaurants serving passable Malay and Chinese food can be found around the market, along and just in from the riverfront.

Information

3 in 1 Services (Shop A1-3, 1st fl, Kompleks Utami Bumiputera; per hr B$1; ⏲8am-5.30pm, closed Sun) Internet access on the 1st floor of the building next to the market (across the pedestrian bridge from the hawker centre).

Bank Islam Brunei Darussalam (⏲8.45am-3.45pm Mon-Thu, 8.45-11am & 2.30-4pm Fri, 8.45-11.15am Sat) The only bank in town's ATM only accepts foreign cards with the cirrus sign (our Visa card didn't work). Non-account holders cannot change money. On the river 150m north of the bridge.

Chop Hock Guan Minimarket (⏲8am-8pm) Exchanges Malaysian ringgits for Brunei dollars. In the first row of shops to the west of Bangar ferry terminal.

Jayamuhibah Shopping Mart Carries some over-the-counter medicines (Temburong District does not have a proper pharmacy). In the second row of shops west of Bangar ferry terminal.

Getting There & Away

BOAT

By far the fastest way to and from BSB is by speedboat (B$7, 45 minutes, hourly from 6am to at least 4.30pm). Bangar's ferry terminal, Terminal Perahu Dan Penumpang, is on the western bank of the river just south of the red bridge.

Boats depart at a scheduled time or when they're full, whichever comes first. When you get to the ticket counters, check which company's boat will be the next to leave and then pay and add your name to the passenger list.

BUS

Buses run by **Jesselton** (☎719 3835, 717 7755, in BSB 718 3838) pick up passengers heading towards Limbang and BSB in the early afternoon; its bus to KK (B$25) and Lawas (B$10) passes through town at about 10am. Buses stop on Jln Labu, just across the bridge on the west side of the river.

TAXI

Bangar doesn't have official taxis, but it's usually not too difficult to hire a car if you ask around under the rain awning in front of the ferry terminal. Drivers may not speak much English. Possible destinations include Limbang in Malaysia (about B$40) and the Peradayan Forest Reserve (Bukit Patoi; about B$30 return).

Taxis do not wait on the Malaysian side of the border, so make sure your transport goes all the way to Limbang

Batang Duri

Batang Duri, 12km south of Bangar, is the jumping-off point for longboat rides to Ulu Temburong National Park. As you head south, the sealed road passes Malay settlements, then Murut (Lun Bawang) hamlets and finally a few partly modern Iban longhouses.

Sleeping

★ **Sumbiling Eco Village** CABIN $$
(☎242 6923, 718 7138; www.borneoguide.com/ecovillage; Kampong Sumbiling Lama, Jln Batang Duri; per person incl breakfast & dinner B$85) If you're looking for Brunei's version of a jungle

camp with basic amenities and a chilled-out atmosphere that encourages slipping into a state of utterly relaxed Zen, come to Sumbiling. This eco-friendly rustic camp in a beautiful riverside location offers tasty Iban cuisine and accommodation in bamboo huts or tents, which have beds, mosquito nets and fans.

When you're not lounging in a hammock there are plenty of outdoor activities on hand (to be booked in advance) including visits to nearby Ulu Temburong National Park, jungle overnights, inner-tubing on the river, night walks and forest hikes.

Sumbiling is run by Borneo Guide (p476) in cooperation with the local community. It's situated a few minutes downstream from Batang Duri. Price includes transport from Bangar jetty.

Ulu Temburong National Park

It's odd that a small, regulated country such as Brunei should contain a sizable chunk of true untamed wilderness. Therein lies the appeal of Ulu Temburong National Park, located in the heart of a 500-sq-km area of pristine rainforest covering most of southern Temburong. It's so untouched that only about 1 sq km of the park is accessible to tourists, who are only admitted as part of guided tour packages. To protect it, the rest is off-limits to everyone except scientists, who flock here from around the world. Permitted activities include a canopy walk, some short jungle walks, and swimming in the cool mountain waters of Sungai Temburong.

The forests of Ulu Temburong are teeming with life, including as many as 400 kinds of butterfly, but don't count on seeing many vertebrates. The best times to spot birds and animals, in the rainforest and along riverbanks, are around sunrise and sunset, but you're much more likely to hear hornbills and Bornean gibbons than to see them.

Activities

Longboat Trip BOAT

One of the charms of Ulu Temburong National Park is that the only way to get there is by *temuai* (shallow-draft Iban longboat). The trip upriver from Batang Duri is challenging even for experienced skippers, who need a variety of skills to shoot the rapids in a manner reminiscent of a salmon: submerged boulders and logs have to be dodged, hanging vines must be evaded and the outboard must be taken out of the water at exactly the right moment.

The journey takes between 25 and 45 minutes, depending on current river conditions. When it rains, the water level can quickly rise by up to 2m, but if the river is low you might have to get out and push (wear waterproof shoes).

Aluminium Walkway CANOPY WALK

The park's main attraction is a delicate aluminium walkway, secured by guy-wires, that brings you level with the jungle canopy, up to 60m above the forest floor. The views of nearby hills and valleys from the walkway are breathtaking, if you can get over the vertigo – the tower, built by Shell using oil-rig scaffolding technology, wobbles in the wind.

In primary rainforests, only limited vegetation can grow on the ground because so little light penetrates, but up in the canopy all manner of life proliferates. Unfortunately there are no explanatory signs here, but a good guide will explain the importance of the canopy ecosystem and point out the huge variety of organisms that can live on a single tree: orchids, bird's-nest ferns and other epiphytes; ants and myriad other insects; amphibians and snakes; and a huge selection of birds.

The trail up to the canopy walk begins near the confluence of Sungai Belalong and Sungai Temburong. It's a short, steep, sweaty walk. If you stay overnight at Ulu Ulu Resort, you can do the canopy walk at sunrise, when birds and animals are most likely to be around.

Rivers & Waterfalls SWIMMING

Places to take a refreshing dip in the park's pure mountain waters include several rivers and waterfalls – your guide can point out the best spots.

At one small waterfall you can stand in a pool and 2cm- to 4cm-long fish will come up and nibble on your feet, giving you a gentle, ticklish pedicure as they feast on the dry skin between your toes. To get there, head downriver about 500m from the park headquarters. Your guide can help find the creek that you need to follow upstream for a few hundred metres.

Sleeping

★ **Ulu Ulu Resort** LODGE $$$

(☎244 1791; www.ululuresort.com; Ulu Temburong National Park; per person standard/superior/deluxe B$275/360/395; ❄) The only accommodation inside the park is an upscale riverside lodge, constructed entirely of hardwood, with some rooms built to resemble 1920s Malaysian-style chalets. Standard rooms are dormitory style with shared bathrooms. Prices include transfers from BSB, meals and activities.

Guests at the resort have a 4.30am wake-up call to see the sunrise at the canopy walk, an unforgettable experience.

In Malay, ulu (as in Ulu Temburong) means 'upriver' and ulu ulu means, essentially, 'back of beyond'. The park's wildness and lack of established trails rules out the possibility of unguided walks, so activities are restricted to an easy-going timetable of kayaking and river swimming during the day and a guided night walk.

Getting There & Away

For all intents and purposes, the only way to visit the park is by booking a tour; several BSB-based agencies (p475) organise tour groups and guides.

BRUNEI SURVIVAL GUIDE

Directory A–Z

CURRENCY

Brunei dollar (B$)

EATING PRICE RANGES

$ less than B$6
$$ B$6 to B$16
$$$ more than B$16

EMERGENCY

Ambulance	991
Police	993
Fire	995
Search & Rescue	998
Directory enquiries	113

PUBLIC HOLIDAYS

Brunei shares major public holidays with Malaysia. Holidays specific to Brunei include **Brunei National Day** (23 February), **Royal Brunei Armed Forces Day** (31 May) and the **Sultan of Brunei's Birthday** (15 July).

TOURIST INFORMATION

Brunei Tourism (www.bruneitourism.travel) is a very useful website, containing information on transport, business hours, accommodation, tour agencies and more.

SLEEPING PRICE RANGES

$ less than B$60
$$ B$60 to B$150
$$$ more than B$150

VISAS

Travellers from the US and European Union, Switzerland and Norway are granted a 90-day visa-free stay; travellers from New Zealand, Singapore and Malaysia, among others, receive 30 days; Japanese and Canadians get 14 free days. Australians can apply for the following visas upon arrival: a 72-hour transit (B$5), a 30-day single-entry (B$20) or a multiple-entry (B$30). Israeli travellers are not permitted to enter Brunei.

CULTURAL & LEGAL MATTERS

In May 2014, Brunei began phasing in a new criminal code based on sharia law. Offenses in this first phase are punishable with a fine, imprisonment or both. Subsequent phases will introduce more severe penalties including corporal and capital punishments. As the laws could be applied to non-Muslims, ensure you're on the right side of them.

Drugs & Alcohol

The sale and public consumption of alcohol is forbidden in Brunei. Non-Muslims can import two bottles of wine or spirits and 12 cans of beer, which must be declared at customs, to consume in private. Keep the customs slip in case of inspection. Drug trafficking is punishable by the death penalty.

LGBT Travellers

Homosexual acts are illegal in Brunei and penalties may include prison sentences.

Smoking

Brunei's tough anti-smoking laws ban puffing not only inside shops and malls but also in outdoor markets and around food stalls. There is no duty-free allowance for tobacco and import tax is payable on every cigarette brought into the country.

Women Travellers

Discreet clothing is appropriate here – you certainly don't have to cover your hair, but walking around in a tank top is a bad idea. Loose fitting clothes that cover the shoulders and knees are best, especially when visiting any kind of official or religious building.

Singapore

☎65 / POP 5.5 MILLION / AREA 718 SQ KM

Includes ➡

Best Places to Eat

- National Kitchen by Violet Oon (p534)
- Ding Dong (p536)
- Momma Kong's (p536)
- Burnt Ends (p537)
- Iggy's (p539)

Best Places to Sleep

- Fullerton Bay Hotel (p530)
- Parkroyal on Pickering (p531)
- Amoy (p531)
- Capella Singapore (p533)
- Adler Hostel (p531)

Why Go?

So much more than just a stopover city, Singapore is a destination in its own right – an ambitious, ever-evolving wonder of sci-fi architecture in billion-dollar gardens, of masterpieces in colonial palaces, and single-origin coffee in flouncy heritage shophouses. From cult-status Aussie chefs to fashion-forward local designers, some of the world's hottest creatives have set up shop on these steamy streets, turning the Little Red Dot into a booming hub for all things hip and innovative. Beyond the new and dynamic simmers the Singapore of old: a spicy broth of Chinese, Malay, Indian and Peranakan traditions, smoky temples, raucous wet markets, and sleepy islands reached by bumboat. Sure, it might be clean, rich and a stickler for rules, but dig a little deeper and you'll uncover a Singapore far more complex than you ever imagined.

When to Go

Singapore

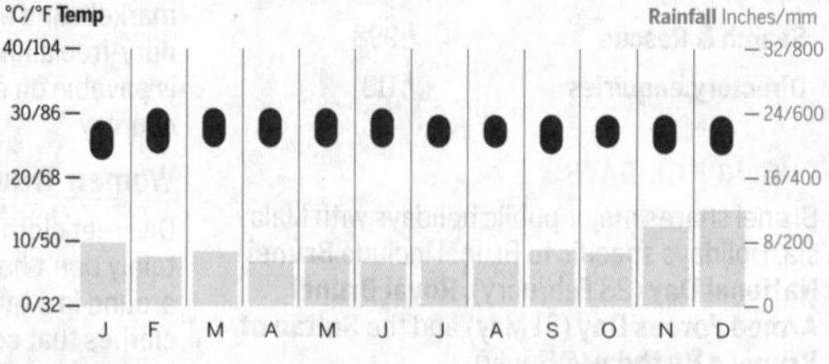

Feb Singapore celebrates Chinese New Year with fireworks, dragon parades and buzzing night markets.

May Bag some grin-inducing bargains at the Great Singapore Sale, launched annually in late May.

Sep Accommodation is scarce and expensive, but speed demons shouldn't miss the Formula One.

History

Chinese traders en route to India had plied the waters around what is now Singapore from at least the 5th century AD, though the records of Chinese sailors as early as the 3rd century refer to an island called Pu Luo Chung, a name reputedly derived from the Malay Pulau Ujong, meaning 'island at the end'.

Landing on its shores in 1819 was Sir Stamford Raffles. Then lieutenant general of Java, Raffles deemed the muddy island an ideal spot for a new British-controlled entrepôt to counter Dutch power in the region. Signing a treaty with the Sultan of Johor and *temenggong* (senior judge), Raffles acquired the use of Singapore in exchange for modest annual allowances to Sultan Hussein and the judge. This exchange ended with a cash buyout of the pair in 1824 and the transfer of Singapore's ownership to Britain's East India Company.

Large waves of immigration soon washed over the free port, driven by thrifty merchants keen to avoid the high tariffs at the competing, Dutch-controlled port of Melaka. Despite a massive fall in rubber prices in 1920, Singapore's prosperity continued, the population soared and millionaires were made almost overnight.

Crashing the party on 15 February 1942 was General Yamashita Tomoyuki and his thinly stretched army, who caught the British rulers by surprise and swiftly wrested control from them, renaming the island 'Syonan' (Light of the South) and interning or executing countless locals, Europeans and Allied POWs. Though the British regained power in 1945, the occupation had eroded Singapore's innate trust in the British empire's protective embrace. New political forces were at work and the road to independence was paved.

If one person can be considered responsible for the position Singapore finds itself in today, it is Lee Kuan Yew (1923–2015). This third-generation Straits-born Chinese was named Harry Lee, and brought up to be, in his own words, 'the equal of any Englishman'. His education at the elite Raffles Institution and Cambridge University equipped him well to deal with both colonial power and political opposition when Singapore took control of its own destiny in the 1960s.

The early years were not easy. Race riots in 1964 and ejection from the Malay Federation in 1965 made Lee's task even harder. Lee used tax incentives and strict new labour laws to attract foreign investment. This, combined with huge resources poured into developing an English-language education system that produced a competent workforce, saw Singapore's economy rapidly industrialise, securing the road to today's affluent, role-model nation.

Sights

Singapore's urban core is located on the south of the island. Here you'll find the Singapore River, flanked by Boat Quay, Clarke Quay and Robertson Quay. South of the river lie the CBD (Central Business District) and Chinatown, while immediately north of the river lies the Colonial (also referred to as the Civic) District. Further north is Little India and Kampong Glam, while east of Kampong Glam are Geylang, Katong (Joo Chiat), East Coast Park and Changi. Northwest of the Colonial District is Orchard Rd, while further west still lie the Singapore Botanic Gardens and the heavily expat district of Dempsey Hill. At the river's mouth is Marina Bay, while further southwest lies Sentosa Island. Central-north Singapore is where you'll find Singapore Zoo and Night Safari, as well as the island's major nature reserves.

Colonial District, the Quays & Marina Bay

The Colonial District brims with iconic heritage architecture and must-see museums. Straddling the river are the eateries, bars and nightspots of Boat Quay, Clarke Quay and Robertson Quay. Further east, the river spills into attention-seeking Marina Bay, home to Marina Bay Sands and Gardens by the Bay.

★**Gardens by the Bay** GARDENS

(Map p494; ☎6420 6848; www.gardensbythebay.com.sg; 18 Marina Gardens Dr; gardens free, conservatories adult/child under 13yr S$28/15; ⏲5am-2am, conservatories & OCBC Skyway 9am-9pm, last ticket sale 8pm; M Bayfront) Singapore's 21st-century botanic garden is a S$1 billion, 101-hectare fantasy-land of space-age biodomes, high-tech Supertrees and whimsical sculptures. The Flower Dome replicates the dry, Mediterranean climates found across the world, while the even more astounding Cloud Forest is a tropical montane affair, complete with waterfall. Connecting two of the Supertrees is the OCBC Skyway, with knockout views of the gardens, city and South China Sea. At 7.45pm and 8.45pm, the

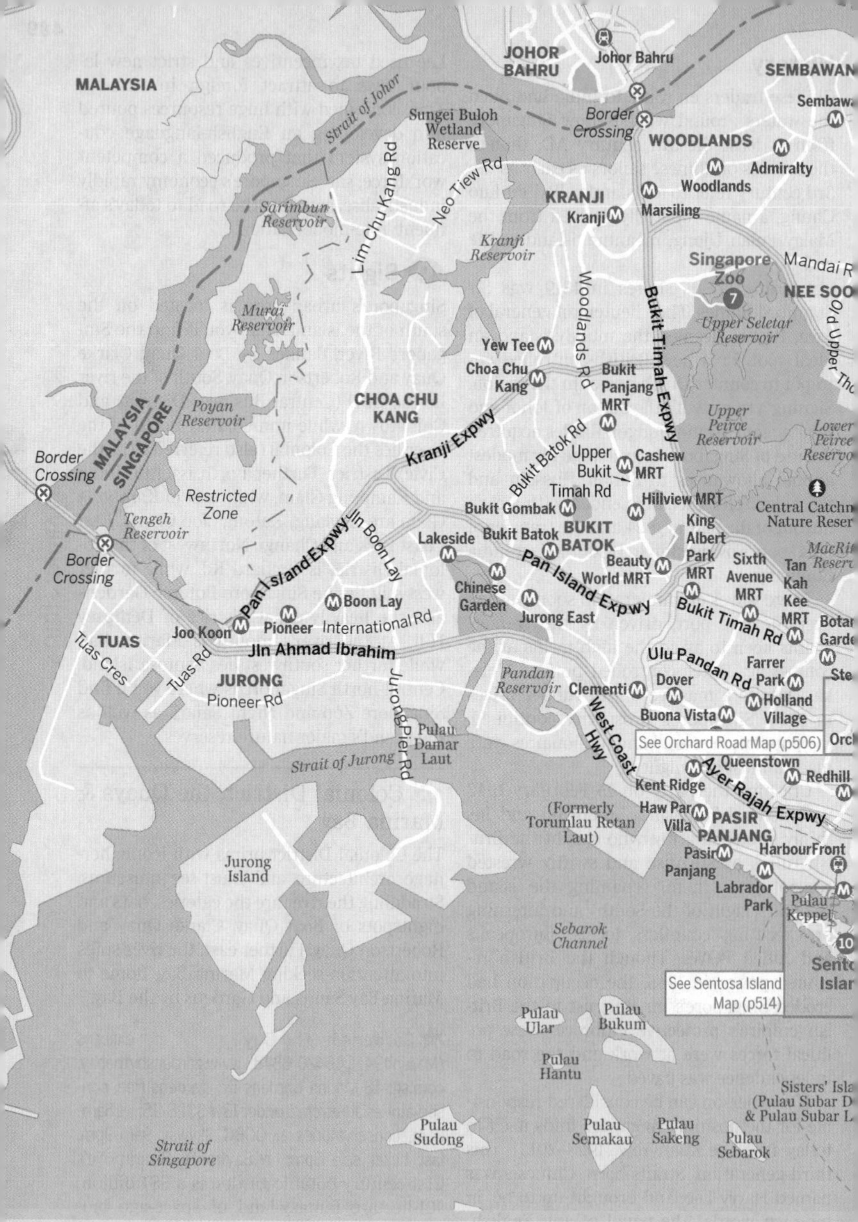

Singapore Highlights

1. Scaling Supertrees and a glass-enclosed mountain at **Gardens by the Bay** (p489).
2. Musing over masterpieces at the extraordinary **National Gallery Singapore** (p492).
3. Reliving Singaporean history at the multisensory **National Museum of Singapore** (p492).
4. Bollyjamming through the crayon-coloured streets of **Little India** (p501).
5. Wining and dining in hot-spot heritage 'hood **Chinatown** (p535).

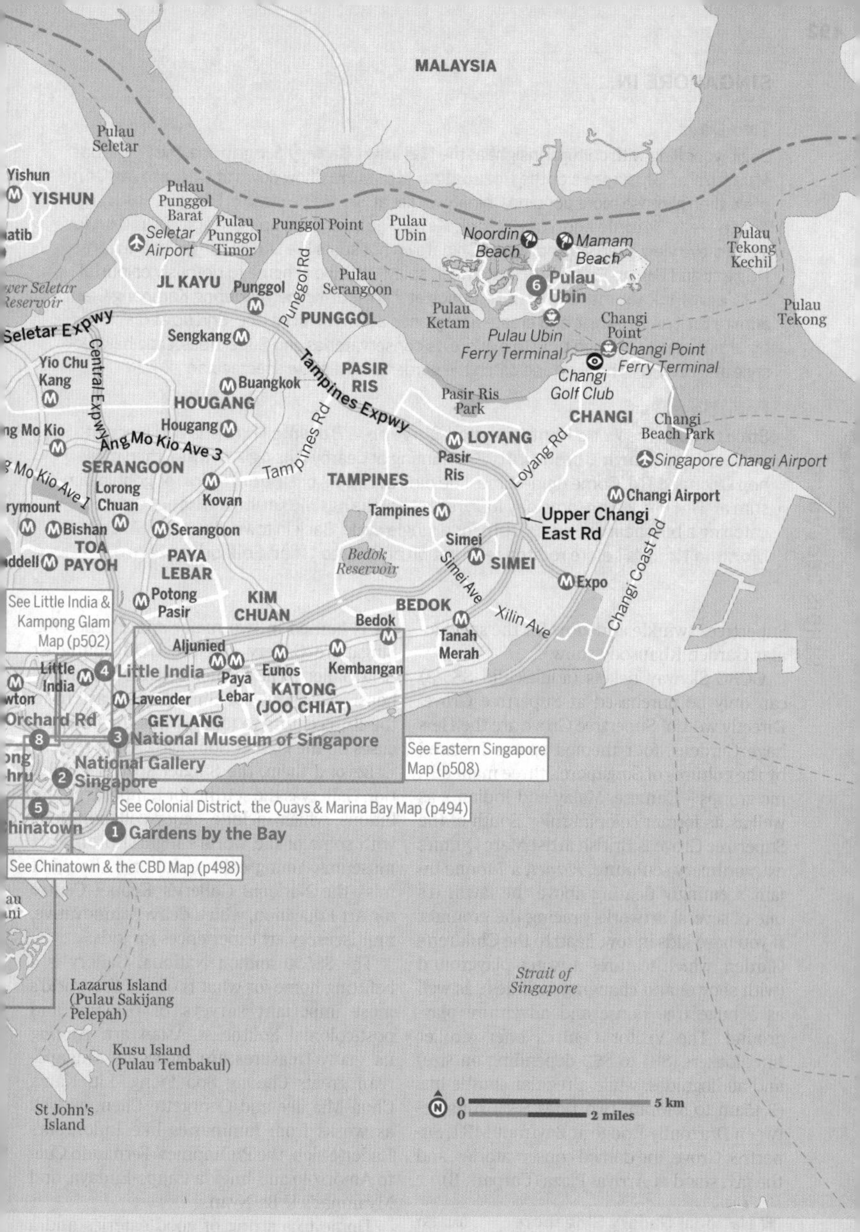

6 Catching a bumboat to bicycle-friendly **Pulau Ubin** (p511).

7 Hanging out with wild ones at showcase **Singapore Zoo** (p509).

8 Mall-hopping along fabled retail strip **Orchard Rd** (p551).

9 Getting your hipster on in low-rise, art deco–styled **Tiong Bahru** (p505).

10 Giving in to a little unadulterated fun on theme-park **Sentosa Island** (p513).

SINGAPORE IN...

Two Days

Begin your fling with cultural insight at the **National Gallery Singapore**, the **National Museum of Singapore** or the **Peranakan Museum**. Chow down at **Chinatown Complex**, then glimpse more genuine Chinatown life at **Sri Mariamman Temple**, **Buddha Tooth Relic Temple** and **Thian Hock Keng Temple**. Head up **Pinnacle@Duxton** for a bird's-eye view, then sip and sup at Chinatown hot spots like **Ding Dong**, **Operation Dagger** and **Burnt Ends**. Start day two in spicy Little India, home to riotously colourful **Sri Veeramakaliamman Temple**. Lunch at **Zam Zam** in neighbouring Kampong Glam, admire **Sultan Mosque** and create a fragrance at **Sifr Aromatics**. End up at **Gardens by the Bay** with enough time to explore its conservatories and Supertrees. Dine hawker-style at **Satay by the Bay** and catch the gardens' light-show spectacular.

Four Days

Stroll through the World Heritage–listed **Singapore Botanic Gardens** and lunch at verdant **Open Farm Community**. Go hunting at nearby **Shang Antique**, then mall-hop **Orchard Rd**. Come dinnertime, fine dine at **Iggy's** or **Buona Terra**, or gobble dim sum at **Tim Ho Wan**. Come day four, reflect at **Changi Museum & Chapel** before catching a bumboat to **Pulau Ubin** for a jungle cycle. Back in town, dig into chilli crab at **Momma Kong's** before rooftop rehydration at **Potato Head Folk** or **Lantern**.

Supertrees twinkle and glow for the spectacular Garden Rhapsody show.

OCBC Skyway tickets (adult/child S$5/3) can only be purchased at Supertree Grove. Directly west of Supertree Grove are the Heritage Gardens, four themed spaces inspired by the cultures of Singapore's three main ethnic groups – Chinese, Malay and Indian – as well as its former colonial ruler. South of the Supertree Grove is British artist Marc Quinn's extraordinary sculpture, *Planet*, a 7-tonne infant seemingly floating above the lawn. It's one of several artworks gracing the grounds. If you have kids in tow, head to the Children's Garden, which features a water playground (with shower and changing facilities), as well as a huge tree house and adventure playground. The Visitor Centres offer stroller hire, lockers (S$1 to S$3 depending on size) and audioguides, while a regular shuttle bus (9.45am to 5.45pm; two rides S$2) runs between Dragonfly Bridge at Bayfront MRT, Supertree Grove, the domed conservatories, and the taxi stand at Arrival Plaza (Carpark B).

★National Gallery Singapore GALLERY

(Map p494; www.nationalgallery.sg; St Andrew's Rd; adult/child S$20/15; ⏲10am-7pm Sun-Thu, to 10pm Fri-Sat; Ⓜ City Hall) Connected by a striking aluminium and glass canopy, Singapore's historic City Hall and Old Supreme Court buildings now form the city's breathtaking National Gallery. Its world-class collection of 19th-century and modern Southeast Asian art is housed in two major spaces, the DBS Singapore Gallery and the UOB Southeast Asia Gallery. The former delivers a comprehensive overview of Singaporean art from the 19th century to today, while the latter focuses on the greater Southeast Asian region.

Beyond them, the Singtel Special Exhibition Gallery is the setting for temporary exhibitions, which include major collaborations with some of the world's highest-profile art museums. Young culture vultures shouldn't miss the National Gallery's Keppel Centre for Art Education, which delivers innovative, multisensory art experiences for kids.

The S$530 million National Gallery is a befitting home for what is one of the world's most important surveys of colonial and post-colonial Southeast Asian art. Among its many treasures are pieces by Singaporean greats Cheong Soo Pieng, Liu Kang, Chua Mia Tee and Georgette Chen, as well as works from luminaries like Indonesia's Raden Saleh, the Philippines' Fernando Cueto Amorsolo and Imelda Cajipe-Endaya, and Myanmar's U Ba Nyan.

Home to a string of good eateries and a gift shop stocked with specially commissioned art books, design pieces and prints, the complex also runs daily guided tours, artist talks, lectures and workshops.

★National Museum of Singapore MUSEUM

(Map p494; www.nationalmuseum.sg; 93 Stamford Rd; adult/student & senior S$10/5; ⏲10am-6pm;

Ⓜ Dhoby Ghaut) Imaginative and immersive, Singapore's rebooted National Museum is good enough to warrant two visits. At once cutting-edge and classical, the space ditches staid exhibits for lively multimedia galleries that bring Singapore's jam-packed biography to vivid life. It's a colourful, intimate journey, spanning ancient Malay royalty, wartime occupation, nation-building, food and fashion. Look out for interactive artwork *GoHead/GoStan: Panorama Singapura*, which offers an audiovisual trip through the city-state's many periods.

★ Asian Civilisations Museum MUSEUM

(Map p494; ☎6332 7798; www.acm.org.sg; 1 Empress Pl; adult/child under 6yr S$8/free, 7-9pm Fri half-price; ⏲10am-7pm Sat-Thu, to 9pm Fri; Ⓜ Raffles Pl) This remarkable museum houses the region's most comprehensive collection of pan-Asian treasures. Recently expanded, its series of thematic galleries explore the history, cultures and religions of Southeast Asia, China, the Asian subcontinent and Islamic West Asia. Exquisite artefacts include glittering Sumatran and Javanese ceremonial jewellery, Thai tribal textiles, Chinese silk tapestries and astronomical treatises from 14th-century Iran and 16th-century Egypt. Among the more macabre objects is a 17th- or 18th-century Tibetan ritual bone apron, made with human and animal bones.

★ Peranakan Museum MUSEUM

(Map p494; ☎6332 7591; peranakanmuseum.org.sg; 39 Armenian St; adult/child under 7yr S$6/free, 7-9pm Fri half-price; ⏲10am-7pm, to 9pm Fri; Ⓜ City Hall) This is the best spot to explore the rich heritage of the Peranakans (Straits Chinese descendants). Thematic galleries cover various aspects of Peranakan culture, from the traditional 12-day wedding ceremony to crafts, spirituality and feasting. Look out for intricately detailed ceremonial costumes and beadwork, beautifully carved wedding beds, and rare dining porcelain. An especially curious example of Peranakan fusion culture is a pair of Victorian bell jars in which statues of Christ and the Madonna are adorned with Chinese-style flowers and vines.

Singapore Art Museum MUSEUM

(SAM; Map p494; ☎6589 9580; www.singaporeartmuseum.sg; 71 Bras Basah Rd; adult/student & senior S$10/5, 6-9pm Fri free; ⏲10am-7pm Sat-Thu, to 9pm Fri; Ⓜ Bras Basah) Formerly the St Joseph's

MARINA BAY SANDS

It's hard to ignore **Marina Bay Sands** (Map p494; www.marinabaysands.com; Marina Bay; Ⓜ Bayfront), the triple-towered, cantilevered behemoth flanking city-centre reservoir Marina Bay. Looking like it's straight out of *The Jetsons*, it's the work of Israeli–North American architect Moshe Safdie, best known for his modular housing complex Habitat 67 in Montreal.

Love it or loathe it, the US$5.5-billion integrated hotel, shopping and entertainment complex is a marvel of modern engineering. Take the record-breaking Sands SkyPark, a 340m-long cantilevered platform, fabricated using over 7000 tonnes of steel, that is long enough to fit four and a half A380 jumbos. How did they do it? By pre-assembling the pieces at ground level and then hoisting them 200m using strand jacks – a 24-hour exercise for each of the 14 pieces.

While the SkyPark's world-famous, 150m-long infinity pool is accessible to hotel guests only, its **observation deck** (Map p494; level 57; adult/child under 13yr S$25/17; ⏲9.30am-10pm Mon-Thu, to 11pm Fri-Sun; Ⓜ Bayfront) is open to all. The deck is completely exposed, so use sunscreen and a hat. An altogether better-value option is the adjoining **Club Lounge bar** (Map p494; 10 Bayfront Ave; ⏲noon-late); entry is via the lifts in the hotel lobby. Although its view is a little more limited, it still takes in all the best bits, including the CBD skyline. And, unlike the observation deck, it offers a close-up view of *that* pool. Entry to the Club Lounge is free, though you'll be expected to make a purchase. Even so, a S$10 juice works out significantly cheaper than admission to the observation deck. Or, for a few dollars more, you can take in the view with a cooling beer or cocktail. Note that a dress code applies for the Club Lounge from 6pm (no shorts, singlets or flip-flops), as well as a cover charge on Friday and Saturday nights from 9pm.

To catch Marina Bay Sands' nightly light and laser spectacular, **Wonder Full** (⏲8pm & 9.30pm Sun-Thu, 8pm, 9.30pm & 11pm Fri & Sat), do your drinking on the other side of Marina Bay, at bars like **Orgo** (p543), **Level 33** (p542) and **Lantern** (p542), which offer clear views of the complex.

Colonial District, the Quays & Marina Bay

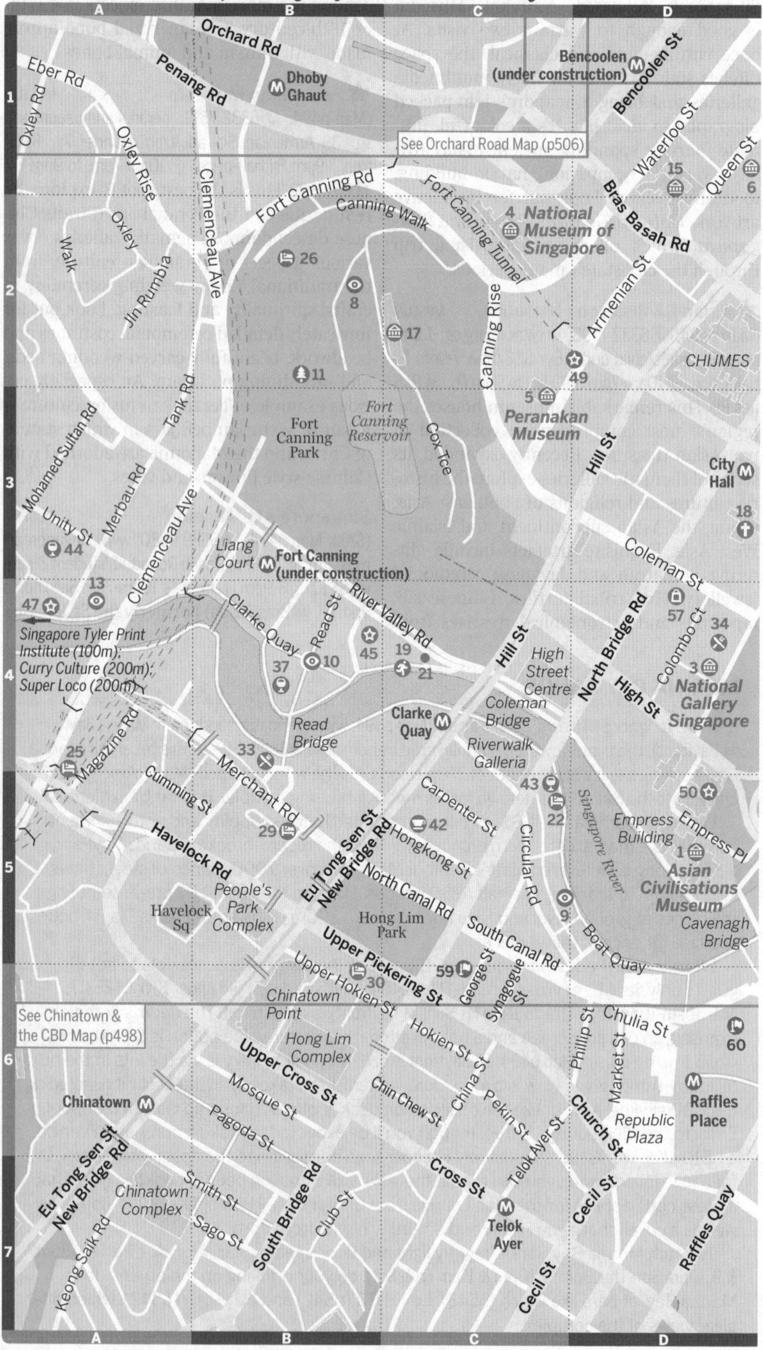

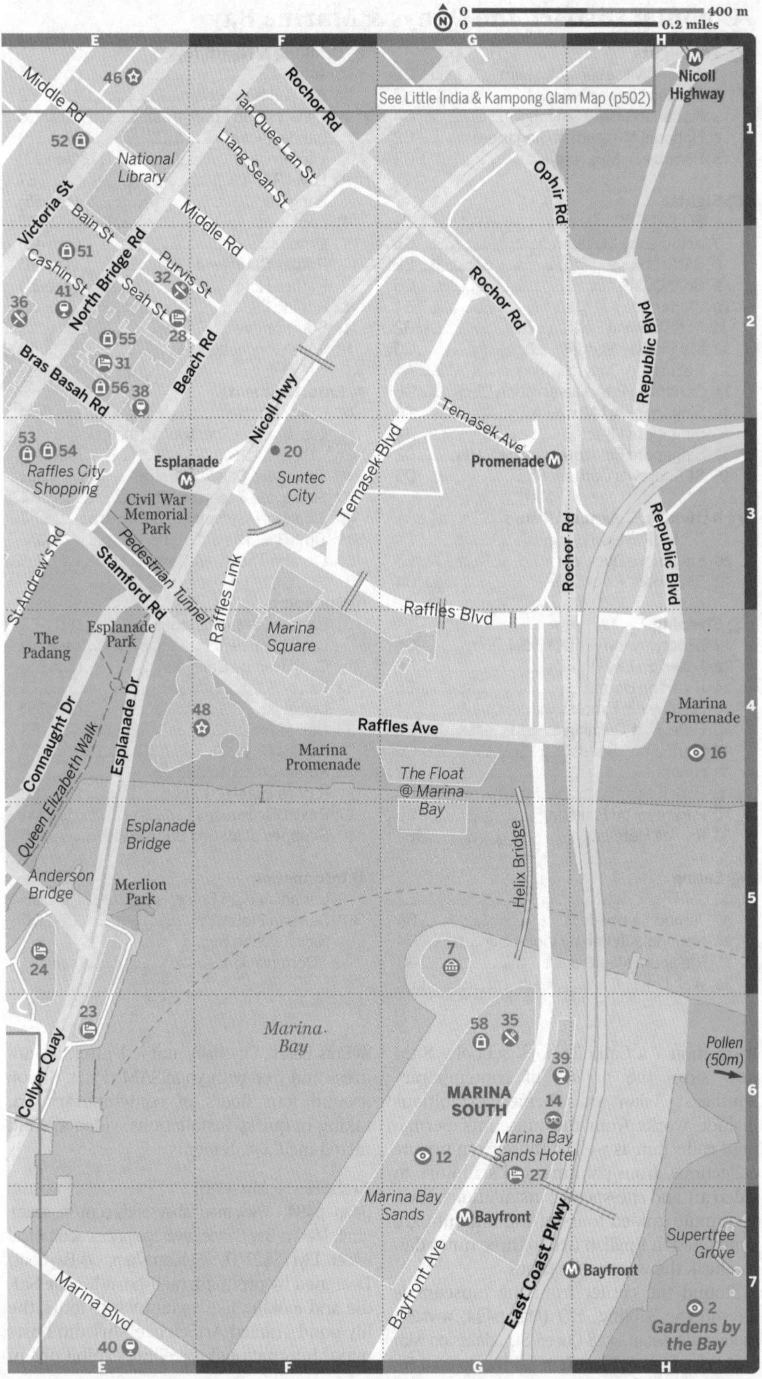
0 400 m
0 0.2 miles
E
F
G
H
1
2
3
4
5
6
7
See Little India & Kampong Glam Map (p502)
Nicoll Highway
Middle Rd
46
52
National Library
Victoria St
Bain St
Tan Quee Lan St
Liang Seah St
Rochor Rd
Ophir Rd
Middle Rd
51
Cashin St
North Bridge Rd
Purvis St
32
Seah St
41
36
28
55
31
Bras Basah Rd
56
38
Beach Rd
Nicoll Hwy
Rochor Rd
Republic Blvd
Temasek Ave
Temasek Blvd
53
54
Raffles City Shopping
Esplanade
20
Suntec City
Promenade
Civil War Memorial Park
Pedestrian Tunnel
Stamford Rd
St Andrew's Rd
Raffles Link
Rochor Rd
Republic Blvd
Raffles Blvd
The Padang
Esplanade Park
Marina Square
48
Raffles Ave
Marina Promenade
16
Connaught Dr
Queen Elizabeth Walk
Esplanade Dr
Marina Promenade
The Float @ Marina Bay
Esplanade Bridge
Helix Bridge
Anderson Bridge
Merlion Park
7
24
23
Marina Bay
58
35
Pollen (50m)
Collyer Quay
39
MARINA SOUTH
14
Marina Bay Sands Hotel
12
27
Marina Bay Sands
Bayfront
East Coast Pkwy
Bayfront Ave
Bayfront
Supertree Grove
Marina Blvd
2
Gardens by the Bay
40
SINGAPORE

Colonial District, the Quays & Marina Bay

Top Sights
1 Asian Civilisations Museum ... D5
2 Gardens by the Bay ... H7
3 National Gallery Singapore ... D4
4 National Museum of Singapore ... C2
5 Peranakan Museum ... C3

Sights
6 8Q SAM ... D1
7 ArtScience Museum ... G5
8 Battlebox ... B2
9 Boat Quay ... C5
10 Clarke Quay ... B4
11 Fort Canning Park ... B2
12 Marina Bay Sands ... G6
13 Robertson Quay ... A4
14 Sands SkyPark Observation Deck ... G6
15 Singapore Art Museum ... D1
16 Singapore Flyer ... H4
17 Singapore Pinacothèque de Paris ... C2
18 St Andrew's Cathedral ... D3

Activities, Courses & Tours
19 G-Max Reverse Bungy ... C4
20 Singapore Ducktours ... F3
21 Singapore River Cruise ... C4

Sleeping
22 5Footway.Inn Project Boat Quay ... C5
23 Fullerton Bay Hotel ... E6
24 Fullerton Hotel ... E5
25 Holiday Inn Express Clarke Quay ... A4
26 Hotel Fort Canning ... B2
27 Marina Bay Sands ... G6
28 Naumi ... E2
29 Park Regis ... B5
30 Parkroyal on Pickering ... B6
31 Raffles Hotel ... E2

Eating
32 Jai Thai ... E2
33 Jumbo Seafood ... B4
34 National Kitchen by Violet Oon ... D4
35 Rasapura Masters ... G6
36 Wah Lok ... E2

Drinking & Nightlife
37 Attica ... B4
38 Bar & Billiard Room ... E2
39 Cé la Vi Club Lounge ... G6
Landing Point ... (see 23)
Lantern ... (see 23)
40 Level 33 ... E7
Long Bar ... (see 55)
41 Loof ... E2
Orgo ... (see 48)
Raffles Courtyard ... (see 31)
Raffles Hotel ... (see 31)
42 Ronin ... C5
43 Southbridge ... C5
44 Wine Connection ... A3

Entertainment
45 Crazy Elephant ... B4
Esplanade – Theatres on the Bay ... (see 48)
46 Singapore Dance Theatre ... E1
47 Singapore Repertory Theatre ... A4
48 Singapore Symphony Orchestra ... F4
49 Timbrè @ The Substation ... D2
50 Victoria Theatre & Concert Hall ... D5

Shopping
51 Basheer Graphic Books ... E2
Cat Socrates ... (see 51)
Chan Hampe Galleries ... (see 55)
52 Kapok ... E1
Leica ... (see 55)
53 Ode to Art ... E3
54 Raffles City ... E3
55 Raffles Hotel Arcade ... E2
56 Raffles Hotel Gift Shop ... E2
57 Roxy Disc House ... D4
58 Shoppes at Marina Bay Sands ... G6

Information
59 Canadian High Commission ... C6
60 German Embassy ... D6
New Zealand High Commission ... (see 59)

Institution – a Catholic boys' school – SAM now sings the praises of contemporary Southeast Asian art. Themed exhibitions include works from the museum's permanent collection as well as those from private collections, from painting and sculpture to video art and site-specific installations. Free, 45-minute guided tours of the museum are conducted in English two to three times daily; check the website for times.

Round the corner from the museum is its younger sibling, **8Q** (Map p494; www.singaporeartmuseum.sg; 8 Queen St; admission with SAM ticket free; ⏲10am-7pm Sat-Thu, to 9pm Fri; Ⓜ Bras Basah, City Hall), named after its address and free with your SAM ticket. Snoop around four floors of contemporary art, taking in quirky installations, video art and mixed-media statements.

ArtScience Museum MUSEUM
(Map p494; www.marinabaysands.com/museum.html; Marina Bay Sands; average prices adult/child under 13yr S$27/17; ⏲10am-7pm; Ⓜ Bayfront) Designed by prolific Israeli-born Moshe Safdie and looking like a giant white lotus, the lily pond–framed ArtScience Museum hosts major international travelling exhibitions in

fields as varied as art, design, media, science and technology. Expect anything from explorations of deep-sea creatures to retrospectives of world-famous industrial designers.

St Andrew's Cathedral CHURCH

(Map p494; www.livingstreams.org.sg; 11 St Andrew's Rd; ⌚9am-5pm; Ⓜ City Hall) FREE Funded by Scottish merchants and built by Indian convicts, this wedding cake of a cathedral stands in stark contrast to the glass and steel surrounding it. Completed in 1838 but torn down and rebuilt in its present form in 1862 after lightning damage, it's one of Singapore's finest surviving examples of English Gothic architecture. Interesting details include the tropics-friendly *porte-cochère* (carriage porch) entrance – designed to shelter passengers – and the colourful stained glass adorning the western wall.

Fort Canning Park PARK

(Map p494; www.nparks.gov.sg; Ⓜ Dhoby Ghaut) When Raffles rolled into Singapore, locals steered clear of Fort Canning Hill, then called Bukit Larangan (Forbidden Hill) out of respect for the sacred shrine of Sultan Iskandar Shah, ancient Singapura's last ruler. These days, the hill is better known as Fort Canning Park, a lush retreat from the hot streets below. Amble through the spice garden, catch an exhibition at Singapore Pinacothéque de Paris (p499) or ponder Singapore's wartime defeat at the **Battle Box Museum** (Map p494; www.battlebox.com.sg; 2 Cox Tce; adult/child S$8/5; ⌚10am-6pm, last entry 5pm; Ⓜ Dhoby Ghaut).

The former command post of the British during WWII, Battle Box's eerie subterranean rooms explore the fateful surrender to the Japanese on 15 February 1942. Japanese Morse codes are still etched on the walls.

Fort Canning Park hosts several outdoor events and concerts throughout the year, including Shakespeare in the Park (April/May), Ballet under the Stars (June/July) and Films at the Fort (August).

QUAYS OF THE CITY

The stretch of the riverfront that separates the Colonial District from the CBD is known as the Quays. The Singapore River, once a thriving gateway for bumboats bearing cargo into the *godown* (warehouses) that lined the riverside, now connects the three quays. A walk through them offers a revealing view of the changes Singapore's trade has weathered over the years: from the dirt and grit of the once-filthy waterways to the gleaming steel and glass of today's financial district.

Boat Quay (Map p494; Ⓜ Raffles Pl, Clarke Quay) Closest to the former harbour, Boat Quay was once Singapore's centre of commerce, remaining an important economic area into the 1960s. By the mid-1980s, many of the shophouses were in ruins, businesses having shifted to high-tech cargo centres elsewhere on the island. Declared a conservation zone by the government, the area has reinvented itself as a major entertainment district packed with touristy bars and smooth-talking restaurant touts. One place worth stopping at is rooftop **Southbridge** (p542), a more discerning bar with OMG! skyline and river views.

Clarke Quay (Map p494; www.clarkequay.com.sg; Ⓜ Clarke Quay) Named after Singapore's second colonial governor, Sir Andrew Clarke, pastel-hued Clarke Quay has reinvented itself as one of Singapore's most popular after-dark haunts. To its critics, this is Singapore at its tackiest and most touristy: a kitschy sprawl of once-dignified shophouses, mediocre eateries and boozy bars packed with lads and ladettes. Whichever way you sway, get messy with scrumptious chilli crab at much-loved **Jumbo Seafood** (p535).

Robertson Quay (Map p494; 🚌 64, 123, 143, Ⓜ Clarke Quay) At the furthest reach of the river, unassuming Robertson Quay was once used for the storage of goods. It's now home to some of the best eateries and bars along the river, including Mexican hipster **Super Loco** (p534) and well-priced vino bar **Wine Connection** (p542). The precinct is also home to the **Singapore Tyler Print Institute** (☎6336 3663; www.stpi.com.sg; 41 Robertson Quay; ⌚10am-7pm Mon-Fri, 9am-6pm Sat, free guided tours 11.30am Tue & Thu, 2.30pm Sat; 🚌 51, 64, 123, 186) FREE, which hosts international and local exhibits showcasing the work of resident print- and paper-makers. The institute's Saturday guided tour takes in the printing workshop itself.

Chinatown & the CBD

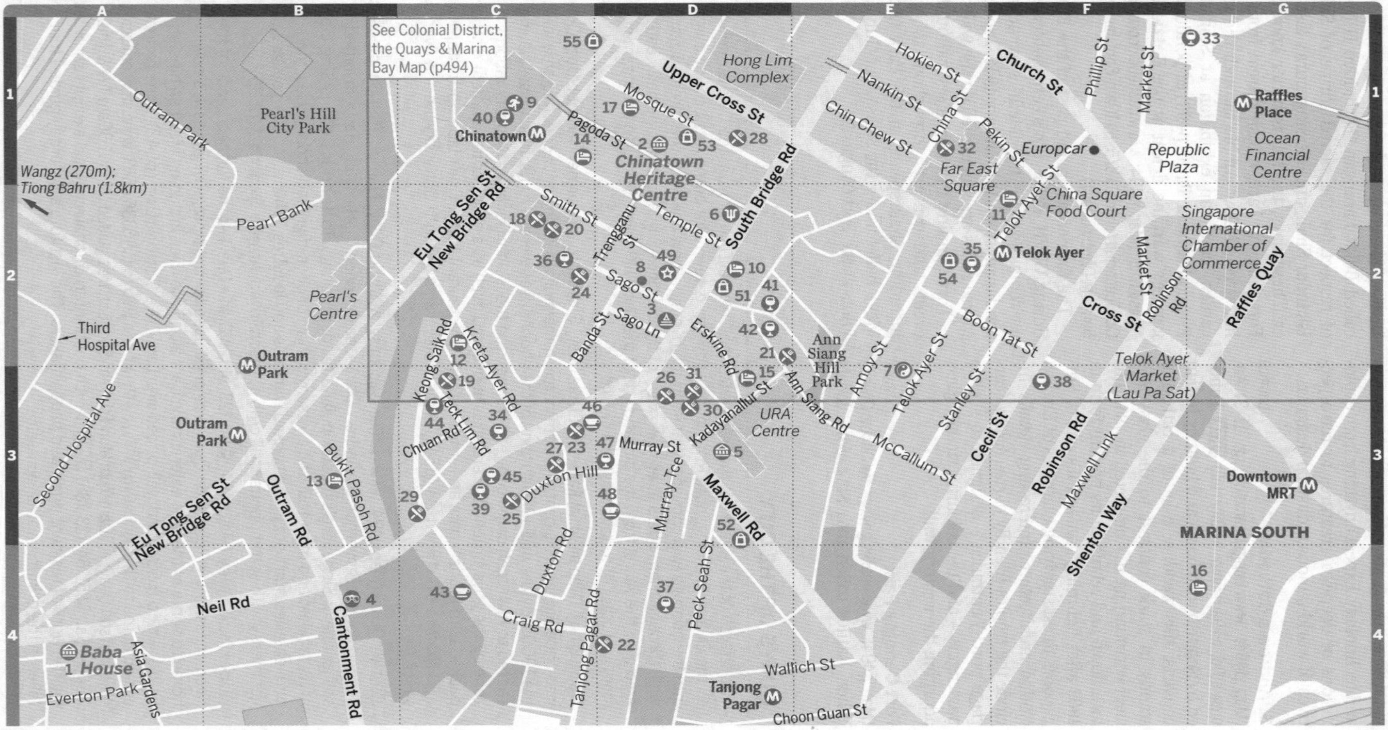

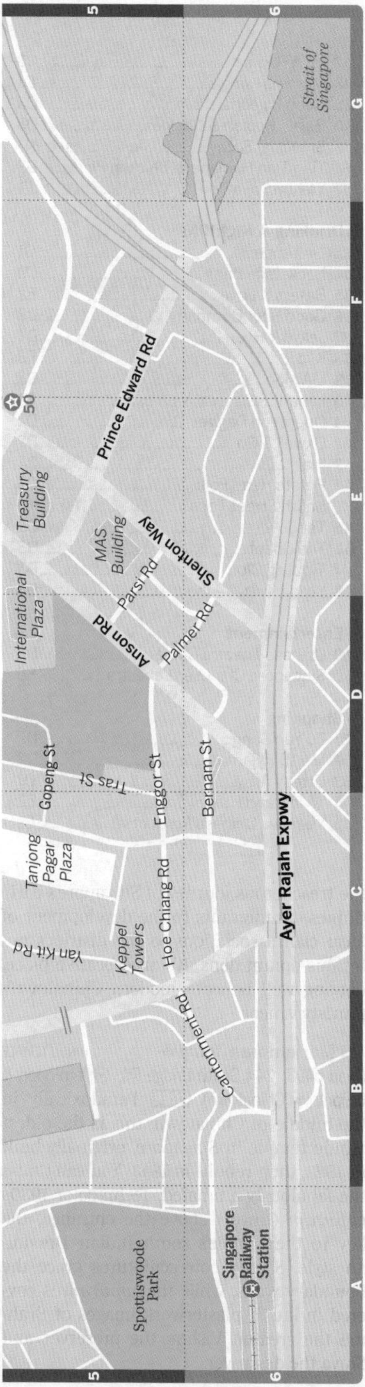

Singapore Pinacothèque de Paris MUSEUM
(Map p494; ☎6883 1588; www.pinacotheque.com.sg; 5 Cox Tce; Heritage Gallery, Graffiti Walk & Garden Walk free, all galleries adult/student/child under 7yr S$28/19/9; ⏰10am-7.30pm Sun-Thu, to 8.30pm Fri & Sat; Ⓜ Dhoby Ghaut) Commanding Fort Canning Park is this offshoot of French private art museum Pinacothèque de Paris. Precious historic Southeast Asian sculpture, jewellery and other artefacts grace the small, free Heritage Gallery, with blockbuster temporary exhibitions (covering a range of themes) held in the Features Gallery. Best of the lot is the Collections Gallery, hung with over 40 rarely seen works from immortals like Rembrandt, Monet, Picasso and Modigliani.

Singapore Flyer FERRIS WHEEL
(Map p494; ☎6333 3311; www.singaporeflyer.com.sg; 30 Raffles Ave; adult/child under 13yr S$33/21; ⏰ticket booth 8am-10pm, wheel 8.30am-10.30pm, last flight 10pm; Ⓜ Promenade) Las Vegas' High Roller may have since stolen its 'World's Biggest Observation Wheel' title, but Singapore's 165m-tall ferris wheel continues to serve up a gob-smacking panorama. On a clear day, the 30-minute ride will have you peering out over the Colonial District, CBD and Marina Bay, the high-rise housing sprawl to the east and out to the ship-clogged South China Sea. The wheel's construction is documented in onsite multimedia display Journey of Dreams. Purchase tickets online for a modest discount.

Chinatown & the CBD

Chinatown's restored shophouses belie the area's rough-and-ready past, a history well documented at the Chinatown Heritage Centre. These days, the neighbourhood delivers a contrasting mix of retro wet markets and hawker centres, heady temples, and hot, hip eateries and bars.

Reaching for the sky between Chinatown and the Singapore River is the Central Business District (CBD), a money-hungry place of dizzying skyscrapers and the odd colonial relic. The finest of the latter is the mighty Fullerton Hotel, housed in the former general post office.

★ **Baba House** MUSEUM
(Map p498; ☎6227 5731; www.nus.edu.sg/cfa/museum/about.php; 157 Neil Rd; ⏰1hr tours 2pm Mon, 6.30pm Tue, 10am Thu, 11am Sat; Ⓜ Outram Park) FREE Baba House is one of Singapore's

Chinatown & the CBD

Top Sights
1 Baba House A4
2 Chinatown Heritage Centre D1

Sights
3 Buddha Tooth Relic Temple D2
4 Pinnacle@Duxton B4
5 Singapore City Gallery D3
6 Sri Mariamman Temple D2
7 Thian Hock Keng Temple E3

Activities, Courses & Tours
8 Food Playground D2
Mr Lim Foot Reflexology .... (see 9)
9 People's Park Complex C1

Sleeping
10 Adler Hostel D2
11 Amoy F2
12 Hotel 1929 .... C2
13 New Majestic Hotel B3
14 Rucksack Inn C1
15 Scarlet D3
16 Westin G4
17 Wink Hostel D1

Eating
18 Bonne Soup C2
19 Burnt Ends C3
20 Chinatown Complex C2
21 Ding Dong D2
22 Ginza Tendon Itsuki D4
23 Jing Hua C3
24 Lian He Ben Ji Claypot Rice C2
Lobby Lounge at The Westin .... (see 16)
25 Lucha Loco C3
26 Maxwell Food Centre D3
27 MEATLiquor C3
28 Momma Kong's D1
29 Neon Pigeon C3
30 Rojak, Popiah & Cockle D3
Shi Xiang Satay .... (see 24)
31 Tian Tian Hainanese Chicken Rice D3
32 Ya Kun Kaya Toast E1

Drinking & Nightlife
33 1-Altitude G1
34 Backstage Bar C3
35 Bitters & Love E2
36 Good Beer Company C2
37 Jekyll & Hyde D4
38 Kyō F3
39 L'Aiglon C3
40 Lepark C1
41 Operation Dagger D2
42 Oxwell & Co D2
43 Plain C4
44 Potato Head Folk C3
Smith Street Taps .... (see 36)
45 Taboo C3
46 Tea Chapter C3
47 Tippling Club D3
48 Yixing Xuan Teahouse D3

Entertainment
49 Chinese Theatre Circle D2
50 Singapore Chinese Orchestra E5

Shopping
51 Eu Yan Sang D2
52 MAAD Pyjamas D3
53 Utterly Art D1
54 Willow and Huxley E2
55 Yue Hwa Chinese Products C1

best-preserved Peranakan heritage homes. Built in the 1890s, it's a wonderful window into the life of an affluent Peranakan family living in Singapore a century ago. Its loving restoration has seen every detail attended to, from the carved motifs on the blue facade down to the door screens. The only way in is on a guided tour, held every Monday, Tuesday, Thursday and Saturday, but the tour is excellent and free. Bookings, by telephone, are essential.

★Chinatown Heritage Centre MUSEUM
(Map p498; ☎6221 9556; www.singaporechinatown.com.sg; 48 Pagoda St; adult/child S$10/6; ⏰9am-8pm; Ⓜ Chinatown) Delve into Chinatown's gritty, cacophonous backstory at the recently revamped Chinatown Heritage Centre. Occupying several levels of a converted shophouse, its interactive exhibitions shed light on numerous historical chapters, from the treacherous journey of Singapore's early Chinese immigrants to the development of local clan associations to the district's notorious opium dens. It's an evocative place, digging well beneath modern Chinatown's touristy veneer.

Sri Mariamman Temple HINDU TEMPLE
(Map p498; 244 South Bridge Rd; ⏰7am-noon & 6-9pm; Ⓜ Chinatown) FREE Paradoxically in the middle of Chinatown, this is the oldest Hindu temple in Singapore, originally built in 1823, then rebuilt in 1843. You can't miss the fabulously animated, Technicolor 1930s *gopuram* (tower) above the entrance, the key to the temple's south Indian Dravidian style. Sacred cow sculptures grace the boundary walls, while the *gopuram* is covered in kitsch plasterwork images of Brahma the creator, Vishnu the preserver and Shiva the destroyer.

Buddha Tooth Relic Temple BUDDHIST TEMPLE
(Map p498; www.btrts.org.sg; 288 South Bridge Rd; 7am-7pm, relic viewing 9am-6pm; M Chinatown) FREE Consecrated in 2008, this hulking, five-story Buddhist temple is home to what is reputedly the left canine tooth of the Buddha, recovered from his funeral pyre in Kushinagar, northern India. While its authenticity is debated, the relic enjoys VIP status inside a 420kg solid-gold stupa in a dazzlingly ornate 4th-floor room. More religious relics await at the 3rd-floor Buddhism museum, while the peaceful rooftop garden features a huge prayer wheel inside a 10,000 Buddha Pavilion.

Thian Hock Keng Temple TAOIST TEMPLE
(Map p498; www.thianhockkeng.com.sg; 158 Telok Ayer St; 7.30am-5.30pm; M Telok Ayer) FREE Surprisingly, Chinatown's oldest and most important Hokkien temple is often a haven of tranquility. Built between 1839 and 1842, it's a beautiful place, and once the favourite landing point of Chinese sailors, before land reclamation pushed the sea far down the road. Typically, the temple's design features are richly symbolic: the stone lions at the entrance ward off evil spirits, while the painted depiction of phoenixes and peonies in the central hall symbolise peace and good tidings respectively.

Pinnacle@Duxton VIEWPOINT
(Map p498; www.pinnacleduxton.com.sg; Block 1G, 1 Cantonment Rd; 50th-floor skybridge S$5; 9am-9pm; M Outram Park, Tanjong Pagar) For killer city views at a bargain S$5, head to the 50th-floor rooftop of Pinnacle@Duxton, the world's largest public housing complex. Skybridges connecting the seven towers provide a 360-degree sweep of city, port and sea. Although a makeshift ticket booth was operating on our last visit, payment is usually by EZ-Link transport card only; simply rest your EZ-Link card on the ticket machine located at the bottom of Block G to pay, then catch a lift up to the 50th floor.

Singapore City Gallery MUSEUM
(Map p498; www.ura.gov.sg/gallery; URA Bldg, 45 Maxwell Rd; 9am-5pm Mon-Sat; M Tanjong Pagar) See into Singapore's future at this interactive city-planning exhibition, which provides compelling insight into the government's resolute policies of land reclamation, high-rise housing and meticulous urban planning. The highlight is an 11m-by-11m scale model of the central city, which shows just how different Singapore will look once all the projects currently under development join the skyline.

Little India

Riotous Little India slaps you across the face with its teeming five-foot ways (covered shophouse walkways), blaring Bollywood tunes and crayon-hued shophouses. Originally a European enclave, the district bloomed into an Indian hub after a Jewish-Indian businessman started farming buffalo here. Today, Little India's heart lies in the incense-scented streets between Serangoon Rd and Jln Besar, stretching from Campbell Lane in the south to Syed Alwi Rd in the north – for the full 'Mumbai' effect, head in on a Sunday afternoon. Just northeast of Little India (and parallel to Jln Besar), Tyrwhitt Rd is the heart of a bite-sized hipster district with all the trimmings, from speciality coffee and craft beer to indie design.

Sri Veeramakaliamman Temple HINDU TEMPLE
(Map p502; www.sriveeramakaliamman.com; 141 Serangoon Rd; 8am-noon & 6.30-9pm Mon-Thu & Sat, 8am-noon & 6-9pm Fri & Sun; M Little India) FREE Little India's most colourful, visually stunning temple is dedicated to the ferocious goddess Kali, depicted wearing a garland of skulls, ripping out the insides of her victims, and sharing more tranquil family moments with her sons Ganesh and Murugan. The bloodthirsty consort of Shiva has always been popular in Bengal, the birthplace of the labourers who built the structure in 1881. The temple is at its most evocative during each of the four daily *puja* (prayer) sessions.

Sri Vadapathira Kaliamman Temple HINDU TEMPLE
(Map p502; 555 Serangoon Rd; 6am-noon & 4.30-9pm Sun-Thu, 6am-12.30pm & 4.30-9.30pm Fri & Sat; M Farrer Park, Boon Keng) FREE Dedicated to

ADDRESSES

Singapore is well laid out, with sign-posted streets and logically numbered buildings. Most addresses are preceded by the number of the floor and then the shop or apartment number. Addresses do not quote the district or suburb. For example, 05-01, the Heeren, 260 Orchard Rd, is outlet No 01 on the 5th floor of the Heeren building at 260 Orchard Rd.

Little India & Kampong Glam

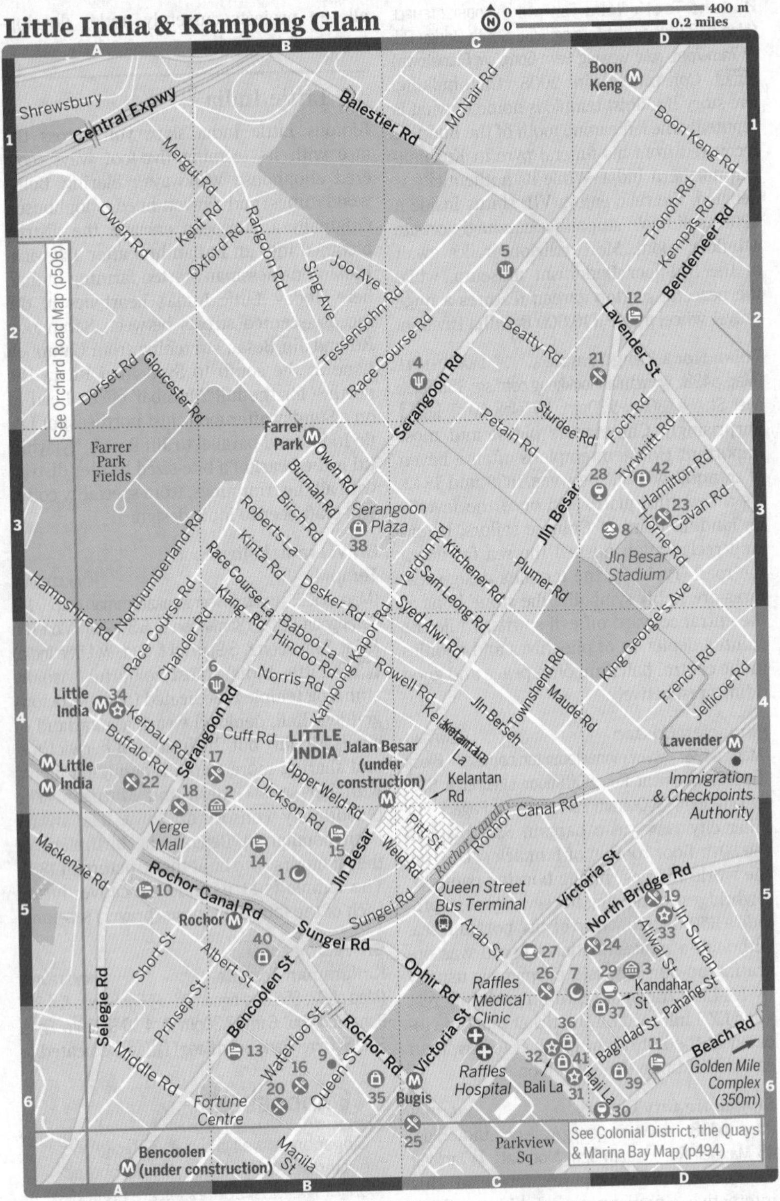

Kaliamman, the Destroyer of Evil, this south Indian temple began life in 1870 as a modest shrine but underwent a significant facelift in 1969 to transform it into the beauty standing today. The carvings here – particularly on the *vimana* (domed structure within the temple) – are among the best temple artwork you'll see anywhere in Singapore.

Abdul Gafoor Mosque MOSQUE

(Map p502; 41 Dunlop St; Ⓜ Rochor, Little India) **FREE** Completed in 1910, the Abdul Gafoor

Little India & Kampong Glam

Sights

1	Abdul Gafoor Mosque	B5
2	Indian Heritage Centre	B4
3	Malay Heritage Centre	D5
4	Sri Srinivasa Perumal Temple	C2
5	Sri Vadapathira Kaliamman Temple	C2
6	Sri Veeramakaliamman Temple	B4
7	Sultan Mosque	C5

Activities, Courses & Tours

8	Jalan Besar Swimming Complex	D3
9	Trishaw Uncle	B6

Sleeping

10	Albert Court Village Hotel	A5
11	Five Stones Hostel	D6
12	Green Kiwi Backpackers Hostel	D2
13	Ibis Singapore on Bencoolen	B6
14	InnCrowd	B5
15	Wanderlust	B5

Eating

16	Ah Heng Curry Chicken Bee Hoon Mee	B6
	Ah-Rahman Royal Prata	(see 22)
	Ananda Bhavan	(see 22)
17	Lagnaa Barefoot Dining	B4
18	Moghul Sweets	A4
19	Nan Hwa Chong Fish-Head Steamboat Corner	D5
	New Rong Liang Ge Cantonese Roast Duck Boiled Soup	(see 16)
20	QS269 Food House	B6
21	Suprette	D2
22	Tekka Centre	A4
23	Two Bakers	D3
24	Warong Nasi Pariaman	D5
25	Ya Kun Kaya Toast	C6
26	Zam Zam	C5

Drinking & Nightlife

27	Artistry	C5
	Chye Seng Huat Hardware	(see 42)
28	Druggists	D3
29	Maison Ikkoku	D5
30	Piedra Negra	D6

Entertainment

31	BluJaz Café	C6
32	Going Om	C6
33	SingJazz Club	D5
34	Wild Rice	A4

Shopping

35	Bugis Street Market	B6
36	Haji Lane	C6
37	Little Shophouse	D6
38	Mustafa Centre	B3
39	Sifr Aromatics	D6
40	Sim Lim Square	B5
41	Tuckshop & Sundry Supplies	C6
42	Tyrwhitt General Company	D3

mosque serves up a storybook fusion of Moorish, southern Indian and Victorian architectural styles. Look out for the elaborate sundial crowning its main entrance, each of its 25 rays decorated with Arabic calligraphy denoting the names of 25 prophets. The sundial is the only one of its kind in the world.

Indian Heritage Centre MUSEUM
(Map p502; ☎6291 1601; www.indianheritage.org.sg; 5 Campbell Lane; adult/child under 7yr S$4/free; ⏰10am-7pm Tue-Thu, to 8pm Fri & Sat, to 4pm Sun; Ⓜ Little India, Rochor) Delve into the heritage of Singapore's Indian community at this showpiece museum. Divided into five themes, its hundreds of historical and cultural artefacts explore everything from early interactions between South Asia and Southeast Asia to Indian cultural traditions and the contributions of Indian Singaporeans in the development of the island nation. Among the more extraordinary objects is a 19th-century Chettinad doorway, intricately adorned with 5000 minute carvings.

Inspired by the *baoli* (Indian stepped well), the museum's architecture is equally intriguing. As night falls, the museum's translucent facade transforms into a giant tapestry of sorts, showcasing the richly coloured mural behind it.

Sri Srinivasa Perumal Temple HINDU TEMPLE
(Map p502; 397 Serangoon Rd; ⏰5.45am-noon & 5-9pm; Ⓜ Farrer Park) FREE Dedicated to Vishnu, this temple dates from 1855, but the striking, 20m-tall *gopuram* (tower) is a S$300,000 1966 add-on. Inside is a statue of Vishnu, his sidekicks Lakshmi and Andal, and his bird-mount Garuda. The temple is the starting point for a colourful, wince-inducing street parade during the Thaipusam festival: to show their devotion, many participants pierce their bodies with hooks and skewers.

Kampong Glam

Compact Kampong Glam is as intriguing as it is incongruous. Not only is it inner Singapore's Muslim heartland – speckled with mosques, shisha-scented cafes, perfume traders, and fabric and rug shops – it also brims with cool-kid cafes and bars, live-music venues and the indie boutiques of Haji Lane. Roughly bounded by Victoria St, Jln Sultan and Beach Rd – all immediately northeast of Bugis MRT – the district's name derives from *kampung* (the Malay word for village) and *gelam*, a type of tree that once grew here.

Sultan Mosque MOSQUE
(Map p502; www.sultanmosque.org.sg; 3 Muscat St; ⏲10am-noon & 2-4pm Sat-Thu, 2.30-4pm Fri; Ⓜ Bugis) FREE Seemingly pulled from the pages of the *Arabian Nights,* Singapore's largest mosque is nothing short of enchanting, designed in the Saracenic style and topped by a golden dome. It was originally built in 1825 with the aid of a grant from Raffles and the East India Company, after Raffles' treaty with the Sultan of Singapore allowed the Malay leader to retain sovereignty over the area. In 1928, the original mosque was replaced by the present magnificent building, designed by an Irish architect.

Non-Muslims are asked to refrain from entering the prayer hall at any time, and all visitors are expected to be dressed appropriately (cloaks are available at the entrance). Pointing cameras at people during prayer time is never appropriate.

Malay Heritage Centre MUSEUM
(Map p502; ☎6391 0450; www.malayheritage.org.sg; 85 Sultan Gate; adult/child under 6yr S$4/free; ⏲10am-6pm Tue-Sun; Ⓜ Bugis) The Kampong Glam area is the historic seat of Malay royalty, resident here before the arrival of Raffles, and the *istana* (palace) on this site was built for the last sultan of Singapore, Ali Iskander Shah, between 1836 and 1843. It's now a museum. Its recently revamped galleries explore Malay-Singaporean culture and history, from the early migration of traders to Kampong Glam to the development of Malay-Singaporean film, theatre, music and publishing.

Orchard Road

What was once a dusty road lined with spice plantations and orchards is now a 2.5km torrent of polished malls, sprawling department stores, and speciality shops – enough to burn out the hardiest shopaholics. But wait, there's more, including the heritage architecture of Emerald Hill Rd and the movie memorabilia of the little-known Cathay Gallery.

Emerald Hill Road ARCHITECTURE
(Map p506; Ⓜ Somerset) Take time out from your shopping to wander up frangipani-scented Emerald Hill Rd, graced with some of Singapore's finest terrace houses. Special mentions go to No 56 (built in 1902, and one of the earliest buildings here), Nos 39 to 45 (with unusually wide frontages and a grand Chinese-style entrance gate), and Nos 120 to 130 (with art-deco features dating from around 1925). At the Orchard Rd end of the hill is a cluster of popular bars housed in fetching shophouse renovations.

Cathay Gallery MUSEUM
(Map p506; www.thecathaygallery.com.sg; 2nd fl, The Cathay, 2 Handy Rd; ⏲11am-7pm Mon-Sat; Ⓜ Dhoby Ghaut) FREE Film and nostalgia buffs will appreciate this pocket-sized silver-screen museum, housed in Singapore's first high-rise building. The displays trace the history of the Loke family, early pioneers in film production and distribution in Singapore and founders of the Cathay Organisation. Highlights include old movie posters, cameras and programs that capture the golden age of local cinema.

Dempsey Hill & Botanic Gardens

★ **Singapore Botanic Gardens** GARDENS
(Map p506; ☎6471 7361; www.sbg.org.sg; 1 Cluny Rd; garden admission free, National Orchid Garden adult/child under 12yr $5/free; ⏲5am-midnight, National Orchid Garden 8.30am-7pm, last entry 6pm, Healing Garden 5am-7.30pm Wed-Mon, Jacob Ballas Children's Garden 8am-7pm Tue-Sun, last entry 6.30pm; 🚌7, 105, 123, 174, Ⓜ Botanic Gardens) Singapore's 74-hectare botanic wonderland is a Unesco World Heritage Site and one of the city's most arresting attractions. Established in 1860, it's a tropical Valhalla peppered with glassy lakes, rolling lawns and themed gardens. The site is home to the National Orchid Garden, as well as a rare patch of dense primeval rainforest, the latter home to over 300 species of vegetation, over half of which are now (sadly) considered rare in Singapore.

The National Orchid Garden itself is the legacy of an orchid-breeding program that began in 1928, and its 3 hectares are home to over 1000 species and 2000 hybrids. Of these, around 600 are on display – the largest showcase of tropical orchids on earth. Located next to the National Orchid Garden is the 1-hectare Ginger Garden, housing over 250

WORTH A TRIP

TIONG BAHRU: SINGAPORE'S HIPPEST 'HOOD

Those with finely tuned hipster radars will most likely end up in Singapore's Tiong Bahru neighbourhood. Yet this epicentre of independent cool is more than just its idiosyncratic boutiques, cafes and bakeries – it's also a rare heritage asset. Distinctly low-rise, the area was Singapore's first public housing estate and its streetscapes of whitewashed, 'walk-up' 1930s Moderne apartment buildings are an unexpected architectural treat.

For a taste of pre-gentrification, scurry into the **Tiong Bahru Market & Food Centre** (83 Seng Poh Rd; ⊙8am-late, individual stalls vary; M Tiong Bahru), old school right down to its orange exterior, the neighbourhood's original hue. Pique your appetite exploring the wet market, then head upstairs to the hawker centre for *shui kueh* (steamed rice cake with diced preserved radish) at **Jian Bo Shui Kueh** (stall 02-05; shui kueh from S$2; ⊙7am-9.30pm; M Tiong Bahru) and luscious *kway teow* (fried noodles with cockles, sliced fish cake and Chinese sausage) at **Tiong Bahru Fried Kway Teow** (stall 02-11; dishes S$2-4; ⊙11am-9.30pm Fri-Tue; M Tiong Bahru).

For new-school style, hit Yong Siak St. It's here that you'll find coffee-geek mecca **40 Hands** (www.40handscoffee.com; 78 Yong Siak St; ⊙8am-7pm Tue-Sun; M Tiong Bahru), one of the first places to introduce Australian-style cafe culture to the island nation. Across the street lies outstanding independent bookshop **BooksActually** (www.booksactually.com; 9 Yong Siak St; ⊙10am-8pm Tue-Sat, to 6pm Mon & Sun; M Tiong Bahru), its savvy selection including art, photography and design tomes, titles on Singapore, and works by Singaporean fiction and non-fiction writers. Don't miss the backroom, where a small, eclectic jumble of knickknacks serves up anything from vintage photographs and teacups to old shop signs. If it's gorgeous children's books you're after, check out **Woods in the Books** (www.woodsinthebooks.sg; 3 Yong Siak St; ⊙11am-8pm Tue-Sat, to 6pm Sun; M Tiong Bahru), a few doors down.

Right in between the bookshops is **Strangelets** (www.strangelets.sg; 7 Yong Siak St; ⊙11am-8pm Mon-Fri, 10am-8pm Sat & Sun; M Tiong Bahru), a sharply curated design store filled with cool and quirky objects from across the globe, such as intriguing sculptural jewellery and lamps, and contemporary Parisian ceramics.

The Gallic connection continues a few streets away at **Tiong Bahru Bakery** (☎6220 3430; www.tiongbahrubakery.com; 01-70, 56 Eng Hoon St; pastries from S$3, sandwiches & focaccias from S$8; ⊙8am-8pm Sun-Thu, to 10pm Fri & Sat; M Tiong Bahru), a laidback bakery-cafe owned by French-born baker Gontran Cherrier. Order a faultless *kouign amann* (Breton-style pastry) and wash it down with smooth coffee from local microroastery Common Man Coffee. Mouth wiped, nip around the corner to **Curated Records** (☎6438 3644; www.facebook.com/curatedrecords; 01-53, 55 Tiong Bahru Rd; ⊙1-8pm Tue-Sun; M Tiong Bahru), a pocket-rocket record shop selling everything from punk and French baroque pop to drone, hip-hop and neo-folk.

To reach Tiong Bahru, catch the MRT to Tiong Bahru station, walk east along Tiong Bahru Rd for 350m, then turn right into Kim Pong Rd.

members of the Zingiberaceae family. Free, themed guided tours of the Botanic Gardens run on Saturday, while the Symphony Lake makes a romantic setting for seasonal opera performances – check the website for details.

Eastern Singapore

Oft overshadowed by Singapore's tourist-trampled central districts, the vibrant eastern neighbourhoods offer an altogether more authentic slice of daily Singaporean life. Motley Geylang serves up temple- and brothel-pimped side streets, as well as street-food hub Geylang Rd. Further east, Katong (Joo Chiat) is famed for its ornate Peranakan terrace houses, craft shops and eateries, while neighbouring East Coast Park straddles the seafront with cycling paths, picnic areas and seafood eateries. The island's laid-back far east is where you'll find the moving Changi Museum & Chapel and *kampong*-like Changi Village, the jumping-off point for time-warped charmer Pulau Ubin.

East Coast Park PARK

(Map p508) This 15km stretch of seafront park is where Singaporeans come to swim,

Orchard Road

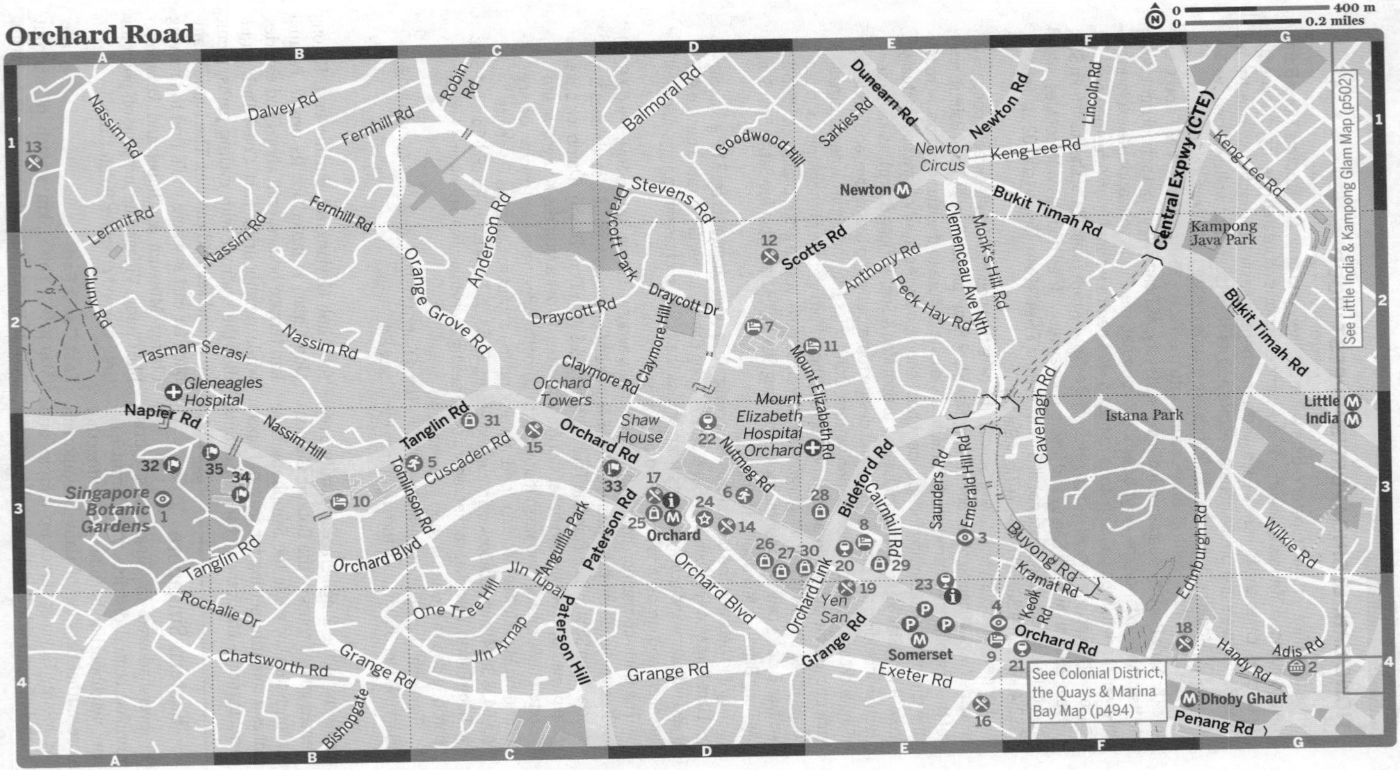

Orchard Road

Top Sights

1 Singapore Botanic Gardens ... A3

Sights

2 Cathay Gallery ... G4
3 Emerald Hill Road ... E3
4 Orchard Rd ... E4

Activities, Courses & Tours

5 Remède Spa ... C3
Spa Esprit ... (see 28)
6 Tomi Foot Reflexology ... D3

Sleeping

7 Goodwood Park Hotel ... D2
8 Holiday Inn Express Orchard Road ... E3
9 Hotel Jen Orchardgateway ... E4
10 Hotel Jen Tanglin ... B3
11 Quincy ... E2

Eating

12 Buona Terra ... D2
13 Casa Verde ... A1
14 Food Republic ... D3
15 Iggy's ... C3
16 Killiney Kopitiam ... E4
17 Paradise Dynasty ... D3
Takashimaya Food Village ... (see 27)
Tambuah Mas ... (see 28)
18 Tim Ho Wan ... F4
19 Wild Honey ... E4

Drinking & Nightlife

20 Bar Canary ... E3
21 KPO ... F4
22 Mezze9 ... D3
23 No 5 ... E4

Entertainment

24 SISTIC ... D3

Shopping

Antiques of the Orient ... (see 31)
Hansel ... (see 19)
Inhabit – The Other Store ... (see 19)
25 ION Orchard Mall ... D3
26 Kinokuniya ... D3
Mandarin Gallery ... (see 19)
27 Ngee Ann City ... D3
28 Paragon ... E3
Raoul ... (see 28)
Reckless Shop ... (see 9)
29 Robinsons ... E3
30 Takashimaya ... E3
31 Tanglin Shopping Centre ... C3

Information

32 Australian High Commission ... A3
33 Dutch Embassy ... D3
Irish Embassy ... (see 33)
34 UK High Commission ... B3
35 US Embassy ... B3

windsurf, wakeboard, kayak, picnic, bicycle, inline skate, skateboard, and, of course, eat. You'll find swaying coconut palms, patches of bushland, a lagoon, sea-sports clubs, and some excellent eateries.

Renting a bike from kiosks like **CycleMax** (Map p508; ☎6445 1147; www.facebook.com/cyclemax.sg; 01-03, 1018 East Coast Parkway; 2hr bike hire S$8; ⏱9am-9pm Mon-Fri, to 10pm Sat, 8am-9pm Sun; Ⓜ Bedok, then bus 197 or 401), enjoying the sea breezes, watching the veritable city of container ships out in the strait, and capping it all off with a beachfront meal is one of the most pleasant ways to spend a Singapore afternoon.

East Coast Park starts at the end of Tanjong Katong Rd in Katong and ends at the National Sailing Centre in Bedok, which is actually closer to the Tanah Merah MRT station. It's connected to Changi Beach Park by the Coastal Park Connector Network (PCN), an 8km park connector running along Changi Coast Rd, beside the airport runway. At the western end of the park, the bicycle track continues right through to Katong, ending at the Kallang River.

From central Singapore, catch bus 36 or 48 to Marine Parade Rd, then walk south one block to East Coast Parkway (ECP), crossing it to East Coast Park via one of the pedestrian underpasses.

Amitabha Buddhist Centre RELIGIOUS SITE
(Map p508; ☎6745 8547; www.fpmtabc.org; 44 Lorong 25A; ⏱10.30am-6pm Tue-Sat, 10am-6pm Sun; Ⓜ Aljunied) Seek inner peace at this seven-storey Tibetan Buddhist centre, which holds classes on dharma and meditation (check its website for the schedule), as well as events during religious festivals. The prayer hall on level four, decorated with colourful *thangkas* (Tibetan Buddhist paintings), statues and offerings, is open to the public. Adjoining it is a small store selling prayer flags, Buddhist literature and other spiritual items.

Pu Ji Si Buddhist Research Centre RELIGIOUS SITE
(Map p508; ☎6746 6211; www.pujisi.org.sg; 39, Lorong 12; ⏱8am-5pm Fri-Wed, to 1pm Thu; Ⓜ Aljunied) Part educational facility, part house of worship, this five-storey spiritual sanctuary

Eastern Singapore

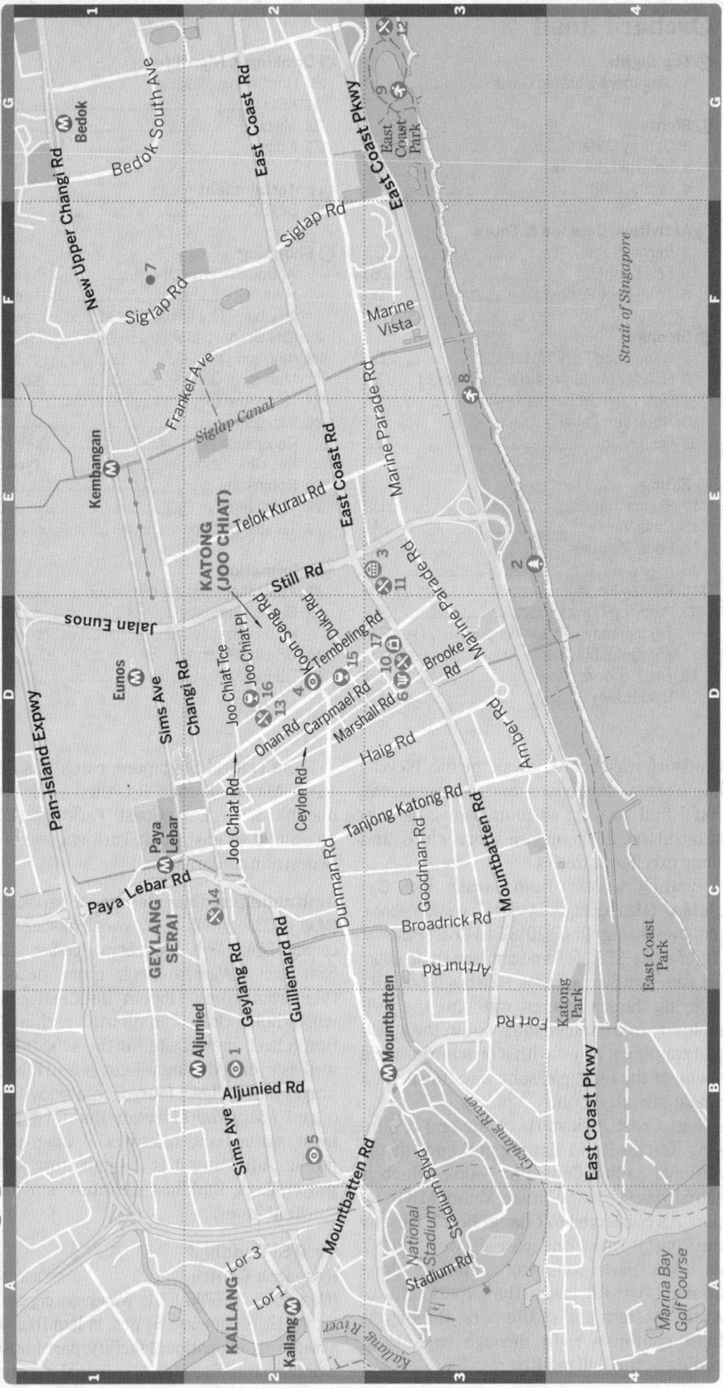

Eastern Singapore

Sights
1 Amitabha Buddhist Centre ... B2
2 East Coast Park ... E3
3 Katong Antique House ... E3
4 Peranakan Terrace Houses ... D2
5 Pu Ji Si Buddhist Research Centre ... B2
6 Sri Senpaga Vinayagar Temple ... D3

Activities, Courses & Tours
7 Cookery Magic ... F1
8 CycleMax ... F3
9 Ski360° ... G3

Eating
10 328 Katong Laksa ... D3
11 Chin Mee Chin Confectionery ... E3
12 East Coast Lagoon Food Village ... G3
13 Long Phuong ... D2
14 Rochor Beancurd ... C2
Smokey's BBQ ... (see 16)

Drinking & Nightlife
15 Cider Pit ... D2
16 Outpost Trading Co ... D2

Shopping
17 Kim Choo Kueh Chang ... D3

includes meditation halls and a seemingly endless well of serenity. Take the elevator up for a seat by the wishing fountain in the modest rooftop garden and ponder the Eternal.

Peranakan Terrace Houses ARCHITECTURE
(Map p508; Koon Seng Rd & Joo Chiat Pl; 16, 33, Eunos) Just off Joo Chiat Rd, these two streets feature Singapore's most extraordinary Peranakan terrace houses, joyously decorated with stucco dragons, birds, crabs and brilliantly glazed tiles. *Pintu pagar* (swinging doors) at the front of the houses are another typical feature, allowing cross breezes while retaining privacy. Those on Koon Seng Rd are located between Joo Chiat and Tembeling Rds, while those on Joo Chiat Pl run between Everitt and Mangis Rds.

Sri Senpaga Vinayagar Temple HINDU TEMPLE
(Map p508; 19 Ceylon Rd; 6.15am-noon & 6.30-9pm; 10, 12, 14, 32, 40) FREE Easily among the most beautiful Hindu temples in Singapore, Sri Senpaga Vinayagar's interior is adorned with wonderfully colourful devotional art, all labelled in various languages. Another feature is the temple's *kamala paatham*, a specially sculpted granite footstone found in certain ancient Hindu temples. Topping it all off, literally, is the roof of the inner *sanctum sanctorum*, lavishly covered in gold.

Katong Antique House MUSEUM
(Map p508; 6345 8544; 208 East Coast Rd; by appointment; 10, 12, 14, 32, 40) Part shop, part museum, the Katong Antique House is a labour of love for owner Peter Wee, a fourth-generation Baba Peranakan. A noted expert on Peranakan history and culture, Peter will happily regale you with tales as you browse an intriguing collection of Peranakan antiques, artefacts and other objets d'art. By appointment only, though it's sometimes open to the public (try your luck).

Changi Museum & Chapel MUSEUM
(6214 2451; www.changimuseum.sg; 1000 Upper Changi Rd N; audioguide adult/child S$8/4; 9.30am-5pm, last entry 4.30pm; Tanah Merah, then bus 2) FREE The Changi Museum & Chapel poignantly commemorates the WWII Allied POWs who suffered horrific treatment at the hands of the invading Japanese. The museum includes full-size replicas of the famous Changi Murals painted by POW Stanley Warren in the old POW hospital and a replica of the original Changi Chapel built by inmates as a focus for worship and as a sign of solidarity.

Northern & Central Singapore

Major sights aside, you'll probably find yourself lingering in Dempsey Hill, a once-crumbling army barracks now graced with trendy eateries, cafes, bars, upmarket antiques and furniture stores, and the odd art gallery.

★ **Singapore Zoo** ZOO
(6269 3411; www.zoo.com.sg; 80 Mandai Lake Rd; adult/child under 13yr S$32/21; 8.30am-6pm; Ang Mo Kio, then bus 138) The line between zoo and botanic oasis blurs at this pulse-slowing sweep of spacious, naturalistic enclosures, freely roaming animals and interactive attractions. Get up close to orangutans, dodge Malaysian flying foxes, even snoop around a replica African village. Then there's *that* setting: 26 soothing hectares on a lush peninsula jutting out into the waters of the Upper Seletar Reservoir.

There are over 2800 residents here, and as zoos go, the enclosures are among the world's most comfortable. Among the highlights is the **Jungle Breakfast with Wildlife** (adult/child S$33/23; ⏲9-10.30am), a morning buffet enjoyed in the company of orang-utans. Come within inches of free-roaming ring-tailed lemurs, lories and tree-hugging sloths at the giant Fragile Forest biodome, or spy on shameless, red-bummed baboons doing things that Singaporeans still get arrested for at the evocative Great Rift Valley exhibit. If you have kids in tow, let them go wild at Rainforest Kidzworld, a wonderland of slides, swings, pulling boats, pony rides and farmyard animals happy for a feed. There's even a dedicated wet area, with swimwear available for purchase if you didn't bring your own.

The zoo ceased offering elephant rides in 2014. However, elephant and other animal shows, which are frowned upon by animal-welfare experts, are held here.

★MacRitchie Reservoir NATURE RESERVE

(☎1800 471 7300; www.nparks.gov.sg; Lornie Rd; ⏲7am-7pm; Ⓜ Toa Payoh, then bus 157) MacRitchie Reservoir makes for a calming, evocative jungle escape. Walking trails skirt the water's edge and snake through the mature secondary rainforest spotted with long-tailed macaques and huge monitor lizards. You can rent kayaks at the **Paddle Lodge** (☎6258 0057; www.scf.org.sg; per hour S$15; ⏲9am-noon & 2-6pm Tue-Sun, last hire 4.30pm; Ⓜ Toa Payoh, then bus 157), but the highlight is the excellent 11km walking trail – and its various well-signposted offshoots. Aim for the **TreeTop Walk** (⏲9am-5pm Tue-Fri, 8.30am-5pm Sat & Sun), the highlight of which is traversing a 250m-long suspension bridge, perched 25m up in the forest canopy.

Trails then continue through the forest and around the reservoir, sometimes on dirt tracks, sometimes on wooden boardwalks. It takes three to four hours to complete the main circuit. From the service centre (which has changing facilities and a small cafe), near where bus 157 drops you off, start walking off to your right (anti-clockwise around the lake) and you'll soon reach the Paddle Lodge. TreeTop Walk is about 3km or 4km beyond this.

Night Safari ZOO

(www.nightsafari.com.sg; 80 Mandai Lake Rd; adult/child under 13yr S$42/28; ⏲7.30pm-midnight, restaurants & shops from 5.30pm; Ⓜ Ang Mo Kio, then bus 138) At Night Safari, electric trams glide past over 130 species, including tigers and elephants, with more docile creatures often passing within inches of the trams. Walking trails lead to enclosures inaccessible by tram, though sighting the animals can be a little hit-and-miss. (In truth, many are better seen at neighbouring Singapore Zoo.) If you've got kids in tow, the 20-minute Creatures of the Night show will thrill. Arrive at the zoo after 9.30pm to avoid the worst queues.

You'll need to catch a bus at around 10.45pm to make the last MRT train from Ang Mo Kio at 11.30pm. Otherwise, there are plenty of taxis out front.

Bukit Timah Nature Reserve NATURE RESERVE

(☎1800 471 7300; www.nparks.gov.sg; 177 Hindhede Dr; ⏲6am-7pm, visitor-centre exhibition 8.30am-5pm; 🚌67, 75, 170, 171, 173, 184, 852, 961, Ⓜ Beauty World) Singapore's steamy heart of darkness is Bukit Timah Nature Reserve, a 163-hectare tract of primary rainforest clinging to Singapore's highest peak, Bukit Timah (163m). The reserve holds more tree species than the entire North American continent, and its unbroken forest canopy shelters what remains of Singapore's native wildlife, including long-tailed macaques, pythons and dozens of bird species. Due to major repair work, only the sealed Summit Trail was accessible when we visited, and only on weekends. Check the website for updates.

Sungei Buloh Wetland Reserve WILDLIFE RESERVE

(☎6794 1401; www.sbwr.org.sg; 301 Neo Tiew Cres; ⏲7.30am-7pm Mon-Sat, 7am-7pm Sun; Ⓜ Kranji, then bus 925) Sungei Buloh's 202 hectares of mangroves, mudflats, ponds and secondary rainforest are a birdspotter's paradise, with migratory birds including egrets, sandpipers and plovers joining locals like herons, bitterns, coucals and kingfishers. The reserve is also a good spot to see monitor lizards, mudskippers, crabs and – if you're very lucky – an estuarine crocodile. Free guided tours run every Saturday at 9.30am.

The reserve is one of the few remaining mangrove areas in Singapore, and its lush, tranquil walking trails – which include a Migratory Bird Trail (1.9km) and a Coastal Trail (1.3km) – are dotted with bird-viewing huts and lookouts. Also on site is a Visitor Centre complete with cafe and mangrove exhibition gallery (open 8.30am to 5.30pm), shedding light on the reserve's wildlife and botany. To

WORTH A TRIP

PULAU UBIN

It may be a quick 10-minute bumboat ride from Changi Village, but Pulau Ubin feels worlds apart from mainland Singapore and its sea of tower blocks. Indeed, it's the perfect day-trip getaway, coloured with unkempt expanses of jungle and sun-bleached, tin-roofed shacks that echo a long-lost era.

Bumboats (one-way S$2.50, bicycle surcharge S$2; ⌚5.30am-9pm) to Pulau Ubin depart from Changi Point Ferry Terminal in Changi Village. There's no timetable: boats depart when 12 people are ready to go, dropping passengers off at **Pulau Ubin Village**. If you're hungry, hit **Season Live Seafood** (☎6542 7627; dishes S$4-30; ⌚11am-7pm Wed-Mon), a no-frills waterside joint offering simple, tasty dishes like butter prawns, fried squid, and sambal sweet-potato leaf.

Food outlets aside, Pulau Ubin Village is the place to rent bikes (around S$8 to S$12 per day for adults and from S$5 for kids). Best of the lot is shop 31, though it always pays to check the brakes and rust levels before agreeing to any particular bike. While clear signboards are dotted around the island, don't be afraid to trundle off on your bike and see where the road takes you.

For those keen on scraping their knees, there's **Ketam Mountain Bike Park**, about 3.4km from the ferry terminal, with a series of trails of varying difficulty. Further along this road, you'll find the quirky **German Girl Shrine**, housed in a wooden hut beside an Assam tree. According to legend, the young German daughter of a coffee-plantation manager was running away from British troops who had come to arrest her parents during WWI when she fell fatally into the quarry behind her house. Somewhere along the way, the Roman Catholic child became a Taoist deity, bestowing good health and fortune. The shrine is now filled with all manner of toys, make-up, folded lottery tickets, even burning candles, joss paper and German beer. One hopes the little *mädchen* (girl) approves; her ghost is said to haunt the area to this day.

If you only have time for one part of Pulau Ubin, make it the **Chek Jawa Wetlands** (⌚8.30am-6pm). Located on the eastern end of the island about 3.5km from the ferry terminal, its 1km coastal boardwalk takes you out over the sea before looping back through the mangrove swamp to the 20m-high Jejawi Tower and its stunning views. You can't bring your bike into the reserve, so make sure the one you've rented comes with a lock so you can secure it to the bike stands at the entrance.

get here, catch bus 925 from Kranji MRT station and alight at Kranji Reservoir Carpark B, directly opposite the reserve's entrance on Kranji Way. On Sunday, bus 925 also stops at the reserve's other entrance on Neo Tiew Cres.

Kranji War Memorial MEMORIAL
(☎6269 6158; 9 Woodlands Rd; ⌚8am-6.30pm; Ⓜ Kranji, then bus 160, 170, 178, 960 or 961) The austere white structures and rolling hillside of the Kranji War Memorial contain the WWII graves of thousands of Allied troops. Headstones, many of which are inscribed simply with the words: 'a soldier of the 1939–1945 war', are lined in neat rows across manicured lawns. Walls are inscribed with the names of over 25,000 men and women who lost their lives in Southeast Asia, and registers are available for inspection.

River Safari ZOO
(www.riversafari.com.sg; 80 Mandai Lake Rd; adult/child under 13yr S$28/18, boat ride adult/child S$5/3; ⌚9am-6pm; Ⓜ Ang Mo Kio, then bus 138) This wildlife park recreates the habitats of numerous world-famous rivers, including the Yangtze, Nile and Congo. While most are underwhelming, the Mekong River and Amazon Flooded Forest exhibits are impressive, their epic aquariums rippling with giant catfish and stingrays, electric eels, red-bellied piranhas, manatees and sea cows. Another highlight is the Giant Panda Forest enclosure, home to rare red pandas and the park's famous black-and-whiters, KaiKai and JiaJia.

Young kids will enjoy the 10-minute Amazon River Quest Boat Ride, a tranquil, theme park–style tour past roaming monkeys, wild cats and exotic birdlife. The ride begins with a big splash, so if you're sitting in the front row, keep feet and bags off the floor.

STROLLING THE SOUTHERN RIDGES

Made up of a series of parks and hills connecting West Coast Park to Mt Faber, the Southern Ridges will have you walking through the jungle without ever really leaving the city. While the entire route spans 9km, the best stretch is from Kent Ridge Park to Mt Faber. Not only is it relatively easy, this 4km stretch offers forest-canopy walkways, lofty skyline vistas, and the chance to cross the spectacular Henderson Waves, an undulating pedestrian bridge suspended 36m above the ground.

Catch the MRT to Pasir Panjang station, from where Kent Ridge Park is a steep but manageable 800m walk up Pepys Rd. At the top of the hill lies **Reflections at Bukit Chandu** (www.nhb.gov.sg; 31K Pepys Rd; adult/child S$2/1; ⌚9am-5.30pm Tue-Sun; Ⓜ Pasir Panjang), a small yet fascinating WWII interpretive centre recounting the brutal fall of Singapore.

Directly behind it is **Kent Ridge Park** and its short forest-canopy walk. The idyllic, leafy shade of Kent Ridge quickly gives way to the themed gardens and prototype glasshouses of **HortPark**. The park is also home to a children's playground, drinking fountains, restrooms and a nursery-cafe.

Cross the leaf-like Alexander Arch bridge from HortPark to the impressive **Forest Walk**, offering eye-level views of the jungle canopy carpeting Telok Blangah Hill. The walkway eventually leads to **Telok Blangah Hill Park**, with its flower-filled terrace garden, and further along to the sculptural **Henderson Waves** pedestrian bridge. The shard-like towers you can see rising above the green form part of Reflections at Keppel Bay, a residential development designed by starchitect Daniel Libeskind.

The final 550m to the summit of **Mt Faber** is a short but reasonably steep climb rewarded with fine city views (skip the average eateries). The **cable car** (www.singaporecablecar.com.sg; adult/child return S$29/18, Sentosa Line only S$13/8; ⌚8.45am-9.30pm) connecting Mt Faber to HarbourFront mall and MRT, and on to Sentosa Island is exorbitantly priced; consider grabbing a taxi (around S$5 to S$7 to HarbourFront or VivoCity) instead.

Boat-ride time slots often fill by 1pm, so go early. River Safari tickets purchased online are subject to a 10% discount.

Southern & Western Singapore

This vast area is home to a handful of lesser-known museums and historic sites, as well as the soothing Southern Ridges walking trail.

Jurong Bird Park BIRD SANCTUARY

(www.birdpark.com.sg; 2 Jurong Hill; adult/child under 13yr S$28/18; ⌚8.30am-6pm; ; Ⓜ Boon Lay, then bus 194 or 251) Home to some 600 species of feathered friends – including spectacular macaws – Jurong is a great place for young kids. Highlights include the wonderful Lory Loft forest enclosure, where you can feed colourful lories and lorikeets, and the interactive High Flyers (11am and 3pm) and Kings of the Skies (10am and 4pm). We must note, however, that some birds are made to perform for humans, which is discouraged by animal-welfare groups.

Young ones can splash about at the Birdz of Play (open 11am to 5.30pm weekdays, 9am to 5.30pm weekends), a wet and dry play area with a shop selling swimwear. There's a guided tram to cart you around the park when energy levels are low.

NUS Museum MUSEUM

(www.nus.edu.sg/museum; University Cultural Centre, 50 Kent Ridge Cres; ⌚10am-7.30pm Tue-Sat, to 6pm Sun; Ⓜ Kent Ridge, then bus A2, the university shuttle bus) FREE Located on the verdant campus of the National University of Singapore (NUS), this museum is one of the city's lesser-known cultural delights. Ancient Chinese ceramics and bronzes, as well as archaeological fragments found in Singapore, dominate the ground-floor Lee Kong Chian Collection; one floor up, the South and Southeast Asian Gallery showcases paintings, sculpture and textiles from the region. The Ng Eng Teng Collection is dedicated to Ng Eng Teng (1934–2001), Singapore's foremost modern artist, best known for his figurative sculptures.

Lee Kong Chian Natural History Museum MUSEUM

(lkcnhm.nus.edu.sg; 2 Conservatory Dr; adult/child under 13yr S$21/12; ⌚10am-7pm Tue-Sun, last entry 5.30pm; Ⓜ Kent Ridge, then bus A2 university shuttle) What looks like a giant rock bursting with greenery is actually Singapore's high-tech, child-friendly natural-history museum. The main Biodiversity Gallery delves into the origin of life using a stimulating combo of fossils, taxidermy and interactive displays. Hard to miss are Prince, Apollonia and Twinky: three 150-million-year-old Diplodocidsauropod dinosaur skeletons, two with their original skull. Upstairs, the Heritage Gallery explores the collection's 19th-century origins, with an interesting section on Singapore's geology to boot.

Haw Par Villa MUSEUM, PARK
(☎6872 2780; 262 Pasir Panjang Rd; ⊙9am-7pm, Ten Courts of Hell exhibit 9am-5.45pm; Ⓜ Haw Par Villa) FREE The refreshingly weird and kitsch Haw Par Villa was the brainchild of Aw Boon Haw, the creator of the medicinal salve Tiger Balm. After Aw Boon Haw built a villa here in 1937 for his beloved brother and business partner, Aw Boon Par, the siblings began building a Chinese-mythology theme park within the grounds. Top billing goes to the Ten Courts of Hell, a walk-through exhibit depicting the gruesome torments awaiting sinners in the underworld.

Gillman Barracks GALLERY
(www.gillmanbarracks.com; 9 Lock Rd; ⊙generally 11am-7pm Tue-Sat, to 6pm Sun; Ⓜ Labrador Park) Built in 1936 as a British military encampment, Gillman Barracks is now a rambling art outpost, with 11 galleries scattered around verdant grounds. Among these is New York's **Sundaram Tagore** (www.sundaramtagore.com; 01-05, Gillman Barracks; ⊙11am-7pm Tue-Sat, to 6pm Sun; Ⓜ Labrador Park) FREE, whose stable of artists includes award-winning photographers Edward Burtynsky and Annie Leibovitz. Also on site is the **NTU Centre for Contemporary Art** (http://ntu.ccasingapore.org; Block 43, Malan Rd; ⊙noon-7pm Tue-Thu, Sat & Sun, to 9pm Fri) FREE, a forward-thinking art-research centre hosting art talks, lectures and contemporary exhibitions from dynamic regional and international artists working in a variety of media.

To reach Gillman Barracks, catch the MRT to Labrador Park station and walk north up Alexandra Rd for 800m; the entry to Gillman Barracks is on your right. A one-way taxi fare from the CBD will set you back around S$10.

Labrador Nature Reserve PARK
(www.nparks.gov.sg; Labrador Villa Rd; ⊙24hr; 🚌408, Ⓜ Labrador Park) Combining forest trails rich in birdlife and a beachfront park, Labrador Park is scattered with evocative British war relics, only rediscovered in the 1980s. Look out for old gun emplacements mounted on moss-covered concrete casements as well as for the remains of the entrance to the old fort that stood guard on this hill. The reserve's hilly terrain sweeps down to the shore, where expansive lawn, shade and the sound of lapping waves invite a lazy picnic.

Sentosa Island

Connected to the 'mainland' by a causeway, Sentosa is essentially one giant Pleasure Island. The choices are head-spinning, from duelling roller-coasters and indoor skydiving to stunt shows, luge racing, Ibiza-style beach bars and a casino. Many of the attractions cost extra, making it easy for a family to rack up a hefty bill in one day. The beaches, however, are completely free and a hit with locals and tourists alike.

★ **SEA Aquarium** AQUARIUM
(Map p514; www.rwsentosa.com; Resorts World; adult/child under 13yr S$32/22; ⊙10am-7pm;

SENTOSA ENTRANCE FEE & TRANSPORT

Sentosa Island charges a small entry fee, based on the form of transport you take. If you walk across from VivoCity, the fee is S$1. If you ride the frequent Sentosa Express monorail, it's S$4, which you can pay using your EZ-Link or Nets transport card. Ride the Mt Faber Line cable car and the entrance fee is included in the price of your cable-car ticket. If arriving by taxi, the fee varies according to the time of day: the peak price is S$6 (2pm to 5pm weekdays, 7am to 5pm weekends).

Once on Sentosa, it's easy to get around, either by walking, taking the Sentosa Express (7am to midnight), riding the free 'beach tram' (shuttling the length of all three beaches, 9am to 10.30pm weekdays, to midnight Saturday) or by using the three free, colour-coded bus routes that link the main attractions (7am to 10.30pm weekdays, to midnight Saturday). The island now also operates a dedicated cable-car line (Sentosa Line), with stops at Siloso Point, Imbiah Lookout and Merlion.

Sentosa Island

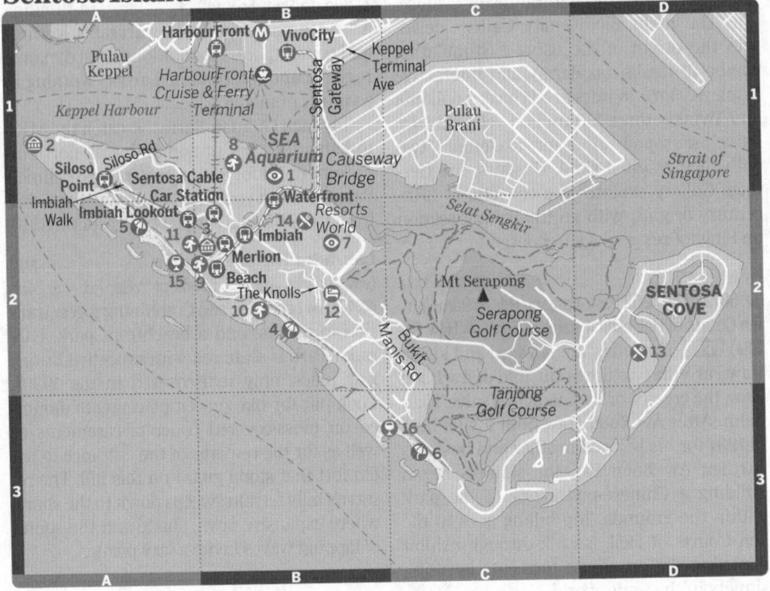

Sentosa Island

Top Sights		**11** Skyline Luge Sentosa	A2
1 SEA Aquarium	B1	Wave House	(see 5)
Sights		**Sleeping**	
2 Fort Siloso	A1	**12** Capella Singapore	B2
3 Images of Singapore Live	B2	**Eating**	
4 Palawan Beach	B2	**13** Kith Cafe	D2
5 Siloso Beach	A2	Knolls	(see 12)
6 Tanjong Beach	C3	**14** Malaysian Food Street	B2
7 Universal Studios	B2	**Drinking & Nightlife**	
Activities, Courses & Tours		**15** Coastes	A2
8 Adventure Cove Waterpark	B1	**16** Tanjong Beach Club	C3
9 iFly	B2		
10 Port of Lost Wonder	B2		

Ⓜ Harbourfront, then monorail to Waterfront) You'll be gawking at over 800 species of aquatic creatures at Singapore's impressive, sprawling aquarium. The state-of-the-art complex recreates 49 aquatic habitats found between Southeast Asia, Australia and Africa. The Open Ocean habitat is especially spectacular, its 36m-long, 8.3m-high viewing panel is one of the world's largest. The complex is also home to an interactive, family-friendly exhibition exploring the history of the maritime Silk Route.

Universal Studios AMUSEMENT PARK
(Map p514; www.rwsentosa.com; Resorts World; adult/child under 13yr S$74/54; ⏲10am-6pm; Ⓜ Harbourfront, then monorail to Waterfront) Universal Studios is the top-drawer attraction in Resorts World. Shops, shows, restaurants, rides and roller-coasters are all neatly packaged into fantasy-world themes based on blockbuster Hollywood films. Crowd favourites include Transformers: The Ride, a next-generation thrill ride deploying 3D animation, and Battlestar Galactica: Human vs Cylon, the world's tallest duelling

roller-coasters. Opening times are subject to slight variations at different times of the year, so always check the website before heading in.

Fort Siloso MUSEUM

(Map p514; www.sentosa.com.sg; Siloso Point; admission free, Surrender Chambers adult/child under 13yr S$6/4.50; ⏲10am-6pm; Ⓜ HarbourFront, then monorail to Beach) Dating from the 1880s, when Sentosa was called Pulau Blakang Mati (Malay for 'the island behind which lies death'), this British coastal fort was famously useless during the Japanese invasion of 1942. Documentaries, artefacts, animatronics and recreated historical scenes take visitors through the fort's history, and the underground tunnels are fun to explore.

Images of Singapore Live MUSEUM

(Map p514; www.imagesofsingaporelive.com; Imbiah Lookout; adult/child under 13yr incl Madame Tussauds S$39/29; ⏲10am-6pm Mon-Fri, to 7.30pm Sat & Sun; Ⓜ HarbourFront, then monorail to Beach) Using actors, immersive exhibitions and dramatic light-and-sound effects, Images of Singapore Live resuscitates the nation's history, from humble Malay fishing village to bustling colonial port and beyond. Young kids will especially love the Spirit of Singapore Boat Ride, a trippy, high-tech journey that feels just a little *Avatar*. Tickets purchased online are S$10 cheaper.

Activities

Adventure Sport

G-Max Reverse Bungy ADVENTURE SPORTS

(Map p494; www.gmax.com.sg; 3E River Valley Rd; adult/student per ride S$45/35, incl GX-5 Extreme Swing S$69/50; ⏲2pm-late; Ⓜ Clarke Quay) Prepare to be strapped into padded chairs inside a metal cage and propelled skyward to a height of 60m at speeds of up to 200km/h before being pulled back down by gravity. Though the ride offers spectacular views to those who can keep their eyes open, it's best avoided by people prone to velocity-induced vomiting.

iFly ADVENTURE SPORTS

(Map p514; www.iflysingapore.com; 43 Siloso Beach Walk; 2 skydives S$119; ⏲9am-9.30pm Mon, Tue & Thu-Sun, 11am-9.30pm Wed; Ⓜ Harbourfront, then monorail to Beach) If you fancy freefalling from 3660m to 914m *without* leaping out of a plane, leap into this indoor-skydiving centre. The price includes an hour's instruction followed by two short but thrilling skydives in a vertical wind chamber. Tickets purchased two days in advance for off-peak times are significantly cheaper. See the website for details.

Skyline Luge Sentosa ADVENTURE SPORTS

(Map p514; www.skylineluge.com; luge & skyride combo from S$17; ⏲10am-9.30pm; Ⓜ HarbourFront, then monorail to Beach) Take the skyride chairlift from Siloso Beach to Imbiah Lookout, then hop onto your luge (think go-cart meets toboggan) and race family and friends through hairpin bends and bone-shaking straights carved through the forest (helmets are provided and mandatory). Young kids will love this. Those with heart conditions or bad backs won't.

Spas & Massage

People's Park Complex MASSAGE

(Map p498; 1 Park Cres; Ⓜ Chinatown) Heady with the scent of Tiger Balm, Singapore's oldest mall is well known for its cheap massage joints. Our favourite is **Mr Lim Foot Reflexology** (Map p498; 03-53 & 03-78 People's Park Complex; 1hr foot reflexology S$25; ⏲10am-11pm), where your robust rubdown comes with televised local and Taiwanese soaps.

SENTOSA BEACHES

Squint hard enough and Sentosa's trio of beaches could pass for a Thai island paradise. The most popular of the three is **Siloso Beach** (Map p514; Ⓜ HarbourFront, then monorail to Beach). A quick walk from Beach monorail station, it's jam-packed with activities, eateries and bars. Further east is **Palawan Beach** (Map p514; Ⓜ HarbourFront, then monorail to Beach), home to water-themed playground **Port of Lost Wonder** (Map p514; www.polw.com.sg; child under 13yr weekday/weekend S$10/15, accompanying adult free; ⏲10am-6.30pm, waterplay area closes 6pm) and popular with families with younger kids. Continue east and you'll reach **Tanjong Beach** (Map p514; Ⓜ HarbourFront, then monorail to Beach), where eye-candy crowds perfect their beach-volleyball moves or simply flirt by the bar. Despite the disconcerting number of cargo ships out at sea, the water at all three beaches is monitored by the National Environment Agency and deemed safe for swimming. To reach Palawan and Tanjong Beaches, catch Sentosa's free beach tram.

Tomi Foot Reflexology MASSAGE
(Map p506; B1-114, Lucky Plaza, 304 Orchard Rd; 30min foot reflexology S$30; ⌚10am-10pm; Ⓜ Orchard) Yes, that's Sting in the photo – even he knows about this no-frills massage joint, lurking in the basement of '70s throwback Lucky Plaza. Head in for one of the best rubdowns in town, provided by a tactile team in matching pink polos. Techniques include acupressure and shiatsu, all approved by Jesus and Mary, hanging on the wall.

Remède Spa SPA
(Map p506; ☎6506 6896; www.remedespasingapore.com; St Regis Hotel, 29 Tanglin Rd; 1hr massage from S$180; ⌚9am-midnight; Ⓜ Orchard) Reputed to have the best masseurs in town, the St Regis Hotel's in-house spa is also home to the award-winning Pedi:Mani:Cure Studio by renowned pedicurist Bastien Gonzalez. Remède's wet lounge – a marbled wonderland of steam room, sauna, ice fountains and spa baths – is a perfect prelude to standout treatments like the 90-minute warm jade stone massage (S$290).

Spa Esprit SPA
(Map p506; ☎6836 0500; www.spa-esprit.com; 05-10, Paragon, 290 Orchard Rd; 1hr massage from S$101.65; ⌚10am-9pm; Ⓜ Somerset) Hip, friendly Spa Esprit is an apothecary and spa in one. Freshly picked ingredients and CPTG (Certified Pure Therapeutic Grade) essential oils are the stars here, deployed in everything from the Zsa Zsa Gabor Hydrating Facial (75 minutes, S$192.60) to the Chavutti Yogic Massage (90 minutes, S$149.80) and the blockbuster Back to Balance body massage (90 minutes, S$235.40).

Swimming

If your hotel is sans pool and the view of cargo ships off Sentosa's beaches leaves you apprehensive, don't fret! Singapore has a plethora of cheap, clean, inviting public pools to cool you down.

Jurong East Swimming Complex SWIMMING
(☎6563 5052; 21 Jurong East St 31; weekdays/weekends S$2/2.60; ⌚8am-9.30pm Tue-Sun; Ⓜ Chinese Garden) This impressive complex includes a massive wave pool, a bubble-jet spa bath, a lazy river, a wading pool, and a tower of three intertwining water slides. If it's just laps you're after, there's an Olympic-size pool too. It gets very busy, especially on weekends. From Chinese Garden MRT station, walk northwest along Boon Lay Way and turn right into Jurong East St 31.

Jalan Besar Swimming Complex SWIMMING
(Map p502; ☎6293 9058; 100 Tyrwhitt Rd; weekdays/weekends S$1.30/1.70; ⌚8am-9.30pm Thu-Tue, 2.30-9.30pm Wed; Ⓜ Lavender) An outdoor swimming complex in hipster enclave Jalan Besar. Facilties include a 50m competition pool and a 25m teaching pool.

Water Sports

Adventure Cove Waterpark WATER PARK
(Map p514; www.rwsentosa.com; Resorts World Sentosa; adult/child under 13yr S$36/26; ⌚10am-6pm; Ⓜ HarbourFront, then monorail to Waterfront) Despite its rides being better suited to kids and families, adult thrill-seekers will appreciate the Riptide Rocket (Southeast Asia's first hydro-magnetic coaster), Pipeline Plunge, and Bluwater Bay, a wave pool with serious gusto. Dolphin Island, charged separately, allows visitors to interact with Indo-Pacific dolphins in a pool. Captive-dolphin swims have been criticised by animal-welfare groups, who claim that captivity is debilitating and stressful for the animals, and that this is exacerbated by human interaction.

Ski360° WATER SPORTS
(Map p508; ☎6442 7318; www.ski360degree.com; 1206A East Coast Parkway; 1hr weekdays/weekends S$38/50, 2hr S$48/64; ⌚10am-7pm Mon, Tue & Thu, noon-9pm Wed & Fri, 9am-10pm Sat & Sun; 🚌36, 196, 197) What better way to cool off than by strapping on some waterskis, a kneeboard or a wakeboard and getting dragged around a lagoon on the end of a cable? From central Singapore, catch bus 196 to Marine Parade Rd, then walk south one block to East Coast Parkway (ECP), crossing it to East Coast Park via one of the pedestrian underpasses.

Wave House SURFING
(Map p514; ☎6238 1196; www.wavehousesentosa.com; Siloso Beach; 30min flowbarrel surf session S$30, 1hr double flowrider surf session from S$35; ⌚10.30am-10.30pm, Double Flowrider 11am-10pm, FlowBarrel 1-10pm Mon, Tue, Thu & Fri, 11am-10pm Wed, Sat & Sun; Ⓜ HarbourFront, then monorail to Beach) Two specially designed wave pools allow surfer types to practise their gashes and cutbacks at ever-popular Wave House. The non-curling Double Flowrider is good for beginners, while the 3m FlowBarrel is more challenging. Wave House also includes beachside eating and drinking options.

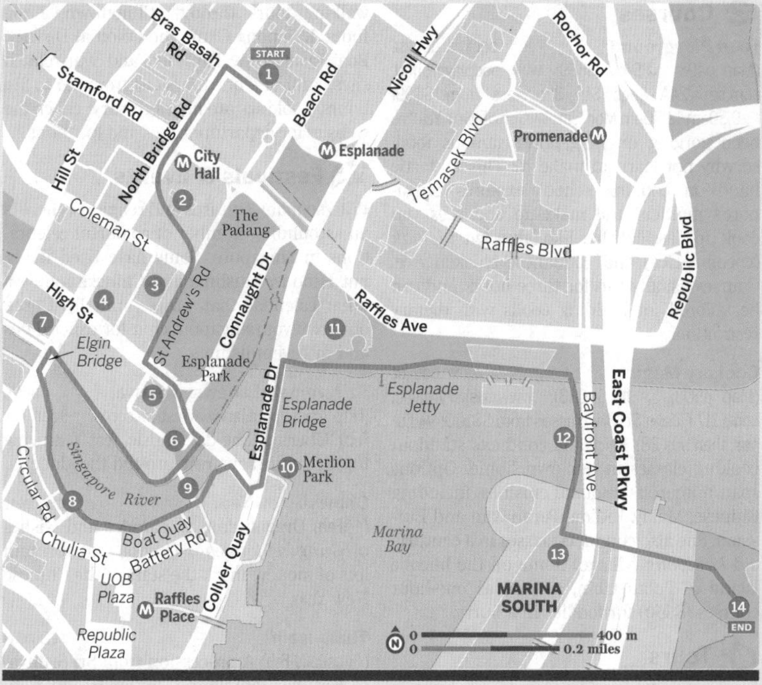

City Walk
Singapore: Colonial to Cutting Edge

START RAFFLES HOTEL
END GARDENS BY THE BAY
LENGTH 4.5KM; FOUR TO FIVE HOURS

Start at 1 **Raffles Hotel** (p530), taking in its elegant colonial arcades and tropical gardens, then head south to 2 **St Andrew's Cathedral** (p497), used as an emergency hospital during WWII. Further south down St Andrew's Rd, City Hall and the Old Supreme Court constitute the new 3 **National Gallery Singapore** (p492). Close by is the 4 **New Supreme Court**, a sci-fi statement co-designed by Sir Norman Foster's firm Foster + Partners. Below where St Andrew's Rd curves to the left, the 5 **Victoria Theatre & Concert Hall**, completed in 1862, was one of Singapore's first Victorian Revivalist buildings. Three years younger is the Empress Building, once the colony's government offices and now the 6 **Asian Civilisations Museum** (p493). Hang a right to walk along the northern bank of the Singapore River, one of the best spots to take in the CBD's powerhouse towers. They're significantly taller than the 7 **Old Hill Street police station** on the corner of Hill St, proclaimed a 'skyscraper' upon completion in 1934. The building houses several high-end art galleries. Cross Elgin Bridge and head down to 8 **Boat Quay** (p497), its riverfront shophouses now home to bars and restaurants. Following the river further east, you'll pass 9 **Cavenagh Bridge**, constructed in Scotland and reassembled in Singapore in 1869. Keeping watch is the Palladian Fullerton Hotel, Singapore's general post office until 1996. Take a 'wacky' photo with the famous 10 **Merlion statue**, then cross the Esplanade Bridge towards Singapore's 'giant durians', 11 **Esplanade – Theatres on the Bay** (p547). Continue east along Marina Promenade to cross the 12 **Helix Bridge**, inspired by the geometric arrangement of DNA. Card decks sparked Moshe Safdie's design concept for the multi-towered 13 **Marina Bay Sands complex** (p493). Turn left and walk along the water to 14 **Gardens by the Bay** (p489), Singapore's Tomorrowland spin on the Botanic Gardens concept.

Courses

Food Playground COOKING COURSE
(Map p498; ☎9452 3669; www.foodplayground.com.sg; 24A Sago St; 3hr class from S$99; ⊙9.30am-12.30pm Mon-Sat; Ⓜ Chinatown) You've been gorging on Singapore's famous food, so why not learn to make it? This fantastic hands-on cooking school explores Singapore's multicultural make-up and sees you cook up classic dishes like laksa, *nasi lemak* (coconut rice) and Hainanese chicken rice. Courses usually run for three hours and can be tailored for budding cooks with dietary restrictions.

Cookery Magic COOKING COURSE
(Map p508; ☎9665 6831; www.cookerymagic.com; 117 Fidelio St; 3hr classes from S$100; Ⓜ Eunos, then bus 28) Ruqxana conducts standout cooking classes in her own home. Options span numerous regional cuisines, including Chinese, Malay, Indian, Peranakan and Eurasian. She also conducts classes in a century-old *kampong* (village) home on the bucolic island of Pulau Ubin, as well as one-hour courses (S$50) for foodies in a hurry.

Tours

Singapore Ducktours BOAT TOUR
(Map p494; ☎6338 6877; www.ducktours.com.sg; 01-330, Suntec City Mall, Nicoll Hwy; adult/child under 13yr $37/27; ⊙10am-6pm; Ⓜ Esplanade) An informative, kid-friendly, one-hour romp in the 'Wacky Duck', a remodelled WWII amphibious Vietnamese war craft. The route traverses land and water, with a focus on Marina Bay and the Colonial District. You'll find the ticket kiosk and departure point in Tower 5 of Suntec City, directly facing the Nicoll Hwy.

Singapore River Cruise BOAT TOUR
(Map p494; ☎6336 6111; www.rivercruise.com.sg; bumboat river cruise adult/child S$25/15; Ⓜ Clarke Quay) Runs 40-minute bumboat tours of the Singapore River and Marina Bay. Boats depart about every 15 minutes from various locations, including Clarke Quay, Boat Quay and Marina Bay. A cheaper option is to catch one of the company's river taxis – commuter boats running a similar route; see the website for stops. River-taxi payment is by EZ-Link transport card only.

Original Singapore Walks WALKING TOUR
(☎6325 1631; www.singaporewalks.com; adult S$35-55, child 7-12yr S$15-30) Conducts irreverent but knowledgeable off-the-beaten-track walking tours through Chinatown, Little India, Kampong Glam, the Colonial District, Boat Quay, Haw Par Villa and war-related sites. Rain-or-shine tours last from 2½ to 3½ hours. Bookings are not necessary; check the website for departure times and locations.

Festivals & Events

With so many cultures and religions, there is an astounding number of colourful celebrations in Singapore. Some have fixed dates, but Hindus, Muslims and Chinese follow a lunar calendar that varies annually. Check out www.yoursingapore.com for exact dates and full event listings.

St Jerome's Laneway Festival MUSIC
(http://singapore.lanewayfestival.com; ⊙Jan or Feb) Uberhip one-day music fest featuring top-tier indie acts from around the globe.

Chinese New Year CULTURAL
(⊙Feb) Dragon dances, parades and wishes of '*Gung hei faat choi*' (I hope that you gain lots of money) mark the start of the Chinese New Year.

Thaipusam RELIGIOUS
(⊙usually Feb) A procession from Sri Srinivasa Perumal Temple to Chettiar Hindu Temple marks this dramatic Hindu festival.

Chingay CULTURAL
(www.chingay.org.sg) Singapore's biggest street parade is held on the 22nd day after the Chinese New Year.

Singapore International Jazz Festival MUSIC
(www.sing-jazz.com; ⊙Mar) Held at Marina Bay Sands, the four-day Sing Jazz presents known and emerging jazz talent from around the world.

Affordable Art Fair ART
(www.affordableartfair.com/singapore; ⊙Apr & Nov) A biannual expo with over 70 local and international galleries showcasing art priced between S$100 and S$10,000 from hundreds of artists. Held at the F1 Pit Building.

Beerfest Asia BEER
(www.beerfestasia.com; ⊙Jun) Held over four days, Asia's biggest beer event (www.beerfestasia.com) pours more than 400 types of brews, from international heavyweights and craft microbreweries. Events include DJs, live music and a beer-pong tournament.

(Continued on page 529)

KONDORUK/GETTY IMAGES ©

The Mega-Diversity Region

Home to thousands of natural species (with more being discovered all the time), Malaysia, Singapore and Brunei are a dream come true for budding David Attenboroughs. Tropical flora and fauna is so abundant that this region is a 'mega-diversity' hot spot. You don't need to venture deep into the jungle to see wildlife either.

Contents

Above Mt Kinabalu (p333)

Jungle Life

The region's lush natural habitats, from steamy rainforests to tidal mangroves, teem with mammals, birds, amphibians, reptiles and insects, many of them found nowhere else on earth. Although vast areas of old growth forest have been cleared, a magnificent few remain, mostly protected within reserves and parks.

Apes & Monkeys

Orangutans, Asia's only great apes, are at the top of many visitors' lists. The World Wildlife Fund (WWF) estimates that between 45,000 and 69,000 live in the dwindling forests of Borneo, a population that has declined by 50% in the last 50 years. Captive orangutans can be viewed at Sabah's Sepilok Orangutan Rehabilitation Centre, the Semenggoh Wildlife Centre in Sarawak, and Singapore Zoo.

The male proboscis monkey is an improbable-looking creature with a pendulous nose and bulbous belly; females and youngsters are more daintily built, with quaint, upturned noses. A beautiful langur is the silvered leaf monkey, whose fur is frosted with grey tips. Macaques are the stocky, aggressive monkeys that solicit snacks from tourists at temples and nature reserves. If you are carrying food, watch out for daring raids and be wary of bites – remember these are wild animals and rabies is a potential hazard.

Tailless and shy gibbons live in the trees, where they feed on fruits such as figs. Their raucous hooting – one of the most distinctive sounds of the Malaysian jungle – helps them establish territories and find mates.

Wild Cats

Species of leopard including the black panther and the rare clouded leopard are found in Malaysia, as well as smaller wild cats, including the bay cat, a specialised fish-eater, and the leopard cat, which is a bit larger than a domestic cat and has spotted fur.

The exact population of Malayan tigers is unknown but considered by WWF to be around 490, the vast majority of which are found in the jungles of Pahang, Perak, Terengganu and Kelantan.

1

1. Female orangutan carrying its baby 2. Baby macaque, Bako National Park (p414) 3. Malayan tiger

3

2

KKSTEVEN/GETTY IMAGES ©

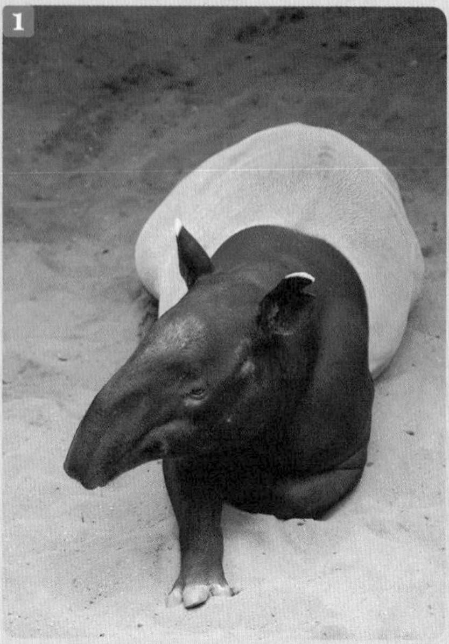

JAYSON PHOTOGRAPHY/GETTY IMAGES ©

1. Malayan tapir 2. Rhinoceros hornbill 3. Pygmy elephants
4. Flying fox

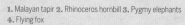

2

REBECCA YALE/GETTY IMAGES ©

4

Elephants, Rhinos & Tapirs

Around 2000 pygmy elephants live in northeastern Borneo, the largest population roaming the forests around Sungai Kinabatangan. It's thought they've lived on the island for at least 18,000 years.

If you're very lucky you may spot wild Asian elephants in Taman Negara. The animal is endangered, with WWF reckoning the population across the region to be between 38,000 and 51,000.

Sadly, according to a Danish study published in 2015, the Sumatran rhinoceros, which previously had been found in isolated areas of Sabah and Endau-Rompin National Park on the peninsula, is now considered extinct in the wild in Malaysia. None have been sighted since 2007.

Similarly under threat from habitat loss is the Malayan tapir, a long-nosed creature with black and white body hair. They can be found living in Taman Negara.

Birds & Bats

Well over a 1000 species of birds can be spotted in this part of the world. The most easily recognisable species in Malaysia are the various types of hornbill, of which the rhinoceros hornbill is the most flashy. Other birds that easily catch the eye include the brightly coloured kingfishers, pitas and trogons as well as the spectacularly named racket-tailed drongo.

The region has more than 100 species of bat, most of which are tiny, insectivorous species that live in caves and under eaves and bark. Flying foxes (fruit bats) are only distantly related to insectivorous bats; unlike them they have well-developed eyes and do not navigate by echolocation.

Aquatic Life

In the region's rivers, lakes and oceans, you'll find a mind-boggling variety of corals, fish and aquatic life. The seas around islands and atolls, including Sipadan, the Perhentians, Tioman and specks off the northeast coast of Sabah, offer some of the finest diving in the world.

Coral Kingdoms

Amid thriving coral – sea fans can grow to 3km – and a wealth of sponges, divers often encounter shimmering schools of jacks, bumphead parrotfish and barracudas, and find themselves making the acquaintance of green turtles, dolphins, manta rays and several species of shark.

Know Your Turtle

Of the world's seven species of turtle, four are native to Malaysia. The hawksbill and the green turtle both have nesting areas within Sabah's Turtle Islands National Park. Both of these species, along with the olive ridley and giant leatherback, also swim in the waters off Peninsular Malaysia's east coast. Here there are beaches which are established turtle rookeries where you may chance upon expectant mother turtles dragging themselves above the high-tide line to bury their eggs.

TOP DIVE SITES

Sipadan Legendary for its deep wall dives, Sipadan is a favoured hangout of turtles, sharks and open-ocean fish.

Layang Layang A deep-ocean island famed for its pristine coral and 2000m drop-off.

Pulau Perhentian Coral reefs surround both islands and some you can even wade out to.

Pulau Redang Corals, green and hawksbill turtles and a rainbow of tropical fish.

Pulau Tioman One of the few places where you stand a good chance of seeing pods of dolphins.

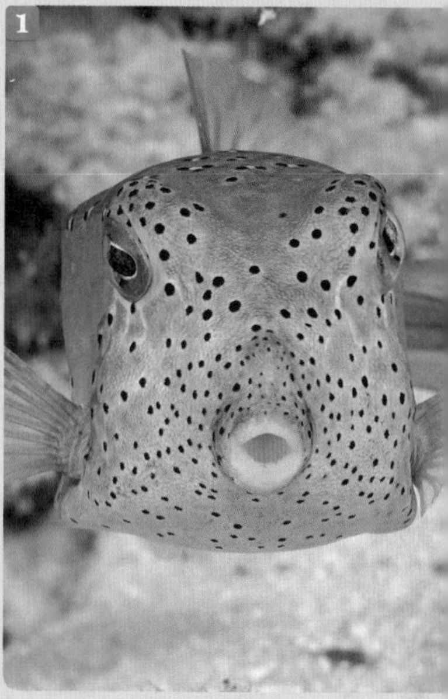

1. Boxfish, Sipadan (p372) 2. Hawksbill sea turtle, Layang Lay (p348) 3. Coral reef, Mabul (p373)

2

BARRETT & MACKAY/GETTY IMAGES ©

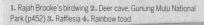

1. Rajah Brooke's birdwing 2. Deer cave, Gunung Mulu National Park (p452) 3. Rafflesia 4. Rainbow toad

PATRICK GIJSBERS/GETTY IMAGES ©

Natural Wonders

Record-breaking plants, geological gems and remarkable creatures big and small are among the multiple natural wonders within the mega-diversity region of Malaysia, Singapore and Brunei.

Rafflesia

A parasite that lacks roots, stems and leaves, this botanical wonder grows up to 1m in diameter. Rafflesias bloom for just three to five days before turning into a ring of black slime. Taman Negara, Cameron Highlands, Royal Belum State Park and the parks of Malaysian Borneo are the places to view these extraordinary specimens.

Deer Cave

Found in Gunung Mulu National Park, the world's largest cave passage open to the public is over 2km in length and 174m in height. It's home to anything between two and three million bats belonging to more than 12 species. They cling to the roof in a seething black mass as they gear up for the evening prowl.

Rainbow Toad

Rediscovered in the jungles of western Sarawak in 2011, after having been thought extinct for almost 90 years, the Sambas stream toad or Bornean rainbow toad, has long limbs and a pebbly back covered with bright red, green, yellow and purple warts. Also endemic of Borneo is the Microhyla nepenthicola, one of the world's tiniest frogs, no bigger than the size of a pea.

Rajah Brooke's Birdwing

Malaysia's national butterfly was discovered on Borneo in 1855 by the explorer and naturalist Alfred Russel Wallace. He named this black and iridescent-green winged beauty after James Brooke, the White Rajah of Sarawak at the time. It can also be found on Peninsular Malaysia below altitudes of 800m and often around hot-spring areas.

Eagle flying above mangroves, Pulau Langkawi (p192)

Diverse Ecosystems

Dense tropical jungle is not the only type of natural habitat you'll encounter in Malaysia. Head to the mountains and coastal regions to see different types of flora and fauna.

Mangroves

These remarkable coastal trees have developed extraordinary ways to deal with an ever-changing mix of salt and fresh water. Uncounted marine organisms and nearly every commercially important seafood species find sanctuary and nursery sites among the mangrove's muddy roots. They also fix loose coastal soil, protecting against erosion and tsunamis. You'll see them on Pulau Langkawi, Bako National Park, Kuching Wetland National Park and Brunei's Temburong District.

Mt Kinabalu

A huge granite dome that formed some nine million years ago, Malaysia's highest mountain is botanical paradise. Over half of the species growing above 900m are unique to the area and include oaks, laurels, chestnuts and a dense rhododendron forest. Elsewhere in the park are many varieties of orchids and insect-eating pitcher plants.

Kerangas

These heath forests, whose name in Iban means 'land that cannot grow rice,' are composed of small, densely packed trees. They also support the world's greatest variety of pitcher plants (nepenthes), which trap insects in chambers full of enzyme-rich fluid and then digest them. There are patches in Sarawak's Bako National Park and Sabah's Maliau Basin Conservation Area.

(Continued from page 518)

Singapore International Festival of Arts CULTURAL
(http://sifa.sg/sifa; ⏰early Aug–mid-Sep) A world-class offering of mostly drama and dance curated by Ong Keng Sen, one of Singapore's most respected theatre practitioners.

Great Singapore Sale SHOPPING
(www.greatsingaporesale.com.sg; ⏰late May-late Jul) Eight credit-crunching weeks of sales across the city. For the best bargains, raid the racks during the first week.

Singapore Food Festival FOOD
(www.yoursingapore.com; ⏰Jul) A two-week celebration of all things edible and Singaporean. Events take place across the city and include tastings, pop-up restaurants and cooking workshops.

Singapore National Day PARADE
(www.ndp.org.sg; ⏰9 Aug) A nationalistic frenzy of military and civilian parades, air-force fly-bys and fireworks. Tickets are snapped up well in advance.

Hungry Ghost Festival CULTURAL
(⏰Aug) Fires, food offerings and Chinese opera honour roaming spirits at this traditional festival.

Singapore Night Festival CULTURAL
(http://nightfest.sg; ⏰Aug) Spectacular light projections, plus interactive installations, performance art, cabaret, comedy and more. Held over two weekends.

Singapore Formula One Grand Prix SPORTS
(www.singapore-f1-grand-prix.com; ⏰late Sep) The F1 night race screams around Marina Bay. Off-track happenings include major international music acts. Book accommodation months in advance.

Deepavali RELIGIOUS
(⏰Oct) Rama's victory over the demon king Ravana is celebrated during the 'Festival of Lights'. Little India is ablaze with lights for a month, culminating in a huge street party on the eve of the holiday.

ZoukOut MUSIC
(http://zoukout.com; ⏰Dec) Singapore's biggest outdoor dance party delivers DJ heavyweights such as Axwell & Ingrosso and Tiësto. Held over two nights on Siloso Beach, Sentosa.

Sleeping

Sleeping in Singapore is expensive. Budget travellers have it best, with hostel rooms as low as S$20 a night and a wave of next-gen hostels cranking up the standards with chicer interiors and added extras. Newer midrange hotels are raising the bar with impressive facilities and good, regular online deals. Luxury digs are expensive but plentiful and among the world's best, with options ranging from the colonial and romantic to the architecturally cutting edge.

You'll find everything from flashpackers and top-notch midrange hotels to a historic luxury icon along the Singapore River. Both luxe and midrange options dot the Colonial District, Marina Bay and CBD, with a plethora of boutique digs and good-quality backpackers in Chinatown. Kampong Glam and Little India are also popular with budget-conscious travellers, while Orchard Rd delivers mostly higher-end chains and trendier boutique options. For a tropical-resort vibe, seek Sentosa.

> **BOOKING ON THE FLY**
>
> If you arrive in Singapore without a hotel booking, the efficient Singapore Hotel Association (www.sha.org.sg) has desks at Changi Airport Terminals 1, 2 and 3. There are dozens of hotels on its lists, ranging from budget sleeps to five-star luxury. There's no charge for the service, and promotional or discounted rates, when available, are passed on to you. You can also book the hotels directly through its affiliate website, www.stayinsingapore.com.

Colonial District, the Quays & Marina Bay

5Footway.Inn Project Boat Quay HOSTEL $
(Map p494; www.5footwayinn.com; 76 Boat Quay; dm from S$20, tw incl breakfast from S$60; ❄@📶; Ⓜ Clarke Quay) Right on Boat Quay, the whitewashed dorms come in two-, three- and four-bed configurations, and though rooms are small (superior rooms have windows), they're modern and comfortable, with white wooden bunks and handy bedside power sockets. Bathrooms are modern, reception operates round-the-clock, and the cheap-chic breakfast lounge comes with river-view balcony seating.

Holiday Inn Express Clarke Quay HOTEL $$
(Map p494; ☎6589 8000; www.hiexpress.com; 2 Magazine Rd; r incl breakfast from S$215; @📶🏊;

Ⓜ Clarke Quay) This smart newcomer delivers modern, earthy-hued rooms with high ceilings, massive floor-to-ceiling windows and comfortable beds with both soft and firm pillows (embroidered on the pillow slip). Small bathrooms come with decent-size showers. Best of all is the rooftop garden, home to a tiny gym and impressive glass-sided pool with spectacular city views. The hotel's self-service laundry room is a handy touch.

Discounted online rates can see rooms offered for under S$200.

Ibis Singapore on Bencoolen HOTEL **$$**
(Map p502; ☎6593 2888; www.ibishotel.com; 170 Bencoolen St; r from S$200; ❄@📶; Ⓜ Bugis) Ibis offers sensible, low-frills comfort, from a generic lobby spiffed up with colourful modular furniture, to smallish, spotless, cookie-cutter rooms with crisp sheets, light wood and peachy hues. Bathrooms are small, clean and modern. Thoughtful extras include complimentary bikes and access to a nearby gym. See the website for regular discounts.

★ **Fullerton Bay Hotel** HOTEL **$$$**
(Map p494; ☎6333 8388; www.fullertonbayhotel.com; 80 Collyer Quay; r from S$600; ❄@📶🏊; Ⓜ Raffles Pl) The Fullerton Hotel's contemporary sibling flanks Marina Bay. It's a light-filled, heavenly scented, deco-inspired number. Rooms are suitably plush, with high ceilings, wood and marble flooring, and warm, subdued hues. Recharge courtesy the in-room Nespresso machine and lather up with Bulgari toiletries; glass panels in the marble bathrooms look into the room and at Marina Bay and beyond.

★ **Raffles Hotel** HOTEL **$$$**
(Map p494; ☎6337 1886; www.raffleshotel.com; 1 Beach Rd; r from S$925; ❄@📶🏊; Ⓜ City Hall) The grand old dame of Singapore's Colonial District has seen many a famous visitor in her time, from Somerset Maugham to Michael Jackson. It's a beautiful place of white colonial architecture, lush pockets of green, and historic bars. Rooms are suitably Old World and elegant, with spacious parlours, polished wooden furniture and floorboards, verandas and lazily swirling ceiling fans.

Fullerton Hotel HOTEL **$$$**
(Map p494; ☎6733 8388; www.fullertonhotel.com; 1 Fullerton Sq; r from S$450; ❄@📶🏊; Ⓜ Raffles Pl) Occupying what was once Singapore's magnificent, Palladian-style general post office, the grand old Fullerton offers classically elegant rooms in muted tones. Entry-level rooms look 'out' into the inner atrium, so consider upgrading to one of the much more inspiring river- or bay-view rooms. A river-and-skyline backdrop awaits at the 25m terrace pool, the hotel's alfresco jewel.

Hotel Fort Canning HOTEL **$$$**
(Map p494; ☎6559 6770; www.hfcsingapore.com; 11 Canning Walk; r from S$380; ❄@📶🏊; Ⓜ Dhoby Ghaut) What was once British military headquarters is now a luxury hideaway surrounded by Fort Canning Park. While we love the mineral water–filled swimming pools, exceptional gym and complimentary evening aperitifs and canapés, the rooms are the star attraction. Gorgeous retreats, they're graced with high ceilings, parquetry flooring, Poltrona Frau chaise longue, Jim Thompson silk bedhead and soothing botanical colours.

Naumi BOUTIQUE HOTEL **$$$**
(Map p494; ☎6403 6000; www.naumihotel.com; 41 Seah St; r incl breakfast from S$400; ❄@📶🏊; Ⓜ City Hall, Esplanade) Slinky Naumi comes with commissioned artwork, playful quotes and a rooftop infinity pool with skyline views. Standard rooms are relatively small but cleverly configured, with 400-thread-count Egyptian-cotton bedlinen, Nespresso machine and complimentary minibar. Shower panels turn opaque at the flick of a switch, with a dramatically lit, stand-alone 'beauty bar' (bathroom counter) in the room itself. Ninth-floor rooms have city views.

Westin HOTEL **$$$**
(Map p498; ☎6922 6888; www.thewestinsingapore.com; Asia Square Tower 2, 12 Marina View; r from S$450; ❄@📶🏊; Ⓜ Downtown) With its lobby on level 32, it's not surprising that Singapore's new Westin offers spectacular views. Peel your eyes away from the windows to appreciate elegant rooms graced with heavenly beds and deep-soaking tubs; a luxurious spa with panoramic hot tubs (accessible to all guests), and a lofty infinity pool that seems to spill straight into the sea below.

Marina Bay Sands HOTEL **$$$**
(Map p494; ☎6688 8888; www.marinabaysands.com; 10 Bayfront Ave; r from S$500; ❄@📶🏊; Ⓜ Bayfront) Part of the ambitious Marina Bay Sands casino-retail complex, the Sands hotel is famed for its extraordinary rooftop infinity pool, which straddles the roofs of the three hotel skyscrapers. Rooms are

modern and comfortable, though generic. A quick walk from Gardens by the Bay, it's a good choice for fans of casinos and high-end shopping sprees. Check online for the best deals.

Park Regis HOTEL $$$
(Map p494; 6818 8888; www.parkregissingapore.com; 23 Merchant Rd; r from S$310; ; Clarke Quay) Regular online offers see this newish, affable place dip into the midrange bracket. Its light-filled rooms are smallish but modern, with window seating and warm, amber accents. The gym is petite but adequate, and overlooks the hotel's fabulous terrace pool, which comes with a cascading waterfall feature and bar.

Staff are wonderfully helpful, and the hotel is an easy walk from both the quays and Chinatown.

Chinatown & the CBD

★Adler Hostel HOSTEL $
(Map p498; 6226 0173; www.adlerhostel.com; 265 South Bridge Rd; cabin s/d S$55/110; ; Chinatown) Hostelling reaches sophisticated new heights at this self-proclaimed 'poshtel'. Chinese antiques grace the tranquil lobby lounge, fresh towels and feather-down duvets and pillows on the beds, and Malin+Goetz products in the bathrooms. Airy, air-conditioned dorms consist of custom-made cabins, each with lockable storage and drawable curtain for privacy. Some even feature king-size beds for couples. Book around three weeks ahead for the best rates.

Wink Hostel HOSTEL $
(Map p498; 6222 2940; www.winkhostel.com; 8 Mosque St; pod s/d S$50/90; ; Chinatown) Located in a restored shophouse in the heart of Chinatown, flashbacker favourite Wink merges hostel and capsule-hotel concepts. Instead of bunks, dorms feature private, sound-proof 'pods', each with comfortable mattress, coloured mood lighting, adjacent locker and enough room to sit up in. Communal bathrooms feature rain shower-heads, while the in-house kitchenette, laundry and lounge areas crank up the homely factor.

Rucksack Inn HOSTEL $
(Map p498; 6438 5146; www.rucksackinn.com/temple-st; 52 Temple St; dm incl breakfast from S$34; ; Chinatown) Travellers' messages are lovingly scrawled all over the streetside columns of this friendly, two-level hostel. Decked out in white-metal bunk beds and quirky wall murals, the dorms come in four, six, eight and 10-bed configurations, with a female-only room. All are clean, modern and cosy, and the communal showers have rain shower-heads. Tech perks include iMacs, Xboxes and Wii consoles.

Hotel 1929 BOUTIQUE HOTEL $$
(Map p498; 6347 1929; www.hotel1929.com; 50 Keong Saik Rd; s/d incl breakfast from S$175/200; ; Outram Park) Occupying a whitewashed heritage building, Hotel 1929 sits on up-and-coming Keong Saik Rd. Rooms are tight, but good use is made of limited space, and interiors are cheerily festooned with vintage designer furniture (look out for reproduction Eames and Jacobsen) and Technicolor mosaic bathrooms.

Rooftop suites spice things up with private, bathtub-graced verandas, and discounts mean you can snag some double rooms for less than S$200.

★Parkroyal on Pickering HOTEL $$$
(Map p494; 6809 8888; www.parkroyalhotels.com; 3 Upper Pickering St; r from S$320; ; Chinatown) Dramatic, cascading gardens, bird-cage cabanas right on the infinity pool and a striking design evocative of terraced paddy fields: this outstanding newcomer is the work of local architecture firm Woha, which designed everything down to the wastepaper baskets. Rooms are light, crisp and contemporary, with natural wood and soothing green hues, high ceilings and heavenly mattresses.

★Amoy BOUTIQUE HOTEL $$$
(Map p498; 6580 2888; www.stayfareast.com; 76 Telok Ayer St; s/d incl breakfast from S$270/325; ; Telok Ayer) Not many hotels are accessed through a historic Chinese temple, but then the Amoy is no ordinary slumber pad. History inspires this contemporary belle, from the lobby feature wall displaying old Singaporean Chinese surnames to custom-made opium beds in the cleverly configured 'Cosy Single' rooms. Plush doubles include Ming-style porcelain basins, and all rooms please with designer bathroom, Nespresso machine and complimentary minibar.

Wangz BOUTIQUE HOTEL $$$
(6595 1388; www.wangzhotel.com; 231 Outram Rd; r incl breakfast from S$275; ; Outram Park) Curvaceous, metallic Wangz is a winner. A quick walk from Tiong Bahru's heritage architecture and hipster hangouts, its 41

rooms are smart and modern, accented with contemporary local art, sublimely comfortable beds, iPod docking stations and sleek bathrooms. Further perks include complimentary non-alcoholic minibar beverages, an in-house gym and a rooftop lounge serving well-mixed drinks. Breakfast is complimentary and the service sterling.

New Majestic Hotel BOUTIQUE HOTEL $$$
(Map p498; ☎6511 4700; www.newmajestichotel.com; 31-37 Bukit Pasoh Rd; r incl breakfast from S$280; ; Outram Park) Still one of the best boutique hotels in Chinatown, offering 30 unique rooms done up in a mix of vintage and designer furniture designed by different Singaporean artists. Among the best are the Attic Loft rooms ('his' and 'hers' vintage bathtubs included), and the fabulous Aqua Room, featuring a glass-encased bathtub as its central feature.

Scarlet BOUTIQUE HOTEL $$$
(Map p498; ☎6511 3333; www.thescarlethotel.com; 33 Erskine Rd; r from S$250; ; Chinatown) Dark, luscious Scarlet offers great service and svelte rooms just around the corner from drinking hot spots Ann Siang Rd and Club St. In colour schemes of teal blue or gold and bronze, the chic rooms feature silky wallpaper, dark Oriental furniture and firm mattresses. The 1st-floor Premium rooms are especially plush and fun, complete with velvety chaise longues.

Little India & Kampong Glam

InnCrowd HOSTEL $
(Map p502; ☎6296 9169; www.the-inncrowd.com; 73 Dunlop St; dm from S$20.50; ; Rochor, Little India) Wildly popular, the InnCrowd is ground zero for Singapore's backpackers. Located right in the heart of Little India, this funkily painted hostel has helpful staff and all the facilities you'd expect of a decent hostel (travel advice, free internet, wi-fi, DVDs, laundry), plus a few you might not expect (a Wii console and kick-scooter city tours!). Bookings essential.

Five Stones Hostel HOSTEL $
(Map p502; ☎6535 5607; www.fivestoneshostel.com; 285 Beach Rd; dm S$30-38, tw/d S$100/115; ; Bugis, Nicoll Hwy) This upbeat, no-shoes hostel comes with polished-concrete floors and both Wii and DVDs in the common lounge, plus complimentary use of washing machines and dryers. While not all dorms have windows, all feature steel-frame bunks, personal power sockets and lamps, and bright, mood-lifting murals depicting local themes. There's an all-female floor, plus private rooms with bunks or a queen-size bed.

Green Kiwi Backpackers Hostel HOSTEL $
(Map p502; ☎9695 9331; www.greenkiwi.com.sg; 280A Lavender St; dm S$22-30; ; Lavender) An easy walk from the hipster pocket of Jalan Besar is this popular, well-air-conditioned option. Low-frills dorms (which include a female-only room) feature red, wooden bunks; the communal bathrooms are reassuringly clean. Perks include laundry service (S$8 per load, wash and dry) and a leafy rooftop garden. The latter is a good spot to neck a beer, on sale at reception.

★ **Wanderlust** BOUTIQUE HOTEL $$
(Map p502; ☎6396 3322; www.wanderlusthotel.com; 2 Dickson Rd; r incl breakfast from S$210; ; Rochor, Bugis) Wanderlust delivers wow factor with its insanely imaginative accommodation, ranging from comic-book 'mono' rooms to options with themes like 'treehouse' and 'spaceship'. Bookings made via the website include complimentary use of a smartphone during your stay, with unlimited local and IDD calls to 15 selected countries and unlimited 3G data. Early bookings and online deals deliver great rates, often below S$200.

Albert Court Village Hotel HOTEL $$
(Map p502; ☎6339 3939; www.stayfareast.com; 180 Albert St; r from S$200; ; Rochor, Little India) A short walk south of Little India is this colonial-era hotel, in a shophouse redevelopment that now shoots up eight storeys. Rooms are classic and spacious, with carved wooden furniture, smallish but spotless bathrooms, and offer a choice of fan or air-con. Service is top-notch and there's wi-fi throughout. You'll find the best deals online.

Orchard Road

Holiday Inn Express Orchard Road HOTEL $$
(Map p506; ☎6690 3199; www.hiexpress.com; 20 Bideford Rd; r incl breakfast from S$240; ; Somerset) Around the corner from Orchard Rd is this crisp, good-value option. The light-filled lobby is upbeat and contemporary, scattered with funky furniture and iMacs. Cookie-cutter rooms are bright and tasteful, with neutral hues, bold yellow lounge chairs, iPod docks and small bathrooms with decent-size showers. Communal

STUCK AT THE AIRPORT?

If you're only in Singapore for a short time or have an endless wait between connections, try the **Ambassador Transit Hotel** (☎ Terminal 2 6542 8122, Terminal 3 6507 9788; www.harilelahospitality.com; s/d/tr S$90/110/135;) . Rates quoted are for the first six hours and each additional hour block thereafter is S$23.54; rooms don't have windows and the budget singles (S$64.74 for six hours) have shared bathrooms. The only swish option at Changi Airport is Terminal 3's **Crowne Plaza Hotel** (☎ 6823 5300; www.ihg.com; 75 Airport Blvd, Changi Airport; d from S$330;), a design-literate, business-oriented place with impressive facilities. Unfortunately, the lack of competition means hiked-up prices; always check online for deals.

washing machines and dryers are a handy touch. Lowest rates usually run Friday to Sunday.

Quincy BOUTIQUE HOTEL **$$$**
(Map p506; ☎ 6738 5888; www.quincy.com.sg; 22 Mount Elizabeth Rd; d from S$350; ; M Orchard) Smart, slimline Quincy offers svelte, Armani-chic rooms, with light-grey walls and high ceilings with fetching back-lighting. TVs are flat, mattresses soft, and charcoal-tiled bathrooms stocked with Molton Brown amenities. Minibars are complimentary, and guests are entitled to two free laundry items per day. The glass-enclosed balcony pool is utterly inviting. Most online deals include breakfast.

Hotel Jen Orchardgateway HOTEL **$$$**
(Map p506; ☎ 6708 8888; www.hoteljen.com/singapore/orchardgateway; 10-01, 277 Orchard Rd; d from S$290; ; M Somerset) Shopaholics will love this fresh, 502-room pad, right above Orchardgateway mall and connected to two other malls and Somerset MRT. Rooms are simple yet stylish, with calming hues and sleep-coaxing beds. Millennial touches include phone-charging lockers and a PressReader app with free access to thousands of online publications. The star attraction, however, is the rooftop pool, with a gorgeous skyline view.

Goodwood Park Hotel HOTEL **$$$**
(Map p506; ☎ 6737 7411; www.goodwoodparkhotel.com; 22 Scotts Rd; r from S$300; ; M Orchard) Dating back to 1900, this wonderful heritage hotel with gracious service feels like an elegant, old-world retreat: the kind of place you just want to hang out in, sinking into a plush sofa with a good book. Deluxe rooms in the main building are impressively spacious; rooms in the newer wing are renovated but smaller. There are two beautiful swimming pools.

Hotel Jen Tanglin HOTEL **$$$**
(Map p506; ☎ 6738 2222; www.hoteljen.com/singapore; 1A Cuscaden Rd; d from S$340; ; 7, 75, 77, 105, 106, 111, 123, 132, 174, M Orchard) Hipster chic underscores Jen's 565 rooms, from the sculptural furniture pieces and funky wallpaper to the mood lighting that makes the ridiculously comfortable beds appear to levitate. Entry-level Club Rooms are small but cleverly designed (we love the bedside USB ports), while the much larger Deluxe Suites come with separate tub and shower. Other perks include pool, gym, spa and self-service laundry.

Sentosa Island

★Capella Singapore RESORT **$$$**
(Map p514; ☎ 6377 8888; www.capellahotels.com/singapore; 1 The Knolls, Sentosa Island; r from S$795, villas from S$1380; ; M HarbourFront, then monorail to Beach) Capella is one of Singapore's A-list slumber numbers, a seductive melange of colonial and contemporary architecture, elegant spa, restaurants, bar and three cascading swimming pools in lush, landscaped gardens. The beautifully appointed rooms are spacious and chic, with king-size beds; earthy, subdued hues; and striking contemporary bathrooms. The villas are even more decadent, each with its own private plunge pool.

Eating

For cheap, authentic local flavours spanning Chinese, Indian, Malay and Peranakan (Malay-style cooking with Chinese ingredients), head to the city's hawker centres and food courts, where memorable meals cost as little as S$3. The general rule: join the longest queues. Beyond these budget staples is a booming restaurant scene, from fine-dining institutions to trendy restaurant-bar hot spots run by innovative local and expat talent. You'll find many of the latter in Chinatown.

Colonial District, the Quays & Marina Bay

You'll find several excellent eating options at Raffles City (p549), most located in the confusing basement warren.

Satay by the Bay HAWKER $

(www.gardensbythebay.com.sg; Gardens by the Bay, 18 Marina Gardens Dr; dishes from S$4; food stalls vary, drinks stall 24hr; M Bayfront) Gardens by the Bay's own hawker centre has an enviable location, alongside Marina Bay and far from the roar of city traffic. Especially evocative at night, it's known for its satay, best devoured under open skies on the spacious wooden deck. As you'd expect, prices are a little higher than at more local hawker centres, with most dishes between S$8 and S$10.

Rasapura Masters HAWKER $

(Map p494; www.rasapura.com.sg; level B2, The Shoppes at Marina Bay Sands, 2 Bayfront Ave; dishes from S$5; M Bayfront) If you prefer your hawker grub with a side of air-con, head down to this bustling, gleaming food court in the basement of the Marina Bay Sands mall. Its stalls cover most bases, from Japanese ramen and Korean kimchi to Hong Kong roast meats and local *bak kut teh* (pork-bone tea soup).

★National Kitchen by Violet Oon PERANAKAN $$

(Map p494; National Gallery Singapore, 1 St Andrew's Rd; S$17-35; 11am-2.30pm & 6-9.30pm; M City Hall) Chef Violet Oon is a national treasure, much loved for her faithful Peranakan (Chinese-Malay fusion) dishes – so much so that she was chosen to open her latest venture inside Singapore's showcase National Gallery. Feast on made-from-scratch beauties like sweet, spicy *kueh pie tee* (prawn- and yam bean–stuffed pastry cups), dry laksa and fried turmeric chicken wings with chinchalok sambal.

Wah Lok CHINESE $$

(Map p494; 6311 8188; Level 2, Carlton Hotel, 76 Bras Basah Rd; dim sum S$4.80-6.90, mains S$12-36; 11.30am-2.15pm & 6.30-10.15pm Mon-Sat, 11am-2.15pm & 6.30-10.15pm Sun; ; M City Hall, Bras Basah) This plush Cantonese classic serves one of Singapore's best dim-sum lunches. There's no trolley-pushing aunties here, just a dedicated yum-cha menu and gracious staff ready to take your order (must-eats include the *xiao long bao* (soup dumplings) and baked barbecued-pork buns). There are two lunch sittings per day on weekends; book three days ahead if heading in then.

Super Loco MEXICAN $$

(6235 8900; http://super-loco.com; 01-13, Robertson Quay; tacos S$9-11, quesadillas S$16-18; 5-10.30pm Mon-Fri, 10am-3.30pm & 5-10.30pm Sat & Sun; 51, 64, 123, 186) The only thing missing is a beach at this breezy hipster cantina, complete with Mexican party vibe, pink-neon lights and playful barkeeps in Cancún-esque shirts. Get the good times rolling with a competent frozen margarita, then lick your lips over the standout ceviche, zingy crab and avocado tostada, and the damn fine *carne asada* (grilled meat) and *pescado* (fish) tacos.

Curry Culture INDIAN $$

(www.thecurryculture.com.sg; 01-10/11, 60 Robertson Quay; mains S$14-28; 5-10.30pm Mon-Thu, 12.30-2pm & 5-10.30pm Fri-Sun; ; 51, 64, 123, 186) Softly lit and semi-alfresco, this outstanding Indian restaurant offers flavour-packed, nuanced dishes like tangy *papdi chaat* (crisp dough wafers topped with spiced potato, yogurt and chutney), seductive *Hyderabadi Baingan* (eggplant in a fresh coconut and peanut sauce), and a spectacular *bhuna gosht* (spiced, slow-cooked lamb with caramelised onion). Cool things down with a soothing ginger *lassi*, made with fried curry leaf for added complexity.

Jai Thai THAI $$

(Map p494; www.jai-thai.com; 27 Purvis St; dishes S$5-18; 11.30am-3pm & 6-9.30pm; M City Hall) On a street studded with reputable eateries, lo-fi Jai Thai serves up cheap, tasty Thai under the gaze of Siamese royalty. Grab a pavement table and channel Bangkok with fragrant green curry chicken or mouth-watering fried prawns in a sweet and sour tamarind sauce. Like it hot? Slurp a bowl of tom yum soup (order the shrimp version). Cash only.

Pollen EUROPEAN $$$

(6604 9988; www.pollen.com.sg; Flower Dome, Gardens by the Bay, 18 Marina Gardens Dr; mains S$32-70, 5-course dinner tasting menu S$170; restaurant noon-2.30pm & 6-9.30pm Wed-Mon, Pollen Terrace cafe 11am-9pm Mon-Thu, 9.30am-9pm Fri-Sun, afternoon tea 3-5pm; M Bayfront)

Right inside Gardens by the Bay's Flower Dome, posh Pollen is the Singapore spin-off of London's lauded Pollen Street Social. Its menus deliver artful, produce-driven European flavours with subtle Asian inflections. The three-course set lunch (S$50, available Wednesday to Monday) is good value, while Pollen's more casual upstairs cafe serves a fine afternoon high tea (book at least a week ahead).

Pollen runs a frequent courtesy buggy service between the restaurant and the Gardens' main Arrival Plaza.

Jumbo Seafood CHINESE **$$$**

(Map p494; ☎6532 3435; www.jumboseafood.com.sg; 01-01/02 Riverside Point, 30 Merchant Rd; dishes from S$12, chilli crab around S$78 per kilogram; ⌚noon-2.15pm & 6-11.15pm; Ⓜ Clarke Quay) If you're lusting after chilli crab – and you should be – this is a good place to indulge. The gravy is sweet and nutty, with just the right amount of chilli. Make sure to order some *mantou* (fried buns) to soak up the gravy. While all of Jumbo's outlets have the dish down to an art, this one has the best riverside location.

One kilo of crab (or 1.5kg if you're especially hungry) should be enough for two. Book ahead if heading in later in the week.

Chinatown & the CBD

★ **Maxwell Food Centre** HAWKER **$**

(Map p498; cnr Maxwell & South Bridge Rds; dishes from S$2.50; ⌚stalls vary; ✍; Ⓜ Chinatown) One of Chinatown's most accessible hawker centres, Maxwell is a solid spot to savour some of the city's street-food staples. While stalls slip in and out of favour with Singapore's fickle diners, enduring favourites include **Tian Tian Hainanese Chicken Rice** (Stall 10; chicken rice from S$3.50; ⌚10am-5pm Tue-Sun) and **Rojak, Popiah & Cockle** (Stall 01-56; popiah S$2.50, rojak from S$3; ⌚noon-10.30pm).

Chinatown Complex HAWKER **$**

(Map p498; 11 New Bridge Rd; dishes from S$3; ⌚stalls vary; Ⓜ Chinatown) Leave Smith St's revamped 'Chinatown Food Street' to the out-of-towners and join old-timers and foodies at this nearby labyrinth. The 25-minute wait for mixed claypot rice at **Lian He Ben Ji Claypot Rice** (Stall 02-198/199; dishes S$2.50-20, claypot rice from S$5; ⌚4.30-10pm Fri-Wed) is worth it, while the rich and nutty satay at **Shi Xiang Satay** (Stall 02-79; satay from S$6; ⌚3.30-9pm Fri-Wed) is insane. For a little TLC, opt for Ten Tonic Ginseng Chicken Soup at **Bonne Soup** (Stall 02-05; soups from S$3.70; ⌚10am-8pm).

A LITTLE AFTERNOON DELIGHT

It's hard to resist a long, slow, naughty session of high tea. Not only is it a civilised antidote to Singapore's high speed and higher temperatures, it's the perfect midafternoon recharge.

Landing Point (Map p494; www.fullertonbayhotel.com; Fullerton Bay Hotel, 80 Collyer Quay; high tea per adult S$45, with glass of Champagne S$65, per child S$22; ⌚9am-midnight Sun-Thu, to 1am Fri & Sat, high tea 3-5.30pm; 📶; Ⓜ Raffles Pl) For a decadent high tea, it's hard to beat the one at this chichi waterside lounge. Book ahead (one day for weekdays, two weeks for weekends), style up, and head in on an empty stomach. Steaming pots of TWG tea are paired with drool-inducing morsels like truffled-egg sandwiches, melt-in-your-mouth quiche, brioche buns topped with duck and blueberries, and caramel-filled dark-chocolate tarts.

You won't be able to stop at one, which is just as well, as your stand will be gladly replenished.

Lobby Lounge at The Westin (Map p498; ☎6922 6888; www.thewestinsingapore.com/en/lobbylounge; level 32, The Westin, Asia Square Tower 2, 12 Marina View; high tea for two S$85; ⌚afternoon high tea 2.30-5pm daily; 📶; Ⓜ Downtown) The Westin's good-value seafood and Champagne high tea is divided into three 'courses', with bites like brioche lobster buns and soft-shell crab with avocado salsa followed by freshly shucked oysters and a whole poached lobster. Your epilogue is a tray of sweet delights, from rich chocolate truffles and chocolate-dipped strawberries to citrusy tarts and dreamy eclairs.

Better still, upgrade your glass of French fizz to a bottle and spend a little longer soaking up that sea, skyline and Sentosa Island view. (Book weekend sessions a fortnight in advance.)

Ginza Tendon Itsuki JAPANESE $

(Map p498; ☎6221 6678; 101 Tanjong Pagar Rd; mains S$12.90-13.90; ⏰11.30am-2.30pm & 5.30-10pm; ✍; Ⓜ Tanjong Pagar) Life's few certainties include taxes, death and a queue outside this dedicated *tendon* (tempura served on rice) eatery. Patience is rewarded with cries of *irrashaimase!* (welcome) and generous bowls of Japanese comfort grub. Both the tempura and rice are cooked to perfection, drizzled in sweet and sticky soy sauce, and served with *chawanmushi* (Japanese egg custard), miso soup and pickled vegetables. A cash-only bargain.

Tip: avoid the longest queues by heading in by noon or 7pm.

Ya Kun Kaya Toast CAFE $

(Map p498; www.yakun.com; 01-01 Far East Sq, 18 China St; kaya toast set S$4.80; ⏰7.30am-7pm Mon-Fri, 8.30am-5.30pm Sat & Sun; Ⓜ Telok Ayer) Though it's now part of a chain, this airy, retro coffeeshop is an institution, and the best way to start the day the Singaporean way. The speciality is buttery *kaya* (coconut jam) toast, dipped in runny egg (add black pepper and a few drops of soy sauce) and washed down with strong *kopi* (coffee).

Jing Hua CHINESE $

(Map p498; ☎6221 3060; 21-23 Neil Rd; dishes S$3-10; ⏰11.30am-3pm & 5.30-9.30pm Thu-Tue; Ⓜ Chinatown) Locals outnumber out-of-towners at halogen-and-laminex Jing Hua. Tuck into a limited yet satisfying repertoire of northern Chinese classics, among them plump pork dumplings, noodles with minced pork and soya-bean sauce, and red-bean-paste pancake. Skip the lacklustre *xiao long bao* for the moreish Chinese pizza, a hearty, deep-fried pastry packed with minced prawn, pork and crab, and spring onion. Cash only.

Lucha Loco MEXICAN $$

(Map p498; www.luchaloco.com; 15 Duxton Hill; tacos S$9-11, quesadillas S$16-19; ⏰5-10.15pm Tue-Thu, 5-10.45pm Fri, 6-10.45pm Sat; Ⓜ Outram Park, Tanjong Pagar) On pumping Duxton Hill, Lucha Loco keeps the crowds purring with its flirtatious barkeeps, effortlessly cool vibe and finger-licking Mexican street food. Though we adore the ceviche, tostaditas and addictive *elotes* (corn rolled in mayonnaise and Cotija cheese), it's the tacos that leave us *loco*, generously topped with fresh, beautiful produce. No reservations, so head in early or late, or grab a Mezcal and wait.

Neon Pigeon JAPANESE $$

(Map p498; ☎6222 3623; www.neonpigeonsg.com; 1 Keong Saik Rd; small dishes S$7-20, large dishes S$13-38; ⏰6-11pm Mon-Thu, to 11.30pm Fri & Sat; 📶; Ⓜ Outram Park) Join the crowd at this graffiti-pimped, cocktail-swilling izakaya for produce-driven, finger-licking Japanese sharing plates. Peck your beak at winners like pillow-soft *tsukune* sliders with pickled *kyuri* and tare aioli; slow-cooked octopus with cauliflower purée and *shichimi*; and dreamy, risotto-like house-smoked bacon with crispy pork scratchings, spring onion and egg yolk. Six small dishes between two should suffice. No bookings.

MEATLiquor AMERICAN $$

(Map p498; ☎6221 5343; meatliquor.com/singapore; 99 Duxton Rd; burgers S$16-24; ⏰5-11pm Mon-Wed, to 1am Thu & Fri, to 2am Sat; Ⓜ Outram Park) Hit this dark, thumping hot spot – the hit British chain restaurant's first opening outside the UK – for messy burgers, expletively good fries, and devil-may-care sides like battered pickles. Sip on an oolong float (ice-cream soda) or reach the point of no return with a Game Over (vodka, gin, rum, tequila, triple sec, pisang ambon, absinthe, fresh lemon juice and Red Bull).

No doubt we'll find you in the photo booth, taking questionable selfies. Head in by 7pm or after 9.30pm to avoid the longest waits.

★ **Ding Dong** SOUTHEAST ASIAN $$$

(Map p498; www.dingdong.com.sg; 23 Ann Siang Rd; dishes S$15-25, 'feed me' menus S$56-80; ⏰noon-2.30pm & 6pm-midnight Mon-Fri, 6pm-midnight Sat; Ⓜ Chinatown) From the graphic bar tiles to the meticulous cocktails to the wow-oh-wow modern takes on Southeast Asian flavours, it's all about attention to detail at this sucker-punch champ. Book a table and drool over zingtastic scallop ceviche with fresh coconut, sultry pork *bao* with smoked hoisin, or 48-hour beef-cheek *rendang* with wild puffed rice and crispy herbs.

Good-value options include a weekday three-course set lunch (S$25) and 'feed me' menus for indecisive gourmets.

★ **Momma Kong's** SEAFOOD $$$

(Map p498; ☎6225 2722; www.mommakongs.com; 34 Mosque St; crab dishes S$48, set menu for two from S$107; ⏰5-10pm Mon-Fri, 11am-10pm Sat & Sun; Ⓜ Chinatown) Small, funky Momma Kong's is run by two young brothers and a cousin obsessed with crab. While the compact menu features numerous finger-licking, MSG-free crab classics, opt for the phenomenal chilli crab, its kick and non-gelatinous gravy are unmatched in this town. One serve of crab and four giant, fresh *mantou* (Chinese bread buns) should happily feed two stomachs.

Unlike many other chilli-crab joints, you'll find fixed prices, which means no unpleasant surprises when it's payment time. Book two days ahead (three days for Friday and Saturday) or take a chance and head in late.

★Burnt Ends BARBECUE **$$$**
(Map p498; ☎6224 3933; www.burntends.com.sg; 20 Teck Lim Rd; dishes S$8-45; ⏰6-11pm Tue, 11.45am-2pm & 6-11pm Wed-Sat; Ⓜ Chinatown, Outram Park) The best seats at this perennial hot spot are at the counter, which offers a prime view of chef Dave Pynt and his 4-tonne, wood-fired ovens and custom grills. The affable Aussie cut his teeth under Spanish charcoal deity Victor Arguinzoniz (Asador Etxebarri), an education echoed in the pulled pork shoulder in homemade brioche, and beef marmalade and pickles on chargrilled sourdough.

The produce-driven, sharing-style menu changes daily, while the drinks list showcases smaller wineries and microbreweries. Walk-ins only after 12.30pm at lunch and 6.30pm at dinner.

Little India & Surrounds

Ananda Bhavan INDIAN **$**
(Map p502; www.anandabhavan.com; block 663, 01-10 Buffalo Rd; dosa S$2.60-4.60, set meals S$6-9; ⏰7am-10pm; 🅥; Ⓜ Little India) This super-cheap chain restaurant is a top spot to sample south Indian breakfast staples like *idly* (fermented-rice cakes) and *dosa* (thin, lentil-flour pancake; spelt 'thosai' on the menu). It also does great-value thali, some of which are served on banana leaves. Other outlets are at 58 Serangoon Rd, 95 Syed Alwi Rd and Changi Airport's Terminal 2.

Tekka Centre HAWKER **$**
(Map p502; cnr Serangoon & Buffalo Rds; dishes S$3-10; ⏰7am-11pm; 🅥; Ⓜ Little India, Rochor) There's no shortage of subcontinental spice at this bustling hawker centre, wrapped around the sloshed guts and hacked bones of the wet market. Queue up for real-deal biryani, *dosa*, *roti prata* and *teh tarik* (pulled tea). Well worth seeking out is **Ah-Rahman Royal Prata** (Stall 01-248; murtabak S$4-8; ⏰7am-10pm, closed alternative Mon), which flips some of Singapore's finest *murtabak* (stuffed savoury pancake).

Two Bakers BAKERY **$**
(Map p502; ☎6293 0329; www.facebook.com/twobakers; 88 Horne Rd; pastries & cakes S$6.80-10.90; ⏰11am-9pm Mon, Wed & Thu, 11am-11pm Fri & Sat, 9am-7pm Sun; Ⓜ Lavender) The bakers at this light, contemporary bakery-cafe earned their stripes at Paris' Cordon Bleu. The result? Irresistible sweet treats and countless broken diets. Which tart to choose: the crowd favourite yuzu lemon or the decadent Purple Gold (lavender-infused chocolate ganache, caramel ganache, caramel tuile and roasted almonds)? What the hell: order both!

Moghul Sweets SWEETS **$**
(Map p502; 48 Serangoon Rd; sweets from S$1; ⏰9.30am-9.30pm; Ⓜ Rochor, Little India) If you're after a subcontinental sugar rush, tiny Moghul is the place to get it. Bite into luscious *gulab jamun* (syrup-soaked fried dough balls), harder-to-find *rasmalai* (paneer cheese soaked in cardamom-infused clotted cream) and *barfi* (condensed milk and sugar slice) in flavours including pistachio, chocolate...and carrot.

★Lagnaa Barefoot Dining INDIAN **$$**
(Map p502; ☎6296 1215; www.lagnaa.com; 6 Upper Dickson Rd; dishes S$6-22; ⏰11.30am-10pm; 📶; Ⓜ Little India) You can choose your level of spice at friendly Lagnaa: level three denotes standard spiciness, level four significant spiciness, and anything above admirable bravery. Whatever level you opt for, you're in for finger-licking good homestyle cooking from both ends of Mother India, devoured at Western seating downstairs or on floor cushions upstairs. If you're indecisive, order chef Kaesavan's famous Threadfin fish curry.

Suprette AMERICAN **$$**
(Map p502; ☎6298 8962; www.suprette.com; 383 Jln Besar; dishes S$10-45; ⏰7.30am-3pm & 6-10.30pm Mon, Wed & Thu, 7.30am-3pm Tue, 7.30am-3pm & 6pm-midnight Fri, 7.30am-4pm & 6pm-midnight Sat, 7.30am-4pm & 6-10.30pm Sun; 📶; 🚌65, 145, 857, Ⓜ Farrer Park) With a look that's part retro diner, part retro shophouse, Suprette serves up American-inspired, globally influenced comfort grub that's fresh and generous. Tuck into luscious breakfast *shakshuka* (eggs poached in spicy tomato sauce with feta and lamb sausage), lunchtime baby-spinach salad with poached egg and

brioche or, come dinner, the devil-may-care, Gruyère-licious Suprette Burger.

Kampong Glam & Surrounds

★Zam Zam MALAYSIAN $
(Map p502; 699 North Bridge Rd; murtabak from S$5, dishes S$4-20; ⏲7am-11pm; Ⓜ Bugis) These guys have been here since 1908, so they know what they're doing. Tenure hasn't bred complacency, though – the touts still try to herd customers in off the street while frenetic chefs inside whip up delicious *murtabak*, the restaurant's speciality savoury pancakes, filled with succulent mutton, chicken, beef, venison or even sardines.

Servings are epic, so order a medium between two.

Warong Nasi Pariaman MALAYSIAN, INDONESIAN $
(Map p502; ☎6292 2374; 742 North Bridge Rd; dishes from S$4.50; ⏲7.30am-2.30pm Mon-Sat; Ⓜ Bugis) This no-frills corner *nasi padang* (rice with curries) stall is the stuff of legend. Top choices include the *belado* (fried mackerel in a slow-cooked chilli, onion and vinegar sauce), delicate *rendang* beef and *ayam bakar* (grilled chicken with coconut sauce). Get here by 11am to avoid the hordes. And be warned: most of it sells out by 1pm (10am Saturday).

QS269 Food House HAWKER $
(Map p502; block 269B, Queen St; ⏲stalls vary; Ⓜ Bugis) This is not so much a 'food house' as a loud, crowded undercover laneway lined with cult-status stalls. Work up a sweat with a bowl of award-winning coconut-curry noodle soup from **Ah Heng Curry Chicken Bee Hoon Mee** (Stall 01-236; dishes from S$4; ⏲8am-4.30pm Sat-Thu) or join the queue at **New Rong Liang Ge Cantonese Roast Duck Boiled Soup** (Stall 01-235; dishes from S$2.50; ⏲7am-8pm), with succulent roast-duck dishes that draw foodies from across the city.

Ya Kun Kaya Toast CAFE
(Map p502; www.yakun.com; B1-11, Bugis Junction, 230 Victoria St; kaya-toast set S$4.80; ⏲7.30am-9.30pm; Ⓜ Bugis) In the basement food hall of Bugis Junction mall, this respected local chain is a solid spot for a traditional local breakfast of *kopi* and *kaya* toast. Don't forget to add a splash of soy sauce and black pepper to the runny eggs before dunking your toast! Don't be put off by the queues – they usually move fast.

Nan Hwa Chong Fish-Head Steamboat Corner CHINESE $$
(Map p502; 812-816 North Bridge Rd; fish steamboats from S$28; ⏲4.30pm-12.15am; Ⓜ Lavender) If you only try fish-head steamboat once, do it at this noisy, open-fronted veteran. Cooked on charcoal, the large pot of fish heads is brought to you in steaming *tee po* (dried flat sole fish) spiked broth. One pot is enough for three or four people, and can stretch to more with rice and side dishes.

There are several fish types to choose from; the grouper is the most popular with locals.

★Kilo FUSION $$$
(☎6467 3987; www.kilokitchen.com; 66 Kampong Bugis; sharing plates S$15-28, mains S$26-48; ⏲6-10.15pm Mon-Sat; Ⓜ Lavender) Despite Singapore's cut-throat restaurant scene, gastro geeks remain loyal to this swinging ode to fusion cooking. Expect the unexpected, from beef-tongue tacos with apple-miso slaw to goat-cheese and ricotta gnocchi in the pan with *maitake*, brown-miso butter and *shiso*. A little tricky to find, the restaurant occupies the 2nd floor of a lone industrial building on the Kallang River; take a taxi.

Bill settled, head up to level eight for cocktails at in-spot Kilo Lounge (p545).

Orchard Road

Burrow into most Orchard Rd malls and you'll find great-value food courts.

Food Republic FAST FOOD $
(Map p506; level 4, Wisma Atria, 435 Orchard Rd; dishes S$4-15; ⏲10am-10pm Sun-Thu, to 11pm Fri & Sat; Ⓜ Orchard) A cornucopia of street food in air-conditioned comfort. Muck in with the rest of the crowd for seats before joining the longest queues for dishes spanning Japan, Korea and Thailand, to India, Indonesia and, quite rightly, Singapore.

Takashimaya Food Village FAST FOOD $
(Map p506; www.takashimaya.com.sg; B2, Takashimaya Department Store, Ngee Ann City, 391 Orchard Rd; dishes S$4-17; ⏲10am-9.30pm; Ⓜ Orchard) In the basement of Japanese department store Takashimaya, this polished, expansive food hall serves up a *Who's Who* of Japanese and other Asian culinary classics. If comfort food is on the agenda, order a fragrant bowl of noodles from the Tsuru-koshi stand. The hall is also home to a large Cold Storage supermarket.

Killiney Kopitiam CAFE $
(Map p506; 67 Killiney Rd; dishes S$1.20-7; ⏲6am-11pm Mon & Wed-Sat, to 6pm Tue & Sun; Ⓜ Somerset) Start the day the old-school way at this veteran coffee joint, pimped with endearingly lame laminated jokes. Order a strong *kopi*, a serve of *kaya* toast, and a side of soft-boiled egg. Crack open the latter, add a dash of soy sauce and pepper, then dip your *kaya* toast in it.

★**Tim Ho Wan** DIM SUM $$
(Map p506; Plaza Singapura, 68 Orchard Rd; dishes from S$3.80; ⏲10am-9.30pm Mon-Fri, 9am-9.30pm Sat & Sun; Ⓜ Dhoby Ghaut) Hong Kong's Michelin-starred dim-sum seller is steaming in Singapore, with the same Mong Kok queues (head in after 8.30pm) and tick-the-boxes order form. While nothing compares to the original (the Singapore branches need to import many ingredients), the recipes are the same and the results still pretty spectacular. Must-trys include the sugary buns with barbecue pork and the perky prawn dumplings.

Paradise Dynasty CHINESE $$
(Map p506; www.paradisegroup.com.sg; 04-12A, ION Orchard, 2 Orchard Turn; dishes S$4-25; ⏲11am-9.30pm Mon-Fri, from 10.30am Sat & Sun; Ⓜ Orchard) Preened staffers in headsets whisk you into this svelte dumpling den, passing a glassed-in kitchen where Chinese chefs stretch their noodles and steam their buns. Skip the novelty flavoured *xiao long bao* (soup dumplings) for the original version, which arguably beat those of legendary competitor Din Tai Fung. Beyond these, standouts include *la mian* (hand-pulled noodles) with buttery, braised pork belly.

Tambuah Mas INDONESIAN $$
(Map p506; ☎6733 2220; www.tambuahmas.com.sg; B1-44, Paragon, 290 Orchard Rd; mains S$7.50-29; ⏲11am-9.30pm; 📶; Ⓜ Orchard) Hiding shyly in a corner of the Paragon's food-packed basement, Tambuah Mas is where Indonesian expats head for a taste of home. Bright, modern and good value for Orchard Rd, it proudly makes much of what it serves from scratch, a fact evident in what could possibly be Singapore's best beef *rendang*. No reservations, so head in early if dining Thursday to Saturday.

Wild Honey CAFE $$
(Map p506; www.wildhoney.com.sg; 03-02, Mandarin Gallery, 333A Orchard Rd; dishes S$12-35; ⏲9am-9.30pm Sun-Thu, to 10.30pm Fri & Sat; 🖉; Ⓜ Somerset) Industrial-style windows, concrete floors and plush designer furniture: airy, contemporary Wild Honey serves scrumptious all-day breakfasts from around the world, from the smoked salmon–laced Norwegian to the *shakshuka*-spiced Tunisian. Other options include muesli, gourmet sandwiches and freshly roasted coffee. Consider booking a day in advance if heading in on weekends. Second branch inside Scotts Square mall, just off Orchard Rd.

★**Iggy's** FUSION $$$
(Map p506; ☎6732 2234; www.iggys.com.sg; level 3, Hilton Hotel, 581 Orchard Rd; 3-course lunch S$85, set dinner menus S$195-275; ⏲noon-1.30pm & 7-9.30pm Mon, Tue & Thu-Sat; 🖉; Ⓜ Orchard) Iggy's dark, slinky design promises something special, and head chef Masahiro Isono delivers with his arresting, poetic takes on fusion flavours. Menus are tweaked according to season, though the knockout capellini with *sakura ebi* (shrimp), *konbu* (kelp) and shellfish oil is always on call to blow gastronomes away. Superlatives extend to the wine list, one of the city's finest.

★**Buona Terra** ITALIAN $$$
(Map p506; ☎6733 0209; www.scotts29.com/buonaterra; 29 Scotts Rd; 3-course set lunch S$38, 3-/4-/5-/6-course dinner S$88/108/128/148; ⏲noon-2.30pm & 6-10.15pm Mon-Fri, 6-10.15pm Sat; 📶; Ⓜ Newton) This intimate, linen-lined Italian is one of Singapore's unsung glories. In the kitchen is young Lombard chef Denis Lucchi, who turns exceptional ingredients into elegant, modern dishes like Parmesan crème brûlée with truffle caviar and yellowtail carpaccio with pomegranate, blood orange and fennel. Lucchi's right-hand man is Emilian sommelier Gabriele Rizzardi, whose wine list, though expensive, is extraordinary.

If you're a gourmand on a budget, opt for the weekday set-lunch menu, which offers three courses for S$38. Book ahead if heading in on Friday or Saturday evening.

Dempsey Hill & Botanic Gardens

PS Cafe INTERNATIONAL $$
(☎9070 8782; www.pscafe.com; 28B Harding Rd; mains S$26-34; ⏲11.30am-3.30pm & 6.30-10.30pm Mon-Fri, 9.30am-3.30pm & 6.30-10.30pm Sat & Sun; 🖉; 🚌7, 75, 77, 105, 106, 123, 174) A chic, light-filled tropical oasis of wooden floorboards, floor-to-ceiling windows and patio tables facing thick tropical foliage. From

brunch to dinner, edibles are beautiful and healthy, whether it's fish croquette Benedict or a 'Morocco miracle stack' of roasted portobello mushroom, grilled vegetables, smoked eggplant and couscous. No bookings taken for weekend brunch; head in at 9.30am to avoid the longest queues.

Casa Verde INTERNATIONAL **$$**
(Map p506; www.casaverde.com.sg; Singapore Botanic Gardens, 1 Cluny Rd; lunch S$9.50-19.50, pizza S$24, dinner mains S$25-35; 7.30am-9.30pm; ; Botanic Gardens) The most accessible restaurant in the Botanic Gardens, 'Green House' serves up acceptable Western grub – pasta, salads, sandwiches – plus woodfired pizzas (not for pizza snobs) and a smattering of local dishes. It's family friendly, too: the lunch menu has a special kids' section, as well as burgers, nuggets, hot dogs and pizzas, and the dinner menu has pasta and pizza options.

Open Farm Community INTERNATIONAL **$$$**
(6471 0306; www.openfarmcommunity.com; 130E Minden Rd; mains S$26-38; noon-2.30pm & 6-10pm Mon-Fri, 11am-10pm Sat & Sun; 7, 75, 77, 105, 106, 123, 174) In a revamped greenhouse scattered with designer furniture and glowing ladies-who-lunch, Open Farm Community puts a tropical spin on the farm-to-table concept. Hand-picked herbs and vegetables from the garden lace a menu of clean, vibrant, comforting creations. From the fermented-carrot tartare to housemade tortellini with pumpkin, pine nuts and local yabbies, dishes sing with intense, natural, life-affirming flavour.

Chopsuey CHINESE **$$$**
(9224 6611; www.chopsueycafe.com; Block 10, Dempsey Rd; dumplings S$7-12; 11.30-4pm & 6.30-10.30pm Mon-Fri, 10.30am-4pm & 6.30-10.30pm Sat & Sun; 7, 75, 77, 105, 106, 123, 174) Swirling ceiling fans, crackly 1930s tunes and ladies on rattan chairs – Chopsuey has colonial chic down pat. It serves revamped versions of retro American-Chinese dishes, but the real highlight is the lunchtime yum cha; standouts include Sichuan pepper-chilli tofu, pumpkin and cod dumplings, and *san choi bao* (minced meat in lettuce cups). The marble bar is perfect for solo diners.

Long Beach Seafood SEAFOOD **$$$**
(6323 2222; www.longbeachseafood.com.sg; 01-01, 25 Dempsey Rd; crab per kilogram around S$72; 11am-12.30am; 7, 75, 77, 105, 106, 123, 174) One of Singapore's top seafood-restaurant chains. Settle in on the veranda, gaze out at the tropical greenery and tackle the cult-status black-pepper crab. The original Long Beach lays claim to inventing the iconic dish, and the version here is fantastically peppery and earthy. Best of all, the kitchen is open later than many restaurants in town.

East Coast

★ **328 Katong Laksa** PERANAKAN **$**
(Map p508; www.328katonglaksa.com.sg; 51/53 East Coast Rd; laksa from S$5; 8am-10pm; 10, 14) For a bargain foodie high, hit this cult-status corner shop. The star is the namesake laksa: thin rice noodles in a light curry broth made with coconut milk and Vietnamese coriander, and topped with shrimps and cockles. Order a side of *otak-otak* (spiced mackerel cake grilled in a banana leaf) and wash it all down with a cooling glass of lime juice.

East Coast Lagoon Food Village HAWKER **$**
(Map p508; 1220 East Coast Parkway; dishes from S$3; generally 1-10pm; 36, 196, 197, 401) There are few hawker centres with a better location. Tramp barefoot off the beach, find a table (note the table number for when you order), then trawl the stalls for staples like satay, laksa, stingray, and the uniquely Singaporean *satay bee hoon* (rice noodles in a chilli-based peanut sauce). Cheap beer and wine (!) available.

Changi Village Hawker Centre HAWKER **$**
(2 Changi Village Rd; dishes from S$3; stalls vary; Tanah Merah, then bus 2) Located in chilled-out Changi Village, this is the most Malay of Singapore's food centres, with locals heading here for one thing: the *nasi lemak* (fragrant coconut rice topped with fried chicken or fish, fried anchovies and sambal chilli). While food bloggers never cease arguing about which stall does it best, the original **International Nasi Lemak** (stall 01-03; nasi lemak from $3; 8am-3pm & 6pm-midnight Mon-Fri, 8.30am-9pm Sat, varies Sun) gets the most loving.

Rochor Beancurd DESSERTS **$**
(Map p508; 745 Geylang Rd; dough sticks S$1, bean curd from S$1.40; 24hr; ; Paya Lebar) This tiny bolthole has an epic reputation. People head here from all over the city for a bowl of its obscenely fresh, silky beancurd (opt for it warm). Order a side of deep-fried dough

sticks and dip to your heart's content. Oh, and did we mention the egg tarts?

Chin Mee Chin Confectionery BAKERY $
(Map p508; 204 East Coast Rd; kaya toast & coffee from S$2.90; 8am-4pm Tue-Sun; ; 10, 12, 14, 32, 40) A nostalgia trip for many older Singaporeans, old-style bakeries like Chin Mee Chin are a dying breed, with their geometric floors, wooden chairs and industrious aunties pouring suckerpunch *kopi*. One of the few Singaporean breakfast joints that still makes its own *kaya*, it's also a good spot to pick up some pastries to go.

Smokey's BBQ AMERICAN $$
(Map p508; 6345 6914; www.smokeysbbq.com.sg; 73 Joo Chiat Pl; mains S$19-43; 3-10pm Tue-Thu, 11.30am-10.30pm Fri-Sun; ; 16, 33, M Eunos) You'll be longing for sweet home Alabama at this breezy, all-American barbecue legend. Californian owner Rob makes all the dry rubs using secret recipes and the meats are smoked using hickory and mesquite woodchips straight from the USA. Start with the spicy buffalo wings with blue-cheese dipping sauce, then stick to slow-roasted, smoked meats like ridiculously tender, fall-off-the-bone ribs.

Long Phuong VIETNAMESE $$
(Map p508; 159 Joo Chiat Rd; dishes S$7-23; 11am-11pm; 33, M Eunos) Yellow plastic chairs, easy-wipe tables and staff shouting out orders: down-to-earth Long Phuong serves up Singapore's best Vietnamese food. The *pho* (Vietnamese noodle soup) is simply gorgeous, its fragrant broth featuring just the right amount of sweetness. Beyond it is a mouthwatering choice of real-deal classics, including mango salad and a very popular *sò huyêt xào sa tê* (cockles with satay). Cash only.

West & Southwest Singapore

Red Baron CAFE $$
(www.redbaronsg.com; 45 Malan Rd; mains S$14-16; 11am-6pm Sat-Thu, to 10pm Fri, kitchen closes 5.30pm; ; M Labrador Park) You'll find this affable, pocket-sized cafe-bakery-bar in the leafy Gillman Barracks gallery district. The menu is small, straightforward and scrumptious, covering all bases from buckwheat pancakes paired with Greek yogurt, mixed-berry compote and agave syrup to a virtuous quinoa *goreng*. Upstaging the lot is a counter of insanely decadent cakes: peanut-butter tart, anyone?

★ Tamarind Hill THAI $$$
(6278 6364; www.tamarindrestaurants.com; 30 Labrador Villa Rd; mains S$22-59, Sun brunch S$60; noon-2.30pm & 6.30-10.30pm; ; 408, M Labrador Park) In a colonial bungalow in Labrador Park, Tamarind Hill sets an elegant scene for exceptional Thai. The highlight is the Sunday brunch (noon to 3pm), which offers a buffet of beautiful cold dishes and salads, as well as the ability to order as many dishes off the à la carte menu as you like (the sautéed squid is sublime). Book ahead.

Sentosa Island

Malaysian Food Street HAWKER $
(Map p514; www.rwsentosa.com; Resorts World; dishes from S$5; 11am-10pm Mon-Thu, 9am-11pm Fri & Sat, 9am-10pm Sun; M HarbourFront, then monorail to Waterfront) With its faux-Malaysian streetscape, this indoor hawker centre beside Universal Studios feels a bit artificial. Thankfully, there's nothing fake about the food, cooked by some of Malaysia's best hawker vendors.

Kith Cafe CAFE $$
(Map p514; www.kith.com.sg; 31 Ocean Way, Sentosa Cove; lunch mains S$15-25, dinner mains S$22-38; 8am-10pm Wed-Mon; ; M HarbourFront, then monorail to Beach) Order a freshly squeezed juice (chia seeds optional), grab a copy of *Kinfolk* and scan the million-dollar yachts moored before you at this breezy, kid-friendly cafe. Ditch the 'egg and optional sides' for bigger, more satisfying offerings like the Kith Breakfast. Beyond these are house-baked cakes, and decent lunch and dinner dishes spanning grilled sandwiches, pastas and Angus rib-eye steak.

★ Knolls EUROPEAN $$$
(Map p514; 6591 5046; www.capellahotels.com/singapore; Capella, 1 The Knolls; Sun brunch from S$128, children from S$48; 7am-11pm, Sun brunch 12.30-3pm; M HarbourFront, then monorail to Imbiah) Free-flow-alcohol Sunday brunch is huge in Singapore, and this posh, secluded spot – complete with strutting peacocks and roaming band – serves one of the best (S$148). Style up and join the fabulous for scrumptious buffet bites like freshly shucked oysters, blue-cheese and pumpkin liégeois, spicy cappellini with quail egg and prawns and foie-gras brûlée. Leave room for Grand Marnier profiteroles and snow eggs. Book one week ahead.

Drinking & Nightlife

You'll find many of Singapore's hottest bars in Chinatown, especially on Club St and Ann Siang Rd, Duxton Hill, and up-and-coming Keong Saik Rd. Chinatown's Neil Rd is home to a handful of swinging gay venues. Other popular drinking spots include bohemian-spirited Kampong Glam, heritage-listed Emerald Hill Rd (just off Orchard Rd), leafy expat enclave Dempsey, and hyper-touristy Boat and Clarke Quays.

Bars generally open around 5pm until at least midnight Sunday to Thursday, and through to 2am or 3am on Friday and Saturday. All prices listed in these reviews exclude taxes.

Most clubs have cover charges of around S$15 to S$40, often including at least one drink; women sometimes pay less (or even nothing!). Also, check out Super 0 (www.super0.sg), which runs pop-up dance parties, usually at the beginning or end of the year. For club events, see www.timeoutsingapore.com/clubs.

Colonial District, the Quays & Marina Bay

★Lantern — BAR

(Map p494; ☎6597 5299; Fullerton Bay Hotel, 80 Collyer Quay; ⏱8am-1am Sun-Thu, to 2am Fri & Sat; Ⓜ Raffles Pl) It may be lacking in height (it's dwarfed by the surrounding CBD buildings) and serves its drinks in plastic glasses (scandalous!), but Lantern remains a magical spot for a sophisticated evening toast. Why? There are the flickering lanterns, the shimmering, glass-sided pool (for Fullerton Bay Hotel guests only), and the romantic views over Marina Bay.

Southbridge — BAR

(Map p494; ☎6877 6965; level 5, 80 Boat Quay; ⏱5-11.30pm; Ⓜ Clarke Quay) Rising above the glut of mediocre Boat Quay bars, this discerning rooftop hangout delivers a panorama guaranteed to loosen jaws. Scan skyline and river with a Lust, Caution (Sichuan pepper–infused gin, Cynar, lemon and soda), or taste-test an interesting selection of spirits that include Nardini grappa and Nikka Taketsuru whisky. Entry is via the back alley, which runs off South Bridge Rd.

Level 33 — MICROBREWERY

(Map p494; www.level33.com.sg; level 33, Marina Bay Financial Tower 1, 8 Marina Blvd; ⏱noon-midnight Sun-Thu, noon-2am Fri & Sat; 📶; Ⓜ Downtown) In a country obsessed with unique selling points, this one takes the cake – no, keg. Laying claim to being the world's highest 'urban craft brewery', Level 33 brews its own lager, pale ale, stout, porter and wheat beer. It's all yours to slurp alfresco with a jaw-dropping view over Marina Bay. Bargain hunters, take note: beers are cheaper before 8pm.

Wine Connection — WINE BAR

(Map p494; www.wineconnection.com.sg; 01-06 Robertson Walk, 11 Unity St; ⏱11am-2am Mon-Thu, to 3am Fri & Sat, to midnight Sun; 📶; 🚌64, 123, 143) Oenophiles love this savvy wine store and bar at Robertson Quay. The team works closely with winemakers across the world, which means no intermediary, an interesting wine list, and very palatable prices: glasses from S$7 and bottles as low as S$30. Edibles include decent salads and tartines, not to mention top-notch cheeses from Wine Connection's fabulously stinky, next-door Cheese Bar.

Zouk — CLUB

(www.zoukclub.com; 17 Jiak Kim St; ⏱Zouk & Phuture 11pm-late Wed, Fri & Sat, Velvet Underground 11pm-late Fri & Sat, Wine Bar 6pm-2am Tue, 6pm-3am Wed-Sat; 🚌5, 16, 75, 175, 195, 970) Set to move to Clarke Quay (at Block C, The Cannery, River Valley Rd) in May 2016, Singapore's premier club draws some of the world's biggest DJs. Choose between the multilevel main club, the hip-hop-centric Phuture or the plush Velvet Underground, slung with original artworks by Andy Warhol, Frank Stella and Takashi Murakami. Take a taxi, and prepare to queue.

Attica — CLUB

(Map p494; www.attica.com.sg; 01-03 Clarke Quay, 3A River Valley Rd; ⏱Level One 10.30pm-4am Wed, Fri & Sat, Level Two 11pm-5am Wed, 11pm-5.30am Fri & Sat, outdoor bar 6pm-late Tue-Sat; Ⓜ Clarke Quay) Attica has secured a loyal following among Singapore's fickle clubbers, modelling itself on New York's hippest clubs but losing the attitude somewhere over the Pacific. Locals will tell you it's where the expats go to pick up on the weekends, mostly in the courtyard. Beats span chart hits, house and R&B; check the website for themed nights.

Loof — BAR

(Map p494; ☎9773 9304; www.loof.com.sg; 03-07 Odeon Towers Bldg, 331 North Bridge Rd; ⏱5pm-1am Mon-Thu, to 2am Fri & Sat; 📶; Ⓜ City Hall) Red neon warmly declares 'Glad you came up' at upbeat Loof, its name the Singlish mangling of the word 'roof'. Sit on the leafy rooftop deck and look out over the Raffles Hotel and Marina Bay Sands with a calamansi-spiked Singapore sour in hand. The great-value weekday happy hour lasts from 5pm to 8pm, with the cheapest drinks early on.

Ronin CAFE
(Map p494; 17 Hongkong St; ⌚8am-6pm Mon-Fri, to 7.30pm Sat & Sun; Ⓜ Clarke Quay) Ronin hides its talents behind a dark, tinted-glass door. Walk through and the brutalist combo of grey concrete, exposed plumbing and low-slung lamps might leave you expecting some tough-talking interrogation. Thankfully, the only thing you'll get slapped with is smooth Australian Genovese coffee and T2 speciality teas. Simple food options include jam and toast and gourmet panini. Cash only.

Orgo BAR
(Map p494; ☎6336 9366; www.orgo.sg; 4th fl, Esplanade Roof Tce, 8 Raffles Ave; ⌚6pm-1.30am; Ⓜ Esplanade, City Hall) It's hard not to feel like the star of a Hollywood rom-com at rooftop Orgo, its view of the skyline so commanding you'll almost feel obliged to play out a tear-jerking scene. Don't. Instead, slip into a wicker armchair, order a vino (you'll get better cocktails elsewhere) and Instagram the view to the sound of soft conversation and sultry tunes.

Raffles Hotel BAR
(Map p494; www.raffles.com; 1 Beach Rd; Ⓜ City Hall) Granted, the prices are exorbitant, but there's something undeniably fabulous about an afternoon cocktail amid white-washed colonial architecture and thick, tropical foliage. Ditch the gloomy, clichéd **Long Bar** (⌚11am-12.30am Sun-Thu, to 1.30am Fri & Sat) for the fountain-graced **Raffles Courtyard** (⌚noon-10.30pm) or sip Raj-style on the veranda at the **Bar & Billiard Room** (⌚5-11pm Tue-Thu, 5pm-1am Fri & Sat, noon-3pm Sun). Tip: pass on the sickly-sweet Singapore sling for something more palatable, like the autumn sling.

Chinatown & the CBD

★ **Operation Dagger** COCKTAIL BAR
(Map p498; operationdagger.com; 7 Ann Siang Hill; ⌚6pm-late Tue-Sat; Ⓜ Chinatown) From the 'cloud-like' light sculpture to the boundary-pushing cocktails, 'extraordinary' is the keyword here. To encourage experimentation, libations are described by flavour, not spirit, the latter shelved in uniform, apothecary-like bottles. Whether you sample the sesame-infused complexity of the Gomashio, the textural surprise of the Hot & Cold or the bar's raw chocolate-infused vino, prepare to fall deeply in love.

★ **Potato Head Folk** COCKTAIL BAR
(Map p498; ☎6327 1939; www.pttheadfolk.com; 36 Keong Saik Rd; ⌚Studio 1939 & rooftop bar 5pm-midnight Tue-Sun; 📶; Ⓜ Outram Park) Offshoot of the legendary Bali bar, this standout, multi-level playground incorporates three spaces, all reached via a chequered stairwell pimped with creepy storybook murals and giant glowing dolls. Skip the Three Buns burger joint and head straight for the dark, plush glamour of cocktail lounge Studio 1939 or the laidback frivolity of the rooftop tiki bar.

Tippling Club COCKTAIL BAR
(Map p498; ☎6475 2217; www.tipplingclub.com; 38 Tanjong Pagar Rd; ⌚noon-midnight Mon-Fri, 6pm-midnight Sat; Ⓜ Outram Park, Tanjong Pagar) Tippling Club propels mixology to dizzying

A CULTURED POUR: CHINATOWN'S TEAHOUSES

For soothing cultural enlightenment, slip into one of Chinatown's atmospheric teahouses.

Yixing Xuan Teahouse (Map p498; www.yixingxuan-teahouse.com; 60 Tanjong Pagar Rd; ⌚10am-9pm Mon-Sat, to 7pm Sun; Ⓜ Tanjong Pagar) Banker-turned-tea purveyor Vincent Low is the man behind this venture, happily educating visitors about Chinese tea and the art of tea drinking. To immerse yourself more deeply, book a tea-ceremony demonstration with tastings (S$25, 45 minutes).

Tea Chapter (Map p498; ☎6226 1175; www.teachapter.com; 9-11 Neil Rd; ⌚teahouse 11am-10.30pm Sun-Thu, to 11pm Fri & Sat, shop 10.30am-10.30pm daily; Ⓜ Chinatown) Queen Elizabeth and Prince Philip dropped by this tranquil teahouse in 1989, and for S$10 you can sit at the table they sipped at. A minimum charge of S$8 per person will get you a heavenly pot of loose-leaf tea, prepared with traditional precision. The selection is excellent and the adjoining shop sells tea and a selection of beautiful tea sets.

heights, with a technique and creativity that could turn a teetotaller into a born-again soak. The best seats are at the bar, where under a ceiling of hanging bottles, passionate pros turn rare and precious spirits into wonders like the Smokey Old Bastard, a mellow concoction of whisky, Peychaud's Bitters, cigar and orange.

L'Aiglon COCKTAIL BAR

(Map p498; ☎6220 0369; www.facebook.com/barlaiglon; 69 Neil Rd; ⊙6pm-1am Mon-Thu, to 2am Fri & Sat; Ⓜ Outram Park, Chinatown) After a stint as a filmmaker and photographer in LA, Frenchman Pierre-Emmanuel Plassart hit Singapore and opened this sultry cocktail joint. Beyond its elegantly crafted, updated classics, the bar offers its own bottled libations. Among these is the ingenious Back Bone Tea, a gingery, gin-based take on *bak kut teh* (pork-bone tea soup), complete with specially ground *bak kut teh* herbs.

Good Beer Company BEER STALL

(Map p498; 02-58, Chinatown Complex, 11 New Bridge Rd; ⊙6-10pm Mon-Sat; Ⓜ Chinatown) Injecting Chinatown Complex with a dose of new-school cool, this hawker-centre beer stall has an impressive booty of bottled craft suds, from Japanese Hitachino Nest to Belgian Trappistes Rochefort. A few stalls down is **Smith Street Taps** (⊙6.30-10.30pm Tue-Sat), run by a friendly dude and offering a rotating selection of craft and premium beers on tap.

Bitters & Love COCKTAIL BAR

(Map p498; ☎6438 1836; www.bittersandlove.com; 118 Telok Ayer St; ⊙6pm-midnight Mon-Thu, to 2am Fri & Sat; Ⓜ Telok Ayer) Look for the bottle-shaped lights, swing open the door and dive into this affable, oft-damn-loud cocktail den, home to some of the city's top barkeeps. Forget the drinks list. Simply rattle off your mood, favourite flavours or spirit base and let the team work their magic. For something local, request a rum-based, tea-infused Kaya Toast.

Jekyll & Hyde COCKTAIL BAR

(Map p498; www.49tras.st; 49 Tras St; ⊙5pm-1am Sun-Thu, to 3am Fri & Sat; Ⓜ Tanjong Pagar) Jekyll & Hyde splits itself into two spaces – buzzing back bar and milder-mannered front space tailored for more tranquil tête-à-têtes. Whichever you choose, expect inspired libations like the strangely seductive Mr Bean (fresh bean curd, vodka, kaya, butterscotch liqueur and Frangelico). For a classic high, order a G&T, made with cognoscenti gins, spiked with rosemary, and served in big, bowl-like glasses.

Oxwell & Co BAR

(Map p498; www.oxwellandco.com; 5 Ann Siang Rd; ⊙11am-midnight; 📶; Ⓜ Chinatown) Laced with cockfighting posters, machinery-turned-furniture and exposed copper pipes, jumping Oxwell & Co feels like a saloon crossed with a vintage workshop. Happy-hour deals (4pm to 8pm daily) include S$10 cocktails on tap. If it's on offer, try the brilliant Gin & Chronic, a sprightly blend of clove- and nutmeg-infused gin, soda water and fresh calamansi.

Other offerings include lesser-known beers, solid wines, and appetite-piquing bar bites like house-marinated olives, Ortiz anchovies and toast, and sambal wings.

1-Altitude BAR

(Map p498; www.1-altitude.com; level 63, 1 Raffles Pl; admission incl 1 drink S$30; ⊙6pm-late; Ⓜ Raffles Pl) Wedged across a triangle-shaped deck 282m above street level, this is the world's highest alfresco bar, its 360-degree panorama taking in soaring towers, colonial landmarks and a ship-clogged sea. Women enjoy free entry and all-night S$10 martinis on Wednesday, while Turn Back Thursday pumps out '80s, '90s and '00s hits. Dress up: no shorts or open shoes, gents.

Kyō CLUB

(Map p498; www.clubkyo.com; B2-01, Keck Seng Tower, 133 Cecil St; ⊙9pm-3am Wed & Thu, 9pm-3.30am Fri, 10.30pm-4.30am Sat; Ⓜ Telok Ayer, Raffles Pl) From boring bank to pulsating hot spot, this sprawling, Japanese-inspired playpen is home to Singapore's longest bar (expect the odd bar-top booty shake), suited eye-candy, and sharp DJs spinning credible electro, house, funk or disco. If you're itching for a little midweek hedonism, you know where to go.

Lepark BAR

(Map p498; www.facebook.com/leparksg; level 6, People's Park Complex, 1 Park Cres; ⊙4-11pm Tue-Fri, 11am-11pm Sat & Sun; Ⓜ Chinatown) After a bargain foot rub on level three of People's Park Complex, head to level six for Singapore's sneakiest rooftop bar, Lepark. A play on the word *lepak* (Malay for 'hanging out'), its caf-style tables, separate bar and food counters and graffiti-sprayed walls scream hipster canteen. Craft beers are the forte, with a huge selection of bottled options and four on tap.

Plain CAFE
(Map p498; www.theplain.com.sg; 50 Craig Rd; 7.30am-5.30pm Mon-Fri, to 7.30pm Sat & Sun; M Tanjong Pagar) A high-cred combo of stark interiors, neatly piled *Monocle* magazines and a Scandi-style communal table, the Plain keeps hipsters and ad-agency types buzzing with Melbourne Genovese coffee, decent all-day breakfasts (from S$4) and sweet treats like salted-caramel brownies. Service is friendly and the vibe refreshingly relaxed.

Backstage Bar BAR, LGBT
(Map p498; www.backstagebar.moonfruit.com; 74 Neil Rd; 6pm-midnight; M Chinatown, Outram Park) Chinatown's veteran gay bar has found new life in a converted Neil Rd shophouse, complete with snug alfresco courtyard and a splash of Broadway posters. Much friendlier than neighbouring gay bar Tantric, it's a top spot to chat, flirt or just sit back and people watch. Entry is via the side alley.

Taboo CLUB, LGBT
(Map p498; www.taboo.sg; 65 Neil Rd; 8pm-2am Wed & Thu, 10pm-3am Fri, 10pm-4am Sat; M Outram Park, Chinatown) Conquer the dance floor at what remains the favourite gay club in town. Expect the requisite line-up of shirtless gyrators, doting straight women and regular racy themed nights. Note: only the chillout lounge is open on Wednesday and Thursday nights.

Kampong Glam & Little India

★**Maison Ikkoku** CAFE, COCKTAIL BAR
(Map p502; www.maison-ikkoku.net; 20 Kandahar St; cafe 9am-10pm Mon-Thu, to midnight Fri & Sat, to 8pm Sun, bar 6pm-1am Mon-Thu, to 2am Fri-Sun; ; M Bugis) Pimped with suspended dressers, Maison Ikkoku's cafe flies the flag for third-wave coffee, with brewing options including Chemex, siphon, cold drip, V60, AeroPress and seasonal-blend espresso. The real magic happens in the upstairs cocktail bar, where a request for something sour might land you a tart, hot combo of spicy gin, grape, lemon and Japanese-chilli threads. Not cheap but well worth it.

★**Kilo Lounge** BAR
(66 Kampong Bugis; 5.30pm-late Tue-Sat; M Lavender) In an isolated, riverside building, six floors above cult-status restaurant Kilo, this is one of Singapore's hottest drinking spots. Elevator doors swing open onto a concrete loft, slung with art and leather lounges, and fuelled by competent cocktails and lush DJ sets (Thursday to Saturday). Genuinely hip and just a little underground.

★**Chye Seng Huat Hardware** CAFE
(Map p502; www.cshhcoffee.com; 150 Tyrwhitt Rd; 9am-7pm Tue-Fri, to 10pm Sat & Sun; M Lavender) An art-deco former hardware store provides the setting and name for Singapore's coolest cafe and roastery, its third-wave offerings including on-tap Nitro Black Matter, a malty, cold-brew coffee infused with CO_2. Get your coffee geek on at one of the cupping sessions (S$25); see www.papapalheta.com/education/classes for details.

Druggists BEER HALL
(Map p502; www.facebook.com/DruggistsSG; 119 Tyrwhitt Rd; 4pm-midnight Tue-Sun; M Lavender) Druggists is indeed addictive for beer aficionados. Its row of 23 taps pour a rotating selection of craft brews from cognescenti brewers like Denmark's Mikkeller and Britain's Magic Rock. The week's beers are scribbled on the blackboard, with the option of 250mL or 500mL pours. Sud-friendly grub is also available, though the place is best for drinking, not eating.

Artistry CAFE
(Map p502; 6298 2420; www.artistryspace.com; 17 Jln Pinang; 9am-11pm Tue-Fri, 9.30am-11pm Sat, 9.30am-4pm Sun; ; M Bugis) Killer coffee, rotating art exhibitions and monthly after-hours events, including singer-songwriter nights: Artistry is a hipster version of the cultural salon. Swig interesting artisanal beers and ciders or tuck into fresh, delicious grub (served till 5pm) like guilt-inducing BRB (blueberry, ricotta and bacon) pancakes or the cross-cultural chilli-crab burger.

Piedra Negra BAR
(Map p502; 6291 1297; www.facebook.com/Piedra.Negra.Haji.Lane; cnr Beach Rd & Haji Lane; noon-12.30am Mon-Thu, noon-2am Fri, 4pm-2am Sat; ; M Bugis) Sexy Latin beats, bombastic murals and tables right on free-spirited Haji Lane, this electric Mexican joint is a brilliant spot for cheapish cocktails and a little evening people-watching. Frozen or shaken, the margaritas pack a punch, and the burritos, quesadillas, tacos and other Tex-Mex staples are filling and delish.

Orchard Road

Mezze9 BAR
(Map p506; Grand Hyatt, 10 Scotts Rd; noon-midnight Sun-Tue, to 1am Wed-Sat; M Orchard)

THE HAPPIEST HOUR OF ALL

Drinking in Singapore can be a sobering experience. A beer at most city bars will set you back between S$10 and S$18, with cocktails commonly ringing in between S$20 and S$30. Thankfully, many bars offer decent happy-hour deals, typically stretching from around 5pm to 8pm, sometimes starting earlier and finishing later. Most deals offer two drinks for the price of one or cheaper 'housepours'. On Wednesday, ladies'-night promotions offer cheaper (sometimes free) drinks to women. Bar Canary (p546), for instance, offers free-flow Veuve for S$50.

Of course, those who don't mind plastic tables and fluorescent lights can always hang out with the locals at hawker centres and coffeeshops, swilling S$6 bottles of Tiger – a tried-and-tested Singaporean tradition.

Hankering for a decent martini? Head here between 6pm and 8pm Monday to Saturday and toast away at half price. Drinks are made with the good stuff, meaning smooth, seamless libations, shaken or stirred, briny or sweet. The half-price deal includes other cocktails and house pours too, keeping all palates pleased.

No 5 BAR
(Map p506; 5 Emerald Hill Rd; noon-2am Mon-Thu, noon-3am Fri & Sat, 5pm-2am Sun; M Somerset) Not much imagination went into naming this long-running boozer, set in a 1910 Peranakan shophouse. Happy-hour deals run for much of the day, with specials including two martinis for S$19 between 9pm and 1am. Sure, it's damned touristy around here, but the cool evening ambience is sweet relief from the Orchard Rd madness.

Bar Canary BAR
(Map p506; http://www.parkhotelgroup.com/orchard; Park Hotel Orchard, 270 Orchard Rd, entry on Bideford Rd; noon-1am Sun-Thu, to 2am Fri & Sat; wi-fi; M Somerset) Canary-yellow beanbags, artificial turf and the sound of humming traffic and screeching birds – alfresco Bar Canary hovers high above frenetic Orchard Rd. It's fab for an evening tipple, with well-positioned fans. Book at least a week ahead for its Wednesday Ladies' Night deal: S$50, plus tax, for free-flow Veuve from 7.30pm to 9pm (S$100 for guys), followed by half-price drinks all night.

KPO BAR
(Map p506; www.imaginings.com.sg; 1 Killiney Rd; 3pm-1am Mon-Thu, to 2am Fri, 6pm-2am Sat; wi-fi; M Somerset) It may no longer be such a see-and-be-seen place, but KPO remains a solid spot to kick back with a beer, especially on the rooftop terrace. It's a contemporary, tropical space, with concrete walls, timber detailing and no shortage of greenery. It's also the only bar in town with an attached post office.

Dempsey Hill & Botanic Gardens

Green Door BAR
(6476 2922; block 13A, Dempsey Rd; 5-11.15pm Mon-Thu, to 1.15am Fri & Sat, 1-11.15pm Sun; wi-fi; bus 7, 75, 77, 105, 106, 123, 174) Wide sky, sinuous palms and the odd frangipani breeze: slip behind the green gate for a little tropical seduction. Under gramophone lights, barkeeps shake and stir twisted classics (think Lillet Blanc–laced Negronis), splashed with herbs and fruit straight from the garden. Happy-hour deals (5pm to 8pm Monday to Saturday, from 1pm Sunday) are decent, pulling in a languid expat crowd.

RedDot Brewhouse MICROBREWERY
(www.reddotbrewhouse.com.sg; 25A Dempsey Rd; noon-midnight Mon-Thu, noon-2am Fri & Sat, 10.30am-midnight Sun; bus 7, 75, 77, 105, 106, 123, 174) In a quiet spot in Dempsey Hill, RedDot has been pouring its own microbrews for years. Ditch the average food and focus on the suds, sipped to the sound of screeching parrots. There are eight beers on tap (from S$6.50 for a half-pint), including an eye-catching, spirulina-spiked green pilsner. Happy hour runs from noon to 7pm, with S$5 half-pints and S$9 pints.

Eastern Singapore

Cider Pit BAR
(Map p508; 328 Joo Chiat Rd; 5pm-1am Mon-Fri, 1pm-1am Sat & Sun; wi-fi; bus 16, 33) Wedged in a nondescript concrete structure, Cider Pit is easy to miss. Don't. The watering hole offers an extensive range of ciders, including Brothers (try the Toffee Apple), and special-

ity beers like Australia's Little Creatures. It's a refreshingly casual, unfussy kind of place, ideal for easygoing drinking sessions among expats in shorts, tees and flip-flops.

Outpost Trading Co BAR

(Map p508; 71 Joo Chiat Pl; 2-10.30pm Tue-Sun; 16, 33, M Eunos) Lined with bottled craft beers, boutique wines and small-batch spirits, this savvy little bottle shop works up a thirst. Thankfully, it also serves well-priced beer on tap (S$8), from the likes of San Diego's Stone Brewing Co and Hong Kong's Big Wave Bay. Perch at a barrel out the front or settle in at next-door Smokey's BBQ, the Californian owner's sensational smokehouse.

Coastal Settlement BAR

(6475 0200; www.thecoastalsettlement.com; 200 Netheravon Rd; 10.30am-midnight Tue-Sun; 29) In a black-and-white colonial bungalow on verdant grounds, this cafe-bar-restaurant is ideal for unhurried idling. It's like a hipster op shop, packed with modernist furniture, the odd Vespa and cabinets filled with retro gizmos. The fresh juices are delicious and the coffee top notch; food options cover most bases, from tacos and pizzas to a wagyu-beef cheeseburger.

Sentosa Island

Tanjong Beach Club BAR

(Map p514; 6270 1355; www.facebook.com/tanjongbeachclub; Tanjong Beach; 11am-11pm Tue-Fri, 10am-midnight Sat & Sun; M HarbourFront, then monorail to Beach) Generally cooler and scenier than the bars on Siloso beach (especially on weekends), Tanjong Beach Club is an evocative spot, with evening torches on the sand, a small, stylish pool for guests, and a sultry lounge-and-funk soundtrack.

Coastes BAR

(Map p514; Siloso Beach; 9am-11pm Sun-Thu, to 1am Fri & Sat; M HarbourFront, then monorail to Beach) More family friendly than many of the other beach venues, Coastes has picnic tables on the palm-studded sand and sunloungers (S$20) by the water. If you're peckish, there's a comprehensive menu of standard offerings, including burgers, pasta and salads.

☆ Entertainment

The city's performing-arts hub is **Esplanade – Theatres on the Bay** (Map p494; 6828 8377; www.esplanade.com; 1 Esplanade Dr; M Esplanade, City Hall), which also hosts regular free music performances. The venue is also home to the Singapore Symphony Orchestra. Broadway musicals take to the stage at Marina Bay Sands, while independent theatre companies like Wild Rice and Singapore Repertory Theatre perform at various smaller venues.

An enthusiastic local music scene thrives (to a point) and homegrown talent is sometimes showcased at unexpected venues, such as cafe Artistry (p545). Clubs, which generally close at 3am and are strictly drug-free, often line up renowned local and visiting DJs.

Tickets to most events are available through **SISTIC** (Map p506; 6348 5555; www.sistic.com.sg). To see what's on, scan Singapore broadsheet *Straits Times* or check www.timeout.com/singapore.

Chinese Opera

Chinese Theatre Circle OPERA

(Map p498; 6323 4862; www.ctcopera.com; 5 Smith St; show & snacks S$25, show & dinner S$40; 7-9pm Fri & Sat; M Chinatown) Teahouse evenings organised by this nonprofit opera company are a wonderful, informal introduction to Chinese opera. Every Friday and Saturday at 8pm there is a brief talk on Chinese opera, followed by a 45-minute excerpt from an opera classic, performed by actors in full costume. You can also opt for a pre-show Chinese meal at 7pm. Book ahead.

Live Music

BluJaz Café JAZZ

(Map p502; www.blujazcafe.net; 11 Bali Lane; admission from $5; noon-1am Mon-Thu, to 2am Fri & Sat; ; M Bugis) Bohemian pub BluJaz is one of the best options in town for live music, with regular jazz jams, and other acts playing anything from blues to rockabilly. Check the website for the list of rotating events, which include DJ-spun funk, R&B and retro nights, as well as 'Talk Cock' open-mic comedy nights on Wednesday and Thursday.

Going Om LIVE MUSIC

(Map p502; www.going-om.com.sg; 63 Haji Lane; 5pm-1am Tue-Thu, to 3am Fri-Sun; M Bugis) FREE A raffish, free-spirited cafe with nightly live music right on Haji Lane. It's an atmospheric spot, peppered with candlelit tables; smooth, acoustic sets (mostly well-executed covers); and no shortage of carefree punters dancing in the laneway. The boho spirit extends to the drinks list, which includes 'chakra' drinks of seven colours (one for each chakra, dude).

SingJazz Club JAZZ
(Map p502; ☎6292 0410; www.eventbrite.sg/o/the-singjazz-club-6628119315; Sultan Hotel, 101 Jln Sultan; ⏰9pm-1am Wed-Sun; Ⓜ Bugis) Good sax, crooners and the occasional dose of soul, funk, Latin and house is what you get at this intimate jazz bar, with both local and visiting acts taking to its red-curtained stage. Leave the shorts and flip-flops at your hotel. Check the club's Eventbrite page for upcoming gigs.

Singapore Symphony Orchestra CLASSICAL MUSIC
(Map p494; www.sso.org.sg; Ⓜ Esplanade) The 1800-seater state-of-the-art concert hall at the Esplanade – Theatres on the Bay (p547) is home to this respected orchestra, which also graces the Victoria Theatre & Concert Hall. It plays at least weekly; check the website for details and book ahead. Discounted student and senior (55-plus) discounts available; kids under six not permitted.

Singapore Chinese Orchestra CLASSICAL MUSIC
(Map p498; ☎6557 4034; www.sco.com.sg; Singapore Conference Hall, 7 Shenton Way; Ⓜ Tanjong Pagar) Using traditional instruments such as the liuqin, ruan and sanxian, the SCO treats listeners to classical Chinese concerts throughout the year. Concerts are held in various venues around the city, with occasional collaborations showcasing jazz musicians.

Timbrè @ The Substation LIVE MUSIC
(Map p494; www.timbre.com.sg; 45 Armenian St; ⏰6pm-1am Sun-Thu, to 2am Fri & Sat; Ⓜ City Hall) Young ones are content to queue for seats at this popular live-music venue, whose daily rotating roster features local bands and singer-songwriters playing anything from pop and rock to folk. Hungry punters can fill up on soups, salads, tapas and passable fried standbys like buffalo wings and truffle fries.

Crazy Elephant LIVE MUSIC
(Map p494; crazyelephant.sg; 01-03/04, Clarke Quay; ⏰5pm-2am Sun-Thu, to 3am Fri & Sat; Ⓜ Clarke Quay) Anywhere that bills itself as 'crazy' should set the alarm bells ringing, but you won't hear them once you're inside. This touristy, graffiti-pimped rock bar is beery, blokey and loud. Music spans rock to deep, funky blues. Rock on!

Theatre & Dance

Wild Rice THEATRE
(Map p502; ☎6292 2695; www.wildrice.com.sg; 65 Kerbau Rd; Ⓜ Little India) Singapore's sexiest theatre group is based in Kerbau Rd but performs shows elsewhere in the city (as well as abroad). A mix of homegrown and foreign work, productions range from farce to serious politics, fearlessly wading into issues not commonly on the agenda in Singapore.

Singapore Repertory Theatre THEATRE
(Map p494; ☎6221 5585; www.srt.com.sg; DBS Arts Centre, 20 Merbau Rd; 🚌64, 123, 143, Ⓜ Clarke Quay) Based at the DBS Arts Centre but also performing at other venues, the SRT produces international repertory standards as well as modern Singaporean plays. The company's annual Shakespeare in the Park series, enchantingly set in Fort Canning Park, is deservedly popular. Check the website for upcoming productions.

Singapore Dance Theatre DANCE
(Map p494; ☎6338 0611; www.singaporedancetheatre.com; level 7, Bugis+, 201 Victoria St; Ⓜ Bugis) This is the HQ of Singapore's premier dance company, which keeps fans swooning with its repertoire of classic ballets and contemporary works, many of which are performed at Esplanade – Theatres on the Bay (p547). The true highlight is the group's Ballet under the Stars season at Fort Canning Park (p497), which usually runs in June or July. See the website for program details.

Shopping

Bangkok and Hong Kong might upstage it on the bargain front, but when it comes to choice, few cities match Singapore. Mall-heavy, chain-centric Orchard Rd is Singapore's retail queen, with no shortage of department stores, luxury boutiques and high-street chains, as well as a smattering of boutiques selling the work of independent local and foreign designers.

For computers and electronics, hit specialist malls like Sim Lim Square (p551).

Good places for antiques include Tanglin Shopping Centre (p552), Dempsey Hill, and Chinatown.

For fabrics and textiles, scour Little India and Kampong Glam. Kampong Glam is also famous for its perfume traders, as well as for independent fashion boutiques (of varying quality) on pedestrianised Haji Lane. Southwest of Chinatown, Tiong Bahru delivers a handful of interesting retailers, selling everything from local literature and art tomes to fashion accessories, homewares and records.

SINGAPORE SHOPPING TIPS

➡ Prices are usually fixed, except at markets and in tourist areas; don't start bargaining if you have no interest in purchasing.

➡ Shop around when buying electronics like computers, tablets and cameras. Researching prices means less chance of getting overcharged. Also, always test the product before making payment.

➡ Especially in smaller shops, ensure international guarantees are filled out correctly, including the shop's name and the item's serial number. When buying antiques, ask for a certificate of antiquity, required by many countries to avoid paying customs duty.

➡ If buying a Blu-ray or DVD player or a gaming system, check that it will play your home country's discs. Also, check the voltage and cycle of electrical goods. Most shops will attach the correct plug for your country if you ask.

➡ Although the annual Great Singapore Sale (p529) spans late May to late July, the best bargains are had during the first week.

➡ In the unlikely case you're ripped off or taken for a ride, contact the Singapore Tourism Board (p556).

Colonial District, the Quays & Marina Bay

Shoppes at Marina Bay Sands MALL
(Map p494; www.marinabaysands.com; 10 Bayfront Ave; ; M Bayfront) From Miu Miu pumps and Prada frocks to Boggi Milano blazers, this sprawling temple of aspiration gives credit cards a thorough workout. Despite being one of Singapore's largest luxury malls, it's relatively thin on crowds – great if you're not a fan of the Orchard Rd pandemonium. The world's first floating Louis Vuitton store is also here, right on Marina Bay.

Raffles City MALL
(Map p494; www.rafflescity.com.sg; 252 North Bridge Rd; M City Hall) Atrium-graced Raffles City includes a three-level branch of fashion-savvy Robinsons department store, flip-flop shop Havaianas, and a string of fashionable bag and luggage retailers, including Coach, Tumi and Kate Spade. You'll find kids' boutiques on level three. For high-end art by established and emerging Asian and Western artists, drop into **Ode to Art** (6250 1901; 01-36, Raffles City; 11am-9pm Sun-Thu, to 10pm Fri & Sat) gallery. Hungry? Trawl the decent basement food court.

Raffles Hotel Arcade MALL
(Map p494; www.raffles.com; 328 North Bridge Rd; M City Hall) Part of the hotel complex, Raffles Hotel Arcade is home to a handful of notable retailers. You'll find quality, affordable souvenirs (the vintage hotel posters are great buys) at **Raffles Hotel Gift Shop** (www.raffleshotelgifts.com; 01-01/03, Raffles Hotel Arcade; 8.30am-9pm) and high-end Singaporean art from emerging talent at **Chan Hampe** (www.chanhampegalleries.com; 01-20/21, Raffles Hotel Arcade; 11am-7pm Tue-Sun; M City Hall). And even if you can't afford its cameras, **Leica** (www.leica-store.sg; 01-18, Raffles Hotel Arcade; 10am-8pm; M City Hall) usually has a free, high-quality photographic exhibition on show.

Roxy Disc House MUSIC
(Map p494; 6336 6192; 03-42, The Adelphi, 1 Coleman St; 1-8pm Mon-Sat, 2-8pm Sun; M City Hall) Squeeze into Roxy's skinny aisles and scan the shelves of top-notch new vinyl as well as CDs. Jazz and blues make up the bulk of the offerings, with both English- and Chinese-language collectors' editions thrown into the mix. You'll find the shop on the 3rd floor of The Adelphi, a lo-fi mall dotted with audio-equipment shops.

Basheer Graphic Books BOOKS
(Map p494; www.facebook.com/BasheerGraphic; 04-19, Bras Basah Complex, 231 Bain St; 10am-8pm Mon-Sat, 11am-6.30pm Sun; M Bugis, City Hall) Spruce up your coffee table at this temple to design books and magazines. Located inside the Bras Basah Complex (locally dubbed 'Book City'), it has everything from fashion tomes to titles on art, architecture and urban planning. The shop also does a brisk mail-order business, so if you're mid-travel and want to have something posted to you, staff are happy to help.

DESIGN HUNTING

Singapore's evolving X-factor is reflected in its ever-expanding booty of locally made design and craft. For a city-wide lisitng of upcoming flea markets, head to www.fleawhere.com.

Kapok (Map p494; ☎6339 7987; www.ka-pok.co; 01-05, National Design Centre, 111 Middle Rd; ⏰shop 11am-9pm; Ⓜ Bugis) Inside the National Design Centre, Kapok showcases beautifully designed products from Singapore and beyond. Restyle your world with local recycled jewellery from ATGAB, artisanal fragrances from Code Deco, and wristwatches from HyperGrand. Imports include anything from seamless Italian wallets to French tees and Nordic courier bags. When you're shopped out, recharge at the on-site cafe.

Tyrwhitt General Company (Map p502; www.thegeneralco.sg; 150A Tyrwhitt Rd; ⏰noon-5pm Tue-Thu, to 7pm Fri-Sun; Ⓜ Lavender) After a caffeine fix at Chye Seng Huat Hardware, duck upstairs to this shop-workshop for hip, beautifully crafted accessories, jewellery and knickknacks from Singapore and beyond. Bag anything from graphic-print ceramics and striking totes to handsome leather wallets. Check the website for upcoming workshops, usually run on Sunday afternoon and mainly focused on leather craft.

MAAD Pyjamas (Market of Artists and Designers; Map p498; www.facebook.com/goMAAD; Red Dot Design Museum, 28 Maxwell Rd; Ⓜ Tanjong Pagar) Held at Singapore's Red Dot Design Museum, this monthly flea market is a showcase for local design, with everything from fashion and homewares to art.

Cat Socrates GIFTS
(Map p494; ☎6333 0870; catsocrates.wix.com/catsocrates; 02-25, Bras Basah Complex, 231 Bain St; ⏰noon-8pm Mon-Sat, 1-7pm Sun; Ⓜ Bugis, Bras Basah) Can't find that retro Chinese toy car? What about Pan-Am wrapping paper? Chances are you'll find them at this quirky shop, inside the bookworm mecca that is Bras Basah Complex. Expect anything from felt laptop sleeves and quirky totes to super-cool Singapore souvenirs like city-themed graphic postcards and neighbourhood sketch books.

Chinatown

★Utterly Art ARTS
(Map p498; ☎9487 2006; www.utterlyart.com.sg; level 3, 20B Mosque St; ⏰usually 2-8pm Mon-Sat, noon-5.30pm Sun; Ⓜ Chinatown) Climb the stairs to this tiny, welcoming gallery for works by contemporary Singaporean, Filipino and, on occasion, Cambodian artists. While painting is the gallery's focus, exhibitions dabble in sculpture and ceramics on occasion, with artworks priced from around S$500 (depending on the exhibition). Opening times can be a little erratic, so always call ahead if making a special trip.

Willow and Huxley FASHION, ACCESSORIES
(Map p498; www.willowandhuxley.com; 20 Amoy St; ⏰9am-8pm Mon-Fri, 11am-3pm Sat; Ⓜ Telok Ayer) Willow and Huxley offers a sharp, vibrant edit of smaller independent labels like Australia's Finders Keepers and Bec & Bridge and Denmark's quirky Baum und Pferdgarten. Jewellery spans vintage to statement, with a small selection of casual, beach-friendly threads for men courtesy of Australia's TCSS and New York's Onia and Psycho Bunny.

Eu Yan Sang CHINESE MEDICINE
(Map p498; www.euyansang.com.sg; 269 South Bridge Rd; ⏰shop 9am-6.30pm Mon-Sat, clinic 8.30am-6pm Mon-Fri, to 7.30pm Sat; Ⓜ Chinatown) Get your *qi* back in order at Singapore's most famous and user-friendly Chinese-medicine store. Pick up some Monkey Bezoar powder to relieve excess phlegm, or Liu Jun Zi pills to dispel dampness. You'll find herbal teas, soups and oils, and you can even consult a practitioner of Chinese medicine at the clinic next door (bring your passport).

Yue Hwa Chinese Products DEPARTMENT STORE
(Map p498; www.yuehwa.com.sg; 70 Eu Tong Sen St; ⏰11am-9pm Sun-Fri, to 10pm Sat; Ⓜ Chinatown) With a deco facade paging Shanghai, this multi-level department store specialises in all things Chinese. Downstairs you'll find medicine and herbs, clothes and cushions. Head up the escalator for silks, food and tea, arts and crafts and household goods, before ending up in a large, cluttered sea of furniture.

Little India, Kampong Glam & Bugis

★Sifr Aromatics BEAUTY
(Map p502; www.sifr.sg; 42 Arab St; ⌚11am-8pm Mon-Sat, to 5pm Sun; Ⓜ Bugis) This Zen-like perfume laboratory belongs to third-generation perfumer Johari Kazura, whose exquisite creations include the heady East (50mL S$140), a blend of oud, rose absolute, amber and neroli. The focus is on custom-made fragrances (consider calling ahead to arrange an appointment), with other heavenly offerings including affordable, high-quality body balms, scented candles, and vintage perfume bottles.

Sim Lim Square ELECTRONICS, MALL
(Map p502; www.simlimsquare.com.sg; 1 Rochor Canal Rd; ⌚10.30am-9pm; Ⓜ Rochor) A byword for all that is cut-price and geeky, Sim Lim is jammed with stalls selling PDAs, laptops, cameras, soundcards and games consoles. If you know what you're doing there are some deals to be had, but the untutored are likely to be out of their depth. Bargain hard (yet politely) and always check that the warranty is valid in your home country.

Little Shophouse HANDICRAFTS
(Map p502; 43 Bussorah St; ⌚10am-5pm; Ⓜ Bugis) Traditional Peranakan beadwork is a dying art, but it's kept very much alive in this quaint shop and workshop. The shop's colourful slippers are designed by craftsman Robert Sng and hand-beaded by his sister, Irene. While they're not cheap (circa S$1000), each pair takes a painstaking 100 hours to complete. You'll also find Peranakan-style tea sets, crockery, vases, handbags and jewellery.

Haji Lane FASHION, HOMEWARES
(Map p502; Haji Lane; Ⓜ Bugis) Narrow, pastel Haji Lane harbours a handful of quirky, indie boutiques. Female fashion blogerati favourites include Dulcetfig, a good spot for cool local and foreign frocks and accessories, including high-end vintage bags and jewellery. Girly threads get a little indie edge at Soon Lee, while concept store Mondays Off stocks anything from contemporary local ceramics and funky cushions to art mags and geometric racks to store them on.

Tuckshop & Sundry Supplies FASHION, ACCESSORIES
(Map p502; 25 Bali Lane; ⌚noon-8pm Mon-Sat, to 6pm Sun; Ⓜ Bugis) A vintage-inspired ode to Americana working-class culture, this little menswear store offers a clued-in selection of rugged threads and accessories, including designer eyewear, grooming products and made-in-house leather goods. Stock up on plaid shirts, sweat tops and harder-to-find denim from brands like Japan's Iron Heart and China's Red Cloud.

Mustafa Centre DEPARTMENT STORE
(Map p502; www.mustafa.com.sg; 145 Syed Alwi Rd; ⌚24hr; Ⓜ Farrer Park) Little India's bustling 24-hour Mustafa Centre is a magnet for budget shoppers, most of them from the subcontinent. It's a sprawling place, selling everything from electronics and garish gold jewellery to shoes, bags, luggage and beauty products. There's also a large supermarket with a great range of Indian foodstuffs. If you can't handle crowds, avoid the place on Sunday.

Bugis Street Market MARKET
(Map p502; www.bugis-street.com; Victoria St; ⌚11am-10pm; Ⓜ Bugis) What was once Singapore's most infamous sleaze pit – packed with foreign servicemen on R&R, gambling dens and 'sisters' (transvestites) – is now its most famous undercover street market, crammed with cheap clothes, shoes, accessories and manicurists especially popular with teens and 20-somethings. In a nod to its past, there's even a sex shop.

Orchard Road

ION Orchard Mall MALL
(Map p506; www.ionorchard.com; 430 Orchard Rd; ⌚10am-10pm; Ⓜ Orchard) Rising directly above Orchard MRT Station, futuristic ION is the cream of Orchard Rd malls. Basement floors focus on mere-mortal high-street labels like Zara and Uniqlo, while upper-floor tenants read like the index of *Vogue*. Dining options span food-court bites to posher nosh, and the attached 56-storey tower offers a top-floor viewing gallery, **ION Sky** (www.ionorchard.com/en/ion-sky.html; ⌚3-6pm, last entry 5.30pm) FREE.

Ngee Ann City MALL
(Map p506; www.ngeeanncity.com.sg; 391 Orchard Rd; ⌚10am-9.30pm; Ⓜ Somerset) It might look like a forbidding mausoleum, but this marble-and-granite behemoth promises retail giddiness on its seven floors. International luxury brands compete for space with sprawling bookworm nirvana **Kinokuniya** (www.kinokuniya.com.sg; 04-20/20B/20C,

Ngee Ann City; ⌚10am-9.30pm Sun-Fri, to 10pm Sat) and upmarket Japanese department store **Takashimaya** (www.takashimaya.com.sg; ⌚10am-9.30pm), home to Takashimaya Food Village, one of the strip's best food courts.

Robinsons DEPARTMENT STORE
(Map p506; www.robinsons.com.sg; 260 Orchard Rd; ⌚10.30am-10pm; Ⓜ Somerset) The flagship for Singapore's top department store offers sharp fashion edits, pairing well-known 'It' labels like Chloe, Bruno Magli and Manolo Blahnik with street-smart cognoscenti brands such as PLAC, Brownbreath and Saturdays NYC. Clothes and shoes aside, you'll find anything from Shinola Detroit leathergoods to Balmain bedlinen.

Tanglin Shopping Centre MALL
(Map p506; www.tanglinsc.com; 19 Tanglin Rd; ⌚10am-10pm; Ⓜ Orchard) This retro mall specialises in Asian art and is *the* place to come for quality rugs, carvings, ornaments, jewellery, paintings, furniture and the like. Top billing goes to **Antiques of the Orient** (www.aoto.com.sg; 02-40, Tanglin Shopping Centre; ⌚10am-6pm Mon-Sat, 11am-4pm Sun), with original and reproduction prints, photographs and maps of Singapore and Asia. Especially beautiful are the richly hued botanical drawings commissioned by British colonist William Farquhar.

Paragon MALL
(Map p506; www.paragon.com.sg; 290 Orchard Rd; ⌚10am-9pm; Ⓜ Somerset) Even if you don't have a Gold Amex, strike a pose inside this Maserati of Orchard Rd malls. Status labels include Burberry, Hermès, Jimmy Choo and Singapore's own **Raoul** (www.raoul.com; 02-49, Paragon), which offers sharp, detailed men's threads and crisp, invigorating womenswear, from classic cropped trousers to sassy cocktail frocks. High-street brands include Banana Republic and G-Star Raw.

Mandarin Gallery MALL
(Map p506; www.mandaringallery.com.sg; 333A Orchard Rd; 📶; Ⓜ Somerset) Rehabilitate your wardrobe at this tranquil, high-end mall. Female fashionistas shouldn't miss local designer Jo Soh's **Hansel** (www.ilovehansel.com; 02-14, Mandarin Gallery), where bold prints and vintage inspiration drive chic yet playful creations. On the same floor, unisex **Inhabit – The Other Store** (02-16, Mandarin Gallery) serves up edgy, contemporary threads from cognoscenti labels like Être Cécile, Soulland and Song for the Mute.

Reckless Shop FASHION
(Map p506; www.recklessericka.com; 02-08/09, Orchard Central, 181 Orchard Rd; ⌚11am-9.30pm; Ⓜ Somerset) Young, talented local designer Afton Chan thrills fashion fiends with her highly creative, affordable pieces. Choose from two labels: Reckless Jersey – delivering fresh, functional maxi frocks and tops for under S$100 – or higher-end Still, known for fashion-forward pieces equally romantic and edgy.

Dempsey Hill & Botanic Gardens

Dempsey Hill, a former British Army barracks, is now a shopping precinct specialising in Kashmiri carpets, teak furniture and antiques.

Shang Antique ANTIQUES
(www.shangantique.com.sg; 18D Dempsey Rd; ⌚10.30am-6.30pm; 🚌7, 75, 77, 105, 106, 123, 174) Specialising in antique religious artefacts from Cambodia, Laos, Thailand, India and Burma, as well as reproductions, Shang has items dating back nearly 2000 years – with price tags to match. Those with more style than savings can pick up old opium pots, beautiful Thai silk scarves or Burmese ornamental rice baskets for under S$30.

Em Gallery FASHION, HOMEWARES
(☎6475 6941; www.emtradedesign.com; block 16, 01-04/05, Dempsey Rd; ⌚10am-7pm Mon, Tue, Thu & Fri, 11am-7pm Sat & Sun; 🚌7, 75, 77, 105, 106, 123, 174) Singapore-based Japanese designer Emiko Nakamura keeps Dempsey's lunching ladies looking whimsically chic in her light, sculptural creations. Emiko also collaborates with hilltribes in northern Laos to create naturally dyed handwoven handicrafts, such as bags and cushions. Other homewares might include limited-edition (and reasonably priced) Khmer pottery from Cambodia.

Eastern Singapore

Kim Choo Kueh Chang FOOD, HANDICRAFTS
(Map p508; www.kimchoo.com; 109 East Coast Rd; ⌚9am-8.30pm; 🚌10, 14, 16, 32) Joo Chiat is stuffed with bakeries and dessert shops, but few equal old-school Kim Choo. Pick up traditional pineapple tarts and other brightly coloured Peranakan *kueh* (bite-sized snacks), and pit stop at the adjoining boutique for colourful Peranakan ceramics, clothing and accessories. Fashion de-

signer Raymond Wong runs four-session Peranakan-beading courses (S$300 to S$350), with each session lasting two hours; email wonjyunyung@hotmail.com.

SINGAPORE SURVIVAL GUIDE

Directory A–Z

ACCOMMODATION

In Singapore's midrange and top-end hotels, room rates are about supply and demand, fluctuating daily. For instance, room rates at business hotels often drop on weekends due to lesser demand. Keep this in mind, especially if you're planning to be here during a major event like the Formula One night race, when rates can skyrocket.

Be aware that top hotels usually add a 'plus plus' (++) after the rate they quote you. Ignore this at your peril. The two plusses are service charge and GST, which together amounts to a breezy 17% on top of your bill. All prices quoted in our listings are from the day of our visit inclusive of the ++ tax; your own price may vary.

CUSTOMS REGULATIONS

You are not allowed to bring tobacco into Singapore unless you pay duty. You will be slapped with a hefty fine if you fail to declare and pay.

You are permitted 1L each of wine, beer and spirits duty free. Alternatively, you are allowed 2L of wine and 1L of beer, or 2L of beer and 1L of wine. You need to have been out of Singapore for more than 48 hours and to anywhere but Malaysia.

It's illegal to bring chewing gum, electronic cigarettes, chewing tobacco, shisha, firecrackers, obscene or seditious material, gun-shaped cigarette lighters, endangered species or their by-products and pirated recordings or publications with you.

DISCOUNTS

If you arrived on a Singapore Airlines or Silk Air flight, you're entitled to discounts (usually 10% to 15%) at selected hotels, attractions, restaurants and shops by presenting your boarding pass. See www.singaporeair.com/boardingpass for information.

Children receive a discount of up to 50% at many tourist attractions, and children six and under are sometimes admitted free. Discounts are often available to visitors over 60. Present your passport or ID with your date of birth on it.

The National Heritage Board's **3 Day Museum Pass** (adult/family S$20/50) offers unlimited admission to six city museums, including the National Museum of Singapore, Asian Civilisations Museum, Peranakan Museum and Singapore Art Museum. Passes can be purchased at the museums.

SLEEPING PRICE RANGES

The following price ranges are for a double room including tax.

$ less than S$100

$$ S$100–250

$$$ more than S$250

ELECTRICITY

Plugs are of the three-pronged, square-pin type used in Malaysia and the UK. Electricity runs at 230V and 50 cycles.

EMBASSIES & CONSULATES

For a full list of foreign embassies and consulates in Singapore, see embassy.goabroad.com/embassies-in/Singapore.

Australian High Commission (Map p506; ☎6836 4100; www.australia.org.sg; 25 Napier Rd; 🚌7, 75, 77, 105, 106, 123, 174)

Canadian High Commission (Map p494; ☎6854 5900; www.singapore.gc.ca; level 11, 1 George St; Ⓜ Clarke Quay, Raffles Pl)

Dutch Embassy (Map p506; ☎6737 1155; www.mfa.nl/sin; level 13, Liat Towers, 541 Orchard Rd; Ⓜ Orchard)

French Embassy (☎6880 7800; www.ambafrance-sg.org; 101-103 Cluny Park Rd; Ⓜ Botanic Gardens)

German Embassy (Map p494; ☎6533 6002; www.singapur.diplo.de; level 12, Singapore Land Tower, 50 Raffles Pl; Ⓜ Raffles Pl)

Irish Embassy (Map p506; ☎6238 7616; www.embassyofireland.sg; level 8, Liat Towers, 541 Orchard Rd; Ⓜ Orchard)

New Zealand High Commission (Map p494; ☎6235 9966; www.nzembassy.com/singapore; level 21, 1 George St; Ⓜ Clarke Quay, Raffles Pl)

UK High Commission (Map p506; ☎6424 4200; www.gov.uk/government/world/singapore; 100 Tanglin Rd; 🚌7, 75, 77, 105, 106, 111, 123, 132, 174)

US Embassy (Map p506; ☎6476 9100; http://singapore.usembassy.gov; 27 Napier Rd; 🚌7, 75, 77, 105, 106, 123, 174)

EMERGENCY

Ambulance, Fire	☎995
Police	☎999

EATING PRICE RANGES

The following ranges indicate the price of a single dish or main course, excluding tax.

$ less than S$10

$$ S$10–30

$$$ more than S$30

FOOD

Bear in mind that most restaurant prices will have 17% added to them at the end: a 10% service charge plus 7% for GST. You'll see this indicated by '++' on menus.

INTERNET ACCESS

➡ Every top hotel has internet access, and the backpacker hostels all offer free internet access and wi-fi.

➡ You will find free wi-fi hot spots at Changi Aiport and in many of Singapore's shopping malls, cafes and pubs.

➡ You can register for a free public wi-fi account at http://wirelesssg.y5zone.sg/registration. Once you're signed up, simply choose wireless@SG where available. In central Chinatown, you'll find free wi-fi hot spots in Trengganu St, Pagoda St, Smith St, Sago St and Kreta Ayer Sq – choose the wireless@chinatown wi-fi network on your device.

LGBT TRAVELLERS

In 2014, the Singapore Supreme Court ruled to uphold section 377A of the country's penal code, which criminalises consensual sex between adult males. The act carries a maximum jail sentence of two years.

In reality, nobody is ever likely to be prosecuted. Singapore has a string of popular LGBT bars and many urbane, well-travelled Singaporeans have relaxed attitudes towards the LGBT community.

A good place to start looking for information is on the websites of **Travel Gay Asia** (www.travelgayasia.com), **PLUguide** (www.pluguide.com) or **Utopia** (www.utopia-asia.com), which provide coverage of venues and events.

LEGAL MATTERS

Singapore's reputation for harsh laws is not undeserved: don't expect any special treatment for being a foreigner. Police have broad powers and you would be unwise to refuse any requests they make of you. If you are arrested, you will be entitled to legal counsel and contact with your embassy. Don't even think about importing or exporting drugs. At best, you'll get a long jail term; at worst, you'll get the death penalty.

Smoking is banned in most public places, including shopping and entertainment centres, restaurants, hawker centres and food courts, public tranport, taxis, and within a 5m radius of most building entrances. The maximum fine for first-time offenders is S$1000. You can smoke on the street (as long as you put your butt in the bin).

Jaywalking (crossing the road within 50m of a designated crossing) and littering could cost you up to S$1000.

MEDICAL SERVICES

Singapore's medical institutions are world class and generally cheaper than private healthcare in the West. This said, travel-insurance cover is advisable. Check with insurance providers what treatments and procedures are covered before you leave home. Note that local GPs also dispense medication on premises.

Clinics

Your hotel or hostel should be able to direct you to a local GP; there are plenty around.

Raffles Medical Clinic (Map p502; ☎6311 2233; www.rafflesmedicalgroup.com.sg; 585 North Bridge Rd; Ⓜ Bugis) A walk-in clinic at Raffles Hospital.

Singapore General Hospital (☎6321 4311; www.sgh.com.sg; block 1, Outram Rd; Ⓜ Outram Park)

Emergency Rooms

Singapore has several 24-hour emergency rooms.

Gleneagles Hospital (Map p506; ☎6473 7222; www.gleneagles.com.sg; 6A Napier Rd; 🚌7, 75, 77, 105, 106, 123, 174)

Mount Elizabeth Hospital Novena (☎6933 0100; www.mountelizabeth.com.sg; 38 Irrawaddy Rd; Ⓜ Novena)

Mount Elizabeth Hospital Orchard (Map p506; ☎6731 2218; www.mountelizabeth.com.sg; 3 Mt Elizabeth Rd; Ⓜ Orchard)

Raffles Hospital (Map p502; ☎6311 1111; www.rafflesmedicalgroup.com.sg; 585 North Bridge Rd; Ⓜ Bugis)

Singapore General Hospital (p554)

MONEY

The country's unit of currency is the Singapore dollar, locally referred to as the 'singdollar', which is made up of 100 cents. Singapore uses 5¢, 10¢, 20¢, 50¢ and S$1 coins, while notes come in denominations of S$2, S$5, S$10, S$50, S$100, S$500 and S$1000. The Singapore dollar is a highly stable and freely convertible currency.

ATMs

Cirrus-enabled ATMs are widely available at malls, banks, MRT stations and commercial areas.

Changing Money

Banks change money, but virtually nobody uses them for currency conversion because the rates are better at the moneychangers dotted all over the city. These tiny stalls can be found in just about every shopping centre (though not necessarily in the more modern malls). Rates can be haggled over a little if you're changing amounts of S$500 or more.

Credit Cards

Widely accepted, except at local hawkers and food courts.

Taxes & Refunds

A 7% goods-and-services tax (GST) is applied to all goods and services. Tax and service charges also apply to room rates. Restaurants charge 17% extra on top of listed prices (7% GST and a 10% service charge).

Departing visitors can get a refund of the 7% GST on their purchases if they have spent a minimum of S$100 at one retailer on the same day for no more than three purchases. The retailer should issue you with an eTRS (Electronic Tourist Refund Scheme) ticket, which you then scan at the eTRS self-help kiosks at the airport or cruise terminal.

If physical inspection of the goods is required, as indicated by the eTRS kiosk, you will have to present the goods, together with the original receipt and your boarding pass, at the Customs Inspection Counter.

Smaller stores may not participate in the GST-refund scheme.

Tipping

Tipping is largely unnecessary and unexpected in restaurants due to the 10% service charge automatically added to your bill. Some restaurants voluntarily omit the charge, leaving a tip to your discretion. Tipping in taxis and hawker centres is not expected. Elsewhere a thank-you tip for good service is discretionary.

OPENING HOURS

Opening hours can vary between individual businesses. General opening hours are as follows.

Banks Monday to Friday 9.30am to 4.30pm – some branches open at 10am and some close at 6pm or later; Saturday 9.30am to noon or later.

Government and post offices Monday to Friday between 8am and 9.30am to between 4pm and 6pm; Saturday between 8am and 9am to between 11.30am and 1.30pm.

Restaurants Top restaurants generally open between noon and 2pm for lunch and 6pm till 10pm for dinner. Casual restaurants and food courts are open all day.

Shops Malls and department stores generally open from 10am to 10pm. Smaller, standalone shops often close earlier (around 7pm or 8pm) and may not trade on Sunday. It's busiest in Little India on Sunday.

POST

Postal delivery in Singapore is very efficient. Call 1605 to find the nearest branch or check www.singpost.com.sg.

PUBLIC HOLIDAYS

New Year's Day 1 January
Chinese New Year Two days in February
Good Friday March/April
Labour Day 1 May
Vesak Day May/June
Hari Raya Puasa July
National Day 9 August
Hari Raya Haji September
Deepavali October/November
Christmas Day 25 December

School Holidays

In Singapore there's a week's holiday towards the end of March, four weeks in June, one week in early September, and a long break from the end of November until the beginning of January.

TELEPHONE

- The country code is 65.
- There are no area codes within Singapore; telephone numbers are eight digits unless you are calling toll-free (1800).
- You can make local and international calls from public phone booths. Most phone booths take phonecards.
- Singapore also has credit-card phones that can be used by running your card through the slot.
- Calls to Malaysia (from Singapore) are considered to be STD (trunk or long-distance)

PRACTICALITIES

- English daily newspapers in Singapore include the broadsheet *Straits Times*, the *Business Times* and the tabloid *New Paper*.
- Pornographic publications are strictly prohibited, but toned-down local editions of *Cosmopolitan* and lads' magazines such as *FHM* and *Maxim* are allowed.
- Singapore uses the metric system for weights and measures. Weights are in grams and kilograms and volume in millilitres and litres.

A WORD OF WARNING

Some travellers have had problems leaving Malaysia if they've entered the country by train from Singapore. Malaysian immigration officials at Singapore's railway station sometimes don't stamp your passport – not a problem as long as you keep your immigration card and your train ticket to show how you entered Malaysia. Your details will have been put into the Malaysian immigration computer and should come up when you exit. Stand your ground if you're asked to pay a fine.

calls. Dial the access code, 020, followed by the area code of the town in Malaysia that you wish to call (minus the leading zero) and then the phone number. Thus, for a call to 346 7890 in Kuala Lumpur (area code 03) you would dial 02-3-346 7890.

Mobile Phones

In Singapore, mobile-phone numbers start with 9 or 8.

You can buy a local SIM card from Changi Recommends stores at Changi Airport (all terminals), as well as from local telco stores, convenience stores and post offices – by law you must show your passport to get one. Cards generally cost S$15 or more, depending on the amount of phone and data credit offered.

M1 (www.m1.com.sg)
SingTel (http://info.singtel.com)
StarHub (www.starhub.com)

TIME

Singapore is eight hours ahead of GMT/UTC (London), two hours behind Australian Eastern Standard Time (Sydney and Melbourne), 13 hours ahead of American Eastern Standard Time (New York) and 16 hours ahead of American Pacific Standard Time (San Francisco and Los Angeles). When it's noon in Singapore, it's 8pm in Los Angeles and 11pm in New York the previous day, 4am in London and 2pm in Sydney.

TOILETS

Toilets in Singapore are Western style. Public toilets are usually very clean and readily available at shopping malls, in hotel lobbies and at tourist attractions.

TOURIST INFORMATION

The **Singapore Tourism Board** (Map p506; ☎1800 736 2000; www.yoursingapore.com; 216 Orchard Rd; ⊙9.30am-10.30pm; 📶; Ⓜ Somerset) provides the widest range of services, including tour bookings and event ticketing. It has a desk at **ION Orchard** (Map p506; level 1, 2 Orchard Turn; ⊙10am-10pm; Ⓜ Orchard). You'll also find tourist-information desks in the arrivals hall of all three terminals at Changi Airport.

TRAVELLERS WITH DISABILITIES

Ramps, lifts and other facilities are common on the island. The footpaths in the city are nearly all immaculate, MRT stations all have lifts and some buses and taxis are equipped with wheelchair-friendly equipment.

The **Disabled People's Association Singapore** (☎6791 1134; www.dpa.org.sg) can provide information on accessibility in Singapore.

Lonely Planet's free Accessible Travel guide can be downloaded at http://lptravel.to/AccessibleTravel.

VISAS

Citizens of most countries are granted 90-day entry on arrival. Citizens of India, Myanmar, the Commonwealth of Independent States and most Middle Eastern countries must obtain a visa before arriving in Singapore. Visa extensions can be applied for at the **Immigration & Checkpoints Authority** (Map p502; ☎6391 6100; www.ica.gov.sg; 10 Kallang Rd; Ⓜ Lavender).

WOMEN TRAVELLERS

Singaporean women enjoy a high degree of autonomy and respect, and the city is one of the safest destinations in Southeast Asia – though some women might be a little uncomfortable in Little India during the weekends, when tens of thousands of men throng the area. Tampons, over-the-counter medications and contraceptive pills are readily available.

ℹ Getting There & Away

Singapore is one of Asia's major air hubs, serviced by both full-service and budget airlines. The city state has excellent and extensive regional and international connections. You can also catch trains and buses to Malaysia and

SINGAPORE TRANSPORT CONNECTIONS

DESTINATION	AIR	BUS
Kuala Lumpur	1hr, from S$40	4-5hr, from S$21
Penang	1hr 20min, from S$45	9-10hr, from S$40

Thailand. Book flights, tours and rail tickets online at lonelyplanet.com/bookings.

AIR

Airports & Airlines

Changi Airport (☎6595 6868; www.changiairport.com), 20km northeast of Singapore Central Business District (CBD), is Singapore's main international airport, with three terminals and a fourth terminal opening in 2017.

It's serviced by an abundance of global carriers and has frequent flights to all corners of the globe. You'll find free internet, courtesy phones for local calls, foreign-exchange booths, 24-hour hotel-reservation counters, medical centres, left luggage, hotels, a movie theatre and children's playground, themed gardens, day spas, showers, a gym, a swimming pool and no shortage of shops.

LAND

The Causeway linking Johor Bahru (JB) with Singapore handles most traffic between the countries. Trains and buses run from all over Malaysia straight through to Singapore, or you can get a taxi or bus to/from JB. There's also a crossing called the Second Link linking Tuas, in western Singapore, with Geylang Patah in Malaysia – some buses to Melaka and Malaysia's west coast head this way.

Bus

Numerous private companies run comfortable bus services between Singapore and many destinations in Malaysia, including Melaka and Kuala Lumpur, as well as to/from destinations such as Hat Yai in Thailand. Many of these services run from **Golden Mile Complex** (5001 Beach Rd; Ⓜ Nicoll Hwy), close to Kampong Glam. The terminal is home to numerous bus agencies specialising in journeys between Singapore and Malaysia and Singapore and Thailand (shop around). You can also book online at www.busonlineticket.com.

Train

Malaysian railway system **Keretapi Tanah Malayu Berhad** (www.ktmb.com.my) operates commuter shuttle trains from **Woodlands Train Checkpoint** (11 Woodlands Crossing; 🚌170, Causeway Link Express from Queen St Bus Terminal) in Singapore to JB Sentral in Johor Bahru (JB) in Malaysia.

Malaysia has two main rail lines: the primary line going from JB to Kuala Lumpur, Butterworth, Alor Setar and then into Hat Yai, Thailand; and a second line branching off at Gemas and going right up through the centre of the country to Tumpat, near Kota Bharu on the east coast.

From Singapore, shuttle trains (S$5) take five minutes to reach JB. Daily services depart at 6.30am, 8am, 9.30am, 5pm, 6.30pm, 8pm and 11pm. Note that shuttle services are not designed to connect with services from JB, so check transit times before travel.

You can book tickets either at the station or via the KTM website (www.ktmb.com.my).

The luxurious **Eastern & Oriental Express** (www.belmond.com/eastern-and-oriental-express) departs Singapore on the two-night, 1943km journey to Bangkok. Don your linen suit, sip a gin and tonic, and dig deep for the fare: from S$3150 per person.

Sea

The following main ferry terminals run services to Malaysia and/or Indonesia.

Changi Point Ferry Terminal (☎6545 2305; 51 Lorong Bekukong; Ⓜ Tanah Merah, then bus 2)

HarbourFront Cruise & Ferry Terminal (Map p514; ☎6513 2200; www.singaporecruise.com; Ⓜ HarbourFront)

Tanah Merah Ferry Terminal (☎6513 2200; www.singaporecruise.com; Ⓜ Tanah Merah, then bus 35)

GETTING TO MALAYSIA: SINGAPORE TO JOHOR BAHRU

Getting to the border The easiest way to reach the border is on the **Causeway Link Express** (www.causewaylink.com.my). Buses run every 15 to 30 minutes between 6am and 11.45pm; fares are S$3.30/RM3.40 one way. There are several routes, with stops including **Queen Street Bus Terminal** (Map p502; cnr Queen & Arab Sts; Ⓜ Bugis), near Bugis and Kampong Glam, Newton Circus, Jurong East Bus & MRT Interchange and Kranji MRT station.

At the border At the Singapore checkpoint, disembark from the bus with your luggage to go through immigration, and reboard the next bus (keep your ticket). After repeating the process on the Malaysian side, it's a quick walk into central JB.

Moving on Most routes also stop at Larkin Bus Terminal (Larkin Sentral), 5km from central JB. From here, long-distance buses depart to numerous Malaysian destinations, including Melaka, Kuala Lumpur and Ipoh.

FERRIES TO RIAU ARCHIPELAGO (INDONESIA)

Direct ferries run between Singapore and the Indonesian islands of Pulau Batam, Pulau Bintan and Pulau Karimun Besar in the Riau Archipelago. The ferries are modern, fast and air-conditioned. The main ferry companies are as follows.

BatamFast (☎HarbourFront terminal 6270 2228, Tanah Merah terminal 6542 6310; www.batamfast.com) Ferries to Batam Centre, Sekupang and Harbour Bay in Pulau Batam depart from HarbourFront Ferry Terminal. Ferries to Nongsapura, also in Pulau Batam, depart from Tanah Merah Ferry Terminal.

Bintan Resort Ferries (☎6542 4369; www.brf.com.sg) Ferries to Bandar Bentan Telani in Pulau Bintan depart from Tanah Merah Ferry Terminal.

Indo Falcon (☎6278 3167; www.indofalcon.com.sg) Ferries to Tanjung Balai depart from HarbourFront Ferry Terminal.

Sindo Ferries (☎HarbourFront terminal 6271 4866, Tanah Merah terminal 6542 7105; www.sindoferry.com.sg) Ferries to Batam Centre, Sekupang, WaterFront and Tanjung Balai depart from HarbourFront Ferry Terminal. Ferries to Tanjung Pinang depart from Tanah Merah Ferry Terminal.

Getting Around

Singapore is the easiest city in Asia to get around.

For online bus information, including the useful IRIS service (which offers live next-bus departure times), see www.sbstransit.com.sg or download the 'SBS Transit iris' app. For train information, see www.smrt.com.sg.

For consolidated transport information, see www.mytransport.sg.

BICYCLE

Singapore's roads are not for faint-hearted cyclists. Fortunately, there's a large network of parks and park connectors and a few excellent dedicated mountain-biking areas, including Pulau Ubin. Indeed, cycling from East Coast Park to Changi Village and then taking the bike over to Pulau Ubin is an excellent adventure.

Only fold-up bikes are permitted on trains and buses, and only during these hours: Monday to Friday 9.30am to 4pm and from 8pm; all day Saturday, Sunday and public holidays. Only ONE fold-up bike is allowed on buses at any time, so you might as well ride if you have to.

Bikes can also be rented at several places along the East Coast Parkway, on Sentosa Island and on Pulau Ubin, with adult prices ranging from S$8 (per day) on Pulau Ubin and S$3 (per hour) at East Coast Park to S$12 (per hour) on Sentosa.

BOAT & FERRY

To reach Singapore's Southern Islands, catch a ferry from **Marina South Pier** (31 Marina Coastal Dr; Ⓜ Marina South Pier). There are regular bumboat services from Changi Point Ferry Terminal to Pulau Ubin (S$2). To reach Changi Point Ferry Terminal, take bus 2 from Tanah Merah MRT.

BUS

Singapore's extensive bus service is clean, efficient and frequent, reaching every corner of the island. The two main operators are **SBS Transit** (☎1800 287 2727; www.sbstransit.com.sg) and **SMRT** (☎1800 336 8900; www.smrt.com.sg). Both offer similar services. For information on routes and fares, see www.mytransport.sg or www.transitlink.com.sg.

Bus fares range from S$1.40 to S$2.50 (less with an EZ-Link card). You can pay by cash (you'll need the exact money, as no change is given), or simply tap your EZ-Link card or Singapore Tourist Pass on the reader as you board, then again when you get off.

SMRT also runs late-night bus services (NightRider) between the city and various suburbs from 11.30pm to 2am on Friday, Saturday and the eve of public holidays. The flat rate per journey is S$4.50. See the SMRT website for route details.

Tourist Buses

SIA Hop-On (☎6338 6877; www.siahopon.com; 24hr ticket Singapore Airlines passengers adult/child S$8/4, non-passengers S$25/15) Singapore Airlines' tourist bus traverses the main tourist arteries every 20 to 30 minutes daily, starting from Singapore Flyer at 9am, with the last bus leaving at 7.40pm and terminating back at Singapore Flyer at 9.10pm. Buy tickets from the driver; see the website for route details.

City Sightseeing (www.ducktours.com.sg/hippo.php; adult/child S$33/23) A double-decker, open-top tourist bus running several tourist routes. Tickets are valid all day, allowing you to hop on and off freely. Buses run every 20 minutes.

CAR & MOTORCYCLE

Singaporeans drive on the left-hand side of the road. It is compulsory to wear seat belts in the front and back of the car.

Motorcycles are held in very low esteem. Be alert when riding.

Driving Licence

If you plan on driving in Singapore, bring your current home driver's licence. Some car-hire companies may also require you to have an international driving permit.

Hire

Given the ease, efficiency and relatively low cost of public transport in Singapore, there's no obvious need to rent a car.

If you do need to rent, rates start from around S$100 a day. Special deals may be available, especially for longer-term rental. If you're going into Malaysia, you're better off renting in Johor Bahru, where the rates are significantly lower (besides, Malaysian police are renowned for targeting Singapore licence plates).

Most rental companies in Singapore require that drivers be at least 23 years old.

The major car-hire companies have booths at Changi Airport as well as in the city.

Avis (☎ 6737 1668; www.avis.com.sg; 01-07 Waterfront Plaza, 390A Havelock Rd; 🚌 5, 16, 75, 175, 195, 970)

Europcar (Map p498; ☎ 6734 3245; www.europcar.com; 3 Church St; Ⓜ Telok Ayer, Raffles Pl)

Hawk (☎ 6466 2366; www.hawkrentacar.com.sg; 01-11, 7 Soon Lee St; Ⓜ Boon Lay)

Hertz (☎ 6542 5300; www.hertz.com; Terminals 2 & 3, Changi Airport)

Restricted Zones & Parking

At various times through the day, from Monday to Saturday, much of central Singapore is considered a restricted zone. Cars are free to enter, but they must pay a toll. Vehicles are automatically tracked by sensors on overhead ERP (Electronic Road Pricing) gantries, so cars must be fitted with an in-vehicle unit, into which drivers must insert a CashCard (available at 7-Eleven and Cheers convenience stores, as well as selected petrol stations). The toll is extracted from the card. The same system is also in operation on certain expressways. Rental cars are subject to the same rules. Check www.onemotoring.com.sg for ERP rates and hours of operation.

Parking in the city centre is relatively easy to find – almost every major mall has a car park. Outdoor car parks and street parking spaces are usually operated by the government – you can buy booklets of parking coupons, which must be displayed in the window, from 7-Eleven, Cheers and selected petrol stations. Many car parks now operate using the same in-vehicle unit and CashCard used for ERP gantries instead of the coupon system. Parking rates are listed at www.onemotoring.com.sg.

MASS RAPID TRANSIT (MRT)

The efficient MRT subway system is the easiest, quickest and most comfortable way to get around Singapore. The system operates from 5.30am to around midnight, with trains at peak times running every two to three minutes, and off-peak every five to seven minutes.

In the inner city, the MRT runs underground, emerging overground out towards the suburban housing estates. It consists of five colour-coded lines: North–South (red), North–East (purple), East–West (green), Circle Line (yellow) and Downtown (blue). Extensions of the Downtown line – known as Downtown 2 and Downtown 3 – are scheduled to open in 2016 and 2017 respectively. You'll find a map of the network at www.transitlink.com.sg.

Eating and drinking is prohibited on trains and on station platforms and concourses.

Fares & Fare Cards

Single-trip tickets cost from S$1.60 to S$2.70, but if you plan to use the MRT and buses

AIRPORT–CITY CONNECTIONS

MODE	AIRPORT TERMINALS	DESTINATION	PRICE	FREQUENCY
Train (MRT)	2 & 3	Extensive island coverage (interchange at Tanah Merah station)	varies, Orchard Rd S$2.50, Clarke Quay S$2.60	every 12min, 5.30am-11.18pm
Taxi	All terminals	Anywhere	varies, around S$20 to S$40	
Bus 36	All terminals	Orchard Rd & Colonial District	varies, around S$2.50	every 6-15min, 6.10am-10.55pm
Airport shuttle	All terminals	Most hotels	adult/child S$9/6	every 15-30min, 24hr

TRISHAWS

Trishaws peaked just after WWII, when motorised transport was practically nonexistent and trishaw drivers could make a tidy income. Today there are only around 250 trishaws left in Singapore, mainly plying the tourist routes. Trishaws have banded together and are now managed in a queue system by **Trishaw Uncle** (Map p502; www.trishawuncle.com.sg; Queen St; 30min tour adult/child from $39/29, 45min tour $49/39; Ⓜ Bugis). Unlike some freelance operators around town, the company has fixed prices, which helps you avoid the possibility of being (figuratively) taken for a ride.

frequently, it's much more convenient to buy a rechargeable EZ-Link card. Alternatively, you can purchase a Singapore Tourist Pass, a special EZ-Link card allowing unlimited travel for one day (S$10), two days (S$16) or three days (S$20). The pass can be bought from the ticket booths at the following MRT stations: Changi Airport, Bayfront, Bugis, Chinatown, City Hall, HarbourFront, Lavender, Orchard and Raffles Place.

TAXI

You can flag down a taxi any time, but in the city centre taxis are technically not allowed to stop anywhere except at designated taxi stands. You will have no luck flagging down a taxi where a road is marked with unbroken yellow double lines (signifying a no-parking zone).

Finding a taxi in the city at certain times is harder than it should be. These include during peak hours, at night, or when it's raining. Many cab drivers change shifts between 4pm and 5pm, making it notoriously difficult to score a taxi then.

The fare system is also complicated, but thankfully it's all metered, so there's no haggling over fares. The basic flagfall is S$3 to S$3.90, then S$0.22 for every 400m.

There's a whole raft of surcharges to note, among them:

- 50% of the metered fare from midnight to 6am.
- 25% of the metered fare between 6am and 9.30am Monday to Friday, and 6pm to midnight daily.
- S$5 for airport trips from 5pm to midnight Friday to Sunday, and S$3 at all other times.
- S$3 city-area surcharge from 5pm to midnight.
- S$3 for trips starting from Resorts World Sentosa and Gardens by the Bay.
- S$2.30 to S$8 for telephone bookings (S$10 to S$18 for limousine taxis).

Payment by credit card incurs a 10% surcharge. Most taxis accept MasterCard, American Express and Diners, though none take Visa. If paying by card, always ask the driver before getting into the vehicle, as some only take cash. You can also pay using your EZ-Link or Nets transport card. For a comprehensive list of fares and surcharges, visit www.taxisingapore.com.

To book a taxi, dial 6-DIAL CAB (6342-5222), and your call will be directed to an available taxi company's call centre.

Taxi companies in Singapore include the following.

Comfort Taxi and CityCab (☎6552 1111)
Premier Taxis (☎6363 6888)
SMRT Taxis (☎6555 8888)

Understand Malaysia, Singapore & Brunei

Malaysia, Singapore & Brunei Today

National tragedies and political troubles have impacted Malaysia in recent years. Passenger airplanes have fallen from the sky, an earthquake struck Sabah, and Prime Minister Najib Razak battled allegations of corruption and a faltering economy. Singapore mourned the death of its founding father Lee Kuan Yew then celebrated its 50th anniversary by re-electing his son as prime minister. Still no elections in the Sultanate of Brunei, but it has introduced sharia laws.

Best in Print: Fiction

The Garden of Evening Mists (Tan Twan Eng; 2012) An elegant, multi-layered narrative that carries the reader from WWII occupied Malaya through to the terrors of the Emergency.

Crazy Rich Asians (Kevin Kwan; 2013) Light entertainment that skewers Singapore's jet-set generation.

Malaysian Tales (ed Daphne Lee; 2011) Local fables, fairy tales, myths and legends re-imagined and retold by contemporary writers.

Devil of a State (Anthony Burgess; 1961) The novel's setting of an imaginary caliphate Dunia is based on Burgess's time in Brunei in the 1950s.

Best on Film

Ilo Ilo (Anthony Chen; 2013) A 2013 Cannes Film Festival award winner, this touching story is about a troubled Chinese-Singaporean boy and his Filipino maid.

Bunohan (Dain Said; 2012) Moody, slow-moving thriller about a kickboxer on the run and troubled family relations on the Kelantan coast.

Sepet (Yasmin Ahmad; 2005) Love across the cultural barriers as a Chinese boy and a Malay girl fall for each other.

Lost Flights & an Earthquake

The discovery in July 2015 of plane debris on the Indian Ocean island of Reunion finally offered conclusive proof about the fate of Malaysian Airlines flight MH370, 18 months after its disappearance. Many questions about the final hours of MH370 and its 239 passengers still remain, not least of which is where the rest of the wreckage is.

The scattered remains of Malaysia Airlines MH17, which crashed on 17 July 2014 in the Donetsk area of Ukraine with a loss of 298 lives, were all too apparent. The official Dutch Safety Board report on the causes of the crash, published in October 2015, confirmed that the flight was shot down by a surface-to-air missile.

Although it was also unexpected, the geological causes of the earthquake that struck Sabah on 5 June 2015 and claimed the lives of 18 people on Mt Kinabalu are not in doubt. This didn't stop some locals believing that the quake, which registered 6.0 on the Richter scale, was the result of the region's animist spirits being angered by the disrespectful behaviour of Western tourists at the summit of the mountain six days earlier.

Najib Under Fire

In July 2015 Malaysia's Prime Minister Najib Razak, already taking the flack for a currency at a 17-year low against the US dollar and the introduction of an unpopular general sales tax, faced a new crisis. The Wall St Journal and other media sources implicated him in a corruption scandal involving the government's 1MBD sovereign investment fund that aims to turn Kuala Lumpur (KL) into a global financial hub. The fund has racked up huge debts at the same time as it appears that nearly US$700 million had been transferred from it into Najib's personal bank accounts.

Najib, who at the time of publication had avoided any formal charges, claims that the transfer was a political donation from undisclosed Middle Eastern supporters. However, public opinion remains highly skeptical – particularly so after the PM sacked his deputy, who had publicly voiced his doubts about the situation, and removed the attorney general who had been conducting an investigation into the affair. That investigation was subsequently suspended. The government also blocked online access to the Sarawak Report (www.sarawakreport.org), which has covered the 1MDB scandal extensively.

Whither Malaysia's Opposition?

The situation appeared to have reached a climax at the end of August 2015 when the Bersih movement organised a rally in KL and several other major cities across Malaysia. Bersih, which means 'clean', consists of 84 nongovernment organisations calling for free and fair elections in Malaysia. Their main demand at the rally was for Najib to resign, a call echoed by former prime minister Mohammad Mahathir who briefly joined the tens of thousands of yellow T-shirt clad Bersih supporters on KL's streets.

The rally passed without any major confrontations, as did a smaller 'red shirt' rally of government supporters on Malaysia Day, 16 September. Bersih supporters are painted predominantly as Chinese, while those on the ruling party side are mainly Malays, which has led to fears of any future demonstration escalating into the kind of ethnic-based riots that shook Malaysia's sense of national cohesion in 1969.

Meanwhile there has been disarray among the political opposition, which in June 2015 splintered when the Democratic Action Party (DAP) pulled out of Pakatan Rakyat (PR), a coalition it had formed with the People's Justice Party (PKR) and the Islamist Parti Islam se-Malaysia (PAS). In September 2015 a new coalition, Pakatan Harapan (PH), was formed by PKR, DAP and the Islamic socialist party Amanah, made up of defectors from PAS. PH's desired prime ministerial candidate for the next general election (most likely to occur in 2018) is Anwar Ibrahim, PKR's former leader. However, it's unclear whether he will have been released by then from jail where he is currently serving time for sodomy, a conviction Anwar and his supporters claim is politically motivated.

Regional Rise of Islam

One of the reasons PAS fell out of the PR coalition was because of its advocacy for harsh Islamic punishments, such as flogging and amputation. Such *hudud* (punishments under Islamic laws) have been approved in PAS-controlled Kelantan, but they will not be imposed as they remain illegal at the national level. Such developments towards a more strictly Islamic country, however, are deeply worrying to non-Muslim Malaysians.

POPULATION:
29.72 MILLION/ 5.4 MILLION/480,000 (MALAYSIA/SINGAPORE/ BRUNEI)

GDP: **US$313.2 BILLION/ $297.9 BILLION/ $16.11 BILLION**

UNEMPLOYMENT:
3.2%/1.9%/6.9%

if Singapore were 100 people

74 would be Chinese
13 would be Malay
9 would be Indian
4 would be other

if Malaysia were 100 people

50 would be Malay
22 would be Chinese
12 would be Orang Asli
7 would be Indian
9 would be other

population per sq km

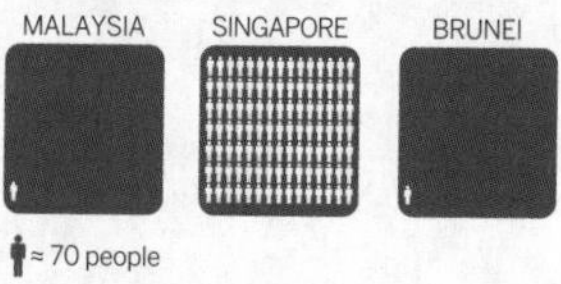

Best in Print: Non-Fiction

Singapore: A Biography (Mark Ravinder Frost & Yu-Mei Balasingamchow; 2010) A well-written and handsomely illustrated history of Singapore.

Malaysia at Random (ed Editions Didier Millet Publishing; 2010) Quirky compendium of facts, quotes and anecdotes.

Malaysia Bagus!: Travels From My Homeland (Sharon Cheah; 2012) Engaging travelogue with stories from all of Malaysia's states plus Singapore.

Best Music

Angin Kencang (Noh Salleh) EP of melodic indie guitar pop by a male vocalist; hailed as one of 2014's best local releases.

Nocturnal (Yuna; www.yunamusic.com) Poster girl for Malaysian young 'hijabsters' with a soulful voice to match her sultry looks.

40th Anniversary Collection (Dick Lee; http://dicklee.com) A Singaporean national treasure, Lee has been making music since the 1970s.

Etiquette

Visiting mosques Cover your head, arms and legs.

Eating Use your right hand only if eating with your fingers.

Modesty Don't embrace or kiss in public.

In Brunei, a tough Islamic Penal Code (sharia laws) started to be phased in from April 2014. It mainly applies to Muslims, however non-Muslims can also be charged for certain offenses including drinking alcohol in public, adultery and homosexual acts. The application of rules regarding Friday prayers and fasting during Ramadan have also been toughened up and will affect visitors.

Having built its economy on oil, the crucial question facing Brunei society is what will happen when this resource runs out. At the current pace of extraction, the sultanate has enough oil left for two decades. Back-up plans for economic diversification remain sketchy, although the construction of a 30km bridge linking Brunei-Maura with Temburong, due to be completed in 2018, may prove a boost to tourism.

Singapore at Fifty

In March 2015, thousands of Singaporeans stood in pouring rain to pay their respects to Lee Kuan Yew as the funeral cortege for the country's first prime minister passed by. Not everyone was sad to see him go: when 16-year-old vlogger Amos Yee was jailed for 53 days for posting offensive comments about Lee on social media it highlighted the country's draconian record on freedom of speech and media censorship.

A few months later everyone reunited in celebration of their country's 50th birthday, proud of Singapore's ascent from a 'little red dot' with rocky prospects, to a global 'it' kid, more than punching its weight when it comes to business, the arts and urban sustainability. The wave of patriotism was one of the factors that is said to have aided the ruling People's Action Party (PAP) in winning 83 out of 89 seats and capturing almost 70% of the vote in the September 2015 general election. This was significantly up from the PAP's record low of 60.1% in 2011 and a severe blow for the opposition who for the first time had fielded candidates in all constituencies.

History

As the countries we know today, Malaysia, Singapore and Brunei have been around since 1963, 1965 and 1984 respectively. The region's history, of course, stretches back much further, although pinning down exactly how far back is tricky due to a lack of archaeological evidence and early written records. Events from the rise of the Melaka Sultanate in the 16th century, however, were well documented locally and by the nations which came to trade with, and later rule over, the peninsula and Borneo.

The Negrito & Early Migrants

Discovered in 1991, the complete 11,000-year-old skeleton, 'Perak Man,' has genetic similarities to the Negrito, ethnic ancestors of the Semang tribe of Orang Asli who still live in the mountainous rainforests of northern Malaysia. The Negrito were joined by Malaysia's first immigrants, the Senoi, from southern Thailand, and later by the Proto-Malay, ancestors of today's Malays, who came by sea from Indonesia between 1500 BC and 500 BC.

By the 2nd century Malaya was known as far away as Europe. Ptolemy, the Greek geographer, labelled it Aurea Chersonesus (Golden Chersonese); Indian traders, who came in search of precious metals, tin and aromatic jungle woods, referred to the land as Savarnadvipa (Land of Gold).

Earliest evidence of human life in the region is a 40,000-year-old skull found in Sarawak's Niah Caves, a period when Borneo was still connected to the Southeast Asian mainland.

Early Trade & Empires

The first formalised religions on the peninsula – Hinduism and Buddhism – arrived with the Indian traders in the 2nd century, giving rise to the first recorded Hindu kingdom on the peninsula, Langkasuka (from the Sanskrit for 'resplendent land').

From the 7th century to the 13th century, the area fell under the sway of the Srivijaya Empire, based in southern Sumatra. This Buddhist empire controlled the entire Malacca Straits, Java and southern Borneo and became fabulously rich through trade with India and China. Under the protection of the Srivijayans, a significant Malay trading state grew up in the Bujang Valley area in the far northwest of the Thai–Malay peninsula.

TIMELINE

c 150 AD

European knowledge of the Malay peninsula is confirmed in Ptolemy's book *Geographia*. It's likely that Romans visited the region during trading expeditions to India and China.

200

Langkasuka, one of the first Hindu-Malay kingdoms, is established on the peninsula around the area now known as Kedah. It lasted in one form or another until the 15th century.

600

From their base in southern Sumatra, most likely around modern-day Palembang, the Buddhist Srivijaya Empire dominates Malaya, Singapore, Indonesia and Borneo for another six centuries.

The growing power of the southern Thai kingdom of Ligor and the Hindu Majapahit Empire of Java finally led to the demise of the Srivijayans in the 14th century.

The Melaka Empire

It's thought that the word Malay (or Melayu) is based on the ancient Tamil word *malia*, meaning 'hill'. Other Malay words like *bahasa* (language), *raja* (ruler) and *jaya* (success) are Sanskrit terms imported to the area by Indian visitors as early as the 2nd century.

The history of the Malay state begins in earnest in the late 14th century when Parameswara, a renegade Hindu prince/pirate from a little kingdom in southern Sumatra, washed up around 1401 in the tiny fishing village that would become Melaka. As a seafarer, Parameswara recognised a good port when he saw it and he immediately lobbied the Ming emperor of China for protection from the Thais in exchange for generous trade deals. Thus the Chinese came to Malaysia.

Equidistant between India and China, Melaka became a major stop for freighters from India loaded with pepper and cloth, and junks from China carrying porcelain and silks, which were traded for local metal and spices. Business boomed as regional ships and *perahu* (small Malay-style boats) arrived to take advantage of trading opportunities. The Melakan sultans soon ruled over the greatest empire in Malaysia's history.

The Portuguese Era

By the 15th century, Europe had developed an insatiable appetite for spices, which were conveyed there via a convoluted trade route through India and Arabia. The Portuguese decided to cut out the middleperson and go directly to the source: Melaka. Reaching the Malay coast in 1509, the Portuguese were greeted warmly by the local sultan, but relations soon soured. The invaders laid siege to Melaka in 1511, capturing the city and driving the sultan and his forces back to Johor.

The Portuguese secured Melaka by building the robust Porta de Santiago (A'Famosa fortress) and their domination lasted 130 years, though the entire period was marked by skirmishes with local sultans. Compared with Indian Muslim traders, the Portuguese contributed little to Malay culture; attempts to introduce Christianity and the Portuguese language were never a big success, though a dialect of Portuguese, Kristang, is still spoken in Melaka.

A History of Malaya by Barbara and Leonard Andaya brilliantly explores the evolution of 'Malayness' in Malaysia's history and the challenges of building a multiracial, post-independence nation.

The Dutch Period

Vying with the Portuguese for control of the spice trade, the Dutch formed an allegiance with the sultans of Johor to oust the Portuguese from Melaka. A joint force of Dutch and Johor soldiers and sailors besieged Melaka in 1641 and wrested the city from the Portuguese. In return for its cooperation, Johor was made exempt from most of the tariffs and trade restrictions imposed on other vassal states. Despite maintaining control of Melaka for about 150 years, the Dutch never really realised

1402

Hindu prince and pirate Parameswara (1344–1414) founds the great trading port and sultanate of Melaka; seven years later he marries a Muslim princess and adopts the Persian title Iskandar Shah.

1446

A naval force from Siam (Thailand) attacks Melaka. Warded off, the Siamese return in 1456 but are again rebuffed. Such attacks encourage Melaka's rulers to develop closer relations with China.

1485

Sultan Bolkiah of Brunei controls land as far south as present-day Kuching in Sarawak and north towards the islands of the Philippines.

1509

Portuguese traders sail into Melaka. Although at first greeted warmly, acting on the advice of his Indian Muslim councillors, the Melakan sultan later attacks the Portuguese ships, taking 19 prisoners.

THE ADOPTION OF ISLAM

Peninsular Malaysia was Buddhist and Hindu for a thousand years before the local rulers adopted Islam. The religion is believed to have spread through contact with Indian Muslim traders; in 1136 the Kedah Annals record that Hindu ruler Phra Ong Mahawangsa converted to Islam and founded the sultanate of Kedah, the oldest on Peninsular Malaysia.

The first sultan of Brunei, Muhammad Shah, converted to Islam in 1363 upon his marriage to a princess from Johor-Temasik. Maharaja Mohammed Shah of Melaka, who reigned between 1424 and 1444, also converted. The maharaja's son, Mudzaffar Shah, later took the title of sultan and made Islam the state religion. With its global trade links, Melaka became a regional hub for the dissemination of Islam and the Malay language.

the full potential of the city. High taxes forced merchants to seek out other ports and the Dutch focused their main attention on Batavia (now Jakarta) as their regional headquarters.

East India Company

British interest in the region began with the need for a halfway base for East India Company (EIC) ships plying the India–China maritime route. The first base was established on the island of Penang in 1786.

Meanwhile, events in Europe were conspiring to consolidate British interests on the Malay peninsula. When Napoleon overran the Netherlands in 1795, the British, fearing French influence in the region, took over Dutch Java and Melaka. When Napoleon was defeated in 1818, the British handed the Dutch colonies back – but not before leaving the fortress of A'Famosa beyond use.

The British lieutenant-governor of Java, Stamford Raffles – yes, *that* Stamford Raffles – soon persuaded the EIC that a settlement south of the Malay peninsula was crucial to the India–China maritime route. In 1819, he landed in Singapore and negotiated a trade deal with Johor that saw the island ceded to Britain in perpetuity, in exchange for a significant cash tribute.

In 1824, Britain and the Netherlands signed the Anglo–Dutch Treaty, dividing the region into two distinct spheres of influence. The Dutch controlled what is now Indonesia, and the British controlled Penang, Melaka, Dinding and Singapore, which were soon combined to create the 'Straits Settlements'.

Sejarah Melayu (Malay Annals), a literary work covering the establishment of the Melaka sultanate and 600 years of Malay history, is believed to have been compiled by Tun Sri Lanang, the *bendahara* (chief minister) of the Johor Royal Court in the early 17th century.

Borneo Developments

Britain did not include Borneo in the Anglo–Dutch treaty, preferring that the EIC concentrate its efforts on consolidating their power on

1511

Following the Portuguese conquest of Melaka, the sultan and his court flee, establishing two new sultanates on the peninsula: Perak to the north and Johor to the south.

1629

The Portuguese in Melaka and the sultanate of Johor unite to successfully defend themselves against the navy of Iskandar Muda, the sultan of Aceh in Sumatra, who had already conquered Kedah.

1641

After a siege lasting several months, the Dutch, with the help of the Johor sultanate, wrest Melaka from the Portuguese. Melaka starts to decline as a major trading port.

1786

Captain Francis Light cuts a deal with the sultan of Kedah to establish a settlement on the largely uninhabited island of Penang. Under a free-trade policy the island's new economy thrives.

the peninsula rather than furthering their geographical scope. Into the breach jumped opportunistic British adventurer James Brooke. In 1841, having helped the local viceroy quell a rebellion, Brooke was installed as raja of Sarawak, with the fishing village of Kuching as his capital.

Through brutal naval force and skillful negotiation, Brooke extracted further territory from the Brunei sultan and eventually brought peace to a land where piracy, headhunting and violent tribal rivalry had been the norm. The 'White Raja' dynasty of the Brookes was to rule Sarawak until 1941 and the arrival of the Japanese.

The White Rajas included tribal leaders in their ruling council, discouraged large European companies from destroying native jungle to plant massive rubber plantations and encouraged Chinese migration.

Meanwhile, the once-mighty empire of Brunei, which had held sway over all the islands of Borneo and much of the present-day Philippines, continued to shrink. In 1865 the American consul to Brunei persuaded the ailing sultan to grant him what is now Sabah in return for an annual payment. The rights eventually passed to an Englishman, Alfred Dent. In 1881, with the support of the British government, Dent formed the British North Borneo Company to administer the new settlement. To prevent a scramble for Brunei's remains, in 1888 the British government acceded to a request by the sultan to declare his territory a British protectorate.

British Malaya

In Peninsular Malaya, Britain's policy of 'trade, not territory' was challenged when trade was disrupted by civil wars within the Malay sultanates of Negeri Sembilan, Selangor, Pahang and Perak. In 1874 the British started to take political control by appointing the first colonial governor of Perak. In 1896 Perak, Selangor, Negeri Sembilan and Pahang were united under the banner of the Federated Malay States, each governed by a British Resident.

THE NAVEL OF THE MALAY COUNTRIES

'It is impossible to conceive a place combining more advantages…it is the Navel of the Malay countries', wrote a delighted Stamford Raffles soon after landing in Singapore in 1819. This statement proves his foresight because at the time the island was an inhospitable swamp surrounded by dense jungle, with a population of 150 fishermen and a small number of Chinese farmers. Raffles returned to his post in Bencoolen, Sumatra, but left instructions on Singapore's development as a free port with the new British Resident, Colonel William Farquhar.

In 1822 Raffles returned to Singapore and governed it for one more year. He initiated a town plan that included levelling a hill to form a new commercial district (now Raffles Place) and erecting government buildings around Forbidden Hill (now Fort Canning Hill). Wide streets of shophouses with covered walkways, shipyards, churches and a botanic garden were all built to achieve his vision of a Singapore that would one day be 'a place of considerable magnitude and importance'.

1790

The sultan of Kedah's attempt to retake Penang from the British fails. He is forced to cede the island to the British East India Company for 6000 Spanish dollars per annum.

1819

By backing the elder brother in a succession dispute in Johor, Stamford Raffles gains sole rights to build a trading base on the island of Singapore.

1823

The Johor sultan fully cedes Singapore to Britain. A year later the Dutch and British carve up the region into what eventually becomes Malaya and Indonesia.

1826

Having swapped Bencoolen on Sumatra for the Dutch-controlled Melaka, the British East India Company combines this with Penang and Singapore to create the Straits Settlements.

Kelantan, Terengganu, Perlis and Kedah were then purchased from the Thais, in exchange for the construction of the southern Thai railway, much to the dismay of local sultans. The 'Unfederated Malay States' eventually accepted British 'advisers,' though the sultan of Terengganu held out till 1919 – to this day, the states of the northeast peninsula form the heartland of the fundamentalist Malay Muslim nationalist movement.

It was British colonial practice across the region to administer the population according to neat racial categories, with the Europeans, Indians, Chinese and Malays living and working in their own distinct quarters.

Creating a Multicultural Nation

Although official British policy was that Malaya belonged to the Malays, colonial rule radically altered the ethnic composition of the country. Chinese and Indian migrant workers were brought into the country in droves, as they shared a similar economic agenda and had less nationalist grievance against the colonial administration than the native Malays.

The Chinese were encouraged to work the mines and the Indians to tap the rubber trees and build the railways. The Ceylonese were clerks in the civil service, and the Sikhs staffed the police force.

Even though the 'better bred' Malays were encouraged to join a separate arm of the civil service, there was growing resentment among the vast majority of Malays that they were being marginalised in their own country. A 1931 census revealed that the Chinese numbered 1.7 million and the Malays 1.6 million. Malaya's economy was revolutionised, but the impact of this liberal immigration policy continues to reverberate today.

By the eve of WWII, Malays from all states were pushing for independence.

WWII Period

A few hours before the bombing of Pearl Harbor in December 1941, Japanese forces landed on the northeast coast of Malaya. Within a few months they had taken over the entire peninsula and Singapore. The poorly defended Borneo states fell even more rapidly.

Singapore Story, the memoirs of Lee Kuan Yew, provides the official account of the birth and rise of the nation by the man who masterminded the whole thing.

Singapore's new governor, General Yamashita, slung the Europeans into the infamous Changi Prison, and Chinese communists and intellectuals, who had vociferously opposed the Japanese invasion of China, were targeted for Japanese brutality. Thousands were executed in a single week. In Borneo, early resistance by the Chinese was also brutally put down.

The Japanese achieved very little in Malaya. The British had destroyed most of the tin-mining equipment before their retreat, and the rubber plantations were neglected. The Malayan People's Anti-Japanese Army (MPAJA), comprising remnants of the British army and Chinese from the fledgling Malayan Communist Party, waged a jungle-based guerrilla struggle throughout the war.

The Japanese surrendered to the British in Singapore in 1945. Despite the eventual Allied victory, Britain had been humiliated by the easy loss

1839

British buccaneer James Brooke lands in Sarawak and helps quell a local rebellion. In gratitude, the Brunei sultanate installs him as the first White Raja of Sarawak two years later.

1874

The British start to take control of Peninsular Malaysia after the Pankor Treaty with the sultan of Perak; Sir James Birch is installed as the Perak's first British Resident.

1888

Having lost much territory to the British Empire, Brunei's sultan signs a treaty to make his country a British protectorate. A British Resident is installed in 1906.

1896

Perak, Selangor, Negeri Sembilan and Pahang join as Federated Malay States; the sultans concede political power to British Residents but keep control of matters relating to Malay traditions and Islam.

THE EMERGENCY

While the creation of the Federation of Malaya appeased Malays, the Chinese felt betrayed, particularly given their massive contribution to the war effort. Many joined the Malayan Communist Party (MCP), which promised an equitable and just society. In 1948 the MCP took to the jungles and embarked on a 12-year guerrilla war against the British. Even though the insurrection was on par with the Malay civil wars of the 19th century, it was classified as an 'Emergency' for insurance purposes.

The effects of the Emergency were felt most strongly in the countryside, where villages and plantation owners were repeatedly targeted by rebels. In 1951 the British high commissioner, Sir Henry Gurney, was assassinated on the road to Fraser's Hill. His successor, General Sir Gerald Templer, set out to 'win the hearts and minds of the people'. Almost 500,000 rural Chinese were forcibly resettled into protected *kampung baru* (new villages), restrictions were lifted on guerrilla-free areas, and the jungle-dwelling Orang Asli were bought into the fight to help the police track down the insurgents.

In 1960 the Emergency was declared over, although sporadic fighting continued and the formal surrender was signed only in 1989.

of Malaya and Singapore to the Japanese, and it was clear that their days of controlling the region were now numbered.

Federation of Malaya

In 1946 the British persuaded the sultans to agree to the Malayan Union, which amalgamated all the peninsular Malayan states into a central authority and offered citizenship to all residents regardless of race. In the process, the sultans were reduced to the level of paid advisers, the system of special privileges for Malays was abandoned and ultimate sovereignty passed to the king of England.

The normally acquiescent Malay population were less enthusiastic about the venture than the sultans. Rowdy protest meetings were held throughout the country, and the first Malay political party, the United Malays National Organisation (UMNO), was formed, leading to the dissolution of the Malayan Union and, in 1948, the creation of the Federation of Malaya, which reinstated the sovereignty of the sultans and the special privileges of the Malays.

F Spencer Chapman's *The Jungle Is Neutral* follows a British guerrilla force based in the Malaysian jungles during the Japanese occupation of Malaya and Singapore.

Merdeka & Malaysia

Malaysia's march to independence from British rule was led by UMNO, which formed a strategic alliance with the Malayan Chinese Association (MCA) and the Malayan Indian Congress (MIC). The new Alliance Party led by Tunku Abdul Rahman won a landslide victory in the 1955 election

1909

Britain does a deal with Thailand to gain control of Kelantan, Terengganu, Perlis and Kedah. Johor succumbs to a British Resident in 1914, completing the set of 'Unfederated Malay States'.

1941

The Japanese land on Malaya's northeast coast. Within a month they've taken Kuala Lumpur, and a month later they are at Singapore's doorstep.

1942

The British suffer a humiliating defeat in February as they capitulate Singapore to the Japanese. The occupiers rename it Syonan (Light of the South).

1944

Z Special Unit parachutes into Sarawak's Kelabit Highlands and wins over the natives. Armed with blowpipes and led by Australian commandos, this unlikely army scores several victories over the Japanese.

and, on 31 August 1957, Merdeka (independence) was declared. Sarawak, Sabah (then North Borneo) and Brunei remained under British rule.

In 1961 Tunku Abdul Rahman proposed a merger of Singapore, Malaya, Sabah, Sarawak and Brunei, which the British agreed to the following year. At the eleventh hour Brunei pulled out of the deal, as Sultan Sri Muda Omar Ali Saifuddien III (and, one suspects, Shell Oil) didn't want to see the revenue from its vast oil reserves channelled to the peninsula.

When modern Malaysia was born in July 1963, it immediately faced a diplomatic crisis. The Philippines broke off relations, claiming that Sabah was part of its territory (a claim upheld to this day), while Indonesia laid claim to the whole of Borneo, invading parts of Sabah and Sarawak before finally giving up its claim in 1966.

The marriage between Singapore and Malaya was also doomed from the start. Ethnic Chinese outnumbered Malays in both Malaysia and Singapore and the new ruler of the island-state, Lee Kuan Yew, refused to extend constitutional privileges to the Malays in Singapore. Riots broke out in Singapore in 1964; in August 1965 Tunku Abdul Rahman was forced to boot Singapore out of the federation.

Noel Barber's *The War of the Running Dogs* is a classic account of the 12-year Malayan Emergency. The title refers to what the communist fighters called the opposition who were loyal to the British.

Ethnic Tensions

Impoverished Malays became increasingly resentful of the economic success of Chinese Malaysians, while the Chinese grew resentful of the political privileges granted to Malays. Things reached breaking point when the Malay-dominated government attempted to suppress all languages except Malay and introduced a national policy of education that ignored Chinese and Indian history, language and culture.

In the 1969 general elections, the Alliance Party lost its two-thirds majority in parliament and a celebration march by the opposition Democratic Action Party (DAP) and Gerakan (The People's Movement) in KL led to a full-scale riot, which Malay gangs used as a pretext to loot Chinese businesses, killing hundreds of Chinese in the process.

Stunned by the savageness of the riots, the government decided that if there was ever going to be harmony between the races then the Malay community needed to achieve economic parity. To this end the New Economic Policy (NEP), a socio-economic affirmative action plan, was introduced. The Alliance Party also invited opposition parties to join them and work from within, and the expanded coalition was renamed the Barisan Nasional (BN; National Front).

Sabri Zain's colourful website Sejarah Melayu: A History of the Malay Peninsula (www.sabrizain.org/malaya) contains a wealth of historical info including a virtual library of nearly 500 books and academic papers.

The Era of Mahathir

In 1981 former UMNO member Mahathir Mohamad became prime minister. Malaysia's economy went into overdrive, growing from one based on commodities such as rubber, to one firmly rooted in industry and

1946
The United Malays National Organisation (UMNO) is formed on 1 March, signalling the rise of Malay nationalism and a desire for political independence from Britain.

1951
Sir Henry Gurney, British high commissioner to Malaya, is assassinated by MCP rebels on the road to Fraser's Hill, a terrorist act that alienates many of the party's moderate Chinese members.

1953
The Parti Perikatan (Alliance Party) is formed, an alliance between UNMO, the Malayan Chinese Association (MCA) and Malayan Indian Congress (MIC). Two years later the party wins Malaya's first national elections.

1957
On 31 August Merdeka (independence) is declared in Malaya; Tunku Abdul Rahman becomes the first prime minister and the nine sultans agree to take turns as the nation's king.

BUMIPUTRA PRIVILEGES

When introduced in 1971, the aim of the New Economic Policy (NEP) was that 30% of Malaysia's corporate wealth be in the hands of indigenous Malays and Orang Asli, or *bumiputra* (princes of the land), within 20 years. A massive campaign of positive discrimination began which handed majority control over the army, police, civil service and government to Malays. The rules extended to education, scholarships, share deals, corporate management and even the right to import a car.

By 1990 *bumiputra* corporate wealth had risen to 19%, but was still 11% short of the original target. Poverty in general fell dramatically, a new Malay middle class emerged and nationalist violence by Malay extremists receded. In the meantime, however, cronyism and discrimination against Indians and Chinese has increased. And even though more Malays are gaining a higher education this is not necessarily translating into jobs: 70% of all jobless graduates in 2010 were *bumiputra*.

Affirmative action remains an integral part of government policy, with the aim of increasing *bumiputra* corporate wealth and control to at least 30% by 2020. However, despite over 40 years of such policies, there is still much to be done to improve the lives of the ethnic minorities of Sabah and Sarawak and the Orang Asli of Peninsular Malaysia, as these *bumiptura* still lag far behind Malays in terms of poverty, employment, education and healthcare.

manufacturing. Government monopolies were privatised, and heavy industries like steel manufacturing (a failure) and the Malaysian car (successful but heavily protected) were encouraged. Multinationals were successfully wooed to set up in Malaysia, and manufactured exports began to dominate the trade figures.

One notable criticism of Mahathir's time as prime minister was that the main media outlets became little more than government mouthpieces. The sultans lost their right to give final assent on legislation, and the once proudly independent judiciary appeared to become subservient to government wishes, the most notorious case being that of Anwar Ibrahim. Mahathir also permitted widespread use of the Internal Security Act (ISA) to silence opposition leaders and social activists, most famously in 1987's Operation Lalang, when 106 people were arrested and the publishing licences of several newspapers were revoked.

Covering events up to 2001, the second edition of Graham Saunder's *History of Brunei* is the only full-length study of how this tiny country came to be formed.

Economic & Political Crisis

In 1997, after a decade of near constant 10% growth, Malaysia was hit by the regional currency crisis. Mahathir blamed it all on unscrupulous Western speculators deliberately undermining the economies of the developing world for their personal gain. He pegged the Malaysian ringgit

1963

In July the British Borneo territories of Sabah and Sarawak are combined with Singapore and Malaya to form Malaysia – a move that sparks confrontations with Indonesia and the Philippines.

1965

In August, following Singapore's refusal to extend constitutional privileges to the Malays on the island and subsequent riots, Singapore is booted out of Malaysia. Lee Kuan Yew becomes Singapore's first prime minister.

1967

Sultan Sri Muda Omar Ali Saifuddien III voluntarily abdicates in favour of his eldest son and the current ruler, the 29th in the unbroken royal Brunei line, Sultan Hassanal Bolkiah.

1969

Following the general election, on 13 March race riots erupt in KL, killing hundreds. In response the government devises the New Economic Policy of positive discrimination for Malays.

to the US dollar, bailed out what were seen as crony companies, forced banks to merge and made it difficult for foreign investors to remove their money from Malaysia's stock exchange. Malaysia's subsequent recovery from the economic crisis, which was more rapid than that of many other Southeast Asian nations, further bolstered Mahathir's prestige.

Anwar Ibrahim, Mahathir's deputy prime minister and heir apparent, was at odds with Mahathir over how to deal with the economic crisis. Their falling out was so severe that in September 1998 Anwar was sacked and soon after charged with corruption and sodomy. Many Malaysians, feeling that Anwar had been falsely arrested, took to the streets chanting Anwar's call for *'reformasi'*. The demonstrations were harshly quelled and, in trials that were widely criticised as unfair, Anwar was sentenced to a total of 15 years' imprisonment. The international community rallied around Anwar, with Amnesty International proclaiming him a prisoner of conscience.

In the following year's general elections BN suffered huge losses, particularly in the rural Malay areas. The gainers were the fundamentalist Islamic party, PAS (Parti Islam se-Malaysia), which had vociferously supported Anwar, and a new political party, Keadilan (People's Justice Party), headed by Anwar's wife Wan Azizah.

Revolusi 48 (http://revolusi48.blogspot.co.uk), the sequel to Fahmi Reza's doco *10 Tahun Sebelum Merdeka* (10 Years Before Merdeka), chronicles the largely forgotten armed revolution for national liberation launched against British colonial rule in Malaya.

BN on the Ropes

Prime minister Mahathir's successor, Abdullah Badawi, was sworn into office in 2003 and went on to lead Barisan Nasional (BN) to a landslide victory in the following year's election. In stark contrast to his feisty predecessor, the pious Abdullah immediately impressed voters by taking a nonconfrontational, consensus-seeking approach. He set up a royal commission to investigate corruption in the police force and called time on several of the massively expensive mega projects that had been the hallmark of the Mahathir era, including a new bridge across the Straits of Johor to Singapore.

Released from jail in 2004, Anwar returned to national politics in August 2008 on winning the bi-election for the seat vacated by his wife. However, sodomy charges were again laid against the politician in June and he was arrested in July.

In the March 2008 election, UMNO and its coalition partners in BN saw their parliamentary dominance slashed to less than the customary two-thirds majority. Pakatan Rakyat (PR), the opposition People's Alliance, led by Anwar Ibrahim, not only bagged 82 of parliament's 222 seats but also took control of four out of Malaysia's 13 states, including the key economic bases of Selangor and Penang. PR subsequently lost Perak following a complex power play between various defecting MPs.

Brunei's ties with its former colonial master remain strong: UK judges sit in the High Court and Court of Appeal and a British Army Gurkha battalion is permanently stationed in Seria.

1974
Following the formation of the Barisan Nasional (BN) in 1973, this new coalition led by Tun Abdul Razak wins the Malaysian general election by a landslide.

1981
Dr Mahathir Mohamad becomes prime minister of Malaysia and introduces policies of 'Buy British Last' and 'Look East' to encourage the country to emulate Japan, South Korea and Taiwan.

1984
A somewhat reluctant Sultan Hassanal Bolkiah leads Brunei to complete independence from Britain. The country subsequently veers towards Islamic fundamentalism, introducing full Islamic law in 1991.

1990
After more than three decades in the job, Lee Kuan Yew steps down as prime minister of Singapore, handing over to Goh Chok Tong.

Abdullah Badawi resigned in favour of his urbane deputy, Mohd Najib bin Tun Abdul Razak (typically referred to as Najib Razak), in April 2008. Son of Abdul Razak, Malaysia's second prime minister after independence and nephew of Razak's successor Hussein Onn, Najib has been groomed for this role ever since he first entered national politics at the age of 23 in 1976.

Amir Muhammad's 2009 documentary *Malaysian Gods* commemorates the decade after the Reformasi movement began with the sacking of Anwar Ibrahim as deputy prime minister in 1998.

Improving International Relations

Ever since Malaysia booted Singapore out of the federation in 1965, leaving Lee Kuan Yew sobbing on camera, the two countries have acted like squabbling siblings. Singapore, the over-achieving youngster with few natural resources beyond its hard-working population, has managed to claw its way from obscurity to world admiration for its rapid and successful industrialisation. Across the causeway big brother Malaysia has achieved a no less impressive economic transformation, albeit one built on prodigious resources, in particular the profits from oil and gas.

Relations between the two reached the heights of touchiness in the 1990s. Former Malaysian prime minister Dr Mahathir and Singapore's 'Minister Mentor' Lee Kuan Yew parried insults back and forth across the Causeway, the former accusing Singaporeans of being the sort of people who 'urinate in lifts' and the latter retorting that the Malaysian town of Johor Bahru was 'notorious for shootings, muggings and car-jackings'.

Recently, however, relations seem to be improving. Persistent squabbles over water (under a 1962 accord, Malaysia supplies Singapore with 250 million gallons of raw water daily) are becoming moot as Singapore develops alternative sources of supply. The 2011 land swap deal that ended a long-running dispute over the KTM railway line in Singapore was also heralded as a breakthrough in attitudes between the two countries.

Relations between Malaysia and Brunei also became a lot more cordial in 2009, when the two signed a deal that ended a 20-year territorial dispute between the neighbouring countries over the land border around Limbang and ownership of offshore gas and oil exploration sites. Malaysian company Petronas is now working with Brunei to develop the sites.

About 30% of the Malaysian government's RM225 billion (US$63 billion) revenue in 2014 was oil-related, including a RM29 billion dividend from Petronas, the national oil and gas company.

GE13 & After

In the months leading up to Malaysia's 13th general election (GE13), on 5 May 2013, opposition parties, political commentators and the public had been calling attention to irregularities and unfairness in Malaysia's electoral system. Unbalanced constituency sizes, lack of access to the media for campaigning, and the possibility of gerrymandering were the main concerns. Major rallies in KL saw tens, if not hundreds, of thousands marching for fair and free elections.

With the results in, BN had lost seven seats in the national parliament but emerged as the majority winner, thus again able to form a govern-

1998
Anwar Ibrahim is sacked, arrested, sent for trial and jailed following disagreements with Dr Mahathir over how to deal with the Asian currency crisis and tackle government corruption.

2003
Having announced his resignation the previous year, Dr Mahathir steps down as prime minister in favour of Abdullah Badawi. He remains very outspoken on national politics.

2004
A month after the election in which BN takes 199 of 219 seats in the Lower House of parliament, Anwar Ibrahim sees his sodomy conviction overturned and is released from prison.

2007
As the country celebrates 50 years since independence it is also shaken by two anti-government rallies in November in which tens of thousands take to the streets of KL to protest.

ment with Najib Razak back as prime minister. The opposition coalition parties in PR won a majority of votes overall, but this counted for little given Malaysia's first-past-the-post election system. PR did, however, hold onto government in Selangor, the state surrounding the federal territory of KL, which it had first captured in the 2008 election.

On 8 May it was reported that 120,000 people gathered at a stadium just outside the city limits to protest the election results. However, a 'Malaysian Spring' (an effort to spread the message of hope and change) was not in the offing. With racially divisive rhetoric in the air (Najib had referred to a 'Chinese tsunami' of voters as being responsible for the coalition's losses) people from all sides called for community harmony and the need to double down on the objectives of the 1Malaysia policy (p580).

Amir Muhammad's *Malaysian Politicians Say the Darndest Things Vols 1 & 2* gathers together jaw-dropping statements uttered by the local pollies over the last three decades. Must be read to be believed.

Death in the Skies

Shortly after midnight on 8 March 2014, Malaysia Airlines flight MH370 took off from KL International Airport bound for Beijing. Less than an hour later, somewhere over the South China Sea, the plane with 239 people aboard lost contact with air traffic control. For the next 18 months nothing more of its whereabouts was known, until a section of its aircraft wing washed up on Reunion Island. At the time of publication, extensive searches of the southern Indian Ocean have turned up no further clues and the exact circumstances of MH370's disappearance remain a mystery.

Malaysia had barely come to terms with the loss of MH370 when on 17 July 2014 another of its national carrier's flights hit the headlines for all the wrong reasons. MH17 became a casualty of the conflict raging between pro-Russian forces and the Ukrainian army in the Donetsk region of Ukraine. Controversy raged over who fired the missile that likely downed the aircraft with a loss of 298 lives, with both sides denying responsibility and pointing the finger at each other.

While Malaysia gained much international sympathy for its handling of the MH17 tragedy, suspicion has lingered that the authorities could have done more in the early hours and days of MH370's disappearance. Confidence in Malaysian Airlines subsequently plummeted, necessitating its nationalisation and a major restructuring with a loss of 6000 jobs. In 2015 its chief executive Christoph Mueller declared the company 'technically bankrupt'.

Lee's Law: How Singapore Crushes Dissent, by Chris Lydgate, is a disturbing account of the rise and systematic destruction of Singapore's most successful opposition politician lawyer, JB Jeyaretnam.

2008

In the March election BN retains power but suffers heavy defeats to the opposition coalition Pakatan Rakyat (PR); in August Anwar Ibrahim becomes PR leader following his re-election to parliament.

2009

In April, Najib Tun Razak succeeds Abdullah Badawi as prime minister; the 1Malaysia policy is introduced to build respect and trust between the country's different races.

2011

Elections in Sarawak return a BN state government but with a reduced majority; tens of thousands rally in KL in support of fairer elections.

2014

Malaysia suffers a double blow as Malaysia Airlines flight MH370 goes missing in March, and flight MH17 is shot down over Ukraine in July.

People, Culture & Politics

There's a strong sense of shared experience and national identity in Malaysia, Singapore and Brunei. Malays, Chinese and Indians live side by side with Peranakan (Straits Chinese) and other mixed-race communities as well as the aboriginal nations – the Orang Asli of Peninsular Malaysia and Borneo's indigenous community. Ethnic diversity and harmony are touted as a regional strength, but none of these multicultural nations is the perfect melting pot. Religious and ethnic tensions remain a fact of life, particularly in Malaysia.

The Region's Peoples

The Malays

Malaysian politicians have been known to call in a *bomoh* (spiritual healer) during election campaigns to assist in their strategy and provide some foresight, or to scare away malicious spirits and bad weather before important events.

All Malays who are Muslim by birth are supposed to follow Islam, but many also adhere to older spiritual beliefs and adat (Malay customary law). With its roots in the Hindu period, adat places great emphasis on collective responsibility and maintaining harmony within the community – almost certainly a factor in the general goodwill between the different ethnic groups in Malaysia.

The enduring appeal of the communal *kampung* (village) spirit shouldn't be underestimated – many an urban Malay hankers after it, despite the affluent Western-style living conditions they enjoy at home. In principle, villagers are of equal status, though a headman is appointed on the basis of his wealth, greater experience or spiritual knowledge. Traditionally the founder of the village was appointed village leader *(penghulu* or *ketua kampung)* and often members of the same family would also become leaders. A *penghulu* is usually a haji, one who has made the pilgrimage to Mecca.

The Muslim religious leader, the imam, holds a position of great importance in the community as the keeper of Islamic knowledge and the leader of prayer, but even educated urban Malaysians periodically turn to *pawang* (shamans who possess a supernatural knowledge of harvests and nature) or *bomoh* (spiritual healers with knowledge of curative plants and the ability to harness the power of the spirit world) for advice before making any life-changing decisions.

Religious customs govern much of the Chinese community's home life, from the moment of birth, which is carefully recorded for astrological consultations later in life, to funerals which also have many rites and rituals.

The Chinese

In Malaysia and Brunei, the Chinese represent the second-largest ethnic group after the Malays. In Singapore they are the largest. The Chinese immigrants are mainly, in order of largest dialect group, Hokkien, Hakka, Cantonese and Wu. They are also predominantly Buddhist but also observe Confuncianism and Taosim, with a smaller number being Christian.

When Chinese people first began to arrive in the region in the early 15th century they came mostly from the southern Chinese province of Fujian and eventually formed one half of the group known as Peranakans. They developed their own distinct hybrid culture whereas later settlers, from Guangdong and Hainan provinces, stuck more closely to the culture of their homelands, including keeping their dialects.

If there's one cultural aspect that all Chinese in the region agree on it's the importance of education. It has been a very sensitive subject among the Malaysian Chinese community since the attempt in the 1960s to phase out secondary schools where Chinese was the medium of teaching, and the introduction of government policies that favour Malays in the early 1970s. The constraining of educational opportunities within Malaysia for the ethnic Chinese has resulted in many families working doubly hard to afford the tuition fees needed to send their offspring to private schools within the country and to overseas institutions.

The Malay surname is the child's father's first name. This is why Malaysians will use your given name after the Mr or Miss; to use your surname would be to address your father.

The Indians

Like the Chinese settlers, Indians in the region hail from many parts of the subcontinent and have different cultures depending on their religions – mainly Hinduism, Islam, Sikhism and Christianity. Most are Tamils, originally coming from the area now known as Tamil Nadu in South India where Hindu traditions are strong. Later, Muslim Indians from northern India followed along with Sikhs. These religious affiliations dictate many of the home-life customs and practices of Malaysian Indians, although one celebration that all Hindus and much of the rest of the region takes part in is Deepaval.

A small, English-educated Indian elite has always played a prominent role in Malaysian and Singaporean society, and a significant merchant class exists. However, a large percentage of Indians – imported as indentured labourers by the British – remain a poor working class in both countries. There's a small population of Indians living in Brunei.

FESTIVALS OF MALAYSIA

One of the most enjoyable ways to tap into the diverse cultures of the region is to attend a local festival. UK-born Keith Hockton spent part of his childhood in the region and now lives in Penang. We caught up with him in George Town to find out more about Malaysia's festivals.

What is particularly interesting about Malaysia's festivals? I began researching festivals when I returned to live in Malaysia in 2010. There were many festivals, Malay in origin, which I knew were taking place more or less in secret these days because of the growing Islamicisation of the country. I wanted to record these before they disappeared completely.

What surprised you in the research? I asked many locals what the most common festivals were about and few were able to answer me or they had very different interpretations. The research took me right across the peninsula and to Sabah and Sarawak where I stayed in longhouses – it was a fascinating journey of discovery. Malays are an extremely fun-loving and jocular people and you generally only get to see this if you spend time in the *kampung* (villages) and attend their festivals.

What are your favourite festivals? Hari Raya Aidilfitri, the breaking of the fast at the end of Ramadan, is a particularly joyous occasion. The Chinese Festival of the Hungry Ghost, when the streets are lit up with paper lanterns, incense and fireworks, is another favourite along with the Buddhist celebration of Songkran – essentially the world's biggest water fight. During the Hindu spring festival of Holi, it's brightly coloured powder that's being chucked around. Thaipusam (p585), another Hindu festival, provides some amazing images for photographers but is certainly not for the squeamish! A great aid to understanding the background and practices of these varied celebrations is *Festivals of Malaysia* (2015).

The Peranakans

Peranakan means 'half-caste' in Malay, which is exactly what the Peranakans are: descendants of Chinese immigrants who from the 16th century onwards principally settled in Singapore, Melaka and Penang and married Malay women.

In December 2013 around 300 migrant labourers from India were involved in a riot in Singapore's Little India following a fatal road accident in which a construction worker from Tamil Nadu was knocked down by a local bus driver.

The culture and language of the Peranakans is a fascinating melange of Chinese and Malay traditions. The Peranakans took the name and religion of their Chinese fathers, but the customs, language and dress of their Malay mothers. They also used the terms Straits-born or Straits Chinese to distinguish themselves from later arrivals from China.

The Peranakans were often wealthy traders who could afford to indulge their passion for sumptuous furnishings, jewellery and brocades. Their terrace houses were brightly painted, with patterned tiles embedded in the walls for extra decoration. When it came to the interior, Peranakan tastes favoured heavily carved and inlaid furniture.

Peranakan dress was similarly ornate. Women wore fabulously embroidered *kasot manek* (beaded slippers) and *kebaya* (blouses worn over a sarong), tied with beautiful *kerasong* (brooches), usually of fine filigree gold or silver. Men – who assumed Western dress in the 19th century, reflecting their wealth and contacts with the British – saved their finery for important occasions such as the wedding ceremony, a highly stylised and intricate ritual dictated by adat.

The Peranakan patois is a Malay dialect but one containing many Hokkien words – so much so that it is largely unintelligible to a Malay speaker. The Peranakans also included words and expressions of English and French, and occasionally practised a form of backward Malay by reversing the syllables.

The Eurasians

If you meet a Singaporean whose surname is Clarke, de Souza or Hendricks, chances are they are Eurasian, a term used to describe people of mixed Asian and European descent. In the early colonial days, the majority of Eurasian migrants arrived from the Malaysian trading port of Melaka, which alongside Goa, Macau and Ceylon (modern Sri Lanka) claimed notable mixed-race communities, a legacy of Portuguese, Dutch and British colonisers marrying local women.

Another name you may hear for the Peranakan is Baba-Nonya, after the Peranakan words for men (baba) and women (nonya). Nonya is also a term to describe Peranakan cuisine.

Shared Christian beliefs and shared cultural traditions created a firm bond between Singapore's British ruling class and the island's Eurasian community, and many Eurasians enjoyed privileged posts in the civil service. The bond would erode after the opening of the Suez Canal, when an increase in European arrivals saw the 'half Europeans' sidelined.

These days, Singapore is home to around 15,000 Eurasians, and the group features prominently in the media and entertainment industries; they even have their own association (www.eurasians.org.sg). The Eurasians' mixed-race appearance is especially appealing to advertisers, who see it as conveniently encompassing Singapore's multiracial make-up. The majority of modern Singaporean Eurasians are of British descent, with English as their first language.

The Orang Asli

The indigenous people of Malaysia – known collectively as Orang Asli (Original People) – played an important role in early trade, teaching the colonialists about forest products and guiding prospectors to outcrops of tin and precious metals. They also acted as scouts and guides for anti-insurgent forces during the Emergency in the 1950s.

Despite this, the Orang Asli remain marginalised in Malaysia. According to the most recent government data published in December 2004, Peninsular Malaysia had just under 150,000 Orang Asli; 80% live below the poverty line, compared with an 8.5% national average. The tribes are generally classified into three groups: the Negrito; the Senoi; and the Proto-Malays, who are subdivided into 18 tribes, the smallest being the Orang Kanak with just 87 members. There are dozens of different tribal languages and most Orang Asli follow animist beliefs, though there are vigorous attempts to convert them to Islam.

Since 1939 Orang Asli concerns have been represented and managed by a succession of government departments, the latest iteration being, an acronym for Jabatan Kemajuan Orang Asli (JAKOA; Orang Asli Development Department; www.jakoa.gov.my), which came into being in 2011. The main goals of JAKOA are to provide protection to the Orang Asli and their way of life from exploitation by external parties and ensure there are adequate facilities and assistance for education, health and socio-economic development.

In the past, Orang Asli land rights have often not been recognised, and when logging, agricultural or infrastructure projects require their land, their claims are generally regarded as illegal. Between 2010 and 2012 the Human Rights Commission of Malaysia (SUHAKAM; www.suhakam.org.my) conducted a national enquiry into the Land Rights of Indigenous Peoples and made various recommendations. This was followed up by government task force to study the finding and look at implementing the recommendations. The report was presented to government in September 2014 but a year later the government was yet to respond.

In Melaka there are around 37,000 Kristang, a group of people with predominantly mixed Portuguese and Malay blood, although a lot of other ethnic heritages are in there due to intermarriages down the generations.

Dayaks & the People of Borneo

The term 'Dayak' was first used by colonial authorities in about 1840; it means upriver or interior in some local languages, human being in others. Not all of Borneo's indigenous tribes refer to themselves as Dayaks but the term usefully groups together peoples who have a great deal in common – and not just from an outsider's point of view.

Sarawak

Dayak culture and lifestyles are probably easiest to observe and experience in Sarawak, where Dayaks make up about 48% of the population.

About 29% of Sarawakians are Iban, a group that migrated from West Kalimantan's Kapuas River starting five to eight centuries ago. Also known as Sea Dayaks for their exploits as pirates, the Iban are traditionally rice growers and longhouse dwellers. A reluctance to renounce head-hunting enhanced the Iban's ferocious reputation.

The Bidayuh (8% of the population), many of whom also trace their roots to what is now West Kalimantan, are concentrated in the hills south and southwest of Kuching. Few Bidayuh still live in longhouses and adjacent villages sometimes speak different dialects.

Upland groups such as the Kelabit, Kayan and Kenyah (ie everyone except the Bidayuh, Iban and coastal-dwelling Melenau) are often grouped under the term Orang Ulu ('upriver people'). There are also the Penan, originally a nomadic hunter-gatherer group living in northern Sarawak.

Some Dayak societies, such as the Iban and Bidayuh, are remarkably egalitarian, while others, including the Kayan, have a strict social hierarchy – now somewhat blurred – with classes of *maren* (nobles), *hipuy* (aristocrats), *panyin* (commoners) and *dipen* (slaves).

Sabah

None of Sabah's 30-odd indigenous ethnicities are particularly keen on the term Dayak. The state's largest ethnic group, the Kadazan-Dusun, make up 18% of the population. Mainly Roman Catholic, the Kadazan and the Dusun share a common language and have similar customs; the former originally lived mainly in the state's western coastal areas and river deltas, while the latter inhabited the interior highlands.

The Murut (3.2% of the population) traditionally lived in the southwestern hills bordering Kalimantan and Brunei, growing hill-rice and

LONGHOUSE LIFE

One of the most distinctive features of Dayak life is the longhouse (*rumah batang* or *rumah panjai*), which is essentially an entire village under one seemingly interminable roof. Longhouses take a variety of shapes and styles, but all are raised above the damp jungle floor on hardwood stilts and most are built on or near river banks.

The focus of longhouse life is the covered verandah, known as a *ruai* to the Iban, an *awah* to the Bidayuh and a *dapur* to the Kelabits; other groups use other terms. Residents use this communal space to socialise, engage in economic activities, cook and eat meals and hold communal celebrations.

One wall of the verandah, which can be up to 250m long, is pierced by doors to individual families' *bilik* (apartments), where there's space for sleeping and storage. If you ask about the size of a longhouse, you will usually be told how many doors – eg family units – it has.

Like the rest of us, Dayaks love their mod-cons, so longhouses where people actually live fuse age-old forms with contemporary conveniences. The resulting mash-up can see traditional bamboo slat floors mixed with corrugated iron, linoleum, satellite dishes and a car park out the front.

Most young Dayaks move away from the longhouse to seek higher education and jobs in the cities, but almost all keep close ties with home, returning for major family and community celebrations.

hunting with spears and blowpipes. They were soldiers for Brunei's sultans, and the last group in Sabah to abandon head-hunting.

Brunei

Indigenous non-Malays, mainly Iban and Kelabit, account for less than 10% of Brunei's population.

Multiculturalism

From the ashes of Malaysia's interracial riots of 1969, when distrust between the Malays and Chinese peaked, the country has managed to forge a more tolerant multicultural society. The emergence of a single 'Malaysian' identity, as espoused by the 1Malaysia policy (www.1malaysia.com.my), continues to be a much-discussed and lauded concept, even if it is far from being actually realised because of strong ethnic loyalties.

The government's *bumiputra* (indigenous Malaysian) policy (p572) has increased Malay involvement in the economy, albeit largely for an elite. This has helped defuse Malay fears and resentment of Chinese economic dominance, but at the expense of Chinese or Indian Malaysians being discriminated against by government policy. The reality is that Malaysia's different ethnic communities mostly coexist rather than mingle, intermarriage being rare. Education and politics are still largely split along ethnic lines.

Young and Malay (2015; ed Ooi Kee Beng and Wan Hamidi Hamid) is a series of essays on what it's like to grow up in multicultural Malaysia.

Singaporean government policy has always promoted Singapore as a multicultural nation in which Chinese, Indians and Malays can live in equality and harmony while maintaining their distinct cultural identities. For example, each Housing Development Board (HDB) public housing complex is subject to ethnic-based quotas that reflect Singapore's demographic mix – one way to prevent the formation of 'ethnic enclaves.' Imbalances in the distribution of wealth and power among the racial groups do exist, but on the whole multiculturalism seems to work much better in small-scale Singapore than it does in Malaysia.

Similarly Brunei's small scale (not to mention great wealth) has allowed all its citizens, 30% of whom are not Muslim, to find common goals and live together harmoniously in a state run according to Islamic laws.

Women in Malaysia, Singapore & Brunei

Women had great influence in pre-Islamic Malay society; there were female leaders and the descendants of the Sumatran Minangkabau in Malaysia's Negeri Sembilan still have a matriarchal society. The arrival of Islam weakened the position of women in the region. Nonetheless, women were not cloistered or forced to wear full purdah as in the Middle East, and today Malay women still enjoy more freedom than their counterparts in many other Muslim societies.

As you travel throughout the region you'll see women taking part in all aspects of society: politics, big business, academia and family life. However, Malaysia's Islamic family law makes it easier for Muslim men to take multiple wives, to divorce them and to take a share of their wives' property (similar laws exist in Brunei, where the Sultan has two wives). Around 40% of women over the age of 15 have been beaten by their partners in Malaysia. While the Domestic Violence Act does provide legal protection for abused women, it does not consider marital rape a crime.

In Chinese-dominated Singapore women traditionally played a small role in public life. In recent years women have started to take up key positions in government and industry. However, as in Malaysia, women make up tiny percentage of the numbers of members of parliament and top positions in companies.

In Islamic Brunei more women wear the *tudong* (headscarf) than in Malaysia. Many work and there are even one or two female politicians. Since 2002 female Bruneians have been able to legally transfer their nationality to their children if the father is not Bruneian.

A 2011 study by the University of Malaya indicated that as many as 93% of Malaysian Muslim women have undergone circumcision. Classified as Female Genital Mutilation (FGM) by the World Health Organisation, the practice isn't illegal in Malaysia, although public hospitals are prevented from offering such procedures.

The Region's Political Systems

Malaysia

Malaysia is made up of 13 states and three federal territories (Kuala Lumpur, Pulau Labuan and Putrajaya). Each state has an assembly and government headed by a *menteri Besar* (chief minister). Nine of the 13 states have hereditary rulers (sultans), while the remaining four have appointed governors as do the federal territories. In a pre-established order, every five years one of the sultans takes his turn in the ceremonial position of Yang di-Pertuan Agong (king). Since December 2011 the king,

TALKING THE TALK: THE REGION'S MANY LANGUAGES

English is widely spoken in the region, but linguists will be pleased to tackle a multitude of other languages spoken here. The national language of Malaysia and Brunei is Bahasa Malaysia. This is often a cause of confusion for travellers, who logically give a literal translation to the two words and call it the 'Malaysian language.' In fact you cannot speak 'Malaysian'; the language is Malay.

Other languages commonly spoken in the region include Tamil, Hokkien, Cantonese and Mandarin, but there are also Chinese dialects, various other Indian and Orang Asli languages and even, in Melaka, a form of 16th-century Portuguese known as Kristang. All Malaysians speak Malay, and many are fluent in at least two other languages.

Even if you stick to English, you'll have to get used to the local patois – Manglish in Malaysia and Brunei, and Singlish (p618) in Singapore – which includes plenty of Mandarin, Cantonese and Tamil words and phrases. Many words are used solely to add emphasis and have no formal meaning, which can make things a little confusing. Used incorrectly, Manglish and Singlish can come across as quite rude, so listen carefully and take local advice before trying it out in polite company.

who is also the head of state and leader of the Islamic faith, has been Sultan Abdul Halim of Kedah. This is the second time the 83-year-old has held the position, the first being from 1970 to 1975.

Borneo's indigenous community is comprised of scores of different tribal groups speaking around well over 100 languages and dialects.

At the time of writing Malaysia's prime minister is Najib Razak, who heads up the Barisan Nasional (BN; National Front), a coalition of the United Malays National Organisation (UMNO) and 13 other parties. The main opposition parties are the Democratic Action Party (DAP); Parti Keadilan Rakyat (PKR), formerly led by the jailed Anwar Ibrahim; and Parti Islam se-Malaysia (PAS). They all sit in a two-house parliament, comprising a 70-member Senate (*Dewan Negara*; 26 members elected by the 13 state assemblies, 44 appointed by the king on the prime minister's recommendation) and a 222-member House of Representatives (*Dewan Rakyat;* elected from single-member districts). National and state elections are held every five years.

An antidemocratic hangover from the 1960s is the lack of local government elections – KL, George Town and Melaka's city councillors have all been government appointees since 1964. Until the BN lose their majority in parliament any changes to this situation are unlikely.

To stem a booming population, Singapore's government encouraged birth control in the 1970s and 1980s. That plan worked so well that it now provides much encouragement, financial and otherwise, for its citizens to have more children.

Singapore

Singapore is a parliamentary republic modelled on the UK's Westminster System. There are numerous political parties in Singapore, but one party, the People's Action Party (PAP), has dominated the political landscape since independence.

The President of Singapore (since 2011, Tony Tan Keng Yam) is the democratically elected head of state, a traditionally ceremonial role that has since 1991 included powers to veto a small number of decisions, largely related to security and the armed service. The president, who serves a six-year term, appoints a prime minister (currently Lee Hsien Loong) as the head of government. Legislative power is vested in both the government and the Parliament of Singapore.

Some critics say the electoral system makes it difficult for opposition parties to gain seats, entrenching the dominance of the PAP. This position is backed up by the strict (by Western standards) controls the government places on political assembly, freedom of expression and behaviours deemed antisocial. This said, the 2015 election, in which the PAP increased its share of the vote by nearly 10% over the 2011 poll, was the first in which opposition candidates were fielded in all constituencies.

Kiasu, a Hokkien word describing Singaporeans, literally means 'afraid to lose', but embraces a range of selfish and pushy behaviour in which the individual must not lose out at all cost.

Brunei

Although internationally classified as a constitutional monarchy, Brunei officially deems itself a *Melayu Islam Beraja* (MIB; Malay Islamic Monarchy) and is, in many ways, an absolute monarchy. Sultan Hassanal Bolkiah has been in power since 1967; he appoints his advisory cabinet, privy council and council of succession. There is a 33-member legislative council, but those members are also appointed by and include the sultan; in 2004 there was talk of holding elections for 15 more seats, but those elections have never materialised.

Religion

Freedom of religion is guaranteed throughout this mainly Islamic region, although in Brunei the Baha'i faith is banned and you are unlikely to encounter practising Jews. Hinduism's roots in the region long predate Islam, and the various Chinese religions are also strongly entrenched. Christianity has a presence, more so in Singapore than Peninsular Malaysia, where it has never been strong. In Malaysian Borneo many of the indigenous people have converted to Christianity, yet others still follow their animist traditions.

Islam

Islam most likely came to the region in the 14th century with South Indian traders. It absorbed rather than conquered existing beliefs, and was adopted peacefully by Malaysia's coastal trading ports. Islamic sultanates replaced Hindu kingdoms – though the Hindu concept of kings remained – and the Hindu traditions of adat continued despite Islamic law dominating.

Malay ceremonies and beliefs still exhibit pre-Islamic traditions, but most Malays are ardent Muslims – to suggest otherwise would cause great offence. With the rise of Islamic fundamentalism, the calls to introduce Islamic law and purify the practices of Islam have increased; yet, while the federal government of Malaysia is keen to espouse Muslim ideals, it is wary of religious extremism.

Sisters in Islam (www.sistersinislam.org.my) is an organisation run by and for Malaysian Muslim women who refuse to be bullied by patriarchal interpretations of Islam.

Key Beliefs & Practices

Most Malaysian Muslims are Sunnis, but all Muslims share a common belief in the Five Pillars of Islam. The first is Shahadah (the declaration of faith): 'There is no God but Allah; Mohammed is his Prophet.' The second is salat (prayer), ideally done five times a day; the muezzin (prayer leader) calls the faithful from the minarets of every mosque. Third is akat (tax), usually taking the form of a charitable donation; and fourth, sawm (fasting), which includes observing the fasting month of Ramadan. The last pillar hajj (the pilgrimage to Mecca), which every Muslim aspires to do at least once in their lifetime.

Muslim dietary laws forbid alcohol, pork and all pork-based products. Restaurants where it's OK for Muslims to dine will be clearly labelled halal; this is a more strict definition than places that label themselves simply 'pork-free'.

A radical Islamic movement has not taken serious root in Malaysia but religious conservatism has grown over recent years. For foreign visitors, the most obvious sign of this is the national obsession with propriety, which extends to newspaper polemics on female modesty and raids by the police on 'immoral' public establishments, which can include clubs and bars where Muslims may be drinking.

Islam in Malaysia: Perceptions & Facts by Dr Mohd Asri Zainul Abidin, the former Mufti of Perlis, is a collection of articles on aspects of the faith as practised in Malaysia.

Chinese Religions

The Chinese in the region usually follow a mix of Buddhism, Confucianism and Taoism. Buddhism takes care of the afterlife, Confucianism looks after the political and moral aspects of life, and Taoism contributes

ISLAMIC FESTIVALS

The high point of the Islamic festival calendar is **Ramadan**, when Muslims fast from sunrise to sunset. Ramadan always occurs in the ninth month of the Muslim calendar and lasts between 29 and 30 days, based on sightings of the moon. Fifteen days before the start of Ramadan, on **Nisfu Night**, it is believed the souls of the dead visit their homes. On Laylatul Qadr (Night of Grandeur), during Ramadan, Muslims celebrate the arrival of the Quran on earth, before its revelation by the Prophet Mohammed.

Hari Raya Puasa (also known as Hari Raya Aidilfitri) marks the end of the month-long Ramadan fast, with two days of joyful celebration and feasting. Hari Raya Puasa is the major holiday of the Muslim calendar and it can be difficult to find accommodation, particularly on the coast. The start of Ramadan and all other Muslim festivals is 11 days earlier every year, as dates are calculated using the lunar calendar.

Other major Islamic festivals celebrated across the region include **Hari Raya Haji**, a two-day festival (in September between 2016 and 2018) marking the successful completion of the hajj (pilgrimage to Mecca). The festival commemorates the willingness of the Prophet Ibrahim (the biblical Abraham) to sacrifice his son. Many shops, offices and tourist attractions close and locals consume large amounts of cakes and sweets.

Awal Muharram, the Muslim New Year, falls in early October in 2016 and September in 2017 and 2018.

animistic beliefs to teach people to maintain harmony with the universe. But to say that the Chinese have three religions is too simplistic a view of their traditional religious life. At the first level Chinese religion is animistic, with a belief in the innate vital energy in rocks, trees, rivers and springs. At the second level people from the distant past, both real and mythological, are worshipped as gods. Overlaid on this are popular Taoist, Mahayana Buddhist and Confucian beliefs.

On a day-to-day level most Chinese are much less concerned with the high-minded philosophies and asceticism of the Buddha, Confucius or Lao Zi than they are with the pursuit of worldly success, the appeasement of the dead and the spirits, and seeking knowledge about the future. Chinese religion incorporates elements of what Westerners might call 'superstition' – if you want your fortune told, for instance, you go to a temple. The other thing to remember is that Chinese religion is polytheistic. Apart from the Buddha, Lao Zi and Confucius, there are many divinities, such as house gods, and gods and goddesses for particular professions.

The most popular Chinese gods and local deities, or *shen*, are Kuan Yin, the goddess of mercy; Kuan Ti, the god of war and wealth; and Toh Peh Kong, a local deity representing the spirit of the pioneers and found only outside China.

Hinduism

Hinduism in the region dates back at least 1500 years and there are Hindu influences in cultural traditions, such as *wayang kulit* (shadow-puppet theatre) and the wedding ceremony. However, it is only in the last 100 years or so, following the influx of Indian contract labourers and settlers, that it has again become widely practised.

Hinduism has three basic practices: puja (worship), the cremation of the dead, and the rules and regulations of the caste system. Although still very strong in India, the caste system was never significant in Malaysia, mainly because the labourers brought here from India were mostly from the lower classes.

Hinduism has a vast pantheon of deities, although the one omnipresent god usually has three physical representations: Brahma, the creator; Vishnu, the preserver; and Shiva, the destroyer or reproducer. All three gods are usually shown with four arms, but Brahma has the added advantage of four heads to represent his all-seeing presence.

Animism

The animist religions of Malaysia's indigenous peoples are as diverse as the peoples themselves. While animism does not have a rigid system of tenets or codified beliefs, it can be said that animists perceive natural phenomena to be animated by various spirits or deities, and a complex system of practices is used to propitiate these spirits.

Ancestor worship is also a common feature of animist societies; departed souls are considered to be intermediaries between this world and the next. Examples of elaborate burial rituals can still be found in some parts of Sarawak, where the remains of monolithic burial markers and funerary objects still dot the jungle around longhouses in the Kelabit Highlands. However, most of these are no longer maintained and they're being rapidly swallowed up by the fast-growing jungle.

Adat, with its roots in the region's Hindu period and earlier, is customary law that places great emphasis on collective rather than individual responsibility and on maintaining harmony.

In Malaysian Borneo, Dayak animism is known collectively as Kaharingan. Carvings, totems, tattoos and other objects (including, in earlier times, head-hunting skulls) are used to repel bad spirits, attract good spirits and soothe spirits that may be upset. Totems at entrances to villages and longhouses are markers for the spirits.

Religious Issues

Freedom of Religon?

Islam is Malaysia's state religion, which has an impact on the cultural and social life of the country at several levels. Government institutions and banks, for example, are closed for two hours at lunchtime on Friday to allow Muslims to attend Friday prayers.

Government censors, with Islamic sensitivities in mind, dictate what can be performed on public stages or screened in cinemas. For example, in 2013, authorities banned US pop star Kesha from performing a

THAIPUSAM

The most spectacular Hindu festival in Malaysia and Singapore is Thaipusam, a wild parade of confrontingly invasive body piercings. The festival, which originated in Tamil Nadu (but is now banned in India), happens every year in the Hindu month of Thai (January/February) and is celebrated with the most gusto at the Batu Caves (p108), just outside Kuala Lumpur.

The greatest spectacle is the devotees who subject themselves to seemingly masochistic acts as fulfilment for answered prayers. Many carry offerings of milk in *paal kudam* (milk pots), often connected to the skin by hooks. Even more striking are the *vel kavadi* – great cages of spikes that pierce the skin of the carrier and are decorated with peacock feathers, pictures of deities, and flowers. Some penitents go as far as piercing their tongues and cheeks with hooks, skewers and tridents.

The festival is the culmination of around a month of prayer, a vegetarian diet and other ritual preparations, such as abstinence from sex, or sleeping on a hard floor. While it looks excruciating, a trance-like state stops participants from feeling pain; later the wounds are treated with lemon juice and holy ash to prevent scarring. As with the practice of firewalking, only the truly faithful should attempt the ritual. It is said that insufficiently prepared devotees keep doctors especially busy over the Thaipusam festival period with skin lacerations, or by collapsing after the strenuous activities.

Thaipusam is also celebrated in Penang at the Nattukotai Chettiar Temple and the Waterfall Hilltop Temple, and in Johor Bahru at the Sri Thandayuthabani Temple. Ipoh attracts a large number of devotees, who follow the procession from the Sri Mariamar Temple in Buntong to the Sri Subramaniar Temple in Gunung Cheroh. In Singapore, Hindus march from the Sri Srinivasa Perumal Temple on Serangoon Rd to the Chettiar Hindu Temple.

concert because of its supposed negative impact on cultural and religious sensitivities.

Sharia (spelt *syariah* in Malay) is the preserve of state governments, as is the establishment of Muslim courts of law, which since 1988 cannot be overruled by secular courts. This has had a negative impact on cases of Muslims wishing to change their religion and to divorced parents who cannot agree on which religion to raise their children by. The end result is that Malaysian Muslims who change their religion or practise no faith at all rarely make their choice official.

Dayak animism considers the hornbill a powerful spirit – the bird is honoured in dance and ceremony and its feathers treasured.

In theory Brunei's constitution also allows for the practice of religions other than the official Sunni Islam. However, as Freedom House (www.freedomhouse.org) reports, proselytising by non-Muslims is prohibited and other forms of Islam are actively discouraged. Christianity suffers censorship. Marriage between Muslims and non-Muslims is not allowed. With permission from the Ministry of Religious Affairs, Muslims can convert their faith, but in reality conversion is practically impossible.

Inter-Religious Relations

In recent years Muslim-Christian relations in Malaysia have been clouded by new laws that forbid Christians from referring to God as 'Allah' in Bahasa Malaysia. In 2013, the Christian Federation of Malaysia (CFM), which represents over 90% of the churches in the country, protested the decision by the Court of Appeal to uphold this ban, saying it neglected the rights of Bahasa Malaysia speaking Christians such as those in Malaysian Borneo and the Orang Asli of Peninsular Malaysia.

Anecdotal evidence from across the region indicates that whereas in the past the various religious communities participated in each other's communal festivities (Hari Raya, Chinese New Year), such easy mingling is becoming less frequent these days, especially among younger people.

Intra-religious relations in Sabah and Sarawak are less fraught than on the mainland but Christians and Chinese (the groups overlap to a certain degree) and Muslim moderates often express concern that the island – especially Sabah – is not immune to the Islamist winds blowing in from other parts of the country.

Anti-Semitism

The only part of the region where you'll find a community of practising Jews is in Singapore. Penang once had a Jewish community large enough to support a synagogue (closed in 1976) and there's been a Jewish cemetery in George Town since 1805. Elsewhere in Malaysia and Brunei, Jewish life is practically unknown.

The Jewish Welfare Board (www.singaporejews.com) contains information about the history of Jews in Singapore as well as details about the current community and its events.

Sadly, anti-Semitism, ostensibly tied to criticism of Israel, is a feature of Malaysia and Brunei. In the region's bookshops it's not difficult to find anti-Semetic publications like *The Protocols of the Elders of Zion*. Former prime minister Mahathir is the most infamously outspoken Malaysian anti-Semite: in 2003 he made a speech to an Islamic leadership conference claiming the US is a tool of Jewish overlords, and he once cancelled a planned tour of Malaysia by the New York Philharmonic because the program included work by a Jewish composer.

A 2014 survey by the US-based Anti-Defamation League (ADL) found that nearly two in three Malaysians admit to being prejudiced against Jews, the highest amount by far in the region.

Israeli passport holders are not permitted to enter Malaysia without clearance from the Ministry of Home Affairs, and very few local Muslims differentiate between Israelis and Jews generally – something worth noting if you're Jewish and travelling in the region.

Arts & Media

Malaysia, Singapore and Brunei are not widely known for their arts, which is a shame as there is much creativity here, particularly in Malaysia and Singapore. Traditional art forms like *wayang kulit* (shadow puppetry) and *mak yong* (dance and music performances) hang on alongside contemporary art, drama and filmmaking. There's a distinctive look to Malaysia's vernacular architecture as well as a daring and originality in modern constructions. The region's authors and visual artists are also gaining attention in the wider world.

Arts

Literature

Writers W Somerset Maugham, Joseph Conrad and Noel Coward were inspired by the region in the early 20th century. The classic colonial expat experience is recounted by Anthony Burgess in *The Malayan Trilogy,* written in the 1950s. In the late 1960s Paul Theroux lived in Singapore, which, together with Malaysia, forms the backdrop to his novel *Saint Jack* (1973) and his short-story collection *The Consul's Wife* (1977). JG Farrell's *The Singapore Grip* (1978) about the decline of British colonialism in the region in the run up to WWII is considered a classic Singapore novel.

Singapore has boosted spending on arts across the board with the aim of making the island state the arts hub of the region, in stark contrast to Malaysia, where very little public money is assigned to the arts.

In recent decades locally born authors have been coming to the fore. Tash Aw's debut novel, *The Harmony Silk Factory,* set in Malaysia during the 1930s and '40s, won the 2005 Whitbread First Novel Award. His latest work, *Five Star Billionaire* (2013), is about four expat Malaysians trying to make a go of it in contemporary Shanghai. Tan Twan Eng's debut novel, *The Gift of Rain,* set in Penang prior to WWII, was long-listed for the Man Booker literature prize. His follow up, *The Garden of Evening Mists,* winner of the Man Asian Literary Prize in 2012, takes the reader deep into the Cameron Highlands and the 1950s era of the Emergency. *Evening Is the Whole Day* (2008), by Preeta Samarasan, shines a light on the experiences of an Indian immigrant family living on the outskirts of Ipoh in the early 1980s.

Catherine Lim's *Little Ironies* (1978) is a series of keenly observed short stories about Singaporeans from a writer who has also published five novels, poetry collections and political commentary. Hwee Hwee Tan pinpoints the peculiar dilemmas and contradictions facing Singaporean youth in her novels *Foreign Bodies* (1999) and *Mammon Inc* (2001). Singapore-born Kevin Kwan has garnered much praise for his witty satire on the lives of the island state's megarich in *Crazy Rich Asians* (2013).

The cartoonist and artist Lat is a national institution in Malaysia. His witty sketches turn up in the *New Straits Times* newspaper, advertisements, and books including *Kampung Boy*.

Other celebrated novels by Singaporean writers include *The Shrimp People* (1991) by Rex Shelly, *Abraham's Promise* (1995) by Philip Jeyaretnam, *Heartland* (1999) by Daren Shiau, and *Ministry of Moral Panic* (2013) by Amanda Lee Koe. More are likely on the way as the National Arts Council of Singapore has beefed up its program with competitions and events such as the annual Singapore Writers Festival (www.singaporewritersfestival.com).

Architecture

Malaysia and Singapore have both made their mark in the world of contemporary architecture with iconic buildings like Kuala Lumpur's Petronas Towers and the Marina Bay Sands complex in Singapore. Other interesting skyscrapers and civic buildings in the cities take inspiration from both local culture and the environment, such as the Tabung Haji and Menara Maybank buildings in KL, both designed by Hijjas Kasturi.

The Minangkabau-style houses found in Negeri Sembilan are the most distinctive of the *kampung* houses, with curved roofs resembling buffalo horns. The design is imported from Sumatra.

Vividly painted and handsomely proportioned, traditional wooden Malay houses are also perfectly adapted to the hot, humid conditions of the region. Built on stilts, with high, peaked roofs, they take advantage of even the slightest cooling breeze. Further ventilation is achieved by full-length windows, no internal partitions, and latticelike grilles in the walls. The layout of a traditional Malay house reflects Muslim sensibilities. There are separate areas for men and women, as well as distinct areas where guests of either sex may be entertained.

Although their numbers are dwindling, this type of house has not disappeared altogether. The best places to see examples are in the *kampung* (villages) of Peninsular Malaysia, particularly along the east coast in the states of Kelantan and Terengganu. Here you'll see that roofs are often tiled, showing a Thai and Cambodian influence. In Melaka, the Malay house has a distinctive tiled front stairway leading up to the front verandah – examples can be seen around Kampung Morten.

Few Malay-style houses have survived Singapore's rapid modernisation – the main place they remain is on Pulau Ubin. Instead, the island state has some truly magnificent examples of Chinese shophouse architecture, particularly in Chinatown, Emerald Hill (off Orchard Rd) and around Katong. There are also the distinctive 'black and white' bungalows built during colonial times; find survivors lurking in the residential areas off Orchard Rd. Around 85% of Singaporeans live in the tower block flats built by the Housing Development Board. These high-density developments have markets, schools, playgrounds, shops and hawker centres hardwired into them.

Despite its oil wealth, there's little that's flashy in the architecture of Brunei's modest capital, Bandar Seri Begawan, where the city's skyline is dominated by the striking Omar Ali Saifuddien Mosque. About 3km outside of the capital is the Sultan's opulent palace Istana Nurul Iman, while at Jerudong is the eye-boggling Empire Hotel.

Silat, or *bersilat*, is a Malay martial art that originated in 15th-century Melaka. Today it is a highly refined and stylised activity, more akin to dance than self-defence.

Drama & Dance

Traditional Malay dances include *menora,* a dance-drama of Thai origin performed by an all-male cast dressed in grotesque masks, and the similar *mak yong,* in which the participants are female. These performances often take place at Puja Ketek, Buddhist festivals held at temples near the Thai border in Kelantan. There's also the *rodat,* a dance from Terengganu, and the *joget,* an upbeat dance with Portuguese origins, often performed at Malay weddings by professional dancers; in Melaka it's better known as *chakunchak.*

When it comes to contemporary drama and dance, Singapore tends to have the edge. There's a lot of interesting work by local theatre companies such as Wild Rice, Necessary Stage and Singapore Repertory Theatre. Singapore's leading dance company, Singapore Dance Theatre, puts on performances ranging from classical ballet to contemporary dance.

Shadow Puppetery

It's in east coast Peninsular Malaysian towns like Kota Bharu and Kuala Terengganu that you're most likely to see *wayang kulit* (shadow-puppet performances), similar to those of Java in Indonesia, which retell tales from Hindu epic the Ramayana. It's a feat of endurance both for performer and audience since the shadow plays, which can take place at weddings or after the harvest, can last for many hours.

There are thought to be no more than 10 practising puppet masters *(dalang)* in Malaysia. The nongovernmental organisation Pusaka is working to keep Malaysian traditional arts, including *wayang kulit,* alive by introducing them to the general public with free shows, and by training a new generation of artists. Shows are by donation and often feature some outstanding older performers and the occasional young phenom.

Music

Traditional & Classical

Traditional Malay music is based largely on *gendang* (drums), but other percussion instruments include the gong and various tribal instruments made from seashells, coconut shells and bamboo. The Indonesian-style *gamelan* (a traditional orchestra of drums, gongs and wooden xylophones) also crops up on ceremonial occasions. The Malay *nobat* uses a mixture of percussion and wind instruments to create formal court music.

Islamic and Chinese influences are felt in the music of *dondang sayang* (Chinese-influenced romantic songs) and *hadrah* (Islamic chants, sometimes accompanied by dance and music). The KL-based Dama Orchestra (www.damaorchestra.com) combines modern and traditional Chinese instruments and play songs that conjure up the mood of 1920s and 1930s Malaysia. In Singapore, catch the well-respected Singapore Chinese Orchestra, which plays not only traditional and symphonic Chinese music but also Indian, Malay and Western pieces.

The standard bearers for Western-style classical music in the region are the Malaysian Philharmonic Orchestra (http://mpo.com.my) and Singapore Symphony Orchestra. Both ensembles include world-class performers.

Popular Music

Snapping at the high heels of demure Malaysian pop songstress Siti Nurhaliza are Zee Avi, who was signed by the US label Bushfire Records for her eponymous debut CD, and Yuna, who has also cut a US record deal and is one of the talented vocalists and songwriters from the new generation of musicians. Also look out for Najwa whose slickly produced EP *Aurora* has garnered positive reviews; the MIA-style rapper Arabyrd; and the more retro guitar jingly pop stylings of Noh Salleh.

In 2015, indie rock band Kyoto Protocol, who have been steadily building their reputation since forming in 2008, finally released a full album, *Catch These Men,* after a series of singles and EPs in the past. A great resource for catching up on other up-and-coming local bands and singers is The Wknd (http://the-wknd.com).

Singapore's pop music scene creates only a small blip internationally. Visitors should look out for local festivals like the annual Baybeats (www.baybeats.com), showcasing alternative singers and bands. Local

CHINESE OPERA

In Malaysia and Singapore *wayang* (Chinese opera) is derived from the Cantonese variety. The performances mix dialogue, music, song and dance, and what they lack in literary nuance, they make up for with garish costumes and the crashing music that follows the action. Scenery and props are minimal; it's the action that is important, and even for the uninitiated it's usually easy to get the gist of the plot.

Performances can go for an entire evening. Even though the acting is very stylised, and the music can be discordant to Western ears, they are worth seeing. Free street performances are held in the Chinatown areas of Kuala Lumpur, Singapore, Melaka and Penang's George Town during important festivals like Chinese New Year (January/February), the Hungry Ghost Festival (August/September) and the Festival of the Nine Emperor Gods (September/October).

TRADITIONAL CRAFTS

The region's crafts have much rustic beauty and incorporate traditional designs.

Batik Produced by drawing or printing a pattern on fabric with wax and then dyeing the material, batik can be made into clothes, homewares, or simply be created as works of art. It's made across Malaysia, but Kelantan and Terengganu are its true homes.

Basketry and weaving The baskets of the Iban, Kayan, Kenyah and Penan are highly regarded. Weaving material include rattan, bamboo, swamp nipah grass and pandanus palms. Related weaving techniques produce sleeping mats, seats and materials for shelters. While each ethnic group has certain distinctive patterns, hundreds or even thousands of years of trade and interaction has led to an intermixing of patterns.

Kain songket This hand-woven fabric with gold and silver threads through the material is a speciality of Kelantan and Terengganu. Clothes made from it are usually reserved for important festivals and occasions. You can also buy pieces of the fabric for decorative purposes.

Kites and puppets The *wau bulan* (moon kite) of Kelantan is a traditional paper and bamboo crescent-shaped kite as large as 3m in length and breadth, while kite makers in Terengganu specialise in the *wau kucing* (cat kite). *Wayang kulit* (shadow puppets) are made from buffalo hide in the shape of characters from epic Hindu legends.

Metalwork Kelantan is famed for its silversmiths, who work in a variety of ways and specialise in filigree and repoussé work. In the latter, designs are hammered through the silver from the underside. Brasswork is an equally traditional skill in Kuala Terengganu. Objects crafted out of pewter (an alloy of tin) are synonymous with Selangor, where you'll find the Royal Selangor Pewter Factory as well as other pewter manufacturers.

Woodcarving The Orang Asli tribe of Hma' Meri, who live in a village on Pulau Carey, off the coast of Selangor, are renowned woodcarving craftspeople. In Malaysian Borneo the Kenyah and Kayan peoples are also skilled woodcarvers, producing hunting-charms and ornate knife-hilts known as *parang ilang*.

artists also show up at music festivals in Malaysia such as Urbanscapes (www.urbanscapes.com.my) and the Rainforest World Music Festival (www.rwmf.net).

Cinema

The heyday of Malaysia's film industry was the 1950s, when P Ramlee dominated the silver screen. This Malaysian icon acted in 66 films, recorded 300 songs and was also a successful film director. His directorial debut, *Penarik Becha* (The Trishaw Man; 1955), is a classic of Malay cinema.

The Brunei Art Forum in Bandar Seri Begawan fosters international links and promotes local contemporary artists (mostly painters) including Zakaria Bin Omar, Haji Padzil Haji Ahmad and Teck Kwang Swee.

Yasmin Ahamad is considered to be the most important Malaysian filmmaker since Ramlee. Her film *Sepet* (2005), about a Chinese boy and Malay girl falling in love, cuts across the country's race and language barriers upsetting many devout Malays, as did her follow up, *Gubra* (2006), which dared to take a sympathetic approach to prostitutes. Causing less of a stir were *Mukshin* (2007), a romantic tale about Malay village life, and *Talentime* (2009), about an inter-school performing arts contest, and what would be Yasmin's final film before her death from a stroke the same year.

Tsai Ming Liang's starkly beautiful but glacially slow interracial romance *I Don't Want to Sleep Alone* (2006) was filmed entirely on location in KL. Set in Kelantan, Dain Said's action-drama *Bunohan* (2012) did well at film festivals around the world, gaining it an international release – rare for a Malaysian movie. At the time of research he was in production for his next movie, *Interchange,* a film noir–style supernatural thriller set in KL.

Singapore's film industry began to gain international attention in the 1990s with movies such as as Eric Khoo's *Mee Pok Man* (1995). Khoo's *12 Storeys* (1997), *Be with Me* (2005), *My Magic* (2008) and the animated drama *Tatsumi* (2011) have since featured in competition at Cannes.

Royston Tan's first feature *15* (2003), about teenage gangsters, fell foul of local censors and had 27 scenes snipped. In response, he produced the hilarious short music video *Cut* (which can be viewed on YouTube). Less controversial was *881* (2007), a campy musical comedy about the *getai* (stage singing) aspirations of two friends.

Anthony Chen's *Ilo Ilo* (2013) explores the relationship between a Singaporean family and their Filipino maid, topical given the recent tension between locals and foreign workers. The film has garnered a number of awards, including the Camera d'Or at Cannes.

Visual Arts

Hoessein Enas was commissioned by Shell Ltd in 1963 to produce a series of portraits celebrating the newly born country. Some of these can be seen in the National Visual Art Gallery in KL, alongside works by Amron Omar who has focused throughout his career on *silat* (a Malay martial art) as a source of inspiration for his paintings.

Among notable contemporary Malaysian artists are Jalaini Abu Hassan ('Jai'), Wong Hoy Cheong, landscape painter Wong Perng Fey, and multimedia artist Yee I-Lann. Work by Malaysian sculptor Abdul Multhalib Musa has won awards and he created several pieces in Beijing for the 2008 Olympics.

In Singapore the visual-arts scene is also vibrant, with painting, sculpture and multimedia the vehicles of choice for dynamic explorations into the tensions between Western art practices and the perceived erosion of traditional values. Highly regarded local artists include Da Wu Tang, Vincent Leow, Jason Lim and Zulkifle Mahmod. The National Gallery Singapore, newly opened in 2015, is aiming to be the region's leading visual arts institution.

Volunteer-run Gerai OA (www.facebook.com/geraioa) sells and promotes crafts by Malaysia's indigenous minorities. Its Facebook page lists the crafts markets in the Kuala Lumpur area and where you'll find them.

Media

Malaysia, Singapore and Brunei all leave much to be desired when it comes to freedom of the press. In the Reports without Borders rankings for 2014, the countries placed 145, 150 and 117 respectively out of the 179 nations surveyed. All the countries have stringent publishing laws with the courts frequently used to silence critics and frighten journalists into self-censorship.

In Malaysia these have been bolstered by a toughened up Sedition Act. It was invoked in 2015 when Malaysian police arrested the publisher of The Edge Media Group, the CEO of the Malaysian Insider news portal, and three editors for publishing articles about a proposal to introduce *hudud* (punishments under Islamic law) in Kelantan state. Malaysia has also blocked access to the news website Sarawak Report, and suspended publication of *Edge* newspapers over their coverage of the troubled state investment fund 1MBD.

Singapore's authorities attracted international criticism for their heavy-handed approach in the case of 16-year-old vlogger Amos Yee who was jailed for 53 days for posting offensive comments about the recently deceased Lee Kuan Yew on social media.

All this said, social media increasingly plays a part in Malaysia and Singapore's mediascape, with local newspapers often quoting bloggers and reporting on issues generated in the blogosphere. Many people also go online to read news they are unlikely to see in print.

Online Arts Resources

Arts Malaysia (www.arts.com.my)

Malaysia Design Archive (www.malaysiadesignarchive.org)

National Arts Council Singapore (www.nac.gov.sg)

Bruneions (www.bruneions.com)

Environment

Many visitors come to Malaysia, Singapore and Brunei to experience first hand the region's amazing natural environment. However, these countries, like others the world over, are grappling with the sometimes conflicting demands of economic development and environmental conservation. Items on the local sustainability agenda include deforestation, a result of the rampant growth of palm-oil plantations in Malaysia; protection of endangered wildlife; cleaning up polluted waterways; and cutting the region's carbon footprint through innovative energy efficiency projects.

Lay of the Land

Large parts of Peninsular Malaysia (132,090 sq km) are covered by dense jungle, particularly its mountainous, thinly populated northern half, although it's dominated by palm-oil and rubber plantations. On the western side of the peninsula there is a long, fertile plain running down to the sea, while on the eastern side the mountains descend more steeply and the coast is fringed with sandy beaches. Jungle features heavily in Malaysian Borneo, along with many large river systems, particularly in Sarawak. Mt Kinabalu (4095m) in Sabah is Malaysia's highest mountain.

Singapore (718 sq km) consists of the main, low-lying Singapore island and 63 much smaller islands within its territorial waters. The central area is an igneous outcrop, containing most of Singapore's remaining forest and open areas. The western part of the island is a sedimentary area of low-lying hills and valleys, while the southeast is mostly flat and sandy. The north coast and the offshore islands are home to some mangrove forests.

The capital of Brunei (5765 sq km), Bandar Seri Begawan, overlooks the estuary of the mangrove-fringed Sungai Brunei (Brunei River), which opens onto Brunei Bay and the separate, eastern part of the country, Temburong, a sparsely populated area of largely unspoilt rainforest. Approximately 75% of Brunei retains its original forest cover.

Online Resources

Sahabat Alam Malaysia (SAM; www.foe-malaysia.org)

Orangutan Foundation (www.orangutan.org.uk)

Wild Singapore (www.wildsingapore.com)

Malaysian Conversation Alliance for Tigers (MYCAT; http://malayantiger.net)

Deforestation

According to WWF Malaysia, just under 60% of Malaysia is covered by forest. However, as the Malaysian Nature Society and others have pointed out, the problem is what this 'forest cover' is comprised of. Currently the government description includes rubber plantations. In many states old-growth forests are being cut down to plant rubber.

There's a disparity between government figures and those of environmental groups, but it's probable that up to 80% of Malaysia's rainforests have been logged. Government initiatives like the National Forestry Policy have led to deforestation being cut to 900 sq km a year, a third slower than previously. The aim is to reduce the timber harvest by 10% each year, but even this isn't sufficient to calm the many critics who remain alarmed at the rate at which Malaysia's primary forests are disappearing.

Environmental groups like TREES (http://trees.org.my) have also been campaigning for the protection of the rainforests and water catchment area along the eastern flank of Selangor. In 2010, 93,000 hectares of these uplands were gazetted as the Selangor State Park making it the peninsula's third-largest protected area of forest after Taman Negara and Royal Belum State Park. Find out more at http://selangorstatepark.blogspot.com.

It's in Sarawak and Sabah that old-growth rainforests are under the most severe threat. To afford a measure of protection, several national parks and reserves have been created or extended, such as the Maliau Basin Conservation Area and the Pulong Tau National Park. In 2005 the Heart of Borneo Initiative (www.heartofborneo.org) was signed by Malaysia, Brunei and Indonesia. The aim is to safeguard Borneo's biodiversity for future generations and ensure indigenous people's cultural survival by protecting 24,000 sq km of interconnected forest land in Sabah, Sarawak, Brunei and Kalimantan – altogether almost a third of the island.

The Sarawak Biodiversity Centre (www.sbc.org.my) carries out research on the state's biodiversity for potential commercialisation. If the multi-million-dollar cure for cancer or AIDS can be found in these forests, it might just be their partial saviour.

In a sharp change of direction from his controversial predecessor Taib Mahmud, the new Chief Minister of Sarawak Adenan Satem has pledged to save the state's remaining rainforests and fight timber corruption. He has also appealed to NGOs to assist his government in these efforts. In the meantime, the detrimental effects of past logging are still clearly being felt in the region, which now suffers unusually long floods during the wet season.

For more on what the government is doing in relation to forest management, see the websites of the forestry departments of Peninsular Malaysia (www.forestry.gov.my), Sarawak (www.forestry.sarawak.gov.my) and Sabah (www.forest.sabah.gov.my). For the alternative point of view, read William W Bevis' award-winning *Borneo Log: The Struggle for Sarawak's Forests* (1995), an evocative narrative that starkly outlines the environmental and human impacts of the logging in Sarawak, and Lukas Straumann's *Money Logging: On the Trail of the Asian Timber Mafia* (2014), a damming account of former Sarawak chief minister Taib's alleged rape of the state's rainforests.

Palm-Oil Plantations

The oil palm, a native of West Africa that was introduced into Malaysia in the 1870s, is probably now the most common tree in Malaysia. The country's first palm-oil plantation was established in 1917. Today, according to the Malaysian Palm Oil Council (www.mpoc.org.my), Malaysia is the world's leading producer of palm oil, accounting for over 40% of global production. The oil is extracted from the orange-coloured fruit, which grows in bunches just below the fronds. It is used primarily for cooking,

WILDLIFE SMUGGLING

Malaysia's Wildlife Conservation Act includes fines of up to RM100,000 and long prison sentences for poaching, smuggling animals and other wildlife-related crimes. Even so, smuggling of live animals and animal parts remains a particular problem in the region. In July 2010 police looking for stolen cars also uncovered an illegal 'mini zoo' in a KL warehouse containing 20 species of protected wildlife, including a pair of rare birds of paradise worth RM1 million.

After serving 17 months of a five year sentence, Malaysia's most notorious animal smuggler Alvin Wong – described as 'the Pablo Escobar of wildlife trafficking' in Bryan Christy's *The Lizard King* – was allegedly back in business in 2013 according to documentary screened by Al Jeezera in 2013.

It's not just live animals that are being smuggled. Malaysia has been fingered as a transit point for illegally traded ivory on its way to other parts of Asia. In August 2015 authorities busted a syndicate in KL that claimed to be trading in tiger and other wildlife parts.

although it can also be refined into biodiesel – an alternative to fossil fuels.

For all the crop's benefits, there have been huge environmental consequences to the creation of vast plantations that have replaced the native jungle and previously logged forests; a UN Environment Program report in 2007 concluded that palm-oil plantations are the leading cause of rainforest destruction in Malaysia. The use of polluting pesticides and fertilisers in palm-oil production also undermines the crop's eco credentials. Palm-oil plantations convert land into permanent monoculture, reducing the number of plant species by up to 90%. Oil palms require large quantities of herbicides and pesticides that can seep into rivers; drainage may lower water tables, drying out nearby peat forests (and releasing huge quantities of greenhouse gases in the process). Plantations also fragment the natural habitats that are especially important to large mammals.

The Clouded Leopard Project (http://cloudedleopard.org) has funded several conservation efforts on Malaysian Borneo for this beautiful animal that may be rarer than the Malayan tiger.

The Palm Oil Action Group (www.palmoilaction.org.au) is an Australian pressure group raising awareness about palm oil and the need to use alternatives. Roundtable on Sustainable Palm Oil (www.rspo.org) tries to look at the issue from all sides while seeking to develop and implement global standards. Proforest (www.proforest.net) has also been working with palm-oil producers in the region, to help growers understand and adopt responsible production practices.

Carbon Emissions & Air Quality

At the 2014 UN Climate Summit, Prime Minister Najib confirmed that Malaysia was well on its way to achieving a 40% reduction in carbon emissions by 2020, a goal set by his government in 2009. Malaysia's average per capita carbon footprint remains around twice that of Thailand and four times higher than Indonesia's or Vietnam's, although it is just half of Singapore's.

To reach its stated goal the federal government has added green technology to the portfolio of the Ministry of Energy & Water and announced the launch of a national green technology policy. Melaka is creating a smart electricity grid with the aim of becoming the country's first carbon-free city by 2020. The Carbon Trust (www.carbontrust.com) is also working with the local government of Petaling Jaya in Selangor to help develop its five-year carbon reduction strategy.

In the meantime, there's an ongoing air-quality threat in the region from 'haze' – smoke from fires set by Indonesian farmers and plantation companies to clear land for agricultural purposes. The haze is usually at its worst in Singapore and parts of Malaysia around March and just before September and October's rainy season; air quality readings for this period in 2015 were among the worst ever.

Pangolins, also known as scaly anteaters, are the most traded species even though they are protected under Malaysian law. Their scales, believed to have medicinal properties, can fetch up to RM800 per kg.

Hydroelectric Dams

Hydroelectric dams are touted as sources of carbon-free energy, but these huge projects often have serious environmental impacts. In addition, indigenous people are often forcibly relocated to areas where they have difficulty earning a living or maintaining their traditions. Such is the case with the Murum Dam, located in a Penan area 60km upriver from Bakun in Sarawak, and the state's controversial Bakun Dam.

In October 2010 the 207m-high Bakun Dam structure began flooding a reservoir that will eventually submerge an area of once-virgin rainforest about the size of Singapore (690 sq km). At full generating capacity, the second-highest concrete-faced rockfill dam in the world will produce 2400MW of emission-free clean energy – 2.5 times as many watts as Sarawak's current peak demand.

THE PLIGHT OF TASIK CHINI

Part of the Sungai Pahang (Pahang River) basin and with a catchment size of 45 sq km, Tasik Chini is Malaysia's sole Unesco Biosphere Reserve. As late as 10 years ago the lake was a major tourist draw for the lotus flowers that practically carpeted its surface. Today pollution of the lake (which is actually a freshwater swamp) has resulted in murky waters and the near extinction of the lotuses.

Problems began in the mid-1980s, when the state government began approving land development schemes around the lake. Things got worse when the federal government built a weir at the end of Sungai Chini in 1995 to facilitate the navigation of tourist boats, despite protests by the Orang Asli who live in six villages around Tasik Chini.

The weir raised the lake by at least 2m, submerging thousands of trees and many stands of rattan by the water's edge, as well as endangering the survival of the lotus plants, which grow best in shallow water. The water, already spoiled by run-off from open-cut iron ore mines as close as 50m from the lake's edge, was further polluted by the methane and hydrogen sulphide that the dead vegetation in the lake produced as it rotted.

With the situation viewed as critical, Transparency International-Malaysia (TI-M) and environmental agencies including WWF Malaysia and Malaysian Nature Society are campaigning to Save Tasik Chini (www.timalaysia-forestwatch.org.my/tchini).

Malaysian and international watchdogs claim the whole Bakun Dam project – including contracts to clear the site of biomass, which involves logging old-growth jungle – has been shot through with corrupt dealings designed to benefit the business associates of local politicians.

Up to three quarters of Kelantan's coast is under attack from erosion; in the worst cases the shoreline is retreating by up to 10m a year.

Rivers

There has been some success in both Penang and Melaka when it comes to cleaning up polluted waterways. The Sungai Pinang that flows through the heart of George Town was once so filthy that it had a Class V classification, meaning it was unable to sustain life and contact with the water was dangerous. The state's clean-up program resulted in the waterway's pollution rating dropping to Class III in 2010, and in 2015, a family of 10 smooth-coated otters were regularly spotted in the river – a sign that fish have also returned to the waters. The long-term goal is to have the river rated Class I.

According to the Malayisan Nature Society, the revival of the once sludgy Sungei Melaka flowing through Melaka is also a model of how a river can be cleaned. Starting in 2005 the city invested about RM100 million in the project, which also included building grassy areas and walking paths along the river banks. A catamaran designed to clean up oil slicks was employed to remove rubbish then compress it into a material that could be used to reinforce the banks. The next step was the beautification of the banks, followed by domestic wastewater and cesspool treatment; reservoirs were built to trap scum, oil and refuse. The project is considered a success and further works, which started in 2013 and are currently ongoing, are aiming to further beautify the riverside areas and improve the water quality.

The Sarawak Report (www.sarawakreport.org) and its sister organisation Radio Free Sarawak (https://radiofreesarawak.org) has called attention to issues such as deforestation and the impact of dam building in Malaysia.

The focus has now turned to KL and the Klang Valley. The literal translation of Kuala Lumpur is 'muddy estuary'; anyone gazing on any of the milk-coffee-coloured waterways that flow through the city would find that name highly appropriate. Following moves in 2010 by the Selangor state government to clean up a 21km stretch of the Sungei Klang around Klang, the much larger River of Life program now focuses antipollution efforts on the river's upper reaches. In 2011 the government allocated RM3 billion for the task of raising the river water quality from

RESPONSIBLE TRAVEL

- Tread lightly and buy locally, avoiding (and reporting) instances where you see parts of or products made from endangered species for sale. On Peninsular Malaysia there's a 24-hour Wildlife Crime Hotline (019 356 4194) you can call to report illegal activities.
- Visit nature sites, hire local trekking guides and provide custom for ecotourism initiatives. By doing so you're putting cash in local pockets and casting a vote for the economic (as opposed to the purely ecological) value of sustainability and habitat conservation.
- Sign up to be a voluntary forest monitor at **Forest Watch** (www.timalaysia-forestwatch.org.my), a project by Transparency International Malaysia.
- Check out projects sponsored and promoted by **Ecotourism & Conservation Society Malaysia** (http://ecomy.org) and **Wild Asia** (www.wildasia.org) to learn more about responsible tourism in the region.
- Keep abreast of and support local campaigns by checking out the websites of organisations like **WWF Malaysia** (www.wwf.org.my) and the **Malaysian Nature Society** (www.mns.org.my).

the current Class III and Class IV (not suitable for body contact) to Class IIb (suitable for body contact and recreational usage) by 2020.

Green, Clean Singapore

Singapore's reputation as an efficiently run, squeaky clean place is well justified. The country has a vision of becoming a 'City in a Garden,' a cutting-edge role model of urban sustainability and biodiversity. A planned 35% improvement in energy efficiency between 2005 and 2030 led the government to introduce a sustainability rating system for buildings – the so-called Green Mark. Since 2008, all construction projects greater than 2000 sq metres (both new and retrofitted) are obliged to meet the Green Mark's minimum standards.

Regional Environmental Awareness Cameron Highlands (REACH; www.reach.org.my) has been working since 2001 to preserve, restore and maintain this region as an environmentally sustainable agricultural area and tourist resort within a permanent nature reserve.

At present, Green Mark–certified buildings account for more than 20% of Singapore's gross floor space. Generous incentive schemes have encouraged an ever-growing number of buildings to incorporate sustainable design features, among them sun-shading exteriors, extensive overhangs, sky gardens, efficient water systems, and computer systems capable of monitoring carbon emissions.

Singapore's incinerated waste is shipped off to Pulau Semakau, an island 8km south of the mainland. The 3.5 sq km landfill here is projected to meet the country's waste needs until 2045. More interestingly, the island itself has been much promoted by the government as an 'eco' hot spot. Rehabilitated mangrove swamps sit next to a coral nursery. In 2005, the island was also opened for recreation activities such as nature walks and fishing.

Though little of Singapore's original wilderness is left, growing interest in ecology has seen bird sanctuaries and parkland areas created, with new parks in the Marina Bay development as well as a series of connectors that link up numerous existing parks and gardens around the island.

Survival Guide

Directory A–Z

See the Directory sections of the Singapore (p553) and Brunei (p487) chapters for further information.

Accommodation

Malaysia's accommodation possibilities range from rock-bottom flophouses to luxurious five-star resorts. Outside the peak holiday seasons (around major festivals such as Chinese New Year in January/February) big discounts are frequently available – it's always worth asking about special offers.

Promotional rates can bring rooms at many top-end hotels into the midrange category. A 6% government tax applies to all hotel rooms (but all budget and many midrange places include this in the quoted rate). Almost all top-end hotels levy an additional 10% service charge on top of this, expressed as ++ on their rates. Credit cards are widely accepted, although at some cheaper places it's cash only.

Warning: bed bug infestations (p613) are common in Malaysia's hotels and are a particular problem at the budget end of the market.

SLEEPING PRICE RANGES

The following price ranges refer to a double room with attached bathroom:

$ less than RM100

$$ RM100–400

$$$ more than RM400

Camping

Many of Malaysia's national parks have official camping grounds and will permit camping in nondesignated sites once you are deep in the jungle. There are also many lonely stretches of beach that are ideal for camping. Likewise, it is possible to camp on uninhabited bays on many of Malaysia's islands. A two-season tent with mosquito netting is ideal. A summer-weight sleeping bag is OK, but the best choice is a lightweight bag-liner, since even the nights are warm.

Homestays

Staying with a Malaysian family will give you a unique experience many times removed from the fast-paced and largely recognisable life of the cities and towns. Enquire with **Tourism Malaysia** (www.tourismmalaysia.gov.my) and each of the state tourism bodies about the homestay programs operating throughout the country in off-the-beaten-track *kampung* (villages). Also see **Go2Homestay.com** (www.go2homestay.com).

Hostels & Guesthouses

At beach resorts and in the main tourist cities you will find a variety of cheap hostels and guesthouses. Dormitory accommodation is usually available. Rooms may be spartan (with flimsy walls and sometimes no window) and have shared bathrooms, but this is the cheapest accommodation option around and a great place to meet fellow travellers. These places offer their customers lots of little extras to outdo the competition, such as free wi-fi, tea and coffee, bicycles and transport. Dorm beds cost anything between RM10 to RM50 depending on the location, a hotel-style room with air-con RM20 to RM100.

Hotels

Standard rooms at top-end hotels are often called 'superior' in the local parlance. Most hotels have slightly more expensive 'deluxe' or 'club' rooms, which tend to be larger, have a better view and include extras such as breakfast or free internet access. Many also have suites.

At the low end of the price scale are the traditional Chinese-run hotels usually offering little more than simple rooms with a bed, table and chair, and sink. The showers and toilets may be down the corridor. Note couples can sometimes economise by asking for a single, since in Chinese-hotel language 'single' means one double bed, and 'double' means two beds. Don't think of this as being tight; in Chinese hotels you can pack as many into one room as you wish.

The main catch with these hotels is that they can sometimes be terribly noisy. They're often on main streets, and the cheapest ones often have thin walls that stop short of the ceiling – great for ventilation but terrible for acoustics and privacy.

Longhouses

A distinctive feature of indigenous Dayak life in Malaysian Borneo is the longhouse (p580) – essentially an entire village under one seemingly interminable roof. Contemporary longhouses fuse age-old forms with highly functional features such as corrugated-iron roofs and satellite dishes. According to longstanding Dayak tradition, anyone who shows up at a longhouse must be welcomed and given accommodation. However, these days turning up at a longhouse unannounced may be an unwelcome imposition on the residents – in short, bad manners. The way to avoid these pitfalls is to hire a locally savvy guide or tour company that can coordinate your visit and make introductions.

Resthouses

A few of the old British-developed resthouses, set up during the colonial era to provide accommodation for travelling officials, are still operating. Many are still government owned but are privately operated. Some have been turned into modern midrange resorts, others retain colonial-era decor. Resthouses typically charge between RM60 and RM150 per room, usually including air-con and attached bathroom.

BOOK YOUR STAY ONLINE

For more accommodation reviews by Lonely Planet authors, check out http://lonelyplanet.com/hotels/. You'll find independent reviews, as well as recommendations on the best places to stay. Best of all, you can book online.

Children

Travelling with the kids in Malaysia is generally a breeze. For the most part, parents needn't be overly concerned, but it pays to lay down a few ground rules – such as regular hand-washing – to head off potential problems. Children should especially be warned not to play with animals, as rabies occurs in Malaysia.

Lonely Planet's *Travel with Children* contains useful advice on how to cope with kids on the road and what to bring along to make things go more smoothly, with special attention paid to travelling in developing countries. Also useful for general advice is www.travelwithyourkids.com.

There are discounts for children for most attractions and for most transport. Many beach resorts have special family lodgings. Cots, however, are not widely available in cheaper accommodation. Public transport is comfortable and relatively well organised. Pushing a stroller around isn't likely to be easy given there are often no level footpaths and kerbs are high.

Baby formula, baby food and nappies (diapers) are widely available. However, it makes sense to stock up on these items before heading to remote destinations or islands.

Customs Regulations

The following can be brought into Malaysia duty free:

- 1L of alcohol
- 225g of tobacco (200 cigarettes or 50 cigars)
- souvenirs and gifts not exceeding RM200 (RM500 when coming from Labuan or Langkawi)

Cameras, portable radios, perfume, cosmetics and watches do not incur duty. Prohibited items include weapons (including imitations), fireworks and 'obscene and prejudicial articles' (pornography, for example, and items that may be considered inflammatory, or religiously offensive) and drugs. Drug smuggling carries the death penalty in Malaysia.

Visitors can carry no more than the equivalent of US$10,000 in ringgit or any other currency in and out of Malaysia.

Electricity

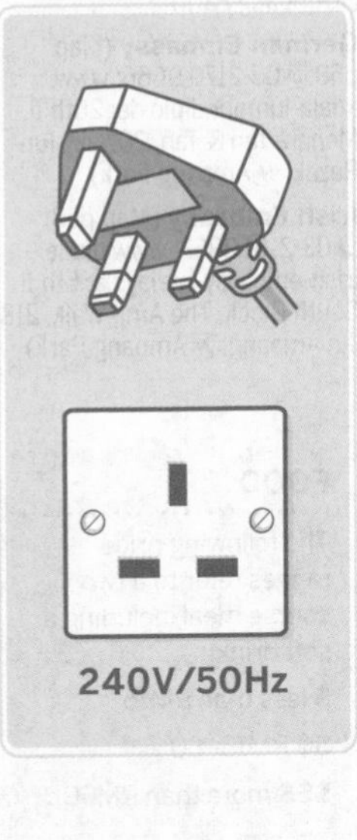

Embassies & Consulates

For a full list of Malaysian embassies and consulates outside the country check out www.kln.gov.my. Most foreign embassies are in Kuala Lumpur and are generally open 8am to 12.30pm and 1.30pm to 4.30pm Monday to Friday.

Australian Embassy (Map p58; ☎03-2146 5555; www.malaysia.highcommission.gov.au/klpr/home.html; 6 Jln Yap Kwan Seng; Ⓜ KLCC)

British Embassy (Map p58; ☎03-2170 2200; www.gov.uk/government/world/organisations/british-high-commission-kuala-lumpur; level 27 Menara Binjai, 2 Jln Binjai; Ⓜ Ampang Park)

Brunei Embassy (☎03-2161 2800; www.mofat.gov.bn/site/Home.aspx; 19-01 Menara Tan & Tan, 207 Jln Tun Razak; Ⓜ Ampang Park)

Canadian Embassy (☎03-2718-3333; www.canadainternational.gc.ca; 17th fl, Menara Tan & Tan, 207 Jln Tun Razak; Ⓜ Ampang Park)

French Embassy (Map p58; ☎03-2053 5500; www.ambafrance-my.org; 196 Jln Ampang; Ⓜ Ampang Park)

German Embassy (Map p58; ☎03-2170 9666; www.kuala-lumpur.diplo.de; 26th fl, Menara Tan & Tan, 207 Jln Tun Razak; Ⓜ Ampang Park)

Irish Embassy (Map p58; ☎03-2161 2963; www.dfa.ie/irish-embassy/malaysia; 5th fl, South Block, The Amp Walk, 218 Jln Ampang; Ⓜ Ampang Park)

FOOD

The following price ranges refer to a two-course meal including a soft drink.

$ less than RM15

$$ RM15–60

$$$ more than RM60

Netherlands Embassy (Map p58; ☎03-2235 3210; http://malaysia.nlembassy.org; 7th fl, South Block, The Amp Walk, 218 Jln Ampang; Ⓜ Ampang Park)

New Zealand Embassy (Map p58; ☎03-2078-2533; www.nzembassy.com/malaysia; Level 21, Menara IMC, 8 Jln Sultan Ismail; monorail Bukit Nanas)

Singapore Embassy (Map p58; ☎03-2161 6277; https://singapore.visahq.com/embassy/malaysia; 209 Jln Tun Razak; Ⓜ Ampang Park)

US Embassy (Map p58; ☎03-2168 5000; http://malaysia.usembassy.gov; 376 Jln Tun Razak; Ⓜ Ampang Park)

LGBT Travellers

Malaysia is a predominantly Muslim country and the level of tolerance for homosexuality is vastly different from its neighbours. It's illegal for men of any age to have sex with other men. In addition, the Islamic sharia laws (which apply only to Muslims) forbid sodomy and cross-dressing. Outright persecution of gays and lesbians is rare.

Nonetheless, LGBT travellers should avoid behaviour that attracts unwanted attention. Malaysians are conservative about all displays of public affection regardless of sexual orientation. Although same-sex hand-holding is fairly common for men and women, this is rarely an indication of sexuality; an overtly gay couple doing the same would attract attention, though there is little risk of vocal or aggressive homophobia.

There's actually a fairly active LGBT scene in KL. Start looking for information on www.utopia-asia.com or www.fridae.com, both of which provide good coverage of LGBT events and activities across Asia.

The **PT Foundation** (http://ptfmalaysia.org/v2) is a voluntary nonprofit organisation providing sexuality and HIV/AIDS education, care and support programs for marginalised communities.

Insurance

It's always a good idea to take out travel insurance. Check the small print to see if the policy covers potentially dangerous sporting activities such as caving, diving or trekking, and make sure that it adequately covers your valuables. Health-wise, you may prefer a policy that pays doctors or hospitals directly rather than your having to pay on the spot and claim later. If you have to claim later, make sure that you keep all documentation. Check that the policy covers ambulances, an emergency flight home and, if you plan on trekking in remote areas, a helicopter evacuation.

A few credit cards offer limited, sometimes full, travel insurance to the holder.

Worldwide travel insurance is available at www.lonelyplanet.com/travel-insurance. You can buy, extend and claim online anytime – even if you're already on the road.

Internet Access

Malaysia is blanketed with hot spots for wi-fi connections (usually free). Internet cafes are less common these days, but do still exist if you're not travelling with a wi-fi enabled device. Only in the jungles and the most remote reaches of the peninsula and Malaysian Borneo are you likely to be without any internet access.

Legal Matters

In any dealings with the local police it will pay to be deferential. You're most likely to come into contact with them either through reporting a crime (some of the big cities in Malaysia have tourist police stations for this purpose) or while driving. Minor misdemeanours may be overlooked, but don't count on it.

Drug trafficking carries a mandatory death penalty. A number of foreigners have been executed in Malaysia, some of them for possession of amazingly small quantities of heroin. Even possession of tiny amounts can bring down a lengthy jail sentence and a beating with the *rotan* (cane). Just don't do it.

Maps

Periplus (http://periplus publishinggroup.com) has maps covering Malaysia, Peninsular Malaysia and KL. Tourism Malaysia's free *Map of Malaysia* has useful distance charts, facts about the country and inset maps of many major cities.

For accurate maps of rural areas contact the **National Survey & Mapping Department** (Ibu Pejabat Ukur & Pemetaan Malaysia; ☎03-2617 0800; www.jupem.gov.my; Jln Semarak, Kuala Lumpur; ⏲7.45am-12.30pm & 2-4.45pm Mon-Thu, 7.45am-noon & 2-4.45pm Fri).

Money

ATMs & Credit Cards

Mastercard and Visa are the most widely accepted brands of credit card. You can make ATM withdrawals with your PIN, or banks such as Maybank (Malaysia's biggest bank), HSBC and Standard Chartered will accept credit cards for over-the-counter cash advances. Many banks are also linked to international banking networks such as Cirrus (the most common), Maestro and Plus, allowing withdrawals from overseas savings or cheque accounts.

If you have any questions about whether your cards will be accepted in Malaysia, ask your home bank about its reciprocal relationships with Malaysian banks.

PRACTICALITIES

Electricity Connect to a reliable supply (220V to 240V, 50 cycles) with a UK-type three-square-pin plug.

Newspapers English-language newspapers include the *New Straits Times* (www.nst.com.my), the *Star* (www.thestar.com.my) and the *Malay Mail* (www.themalaymailonline.com). In Malaysian Borneo you'll also find the *Borneo Post* (www.theborneopost.com), the *New Sarawak Tribune* (www.newsarawaktribune.com) and the *New Sabah Times* (www.newsabahtimes.com.my).

Radio Listen to channels Traxx FM (http://traxxfm.rtm.gov.my; 90.3FM), HITZ FM (www.hitz.fm; 92.9FM) and MIX FM (www.mix.fm; 94.5FM) for pop music, and BFM (www.bfm.my; 89.9FM) or Fly FM (www.flyfm.com.my; 95.8FM) for news.

TV Watch Malaysia's two government channels (TV1 and TV2), four commercial stations (TV3, NTV7, 8TV and TV9) as well as a host of satellite channels.

Weights & Measures Use the metric system.

Contact details for credit card companies in Malaysia:

American Express (☎03-2031 7888, 1800 88 9559; https://network.americanexpress.com/my/en/homepage)

Diners Card (☎03-2730 3388; www.diners.com.my)

MasterCard (☎1800 804 594; www.mastercard.com/sea)

Visa (☎1800 802 997; www.visa-asia.com)

Currency

The ringgit (RM) is made up of 100 sen. Coins in use are 1 sen (rare), 5 sen, 10 sen, 20 sen and 50 sen; notes come in RM1, RM5, RM10, RM20, RM50 and RM100.

Older Malaysians sometimes refer to ringgit as 'dollars' – if in doubt ask if people mean US dollars or 'Malaysian dollars' (ie ringgit).

Be sure to carry plenty of small bills with you when venturing outside cities – in some cases people cannot change bills larger than RM10.

Taxes & Refunds

Since 2015 a goods and sales tax (GST) of 6% has been levied on most goods and services in Malaysia. There are some exemptions (mainly for fresh and essential foods) but generally you'll now find this tax added to most things you buy including restaurant meals and souvenirs. Some establishments, if their turnover is low or if they have decided to absorb the GST into their regular prices, will not add the tax on top of the bill – it's always worth checking in advance if you're unsure.

If you spend in excess of RM300 at any one government-approved outlet, it is possible for international visitors to claim a refund of GST on certain goods they are taking out of the country. Full details of how to do this can be found at http://gst.customs.gov.my.

Travellers Cheques & Cash

Banks in the region are efficient and there are plenty of moneychangers. For changing cash or travellers cheques, banks usually charge a commission (around RM10 per transaction, with a possible small fee per cheque), whereas moneychangers have no charges

CALCULATING HOLIDAY DATES

Muslims holidays follow a lunar calendar, while dates for Chinese and Hindu religious festivals are calculated using the lunisolar calendar. Muslim holidays fall around 11 days earlier each year, while Hindu and Chinese festivals change dates but fall roughly within the same months.

but their rates vary more. Compared with a bank, you'll generally get a better rate for cash at a moneychanger – it's usually quicker too. Away from the tourist centres, moneychangers' rates are often poorer and they may not change travellers cheques.

All major brands of travellers cheques are accepted across the region. Cash in major currencies is also readily exchanged, though like everywhere else in the world the US dollar has a slight edge.

Opening Hours

Banks 10am–3pm Monday to Friday, 9.30am–11.30am Saturday

Bars & clubs 5pm–5am

Cafes 8am–10pm

Restaurants noon–2.30pm and 6pm–10.30pm

Shops 9.30am–7pm, malls 10am–10pm

Photography

Malaysians usually have no antipathy to being photographed, although of course it's polite to ask permission before photographing people and taking pictures in mosques or temples. For advice on taking better photos, see Lonely Planet's *Travel Photography: A Guide to Taking Better Pictures*, written by travel photographer Richard I'Anson.

Post

Pos Malaysia Berhad (☎1300 300 300; www.pos.com.my) runs an efficient postal system. Post offices are open 8am to 5pm from Monday to Saturday, but closed on the first Saturday of the month and public holidays.

Aerograms and postcards cost 50 sen to send to any destination. Letters weighing 20g or less cost 1.20 sen to Brunei, Singapore, Cambodia, Indonesia, Laos, Myanmar, Philippines, Thailand and Vietnam; RM1.40 to other Asia-Pacific countries including Australia or New Zealand; and RM2 to all other countries. Parcel rates range from around RM20 to RM60 for a 1kg parcel, depending on the destination.

Main post offices in larger cities sell packaging materials and stationery.

Public Holidays

As well as fixed secular holidays, various religious festivals (which change dates annually) are national holidays. These include Chinese New Year (in January/February), the Hindu festival of Deepavali (in October/November), the Buddhist festival of Wesak (April/May) and the Muslim festivals of Hari Raya Haji, Hari Raya Puasa, Mawlid al-Nabi and Awal Muharram (Muslim New Year). See p25 for dates and more information.

Fixed annual holidays include the following:

New Year's Day 1 January

Federal Territory Day 1 February (in Kuala Lumpur and Putrajaya only)

Good Friday March or April (in Sarawak & Sabah only)

Labour Day 1 May

Yang di-Pertuan Agong's (King's) Birthday 1st Saturday in June

Governor of Penang's Birthday 2nd Saturday in July (in Penang only)

National Day (Hari Kebangsaan) 31 August

Malaysia Day 16 September

Christmas Day 25 December

School Holidays

Schools break for holidays five times a year. The actual dates vary from state to state but are generally in January (one week), March (two weeks), May (three weeks), August (one week) and October (four weeks).

Safe Travel

Animal Hazards

Rabies does occur in Malaysia, so any bite from an animal should be treated very seriously. In the jungles and mangrove forests, living hazards include leeches (annoying but harmless), snakes (some kinds are highly venomous), macaques (prone to bag-snatching in some locales), orangutans (occasionally aggressive) and, in muddy estuaries, saltwater crocodiles (deadly if they drag you under).

Theft & Violence

Theft and violence are not particularly common in Malaysia and compared with Indonesia or Thailand it's extremely safe. Nevertheless, it pays to keep a close eye on your belongings, especially your travel documents (passport, travellers cheques etc), which should be kept with you at all times.

Muggings do happen, particularly in KL and Penang, and physical attacks have been known to occur, particularly after hours and in rundown areas of cities. Thieves on motorbikes particularly target women for grab raids on their handbags. Also keep a watch out for sleazy local 'beach boys' in Langkawi and the Perhentians.

Credit-card fraud is a growing problem in Malaysia. Use your cards only at established businesses and guard your credit-card numbers closely.

A small, sturdy padlock is well worth carrying, especially if you are going to be staying at any of the cheap huts found on Malaysia's beaches, where flimsy padlocks are the norm.

Telephone

Landline services are provided by the national monopoly **Telekom Malaysia** (TM; www.tm.com.my).

Fax

Fax facilities are available at TM offices in larger cities and at some main post offices. If you can't find one of these, try a travel agency or large hotel.

International Calls

The easiest and cheapest way to make international calls is to buy a local SIM card for your mobile (cell) phone. Only certain payphones permit international calls. You can make operator-assisted international calls from local TM offices. To save money on landline calls, buy a prepaid international calling card (available from convenience stores).

Local Calls

Local calls cost 8 sen for the first two minutes. Payphones take coins or prepaid cards which are available from TM offices and convenience stores. Some take international credit cards. You'll also find a range of discount calling cards at convenience stores and mobile-phone counters.

Mobile (Cell) Phones

If you have arranged global roaming with your home provider, your GSM digital phone will automatically tune into one of the region's networks. If not, buy a prepaid SIM card (passport required) for one of the local networks on arrival. The rate for locals calls and text messages is around 36 sen.

There are three main mobile-phone companies, all with similar call rates and prepaid packages:

Celcom (www.celcom.com.my) This is the best company to use if you'll be spending time in remote regions of Sabah and Sarawak.

DiGi (www.digi.com.my)

Maxis (www.maxis.com.my)

Time

Malaysia is eight hours ahead of GMT/UTC, two hours behind Australian Eastern Standard Time, 13 hours ahead of American Eastern Standard Time.

Toilets

Although there are still some places with Asian squat-style toilets, you'll most often find Western-style ones these days. At public facilities toilet paper is not usually provided. Instead, you will find a hose which you are supposed to use as a bidet or, in cheaper places, a bucket of water and a tap. If you're not comfortable with this, take tissues or toilet paper wherever you go.

Tourist Information

Tourism Malaysia (www.tourism.gov.my) has a good network of overseas offices, which are useful for pre-departure planning. Unfortunately, its domestic offices are less helpful and are often unable to give specific information about destinations and transport. Nonetheless, they do stock some decent brochures as well as the excellent *Map of Malaysia*.

Within Malaysia there are also a number of state tourist-promotion organisations, which often have more detailed information about specific areas. These include:

Sabah Tourism (www.sabahtourism.com)

Pahang Tourism (www.pahangtourism.org.my)

Perak Tourism (www.peraktourism.com.my)

Sarawak Tourism (http://sarawaktourism.com)

Penang Tourism (www.visitpenang.gov.my)

Tourism Selangor (www.tourismselangor.my)

Tourism Terengganu (http://tourism.terengganu.gov.my)

Travellers with Disabilities

For the mobility impaired, Malaysia can be a nightmare. In most cities there are often no footpaths, kerbs are high, construction sites are everywhere, and crossings are few and far between. On the upside, taxis are cheap and both Malaysia Airlines and KTM (the national rail service) offer 50% discounts on travel for travellers with disabilities.

TRAVEL ADVISORIES

For the latest travel advisories check the following websites:

Australia (www.smartraveller.gov.au)

Canada (www.voyage.gc.ca)

New Zealand (www.safetravel.govt.nz)

UK (www.gov.uk/foreign-travel-advice)

USA (http://travel.state.gov/content/travel/eng.html)

Before setting off get in touch with your national support organisation (preferably with the travel officer, if there is one).

Visas

Visitors must have a passport valid for at least six months beyond the date of entry into Malaysia. The following gives a brief overview of other requirements – full details of visa regulations are available at www.kln.gov.my.

Nationals of most countries are given a 30- or 60-day visa on arrival, depending on the expected length of stay. As a general rule, if you arrive by air you will be given 60 days automatically, though coming overland you may be given 30 days unless you specifically ask for a 60-day permit. It's possible to get an extension at an immigration office in Malaysia for a total stay of up to three months. This is a straightforward procedure that is easily done in major Malaysian cities.

Only under special circumstances can Israeli citizens enter Malaysia.

Both Sabah and Sarawak retain a certain degree of state-level control of their borders. Tourists must go through passport control and have their passports stamped whenever they:

- arrive in Sabah or Sarawak from Peninsular Malaysia or the federal district of Pulau Labuan
- exit Sabah or Sarawak on their way to Peninsular Malaysia or Pulau Labuan
- travel between Sabah and Sarawak

When entering Sabah or Sarawak from another part of Malaysia, your new visa stamp will be valid only for the remainder of the period left on your original Malaysian visa. In Sarawak, an easy way to extend your visa is to make a 'visa run' to Brunei or Indonesia (through the Tebedu–Entikong land crossing).

Volunteering

There are myriad volunteering organisations in the region, but be aware that so-called 'voluntourism' has become big business and that not every organisation fulfils its promise of meaningful experiences. Experts recommend a minimum commitment of three months for positions working with children.

Lonely Planet does not endorse any organisations that we do not work with directly, so it is essential that you do your own thorough research before agreeing to volunteer with any organisation.

All Women's Action Society Malaysia (www.awam.org.my) Aims to improve the lives of women in Malaysia by lobbying for a just, democratic and equitable society with respect and equality for both genders.

Ecoteer (www.ecoteerresponsibletravel.com) Offers various volunteer projects including ones relating to orangutan conservation.

Eden Handicap Service Centre (www.edenhandicap.org) Christian-run organisation caring for people with disabilities in Penang; volunteers are needed to help with a variety of activities.

The Great Projects (www.thegreatprojects.com) Organisation that places paying volunteers at the Matang Wildlife Centre in Sarawak as well as on other wildlife conservation projects around Malaysia.

Lang Tengah Turtle Watch (http://langtengahturtlewatch.org; Turtle Bay; per week US$240) Help safeguard the turtles that come to lay their eggs on this Peninsula East Coast island.

LASSie (www.langkawilassie.org.my) Dog and cat lovers can help out at the Langkawi Animal Shelter & Sanctuary Foundation.

Malaysian Nature Society (www.mns.org.my) Check its website or drop them a line to find out ways you can get involved in helping preserve Malaysia's natural environment.

Miso Walai Homestay Program (www.misowalaihomestay.com) Gets travellers involved with local wetlands restoration projects.

PAWS (www.paws.org.my) Animal rescue shelter in Subang, about 30 minutes from central KL.

Regional Environmental Awareness Cameron Highlands (www.reach.org.my) Take part in reforestation and recycling programs in the Cameron Highlands.

Sepilok Orangutan Rehabilitation Centre (p355) Has one of Malaysia's best established volunteer programs for animal lovers.

Wild Asia (www.wildasia.org) A variety of volunteer options generally connected with the environment and sustainable tourism in the region.

Women Travellers

Dressing modestly and being respectful, especially in areas of stronger Muslim religious sensibilities such as the northeastern states of Peninsula Malaysia, will ensure you travel with minimum hassle. When visiting mosques, cover your head and limbs with a headscarf and sarong (many mosques lend these out at the entrance). At the beach, most Malaysian women swim fully clothed in T-shirts and shorts, so don't even think about going topless.

Be proactive about your own safety. Treat overly friendly strangers, both male and female, with a good deal of caution. Take taxis after dark and avoid walking alone at night in quiet or seedy parts of town.

Transport

See the Transport sections of the Singapore (p556) and Brunei (p480) chapters for further information.

GETTING THERE & AWAY

Entering Malaysia

The main requirements are a passport that's valid for travel for at least six months, proof of an onward ticket and adequate funds for your stay, although you will rarely be asked to prove this.

Flights, tours and rail tickets can be booked online at www.lonelyplanet.com/bookings.

Air

Airports & Airlines

The bulk of international flights arrive at Kuala Lumpur International Airport (KLIA), 75km south of Kuala Lumpur (KL); it has two terminals with KLIA2 being used mainly by budget airlines (KLIA2 is AirAsia's hub). There are also direct flights from Asia and Australia into Penang, Kuching, Kota Kinabalu and a few other cities.

Tickets

When shopping for a ticket, compare the cost of flying into Malaysia versus the cost of flying into Singapore. From Singapore you can travel overland to almost any place in Peninsular Malaysia in less than a day, and Singapore also has direct flights to Malaysian Borneo and Brunei. KL and Singapore are also good places to buy tickets for onward travel.

Land

Brunei

Border crossings are possible into Brunei from Sarawak.

Indonesia

Several express buses run between Pontianak in Kalimantan and Kuching and Miri in Sarawak, as well as Kota Kinabalu in Sabah. The bus crosses at the Tebedu–Entikong border.

Singapore

The Causeway linking Johor Bahru with Singapore handles most traffic between the countries. Trains and buses run from all over Malaysia straight through to Singapore, terminating at Woodlands, or you can take a bus to JB and get a taxi or one of the frequent buses from JB to Singapore.

A shuttle train (RM5/S$5, five minutes) operated by Malaysia's Keretapi Tanah Melayu (KTM) ferries commuters between the Woodlands Checkpoint and JB Sentral seven times a day.

A good website with details of express buses between Singapore, Malaysia and Thailand is the **Express**

CLIMATE CHANGE & TRAVEL

Every form of transport that relies on carbon-based fuel generates CO_2, the main cause of human-induced climate change. Modern travel is dependent on aeroplanes, which might use less fuel per kilometre per person than most cars but travel much greater distances. The altitude at which aircraft emit gases (including CO_2) and particles also contributes to their climate change impact. Many websites offer 'carbon calculators' that allow people to estimate the carbon emissions generated by their journey and, for those who wish to do so, to offset the impact of the greenhouse gases emitted with contributions to portfolios of climate-friendly initiatives throughout the world. Lonely Planet offsets the carbon footprint of all staff and author travel.

SUSTAINABLE TRAVEL

Carbon-cutting overland travel to Peninsular Malaysia from Europe and most parts of Asia is possible as long as you're not in a hurry. See **Man in Seat 61** (www.seat61.com/malaysia.htm) for how to reach KL from London by a combination of trains and buses in three and a half weeks.

Once in the region consider taking part in a homestay program, hiring local hiking guides and supporting traditional craft industries when buying souvenirs. See our sustainable picks throughout the guide (indicated by 🍃).

Bus Travel Guide (www.singaporemalaysiabus.com).

There is also a causeway linking Tuas, in western Singapore, with Geylang Patah in JB. This is known as the Second Link, and some bus services to Melaka and up the west coast head this way; be prepared for delays at the immigration section on the Singapore side. If you have a car, tolls on the Second Link are much higher than those on the main Causeway.

Thailand

BUS & CAR

You can cross the border by road into Thailand at Padang Besar, Bukit Kayu Hitam, Rantau Panjang (Sungai Golok on the Thai side) and Pengkalan Kubor.

TRAIN

The rail route into Thailand is on the Butterworth–Alor Setar–Hat Yai route, which crosses into Thailand at Padang Besar. You can take the International Express from Butterworth all the way to Bangkok. Trains from KL and Singapore are timed to connect with this service.

From Butterworth to Hat Yai the 2nd-class fare is upper/lower berth RM35/39, to Bangkok RM104/112.

From Alor Setar there's one daily northbound train to Hat Yai (RM9 to RM48) and one to Bangkok(upper/lower berth RM97/105)

From KL there is one through service daily (the Senandung Langkawi) to Hat Yai (seat/upper berth/lower berth RM44/54/60).

From Hat Yai there are frequent train and bus connections to other parts of Thailand.

The opulent **Eastern & Oriental Express** (www.belmond.com/eastern-and-oriental-express) also connects Singapore and Bangkok, making stops in KL and Butterworth (for Penang).

Sea

Brunei

Boats connect Brunei to Pulau Labuan, from where boats go to Sabah. All international boats depart from Muara, 25km northeast of Bandar Seri Begawan, where Brunei immigration formalities are also handled.

Indonesia

The following are the main ferry routes between Indonesia and Malaysia:

- Bengkalis (Sumatra) to Melaka
- Pulau Batam to Johor Bahru
- Dumai (Sumatra) to Melaka
- Medan (Sumatra) to Penang
- Pekanbaru (Sumatra) to Melaka
- Tanjung Pinang Bintan to Johor Bahru
- Tanjung Balai (Sumatra) to Pelabuhan Klang and Kukup
- Tarakan (Kalimantan) to Tawau

Philippines

Weekly ferries link Sandakan with Zamboanga, on the Philippine island of Mindanao.

Singapore

Singapore has a number of regular ferry connections to Malaysia. Cruise trips in the region are also very popular with locals.

Thailand

Ferries connect Kuah on Pulau Langkawi with Satun on the Thai coast and, from November to mid-May, with Ko Lipe; make sure you get your passport stamped going in either direction.

GETTING AROUND

Air

Airlines in Malaysia

The two main domestic operators are **Malaysia Airlines** (MAS; ☎1300 883 000, international 03-7843 3000; www.malaysiaairlines.com) and **AirAsia** (☎600 85 8888; www.airasia.com).

The MAS subsidiary **Firefly** (☎03-7845 4543; www.fireflyz.com.my) has flights from KL (SkyPark Subang Terminal) to Ipoh, Johor Bahru, Kerteh, Kota Bharu, Kuala Terengganu, Langkawi and Penang. It also runs connections between Penang and Langkawi, Kuantan and Kota Bharu, Ipoh and JB, and JB and Kota Bharu.

Malindo Air (☎03-7841 5388; www.malindoair.com) also has a wide range of connections between many Malaysian cities and towns.

In Malaysian Borneo, Malaysia Airlines' subsidiary **MASwings** (☎1300-88 3000; www.maswings.com.my) offers local flights within and between Sarawak and Sabah; it's main hub is Miri. These services, especially those handled by 19-seat Twin Otters, are very much reliant on the vagaries of the weather. In the wet season (October to March in Sarawak and on Sabah's northeast coast; May to November on Sabah's west coast), places like Bario in Sarawak can be isolated for days at a time, so don't venture into this area if you have a tight schedule. These flights are completely booked during school holidays. At other times it's easier to get a seat at a few days' notice, but always book as far in advance as possible.

Discounts

All the airlines offer discounted tickets online, depending on how far in advance you book. A variety of other discounts (typically between 25% and 50%) are available for flights around Malaysia on Malaysia Airlines, including for families and groups of three or more – it's worth inquiring when you book tickets in Malaysia. Student discounts are available, but only for students enrolled in institutions that are in Malaysia.

Bicycle

Bicycle touring around Malaysia and neighbouring countries is an increasingly popular activity. The main road system is well engineered and has good surfaces, but the secondary road system is limited. Road conditions are good enough for touring bikes in most places, but mountain bikes are recommended for forays off the beaten track.

Top-quality bicycles and components can be bought in major cities, but generally 10-speed (or higher) bikes and fittings are hard to find. Bringing your own is the best bet. Bicycles can be transported on most international flights; check with the airline about extra charges and shipment specifications.

Useful websites include:

Kuala Lumpur Mountain Bike Hash (http://klmbh.org) Details of the monthly bike ride out of KL.

Bicycle Touring Malaysia (www.bicycletouringmalaysia.com) A mine of information about cycling around the region, run by Mr David and his son Suresh, who also offer tour packages.

Malaysia Cycling Events & Blogs (malaysiacycling.blogspot.co.uk) Includes listings of cycle shops around the country.

Cycling Kuala Lumpur (http://cyclingkl.blogspot.co.uk) A great resources for cycling adventures in and around KL

Boat

There are no services connecting Peninsular Malaysia with Malaysian Borneo. On a local level, there are boats and ferries between the peninsula and offshore islands, and along the rivers of Sabah and Sarawak. Note that some ferry operators are notoriously lax about observing safety rules, and local authorities are often nonexistent. If a boat looks overloaded or otherwise unsafe, *do not board it* – no one else will look out for your safety.

Bus

Bus travel in Malaysia is economical and generally comfortable. Seats can be paid for and reserved either directly with operators or via online sites such www.easybook.com. Some bus drivers speed recklessly, resulting in frequent, often fatal, accidents.

Konsortium Transnasional Berhad (www.ktb.com.my) is Malaysia's largest bus operator running services under the **Transnasional** (☎1300 888 582; www.transnasional.com.my), **Nice** (☎013-220 7867; www.nice-coaches.com.my; 🚇Kuala Lumpur), **Plusliner** (☎013-220 7867; www.plusliner.com.my) and **Cityliner** (☎03-4047 7878; www.cityliner.com.my) brands. Its services tend to be slower than rivals, and its buses have been involved in several major accidents. It has competition from a variety of privately operated buses on the longer domestic routes, including **Aeroline** (www.aeroline.com.my) and **Supernice** (www.supernice.com.my). There are so many buses on major runs that you can often turn up and get a seat on the next bus.

Most long-distance buses have air-con, often turned to frigid so bring a sweater!

In larger towns there may be a number of bus stations; local/regional buses often operate from one station and long-distance buses from another; in other cases, KL for example, bus stations are differentiated by the destinations they serve.

Bus travel off the beaten track is relatively straightforward. Small towns and *kampung* (villages) all over the country are serviced by public buses, usually rattlers without air-con. Unfortunately, they are often poorly signed and sometimes the only way to find your bus is to ask a local. These buses are invariably dirt cheap and provide a great sample of rural life. In most towns there are no ticket offices, so buy your ticket from the conductor after you board.

Car & Motorcycle

Driving in Malaysia is fantastic compared with most Asian countries. There has been a lot of investment in the country's roads, which are generally of a high quality. New cars for hire are commonly available and fuel is inexpensive (RM1.95 per litre).

It's not all good news though. Driving in the cities, particularly KL, can be a nightmare, due to traffic and confusing one-way systems. Malaysian drivers aren't always the safest when it comes to obeying road rules – they mightn't be as reckless as drivers elsewhere in Southeast Asia, but they still take risks. For example, hardly any of the drivers keep to the official 110km/h speed limit on the main highways and tailgating is a common problem.

The Lebuhraya (North–South Hwy) is a six-lane expressway that runs for 966km along the length of the peninsula from the Thai border in the north to JB in the south. There are quite steep toll charges for using the expressway and these vary according to the distance travelled. As a result the normal highways remain crowded while traffic on the expressway is light.

Bringing Your Own Vehicle

It's technically possible to bring your vehicle into Malaysia, but there are reams of red tape and the costs are prohibitively expensive – a hire car is a much better proposition.

Driving Licence

A valid overseas license is needed to rent a car. An International Driving Permit (a translation of your state or national driver's license and its vehicle categories) is usually not required by local car-hire companies, but it is recommended that you bring one. Most rental companies also require that drivers are at least 23 years old (and younger than 65) with at least one year of driving experience.

Hire

Major rent-a-car operations include **Avis** (www.avis.com.my), **Hertz** (www.simedarbycarrental.com), **Mayflower** (www.mayflowercarrental.com.my) and **Orix** (www.orixcarrentals.com.my). There are many others though, including local operators only found in one city.

Unlimited distance rates for a 1.3L Proton Saga, one of the cheapest and most popular cars in Malaysia, are posted at around RM190/1320 per day/week, including insurance and collision-damage waiver. The Proton is basically a Mitsubishi assembled under licence in Malaysia.

You can often get better prices, either through smaller local companies or when the major companies offer special deals. Rates drop substantially for longer rentals. The advantage of dealing with a large company is that it has offices all over the country, giving better backup if something goes wrong and allowing you to pick up in one city and drop off in another.

The best place to look for car hire is KL, though Penang is also good. In Sabah and Sarawak there is less competition and rates are higher, partly because of road conditions; there's also likely to be a surcharge if you drop your car off in a different city from the one you rented it in.

Insurance

Rental companies will provide insurance when you hire a car, but always check what the extent of your coverage will be, particularly if you're involved in an accident. You might want to take out your own insurance or pay the rental company an extra premium for an insurance excess reduction.

Road Rules

- Cars are right-hand drive, and you drive on the left side of the road.
- The speed limit is 110km per hour on expressways, 50km per hour on *kampung* (village) back roads.
- Wearing safety belts is compulsory.
- Watch out for stray animals, wandering pedestrians and the large number of motorcyclists.
- Malaysia drivers show remarkable common sense compared to other countries in the region. However, there are still plenty of drivers who take dangerous risks. Lane-drift is a big problem and signalling, when used at all, is often unclear. Giving a quick blast of the horn when you're overtaking a slower vehicle is common practice and helps alert otherwise sleepy drivers to your presence.

Hitching

Keep in mind hitching is never entirely safe, and we don't recommend it. Travellers who decide to hitch should understand that they are taking a small but potentially serious risk. People who do choose to hitch will be safer if they travel in pairs and let someone know where they are planning to go.

This said, Malaysia has long had a reputation for being a great place for hitchhiking, and it's generally still true, though with inexpensive bus travel most travellers don't bother. Note that hitchers are banned from expressways.

Local Transport

Taxis are found in all large cities, and most have meters – although you can't always rely on the drivers to use them.

Bicycle rickshaws (trishaws) supplement the taxi service in George Town and Melaka and are definitely handy ways of getting around the older parts of town, which have convoluted and narrow streets.

In major cities there are also buses, which are extremely cheap and convenient once you figure out which one is going your way. KL also has commuter trains, a Light Rail Transit (LRT) and a monorail system.

In Malaysian Borneo, once you're out of the big cities, you're basically on your own and must either walk or hitch. If you're really in the bush, of course, riverboats and airplanes are the only alternatives to lengthy jungle treks.

Long-Distance Taxi

As Malaysia has become a wealthier country, with more people owning their own cars, the long-distance taxi is becoming less of a feature of the transport landscape. However, in major towns and cities there will be a *teksi* stand for long distance travel.

Taxis are available on a share basis for up to four people. As soon as a full complement of passengers turns up, off you go; alternatively, you can charter the whole taxi which is four times the single-fare rate. Early morning is generally the best time to find people to share a taxi, but enquire at the taxi stand the day before as to the best time to turn up.

Fares are generally about twice the comparable bus fares. If you want to charter a taxi to an obscure destination, or by the hour, you'll probably have to do some negotiating. On the peninsula you're likely to pay around 50 sen per kilometre. In Sarawak, the taxi metre price (for kilometres beyond the first 3km which is RM10) is RM1.20 per km.

Taxi drivers often drive at frighteningly high speeds. They don't have as many head-on collisions as you might expect, but closing your eyes at times of high stress certainly helps! You also have the option of demanding that the driver slow down, but this can be met with varying degrees of hostility.

Train

Malaysia's national railway company is **Keretapi Tanah Melayu** (KTM; ☎1300 885 862; www.ktmb.com.my). It runs a modern, comfortable and economical railway service, although there are basically only two lines and for the most part services are slow.

One line runs up the west coast from Singapore, through KL, Butterworth and on into Thailand. The other branches off from this line at Gemas and runs through Kuala Lipis up to the northeastern corner of the country near Kota Bharu in Kelantan. Often referred to as the 'jungle train,' this line is properly known as the 'east-coast line.'

In Sabah the **North Borneo Railway** (www.suteraharbour.com/north-borneo-railway), a narrow-gauge line running through the Sungai Padas gorge from Tenom to Beaufort, offers tourist trips lasting four hours on Wednesday and Saturday.

Services & Classes

There are two main types of rail services: express and local trains. Express trains are air-conditioned and have 'premier' (1st class), 'superior' (2nd class) and sometimes 'economy' (3rd class) seats and, depending on the service, sleeping cabins. Local trains are usually economy class only, but some have superior seats.

Express trains stop only at main stations, while local services, which operate mostly on the east-coast line, stop everywhere, including the middle of the jungle, to let passengers and their goods on and off. Consequently local services take more than twice as long as the express trains and run to erratic schedules, but if you're in no hurry they provide a colourful experience and are good for short journeys.

Train schedules are reviewed a few times a year, so check the KTM website, where you can make bookings and buy tickets.

Health

BEFORE YOU GO

- Take out health insurance.
- Pack medications in their original, clearly labelled containers.
- Carry a signed and dated letter from your physician describing your medical conditions and medications, including their generic names.
- If you have a heart condition bring a copy of your ECG taken just prior to travelling.
- Bring a double supply of any regular medication in case of loss or theft.

Recommended Vaccinations

Proof of yellow fever vaccination will be required if you have visited a country in the yellow-fever zone (such as Africa or South America) within the six days prior to entering the region. Otherwise the World Health Organization (WHO) recommends the following vaccinations:

Adult diphtheria & tetanus Single booster recommended if none have been had in the previous 10 years.

Hepatitis A Provides almost 100% protection for up to a year. A booster after 12 months provides at least another 20 years' protection.

Hepatitis B Now considered routine for most travellers. Given as three shots over six months. A rapid schedule is also available, as is a combined vaccination with Hepatitis A.

Measles, mumps & rubella (MMR) Two doses of MMR are required unless you have had the diseases. Many young adults require a booster.

Polio There have been no reported cases of polio in recent years. Only one booster is required as an adult for lifetime protection.

Typhoid Recommended unless your trip is less than a week and is only to developed cities. The vaccine offers around 70% protection, lasts for two to three years and comes as a single shot. Tablets are also available but the injection is usually recommended as it has fewer side effects.

Varicella If you haven't had chickenpox, discuss this vaccination with your doctor.

Online Resources

Centres for Disease Control & Prevention (CDC; www.cdc.gov) Check health conditions in all destinations and get up-to-date travel advice.

World Health Organization (WHO; www.who.int/ith) Has links to national travel and health websites.

HEALTH ADVISORIES

It's usually a good idea to consult your government's travel-health website, if one is available, before departure:

Australia (http://smartraveller.gov.au)

Canada (www.phac-aspc.gc.ca)

New Zealand (www.safetravel.govt.nz)

UK (www.gov.uk/foreign-travel-advice)

USA (http://wwwnc.cdc.gov/travel)

IN MALAYSIA, SINGAPORE & BRUNEI

Availability & Cost of Health Care

Malaysia The standard of medical care in the major centres is good, and most problems can be adequately dealt with in Kuala Lumpur.

Singapore Excellent medical facilities. You cannot buy medication over the counter without a doctor's prescription.

Brunei General care is reasonable. There is no local medical university, so expats and foreign-trained locals run the health-care system. Serious or complex cases are better managed in Singapore, but adequate primary health care and stabilisation are available.

DRINKING WATER

- Never drink tap water unless you've verified that it's safe (many parts of Malaysia, Singapore and Brunei have modern treatment plants).
- Bottled water is generally safe – check the seal is intact at purchase.
- Avoid ice in places that look dubious.
- Avoid fruit juices if they have not been freshly squeezed or you suspect they may have been watered down.
- Boiling water is the most efficient method of purification.
- The best chemical purifier is iodine. It should not be used by pregnant women or those with thyroid problems.
- Water filters should also filter out viruses. Ensure your filter has a chemical barrier such as iodine and a small pore size (eg less than 4 microns).

Infectious Diseases

The following are the most common for travellers:

Dengue fever Increasingly common in cities. The mosquito that carries dengue bites day and night, so use insect avoidance measures at all times. Symptoms can include high fever, severe headache, body ache, a rash and diarrhoea. There is no specific treatment, just rest and paracetamol – do not take aspirin as it increases the likelihood of hemorrhaging.

Hepatitis A This food- and water-borne virus infects the liver, causing jaundice (yellow skin and eyes), nausea and lethargy. All travellers to the region should be vaccinated against it.

Hepatitis B The only sexually transmitted disease (STD) that can be prevented by vaccination, hepatitis B is spread by body fluids, including sexual contact.

Hepatitis E Transmitted through contaminated food and water and has similar symptoms to hepatitis A, but it is far less common. It is a severe problem in pregnant women and can result in the death of both mother and baby. There is currently no vaccine, and prevention is by following safe eating and drinking guidelines.

HIV Unprotected heterosexual sex is the main method of transmission.

Influenza Can be very severe in people over the age of 65 or in those with underlying medical conditions such as heart disease or diabetes; vaccination is recommended for these individuals. There is no specific treatment, just rest and paracetamol.

Malaria Uncommon in the region and antimalarial drugs are rarely recommended for travellers. However, there may be a small risk in rural areas. Remember that malaria can be fatal. Before you travel, seek medical advice on the right medication and dosage for you.

Rabies A potential risk, and invariably fatal if untreated, rabies is spread by the bite or lick of an infected animal – most commonly a dog or monkey. Pre-travel vaccination means the post-bite treatment is greatly simplified. If an animal bites you, gently wash the wound with soap and water, and apply iodine based antiseptic. If you are not pre-vaccinated you will need to receive rabies immunoglobulin as soon as possible.

Typhoid This serious bacterial infection is spread via food and water. Symptoms include high and slowly progressive fever, headache, a dry cough and stomach pain. Vaccination, recommended for all travellers spending more than a week in Malaysia, is not 100% effective so you must still be careful with what you eat and drink.

Traveller's Diarrhoea

By far the most common problem affecting travellers and commonly caused by a bacteria. Treat by staying well hydrated, using a solution such as Gastrolyte. Antibiotics such as Norfloxacin, Ciprofloxacin or Azithromycin will kill the bacteria quickly.

Loperamide is just a 'stopper,' but it can be helpful in certain situations, such as if you have to go on a long bus ride. Seek medical attention quickly if you do not respond to an appropriate antibiotic.

Giardiasis is relatively common. Symptoms include nausea, bloating, excess gas, fatigue and intermittent diarrhoea. The treatment of choice is Tinidazole, with Metroniadzole being a second option.

Environmental Hazards

Air Pollution

If you have severe respiratory problems, speak with your doctor before travelling to any heavily polluted urban

LEECHES

You may not encounter any of these slimy little vampires while walking through the region's jungle, but if the trail is leafy and it's been raining, chances are you'll be preyed upon.

The local leeches are so small they can squeeze through tight-knit socks. They don't stay tiny for long, however, since once a leech has attached to your skin, it won't let go until it has sucked as much blood as it can hold.

Two species are common: the brown leech and the tiger leech. The tiger leech is recognisable by its cream and black stripes, but you'll probably feel one before you see it. Unlike the brown leech, whose suction is painless, tiger leeches sting a bit. Brown leeches hang around on, or near, the forest floor, waiting to grab onto passing boots or pants. Tiger leeches lurk on the leaves of small trees and tend to attack between the waist and neck, and that can mean any orifice there and around. Keep your shirt tucked in.

Leeches are harmless, but bites can become infected, so it's best to prevent them becoming attached in the first place. Insect repellent on feet, shoes and socks works temporarily; loose tobacco or washing powder in your shoes and socks is also said to help. Better yet, invest in some leech-proof socks that cover the foot and boot heel and fastens below the knees.

Safe and effective ways to dislodge leeches include flicking them off – try using a credit card to do this and aim for the mouth end as pulling a leech off by the tail can make it dig in harder. Tiger balm, iodine or medicated menthol oil will also get leeches off. Otherwise, succumb to your fate as a reluctant blood donor and they will eventually drop off.

centres. If troubled by the pollution, leave the city for a few days to get some fresh air. Consult the **Air Polutant Index of of Malaysia** (http://apims.doe.gov.my/v2) for current situation across region.

Diving & Surfing

If planning on diving or surfing, seek specialised advice before you travel to ensure your medical kit also contains treatment for coral cuts and tropical ear infections. Have a dive medical before you leave your home country – there are certain medical conditions that are incompatible with diving. Hyberbaric chambers are located in Kuantan and Lumut on Peninsular Malaysia, Labuan on Malaysian Borneo, and Singapore.

Heat

It can take up to two weeks to adapt to the region's hot climate. Swelling of the feet and ankles is common, as are muscle cramps caused by excessive sweating. Prevent these by avoiding dehydration and excessive activity in the heat.

Dehydration is the main contributor to heat exhaustion. Symptoms include feeling weak, headache, irritability, nausea or vomiting, sweaty skin, a fast, weak pulse, and a normal or slightly elevated body temperature. Treat by getting out of the heat, applying cool, wet cloths to the skin, laying flat with legs raised, and rehydrating with water containing a quarter of a teaspoon of salt per litre.

Heat stroke is a serious medical emergency. Symptoms come on suddenly and include weakness, nausea, a body temperature of over 41°C, dizziness, confusion, loss of coordination, fits and, eventually, collapse and loss of consciousness. Seek medical help and commence cooling by getting out of the heat, removing clothes, and applying cool, wet cloths or ice to the body, especially to the groin and armpits.

Prickly heat – an itchy rash of tiny lumps – is caused by sweat being trapped under the skin. Treat by moving out of the heat and into an air-conditioned area for a few hours and by having cool showers. Creams and ointments clog the skin so they should be avoided.

Insect Bites & Stings

Lice Most commonly inhabit your head and pubic area. Transmission is via close contact with an infected person. Treat with numerous applications of an anti-lice shampoo such as Permethrin.

Ticks Contracted after walking in rural areas. If you are bitten and experience symptoms – such as a rash at the site of the bite or elsewhere, fever or muscle aches – see a doctor. Doxycycline prevents tick-borne diseases.

Leeches Found in humid rainforest areas. Don't transmit any disease but their bites can be itchy for weeks afterwards and can easily become infected. Apply an iodine-based antiseptic to any leech bite to help prevent infection.

Bees or wasps If allergic to their stings, carry an injection of adrenaline (eg an Epipen) for emergency treatment.

Jellyfish Most are not dangerous. If stung, pour vinegar onto the affected area to neutralise the poison. Take painkillers, and seek medical advice if your condition worsens.

Skin Problems

There are two common fungal rashes that affect travellers in the Tropics. The first occurs in moist areas that get less air, such as the groin, armpits and between the toes. It starts as a red patch that slowly spreads and is usually itchy. Treatment involves keeping the skin dry, avoiding chafing and using an antifungal cream such as Clotrimazole or Lamisil. Tinea versicolour is also common – this fungus causes small, light-coloured patches, most commonly on the back, chest and shoulders. Consult a doctor.

Take meticulous care of any cuts and scratches to prevent infection. Immediately wash all wounds in clean water and apply antiseptic. If you develop signs of infection (increasing pain and redness), see a doctor. Divers and surfers should be particularly careful with coral cuts.

Snakes

Assume all snakes are poisonous. Always wear boots and long pants if walking in an area that may have snakes. First aid in the event of a snake bite involves pressure immobilisation via an elastic bandage firmly wrapped around the affected limb, starting at the bite site and working up towards the chest. The bandage should not be so tight that the circulation is cut off; the fingers or toes should be kept free so the circulation can be checked. Immobilise the limb with a splint and carry the victim to medical attention. Don't use tourniquets or try to suck out the venom. Antivenin is available for most species.

Sunburn

Even on a cloudy day, sunburn can occur rapidly. Always use a strong sunscreen (at least SPF 30), making sure to reapply after a swim, and always wear a wide-brimmed hat and sunglasses outdoors. Avoid lying in the sun during the hottest part of the day (10am to 2pm). If you're sunburnt, stay out of the sun until you've recovered, apply cool compresses and take painkillers for the discomfort. Applied twice daily, 1% hydrocortisone cream is also helpful.

Travelling with Children

There are specific issues you should consider before travelling with your child:

- All routine vaccinations should be up to date, as many of the common childhood diseases that have been eliminated in the West are still present in parts of Southeast Asia. A travel-health clinic can advise on specific vaccines, but think seriously about rabies vaccination if you're visiting rural areas or travelling for more than a month, as children are more vulnerable to severe animal bites.
- Children are more prone to getting serious forms of mosquito-borne diseases such as malaria, Japanese B encephalitis and dengue fever. In particular, malaria is very serious in children and can rapidly lead to death – you should think seriously before taking your child into a malaria-risk area. Permethrin-impregnated clothing is safe to use, and insect repellents should

DON'T LET THE BEDBUGS BITE

Bedbugs live in the cracks of furniture and walls, and migrate to the bed at night to feed on you. They are a particular problem in the region and are more likely to strike in high-turnover accommodation, especially backpacker hostels, though they can be found anywhere. The room may look very clean but they can still be there. Protect yourself with the following strategies:

- Ask the hotel or hostel what they do to avoid bed bugs. It's a common problem and reputable establishments should have a pest-control procedure in place.
- Keep your luggage elevated off the floor to avoid having the critters latch on – this is one of the common ways bedbugs are spread from place to place.
- Check the room carefully for signs of bugs – you may find their translucent light brown skins or poppy seed–like excrement. Pay particular attention to places less likely to have seen a dusting from cleaning staff.

If you do get bitten:

- Treat the itch with antihistamine.
- Thoroughly clean your luggage and launder all your clothes, sealing them after in plastic bags to further protect them.
- Be sure to tell the management – if they seem unconcerned or refuse to do anything about it, complain to the local tourist office.

contain between 10% and 20% DEET.

➡ Diarrhoea can cause rapid dehydration and you should pay particular attention to keeping your child well hydrated. The best antibiotic for children with diarrhoea is Azithromycin.

➡ Children can get very sick, very quickly so locate good medical facilities at your destination and make contact if you are worried – it's always better to get a medical opinion than to try to treat your own children.

Women's Health

➡ In urban areas, supplies of sanitary products are readily available. Birth-control options may be limited so bring adequate supplies of your own form of contraception.

➡ Heat, humidity and antibiotics can all contribute to thrush. Treatment is with antifungal creams and pessaries such as clotrimazole. A practical alternative is a single tablet of Fluconazole (Diflucan).

➡ Urinary-tract infections can be precipitated by dehydration or long bus journeys without toilet stops; bring suitable antibiotics.

Pregnancy

➡ Find out about quality medical facilities at your destination and ensure you continue your standard antenatal care at these facilities. Avoid travel in rural areas with poor transport and medical facilities.

➡ Ensure travel insurance covers all pregnancy-related possibilities, including premature labour.

➡ Malaria is a high-risk disease in pregnancy. The World Health Organization recommends that pregnant women do not travel to areas with malaria resistant to chloroquine. None of the more effective antimalarial drugs is completely safe in pregnancy.

➡ Traveller's diarrhoea can quickly lead to dehydration and result in inadequate blood flow to the placenta. Many of the drugs used to treat various diarrhoea bugs are not recommended in pregnancy. Azithromycin is considered safe.

Traditional & Folk Medicine

Throughout Asia, traditional medical systems are widely practised. There is a big difference between these traditional healing systems and 'folk' medicine. Folk remedies should be avoided, as they often involve rather dubious procedures with potential complications. In comparison, traditional healing systems, such as traditional Chinese medicine, are well respected, and aspects of them are being increasingly utilised by Western medical practitioners.

All traditional Asian medical systems identify a vital life force, and see blockage or imbalance as causing disease. Techniques such as herbal medicines, massage and acupuncture bring this vital force back into balance or maintain balance. These therapies are best used for treating chronic disease such as chronic fatigue, arthritis, irritable bowel syndrome and some chronic skin conditions. Traditional medicines should be avoided for treating serious acute infections such as malaria.

Be aware that 'natural' doesn't always mean 'safe,' and there can be drug interactions between herbal medicines and Western medicines. If you are using both systems, ensure you inform both practitioners of what the other has prescribed.

Language

The national language of Malaysia is Malay, also known as Bahasa Malaysia. It's spoken with slight variations throughout Malaysia, Singapore and Brunei, although it's by no means the only language. Various dialects of Chinese are spoken by those of Chinese ancestry, and Mandarin is fairly widely used. Indian Malaysians also speak Tamil, Malayalam and other languages. In Singapore, the official languages alongside Malay (which is mostly restricted to the Malay community) are Tamil, Mandarin and English.

You'll find it easy to get by with English not only in Singapore and on mainland Malaysia, but also in Malaysian Borneo (Sabah and Sarawak) and Brunei. English is the most common second language for Borneo's ethnic groups and is often used by people of different backgrounds, like ethnic Chinese and ethnic Malays, to communicate with one another.

In Bahasa Malaysia, most letters are pronounced more or less the same as their English counterparts, except for the letter *c* which is always pronounced as the 'ch' in 'chair'. Nearly all syllables carry equal emphasis, but a good approximation is to lightly stress the second-last syllable.

Pronouns, particularly 'you', are rarely used in Bahasa Malaysia. *Kamu* is the egalitarian form designed to overcome the plethora of terms relating to a person's age and gender that are used for the second person.

BASICS

Hello.	*Helo.*
Goodbye.	*Selamat tinggal/jalan.* (said by person leaving/staying)
How are you?	*Apa kabar?*
I'm fine.	*Kabar baik.*
Excuse me.	*Maaf.*
Sorry.	*Maaf.*
Yes./No.	*Ya./Tidak.*
Please.	*Silakan.*
Thank you.	*Terima kasih.*
You're welcome.	*Sama-sama.*
What's your name?	*Siapa nama kamu?*
My name is ...	*Nama saya ...*
Do you speak English?	*Adakah anda berbahasa Inggeris?*
I don't understand.	*Saya tidak faham.*

ACCOMMODATION

Do you have any rooms available?	*Ada bilik kosong?*
How much is it per day/person?	*Berapa harga satu malam/orang?*
Is breakfast included?	*Makan pagi termasukkah?*
campsite	*tempat perkhemahan*
guesthouse	*rumah tetamu*
hotel	*hotel*
youth hostel	*asrama belia*
single room	*bilik untuk seorang*
room with a double bed	*bilik untuk dua orang*
room with two beds	*bilik yang ada dua katil*

QUESTION WORDS

How?	*Berapa?*
What?	*Apa?*
When?	*Bilakah?*
Where?	*Di mana?*
Who?	*Siapakah?*
Why?	*Mengapa?*

KEY PATTERNS

To get by in Malay, mix and match these simple patterns with words of your choice:

When's (the next bus)?
Jam berapa (bis yang berikutnya)?

Where's (the station)?
Di mana (stasiun)?

I'm looking for (a hotel).
Saya cari (hotel).

Do you have (a local map)?
Ada (peta daerah)?

Is there a (lift)?
Ada (lift)?

Can I (enter)?
Boleh saya (masuk)?

Do I need (a visa)?
Saya harus pakai (visa)?

I'd like (the menu).
Saya minta (daftar makanan).

I'd like (to hire a car).
Saya mau (sewa mobil).

Could you (help me)?
Bisa Anda (bantu) saya?

air-con	*pendingin udara*
bathroom	*bilik air*
mosquito coil	*obat nyamuk*
window	*tingkap*

DIRECTIONS

Where is ...?	*Di mana ...?*
What's the address?	*Apa alamatnya?*
Could you write it down, please?	*Tolong tuliskan alamat itu?*
Can you show me (on the map)?	*Tolong tunjukkan (di peta)?*
Turn left/right.	*Belok kiri/kanan.*
Go straight ahead.	*Jalan terus.*
at the corner	*di simpang*
at the traffic lights	*di tempat lampu isyarat*
behind	*di belakang*
far (from)	*jauh (dari)*
in front of	*di depan*
near (to)	*dekat (dengan)*
opposite	*berhadapan dengan*

EATING & DRINKING

A table for (two), please.	*Meja untuk (dua) orang.*
What's in that dish?	*Ada apa dalam masakan itu?*
Bring the bill, please.	*Tolong bawa bil.*
I don't eat ...	*Saya tak suka makan ...*
chicken	*ayam*
fish	*ikan*
(red) meat	*daging (merah)*
nuts	*kacang*

Key Words

bottle	*botol*
breakfast	*sarapan pagi*
cold	*sejuk*
cup	*cawan*
dinner	*makan malam*
food	*makanan*
fork	*garfu*
glass	*gelas*
hot	*panas*
knife	*pisau*
lunch	*makan tengahari*
market	*pasar*
menu	*menu*
plate	*pinggan*
restaurant	*restoran*
spicy	*pedas*
spoon	*sedu*
vegetarian	*sayuran saja*
with	*dengan*
without	*tanpa*

Meat & Fish

beef	*daging lembu*
chicken	*ayam*
crab	*ketam*
fish	*ikan*
lamb	*anak biri-biri*
mussels	*kepah*
pork	*babi*
shrimp	*udang*

Fruit & Vegetables

apple	*epal*
banana	*pisang*
carrot	*lobak*

cucumber	*timun*
jackfruit	*nangka*
mango	*mangga*
orange	*jeruk oren*
peanut	*kacang*
starfruit	*belimbing*
tomato	*tomato*
watermelon	*tembikai*

Other

bread	*roti*
cheese	*keju*
egg	*telur*
ice	*ais*
rice	*nasi*
salt	*garam*
sugar	*gula*

Drinks

beer	*bir*
bottled water	*air botol*
citrus juice	*air limau*
coffee	*kopi*
milk	*susu*
tea	*teh*
water	*air*
wine	*wain*

EMERGENCIES

Help!	*Tolong!*
Stop!	*Berhenti!*
I'm lost.	*Saya sesat.*
Go away!	*Pergi!*
There's been an accident.	*Ada kemalangan.*
Call the doctor!	*Panggil doktor!*
Call the police!	*Panggil polis!*
I'm ill.	*Saya sakit.*
It hurts here.	*Sini sakit.*
I'm allergic to (nuts).	*Saya alergik kepada (kacang).*

SHOPPING & SERVICES

I'd like to buy ...	*Saya nak beli ...*
I'm just looking.	*Saya nak tengok saja.*
Can I look at it?	*Boleh saya tengok barang itu?*
How much is it?	*Berapa harganya?*
It's too expensive.	*Mahalnya.*
Can you lower the price?	*Boleh kurang?*
There's a mistake in the bill.	*Bil ini salah.*

ATM	*ATM ('a-te-em')*
credit card	*kad kredit*
internet cafe	*cyber cafe*
post office	*pejabat pos*
public phone	*telpon awam*
tourist office	*pejabat pelancong*

TIME & DATES

What time is it?	*Pukul berapa?*
It's (seven) o'clock.	*Pukul (tujuh).*

NUMBERS

1	*satu*
2	*dua*
3	*tiga*
4	*empat*
5	*lima*
6	*enam*
7	*tujuh*
8	*lapan*
9	*sembilan*
10	*sepuluh*
11	*sebelas*
12	*dua belas*
20	*dua puluh*
21	*dua puluh satu*
22	*dua puluh dua*
30	*tiga puluh*
40	*empat puluh*
50	*lima puluh*
60	*enam puluh*
70	*tujuh puluh*
80	*lapan puluh*
90	*sembilan puluh*
100	*seratus*
200	*dua ratus*
1000	*seribu*
2000	*dua ribu*

It's half past (one).	*Pukul (satu) setengah.*	**yesterday**	*semalam*
		today	*hari ini*
in the morning	*pagi*	**tomorrow**	*esok*
in the afternoon	*tengahari*	**Monday**	*hari Isnin*
in the evening	*petang*	**Tuesday**	*hari Selasa*
		Wednesday	*hari Rabu*

SINGLISH

One of the most intriguing things the visitor to Singapore will notice is the strange patois spoken by the locals. Nominally English, it contains borrowed words from Hokkien and Malay, such as *shiok* (delicious) and *kasar* (rough). Unnecessary prepositions and pronouns are dropped, word order is flipped, phrases are clipped short, and stress and intonation are unconventional, to say the least. The result is known locally as Singlish. Singlish is frowned upon in official use, though you'll get a good idea of its pervasive characteristics of pronunciation if you listen to the news bulletins on TV or the radio.

There are a number of interesting characteristics that differentiate Singlish from standard English. First off, there's the reverse stress pattern of double-barrelled words. For example, in standard English the stress would be '*fire*-fighter' or '*theatre* company' but in Singlish it's 'fire-*fighter*' and 'theatre *company*'. Word-final consonants – particularly *l* or *k* – are often dropped, and vowels are often distorted; a Chinese-speaking taxi driver might not understand 'Perak Road' since they pronounce it 'Pera Roh'. The particle *-lah* is often tagged on to the end of sentences as in, 'No good, *lah*', which could mean (among other things) 'I don't think that's such a good idea'. Requests or questions will often be marked with a tag ending, since direct questioning is considered rude. So a question such as 'Would you like a beer?' might be rendered as 'You want beer or not?', which, ironically, might come across to speakers of standard English as being rude. Verb tenses tend to be nonexistent – future, present or past actions are all indicated by time phrases, so in Singlish it's 'I go tomorrow' or 'I go yesterday'.

The following are some frequently heard Singlishisms:

ah beng – unsophisticated person with no fashion sense or style; redneck

Aiyah! – 'Oh, dear!'

Alamak! – exclamation of disbelief, frustration or dismay, like 'Oh my God!'

ayam – Malay word for chicken; adjective for something inferior or weak

blur – a slow or uninformed person

buaya – womaniser, from the Malay for 'crocodile'

Can? – 'Is that OK?'

Can! – 'Yes! That's fine.'

char bor – babe, woman

cheena – old-fashioned Chinese in dress or thinking (derogatory)

go stan – to reverse, as in 'Go stan the car' (from the naval expression 'go astern'; pronounced 'go stun')

heng – luck, good fortune (from Hokkien)

hiao – vain

inggrish – English

kambing – foolish person, literally 'goat' (from Malay)

kena ketuk – ripped off, literally 'get knocked'

kiasee – scared, literally 'afraid to die'; a coward

kiasu – selfish, pushy, always on the lookout for a bargain, literally 'afraid to lose'

lah – generally an ending for any phrase or sentence; can translate as 'OK', but has no real meaning; added for emphasis to just about everything

looksee – take a look

malu – embarrassed

minah – girlfriend

Or not? – general tag for questions, as in 'Can or not?' (Can you or can't you?)

see first – wait and see what happens

shack – tired

shiok – good, great, delicious

steady lah – well done, excellent; expression of praise

Wah! – general exclamation of surprise or distress

ya ya – boastful, as in 'He always *ya ya*'

Thursday	*hari Kamis*
Friday	*hari Jumaat*
Saturday	*hari Sabtu*
Sunday	*hari Minggu*

January	*Januari*
February	*Februari*
March	*Mac*
April	*April*
May	*Mei*
June	*Jun*
July	*Julai*
August	*Ogos*
September	*September*
October	*Oktober*
November	*November*
December	*Disember*

TRANSPORT

At what time does the ... leave?	*Pukul berapa ... berangkat?*
boat	*kapal*
bus	*bas*
plane	*kapal terbang*
train	*kereta api*

I want to go to ...	*Saya nak ke ...*
Does it stop at ... ?	*Berhenti di ...?*
How long will it be delayed?	*Berapa lambatnya?*
I'd like to get off at ...	*Saya nak turun di ...*
Please put the meter on.	*Tolong pakai meter.*
Please stop here.	*Tolong berhenti di sini.*

I'd like a ... ticket.	*Saya nak tiket ...*
1st-class	*kelas pertama*
2nd-class	*kelas kedual*
one-way	*sehala*
return	*pergi balik*

the first	*pertama*
the last	*terakhir*
the next	*berikutnya*

SIGNS

Buka	Open
Dilarang	Prohibited
Keluar	Exit
Lelaki	Men
Masuk	Entrance
Perempuan	Women
Tandas	Toilets
Tutup	Closed

bus station	*stesen bas*
bus stop	*perhentian bas*
cancelled	*dibatalkan*
delayed	*lambat*
platform	*landasan*
ticket office	*pejabat tiket*
ticket window	*tempat/kaunter tikit*
timetable	*jadual waktu*
train station	*stesen keretapi*

I'd like to hire a ...	*Saya nak menyewa ...*
bicycle	*basikal*
car	*kereta*
jeep	*jip*
motorbike	*motosikal*

diesel	*disel*
helmet	*topi keledar*
leaded petrol	*petrol plumbum*
unleaded petrol	*tanpa plumbum*
petrol	*petrol*
pump	*pam*
Is this the road to ...?	*Ini jalan ke ...?*
Where's a petrol station?	*Stesen minyak di mana?*
(How long) Can I park here?	*(Beberapa lama) Boleh saya letak kereta di sini?*
I need a mechanic.	*Kami memerlukan mekanik.*
The car has broken down at ...	*Kereta saya telah rosak di ...*
I have a flat tyre.	*Tayarnya kempis.*
I've run out of petrol.	*Minyak sudah habis.*
I've had an accident.	*Saya terlibat dalam kemalangan.*

GLOSSARY

adat – Malay customary law

adat temenggong – Malay law with Indian modifications, governing the customs and ceremonies of the sultans

air – water

air terjun – waterfall

alor – groove; furrow; main channel of a river

ampang – dam

ang pow – red packets of money used as offerings, payment or gifts

APEC – Asia-Pacific Economic Cooperation

arak – Malay local alcohol

arrack – see arak

Asean – Association of Southeast Asian Nations

atap – roof thatching

Baba-Nonya – descendants of Chinese immigrants to the Straits Settlements (namely Melaka, Singapore and Penang) who intermarried with Malays and adopted many Malay customs; also known as Peranakan, or Straits Chinese; sometimes spelt Nyonya

Bahasa Malaysia – Malay language; also known as Bahasa Melayu

bandar – seaport; town

Bangsawan – Malay opera

batang – stem; tree trunk; the main branch of a river

batik – technique of imprinting cloth with dye to produce multicoloured patterns

batu – stone; rock; milepost

belukar – secondary forest

bendahara – chief minister

bendang – irrigated land

bomoh – spiritual healer

British Resident – chief British representative during the colonial era

bukit – hill

bumboat – motorised sampan

bumiputra – literally, sons of the soil; indigenous Malays

bunga raya – hibiscus flower (national flower of Malaysia)

dadah – drugs

dato', datuk – literally, grandfather; general male nonroyal title of distinction

dipterocarp – family of trees, native to Malaysia, that have two-winged fruits

dusun – small town; orchard; fruit grove

genting – mountain pass

godown – river warehouse

gua – cave

gunung – mountain

hilir – lower reaches of a river

hutan – jungle; forest

imam – keeper of Islamic knowledge and leader of prayer

istana – palace

jalan – road

kain songket – traditional Malay handwoven fabric with gold threads

kampung – village; also spelt kampong

kangkar – Chinese village

karst – characteristic scenery of a limestone region, including features such as underground streams and caverns

kedai kopi – coffee shop

kerangas – distinctive vegetation zone of Borneo, usually found on sandstone, containing pitcher plants and other unusual flora

khalwat – literally, close proximity; exhibition of public affection between the sexes, which is prohibited for unmarried Muslim couples

kongsi – Chinese clan organisations, also known as ritual brotherhoods, heaven-man-earth societies, triads or secret societies; meeting house for Chinese of the same clan

kopitiam – coffee shop

kota – fort; city

kramat – Malay shrine

KTM – Keretapi Tanah Melayu; Malaysian Railways System

kuala – river mouth; place where a tributary joins a larger river

laksamana – admiral

langur – small, usually tree-dwelling monkey

laut – sea

lebuh – street

Lebuhraya – expressway or freeway; usually refers to the North–South Highway, which runs from Johor Bahru to Bukit Kayu Hitam at the Thai border

lorong – narrow street; alley

LRT – Light Rail Transit (Kuala Lumpur)

lubuk – deep pool

macaque – any of several small species of monkey

mandi – bathe; Southeast Asian wash basin

masjid – mosque

MCP – Malayan Communist Party

Melayu Islam Beraja – MIB; Brunei's national ideology

merdeka – independence

Merlion – half-lion, half-fish animal; symbol of Singapore

MRT – Mass Rapid Transit (Singapore)

muara – river mouth

muezzin – mosque official who calls the faithful to prayer

negara – country

negeri – state

nonya – see Baba-Nonya

orang asing – foreigner

Orang Asli – literally, Original People; Malaysian aborigines

Orang Laut – literally, Coastal People; Sea Gypsies

Orang Ulu – literally, Upriver People

padang – grassy area; field; also the city square

pantai – beach

PAP – People's Action Party

parang – long jungle knife

PAS – Parti Islam se-Malaysia

pasar – market

pasar malam – night market

Pejabat Residen – Resident's Office

pekan – market place; town

pelabuhan – port

pencak silat – martial-arts dance form

penghulu – chief or village head

pengkalan – quay

Peranakan – literally, half-caste; refers to the Baba-Nonya or Straits Chinese

PIE – Pan-Island Expressway, one of Singapore's main road arteries

pua kumbu – traditional finely woven cloth

pulau – island

puteri – princess

raja – prince; ruler

rakyat – common people

rantau – straight coastline

rattan – stems from climbing palms used for wickerwork and canes

rimba – jungle

rotan – cane used to punish miscreants

roti – bread

sampan – small boat

samsu – Malay alcohol

sarong – all-purpose cloth, often sewn into a tube, and worn by women, men and children

seberang – opposite side of road; far bank of a river

selat – strait

semenanjung – peninsula

silat – see pencak silat

simpang – crossing; junction

songkok – traditional Malay headdress worn by males

Straits Chinese – see Baba-Nonya

sungai – river

syariah – Islamic system of law

tambang – river ferry; fare

tamu – weekly market

tanah – land

tanjung – headland

tasik – lake

teluk – bay; sometimes spelt telok

temenggong – Malay administrator

towkang – Chinese junk

tuai rumah – longhouse chief (Sarawak)

tuak – local 'firewater' alcohol (Malaysian Borneo)

tunku – prince

ujung – cape

UMNO – United Malays National Organisation

warung – small eating stalls

wayang – Chinese opera

wayang kulit – shadow-puppet theatre

wisma – office block or shopping centre

yang di-pertuan agong – Malaysia's head of state, or 'king'

yang di-pertuan besar – head of state in Negeri Sembilan

yang di-pertuan muda – under-king

yang di-pertuan negeri – governor

Behind the Scenes

SEND US YOUR FEEDBACK

We love to hear from travellers – your comments keep us on our toes and help make our books better. Our well-travelled team reads every word on what you loved or loathed about this book. Although we cannot reply individually to your submissions, we always guarantee that your feedback goes straight to the appropriate authors, in time for the next edition. Each person who sends us information is thanked in the next edition – the most useful submissions are rewarded with a selection of digital PDF chapters.

Visit **lonelyplanet.com/contact** to submit your updates and suggestions or to ask for help. Our award-winning website also features inspirational travel stories, news and discussions.

Note: We may edit, reproduce and incorporate your comments in Lonely Planet products such as guidebooks, websites and digital products, so let us know if you don't want your comments reproduced or your name acknowledged. For a copy of our privacy policy visit lonelyplanet.com/privacy.

OUR READERS

Many thanks to the travellers who used the last edition and wrote to us with helpful hints, useful advice and interesting anecdotes: A Adelien Vandeweghe, Ali Thorn, Ankur Agarwal, Anne & David Brock, Anouk van Lammeren **B** Bas Zeper **C** Christopher Moore **D** Dave Krantz **E** Eamon McCann, Erik Eskin **F** Frank Genghis **J** Jan Timmermans, Jan van den Heuij, John Bone, Jurgen Bruyninx **K** Karri Viitala & Maiju Monto **M** Marcus Feaver, Mark Cohen, Melissa & Dominic Pepper **O** Oscar Page **P** Peter Daemen **R** Remko Donga, Roger Lewis **S** Samuel Wainstein, Sapideh Gilani, Soren Braun, Stéphanie Visser **T** Tarsis Arroo **W** Wilfried Vancraeynest

AUTHOR THANKS

Isabel Albiston

Thanks to everyone who helped out along the way, especially Narelle McMurtrie, Mrs Lee, Stephen Baya and Tine Hjetting, Mado in Pa Lungan, Dina Bailey, Chongteah Lim, Leslie Chiang, Anthony Chieng, Polycarp Teo Sebum and Louise, Jacqueline Fong and Jo-Lynn Liao. Cheers also to Stefan Arestis and Sebastien Chaneac for making me laugh and to my friends and family for their love and support. Lastly, huge thanks to Sarah and Simon.

Brett Atkinson

Terima kasih to a whole cast of characters who assisted me on this trip. In Kota Bharu, cheers to Zeck and Bob, and on the Perhentian islands, thank you to Neil, Shauna – especially for the scissors – Raymond and Seh Ling. In Kuala Terengganu, many thanks to Alex and Maslina for the company and conversation. Thanks to Sarah Reid and the wider editorial and cartography team, and final thanks to Carol and my family back home in Selandia Baru.

Greg Benchwick

Huge thanks to my Destination Editor Sarah for putting her faith in me on this project (my first in the region). The people of Malaysia are super friendly. I really want to thank Joe at the Kuantan Visitor Center, and the entire crew of rip-roarious irregulars at EcoBar in Cherating. And first and always, thank you my darling Violeta for making my life so rich. Love, Daddy.

Cristian Bonetto

A heartfelt thankyou to Helen Burge, Craig Bradbery, Honey Lee, Carolyn Ng, Sharon Vu, Myra Tan, Andy Yeo, Michelle Chua, Richie Raupe, Seb Neylan, Stephane Hasselsweiler and Dean Brettschneider. Many thanks also to my patient, supportive family and to Sarah Reid for the commission.

Austin Bush

Thanks to the kind folks on the ground in Malaysia and abroad including Joann Khaw, Bee Yinn Low, Narelle McMurtrie, Chris Ong, Wanida Razali, Khoo Salma and Ernest Zacharevic.

Anita Isalska

My research was much richer thanks to Mr David at Sekeping Kong Heng, Noor Rashiela Binti Mohd Salleh and the Tourism Malaysia team, Steve Khong, Shaukani Abbas, K Rajasegaran, Jek Yap, Jay and the Father's Guesthouse crew. Big thanks to Seow Wei Tang and family for tips and karaoke, and Simon Richmond for thoughtful guidance. Nora, who gave me cola when I was slipping unconscious with Jerantut nausea, danke. And Normal Matt, for KL rooftop cocktails and boundless cheer.

Robert Scott Kelly

For this book, the dedications are simple. All my love and thanks go to Tania Simonetti, wife and companion on my most important travels in this world, and to our infant son, Robin Francesco, born beautiful and healthy on 20 July 2015, while this guidebook was taking shape.

Simon Richmond

Terima kasih to the following: Nozara Yusof, Alex Yong, Andrew Sebastian, Narelle McMurtrie, Gregers Reimann and Scott Dunn.

Richard Waters

Sincere thanks to Eljer for his patience and skill, Daniken for keeping my dinner warm, Diana without whose help much of this trip would have been so much harder, Arwen, Walter and staff, Kurt (easily the best wildlife guide in 15 years' travel writing), Mr Reward and brother James Bond, tireless Bobby who braved the mudslides and aftershocks to take me to Mt K, Charlie and Jess for all their fabulous help, Brodie, Emma and Sadie for their lovely co, Jan for his hospitality and Ellen for her reef, Tom, Fanny and finally Carmalita, Mr Robin and May at Sabah Tourism for their fantastic support.

ACKNOWLEDGEMENTS

Climate map data adapted from Peel MC, Finlayson BL & McMahon TA (2007) 'Updated World Map of the Köppen-Geiger Climate Classification', Hydrology and Earth System Sciences, 11, 163344.

Cover photograph: Food market in Kota Bharu, Peter Adams/AWL ©

THIS BOOK

This 13th edition of Lonely Planet's *Malaysia, Singapore & Brunei* guidebook was researched and written by Isabel Albiston, Brett Atkinson, Greg Benchwick, Cristian Bonetto, Austin Bush, Anita Isalska, Robert Scott Kelly, Simon Richmond and Richard Waters. The previous edition was written by Simon Richmond, Cristian Bonetto, Celeste Brash, Joshua Samuel Brown, Austin Bush, Adam Karlin and Daniel Robinson. This guidebook was produced by the following:

Destination Editor Sarah Reid

Product Editor Kathryn Rowan, Elizabeth Jones

Senior Cartographer Julie Sheridan

Book Designer Mazzy Prinsep

Assisting Editors Sarah Bailey, Melanie Dankel, Carly Hall, Gabrielle Innes, Rosie Nicholson, Charlotte Orr, Kirsten Rawlings, Fionnuala Twomey, Simon Williamson

Cartographer Michael Garrett

Assisting Book Designer Wibowo Rusli

Cover Researcher Naomi Parker

Thanks to Anita Banh, Carolyn Boicos, Grace Dobell, Ryan Evans, Andi Jones, Anne Mason, Kate Matthews, Jenna Myers, Wayne Murphy, Catherine Naghten, Karyn Noble, Vicky Smith, Lauren Wellicome

Index

Map Pages **000**
Photo Pages **000**

Map Pages **000**
Photo Pages **000**

Map Pages **000**
Photo Pages 000

N

O

P

Map Pages **000**
Photo Pages **000**

T

lonely planet
40 YEARS
Japan
Tokyo
pull-out map

Map Legend

Sights
- Beach
- Bird Sanctuary
- Buddhist
- Castle/Palace
- Christian
- Confucian
- Hindu
- Islamic
- Jain
- Jewish
- Monument
- Museum/Gallery/Historic Building
- Ruin
- Shinto
- Sikh
- Taoist
- Winery/Vineyard
- Zoo/Wildlife Sanctuary
- Other Sight

Activities, Courses & Tours
- Bodysurfing
- Diving
- Canoeing/Kayaking
- Course/Tour
- Sento Hot Baths/Onsen
- Skiing
- Snorkelling
- Surfing
- Swimming/Pool
- Walking
- Windsurfing
- Other Activity

Sleeping
- Sleeping
- Camping

Eating
- Eating

Drinking & Nightlife
- Drinking & Nightlife
- Cafe

Entertainment
- Entertainment

Shopping
- Shopping

Information
- Bank
- Embassy/Consulate
- Hospital/Medical
- Internet
- Police
- Post Office
- Telephone
- Toilet
- Tourist Information
- Other Information

Geographic
- Beach
- Gate
- Hut/Shelter
- Lighthouse
- Lookout
- Mountain/Volcano
- Oasis
- Park
- Pass
- Picnic Area
- Waterfall

Population
- Capital (National)
- Capital (State/Province)
- City/Large Town
- Town/Village

Transport
- Airport
- Border crossing
- Bus
- Cable car/Funicular
- Cycling
- Ferry
- Metro/MRT/MTR station
- Monorail
- Parking
- Petrol station
- Skytrain/Subway station
- Taxi
- Train station/Railway
- Tram
- Underground station
- Other Transport

Note: Not all symbols displayed above appear on the maps in this book

Routes
- Tollway
- Freeway
- Primary
- Secondary
- Tertiary
- Lane
- Unsealed road
- Road under construction
- Plaza/Mall
- Steps
- Tunnel
- Pedestrian overpass
- Walking Tour
- Walking Tour detour
- Path/Walking Trail

Boundaries
- International
- State/Province
- Disputed
- Regional/Suburb
- Marine Park
- Cliff
- Wall

Hydrography
- River, Creek
- Intermittent River
- Canal
- Water
- Dry/Salt/Intermittent Lake
- Reef

Areas
- Airport/Runway
- Beach/Desert
- Cemetery (Christian)
- Cemetery (Other)
- Glacier
- Mudflat
- Park/Forest
- Sight (Building)
- Sportsground
- Swamp/Mangrove

Austin Bush

Penang Austin came to Thailand in 1999 on a language scholarship, and has remained in Southeast Asia ever since. This is his second time contributing to *Malaysia, Singapore & Brunei*, a gig that is arguably Lonely Planet's most delicious. Austin is a native of Oregon and a writer and photographer who often focuses on food; samples of his work can be seen at www.austinbushphotography.com. Autin also wrote the Eat Like a Local and Regional Specialities features of this book.

Read more about Austin at: https://auth.lonelyplanet.com/profiles/osten_th

Anita Isalska

Melaka, Perak Anita is a freelance travel journalist, editor and copywriter. Formerly a Lonely Planet digital editor, Anita surprised no one when she swapped office life for taste-testing street food and prowling beach resorts. Previous Malaysia travels took Anita from leechy Sabah hikes to Ipoh's red bean frappés. Returning to research her most-adored regions, Perak and Melaka, was a joy. Anita writes about travel, adventure, food and culture for a host of international publications; check out some of her work at www.anitaisalska.com.

Read more about Anita at: https://auth.lonelyplanet.com/profiles/anitatravels

Robert Scott Kelly

Selangor & Negeri Sembilan A resident of Kuala Lumpur since 2013, Robert enjoyed the opportunity to explore the states surrounding his home in more detail to update this guidebook. His favourite discoveries: the megaliths of Negeri Sembilan and the traditional wood houses of Kampung Pantai. Robert, a freelance writer, photographer, documentary filmmaker and, now, fledgling podcaster, has also contributed to Lonely Planet titles including Kuala Lumpur, Taiwan, China, Alaska, and Tibet. Check out his latest work on www.robertscottkelly.com.

Read more about Robert at: https://auth.lonelyplanet.com/profiles/RobertScottKelly

Simon Richmond

Kuala Lumpur Simon first travelled in the region back in the early 1990s. A lot has changed since, but both Malaysia and Singapore remain among Simon's favourite destinations for their easily accessible mix of cultures, landscapes, adventures and, crucially, delicious food. This is the fifth time the award-winning travel writer and photographer has written for Lonely Planet's *Malaysia, Singapore & Brunei* guide. He's also the author of Lonely Planet's *Kuala Lumpur, Melaka & Penang* guide as well as a shelf-load of other titles for this and other publishers. Read more about Simon's travels at www.simonrichmond.com and on Twitter and Instagram @simonrichmond. Simon also wrote most of the Plan Your Trip section and the Understand and Survival Guide sections of this book.

Read more about Simon at: https://auth.lonelyplanet.com/profiles/simonrichmond

Richard Waters

Sabah Richard is an award-winning journalist and writes about travel for *The Daily Telegraph, The Independent* and *Sunday Times, Sunday Times Travel Magazine, Elle* and *National Geographic Traveller*. He lives with his family in the Cotswolds, UK, and when he's not travelling, loves surfing and diving. Exploring Sabah was an absolute joy, his favourite moments being watching sharks in Sipadan, and seeing the sun rise over the jungle in the Danum Valley. He also writes a family wellbeing, adventure blog called Soul Tonic for Sanlam Bank. Check it out on: www.sanlam.co.uk/Media/Blogs/Soul-Tonic.asp

OUR STORY

A beat-up old car, a few dollars in the pocket and a sense of adventure. In 1972 that's all Tony and Maureen Wheeler needed for the trip of a lifetime – across Europe and Asia overland to Australia. It took several months, and at the end – broke but inspired – they sat at their kitchen table writing and stapling together their first travel guide, *Across Asia on the Cheap*. Within a week they'd sold 1500 copies. Lonely Planet was born.

Today, Lonely Planet has offices in Franklin, London, Melbourne, Oakland, Beijing and Delhi, with more than 600 staff and writers. We share Tony's belief that 'a great guidebook should do three things: inform, educate and amuse'.

OUR WRITERS

Isabel Albiston

Langkawi, Kedah & Perlis; Sarawak; Brunei Since her first trip to Malaysia, travelling the length of the peninsula by train on an overland journey from Singapore to Nepal, Isabel has grown to love shimmying across rickety bamboo bridges on rainforest hikes. The pursuit of laksa keeps luring her back and she can now confirm Sarawak to be the clear winner in the countrywide contest for the best broth. Isabel is a journalist who has written for a number of newspapers and magazines including the UK's *Daily Telegraph*.

Read more about Isabel at: https://auth.lonelyplanet.com/profiles/IsabelAlbiston

Brett Atkinson

East Coast Islands, Kelantan & Terengganu Following past sojourns in the west of Malaysia, this was Brett's first exploration of the peninsula's eastern edge. Highlights included island hopping from the Perhentians to Pulau Kapas, the street food and night markets of Kota Bharu, and the compact heritage appeal of Chinatown in Kuala Terengganu. Brett is based in Auckland, New Zealand and has covered more than 50 countries as a guidebook author and travel and food writer. See www.brett-atkinson.net for his most recent work and upcoming travels.

Read more about Brett at: https://auth.lonelyplanet.com/profiles/BrettAtkinson

Greg Benchwick

Johor, Pahang & Tioman Island Greg's been writing about travel both near and far for the better part of the past two decades. He's written dozens of travel guides for Lonely Planet, and is a recognised expert on sustainable tourism. For this edition, he jungle-boated down from Taman Negara, got nuclear drunk in his search for the perfect bar in Cherating and nearly fell off the planet in Tioman.

Read more about Greg at: https://auth.lonelyplanet.com/profiles/gregbenchwick

Cristian Bonetto

Singapore Cristian has been chowing his way across Singapore for well over a decade. Countless calories later, the Australian-born writer remains deeply fascinated by the Little Red Dot's dramatic evolution. To date, Cristian has contributed to more than 30 Lonely Planet guides, including *New York City*, *Italy*, *Denmark* and both the Singapore city and pocket guides. His musings have also appeared in a string of publications, including Britain's *The Telegraph* and San Francisco's *7X7*. Follow Cristian on Twitter (@CristianBonetto) and Instagram (rexcat75).

Read more about Cristian at: https://auth.lonelyplanet.com/profiles/CristianBonetto

OVER PAGE MORE WRITERS

Published by Lonely Planet Publications Pty Ltd
ABN 36 005 607 983
13th edition – August 2016
ISBN 978 1 74321 029 1

10 9 8 7 6 5 4 3 2 1
Printed in China